**SOCIAL PROBLEMS
IN CORPORATE
AMERICA**

Social Problems in Corporate America

Edited by
HELEN ICKEN SAFA
GLORIA LEVITAS
Rutgers University

A *trans*action/**Society** TEXTBOOK

Harper & Row, Publishers
New York, Evanston, San Francisco, London

Acknowledgments

Acknowledgment is gratefully given to the following individuals and organizations for permission to use their photographs.

Page: 24 Ken Heyman; 33 Verna M. Fausey; 39 Burk Uzzle, Magnum; 46 Arthur Tress; 49 Neil Benson; 63 Steve Eagle; 68 Neil Benson; 71–79 Ken Heyman; 80–94 Joan Dufault; 96 B. D. Vidibor; 98–100 Donald Greenhaus; 111 Ken Heyman; 117 Nathan Farb; 128 Arthur Tress; 130 Lynn McLaren, Rapho Guillumete; 135 Charles Harbutt, Magnum; 150 Bob Adelman, Magnum; 157 George Ballis © All rights reserved; 162–171 The Bettmann Archive; 173 Bruce Davidson, Magnum; 180–181 UPI; 190 Neil Benson; 209 Historical and Philosophical Society of Ohio; 215 UPI; 224 Patricia Hollander Gross, Stock, Boston; 231 Eve Arnold, Magnum; 233 Ken Heyman; 234 Eve Arnold, Magnum; 252 Charles Harbutt, Magnum; 260 C. R. Moore © 1972; 264–267 Nathan Farb; 275 Herb Bettin; 306 Neil Benson; 309 Burk Uzzle, Magnum; 314 Neil Benson; 322 Margot Granitsas; 330 Herb Bettin; 343 Jim Colman; 345 Bruce Davidson, Magnum; 350–355 Shelly Rusten; 357 Ken Heyman; 359 Jim Colman; 362 Neil Benson; 373 Bill Owens; 379 Jim Colman; 380 Nathan Farb; 384 Neil Benson; 386 Peter N. Gold; 388 Nathan Farb; 390 Margot Granitsas © 1971; 395–405 Ken Heyman; 409 Nathan Farb; 413–416 Ken Heyman; 421 Charles Gatewood © All rights reserved; 422 Joan Dufault; 423 Nathan Farb; 428 (top) Joan Dufault; 428 (bottom) Benedict Fernandez; 429 Danny Lyon, Magnum; 434 Henry Gutwirth; 459 UPI; 470 Roger Malloch, Magnum; 473–474 (top) Philip Jones Griffiths, Magnum; 474 (bottom) UPI; 486 Erick C. Schreiber; 494 Irving Louis Horowitz; 495–497 Neil Benson; 498 Irving Louis Horowitz; 506 Neil Benson; 507 Nathan Farb; 511 Leonard Freed, Magnum; 512 Joan Dufault

Sponsoring Editor: Ronald K. Taylor
Project Editor: Ellen Meek
Production Supervisor: Stefania J. Taflinska

SOCIAL PROBLEMS IN CORPORATE AMERICA

Library of Congress Cataloging in Publication Data

Safa, Helen Icken, comp.
    Social problems in corporate America.

    (A Transaction/Society textbook)
    A collection of articles from Trans-action and Society.
    1. United States—Social conditions—1960–   —Addresses, essays, lectures. 2. Social problems—Addresses, essays, lectures. I. Levitas, Gloria B., joint comp. II. Trans-action. III. Society.
IV. Title.
HN65.S26   309.1′73   74-11771
ISBN 0-06-046638-3

Contents

Foreword

Nearly a decade ago I wrote a paper on "The Sociology of Social Problems: A Study in the Americanization of Ideas." In it I pointed out somewhat acrimoniously that:

> The study of social problems is marred by intellectual timidity and mired in moral ambiguity. Of all areas and aspects of sociology as it is currently practiced, none seems at one and the same time more pervasive and parochial—pervasive in the sense that all sociologists acknowledge that there are indeed social problems and these ought to be removed; parochial in the sense that this concern for the importance of social problems seems so confined to the United States. Even when issues normally covered by a social problems orientation in the United States are handled by European scholars, they are cast in different terms—as anything from social welfare to social policy. The concept of a social problem is therefore far from self-evident. All that can be said for certain is that the social problems approach is a challenge to the sanitized world of value-suspending social science approaches.

It is both exciting and amazing to report, less than ten years later, that a considerable amount of that timidity and ambiguity has been pushed aside by an extraordinary output of work in the area of social problems. The work of Helen Icken Safa and Gloria Levitas in organizing these materials for and from *trans*action/**Society** convinces me that they are indeed representative of a new breed of social researcher with a level of conscience and courage equal to the task of de-parochializing this area.

The efforts herein contained have, however, been preceded by, or have run parallel with attempts to locate social problems in a structured text that has to do with the nature of the social system rather than demands for therapeutic relief. The efforts of such people as Johnathan H. Turner, Maurice Zeitlin, and Richard Quinney, following in the footsteps of a slightly older generation of scholars—people like Elliot Liebow, Lee Rainwater, and Howard Becker, to name but a few—have transformed the area of social problems. No longer is it a desultory field which assumes the health of society and the sickness of individuals and which assumes personal deviation is itself a social problem. These people have stood the world on its head, or perhaps, more sagaciously, stood the people most directly involved, those victimized by the social system, back on their feet.

The solutions and organization of *Social Problems in Corporate America* reveal how far the social sciences have come from only a decade ago, when the dominant view was based on a formula of equilibrium in which social problems emerge when social formulas break down. In other words, the volume by Safa and Levitas must be considered a contribution to structural analysis quite beyond functional analysis: a work in which few metaphysical assumptions are made concerning what is normative and what is deviant, what is right and what is wrong. If anything, the editors and the essays themselves for the most part presume individuals rather than societies to be the more important.

In all studies of social problems an enormous decision must be made by researcher, teacher, and students alike; namely, where does one allocate blame and responsibility? Who has rights and who has obligations; or better, what are the rights and obligations of individuals with respect to systems? There is no metaphysical response possible and yet the entire history of social problems texts is laden with the presumption that systems have rights and individuals have responsibilities. It is a measure of how far we have come that a text such as *Social Problems in Corporate America* puts this entire framework out of the way and places the very notion of obligations and rights in a larger context of the social order and what it *has done* to people rather than what it *might* do for them.

A great merit of this reader, as well as the introductory statements, is that Safa and Levitas do not make the opposite mistake. They do not oversimplify the issues and merely assume society is an instrument bearing all obligations while individuals retain all rights. This work must thus be considered a part of the new mainstream in the study of social problems and analysis that leaves open ultimate questions of rights and responsibilities, and rather seeks a solution in changing, as well as understanding, the main categories of poverty, race, economy, and politics as they affect individual behavior. Indeed, the fact that politics has joined the long list of social problems is itself a major aspect of this volume, and deserves special attention. The social scientists involved, both as editors and authors of this reader, have gone beyond observation, and have entered into the vital and difficult tasks of interpretation and explanation. *Social Problems in Corporate America* has defined issues in a way that makes solutions possible. It seeks to provide answers as well as to ask the right questions. Thus, this text is dedicated not simply to highlighting social problems for students already inundated with such an awareness; but far more important, to establishing guidelines for social solutions based on the social sciences.

Irving Louis Horowitz
Editor-in-Chief
*trans*action/**Society**

June 28, 1974

1. Introduction

Of the many books on social problems published in the United States, some of them, like this one, have confined themselves to domestic problems; others have adopted a wider lens, focusing on a range of world problems. Why, then, yet another book on social problems? What makes this one different?

First, this is a book based entirely on articles drawn from *trans*action/ **Society** magazine—primarily articles which have appeared during the last five years (1968–1973). As its readers know, **Society** is no ordinary social science journal. It seeks to communicate not only with the professional audience of social scientists, but also with a broader public. It numbers among its readers practitioners and policymakers responsible for developing and implementing America's social programs. Thus, it has attempted to make use of the tools of social science for the analysis of vital contemporary issues which concern a broad spectrum of the American public. Its intention has been inclusive rather than exclusive: to make social science intelligible to all rather than to confine itself to the social science élite. **Society** has, therefore, concentrated upon problems of more than abstract theoretical interest; its articles strive to join theory with action, to suggest solutions or to present alternatives which may be of value to the planner and policymaker as well as the social scientist.

Second, this volume obviously reflects the editors' own predilections, observable not only in the articles chosen but in the topics which we feel most accurately portray the most vital contemporary issues in American society. While most readers on social problems are written or edited by sociologists, we are both anthropologists. We feel that our anthropological training strongly influenced our way of perceiving and analyzing problems whether we are dealing with Australian aborigines or contemporary American society. How?

There are at least three hallmarks to the anthropological tradition reflected in this volume. First, our emphasis is upon a holistic approach to contemporary social problems. We recognize from the outset that no one problem can be divorced from another, nor from the societal context in which each occurs. Thus we see both poverty and racism as the outgrowth of the structural and social inequality embedded in "the American way of life." Inequality, in turn, is a product of our economic system with its emphasis on material wealth and production rather than human needs and social welfare. Although both poverty and racism may derive from the same source, it is a mistake to equate them and to argue, as some have done, that blacks are poor simply because they are black—as if a biological principle, race, could explain socioeconomic inequality.

Why racial minorities like blacks tend to constitute such a large segment of the American poor can best be explained by historical analysis—a second hallmark of the anthropological method. Most Americans know that blacks were brought to this country as slaves, but they do not know how the rural Southern plantation and the Northern urban ghetto have perpetuated the pattern of subordination and exploitation initiated under slavery. Like poverty or racism, most contemporary social problems can be understood more clearly if looked at in historical perspective. Thus, Gutman's article "Industrial Invasion of the Village Green" and Sennett's article "Genteel Backlash: Chicago 1886" illustrate how nineteenth-century American cities reacted to rapid economic change and a challenge to the status quo, and how similar these reactions are to the hostility and hysteria which have overcome many of the older residents of the inner city today (e.g., Conforti's article "Newark: Ghetto or City?").

Third, anthropologists have always strived to adopt a comparative perspective, to shed themselves of ethnocentric bias, and to view each culture on its own merits. We have deliberately limited the range of our comparison here to internal American problems and have avoided dealing with issues such as the Vietnam war, the monetary crisis, or other international problems which have had a profound impact on the United States in recent years. These are topics for another book, and we chose to confine ourselves here to articles which could be analyzed within a domestic framework. The incredible diversity of the American people—by race, religion, region, class, ethnic background—provides a vast range of comparative materials. This diversity is especially apparent in the American underclass, among the poor, blacks, Chicanos, Puerto Ricans, Indians, as well as older European ethnic urban groups. Even the middle class has its significant divisions: despite the fears of "mass homogenization" voiced by intellectuals as they attempt to assess the impact of the exodus to the suburbs, the pervasive influence of the mass media, and other standardizing mechanisms, it appears that the tendency towards diversity is as strong as ever. This is especially true among the young, women, and other marginal groups whose refusal to conform to the American mold has led to a good deal of experimentation with social relationships. Our section on Changing Life-Styles provides graphic examples of this new diversity in sex styles, family life, economic arrangements, and even religious belief.

The anthropologist's holistic, historical, and comparative view of society leads to a view of problems—and of change—which is often different from that held in other social sciences. The anthropologist's respect for and concern with cultural diversity makes him ask why a particular value or behavior pattern—though different from the norm—is maintained. He is less likely to dismiss behavioral variation by labeling it as "deviant" and pathological. In the anthropological view, differences are good—adding to the richness of human experience and to the variety of human alternatives. Anthropological sympathy with "deviance" is not surprising: one of the prime goads to the anthropological career has been the anthropologist's dissatisfaction with his own culture. This cultural alienation has sent anthropologists in pursuit of alternatives, but it has often allowed anthropologists to retreat from the problems in their own society by withdrawing into studies of other cultures. In recent years, anthropologists have begun to turn their attention to American society. This interest has grown as primitive people and peasants gradually disappeared, as new Third World nations threatened by outsiders increasingly bar or restrict research, and as awareness by anthropologists of their role as Western culture brokers has increased.

The anthropological perspective on social problems demonstrates that how a social scientist defines a social problem clearly depends upon his values, his training, and the model of reality current in his profession. Science is not a product but a process which attempts to develop better understanding of the world in which we live. Scientists build models of reality and then test them. As long as their models work—that is, as long as the scientist finds a good fit between his model and reality—scientists have little to do but to keep testing cases against their theories. If, however, their tests do not support their theories, then scientists, like other people, engage in conflict. Some are conservative and will try to "save the model." Like reformists and politicians who prefer to alter the deviants rather than the system, they correct their procedure and try again. Others strike out in a new direction and try to create a new model that better reflects the reality they have found. The two groups may battle vigorously, but their weapons are generally words and experiments. The conflict generally ends when one group successfully proves to the other that its model is better— that is, explains more of the facts more satisfactorily. The new model will be used until it, too, is superseded.

In this book, we have systematically attempted to present our own model of American reality, and to destroy the concept that the poor, the minorities, or any other social group is responsible for past or present social problems in America. The emphasis is not on the social pathology of persons who may, at this particular historical moment, be experiencing or producing problems in American society, but on society's inability to cope with these problems. We see the root of these problems not in the people themselves but in the external forces to which these people are subject.

In the United States, these external forces have been increasingly the dual dominance of big business and unrepresentative government. America is no longer the land of the laissez-faire, independent, small-scale entrepreneur enshrined in the persons of Horatio Alger, the pioneer, the cowboy, and the immigrant, all in pursuit of the American dream. We are living in a highly complex, bureaucratic society, controlled by a vast state machinery, and with huge sums of wealth concentrated in the hands of mammoth multinational corporations. The avenues to upward mobility are no longer open to the independent entrepreneur—the retail store, the small factory, the farm. Success is achieved primarily through the hierarchies in these large private and public bureaucracies—the corporation, the civil service, and even the universities. The more complex and controlled American society becomes, the more circuitous and narrow becomes the avenue to success— particularly for those who must start from the bottom. Our society demands a high level of skill and knowledge even for those exercising routine tasks.

Yet the mythology of an open society persists in the United States and continues to condition our view of social problems and how they should be solved. We continue to believe that the problems emanate from the poor, the blacks, and other "deviant" minorities because they have not made it in American society. We condemn those who are the victims of our society's malfunctions because they are too powerless to defend their own interests and to demand a just share of the society's resources.

Increasingly it is no longer only the poor and powerless who are the victims of society's greed and injustice. As shown in the section on The Changing Economy the middle class too is beginning to feel the strains of unemployment, of constant uprooting and mobility, and of heavy taxation and poor public services. Like the poor, the middle class is becoming a pawn in the games played by the "power élite" who selfishly strive only to protect their own vested interest.

As long as the primary goal of American society remains greater production and greater wealth, as long as we measure our prestige and strength in global terms solely by the size of our defense establishment and the value of the dollar, the social problems undermining the fabric of American society will continue to expand. What then is the solution? What strategies for change can we suggest to reduce the inequities of present-day American society?

To correct the problems of our cities, of the poverty, racism, violence, crime, and other social ills which now beset American society, we must begin to ask how we can reorder our present system of priorities to achieve a more equitable distribution of wealth and resources. We must demand that the government use its power to redistribute our wealth—not simply through the demeaning and inadequate welfare measures now in operation, but through public guarantees of *optimal* rather than *minimal* standards of health, housing, education, income, and other necessities. We must demand that the government accept greater responsibility for the welfare of all its citizens and not simply defend the interests of big business.

We increasingly hear calls for a guaranteed national income, a national health service, or nationalized housing, as indicated by several of the authors in this volume. Clearly, state and local governments can no longer absorb these costs, even with heavy federal subsidies. Yet we cling to an outworn concept of social welfare, which views aid as demeaning or at best rehabilitative, and therefore best administered by local communities with direct measures of social control.

At a time of rapid technological change, when automation threatens even the highly skilled worker, we can no longer rely on these stopgap measures. We must move toward guaranteeing *every* citizen an adequate level of housing, health, and income, much as we now accept free public education. Undoubtedly inequities will persist, as our educational system amply demonstrates. However, we will at least have eliminated the *idea* that basic necessities such as health and housing are commodities to be purchased on the private market rather than the rights due any citizen in a democracy. As Heilbroner notes in his article in Section 3, several European capitalist countries have accepted this notion within the framework of bourgeois democracy. It is our sanctioned notions of individualism and competition, not democracy, which are threatened by such humanitarian measures.

To the radical, these measures may seem reformist—and indeed they are. They will not wipe out the inequities inherent in a capitalist system where well-being is still primarily determined by one's purchasing power. However, we feel that the realities of American society preclude the possibility of a socialist revolution at this stage of our history. Even the reformist measures suggested above have lacked electoral support because those sectors of American society most affected—the poor, blacks, women, and other minorities—have been effectively disenfranchised. They may have a vote, but they lack a voice where the real decisions governing the society are made. It is only through the increased politicalization of such groups and their effective participation in the power structure that a radical transformation of American society may come about.

2. The Urban Crisis

No discussion of social problems in corporate America would be complete without an analysis of the urban crisis. Though clearly not confined to cities, social problems such as poverty, racism, unemployment, or crime are most visible and most explosive in our teeming metropolises.

Is urban life itself responsible for these problems? Is there something inherent in the nature of cities that breeds social disorganization and delinquency? Much public opinion as well as social research in the United States tends to support this view. We have a traditional antiurban ethos in the United States which has crept into the writing of such eminent social scientists as Louis Wirth, Robert Redfield, and Lewis Mumford. These writers viewed the modern city as a center of anomie and social disorganization while they romanticized the rural area as an organized and harmonious setting for intimate personal relationships. Wirth's classic essay on "Urbanism as a Way of Life" identified urbanism with specific sociocultural criteria such as impersonality, heterogeneity, and disorganization which influenced (and continues to influence) a whole generation of urban sociologists, just as Redfield's image of peasant society as homogeneous, highly personalistic, and stable spurred much anthropological research into cross-cultural studies of the peasantry. Most of this research tended to reinforce the rural—urban dichotomy since the research by urban sociologists focused upon rapid social change and social pathology, while the work of anthropologists, at least till recently, emphasized the stability and cohesiveness of traditional peasant society.

However, an alternative explanation for the urban crisis is possible. The cities have not been so much the cause of social problems, as the *locus* of political and economic forces in American society which have brought about conflict, change, and disorganization. Cities have traditionally been centers of power. Even in prehistoric times their influence expanded and waned with the power of the state (cf. R. Mc C. Adams 1966). It was in cities that the full range of social stratification first developed, since even today rural peasant communities are composed largely of one class of cultivators. From their early beginnings, cities were associated with the need for an increasing specialization and division of labor; with competition for control of resources; and with ethnic heterogeneity resulting from conquest, immigration, slavery, and other historic phenomena which moved people across national boundaries.

The new technology introduced by industrialization in the nineteenth and twentieth centuries accelerated these trends established in earlier patterns of urbanization. Cities are still centers of power, competition, and ethnic and class conflict. Industrial cities intensified the relationships between economic class, social status, and power. After the Industrial Revolution, the basic source of wealth was transferred from land to manufacturing, mining, finance, commerce, and other potential sources of profit. However, since industrialization was developed in a free enterprise, capitalist economy, this wealth continued to be concentrated in a few hands, much as land had been earlier. Industrialization promoted the growth of a middle class, which, however, never controlled the basic means of production but found economic niches in petty business and trade and expanding professional and clerical white-collar occupations. Industrialization was responsible for the growth of an urban proletariat, employed first in factories and later in the expanding service occupations which catered to the needs of urban residents.

Gutman's article on the "Industrial Invasion of the Village Green" documents the resistance to factory owners in the nineteenth-century American mill towns of the East. The resistance stemmed not just from workers, but from older ruling groups—local politicians and nonindustrial property owners who resented the new, hard-cutting competitive wages of the industrialists and often backed workers in their demand for higher wages and better working conditions.

As Gutman points out, the degree of local autonomy enjoyed by these mill towns enabled the resistance to new industrialists to be successful, if only temporarily. The resistance by the older nonindustrial ruling groups can be interpreted as a vain attempt to protect this autonomy since many foresaw that industrialization would necessitate the forging of new political and economic links across community boundaries and the loss of local community control. The nature of the industrial productive process demands a wider scale of operation, involving not only larger sources of capital and labor, but more extensive financing, marketing, etc.

As the scale of industrialism grew in the United States in the early twentieth century, attempts were made to curb this monopolistic trend of big business by antitrust legislation and the institution of such redistributive measures as a progressive income tax. However, this did not prevent the growth of "monopoly capitalism," as the new industrial giants of the twentieth century came to be known. Whitt's article on "Californians, Cars and Technological Death" demonstrates the impotence of ordinary citizens and consumers against these powerful, organized and well-financed vested interests in the defeat of Proposition 18 in California, a measure designed to alleviate pollution and create additional funds for mass transit. Opposition to Proposition 18 came especially from an interlocking directorate of oil, automobile, and banking interests, which launched a vigorous and well-publicized campaign against the amendment. Though pollution could not force us to reduce wanton use of the private automobile, the energy crisis may. Till now, however, the result of the energy crisis has been rapidly rising profits for oil corporations and the relaxation of pollution standards to "conserve" energy. As usual, it is the consumer who suffers.

Industrialism signified not merely a change in the economic structure of the United States, but in its political forces as well. The growth of "big business" necessitated the growth of "big government" to cope with the

6

increasing complexity and scale of the American economy and society. The struggle for local autonomy was fought not only at the community level but by states and cities as well. In the period following the Civil War, the federal government became increasingly powerful through new legislation, federal agencies, Supreme Court decisions, etc. The authority of the federal government was reinforced by the increasing dependence of states, cities, and local communities on financial aid from the federal government to cope with mounting social welfare and other public expenditures.

Greer's article on "The 'Liberation' of Gary, Indiana," demonstrates how cities are caught in a vise between business and government which severely limits their alternatives and freedom of action. Gary, Indiana, the home of U.S. Steel, is the largest of all company towns in the United States and virtually the entire business community is a "de facto fief of the corporation." Local government was weak, corrupt, and highly fragmented, without adequate legal and financial authority to carry out municipal functions. Racism was evident both in the corporation's employment practices and in the grossly inadequate public services provided to the black community, which eventually grew to a majority of the population. On the basis of these grievances, Hatcher was able to develop a black united front and to be elected Gary's first black mayor. However, the apparent victory of blacks was short-lived, for Hatcher and his staff found themselves dependent on an old, largely white bureaucracy, which balked at many of his reforms, and on federal aid to carry out many of the social welfare programs he had promised. The regulations involving federal aid reduced even further Hatcher's freedom to respond to the needs of the black community.

Reforms carried out in the name of good government often tend to undermine even further the attempts by blacks and other low-income groups to establish a local power base in their own communities. Metro-government, for example, certainly appears rational and progressive in view of the need for cities to expand their tax base and to consolidate the provision of public services such as transportation, water, electricity, etc. However, as Sloan and French demonstrate in their article "Black Rule in the Urban South?" the move to consolidate the inner city with the surrounding suburbs, as in Jacksonville, is often a calculated strategy on the part of the white community to curb black attempts at gaining some measure of political power and community control. Actually, as Sloan and French point out, most black leaders in Jacksonville supported consolidation, which was approved by a "healthy majority" of black voters, since the gains in terms of a widened tax base and representation on the new community council were seen to outweigh the disadvantages in terms of a weakening of black control. By this time blacks realized that to control a bankrupt inner city with a diminishing tax base and an increasing tax burden represented a hollow victory.

Newark represents probably the most severe case of economic bankruptcy with its high incidence of deteriorated and abandoned housing, rising welfare rolls, and fleeing industry. As Conforti writes in his article, Newark "symbolizes all that is wrong with cities in America." His historical documentation of Newark's steady decline parallels those of many other old American industrial cities, particularly in the Northeast. In contrast to Suttles, who limits his analysis of interethnic relationships to the slum community of Chicago, Conforti describes how the ethnic pecking order of Newark affects the entire city, with blacks and Italians vying for control of the construction industry, poverty programs, political posts, etc. "There continues to be a scramble for the spoils, and the spoils continue to diminish." This continued even after the election of Kenneth Gibson as the city's first black mayor and according to Conforti, Gibson may well find himself heading the "first major urban welfare reservation in the United States."

Thus, the problems of American cities have been intensified by industrialization and the growth of giant corporations and the bureaucratic state. Cities have been the arena in which the contest between public gain and private interest has been most bitterly fought. This has engendered racism, poverty, ethnic and class conflict, and an increasing sense of powerlessness, particularly on the part of the poor, blacks, and other racial minorities.

Suttles, in his description of an ethnically heterogeneous slum neighborhood in "Anatomy of a Chicago Slum," suggests ways in which this competition and conflict among the poor may be reduced. Apparently, in older established urban neighborhoods, where each ethnic group has found its ecological niche, extending the gamut of residences, stores, churches, clubs, etc., tensions and potential conflict among ethnic groups are reduced. However, as we know from many other studies, (e.g., Gans' *The Urban Villagers*), these older neighborhoods are being systematically destroyed, either through urban renewal or the invasion of new ethnic groups which upset the delicate ecological balance.

What, then, is the solution to the social and physical deterioration of our cities? Must we abandon the city, as so many of the white middle class have done, and attempt to develop a new life-style in the suburbs, free of congestion, noise, violence, and the other ills commonly associated with the city? Clearly suburbanization, since it is an alternative open only to mobile élites, only intensifies the structural inequalities in our society and reinforces the isolation of the urban poor into "dark ghettos."

The solution to the problem of American cities lies not in the abandonment of the inner city and the flight to the suburbs, nor even in more novel approaches such as the construction of new towns or metro-government. New planned communities tend to replicate segregated suburban patterns, both in terms of race and class, as the experiments in Columbia, Maryland and Reston, Virginia demonstrate. Blacks are now constructing their own new town in Soul City, North Carolina with aid from the federal government. However, the ability of these new towns to attract industry and other sources of taxation and employment is questionable, and they may therefore be reduced to residential suburbs, still dependent on outside sources of employment.

Urban planning in the United States has concentrated upon measures which will take people out of the city—new towns, suburbs, highways, outlying industrial zones, branch stores, and shopping centers. We have abandoned the inner city to the blacks and the poor, and to the commercial interests that need to remain at the core, such as banks, insurance companies, and corporate headquarters. In an effort to retain this business, higher priority is assigned to downtown civic centers and shopping malls than to low-income housing, better schools, or more parks and recreation facilities. We consistently favor private gain above the general public welfare, on the theory that the profits from increased private investment will eventually trickle down and benefit all.

We are not advocating that all public money be spent on social goals, but certainly a better balance could be struck between the needs of the people and those of private business. We also need to give the people who live in the inner city a greater voice in city governance, not just through elections or public hearing, but through meaningful community control and government decentralization. Citizen interest in the recent experiment in little city halls through the Office of Neighborhood Government in New York City suggests that we are not dealing with a totally apathetic public, as many would have us believe. On the contrary, the bitter struggle fought by blacks and Puerto Ricans for school decentralization in New York City indicates their desire to obtain greater control over their own institutions. Community control increases citizen sense of self-esteem and self-confidence as they become active participants in the political process. Community control and greater citizen participation would also assure the expression of a greater diversity of interests among different ethnic and racial groups, classes, and ages. We need special programs designed for a variety of needs, not an abstractly defined public interest. To design such programs, these community boards must have real fiscal control and not simply serve in an advisory capacity.

So far these experiments in community control have not been very successful because they face the entrenched opposition of powerful bureaucracies, political parties, real estate interests, as well as factionalism within the community. Community control is not an easy way out as the difficulties of "maximum feasible participation" under OEO pointed out. However, it could help considerably to politicize the urban population and make neighborhood groups aware of the issues affecting them. Community boards could serve as a powerful counter-group to the vested interests now controlling our cities.

HERBERT G. GUTMAN

Industrial Invasion of the Village Green

Apart from the dislocations of the Civil War, the economic and social history of the United States in the second half of the last century—both the glory and the agony—is in large part the histories of the booming and changing industrial cities.

No place felt the radical and far-reaching effects of the post-1850 industrial boom more than the mill towns of the East. Peaceful villages, proud of their green spaces and leisurely ways, saw great factories and towering smokestacks rise to dominate their skylines and atmospheres in a few short years. Their populations often doubled and even tripled in a single decade as propertyless workers, many of them immigrants, jammed together in what soon became tenements, slums, and shacks. Their economies came under the domination of hard-driving manufacturers, many from out of town, who were used to playing rough with competition and opposition and were careless or contemptuous of the old ways.

Historians—conservative or liberal, the chroniclers of business as well as of labor and the city—exhibit rare agreement about what life in those mill towns was like. From the *start,* they imply, the industrialists had the social and political power and prestige to match their economic force, and controlled the towns. Local politics zigged and zagged according to their interests. Other property owners—especially small businessmen and professionals—identified with them, applauded their innovations and successes, and made common cause; and the factory workers almost inevitably found themselves totally alienated from the general community, practically helpless before their all-powerful employers. Stated in another fashion, from the beginning there existed a close relationship between economic class, social status, and power, and that control over "things"—most especially industrial property and machinery—was transformed quickly and with relative ease into legitimate authority so that industrialists could do little wrong.

This picture is distorted. These historians have accepted much too uncritically a misleading generalization. They have made too much of the early New England textile towns as later "models" or have drawn inaccurate parallels with large cities. As a result they have tended to bypass the actual histories of the mill towns they describe. Detailed study of the history of almost any victorian American mill town reveals these errors.

Throughout their early years for at least a generation the large impersonal corporations, the new factories with their new methods, and the wage earners, remained unusual and even alien elements in the industrial town. They disrupted tradition, challenged the accepted and respected modes of thought, and threatened the old ruling groups. How then could the mill owners *from the first* have dominated the social and political structures?

Conservatism is not always automatic obeisance to wealth; it is more often resistance to change and challenge. The industrialists had great economic power and influence over *things;* but in my studies I have found that often they

"Mill town economies came under the domination of hard-driving manufacturers who were used to playing rough with competition and opposition and were careless or contemptuous of the old ways." (Officers, Dexter, Lambert & Co., Paterson, New Jersey.)

could not even control the public decisions and judgments that directly affected their own economic welfare. The non-industrial property owners often opposed them; they did not dominate the government; and the professional groups and middle-classes frequently criticized them and rejected their leadership. Even the apparently resourceless workers were able to find friends and support where their employers could not, in spite of the lack of strong unions.

Take as an example the industrial city of Paterson, New Jersey, with its highly suggestive official motto, *Spe et*

"Paterson was regarded by New Yorkers, only fourteen miles away, as an 'up-country hamlet, chiefly noted for fine waterfall and valuable waterpower.' "

Labore (With Hope and Labor). Its development provides clear examples of the early, frustrated search for status and unchallenged authority by big mill and factory owners.

THE SILKEN THREAD OF POWER

The history of an industrial town can often be divided into two almost distinct stories: what happened in the more isolated village before the large factories came, and what happened after. Until 1850 Paterson's growth was fitful and relatively slow, its industry (mostly cotton textiles) not very efficient. As late as 1838 it was regarded by New Yorkers, only fourteen miles away, as an "up-country hamlet, chiefly noted for its fine waterfall and valuable waterpower."

But its closeness to a market and to a port, that "valuable waterpower," and the skilled machinists and machine shops that the cotton mills had attracted, made it very attractive to industry in the booming years before, during, and just after the Civil War.

By the early 1870's Paterson was a major American industrial city, producing one-fourth of the nation's locomotives, and much of the ironwork used in the great public buildings and bridges in New York and Pennsylvania. It led the country in silk textile production, and its jute, flax, and mosquito net mills were the largest of their kinds in the nation. Since most of these mills were founded after 1850 and the others had had their greatest growth in the same period, the older inhabitants of Paterson saw a new city they hardly recognized spring up around them between 1850 and 1870. The first locomotive shop was founded in 1836; by 1873 three large locomotive works employed 3000 men. A machine shop which had ten workers in 1845 employed 1100 in 1873. The textile factories, taking advantage of the water power, cheap mills, and help left behind by the declining cotton industry, rose even faster. In 1860 four silk mills employed 590 workers; just sixteen years later fourteen silk factories employed 8000.

Although small spinning and weaving shops started in the 1840's, the great stimulus to the textile industry came from outside the city in the 1860's when New York and Boston textile manufacturers and importers moved their mills to Paterson or built new ones there. A Coventry Englishman brought his silk mill from New York in 1860. Two years later, the nation's leading importer of tailor trimmings moved there from Boston. In 1868, a great New York silk importer came to Paterson. Eighty-one years after its founding in Northern Ireland, Barbour Brothers opened a linen factory that quickly became one of Paterson's great mills. From the start, these men of wealth constructed large mills, introduced power machinery, and made other significant innovations. One even imported an entire English factory. A new industrial leadership alien to the older city, these men represented a power unknown in earlier years. And they transformed the city.

In 1846 Paterson had 11,000 inhabitants; by 1870 it had 33,000. More than a third of these—a group larger than the whole 1846 population—were European immigrants, including skilled silk workers from France, Germany, and England. Large numbers of unskilled Irish laborers came, too. The booming city offered employment to whole families. Iron factories hired only men, and textile mills relied mainly on female and child labor. Two-thirds of the silk workers in 1876 were women, and one of every four workers under 16 years of age. Small business also prospered: from 1859 to 1870 the number of grocers more than doubled, and saloonkeepers increased from 46 to 270.

The social dislocations were severe, but prosperity was general—until the depression of 1873-1878.

The decline then was almost as extreme as the rise had been. The economy was crippled. "Among all classes (in 1873) there is a feeling of gloom and intense anxiety in regard to the future." In three years these fears had been realized, and a silk worker reported that "Paterson is in a deplorable condition." The production of locomotives fell off by five-sixths. Wages paid locomotive workers in 1873 amounted to $1,850,000; by 1877 they had fallen to $165,000. The unemployed overtaxed all available charities and even paraded in the streets demanding public works. In 1876 a *New York Sun* reporter called Paterson an industrial ghost town, and compared it to a Southern city after Lee's surrender.

Generally, historians contend that the depression of 1873-78, because of the great suffering and insecurity it caused, broke the back of labor's independence and immeasurably strengthened employers. Again, this narrow economic interpretation ignores the total reality. The workers were not the only ones put to the test. The city government, the middle class, and the older inhabitants also faced grave problems. So did the new industrialists. Trying to meet the economic crises resulting from declining markets, declining profits, and strikes, they needed support and help at critical times from the community and its leaders. Did they always get it?

Four conflicts involving the mill owners occurred between 1877 and 1880—two textile strikes and two libel suits against a newspaper editor. They tell the story pretty well. They reveal much about the actual prestige and political influence the owners had at that time.

Revolt of the Ribbon Weavers

In June of 1877, immigrant silk-ribbon weavers struck because of a 20 percent wage cut and an irksome contract. At its height the strike was Patterson's largest up to then: it idled 2000 workers and closed down the mills.

The workers had no union to speak of; they had endured forty-four months of depression. They showed great staying power, but in practical economic terms they had very little to bargain with. Yet after ten weeks the employers accepted a compromise which rescinded the wage cut and ended the strike. Why?

Local people refused to give their approval and support to the mill owners. Elected city officials either supported the strikers, or, even more significantly, refused to bow to pressures and "commands" from owners.

A few examples: small shopkeepers gave credit and raised money for the strikers; the daily newspapers, though critical of the strikers too, urged the employers to use "conscience as well as capital." The courts remained independent. Weavers on trial for disorderly conduct went free or received small fines. When a manufacturer successfully prosecuted two weavers for violating contracts, city officials, including the mayor, persuaded a local judge to postpone forty similar trials indefinitely.

Republican Mayor Benjamin Buckley and the Democratic-controlled board of aldermen gave the manufacturers their greatest trouble. The aldermen were mostly self-made men: skilled workmen of independent means, retail shopkeepers, and professionals, their number included neither factory workers nor large manufacturers. Mayor Buckley personified the pre-corporate American dream. Born in England in 1808, he had come to Paterson as a young man, worked first in a cotton factory, and then achieved much. By 1877, he owned a small spindle factory, headed a local bank, and thrived in Republican politics, serving several terms in the state legislature before winning the 1875 mayoralty election.

Buckley believed his primary duty was to maintain order, and he used his small police force with great skill and tact, but only to stop open conflict. He would not suppress the strikers or their leaders. This infuriated the industrialists, who insisted that the mayor's inaction allowed a few agitators to dominate hundreds of workers. The Paterson Board of Trade, controlled by the largest mill owners, charged

"Paterson produced one-fourth of the nation's locomotives and much ironwork used in the great public buildings and bridges in New York and Pennsylvania."

that "the laws of the land are treated with contempt and trampled upon by a despotic mob" led by immigrant radicals and "Communists." (This in 1877.) They tried to pressure the city authorities to enlarge the police force and declare a state of emergency that would severely hamper the strikers. A manufacturer warned that unless the authorities put down these troublemakers, the city would be left "with nothing . . . but the insignificant industries of an unimportant town." One urged that strike leaders be "taken out and shot"; another offered to finance a private militia.

Mayor Buckley refused all these demands. He charged that the Board of Trade did "great injury to the credit of the city," and commended "the good sense of the working people." All elected city officials, Republican and Democratic, were property owners, but they remained independent, and rejected the claim that the Board of Trade was "best able to judge what the city needed to protect it." The Democratic-controlled Board of Aldermen unanimously commended Republican Mayor Buckley's "wise and judicious course" and added insult to injury by passing a resolution urging immediate prosecution of mill owners who violated local fire-escape ordinances. No wonder iron manufacturer Watts Cooke lamented: "All the classes of the community are coming to lean towards and sympathize with the men rather than the employers."

After the strike the manufacturers turned away from politics and raised a private militia. The Board of Trade listened approvingly to a member who found "more virtue in one well-drilled soldier than in ten policemen, or in one bullet than in ten clubs in putting down a riot." Money was quickly collected and 120 militiamen quickly recruited. But for ten years after the strike the ratio of *policemen* to population remained the same. Clearly it was easier to get up money for a private militia than to "reform" the stubborn city government. And the fact that the mill owners were forced to raise this militia was a measure of their local weakness, not of their strength.

The Adams Company Strike

A year after the ribbon weaver's strike was settled, 550 more unorganized textile workers, mostly women and children, reacted to their third wage cut in a year by striking the factories of Robert and Henry Adams, the largest manufacturers of mosquito netting in the country.

More unequal adversaries could hardly be imagined. The Adams brothers had brought a small factory from New York in 1857, and in twenty years had added several large and efficient mills to it, so that by 1878 they were practically dominating their industry, exporting huge quantities of mosquito netting to Africa and Asia. Yet after a strike of nine months, they conceded defeat. The senior partner, Robert Adams, bitterly quit the firm and left Paterson.

It was he, not the strikers, who had fought the lonely and friendless battle. No one publicly protested his repeated threats to move the mills. The press stayed neutral. With only one exception, he got no encouragement from other manufacturers, retail businessmen, or professionals. He even was forced to fire some of his own foremen for defending the strikers.

On the other hand, strikers received much support. Some took jobs in other mills. Strike funds were collected from other workers—and especially from shopkeepers and merchants. Concerts and picnics were given in their honor and to their benefit. Street demonstrations supported them; more than one-eighth of all Patersonians signed petitions attacking the Adams brothers.

"Two-thirds of the silk workers in 1876 were women, and one of every four workers was under sixteen years of age."

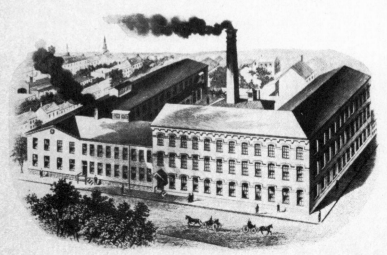

An outspoken Irish Socialist, Joseph P. McDonnell, came to Paterson from New York to support the strikers and to successfully organize them. He found a socialist weekly, the Paterson *Labor Standard*. The front pages quoted Karl Marx, and called Robert Adams "Lucifer" and his mills "a penitentiary." But the back pages carried advertisements from forty-five retail enterprises, which kept it going.

When Adams recruited new workers from nearby towns, they were met at the rail depot or in the streets by as many as 2000 strikers and sympathizers, and persuaded to go back. The strikers had full use of the streets. The city authorities arrested a few workers when tempers flared, but quickly released them and did not restrain them so long as they stayed peaceful. By carefully discriminating between peaceful coercion and "violence," the authorities effectively (even if unintentionally) strengthened the strikers. Adams had only his firm's money with which to fight, and it was limited. His power was checked, his impotence revealed, and he was forced to surrender and leave the city.

The Libel Trials—I

Socialist Joseph P. McDonnell, though only thirty-two years old when he came to Paterson, already had a long and active career in political agitation. He had edited Irish nationalist newspapers, engaged in Fenian "conspiracies," represented Ireland at the 1872 Hague Congress of the First International (siding with the Marxists), helped organize several huge London labor demonstrations and served four prison terms before coming to the United States. In this country he indignantly exposed the steerage conditions of his passage, edited a New York Socialist weekly, and traveled the East denouncing capitalism and organizing weak Socialist-led trade unions. According to the usual historical stereotypes, he should have been a pariah to almost all Patersonians and easy game for his opponents. But even though he did have trouble and went to prison, he and his newspaper nevertheless soon won acceptance and popularity.

His legal difficulties started with the first issue of the *Labor Standard* and lasted for eighteen months. He called some loyal Adams workers "scabs"; they filed a formal complaint and he was indicted, convicted, and fined $500 and costs. He narrowly averted a second libel indictment a few months later. But in the fall of 1879 he was indicted again, this time for publishing a bitter letter by a brickyard worker, denouncing working and living conditions in a Passaic River brickyard. Both he and the worker were found guilty and sent to the Passic County Jail for three months.

Did these convictions illustrate the power of "capital" and the supineness of judges before it? Not entirely, if at all.

At his first trial McDonnell was still a newcomer and radical and controversial; nevertheless his lawyer was an old Patersonian, wealthy in real estate, father of the state's first ten-hour law and important banking reforms, organizer of the city's waterworks, and a prominent Republican for twenty years before standing as Greenback candidate for New Jersey governor. Predictably, the prosecutor castigated McDonnell as a "woman libeler," a threat to established order, and a "foreign emissary" sent by English manufactures to "breed discontent" in America. Nevertheless, the jury stayed deadlocked for three days and nights and only unusual pressure from the judge brought in a conviction. Even then, another judge, himself originally a Lancashire worker and then the owner of a small bobbin pin factory, convinced the presiding judge to go easy, and the $500 fine was a great deal less than the $2000 and two years in prison that could have been assessed.

Workers crowded the courtroom to cheer McDonnell, and after conviction quickly raised the fine and costs, hoisted their hero aloft, and carried him triumphantly through the streets. Storekeepers and merchants contributed handsomely to a defense fund. The trial occurred during the bitter 1878 Congressional election, and the prosecutor suddenly found himself surrounded by hostile voters. Workers, supported by sympathetic shopkeepers, jammed the Democratic meetings, and demonstrated against him or walked out when he tried to speak. Politicians got the point. A Republican argued that only free speech and a free press could preserve American liberty. The Democrats defended the right to strike and one declaimed: "Away with the government of the aristocracy! Away with legislators only from the wealthy classes! We have had enough of them!" A nearby non-Socialist newspaper concluded: "In Paterson he (McDonnell) is stronger than his accusers. Today he has the sympathy of the people."

The Libel Trials—II

The second trial—and the imprisonment—were, paradoxically, even greater triumphs for McDonnell. Outside the courtroom, no one publicly attacked him. The decision was severely criticized. The judge justified the prison sentence only because he felt that a fine would, again, be paid by others. McDonnell's support was overwhelming and bipartisan. His lawyers were the son of a former Democratic mayor, and Socrates Tuttle, Paterson's most respected attorney and Republican ex-Mayor. Tuttle called the trial an attack on a free press and on the right of workers to protest. Two former silk factory foremen, one German and the other English, led McDonnell's sympathizers and got help from a Baptist and a Methodist clergyman, the latter active in Republican politics and Paterson's most popular preacher. Several aldermen, former aldermen, and county freeholders visited him in prison. Even a nephew of Robert Adams, McDonnell's 1878 adversary, gave the Socialist $20 and visited him in jail. Garrett A. Hobart, a rising corporation lawyer, president of the New Jersey State Senate and chairman of the Republican State Committee, (later to be Vice President of the United States), sent ten dollars for McDonnell's defense, offered "to do his best," and tried to get the state libel law changed. (During the 1896 national election, McDonnell's paper still carried Karl Marx's

THE ATTEMPT TO CRUSH LABOR.

The Memorable Blood-Money Bill.

"Joseph McDonnell, with a long career in political agitation, edited his newspaper and organized a national campaign of protest from his prison cell."

words on its masthead. Though a strong foe of McKinley conservatism, the *Labor Standard* said of Hobart: "a rare specimen of manhood in the class in which he moves . . . to know him is to like him whether you agree with his opinions or not.")

McDonnell's jail experience is one of the most unusual in American penal history. Warden Buckley, the former mayor's son, did his best to assure the comfort and freedom for his guest. McDonnell edited his newspaper and organized a national campaign of protest from his cell. He received his visitors (and their children) daily in the warden's office—one day he entertained twenty-one visitors. His meals came from outside the jail, and saloon and boarding house keepers overstocked him with cigars, wines, and liquors. Others brought fresh fruit, cakes, and puddings. Shamrocks came on St. Patrick's Day, and two fancy dinners on his birthday. Released ten days early, McDonnell had the warden's personal commendation for good behavior.

On his release, 15,000 persons greeted him in Paterson's greatest demonstration. He went on to found the New Jersey Federation of Trades and Labor Unions in 1883, and to push for protective labor legislation. Less than six years after coming to Paterson, and four years after release from prison, a Democratic governor appointed him New Jersey's first Deputy Inspector of Factories and Workshops. The prosecutor who had convicted him advertised his legal services in McDonnell's paper; the City of Paterson brought space for its official announcements. The paper survived and prospered until his death in 1908.

A NATIONAL PATTERN

Was this general pattern of events confined to Paterson? Not at all. It was, instead, typical of the history of many factory towns during that period. The examples are common: the merchant mayor of an Illinois mining town disarmed Pinkerton police imported to guard an operator's properties; Ohio Valley newspapers condemned iron manufacturers for arming strikebreakers; northern Pennsylvania merchants housed striking, evicted coal miners.

The pattern had recognizable and common elements. Poorly organized and unorganized workers displayed surprising staying power and received much sympathy from non-workers. Local politicians often rejected or at least modified pressures from industrialists. Most surprising, and most significant, were the attitudes of the non-industrial property owners. They enjoyed "traditional" prestige and power; they believed in competitive free enterprise and used it for their own enrichment; nevertheless they responded equivocally or critically to the practices of the new industrialists.

How can these facts, so contrary to the usual historical interpretations, be explained? First, we must rid ourselves of some misconceptions. One, that the new industrialist and his power achieved standing and acceptance quickly and easily in the local communities; in most cases they did not. Two, that all urban property owners share common attitudes, interests, and prejudices. Grocers—or even local bankers—are not the same as factory owners. Because Andrew Carnegie applauded Herbert Spencer, it does not mean that all urban property owners cheered along, too. Three, we cannot equate the patterns in mill towns with those occurring in large cities, states, or even the nation. Congress gave huge land grants to railroads and state governors frequently supplied militia to "settle" strikes; but paradoxically, it does not necessarily follow that mill owners commanded equivalent power and prestige in their own towns.

What then is the explanation?

■ It must be emphasized again that in nineteenth century America power and standing had meaning almost entirely within a given community—at least as far as that community was concerned. The new industrialist—especially if he came from elsewhere—was an outsider and a disruptive one. He found a more or less static city which thrived on small and personal workshops and an intimate and personal way of life. It was not ideal, but it was settled and familiar. He brought in radical new ways of making things and using people. Where he violated community traditions or made extreme or new demands—such as the special use of a police force or the suppression of a newspaper—he often provoked opposition.

■ In the smaller towns change—and power—were more visible and vulnerable than in the large, complex cities.

Since relationships tended to be personal, the middle class and the older residents could themselves see and understand what was happening to the town and the workers instead of accepting second-hand information through the opaque filter of *laissez-faire* economic thought or pseudo-Darwinian ideology.

■ In the factory town, the worker had more economic and political power than in the metropolis. A larger percentage of grocers, saloon-keepers, and other shopkeepers depended on him and knew it; his vote meant much more in Paterson than it would have in New York, and the politicians knew that, too.

■ Strangely, the rapid growth of the mill town, which the industrialists had themselves brought about, weakened their chances for civic and police control. A number of studies of the mobility patterns of Paterson men show that the more ambitious and able workers found expanding opportunities outside the factories in small retail business, politics, and the police force—the very areas in which the industrialists demanded cooperation or control. Conservative in many ways, these men had a "stake" in the new society. But they still had memories, roots, and relatives among the workers. They had, in fact, often suffered from the same employers they were now called on to protect. During strikes and other crises the industrialists could not expect unswerving loyalty or approval from them; nor did they get it.

Wealth does talk; and eventually it will be heard. The factories and their owners dug deeper and deeper into the lives of the mill towns and became more and more accepted and powerful. Yesterday's innovators became today's watchdogs of tradition. The old middle class, and those who remembered and revered the old, pre-corporate towns, lost influence and died off; they were replaced by others closer to the corporate image. The city governments became more bureaucratic, less responsive to "popular" pressures.

But the notion that the 19th century factory owners moved into overnight control of the industrial towns is a myth that must be discarded in order to understand the real nature of these twentieth century changes.

FURTHER READING

Sister Carrie by Theodore Dreiser (New York: Holt, Rinehart and Winston, 1957). One of Dreiser's best novels based in Chicago during a period of especially rapid growth.

We Shall Be All: A History of the Industrial Workers of the World by Melvyn Dubofsky (New York: Chicago: Quadrangle, 1969). An outstanding history of a nineteenth-century American labor movement whose leader, Big Bill Haywood, led a textile strike in Paterson, New Jersey.

The Jungle by Upton Sinclair (New York: New American Library, 1964). The trials and radicalization of an immigrant in Chicago.

Images of the American City by Anselm Strauss (New York: Free Press, 1961).

J. ALLEN WHITT

Californians, Cars and Technological Death

The freeways, like the vehicles that cruise them, are anything but free. The price in misallocation of resources, in deaths, in pollution and environmental disruption are enormous. These costs are social, borne not by auto manufacturers and motorists alone but by society at large. Since California is popularly held to be two years ahead of the rest of the country in social trends it is already in an advanced state of auto-addiction and is a logical proving ground for would-be social solutions to the auto problem.

Little wonder, then, that supporters of one such plan—a measure to fight auto pollution and improve mass transit—were confident that their proposal would be readily approved by the electorate. If anything, Proposition 18, as the measure was known, was felt by its supporters to be too modest an attempt at reform. It had but two provisions: that an unspecified amount of the revenue from gasoline taxes and license fees would go to control environmental pollution caused by motor vehicles; and that local voters could use up to 25 percent of their county's revenues for improving mass transit systems.

But the environmental groups and urban transit interests which supported Proposition 18 had badly misjudged the strength of the highway lobby; the measure never stood a chance. Proposition 18's author, Senator James Mills, later wrote that he was surprised that the bill got as far as the ballot. In fact, on the day it was due to come to a vote he left the Assembly early, "thinking the bill had died." Perhaps some assemblymen voted for Proposition 18 since they were certain it would fail anyway but felt that a token pro-ecology vote would be politically astute. Whatever the reason, Proposition 18 made it through the legislature and was scheduled to appear, just 11 weeks later, on the November 1970 ballot as a referendum. The life history of Proposition 18—certainly a small-scale attempt to mitigate certain of the social costs of the automobile transport system—can prepare us for the course of future contests between environmentalists and their economic and political enemies.

The Campaign

Proponents of the proposition formed an organization called Californians Against Smog. Aided by a $10,000 contribution from the Tuberculosis and Respiratory Disease Association of California (TARDAC) and with active support from the Sierra Club and other environmental groups, Californians Against Smog began to try to raise money for campaign expenses. Also allied with pro-18 groups was the Citizen's Transportation Committee in Los Angeles, which had succeeded in raising around $400,000 for a rapid transit campaign in 1968. CTC spokesman told Proposition 18 proponents: "You are a real army. Your foot soldiers should get the message to the grassroots. . . . You only need $200,000 this time. Eighteen's a good issue. That's all it'll take."

Meanwhile, opponents of Proposition 18 had established a group called Californians Against the Street and Road Tax Trap. Its purpose was to gather forces for a media blitz.

The contest which followed was replete with rhetoric, denunciations, protest, law suits, charges of prevarication and perfidy, and disillusionment.

Proponents of Proposition 18 argued that building more highways cannot solve traffic problems since new roads are overrun by autos as soon as they open, and that funds produced by the automobile should logically be used to control air pollution—also produced by the automobile. Citing studies which were said to show that "up to 87 percent of the travel on State highways terminates within the county of origin," they maintained that the state road system was basically a local transportation system. It followed that local voters should be able to determine the kind of local system of transport they desire. Earmarking of highway funds leads, they argued, to inflexibility and inequality of funding state projects. Under Proposition 18 benefits would also accrue to rural residents, because they would be able to use their 25 percent of highway revenues for the construction and maintenance of local roads, if they so voted. Federal matching funds for rapid transit would become available, easing the present burden of property taxes to pay for such transit. Proponents also argued that the availability of rapid transit facilities would help reduce traffic congestion on the freeways and would decrease air pollution.

Opponents of Proposition 18 countered that the "freeway master plan, adopted by the Legislature in 1959, is only about 36% developed to freeway standards and the remainder of that system may never be finished if highway gasoline tax money is used to finance rapid transit." Rapid transit, they said, is very expensive and will not be able to compete successfully with automobile transportation. Moreover, "it is unfair and economically unsound to impose a tax burden upon one form of transportation to finance another." The building of highways, they continued, is a very complex and long-range process. "The very nature of this type of program demands a predictable, steady, and assured source of revenue, making a special purpose fund and tax source highly desirable." Noting that highway funds were already available for the support of State Air Resources Board and air pollution research, they said that it was not necessary to amend the Constitution for this purpose. Final-

ly, they argued that by the time rapid transit systems could be built, "much will have been accomplished through engine and fuel modifications in the elimination of automobile air pollution."

Early in the campaign, various organizations and individuals went on record as being for or against Proposition 18. Governor Reagan was at first publicly opposed to the bill "because it would endanger the state highway system." Yet by election time, Reagan was *for* the amendment, saying that it gave the people the right to say how public funds should be spent. Reagan's opponent in the November election, Jesse Unruh, called the governor's stand "hypocritical," noting that oil companies had contributed more than $100,000 to Reagan's campaign, and drawing attention to Standard Oil of California's bad record as a polluter.

Declared opponents of Proposition 18 included the Automobile Club of Southern California, California State Automobile Association, the Teamsters Union, California Trucking Association, California State Chamber of Commerce, County Supervisors Association of California, Atlantic-Richfield Company, E.P. DuPont de Nemours & Company, Ethyl Corporation, Gulf Oil Corporation, Humble Oil & Refining Company, Mobil Oil Corporation, Phillips Petroleum Company, Standard Oil of California, Union Oil Company of California, California Taxpayers' Association, California State Employees Association, California Farm Bureau, California Real Estate Association, and the Property Owners' Tax Association of California.

To run their media campaign, opponents of Proposition 18 hired Milton Kramer, a political consultant from suburban Los Angeles who had waged a successful campaign a few months before against a ballot proposition that would have shifted education costs to the state.

Billboard Propaganda

During the second week in October, Kramer saturated the state with billboards reading "More taxes? No No. 18." The 700 billboards were placed to achieve a "100 percent showing"; that is, every person in the state should theoretically have seen such a billboard at least once before election time (except in those few counties, such as Santa Barbara, that ban billboards). The opponents argued that such slogans were justified since the state highway system was already behind schedule, revenues were inadequate to meet the need for highways, and any diversion of monies from the highway trust fund would have to be compensated for by an increase in taxes.

Proponents of 18 cried out in anguish against the contention that the amendment would raise taxes, pointing out that only a *diversion* of money was involved. As campaign rhetoric became more heated, nearly all of the major newspapers in the state announced support for Proposition 18. In endorsing 18, the *Sacramento Bee* said:

> This modest step is too much for the highway lobby, an aggregation of oil companies, cement firms, automobile clubs, truckers, contractors, and others with vested interests in restricting the use of gasoline tax revenue for highway purposes.

The *Los Angeles Times* called the opposition campaign by "powerful special interests" one of "deliberate confusion and misinformation" designed to deceive the voters.

Yet the media campaign was only one impediment that Proposition 18 supporters had to overcome. As organizations and individuals that proponents had counted on for support let them down, it became increasingly apparent during the month of October that their initial optimism was not justified. Californians Against Smog had counted on the aluminum industries to support Proposition 18 since they stood to profit from mass transit systems (Bay Area Rapid Transit, for example, is expected to use two million pounds of Alcoa aluminum) but they proved to be ambivalent towards the amendment since they also have big interests in highway construction and maintenance and in auto manufacture.

Money sources for the measure virtually dried up. Businessmen united with what one supporter of the proposition called "interlocking corporate good will" and spread the word that 18 was bad for business. Quasi-environmentalist organizations like the Los Angeles County Environmental Quality Control Committee voted not to support 18. The Los Angeles Chamber of Commerce did endorse 18, but weakly and very late in the campaign. The San Francisco Chamber of Commerce went on record against 18, though Mayor Joseph Alioto stated he was appalled at their position on an issue that would bring San Francisco between $72 and $90 million to aid the Municipal Railway "as well as fighting pollution." According to Sierra Club president Phillip Berry, the decision of the Chamber was the direct result of pressure from Standard Oil of California, an accusation which, says Berry, "Interestingly, Standard never denied. . . ."

Proponents of Proposition 18 also saw opposition voiced against their amendment in "unofficial" ways. The Freeway Support Committee of the State Chamber sponsored a six-page supplement which appeared in the *Los Angeles Times* one week before the election. Although the $14,000 supplement did not mention Proposition 18, thus qualifying for the lower "educational" rate rather than the "political" rate, the supplement eulogized the state highway system in pictures and text, and provided a card for registering reader approval. The chairman of the Freeway Support Committee was also president of the Automobile Club of Southern California.

Not unexpectedly, the auto club was opposed to Proposition 18, as was the California State Automobile Association (both affiliates of the American Automobile Association). It has been estimated that the club spends from $30,000 to $35,000 a year lobbying in Sacramento. The club magazines were another source of "unofficial" opposition to the measure. With a combined membership of approximately two and a half million, the clubs may have significantly influenced the final vote.

Most auto club members are concerned only with the road services that such associations offer, services that are generally of a high order. Member apathy is conducive to oligarchical control. Ralph Nader and other critics have charged that the American Automobile Association is not adequately meeting member needs and has extensive ties with the highway lobby. Local auto clubs are also big business. Many sell tires, batteries and automobile insurance. The California State Automobile Association, for example, reported that it wrote more than $120 million worth of insurance in 1970.

Supporters of Proposition 18 were severely hampered by their lack of campaign money. Endorsements by Sugar Ray Robinson, Carol Burnett and Jack Lemmon were taped, but there was too little money to buy time to broadcast them. Two full-time staff members had to be let go and the campaign ran on the efforts of 2,000 to 4,000 volunteers.

In contrast, opponents of 18 were well financed. Expenditures by both sides for their media campaigns have been estimated as follows:

	Opponents	Proponents
Billboards	$123,000	—
Television	60,000	$1,400
Newspaper	17,000	1,456
Radio	15,000	2,401
Total	$215,000	$5,257

The advantage of the opposition is even more overwhelming considering that these are the official expenses; not included is the "unofficial" assistance to the opposition campaign by the California State Chamber of Commerce in its mailings to local government officials, nor the newspaper supplement by the Freeway Support Committee, nor the articles against Proposition 18 which appeared in auto club publications. Moreover, there was an enormous organizational advantage on the side of opponents. As E.E.Schattschneider has observed:

> . . . businessmen collectively constitute the most class-conscious group in American society. As a class they are the most highly organized, more easily mobilized, have more facilities for communication, are more like-minded, and are more accustomed to stand together in defense of their privileges than any other group.

About four months before the campaign started, a

state-wide attitudinal survey found that 77 percent of California adults favored "spending some of that state gas money (i.e., that currently spent for highways) for smog or air pollution research." Only 17 percent expressed disapproval. About five months later, just before the billboards of the anti-18 forces were erected, the Field poll discovered that only about one in three voters in the state had heard of Proposition 18. However, when they were given a copy of the measure as it was to appear on the ballot, 64 percent said they would vote yes. Twenty-two percent were opposed. It looked as though 18 would pass. Another Field poll was taken a week before the election, after the measure had been more publicized. Still, only 57 percent had seen or heard about Proposition 18. The ballot statement was read to those who had not heard anything about the measure, and 56 percent of that group were in favor. Twelve percent were opposed. On the other hand, 53 percent of those who were previously aware of the issue said they would vote yes, while 29 percent said they would vote no. Among all voters, potential support for the amendment had declined to 52 percent, a drop of 12 percentage points in approximately one month. Since the main voices for and against the measure had been, up until that time, the major newspapers and the billboards, respectively, it must be assumed that the disingenuous message of the laconic billboards was having the greater influence.

During the last days of the campaign, anti-18 forces waged a weekly saturation campaign on television, newspapers and radio. These advertisements, supporters say, were filled with distortions. The central theme was that Proposition 18 would increase taxes. It was suggested that toll booths would appear on freeways if money were diverted from highways.

This ad campaign was as effective as it was misleading: although 52 percent of those surveyed had approved of Proposition 18 one week before the election, on November 3 the amendment was defeated by a vote of 2.7 million (45.9 percent) to 3.2 million (54.1 percent). Proposition 18 passed in only eight of the 58 counties.

Further indication of the last-minute success of the opposition campaign is revealed by the absentee ballots. By law absentee ballots in the state may be requested between seven and 29 days before the election. That means that such ballots could have been filled out as early as October 5, 1970, well before the media blitz at the end of the campaign. Absentee voting figures are available for 35 of the 58 counties, the rest having been combined with general election totals. The total absentee vote in the 35 counties was *favorable* to the measure: 90,148 (58.7 percent) versus 63,480 (41.3 percent). General election totals for the amendment in those counties were close to the statewide percentage (46.2 percent versus 45.9 percent). Assuming that these 35 counties are a representative sample, a comparison of the absentee vote with

the general election vote indicates a highly significant relationship between voting absentee and voting for Proposition 18. While we cannot be certain, of course, that other temporal factors were not at work here, there can be little doubt that the opposition media campaign was decisive in the defeat of Proposition 18.

Contributions

More precise identification of the proponents and opponents of Proposition 18 is contained in the campaign contribution reports filed with the secretary of state. It is not possible to determine just how accurate these reports may be, especially since none of them was verified under penalty of perjury as required by the California Elections Code, but they are at least *minimal* indices of the nature of the forces for and against the amendment.

According to these reports, opponents spent about 15 times as much as proponents ($335,445.69 versus $22,721.81). Total contributions for and against 18 were $348,830.00 and $17,714.20, respectively. It is obvious that money was overwhelmingly on the side of the opposition. Those who contributed $10,000 or more to oppose Proposition 18 were:

1.	Standard Oil of California	$75,000
2.	Shell Oil Company	50,000
3.	Mobil Oil	30,000
4.	Automobile Club of Southern California	22,000
5.	Gulf Oil	20,000
6.	Texaco	20,000
7.	Union Oil Company of California	20,000
8.	Sully Miller Company	15,000
9.	Phillips Oil	15,000
10.	Humble Oil and Refining Company	12,000
11.	California State Automobile Association	11,000
12.	Interinsurance Bureau, Los Angeles	10,000

By contrast, supporters of the amendment received only three contributions of more than $1,000. They were from two companies with mass transit interests, Kaiser Industries ($2,500) and Rohr Corporation ($2,000), and from the Citizens Transportation Committee ($3,345.98). The CTC money represented that group's working capital.

Opposition money came primarily from large contributions, while money for 18 came from small donations: the median contribution for the anti-18 campaign was $500; the median contribution for the pro-18 campaign was $5. More than three-fourths of the opposition money came from oil companies. Other anti-18 interests were (in order of contribution): automobile clubs and their insurance bureaus; highway equipment and construction companies; trucking and taxi companies; labor unions representing highway construction employees; forest products and land companies; tire and rubber companies; and individuals.

The full involvement of oil companies in the campaign had not been immediately apparent. The opposition's contribution report, filed about three weeks after the election, listed four "anonymous" donations totaling $95,000.

Kramer, the opposition's campaign manager, had wanted $600,000 with which to conduct a proper campaign. He complained that he did not have enough money for the final weekend media campaign he had been planning. The events of the last week before the election are described by the *Washington Post:*

> The way Kramer tells it, four unidentified cashiers' checks turned up at the committee's Los Angeles offices while he was away in Sacramento. . .the total—$95,000—was put toward a final weekend media blitz, including $60,000 in television spots. . . .

Secretary of State-elect Edmund G. Brown, Jr., decided to force the issue. He sent a letter to the District Attorney of Sacramento County, demanding that he

> . . .launch an immediate investigation and also inquire of each committee member (Californians Against the Street and Road Tax Trap) concerning his knowledge of these anonymous donations to determine whether there has been a violation of the Elections Code through failure to disclose the donors' true identity.

One week later, Mobil Oil Corporation admitted in a letter to Sullivan that it was one of the anonymous donors, its contribution of $30,000 having been made on October 28, five days before the election. The company said that it gave the money in good faith and never asked for anonymity.

When the next campaign expenditure report was filed near the end of December, the three remaining anonymous donations were listed: Anonymous—Mellon National Bank—cashier's check—$20,000.00; Anonymous—California Bank NA,SF—cashier's check—$25,000.00; Anonymous—California Bank NA,SF—cashier's check—$20,000.00.

Another month passed. On January 26, 1971, Brown filed suit in Los Angeles asking permission to subpoena bank records to determine the identities of the contributors. The next day, Gulf Oil confessed that it had given $20,000 to oppose 18. Brown observed, "A Gulf spokesman says the company never requested anonymity, but I am highly suspicious of the circumstances surrounding this matter."

One day later, Standard Oil of California, a company which had already contributed $30,000, admitted that the two remaining anonymous contributions of $20,000 and $25,000 were its own. Standard's story was much like that of Mobil and Gulf. A spokesman said, "There never was any intention on our part to conceal the contribution. It was the responsibility of the campaign organization to make the report, not us."

After these disclosures, Brown continued with his civil suit. The suit asked a $1,000 penalty from each defendant: Standard, Mobil, Gulf, Kramer, Californians Against the Street and Road Tax Trap, and two of its officers. The Sacramento County district attorney had rejected Brown's demand for an investigation. Moreover, the Sacramento County grand jury indicated little interest in the case. A Los Angeles Superior Court judge ruled that Brown's suit was unconstitutional: the election code laws requiring the disclosure of contributions to defeat or pass ballot measures were discriminatory because such requirements were not placed upon donors to the campaigns of individual candidates. Brown persisted. The State Supreme Court overturned the lower court ruling and authorized a continuation of the suit. On January 30, 1972, Brown announced a settlement with one of the defendants. Gulf Oil Corporation agreed to donate $25,000 to the Air Pollution Research Center at the University of California, Riverside.

Oil's Role

There can be little doubt that oil companies played a major part in the defeat of Proposition 18. Their contributions were apparently coordinated by the Western Oil and Gas Association (WOGA). Harry Morrison, general manager of WOGA, says that some oil companies asked him what their "fair share" of contributions against Proposition 18 would be. He maintains he asked the campaign manager how much the anti-18 campaign would need. Kramer told him between $600,000 and $1.25 million. Morrison says that he then calculated that contributions from oil companies totaling $175,000 (the actual oil contributions amounted to $240,000) would be appropriate, "if they were going to give." The sum was apportioned among the various companies on the basis of their "gallonage" sold in California.

When asked why oil companies such as Sun Oil (headquartered in Philadelphia and having no service stations in California) and Standard of Indiana saw fit to donate money to oppose 18, Morrison responded that the oil industry saw the campaign as a very important one. If diversion of gas taxes could happen in California, it "could happen anywhere." A spokesman for an oil company that requested anonymity agreed with Morrison's interpretation: he called the issue a "bellwether nationally" as far as oil companies were concerned.

Even so, one major oil company doing business in California, Atlantic-Richfield, did not (apparently) contribute money to the opposition campaign. ARCO is not listed on the contribution lists although the company was reported early in the campaign to be opposed to Proposition 18. This was confirmed after the election by a company spokesman. An oil company executive later admitted that "not all companies wanted to go along," fearing a bad press. The *Los Angeles Times* quotes one

Californians, Cars and Technological Death

21

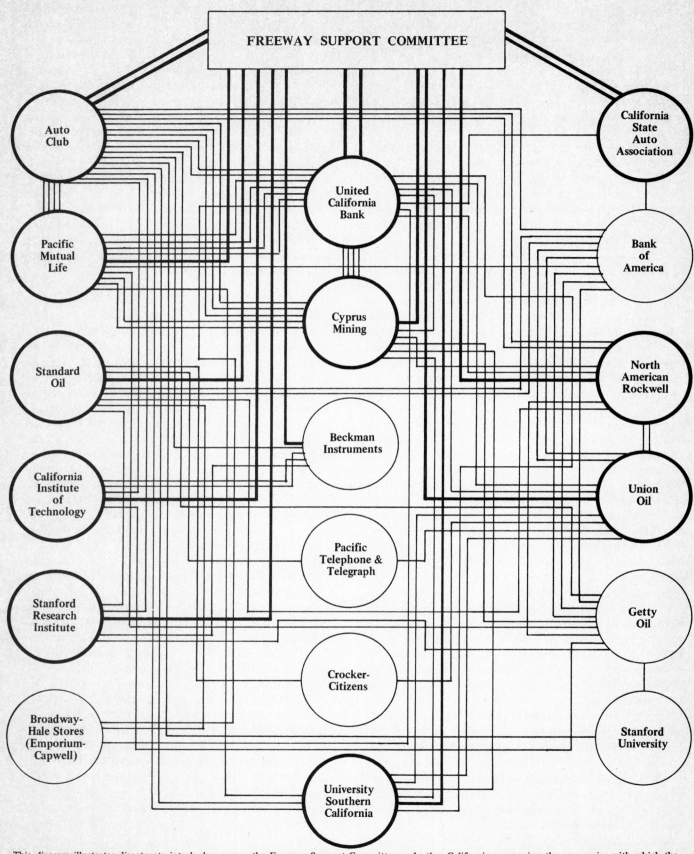

This diagram illustrates directorate interlocks among: the Freeway Support Committee and other California companies; the companies with which the Freeway Support Committee was linked; and several miscellaneous firms, associations and universities. Each line represents one director.

Source: *Poor's Register of Corporations, Directors and Executives* (1970, 1971); *Moody's Industrial Manual* (1970, 1971); *Moody's Banking and Finance Manual* (1971); *Dun & Bradstreet Million Dollar Directory* (1971); corporation files from the office of the California Secretary of State.

Asking people to vote against the pollution initiative is like asking them to vote against motherhood. . . .only *after* people have been personally hurt by loss of jobs, by increased prices and shortages of food and fiber, and by disease epidemics, will its folly become apparent. . . .If they are informed of the facts. . . .the people of California can distinguish between motherhood and suicide. If the issues are understood, the people of California will vote NO on the pollution initiative.

from an anti-18 campaign booklet

source in the oil industry as saying:

Some of us . . . wanted to stay neutral. But [Otto] Miller [chairman of the board of Standard Oil of California] and [Fred] Hartley [head of Union Oil] reminded us persuasively of all the joint ventures in exploration where we worked with their companies.

Interlocks

In addition to the unity of purpose brought about by common interests, the business community had more direct means of coordination. The California State Chamber of Commerce, for example, was a primary agent in the planning and execution of the anti-18 strategy. Interlocking boards of directors constitute a second means of coordination. The connections between the Automobile Club of Southern California and other businesses are more impressive than those links between the California State Automobile Association (CSAA) and business. CSAA is interlocked with the Freeway Support Committee (two mutual directors), United California Bank (one) and Bank of America (one). The Automobile Club of Southern California, on the other hand, shares directors with the Freeway Support Committee (two), United California Bank (two), Bank of America (one), Cyprus Mining (three), North American Rockwell (two), Beckman Instruments (one), Getty Oil (one), Stanford University (one), Pacific Mutual Life Insurance (four), University of Southern California (two), California Institute of Technology (one) and Stanford Research Institute (one). All three California oil companies, Getty, Standard and Union, are linked to the Stanford Research Institute, the California Institute of Technology and Bank of America. Some of the links between corporations bind them together very tightly. For example, one person, Asa V. Call, links together the Automobile Club of Southern California, United California Bank, Cyprus Mining, University of Southern California and Pacific Mutual Life Insurance Company.

It is obvious that such interlocks were not without effect in the Proposition 18 campaign. At a minimum, they facilitated communication and coordination among anti-18 forces. More likely they constituted a significant web of influence among the largest corporations in the state which effectively suppressed potential support for Proposition 18 among business interests.

Power to the Automobile

The automobile transportation system produces enormous private profits and massive social costs. Proposition 18 was a mild attempt to reduce these social costs. Not surprisingly, the highway and automotive interests—with their money, organization and economic influence—overwhelmed the poorly funded, loosely organized coalition of rapid-transit interests and environmental associations.

The power of the auto interest is such that even public outrage generated by a barrage of adverse publicity following the defeat of Proposition 18 did not stop Standard Oil of California from blatantly funding a campaign to defeat a similar anti-pollution measure in 1972. For the auto interests in California it will be business as usual for some time to come.

EDWARD GREER

The "Liberation" of Gary, Indiana

In silhouette, the skyline of Gary, Indiana, could serve as the perfect emblem of America's industrial might—or its industrial pollution. In the half-century since they were built, the great mills of the United States Steel Corporation —once the largest steel complex on earth—have produced more than a quarter-trillion tons of steel. They have also produced one of the highest air pollution rates on earth. Day and night the tall stacks belch out a ruddy smoke that newcomers to the city find almost intolerable.

Apart from its appalling physical presence, the most striking thing about Gary is the very narrow compass in which the people of the city lead their lives. Three-quarters of the total work force is directly employed by the United States Steel Corporation. About 75 percent of all male employment is in durable goods manufacture and in the wholesale-retail trades, and a majority of this labor force is blue-collar. This means that the cultural tone of the city is solidly working-class.

But not poor. Most Gary workers own their own homes, and the city's median income is 10 percent above the national average. The lives of these people, however, are parochial, circumscribed, on a tight focus. With the exception of the ethnic clubs, the union and the Catholic church, the outstanding social edifices in Gary are its bars, gambling joints and whorehouses.

Company Town

The city of Gary was the largest of all company towns in America. The United States Steel Corporation began construction in 1905, after assembling the necessary parcel of land on the Lake Michigan shore front. Within two years, over $40 million had been invested in the project; by now the figure must be well into the billions.

Gary was built practically from scratch. Swamps had to be dredged and dunes leveled; a belt-line railroad to Chicago had to be constructed, as well as a port for ore ships and of course a vast complex of manufacturing facilities including coke ovens, blast furnaces and an independent electrical power plant. The city was laid out by corporation architects and engineers and largely developed by the corporation-owned Gary Land Company, which did not sell off most of its holdings until the thirties. Even though the original city plan included locations for a variety of civic, cultural and commercial uses (though woefully little for park land), an eminent critic, John W. Reps, points out that it "failed sadly in its attempt to produce a community pattern noticeably different or better than elsewhere."

The corporation planned more than the physical nature of the city. It also had agents advertise in Europe and the South to bring in workers from as many different backgrounds as possible to build the mills and work in them. Today over 50 ethnic groups are represented in the population.

This imported labor was cheap, and it was hoped that cultural differences and language barriers would curtail the growth of a socialist labor movement. The tough, pioneer character of the city and the fact that many of the immigrant workers' families had not yet joined them in this country combined to create a lawless and vice-ridden atmosphere which the corporation did little to curtail. In much more than its genesis and name, then, Gary is indelibly stamped in the mold of its corporate creators.

Labor and the Left

During the course of the First World War, government and vigilante repression broke the back of the Socialist party in small-town America, though it was not very strong to begin with. Simultaneously, however, the Left grew rapidly as a political force among the foreign-born in large urban centers. As the war continued, labor peace was kept by a combination of prosperity (full employment and overtime), pressures for production in the "national interest," and Wilsonian and corporate promises of an extension of democracy in the workplace after the war was over. The promises of a change in priorities proved empty, and in 1919 the long-suppressed grievances of the steelworkers broke forth. Especially among the unskilled immigrant workers, demands for an industrial union, a reduction of the workday from 12 to eight hours and better pay and working conditions sparked a spontaneous movement for an industry-wide strike.

For a time it appeared that the workers would win the Great Steel Strike of 1919, but despite the capable leadership of William Z. Foster the strike was broken. The native white skilled labor aristocracy refused to support it, and the corporation imported blacks from the South to scab in the mills. This defeat helped set back the prospect of militant industrial trade unionism for almost a generation. And meanwhile, racism, a consumer-oriented culture (especially the automobile and relaxed sexual mores) and reforms from above (by the mid-twenties the eight-hour day had been voluntarily granted in the mills) combined to prevent the Left from recovering as a significant social force.

It was in this period between World War I and the depression that a substantial black population came to Gary. Before the war only a handful of black families lived there, and few of them worked in the mills. During World War I, when immigration from abroad was choked off, blacks were encouraged to move to Gary to make up for the labor shortage caused by expanding production. After the war this policy was continued, most spectacularly during the strike, but rather consistently throughout the twenties. In 1920 blacks made up 9.6 percent of the population; in 1930 they were 17.8 percent—and they were proportionately represented in the steel industry work force.

When the CIO was organized during the depression, an interracial alliance was absolutely essential to the task. In Gary a disproportionate number of the union organizers were black; the Communist party's slogan of "black and white unite and fight" proved useful as an organizing tactic. Nevertheless, it was only during World War II (and not as the result of the radicals' efforts) that black workers made a substantial structural advance in the economy. Demography, wartime full employment and labor shortages proved more important to the lot of black workers than their own efforts and those of their allies.

As after the First World War, so after the second, there came a repression to counter the growth of the Left. The Communist component of the trade union movement was wiped out, and in the general atmosphere of the early cold war black people, too, found themselves on the defensive. At the local level in Gary, the remaining trade union leaders made their peace with the corporation (as well as the local racketeers and Democratic party politicians), while various campaigns in the forties to racially integrate the schools and parks failed utterly.

Finally, in the early fifties, the inherently limited nature of the trade union when organized as a purely defensive institution of the working class—and one moreover that fully accepts capitalist property and legal norms—stood fully revealed. The Steelworkers Union gave up its right to strike over local grievances, which the Left had made a key part of its organizing policy, in return for binding arbitration, which better suited the needs and tempers of the emerging labor bureaucrats.

Corporate Racism

The corporation thus regained effective full control over the work process. As a result, the corporation could increase the amount of profit realized per worker. It could also intensify the special oppression of the black workers; foremen could now assign them discriminatorily to the worst tasks without real union opposition. This corporate racism had the additional benefit of weakening the workers' solidarity. For its part, the union abolished shop stewards, replacing them with one full-time elected "griever." This of course further attenuated rank-and-file control over the union bureaucracy, aided in depoliticizing the workers and gave further rein to the union's inclination to mediate worker/employer differences at the point of production, rather than sharpen the lines of struggle in the political economy as a whole.

The corporate and union elites justified this process by

substantial wage increases, together with other benefits such as improved pension and welfare plans. For these gains a price was paid. Higher product prices, inflation and a rising tax burden on the workers all ensued from the union's passive acceptance of corporate priorities.

There were extremely important racial consequences as well. For as the union leadership was drawn further and further into complicity with corporate goals, a large segment of the industrial working class found itself in the apparently contradictory position of opposing the needs of the poorest workers for increased social welfare services. A large part of the material basis for white working-class racism originates here. Gary steelworkers, struggling to meet their home mortgage payments, are loath to permit increased assessments for additional municipal services which they view as mostly benefitting black people.

United States Steel

Needless to say, the corporation helped to develop, promote and protect the Gary working class's new ways of viewing itself and its world.

In the mill, the corporation systematically gave the black workers the dirtiest jobs (in the coke plants, for example) and bypassed them for promotion—especially for the key skilled jobs and as foremen. Nor has that policy changed. Although about a third of the employees in the Gary Works are black, and many of them have high seniority, and although virtually all the foremen are promoted directly from the ranks without needing any special qualifications, there are almost no black (or Spanish-speaking) foremen. According to figures submitted by the United States Steel Corporation to the Gary Human Relations Commission, as of 31 March 1968, out of a total of 1,011 first-line supervisors (foremen) only 22 were black.

The corporation not only practices racism directly, it also encourages it indirectly by supporting other discriminatory institutions in Gary. Except for some free professionals and small business, the entire business community is a de facto fief of the corporation. The Gary Chamber of Commerce has never to my knowledge differed from the corporation on any matter of substance, though it was often in its economic self-interest to do so. This has been true even with regard to raising the corporation's property assessment, which would directly benefit local business financially. And in its hiring and sales practices, as well as in its social roles, this group is a leading force for both institutional racism and racist attitudes in the community. For instance, it is well known that the local banks are very reluctant to advance mortgage money in black areas of town, thus assuring their physical decline. White workers then draw the reasonable conclusion that the movement of blacks into their neighborhoods will be at the expense of the value of their homes and react accordingly. The local media, completely dependent financially on the local business community, can fairly be described as overtly racist. The story of the voting fraud conspiracy to prevent the election of the present mayor, Richard Hatcher, a black

man, didn't get into the local paper until days after it made the front page of the *New York Times*.

The newspaper publisher is very close to the national Catholic hierarchy and the local bishop, who in turn is closely linked to the local banks. The church is rhetorically moderately liberal at the diocesan level, but among the ethnic parishes the clergy are often overtly racist.

Political Considerations

While the United States Steel Corporation has an annual budget of $5 billion, the city of Gary operates on some $10 million annually. (This figure applies only to municipal government functions; it excludes expenditures by the schools, welfare authorities, the Sanitary Board and the Redevelopment Commission.)

And the power of the city government, as is usually the case in this country, is highly fragmented. Its legal and financial authority is inadequate to carry out the public functions for which it bears responsibility. The power of the mayor is particularly limited. State civil service laws insulate school, welfare, fire and police personnel from the control of City Hall. Administrative agencies control key functions such as urban renewal, the low income housing authority, sanitation, the park system and the board of health. Appointive boards, with long and staggered terms of tenure, hire the administrators of these agencies; and although in the long run a skillful mayor can obtain substantial control over their operations, in the short run (especially if there are sharp policy differences) his power may well be marginal.

Two other structural factors set the context in which local government in Gary—and in America generally—is forced to operate. First, key municipal functions increasingly depend upon federal aid; such is the case with the poverty program, urban renewal, low income housing and, to a substantial degree, welfare, education and even police and sanitation. Thus, the priorities of the federal government increasingly shape the alternatives and options open to local officials, and their real independence is attenuated.

Second, the tax resources of local governments—resting for the most part on comparatively static real estate levies—are less and less able to meet the sharply rising costs of municipal services and operations. These costs reflect the increased social costs of production and welfare, costs that corporations are able to pass on to the general public.

This problem is particularly acute in Gary because of the ability of the corporation to remain grossly underassessed. As a result, there are implacable pressures to resist expansion of municipal services, even if the need for them is critical. In particular, since funds go to maintain existing services, it is virtually impossible for a local government to initiate any substantive innovations unless prior funding is assured. In this context, a sustained response to the urban crisis is prevented not only by a fragmentation of power but also by a lack of economic resources on a scale necessary to obtain significant results.

For the city of Gary, until the election of Mayor Hatcher, it was academic to talk about such considerations as the limits of local government as an instrument of social change and improvement of the general welfare. Before him, municipal government had been more or less content simply to mediate between the rackets on the one hand and the ethnic groups and business community on the other.

The Democratic party, structured through the Lake County machine, was the mechanism for accomplishing a division of spoils and for maintaining at least a formal legitimacy for a government that provided a minimum return to its citizenry. Left alone by the corporation, which subscribed to an inspired policy of live and let live where municipal politics were concerned, this political coalition governed Gary as it saw fit.

In return for the benevolent neutrality of the corporation toward its junior partner, the governing coalition refrained from attempting to raise the corporation's tax assessments or to otherwise insinuate itself into the absolute sovereignty of the corporation over the Gary Works. Air pollution activities were subjected only to token inspection and control, and in the entire history of the city the Building Department never sent an inspector into the mill. (These and other assertions about illegal or shady activities are based on reports from reliable informants and were usually verified by a second source. I served under Mayor Hatcher as director of the Office of Program Coordination until February 1969.)

In this setting—particularly in the absence of a large middle class interested in "good government" reform—politics was little more than a racket, with the city government as the chief spoils. An informal custom grew up that representatives of different ethnic minorities would each hold the mayor's office for one term. The mayor then, in association with the county officials, would supervise the organized crime (mostly gambling, liquor and prostitution) within the community. In effect, the police force and the prosecutor's office were used to erect and centralize a protection racket with the mayor as its director and organized crime as its client. Very large sums of money were involved, as indicated by the fact that one recent mayor was described by Internal Revenue officials as having an estimated annual income while in office of $1.5 million.

Besides the racket of protecting ciminal activity, other sources of funds contributed to the large illicit incomes of city officials. There were almost 1,000 patronage jobs to distribute to supporters or sell to friends. There were proceeds from a myriad of business transactions and contracts carried out under municipal authority. Every aspect of municipal activity was drawn into the cash nexus.

For instance, by local ordinance one had to pass an examination and pay a $150 fee for a contractor's license to do repair or construction work within city limits. The licensing statute was enacted to maintain reasonable standards of performance and thus protect the public. In reality, as late as 1967, passing the exam required few skills, except the ability to come up with $1,200 for the relevant offi-

cials, or $1,500 if the applicant was unfortunate enough to have black skin.

Gary municipal affairs also had a racist quality. The black population continued to rise until in the early sixties it composed an absolute majority. Yet the benefits of the system just outlined were restricted to the less scrupulous of the leaders of other ethnic groups, which constituted altogether only 40 percent of the population. The spoils came from all; they were distributed only among whites.

And this was true not only for illegal spoils and patronage but also for legitimate municipal services. As one example, after Hatcher became mayor, one of the major complaints of the white citizenry concerned the sharp decline in the frequency of garbage collection. This resulted, not from a drop in efficiency of the General Services division, as was often charged, but from the fact that the garbage routes were finally equalized between white and black areas.

In short, the city government was itself just another aspect of the institutionalized structure of racism in Gary. To assure the acquiescence of Gary's blacks to the system, traditional mechanisms of repression were used: bought black politicians and ward leaders, token jobs, the threat of violence against rebels and the spreading of a sense of impotence and despair. For instance, it was a Gary tradition for the Democratic machine to contribute $1,500 each week to a black ministers' alliance for them to distribute to needy parishioners—with the tacit understanding that when elections came around they would help deliver the vote.

Hatcher's Campaign

The successful insurgency of Richard Gordon Hatcher destroyed the core of this entire relationship.

Hatcher developed what can best be described as a black united front, inasmuch as it embraced all sectors of the black community by social class, occupation, ideology and temperament. The basis of this united front was a commonly held view that black people as a racial group were discriminated against by the politically dominant forces. Creating it required that Hatcher bridge existing divisions in the black community, which he did by refusing to be drawn into a disavowal of any sector of the black movement either to his left or right—except for those local black politicians who were lackeys of the Democratic machine. Despite immense public pressure, for example, Hatcher refused to condemn Stokley Carmichael, even though scurrilous right-wing literature was widely circulated calling him a tool of Carmichael and Fidel Castro. Actually, the rumor that hurt Hatcher the most was the false assertion that he was secretly engaged to a white campaign worker—and it was so damaging in the black community that special pains had to be taken to overcome it.

Muhammad Ali was brought to the city to campaign for Hatcher, but Hubert Humphrey was not invited because of the bitter opposition of white antiwar elements within his campaign committee. It is worth noting that a substantial portion of Hatcher's financial and technical assistance came from a very small group of white liberals and radicals, who, while they played a role disproportionate to their numbers, suffered significant hostility from their white neighbors for involving themselves openly with Hatcher. Their support, however, made it possible for the campaign to appeal, at least rhetorically, to all the citizens on an interracial basis.

Of course, this support in the white community did not translate into votes. When the count was complete in the general election, only 13 percent of Gary's overwhelmingly Democratic white voters failed to bolt to the Republicans; and if one omits the Jewish professional and business section of town, that percentage falls to 6 percent (in blue-collar Glen Park)—a figure more explicable by polling booth error than goodwill.

Even in the Democratic primary against the incumbent mayor, Hatcher barely won, although he had the support of a large majority of the Spanish-speaking vote and overwhelming support (over 90 percent) of the black vote. His victory was possible, moreover, only because the white vote was split almost down the middle due to the entry of an insurgent and popular "backlash" candidate.

Hatcher's primary victory was particularly impressive given the obstacles he had to face. First, his entire primary campaign was run on less than $50,000, while the machine spent an estimated $500,000 in cash on buying black votes alone. Second, the media was openly hostile to Hatcher. And third, efforts were made to physically intimidate the candidate and his supporters. Death threats were common, and many beatings occurred. Without a doubt, the unprecedented action of the Hatcher organization in forming its own self-defense squads was essential in preventing mass intimidation. It was even necessary on primary day for armed groups to force open polls in black areas that would otherwise have remained inoperative.

These extraordinary methods demonstrated both how tenuous are the democratic rights of black people and what amazing organization and determination are necessary to enforce them when real shifts of power appear to be at stake. When the primary results came in, thousands of black citizens in Gary literally danced in the streets with joy; and everyone believed that the old Gary was gone forever.

Hatcher's Temptations

Immediately after the primary victory, the local alignment of forces was to some degree overshadowed by the rapid interposition of national ones. Until Hatcher won the primary, he was left to sink or swim by himself; after he established his own independent base of power, a new and more complex political process began: his reintegration into the national political system.

The county Democratic machine offered Hatcher a bargain: its support and $100,000 for the general election campaign in return for naming the chief of police, corporation counsel and controller. Naturally, Hatcher refused to accept a deal that would have made him a puppet of the corrupt elements he was determined to oust from power. Thereupon the county machine (and the subdistrict direc-

tor of the Steelworkers Union) declared itself for, and campaigned for, the Republican.

But the question was not left there. To allow the Democratic party to desert a candidate solely because he was black would make a shambles of its appeal to black America. And dominant liberal forces within the Democratic party clearly had other positive interests in seeing Hatcher elected. Most dramatically, the Kennedy wing of the Democratic party moved rapidly to adopt Hatcher, offering him sorely needed political support, financial backing and technical assistance, without any strings attached. By doing this, it both solidified its already strong support from the black community and made it more reasonable for blacks to continue to place their faith in the Democratic party and in the political system as a whole.

As a necessary response to this development (although it might have happened anyway), the Johnson-Humphrey wing of the Democratic party also offered support. And this meant that the governor of Indiana and the Indiana State Democratic party endorsed Hatcher as well—despite the opposition of the powerful Lake County machine. Thus Hatcher achieved legitimacy within the political system—a legitimacy that he would need when it came to blocking a serious voting fraud plot to prevent his winning the election.

Despite clear evidence of what was happening, the Justice Department nevertheless refused to intervene against this plot until Hatcher's campaign committee sent telegrams to key federal officials warning them that failure to do so would result in a massive race riot for which the federal officials would be held publicly responsible. Only by this unorthodox maneuver, whose credibility rested on Hatcher's known independent appeal and constituency, was the federal executive branch persuaded to enforce the law. Its intervention, striking 5,000 phony names from the voters rolls, guaranteed a Hatcher victory instead of a Hatcher defeat.

The refusal of the Justice Department to move except under what amounted to blackmail indicated that the Johnson-Humphrey wing of the party was not enthusiastic about Hatcher, whose iconoclastic and often radical behavior did not assure that he would behave appropriately after he was in power. But its decision finally to act, together with the readiness of the Kennedy forces to fully back Hatcher, suggests that there was a national strategy into which the Hatcher insurgency could perhaps be fitted.

My own view of that national strategy is that the federal government and the Democratic party were attempting to accommodate themselves to rising black insurgency, and especially electoral insurgency, so as to contain it within the two-party system. This strategy necessitated sacrificing, at least to a degree, vested parochial interests such as entrenched and corrupt machines.

Furthermore, black insurgency from below is potentially a force to rationalize obsolete local governments. The long-term crisis of the cities, itself reflecting a contradiction between public gain and private interest, has called forth the best reform efforts of the corporate liberal elite. Centered in the federal government, with its penumbra of foundations, law firms and universities, the political forces associated with this rationalizing process were most clearly predominant in the Kennedy wing of the Democratic party.

The economic forces whose interests are served by this process are first the banks, insurance companies and other sections of large capital heavily invested in urban property and, more generally, the interests of corporate capital as a whole—whose continued long-range profit and security rest on a stable, integrated and loyal population.

Thus the support given to Hatcher was rational to the system as a whole and not at all peculiar, even though it potentially implied economic and political loss for the corporation, United States Steel, whose operations on the spot might become more difficult. The interests of the governing class as a whole and of particular parts of it often diverge; this gap made it possible for Hatcher to achieve some power within the system. How these national factors would shape the amount and forms of power Hatcher actually obtained became quite evident within his first year of office.

Mosaic of Black Power

When I arrived in the city five months after the inauguration, my first task was to aid in the process of bringing a semblance of order out of what can fairly be described as administrative chaos.

When the new administration took over City Hall in January 1968 it found itself without the keys to offices, with many vital records missing (for example, the file on the United States Steel Corporation in the controller's office) and with a large part of the city government's movable equipment stolen. The police force, for example, had so scavenged the patrol cars for tires and batteries that about 90 percent of them were inoperable. This sort of thing is hardly what one thinks of as a normal process of American government. It seems more appropriate to a bitter ex-colonial power. It is, in fact, exactly what happened as the French left Sekou Toure's Guinea.

There were no funds available. This was because the city council had sharply cut the municipal budget the previous summer in anticipation of a Hatcher victory. It intended, if he lost, to legislate a supplemental appropriation. But when he won without bringing in a council majority with him, its action assured that he would be especially badly crippled in his efforts to run the city government with a modicum of efficiency. Moreover, whenever something went wrong, the media could and did blame the mayor for his lack of concern or ability.

Not only did Richard Hatcher find his position sabotaged by the previous administration even before he arrived, but holdovers, until they were removed from their positions, continued to circumvent his authority by design or accident. And this comparatively unfavorable situation extended to every possible sphere of municipal activities.

Another problem was that the new administrators had to take over the management of a large, unwieldly and obsolete municipal system without the slightest prior executive experience. That there were no black people in Gary with such experience in spite of the high degree of education and intelligence in the black community is explicable only in terms of institutionalized racism—blacks in Gary were never permitted such experiences and occupational roles. Hatcher staffed his key positions with black men who had been schoolteachers, the professional role most closely analogous to running a government bureaucracy. Although several of these men were, in my view, of outstanding ability, they still had to learn everything by trial and error, an arduous and painful way to maintain a complex institution.

Furthermore, this learning process was not made any easier by the unusually heavy demands placed on the time of the mayor and his top aides by the national news media, maneuvering factions of the Democratic party, a multiplicity of civil rights organizations, universities and voluntary associations and others who viewed the mayor as a celebrity to be importuned, exploited or displayed. This outpouring of national interest in a small, parochial city came on top of and was almost equal to, the already heavy work load of the mayor.

Nor were there even clerical personnel to answer the mail and phone calls, let alone rationally respond to the deluge. The municipal budget provided the mayor with a single secretary; it took most of the first summer to make the necessary arrangements to pay for another two secretaries for the mayor's own needs. One result was that as late as June 1968 there was still a two-month backlog of personal mail, which was finally answered by much overtime work.

In addition to these problems there were others, not as common to American politics, such as the threat of violence, which had to be faced as an aspect of daily life. The problem of security was debilitating, especially after the King and Kennedy assassinations. In view of the mayor's aggressive drive against local organized crime, the race hatred whipped up during and after the campaign by the right wing and the history of violence in the steel town, this concern with security was not excessive, and maintaining it was a problem. Since the police were closely linked with the local Right, it was necessary to provide the mayor with private bodyguards. The presence of this armed and foreboding staff impaired efficiency without improving safety, especially since the mayor shrugged off the danger and refused to cooperate with these security efforts.

In addition, the tremendous amounts of aid we were offered by foundations, universities and federal officials proved to be a mixed blessing. The time needed to oversee existing processes was preempted by the complex negotiations surrounding the development and implementation of a panoply of new federal programs. There had never been a Concentrated Employment Program in Gary, nor a Model Cities Program, nor had the poverty program been locally controlled. Some of these programs weren't only new to Gary, they hadn't been implemented anywhere else either.

The "Liberation" of Gary, Indiana

The municipal bureaucracy, which under previous administrations had deliberately spared itself the embarrassment of federal audits, didn't have the slightest idea as to how to utilize or run these complex federal programs. Moreover, none of the experts who brought this largesse to Gary had a clear understanding of how it was to be integrated into the existing municipal system and social structure. These new federal programs sprang up overnight—new bureaucracies, ossified at birth—and their actual purposes and effects bore little relation to the legislative purposes of the congressional statutes that authorized them.

Needless to say, ordinary municipal employees experienced this outside assistance as a source of confusion and additional demoralization, and their efficiency declined further. Even the new leadership was often overwhelmed by, and defensive before, the sophisticated eastern federal bureaucrats and private consultants who clearly wanted only to help out America's first black mayor. The gifts, in other words, carried a fearful price.

Bureaucratic Enemies

Except for the uniformed officials and the schools, which were largely outside the mayor's control, the standing city bureaucracy was a key dilemma for Mayor Hatcher.

The mayor had run on a reform program. His official campaign platform placed "good government" first, ahead of even tax reform and civil rights. Hatcher was deeply committed to eliminating graft and corruption, improving the efficiency of municipal government—especially the delivery of services to those sectors of the citizenry that had been most deprived—and he did not view his regime as merely the substitution of black faces for white ones in positions of power.

But he also had a particular historic injustice to rectify: the gross underrepresentation of blacks in the city government, and their complete exclusion from policy-making positions. Moreover, implicit in his campaign was a promise to reward his followers, who were mostly black. (At least most participants in the campaign assumed such a promise; Hatcher himself never spoke about the matter.)

Consequently, there was tremendous pressure from below to kick out everyone not covered by civil service protection and substitute all black personnel in their places. But to do so would have deepened the hostility of the white population and probably weakened Hatcher's potential leverage in the national Democratic party. He resisted this pressure, asserting that he believed in an interracial administration. However, in addition to this belief (which, as far as I could determine, was genuine), there were other circumstances that dictated his course of action in this matter.

To begin with, it was always a premise of the administration that vital municipal services (police and fire protection, garbage collection, education, public health measures) had to be continued—both because the people of Gary absolutely needed them and because the failure to maintain

them would represent a setback for black struggles throughout the country.

It also appeared that with a wholesale and abrupt transition to a totally new work force it would be impossible to continue these services, particularly because of a lack of the necessary skills and experiences among the black population—especially at the level of administration and skilled technical personnel. In this respect Hatcher faced the classic problem faced by all social revolutions and nationalist movements of recent times: after the seizure of power, how is it possible to run a complex society when those who traditionally ran it are now enemies?

The strategy Hatcher employed to meet this problem was the following. The bulk of the old personnel was retained. At the top level of the administration (personal staff, corporation counsel, chief of police, controller) new, trustworthy individuals were brought in. Then, gradually, new department heads were chosen, and new rank-and-file people included. If they had the skill already, they came at the beginning; if they didn't, they were brought in at a rate slow enough to provide for on-the-job training from the holdovers, without disrupting the ongoing functions of the particular department.

The main weakness of this gradualist strategy was that it permitted the old bureaucracy to survive—its institutional base was not destroyed.

The result was that the new political priorities of the administration could not be implemented with any degree of effectiveness in a new municipal political practice. City government remained remarkably like what it had been in the past, at least from the perspective of the average citizen in the community. While the political leadership was tied up with the kinds of problems I noted earlier, the bureaucracy proceeded on its own course, which was basically one of passive resistance. There were two aspects to this: bureaucratic inertia, a sullen rejection of any changes in established routine that might cause conflicts and difficulties for the employees; and active opposition based on politics and racism, to new methods and goals advocated by the mayor.

To cite just one example, the mayor decided to give a very high priority to enforcement of the housing codes, which had never been seriously implemented by preceding administrations. After much hard work, the Building Department was revamped to engage in aggressive inspection work. Cases stopped being "lost," and the number of inspections was increased by 4,000 percent while their quality was improved and standardized. Then it was discovered that cases prepared for legal enforcement were being tabled by the Legal Department on grounds of technical defects.

I personally ascertained that the alleged legal defects were simply untrue. I then assumed that the reason for the legal staff's behavior was that they were overburdened with work. Conferences were held to explain to them the mayor's priorities so they could rearrange their work schedule. Instead, a series of bitter personal fights resulted, culminating in my removal from that area of work since the staff attorneys threatened to resign if there were continued interference with their professional responsibility. In the course of these disputes, both black and white attorneys expressed the opinion that they did not consider themselves a legal aid bureau for Gary's poor, and furthermore the root of the city's housing problem was the indolent and malicious behavior of the tenants. In their view, it was therefore unjust to vigorously enforce the existing statutes against the landlords. Thus, despite the administration's pledge, black ghetto residents did not find their lives ameliorated in this respect.

Gradually, then, the promise of vast change after the new mayor took office came to be seen as illusory. Indeed, what actually occured was much like an African neocolonial entity: new faces, new rhetoric and people whose lives were scarcely affected except in their feelings towards their government.

This outcome was not due to a failure of good faith on the part of the Hatcher administration. Nor does it prove the fallacious maximalist proposition that no amelioration of the people's conditions of life is possible prior to a revolution. Instead, it was due to the decline of the local mass base of the Hatcher administration and the array of national political forces confronting it.

Most black people in Gary were neither prepared nor able to take upon themselves the functions performed for them by specialized bureaucracies. They relied upon the government for education, welfare, public health, police and fire protection, enforcement of the building codes and other standards, maintenance of the public roads and the like. Unable to develop alternative popularly based community institutions to carry on these functions by democratic self-government, the new administration was forced to rely upon the city bureaucracy—forced to pursue the option that could only result in minor changes.

Aborted Liberation

The most significant consequence of the Hatcher administration's failure to transcend the structural terrain on which it functioned was political, the erosion of popular support after the successful mobilization of energies involved in the campaign. The decline of mass participation in the political process contributed in turn to the tendency of the new regime to solve its dilemmas by bureaucratic means or by relying on outside support from the federal government.

The decline in mass support ought not to be confused with a loss of votes in an election. Indeed, Hatcher is now probably as secure politically as the average big city mayor. The point is that the mass of the black population is not actively involved in helping to run the city. Thus, their political experiences are not enlarged, their understanding of the larger society and how it functions has not improved, and they are not being trained to better organize for their own interests. In short, the liberating process of the struggle

for office was aborted after the initial goal was achieved—and before it could even begin to confront the profound problems faced by the mass of urban black Americans.

For example, after the inauguration, old supporters found themselves on the outside looking in. For the most part, since there was no organized effort to continue to involve them (and indeed to do so could not but conflict with the dominant strategy of the administration), they had to be content to remain passive onlookers. Moreover, the average citizen put a lot of faith in the mayor and wanted to give him an opportunity to do his job without intruding on the process.

Even among the most politicized rank-and-file elements there was a fear of interfering. Painfully conscious of their lack of training and experience, they were afraid of "blowing it." Instead they maintained a benevolent watchfulness, an attitude reinforced by the sense that Hatcher was unique, that his performance was some kind of test of black people as a race. (Whites were not the only people encouraged by the media to think in these terms.) There were of course some old supporters who were frankly disillusioned: they did not receive the patronage or other assistance they had expected: they were treated rudely by a bureaucratic holdover or were merely unable to reach the ear of a leader who was once accessible as a friend.

The ebbing away of popular participation could be seen most markedly in the Spanish-speaking community, which could not reassure itself with the symbolic satisfaction of having a member of its group in the national spotlight. With even less education and prior opportunity than the blacks, they found that the qualifications barrier to municipal government left them with even less patronage than they felt to be their due reward. This feeling of betrayal was actively supported by the former machine politicians and criminal elements, who consciously evoked ethnic prejudices to isolate the mayor and weaken his popular support.

What happened in the first year of the new administration, then, was a contradiction between efficiency and ethnic solidarity. At each point the mayor felt he had to rely upon the expert bureaucracy, even at the cost of increasing his distance from his mass base. And this conflict manifested itself in a series of inexorable political events (the appointment of outside advisors, for example), each of which further contributed to eroding the popular base of the still new leadership.

As Antonio Gramsci pointed out, beneath this contradiction lies a deeper one: a historic class deprivation—inflicted on the oppressed by the very structure of the existing society—which barred the underclass from access to the skills necessary for it to run the society directly in its own interests and according to its own standard of civilization. Unless an oppressed social group is able to constitute itself as what Gramsci characterizes as a counterhegemonic social bloc, its conquest of state power cannot be much more than a change in leaders. Given the overall relation of forces in the country at large, such an undertaking was beyond the power of the black community in Gary in 1968. Therefore, dominant national political forces were able quickly to reconstitute their overall control.

National Power

What happened to Richard Hatcher in Gary in his first year as mayor raises important questions—questions that might be of only theoretical interest if he were indeed in a unique position. He is not. Carl Stokes, a black, is mayor of Cleveland. Charles Evers, a black, is mayor of Fayette, Mississippi. Thomas Bradley, a black, very nearly became mayor of Los Angeles. Kenneth Gibson, a black, is now mayor of Newark. The list will grow, and with it the question of how we are to understand the mass participation of blacks in electoral politics in this country and the future of their movement.

I believe that until new concepts are worked out, the best way of understanding this process is by analogy with certain national liberation movements in colonial or neocolonial countries. Of course, the participants—in Gary as in Newark—are Americans, and they aren't calling for a UN plebiscite. But they were clearly conscious of themselves as using elections as a tool, as a step toward a much larger (though admittedly ill-defined) ultimate goal—a goal whose key elements of economic change, political power, dignity, defense of a "new" culture and so forth are very close to those of colonial peoples. It is because Hatcher embraced these larger objectives (without, of course, using precisely the rhetoric) that his campaign can be thought of as part of a nationalist process that has a trajectory quite similar to that of anticolonial liberation movements.

In its weakened local posture, the Hatcher administration was unable to resist successfully a large degree of cooptation by the national political authorities. Despite a brave vote at the Democratic National Convention for Reverend Channing Philips, Hatcher was essentially forced to cooperate with the national government and Democratic party—even to the extent of calling on the sheriff of Cook County to send deputies to reinforce the local police when a "mini-riot" occurred in the black ghetto.

Without either a nationally coordinated movement or an autonomous base of local insurgency—one capable of carrying out on a mass scale government functions outside the official structure—Hatcher's insurgency was contained within the existing national political system. Or, to express it somewhat differently, the attempt by black forces to use the electoral process to further their national liberation was aborted by a countervailing process of neocolonialism carried out by the federal government. Bluntly speaking, the piecemeal achievement of power through parliamentary means is a fraud—at least as far as black Americans are concerned.

The process by which the national power maintained itself, and even forced the new administration to aid it in doing so, was relatively simple. As the gap between the popular constituency and the new government widened, like many another administration, Hatcher's found itself increasingly forced to rely upon its "accomplishments" to maintain its popularity and to fulfill its deeply held obligation to aid the community.

Lacking adequate autonomous financial resources—the mill remained in private hands, and it still proved impossible to assess it for tax purposes at its true value—accomplishments were necessarily dependent upon obtaining outside funds. In this case, the funds had to come from the federal government, preferably in the form of quick performance projects to maintain popular support and to enable everyone to appear to be doing something to improve matters.

These new programs injected a flow of cash into the community, and they created many new jobs. In his first year in office, the mayor obtained in cash or pledges more federal funds than his entire local budget. Hopes began to be engendered that these programs were the key to solving local problems, while the time spent on preparing them completed the isolation of the leadership from the people.

Then, too, the stress of this forced and artificial growth created endless opportunities for nepotism and even thievery. Men who had never earned a decent living before found themselves as high-paid executives under no requirement to produce any tangible results. Indeed, federal authorities seemed glad to dispense the funds without exercising adequate controls over their expenditures. A situation arose in which those who boasted of how they were hustling the system became prisoners of its largesse.

Even the most honest and courageous leader, such as Mayor Hatcher, could not help but be trapped by the aid offered him by the federal authorities. After all, how can any elected local executive turn down millions of dollars to dispense with as he sees fit to help precisely those people he was elected to aid: The acceptance of the help guaranteed the continuation of bonds of dependence. For without any real autonomous power base, and with new vested interests and expectations created by the flow of funds into the community, and with no available alternate path of development, the relation of power between the local leader and the national state was necessarily and decisively weighted toward the latter.

In Gary, Indiana, within one year after the most prodigious feat in the history of its black population—the conquest of local political power—their insurgency has been almost totally contained. It is indeed difficult to see how the existing administration can extricate itself from its comparative impasse in the absence of fresh national developments, or of a new, more politically coherent popular upsurge from below.

There is, however, no doubt that the struggle waged by the black people of Gary, Indiana, is a landmark on their road to freedom; for the experiences of life and struggle have become another part of their heritage—and thus a promise for us all.

LEE SLOAN AND ROBERT M. FRENCH

Black Rule in the Urban South?

Jacksonville is a major commercial and financial city in northeast Florida, a regional center for banking and insurance. As a port city with access to the Atlantic, it serves as a major transfer point. But, like many cities, Jacksonville was caught in the familiar cycle of urban decay and suburban exodus. For Jacksonville this has meant racial transition as well. As affluent whites fled to suburban Duval County, low-income blacks crowded Jacksonville's central city. As the nonwhite population of Jacksonville approached the 50 percent mark, area whites saw a need for change. Whether racial imbalance was seen as a problem in itself or as an indicator of deeper troubles is unclear. In any case, a group of reformers proposed a solution to the city's problems—to consolidate the government of Jacksonville with that of Duval County.

City-County consolidation or "Metrogovernment" has often been proposed, but has rarely been achieved. Prior to the 1967 merger in Jacksonville-Duval, the most prominent recent instance involving major governmental reorganization was the 1962 merger of Nashville and Davidson County in Tennessee.

Those supporting consolidation have always presented their case in terms of "good government" reform. The reformers stress that consolidation will result in the establishment of a "rational" government which will provide increased governmental efficiency, greater economy, expanded and improved services, greater accountability of public officials, the elimination of overlapping jurisdictions and the duplication of services, the elimination of corruption, and so forth. Further, reformers claim that consolidation facilitates the expression of a "public interest" thus guaranteeing, as Michael Danielson has expressed it, that "the metropolis will be governed in the interest of the whole rather than in the conflicting interests of its many parts."

Yet conflicting interests, and particularly racial interests, may be crucial in determining whether or not consolidation is achieved and, if so, its specific form. Racial transition in metropolitan areas concentrating blacks in the central core of the city and whites in the surrounding suburbs may lead to a point in time when tolerance for existing governmental arrangements is drastically reduced—a kind of political "tip point." Though the political tip point is analogous to neighborhood or school tip points, its accompanying problems are less easily resolved. Many whites cope with racial transition in both neighborhoods and schools by simply moving out. It may be, however, that simple evasion does not truly resolve racial problems centered in residential neighborhoods and the schools, but simply buys some time before the problems must be confronted in the political realm. It is becoming increasingly evident that whites moving out may be forfeiting political control to the blacks who are left behind. Already black mayors have been elected in Cleveland, in Gary, and most recently, in Newark. Furthermore, in Los Angeles, Tom Bradley ran first in the primary election for mayor in 1969, though he failed to obtain an absolute majority. He subsequently lost in the run-off election to the incumbent mayor, Sam Yorty.

Holding the line against black power seems to be a growing problem for metropolitan white America. Resolving it will often involve *redefining political boundaries so that the proportion of blacks within the new political unit is drastically decreased.* This can assume the forms of gerrymandering or annexation, and the at-large election is a variation of the theme. Gerrymandering is a time honored means of limiting or controlling such minority-group political power. But in recent years, court decisions regarding compliance with the one man—one vote principle have undermined the effectiveness of the gerrymander.

Annexation, the formal addition of new territory to an existing governmental unit, too has provided a means of coping with the concentration of blacks in urban centers. Though race is surely not the only motivating force behind annexation movements, the addition of outlying areas to the city oftentimes reduces the relative size of the black population, for those areas annexed are often predominantly white. The white doughnut, then, becomes a formal part of the black center, thus reducing the relative power of the center's black citizens over their destiny. Though those whites who moved to the suburbs to escape the problems of the city will not see annexation as a panacea, the risk of forfeiting the city's government to blacks may well be sufficient to swing many white suburbanites to a pro-annexation position.

The at-large electoral system also may be used to limit or control black political power. In cities where blacks still constitute a numerical minority, an at-large (as opposed to a ward or district) electoral system offers assurance that the black community will either be unable to elect a black representative, or white leaders will see to it that blacks have but token conservative representation. Under an at-large system, black candidates cannot expect to win election without the financial support of white leaders and the endorsement of civic associations. Of course, if blacks become a numerical majority of the electorate, then the at-large system could work to their advantage.

Now in metropolitan areas, governmental consolidation may be emerging as a new means of dealing with the growing black threat to the existing political structure. While accomplishing the same racial goal as other techniques, it holds the promise of coping with other problems related to interdependency. Our argument should not be interpreted to imply that race is the only factor leading the residents of metropolitan areas (in Jacksonville or elsewhere) to contemplate or actually adopt a metropolitan area-wide government. There are other reasons, many of which we ourselves would recognize as valid. Still we are convinced that local political elites may be deceiving themselves as well as others in failing to face the racial realities behind governmental reorganization.

Jacksonville and Duval—The Setting

At the time of consolidation, the citizens of Jacksonville and of Duval County were beset with many governmental problems, some related to governmental structure and others to governmental inaction in the past. The city charter was 50 years old, and provided for a uniquely inefficient governmental structure. An elected five-member city commission was the major administrative body, although additional elected officials and independent boards shared administrative functions. The elected mayor, who sat on the commission, had relatively little power. Theoretically, an elected city council served as the city's legislative body. But in actuality, the commission, other elected officials and the various independent boards all encroached upon the policy-making authority of the council. Under this complex arrangement, power and authority were so diffused that it was difficult, if not impossible, to establish governmental responsibilities.

Jacksonville's history provides a dismal record of governmental corruption. The citizens of the city have spoken for years of a machine government. Richard Martin reports that for a city of its size in 1966, Jacksonville had the largest number of full-time employees and the highest monthly payroll in the nation.

The governmental structure of Duval County provided even greater problems. The elected five-member county commission was really an administrative arm of the state government. Legislative authority rested not with the commission nor with the other 69 elected county officials, but rather with the state legislature which meant, in effect, the Duval County legislative delegation. Until Florida's new constitution went into effect in 1969, local bills pertaining to Duval could be passed only during a 60-day period every other year. Because of the tradition of "local bill courtesy" and the fact that for many years Duval County had only one state senator, that one person actually possessed veto power over all legislative matters. In brief, the county government was without the power and authority to meet the problems of an essentially urban and suburban population.

Not only were city and county governments unable to handle their own respective problems, but city-county cooperation was nearly impossible. As Martin points out, as many as four governmental bodies were required to have a say in any city-county project: the city council and city commission, the Duval legislative delegation and the county commission.

Population growth was at the root of many problems in Jacksonville and Duval. Total county population doubled between 1930 and 1950, but the increase was very uneven. The growth rate in the decade of the forties, for example, was only 18.2 percent in Jacksonville but 168.4 percent in the remainder of the county. Comparable figures for the decade of the fifties were -1.7 percent and 155.6 percent. By the mid-sixties Jacksonville had an estimated population of 196,000, while the county population outside the city was estimated at 327,000.

As in most large metropolitan areas, a rapidly growing nonwhite population was centered in the core of the city. According to the 1966 Local Government Study Commission, Jacksonville ranked third in the nation in percentage of total population nonwhite for cities of over 100,000. But nonwhite population outside the city limits in Duval was only 9.2 percent of the total.

The area was also plagued by economic problems. Within the city, 31 percent of all families earned less than $3,000 according to the 1960 census. The same source classified over 30 percent of Jacksonville's housing units as in either deteriorating or dilapidated condition. The schools were similarly rundown and their condition, combined with a tradition of political meddling in educational affairs, led to disaccreditation of every senior high school in the county in 1964. Adding to the list of area problems were pollution of air and water, lack of adequate county police and fire protection, soaring taxes, a rising crime rate and an economic slowdown. As Martin points out, concern over these conditions made the move to consolidation more popular.

By the mid-sixties, both blacks and whites were aware that approximately 44 percent of the city's population was black. *The Report of the National Advisory Commission on Civil Disorders* estimated that if current trends continued, a majority of Jacksonville's citizens would be black by 1972. Martin writes that:

The specter of a Negro mayor and of a government dominated by Negroes became a subject of growing concern for all citizens whose thoughts ran in such directions, and there were many. In 1966 the Community Development Action Committee . . . noted tactfully that the movement of the young and higher income groups out of the city was putting Jacksonville "under the potential control of lower income groups who may not have a feeling of responsibility toward local government."

This racial transition was surely one of the more crucial factors leading to popular referenda to annex in both 1963 and 1964. In both instances, voters in the outlying areas voted against their being annexed.

A few black leaders in Jacksonville argued that these trends would lead inevitably to the day when black voters would outnumber whites and it would be possible to elect a black mayor and a black council. From the perspective of these persons, consolidation would lead to the dilution of the black vote just when the establishment of black political power was a distinct possibility. One black leader argued that under the old city government, all candidates for the council had to appeal to the black electorate. He argued that black voters, representing approximately 42 percent of the total, would be foolish to support consolidation which would reduce their share of the total electorate to approximately 19 percent. As the most vocal black leader opposing consolidation, he charged that the black leaders supporting consolidation "sold out" the black community. This individual was generally identified as the old line, traditional Negro leader, and he had been tied to the political machine in Jacksonville for years. Other blacks believed that he opposed consolidation because the machine opposed it and because he reaped economic benefits from his promises to deliver the Negro vote, despite the widespread belief that he could no longer, in fact, deliver it.

Very few black leaders openly opposed consolidation, but the dilution argument was the basis of their opposition. These persons also argued that consolidation would not lead to governmental economy, but this was a minor theme. Several of those who originally opposed consolidation were eventually neutralized or converted during the course of the consolidation movement. At any rate, only two black leaders of stature took strong positions opposing consolidation, and the other opponent was also considered to be tied to the old machine government.

Most of Jacksonville's black leaders recognized well that dilution would indeed be a consequence of consolidation, but they still found reasons to support consolidation. Foremost among those black leaders supporting consolidation was a lawyer viewed by others as moderate even though his office was noted for playing a strong role in civil rights cases. He had made a very favorable impression on both blacks and white liberals in a losing campaign for a seat in the state legislature. Even though he probably had the best chance of becoming Jacksonville's first black mayor, he expressed his position as follows:

I argued that such a town as Jacksonville was becoming couldn't hope to attract industry or new blood. And that if that was the case, the black man obviously had more to lose than anybody else. All of the wealth in the community was outside the corporate limits. The young folks—black and white—were pretty much outside the corporate limits. All of the innovators and the creators were moving into the suburbs. That's where the industry and business was, except for a few little stores—and Main Street was declining. Main Street was a street of black faces and store windows, shop windows. The educated were in the suburbs and not in the corporate limits. Jacksonville was being run from! It would do me no good to be mayor of such a town as Jacksonville was becoming. There would certainly be no interest on the part of the people sitting out there in the suburbs if they were fighting coming in all the while.

Jacksonville's black leaders were convinced that whites were not going to allow the day to come when they would have to accept a black mayor. One embittered black leader said that whites "would have resorted to any means to prevent black control of the city." Most black leaders were convinced that the future held either consolidation or annexation, either of which would have diluted Negro voting strength. Many, though not all black leaders, were aware that the Duval legislative delegation could have annexed by merely passing a local bill, thus bypassing a popular referendum. And most were fairly certain that if consolidation failed, the delegation indeed would have passed annexation by decree.

Most black leaders, then, saw consolidation as the lesser of two evils. Recognizing that white pro-consolidation leaders felt they needed to prevent a heavy negative vote in the black community, black leaders sought the best deal they could get. From the perspective of these individuals, the most important feature of the proposed charter was the provision for a council with 14 of 19 members elected by district. District lines were drawn to assure the election of three blacks to the council, and it was argued that blacks could also be elected to the five at-large seats. Some black leaders even felt they had promises from white leaders to support black candidates in the at-large elections. A charter requirement for regular reapportionment and compliance with the principle of one man—one vote representation also reassured black leaders.

The significance of the districting provision lies in the fact that the entire council under the old Jacksonville government had been elected at large. Nearly twenty years earlier, Jacksonville had moved from district to at-large council elections, and most observers are convinced that the rapid increase of black voters was a crucial factor in that change. It was only in the last election held under the old government that the black community succeeded in placing the first blacks on the council (in this century). Two black women, with vastly different kinds of appeal within the black community, were elected to the council as a part of a reform government. But many black leaders were quick to observe that there was no guarantee that black candidates could continue to win at-large elections.

One might be tempted to label the districting under consolidation as "benign gerrymandering" since lines were drawn so as to assure representation of blacks in proportion to their county population, at least so far as district seats were concerned. White leaders who wrote the charter were of the opinion that this was a major step toward justifying the support of consolidation by black leaders. However, the authors were also aware of an ideological commitment to local representation among whites which also favored district seats on the council. Since the provision of black seats on the council may also be viewed as a concession made to assure continued white political control, however, the gerrymandering was not totally benign.

The major argument used by black leaders to support consolidation, then, stressed the assurance of black representation on the new council. These leaders discounted the election of the two Negro councilwomen under the old Jacksonville government, emphasizing that there was no guarantee that black candidates could win again at large. Parris N. Glendening and John Wesley White expressed well the rationale of those black leaders supporting consolidation: "A possibility of future Negro political power of undertermined strength was, apparently, traded for immediate power of limited strength in Duval County." From their perspective, the black community stood to gain a voice in government where they had had none in the past. This argument was strengthened by black leaders' certainty that Jacksonville and Duval County whites would not have allowed a black take-over of Jacksonville government.

Representation was not the only factor leading black leaders to support consolidation. These leaders also advanced the general argument that they had not fared well under the old governmental system. Many felt that in years past, white political leaders had maintained a machine government largely on the strength of black votes purchased cheaply at election time. One leader respected by the rank-and-file within the black community observed that consolidation would eliminate a lot of the problems blacks

had lived under. "This city has suffered from political boondoggling, financial irresponsibility and a high crime rate," he said, "and when the city suffers, the black man suffers the most."

Clean Government Campaign

Pro-consolidation blacks argued that the old government was corrupt through and through, and they had plenty of evidence to back them up. Since 1965 a local TV station, through documentaries and editorials, had exposed local governmental corruption. As a result of the station's efforts a grand jury called in 1966 indicted two of five city commissioners, four of nine city councilmen, the city auditor and the recreation chief. Charges included larceny, grand larceny, conspiracy, perjury and the acceptance of bribes. Media reports of the trial proceedings led the public to believe that other officials avoided indictments merely because they had more cleverly covered their tracks. Thus pro-consolidationists could turn the movement into a "throw the rascals out" kind of campaign, and blacks as well as whites were influenced by this appeal.

In addition to the issues of representation and governmental corruption, black pro-consolidationists stressed the minor themes that the new system would yield: 1) greater employment opportunities for blacks in government, 2) tax resources from affluent suburban whites, 3) elimination of duplication of services and the overlapping of jurisdictions, 4) improved municipal services at greater economy, and 5) solutions for problems related to disaccreditation and segregation in the schools.

The arguments of the pro-consolidation forces proved convincing. In August of 1967, 63.9 percent of the more than 86,000 Duval County voters who voted approved governmental consolidation. This was indeed an impressive victory. In the Nashville consolidation in 1962, only 56.8 percent of the voters favored Metro, and the reformers there had lost the first referendum in 1958. And just two months prior to the victory in Jacksonville, voters in Tampa and Hillsborough County had soundly defeated a consolidation proposal.

Aggregate voting statistics in previous consolidation referenda show Negro precincts returning heavier anti-consolidation votes than white precincts. This pattern held also in Duval, but *a healthy majority of black voters still approved consolidation.* The Jacksonville data conflict with Grubbs' study of the 1958 Nashville referendum which concluded that "the Negroes on the whole did not favor the charter and that the higher the proportion of Negroes the less the support for the charter." (See Table 1.)

The difference notwithstanding, there are some striking similarities in the two successful consolidation movements in Jacksonville and Nashville. Both metropolitan areas were confronted with a rapidly growing Negro population. The threat of growing black political power, as we have seen, was a crucial factor leading Jacksonville and Duval County influentials to push for a consolidated government. Nashville whites felt similarly threatened. During the decade of the fifties, the percentage of nonwhites in the city grew from 31.4 percent to 38.1 percent. Though the first consolidation referendum was defeated in 1958, the city council passed annexation bills in 1958 and 1960 without referenda. Annexation reduced the percentage of nonwhites within the city to 27.6 percent, a figure actually lower than that in the 1940 census.

A second major similarity between Nashville and Jacksonville is that in both cities, black leaders perceived themselves to be confronted with the dilemma of choosing between consolidation and annexation. We have just observed that the defeated '58 referendum in Nashville led to hasty annexation which diluted black voting strength. In Jacksonville, two annexation referenda were voted down in the years immediately prior to the consolidation movement. But most Jacksonville black leaders were convinced that a defeat of consolidation would be followed by annexation, perhaps accomplished by the Duval legislative delegation without a referendum. Especially in Jacksonville, but also in Nashville, many black leaders reached the judgment that the probabilities of maximizing gains and minimizing losses lay in support of consolidation. It is especially interesting to note that in Nashville, the 1958 charter assured blacks of only two of 21 seats on the new council, but the 1962 charter assured blacks of six of 40 seats. In Jacksonville also, there is reason to believe that blacks were assured seats on the new council in the hope of preventing a heavy anti-consolidation vote among blacks.

A third similarity between the two cities shows the success reformers had in using consolidation as an anti-status quo movement. This strategy was employed in both cities. Apparently in Jacksonville, both black and white citizens—and perhaps especially whites in the suburbs—were influenced by the timely exposure of extensive governmental corruption. In Nashville, most observers felt that white suburbanites threw their support to Metro because they were opposed to accomplished and anticipated annexations, and because they opposed the city government's tax upon cars operated in the city by suburban residents. Nashville's mayor Ben West provided a convenient scapegoat for the frustrations of suburban residents. For many, a vote for Metro was a vote against the city machine and the referendum served as a purification rite.

The reform theme was missing in both the unsuccessful movements in St. Louis and Cleveland. Scott Greer concluded that "The decision not to attack incumbent officials and existing governments for their incompetence and inability weakened the hands of the crusaders." Greer also notes that there had been some "extreme dissatisfaction" with the government of Miami, which in 1957 adopted a "federalized" form of consolidation (and thus a much weaker form of consolidation than in either Jacksonville or Nashville).

There were further dissimilarities between Jacksonville and the unsuccessful efforts to consolidate in St. Louis and Cleveland where, according to Greer, Negro wards voted almost solidly against reform. Greer cites three major reasons for black opposition to consolidation in those cities. Probably of most importance, in both St. Louis and Cleveland, blacks were fearful of losing representation in the central city councils. A black leader in Cleveland argued that Negroes could elect two and only two representatives under the proposed system, while in Jacksonville, blacks were guaranteed greater representation under consolidation.

Greer also reported that reformers in St. Louis neglected

Precincts by Racial Composition	Total County Vote
	%
Less than 5% Negro (122)*	36.3
5–24% Negro (21)	41.6
25–49% Negro (9)	46.9
50–94% Negro (7)	43.8
95–100% Negro (28)	40.1

TABLE 1
ANTI-CONSOLIDATION VOTE BY RACE-JACKSONVILLE

*Figures in parentheses indicate the number of precincts in each category.
Source: Glendening and White, 1968:3.

to consult leaders from the black community. As a result black leaders made a pact *not to support anything they had had nothing to do with formulating.*

In Cleveland, black leaders were approached, but the nature of the approach led black leaders to oppose reform. Greer quotes one black leader's sentiments:

> We have just got to stop this business of the white people treating us without any respect. Lindseth (leader of the charter campaign) came down to us, to the assembled Negro community political leaders, and he said: 'Gentlemen, what is this going to cost us?'

In Jacksonville, on the other hand, white leaders supporting consolidation worked with and through black leaders in their attempt to win black pro-consolidation votes. The Duval County legislative delegation saw to it that four Negroes were appointed to the study commission which was responsible for drafting the new charter. One of those four, the prominent and respected attorney discussed above (who was later to be elected at-large to the new Jacksonville council), was appointed secretary of the commission and served as the major voice of the black community.

Another successful tactic used by Jacksonville reformers was to provide civil service job protection under consolidation. Greer notes that the failure of Cleveland to make such a guarantee led to fears such as those expressed by one black leader:

> The charter would write the protection out of civil service and you know how important civil service is to my people. They have a better shake there than in industry. They have better jobs and if you put those jobs into a county government without civil service, the chances are that a lot of people will lose their jobs.

These differences between Jacksonville's approach to reform versus that of St. Louis and Cleveland go far in explaining the differences in the extent of black support for consolidation. Blacks in Jacksonville perceived potential gains under consolidation because they had so little under the old system of government, and thus a majority of them supported consolidation. Blacks in St. Louis and Cleveland perceived potential losses under consolidation because they had something to lose, and thus they cast heavy votes against consolidation.

The history of governmental reorganization through consolidation is largely one of failure—there are few success stories. But perhaps the next few decades will change that. Since the first writing of this article, Indianapolis and Marion County in Indiana were consolidated (by state legislation, bypassing a referendum).

There are indications that governmental consolidation is currently being discussed in the following southern cities: Atlanta, Macon, Savannah, and Brunswick (all in Georgia); Charlottesville, Richmond and Roanoke, in Virginia; Charleston, South Carolina; Charlotte, North Carolina; Tampa, Pensacola, and Tallahassee in Florida; and Chattanooga, Tennessee.

If consolidation does become more widespread in the near future, we suspect that racial conflict will play a crucial role in the change. We would hypothesize that consolidation movements will be likely to emerge in those metropolitan areas where the proportion of blacks within the corporate limits of the city 1) is growing rapidly, and especially where it is 2) approaching 40 or 50 percent.

This may well be a movement which initially will be restricted to southern cities. In most northern cities, a proposal of consolidation would pit the Democratic central city against the Republican suburbs. As Edward C. Banfield observed over a decade ago, "advocates of consolidation schemes are asking the Democrats to give up their control of the central cities or, at least, to place it in jeopardy." Furthermore, as Glendening and White observed, "all of the post-1945 reorganization plans for area-wide government that have been accepted by the voters have been in the one-party South."

The "urge to merge" through consolidation can also be expected as a response to the election of black mayors in a number of cities and to the continuing development of Black Power with its emphasis on community control. Consolidated metropolitan government may well become a part of the backlash to the ideology and potential reality of Black Power. The major dilemma for black leaders faced with a consolidation movement becomes that stated by the black attorney in Jacksonville: to fight consolidation in the hopes of capturing the government of a dying city or to support consolidation and bring the taxes of white suburbanites back into the city. It is reported by Michael Lipsky and David J. Olson that this was also the major divisive issue in the deliberations on Newark by the Governor's Select Commission on Civil Disorders of New Jersey:

> One-half of the commissioners argued that political consolidation was the only means of establishing a tax base that would allow Newark to solve its problems. They argued that in the long run this would yield the greatest benefit to Negroes in Newark. Other commissioners argued against political consolidation on the grounds that this would, in effect, disenfranchise black people in Newark precisely at the time when their numbers had grown to constitute a majority of the city electorate. The first argument risked disturbing white suburbanites upon whom the commission felt dependent for implementation of recommendations directed at the state government. The second argument risked assuring Negroes of electoral success without the resources to provide basic services.

Newark did not consolidate, and Newark now has Kenneth Gibson as its own black mayor. No doubt some black leaders in Jacksonville still feel that one of their own could be the mayor of their city some day soon had they fought consolidation. But most of Jacksonville's black leaders were convinced that whites would not have allowed such a development under any conditions, and they cast their lot with consolidation knowing that it destroyed any chance of their electing a black mayor—though it may have guaranteed black representation on the commission. Whether blacks should have supported consolidation or whether they got enough in return for their support are difficult judgments.

Middle-Class Political Style

The rhetoric of the middle-class political style, of course, avoids the nastiness of racial conflict. A review of the public record of the consolidation movement in Jacksonville would not lead one to suspect that race was a crucial factor. Jacksonville's white elite used the good government reform rhetoric, thus avoiding the mention of race, and still got their message of the significance of race across to those who were attuned. This was beautifully illustrated in the Community Development Action Committee's warning that Jacksonville could come "under the potential control of lower income groups who may not have a feeling of responsibility toward local government." Anyone clever enough to know what "law and order" says of contemporary race relations is also clever enough to know the identity of the lower-income groups under discussion.

What happened in Jacksonville is an old story. At precisely that point in time when blacks threatened to wrest their share of political power from others, the rules of the game were changed. Black Americans may well be justified in concluding that the history of urban governmental reform reveals ever-changing attempts to conform to good government while at the same time avoiding what white Americans see as the detrimental consequences of democracy.

FURTHER READING

Community Control and the Black Demand for Participation in American Cities by Alan Altshuler (New York: Pegasus, 1970).

The Moral Basis of a Backward Society by Edward C. Banfield (Glencoe: The Free Press, 1958).

The Unheavenly City by Edward C. Banfield (Boston: Little, Brown, 1970). A highly controversial book challenging black power and often attacked as racist.

Nashville Metro: The Politics of City-County Consolidation by Brett W. Hawkins (Nashville, Tenn.: Vanderbilt University Press, 1966).

Consolidation: Jacksonville-Duval County by Richard Martin (Jacksonville, Fla.: Crawford, 1968).

Negroes in Cities: Residential Segregation and Neighborhood Change by Carl E. and Alma A. F. Taeuber (Chicago: Aldine, 1965).

Millhands and Preachers: A Study of Gastonia by Liston Pope (New Haven, Conn.: Yale University Press, 1965).

JOSEPH M. CONFORTI

Newark: Ghetto or City?

Get off the train at Newark's Penn Station, go to the front of the station, look across the street and view the new Newark. There you will see the sparkling new Gateway Center: lean office towers, a modern hotel, enclosed shopping arcade and underground parking garage, all dramatically connected to Penn Station by a glass enclosed bridge—the final elegant touch in a chamber of commerce dream? Or is it an architectural tribute to racist urban polarization?

That is the strange question posed by new development in Newark. A perverse kind of question? Gateway is after all a substantial development, an improvement over the depressing skid row it replaced, a symbol of faith backed by substantial investment, a stimulus to further growth. Certainly it is all these things. But the street between Penn Station and Gateway is not very wide, and there is a traffic light at the corner. So why build a bridge? Because the bridge is comforting, reassuring, a guarantee that you can come to work in an office or stay in a hotel in Newark without fear of ever having to walk on the city's streets. You can be safely enclosed from the time you board a train in suburbia until you settle in your office or hotel room, you will hardly know that you are in Newark.

You won't even have to go out to see a current movie, for the Gateway's hotel boasts that it is the "first hotel in the world to offer guests current feature movies in their rooms." You won't have to walk the few blocks to "The Four Corners," the city's main intersection of Broad and Market streets, where 20 or 30 years ago a visitor might have gone to select an evening's entertainment from among the 20 or so theaters in the area. Late night disk jockeys used to have a standard joke—"Go down to Broad and Market please, they're running out of pedestrians." It is no longer funny—Newark itself has become a joke for many people, in the genre of the Polish joke. So much so that one Newark bank president, Paul Stillman, defensively took out full page ads in the *New York Times* during 1969 to proclaim "It's the 'in' thing to knock Newark, but it's the *wrong* thing." He sought to highlight the most positive achievements of Newark in such areas as housing, education and health, but above all else, to stress that all is not wrong with Newark.

It didn't work. Newark had already come to symbolize too well all that is wrong with cities in America, a distinction not easily shed. But more than serving as a symbol of what is wrong with cities, Newark has also raised the question of whether or not it is the bellwether city, an ominous possibility posed by Mayoral Assistant Donald Malafronte in 1966 when he began Newark's Model Cities application with the words "Wherever America's cities are going, Newark will get there first."

If Newark is where America's cities are going, few will take comfort in the urban future, for Newark presents a bleak prospect. A city that at night has few pedestrians on feared streets lighted only by street lamps; where you can do little window shopping in the evening because many stores bar their windows with opaque steel; a city that has a severe housing shortage amidst thousands of abandoned houses; a geographically small city with huge empty (urban renewal) lots that, together with the abandoned housing, create a bombed out appearance; a city where the German shepherd population rises faster than new office buildings; where there is a cop, public or private, for every 150 residents; where one out of every ten residents lives in a public housing project; one out of three is on welfare and where urban pathologies can be described only in superlatives.

How does a major city in the richest nation in the world come to this, and what does it mean for the future of urban America? It is a long story in terms of Newark's age, being the third oldest of America's large cities, pre-dated only by Boston and New York. A century before the United States, in 1666, Newark began. It grew rapidly as an Anglo-Saxon Protestant theocracy, spreading out for more than 100 square miles of mostly agricultural land. But unlike other cities that grew larger, Newark grew smaller, reduced to less than 20 square miles by 1810, as areas seceded to form new townships. Originally slaves, Newark's earliest black settlers were free men by 1810—free to pay taxes, that is, not to vote. Despite its small size the city was an established commercial and manufacturing center by 1825, complete with newly arrived Irish immigrants who worked on the Morris Canal, the city's newest source of pride, which connected Newark to Pennsylvania's coal fields. The Irish and later the Germans, joined the city's blacks in reassuring the older English and Dutch residents of their self-proclaimed superiority.

By the eve of the Civil War the city's future economic character was well established. The railroads dominated transportation while the steam engine powered industry; the Germans built breweries, though outdone by a Scot, Peter Ballantine, who built the largest brewery; the insurance companies, led by Mutual Benefit, were established; leather and chemicals led a list of manufactured commodities that was characterized above all by diversity. Newark's highly skilled labor force and industrial diversity attracted many inventor-entrepreneurs like Edison, Weston and Hyatt whose work further spurred industrial growth.

But Newark's rapid and dramatic growth was basically quantitative—more and more in the same economic pattern. Newark continued to be overshadowed by its much larger and faster-growing

neighbor New York, a city too short a distance away to give Newark any sense of emerging metropolitan grandeur, even as it became an industrial giant.

Newark had also changed demographically, largely through growth. New waves of immigrants arrived, replacing the previous immigrants in the oldest, least desirable housing and jobs. Older immigrants, who by this point preferred to call themselves native Americans, moved on to the newer housing and better jobs, thereby establishing an ethnic (religious and racial) pecking order.

To the extent that the various immigrant groups formed ghettos where they settled, as was typically the case, there existed caste opportunities for advancement. Small elites of doctors, lawyers, importers, newspaper editors and other specialists were able to rise above their countrymen by providing them with specialized services otherwise unavailable. This was possible because the melting pot did not happen in Newark, not even in the polygenetic Ironbound district, where the commonality of Catholicism would have seemed a binding force. Rather than bind, the Catholic church multiplied in Ironbound with each ethnic group building at least one church, leaving only the less numerous parochial schools to forge some semblance of a Catholic community.

If caste was a characteristic of the emergent white ethnic ghettos, it was even more emphatically a condition of life for the city's growing black population. Although the blacks were among Newark's earliest settlers, they were at the bottom of the ethnic pecking order. Working largely as servants and porters and in other unskilled, undesirable work, few blacks achieved managerial or professional positions, nor were many successful as small entrepreneurs. Unlike the more recently arrived European immigrants, the blacks did not suffer language problems or cultural dissonance. Their experience had long been American and many had long lived in the city, alleviating the rural to urban adjustment that might have explained their lack of success. A single factor, white racism, exercised in terms of discrimination would better explain it. Blacks settled in two areas of Newark, the lower end of the near Southside and the near Eastside. In a few instances they were able to find housing in the oldest and least desirable sections of East Orange and Montclair, two of the nearby old established suburbs populated by affluent WASPs, for whom blacks worked as house servants.

By the 1920s Newark was booming. World War I had served as a further spur to its factories and the Depression was not yet in sight. The boom was reflected in the construction of skyscraper office buildings along Broad Street, crowded department stores, the clutter of automobile traffic, new high-rise apartment houses, an airport and two of the nation's first radio stations. Like so many other things that might have given Newark greater stature, the radio stations were quickly moved over to New York, leaving Newark the nuts-and-bolts end of the glamorous new medium—manufacture of the radio receivers.

The Prohibition era was also a time when organized crime flourished as an industry. In Newark this meant ethnic struggle too, as Jews and Italians competed for control. Abner (Longie) Zwillman, leading the Jewish forces of the Third Ward (near Southside) and Ruggerio (The Boot) Boiardo, leading the Italian forces of the First Ward (near Northside), fought for years to control bootlegging in and around Newark (and much of the East Coast), until they made peace by dividing the distribution territories.

The 1920s seemingly marked an end to further change in the composition of Newark's population when America's earlier immigrants legislatively closed the doors to any more of their brothers. Only small numbers of Spaniards and Portugese settling in Ironbound represented any immediate change in the city's huge population of European immigrant residents. Largely unnoticed at the time, however, was a new stream of migrants who would replace the Europeans—rural Americans displaced by the growing technology of agriculture.

Also unnoticed was the fact that the rapidly growing American economy, on which Newark had thrived, was about to collapse. Factories began dismissing workers and had to close. By 1930 almost 10 percent of the city's population was on relief and that number tripled within five years. As the Depression approached, the city's population growth slowed almost to a halt, but Newark's economy did not completely collapse. Some new office buildings were finished thanks to the sudden abundant supply of cheap labor, and the WPA programs generated work as sewer lines were completed, a new airport terminal building was constructed, streets were hand-paved with bricks, and Branch Brook Park was extended to the city's border. The municipal government also took advantage of the labor surplus by using men rather than machines to enlarge the old Morris Canal bed, transforming it into the main downtown tunnel of a new subway system terminating at the new Pennsylvania Railroad Station, also under construction.

Newark WASPs suffered least in the Depression and were able to take advantage of low-wage surplus labor and accumulated savings to have new houses built in the city's outskirts and adjoining suburbs. Those who suffered most were at the other end of the pecking order, especially blacks, whose numbers in Newark had doubled between 1920 and 1930. As in other times, blacks lost jobs before whites and were hired after whites. Some of the most recent European immigrants tried to weather the storm by returning to Europe. The rest of the population sought only to avoid having to go on relief, a shameful fate for an immigrant population still largely tied to a peasant cultural background.

The repeal of Prohibition in 1933 seemed a bright sign for the city. The reopening of the breweries, together with the construction of office buildings, an airport terminal, a new subway, a railroad station might even have reassured Newark that the city was continuing its growth. But these projects were begun for the most part in the prosperous 1920s and proved to be the last remnants of a period of growth. The National Housing Act of 1937 and subsequent housing legislation would have an enormous impact on the city, an impact that residents could not foresee. The immediate visible consequence was limited to the construction of the James Baxter Terrace—one of the first low-income public housing projects to be built in America, which was racially segregated like many facilities in the city.

As elsewhere in America, World War II served as the prime basis of economic recovery. Newark factories began humming in 1940 with army orders and shortly thereafter the shipyards began operating around the clock. There was more than enough work for all the Newarkers who did not put on a uniform, and those who did were readily replaced by new black migrants from the South and white migrants from Pennsylvania who came to Newark to work in the war industries. It was a time when even the proverbial melting pot seemed possible, for there was enough work for everyone and the federal government sought to bind the population into a unified patriotic war effort, supplying official enemies toward whom racial hatred could legitimately be directed. (In Newark this hatred was especially reserved for Japan, which had sent far fewer immigrants to the city than either Germany or Italy.)

The end of the war brought wild celebration to the streets of Newark, but it was an ironic celebration, for the city's war-stimulated economy was about to wind down. The process was forestalled only by the postwar surge in consumption. The economy in Newark did not collapse immediately after the war. But it began to move to the suburbs along with the ethnic groups at the top of the hierarchy.

Factories had deteriorated because of the strain placed on them by the wartime storming. The war had caused a critical deterioration of the city's housing too, much of which was wooden and hadn't been maintained through the war and depression years. Overcrowding was another problem, particularly in the substandard tenements that continued to be put to heavy use during the influx of war industry workers. These factors, together with the growing popularity of the automobile, made the suburbs attractive to residents and industry alike.

Those at the top of the ethnic pecking order—the WASPs—were the first to leave followed by the old German and Irish populations. There was much reshuffling of neighborhoods among those that remained, as middle-class groups moved into housing vacated by the fleeing WASPs and other ghettos expanded to annex the territory vacated by whatever group above them had moved. At the same time, the economic status of white Newarkers moving to the suburbs resulted in a new phenomenon—the lower-middle-class, blue-collar suburb.

Blacks remained in the expanding ghetto of the Third Ward. Blacks in smaller numbers also moved to the near Northside and to Ironbound. More affluent blacks moved in small but increasing numbers to the suburbs of East Orange and Montclair. The increased amount of federal mortgage money made available in 1954 for suburban housing construction meant that even more people were likely to move out of the geographically small city.

Still the heterogeneous ethnic character of the city remained intact. This was evident in the political arena where Newarkers had long voted along ethnic lines and the municipal administration's ethnic composition reflected, with some lag, the city's ethnic composition in general. The Germans had given way to the Irish, who in 1950 shared political power with an Italian and a Jew. The ethnic division of the city could also be observed less directly. Many occupations were ethnically identifiable: the police and fire departments were overwhelmingly Irish, the construction trade was Italian, the merchants were largely Jewish, the small luncheonettes were Greek, the large businesses were owned and managed by WASPs, skilled craftsmen were likely to be German and the factory operatives were Irish, Polish and Italian. Even the city's taxicabs had ethnic identifications. Yellow cabs were operated by the Irish, 20th Century cabs by Jews, Brown and White cabs by Italians and Green cabs by blacks.

The city had lost a significant amount of industry and retail commerce by 1950 and that began to worry both the politicians and the businessmen. But what worried them more was the changing composition of the city's population, for as the 1950s wore on they observed the movement in ever increasing numbers of Newark's most affluent residents to the suburbs. While this was not a new phenomenon for cities such as Newark, the process in the latter 1950s did contain elements that indicated a more significant change than had been occurring through suburbanization in the past.

A basic consequence of this process was that the city was experiencing not only another ethnic change in its population, as had long been its experience, but also a dramatic change in its economic composition. In the past the relatively small population of recently arrived poor migrants was able to survive and progress in the city as a result of having the cost of its limited needs for public services met by a larger and more affluent population. What was occurring in the 1950s was that the larger more affluent population was leaving the city almost in its entirety, being replaced by an overwhelmingly poorer population with extensive demands for public services. The decreasing employment opportunities for unskilled workers, even in as industrial an area as Newark, left the poor population ever more dependent upon the structure of public services, including health, education, fire, police, housing and welfare facilities, while the ratio of the dependent to the taxpayers grew.

While Newark was becoming an increasingly blacker city, that segment of the white population that had arrived most recently, the Italian population, was becoming the majority population in the city.

These developments contained the seeds of conflict for two reasons: the Italians, more than any other white group, attached great importance to the territorial integrity of their community and Italians held more than their share of the city's lower-skill jobs. That other whites, ensconced in restricted suburbs and more secure jobs, would support black demands for jobs and housing—demands that threatened Italians more than other whites—disposed Italians to view themselves as unjustly caught in the middle, a viewpoint that encouraged a reactionary-racist stance.

During the 1960s these developments accelerated further. Newark was becoming a tense city of poor people, the first such city in the United States. In this process the city confronted its increasing fiscal problems (including a growing population of city employees demanding more pay) through static maintenance of public facilities. The city's black population, which suffered most, took this condition stoically, not having much choice. To recent migrants, Newark still represented an improvement over past housing and job opportunities. Nevertheless Newark blacks were plagued by economic frustrations. There weren't enough good jobs for everyone, and housing and consumer goods were overpriced. For those who could afford it, housing in decent neighborhoods with good schools was unattainable because of discrimination.

Some of these frustrations became manifested in racial conflicts in Newark in the early 1960s. For example, after blacks began to move to the Clinton Hill section on the Southside of the city, they sought to rehabilitate and improve their homes only to find that the area had been "blacklisted" for mortgage loans by the local banks. After mortgage money finally became available and houses were improved in Clinton Hill, the city's housing authority (urban renewal division) proclaimed in 1961 that Clinton Hill would become the site of an urban renewal project, slated for the construction of light industry. In view of the fact that there were other areas of the city far more deteriorated that could better be put to use as light industrial renewal areas and particularly since they had invested money in the improvement of their homes, the most affluent black Newarkers felt deepening frustration about their future in the city. This caused them to follow increasingly in the footsteps of their white counterparts and move to the suburbs, particularly East Orange where substantial numbers of Newark's middle-class blacks have settled.

In 1963 racial confrontations arose in relation to the construction of a new Barringer High School in Newark. The conflict revolved about the employment of blacks among the construction workers on the project, an issue that would arise at other sites of construction throughout Newark in the following years. Construction was one of the fields which relatively unskilled blacks could potentially enter without having to meet rigorous education or skill requirements. By 1963 the industry was generally enclosed in an exclusive set of guildlike unions by whites who themselves felt economically insecure. This was particularly volatile in Newark where the industry was dominated by Italians who, not having yet experienced much economic mobility, claimed a proprietary right to this avenue of opportunity which they had cornered.

In 1964 Tom Hayden, a founder of Students for a Democratic Society (SDS), came to Newark to establish a liaison group with the Clinton Hill community, which then evolved into the Newark Community Union Project (NCUP). This was one of several projects that SDS had undertaken throughout the United States and its objective in Newark, as elsewhere, was to organize poor people as both a political and economic force within the city. Upon his entry into the city Hayden, as a result of previous publicity received by the SDS, was given a less than welcome reception by the city's administration and police force. NCUP itself accomplished relatively little for blacks in the Clinton Hill area, except in the opinion of its enemies, such as Captain Charles Kinney of the Newark police department, who felt it should accomplish nothing. On the other hand, they were stimulating the kind of self-help/self-interest community action that was being organized in New York and some other cities, but not otherwise being developed in Newark.

Among the frustrations faced by the black population in Newark in the mid-1960s was that of contending with what was perceived as widespread corruption among whites in general and Italians in particular. Organized crime had long been an open secret in Newark and was dominated by Italian names. Corruption was believed to permeate the municipal government as well, also dominated by Italian names. This suspicion, combined with the domination of construction unions by Italians, a bigoted police force which was mainly Italian and a residential population that was predominately Italian, led to a general black hostility toward Italians, equivalent to the more highly publicized black anti-Semitism observed in New York at the same time. Further, blacks couldn't help but resent the fact that though they made up half the population, there were only a few blacks in the city government. Newark's Italians in turn resented blacks for their failure to abide by Newark's unwritten rules of ethnic group ascendancy—it was not yet their turn to take over. A long power struggle began.

The first bone of contention was control of the city's poverty program. The federally funded community action program, called the United Community Corporation in Newark, was organized outside the traditional political structures by a coalition of blacks and whites. A frightened city hall began making charges of inefficiency, waste, favoritism and political activism and suggested that the poverty program be brought under jurisdiction of the municipal government.

Similar efforts undertaken by municipal governments throughout the country to co-opt this program succeeded in 1967 and Congress shifted resources to the new municipally administered Model Cities program. Black leaders in Newark turned their efforts toward capturing the municipal government and particularly its largest patronage pool, the quasi-autonomous board of education.

Control of the school system was more than a political plum. It was also an institution that had grown significantly in importance in American society and, in Newark, an institution that was poorly serving a mainly black student body while overwhelmingly staffed by whites and where anyone who tried to change the system was fired.

When, in May of that year, Mayor Hugh Addonizio proposed the appointment of a white city councilman as secretary of the board of education, blacks went to stormy board meetings in large numbers to insist upon the appointment of Wilbur Parker, the black city budget director who was much more highly qualified for the position. But the issue was temporarily defused by the current secretary agreeing to stay in the position for another year.

Urban renewal policies were another racial issue. Blacks saw the policies of the Newark Housing Authority (the first such agency in the country) as Negro removal and whether it was conscious or not the agency had concentrated poor blacks in limited areas while demolishing their homes to make the sites available to affluent whites. The sites cleared in the First Ward for a luxury apartment complex were damning evidence of NHA's policies.

Meanwhile in 1966, Kenneth Gibson, then a city engineer, entered the mayoralty race in an effort to rally the black vote. Although he entered the campaign late and didn't win the election, Gibson acquired enough votes to force a runoff between Addonizio and runner-up Leo Carlin, a previous mayor of Newark.

Newark was rapidly becoming an evil word in itself, independent of any particular manifestation such as deteriorated housing or dirty streets. Whites left in droves, taking their commercial, cultural and industrial facilities with them to the suburbs. There they found that Newark's stigma had followed them. Former Newarkers in the suburbs were called Newarkies, Nicky Newark or greasers. Suburbanites used Newark as a negative adjective, describing deteriorating areas of their communities as "beginning to look Newarkish" or warning that if action were not rapidly taken on a local issue, their town could become "another Newark."

As a result, Newark was becoming ever more of a ghost city. Theaters and restaurants no longer remained open after dark; downtown department stores reduced their evening hours; the city center became desolate at dusk. For many people living in the area, Newark had been reduced to a necessary economic evil, a place where money could still be made, but to be otherwise avoided.

For the city's blacks the growing political activism that began in 1965 was becoming an exercise in futility by 1967. The poverty program remained in the hands of blacks, but was becoming irrelevant as funds

Newark: Ghetto or City?

diminished; a functionally illiterate generation of youth was graduating from school; a 150-acre site was being surveyed for condemnation to make way for a new medical school; the board of education had retained a white secretary and a white majority on the board itself, in a city with a 75 percent black student body; and municipal elections had just returned whites to office in a city that was at least 50 percent black but could count only two (out of nine) black councilmen and no blacks in strategic administrative positions in the city's government. Further, whatever hopes blacks may have had of inheriting the city were dampened by the wholesale flight of whites and the economic interests they represented.

Newark's rebellion in the summer of 1967 had been anticipated for years, ever since rioting began in cities like Rochester and Cleveland. The governmental response in Newark was intense. Armed state and local police and the national guard were brought in. Heavy war machinery including armored tanks and even army helicopters were deployed. The resultant battle was a brutal one and served to intensify emergent black power and separatism. Its focal point was the ghetto school. Shortly after the rebellion the city's own teachers' union criticized the school system as second rate, deteriorating and a cause of the rebellion. Based on a survey made by the Governor's Select Commission on Civil Disorder the state pronounced the Newark school system "in a state of educational crisis" and proposed that the state take over the administration of the schools.

The rebellion and its aftermath had an almost predictable impact upon the white population remaining in Newark. A vigilante group developed on the Northside, and soon groups of vigilantes were patrolling white neighborhoods all over the city in their own radio cars. Anthony Imperiale, head of the North Ward Citizens Committee, emerged as their leader. The extensive media coverage given this movement exacerbated the polarization of blacks and whites in Newark by stressing Imperiale and Imamu Amiri Baraka (LeRoi Jones) as the leaders of "the two constituencies" in the city. The publicity did Imperiale no harm in his political ambitions, for he won election as councilman-at-large in 1968.

A more official response to the rebellion consisted of government demolition of the riot-torn blocks in the Central Ward, giving it the appearance of a bombed out city in postwar Japan or Germany. Needless to say, the negative image of Newark increased even further after 1967. As an extraordinary example of how far this phenomenon extended, the *Newark Evening News* and *Newark Star-Ledger,* the city's two daily newspapers, each of which had been in the city for about 100 years dropped *Newark* from their mastheads. Newark was a desperate city after the rebellion.

In 1968, following the assassination of Dr. Martin Luther King, Jr., there was limited (largely potential) violence in the streets, as there was again in the summer of 1969 following the killing of a youth by a policeman. The school situation worsened: schools were so crowded that if all students appeared at school on a given day, 10,000 would be without seats; violence began breaking out in the high schools, parents began boycotting schools; rival teachers' organizations quarreled about jurisdiction over the system's teachers; the issue of community control began to arise. The school crises drove even more whites out into what have become ethnic suburbs.

After the summer of 1967, two official investigating bodies, the Governor's Select Commission on Civil Disorder and the federal Kerner Commission reported on the causes of the riot. Though basically inconclusive, the reports included among "official" assessments of Newark the fact that there existed "a pervasive feeling of corruption" in the city. The investigations thus stimulated resulted in the indictment of Addonizio in 1969, together with the two white councilmen, Lee Bernstein and Frank Addonizio, who were allies of the mayor and had continually challenged the anti-poverty program; the city's two black councilmen, Irvine Turner and Calvin West; former city councilman James Callaghan, who was a central figure in the conflict over appointment of a new secretary to the board of education in 1967; four other city officials; and three others not in the city government, including Anthony Boiardo, son of Ruggerio Boiardo and a reputed Mafia member. They were charged with various counts of extortion and tax evasion.

The indictments not only dealt a shattering blow to Addonizio's personal political career but more important to the political hopes of Italians as a group. That the indictments tied the Addonizio administration to reputed Mafia figures and that it occurred amidst other highly publicized investigations into organized crime in and around Newark lent substance to the claims of black leaders that the city in general was corrupt and that the Mafia played a significant role in Newark affairs and reduced the probability that the Italians would retain control of the city. Italian fears were confirmed in the 1969 mayoralty runoff election when the moderate candidates threw their support to Gibson, thus assuring a black victory.

The racial reactions to the election were immediately apparent. The downtown streets of the city were filled with throngs of jubilant blacks in numbers that had not been seen there since the end of World War II. The celebration went on for hours with shouts of "right on," horn blowing and dancing in the streets. Whites were on the streets too that night, particularly on the Italian Northside where Addonizio's vote-counting headquarters were established. They were not celebrating. Their faces expressed shock and, above all, fear. Although the runoff election resulted in a city council composed of three blacks and six Italians, the Italians viewed the ascendancy of a black to the executive position as marking an end to the short reign of Italians in the city.

The defeat of Addonizio and his subsequent conviction would serve to demonstrate to the average Newark Italian that Addonizio's administration had, in the last analysis, done little for Italians. The Newark Italian remained a man in the middle: not affluent enough to enjoy the security and comforts of American society, yet not poor enough to qualify for welfare or poverty program assistance. Added to this frustration was resentment based on the feeling they had done all the things American society said were the proper things to do. They had worked hard, seldom if ever asked for charity, kept their families intact, maintained their houses and neighborhoods and went to church. But what they did not notice was that the rules had changed and the skills and talents they had cultivated for participation in a blue-collar society were increasingly superfluous. They were ill-prepared for a society in which white-collar credentials were increasingly important. That there were just enough successful Italians to preclude viable charges of discrimination compounded their frustration.

Among the consequences of Italians' retention of cultural norms that failed to meet contemporary needs was their maintenance of a distrust of things intellectual. As a result, the leadership potential of the many Italians in academic institutions had not been realized and in turn Italian intellectuals, unlike Jewish or black intellectuals, tended not to identify with the Italian community. This phenomenon was also reflected in the ambivalence with which Italian parents sent their children off to college, in keeping with their effort to do the things America said were appropriate and yet fearing the corrupting influences college would have upon their children's loyalties to family and tradition. In the absence of leadership from Italian intellectuals, the church or even such traditional middle-class Italian organizations as UNICO or the Columbians (which Italian professionals and politicians have long maintained as bourgeois fraternities) the most effective rallying groups for proletarian Italians were organized by reputed Mafia leaders Joe Columbo (Italian-American Civil Rights League) and the late Joe Gallo (Americans of Italian Descent). Italian frustration was readily transformed into hostility toward blacks. And since blacks in turn blamed Italians for their seeming lack of progress in their struggle for majority rule, the hostilities increased.

Further, the teachers' strike settlements of 1970 and 1971 left the black community even more frustrated and stimulated further efforts to make the school system sensitive to the needs of black students. Some of the endeavors have been symbolic in nature, such as the renaming of schools in honor of such historic black figures as Harriet Tubman, Dr. Martin Luther King, Jr. and Marcus Garvey. This is part of a larger effort to change some of the symbols of Newark from white to black—including street names and even the city seal. This effort is unprecedented in Newark, since few street, school or other names have been changed in the course of the city's history from those given by the city's WASP founders. The effort, emanating from Baraka's Committee for a Unified Newark, follows in the course of continual efforts to rename the city itself, from Newark to New Ark. One symbolic effort, to have black liberation flags flown in all Newark schools with an enrollment of at least 50 percent black students, resulted in a storm of reaction from whites and was ultimately ruled out by the state.

The quasi-formal base of a political machine was secured through the success of the Black and Puerto Rican Convention resulting in the election of Kenneth Gibson and others on the "community's choice" ticket. If Baraka's organizational effort served as a base for Gibson's success, then Gibson's subsequent successes cannot be easily dissociated from Baraka's political potential. In this respect Gibson's appointments to the board of education, coupled with other appointments and community action that have been inspired by Baraka, suggest that black control of the school system has been progressing, however slowly. Baraka's chief associate, David Barrett, is head of the United Community Corporation.

The city's powerful Newark Housing Authority has emerged as another arena of racial competition, and again one that pits blacks against Italians. The authority has extensive control over all aspects of redevelopment in Newark, as well as the vast low-income public housing, which represents a significant (if potentially waning) patronage plum. Still another conflict is occurring over the reorganization of the Model Cities Program that would expand the program to the entire city. Extending to the entire city a program with millions of dollars of federal funds simultaneously constitutes revenue sharing and another large patronage pie. The city council, which must approve the city's application for the program, has been uncooperative, not willing to let the mayor, whose office administers the Model Cities Program, get the new resources unless they are split with the (Italian) city council and its constituency.

Still another conflict of this type has taken shape in terms of congressional elections. Blacks, led by Baraka and State Assemblyman George Richardson, had been striving to have Newark designated a congressional district in itself. Newark has been divided into two districts, each attached to surrounding suburbs and each represented by an Italian. After the New Jersey legislature failed to agree on redrawn congressional districts, a panel of federal judges established the new districts. They made Newark a single district, attaching to it the City of East Orange (50 percent white and 50 percent black) and the small towns of Harrison and Glen Ridge (both overwhelmingly white), resulting in a Democratic district composed of approximately half blacks and half whites (among which Italians predominate).

Baraka, following the success of the city's Black and Puerto Rican Convention, organized a county black convention that led to the selection of the mayor

Newark: Ghetto or City?

of East Orange, William Hart, as the black congressional candidate. Assemblyman George Richardson, however, declared his own candidacy, thus providing black competition, as he had in the mayoralty race in Newark. Running against the black candidates was Peter Rodino, who had long represented one of Newark's congressional districts. While this was in one sense another example of the competition between Italians and blacks for power in Newark, it was also an ironic one, for there was seeming agreement between blacks and Italians that Peter Rodino had been an outstanding congressman and that Newark should have a black representative in Congress. Since Rodino apparently aspires to the governorship, an alliance of blacks and Italians could easily have produced an Italian governor and a black congressman from Newark. But such an alliance did not materialize and Rodino was re-elected.

Racial conflict in Newark is not limited to that between blacks and whites. A Newark Italian, Ron Porambo, recently published a book painstakingly detailing the killing of blacks by Newark policemen and became himself the target of an assassin's bullets, some of which found their mark—though not fatally.

A group of black Newark ministers has recently instituted itself as a community watchdog, charging a variety of heavy-handed activities to Baraka and his associates. Some of the racial division is simply accommodated: last Christmas Bamberger's department store had dual Santa Clauses, black and white, next to each other.

Nevertheless, there continues to be a scramble for the spoils, and the spoils continue to diminish. Stores continue to close, industrial and commercial firms relocate or go out of business, as the huge Ballantine brewery recently did, throwing over 2,000 employees out of work and out of pensions. Of the 750 land parcels put up for bids by the city last year, not one was sold, and more are accumulating as fires and abandonment continue to decrease the housing supply.

Are these the symptoms of a dead or dying city? Certainly not a dead city, a dead city would not have traffic jams; not even a dying city, not with new office buildings still going up, new high-rise apartment houses and new college campuses, even if the gains lag behind the losses. No, Newark is not a city in its death throes; it is a city undergoing changes that are both qualitatively and quantitatively unprecedented in recent urban experience, changes that portend a new kind of city—and the form it will take is not yet clear. Several possibilities loom as alternative futures.

Newark could be the first major commercial center to be wholly relocated, a prospect that looms in spite of the further development of the central business center. One of the demands made by some black leaders, that the downtown business interests turn more of their earnings back to the city (especially the giant Prudential Insurance Company) places these companies under pressure that their national competitors do not have. In the face of such a competitive disadvantage, relocation is a viable solution, particularly in view of other factors like the large, car-oriented labor pool in the suburbs. Since Newark has no captive economic base equivalent to Boston's education plant or New York's national business stature, everything in the city is subject to relocation. As Newark's metropolitan position becomes less viable, its remaining metropolitan functions do tend to shift to Manhattan (or the suburbs), not because Newark is a satellite of New York as some observers believe, but because it is a poor competitor with the urban colossus only nine miles away when it is as easy to commute from the suburbs to New York as to Newark.

As the largest self-ruling city in the United States with a predominantly black population, it would seem that Newark could become the center of black life in America. This is not likely, however, in view of the black talents concentrated in cities such as Chicago or New York each of which houses a black population several times the size of Newark's black population—populations that are far more affluent.

That Newark's black population is not affluent, that whites continue to leave the city and that the, Puerto Ricans and whites who remain in Newark to complement the blacks are also relatively poor, raises the possibility that Newark could become the first major urban welfare reservation in the United States. Ten percent of the population already lives in public housing projects and there is no likelihood at all that the private market will provide new housing for low-income families. Despite a moratorium on the further construction of public housing projects in Newark (except for the aged) and a growing movement to have some of the existing high-rise projects torn down, the supply of low-income public housing is proportionally increasing through rent subsidizations for welfare families in private housing and FHA subsidized mortgage purchases of private housing by low-income families.

City as Reservation

Other dimensions of a growing welfare reservation include: the proliferation of alphabet agencies serving various poverty needs, the construction of very permanent community centers, a severe decline in private medical services and private schools with a corresponding increase in demands upon public facilities in these areas, together with the yet-to-be-addressed problems of man—malnutrition and drug addiction that will require still more public facilities.

On the other hand, it is not inconceivable that the federal government will undertake to establish a domestic version of "new life" centers in rural areas, to which the dependent population would be "induced" to move. The introduction of mobile homes by the New York City Housing Authority in the Brownsville area of Brooklyn suggests an interim phase of such a possibility. This would serve two purposes. It would provide the streamlining of control to which so many Americans are disposed in dealing with the poor and a device for contending with the suburban "invasion" of the poor, now being combatted through zoning ordinances. It would also facilitate the clearing of Newark to make it available as a desirable central location for further suburban "development." This ominous possibility could prove especially attractive to state-level developers should their plans to build a new city in the Hackensack Meadows across from Manhattan prove infeasible.

One of the problems confronting Newark and other Northern New Jersey cities has been the retention of Manhattan as a model of spatial form over the suburbs as a model of spatial organization like that of Los Angeles that has given the West certain growth advantages. If the federal government were willing to pay the cost of such an adventure, the state government would have the opportunity to forge for New Jersey the Los Angeles it is so anxious to build at the breast of Manhattan.

Still another possibility looms—that of the city's being rebuilt, just as Stuttgart and Hiroshima were rebuilt. Surely if Newark had been bombed to its present condition, it would have been rebuilt immediately.

This brings us back to the question of whether Newark is where American cities are headed. The answer has to be a mixed yes and no, for Newark serves well as a model only for those cities that resemble it, primarily the cities along the northeastern coast and along the Great Lakes. What they have in common with Newark is old age, development anteceding the emergence of automobiles, ethnic and racial heterogeneity, a high percentage of rental housing, established autonomous suburbs on their borders resistant to annexation and an aura as undesirable low-status places in which to reside. These factors interact with unique characteristics to differentiate the rate of change in specific cities. Boston's huge youth population, tied to the area's colleges, has served as a significant factor in retaining that city's large Back Bay area as a viable high-rent district. Analogously, New York City's rent-control program has locked large numbers of white middle-class families into low-rent apartments, families that would probably have moved to suburbs if their apartment rents were controlled by market forces. Cities in the West and South, on the other hand, tend overwhelmingly toward the opposite pole of the continuum implied by the characteristics of Newark.

Newark: Ghetto or City?

Size alone is a significant factor. No major city in the United States is as small as Newark. If Newark covered an area as large as Houston or Dallas, it would probably have a composition not unlike the composition it had in 1950 or 1940, and would be larger than either of those cities. Another characteristic that makes Newark somewhat unique is its relationship to New York. Only Oakland, California, East St. Louis, Illinois and Gary, Indiana come close to being overshadowed by a larger city in the manner of Newark and even then it is not a shadow cast by *the* largest city, nor are they cast in such shadows while struggling to remain the metropolitan center of their respective states.

While many of the large, young, homogeneous cities of the West and South continue to blossom successfully in the model of Los Angeles, such old cities as Baltimore, New York, Philadelphia, Cleveland, Detroit, St. Louis and Chicago would appear the most likely to follow the Newark model, unless the prospect becomes more costly than the country finds it can afford, or more embarrassing than a major urban-industrial nation's ego can tolerate.

FURTHER READING

City Politics by Edward C. Banfield and James Q. Wilson (New York: Vintage Books, 1963).

Raise Race Rays Raze by Imamu Amiri Baraka (New York: Random House, 1971). A collection of essays that address Newark as an arena for black experience.

Newark by John T. Cunningham (Newark: New Jersey Historical Society, 1966). Newark's first 300 years with emphasis on economic development.

Report for Action by the Governor's Select Commission on Civil Disorders, State of New Jersey, February 1968. Chronology of events before, during, and after the civil disorders of the summer of 1967.

Rebellion in Newark by Tom Hayden (New York: Vintage, 1967). A first-hand analytic description of the 1967 rebellion, including a detailed listing of those killed in the course of its violence.

The Death and Life of Great American Cities by Jane Jacobs (New York: Random House, 1961). A classic study by a well-known architect analyzing America's urban ills.

Urban Renewal Politics: Slum Clearance in Newark by Harold Kaplan (New York: Columbia University Press, 1963). Politics of the Newark Housing Authority's urban renewal program in the years before the Addonizio administration. Informative material on the downtown business community and the Carlin administration.

No Cause for Indictment: An Autopsy of Newark by Ron Porambo (New York: Holt, Rinehart and Winston, 1971). A journalistic diary in the muckraking tradition that describes Newark as a center of violence, corruption, and brutality. A carefully detailed examination of the killing of blacks by police.

Governing New York City by Wallace S. Sayre and Herbert Kaufman (New York: Norton, 1965). A classic analysis from the pluralist school of political scientists.

The Tenement Landlord by George Sternlieb (New Brunswick, N.J.: Rutgers University Press, 1966). A study of the reasons behind landlord abandonment of urban tenements.

Ready to Riot by Nathan Wright, Jr. (New York: Holt, Rinehart and Winston, 1968). Social, political, and economic conditions in Newark during the period immediately preceding the 1967 rebellion.

GERALD D. SUTTLES

Anatomy of a Chicago Slum

In its heyday, the Near West Side of Chicago was the stronghold of such men as Al (Scarface) Capone and Frank (The Enforcer) Nitti, and served as the kindergarten for several figures still active in the underworld. For convenience, I will call this part of Chicago the Addams area —after Jane Addams, who founded Hull House there. The name is artificial, since it is never used by the local residents.

The Addams area is one of the oldest slums in Chicago, and researchers have invaded it almost as often as new minority groups have. Like most slums, it remains something of a mystery. In some ways it is easiest to describe the neighborhood by describing how its residents deviate from the public standards of the wider community. The area has, for example, a high delinquency rate, numerous unwed mothers, and several adolescent "gangs." It is tempting to think that the residents are simply people suffering from cultural deprivation, unemployment, and a number of other urban ills. And if the residents insist upon the irrelevance of the standards of the wider community and the primacy of their own, this can be dismissed as sour grapes or an attempt to make of necessity a virtue.

Seen from the inside, however, Addams area residents require discipline and self-restraint in the same way as the wider community does. Conventional norms are not rejected but emphasized differently, or suspended for established reasons. The vast majority of the residents are quite conventional people. At the same time, those who remain in good standing are often exceptionally tolerant of and even encouraging to those who are "deviant."

Certainly the social practices of the residents are not just an inversion of those of the wider society, and the inhabitants would be outraged to hear as much. Nor is the neighborhood a cultural island with its own distinct and imported traditions. The area's internal structure features such commonplace distinctions as age, sex, territoriality, ethnicity, and personal identity. Taken out of context, many of the social arrangements of the Addams area may seem an illusory denial of the beliefs and values of the wider society. But actually the residents are bent on ordering local relations because the beliefs and evaluations of the wider society do not provide adequate guidelines for conduct.

In anthropology, territorial grouping has been a subject of continued interest. Most anthropological studies begin by focusing upon social groupings that can be defined by their areal distribution. In turn, many of the social units singled out for particular attention—the domestic unit, the homestead, the tribe, and so forth—frequently have locality as one of their principles of organization. And where locality and structural forms do not coincide, anthropologists have regarded this discrepancy as a distinct problem that raises a number of theoretical and methodological issues.

The most obvious reason for focusing on locality groups is that their members cannot simply ignore one another. People who routinely occupy the same place must either develop a moral order that includes all those present or fall into conflict. And because almost all societies create a public morality that exceeds the capabilities of some of its members, territorial groups are always faced with the prospect of people whose public character does not warrant trust. In the United States a very large percentage of our population fails to meet the public standards we set for measuring someone's merit, trustworthiness, and respectability.

Many groups have avoided compromising these ideals of public morality by territorial segregation. More exactly, they have simply retreated and left valuable portions of the inner city to those they distrust. Obviously, this practice has its limits—it tends to aggregate those who are poor, unsuccessful, and disreputable in the same slum neighborhoods. These people must compromise the ideals of public morality or remain permanently estranged from one another.

In slum neighborhoods, territorial aggregation usually comes before any common social framework for assuring orderly relations. After all, ethnic invasion, the encroachment of industry, and economic conditions constantly reshuffle slum residents and relocate them around new neighbors. Since the residents lack obvious grounds for assuming mutual trust, a combination of alternatives seems to offer the most promising course:

■ Social relations can be restricted to only the safest ones. Families can withdraw to their households, where they see only close relatives. Segregation by age, sex, and ethnicity are maneuvers that will prevent at least the most unfair and most likely forms of conflict and exploitation. Remaining close to the household cuts down on the range of anonymity and reduces the number of social relations. The general pattern, then, should be a fan-shaped spatial arrangement, with women and children remaining close by the house while males move progressively outwards, depending on their age.

■ Slum residents can assuage at least some of their apprehensions by a close inquiry into one another's personal character and past history. Communication, then, should be of an intimate character and aimed toward producing personal rather than formal relations. In turn, social relations will represent a sort of private compact in which particular loyalties replace impersonal standards of worth.

Neither of these patterns will immediately produce a comprehensive framework within which a large number of slum residents can safely negotiate with one another. The segregation by age, sex, and territorial groups, however, does provide a starting point from which face-to-face relations can grow and reach beyond each small territorial aggregation. The development of personal relations furnishes both a moral formula and a structural bridge between

groups. Within each small, localized peer group, continuing face-to-face relations can eventually provide a personalistic order. Once these groups are established, a single personal relation between them can extend the range of such an order. Thus, with the acceptance of age-grading and territorial segregation, it becomes possible for slum neighborhoods to work out a moral order that includes most of their residents.

The Addams area actually consists of four different sections, each occupied predominantly by Negroes, Italians, Puerto Ricans, and Mexicans. And each of these sections falls into a somewhat different stage in its development of a provincial order.

Despite this difference and others, all four ethnic sections share many characteristics and seem headed along the same social progression. The overall pattern is one in which age, sex, ethnic, and territorial units are fitted together like building blocks to create a larger structure. I have termed this pattern "ordered segmentation" to indicate two related features: (1) the orderly relationship between groups; and (2) the order in which groups combine in instances of conflict and opposition. This ordered segmentation is not equally developed in all ethnic sections but, in skeletal outline, it is the common framework within which groups are being formed and social relations are being cultivated.

My own experiences within the Addams area and the presentation of this volume are heavily influenced by the ordered segmentation of the neighborhood. I took up residence in the area in the summer of 1963 and left a little fewer than three years later.

Methodology

Gerald D. Suttles spent three years in the Near West Side of Chicago making a study of a multiethnic community that includes Italians, Mexicans, Negroes and Puerto Ricans. He took up residence in the area in the summer of 1963 and did not leave until almost three years later. It took him a year or more to acquire friends and enter the private worlds of families, social-athletic clubs and other groups. The findings of his study are published in *The Social Order of the Slum* from which *Trans*-action has taken excerpts—chiefly from materials on the Italian population. The book in its entirety shows that there are broad structural similarities between all the ethnic groups—Italian, Mexican, Negro and Puerto Rican, although this structure is more clearly developed among the Italians. The excerpts draw on some of Suttles' more general observations rather than his detailed empirical findings.

As I acquired friends and close informants, my own ethnicity became a serious problem. A few people worked over my genealogy trying to find some trace that would allot me to a known ethnic group. After close inquiry, one old Italian lady announced with peals of laughter, "Geraldo, you're just an American." She did not mean it as a compliment, and I remember being depressed. In the Addams area, being without ethnicity means there is no one you can appeal to or claim as your own.

Only after a year or more in the Addams area was I able to penetrate the private world of its families, street-corner groups, and insular establishments. These are the groupings within which Addams area residents are least cautious and most likely to expose themselves. In large part my experience with these groups is limited to many adolescent male street-corner groups and my own adult friends, who formed a group of this type.

By far the most striking contrast is between the Negro and the Italian sections. For instance, almost all the Negroes live in public housing; the Italians usually control both their households and commercial establishments. The Negroes have very similar incomes and almost no political power; among the Italians, there *is* some internal differentiation of income and political power. Such differences draw the Italians and Negroes apart and generate radically different styles of life.

In most ways, the Puerto Rican section is the least complex of those in the Addams area. There are no more than 1100 Puerto Ricans in the section and, within broad age ranges, most of them know one another. Until 1965, no named groups had emerged among the Puerto Ricans.

The Mexicans are more numerous, and several named groups have developed among the teenagers. Unlike the Italians, however, the Mexican groups have not survived into adulthood. The Mexicans seem to have much in common with the Italians, and frequently their relationships are congenial. What gives the Mexicans pause is the occasional necessity to divide their loyalties between the Italians and the Negroes.

Although one must not overemphasize the extent of differences between all these ethnic sections, such differences as do occur loom large in the Addams area. The residents are actively looking for differences among themselves. The ethnic sections in the area constitute basic guidelines from which the residents of each section can expect certain forms of reciprocity, and anticipate the dangers that may be in store elsewhere.

The portion of the Addams area now controlled by the Italians is only a residue from the encroachments of the three other ethnic groups. But in total land space, it is the largest of any controlled by a single ethnic group. In population, it is not exceptionally big, though, and throughout the section an unusually high percentage of Mexicans have been accepted by the Italians as neighbors.

What the Italians lack in numbers, they often make up for by their reputation for using sheer force and for easy access to "influence" or "connections." It is said, for example, that many of the Italians are "Outfit people," and that many more could rely on mobsters if they needed help. Also, it is the general view that the Italians control both the vice and patronage of the First Ward, a political unit that includes the spoils of the Loop—downtown Chicago.

There are some very famous Italians in the Addams area, and they frequently get a spread in the city newspapers. There are many others not nearly so prominent but whose personal histories are still known in the neighborhood. At least five Italian policemen live in the area, and a few more who grew up there are assigned to the local district. The other ethnic groups have not a single

resident or ex-resident policeman among them. Most of the precinct captains are also Italian; and, outside the projects, the Italians dominate those jobs provided by public funds. There are a number of Italian businessmen, each of whom controls a few jobs. It is also widely believed that they can "sponsor" a person into many of the industries of the city —the newsstands in the Loop, the city parks, the beauty-culture industry, a large printing company, and a number of clothing firms.

While there is some substance to this belief in Italian power and influence, it is actually quite exaggerated. Many of the Italian political figures seem to have little more than the privilege of announcing decisions that have been made by others. In most of the recent political actions that have affected the area, they have remained mute and docile. When the Medical Center was built and then extended, they said nothing. The Congress and the Dan Ryan Expressways were constructed with the local politicians hardly taking notice. Finally, when the University of Illinois was located at Congress Circle, the politicians, mobsters, and—indeed—all the male residents accepted it without even a show of resistance. In fact, only a group of Italian and Mexican housewives took up arms and sought to save some remnant of the neighborhood.

The Italians' notoriety for being in the rackets and having recourse to strong-arm methods is also a considerable exaggeration, or at least a misinterpretation. The majority of the local Italians are perfectly respectable people and gain nothing from organized crime. Yet, many of the common family names of the area have been sullied by some flagrant past episode by a relative. And in the area, family histories remain a basis for judging individual members and are extended to include all persons who share the same name. In another neighborhood, this information might be lost or ignored as improper; in the Addams area, it is almost impossible to keep family secrets, and they are kept alive in the constant round of rumor and gossip.

The local Italians themselves contribute to their reputation—because on many occasions they find it advantageous to intimate that they have connections with the Outfit. For example, outsiders are often flattered to think that they are in the confidence of someone who knows the underworld. Also, it is far more prestigious to have other people believe that one's background is buried in crime and violence than in public welfare. In America, organized crime has always received a certain respect, even when this respect had to be coerced. A recipient of public welfare is simply dismissed as unimportant. And during the Depression many of the Italians went on welfare.

"Right People" Can Protect Them

In addition, some of the Italians feel that a reputation of being in with the "right people" can in some circumstances ensure them against victimization. They often hint about their connections with the Outfit when facing the members of another ethnic group under uncertain odds, or when in an argument among themselves. Yet with friends and relatives, the Italians often complain bitterly of how they are maligned by the press and by their neighbors.

Ironically, the Italians are cautious in their dealings with one another; more than any other group, they are intimidated by the half-myth that is partly of their own creation. And indirectly this myth gives them considerable cohesion, and a certain freedom from the judgments and actions of the wider society. It is almost impossible to persuade one of them to make a complaint to the police, for instance, because of their fear of the Outfit; indeed, they shun all public sources of social control. They handle grievances, contracts, and exchanges in a very informal manner, usually limited to the immediate parties. If in need, they exact aid in the form of favors and generally ignore sources available to the general public. As a result, the Italians have been able to sustain among themselves the image of an independent, powerful, and self-confident people.

Behind the Scenes Bargaining

Yet the cohesion and solidarity of the Italians are very limited. They are based primarily on the suspicion that social arrangements are best made by private settlements. This suspicion, in turn, is based on the assumption that recourse to public means can do little more than excite retaliation and vengeance. These same suspicions and doubts undermine the possibilities of a unified and explicit stance by the Italians toward the wider community and political organization. First, very few of them believe that the others will cooperate in joint efforts unless it is to their personal advantage or they are under some dire threat. Second, the Italians simply fear that a united public stand will elicit a similar posture on the part of their adversaries and eliminate the opportunity for private negotiations. Accordingly, the Italians either shun public confrontations or slowly draw away, once so engaged. In retrospect, the spirit of *omerta* seems ineffectual when it confronts the explicit efforts of the wider community. (Literally, *omerta* means a conspiracy between thieves. The Italians use it to mean any private agreement that cannot be safely broached before the general public.)

The inability of the Italians to accept or engage in public appeals leaves them somewhat bewildered by the Negroes' civil-rights movement. By the Italians' standards, the Negroes are "making a federal case" out of something that should be handled by private agreement. Indeed, even those who accept the justice of the Negroes' cause remain perplexed by the Negroes' failure to approach *them* in some informal manner. Throughout the summer of 1964, when demonstrators were most active, the Italians always seemed aggrieved and surprised that the Negroes would "pull such a trick" without warning. The Negroes took this view as a "sham" and felt that the Italians had ample reason to anticipate their demands. To the Italians this was not the point. Of course, they knew that the Negroes had many long-standing demands and desires. What struck the Italians as unfair about the Negroes' demonstrations was their tactics: sudden public confrontations, without any chance for either side to retreat or compromise with grace.

Ultimately, both the Italians and Negroes did take their differences behind closed doors, and each settled for something less than their public demands. The main bone of contention was a local swimming pool dominated by the Italians and their Mexican guests.

In the background, of course, was the oppressive belief that the benefits of social life make up a fixed quantity and are already being used to the maximum. Thus, even the most liberal Italians assume that any gain to the Negroes must be their loss. On their own part, the Negroes make the same assumption and see no reason why the Italians should give way without a fight. Thus, whatever good intentions exist on either side are overruled by the seeming impracticality or lack of realism.

The Italians' career in the Addams area has been shaped by a traditional world view that relies heavily on a belief in "natural man." For example, it is felt to be "natural" for men to be sexual predators; for mothers to love their children, regardless of what their children do; for girls to connive at marriage; for boys to hate school; for a businessman to cheat strangers; and for anyone to choose pleasure in preference to discipline and duty. Implicit in the concept of natural man is the conviction that moral restraints have little real power in a situation in which they contradict man's natural impulses. Civilization is a mere gloss to hide man's true nature.

Often, although not always, man's natural impulses are at odds with his moral standards. Indeed, otherwise there would be no need for the church, the police, the government, and all other bodies of social control. But it is not always possible for these external bodies of social control to keep track of what people are doing. Inevitably, then, there will be occasions when people are free to choose between acting naturally and acting morally. For their own part, the Italians may have considerable conviction of their personal preferences for morality. In their dealings with other people, however they have little faith in this thin thread of individual morality. Correspondingly, to them their own personal morality becomes utterly impractical and must be replaced by whatever amoral expedient seems necessary for self-defense.

The general outcome seems to be an overwhelming distrust of impersonal or "voluntary" relationships. The other side of the coin is an equally strong tendency to fall back on those relationships and identities where one's own welfare is guaranteed by "natural inclinations." For the most part these are kin relations, close friendship, common regional origins *(paesani)*, joint residential unity, and sacred pledges like marriage, God, parenthood, etc. Thus, the Italians in the Addams area have tended to turn in upon themselves and become a provincial moral world.

Actually, many of the Italians are quite "Americanized." Frequently, though, these people lead something of a double life. During the daytime they leave the neighborhood and do their work without much thought of their ethnicity. When they come home in the evening, they are obliged to reassume their old world identity. This need not be so much a matter of taste as necessity. Other people are likely to already know their ethnicity, and evasions are likely to be interpreted as acts of snobbery or attempts at deception. Moreover, members of the other three ethnic groups refuse to accept such a person's Americanization, no matter how much it is stressed. To others, an attempt to minimize one's ethnicity is only a sly maneuver to escape responsibility for past wrongs or to gain admission into their confidence.

Finally, there are still many old-timers in the neighborhood, and it would be very ill-mannered to parade one's Americanism before them. Thus, within the bounds of the local neighboorhood, an Italian who plays at being an "American" runs the risk of being taken as a snob, phony, opportunist, coward, or fink.

Among the Italians themselves, notions of ethnicity are particularly well-elaborated. For the most part, these internal subdivisions are based on regional origins in Italy. By contrast, the other ethnic groups have very little internal differentiation. The Negroes make only a vague distinction between those raised in the South and those raised in the North. Among the former, Mississippians are sometimes singled out for special contempt. However, none of these divisions lead to cohesive social unities. But among the Italians their *paesani* (regional origins) take on great importance, and it remains the first perimeter beyond the family within which they look for aid or feel themselves in safe hands. Most *paesani* continue to hold their annual summer picnics and winter dance. Some have grown into full-scale organizations with elected officers, insurance plans, burial funds, and regular poker sessions.

Of all the ethnic groups in the Addams area, the Italians still have the richest ceremonial life. Aside from the annual *paesani* dances and picnics, there are parades, *feste*, and several other occasions. In the summer, their church holds a carnival that duplicates much of the Italian *feste*. On Columbus Day there is a great parade in the Loop, exceeded in grandeur only by the one held by the Irish on St. Patrick's Day. During Lent there are several special religious events and afterwards a round of dances, parties, and feasts. Throughout the summer a local brass band periodically marches through the streets playing arias from Puccini and Verdi. Sidewalk vendors sell Italian lemonade, sausages, and beef sandwiches. Horsedrawn carts go about selling grapes during the fall winemaking season, tomatoes when they are ready to be turned to paste, and fruit and vegetables at almost any time of the year.

Communal Ceremonies and Festivities

Even weddings, communions, funerals, and wakes maintain some of their communal nature. Weddings are usually known of beforehand and often attract a number of onlookers as well as those invited. Afterwards the couple and their friends drive around the neighborhood in decorated cars, honking their horns at one another and whomever they recognize on the streets. Parochial-school children usually receive first communion as a group and attract a good deal of attention. Wakes are also open to almost anyone, and funeral processions often tour a portion of the neighborhood. On this sort of occasion, the Mexicans follow much the same practice, although they lack full control of a local church where they can carry out these affairs to the same extent as the Italians. Among the Negroes and Puerto Ricans, weddings, funerals, and religious events tend to be quite private affairs, open through invitation alone.

The Italians are also favored by the relatively long period over which many of them have been able to know one another and to decide upon whom they can or cannot trust. Over time, a considerable amount of information has been accumulated on many people, and this circulates in such a way as to be available to even a fairly recent resident. Moreover, the intertwining of social relations has become so extensive that contact with one person often opens passage to many others. In this sense, "getting acquainted" is almost unavoidable for a new resident.

The forms of social organization in the Italian section are far more extensive and complicated than those of the other ethnic groups. At the top are two groups, the "West Side Bloc" and the "Outfit," which share membership and whose participants are not all from the Addams area. The West Side Bloc is a group of Italian politicians whose constituency is much larger than the Addams area but which includes a definite wing in the area. Generally its members are assumed to belong to or to have connections with the Outfit. A good deal of power is attributed to them within the local neighborhood, city, state, and nation. The Outfit, more widely known as the Syndicate, includes many more people, but it is also assumed to reach beyond the Addams area. Locally, it is usually taken to include almost anyone who runs a tavern or a liquor store, or who relies on state licensing or city employment. A few other businessmen and local toughs are accredited with membership because of their notorious immunity to law enforcement or their reputed control of "favors."

Indirectly, the Outfit extends to a number of adult social-athletic clubs (s.a.c.'s). These clubs invariably have a storefront where the members spend their time in casual conversation or drink, or play cards. A few of their members belong to the Outfit, and a couple of these clubs are said to have a "regular game" for big stakes. Each group is fairly homogeneous in age, but collectively the groups range between the late 20's up to the late 60's.

Below these adult s.a.c.'s are a number of other s.a.c.'s that also have a clubhouse, but whose members are much younger. As a rule, they are somewhat beyond school age, but only a few are married, and practically none have children. To some degree, they are still involved in the extra-familial life that occupies teenagers. Occasionally they have dances, socials, and impromptu parties. On weekends they still roam around together, attending "socials" sponsored by other groups, looking for girls or for some kind of "action." Within each young man's s.a.c., the members' ages cover a narrow range. Together, all the groups range between about 19 and the late 20's. They form a distinct and well-recognized age grade in the neighborhood because of their continuing involvement in those cross-sexual and recreational activities open to unmarried males.

Nevertheless, these young men's s.a.c.'s are somewhat outside the full round of activities that throw teenagers together. A good portion of their time is spent inside their clubhouse out of sight of their rivals or most bodies of social control. Most members are in their 20's and are able to openly enjoy routine forms of entertainment or excitement that the wider community provides and accepts. When they have a dance or party, it is usually restricted to those whom they invite. Being out of school, they are not forced each day to confront persons from beyond their neighborhood. Since many of them have cars, they need not trespass too much on someone else's domain.

Anatomy of a Chicago Slum

These s.a.c.'s are not assumed to have any active role in the Outfit. At most, it is expected that they might be able to gain a few exemptions from law enforcement and an occasional "favor," e.g., a job, a chance to run an illegal errand, a small loan, someone to sign for their clubhouse charter (required by law); and the purchase of stolen goods or of anything else the boys happen to have on hand. It is assumed that they could solicit help from the Outfit if they got into trouble with another group, but very rarely are they drawn into this type of conflict. Almost invariably the opponent is a much younger "street group" that has encroached on what the s.a.c. considers its "rights"—e.g., tried to "crash" one of their parties, insulted them on the streets, made noise nearby, or marked up their clubhouse. Even at these times, their actions seem designed to do little more than rid themselves of a temporary nuisance. Once rid of their tormentors, they usually do not pursue the issue further, and for good reason. To charter such a club requires three cosigners, and these people may withdraw their support if the group becomes too rowdy. Also, they have a landlord to contend with, and he can throw them out for the same reason. Finally, they cannot afford to make too many enemies; they have a piece of property, and it would be only too easy for their adversaries to get back at them. Unlike all the groups described in the other three sections, they have a stake in maintaining something like law and order.

All the remaining Italian groups include members who are of high-school age. While they too call themselves s.a.c.'s, none of them have a storefront. All of them do have an established "hangout," and they correspond to the usual image of a street-corner group.

While the street groups in this section of the area often express admiration for the adult s.a.c.'s, they seldom develop in an unbroken sequence into a full-fledged adult s.a.c. Usually when they grow old enough to rent a storefront they change their name, acquire new members from groups that have been their rivals, and lose a few of their long-term members. Some groups disband entirely, and their members are redistributed among the newly formed s.a.c.'s. Of the 12 young men's and adult s.a.c.'s, only one is said to have maintained the same name from the time it was a street-corner group. Even in this case some members have been added and others lost. Together, then, the Italian street-corner groups make up the population from which future young men's s.a.c.'s are drawn, but only a few street-corner groups form the nucleus of a s.a.c.

Conceptually, the Italian street groups and the older s.a.c.'s form a single unity. In the eyes of the boys, they are somewhat like the steps between grammar school and college. While there may be dropouts, breaks, and amalgamations, they still make up a series of steps through which one can advance with increasing age. Thus, each street group tends to see the adult s.a.c.'s as essentially an older and more perfect version of itself. What may be just as important is their equally strong sense of history. Locally, many of the members in the street groups can trace their group's genealogy back through the Taylor Dukes, the 40 game, the Genna Brothers, and the Capone mob. Actually, there is no clear idea of the exact order of this descent line; some people include groups that others leave out. Moreover, there is no widespread agreement on which specific group is the current successor to this lineage. Nonetheless, there is agreement that the groups on Taylor Street have illustrious progenitors. On some occasions this heritage may be something of a burden, and on others a source of pride. In any case, it is unavoidable, and usually the Italian street group preface its own name with the term "Taylor." Among the younger groups this is omitted only when their name is an amalgam made up from a specific street corner or block. Only the adult s.a.c.'s regularly fail to acknowledge in their name the immediate territory within which they are situated.

Direct Line of Succession from the Outfit

Since they see themselves in a direct line of succession to groups reputed to be associated with the Outfit, these street-corner groups might be expected to have a strong criminal orientation. In the Addams area, however, the Italian groups are best known for their fighting prowess, and their official police records show no concentration on the more utilitarian forms of crime. The fact is that, like the other adolescent groups in the area, the Italian boys are not really free to choose their own goals and identities. Territorial arrangements juxtapose them against similar groups manned by Negro and Mexican boys. If the Italian street-corner groups fail to define themselves as fighting groups, their peers in the other ethnic groups are certainly going to assume as much.

There is also considerable rivalry between Italian street-corner groups of roughly the same age. Commonly they suspect each other of using force to establish their precedence. In turn, each group seems to think it must at least put on a tough exterior to avoid being "pushed around." Privately there is a great deal of talk among them about the Outfit and about criminal activities, but it is academic in the sense that there is no strong evidence that their behavior follows suit.

It is interesting that the adult s.a.c.'s that actually have members in the rackets avoid any conspicuous claims about their criminal activities or fighting abilities. Their names, for example, are quite tame, while those of the street groups tend to be rather menacing. And their dances, leisure-time activities, and interrelationships are quite private and unpretentious. Unlike the street groups, they never wear clothing that identifies their group membership. The older men in the s.a.c.'s make no apparent attempt to establish a publicly-known hierarchy among themselves. Other people occasionally attribute more respect to one than another of them, but there seems to be little consensus on this. On their own part, the older groups seem to pay little attention to their relative standing and to be on fairly good terms. During my three years in the area, I never heard of them fighting among themselves.

Unlike the Negro and Mexican ethnic sections, there are no female counterparts to the named Italian street-corner groups. A very few Italian girls belong to two Mexican girls' groups that "hung" in the Mexican section. This, in itself, was exceptional; almost always the minority members in a street group are from a lower-ranking ethnic group.

The Italian girls, however, are under certain constraints that may be lacking for those in the other ethnic groups. Naturally, their parents disapprove of such a blatant display of feminine unity. The Italian parents may gain stature by their power and precedence in comparison to the Negro and Mexican adults. Yet what seems far more significant is the general form that boy-girl relationships take among the Italians. On either side, the slightest hint of interest in the other sex is likely to be taken in the most serious way; as either a rank insult or a final commitment. Thus, any explicit alliance between a boys' and girls' group can be interpreted in only one of two ways: (1) all the girls are "laying" for the boys, or (2) they are seriously attached to each other. Neither side seems quite willing to betray so much and, thus, they avoid such explicit alliances.

This dilemma was quite evident on many occasions while I was observing the Italian boys and girls. The girls seemed extraordinarily coy when they were in a "safe" position—with their parents, in church, etc. When alone and on their own they became equally cautious and noncommittal. On public occasions, the boys seemed almost to ignore the girls and even to snub them. On Taylor Street, for instance, an Italian boys' group and an Italian girls' group used to hang about 10 feet from each other. Almost invariably they would stand with their backs to each other, although there were many furtive glances back and forth. During almost two years of observation, I never saw them talk. Later, I was surprised to learn that everyone in each group was quite well-known to the other. For either of them to have acknowledged the other's presence openly, however, would have been too forward. The boys are quite aware of this dilemma and complain that the girls are not free enough to be convenient companions. This, they say, is one reason why they have to go elsewhere to date someone. At the same time, they perpetuate the old system by automatically assuming that the slightest sign of interest by a girl makes her fair game. Out of self-defense, the girls are compelled to keep their distance. On private occasions, of course, there are many Italian boys and girls who sneak off to enjoy what others might consider an entirely conventional boy-girl relationship (petting, necking). In public, though, they studiously ignore each other. Throughout my time in the area I never saw a young Italian couple hold hands or walk together on the sidewalk.

The Barracudas were the first Mexican street-corner group to emerge in the Italian section. They first became a named group in the spring of 1964, and all members were Mexican.

Once established, the Barracudas installed themselves in the northwest corner of Sheridan Park. Virtually every Italian street group in the area makes use of this park, and several have their hangout there. Other people in turn refer to the Italian groups collectively as "the guys from the Park." The park itself is partitioned into a finely graduated series of more or less private enclosures, with the most private hangout going to the reigning group and the least private to the weakest group. The northwest corner of the park is the most exposed of any portion, and this is where the Barracudas installed themselves. Even in this lowly spot, they were much resented by the other groups. To the Itali-

ans the Park was almost a sacred charge, and the Mexicans' intrusion was a ritual pollution. The Barracudas were harassed, ridiculed, and insulted. On their own part, they became belligerent and vaunted all sorts of outrageous claims about themselves. Soon the situation deteriorated and the Italian groups became extremely harsh with the Barracudas. Since the Barracudas were no match for even some of the younger Italian groups, they removed themselves to one member's house.

Their new hangout placed them in an anomalous position. Ethnically they were identified as a Mexican group. Yet they were located in a part of the area that had been conceded to the Puerto Ricans. And individually most of them continued to reside in the Italian section. The general result seems to have been that the Barracudas were isolated from any of the other group hierarchies and placed in opposition to every group in the area. Within a year every white group was their enemy, and the Negroes were not their friends. The Barracudas responded in kind and became even more truculent and boastful. More than any group in the area, they openly embraced the stance of a fighting group. They wrote their name all over the neighborhood and even on some of the other groups' hangouts. In the meantime, they made a clubhouse out of a lean-to adjacent to a building on Harrison Street. Inside they installed a shield on which they wrote "hate," "kill," and other violent words. Carrying a weapon became almost routine with them, and eventually they collected a small arsenal. In time they had several small-scale fights with both the Italians from the Park and the Mexicans around Polk and Laflin. In due course, they acquired so many enemies that they could hardly risk leaving the immediate area of their hangout. At the same time, some of them began to go to Eighteenth Street, where they had "connections"—relatives. This only brought them into conflict with other groups in this neighborhood. By the summer of 1965, the Barracudas were as isolated and resentful as ever.

"Incognitos" and the "Pica People"

There are two other groups in the Italian section, the Pica People and the Incognitos. The groups' names are themselves an expression of their isolation. The Incognitos self-consciously avoided comparison with the other groups: They did not hang in the Park, hold socials, or become involved in any of the local sidewalk confrontations. About the same age as the Contenders, the Incognitos were notably different in their exclusion from the local round of praise and recriminations.

"Pica People" is a derisive name meant as an insult for five young men about 19 to 25 years of age. Although these five individuals associate regularly, they claim no group identity and become angry when called the Pica People. Unlike the Incognitos, the Pica People are well-known and often accused of some predatory display. They do not fight for group honor, but there is friction between them and all the other street-corner groups in the Addams area.

It was impossible to determine how these two groups came into existence. (I talked only twice with the Incognitos, who simply said they "grew up together." Local people started calling the Pica People by that name after a movie in which the "Pica People" were sub-humans. I knew some of the members of this group, but they became so angry at any mention of the name that I could not discuss it with them.) What is known of their composition may throw some light on why they were excluded from the structure of the other groups. All informants described the Incognitos as "good guys," still in school and no trouble to anyone. They were not considered college boys but, if asked, most informants said they thought some of them might go to college. Local youth agencies made no attempt to work with them, and the entire neighborhood seemed to feel they were not dangerous. Other street-corner groups in the Italian section did not look down on them, but they did exempt them from the ambitions that brought other groups into opposition.

The Pica People were just the opposite. All members were boastful of their alleged Outfit connections and their ability to intimidate other people. But the Pica People possessed so many personal flaws that they were rather useless to the Outfit. One member was slightly claustrophobic. Another was so weak that even much younger boys pushed him around. A third had an exceedingly unfortunate appearance. Under the circumstances, their pretensions became laughable.

Extremes of Street Corner Groups

The Incognitos and the Pica People seem to represent the extremes of a range in which the street-corner group is considered the normal adolescent gathering. Modest and well-behaved youngsters are excluded as exceptions, as are criminally inclined but unsuccessful young men. Both of these groups fell outside the range considered normal by the local residents and were thereby dissociated from the total group hierarchy.

The social context of the Italian street groups is somewhat different from that of the street groups in the other three ethnic sections. Among the Italians, the major share of coercive power still remains in adult hands. The wider community may not be very pleased with the form *their* power takes, but it is the only case where the corporate power of the adolescents is tempered by that of the adults. Also, since many of the same adults have an active role in distributing some of the benefits that are held in store by the wider community, their power is augmented. Perhaps the most obvious result of the adults' ascendency is that the adolescents do not simply dismiss them or adulthood as unimportant. A more immediate consequence is to give many of the adults the prerogative of exacting considerable obedience from the local adolescents. It is not all uncommon to see an Italian adult upbraid and humble one of the local youths. Not all adults have this privilege; but many do, and their example provides a distinct contrast to the other ethnic groups where similar efforts would be futile.

In the long run, the effectiveness of these coercive controls among the Italians may do little more than confirm their convictions that, outside of natural tendencies, there is no guarantee to moral conduct except economic and numerical strength. Within their own little world, however, such coercive measures constitute a fairly effective system of social control. Personal privacy and anonymity are almost impossible. In turn, each person's known or assumed connections dampen most chances at exploitation because of the fear of unknown consequences. Thus, the opportunities for immorality presented by transient relations and "fair game" are fairly rare. Within these limits, such an authoritarian system of social control will work. Outside their own section, of course, these conditions do not hold; and the Italian boys find themselves free to seize whatever advantages or opportunities present themself. Among themselves, they are usually only a rowdy and boisterous crowd. With strangers or in other parts of the Addams area, they become particularly arrogant and unscrupulous.

With these qualifications, it appears that well-established adolescent street-corner groups are quite compatible with strong adult authority and influence. In fact, judging from the Italian section, these adolescent street-corner groups seem to be the building blocks out of which the older and more powerful groups have originated. The younger groups continue to replenish the older ones and help maintain the structure within which adults are shown deference.

Moreover, the total age-graded structure of groups in the Italian section relates youngsters to the wider society both instrumentally and conceptually. The Italian street groups see themselves as replacements in an age structure that becomes progressively less provincial. At the upper age level, groups even stop prefacing their name with the term "Taylor"; and a few of their members have a place in the wider society through the Outfit and West Side Bloc. The relationship between these age grades also provides a ladder down which favors and opportunities are distributed. The wider community may hesitate at accepting the legitimacy of these transactions, but they are mostly of a conventional form. The "Outfit" and the "West Side Bloc" have a strong interest in maintaining a degree of social order, and the sorts of wanton violence associated with gangs do not at all fit their taste.

In Conclusion

The Addams area is probably a more orderly slum than many others, and it departs sharply from the common image of an atomized and unruly urban rabble. For all its historical uniqueness, the neighborhood does establish the possibility of a moral order within its population. The recurrence of the circumstances that led to its organization is as uncertain as the future of the Addams area itself. In spite of all these uncertainties, the Addams area shows that slum residents are intent upon finding a moral order and are sometimes successful in doing so.

Gerald D. Suttles is assistant professor of sociology at the University of Chicago. His article is an excerpt from his book *The Social Order of the Slum: Ethnicity and Territoriality in the Inner City* published by the University of Chicago Press, © 1968, all rights reserved by the University of Chicago Press.

3. Poverty and Social Inequality

The War on Poverty, in effect, died with the end of the Johnson presidency in 1968. Much has been written about the mistakes that were made, the limitations of the program, and how it could have been improved. While we shall not attempt to review this literature here, it should be noted that the War on Poverty personified the persistent errors the United States government makes in addressing the issue of poverty in America.

The emphasis in the War on Poverty was on the provision of social services designed to alleviate the most acute symptoms of poverty in the United States. It led to a huge increase in government expenditures, little of which was channeled directly to the poor. Instead, much of it was used to staff a whole new government bureaucracy, some recruited from disadvantaged ethnic groups, who found a new avenue of upward mobility (which today is fast vanishing). It also reinforced the dependency of the poor on an array of social services now being withdrawn or drastically reduced. The War on Poverty neglected the basic issue of the unequal distribution of wealth and resources in American society and the concentration of power in the hands of a few élite groups. It attacked poverty but not inequality, which requires a redistribution of wealth and power in the society. Inequality inevitably demands a political solution designed to reduce the powerlessness of the poor as well as raise their low income.

The politicalization of the poor in the United States is just beginning. As Heilbroner points out in his article "Benign Neglect in the United States," we do not even have a social democratic tradition in the United States such as grew up around working class movements in Europe. Just as the trade union movement in this country was gaining a strong foothold, it was seized with the anti-Communist hysteria that swept the nation following the Russian revolution. As a result, organized labor never attempted to create a mass political party of its own addressed to the needs of the working class, but was co-opted into the more moderate reformist tradition of the Democratic Party.

Heilbroner notes that we do not even compare favorably with other advanced capitalist countries like Sweden, England, or Canada in terms of such indexes as housing, public health, and criminal justice. The reasons,

Heilbroner feels, lie in our democratic distrust of government and the restricted reach of concern stemming from the "frontier spirit" of egalitarian individualism. The tremendous economic growth of the United States with its expanding possibilities for social mobility reinforced the Social Darwinistic belief that the poor are themselves to blame for their failure to take advantage of these opportunities. As a result, Heilbroner notes, ". . . the American experience made Americans loath to acknowledge the social causes of neglect and reluctant to use public authority to attend to them."

The view that the poor are themselves to blame for their problems continues to influence much of the social science literature on poverty. The poor are seen as distorted, deviant, and pathological versions of middle-class "normalcy," as shown by the high incidence of crime, juvenile delinquency, illegitimacy, and other indexes of social disorganization in poverty areas. McClellan points to the lack of "need achievement" among the poor, while Banfield goes so far as to advocate the removal of children from poor families as a "preventive" measure. Even Oscar Lewis' vivid description of the death of a poor Puerto Rican woman in "The Death of Dolores" in this section focuses largely upon the pathology of shantytown life and the bitter human relationships it breeds. While Lewis' culture-of-poverty thesis acknowledges the importance of external conditions such as a capitalistic class structure in the development of the subculture, his focus upon the pathology of the poor themselves leads the reader to dwell on this as a causal factor.

In the view of most authors assembled here, however, poverty is not the fault of the poor, but of the institutions of the larger society which exploit and oppress them. The life of the poor is seen as an adaptation to substandard conditions restricting their upward mobility, such as unemployment, welfare, illness, poor education, and housing. From this perspective, the solution to poverty lies not in changing the values and life-styles of the poor, as Banfield and McClellan would have us do, but in changing the conditions in the larger society which sustain poverty and inequality.

The articles in this section point to the diversity of the American poor. Contrary to popular misconception, they are not just blacks and other minorities living in crowded, inner-city ghettos (a subject which will be treated more fully in the next section on racism and repression); the poor include the aged, migrant workers, abandoned mothers with children living on welfare, and the old-time rural residents of depressed areas like Appalachia. The reason why such groups are often overlooked in discussions of the poor are that they tend to be "invisible," as Nelkin puts it—shut off from the mainstream of American society in camps, institutions, and remote areas of the country (like Appalachia). Confinement or concealment has always been a convenient way of dealing with the poor, dating from the early English poorhouse, since it not only reduces the society's sense of shame or guilt, and possible "contagion" from these deviant elements, but also reduces the poor's ability to bring pressure upon the larger society to redress these injustices.

Nelkin's article on "Invisible Migrant Workers" documents how the totally isolated and stigmatized position of migrants adds to the difficulties of organization or self-help activities. The same is noted by Jackson in his article "In the Valley of the Shadows: Kentucky"; he demonstrates how the total dependency of the Appalachian poor on outside resources—jobs, welfare, or public services—effectively stymied the attempt by the Appalachian volunteers to organize the community against exploitation by the larger society.

The low status of the poor in American society not only renders them powerless, but reinforces their own lack of self-esteem and self-confidence. This is most poignantly demonstrated in Markson's article on the aged, in which she describes how the chronically ill are often assigned to state mental hospitals, not because of any basic psychiatric disorder but in order to be given "A Hiding Place to Die." She notes, "The old are already socially dying through relinquishment of roles; as they have little future before them, their lives are considered to have little social worth." Even their families prefer to be relieved of the burden. In a capitalist society, where status is measured in terms of productivity, property ownership, and other material assets, the aged, most of whom are poor and in failing health, can have little sense of worth.

Another large category of the poor in American society who are also considered socially unproductive are mothers with dependent children. As Piven and Cloward point out in their article "The Relief of Welfare" the Aid to Families with Dependent Children (AFDC) is currently our major relief program and is growing constantly, even in periods of high employment. Piven and Cloward demonstrate that welfare, far from constituting a public dole or charity, actually performs an essentially labor-regulating function in capitalist society. Welfare maintains the status quo by supporting the unemployed at times when mass unemployment might lead to protest, and expelling them when a cheap labor reserve is again needed. The stigma of welfare also reinforces the much-lauded "work ethic" in American society for "to demean and punish those who do not work is to exalt by contrast even the meanest labor at the meanest wages."

Because of growing welfare budgets, particularly among AFDC recipients, and the feeling among officials and the general public that many mothers are simply taking advantage of these benefits, there has been increasing emphasis on pushing relief clients to work. The most serious obstacle in the case of AFDC recipients is the care of the children, leading to the initiation of the first large-scale federal sponsorship of day-care centers described by Steiner in his article "Day Care Centers: Hype or Hope?" These centers meet a great need, not only among AFDC recipients, but among many working mothers who have long struggled to provide adequate care for their children during working hours. In fact, the rather broad base of support for day care centers lies in their appeal to the middle class where there is also a high percentage of women employed. Programs which do not cater exclusively to the needs of the poor generally fare more successfully in American society, as witness social security and unemployment compensation which were considered radical when first proposed in the 1930s, and now are accepted as the minimal security due any citizen in a democracy. However, contrary to socialist or even social democratic countries like Sweden, we are still unable to accept the notion that the state should take any responsibility for child care, since this is considered the mother's primary responsibility (and also becomes a convenient device for keeping women out of the labor force). As a result, Steiner points out, most federal support for day care centers has now been severely curtailed, leaving many working mothers without any suitable alternative.

We have also consistently refused to support federal aid for health care, except for the ground-breaking programs of Medicare and Medicaid, limited to the aged and the very poor. Providing health care to the chronically ill, such as those suffering from kidney disease, represents an enormous burden even to the middle class, as Suczek's article on "Chronic Medicare" demonstrates. Kidney transplants are still of limited success, and the cost of long-term dialysis is not covered by most private health insurance policies. As a result, even some physicians and politicians are beginning to look toward the federal government to meet this clearly emerging need.

Opponents of federal programs in health, day care, housing, and other areas argue that our "free enterprise" economy is so strong that aid is unnecessary for all but the disabled, the aged, and others unable to work. They preserve the myth of an open society which provides opportunities for everyone who wishes to work hard to get ahead. Education has long been considered the "great equalizer" in American society and the quickest avenue to upward mobility. However, Bowles' article "Unequal Education and the Reproduction of the Class Structure" demonstrates how schools actually maintain the status quo of American society by legitimizing and reproducing the current class structure. Bowles shows how both the quantity and quality of education is differentiated among the rich and the poor, extending even to the attitudes conveyed in the classroom where the élite are taught self-reliance while the poor are trained in conformity and obedience. Just as welfare performs a labor-regulating function in capitalist society, schools help meet the needs of capitalist employers for a disciplined and skilled labor force, at the same time that they legitimize this order and thus act as a mechanism for social control and political stability. As a result, Bowles notes, attempts at reducing inequality in education, as in other areas, generally fail because none of these reforms challenge the basic class structure of American society. On the contrary, most reforms are designed to keep the system operating by placating the poor without endangering the vested interests of the élite.

Housing reforms suffer from the same limitation. Stegman's article "The New Mythology of Housing" points out how all of the current proposals for housing reform, including home ownership for the poor, self-help housing employing ghetto residents, and the more sophisticated systems approach, fail to attack the basic issue of the maldistribution of wealth and income in the United States, from which all of the problems of poverty ultimately stem. Stegman suggests—as a last resort—declaring substandard housing a public utility, in short, nationalizing at least part of the housing industry. Though this has been done quite successfully in most socialist and some social democratic countries, it stands little chance of success here because nationalized housing strikes at the very core of the concept of private ownership so sacred to the capitalist system. Even public housing which retains state ownership of property with subsidized rental for the poor has had little public support.

The minimal federal support now provided for health, housing, welfare, and other needs has, in effect, created a dual system of social services in the United States, one provided by the private market and another by the public sector, usually at far lower standards. This system of social services has thus intensified the structural inequalities of American society and added to the degradation and shame suffered by those who must rely on public aid. Other social welfare measures—unemployment compensation, social security, and AFDC—have not helped to reduce inequality, but serve primarily to maintain a cheap labor reservoir for use by private business in times of high demand and productivity. Programs designed ostensibly for the public welfare are used to underwrite the capricious labor needs of big business.

The solution to poverty and inequality in American society clearly lies in a basic redistribution of resources which would fundamentally alter the present class structure. Full-scale federal programs in health, housing, day care, as well as the various proposals for a guaranteed national income (discussed in Gans' article in Section 7) clearly represent a step in this direction. But they have lacked the electoral support which the poor and the working class, acting out of their own self-interest, should provide. Till now, organized labor has concentrated chiefly on their own union programs in health, housing, education, etc., financed through union funds with limited public support. Organized labor, including not only the "hard hats" but professional unions of teachers and other white-collar workers, has refused to accept responsibility for the "undeserving poor."

A fundamental obstacle to working class unity in the United States, as Heilbroner points out, is that we have tended to identify poverty with race. Organized labor generally has been more concerned with maintaining relatively privileged status and with distinguishing themselves from the inner city ghetto poor (blacks and other racial minorities) than with building political movements addressed to all workers, regardless of race. They still believe in the myth of an open society and in individual mobility.

As job markets tighten and the burden of providing adequate education, health, housing, and other needs increases, even for the middle class, we may find increasing support for federal programs in these areas. The proposed programs in federal health care, brought on by astronomically rising costs, certainly point in this direction. However, we have a long way to go to approximate the standards of other advanced capitalist nations.

ROBERT L. HEILBRONER

Benign Neglect in the United States

The United States is by all conventional measures the wealthiest nation in the world. Why is it not at the same time the most socially advanced? To put the question differently, why is it that a nation that could afford to remove social and economic inequities more easily than any other has been so laggard in doing so?

Note that my question hinges on the *comparative* performance of the United States. I am not concerned with measuring the absolute level of neglect in America, or assessing the trend of that neglect or trying to estimate by how much it could or should be reduced in the future. My problem here is broader and more far-reaching, and perhaps correspondingly more difficult. It is why social neglect in the United States is greater than in other nations with similar institutions, such as Norway, Sweden, Denmark, Switzerland, New Zealand, England or Canada. In the end, of course, the matter that concerns us is the alleviation of

neglect in this country—a matter to which I shall turn at the end of this essay—but the primary focus of my inquiry lies in the roots of the problem rather than in the specifics of its remedy.

Let me begin by documenting briefly the premise from which I start. I shall do so in broad brush strokes, partly because the statistical information is lacking to make finer comparisons, and partly because I do not think the basic evidence is apt to be called into question.

I start with habitat itself. It is not a simple matter to make precise comparisons of social neglect with regard to housing and living environment among nations, because accepted standards differ from one country to the next.

Swedish housing projects, for example, have fewer rooms per family and less room space per person than similar projects in the United States, while in Japan only 13 percent of all urban and less than 2 percent of all rural dwellings have flush toilets, a condition that in the United States is virtually prima facie evidence of extreme social disrepair. Thus the unwary statistical comparison shopper could easily come to the conclusion that American housing projects are better than Swedish, or that the vast bulk of Japanese live in conditions similar to those of the worst of our slums.

Such considerations make it exceedingly difficult, or even impossible, to arrive at a simple ranking of living habitats that will disclose where the United States belongs on an international spectrum of neglect. Hence I shall content myself with two generalizations based on personal observations at home and abroad. First, I believe that in no large city in the United States do we find a concern for the living habitat comparable to that commonly found in the cities of such nations as the Netherlands, Switzerland or the countries of Scandinavia; and second, I maintain that to match the squalor of the worst of the American habitat one must descend to the middle range of the underdeveloped lands. These are, I repeat, "impressionistic" statements, for which quantitative documentation is lacking, but I do not think they will be challenged on that account.

Let me now turn to a second and somewhat more objective indicator of the comparative performance of the United States with regard to social well-being—the neglect of poverty. Here again, however, a degree of statistical prudence is necessary. The income of a family of four at the "official" threshold of poverty in the United States is roughly $3,500. This is an income approximately equivalent to that of a family in the middle brackets in Norway. Poverty is therefore a matter of relative affluence quite as much as absolute income. Nevertheless, just as the definition of poverty reflects the differing levels of productivity of different countries, so the neglect of poverty also mirrors the differing capabilities of nations to create a surplus that can be transferred to those in need. Thus, a rich nation may define its level of need higher than its poor neighbor, but it should also be in a better position to devote more of its income to the remedy of that need.

Unfortunately, we do not have detailed statistics that allow us to match the specific antipoverty efforts of different nations, as percentages of their national incomes. But as a very rough indicator of the allocation of resources for this purpose we can turn to the percentage of Gross National Product used for income transfers of all kinds. In the 1960s, for the nations of the European Economic Community the average ratio of social security expanditure to GNP was approximately 14 percent; for the Scandinavian trio it was around 12 to 13 percent; for Canada 9.9 percent. In the United States the ratio was 6.5 percent, barely above the level for Portugal.

Furthermore, to this general indicator of comparative per-

formance we can add a second consideration. The existential quality of poverty is profoundly affected by the surrounding conditions in which it is experienced. The difference between "genteel" and "degrading" poverty is not alone one of private income but of public environment. Thus, a factor worsening the relative neglect of poverty in the United States is that it is here concentrated in the noisome slums of our cities or rural backwaters, rather than being alleviated, as in the Scandinavian or better European nations, by clean cities, attractive public parks and a high general level of basic life support.

Another related, and yet distinct, area of social neglect is that of public health. Here we possess the most detailed statistics of international performance, but once again the results are not comforting for the United States.

Just Above Hong Kong

At first blush, one would expect to find the United States as a world leader in the field of health. No nation devotes as large a fraction of its gross output—some 6.5 percent—to health services. None has produced more important advances in drugs or medical techniques or spent more on basic research. Yet the comparative showing of the United States can only be described as disastrous. In 1950 the United States ranked fifth safest in the world in risk of infant mortality. This less-than-best rating could perhaps be explained by the generally admitted inferior health services provided the Negro population, much of which still lived in rural areas in the South. Since then, however, the Negro has moved northward and to the cities, but despite (or because of?) this migration, our infant mortality rate has steadily worsened. By 1955 we had fallen to eighth place; by 1960, to 12th. Today it is estimated that we rank 18th, just above Hong Kong.

It is not only in infant mortality that comparative neglect in matters of health is visible in the United States. Despite our overall expenditure on health services, we ranked only 22nd in male life expectancy in 1965 (down from 13th in 1959) and tenth in female life expectancy (down from seventh in 1959). Our death rates from pneumonia and TB are far from the best. Diseases of malnutrition, including kwashiorkor—long considered a disease specific to underdeveloped areas—have been discovered in the United States.

The causes for this deplorable showing are complex and involve many cultural attributes of Americans, who overeat and oversmoke, as well as reflecting the effects of sheer neglect. But the steady deterioration of our comparative showing does not result from an absolute impairment of American health (with minor exceptions) as much as from the spectacular successes of other nations in applying social effort to the improvement of their national health. Judged against this steady comparative decline, the finding of extreme social neglect in the area of health seems inescapable.

Last, let me direct attention to a somewhat unrelated but

surely no less important area of social concern. This is the manner in which we and other advanced nations treat that aberrant fraction of the population that is apprehended for criminality. I put the matter this way since it is well known that the infringement of laws is much more widespread than the prosecution of illegality. Estimates of crimes committed, but unreported, range from twice the number of recorded instances of criminality to much larger than that. Indeed, a recently reported survey of 1,700 adults without criminal records brought out that 99 percent of them had committed offenses for which they could have ended in prison. Furthermore, it is clear that among those who do commit crimes, it is the economically and socially least privileged that bear by far the heaviest incidence of prosecution and punishment. In 1967 the President's Crime Commission reported that 90 percent of American youth had done something for which they could have been committed by a juvenile court. Yet only 5 percent of the children in institutions for juvenile delinquency come from families in "comfortable circumstances."

I have no evidence to indicate that this differential apportionment of punishment is more pronounced in this nation than in others. But I have some distressing statistics with regard to the measures taken by our nation in its treatment of the "criminal" stratum compared with the measures taken by other nations. The total population of Sweden, for example, is about half that of California. Yet her prison population is only one-fifth that of California's, and one-third of that prison population is in small light-security camps enjoying "open" conditions. In the United States, such work-release camps are available only in four states. The caseloads of prison psychologists in Denmark average 20 to 30 per doctor; in the United States the average ratio of psychiatrists or trained therapists per inmate is one to 179, and this ratio is for our federal penal institutions which are far superior to our state institutions. In no Scandinavian (or European) country have prison camps or institutions been reported that can match for brutality the conditions recently discovered at the Arkansas state farm. All this must have some bearing on the fact that 20 to 40 convicted persons out of 100 in Scandinavia go back to jail for some other offense, while an average of 73 out of 100 do so in the United States.

Capitalism and Character

It would not be difficult to add evidence of neglect in other areas of American social life. One thinks, for example, of the niggardliness of American social security payments as a percentage of preretirement earnings compared with those of Sweden, or of the greater American than European indifference with regard to the protection of the consumer in many areas. But I think the basic premise does not require further detailed argument. Instead, let us now turn to the central and critical question with which we began. How can we account for the anomaly that the United States, which among all nations can most easily afford to remedy social neglect, has been so lax in doing so?

We move now from the reasonably solid ground of evidence to the quicksands of explanation. Any effort to unravel the problem of American relative social backwardness must be suppositive and conjectural. But let me begin by stressing an essential aspect of this inquiry. It is that the terms of the problem, as we have posed it, make it impossible simply to declare that the social neglect all too visible in America is nothing but the "natural" result of the class stratification, the hegemony of property interest or the blind play of market forces characteristic of capitalism. Speaking of the failure of American society to provide low-cost housing, two radical critics, Paul Baran and Paul Sweezy, have declared: "Such planning and such action [that is, the provision of low-rent housing] will never be undertaken by a government run by and for the rich, as every capitalist government is and must be." The trouble with such an explanation is that it overlooks the fact that there is no significant difference in income distribution, concentration of private or corporate wealth or play of market forces among the various countries that we have used to establish the laggard social record of the United States. The top 5 percent of income receivers in Denmark received 17.5 percent of national income in 1955; 19 percent in (urban) Norway in 1948; 24 percent in Sweden in 1945; 20 percent in the United States in 1955–59 (before tax). Concentration of corporate assets and sales among all capitalist nations is also roughly similar. Nor does the degree of intervention into the market seem inordinately different as between, say, Switzerland on the one hand and the United States on the other. It may very well be that the institutions and ideologies of capitalism place fundamental inhibitions on the reach of social amelioration in all capitalist nations, but the problem remains as to why the United States has not reached the limits of improvement that have been attained by other nations in which the same basic inhibitions exist.

This initial orientation to our inquiry suggests that the reasons must be sought in the most treacherous of all quicksand regions—those that account for the subtle differences in basic institutions, attitudes or responses that we call "national character." Evidently factors and forces in the American past made American capitalism less attentive, or less responsive, to large areas of social neglect than was the case with her sister societies abroad. What might these elements have been?

We might start by considering what is perhaps the most obvious difference between the United States and the European nations—the matter of size. One hypothesis would then be that the higher level of American neglect could be ascribed to social changes induced by the larger scale of our continent, with its obvious spatial obstacles in the way of creating a tight-knit society with a strongly felt sense of communal responsibility and concern.

The hypothesis is a tempting one and perhaps contains a modicum of explanatory power. Sheer distance undoubtedly works against the growth of community spirit. But the effects of scale cannot possibly bear the whole burden of the problem. Canada, with a better record of legislative social concern than we, has an even larger territory. More to the point, the density of population per square mile, which is perhaps the most important way in which scale becomes translated into human experience, is not markedly different in the United States than in many smaller nations. The United States averages 55 persons per square mile; Sweden averages 44; Norway, 31; New Zealand, 26; Canada, 5. Thus the effects of scale in separating man from man, and presumably thereby reducing the level of shared concerns and mutual responsibilities, should operate in the opposite direction, toward a higher level of concern in the United States than in any of the above countries.

A second intuitive possibility seems more convincing. If size does not provide a convincing answer to the problem of why America lacks a relatively high-ranking program of social repair, the striking diversity of the American scene may serve as a better reason. In the heterogeneity of the American population there would seem to be a prima facie cause for its lack of community feeling.

As with the matter of size, it may be that heterogeneity has its role to play, but—with one special exception to which I will shortly turn—I do not believe it can be made a central causative factor. There is, to begin with, the awkward fact that the most heterogenous of all European nations—Switzerland with its three language groups—is certainly one with a high level of public amenities. Canada is another example of a culturally diverse nation, in which political frictions have not stood in the way of the development of an advanced welfare system. Perhaps even more telling, we cannot easily establish within the United States any strong association between homogeneity of culture and community concern. The high level of social neglect among the white population of the southern states and the inattention paid to the decline of Appalachia by its white kinsmen in more affluent areas of that region are cases in point.

However, if homogeneity, in itself, seems an uncertain source of social concern, there is no doubt that the special case of racial heterogeneity is an all too certain cause of social neglect. The problem of racial animosity is by no means confined to this country and wherever it appears greatly intensifies the problem of neglect: witness the Maori in New Zealand and the Ainu in Japan. But there is no parallel to the corrosive and pervasive role played by race in the problem of social neglect in the United States. It is an obvious fact that the persons who suffer most from the kinds of neglect we have mentioned—residents of the slums, recipients of welfare payments, the medically deprived and the inmates of prisons—are disproportionately Negro. This merging of the racial issue with that of ne-

glect serves as a rationalization for the policies of inaction that have characterized so much of the American response to need. Programs to improve slums are seen by many as programs to "subsidize" Negroes; proposals to improve the conditions of prisons are seen as measures to coddle black criminals, and so on. In such cases, the fear and resentment of the Negro take precedence over the social problem itself. The result, unfortunately, is that society suffers from the results of a failure to correct social evils whose ill effects refuse to obey the rules of segregation.

If the subject of race is discouraging, at least it gives us a clue as to where to search for the causes of the comparative social neglect in the United States. For the important role played by race in the etiology of the problem gives us one clear-cut reason why the institutions of capitalism in America have failed to develop in the same way as in other nations. Moreover, the importance of this special factor in our past suggests that other distinctively "American" facets of our history should also be examined to see if they too bear on the problem.

Whoever searches for such distinctive shaping forces of our past quickly fastens on two: the unique role of democracy and the extraordinary success of the economic system in shaping the American heritage. But if democracy and economic success are familiar touchstones in our history, they are surely disconcerting candidates for the role of social retardants. We are accustomed to pointing to our strong egalitarian sentiments and to the exuberant pace of economic progress when asked why we did so much "better" than Europe in the nineteenth century, not why we are doing so much "worse" in the twentieth century. To consider the possibility that these very elements of our past success may now act as social retardants would seem to require us to reverse the verdict of considered historical judgment.

That is not, however, what I intend. My thought, rather, is to suggest that the traits and institutions that admirably served the needs of one period may not be equally well suited to those of another. Consider, to begin with, the much-admired democratic cast of American political thought. This is usually extolled for the impetus it gave to self-government, the limits it established against tendencies to tyranny and so forth. That judgment remains valid. But the democratic bias of American thought can also be seen in another light, when we consider it as a background factor that has conditioned our attitude to social need. The idea of the self-government of equals, as has often been remarked, has brought with it a deep suspicion of government for any purposes other than to facilitate the intercourse of the (presumably) successful majority. And beyond that it has meant as well a denigration of an important aspect of the more ancient conception of a government of unequals—namely, that one of the justifications of government was the dispensation of charity and social justice to the neediest by those entrusted with state power.

Antiwelfare

I have no wish to romanticize this elitist ideal of government. Indeed, it is probable that the homely realities of American democratic social justice were preferable by far to those of the "benevolence" of the rulers of nineteenth century Europe. Nonetheless there remained within the older "feudal" conception of government a latent legitimization of authority that, once given the changed mandates of the twentieth century, provided the basis for a much stronger and more penetrating attack on social neglect than did the much more restricted democratic concept. In a word, the elitist tradition was ultimately more compatible with the exercise of a compassionate and magnanimous policy than was the democratic.

As always, Alexis de Tocqueville sensed the difference. "The bonds of human affection," he wrote, "with regard to the democratic state, are wider but more relaxed" than those of the aristocratic:

Aristocracy links everybody, from peasant to king, in one long chain. Democracy breaks the chain and frees each link. As social equality spreads there are more and more people who, though neither rich nor powerful enough to have much hold over others, have gained or kept enough wealth and enough understanding to look after their own needs. Such folk owe no man anything and hardly expect anything from anybody. They form the habit of thinking of themselves in isolation and imagine that their whole destiny is in their own hands. Thus, not only does democracy make men forget their ancestors, it also clouds their view of their descendants, and isolates them from their contemporaries. Each man is forever thrown back on himself alone, and there is danger that he may be shut up in the solitude of his own heart.

What Tocqueville alerts us to is a restriction of the reach of concern in democratic societies—a tendency to cultivate a general solicitude for those who remain within a few standard deviations from the norm of success, but that ignores those who drop beyond the norm into the limbo of failure.

In its general antipathy for government policies that transgressed these narrow boundaries of social concern, the "antiwelfare" animus of American democracy was further abetted by two other attributes of our experience. One of these was the frontier spirit with its encouragement of extreme individualism and self-reliance. The other was the enormous influence of economic growth. What E. H. Kirkland has called "that great human referendum on human conditions, the number of immigrants" provided striking confirmation throughout the late nineteenth and early twentieth centuries of the relative superiority of life chances in America to those elsewhere, including the Scandinavian countries that now appear as paragons of capitalism. This vast encouragement in the field of economic life powerfully

reinforced the prevailing political belief that those who failed to reach the general level of average well-being had no one to blame but themselves. Not only among the upper classes, but in the middle and working classes as well, the conviction was gained that social failure was more a matter for scolding than for indignation. Thus the rampage of Social Darwinism in late nineteenth-century America, with its long-abiding legacy of antiwelfare attitudes in the twentieth, cannot be divorced from the myth (and the reality) of the frontier or the facts of economic life itself.

The result was a peculiarly American anesthetizing of the public's social conscience which, coupled with its profound suspicions of government "from above," led toward a mixed indifference and impotence with regard to social neglect. This is not to say that American culture produced a people that was less sensitive to suffering than other peoples; on the contrary, Americans have shown their quick human sympathies more readily than many other nationalities, especially for victims of misfortune in other parts of the world. It is, rather, that the ingredients of the American experience made Americans loath to acknowledge the social causes of neglect and reluctant to use public authority to attend to them.

Middle-Class Attitudes

It is informative in this regard to reflect on how much of the social legislation in America has come about as the result of determined work by the "aristocrats" of the system, against the opposition of the middle classes. Today as well, proposals for the elimination of social grievances receive much more support from the elites of national government than from the county administrators, state legislators or small-town congressmen who continue to express the traditional philosophy of the American past. When it comes to the alleviation of the specific forms of neglect we have discussed in this essay, it is not a pinch on the profits of the great corporations but a pinch on the principles of middle-class Americans that often stands in the way.

To this enthronement of middle-class attitudes must be added one last and exceedingly important supplement. This is the combined efficacy of the American democratic ethos and the American economic élan in preventing the socialist movement from gaining a foothold in the United States.

On the one hand, as Leon Samson has pointed out, the political ideology of America, with its stress on equality, came very close to that of socialism, to the detriment of the special appeal of the latter less democratic milieux. On the other hand, the sheer economic advance of the United States greatly lessened the traditional appeal of socialism in terms of its promised economic benefits. As Werner Sombart remarked crudely but tellingly: "On the reefs of roast beef and apple pie, socialist Utopias of all sorts are sent to their doom."

The absence of a socialist movement in turn exerted two

effects. First, it removed from American political life the abrasive frictions of a class-oriented politics that proved the undoing of parliamentary government in many nations of Europe. That was sheer gain. Second, however, it also removed the combination of working-class political power and intellectual concern for social reform that provided the moving force behind much of the reform legislation that eventually emerged in the rest of the Western world. If there seems to be one common denominator within the variety of capitalist governments that have developed a high level of response to social neglect, it is the presence within all of them of powerful social democratic parties combining trade union strength and moderate socialist ideology. Per contra, one cause for the relative neglect of social ills in this country seems to be the failure of a comparable alliance to emerge in America.

In focusing attention on the roles played by the democratic and economic elements of American history in giving rise to her present condition of relative social backwardness, I do not wish to overlook consideration of numerous other factors that we have not considered, primary among them the peculiarly tangled and ineffective structure of American political power. The impotence of city government, the rivalry of the states, the power of sabotage inherent in the seniority system in Congress—all these and still other factors surely deserve their places in an examination of the

roots of social neglect. Nevertheless, with all the risks inherent in an effort to simplify a multicausal phenomenon, I believe that we can offer a reasonably cogent answer to the question with which we began: why has American capitalism lagged behind other capitalist nations in the repair of its social defects?

The reasons, as I see them, are threefold. First, the remedy of neglect has been stymied because of the identification of need with race and the unwillingness to take measures of which a principal effect would have to be a marked improvement in the condition of the Negro. Second, social reform has been retarded due to the lingering heritage of the democratic conception of limited government and to its lack of the ideal of social magnanimity. Finally, social neglect has persisted because the American credo and the American experience have inhibited the formation of a social-democratic, working-class party dedicated to the improvement of the lower classes.

Is it possible to go beyond diagnosis to prognosis? Can an examination of the roots of American inertia give us some clues as to the chances of remedying the neglect from which the country suffers? From the material we have covered I shall venture a few comments that may seem surprising, for in an age of general pessimism they carry a message of qualified optimism. By this I mean that new social forces capable of bringing about a substantial betterment of the prevailing level of social neglect seem to me to be at hand, but that we cannot yet say whether the potential for change inherent in these forces will be allowed to exert its influence.

A New New Deal?

Few would deny the presence of the first force. It is the belated arrival on the American scene of significant improvement in the relative economic well-being of the Negro community. Median incomes of black families, which averaged 55 percent of white incomes at the beginning of the decade, moved up to 63 percent at the end. Moreover, the preconditions for further increases are present in the existence of legislative measures that, however inadequately, bring some power of remedy against the remaining barriers of discrimination. I do not wish in any way either to exaggerate the progress of the average black family, which is still much too little, or to brush aside as inconsequential the obstacles to social equality that remain, which are immense, but only to state as an indisputable fact that a beginning has been made, and that it seems unlikely that it will come to a halt.

My second cause for qualified optimism is the tardy arrival of another necessary force for the repair of social neglect in America. This is the basis for a possible new New Deal—that is, for a second great massing of public energies for the improvement of social conditions in the United States. Here, the stimulus is provided by the challenge of the ecological crisis which, in the short run, threatens the comfort, decency and convenience of life in America and in the long run imperils its very continuance. There is no doubt that the reckless abuse of the environment must come to an end and that the present mindless extraction of raw materials and heedless disposal of wastes must give way to an orderly administration of the entire economic process from start to finish. In this imperious requirement, imposed on us not by a division within society but by a potentially fatal imbalance between the system as a whole and its adjustment to nature, there lies an issue that may be sufficiently impelling—and yet also homely and personal enough—to bring about the needed public acquiescence in the bold use of government authority for social ends. What the ecological crisis offers is the basis for a new reform movement in America whose potential for improving our habitat, health and general well-being could be very great.

My third cause for qualified optimism lies in the presence of still a last necessary ingredient for social change. This is the discovery in our midst of a social force that may provide a substitute for the social-democratic political conscience that has been missing from the American experience. That substitute is the party of the young.

I am aware that the young are not currently in full favor with other Americans, and I shall have something to say about their shortcomings. But at this juncture, while we are looking for possible counterforces against the tradi-

tional American inertia in the face of social neglect, surely we must count the energy and idealism of the youth movement as one of these. Whatever their faults, the vanguard of angry young people has succeeded, where all else has failed, in causing Americans to reexamine the condition of their own house. Do not forget that the movement for civil rights was begun by the young, that the opposition to the war has been led by them, that the "discovery" of the ecological crisis was and is their special concern. It would be foolish to glorify everything that the youth movement has produced in America, but it would be wrong to deny the role that the young have played as the enforcement agents for the nation's conscience.

The presence within contemporary America of the first real signs of racial improvement, of the basis for a new New Deal and of a corps of idealistic and determined youth constitutes new and promising possibilities for the repair of social neglect. Yet I would be remiss if I did not make clear the basis for the qualifications that I must also place against these optimistic possibilities.

The Failure of Success

Let me begin with the risks that must be faced in the rise of black well-being. They derive from the fact that we cannot expect a continued improvement in the social neglect suffered by blacks to follow "automatically" from the workings of a growing economy, or even from a rise in the average income of blacks. On the contrary, the past decade of "average" improvement tells us that the deprivations of black ghetto life, the prison brutalities suffered by blacks, the terrible differentials in conditions of health or the persistent poverty of the black fatherless slum family will not melt away quickly even under the warming sun of a general rise in relative Negro incomes. To repair these resistant areas of social failure will require continued agitation on the part of the black community to bring its neglect incessantly and insistently before the attention of the white community. The prerequisite for improvement, in a word, is a continuation of black militancy, meaning by this demonstrations, confrontations and the like.

The dangers here are twofold. On the one hand, the prospect of a decade or more of continual turmoil and pressure from the black minority hardly promises a peaceful or easy political atmosphere for the nation as a whole. More ominous, there is the risk that black militancy, if pushed beyond the never clearly demarcated line of social tolerance, may result in white countermilitancy, with the possibility of an annulment of black gains, or even of a retrograde movement. If the rise of black power thus opens the way to a long overdue repair of the single greatest source of social neglect in America, it also holds the worrisome prospect of a polarization of race relations that could result in a major social catastrophe, for whites as well as blacks.

Second, the possible basis for a new New Deal, based on the need to work toward an intelligent management of our economy, carries a considerable price. For the achievement of an ecological balance in America will not be won by the imposition of a few antipollution measures. In the long run it will require an unremitting vigilance over and a penetrating regulation of large areas of both production and consumption. In a word, the functional requirements of a new New Deal must include a far-reaching system of national planning.

Is it possible that such a profound change in the structure of the American economy will be easy to achieve? The experience of the first New Deal is hardly reassuring in this regard. Yet the problem this time may not lie at first with the recalcitrance of business management—it is significant that two major corporate leaders, Robert W. Sarnoff of RCA and Thomas J. Watson, Jr., of IBM, have already called for national planning as the necessary first step if we are to exert effective control over the future. The difficulties may lie, instead, with the unwillingness of the great mass of average Americans to give up the easy freedom of an unrestrained economic carnival for the much more self-denying life style necessary for a truly balanced economic equilibrium. And beyond that lies the still more difficult problem of reorienting our whole economic system away from its accustomed goals of growth to new goals of a cautiously watched relationship with nature itself. In the end, the demands placed on the adaptive powers of the system by the requirements of ecology may constitute the life-or-death test of capitalism itself.

Finally, there are the qualifications with regard to the young. These are of two kinds. The first I need not dwell upon. It is the risk that the energies and idealism of the young will focus on petty issues rather than central ones, will be directed to rhetoric rather than remedies, or will culminate in a senseless fury that will only bring upon itself the repressive countermeasures of their elders. The second danger is perhaps even greater, although it is one to which we usually pay less attention. It is simply that the party of the young will vitiate its strength in internecine quarrels, as have so many parties of reform, or will become a party of the few rather than one of the many. The danger, in a word, is that the present energy and idealism of the young will peter out into exhaustion and futility. There are those in the older generation, I know, who would welcome such a disappearance of youthful activism. But where, we must ask ourselves, would we then find an equally effective force of conscience in America?

Offsets to Optimism

All these qualifications come as chastening offsets to the optimism offered by the advent of new forces for social change. The threat of the difficult adjustments, clashes and crises that seem certain to arise from the need for continued black militancy, for expanded government planning, and from uncertain temper, appeal or staying power of youth, which makes it impossible to look forward to a smooth transition from a relatively neglectful America to a relatively concerned one. Indeed, it is entirely possible that the decade ahead will not be one of improvement at all, but only one of growing tensions between the forces for change and those of indifference or inertia, and that the indices of social neglect will show little or no gain. In a word, America ten or 20 years hence may be as ugly, slum-ridden, unconcerned with poverty, unhealthy, negligent in her treatment of criminals—in short, as laggard with regard to her social problems—as she is today.

Before this indeterminate outlook, predictions can only be fatuous. More important, they are beside the point. For what our diagnosis has brought to the fore is a recognition that social neglect in America is but the tip of an iceberg of attitudes and institutions that deter our society, not alone in dealing generously with respect to its least fortunate members, but in dealing effectively with respect to the most pressing issues—racial, ecological, ideological—of our times. In this sense, the remedy of neglect in America comes as a challenge much larger than the immediate problems to which it addresses itself. What is at stake is not only whether the richest nation in the world will finally become the most decent but whether a nation whose very greatness is now in jeopardy can recognize—and thus perhaps begin to remedy—the degree to which its present failures are rooted in its past success.

FURTHER READING

Urban Poverty in a Cross-Cultural Context by Edwin Eames and Judith G. Goode (New York: Free Press, 1973).

From Poverty to Dignity: A Strategy for Poor Americans by Charles Hamden-Turner (Garden City, N.Y.: Anchor Books, 1974).

Structured Social Inequality edited by Celia S. Heller (New York: Macmillan, 1969).

Between Capitalism and Socialism by Robert Heilbroner (New York: Random House, 1970).

Wealth and Power in America by Gabriel Kolko (New York: Praeger, 1962).

The First New Nation by Seymour Martin Lipset, New York: Basic Books, 1963).

The Future of Inequality by S. M. Miller and Pamela Roby (New York: Basic Books, 1970).

Toward Understanding Poverty: Perspectives From the Social Sciences edited by Daniel P. Moynihan, New York: Basic Books, 1969).

Poverty and Progress by Stephan Thernstrom (Cambridge, Mass.: Harvard University Press, 1964).

Issues in Social Inequality edited by Gerald N. Thielbar and Saul D. Feldman (Boston: Little, Brown, 1972).

Toward A Social Report (Washington, D.C., Department of Health, Education and Welfare, 1960).

OSCAR LEWIS

The Death of Dolores

In June, 1963, when I began my study of her family, Dolores Corrado was 36 years old. She lived in the San Juan slum I have called La Esmeralda, in a flimsy two-room shack at the edge of the sea; there was an ever-present danger of being swept away by high waves. Dolores had bought the little house for $450 with money she won in the lottery. She used the rest of her winnings to install electricity, running water, a tiny toilet, a refrigerator, and a few pieces of shabby second-hand furniture. Dolores lived with her fourth husband, Arturo, her nine-year-old son Millo, of a previous marriage, her mother Doña Carmen and a young man, Araceli, who was a boarder.

Dolores had formerly been the economic mainstay of her mother and son, but she was now too ill to work. The family income was very meagre and sporadic. Arturo, who often disappeared for days, would give Dolores a few pesos

now and then. Millo's earnings as a shoeshine boy at that time rarely exceeded a dollar or two a day. Doña Carmen had a steady but small income of $7.50 a month from relief, and Araceli, who contributed only when he was working, gave just enough to pay for his food and for Dolores' daily supply of cigarettes and beer.

From the tender age of six or seven, Dolores had worked as a coffee-picker, a charcoal burner, and a domestic servant in the hill country of Jayuya. She never attended school and was still illiterate. At age 15 she left the country for San Juan, where she worked as a housemaid and a kitchen helper until age 21, when she became pregnant and was married. Abandoned by her husband after the birth of her second child, Dolores went back to work, but was unable to hold a job because of severe asthma attacks. When she and her mother and children were on the verge of starvation, she took up prostitution.

Dolores was pretty and spirited but the harsh experience of her profession, the death of a son, and her own explo-

sive, violently self-destructive personality, undermined her health. When I met her, she was pale, emaciated, almost bedridden and obviously very ill. She was an erratic informant, but when she felt well she told her story with enjoyment and with lively humor. Dolores died of tuberculosis five months after my last interview with her.

The following excerpt is from my forthcoming book, Six Women: A Study of Three Generations in a Puerto Rican Family. *It is narrated by Magdalena, the eldest of Doña Carmen's five daughters.*

FROM MY HOUSE I could look down the alleyway to the left and see Lola's house. I used to watch her sitting by her window, looking out at the sea. When she left the sanatorium in April she promised to return, but she never did. She stayed home with her son Millo and was taking her medicine, and after about a month she began to feel a little better. She had been to the public health clinic a few times and told *mamá* that she had another appointment in July. She had hopes of being cured. Of course, she did!

Lola's husband, Arturo Hoyos, hadn't shown up for over a month. He was living with another woman, and the only reason Lola wasn't short of money was because Millo brought her what he earned by shining shoes. Why, that boy brought her seven or eight dollars a day. Every single day! Think of it! She forced him to bring her all that money. I'd say to her, "Forgive me, *comai* (my friend), but it isn't right to make the kid bring you so much. You know a shoeshine boy can't earn more than two or three dollars a day, even if he kills himself working. It's us mothers who are to blame when a child steals, because if I tell my sons, 'Unless you bring me such-and-such an amount of money, I'll kill you,' the kid will do anything to save his skin."

Lola's answer to that was, "Ah, let him steal. Let him do whatever he pleases! Better he should hold up a bank than bring me a few measly dollars. Money, lots of money, that's what I want!"

Lola needed money to pay for her vices. She drank a dollar's worth of beer every day, besides a pint of rum with anise which cost another seventy-five cents. She'd also give me a dollar or two a day to cook for her kid, as well as for mine.

On the Monday before Mother's Day, comai Lola wasn't feeling too good, but she joked and teased as usual. After kidding around for a while, she said she wanted a mango, the real meaty kind they call "bull's balls." It was a craving she had, I guess. I managed to get one for her and she ate every bit of it. Later that week she even ate some chopped ham.

Mamá visited Lola a lot. She was living with my sister Sofía and her husband Antonio, and they were only a four or five minute walk from Lola's house. On Mother's Day in the morning, mamá went to take Lola some pigeon broth. Lola didn't have a gift for her so she said, "Mami,

there's some soap and a bottle of perfume on the shelf. Take them, they're too sweet and the smell makes me sick." Mamá pretended not to hear and went right on talking. When she went away she left the things there. By then Lola was looking better; she was expecting me to come over with a cup of coffee. But before I got there, along came that husband of hers, drinking beer. He said, "I'd like to smash this bottle in your face, but rather than land in jail for just hurting you, I might as well kill you and have done with it. Anybody with TB should be killed." Then he pulled out a gun and put it up against Lola's head, saying, "Look, here's my gift to you!" Lola screamed, "Dear God, help me!" Then Arturo wheeled around and took a shot at the electric light cables in front of the house. Lola begged him to stop because he might start a

---

CAST OF CHARACTERS

Doña Carmen	*age 71*	*The mother*
Dolores (Lola)	*age 39*	
Eva	*age 30*	
Alicia	*age 28*	*Daughters of Doña Carmen*
Sofía	*age 26*	
Magdalena	*age 42*	
Esteban	*age 47*	*Magdalena's husband*
Arturo Hoyos	*age 44*	*Dolores's husband*
Chango	*age 28*	*Alicia's husband*
Antonio	*age 26*	*Sofía's husband*
Robert	*age 14*	
Danny	*age 11*	*Magdalena's sons*
Carlitos	*age 9*	
Millo	*age 11*	*Dolores's son*

---

fire and burn us all to death. Arturo told her, "As long as I save my own skin, you and your family can go fuck yourselves and shit on your mother because you're nothing but a bunch of no-good whores."

Lola said to him, "Go ahead, Arturo, sink half the world if you like—you'll get pulled into jail before you know how you got there."

"Is that right?" he said, "Then I might as well kill you first."

"You aren't man enough to kill me," said Lola, and she began to cry. She cried and cried like a Mary Magdalene. Arturo was gone when I came, and Lola said, "Comai, Arturo is giving me a bad time and God only knows how I'm going to defend myself. I wish I could kill that man!" When Millo came back from shining shoes and saw her crying he went to mamá's house looking for a weapon to kill Arturo.

Poverty and Social Inequality

Arturo showed up at mamá's first with a story about how he'd offered Lola three dollars and she had refused it, saying she wasn't a beggar. While he was speaking, Millo came in and Arturo started backing down the stairs as soon as he caught sight of the boy. Millo made signs to mamá, asking for a knife. Mamá said to Arturo, "All right, *compai* (my friend), with your permission, I can't stand here making conversation with you any longer. You've no call to come gossiping about a sick woman who doesn't bother you nor anybody else either."

"Oh, never mind," Arturo answered, "I won't be talking anymore because I'm going."

"I won't miss you any," mamá said.

I stayed with Lola until she got over her crying spell. When Millo came back I left. But she must have cried again that night because in the morning, after Esteban got up to go to work, Millo called to me that she was coughing up blood. What I think is that Arturo's behavior brought on the haemoptysis.

When I got there, comai Lola was crouching over the basin which was already half full of blood. I helped her stand up and get into bed. She was in pretty bad shape.

I went over to Sofía's to tell mamá about Lola. Mamá was doing the dishes when I arrived and I said, "Mamá, do you know why I came?"

"How would I know, child? Can it be to tell me Lola is dead?"

"She had an attack of haemoptysis last night that practically finished her."

Mamá said, "Ay, Dios," and she ran to Lola's house.

I had to go back home and get my boys off to school but I went over to Lola's every little while to rub her chest with bay rum. That was the only thing to do because she had a bad pain in the chest and could hardly breathe. By evening she was better.

On Tuesday I had to take my son Robert to the Puerta de Tierra clinic because he'd been having the earache so bad that he hadn't let me get any sleep for three nights. I was waiting for Robert's turn at the clinic when compai Ismael came in and told me that Lola had gotten another attack of haemoptysis and was all alone. I phoned Chango, Alicia's husband, at the La Esmeralda dispensary and asked him to send word to mamá that Lola was very sick and that she should go stay with her until I could get there.

I had to wait a long time at the clinic for Robert's turn, but when I got to Lola's, mamá was sitting by the bed fanning her. Lola was gasping and choking and too weak to get up. "Look, child," mamá said to her, "you know that when someone's sick in bed, whether they are getting better or worse, they should have a priest."

"But there's no one to fetch one for me."

"I'm ready to do it," said mamá. So she went right away and got a priest at a church over in Tanca Street. He said, "I'll come at about four."

Antonio, Sofía, and Alicia arrived while the priest was there. He asked everybody to clear out so Lola could confess her sins. Then he rubbed Holy Oil on her but he said he couldn't give her communion because of the blood she was spitting. After the priest left, Lola told me, "Comai, the first thing I spoke about to the priest were the quarrels you and I had, because it would hurt too much to go without being forgiven by you."

"I have always forgiven you," I said, "and, anyway, you're going to last longer than me." But she answered, "No, I'm dying. The one I want to see is comai Eva."

Lola seemed to get better later so mamá went home. That night, around ten, Lola had a lot of visitors, mostly people who came to say goodbye to her. Her little boy, Millo, being sort of wrong in the head like he is, was jumping and dancing around in the crowd while she coughed up blood, as if seeing his mother like that made him happy.

All of a sudden Lola let out a yell, "Ayyy, I'm choking!" We brought her a basin to spit into and then right away we had to bring another to put under the first one. We had to keep changing basins because Lola coughed up so much blood she fairly emptied herself out. Right in the middle of everything she begged us to send for Eva. She was white as a sheet. My husband Esteban was holding her up but he was drunk and pressed her real hard to help her get the blood out. He only made her choke more and I made him change places with me. But first I had to wipe Lola's blood from his arms. The bleeding wouldn't stop and I got blood on my hands too. I wasn't afraid though— why should I be afraid of my own sister? Lola finally fell back in my arms, fainting. For more than an hour she leaned against my left shoulder. She looked dead, completely dead; cold, as if she'd been put on ice. I got icy cold myself, holding her.

When Lola came to, the first thing she did was beg us to send for Eva. She wanted to be forgiven for having married Arturo, who was her compai and Eva's ex-husband. Sofía rushed home like a madwoman to get some money from mamá to send a cablegram to New York asking Eva to come. Mamá gave her the money but the cablegram was returned because we put the wrong address on it. So then Antonio wrote out the address on an envelope and sent her a letter instead.

Lola was getting worse. I couldn't take care of her myself because I can't lose my sleep at night. There was no extra bed in her house and I'd have to sleep on the floor. Besides, I have kids to take care of. With so many thieves and criminals around, I was afraid someone might break into my house to steal and maybe even hurt the kids or something. I said mamá could stay with Lola, but Alicia and Sofía wouldn't hear of it! They said, "If mamá stays we'll wind up with two corpses on our hands." So we asked Lola if she wanted us to take her to Alicia's house. "If that's where you want me to go, I'm willing," she said. Antonio picked her up and carried her all the way there in his arms. They sat up with her until midnight, then mamá took over and watched her till morning.

Lola said to mamá, "Listen, you and I have a promise to fulfill; I'm going to take you with me when I die."

"Yes, I remember and I'm expecting you to keep your word," mamá said.

Seven nights they took turns like that, so there was always someone awake and looking after her until daybreak. I couldn't take care of her but as long as she was at Alicia's house, I kept visiting her. She would lie there chatting with us as if nothing had happened, but every time she coughed, she spat out blood by the mouthful. And when she saw Alicia working so hard in the house she gave her money to send out the ironing. She said, "I won't live long enough to eat my way through this money, anyway. My days are numbered."

One night when mamá was sitting with her, Lola said, "Mamá, get somebody to write down on a paper for me to sign that I'm leaving the house to my son. Then sell it and put the money into the bank for him." But nobody who could do it showed up.

THEN LOLA GOT it into her head that she wanted to take the boy with her. She'd say to him, "Damn you, I'm going to take you with me. Come and stand here beside me so I can kill you!" She tried to bribe Alicia's little girl to bring her a knife. She said she didn't want to leave Millo an orphan and risk his turning into a thief. But Alicia sent Millo to school and told Lola to ask God's forgiveness and to beg Him for strength to leave her son behind.

On Thursday her husband Arturo showed up. He was standing just outside the front door and when Lola heard his voice, she said, "Don't let him in, Alicia." So, when Arturo asked, Alica said, "No, Lola doesn't want you here."

"I'm not all that bad," he said.

"It's you that brought this illness upon her, threatening her with a gun," Alicia said.

Arturo denied it, "Say what you like," he said, "but it's still a lie. I never pulled a gun on her."

Then mamá told him, "Never again will you be allowed to set foot in this house. As long as you live you have no right to come here. You and I have a little quarrel to settle; the time will come when we'll have it out."

"There's no time like the present," said Arturo, "but suit yourself." So they left it at that.

Eva arrived from New York on Saturday and she and Lola fell into each other's arms. Eva was weeping and wailing, "Ay, comai Lola of my soul!" Lola threw herself on the floor and groveled like a worm until we picked her up and laid her on the sofa again. Ay, bendito (Oh, Jesus!), it was pitiful.

Lola had two more attacks there at Alicia's. After the first one, she got better. According to mamá, she began to joke again. She'd smile and say, "Ay, mamá, you've got a

face like a cunt!" Sick as she was, she was happy and good humored. On Monday she was terribly upset because of a complaint that Millo had been stealing.

Millo had a little silver hand, the kind they call the Hand of God, that he said he'd bought at Santos' store for a quarter. A few days later, he brought home a good gold ring. He kept bringing home things like that. Then one day, while he was shining shoes at the docks, a man who had an office there caught sight of the silver hand and called a cop. He said a little hand like that and several other things were missing from his office.

Millo didn't give the cop his right address because of Lola and took him to his godmother's house instead. But the cop said, no, that wouldn't do, and Millo had to take him home. When Lola heard what had happened, she said, "It's you cops who are to blame for kids growing up to be thieves and drug addicts because if a mother beats up her child you arrest her and make her pay a fine. So how can you expect a mother to correct her children?"

"You can kill the kid and eat him, for all I care," the cop answered. At that, Lola got up, grabbed a stick and tried to beat Millo, but she was too tired and sick. She got an asthma attack and had to lie down again. The asthma brought on another hemorrhage. She cried out, "Ay, mamá," and she died there, in mamá's arms. But our screams and wails brought her back. Eva kept bawling, "Dear God, don't take my sister away. Oh, sister of my heart." That's what brought the woman back. Lola opened her eyes, looked all around, and said, "I can't go; I can't go." Twice, like that. It was us sisters crying that wouldn't let her go in peace! What we did was make her so desperate that she couldn't go through her change.

Alicia said, "Eva hasn't pardoned comai Lola, that's what's keeping her there on that bed!" Eva wanted to pardon Lola just before she went back to New York but Alicia said Lola wasn't going to last that long. "The only thing that's keeping her alive is that she wants your forgiveness." Eva went to ask her mother-in-law, Bertha, her opinion. Bertha said to her, "If Alicia advises it, you'd better do it." Eva still didn't believe it, so she went to the priest. He said, "I've done all I can so that the Lord would receive your sister in His arms. Now you should pardon her as Alicia advises."

So Eva went to Lola and asked her, "Comai, is it my forgiveness you are waiting for?" Lola opened her eyes wide and said, "That's what I'm waiting for." Then Eva knelt and pressed her hand and said, "Comai, you are forgiven." Lola couldn't speak after that. She lost her voice.

When I left that night, Lola was in a bad way. She couldn't swallow anything, not even water. Mami would say, "Child, would you like some water?" and she'd make signs that she wanted mami to moisten her mouth with a bit of wet cotton. Mamá kept on doing that until the spirit came down to Lola about half past eight it was, and

she sat up in her bed. That brought on a fit of coughing and spitting blood. She coughed so hard that she fell off the bed. Then, with the blood running from her mouth, she screamed, "Ay, a taxi, a taxi! Take me to the hospital. I don't want to die here. Mami, don't be so tight. There's money here!" After having spent so much, Lola still had forty dollars under her mattress.

Antonio flew to get a taxi while the others stayed with Lola. She kind of said goodbye to them then. Millo was hanging about, near the door, and Lola beckoned to him. She kissed him and gave him a long look, as if saying, "This is the last time I'll ever see him."

Antonio came back and said he had a taxi waiting. He took her in his arms, just as she was, in nothing but a nightgown, and carried her up to the Boulevard.

At the hospital they took Lola to the ward and mamá, Eva, Sofía, and Antonio went with her. The doctor ordered the nurse to give her two bottles of serum but after about fifteen minutes he touched her and said, "Take the serum away." By that time, her skin was punctured all over from so many injections. But she felt strong enough to talk and told the doctor, "Those tubes in my nose are choking me to death." So the doctor had them taken away, the oxygen too. "She's done for," he said.

"Done for? What a thing to say!" mamá protested. That made the doctor get into an argument with her. Finally he told the nurse, "Take out the old lady and the girl." After mamá and Sofía left, he said to Antonio, "She's got about half an hour more to live." Antonio rushed out of the room crying. Mamá began to scream and Eva was screaming like crazy too. The doctor came and gave them an injection to quiet them down. "We are women, all of us," Antonio said, "because the old lady is crying, comai is crying, and I'm crying too, I'm too tender-hearted to take it."

When they said goodbye to Lola, she begged them, "Take good care of Millo for me," and then, "Mami, a kiss for each of you."

"Don't worry," mamá told her, "think of God and the Virgin Mary. They are the ones you should turn to now, not anybody here on earth. May God and the Virgin forgive you for the wrong you have done and forgive all those who have wronged you." They went away then, still weeping but feeling much calmer because of the injections. That night mamá couldn't sleep. She was up before anyone else. Then she got a note from the sanatorium saying, "Urgent, for the relatives of Dolores Figueroa."

"That must mean she's dead," Sofía told mamá, "be-

The Death of Dolores

cause if it was to ask for a blood donor or something, they would have sent another kind of note."

Mamá went over to the dispensary to call the hospital and they told her that Lola was on the list of the dead and that some member of the family should go there and get her. Mamá rushed back home like a madwoman. When she told Antonio he acted crazy too, sticking his feet into his bedroom slippers without looking, and putting on a dirty shirt and rushing out like that.

When they told Millo his mother was dead, he cried and screamed. He rushed outside and they went after him and found him all stiff, like his nerves were all twisted up. He was crying, "My mami's dead, mami's dead . . . what will become of me now?" Mamá said to him, "Don't worry, son, no matter what anybody says, I'm here and you can count on me."

I had been sleeping and didn't know anything about Lola's death that morning until Millo came and I heard him ask Rafael García, "Is Auntie there?"

"Yes, she is."

"Tell her that mami died, will you?"

That kid didn't seem to have any feelings at all about anything. He said 'Mami died' as calmly as if she'd been no relative of his. I was paralyzed when I heard the news, because of that nervous illness of mine. Not one tear came at the moment. I just started trembling and trembling, but after the first sob, I cried so hard that Rafael said, "If you keep on crying like that, I'll go back home and leave your house with nobody to take care of it. What you should do is go over there." But I couldn't go yet because I didn't have a black dress to wear. I sent my boy to borrow one for me and he didn't get back until after three.

Eva went to shop for some clothes to bury Lola in and she took Millo with her. When he came back he asked mamá, "Grandma, will they bury mami soon? I'm going to New York with auntie."

Mamá asked Eva, "Did you tell him that?"

"Yes, I asked him to go with me."

Mamá said to her, "Well, daughter, that's your lookout. You know that he isn't what you'd call a good boy, but he isn't a bad boy either. He's a little of both." She wanted to keep Millo but Antonio didn't like to have him around because of Ruby. The two of them are like wasps, they fight all the time. So, it was better to have Millo in New York. What the eyes don't see, the heart doesn't feel. If someone hit him up there, he could hit back. He was big enough now.

About one o'clock in the afternoon Antonio returned from the hospital and told mamá that they already did an autopsy on Lola and that we had to buy her a coffin. So each of us went around to collect money. It was the only thing I could do for Lola after she died. I collected very little, about six-fifty or seven dollars, from neighbors and

from friends in San Juan. I couldn't walk much because ever since Lola had leaned against my shoulder when she was sick, my legs swelled up and my whole left side felt numb. But with the money I bought a large tin of crackers, a pound of coffee, two pounds of sugar and half a cheese and sent it all to Alicia's house.

Antonio wrote out a paper asking the neighbors to help pay for the funeral and Alicia sent her husband Chango to show it around and collect some money. The people who read the paper began to joke about it. They said that the lady hadn't really died but had made up that story herself to raise money to buy rum. Chango answered that the paper said plain as plain that she was dead. So then they told him to go and get the money from Doña Felisa, the mayoress. Chango had to control himself because those people were all acting disrespectful to comai Lola and to Millo, saying the kid was a thief. Chango said they could do just as they pleased, but they were all invited to come and see the dead woman if they had any doubts. Then he went back home, mad as anything.

Millo kept asking him to go out to raise more money, but Chango said no, he wasn't going to be embarrassed like that again. Millo asked Arturo for money and Arturo came crying and making a fool of himself. He had no call to be weeping like a hypocrite, when he was the one that killed Dolores. He ran off to rent a niche in the churchyard for her and didn't show up again until that night, when he came in beating his breast.

He asked Alicia for permission to bring his wife. "Never!" she said, "That wife of yours is as much your mistress as comai Lola was. If you come to the wake with her, people will talk."

They didn't let Arturo go to the wake and he came to my house looking for me. He told me, "I just had to go to Lola's house. I still love her."

"But you didn't know how to keep her love," I said. "The truth is, you didn't love her. If you had been a man of dignity and worthy of respect, you would not have abandoned her, no matter how she talked and quarreled with you. Knowing she was sick, you should have let her tongue run on and not paid any attention. You would have stuck by your wife, and then she could have died in your arms, under your care." When he heard that, Arturo burst into tears. He pulled out his handkerchief, wiped his eyes, and walked out.

Later that afternoon Antonio and mamá went to Morovis to get a *rezador* (one who prays) to lead the prayers at the wake. He wanted ten dollars but they paid him five. They told him they couldn't lay their hands on any more money. He stayed all night, praying.

They brought Lola from the hospital to Alicia's house and laid her out there. Four people carried her coffin and one person got underneath and lifted it up. According to mamá everybody was crying, but when I got there at three-

Poverty and Social Inequality

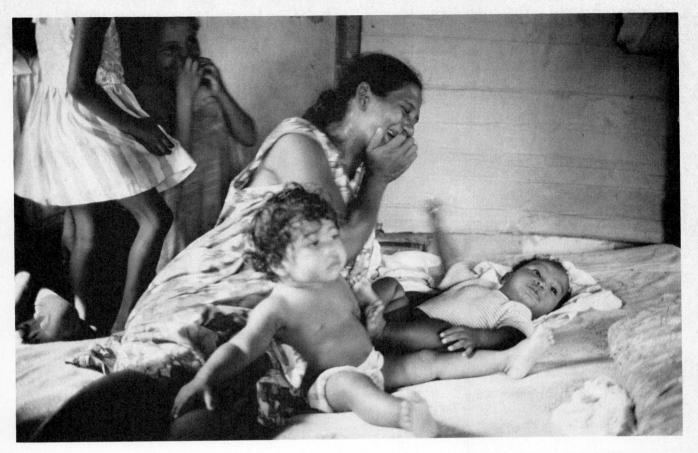

thirty, my sisters looked perfectly calm and happy. Mamá had her head bent but she wasn't crying. I saw Lola there in her coffin and that's when I really cried. She looked as beautiful as the Virgin Mary because they had made up her face. She looked real young, absolutely lovely, like an image of the Virgin. Oh, that's when I really cried, remembering all the fights we'd had and all we had been through together and our games and jokes and everything It broke my heart and wrung my soul to see her go like she did.

They had taken a photo of her lying there, and another with mamá, Sofía, Alicia, and Millo standing beside the coffin. Then Antonio came and said they shouldn't have opened the box because the infection was shut up inside it, but mamá told him the more one tried to protect oneself, the quicker one caught the infection. It's true. After all, everyone of us has worn clothes left by cousins who had died of the chest sickness like Lola, yet, thank God, we all came out all right.

It made me sad to see that Millo didn't feel his mother's death any more than if she had been a stranger to him. And to think that all her worries and sorrow had been over leaving him! She kept begging mamá and me to take good care of the child and look after him. Yet there was Millo, laughing and dancing and joking with Alicia's little girls. The oldest girl said, "Don't act like that. You've just lost your mother and you shouldn't be happy."

"Oh, I still have grandmother," he answered, and Alicia came right back at him and said, "Well, your grandmother is going the same way your mother went, so quit horsing around. Show more respect and be sad for a while."

The way that kid acted! He's crazy or something. He was so happy over the trip to New York that Eva had cooked up for him. He kept repeating, "Ay, how wonderful, I'm going to New York!" as if Lola hadn't meant a thing to him. Some of us suspect (we wouldn't dream of mentioning this to mamá) that maybe the child wasn't too fond of his mother because she treated him pretty badly. The black and blue marks from her last beating were still on him, may God forgive her. Lola had such a long, boring illness, you see, that she took it out on the kid.

As long as she lived, Lola had friends but after she was dead there wasn't anybody to speak of who went to see her.

I didn't stay long at the wake because I wasn't feeling well. Only mamá and my sisters were there to pray the rosaries all night. Everybody else stayed away; they left her alone, absolutely alone—she, who had had so many friends in San Juan! Not even her husband was there.

Everything went smoothly until around 5 A.M. when a gang of boys came in and began making jokes about the corpse. They'd run in yelling, "Catch 'em, corpse!" and then run out again, laughing. When Alicia had all she could take she said, "Those boys don't deserve to be treated with respect. I'm going to tell them off." So she stood up and yelled, "What do you think this is, a ball? If you guys are scared of the dead, stay away from wakes. Don't come here and interrupt our prayers with your horseplay!" After that, they all went away.

For the funeral I rented a car for those who were to go with me. My car was full. Cheo, the *comisario de barrio* (justice of the peace), came to represent the Popular Party and he took some people in his car. The man next door to mamá did too. There were five cars in all, costing ten dollars each. We all rode behind the hearse to Monacillo cemetery. Bebo is buried there too.

At the cemetery mamá didn't cry out loud. She just stood there, with the tears running down her face. She is a sick woman; she suffers from heart trouble. But mamá even tried to comfort me saying, "Don't cry child, that will only give Lola more pain." But when we got to the grave, I don't know . . . I was carrying a wreath in one hand and was leading my youngest child with the other and suddenly my hands were empty without my having noticed who took the wreath or the child.

When they were lowering Lola into the grave and taking more photographs, mamá cried out, "Ay, my child, you promised to take me with you but you didn't. You abandoned me and left me here in this world." And then she fell down in a fit. None of the people there had the courage to grab hold of her except me. I was nervous anyway and couldn't cry, so I grabbed her to keep her from falling. But my own mind failed, too, and I didn't realize what was going on. Why, I didn't even see when they covered Lola with earth. They gave mamá an injection and put me into the car I had hired.

After that mamá didn't feel a thing. She saw things happen and nothing seemed to matter to her. She didn't even know how the burial went. That night Antonio hired a car to take Eva and Millo to the airport and mamá didn't notice that either. It was only later that she was told Eva had to go right back because she's on relief and wasn't supposed to be away from New York.

In the end, it was Antonio who paid the expenses with money he had saved in the bank to buy a house. He even went and bought Millo a plane ticket to New York because Eva was broke; she had gotten her own ticket on credit. Antonio is only a brother-in-law but he paid for everything. According to what they told me, the coffin and everything cost over two hundred dollars. He's still paying the installments to the funeral parlor but mamá is paying him back for the coffin by renting out Lola's house for $15 a month and turning over the money to him.

Arturo stayed away for three whole days after Lola was buried. That's how bad he is. Then he got high on beer and came over to see mamá. He said to her, "You've been going around saying I only gave three dollars for Lola's funeral. I gave twenty-five."

Mamá said to him, "Well, maybe you did start out with twenty-five but all I got was three. You must have been playing with yourself on the way over and got your fingers so sticky that the rest of the money stuck to your fist."

"Now look, if it comes to that, how do I know you didn't pinch it yourself?"

"You miserable thief!" said mamá, "you're the one who steals, not me. You steal over at the docks. I never go to the docks and I've got a clean record everywhere." Then she called Alicia. "Alicia, how much money did compai Arturo hand over to me in front of Chango and you?"

"Three dollars," she said.

"You stole the rest between you," Arturo yelled. Alicia is a redhead and has a temper to match. She flared up and grabbed Chango's policeman's billy and started to call Arturo names . . . *cabrón,* (cuckold) good-for-nothing, pitiful-excuse-of-a-man, and a few others as well. It's a good thing Arturo didn't try to hit her. He just said, "Oh, shut up! I don't want to get mixed up in any more quarrels with you people. Just tell me whether you want friendliness or unfriendliness between you and me."

"Unfriendliness!" mamá said. "What do we want your dirty friendship for?" Mamá swears she's going to get even with Arturo someday, that as long as they both live, there's a quarrel between them. Mamá told him she hoped he dropped dead.

Then he came wandering around near Lola's house, like a stray mongrel puppy. But he got kind of fresh with me, touching my face and so on, so I told him off too. I said, "The dead woman is my sister and I at least, may God forgive her, respect my *compadres* (fellowmen). So stop fooling around, see?" I haven't been bothered by him since.

I DON'T KNOW about my sisters, but as for myself, I seemed to have lost my mind in those days. I was in such a state of mind that once I took a bottle of water to put in the refrigerator and instead I stuck it among the clothes in that rickety old thing we call a wardrobe. My mind still wanders, and I still hear Lola. I hear her laughing and joking and whistling to me. My kids, too, say they hear and see her all the time. And when I'm going to do something, Lola's the first person I mention. Like the other day, I made plantain dumplings and, meaning to send some to comai Sofía, I said to Danny, "Here, take this to comai Lola. I have Lola on my mind. And that's the way it goes."

Mamá began saying that the dead don't come back because Lola's had plenty of time to appear and so far she hasn't. Mamá swears she hasn't heard any noises even. She went to a spiritist who told her, "Your daughter is full of life. She's happy and grateful because her little boy went to New York." So mamá is calmer about her now.

But I am not at ease about comai Lola because it seems to me she is still suffering. She owes a month, or maybe two, on her vow to wear Our Lady of Carmel's habit and I think Lola wants me to pay the Virgin by wearing the habit myself. Last night I had a kind of revelation about it. I dreamed that mamá had brought in the can of slop for the pigs while I was watching television. As she passed, I grabbed a piece of fatback that was on top and I began to chew on it. Suddenly I saw Lola at the window, with her arms crossed on the sill, just like she used to do. She says to me, "What a slop you are, eating that fatback from the pigs' dinner!" I said, "Ah . . ." and then I couldn't get out another word. I was paralyzed and struck dumb, seeing her there, rubbing her eyes as if she just woke up. I made signs to mamá to come over, because my throat was completely paralyzed. I made signs to the neighbors too. Everybody saw Lola. I felt like laughing but Lola said, "Don't anybody laugh at me now or you'll see what I'll do to you!" She shut the window quickly, got down and walked into my parlor. Then she tried to grab me, mamá, and Esteban by the legs. My neighbor, Doña Laura, said to her, "Now look here, don't do that. You are dead now. If you keep this up you will kill your sister and mother and brother-in-law. Can't you see that you are a dead woman?"

"Ah, that's what you think," Lola said, "I'm not a bit dead. I'm more alive than any of you!" Then, suddenly, she stood up and ran into the bedroom in desperation. She yelled to my son, "Carlitos, come here. Carlitos, come here!" She wanted Carlitos to lift her nightgown and scratch her back. I said to her, "No, no! My little boy

can't look at your back; you are dead. You're a ghost, so stop horsing around like that. You're only smoke and you shouldn't be coming here." At that she sort of evaporated. But later that night I felt as if somebody were touching me from head to foot.

I know my sister is not happy. I mean to go to a spiritist to find out if Lola wants me to pay off her vow to the Virgin of Carmel. If I have to wear that habit for two months, I'll do it. I'll do that and anything more to bring her peace.

FURTHER READING

The Culture of Poverty: A Critique edited by Eleanor Leacock (New York: Simon & Schuster, 1971). A critique of Lewis by anthropologists in the field of the urban poor.

The Urban Poor of Puerto Rico: A Study in Development and Inequality by Helen Safa (New York: Holt, Rinehart and Winston, 1974). A study of an urban shantytown in San Juan, depicting changes brought about by Operation Bootstrap.

Down These Mean Streets by Piri Thomas (New York: Knopf, 1967). A novel by a Puerto Rican novelist based on Puerto Rican slum life in New York City.

Culture and Poverty by Charles Valentine (Chicago: University of Chicago Press, 1968). A critique of Frazier, Moynihan, Oscar Lewis, and other theorists of poverty.

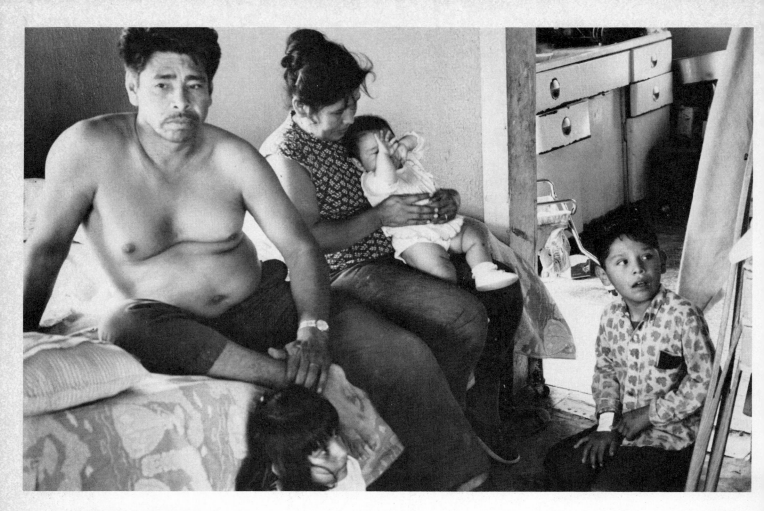

DOROTHY NELKIN

Invisible Migrant Workers

Early last summer, the soft earth of a California peach orchard yielded the bodies of 25 nameless murder victims. Their anonymity was made less astonishing by the discovery that all the dead men were migrant farm workers—a group whose isolation from society is well known. Indeed, the accounts of the lives of migratory workers from *Grapes of Wrath* to *Harvest of Shame* have described these people as invisible to the rest of American society. But are they invisible even to each other? Was there no one to miss the slain men? Surely no group can be so alienated as to accept murder rather than call the police—or can it?

To discover just what social forces could account for the namelessness of migrant faces, a four-year participant-observation study was made of black migrant farm workers in the northeastern United States. The findings suggest that migrant invisibility is systematic—that it is controlled by mechanisms both from within and without the migrant group.

Though the migrant worker may live in a camp five months out of a year, his communication with the permanent community is kept at a minimum. First, he is often physically isolated. Camps are usually located in

out-of-the-way sites several miles from the nearest town. And since most migrants were brought North on a bus by a crew leader, they rarely have their own means of transportation. If community facilities near camps are used there are often separate stores and laundromats so that migrants are segregated from local residents. Other more subtle barriers also separate the migrants from local populations. For example, the illegal sale of alcohol in camps is not only ignored, but sometimes encouraged in the hope that the migrants will drink in camp rather than in the town bars.

Sodus Village is the center of one such agricultural area; there are 50 labor camps in the township with facilities for housing about 1,000 workers. Many of their employers live in the village, which has a population of 1,233 of age 14 or over. Even though migrants use the town laundromats and gas stations, shop in the stores and drink at the local bar, a random sampling of the townspeople showed that over two-thirds had no direct contact with the workers. Nearly 10 percent said they had never noticed a labor camp nearby. Even among the majority who were aware of the camps, having noticed them from the highway, knowledge of life within the camps was vague or nonexistent. Despite their physical presence in the community they are not a part of it. The migrant is an outsider, an element to be dealt with as a problem.

An agricultural community may have church or lay groups concerned with migrant welfare. Their interest ranges broadly from prayer and indignation to the management of day schools and child-care centers. Old clothes, money and transportation services are often provided when there are people with the energy and ability to organize collections. It was found, however, that the clergy were more interested in social action programs than were their parishioners. One minister had been working with migrants for several years and, despite a highly conservative parish consisting largely of growers, devoted considerable energy to providing social services in nearby labor camps. His parishioners had not complained about his activities with the migrant workers, but they did not volunteer to participate personally in his programs. Torn between his desire to help the migrants and his obligations to his parish, he hesitated to spend much time on migrant-worker problems. When asked if his parishioners would mind if migrants came to the church, he replied that the question never came up. Since there was absolutely no social contact between the two groups, the migrants would "just not be interested in coming." He strongly asserted that migrants "do better in their own situation," and that he would not consider encouraging a migrant to attend services in his church. His activities consisted primarily of showing films and bringing athletic equipment to the camp. But the migrants were apathetic toward his efforts, and he felt that he had failed to accomplish anything of significance. Totally frustrated, he was waiting for mechanization to solve the problem by drying up the migrant labor stream.

The habit of ignoring controversial or disturbing problems in a community is seldom a conscious one but may surface during a crisis. In one agricultural area, a migrant child-care center was about to close in the middle of the summer because the public-school building in which it was located was no longer available. A local minister was under pressure to find an alternate location. When asked about the possibility of using his Sunday-school building, he said it would be impossible since there was a very small septic tank and the system would be ruined if more people used the toilets. He finally admitted, however, that the vestry was more liberal than the parishioners, who were quite willing to supply old clothes as long as the migrants remained in their camps; caring for their children on church property was another matter.

Unwelcome Offerings

The success of other agencies concerned with migrant welfare has been similarly limited. State and federally sponsored antipoverty programs have been organized to change the migrant labor situation, but social workers have had difficulty in communicating with their clients and arousing interest in the programs provided. Social workers tend to assume that the value of their offerings is self-evident, that they need only bring what they think is necessary into the camps, and the migrants will welcome them. They are often dismayed to discover this is not the case. There are a number of possible reasons for this

breakdown in communications: the attitude of migrants commonly labeled apathy, the irrelevance of the particular program offered and the fear that outsiders are only introducing one more exploitative mechanism.

A more important factor in the failure of most programs, however, is that client invisibility is built into the sponsoring organizations themselves. The experience of one social-work organization will serve as an example. Though its stated purpose was to improve conditions for migrants and to enable them to deal knowledgeably and effectively with society, agency staff members indicated that they were perpetually frustrated by lack of rapport with migrants in the camps they visited. The director of this agency knew little about his clients and seldom visited the camps in which his program operated, working instead through subordinate field instructors. In spite of his limited activity in the field, he ran the program in a centralized and authoritarian manner, and the field instructors, who had day-to-day familiarity with the camps, often found themselves disagreeing with his decisions.

For the most part, field instructors occupied their time playing with children and showing films, many of which were inappropriate to the audience. For example, one oil-company advertisement exalted the American farmer and pictured him as a national hero, fair and blond, driving his tractor across the many acres of his farm. Another was a sex education film originally developed for a middle-class school audience.

Field instructors were constrained by the centralization of decision-making in the organization and by inadequate preparation for work with migrants. Training sessions had been conducted by teachers who had experience in industrial personnel work, but who had no knowledge of problems peculiar to the migrant system. Thus, much energy was deflected to handling problems within the organization itself.

This agency and others are hampered by their dependence on local authorities. They must adjust their activities more to established community interests than to the migrants who make few conspicuous demands. Thus, their primary goals become the avoidance of disruption and the maintenance of a level of satisfaction which will minimize demands. At the same time they must make sure that educational programs, health care and other activities do not interfere with the harvest.

National or statewide church organizations occasionally employ social workers to deal with migrant labor problems. They select personnel who will work quietly, offering services that will keep the migrants happily ensconced in the camps. One social worker regularly tried to call attention to problems in the camp. His organization disapproved, and he was eventually asked to submit his resignation.

Other programs have been hampered by the insensitivity of social workers themselves, some of whom have been observed conducting themselves in camps as if their clients were not there. One such worker talked to a friend while showing movies one evening. He was unaware that their conversation was interfering with the sound track. The viewers, distracted by the voices, kept looking back, but the two men continued to talk in a normal tone until the end of the film. In another case, a social worker invited a researcher to see some migrant rooms. When knocking produced no response from the occupant of one room, he went in anyway. He asked another woman if he could show her room to the observer but had opened the door and was inside before she had a chance to answer. The woman said nothing. It did not occur to him that his actions were an invasion of privacy and later, oblivious to the people nearby, he declared that this was his favorite camp because "people are very friendly and there is never any threat of trouble."

Even genuinely concerned volunteers find themselves constrained by community pressures. One woman had written a letter to the welfare department concerning incidents in which migrants were refused medical attention. When inspectors were sent to investigate the matter, delegations of concerned citizens visited her home to ask her to retract her statements. Other outspoken volunteers have been effectively controlled by their organizations and reassigned to innocuous jobs. One black social worker described by his co-workers as "not very well liked here" was under pressure from colleagues who feared he would "cause trouble." He had been critical of interminable meetings and of other social workers who avoided going to the camps. In the camps, however, where he distributed Social Security cards and dispensed information about jobs and events outside the camp, observers noted that he was more effective and had closer rapport with the migrants than had any of the other social workers. He eventually left the organization.

Because they find it difficult to work without an organizational base and equally difficult to work within the existing ones, many of the most concerned and active people drop out of migrant work altogether. For most social work activities are directed only toward making the migrant situation more bearable and not to changing it—films and old clothes are brought to the camps, women are trained to prepare surplus food and people are taught their rights *as migrants*. These activities are indeed important, but only help migrants adapt more efficiently to their present circumstances. Relatively few programs in the North are specifically directed toward training people for jobs out of the migrant labor stream. The experience of participants and observers alike in the study provides a strong indication that the invisibility of migrants is built into the very institutions created to deal with them.

Crew Leader System

Migrant invisibility is evident in the recruitment process itself. Arrangements for recruiting agricultural labor are handled through the farm labor division of the state employment services. For example, the grower makes his manpower needs known in the early spring and contracts are negotiated with crew leaders via the Farm Labor Service in Florida to transport a specified number of workers North on a specified date. Here the responsibility of the employment service and often of the grower ends. The migrant himself in involved only when he is signed up by the crew leader, who acts as intermediary throughout the season. Growers provide camps and work sites, but many prefer to leave all dealings with the migrants themselves to the crew leaders. For example, 67 percent of 119 migrants inter-

viewed had never been directly supervised by a grower. This avoidance of contact is often maintained at the expense of efficiency.

The crew leader system, developed from the delegation of employment responsibility, perpetuates migrant invisibility. It is the crew leader who assumes all responsibility, not only for recruitment and work supervision, but also for the sustenance of his crew, the policing of the camp, transportation and the provision of other services normally provided by a community. However, he is not accountable to outside authorities for these maintenance activities and may even have a stake in concealing how they are carried out—a point suggested by the threats made against farm workers who agree to testify before an investigating committee.

The desire of growers to minimize public awareness of their labor camps was apparent in the no trespassing signs found at the entrance of many camps, the difficulties encountered by VISTA volunteers who found themselves barred from some camps and problems in attempting to place students in camps for research purposes. One grower, who is in fact active on several migrant service committees, contends that the condition of migrants has greatly improved, but the problem now is that there are far too many social agencies involved. According to this grower, social workers do not recognize that migrants have different cultural backgrounds and that "they do not need the same things we do." From his perspective, most social work activities are destructive because they create unfavorable publicity. The growers' position is understandable in light of their vested interest in leaving things as they are. The subtle pervasiveness of this tendency is better illustrated by groups whose self-interest is less obvious.

Government inspectors are responsible for deciding whether or not migrant camps meet minimum standards. The main inspection occurs prior to the season, before the occupants of the camp arrive. Subsequent inspections, if they occur at all, are cursory. There are complex structural problems in the current system of inspection in New York State which hamper its effectiveness. The New York State Joint Legislative Committee Report in 1967 noted that local county health officers were not adequately enforcing the state sanitary code. "It is the opinion of this Committee that the County health officers and their assistants are too close to the leadership structure in the county, where the migrants are non-voters and have no representation in the power structure of these counties." As members of the local community, inspectors are often friends of growers and see them regularly the year round which may make it more difficult for them to enforce regulations. One inspector asserted in an interview that there was no exploitation in labor camps and that most migrants have too many expectations. He suggested that a large, self-contained labor camp be built with complete service facilities, including stores, clinics and child-care centers. This would avoid scattering people in tenant houses and small camps throughout agricultural communities. While such an arrangement might be convenient in terms of the availability of services, it is a solution that would further reduce migrant visibility.

Although enforcement problems are ubiquitous, legisla-

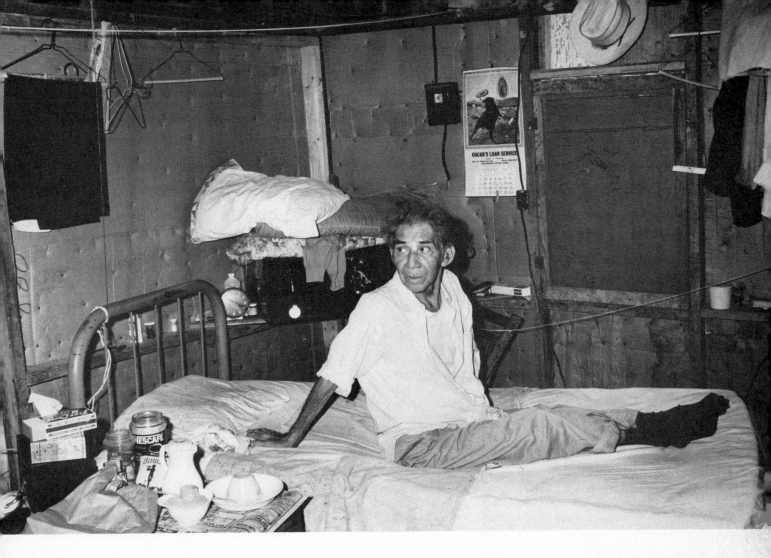

tion concerning labor camps places the burden of responsibility on the individual inspector. A content analysis of the New York State Health Code introduced in March 1968 reveals that in 16 items, the decision on the acceptability of a given condition is left to the discretion of the permit-issuing official. Other aspects of this legislation, intended to improve the situation, reveal an ignorance of the social realities in the camps and demonstrate the dangers of piecemeal improvement of a fundamentally poor situation. The vagueness of the earlier legislation had given the migrant a certain degree of independence from the crew leader. For example, because he was allowed to cook food in his room, he could avoid paying for prepared meals. Ironically, the new legislation, intended to improve fire safety, set minimum standards for cooking areas and left no alternative but to buy meals from the crew leader, thereby reinforcing his control. The intended solution of one problem only served to exacerbate another.

Camp conditions were the focus of a crisis that occurred when an organizer convinced a migrant to discuss the problems of farm labor on the radio. He described the decrepit buildings, the lack of sufficient water supply and the inadequate cooking and bathroom facilities. Despite the fact that the program was broadcast on an FM station with relatively few listeners, the publicity was sufficient to arouse not only local growers, but also community groups ostensibly concerned with improving just those conditions criticized. The next morning the grower, an inspector and the crew leader questioned the migrant who had appeared on the program and asked him to leave the camp. He went to town to rent a trailer, but later when he returned for his clothes, he was discouraged from leaving by the grower who feared further publicity.

One irate official at the government employment office complained that such publicity calls attention only to the worst camps, while ignoring all the positive changes in the migrant situation. The organizer, he felt, was interfering in what was none of his business. A church volunteer criticized the organizer, saying that he had angered a lot of people by intruding too aggressively; this would do more harm than good, for it would be damaging to social work programs in the area. The migrant who participated in the broadcast was spoken of with disdain ("he brought his own Beautyrest mattress North"), suggesting that he was not a real migrant because he showed concern for his own comfort.

A more serious incident revealed the extent and consequences of the invisibility of the migrant laborers. During the summer of 1966, a group of migrants in an agricultural community marched into town as a protest against their

Invisible Migrant Workers

conditions, and fear of a riot was expressed. The event shocked community officials who had assumed that the migrants were well satisfied with the circumstances in which they lived. "Why," said the mayor, "they walked by here on the road and I waved to them and they laughed and smiled . . . real happy, you know." And the wife of the police chief noted, "this place is a paradise compared to what they are used to living in. Of course you or I wouldn't want to live that way, but I believe they like it fine."

Such a total lack of communication with the migrants is not entirely the fault of the community. The migrants themselves, as an outgroup subject to external pressures, control their visibility for purposes of protection in somewhat the same way as gypsies have developed subtle and complex mechanisms for maintaining a mystique of obscurity. Gypsies know back roads and inconspicuous gathering places, employ a private language and use decoys and facades such as fortune-telling; the latter diverts attention from what they consider to be the really important aspects of their culture. Invisibility permits autonomy and limits interference.

Migrants too are concerned primarily with self-protection. Living in the North for only part of the year and unfamiliar with many physical and social aspects of their environment, they feel isolated and alien. One articulate individual described his discomfort. In the South he knew where he could go and what he could do without getting into trouble; in the North he was never certain and he never knew what people were thinking. "Here people don't know where they stand and they are self-conscious all the time."

A second incentive for controlling visibility lies in the migrant's lack of autonomy. Control comes from outside the group and from such unpredictable sources as the weather and "the Man." Invisibility allows a sense of independence: "I don't drink. I mind my own business. It depends on how you act. If you're careful there'll be no trouble."

Finally, it is often pragmatically convenient to be invisible. Families needing income from their children's labor, for example, must be sensitive to their visibility when inspectors come to the fields.

Disappearing Acts

Children working illegally often disappear from view as soon as state-government license plates are spotted. In one case, researchers using state vehicles found that their cars had to be relicensed or many people in the camps would disappear upon their arrival.

In many cases, crew leaders conceal overcrowded camp conditions. In one camp, approved for 86 occupants, there were 120 people, a discrepancy never noticed until a count was required for purposes of allocating government food during a time when there was no work. When the situation of overcrowding became visible, the crew leader with a logic clear only to himself eliminated 34 names, claiming that exactly 86 people were eligible. In effect he was able to make more than one-fourth of his crew disappear.

Certain aspects of migrant behavior correspond strikingly to the process of information control that Erving Goffman has described as "stigma management." To maintain invisibility in Goffman's terms, it is necessary to avoid any action which might violate the expectations of others. This is an important group norm in migrant camps. There is considerable pressure to avoid arguing with a farmer or supervisor regardless of provocation. When one man spoke back to a farmer in a mildly facetious manner, he was immediately rebuked by the group for acting in this unexpected and therefore conspicuous fashion. Similarly, there are normative sanctions against picking too rapidly or too slowly. One must not stand out by working apart from the group and thereby possibly calling attention to the pace of others. Norms against ratebusting are of course not unique to this group, but they are particularly salient in this case because of the limited channels through which individuals may achieve mobility.

Similarly, group norms tend to level participants, to put down those who want to assume leadership. The outside society which perceives migrants as an undifferentiated group reinforces this leveling tendency and thus perpetuates stagnation.

Field researchers were struck by the dual personality exhibited by many migrants who assumed a meek demeanor in the presence of white people, but who were aggressive among their peers. To remain inconspicuous, these migrants had learned to assume different styles of behavior that meshed with the expectations of others. Thus, they manage the information that others receive about them.

A visitor to a migrant camp will often find himself next to a juke box turned up to full volume or faced with other means to limit communication, such as garbled accents, hand over mouth or silence. When not confronted directly, migrants maintain invisibility by simply avoiding outsiders.

Since there are few visitors, migrants remain unseen simply by staying in the camps. Certain people, primarily older workers, chose to stay out of town even when a ride was available. Younger people appeared less concerned, but when they did go to town they avoided unfamiliar areas. Once in the public eye, normative constraints against calling attention to the group were in operation. One young shoplifter was warned repeatedly, "don't cause trouble." Migrants hesitated to enter stores. In one case, a man who tried on a pair of shoes was afraid not to buy them. Although he did not want the shoes, he felt it would be less conspicuous to buy them than to leave without a purchase. A group of migrants on a truck being serviced at a garage would not ask for the key to the rest room, nor would they go into the station to buy soda.

The reluctance to call on outside authority is another symptom of the desire to maintain invisibility. Police are rarely requested to manage internal problems. Since migrants tend to distrust police authority, crew leaders prefer to maintain control themselves. When a police inquiry does take place, it is usually at the instigation of outsiders. For example, one man alienated several people in his camp and, afraid they would beat him, fled the camp. Local white residents who were concerned by his presence in their neighborhood initiated a police inquiry.

The police prefer to avoid involvement. A police officer, interviewed about his investigation of a fight between two migrants that occurred in the town, said that he instructed a group of migrants who had observed the fight to take care of the problem. "These are your people, you take care of them." They obliged by driving the men back to the camp. The officer claimed that he liked to avoid arresting migrants since it would keep them out of work. He preferred to ignore incidents and just to "quiet things down." Those migrants who do want police protection resent such an attitude, though they have come to expect it.

Migrant invisibility, then, is fostered both by the migrants themselves in an effort to adapt to their particular circumstances as well as by employers and social work groups and poverty organizations seeking to improve the situation. Groups seeking change share the preconception that while there are many problems, there are no alternatives to present arrangements. Solutions to problems are seen to lie in small, nonstructural changes. The primary concern is to avoid disturbing incidents which might in any way threaten the existing system. The tendency is to isolate migrants, to keep them in the camps where there is minimum visibility and limited contact with the outside community.

To render the migrant visible would expose the depths of the problem and certainly jeopardize the interests of those who have a stake in the system as it presently operates. Open acknowledgement of the existence of a social situation that is dissonant with basic social values would call these conditions into question. As long as the migrant remains out of sight, he is also out of mind. Disturbance may be minimized, but the obvious question remains: Can an invisible problem be resolved?

FURTHER READING

Migrants, Sharecroppers and Mountaineers: Children of Crisis, vol. 2 by Robert Coles (Boston: Little, Brown, 1972).

Migrant: Agricultural Workers in America's Northeast by William H. Friedland and Dorothy Nelkin (New York: Holt, Rinehart and Winston, 1972).

Migrant and Seasonal Farmworker Powerlessness, Hearings in U.S. Senate, Committee on Labor and Public Welfare, Subcommittee on Migratory Labor, 91st Congress (Washington, D.C.: USGPO, 1970).

BRUCE JACKSON

In the Valley of the Shadows: Kentucky

Along the roadsides and in backyards are the cannibalized cadavers of old cars: there is no other place to dump them, there are no junkyards that have any reason to haul them away. Streambeds are littered with old tires, cans, pieces of metal and plastic. On a sunny day the streams and creeks glisten with pretty blue spots from the Maxwell House coffee tins and Royal Crown cola cans. For some reason the paint used by Maxwell House and Royal Crown doesn't wear off very quickly, and while the paint and paper on other cans are peeling to reveal an undistinctive aluminum color, the accumulating blues of those two brands make for a most peculiar local feature.

Winter in eastern Kentucky is not very pretty. In some places you see the gouged hillsides where the strip and auger mines have ripped away tons of dirt and rock to get at the mineral seams underneath; below the gouges you see the littered valleys where the overburden, the earth they have ripped and scooped away, has been dumped in spoil banks. The streams stink from the augerholes' sulfurous exudations; the hillsides no longer hold water back because the few trees and bushes are small and thin, so there is continual erosion varying the ugliness in color only.

Most of the people around here live outside the town in hollers and along the creeks. Things are narrow: the hills rise up closely and flatland is at a premium. A residential area will stretch out for several miles, one or two houses and a road thick, with hills starting up just behind the outhouse. Sometimes, driving along the highway following the Big Sandy river, there is so little flat space that the highway is on one side of the river and the line of houses is on the other, with plank suspension bridges every few miles connecting the two. Everything is crushed together. You may ride five miles without passing a building, then come upon a half-dozen houses, each within ten feet of its neighbor. And churches: the Old Regular Baptist church, the Freewill Baptist church, the Meta Baptist church. On the slopes of the hills are cemeteries, all neatly tended; some are large and old, some have only one or two recent graves in them.

In winter, when the sun never rises very far above the horizon, the valley floors get only about four hours of direct sunlight a day; most of the days are cloudy anyhow. One always moves in shadow, in greyness. Children grow up without ever seeing the sun rise or set.

The day of the company store and company house is gone. So are most of the big companies around here. This is small truck mine country now, and operators of the small mines don't find stores and houses worth their time. The old company houses worth living in have been bought up, either as rental property or for the new owner's personal use; the company houses still standing but not worth living in comprise the county's only public housing for the very poor.

At the end of one of the hollows running off Marrowbone Creek, three miles up a road you couldn't make, even in dry weather, without four-wheel drive, stands an old cabin. It is a log cabin, but there is about it nothing romantic or frontiersy, only grimness. Scratched in the kitchen window, by some unknown adult or child, are the crude letters of the word victory. Over what or whom we don't know. It is unlikely anyway. There are no victories here, only occasional survivors, and if survival is a victory it is a mean and brutal one.

Inside the cabin a Barbie doll stands over a nearly opaque mirror in a room lighted by a single bare 60-watt bulb. In the middle of the room a coal stove spews outrageous amounts of heat. When the stove is empty the room is cold and damp. There is no middle area of comfort. The corrugated cardboard lining the walls doesn't stop drafts very well and most of the outside chinking is gone. On one side of the room with the stove is the entrance to the other bedroom, on the other side is the kitchen. There are no doors inside the house. A woman lives here with her nine children.

If all the nine children were given perfectly balanced full meals three times a day from now on, still some of them would never be well. A 15-year-old daughter loses patches of skin because of an irreversible vitamin deficiency, and sometimes, because of the supporations and congealing, they have to soak her clothing off when she comes home from school. Last month the baby was spitting up blood for a while but that seems to have stopped.

It might be possible to do something for the younger ones, but it is not likely anyone will. The husband went somewhere and didn't come back; that was over a year ago. The welfare inspector came a few months ago and found out that someone had given the family a box of clothes for the winter; the welfare check was cut by $20 a month after that. When the woman has $82 she can get $120 worth of food stamps; if she doesn't have the $82, she gets no food stamps at all. For a year, the entire family had nothing for dinner but one quart of green beans each night. Breakfast was fried flour and coffee. A friend told me the boy said he had had meat at a neighbor's house once.

Bony Hills

This is Pike County, Kentucky. It juts like a chipped arrowhead into the bony hill country of neighboring West Virginia. Pike County has about seventy thousand residents and, the Chamber of Commerce advertises, it produces more coal than any other county in the world. The county seat, Pikeville, has about six thousand residents; it is the only real town for about 30 miles.

The biggest and bitterest event in Pike County's past was sometime in the 1880s when Tolbert McCoy killed Big Ellison Hatfield: it started a feud that resulted in 65 killed, settled nothing and wasn't won by either side. The biggest and bitterest thing in recent years has been the War on Poverty: it doesn't seem to have killed anyone, but it hasn't settled anything or won any major battles either.

About seventy-five hundred men are employed by Pike County's mines: one thousand drive trucks, five hundred work at the tipples (the docks where coal is loaded into railway cars) and mine offices, and six thousand work inside. Most of the mines are small and it doesn't take very many men to work them: an automated truck mine can be handled by about eight men. Some people work at service activities: they pump gas, sell shoes, negotiate contracts (there are about *40* lawyers in this little town), dispense drugs, direct traffic, embalm—all those things that make an American town go. There are six industrial firms in the area; two of them are beverage companies, one is a lumber company; the total employment of the six firms is 122 men and women.

A union mine pays $28-$38 per day, with various benefits, but few of the mines in Pike County are unionized. The truck mines, where almost all the men work, pay $14 per day, with almost no benefits. The United Mine Workers of America were strong here once, but when times got hard the union let a lot of people down and left a lot of bitterness behind. Not only did the union make deals with the larger companies that resulted in many of its own men being thrown out of work (one of those deals recently resulted in a $7.3 million conspiracy judgment against the UMWA and Consolidation Coal Company), but it made the abandonment complete by lifting the unemployed workers' medical cards and shutting down the union hospitals in the area. For most of the area, those cards and hospitals were the only source of medical treatment. There has been talk of organizing the truck mines and someone told me the UMW local was importing an old-time firebreathing organizer to get things going, but it doesn't seem likely the men will put their lives on the line another time.

With Frederic J. Fleron, Jr., an old friend then on the faculty of the University of Kentucky in Lexington, I went to visit Robert Holcomb, president of the Independent Coal Operator's Association, president of the Chamber of Commerce and one of the people in the county most vocally at war with the poverty program. His office door was decorated with several titles: Dixie Mining Co., Roberts Engineering Co., Robert Holcomb and Co., Chloe Gas Co., Big Sandy Coal Co. and Martha Colleries, Inc.

One of the secretaries stared at my beard as if it were a second nose; she soon got control of herself and took us in to see Holcomb. (Someone had said to me the day before, "Man, when Holcomb sees you with that beard on he's gonna be sure you're a communist." "What if I tell him I'm playing Henry the Fifth in a play at the university?" "Then he'll be sure Henry the Fifth is a communist too.") Holcomb took the beard better than the girl had: his expression remained nicely neutral. He offered us coffee and introduced us to his partner, a Mr. Roberts, who sat in a desk directly opposite him. On the wall behind Roberts' head was a large white flying map of the United States with a brownish smear running over Louisiana, Mississippi and most of Texas; the darkest splotch was directly over New Orleans. The phone rang and Roberts took the call; he tilted back in his chair, his head against New Orleans and Lake Pontchartrain.

Holcomb was happy to talk about his objections to the poverty program. "I'm a firm believer that you don't help a man by giving him bread unless you give him hope for the future, and poverty programs have given them bread only." The problem with the Appalachian Volunteers (an anti-poverty organization partially funded by OEO, now pretty much defunct) was "they got no supervision. They brought a bunch of young people in, turned 'em loose and said, 'Do your thing' . . . . I think they have created a disservice rather than a service by creating a lot of disillusionment by making people expect things that just can't happen."

Expanding and Wrecking

He told us something about what was happening. The coal industry had been expanding rapidly. "Over the last eight years the truck mining industry has created an average of 500 new jobs a year." He sat back. "We're working to bring the things in here that will relieve the poverty permanently." He talked of bringing other kinds of industry to the area and told us about the incentives they were offering companies that were willing to relocate. "We know a lot of our people are not fitted for mining," he said.

(It is not just a matter of being "fitted" of course. There is the problem of those who are wrecked by silicosis and black lung who can do nothing but hope their doctor bills won't go up so much they'll have to pull one of the teenage kids out of school and send him to work, or be so screwed by welfare or social security or the UMW pension managers or the mine operators' disability insurance company that the meager payments that do come into some homes will be stopped.)

The truck mines play an ironic role in the local economy: half the men working in them, according to Holcomb, cannot work in the large mines because of physical disability. The small mines, in effect, not only get the leftover coal seams that aren't fat enough to interest Consol or U.S. Steel or the other big companies in the area, but they also get the men those firms have used up and discarded.

From Holcomb's point of view things are going pretty well in Pike County. In 1960 there were $18 million in deposits in Pikeville's three banks; that has risen to $65 million. There are 700 small mines in the county, many of them operated by former miners. "This is free enterprise at its finest," he said.

The next morning he took us on a trip through the Johns Creek area. As we passed new houses and large trailers he pointed to them as evidence of progress, which they in fact are. In the hollers behind, Fred and I could see the shacks and boxes in which people also live, and those Holcomb passed without a word. I suppose one must select from all the data presenting itself in this world, otherwise living gets awfully complex.

We drove up the hill to a small mine. Holcomb told us that the eight men working there produce 175 tons daily, all of which goes to the DuPont nylon plant in South Carolina.

A man in a shed just outside the mine mouth was switching the heavy industrial batteries on a coal tractor. The miner was coated with coal dust and oil smears. He wore a plastic helmet with a light on it; around his waist was the light's battery pack, like a squashed holster. He moved very fast, whipping the chains off and on and winding the batteries out, pumping the pulley chains up and down. Another mine tractor crashed out of the entrance, its driver inclined at 45 degrees. The tractor is about 24 inches high and the mine roof is only 38 inches high, so the drivers have to tilt all the time or get their heads crushed. Inside, the men work on their knees. The tractor backed the buggy connected to it to the edge of a platform, dumped its load, then clanked back inside.

I went into the mine, lying on my side in the buggy towed by the tractor with the newly charged batteries.

Inside is utter blackness, broken only by the slicing beams of light from the helmets. The beams are neat and pretty, almost like a lucite tube poking here and there; the prettiness goes away when you realize the reason the beam is so brilliant is because of the coal and rock dust in the air, dust a worker is continually inhaling into his lungs. One sees no bodies, just occasional hands interrupting the moving lightbeams playing on the timbers and working face. Clattering noises and shouts are strangely disembodied and directionless.

Outside, I dust off and we head back towards town in Holcomb's truck.

"The temperature in there is 68 degrees all the time," he says. "You work in air-conditioned comfort all year 'round. Most of these men, after they've been in the mine for awhile, wouldn't work above ground." (I find myself thinking of Senator Murphy of California who in his campaign explained the need for bracero labor: they stoop over better than Anglos do.) The miners, as I said, make $14 a day.

"When you see what's been accomplished here in the last ten years it makes the doings of the AVs and the others seem completely insignificant. And we didn't have outside money." The pitted and gouged road is one-lane and we find ourselves creeping behind a heavily loaded coal truck heading toward one of the tipples up the road. "We think welfare is fine, but it should be a temporary measure, not a permanent one. And any organization that encourages people to get on welfare is a detriment to the community." The truck up front gets out of our way, Holcomb shifts back to two-wheel drive, we pick up speed. "These poverty program people, what they tried to do is latch on to some mountain customs and try to convince people they have come up with something new."

He believes business will help everybody; he believes the poverty program has been bad business. He is enormously sincere. Everyone is enormously sincere down here, or so it seems.

So we drove and looked at the new mines and tipples and Robert Holcomb told us how long each had been there and what its tonnage was and how many people each mine employed and how many mines fed into each tipple. One of his companies, he told us, produced 350,000 tons of coal last year and operated at a profit of 15.7 cents per ton.

Hospital death certificates cite things like pneumonia and heart disease. There is no way of knowing how many of those result from black lung and silicosis. The mine owners say very few; the miners and their families say a great many indeed. A lot of men with coated lungs don't die for a long time, but they may not be good for much else meanwhile. Their lungs won't absorb much oxygen, so they cannot move well or fast or long.

"This is a one-industry area," Holcomb had said, "and if you can't work at that industry you can't work at anything." Right. And most of the residents—men wrinkled or contaminated, widows, children—do not work at anything. Over 50 percent of the families in Pike County have incomes below $3,000 per year. Like land torn by the strip-mining operations, those people simply stay back in the hollers out of sight and slowly erode.

We talked with an old man who had worked in the mines for 28 years. He told us how he had consumed his life savings and two years' time getting his disabled social security benefits.

"See, I got third-stage silicosis and I've got prostate and gland trouble, stomach troubles, a ruptured disc. Now they say that at the end of this month they're gonna take the state aid medical card away. And that's all I've got; I've got so much wrong with me I can't get no insurance. I've had the card two years and now they say I draw too much social security because of last year's increase in social security benefits and they're gonna have to take my medical card away from me after this month. I don't know what in the hell I'm gonna do. Die, I reckon."

"Yeah, yeah," his wife said from the sink.

"It don't seem right," he said. "I worked like hell, I made good money and I doublebacked. Because I worked a lot and draw more social security than lots of people in the mines where they don't make no money, I don't see where it's right for them not to allow me no medical card."

He opened the refrigerator and showed us some of the various chemicals he takes every day. In a neat stack on the table were the month's medical receipts. He said something about his youth, and I was suddenly stunned to realize he was only 51.

"You know," he said, "sand's worse than black lung. Silicosis. It hardens on the lung and there's no way to get it off. In West Virginia I worked on one of those roof-bolting machines. It's about eight, nine-foot high, sandstone top. Burn the bits up drillin' holes in it. And I'd be there. Dust'd be that thick on your lips. But it's fine stuff in the air, you don't see the stuff that you get in your lungs. It's fine stuff. Then I didn't get no pay for it."

"You got a thousand dollars," his wife said.

"A thousand dollars for the first stage. They paid me first stage and I just didn't want to give up. I kept on workin', and now I got third stage . . . . I just hated to give up, but I wished I had of. One doctor said to me, 'If you keep on you might as well get your shotgun and shoot your brains out, you'd be better off.' I still kept on after he told me that. Then I got so I just couldn't hardly go on. My clothes wouldn't stay on me."

The woman brought coffee to the table. "He draws his disabled social security now," she says, "but if he was to draw for his black lung disease they would cut his social security way down, so he's better off just drawing his social security. There's guys around here they cut below what they was drawing for social security. I don't think that's right."

It is all very neat: the black lung, when a miner can force the company doctors to diagnose it honestly, is paid for by company insurance, but payments are set at a level such that a disabled miner loses most of his social security benefits if he takes the compensation; since the compensation pays less than social security, many miners don't put in their legitimate claims, and the net effect is a government subsidy of the insurance companies and mine owners.

Mary Walton, an Appalachian Volunteer, invited Fred and me to dinner at her place in Pikeville one night during our stay. It turned out Mary and I had been at Harvard at the same time and we talked about that place for a while, which was very strange there between those darkening hills. Three other people were at Mary's apartment: a girl named Barbara, in tight jeans and a white shirt with two buttons open and zippered boots, and two men, both of them connected with the local college. One was working with the Model Cities project, the other worked in the college president's office; one was astoundingly tall, the other was built like a wrestler; they all looked aggressively healthy. Barbara's husband worked for the Council of the Southern Mountains in Berea.

The fellow who looked like a wrestler told me at great length that what was going on in Pikeville wasn't a social or economic attack on the community structure, but rather an attack on the structure of ideas and only now was everyone learning that. I asked him what he meant. He said that the poverty workers had once seen their job as enlightening the masses about how messed up things were. "We were ugly Americans, that's all we were. That's why we weren't effective. But now we've learned that you don't change anything that way, you have to get inside the local community and understand it first and work there."

I thought that was indeed true, but I didn't see what it had to do with the structure of the community's ideas; it had to do only with the arrogance or naivete of the poverty workers, and that was awfully solipsistic. He hadn't said anything about his clients—just himself, just the way his ideas were challenged, not theirs.

The apartment was curiously out of that world. On the walls were posters and lithos and prints and pictures of healthy human bodies looking delicious. The record racks contained the Stones and *Tim Hardin No. 3* and a lot of Bach. Many of the recent books we'd all read and others one had and the others meant to, and Mary and I talked about them, but there was something relative, even in the pleasantness, as if it were an appositive in the bracketing nastiness out there.

When we got back to the car I took from my jacket pocket the heavy and uncomfortable shiny chromeplated .380 automatic pistol someone had once given me in San Antonio. I put it on the seat next to Fred's .357 revolver. They looked silly there; real guns always do. But people

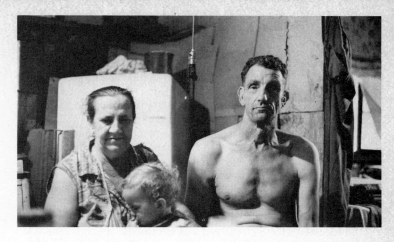

kept telling us how someone else was going to shoot us, or they recounted the story of how Hugh O'Connor, a Canadian film producer down in the next county the year before to make a movie, was shot in the heart by a man with no liking for outsiders and less for outsiders with cameras, and it did seem awfully easy to be an outsider here.

We went to see Edith Easterling, a lifelong Marrowbone Creek resident, working at that time for the Appalachian Volunteers as director of the Marrowbone Folk School. "The people in the mountains really lives hard," Edith said. "You can come into Pikeville and go to the Chamber of Commerce and they'll say, 'Well, there's really no poor people left there. People are faring good.' Then you can come out here and go to homes and you'd just be surprised how poor these people live, how hard that they live. Kids that's grown to 15 or 16 years old that's never had a mess of fresh milk or meats, things that kids really need. They live on canned cream until they get big enough to go to the table and eat beans and potatoes."

She told us about harassment and redbaiting of the AVs by Robert Holcomb, Harry Eastburn (the Big Sandy Community Action Program director, also funded by OEO, a bitter antagonist of any poverty program not under his political control), and Thomas Ratliff, the commonwealth's attorney (the equivalent of a county prosecutor).

Some of the AVs came from out of state, especially the higher paid office staff and technical specialists, but most of the 14 field workers were local people, like Edith. Since becoming involved with the poverty program Edith has received telephone threats and had some windows shot out. The sheriff refused to send a deputy to investigate. Occasionally she gets anonymous calls; some are threats, some call her "dirty communist." She shrugs those away: "I'm a Republican and who ever seen a communist Republican?"

Changing a Way of Life

The Appalachian Volunteers began in the early 1960s as a group of students from Berea College who busied themselves with needed community band-aid work: they made trips to the mountains to patch up dilapidated schoolhouses, they ran tutorial programs, they collected books for needy schools. The ultimate futility of such work soon became apparent and there was a drift in the AV staff toward projects that might affect the life style of some of the mountain communities. In 1966 the AVs decided to break away from their parent organization, the conservative

Council of the Southern Mountains. The new, independent Appalachian Volunteers had no difficulty finding federal funding. During the summers of 1966 and 1967 the organization received large OEO grants to host hundreds of temporary volunteer workers, many of them VISTA and Peace Corps trainees. According to David Walls, who was acting director of the AVs when I talked with him, the organization's mission was to "create effective, economically self-sufficient poor people's organizations that would concern themselves with local issues, such as welfare rights, bridges and roads, water systems and strip mining."

It didn't work, of course it didn't work; the only reason it lasted as long as it did was because so much of the AV staff was composed of outsiders, people who had worked in San Francisco and Boston and New York and Washington, and it took a long time before the naivete cracked enough for the failure to show through.

The first consequence of creating an organization of the impoverished and unempowered is not the generation of any new source or residence of power, but rather the gathering in one place of a lot of poverty and powerlessness that previously were spread out. In an urban situation, the poor or a minority group may develop or exercise veto power: they can manage an economic boycott, they can refuse to work for certain firms and encourage others to join with them, they can physically block a store entrance. It is only when such efforts create a kind of negative monopoly (a strike line no one will cross or a boycott

others will respect) that power is generated. When that negative monopoly cannot be created, there is no power— this is why workers can successfully strike for higher wages but the poor in cities cannot get the police to respect their civil liberties enough to stop beating them up; if everyone refuses to work at a factory, the owner must cooperate or close down, but there is nothing anyone can refuse a policeman that will remove the immediate incentive for illegal police behavior. The poor in the mountains cannot strike—they are unemployable anyway, or at least enough of them are to make specious that kind of action. Even if they were to get something going the UMW would not

support them. The poor cannot start an economic boycott: they don't spend enough to hold back enough to threaten any aspect of the mountain coal economy. (there have been a few instances of industrial sabotage—I'll mention them later on—that have been dramatic, but pitifully ineffective.) One of the saddest things about the poor in the mountains is they have nothing to deny anyone. And they don't even have the wild hope some city poor entertain that something may turn up; in the mountains there is nothing to hope for.

Another problem with organizations of the very poor is they do not have much staying power: the individual participants are just too vulnerable. So long as the members can be scared or bought off easily, one cannot hope for such groups to develop solidarity. In Kentucky, where welfare, medical aid, disability pensions and union benefits all have a remarkable quality of coming and going with political whims, that is a real problem. Edith Easterling described the resulting condition: "These people are scared people, they are scared to death. I can talk to them and I can say, 'You shouldn't be scared, there's nothing to be scared about.' But they're still scared."

"What are they scared of," Fred asked her, "losing their jobs?"

"No. Some of 'em don't even have a job. Most of the people don't have jobs. They live on some kind of pension. They're scared of losing their pension. If it's not that, they're scared someone will take them to court for something. 'If I say something, they're going to take me to court and I don't have a lawyer's fee. I don't have a lawyer, so I'd rather not say nothing.' When you get the people to really start opening up and talking, that's when the county officials attack us every time with something."

Publicity and Revenge

For someone who brings troublesome publicity to the community, there are forms of retaliation far crueler than the mere cutting off of welfare or unemployment benefits. One poverty worker told of an event following a site visit by Robert Kennedy a few years ago: "When Kennedy was down for his hearings one of his advance men got in contact with a friend of ours who had a community organization going. They were very anxious to get some exposure, to get Kennedy involved in it. They took the advance men around to visit some families that were on welfare. He made statements about the terrible conditions the children there in two particular homes had to live under. He wasn't indicting the families, he was just talking about conditions in general. These were picked up by the local press and given quite a bit of notoriety—Kennedy Aide Makes the Scene, that sort of thing. After he left, about three days later, the welfare agency came and took away the children from both of those families and put them in homes . . . . This is the control that is over people's lives."

The group with the potential staying power in the mountains is the middle class, the small landowners. They have concrete things to lose while the poor (save in anomalous atrocities such as the one with the children mentioned above) have nothing to lose, they only have possible access to benefits that someone outside their group may or may not let them get. There is a big difference in the way one fights in the two situations. Something else: it is harder to scare the middle class off, for it has not been conditioned by all those years of humiliating control and dependency.

One Appalachian Volunteer, Joe Mulloy, a 24-year-old Kentuckian, realized this. He and his wife decided to join a fight being waged by a Pike County landowner, Jink Ray, and his neighbors, against a strip-mine operator who was about to remove the surface of Ray's land.

Rights for Pennies

The focus of the fight was the legitimacy of the *broadform* deed, a nineteenth century instrument with which landowners assigned mineral rights to mining companies, usually for small sums of money (50 cents per acre was common). When these deeds were originally signed no landowner had any thought of signing away all rights to his property—just the underground minerals and whatever few holes the mining company might have to make in the hillside to get at the seams. In the twentieth century the coal companies developed the idea of lifting off all the earth and rock above the coal, rather than digging for it, and since the broadform deed said the miner could use whatever means he saw fit to get the coal out, the Kentucky courts held that the miners' land rights had precedence over the surface owners'—even though that meant complete destruction of a man's land by a mining process the original signer of the deed could not have imagined. The strip miners are legally entitled, on the basis of a contract that might be 90 years old, to come to a man's home and completely bury it in rubble, leaving the owner nothing but the regular real estate tax bill with which he is stuck even though the "real estate" has since been dumped in the next creekbed. First come the bulldozers to do the initial clearing (a song I heard in West Virginia, to the tune of "Swing Low, Sweet Chariot," went: "Roll on, big D-9 dozer, comin' for to bury my home/ I'm getting madder as you're gettin' closer, comin' for to bury my home."), then they roll in the massive shovels, some of which grow as large as 18.5 million pounds and can gobble 200 tons of earth and rock a minute and dump it all a city block away. Such a machine is operated by one man riding five stories above the ground.

On June 29, 1967, Jink Ray and some neighbors in Island Creek, a Pike County community, blocked with their bodies bulldozers that were about to start stripping Ray's land. With them were Joe and Karen Mulloy. The people themselves had organized the resistance; the Mulloys were simply helping.

With the strip-mining fight on the mountain, the AVs were for the first time involved in something significant. It was also dangerous: the members of the Island Creek group were challenging not only the basis of the local economy, but the federal government as well: the big mines' biggest customer is the Tennessee Valley Authority, and the Small Business Administration supports many of the smaller mine operators. The poverty program and other federal agencies were moving toward open conflict.

What happened was that the poverty program backed down and the local power structure moved in. Eleven days after Governor Edward Breathitt's August 1 suspension of the strip-mine company's Island Creek permit (the first and only such suspension), Pike County officials arrested the Mulloys for sedition (plotting or advocating the violent overthrow of the government). Arrested with them on the same charge were Alan and Margaret McSurely, field workers for the Southern Conference Educational Fund (SCEF), a Louisville-based civil rights organization. McSurely had been hired as training consultant by the AV's during the spring of 1967, but the real reason he had been hired was to restructure the cumbersome organization. One of the first things he did was get the AVs to allow local people on the board of directors; he was fired in a month and went to work for SCEF; they even arrested Carl Braden (SCEF's executive director) and his wife, Anne. Anne Braden had never been in Pike County in her life; the first time Carl Braden had been there was the day he went to Pikeville to post bail for McSurely on the sedition charge.

In Washington, the response to the arrests was immediate; Sargent Shriver's office announced that AV funds would be cut off; no funds previously granted were taken away, but no new money was appropriated after that.

The Pike County grand jury concluded that "A well-organized and well-financed effort is being made to promote and spread the communistic theory of violent and forceful overthrow of the government of Pike County." The grand jury said also that "Communist organizers have attempted, without success thus far, to promote their beliefs among our school children by infiltrating our local schools with teachers who believe in the violent overthrow of the local government." Organizers were "planning to infiltrate local churches and labor unions in order to cause dissension and to promote their purposes." And, finally, "Communist organizers are attempting to form community unions with the eventual purpose of organizing armed groups to be known as 'Red Guards' and through which the forceful overthrow of the local government would be accomplished."

Untouchable Volunteers

The AVs came unglued. The Mulloys became pariahs within the organization. "We spent that whole summer and no AV came to see us at all in Pike County," Joe Mulloy said. "Once they came up to shit on us, but that was the only time. Then the thing of our getting arrested for sedition was what just really flipped everybody . . . . This was a real situation that you had to deal with, it wasn't something in your mind or some ideological thing. It was real. Another person was under arrest. I think that the feeling of a number of people on the staff was it was my fault that I had been arrested because I had been reckless in my organizing, that I had been on the mountain with the fellas and had risked as much as they were risking and I deserved what I got, and that I should be fired so the program would go on; that was now a detriment."

That fall, a special three judge federal court ruled the Kentucky sedition law unconstitutional so all charges against the Mulloys, the Bradens and the McSurelys were wiped out. But the AVs were still nervous. "After the arrests were cleared away," Mulloy said, "things started to happen to me on the staff. I was given another assignment.

I was told that I couldn't be a field man any more because I was a public figure identified with sedition and hence people would feel uneasy talking to me, and that I should do research. My truck was taken away and I was given an old car, and I was given a title of researcher rather than field man. It took away considerable voice that I had in the staff until then."

Karen Mulloy said she and Joe really had no choice. "If we had organized those people up there, with possible death as the end result for some of them—fortunately it was kept nonviolent—and if we weren't with them they wouldn't have spoken to us. We took as much risk as they did. We said to them, 'We're not going to organize something for you that we won't risk our necks for either.' An organizer can't do that."

"These people have gone through the whole union experience and that has sold them out," Joe said. "And a great number of people have gone through the poverty war experience and that hasn't answered anybody's problems, anybody's questions. Getting together on the strip-mining issue—if there was ever one issue that the poverty war got on that was good, that was it. It all fell through because when we started getting counterattacked by the operators the poverty war backed up because their funds were being jeopardized. The whole strip-mining issue as an organized effort has collapsed right now and the only thing that's going on is individual sabotage. There's a lot of mining equipment being blown up every month or so, about a million dollars at a time. These are individual or small group acts or retaliation, but the organized effort has ceased."

(Later, I talked with Rick Diehl, the AV research director, about the sabotage. He described two recent operations, both of them very sophisticated, involving groups of multiple charges set off simultaneously. The sheriff didn't even look for the dynamiters: he probably wouldn't have caught them and even if he had he wouldn't have gotten a jury to convict. "And that kind of stuff goes on to some degree all the time," Diehl said. "There's a growing feeling that destroying property is going to shut down the system in Appalachia. The people don't benefit from the coal companies at all, 'cause even the deep mines don't have enough employees. The average number of employees in a deep mine is 16 people. So, you can see, there is nothing to lose. It's that same desperation kind of thing that grips people in Detroit and Watts.")

Organizing Outrage

Even though the sedition charges were dropped, the Mulloys and McSurelys weren't to escape punishment for their organizing outrages.

One Friday the 13th Al McSurely came home late from a two or three day trip out of town, talked with his wife a little while, then went to bed. Margaret went to bed a short time later. "I wasn't asleep at all," she said, "but he was so tired he went right to sleep. I heard this car speed up. Well, I had got into the habit of listening to cars at night, just because we always expected something like this to happen. And sure enough, it did. There was this blast. The car took off and there was this huge blast, and glass and dirt and grit were in my mouth and eyes and hair, and the baby was screaming. So I put on my bathrobe and ran across the street with the baby."

"The state trooper was pretty good," Alan said. "He gave me a lecture: 'The next time this happens call the city police first so they can seal off the holler. They can get here much faster than I can.' I said, 'I'll try and remember that.'"

Joe Mulloy was the only AV with a Kentucky draft board; he was also the only AV to lose his occupational deferment and have his 2-A changed to 1-A. Mulloy asked the board (in Louisville, the same as Muhammed Ali's) for a rehearing on the grounds of conscientious objection, and he presented as part of his evidence a letter from Thomas Merton saying he was Mulloy's spiritual adviser (the two used to meet for talks in Merton's cabin in the woods) and could testify to the truthfulness of Mulloy's C.O. claim. The board refused to reopen the case because, they said, there was no new evidence of any relevance or value. In April 1968 Mulloy was sentenced to five years in prison and a $10,000 fine for refusing induction.

He was fired immediately by the Appalachian Volunteers. Some wanted him out because they honestly thought his draft case would be a major obstacle to his effectiveness with the oddly patriotic mountain people. (In the mountains you can be against the war, many people are, but if your country calls you, you go. It would be unpatriotic not to go. The government and the country are two quite independent entities. The government might screw up the poverty program, run that bad war, work in conjunction with the mine owners and politicians, but it isn't the government that is calling you—it is the country. Only a weirdo would refuse that call. But once you're in you are working for the government, and then it is all right to desert.) Others on the AV staff objected to Mulloy's getting involved in issues that riled up the authorities. The staff vote to get rid of him was 20 to 19.

What the AVs failed to admit was that the changing of Mulloy's draft status was an attack on them as well: the only reason for the change was the strip-mine fight. The draft board had joined the OEO, the TVA, the mine owners, the political structure of the state and the UMW in opposition to effective organization of the poor in the mountains.

I asked Joe how he felt about it all now. "I don't know if I can really talk about this objectively," he said. "I feel in my guts as a Kentuckian a great deal of resentment against a lot of these people. And some of them are my friends that have come in and stirred things up and then have left. The going is really tough right now. I'm still here, all the people that have to make a living out in those counties are still there with their black lung. I don't think anything was accomplished. It's one of those things that's going to go down in history as a cruel joke: the poverty war in the mountains."

The two bad guys of the story, I suppose, should be Robert Holcomb, spokesman for the mine owners in the county, and commonwealth's attorney Thomas Ratliff, the man who handled the prosecution in the sedition and who was (coincidentally, he insists) Republican candidate for lieutenant governor at the time; Ratliff got rich in the mine business, but is now into a lot of other things. Like most

bad guy labels, I suspect these are too easy. I'll come back to that.

I rather liked Ratliff even though there were things I knew about him I didn't like at all. It is quite possible he really does believe, as he said he does, that the McSurelys and the Bradens are communist provocateurs; there are people in America who believe such menaces exist, though not very many of them are as intelligent as Ratliff.

He claims the defendants in the sedition case had "a new angle on revolution—to do it locally and then bring all the local revolutions together and then you got a big revolution. Now whether it would have succeeded or not I don't know. I think it possibly could have, had they been able to continue to get money from the Jolly Green Giant, as they call Uncle Sam. I certainly think with enough money, and knowing the history of this area, it was not impossible."

What seems to have bothered him most was not the politics involved but the bad sportsmanship: "The thing that rankled me in this case, and it still does, this is really what disturbed me more about this thing than anything else, was the fact that . . . they were able to use federal money . . . to promote this thing. Frankly, I would be almost as opposed to either the Republican party or the Democratic party being financed by the federal money to prevail, much less a group who were avowed communists, made no bones about it that I could tell, whose objective was revolution, the forceful and violent overthrow of the local government and hopefully to overthrow the federal government, and it was being financed by federal tax money!"

Once Ratliff got off his communist menace line, I found myself agreeing with him as much as I had with some of the remarks Joe Mulloy had made. Ratliff spoke eloquently on the need for a negative income tax, for massive increases on the taxes on the mine operators, things like that. (Whether he meant the things he said is impossible to tell; one never knows with politicians, or anyone else for that matter.)

"It's the reaction to this sort of situation that really bothers me," he said, "because—there is no question about it—there is some containment of free speech, free expression, when you get a situation like this. People become overexcited and overdisturbed. And the laws of physics play in these things: for every action there's a reaction, and the reaction, unfortunately, is often too much in this kind of situation. You begin seeing a communist behind every tree. That's bad. Because there isn't a communist behind every tree, or anything like that.

"But I think they've accomplished one thing, not what they thought they would . . . . That's the tragic part of it, I don't think they've uplifted anybody. I think they have left a lot of people disappointed, frustrated . . . . But I think they have scared the so-called affluent society into doing something about it. Maybe. I think there are people more conscious of it because of that."

It is so easy to write off Holcomb or Ratliff as evil men, grasping and groping for whatever they can get and destroying whatever gets in the way; for a poverty worker it is probably necessary to think such thoughts, that may be the mental bracing one needs to deal as an opponent.

But I think it is wrong.

Holcomb is an ex-miner who made it; uneducated and

not particularly smart, he somehow grooved on the leavings in that weird economy and got rich. He thinks what he did is something anyone ought to be able to do: it is the American dream, after all. His failure is mainly one of vision, a social myopia hardly rare in this country. From Holcomb's point of view, those people stirring up the poor probably are communist agitators—why else would anyone interfere with the "free enterprise system at its best"? If you tried to tell him that a system that leads to great big rich houses on one side of town and squalid leaky shacks on the other might not be the best thing in this world he'd think you were crazy or a communist (both, actually) too. And Thomas Ratliff is hardly the simple Machiavelli the usual scenario would demand.

Picking out individuals and saying the evil rests with them is like patching schoolhouses and expecting the cycle of poverty to be broken. Even when you're right you're irrelevant. What is evil in the mountains is the complex of systems, a complex that has no use or place or tolerance for the old, the wrecked, the incompetent, the extra, and consigns them to the same gullies and hollers and ditches as the useless cars and empty Maxwell House coffee tins and Royal Crown cola cans, with the same lack of hate or love.

The enemies of the poverty program, malicious or natural, individual or collective, turn out to be far more successful than they could have hoped or expected. One reason for that success is the cooperation of the victims: groups like the AVs become, as one of their long-time members said, "top-heavy and bureaucratic, a bit central office bound. We are . . . worried about maintaining the AV structure, and responding to pressures from foundations and OEO, rather than from community people." The federal government, presumably the opponent of poverty here, plays both sides of the fence: it supports activities like the AVs (so long as they are undisturbing), but it also supports the local Community Action Program, which is middle-class dominated and politically controlled; it created a generation of hustlers among the poor who find out that only by lying and finagling can they get the welfare and social security benefits they legitimately deserve; it strengthens the local courthouse power structures by putting federal job programs in control of the county machines and by putting the Small Business Administration at its disposal; it commissions studies to document the ill effects of strip mining and simultaneously acts, through TVA, as the largest consumer of the product.

The mood is much like the McCarthy days of the early 1950s: actual legal sanctions are applied to very few people, but so many others are smeared that other people are afraid of contagion, of contamination, even though they know there is nothing to catch. They avoid issues that might threaten some agency or person of power, they stop making trouble, stop looking for trouble, they keep busy, or they stay home—and no one ever really says, when faced by the complex, "I'm scared."

Everyone has something to do: busy, busy, busy. I remember a visit to the AV office in Prestonsburg; they had there what must have been one of the largest Xerox machines in the state of Kentucky; it was used for copying newspaper articles; someone on the staff ran it. There was an AV magazine assembled by a staff member who, if some of the foundations grants had come through, would have

gotten a full-time assistant. The mining went on; the acting director of the AVs, Dave Walls, went about hustling private foundations grants and being sociable and vague and disarming to visitors, and not much of anything really happened.

I visited eastern Kentucky again a short time ago. There were some changes. The weather was softer and some leaves were on the trees, so you couldn't see the shacks back in the hollers unless you drove up close; you couldn't see the hillside cemeteries and junkyards at all.

I found out that Governor Louis Nunn had blocked any new AV funds and most of the other money had gone, so there were ugly battles over the leavings, mixed with uglier battles over old political differences within the organization itself.

Edith Easterling was fired; she now has a Ford grant to travel about the country and look at organizing projects. Rick Diehl has gone somewhere else. Mary Walton is now a staff reporter for the Charleston (W. Va.) *Gazette*. The Prestonsburg AV office is still open—with a small group of lawyers working on welfare rights problems; that is the only AV activity still alive and no one knows how much longer there will be any money for that.

I ran into Dave Walls in a movie house in Charleston. The show was *Wild River* with Montgomery Clift and Lee Remick, and it was about how good TVA is and what a swell guy Montgomery Clift is and how homey and true mountain girl Lee Remick is. Anyway, I saw Dave there and we talked a moment during intermission. He still draws a subsistence salary from the AVs, still lives in Berea, over in the Bluegrass country far and nicely away from it all. He is going to school at the University of Kentucky in Lexington, doing graduate work in something. He looked just the same, no more or less mild. Someone asked him, "What's going on in the mountains now? What happened to everything?" He shrugged and smiled, "I don't know," he said, "I haven't gone to the mountains in a long time."

Well, for the other people, the ones who were there before, things are pretty much the same. That woman and her nine children still live in that shack in Poorbottom. The man who worked the mines for 28 years is still kept marginally alive by the chemical array in his refrigerator he still somehow manages to afford.

A Distrust of Strangers

Jink Ray, the man who faced down the bulldozers, I met on that recent trip. When we drove up he had just put out some bad honey and the bees were a thick swarm in the front of the house. We went into a sitting room-bedroom where his wife sat before an open coal fire and each wall had one or two Christs upon it. We talked about the strip-mine fight. On one wall was a photo of him with Governor Breathitt the day the governor came up to stop the strippers. We went outside and talked some more, standing by the overripe browning corn standing next to a patch of corn just about ripe, the hills thickly coated and overlapping to form a lush box canyon behind him. He pointed to the hillside the other side of the road and told us they'd been augering up there. "You can't see it from down here this time of year, but it's bad up there." The seepage killed the small streams down below: nothing lives in those streams anymore. "We used to get bait in them streams, nothing now, and fish used to grow there before they went to the river. Not now." Suddenly his face hardened, "Why you fellas asking me these questions?" We told him again that we were writing about what had happened in Pike County. "No," he said, "that ain't what you are. I believe you fellas are here because you want to get stripping going again, you want to know if I'll back off this time." He talked from a place far behind the cold blue eyes that were just so awful. We protested, saying we really were writers, but it didn't work—it's like denying you're an undercover agent or homosexual, there's no way in the world to do it once the assumption gets made, however wrong. He talked in postured and rhetorical bursts awhile and it seemed a long time until we could leave without seeming to have been run off. Leaving him standing there looking at the yellow Hertz car backing out his driveway, his face still cold and hard, polite to the end, but . . . But what? Not hating, but knowing: he knows about strangers now, he knows they are there to take something away, to betray, to hustle, he knows even the friendly strangers will eventually go back wherever strangers go when they are through doing whatever they have come down to do, and he will be just where he is, trying with whatever meagre resources he's got to hold on to the small parcel of land he scuffled so hard to be able to own. He'll not trust anyone again, and for me that was perhaps the most painful symptom of the failure and defeat of the poverty program in the mountains.

The others: Joe Mulloy, after about two years in the courts, finally won the draft appeal he should never have had to make in the first place; Al and Margaret McSurely were sentenced to prison terms for contempt of Congress after they refused to turn over their personal papers to a Senate committee investigating subversion in the rural South. Tom Ratliff is still commonwealth's attorney, there in the county of Pike, in the state of Kentucky. And Robert Holcomb still has his mines, his colleries, his offices, and his fine and unshaken belief in the American Way.

FURTHER READING

Let Us Now Praise Famous Men by James Agee and Walker Evans (Boston: Houghton Mifflin, 1960) is the most poetic document for an outsider who wants a sense of rural poverty in America; it isn't dated yet.

My Land Is Dying by Harry Caudill (New York: Dutton, 1973).

Night Comes to the Cumberlands by Harry Caudill (Boston: Little, Brown, 1963) is the best book for any outsider who wants a sense of the space and anguish of Appalachia.

The Senators From Slaughter County by Harry Caudill (Boston: Little, Brown, 1973).

Stinking Creek by John Fetterman (New York: Dutton, 1970).

The People of Coaltown by Herman R. Lantz (New York: Columbia University Press, 1958).

Coal Town Revisited: Appalachian Notebook by William Peterson (Chicago: Regnery, 1972).

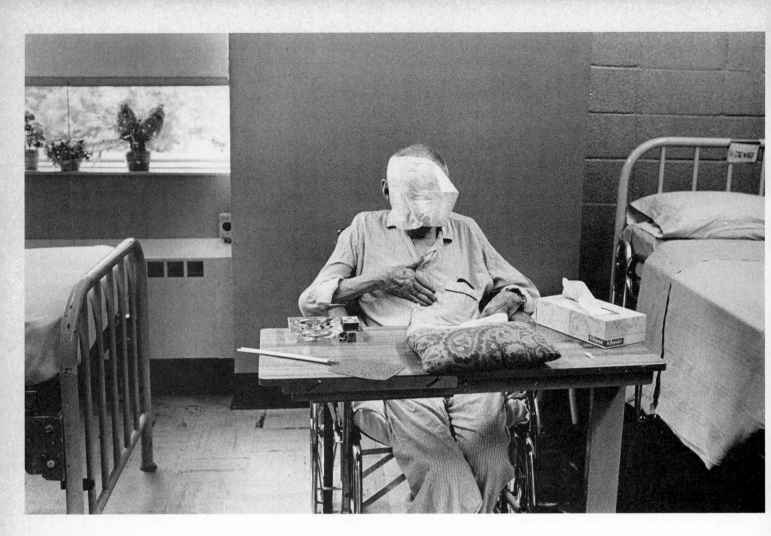

ELIZABETH MARKSON

A Hiding Place to Die

Francis Bacon said, "Men fear death as children fear to go in the dark; and as that natural fear in children is increased with tales, so is the other." Much of this fear of death is valuable for survival, but it has also tended to obscure the actual conditions under which people die. Death has either been romanticized, the Victorian solution, or minimized, as in the United States today. The elaborate American funeral rituals described in Evelyn Waugh's *The Loved One* and Jessica Mitford's *The American Way of Death* are not contradictory evidence on this point, for the actual *act of dying* is shunned and much of the ceremony seems designed to deny that death has really occurred.

Few tales of death have been told by anyone, including social scientists, but the recent work of Barney G. Glaser and Anselm L. Strauss in *Awareness of Dying* and *Time for Dying* and other studies marks the opening of this area of inquiry. The study reported on here supports the idea, first suggested by Glaser and Strauss, that the anathema of dying

is not only a problem for lay people, but also for health professionals, and describes one way in which professionals attempt to avoid the dying. Their success in doing so, it appears, depends on the relative status of the dying person.

There is a norm, subscribed to by at least some professionals, that old people should be allowed to die at home, but in fact most people die in hospitals or other institutions. It is suggested here that though it is desirable to die at home, for it is more comfortable, such comfortable deaths are a privilege accorded only to higher status people. Put another way, the lower the status of the dying person, the less likely are those around him to want to participate in his death.

It is well known that older patients who enter state mental hospitals have an excessive death rate. It has been suggested that this is because they are already dying when they are sent there, the early signs of impending death having been mistaken for insanity. Data gathered in New

York State reveal, moreover, that older people tend to have higher death rates in both the state mental hospitals and county infirmaries than they do in any other kind of psychiatric treatment facility. Even those older people who are being treated in general hospital emergency rooms are less likely to die within six months of treatment than are those entering state and county hospitals.

These findings tend to confirm the idea put forward by a number of students of death that the old are sent to lower status institutions, particularly mental hospitals, to die. The following study of deaths of the aged at a state mental hospital will postulate the processes by which both the laity and professionals make the decision to send patients to mental hospitals when they are not mentally ill, but are simply taking too long to die.

This study of whether those who send geriatric patients to state mental hospitals know of the excessive risk of death is founded on an examination of the medical records of 174 elderly patients who were admitted to Fairview State Hospital during an eight-month period in 1967. The hospital serves two boroughs of New York City and their suburbs and is located near a suburban community. During the period studied, the hospital admitted all patients who applied. The medical and nursing staff supported this open-door policy on the grounds that denial of admission to any geriatric patient would be a disservice to both the patient and the community.

The physical illnesses of the 174 patients detected at the post-admission physical examination (Table l) make it clear that elderly people with a multiplicity of serious physical illnesses, primarily heart and circulatory diseases, either alone or in combination with other disorders, were being sent to the hospital. Indeed, 44 of the 174 (25 percent) died within 30 days of admission. Those patients with one or more severe physical illnesses included proportionately more of those who died within one month than of those who survived, and this difference is statistically significant.

The old people in this study were not only physically ill, but also grossly impaired. Less than half the group were able to walk without assistance. One quarter were described as "feeble," 11 percent were in wheelchairs and 19 percent were on stretchers, including 6 percent who were comatose. Those patients who were mobile were strikingly less likely to die than those who were feeble or worse at admission. Of the mobile group, only 9.1 percent had died within a month of admission; the figure for the incapacitated group was 38.9 percent.

While it seems evident that moribund patients were being sent to this hospital for the mentally ill, it is possible that these patients were referred to psychiatric care because their behavior mimicked mental illness, as suggested earlier. It might be expected that the dying would resemble at least a portion of those who have an organic brain syndrome but do not die, for both have symptoms of organic origin. To test this hypothesis, the reasons for referral recorded by Fairview's admitting psychiatrists were examined. Virtually

TABLE 1 PHYSICAL DISEASES AND DEATHS

Diseases	All Admitted	All Dying Within Month	Dying of Detected Disease
Cancer, all types	7	4	3
alone	2	1	0
with heart and/or circulatory diseases	3	3	3
with digestive and/or genitourinary diseases	2	0	0
with respiratory diseases	0	0	0
Heart and circulatory diseases, all types	85	24	17
alone	58	13	7
with respiratory diseases	8	6	6
with digestive and/or genitourinary diseases	13	2	1
with respiratory and digestive or genitourinary diseases	6	3	3
Respiratory diseases	5	1	1
alone	4	1	1
with digestive and/or genitourinary diseases	1	0	0
Digestive and/or genitourinary diseases alone	15	6	0
None of the above	62	9	0

The two major causes of death listed on death certificates were heart and circulatory disease and respiratory diseases. There is general agreement that such illnesses are often related.

The totals given for each broad disease type, with the exception of cancer, do not include everyone with that disease, since combinations are given. Thus, the table shows 88 patients with heart disease, 85 in that category plus 3 who also have cancer.

TABLE 2 PHYSICAL IMPAIRMENT AND DEATHS

Impairment	All Admitted	All Dying Within Months	
		N	%
None, walked without help	77	7	9.1
Feeble	43	12	27.9
In wheel chair	19	10	52.6
On stretcher	33	15	45.5
Not ascertained	2	0	—
All patients	174	44	25.3

The difference in death rates between patients on stretchers and those in wheelchairs is not statistically significant. It is possible that some patients who might otherwise have been on stretchers were propped up in wheelchairs for convenience in moving them.

A Hiding Place to Die

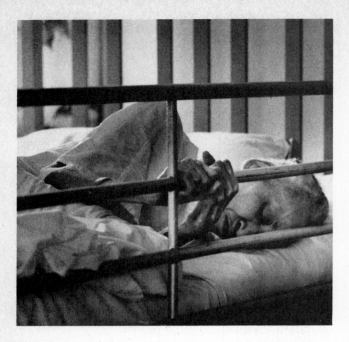

all the complaints made about these patients by their families or others interested in having them committed concerned either senile behavior alone or in combination with such major psychiatric symptoms as delusions, hallucinations or depression, but this was equally true of those who died within a month and those who survived with one exception: the ten comatose patients who could not be examined by the psychiatrist. Six of the eight men and one of the two women in this group died shortly after admission.

TABLE 3   PRESSURE FOR ADMISSION AND DEATHS

Agents referring patients for admission	All Admitted	All Dying Within Month	
		N	%
Male	69	24	34.8
Formal agents only	19	5	26.3
Informal agents	34	16	47.1
Family only	28	13	46.4
Family and/or community agents	6	3	50.0
Formal and informal agents	11	2	18.2
Agents unknown	5	1	20.0
Female	105	20	19.1
Formal agents only	18	4	22.2
Informal agents	70	13	18.6
Family only	58	10	17.2
Family and/or community agents	12	3	25.0
Formal and informal agents	17	3	17.7
Agents unknown	0	0	—
All patients	174	44	25.3

In sum, it appears that no premonitory or prodromal signs of death that could be distinguished from psychiatric symptoms were detected among this group of old people, even in psychiatric examination. This is particularly interesting in view of Morton Lieberman's finding that specific personality changes occur among old people several months prior to death. Lieberman was studying a nursing home population, however, which may have differed considerably from the group of elderly mental hospital patients studied here. Further, since our data are drawn from case reports, personality differences associated with either dying or psychosis may have been obscured by inadequate descriptions.

Psychiatric diagnosis at the hospital was apparently routine and cursory. Organic brain syndrome with psychosis was the designation given 114 patients in our study. In more than 88 percent of the cases, this diagnosis differed in either degree or kind from that made by the referring hospital. Follow-up data on patients who survived more than a month showed that more than one third of those diagnosed at admission as suffering organic brain syndrome with psychosis were found to have had no symptoms whatsoever, or to have been only apathetic, with no impairment of memory or confusion. Thus, it might be said that prodromal signs of death were missed in these cursory examinations, perhaps because the examining psychiatrists were aware that psychiatric treatment for the aged was less important than providing a place to die. Granting these reservations, however, the present data suggest that most patients were known or thought to be dying when referred to Fairview.

What seems crucial is that little effort was made to distinguish between symptoms reflecting an acute physical condition as opposed to chronic disorders of aging.

Some psychiatric hospitals have geriatric treatment programs aimed at helping patients get the most out of life, but Fairview's programs were marked by a fatalism that suggests that old people are expected to do nothing more than die. No physical examinations prior to admission were required, although elsewhere in the state such examinations have been shown to reduce inappropriate admissions. In fact, at the time of the study, deaths of those admitted *as well as those refused admission* at a sister hospital with a stringent screening program were only half as great as those at Fairview. This suggests that those responsible for referring the elderly for psychiatric care had learned where to send their dying patients.

Death As a Career

The Fairview program structured the patient's career as one of dying rather than of active physical or psychiatric treatment. While the post-admission physical examination is routinely performed, almost all geriatric patients are classified as being of "failing status because of age and general debility." This designation seems to be applied almost automatically. It certainly is not associated with the presence of physical illness, ability to walk or chronological age. The role of the physician on Fairview's geriatric wards appeared to be to regularize the patients' deaths by tacitly legitimating the actions of the referring hospital. Thus, the high death rate among old people admitted to the hospital is made to seem part of the "natural" process of dying.

The physical disabilities of those who died within a month of admission are so similar to those of the survivors that the mental disability of *most* of the old people admitted may reflect physical problems. In other words, the admission of *most* of the elderly people to Fairview was probably inappropriate; instead they should have been receiving medical treatment or terminal care for their physical disorders in a general hospital ward.

As for the argument that a sick, confused person is easily mistaken for a mentally ill person, it is significant that young patients are never sent to state hospitals in the moribund condition described above. Patients aged 35, on stretchers, in comas or with intravenous tubes running are unlikely to be found applying for admission to Fairview. Yet such patients exist and often display toxic confusions similar to those of the older patients. The older patient is selected for transfer to the state mental hospital because he is considered in hopeless condition by family and physicians, because of the extreme pressure for hospital beds and because he has compounded the low status of old age with illness, and often poverty. The evidence for these conclusions is reported below.

The pressure that ends with an elderly person being sent to a state mental hospital seems to be begun by the family. Old people coming to Fairview were usually first defined as physically or mentally ill by their families or other community members, usually after a specific health crisis. The patient was either sent directly to the state hospital, or taken first to a medical hospital or nursing home for treatment, depending on available facilities and the attitudes of those in close contact with him.

Among the elderly sent to Fairview, the dying men are somewhat younger than women. The median age for men at death was 74.5; for women it was 78.7. This was not particularly surprising, given the greater life expectancy of women in general. What is surprising, however, is that men whose families have pressed for their admission are more likely to die within a month than men referred only by formal agents such as a nursing home or those referred both by their families and such formal agents. For elderly women, however, this does not seem to be true. There are two factors which may explain this difference. First, there is some reason to believe, from other work I've been doing, that elderly men consistently overrate their health and independence, while elderly women tend to underrate themselves—perhaps a last holding on to the remnants of an

instrumental "fit," able-bodied role by the men; women, having greater expressive latitude, can legitimately complain more. Following this line of reasoning, elderly men would perhaps try to compensate and conceal their illness until it became very serious; women, on the other hand, would complain earlier. As soon as complaints become frequent, the family responds by sending the patient to a hospital; men, complaining later, would be in more risk of dying than the female early complainers.

A second factor is differences in family structure. Only 36 percent of the men in the study were still married, but 54 percent of the men who died were married. Women in the study were most likely to be widowed (61.9 percent) and of those who died, 55 percent were widows. Put differently, dying men are most likely to be admitted to Fairview when they become ill and are a burden to their wives who have themselves limited physical (or emotional) strength to deal with an old sick husband who requires nursing care or constant attention. Women, on the other hand, generally outlive their husbands and are most likely to be sent to mental hospitals when they present any kind of management problem, not just terminal illness, to children, other relatives, or to an institution.

Where Are The Children?

It has been observed that having one or more children tends to insulate old people against illness and relatively early death. It might also be expected that parenthood might protect the aged from commitment to a mental hospital for terminal care. This did not prove to be the case at Fairview. While 40 percent of the men and 30 percent of the women admitted had no living children, the likelihood of death within one month was the same for this group as for the group having one or more living children. Nor did the number of children living change the odds. This may mean that once a family has decided to send the patient to the hospital, their contact with him is reduced by distance. Or, the decision to send him to the hospital may result from previous difficulty in getting along with the patient, unusual family relationships or other situations reducing the basis for close ties with the old person. At any rate, in such situations the power the children might have had to postpone their aging parent's death is dissipated. The patient is already socially dead. Only his physical death is lacking.

Most patients did not arrive at Fairview from their own homes, however. Five of six came there from other institutions, most often hospitals. A hospital that is being fully utilized is always in the process of an informal review of patients, seeking out those who can be sent home or referred elsewhere. Combined with this pressure is a feeling, shared by the general public, that general hospital beds are expensive while mental hospitals beds are cheap. Whatever the source of this reasoning, it does not apply to these patients. They are suffering serious, often terminal, illnesses; the care they need will cost the same in any setting that shares the same labor market.

Of the patients sent to Fairview from other hospitals, about half were referred by receiving hospitals, that is, general hospitals with psychiatric service designated as reception centers for the mentally ill. Receiving hospitals in New York City have been the traditional route into state mental hospitals. They are overcrowded and there is considerable pressure to make a quick disposition of patients without concern for the refinements of the individual patient's situation. This may be particularly true for the elderly, whose physical condition is often ignored when a disposition is made. For example, one elderly male patient in the study had been taken to a receiving hospital in the city by his daughter, who stated that he urinated in the hallway and that she "could no longer care for his needs." He was sent to Fairview on a stretcher from the receiving hospital, which had neither admitted nor even examined him. According to the admitting psychiatrist's report, the patient had bedsores, indicating that his problems were long-standing. The psychiatrist observed:

> He did not indulge in any spontaneous acts . . . . The eyes were open and vision was intact as he blinked when fingers were brought close to his eyes. He showed fixed gazing and his eyes did not follow any moving object . . . . Patient showed no response to demands and showed no withdrawal from pain . . . . He retained food in his mouth and wet and soiled. He was mute and only made sounds in his throat.

Seventeen days after admission to Fairview, this patient died of bronchopneumonia. This not atypical case illustrates that many old people are sent away without adequate social and medical histories from receiving hospitals and in such impaired physical condition that it is difficult to determine whether or not they are mentally ill.

The remainder of the patients admitted to Fairview from hospitals have been in the medical wards of general hospitals. Like those from receiving hospitals, they often appear to have been sent to Fairview because they failed to respond to treatment or failed to die within a short period after being put on terminal care. For example, a 74-year-old man with an indwelling catheter was transferred from a medical ward to Fairview on a stretcher. The admitting psychiatrist reported:

> He was transferred from . . . General Hospital on a health officer's certificate because of increasing obtundation (dullness). The patient was noted to be . . . breathing heavily and in some distress . . . . He was able to respond only to pain and contact with the patient was impossible.

This patient's physical examination after admission indicated merely that he was dehydrated. Five days after admission, he died of congestive heart failure and bronchopneumonia.

Geriatric patients with their numerous medical complaints and limited future are not the favored patients of general hospital personnel, as has been shown by Glaser and Strauss and others. There are, however, institutions like nursing homes specializing in the care of terminal patients. Only five women and five men in the group studied had been sent to Fairview from nursing homes. The cause, ordinarily, was some kind of disruptive behavior. One elderly man who died within a month of arriving at Fairview was admitted from a nursing home with lung cancer and malignant lesions of the brain and bones. While the nursing home had had no difficulty in giving him minimal physical care and controlling his pain, they became upset and turned to Fairview when he threatened to commit suicide. (Upon checking with an internal medical specialist, I was assured that this patient was *under*medicated for pain—dosage limited to prevent addiction in a dying patient! Motive for suicide?)

Unlike the general hospital, the nursing home does not seem to be concerned with freeing beds occupied by old people. Nor does the threat of death seem to concern them, but rather deviance. They do not like any threat to orderly and routine dying. For example, nursing home patients who survived more than a month of Fairview often had been sent for similar reasons: One female paraplegic cancer patient had been referred because she had tried to set her bed on fire.

It seems obvious that this state hospital functions as a geriatric house of death to which the elderly are relegated because of the despair of their families and the pressure on general hospital beds. There seem to be three elements that establish the pattern of withdrawal of interest and abandonment of the aged to a state mental hospital. One of these is old age itself. The old are already socially dying through relinquishment of roles; as they have little future before them, their lives are considered to have little social worth. But being old in itself is not enough; most old people do not die in state mental hospitals.

The second element is the high probability of dying, though this alone does not automatically lead to Fairview. Young patients who have terminal illnesses are more likely to be sent home for short periods of time and to return to die in the hospital.

The third element is low social status and lack of power. It has often been shown that the poor and powerless of any age are generally considered to have less moral worth than those with more money or those with access to the ear of those with money. The patients in this study were not only seriously ill and old, they were also from mostly working-class and lower-class backgrounds. Only five had had professional occupations and only 29 had a tenth-grade or better education. When old age and relatively low socio-economic status are merged, the person is doubly worthless for he is neither productive nor does he have the reputation for past productivity. A combination of great age, powerlessness *and* terminal illness makes one despised by medical and lay people alike and, unless death comes on schedule, suggests transfer to a state mental hospital. Here the old are

hidden away, or taken away, from all that is familiar to them and left to await death. Death here, as Rilke observed, is "factory-like, of course. Where production is so enormous, an individual death is not so nicely carried out, but then that doesn't matter. It is quantity that counts."

Death Rights

The general lack of concern for the way old, sick people die is clearly a disavowal of any right to a death in stable and comfortable surroundings where opportunities for physical, psychological and spiritual comfort are protected. To some extent this is changing. All mental hospitals in New York State, for instance, have recently introduced geriatric screening programs designed specifically to exclude those patients who are dying or whose physical condition is the prime reason for their referral. These screening programs have already enabled some geriatric services to become active psychiatric treatment centers rather than houses of death. But where the old, sick, powerless people who might have died at Fairview will die now remains unresolved.

FURTHER READING

The Dying Patient edited by Orville Brim, Jr., Howard Freeman, Sol Levine, and Norman Scotch (New York: Russell Sage, 1970).

Asylums by Erving Goffman (Garden City, N.Y.: Anchor, 1961).

Research Planning and Action for the Elderly edited by Donald Kent, Robert Kastenbaum, and Sylvia Sherwood (New York: Behavioral Publications, 1972).

Death and Dying: Current Issues in the Treatment of the Dying Person edited by Leonard Pearson (Cleveland, Ohio: University of Case-Western Reserve, 1969).

Old People in Three Industrial Societies by Ethel Shanus et al. (Chicago: Aldine, 1968).

Crisis and Intervention edited by Alexander Simon, Marjorie Fiske Lowenthal, and Leon Epstein (San Francisco, Calif.: Jossey-Bass, 1970).

Passing On by David Sudnow (Englewood Cliffs, N.J.: Prentice-Hall, 1967).

FRANCES FOX PIVEN AND RICHARD A. CLOWARD

The Relief of Welfare

Aid to Families with Dependent Children (AFDC) is our major relief program. It has lately become the source of a major public controversy, owing to a large and precipitous expansion of the rolls. Between 1950 and 1960, only 110,000 families were added to the rolls, yielding a rise of 17 percent. In the 1960s, however, the rolls exploded, rising by more than 225 percent. At the beginning of the décade, 745,000 families were receiving aid; by 1970, some 2,500,000 families were on the rolls. Still, this is not the first, the largest or the longest relief explosion. Since the inauguration of relief in Western Europe three centuries ago, the rolls have risen and fallen in response to economic and political forces. An examination of these forces should help to illuminate the meaning of the current explosion, as well as the meaning of current proposals for reform.

Relief arrangements, we will argue, are ancillary to economic arrangements. Their chief function is to regulate labor, and they do that in two general ways. First, when mass unemployment leads to outbreaks of turmoil, relief programs are ordinarily initiated or expanded to absorb and control enough of the unemployed to restore order; then, as turbulence subsides, the relief system contracts, expelling

those who are needed to populate the labor market. Relief also performs a labor-regulating function in this shrunken state, however. Some of the aged, the disabled and others who are of no use as workers are left on the relief rolls, and their treatment is so degrading and punitive as to instill in the laboring masses a fear of the fate that awaits them should they relax into beggary and pauperism. To demean and punish those who do not work is to exalt by contrast even the meanest labor at the meanest wages. These regulative functions of relief are made necessary by several strains toward instability inherent in capitalist economics.

Labor and Market Incentives

All human societies compel most of their members to work, to produce the goods and services that sustain the community. All societies also define the work their members must do and the conditions under which they must do it. Sometimes the authority to compel and define is fixed in tradition, sometimes in the bureaucratic agencies of a central government. Capitalism, however, relies primarily upon the mechanisms of a market—the promise of financial rewards or penalties—to motivate men and women to work and to hold them to their occupational tasks.

But the development of capitalism has been marked by

periods of cataclysmic change in the market, the main sources being depression and rapid modernization. Depressions mean that the regulatory structure of the market simply collapses; with no demand for labor, there are no monetary rewards to guide and enforce work. By contrast, during periods of rapid modernization—whether the replacement of handicraft by machines, the relocation of factories in relation to new sources of power or new outlets for distribution, or the demise of family subsistence farming as large-scale commercial agriculture spreads—portions of the laboring population may be rendered obsolete or at least temporarily maladjusted. Market incentives do not collapse; they are simply not sufficient to compel people to abandon one way of working and living in favor of another.

In principle, of course, people dislocated by modernization become part of a labor supply to be drawn upon by a changing and expanding labor market. As history shows, however, people do not adapt so readily to drastically altered methods of work and to the new and alien patterns of social life dictated by that work. They may resist leaving their traditional communities and the only life they know. Bred to labor under the discipline of sun and season, however severe that discipline may be, they may resist the discipline of factory and machine, which, though it may be no more severe, may seem so because it is alien. The process of human adjustment to such economic changes has ordinarily entailed generation of mass unemployment, distress and disorganization.

Now, if human beings were invariably given to enduring these travails with equanimity, there would be no governmental relief systems at all. But often they do not, and for reasons that are not difficult to see. The regulation of civil behavior in all societies is intimately dependent on stable occupational arrangements. So long as people are fixed in their work roles, their activities and outlooks are also fixed; they do what they must and think what they must. Each behavior and attitude is shaped by the reward of a good harvest or the penalty of a bad one, by the factory paycheck or the danger of losing it. But mass unemployment breaks that bond, loosening people from the main institution by which they are regulated and controlled.

Moreover, mass unemployment that persists for any length of time diminishes the capacity of other institutions to bind and constrain people. Occupational behaviors and outlooks underpin a way of life and determine familial, communal and cultural patterns. When large numbers of people are suddenly barred from their traditional occupations, the entire network of social control is weakened. There is no harvest or paycheck to enforce work and the sentiments that uphold work; without work, people cannot conform to familial and communal roles; and if the dislocation is widespread, the legitimacy of the social order itself may come to be questioned. The result is usually civil disorder—crime, mass protests, riots—a disorder that may even threaten to overturn existing social and economic arrangements. It is then that relief programs are initiated or expanded.

Western relief systems originated in the mass disturbances that erupted during the long transition from feudalism to capitalism beginning in the sixteenth century. As a result of the declining death rates in the previous century, the population of Europe grew rapidly; as the population grew, so did transiency and beggary. Moreover, distress resulting from population changes, agricultural and other natural disasters, which had characterized life throughout the Middle Ages, was now exacerbated by the vagaries of an evolving market economy, and outbreaks of turbulence among the poor were frequent. To deal with these threats to civil order, many localities legislated severe penalties against vagrancy. Even before the sixteenth century, the magistrates of Basel had defined twenty-five different categories of beggars, together with appropriate punishments for each. But penalties alone did not always deter begging, especially when economic distress was severe and the numbers affected were large. Consequently, some localities began to augment punishment with provisions for the relief of the vagrant poor.

Civil Disorder and Relief

A French town that initiated such an arrangement early in the sixteenth century was Lyons, which was troubled both by a rapidly growing population and by the economic instability associated with the transition to capitalism. By 1500 Lyons' population had already begun to increase. During the decades that followed, the town became a prosperous commercial and manufacturing center—the home of the European money market and of expanding new trades in textiles, printing and metalworking. As it thrived it attracted people, not only from the surrounding countryside, but even from Italy, Flanders and Germany. All told, the population of Lyons probably doubled between 1500 and 1540.

All this was very well as long as the newcomers could be absorbed by industry. But not all were, with the result that the town came to be plagued by beggars and vagrants. Moreover, prosperity was not continuous: some trades were seasonal and others were periodically troubled by foreign competition. With each economic downturn, large numbers of unemployed workers took to the streets to plead for charity, cluttering the very doorsteps of the better-off classes. Lyons was most vulnerable during periods of bad harvest, when famine not only drove up the cost of bread for urban artisans and journeymen but brought hordes of peasants into the city, where they sometimes paraded through the streets to exhibit their misfortune. In 1529 food riots erupted, with thousands of Lyonnais looting granaries and the homes of the wealthy; in 1530, artisans and journeymen armed themselves and marched through the streets; in 1531, mobs of starving peasants literally overran the town.

Such charity as had previously been given in Lyons was primarily the responsibility of the church or of those of the more prosperous who sought to purchase their salvation through almsgiving. But this method of caring for the needy

The Relief of Welfare

obviously stimulated rather than discouraged begging and created a public nuisance to the better-off citizens (one account of the times describes famished peasants so gorging themselves as to die on the very doorsteps where they were fed). Moreover, to leave charity to church or citizen meant that few got aid, and those not necessarily according to their need. The result was that mass disorders periodically erupted.

The increase in disorder led the rulers of Lyons to conclude that the giving of charity should no longer be governed by private whim. In 1534, churchmen, notables and merchants joined together to establish a centralized administration for disbursing aid. All charitable donations were consolidated under a central body, the "Aumone-Generale," whose responsibility was to "nourish the poor forever." A list of the needy was established by a house-to-house survey, and tickets for bread and money were issued according to fixed standards. Indeed, most of the features of modern welfare—from criteria to discriminate the worthy poor from the unworthy, to strict procedures for surveillance of recipients as well as measures for their rehabilitation—were present in Lyons' new relief administration. By the 1550s, about 10 percent of the town's population was receiving relief.

Within two years of the establishment of relief in Lyons, King Francis I ordered each parish in France to register its poor and to provide for the "impotent" out of a fund of contributions. Elsewhere in Europe, other townships began to devise similar systems to deal with the vagrants and mobs cast up by famine, rapid population growth and the transition from feudalism to capitalism.

England also felt these disturbances, and just as it pioneered in developing an intensively capitalist economy, so it was at the forefront in developing nation-wide, public relief arrangements. During the closing years of the fifteenth century, the emergence of the wool industry in England began to transform agricultural life. As sheep raising became more profitable, much land was converted from tillage to pasturage, and large numbers of peasants were displaced by an emerging entrepreneurial gentry which either bought their land or cheated them out of it. The result was great tumult among the peasantry, as the Webbs were to note:

When the sense of oppression became overwhelming, the popular feeling manifested itself in widespread organised tumults, disturbances and insurrections, from Wat Tyler's rebellion of 1381, and Jack Cade's march on London of 1460, to the Pilgrimage of Grace in 1536, and Kett's Norfolk rising of 1549—all of them successfully put down, but sometimes not without great struggle, by the forces which the government could command.

Early in the sixteenth century, the national government moved to try to forestall such disorders. In 1528 the Privy Council, anticipating a fall in foreign sales as a result of the war in Flanders, tried to induce the cloth manufacturers of Suffolk to retain their employees. In 1534, a law passed

under Henry VIII attempted to limit the number of sheep in any one holding in order to inhibit the displacement of farmers and agricultural laborers and thus forestall potential disorders. Beginning in the 1550s the Privy Council attempted to regulate the price of grain in poor harvests. But the entrepreneurs of the new market economy were not so readily curbed, so that during this period another method of dealing with labor disorders was evolved.

Early in the sixteenth century, the national government moved to replace parish arrangements for charity with a nation-wide system of relief. In 1531, an act of Parliament decreed that local officials search out and register those of the destitute deemed to be impotent and give them a document authorizing begging. As for those who sought alms without authorization, the penalty was public whipping till the blood ran.

Thereafter, other arrangements for relief were rapidly instituted. An act passed in 1536, during the reign of Henry VIII, required local parishes to take care of their destitute and to establish a procedure for the collection and administration of donations for that purpose by local officials. (In the same year Henry VIII began to expropriate monasteries, helping to assure secular control of charity.) With these developments, the penalties for beggary were made more severe, including an elaborate schedule of branding, enslavement and execution for repeated offenders. Even so, by 1572 beggary was said to have reached alarming proportions, and in that year local responsibility for relief was more fully spelled out by the famous Elizabethan Poor Laws, which established a local tax, known as the poor rate, as the means for financing the care of paupers and required that justices of the peace serve as the overseers of the poor.

After each period of activity, the parish relief machinery tended to lapse into disuse, until bad harvests or depression in manufacturing led again to widespread unemployment and misery, to new outbreaks of disorder, and then to a resuscitation and expansion of relief arrangements. The most illuminating of these episodes, because it bears so much similarity to the present-day relief explosion in the United States, was the expansion of relief during the massive agricultural dislocations of the late eighteenth century.

Most of the English agricultural population had lost its landholdings long before the eighteenth century. In place of the subsistence farming found elsewhere in Europe, a three-tier system of landowners, tenant farmers and agricultural workers had evolved in England. The vast majority of the people were a landless proletariat, hiring out by the year to tenant farmers. The margin of their subsistence, however, was provided by common and waste lands, on which they gathered kindling, grazed animals and hunted game to supplement their meager wages. Moreover, the use of the commons was part of the English villager's birthright, his sense of place and pride. It was the disruption of these arrangements and the ensuing disorder that led to the new expansion of relief.

By the middle of the eighteenth century, an increasing

population, advancing urbanization and the growth of manufacturing had greatly expanded markets for agricultural products, mainly for cereals to feed the urban population and for wool to supply the cloth manufacturers. These new markets, together with the introduction of new agricultural methods (such as cross-harrowing), led to large-scale changes in agriculture. To take advantage of rising prices and new techniques, big landowners moved to expand their holdings still further by buying up small farms and, armed with parliamentary Bills of Enclosure, by usurping the common and waste lands which had enabled many small cottagers to survive. Although this process began much earlier, it accelerated rapidly after 1750; by 1850, well over 6 million acres of common land—or about one-quarter of the total arable acreage—had been consolidated into private holdings and turned primarily to grain production. For great numbers of agricultural workers, enclosure meant no land on which to grow subsistence crops to feed their families, no grazing land to produce wool for home spinning and weaving, no fuel to heat their cottages, and new restrictions against hunting. It meant, in short, the loss of a major source of subsistence for the poor.

New markets also stimulated a more businesslike approach to farming. Landowners demanded the maximum rent from tenant farmers, and tenant farmers in turn began to deal with their laborers in terms of cash calculations. Specifically, this meant a shift from a master-servant relationship to an employer-employee relationship, but on the harshest terms. Where laborers had previously worked by the year and frequently lived with the farmer, they were now hired for only as long as they were needed and were then left to fend for themselves. Pressures toward short-term hiring also resulted from the large-scale cultivation of grain crops for market, which called for a seasonal labor force, as opposed to mixed subsistence farming, which required year-round laborers. The use of cash rather than produce as the medium of payment for work, a rapidly spreading practice, encouraged partly by the long-term inflation of grain prices, added to the laborer's hardships. Finally the rapid increase in rural population at a time when the growth of woolen manufacturing continued to provide an incentive to convert land from tillage to pasturage produced a large labor surplus, leaving agricultural workers with no leverage in bargaining for wages with their tenant-farmer employers. The result was widespread unemployment and terrible hardship.

None of these changes took place without resistance from small farmers and laborers who, while they had known hardship before, were now being forced out of a way of life and even out of their villages. Some rioted when Bills of Enclosure were posted; some petitioned the Parliament for their repeal. And when hardship was made more acute by a succession of poor harvests in the 1790s, there were widespread food riots.

Indeed, throughout the late eighteenth and early nineteenth centuries, the English countryside was periodically beseiged by turbulent masses of the displaced rural poor and the towns were racked by Luddism, radicalism, trade-unionism and Chartism, even while the ruling classes worried about what the French Revolution might augur for England. A solution to disorder was needed, and that solution turned out to be relief. The poor relief system—first created in the sixteenth century to control the earlier disturbances caused by population growth and the commercialization of agriculture—now rapidly became a major institution of English life. Between 1760 and 1784, taxes for relief—the poor rate—rose by 60 percent; they doubled by 1801, and rose by 60 percent more in the next decade. By 1818, the poor rate was over six times as high as it had been in 1760. Hobsbaum estimates that up to the 1850s, upwards of 10 percent of the English population were paupers. The relief system, in short, was expanded in order to absorb and regulate the masses of discontented people uprooted from agriculture but not yet incorporated into industry.

Relief arrangements evolved more slowly in the United States, and the first major relief crisis did not occur until the Great Depression. The inauguration of massive relief-giving was not simply a response to widespread economic distress, for millions had remained unemployed for several years without obtaining aid. What finally led the national government to proffer aid was the great surge of political disorder that followed the economic catastrophe, a disorder which eventually led to the convulsive voting shifts of 1932. After the election, the federal government abandoned its posture of aloofness toward the unemployed. Within a matter of months, billions of dollars were flowing to localities, and the relief rolls skyrocketed. By 1935, upwards of 20 million people were on the dole.

The contemporary relief explosion, which began in the early 1960s, has its roots in agricultural modernization. No one would disagree that the rural economy of America, especially in the South, has undergone a profound transformation in recent decades. In 1945, there was one tractor per farm; in 1964 there were two. Mechanization and other technological developments, in turn, stimulated the enlargement of farm holdings. Between 1959 and 1961, one million farms disappeared; the 3 million remaining farms averaged 377 acres in size—30 percent larger than the average farm ten years earlier. The chief and most obvious effect of these changes was to lessen the need for agricultural labor. In the years between 1950 and 1965 alone, a Presidential Commission on Rural Poverty was to discover, "New machines and new methods increased farm output in the United States by 45 percent, and reduced farm employment by 45 percent." A mere 4 percent of the American labor force now works the land, signalling an extraordinary displacement of people, with accompanying upheaval and suffering. The best summary measure of this dislocation is probably the volume of migration to the cities; over 20 million people, more than 4 million of them black, left the land after 1940.

Nor were all these poor absorbed into the urban economic system. Blacks were especially vulnerable to unemployment. At the close of the Korean War, the national nonwhite unemployment rate leaped from 4.5 percent in 1953 to 9.9 percent in 1954. By 1958, it had reached 12.6 percent, and it fluctuated between 10 and 13 percent until the escalation of the war in Vietnam after 1964.

These figures pertain only to people unemployed and looking for work. They do not include the sporadically unemployed or those employed at extremely low wages. Combining such additional measures with the official unemployment measure produces a subemployment index. This index was first used in 1966—well after the economic downturns that characterized the years between the end of the Korean War and the escalation of the war in Vietnam. Were subemployment data available for the "Eisenhower recession" years, especially in the slum-ghettoes of the larger central cities, they would surely show much higher rates than prevailed in 1966. In any event, the figures for 1966 revealed a nonwhite subemployment rate of 21.6 percent compared with a white rate of 7.6 percent.

However, despite the spread of economic deprivation, whether on the land or in the cities, the relief system did not respond. In the entire decade between 1950 and 1960, the national AFDC caseload rose by only 17 percent. Many of the main urban targets of migration showed equally little change: the rolls in New York City moved up by 16 percent, and in Los Angeles by 14 percent. In the South, the rolls did not rise at all.

But in the 1960s, disorder among the black poor erupted on a wide scale, and the welfare rolls erupted as well. The welfare explosion occurred during several years of the greatest domestic disorder since the 1930s—perhaps the greatest in our history. It was concurrent with the turmoil produced by the civil-rights struggle, with widespread and destructive rioting in the cities, and with the formation of a militant grassroots movement of the poor dedicated to combating welfare restrictions. Not least, the welfare rise was also concurrent with the enactment of a series of ghetto-placating federal programs (such as the antipoverty program) which, among other things, hired thousands of poor people, social workers and lawyers who, it subsequently turned out, greatly stimulated people to apply for relief and helped them obtain it. And the welfare explosion, although an urban phenomenon generally, was greatest in just that handful of large metropolitan counties where the political turmoil of the mid- and late 1960s was the most acute.

The magnitude of the welfare rise is worth noting. The national AFDC caseload rose by more than 225 percent in the 1960s. In New York City, the rise was more than 300 percent; the same was so in Los Angeles. Even in the South, where there had been no rise at all in the 1950s, the rolls rose by more than 60 percent. And most significant of all, the bulk of the increase took place after 1965—that is, after disorder reached a crescendo. More than 80 percent of the national rise in the 1960s occurred in the last five years of the decade. In other words, the welfare rolls expanded, today as at earlier times, only in response to civil disorder.

While muting the more disruptive outbreaks of civil dis-

order (such as rioting), the mere giving of relief does nothing to reverse the disintegration of lower-class life produced by economic change, a disintegration which leads to rising disorder and rising relief rolls in the first place. Indeed, greatly liberalized relief-giving can further weaken work and family norms. To restore order in a more fundamental sense the society must create the means to reassert its authority. Because the market is unable to control men's behavior a surrogate system of social control must be evolved, at least for a time. Moreoever, if the surrogate system is to be consistent with normally dominant patterns, it must restore people to work roles. Thus even though obsolete or unneded workers are temporarily given direct relief, they are eventually succored only on condition that they work. As these adjustments are made, the functions of relief arrangements may be said to be shifting from regulating disorder to regulating labor.

Restoring Order by Restoring Work

The arrangements, both historical and contemporary, through which relief recipients have been made to work vary, but broadly speaking, there are two main ways: work is provided under public auspices, whether in the recipient's home, in a labor yard, in a workhouse or on a public works project; or work is provided in the private market, whether by contracting or indenturing the poor to private employers, or through subsidies designed to induce employers to hire paupers. And although a relief system may at any time use both of these methods of enforcing work, one or the other usually becomes predominant, depending on the economic conditions that first gave rise to disorder.

Publicly subsidized work tends to be used during business depressions, when the demand for labor in the private market collapses. Conversely, arrangements to channel paupers into the labor market are more likely to be used when rapid changes in markets or technology render a segment of the labor supply temporarily maladapted. In the first case, the relief system augments a shrunken labor market; in the other, its policies and procedures are shaped to overcome the poor fit between labor demand and supply.

Public work is as old as public relief. The municipal relief systems initiated on the Continent in the first quarter of the sixteenth century often included some form of public works. In England, the same statute of 1572 that established taxation as the method for financing poor relief charged the overseers of the poor with putting vagrants to work. Shortly afterwards, in 1576, local officials were directed to acquire a supply of raw goods—wool, hemp, iron—which was to be delivered to the needy for processing in their homes, their dole to be fixed according to "the desert of the work."

The favored method of enforcing work throughout most of the history of relief was the workhouse. In 1723, an act of Parliament permitted the local parishes to establish workhouses and to refuse aid to those poor who would not enter; within ten years, there were said to be about fifty workhouses in the environs of London alone.

The destitute have also sometimes been paid to work in the general community or in their own homes. This method of enforcing work evolved in England during the bitter depression of 1840–1841. As unemployment mounted, the poor in some of the larger cities protested against having to leave their communities to enter workhouses in order to obtain relief, and in any case, in some places the workhouses were already full. As a result, various public spaces were designated as "labor yards" to which the unemployed could come by the day to pick oakum, cut wood, and break stone, for which they were paid in food and clothing. The method was used periodically throughout the second half of the nineteenth century; at times of severe distress, very large numbers of the able-bodied were supported in this way.

The first massive use of public work under relief auspices in the United States occurred during the 1930s when millions of the unemployed were subsidized through the Works Progress Administration. The initial response of the Roosevelt administration was to appropriate billions for direct relief payments. But no one liked direct relief—not the president who called for it, the Congress that legislated it, the administrators who operated it, the people who received it. Direct relief was viewed as a temporary expedient, a way of maintaining a person's body, but not his dignity; a way of keeping the populace from shattering in despair, discontent and disorder, at least for a while, but not of renewing their pride, of bringing back a way of life. For their way of life had been anchored in the discipline of work, and so that discipline had to be restored. The remedy was to abolish direct relief and put the unemployed to work on subsidized projects. These reforms were soon instituted—and with dramatic results. For a brief time, the federal government became the employer of millions of people (although millions of others remained unemployed).

Quite different methods of enforcing work are used when the demand for labor is steady but maladaptions in the labor supply, caused by changes in methods of production, result in unemployment. In such circumstances, relief agencies ordinarily channel paupers directly into the private market. For example, the rapid expansion of English manufacturing during the late eighteenth and early nineteenth centuries produced a commensurately expanded need for factory operatives. But it was no easy matter to get them. Men who had been agricultural laborers, independent craftsmen or workers in domestic industries (i.e., piecework manufacturing in the home) resisted the new discipline. Between 1778 and 1830, there were repeated revolts by laborers in which local tradesmen and farmers often participated. The revolts failed, of course; the new industry moved forward inexorably, taking the more dependent and tractable under its command, with the aid of the relief system.

The burgeoning English textile industry solved its labor problems during the latter part of the eighteenth century by using parish children, some only four or five years old, as factory operatives. Manufacturers negotiated regular bargains with the parish authorities, ordering lots of fifty or more children from the poorhouses. Parish children were an ideal labor source for new manufacturers. The young paupers could be shipped to remote factories, located to take advantage of the streams from which power could be drawn. (With the shift from water power to steam in the nineteenth century, factories began to locate in towns where they could employ local children; with that change, the system of child labor became a system of "free" child labor.) The children were also preferred for their docility and for their light touch at the looms. Moreover, pauper children could be had for a bit of food and a bed, and they provided a very stable labor supply, for they were held fast at their labors by indentures, usually until they were twenty-one.

Sometimes the relief system subsidizes the employment of paupers—especially when their market value is very low—as when the magistrates of Lyons provided subsidies to manufacturers who employed pauper children. In rural England during the late eighteenth century, as more and more of the population was being displaced by the commercialization of agriculture, this method was used on a very large scale. To be sure, a demand for labor was developing in the new manufacturing establishments that would in time absorb many of the uprooted rural poor. But this did not happen all at once: rural displacement and industrial expansion did not proceed at the same pace or in the same areas, and in any case the drastic shift from rural village to factory system took time. During the long interval before people forced off the land were absorbed into manufacturing, many remained in the countryside as virtual vagrants; others migrated to the towns, where they crowded into hovels and cellars, subject to the vicissitudes of rapidly rising and falling markets, their ranks continually enlarged by new rural refugees.

These conditions were not the result of a collapse in the market. Indeed, grain prices rose during the second half of the eighteenth century, and they rose spectacularly during the Revolutionary and Napoleonic wars. Rather, it was the expanding market for agricultural produce which, by stimulating enclosure and business-minded farming methods, led to unemployment and destitution. Meanwhile, population growth, which meant a surplus of laborers, left the workers little opportunity to resist the destruction of their traditional way of life—except by crime, riots and incendiarism. To cope with these disturbances, relief expanded, but in such a way as to absorb and discipline laborers by supporting the faltering labor market with subsidies.

The subsidy system is widely credited to the sheriff and magistrates of Berkshire, who, in a meeting at Speenhamland in 1795, decided on a scheme by which the Poor Law authorities would supplement the wages of underemployed and underpaid agricultural workers according to a published scale. It was a time when exceptional scarcity of food led to riots all over England, sometimes suppressed only by calling out the troops. With this "double panic of famine and revolution," the subsidy scheme spread, especially in counties where large amounts of acreage had been enclosed.

The local parishes implemented the work subsidy system in different ways. Under the "roundsman" arrangement, the parish overseers sent any man who applied for aid from house to house to get work. If he found work, the employer was obliged to feed him and pay a small sum (6 d) per day, with the parish adding another small sum (4 d). Elsewhere, the parish authorities contracted directly with farmers to have paupers work for a given price, with the parish paying the combined wage and relief subsidy directly to the pauper. In still other places, parish authorities parcelled out the unemployed to farmers, who were obliged to pay a set rate or make up the difference in higher taxes. Everywhere, however, the main principle was the same: an underemployed and turbulent populace was being pacified with public allowances, but these allowances were used to restore order by enforcing work, at very low wage levels. Relief, in short, served as a support for a disturbed labor market and as a discipline for a disturbed rural society. As the historians J. L. Hammond and Barbara Hammond were to say, "The meshes of the Poor Law were spread over the entire labour system."

The English Speenhamland plan, while it enjoys a certain notoriety, is by no means unique. The most recent example of a scheme for subsidizing paupers in private employ is the reorganization of American public welfare proposed in the summer of 1969 by President Richard Nixon; the general parallel with the events surrounding Speenhamland is striking. The United States relief rolls expanded in the 1960s to absorb a laboring population made superfluous by agricultural modernization in the South, a population that became turbulent in the wake of forced migration to the cities. As the relief rolls grew to deal with these disturbances, pressure for "reforms" also mounted. Key features of the reform proposals included a national minimum allowance of $1,600 per year for a family of four, coupled with an elaborate system of penalities and incentives to force families to work. In effect, the proposal was intended to support and strengthen a disturbed low-wage labor market by providing what was called in nineteenth century England a "rate in aid of wages."

Enforcing Low Wage Work During Periods of Stability

Even in the absence of cataclysmic change, market incentives may be insufficient to compel all people at all times to do the particular work required of them. Incentives may be too meager and erratic, or people may not be sufficiently socialized to respond to them properly. To be sure, the productivity of a fully developed capitalist economy would allow for wages and profits sufficient to entice most of the population to work; and in a fully developed capitalist society, most people would also be reared to want what the market holds out to them. They would expect, even sanctify, the rewards of the market place and acquiesce in its vagaries.

But no fully developed capitalist society exists. (Even today in the United States, the most advanced capitalist country, certain regions and population groups—such as southern tenant farmers—remain on the periphery of the wage market and are only partially socialized to the ethos of the market.) Capitalism evolved slowly and spread slowly. During most of this evolution, the market provided meager rewards for most workers, and none at all for some. There are still many for whom this is so. And during most of this evolution, large sectors of the laboring classes were not fully socialized to the market ethos. The relief system, we contend, has made an important contribution toward overcoming these persisting weaknesses in the capacity of the market to direct and control men.

Once an economic convulsion subsides and civil order is restored, relief systems are not ordinarily abandoned. The rolls are reduced, to be sure, but the shell of the system usually remains, ostensibly to provide aid to the aged, the disabled and such other unfortunates who are of no use as workers. However, the manner in which these "impotents" have always been treated, in the United States and elsewhere, suggests a purpose quite different from the remediation of their destitution. These residual persons have ordinarily been degraded for lacking economic value, relegated to the foul quarters of the workhouse, with its strict penal regimen and its starvation diet. Once stability was restored, such institutions were typically proclaimed the sole source of aid, and for a reason bearing directly on enforcing work.

Conditions in the workhouse were intended to ensure that no one with any conceivable alternatives would seek public aid. Nor can there by any doubt of that intent. Consider this statement by the Poor Law Commissioners in 1834, for example:

Into such a house none will enter voluntarily; work, confinement, and discipline will deter the indolent and vicious: and nothing but extreme necessity will induce any to accept the comfort which must be obtained by the surrender of their free agency, and the sacrifice of their accustomed habits and gratifications. *Thus the parish officer, being furnished an unerring test of the necessity of applicants, is relieved from his painful and difficult responsibility: while all have the gratification of knowing that while the necessitous are abundantly relieved, the funds of charity are not wasted by idleness and fraud.*

The method worked. Periods of relief expansion were generally followed by "reform" campaigns to abolish all "outdoor" aid and restrict relief to those who entered the workhouse—as in England in 1722, 1834 and 1871 and in the United States in the 1880s and 1890s—and these campaigns usually resulted in a sharp reduction in the number of applicants seeking aid.

The harsh treatment of those who had no alternative except to fall back upon the parish and accept "the offer of the House" terrorized the impoverished masses in another way as well. It made pariahs of those who could not support themselves; they served as an object lesson, a means of celebrating the virtues of work by the terrible example of their agony. That, too, was a matter of deliberate intent. The workhouse was designed to spur men to contrive ways of supporting themselves by their own industry, to offer themselves to any employer on any terms, rather than suffer the degraded status of pauper.

All of this was evident in the contraction of relief which occurred in the United States at the close of the Great Depression. As political stability returned, emergency relief and work relief programs were reduced and eventually abolished, with many of those cut off being forced into a labor market still glutted with the unemployed. Meanwhile, the Social Security Act had been passed. Widely hailed as a major reform, this measure created our present-day welfare system, with its categorical provisions for the aged, the blind and families with dependent children (as well as, in 1950, the disabled).

The enactment of this "reform" signalled a turn toward the work-enforcing function of relief arrangements. This became especially evident after World War II during the period of greatly accelerated agricultural modernization. Millions were unemployed in agriculture; millions of others migrated to the cities where unemployment in the late 1950s reached extremely high levels. But few families were given assistance. By 1960, only 745,000 families had been admitted to the AFDC rolls. That was to change in the 1960s, as we have already noted, but only in response to the most unprecedented disorder in our history.

That families without jobs or income failed to secure relief during the late 1940s and the 1950s was in part a consequence of restrictive statutes and policies—the exclusion of able-bodied males and, in many places, of so-called employable mothers, together with residence laws, relative responsibility provisions and the like. But it was also—perhaps mainly—a consequence of the persistence of age-old rituals of degradation. AFDC mothers were forced to answer questions about their sexual behavior ("When did you last menstruate?"), open their closets to inspection ("Whose pants are those?"), and permit their children to be interrogated ("Do any men visit your mother?"). Unannounced raids, usually after midnight and without benefit of warrant, in which a recipient's home is searched for signs of "immoral" activities, have also been part of life on AFDC. In Oakland, California, a public welfare caseworker, Bennie Parish, refused to take part in a raid in January 1962 and was dismissed for insubordination. When he sued for reinstatement, the state argued successfully in the lower courts that people taking public assistance waive certain constitutional rights, among them the right to privacy. (The court's position had at least the weight of long tradition, for the withdrawal of civil rights is an old feature of public relief. In England, for example, relief recipients were denied the franchise until 1918, and as late as 1934 the constitutions of fourteen American states deprived recipients of the right to vote or hold office.)

The main target of these rituals is not the recipient who ordinarily is not of much use as a worker, but the able-bodied poor who remain in the labor market. It is for these people that the spectacle of the degraded pauper is intended. For example, scandals exposing welfare "fraud" have diffuse effects, for they reach a wide public—including the people who might otherwise apply for aid but who are deterred because of the invidious connotations of being on welfare. Such a scandal occurred in the District of Columbia in 1961, with the result that half of all AFDC mothers were declared to be ineligible for relief, most of them for allegedly "consorting with men." In the several years immediately before the attack, about 6,500 District of Columbia families had applied for aid annually; during the attack, the figure dropped to 4,400 and it did not rise for more than five years—long after that particular scandal itself had subsided.

In sum, market values and market incentives are weakest at the bottom of the social order. To buttress weak market controls and ensure the availability of marginal labor, an outcast class—the dependent poor—is created by the relief system. This class, whose members are of no productive use, is not treated with indifference, but with contempt. Its degradation at the hands of relief officials serves to celebrate the virtue of all work and deters actual or potential workers from seeking aid.

The Current Call for Reform

From our perspective, a relief explosion is a reform just because a large number of unemployed or underemployed people obtain aid. But from the perspective of most people, a relief explosion is viewed as a "crisis." The contemporary relief explosion in the United States, following a period of unparalleled turbulence in the cities, has thus resulted in a clamor for reform. Similar episodes in the past suggest that pressure for reform signals a shift in emphasis between the major functions of relief arrangements—a shift from regulating disorder to regulating labor.

Pressure for reform stems in part from the fiscal burden imposed on localities when the relief rolls expand. An obvious remedy is for the federal goverment to simply assume a greater share of the costs, if not the entire cost (at this writing, Congress appears likely to enact such fiscal reform).

However, the much more fundamental problem with which relief reform seeks to cope is the erosion of the work role and the deterioration of the male-headed family. In principle, these problems could be dealt with by economic policies leading to full employment at decent wages, but there is little political support for that approach. Instead, the historic approach to relief explosions is being invoked, which is to restore work through the relief system. Various proposals have been advanced: some would force recipients to report regularly to employment offices; others would provide a system of wage subsidies conditional on the recipient's taking on a job at any wage (including those below the federal minimum wage); still others would inaugurate a straight-forward program of public works projects.

The Relief of Welfare

We are opposed to any type of reform intended to promote work through the relief system rather than through the reform of economic policies. When similar relief reforms were introduced in the past, they presaged the eventual expulsion of large numbers of people from the rolls, leaving them to fend for themselves in a labor market where there was too little work and thus subjecting them once again to severe economic exploitation. The reason that this happens is more than a little ironic.

The irony is this: when relief is used to enforce work, it tends to stabilize lower-class occupational, familial and communal life (unlike direct relief, which merely mutes the worst outbreaks of discontent). By doing so, it diminishes the proclivities toward disruptive behavior which give rise to the expansion of relief in the first place. Once order is restored in this far more profound sense, relief-giving can be virtually abolished as it has been so often in the past. And there is always pressure to abolish large-scale work relief, for it strains against the market ethos and interferes with the untrammeled operation of the market place. The point is not just that when a relief concession is offered up, peace and order reign; it is, rather, that when peace and order reign, the relief concession is withdrawn.

The restoration of work through the relief system, in other words, makes possible the eventual return to the most restrictive phase in the cycle of relief-giving. What begins as a great expansion of direct relief, and then turns into some form of work relief, ends finally with a sharp contraction of the rolls. Advocates of relief reform may argue that their reforms will be long-lasting, that the restrictive phase in the cycle will not be reached, but past experience suggests otherwise.

Therefore, in the absence of economic reforms leading to full employment at decent wages, we take the position that the explosion of the rolls is the true relief reform, that it should be defended, and that it should be expanded. Even now, hundreds of thousands of impoverished families remain who are eligible for assistance but who receive no aid at all.

FURTHER READING

Aid to Dependent Children by Winifred Bell (New York: Columbia University Press, 1965). The best and most candid account of this American relief program which has lately become so controversial.

The Village Labourer by J. L. and Barbara Hammond (London: Longmans, Green, 1948). Contains evidence from English history on the relationship of economic change to the rise of disorder and on the role of relief-giving in moderating disorder.

Captain Swing by E. J. Hobsbawm and George Rude (New York: Pantheon Books, 1968). A detailed study of one series of English rural disorders in the 1830s.

Welfare Mothers Speak Out by Milwaukee County Welfare Rights Organization (New York: Norton, 1972).

Regulating the Poor: The Functions of Public Welfare by Frances Fox Piven and Richard Cloward (New York: Pantheon, 1971).

Blaming the Victim by William Ryan (New York: Vintage, 1971).

GILBERT Y. STEINER

Day Care Centers: Hype or Hope?

By the end of the 1960s it was evident that under the most prosperous of conditions, public assistance was not about to wither away. A considerable fraction of the population was still outside the sweep of social security's old age pensions, survivors' benefits, or disability insurance, and also outside the sweep of the country's prosperity. "It becomes increasingly clear," the *New York Times* editorialized after the overall level of unemployment in New York City declined to 3.2 percent of the civilian labor force while at the same time the number of welfare clients in the city climbed to one million, "that the welfare rolls have a life of their own detached from the metropolitan job market."

It is detached from the national job market as well. In 1961, when there were 3.5 million AFDC recipients, unemployment as a percent of the civilian labor force nationally was a high 6.7 percent. By 1968 the national

This article is an excerpt from *The State of Welfare* by Gilbert Y. Steiner, ©1971 The Brookings Institution, 1771 Massachusetts Ave., N.W., Washington, D. C. 20036

unemployment figure was hovering around a record low 3.4 percent, and there was serious talk among economists about the possible need for a higher rate of unemployment to counteract inflation. But the average monthly number of AFDC recipients in 1968 was up to 5.7 million, almost 4.4 million of whom were children. In 1969 the monthly recipient total averaged 6.7 million, and for the first six months of 1970 it was 7.9 million.

Public assistance also has a separate life outside the growth of the economy. The gross national product was $520 billion in 1961; in 1969 it was $932 billion. One of the things not expected to rise under those prosperous conditions was payments to relief recipients. Yet total payments in AFDC alone in 1961 were $1,149 million; in 1969 total payments were $3,546 million and rising rapidly.

To put all this another way, it is roughly accurate to say that during the 1960s the unemployment rate was halved, AFDC recipients increased by almost two-thirds, and AFDC money payments doubled. Whatever the relationship between workfare and welfare, it is not the simple one of reduced unemployment making for reduced dependency. How has government responded to this confounding news?

For the most part over the past ten years it has responded by tirelessly tinkering with the old welfare system. Special emphasis has been placed on preparing the welfare population emotionally and vocationally for participation in the labor market, thereby enjoying not only the economic security provided by employment itself, but also the unemployment insurance and survivors' insurance, if needed, which employment gives access to. The first such effort—the professional social service approach characterized by a stated plan emphasizing services over support and rehabilitation over relief—showed no progress after running its full five-year trial period from 1962 to 1967. And so, in 1967 a series of programs was invented in order to push relief clients to work. Work experience, work training, work incentives—whatever the titles and whatever the marginal differences in program content—were all designed, in the catch phrase often used, to move people off the relief rolls and onto the tax rolls. Each program assumed that the gulf between labor force participation with accompanying economic security benefits, on the one side, and relief status, on the other side, was bridgeable.

It was not until 1967, however, that it came to be perfectly acceptable to think of mothers with dependent small children as proper objects of the effort to get the very poor off the relief rolls and onto the tax rolls.

Agreement on this question resulted from the confluence of two separate concerns. One concern was with costs and criticisms. Representative Wilbur Mills, powerful leader of the crucial House Ways and Means Committee, viewed with alarm the costs of an unchecked public assistance program:

I am sure it is not generally known that about 4 or 5 years hence when we get to the fiscal year 1972, the figure will have risen by $2.2 billion to an amount of $6,731,000,000 . . . . If I detect anything in the minds of the American people, it is this. They want us to be certain that when we spend the amounts of money that we do, and of necessity in many cases have to spend, that we spend it in such a way as to promote the public interest, and the public well-being of our people.

Is it . . . in the public interest for welfare to become a way of life?

A different concern motivated an HEW task force, department officials, and some of Mills' legislative colleagues. The task force showed little worry over how many billions of dollars public relief was costing, but did concern itself with the turmoil and deprivation that beset recipients in depressed rural areas and in urban ghettos. Thus, to the Mills conclusion that the costs are prohibitive, there was joined a related HEW conclusion, shared by some members of Congress, that the quality of life on welfare was intolerable.

One congressman with such a view is the only lady member of the Ways and Means Committee, Martha Griffiths. Mrs. Griffiths was especially indignant over the conditions imposed on AFDC mothers.

I find the hypocrisy of those who are now demanding freedom of choice to work or not to work for welfare mothers beyond belief. The truth is these women never have had freedom of choice. They have never been free to work. Their education has been inadequate and the market has been unable to absorb their talents . . . .

Can you imagine any conditions more demoralizing than those welfare mothers live under? Imagine being confined all day every day in a room with falling plaster, inadequately heated in the winter and sweltering in the summer, without enough beds for the family, and with no sheets, the furniture falling apart, a bare bulb in the center of the room as the only light, with no hot water most of the time, plumbing that often does not work, with only the companionship of small children who are often hungry and always inadequately clothed—and, of course, the ever-present rats. To keep one's sanity under such circumstances is a major achievement, and to give children the love and discipline they need for healthy development is superhuman. If one were designing a system to produce alcoholism, crime, and illegitimacy, he could not do better.

Whatever the differing motivation, HEW's task force, Mills and Mrs. Griffiths all pointed in the direction of change from the status quo. And the change agreed upon was abandonment of the heretofore accepted idea that the only employable AFDC recipients were unemployed fathers.

In 1967 the Ways and Means Committee unveiled its social security and welfare bill at about the same time that HEW Secretary John Gardner unveiled his reorganization of the welfare agencies in his department. That reorganization merged the Welfare Administration, the Administration on Aging, and the Vocational Rehabilitation Service into a new agency called the Social and Rehabilitation Service (SRS). To run it, Gardner named Mary Switzer, a veteran commissioner of vocational rehabilitation who was aptly described by a local journalist as "a diligent disciple of work." This bit of tinkering was designed to send the message through the federal welfare bureaucracy that the secretary was receptive to policy change, apparently including a new work emphasis. The great drive to employ dependent mothers and provide day care for their children thus began both in the administration and in Congress two years before President Nixon discovered it anew.

Day Care

Despite an announcement by Miss Switzer in April 1969 that a reduction in the number of people on the welfare rolls is "a top priority of the Social and Rehabilitation Service" which she asked state welfare admistrators "to make yours as well," it was really beyond the power of either Miss Switzer or the state administrators to effect a big breakthrough in the AFDC problem. The key to moving some people off the rolls is employment for the AFDC employable parent. The rub is that even training for employment, a first step, requires an expensive new industry—day care—which now lacks organization, leadership, personnel and money for construction of facilities. Moreover, once the realities of work training and day care programs are examined, it becomes evident that there is not much incentive for a poorly educated AFDC mother to accept training for herself and day care service of uncertain quality for her children.

Training AFDC mothers for employment, actually finding jobs for them, and providing day care facilities for their children present formidable problems. A recent survey of the AFDC population found that 43 percent of the mothers had gone no further than the eighth grade, including 10.6 percent with less than a fifth grade education. Work training that leads to employment at wages adequate to support a family is likely to be prolonged, at best, for this undereducated group.

The realities of the coming crunch in day care are even more troublesome. Day care provisions accompanying the 1967 work incentive (WIN) legislation did not extend to the creation of a federal program authorizing funds for new facilities. There are approximately 46,300 licensed facilities caring for 638,000 children. If every place in every licensed day care facility in the United States were to be reserved for an AFDC child under the age of six, there would be more than one million AFDC children in that age group with no place to go. There would also be consternation among the thousands of non-AFDC mothers with children of that age level who are already in day care centers.

In short, there are not enough facilities—good, bad or indifferent—to accomplish the day care job envisioned by the congressional and administration planners who still talk of moving parents from welfare rolls to payrolls. Representative Fernand St. Germain was undoubtedly right in stating in 1969 that "costs of new facilities are too much for the states to bear alone; centers will only be built in numbers that have any relation to the critical need if federal assistance is forthcoming." No one seems to have foreseen this in 1967, however, and the point never got into the HEW program memorandum that influenced the employable mother discussions and proposals of the House Ways and Means Committee.

But the day care problem goes beyond the matter of adequate space to an important philosophical and political question regarding the appropriate clientele for the service.

There is no political conflict over the proposition that a young mother suddenly widowed and left dependent on social security survivors' benefits should be supported with public funds so that she can stay home and take care of her children. Nor is there congressional discussion or any HEW proposal for day care for those children. If 94.5 percent of AFDC dependency were attributable to death of the father, there would be no congressional interest in day care to speak of.

But, in fact, 94.5 percent of AFDC dependency is not attributable to death of the father; only 5.5 percent is. Most of the political conflict and a good deal of the interest in day care is over whether the public should subsidize those women whom Senator Russell Long once called "brood mares" to stay home, produce more children—some of them born out of wedlock—and raise those children in an atmosphere of dependency.

While medical authorities and professional social workers are still divided philosophically over how accessible day care should be and to whom, Congress in 1967 and President Nixon in 1969 simply embraced the possibility of putting day care to work in the cause of reducing public assistance costs. In other words, political attention has focused less on the practical limits of day care and more on its apparent similarities to baby sitting.

Day care was simply not ready to assume the responsibilities thrust on it by the welfare legislation adopted in 1967, and it was not ready for President Nixon's proposal to expand it in 1969. Whether day care is a socially desirable or even an economical way of freeing low income mothers with limited skills and limited education for work or work training still has not been widely considered. In the few circles where it has been considered, there is no agreement. Both the 1967 legislation and the Nixon proposal for escalation should have been preceded by the development of publicly supported, model day care arrangements that could be copied widely; by attention to questions of recruitment and appropriate educational training for day care personnel; by an inventory of available and needed physical facilities; by the existence of a high-spirited and innovative group of specialists in government or in a private association or both; and by enough experience to expose whatever practical defects may exist in day care as a program to facilitate employment of low income mothers. Instead of meeting these reasonable conditions for escalation, public involvement in day care programs for children, a phenomenon especially of the last ten years, remains unsystematic, haphazard, patchworky.

The Children's Bureau Approach

For many years before 1969, the HEW Children's Bureau ran the bulk of the federal day care program. It did not encourage an approach that would make day care readily available on demand. Stressing that day care can be harmful unless it is part of a broader program overseen by a trained social worker, the bureau defined day care as a child welfare service offering "care and protection." The child in need of day care was identified as one who "has a family problem which makes it impossible for his parents to fulfill their parental responsibilities without supplementary help." The social worker was seen as necessary to help determine whether the family needs day care and if so to develop an appropriate plan for the child, to place the child in a day care program, to determine the fee to be paid by the parents and to provide continuing supervision.

Change comes slowly to child welfare—as to other specialists. Those in the Children's Bureau found it difficult to adjust to the idea of day care available to all comers and especially to low income working mothers. On the one hand, the talk from the top of the bureau has been about the need to face reality in the day care picture—"when," as one bureau chief put it as early as 1967, "thousands of infants and young children are being placed in haphazard situations because their mothers are working." On the other hand, down the line at the bureau the experts continued to emphasize the importance of the intake procedure to insure that children placed in day care "need" the service.

With this approach it might be expected that while the day care expansion movement has ground along slowly, it has ground exceedingly fine. Day care undoubtedly is a risky enterprise. Every center should have a genuinely high-quality, sympathetic environment; no center should be countenanced without clear evidence that such an environment is being created, and all centers that do not give such evidence should be discouraged. The payoff, therefore, for what might seem to be excessive caution by the Children's Bureau could have been a jewel of a limited program and no second or third rate imitations. Then, when money and will were at hand, the jewel could be reproduced.

In fact, no day care activity was discouraged, whether of low quality or not. Caution on the subject of quantity did not work to guarantee quality. Whether or not there would be any day care activity depended on the states, and the federal agency was accommodating, both because it was hard to interest the states in day care at all, and because Congress provided money in fits and starts, rather than in a steady flow. When the money did come, there was an urgent need to spend it.

Funding

Between 1962 and 1965, HEW had only $8.8 million to parcel out to the states for day care. Moreover, it was never able to count on having anything from year to year, so that it is understandable that the federal agency was in no position to threaten the states about the quality of service. The 1962 law required that federal day care money go only to facilities approved or licensed in accordance with state standards. The law said nothing about minimum federal standards. In 1962 a number of states had no day care licensing programs at all; among the states that did, the extent of licensing and the standards used varied considerably. The Children's Bureau's own guidelines were little more than advisory. To raise the quality of day care nationally, the bureau had to fall back on persuasion and consultation, weak tools compared to money.

Licensing

One certain effect of the 1962 requirement that the available federal money go only to licensed facilities was to divert a substantial part of the funds into licensing activity itself and away from actual day care services. For fiscal 1965, for example, 43 percent of the $4 million appropriated for day care was spent on personnel engaged in licensing, while only 36 percent was used to provide day care services in homes or centers. This increased licensing activity has the effect of distorting the picture of growth of day care facilities. In 1960, licensed day care facilities had a reported total capacity of 183,332; in 1965 this had increased to 310,400; in 1967 the figure was up to 473,700; in 1968 to 535,200; and in 1969 to 638,000. There is universal agreement, however, that the growth figure is mostly illusory, a consequence of formerly unlicensed facilities now being licensed.

Moreover, there is more form than substance to licensing decisions. The fact that a day care facility is licensed cannot yet be taken to mean that its physical plant and personnel necessarily satisfy some explicitly defined and universally accepted standards. Like "premium grade" automobile tires, licensed day care facilities can differ sharply in quality—and for the same reason, the absence of industry-wide standards. Licensing studies by public welfare agencies are invariably assigned to new and untrained caseworkers. The results are unpredictable and there is no monitoring

body able and authorized to keep a watchful eye on who is being licensed.

Even from those who accept the simplistic assumption that only the absence of child care services and of job or training opportunities preclude AFDC recipients from becoming wage earners, there is no suggestion that just any kind of child care will do. Yet the state of the art in day care is not sufficiently advanced to make it reasonable to expect that states can meet the requirement to provide day care services other than in makeshift, low quality programs. There is clear validity in the complaint of the National Committee for the Day Care of Children that the 1967 legislation was not designed to help children develop mentally and physically, but was "a hastily put together outline for a compulsory, custodial service which is not required to maintain even minimal standards of adequacy."

Challenge from Head Start

Only a month after taking office, President Nixon called for a "national commitment to providing all American children an opportunity for healthful and stimulating development during the first five years of life." A few weeks later secretary of HEW Robert Finch welcomed the delegation of the Head Start program to HEW as the occasion for a new and overdue national commitment to child and parent development. Finch indicated publicly that he was not inclined to put Head Start in the Children's Bureau and instead placed it in a new HEW Office of Child Development (OCD) where the Children's Bureau was also transferred. Social planners in HEW, the Bureau of the Budget and the White House envisioned a new era: day care programs for low income children would be modeled on Head Start; simple custodial arrangements would not be tolerated; parents would be involved. The way for this happy outcome had already been paved by issuance of the Federal Interagency Day Care Requirements, a joint product of HEW and OEO, approved in the summer of 1968.

Things have not worked out. Whatever Finch's initial intention, the day care programs operated by the Children's Bureau never made it to the OCD. In September 1969 a new Community Services Administration was created within the Social and Rehabilitation Service to house all service programs provided public assistance recipients under social security. The Head Start bureau of the OCD, according to the terms of the reorganization, was given some responsibility in Social Security Act day care programs—to participate in policy making and to approve state welfare plans on day care. But effective control of the money and policy in the day care programs remains with the Social and Rehabilitation Service. President Nixon's "commitment to providing all American children an opportunity for healthful and stimulating development during the first five years of life" has so far produced more talk than money.

A High Cost Service

There has simply not been enough thinking about the benefits and costs of a good day care program to merit the faith political leaders now express in day care as a dependency-reducing mechanism. Federal day care program requirements are, for the most part, oriented to the idea of day care as a learning experience. They are, therefore, on a collision course with supporters of mass day care as an aspect of the struggle to reduce welfare costs. The high-quality program requirements reject simple warehousing of children, but the prospects for meeting high standards are not good. It seems inevitable that there will be disappointment both for those who think of day care as a welfare economy and for those who think of day care for AFDC children as an important social and educational advance.

Consider the situation in the District of Columbia, which is reasonably typical of the day care problem in large cities. The District Public Welfare Department (DPW) in May 1969 was purchasing child care for 1,056 children, of whom about 400 were children of women in the WIN program. Of the total 1,056 children, 865 were in day care centers, 163—primarily infants too young to be placed in centers—were in family day care homes, and 28 were in in-home care arrangements, a service considered practical only for large families. The total anticipated day care load for the end of fiscal 1969 was 1,262. District day care personnel estimated that 660 AFDC mothers to be referred to WIN during fiscal 1970 (on the basis of 55 per month) would need, on the average, day care for 2 children. These additional 1,320 children would bring the likely number for whom the District would be paying for care to 2,582 by July 1, 1970. Budget requests for day care for fiscal 1970 totaled $3,254,300 in local and federal funds ($1,148,000 of local funds brings $2,106,300 in federal money). Of this amount, about $3 million is for purchase of care, the remainder for administrative expenses. If budget requests were met, the purchase cost of day care in the District would thus be expected to average almost $1,200 per child. Costly as that may seem to be, it represents only a little more than half the actual cost.

It is the beginning of day care wisdom to understand that it is an expensive mechanism and to understand that there are qualitative differences in the care provided. The elegantly stated effort of the DPW is to secure "in addition to good physical care, the kind of exceptionally enriched day care experience that is specifically designed and programmed to stimulate and promote the maximum in emotional, physical, and educational growth and development of the child." Alas, one-third of the centers with which the DPW contracts only "offer primarily custodial and protective care," a code phrase for warehousing. Fees paid day care centers by the District Welfare Department are supposed to be a function of the quality of services offered. Grade A centers are paid $4.00 a day, B centers $3.00 a day, and C centers $2.50 a day. The department's Standards for Day Care Centers say that it uses a fee schedule for two reasons: "to assure that proper value is received for each dollar spent and, secondly, to provide a monetary stimulus to contract day care facilities to up-grade the quality of their services to meet the Department's maximum expectations." Each center's "rating," known only to it and to the Welfare Department, is for "internal use" and is not revealed to the welfare mother because, according to department officials, it would not be fair to the center to do so. A more pertinent question is whether it is fair to the mother, since 25 of the 55 centers from which day care is purchased are graded B or C, and

since half of all placements are in B or C centers.

All centers—whether A, B or C—must meet the Health Department's licensing requirements, as well as additional specific standards set down by the Welfare Department in the areas of educational qualifications of personnel, program content, and equipment and furnishings. Yet there are two problems with this seemingly tidy picture. The first is the insistence of close observers that while the Welfare Department's standards for centers look satisfactory on paper, they have not been put into practice very consistently. The second is that even the paper standards will not do when the federal interagency standards become effective July 1, 1971. Spokesmen for the National Capital Area Child Day Care Association (NCACDCA) and District Health Department licensing personnel are critical of the Welfare Department's day care operation. Both suggest there is a lack of awareness in the Welfare Day Care Unit of what constitutes good day care. That high ranking is reserved, in the judgment of these people, for the centers operated by NCACDCA. The critics complain that only the NCACDCA centers can legitimately meet the Welfare Department's own A standards and maintain that the other A centers simply do not meet them. They claim, for example, that one way these latter centers "meet" the educational qualifications for personnel is to list as a director an "absentee"—perhaps a kindergarten teacher in the District of Columbia school system or that of a neighboring county.

No one disputes that most centers in the District cannot meet the Federal Interagency Day Care Requirements—particularly the child-adult ratios and the educational qualifications for staff. Even a good number of the A centers do not meet the child-adult ratio requirements, and the B and C centers meet neither the staff educational qualifications nor the child-adult ratios of the federal requirements. If the day care centers have not met the federal standards by July 1, 1971, DPW cannot continue making payments on behalf of children for whom it receives federal matching funds. But in the District Welfare Department the view is that the requirements are unrealistic and that widespread complaints from private users who cannot afford the costs involved may result in a lowering of standards.

All the evidence suggests that day care is expensive whether the auspices are public, private or mixed. In a curiously chosen experiment, the Department of Labor decided in 1969 to fund an experimental day care program for its own employees at a time when emphasis was presumably being placed on supporting day care for the welfare poor. Its estimated budget for the first full year of care for 30 children was $100,000, one-third of which was for nonrecurring development costs, including renovation for code compliance, equipment and evaluation. Tuition from the group of working mothers involved amounted to only $7,300, leaving $59,600 of public funds necessary to provide care for 30 children—a subsidy of almost $2,000 per child without considering nonrecurring cost items. Doubling the number of children served the second year would require a budget of $100,000, resulting in an average annual per child cost over the two years of $1,850, or of $2,225, if the renovation and equipment items are not dismissed as readily as the department sought to dismiss them in its official explanation.

The National Capital Area Child Day Care Association estimates costs at almost $2,400 per child per 50-week year. Its standard budget for a 30-child center exceeds $71,000. Tight-fisted budget examiners might effect reductions, but they cannot be consequential unless the pupil teacher ratio is drastically revised. Morever, NCACDCA salary figures are unrealistically low. Head teachers for a 30-child center are hard to come by at $7,300. (See table.)

If these per child costs of desirable day care are projected nationally, the annual bill for all preschool AFDC children must be figured conservatively at $3 billion.

Client Arithmetic

Most women in the District of Columbia WIN program are being trained in clerical skills in anticipation that they will take jobs with the federal government as GS-2s. This is an optimistic view since most trainees have ninth to eleventh grade educations while a GS-2 needs a high school diploma or equivalency or six months' experience and the ability to pass a typing test. That problem aside, the District AFDC mother who completes work incentive training and is placed in a GS-2 job will be better off financially than the mother who stays on welfare. Her gain will be greater the smaller the size of her family. She will have fewer children to support on her fixed earnings, whereas the larger the family on AFDC, the larger the grant.

For many a female head of a family of four in the spring of 1970, however, the work and day care arithmetic was not encouraging as the following illustration shows. If the GS-2 mother has three children and claims four exemptions, about $39 of her monthly salary of $385 is deducted for retirement ($18.50) and for federal ($17) and local ($3.50) taxes, leaving a take home pay of about $346 a month. If two of the three children are in Welfare Department child care arrangements, placed there when the mother entered the WIN program, the mother would pay the department about $6.00 a week toward their care; if the mother had only one child in care, she would pay $5.50. Assuming two children in care, the mother's monthly cost would be about $26, lowering her net earnings to $320.

Suppose, however, that the woman stayed on AFDC. The average benefit for a four-person family on AFDC in the District would bring her $217 monthly. Both the welfare mother and the working mother would be eligible for Medicaid, but only the welfare mother would be eligible for food stamps. For $60 a month she could receive $106 in food stamps, a gain of $46. The welfare mother's child could also receive free lunches at school while the working mother's could not. (The working mother is considerably above the income scale used to determine eligibility for free lunches, although in cases where it is felt children are going hungry, exceptions to the income scale can be made.) A school lunch costs 25 cents in the District's elementary schools. If the welfare child took advantage of the free lunch the mother would save about $5 a month. Thus, the welfare mother would end up with a total of about $268 in welfare, food stamps and school lunches while the working

Standard Day Care Center Budget for Thirty Children for One Year

A. *Personnel*	
3 Full-time teachers (head teacher, $7,300; teacher, $7,000; teacher assistant, $4,700)	$19,000
2 Full-time aides ($4,140 each)	8,280
1 Half-time clerk	2,400
Part-time maintenance help (cook, $2,610; janitor, $2,024)	4,634
Substitute (teacher aide, $4,300) and part-time student aide ($1,214)	5,514
Subtotal	$39,828
Fringe benefits (11 percent)	4,381
Total	$44,209
B. *Consultant and Contract Services*	
Part-time social worker ($2,500), psychiatric consultant ($5,000), and educational consultant ($1,000)	$8,500
Dietitian	500
Dental and emergency medical service	450
Total	$9,450
C. *Space*	
Rent ($1,800); custodial supplies and minor repairs ($1,800)	$3,600
D. *Consumable Supplies*	
Office, postage, and miscellaneous (blankets, towels, etc.)	$450
Educational ($400) and health supplies ($30)	430
Food and utensils	4,674
Total	$5,554
E. *Rental, Lease, or Purchase of Equipment*	
Children's furniture ($3,000) and office equipment ($200)	$3,200
Equipment: basic (easels, blocks, etc., $1,500); expendable (dolls, puzzles, books, etc., $700); outdoor, with storage ($1,000)	3,200
Total	$6,400
F. *Travel*	
Staff ($240) and children's trips ($720)	$960
G. *Other*	
Telephone ($36 a month; installation $50)	$482
Insurance (liability, property, and transportation liability)	$700
Total	$1,182
Total project cost	$71,355
Child cost per year	$2,378

Source: Derived from budget of National Capital Area Day Care Association, Inc., Washington, D.C., August 1968.

mother would have about $320 a month. In addition, the 1967 welfare amendments allow a welfare mother to earn $30 per month without loss of benefits. The net gain for working full time compared to working only 19 hours a month at the minimum wage is thus reduced to $22. From this, the working mother would have expenses to cover such items as transportation and extra clothes for herself and might have to make some after school care arrangement for her third (school-aged) child.

City Arithmetic

How much work training and day care can save the District of Columbia will depend on how many trainees complete training successfully, get a job and keep it, and on how many children of trainees need child care. The Welfare Department will benefit financially by the AFDC mother's entering a training program and becoming employed as a GS-2 unless the mother has four or more children in day care—which would be most unusual. While it might give the AFDC mother of three $217 each month, the department would pay only part of her day care cost once she begins working (the department pays all costs for the first three months). With an average cost to the department for day care of $17.50 per child per week, using our hypothetical GS-2 mother with two children in day care and one in elementary school, the mother would pay $6 a week and the Welfare Department $29 a week for day care. This working mother thus represents a monthly saving to the department of about $56. If, however, the AFDC mother had four children in day care centers and one in elementary school, the mother would pay $6.50 a week toward their care (this figure is the same for three or more children) and the department $63.50. The department would thus spend $273 a month for child care—and save nothing compared to what it would have given her on AFDC to care for her own children at home.

Prospects

What are the prospects for success in turning day care into a program that will reduce the costs of AFDC? They hinge, first, on large numbers of AFDC mothers actually turning out to be trainable and able to be placed in jobs under any conditions and, second, on finding some cheaper substitute for traditional day care centers.

The difficulty in securing the physical facilities and staff needed to develop the traditional centers looked overwhelming to state welfare administrators examining the day care problem in 1967. They did, however, see some hopes for neighborhood day care, a kind of glorified, low income equivalent of the middle class baby-sitting pool. Stimulated by OEO's success in involving poor people in poverty programs, HEW early in 1967 started pushing neighborhood day care demonstration projects using welfare mothers to help care for other welfare mothers' children. This seemingly ideal solution has its own problems. One of them is sanitary and health requirements that, if enforced, disqualify the substandard housing used by many recipients. The unknown emotional condition of the AFDC mother is an equally important problem in this use of the neighborhood care idea. A spokesman for the Welfare Rights Organization warns:

> Do not force mothers to take care of other children. You do not know what kind of problem that parent might have. You do not know whether she gets tired of her own children or not but you are trying to force her to take care of other people's children and forcing the parents to go out in the field and work when you know there is no job.
>
> This is why we have had the disturbance in New York City and across the country. We, the welfare recipients, have tried to keep down that disturbance among our people but the unrest is steadily growing. The welfare recipients are tired. They are tired of people dictating to them telling them how they must live.

Not surprisingly, day care and work training through WIN are lagging as the hoped-for saving graces of public assistance. New York City's experience is instructive. In 1967 the City Council's finance committee concluded that an additional expenditure of $5 million for 50 additional day care centers to accommodate 3,000 additional children was warranted. "The Committee on Finance is informed," said its report, "that many (welfare) mothers would seek employment if they could be assured of proper care of their children while at work. We feel that expansion . . . on a massive scale is called for." The mayor's executive expense budget for day care was thereupon increased by about 60 percent and appropriations in subsequent years have continued at the higher level. But the New York City Department of Social Services—like the U.S. Department of Health, Education, and Welfare—lacks a program for such a rapid expansion of day care. Actual expenditures have lagged. In contrast to the anticipated 50 new centers caring for 3,000 additional children, it was reported in June 1969 that 19 new centers accommodating 790 children had been established.

The national figures resulting from the 1967 amendments are no more encouraging. Like New York City, the federal government has not been able to shovel out the available money. Consider the situation around the time of the Nixon family assistance message. Of a projected June

1969 goal of 102,000 WIN enrollees, only 61,847 were in fact enrolled by the end of that month. Of a projected 100,000 child care arrangements, only about 49,000 children were receiving care at the end of June 1969, and 50 percent of them were receiving care in their own homes. Thus, when President Nixon proposed 150,000 new training slots and 450,000 new day care places in his August 1969 welfare message, the Labor Department and HEW had already found that 18 months after enactment of the 1967 legislation they were unable to meet more than 60 percent of their modest work and training goals or more than 50 percent of their even more modest day care goals.

WIN Loses

The gap between original projections and depressing realities held constant into 1970. The Labor Department first estimated a WIN enrollment level of 150,000 at the close of fiscal 1970, later scaled the figure down to 100,000. And as of February 1970 the cumulative WIN data took the shape of a funnel:

Welfare recipients screened by local agencies for possible referral	1,478,000
Found appropriate for referral to WIN	301,000
Actually referred to WIN	225,000
Enrolled in WIN program	129,000
Employed	22,000

As for day care, 188,000 children were initially expected to be receiving "child care"—which includes care in their own homes by grandmothers or other relatives—on June 30, 1970. The target later was dropped to a more modest 78,000. In May 1970 there were just 61,000 reported in child care, and only about one-fifth of these children were really cared for in a day care facility. Approximately one-half were cared for in their own homes, one-tenth in a relative's home, and the last one-fifth were reported to have "other" arrangements—a category that actually includes "child looks after self."

By July 1970 the House Labor-HEW appropriations subcommittee was discouraged about the progress of work training-day care activity. "It doesn't sound too good," said Chairman Dan Flood (Democrat of Pennsylvania) after hearing the WIN program statistics. The committee proposed a reduction of $50 million from the administration's request for $170 million in 1971 work incentive funds. There was no confusion about either the purpose of the program or its lack of accomplishment:

> The objective of the work incentives program is to help people get off the welfare rolls and to place them in productive jobs. While the committee supports the program, it has just not been getting off the ground for several reasons, such as poor day care standards for children.

Unfortunately, the sorry history and the limitations of day care and work training as solutions to the welfare problem could not be faced by the administration's welfare specialists in 1970 because all of their energies were directed toward support for the Nixon family assistance plan. But after a few years it will inevitably be discovered that work training and day care have had little effect on the number of welfare dependents and no depressing effect on public relief costs. Some new solution will then be proposed, but the more realistic approach would be to accept the need for more welfare and to reject continued fantasizing about day care and "workfare" as miracle cures.

FURTHER READING

Security and Services for Children by Robert H. Bremner, Sanford N. Katz, Rachel Marks, and William M. Schmidt, M.D. (New York: Arno Press, 1974).

Children Are the Revolution: Day Care in Cuba by Marvin Leiner (New York: Viking, 1974).

Child Care: Who Cares? by Pamela Roby (New York: Basic Books, 1972).

Women and Child Care in China by Ruth Sidel (New York: Hill & Wang, 1972).

BARBARA SUCZEK

Chronic Medicare

What is a human life worth? For a people readily moved to personal generosity when catastrophe hits friend or stranger we are strangely reluctant to commit ourselves to the expense of instituting a federally financed health-care policy. One result of this fear of changing the social system is that the life of a victim of a chronic ailment is virtually price-tagged at whatever the cost of treatment is. In the case of renal failure (kidney disease) victims, this figure is at least several thousand dollars a year— the cost of hemodialysis, the process of filtering toxic substances which accumulate in a renal patient's blood. Despite its time-consuming and psychologically demanding nature, dialysis holds out dramatic hope to chronic renal failure victims. But the same society whose technology offers this life-sustaining promise cruelly impedes its fulfillment with random, arbitrary methods of making funds available to those who need treatment.

Regardless of his economic status, the chronic renal failure patient—sick and worried—is forced to chart a perilous physical and financial course. Unfortunately, the physically healthy seem to lack the imagination, the time and the emotional energy to sustain any deep in-

volvement with seemingly interminable medical problems. Bolstered by a proud but largely unexamined assumption that "we," as Americans, are probably doing as well as can be expected in providing for general health care, the chronically sick and those intimately involved with their care are essentially left to cure their own financial ills.

The two major phases of the illness trajectory—the acute, or *rescue* period and the chronic, or prolonged *maintenance* period—are each accompanied by their own special funding problems. Since the latter phase may extend over an entire lifetime, it will almost certainly be accompanied by a sequential depletion of funding sources—each failure initiating a new crisis that propels the patient into a search for new funds.

Without public monies the fund-raising process takes on the ongoing, never-consummated quality of running on a treadmill. A successful kidney transplant may seem the only real hope for escape. Such an escape is not, unfortunately, a panacea. It involves massive problems of its own, such as locating donors, the inevitable risks associated with major surgery and the hovering possibility

Author's note:

On July 1, 1973 new provisions for funding hemodialysis went into effect under Medicare. Such provisions offer some hope for easing the financial burden of many chronic renal failure victims. What the actual effect will be, of course, nobody knows, but professionals with whom I have spoken are cautiously optimistic. At the very least this sort of funding proves

that efforts *are* being made in response to lobbying pressure.

Despite the fact that this article was written prior to the new rulings, none of its basic points has been invalidated. The new guidelines simply demonstrate the ongoing struggle over funding which will not, I am convinced, reach any satisfactory resolution until we face the need to socialize medical services for all.

of organ rejection. Though it is also an expensive procedure, its financial advantage lies in the fact that the costs involved are circumscribed and at least roughly calculable. If it is successful, there is hope for genuine relief at the economic as well as the physical level. If it is unsuccessful, the patient returns to the treadmill.

Originally, at least, the victim of chronic renal failure who has health insurance coverage may be saved from financial worries. Although the costs of the rescue period will probably be higher than those of subsequent phases, the patient may actually experience less financial distress than later in his illness since health insurance generally cushions the initial blow.

Health insurance as it now stands, however, falls far short of meeting the funding needs of dialysis patients. Since health insurance policies are primarily geared to protect the insured against the cost of acute illness, they are rarely adequate for coping with the long-term financial drain associated with chronic illness.

Essentially, health insurance coverage may determine which renal failure victims live and which die. About 80 percent of survivors (those stabilized and on dialysis) carry some sort of major medical coverage at the onset of illness. This figure is higher than the national average. Without recourse to the lifesaving machines or sufficient funds to pay for using the machines, renal failure victims die early in the course of their illness. Many more renal failure victims die than are saved. Of those who die, many could be saved.

Competing for Dialysis

Those who live—even though semi-permanently attached to a dialysis machine—are not randomly selected. As a group they have four outstanding characteristics: urbanity, respectability, affiliation and a record of fairly steady employment.

Urbanity is intended in both its geographical and psychological sense. It takes an urbane, sophisticated know-how to locate sources of funds. Further, dialysis units are almost exclusively located in large urban centers so patients must live in or within commuting distance of the city. Even patients on home dialysis must have some means of reaching the city for the six-week training period, for periodic checkups and for medical and mechanical emergencies. There are, moreover, rural areas that are not suited to the installation or operation of dialysis machinery.

Respectability is less an inherent personal trait than a value judgment made by others who must choose among patients competing for limited medical facilities. Persons who are viewed as "unbalanced" or socially irresponsible are obviously less likely to qualify for selection.

Affiliation, that is, whether the patient has recourse to a social network, will also have bearing on alternatives available to him, especially on the choice between center- and home-based dialysis. Home care is possible only if the patient has a responsible person available to help him use the machine. There are, at present, no trained professional assistants.

A steady employment record is necessary because health insurance policies are frequently sponsored by labor groups or business organizations and are, as such, available only to employees in good standing: and because—regardless of sponsorship—some stable base of income is obviously needed in order to meet a schedule of regular payments.

There is little that can be confidently stated with regard to the overall health insurance picture. Not only do various plans differ widely from one another in the kinds and amounts of benefits they offer, but even within the framework of a specific plan there are wide disparities in coverage, varying according to such criteria as the relationship of the patient to the policyholder (in cases where dependents are covered), type of facility used (many policies will cover hospital treatment but will not pay for outpatient or home care—a source of running dispute, incidentally, between an organization of New York kidney disease victims and New York City Blue Cross), length of time the policy has been in effect (the Kaiser health plan stipulates, for example, that the claimant must have been a member of the plan for at least two years prior to qualifying for prepaid dialysis). Nearly all policies carry clauses that specifically limit the liability of the carrier to prestated amounts. The relationship of the patient to the subscriber, the particular and peculiar conjunction of points in personal, occupational and disease careers, the site and type of available treatment all have their bearing on how the terms of a specific policy will be interpreted.

Coding categorical differences is not the major difficulty, although it is true that here—as in any coding operation—there will be cases whose disposition is not readily clear and apparent. Rather, the major source of confusion stems from a seemingly universal effort to evade the issue of financial responsibility.

Health insurance policies are formulated and contracts negotiated in an atmosphere of uncertainty. One side does not know what reasonably to demand; the other does not know what to refuse. The central issue is the extent to which the surety shall be liable for claims that were unforseeable at the time of contract. Little more than a decade ago the alternative of hemodialysis did not exist in the treatment of kidney failure, and its effect, therefore, could not be anticipated in actuarial calculations. There seems no reason to assume that the present procedure and its attendant costs will long endure; the probability is that any day now some new technological breakthrough will render them both obsolete.

One tactic insurance companies might adopt would be to refuse to honor any claim based on future technological developments. But such a policy could be strategically inadvisable since business competitors might be able to exploit that stand to their own advantage.

Liability Loopholing

Corporate tradition dictates that the problem of competition could be resolved by collusion were it not for the spectre of that anathema to insurance companies—socialized medicine. Certainly it would seem imprudent for anyone with a vested interest in private enterprise to pursue a course that might tip the balance of public sentiment in the direction of state-financed medical care.

The fear of making firm, definitive statements that might inadvertently establish precedents leads both sides to a vagueness of position. The result is that there is a wide area for loopholing for both claimant and corporation.

Further adding to the confusion is the fact that the claimant may be simply and overwhelmingly ignorant. It is a rare person who has the slightest idea what his insurance can be expected to cover. There is simply no way for an individual to be able to anticipate all eventualities and their consequences. Who could have guessed a few years ago that even "forever" might be barely adequate as a time stipulation? Yet this is only a slight overstatement of what has become a fact of life for thousands of victims of renal failure.

A policy carrying a $20,000 liability limitation may seem, to the healthy, more than adequate to protect a family from the costs of even major illnesses. However, in the case of one young woman—a wife and mother—who was stricken with kidney failure, $13,000 of such a policy was consumed in less than four months. This amount covered only 80 percent of her overall medical expense. Thus, the family was already more than $2,000 out of pocket, the insurance was 65 percent depleted and there was still a lifetime of expense ahead which, for a woman of 27, might be expected to extend for upwards of 50 years. This young and previously prospering family watched a carefully planned insurance program melt away before their eyes, carrying with it many of their hopes and plans for the future.

The simple truth is that, for many individuals, health insurance seems to function like ritual magic: they trust that the powers-that-be, having been duly placated by the proper observances and offerings, will come to their rescue in time of need.

Ignorance of content is often accompanied by ignorance of procedure. For patients who are unfamiliar with the intricacies of bureaucratic paperwork or for those who are too sick to concern themselves with it, filling out the required forms according to prescribed time schedules may present an almost insurmountable problem. One patient reported:

I owe about $300 in hospital bills that I'll have to pay for myself. I didn't fill out the state disability form so the insurance doesn't cover it. I'm just out of pocket. I was too sick to deal with that. I didn't know *anything* for two weeks and that was when I was supposed to fill out the form. After I was well I called them about it but I found out it was too late. . . .

Diffidence can also limit the patient's knowledge: "I don't know why it's taking so long. I'd kind of like to know, but. . . well, I don't like to call them . . . . Oh, I hate to go causing people trouble."

It seems clear that there are various reasons that patients may need help with insurance formalities. At present, responsiblity for assisting patients falls to a motley crew of agents whose efforts are not necessarily closely coordinated.

The hospital employs social workers, administrators and other professionals to recover costs that the institution cannot afford to absorb. There are also unofficial assistants—often nurses and doctors whose work brings them into close and frequent contact with individual patients—who, in addition to their regular duties, may find themselves involved in efforts to unsnarl a patient's financial difficulties. There are two basic reasons for this sort of involvement: first, since effective functioning of the treatment process can be seriously impeded by recurring financial problems, frustrated professionalism may demand their solution by whatever or whosoever intervention seems most expedient; second, the close association between dialysis patients and the professionals who supervise their care often leads to a sympathetic involvement with the patient's affairs. Dialysis room concern often manifests itself in efforts above and beyond the normal call of professional duties. No one, anywhere, serves primarily to help the patient understand and order his financial affairs strictly in accordance with his own needs and interests.

Rejected Claims

The usual procedure followed by insured patients seems to be that of submitting claims on an *ad hoc* basis until such time as payment is refused. If refusal is based on a technicality, a running dispute with the company may ensue:

I had trouble with the insurance company, but Dr. A. finally got it settled. They wouldn't pay for the dialysis unless you spent the night in the hospital and the dialysis unit here isn't open at night. It just didn't make sense . . . all through October and November it was under debate: Dr. A., the hospital and the insurance company. Finally I guess Dr. A. convinced them . . . since December the insurance company has started paying . . . but I think the hospital took the loss.

If refusal is based on the fact that the company's liability is spent—that the source of funds is exhausted—a new crisis is precipitated. Rarely does a patient make any advance plans for dealing with the crisis. "I just don't know *what* I'll do when the insurance runs out!" is a typical comment. This is undoubtedly because there are few—terrifyingly few—available options. The patient, helpless and bewildered, simply drifts into crisis, hoping that, when the point is reached, some solution will present itself.

Rescue Efforts

Individuals are occasionally rescued by charitable intervention: organizations and groups may have funds available or may undertake fund-raising drives in a patient's behalf. Appeals through the media sometimes meet with surprisingly generous public response. In such cases, however, novelty is a powerful ally. Every fund drive that depends on a human interest motif to insure its success probably serves, in a degree, to desensitize its audience and may decrease the chance that such drives will be similarly successful in the future. A time of increasing need, therefore, may unfortunately be merging with a period of diminishing returns.

It is also true that fund-raising ventures probably do better when it is possible to define a single, specific objective—some indicator that can be used both as the measure of success and the end of the project. Interest and energy flag in confrontation with the demoralizing drain of unremitting need. The renal failure patient thus has a much better chance of receiving aid in some specific amount—the sum needed to defray the cost of a heroic rescue, for example, or to buy a machine for home use—than he has of tapping charitable or voluntary resources for long-term maintenance.

The prolonged maintenance period is one in which the renal failure patient's condition has stabilized. Although

---

The patient has a better chance of receiving the sum needed to defray the cost of an heroic rescue than he has of tapping charitable or voluntary resources for long-term maintenance.

---

it is impossible to keep the body chemistry in perfect balance—there will always be periodic flurries and alarms and medical supervision must be regularly maintained—the physical condition is basically under control and the situation permits some opportunity for predicting and planning of future needs. Despite this, however, the period is characterized by a series of funding crises. While it is presumably true that in California, for example, since the state offers funds under the provisions of MediCal, no Californian need die for lack of money for treatment, there is so much personal misery and financial distress entailed in accepting state medical aid that recourse to public funds will almost certainly be postponed as long as possible.

How early and to what extent an individual will experience the treadmill effect of the prolonged maintenance period hinges on many contingencies. It makes a critical difference, for example, whether a patient is financially dependent, self-supporting or the breadwinner for a family. The most difficult position is that of the afflicted person who must earn a living.

Renal failure is hardest on the breadwinner for three reasons. First, the time needed for dialysis may cut seriously into working hours. Second, physical debility not only hampers productivity and overall efficiency but also limits the sort of work that can be undertaken. Occupations that involve a considerable outlay of physical energy or require extensive travelling, for example, may have to be abandoned. Third, it may be difficult to find any sort of suitable work since employment policies are frequently associated with insurance regulations that will, almost certainly, reject persons suffering from serious chronic disease.

Early retirement is a frequent solution among those whose age and seniority status permit them that alternative. The person who can retire on a pension and is qualified to receive help from Medicare is in a relatively good financial position, providing there are no extraneous complicating factors. Under other circumstances, however, retirement—by cutting down income and changing insurance status—may be extremely threatening. Consider, for example, the plight of a man who had reached the compulsory retirement age but whose wife—20 years his junior—was on hemodialysis that was being funded through his occupational insurance.

Medical Aid

The Californian who is already on welfare at the time of kidney failure—if he survives the many hazards in the path to rescue—will, theoretically, qualify by definition for medical aid from MediCal. Ironically, such patients are often among those whose treatment is the most expensive to maintain since they lack the stable conditions necessary to qualify them for home care.

In California, the whole issue of state-financed medical help is fraught with bitterness and altercation, and the financing of renal failure—because of its chronic nature and its extraordinarily high cost—is a particularly touchy point.

There are three sources of major dispute: welfare restrictions, governmental responsibility and administrative red tape.

Welfare Restrictions. In order to qualify for funds from MediCal, a patient must divest himself of any personal property or income he may have in excess of that permitted to recipients of state welfare. The MediCal plan is apparently so designed in order to insure that an individual will not freeload at the taxpayers' expense—that he will assume liability and share the cost of his illness. In operation it is like a deductible clause that is based on the patient's income. A single person, for example, with an income of $500 a month may be permitted a maintenance need allowance of $110 a month (the fact that specifications are subject to unpredictable change is another source of ambiguity and worry); all income above that amount must be used for medical expenses before MediCal will intervene. In addition, according to its policy, MediCal will not assist anyone who owns cash or property in excess of a value of $1,200 (personal dwelling excepted) and/or cash value of life insurance over $100 per dependent. Thus, if the patient has been fortunate enough or foresighted enough to be able to provide some security for his family, he is expected to see to the dispersal of that security before he can apply to MediCal for the funds needed to save his life. To lose one's financial foothold is never a happy eventuality, but to do so at a time when the physical realities of illness are making the course of the future extremely uncertain is particularly distressing. Once he has been reduced to the welfare level, there seems little likelihood that a patient can find the means to regain his independence.

To many persons involved in it—patients and professionals alike—the situation seems not only unfortunate but contrary to American principles and goals. Such prescriptions may even be generating a *welfare race* of persons who no longer have any incentive to self-help. That a victim of illness through no perceivable fault of his own should be reduced to such a plight is thoroughly unjust. In the words of one administrator:

Most people are not millionaires. Most people are middle income—six to ten thousand dollars a year. I, myself, just don't think it's worth all that hassle. Especially when you stop to think that these people never feel very good—well, you get accustomed to feeling half-good . . . . But when you work all your life and you pay taxes all your life and taking care of yourself has always been a source of pride to you, and then you get turned down because *you've got too much!* Well, it's demoralizing.

To lose one's financial foothold is never a happy eventuality but to do so at a time when illness is making the course of the future uncertain is particularly distressing.

Governmental Responsibility. California's state legislature is caught in a crossfire of constituent demands: reconciliation of public and private interests is not often reached at a single bound. Simultaneously pressured by demands for increased assistance, lower taxes, less governmental intervention and universal health benefits, the result is, not surprisingly, lacking in clarity and direction. The fight over hemodialysis is a case in point:

The whole dialysis issue is a big problem in Sacramento—an embarrassment. The legislature didn't really want to pay for dialysis. But dialysis, after all, came into being here—here and at a sister center in Seattle. There was a sort of local proprietary pride . . . . And then it turned out there wasn't enough insurance to go around, so great pressure was put on the Reagan administration to accept hemodialysis. This was in 1967. Now they regret it. They didn't know what they were getting into. The State Department of Public Health estimates that by 1977 there will be 3,000 people on chronic dialysis in California. The money men say, "My God! Who's going to support their habit?"

While the legislature allegedly regrets its decision, lobbies of patients and/or professionals fight desperately to maintain and increase their financial foothold—frustration and exasperation with the ins and outs of bureaucratic evasion sometimes leading to unexpected political and ideological configurations. Because there seems to be no source of funds other than the federal government that is capable of absorbing the potential burden of technological medicine, physicians and other professionals who, in different circumstances, might have been expected to form a bulwark of resistance to socialized medicine may now—for both humane and career reasons—begin to agitate in its favor.

Administrative Red Tape. The organization and distribution of state health-care funds is apparently so tangled in a web of duplication, evasion and conflicting purpose that the overall result is mass confusion. Presumably the outgrowth of legislative ambivalence, the present situation seems to be characterized by overlapping jurisdiction, conflict of policy, bureaucratic shuffling of responsibility, and a general lack of coordination and accountability. The following is a description given by a representative of a community hospital:

We've had reforms and we've reformed the reforms . . . . The providers are so entangled in confusion it is virtually impossible to get reimbursed. Blue Cross pays for MediCal. Welfare establishes eligibility. But the criteria of the Department of Health say *everybody* is eligible. These two agencies controvert each other. So they spend now and eligibility may be established six months from now, but the provider doesn't know whether it will be or not . . . . There's a subtle move—not to *refuse*—but to pressure the provider: 45% of the applications "disappear" or are returned for no valid reason and usually too late to resubmit them. Do you know that there are *218* reasons why a thirty-four item form can be returned? And after that there's "Other"! . . . I think they're deliberately stalling . . . . The provider is caught in a bind . . . . Eventually *somebody* has to reimburse *somebody!*

Loopholing is an informal device whereby officially proscribed actions may be unofficially redefined in terms that permit their accomplishment without open infraction of rules. There is considerable evidence to suggest that—even as lack of clear definition in the private insurance transaction sometimes leads to exploitable loopholes—confusion and ambiguity at the state level inadvertently leaves gaps whereby patients may escape some of the more devastating effects of eligibility rulings.

Paper Statements

Because loopholing must, of necessity, be evasive in method as well as in goal, it entails some special problems. In the case of dialysis patients, for instance, the medical staff or a case worker may point out the possibility of making "paper statements" that will indicate intent but may not be binding in actual commission. This is a task of considerable delicacy: such patterns of evasion are usually couched in subtle terms as a protection against the danger of legal and political repercussions.

. . . the social workers can't say right out what is going on. They have to hope the patients will catch on when they say things like, "Well, in your case I wouldn't worry too much!" Once in a while but not very often, they'll just come right out with it. But this is dangerous.

Some persons take loopholing easily in stride, seeing it in the light of a sensible and innocuous business arrangement—like maneuvering all possible personal advantages from income tax regulations—or as a more-or-less empty ritualistic gesture. Others view it as simple dishonesty and suffer accordingly—either because desperation leads them to comply with evasionary tactics

against the dictates of their scruples, in which case they suffer from the demeaning pangs of bad conscience, or because they do not, and bear, in consequence, the effects of financial anguish.

Patients as Prisoners

Loopholing can sometimes be accomplished by making a change in legal status (a device not infrequently employed by the urban poor). One such case was reported by a social worker:

The husband, who was the patient, was in his fifties but he had a young family from a second marriage . . . . It was a working class family: the mother had a job as a salesgirl and he was a garage attendant. When they applied for MediCal, the welfare guidelines for a family of their size were just impossible—if they kept their combined income they would just be working for the state. It was a total mess! Well, the upshot of the matter was that after he had been on dialysis for a month, the marriage broke up. They got a divorce. It was the only way to save the income . . . . The woman continued to take care of him and was obviously very fond of him.

To be successful, loopholing ususally depends upon an alliance of, for example, patient, case worker and eligibility worker. If participants do not share understandings of need or definitions of loyalty the situation may dissolve into one of personal rancor and agency infighting, with counter-attributions of bureaucratic inhumanity and fiscal irresponsibility being hurled back and forth to the apparent benefit of no one.

The patient, meanwhile, stands helplessly by. He is like a prisoner at the bar waiting for the result of adversary action to decide his fate: in this case, a negative decision will condemn him to the humiliation and distress of ultimate financial wipeout.

At present several treatment alternatives exist for dealing with chronic renal failure. Chief among these are center-based hemodialysis, home-based hemodialysis and kidney transplant. Each has major drawbacks and each offers its own special advantages. The patient is not likely to have much of a say in deciding on a method, first because he usually inherits certain preselected programs and equipment along with the physician and/or institution which circumstances have assigned him; second, because personal limitations—physical, social and economic—dictate what alternative may be practical or even possible in an individual case; and third, because medical paternalism is such that the situation of the patient as it is perceived by persons in decision-making relationships to him will greatly influence what choices are brought to his attention.

For center-based dialysis the patient comes to a central unit two or three times a week for treatment. There are four major advantages to this arrangement: constant supervision by personnel trained and equipped to deal with emergencies; relief for family members from some of the burden of work and anxiety; availability to many persons who lack a suitable home or who do not have a responsible assistant regularly available; usefulness in transient holding cases—patients awaiting a transplant, for example—where investment for home equipment would be impractical.

The chief disadvantages of center-based dialysis are higher cost, transportation problems and loss of independence. The high cost of center-based as compared with home-based dialysis is an interesting problem. In theory, centralization of services and multiple use of equipment suggest an economic efficiency that should produce the opposite effect. In practice, however, high hospital overhead, inefficient administrative practices (few centers, for example, are operated on a 24-hour schedule), a certain degree of professional and institutional profiteering, and competition among providers combine to make centralization more costly. The fact that dialysis centers have no assurance as to time or extent of reimbursement for their services makes it even harder to cut costs.

Home-based dialysis was initially designed as a program to reduce operating costs and to reach patients otherwise inaccessible for treatment—goals it has achieved with some success. Home dialysis does not eliminate the need for the center, which still provides training, medical—and sometimes mechanical—supervision and emergency care. In addition, it is customary for the patient to return to the center at specific intervals —perhaps four times a year—for a period of followup study and medical workup.

The chief drawback to home dialysis is probably the patient's need for a qualified home helper, one who can bear the physical, emotional and temporal burdens and meet high standards of intelligence, character and training. In addition, even well-qualified helpers are not unfailingly reliable: they fall ill themselves; they leave to get married; they simply grow tired of it all and quit. Their places are not readily filled.

Another problem that may beset the home-dialysis candidate is the fact that his insurance may not cover outpatient care. Unless he can convince his insuror that home dialysis is not in that category, the patient may have no choice but to accept center-based treatment, with all the irony of its additional cost.

A machine for home use can be either purchased or rented. Unless the patient has reason for anticipating an early release—by transplant, for example—it is cheaper to buy it. Once he has paid for the machine (an expense of, roughly, $4,000) and has completed the launching period of physical stabilization and home training (altogether, perhaps, a matter of $12,000) a patient's home dialysis expenses will probably range from $2,500 to $3,000 a year (as compared with estimates of center-based costs that run from $22,000 to $30,000 annually).

The funding process for home dialysis follows the pattern for center-based dialysis. There is an initial high cost period that may be cushioned by insurance as the patient is rescued and launched into his home-dialysis career. This is followed by a period of somewhat lower and more predictable cost for prolonged maintenance. Treadmilling problems typically attend this situation of continuing need and diminishing supply.

Kidney transplant, the only alternative to dialysis, is the most dramatic and theoretically the most promising of the solutions now available for chronic renal failure. Although an enormously expensive process, like any major surgery, the cost of transplant in no way compares with the financial burden imposed by a lifetime of dialysis. Furthermore, such expenses are often covered by major medical insurance policies, with the unfortunate exclusion of the financial burden of the donor. These latter can be considerable: the surgical process involved in removing a kidney is more difficult than that required for implanting one. However, there are a number of possibilities for defraying donor expenses, including such resources as personal savings, personal loans and charitable subscription.

Unfortunately, the possibility of rejection is high. Figures based on a one-year success rate suggest, very roughly, a 70 percent success with transplants from live

It is cheaper to buy a kidney machine than to rent one. After the initial purchase price (roughly $4,000) is paid and a launching period of physical stabilization and home training is completed (at a cost of about $12,000) a patient's home dialysis expenses range from $2,500 to $3,000 a year versus estimated center-based costs of $22,000 to $30,000 annually.

donors and a 50 percent or less chance with cadaver kidneys. Further, the antirejection regimen is itself unpleasant and restrictive. If rejection occurs, the patient is once more caught up on the treadmill—searching for funds and probably for kidney donors as well.

Groups of enterprising patients occasionally organize themselves into kidney clubs, which are usually oriented to consumer activities such as group buying in order to reduce the cost of supplies, pressuring insurance companies for certain policy redefinitions, challenging doctors on details of care, small-scale legislative lobbying and fund-raising for specific purposes. (One such project involved an effort to provide flight money for members in the event that an individual awaiting a transplant is suddenly informed, by computerized matching service, that a suitable kidney is available in a distant city.) The effectiveness of such organizations is seriously hampered by basic lack of group cohesion. Since the membership is composed of persons who are chronically ill, there is a marked dearth of the physical energy and stamina needed to sustain a concerted drive towards large objectives. Additionally, members, by and large, are committed to one another only at the financial level. For many, particularly those who exhibit the most vitality and talent for leadership, there seems to be a tendency to disavow the invalid identity and therefore resist any real involvement with persons who are ill, maintaining their own membership only as long as it seems to provide personal, material advantages. Participation in the group is thus apt to be ambivalent and transitory: members who, by good fortune or good management, find better solutions for their problems, typically withdraw from the club.

There are some who object to the present emphasis on the treatment of chronic renal failure, arguing that research might more profitably be directed towards prevention than toward cure. A spokesperson for the Northern California Kidney Foundation argues, for example, that a program of periodic urinalysis among school children might provide an effective early warning system, predicting potential renal failure at a phase in its trajectory when it may still be reversible.

Such views are, at present, much overshadowed by public and professional interest in the more dramatic possibilities of artificial organs and transplant. In addition, research findings tend to rule out the effectiveness of any single preventative program.

There is a significantly higher incidence of suicidal behavior among chronic renal failure patients than for the population at large or even as compared with victims of other chronic disease. Suicidal behavior refers both to deliberate action taken by the patient to terminate his own life and to his refusal to undergo treatment with an intent to accomplish the same end.

Over the past few years considerable attention has been directed to identifying predisposing psychological factors that may contribute to the self-destructive impulse. Personality variables such as ego strength and self-esteem have been defined and measured as factors controlling the suicidal tendency. It may be that being in bondage to the machine sends those patients with unresolved dependency conflicts into a state of suicidal despair.

The conditioning effect that circumstance and status can exert on the direction of personal decision is demonstrated in the following examples. The first was reported by the administrator of a dialysis center:

There are lots of cases where patients just haven't showed up. Patients have been referred to private centers, say, where they demand a deposit of $10,000, and they just toss in the towel. One man I know of personally—thirty-seven years of age with three children and $19,000 in the bank—elected to die. He was perfectly frank. He said if he went into treatment he would destroy his family.

Another patient—a 27-year-old father of two young children—faced a different situation and, in accordance with his perception of it, reached a different decision:

. . . the way I see it, I'm going to be in the hole all my life. I worry about bills. I worry about a change in the laws that will cut off what we're getting now. Most of my worry is money . . . . It's my kids. They're forcing me to stay alive. I keep seeing myself caring for them until they're on their own. I imagine what it will be like for them if I die. They'll hardly have anything. My wife didn't even finish high school and she wouldn't be able to take care of them . . . . They'd hardly get anything to eat, maybe. The thought keeps me going. I want to live . . . .

In neither of these cases did the patient—by demeanor or behavior—manifest lack of self-esteem or neurotic fear of dependency. Opposite decisions were apparently reached according to real differences in external conditions.

The funding process pursued by the renal failure patient dramatically highlights, by the urgency of its precarious balance between financial wipeout and death, a course that is probably typical of that to which desperate persons may, in the end, be always reduced—including crisis-oriented, *ad hoc* decision-making and rule-evading loopholing tactics that undermine personal morale, social values and, possibly, in the end, established social systems.

Future Proposals

A number of proposals for alleviating the distress of chronic renal failure patients have emerged from our study of the problem:

☐ That insurance carriers reimburse claimants for outpatient treatment.

☐ That unions assign trained persons to act as insurance advisors to their members, on an individual basis.

☐ That providers of dialysis treatment work together to relieve expensive duplication and overlap that often result from competitive efforts.

☐ That dialysis centers be operated on a 24-hour basis.

☐ That paramedical personnel be trained in hemodialysis techniques in order to assist home-care patients, if not on a regular, at least on an emergency basis.

☐ That prepaid transportation service be provided for center-based patients—urban, suburban and interurban.

☐ That some relaxation be made in insurance regulations in order to encourage businesses to employ chronically ill individuals who are able and willing to work.

☐ That state health insurance policies and their administration be completely reorganized in order to cut red tape, to give health care providers a reasonable basis for predicting the time and extent of reimbursement for services rendered, and to remove health care assistance from the restrictions of welfare eligibility rules.

The implementation of any or all such suggestions would bring some measure of relief to the individual patient. It would not, however, eliminate the basic problem and the crisis-to-crisis course of the funding process. That will happen only when we are ready to take the financial responsibility for our espoused humanitarianism and pay for a federal health care program.

FURTHER READING

"Psychosocial Aspects of Hemodialysis" by George L. Bailey in *Hemodialysis: Principles and Practice* (New York: Academic, 1973).

Health and the Family edited by Charles Crawford (New York: Macmillan, 1971). A collection of essays describing the relationships between health and family functions.

"Help Patterns in Severe Illness: The Roles of Kin Network, Non-Family Resources and Institutions" by Sydney H. Croog, Alberta Lipson and Sol Levine, *Journal of Marriage and the Family*, February 1972.

Sickness and Society by Raymond Deff and August Hollingshead (New York: Harper & Row, 1968).

Cancer Ward by Alexander Solzhenitsyn (New York: Dial, 1968).

"Funding for End-Stage Renal Patients" by Margaret B. Wilkins in *Hemodialysis: Principles and Practice*, ed. George L. Bailey (New York: Academic, 1973).

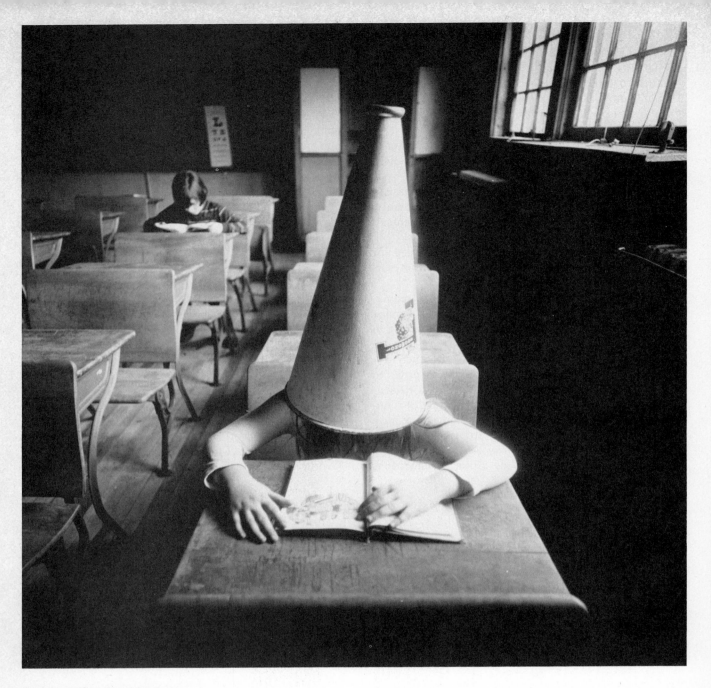

SAMUEL BOWLES

Unequal Education and the Reproduction of the Class Structure

Education has long been the chosen instrument of American social reformers. Whatever the ills that beset our society, education is thought to be the cure. Most Americans share the faith—voiced by Horace Mann over a century ago—that education is the "great equalizer." With access to public schools, the children of every class and condition have an equal chance to develop their talents and make a success of themselves. It is our public system of education—so the conventional wisdom goes—that guarantees an open society where any citizen can rise from the lowliest background to high social position according to his ability and efforts.

The record of educational history in the United States and scrutiny of the present state of our colleges and schools lend little support to this comforting optimism. Rather, the available data suggest an alternative interpretation. Apparently our schools have evolved not as part of a pursuit of equality but rather to meet the needs of capitalist employers for a disciplined and skilled labor force and to provide a mechanism for social control in the interests of political stability. As the economic importance of skilled and well-educated labor has grown, inequalities in the school system have become increasingly important in reproducing the class structure from one generation to the next. In fact, the United States school system is pervaded by class inequalities which have shown little sign of diminishing over the last half-century. The evidently unequal control over school boards and other decision-making bodies in education does not provide a sufficient explanation of the persistence and pervasiveness of these inequalities. Although the unequal distribution of political power serves to maintain inequalities in education, their origins are to be found outside the political sphere in the class structure itself and in the class subcultures typical of capitalist societies. Thus unequal education has its roots in the very class structure which it serves to legitimize and reproduce.

In colonial America, as in most pre-capitalist societies of the past, the basic productive unit was the family. For the vast majority of male adults, work was self-directed and was performed without direct supervision. Though constrained by poverty, ill health, the low level of technological development and occasional interferences by the political authorities, a man had considerable leeway in choosing his working hours, what to produce and how to produce it. While great inequalities in wealth, political power and other aspects of status normally existed, differences in the degree of autonomy in work were relatively minor, particularly when compared with what was to come.

Parents as Teachers

Transmitting the necessary productive skills to the children as they grew up proved to be a simple task, not because the work was devoid of skill, but because the quite substantial skills required were virtually unchanging from generation to generation, and because the transition to the world of work did not require that the child adapt to a wholly new set of social relationships. The child learned the concrete skills and adapted to the social relations of production through learning by doing within the family.

All of this changed with the advent of the capitalist economy in which the vast majority of economically active individuals relinquished control over their labor power in return for wages or salaries and in which the non-labor means of production were privately owned. The extension of capitalist production (particularly the factory system) undermined the role of the family as the major unit of both socialization and production. Small farmers were driven off the land or competed out of business. Cottage industry was destroyed. Ownership of the means of production became heavily concentrated in the hands of the owners of capital and land. Increasingly, production was carried on in large organizations in which a small management group directed the work activities of the entire labor force. The social relations of production—the authority structure, the prescribed types of behavior and response characteristic of the work place—became increasingly distinct from those of the family.

The divorce of the worker from control over production—from control over his own labor—is particularly important in understanding the role of schooling in capitalist societies. The resulting social division of labor between controllers and the controlled is a crucial aspect of the class structure and will be seen as an important barrier to the achievement of social-class equality in schooling.

While undermining both family and church—the main institutions of socialization—the development of the capitalist system created at the same time an environment which would ultimately challenge the political order. Workers were thrown together in oppressive factories, and the isolation which had helped to maintain quiescence in earlier, widely dispersed peasant populations was broken down. With an increasing number of families uprooted from the land, the workers' search for a living resulted in large-scale labor migrations. Transient (and even foreign) elements came to constitute a major segment of the population and began to pose seemingly insurmountable problems of assimilation, integration and control. Inequalities of wealth became more apparent and were less easily justified and less readily accepted. The simple legitimizing ideologies of the earlier period—for example, the divine right of kings and the divine origin of social rank—fell under the capitalist attack on the royalty and the traditional landed interests. The broadening of the electorate, first sought by the capitalist class in the struggle against the entrenched interests of the pre-capitalist period, soon threatened to become an instrument for the growing power of the working class. Having risen to political power, the capitalist class sought a mechanism to insure social control and political stability.

An institutional crisis was at hand. The outcome, in virtually all capitalist countries, was the rise of mass education. In the United States, the many advantages of schooling as a socialization process were quickly perceived. The early proponents of the rapid expansion of schooling argued that education could perform many of the socialization functions which earlier had been centered in the family and to a lesser extent in the church.

An ideal preparation for factory work was found in the social relations of the school, specifically in its emphasis on discipline, punctuality, acceptance of authority outside the family and individual accountability for one's work. A manufacturer writing to the Massachusetts State Board of Education from Lowell in 1841 commented:

> I have never considered mere knowledge. . .as the only advantage derived from a good education. . . . [Workers with more education possess] a higher and better state of morals, are more orderly and respectful in their deportment, and more ready to comply with the wholesome and necessary regulations of an establishment. . . . In times of agitation, on account of some change in regulations or wages, I have always looked to the most intelligent, best educated and the most moral for support. The ignorant and uneducated I have generally found the most turbulent and troublesome, acting under the impulse of excited passion and jealousy.

The social relations of the school would replicate the social

Unequal Education and the Reproduction of the Class Structure

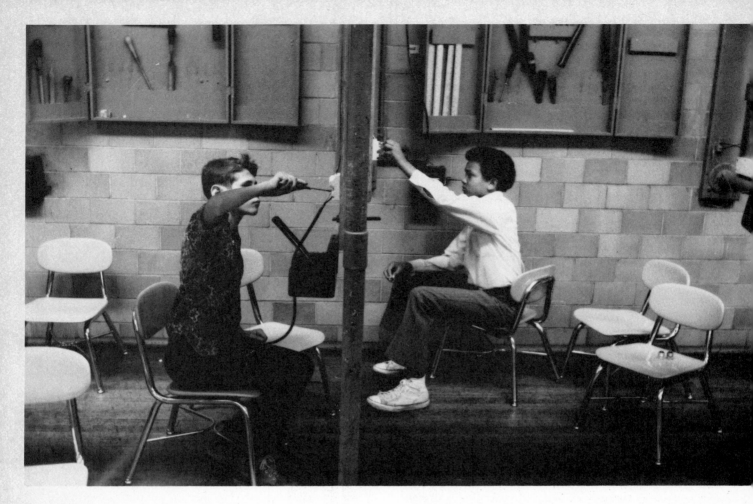

relations of the workplace and thus help young people adapt to the social division of labor. Schools would further lead people to accept the authority of the state and its agents—the teachers—at a young age, in part by fostering the illusion of the benevolence of the government in its relations with citizens. Moreover, because schooling would ostensibly be open to all, one's position in the social division of labor could be portrayed as the result not of birth, but of one's own efforts and talents. And if the children's everyday experiences with the structure of schooling were insufficient to inculcate the correct views and attitudes, the curriculum itself would be made to embody the bourgeois ideology. Thomas Cooper, an American economist, wrote in 1828:

> Education universally extended throughout the community will tend to disabuse the working class of people in respect of a notion that has crept into the minds of our mechanics and is gradually prevailing, that manual labor is at present very inadequately rewarded, owing to combinations of the rich against the poor; that mere mental labor is comparatively worthless; that property or wealth ought not to be accumulated or transmitted; that to take interest on money lent or profit on capital employed is unjust. . . . The mistaken and ignorant people who entertain these fallacies as truths will learn, when they have the opportunity of learning, that the institution of political society originated in the protection of property.

The movement for public elementary and secondary education in the United States originated in the nineteenth century in states dominated by the burgeoning industrial capitalist class, most notably in Massachusetts. It spread rapidly to all parts of the country except the South. In Massachusetts the extension of elementary education was in large measure a response to industrialization and to the need for social control of the Irish and other non-Yankee workers recruited to work in the mills. The fact that some working people's movements had demanded free instruction should not obscure the basically coercive nature of the extension of schooling. In many parts of the country, schools were literally imposed upon the workers.

A system of class stratification developed within this rapidly expanding educational system. Children of the social elite normally attended private schools. Because working-class children tended to leave school early, the class composition of the public high schools was distinctly more elite than that of the public primary schools. And as a university education ceased to be merely training for teaching or the divinity and became important in gaining access to the pinnacles of the business world, upper-class families increasingly used their money and influence to get their children into the best universities, often at the expense of the children of less elite families.

Around the turn of the century, large numbers of working-class (and particularly immigrant) children began attending high schools. At the same time, a system of class stratification developed within secondary education.

The older democratic ideology of the common school—

In a well-integrated high school in the Boston area, a part of the training for the boys is "electrical shop." They learn how to repair switches, junction boxes and so forth. Here they are practicing on a switchboard.

that the same curriculum should be offered to all children—gave way to the "progressive" insistence that education should be tailored to the "needs of the child." The superintendent of the Boston schools summed up the change in 1908:

> Until very recently [the schools] have offered equal opportunity for all to receive *one kind* of education, but what will make them democratic is to provide opportunity for all to receive such education as will fit them *equally well* for their particular life work.

In the interests of providing an education relevant to the later life of the students, vocational schools and tracks were developed for the children of working families. The academic curriculum was preserved for those who would later have the opportunity to make use of book learning either in college or in white-collar employment. This and other educational reforms of the progressive education movement reflected an implicit assumption of the immutability of the class structure.

Tracking by Social Class

The frankness with which students were channeled into curriculum tracks on the basis of their social-class background raised serious doubts concerning the openness of the class structure. The apparent unfairness of the selection and tracking procedures was disguised (though not mitigated much) by another "progressive" reform—"objective" educational testing. Particularly after World War I, the capitulation of the schools to business values and the cult of efficiency led to the increased use of intelligence and scholastic achievement testing as an ostensibly unbiased means of measuring school outputs and classifying students. The complementary growth of the guidance counseling profession allowed much of the channeling to proceed from the students' own well-counselled choices, thus adding an apparent element of voluntarism to the mechanisms perpetuating the class structure.

As schooling became the standard for assigning children positions in the class structure, it played a major part in legitimizing the structure itself. But at the same time it undermined the simple processes by which the upper class had preserved its position from one generation to the next—the inheritance of physical capital. When education and skills play an important role in the hierarchy of production, the inheritance of capital from one generation to the next is not enough to reproduce the social division of labor. Rather skills broadly defined and educational credentials must somehow be passed on within the family. It is in furthering this modern form of class structure that the school plays a fundamental role. Children whose parents occupy positions at the top of the occupational hierarchy receive more and better schooling than working-class children. Inequalities in years of schooling are particularly evident. My analysis of United States Census data indicate that if we define social-class standing by the income, occupation and educational level of the parents, a child from the 90th percentile in the class distribution may expect on the average to achieve over four-and-a-half more years of schooling than a child from the tenth percentile.

Even among those who had graduated from high school, children of families earning less than $3,000 per year were over six times as likely not to attend college as were the children of families earning over $15,000.

Because schooling is heavily subsidized by the general taxpayer, the longer a child attends school, the more public resources he has access to. Further, public expenditure per student in four-year colleges greatly exceeds that in elementary schools; those who stay in school longer receive an increasingly large *annual* public subsidy. In the school year 1969-70, per-pupil expenditures of federal, state and local funds were $1490 for colleges and universities and $747 for primary and secondary schools. Even at the elementary level, schools in low income neighborhoods tend to be less well endowed with equipment, books, teachers and other inputs into the educational process.

The inequalities in schooling go deeper than these simple measures. Differences in rules, expected modes of behavior and opportunities for choice are most glaring when we compare levels of schooling. Note the wide range of choice over curriculum, life style and allocation of time afforded to college students compared with the obedience and respect for authority expected in high school. Differentiation also occurs within each level of schooling. One needs only to compare the social relations of a junior college with those of an elite four-year college, or those of a working-class high school with those of a wealthy suburban high school, for verification of this point. It is consistent with this pattern that the play-oriented, child-centered pedagogy of the progressive movement found little acceptance outside of private schools and public schools in wealthy communities.

Mirror of the Factory

These differences in socialization patterns do not arise by accident. Rather, they are the product of class differences in educational objectives and expectations held by parents and educators alike and of differences in student responsiveness to various patterns of teaching and control. Further, a teacher in an understaffed, ill-equipped school may be compelled to resort to authoritarian tactics whether she wants to or not. Lack of resources precludes having small intimate classes, a multiplicity of elective courses, specialized teachers (except disciplinary personnel), free time for the teachers and the free space required for a more open, flexible educational environment. Socialization in such a school comes to mirror that of the factory; students are treated as raw materials on a production line. There is a high premium on obedience and punctuality and there are few opportunities for independent, creative work or individualized attention by teachers.

Even where working-class children attend a well-financed school they do not receive the same treatment as the children of the rich. Class stratification within a given school is achieved through tracking and differential participation in extracurricular activities; it is reinforced by attitudes of teachers and particularly guidance personnel who expect working-class children to do poorly, to terminate schooling early and to end up in jobs similar to their parents.

Not surprisingly, the results of schooling differ greatly

for children of different social classes. On nationally standardized achievement tests, children whose parents were themselves highly educated outperform by a wide margin the children of parents with less education. A recent study revealed, for example, that among white high school seniors, those whose parents were in the top education decile were on the average well over three grade levels ahead of those whose parents were in the bottom decile.

Given class differences in scholastic achievement, class inequalities in college attendance are to be expected. Thus one might be tempted to argue that the data in Table I are simply a reflection of unequal scholastic achievement in high school and do not reflect any additional social-class inequalities peculiar to the process of college admission. This view, so comforting to the admissions personnel in our elite universities, is unsupported by the available data, some of which is presented in Table 2. Access to a college education is highly unequal, even for students of the same measured academic ability.

And inequalities of educational opportunity show no signs of abatement. In fact, data from a recent United States Census survey reported in Table 3 indicate that graduation from college is at least as dependent on one's class background now as it was 50 years ago. Considering access to all levels of education, the data suggest that the number of years of schooling attained by a child depends upon the social-class standing of the father slightly more in the recent period than it did at the beginning of the century.

The pervasive and persistent inequalities in the United States system of education pose serious problems of interpretation. If the costs of education borne by students and their families were very high, or if nepotism were rampant, or if formal segregation of pupils by social class were practiced, or if educational decisions were made by a select few whom we might call the power elite, it would not be difficult to explain the continued inequalities in the system. The problem is to reconcile the above empirical findings with the facts of our society as we perceive them: public and virtually tuition-free education at all levels, few legal instruments for the direct implementation of class segregation, a limited role for contacts or nepotism in the achievement of high status or income, a commitment (at the rhetorical level at least) to equality of educational opportunity and a system of control of education which if not particularly democratic extends far beyond anything

Table 1 — College Attendance in 1967 among High School Graduates, by Family Income

Family income	Percent who did not attend college
Total	53.1
under $3,000	80.2
$3,000 to $3,999	67.7
$4,000 to $5,999	63.7
$6,000 to $7,499	58.9
$7,500 to $9,999	49.0
$10,000 to $14,999	38.7
$15,000 and over	13.3

Refers to high school seniors in October 1965 who subsequently graduated. Bureau of the Census, *Current Population Report,* 1969. College attendance refers to both two- and four-year institutions.

Table 2 — Probability of College Entry for a Male Who Has Reached Grade 11

		Socioeconomic quartiles			
		Low			High
		1	2	3	4
	1 Low	.06	.12	.13	.26
Ability	2	.13	.15	.29	.36
quartiles	3	.25	.34	.45	.65
	4 High	.48	.70	.73	.87

Based on a large sample of U.S. high school students studied by Project Talent at the University of Pittsburgh, 1966.
The socioeconomic index is a composite measure including family income, father's occupation and education, mother's education and so forth. The ability scale is a composite of tests measuring general academic aptitude.

resembling a power elite. The attempt to reconcile these apparently discrepant facts leads us back to a consideration of the social division of labor, the associated class cultures and the exercise of class power.

The social division of labor—based on the hierarchical structure of production—gives rise to distinct class subcultures, each of which has its own values, personality traits and expectations. The social relations of production characteristic of advanced capitalist societies (and many socialist societies) are most clearly illustrated in the bureaucracy and hierarchy of the modern corporation. Occupational roles in the capitalist economy may be grouped according to the degree of independence and

Table 3 — Among Sons Who Had Reached High School, Percentage Who Graduated from College, By Son's Age and Father's Level of Education

			Father's Education					
	Likely dates of	Less than 8 years	Some high school		High school graduate		Some college or more	
Son's age in 1962	college graduation		Percent graduating	Ratio to less than 8 years	Percent graduating	Ratio to less than 8 years	Percent graduating	Ratio to less than 8 years
25-34	1950-1959	07.6	17.4	2.29	25.6	3.37	51.9	6.83
35-44	1940-1949	08.6	11.9	1.38	25.3	2.94	53.9	6.27
45-54	1930-1939	07.7	09.8	1.27	15.1	1.96	36.9	4.79
55-64	1920-1929	08.9	09.8	1.10	19.2	2.16	29.8	3.35

Based on U.S. Census data for 1962 as reported in William G. Spady, "Educational Mobility and Access: Growth and Paradoxes," *American Journal of Sociology,* November 1967.
Assumes college graduation at age 22.

control exercised by the person holding the job. The personality attributes associated with the adequate performance of jobs in occupational categories defined in this broad way differ considerably, some apparently requiring independence and internal discipline, and others emphasizing such traits as obedience, predictability and willingness to subject oneself to external controls.

These personality attributes are developed primarily at a young age, both in the family and to a lesser extent in secondary socialization institutions such as schools. Daily experience in the work place reinforces these traits in adults. Because people tend to marry within their own class, both parents are likely to have a similar set of these fundamental personality traits. Thus children of parents occupying a given position in the occupational hierarchy grow up in homes where child-rearing methods and perhaps even the physical surroundings tend to develop personality characteristics appropriate to adequate job performance in the occupational roles of the parents. The children of managers and professionals are taught self-reliance within a broad set of constraints; the children of production-line workers are taught conformity and obedience.

Melvin Kohn summarizes his extensive empirical work on class structure and parental values as follows:

> Whether consciously or not, parents tend to impart to their children lessons derived from the condition of life of their own class—and thus help to prepare their children for a similar class position. . . . The conformist values and orientation of lower- and working-class parents are inappropriate for training children to deal with the problems of middle-class and professional life. . . . The family, then, functions as a mechanism for perpetuating inequality.

This relation between parents' class position and child's personality attributes is reinforced by schools and other social institutions. Teachers, guidance counselors and school administrators ordinarily encourage students to develop aspirations and expectations typical of their social class, even if the child tends to have deviant aspirations.

It is true that schools introduce some common elements of socialization for all students. Discipline, respect for property, competition and punctuality are part of implicit curricula. Yet the ability of a school to appreciably change a child's future is severely limited. However, the responsiveness of children to different types of schooling seems highly dependent upon the personality traits, values and expectations which have been developed through the family. Furthermore, since children spend a small amount of time in school—less than a quarter of their waking hours over the course of a year—schools are probably more effective where they complement and reinforce rather than oppose the socialization processes of the home and neighborhood. Not surprisingly, this relationship between family socialization and that of the schools reproduces patterns of class culture from generation to generation.

Among adults the differing daily work experiences of people reinforce these patterns of class culture. The reward structure of the workplace favors the continued development of traits such as obedience and acceptance of authority among workers. Conversely, those occupying directing roles in production are rewarded for the capacity to make decisions and exert authority. Thus the operation of the incentive structure of the job stabilizes and reproduces patterns of class culture. The operation of the labor market translates these differences in class culture into income inequalities and occupational hierarchies. Recent work by Herbert Gintis and other economists shows that the relation between schooling and economic success cannot be explained by the effect of schooling on intellectual capacity. Rather, the economic success of individuals with higher educational attainments is explained by their highly rewarded personality characteristics which facilitate entry into the upper echelons of the production hierarchy. These personality characteristics, originating in the work experiences of one's parents, transmitted in turn to children through early socialization practices and reinforced in school and on the job are an important vehicle for the reproduction of the social division of labor.

But the argument thus far is incomplete. The perpetuation of inequality through the schooling system has been represented as an almost automatic, self-enforcing mechanism, operating through the medium of class culture. An important further dimension is added to this interpretation if we note that positions of control in the productive hierarchy tend to be associated with positions of political influence. Given the disproportionate share of political power held by the upper classes and their capacity for determining the accepted patterns of behavior and procedures, to define the national interest and to control the ideological and institutional context in which educational decisions are made, it is not surprising to find that resources are allocated unequally among school tracks, between schools serving different classes and between levels of schooling. The same configuration of power results in curricula, methods of instruction and criteria which, though often seemingly innocuous and ostensibly even egalitarian, serves to maintain the unequal system.

Illusion of Fair Treatment

Take the operation of one of these rules of the game—the principle that excellence in schooling should be rewarded. The upper class defines excellence in terms on which upper-class children tend to excel (for example, scholastic achievement). Adherence to this principle yields inegalitarian outcomes (for example, unequal access to higher education) while maintaining the appearance of fair treatment. Those who would defend the "reward excellence" principle on the grounds of efficient selection to ensure the most efficent use of educational resources might ask themselves this: why should colleges admit those with the highest college entrance examination board scores? Why not the lowest or the middle? According to conventional standards of efficiency, the rational social objective of the college is to render the greatest increment in individual capacities ("value added," to the economist), not to produce the most illustrious graduating class ("gross output"). Thus the principle of rewarding excellence does not appear to be motivated by a concern for the efficient use of educational resources. Rather it serves to legitimize the unequal consequences of schooling.

Though cognitive capacities are relatively unimportant in the determination of income and occupational success, the reward of intellectual ability in school plays an important role. The "objective" testing of scholastic achievement and relatively meritocratic system of grading encourages the illusion that promotion and rewards are distributed fairly. The close relationship between educational attainments and later occupational success further masks the paramount importance of race and social-class background for getting ahead.

At the same time, the institution of objectively administered tests of performance serves to allow a limited amount of upward mobility among exceptional children of the lower class, thus providing further legitimation of the operations of the social system by giving some credence to the myth of widespread mobility.

The operation of the "reward excellence" rule illustrates the symbiosis between the political and economic power of the upper class. Adherence to the rule has the effect of generating unequal consequences via a mechanism which operates largely outside the political system. As long as one adheres to the reward (academic) excellence principle, the responsibility for unequal results in schooling appears to rest outside the upper class, often in some fault of the poor—such as their class culture—which is viewed as lying beyond the reach of political action or criticism.

Thus it appears that the consequences of an unequal distribution of political power among classes complement the results of class culture in maintaining an educational system which has thus far been capable of transmitting status from generation to generation, and capable in addition of political survival in the formally democratic and egalitarian environment of the contemporary United States.

The role of the schools in reproducing and legitimizing the social division of labor has recently been challenged by popular egalitarian movements. At the same time, the educational system is showing signs of internal structural weakness. I have argued elsewhere that overproduction of highly educated workers by universities and graduate schools and a breakdown of authority at all levels of schooling are not passing phenomena, but deeply rooted in the pattern of growth and structural change in the advanced capitalist economy. These two developments suggest that fundamental change in the schooling process may soon be possible.

But it should be clear that educational equality cannot be achieved through changes in the school system alone. Attempts at educational reform may move us closer to that objective (if, in their failure, they lay bare the unequal nature of our school system and destroy the illusion of unimpeded mobility through education). Yet if the record of the last century and a half of educational reforms is any guide, we should not expect radical change in education to result from the efforts of reformers who confine their attention to the schools. My interpretation of the educational consequences of class culture and class power suggests that past educational reform movements failed because they sought to eliminate educational inequalities without challenging the basic institutions of capitalism.

Efforts to equalize education through changes in school finance, compensatory education and similar programs will at best scratch the surface of inequality. As long as jobs are structured so that some have power over many and others have power over nothing—as long as the social division of labor persists—educational inequality will be built into U.S. society.

FURTHER READING

"Contradictions in U.S. Higher Education" by Samuel Bowles in *Political Economy: Radical vs. Orthodox Approaches*, edited by James Weaver (Boston: Allyn & Bacon, 1972).

The Student as Nigger by Jerry Farber (New York: Pocket Books, 1970).

Pedagogy of the Oppressed by Paulo Freire (St. Louis, Mo.: Herder, 1972).

The New Assault on Equality: IQ and Social Stratification edited by Alan Gartner, Colin Greer, and Frank Riessman (New York: Harper & Row, 1974).

Culture Against Man by Jules Henry (New York: Random House, 1963).

Inequality: A Reassessment of the Effect of Family and Schooling in America by Christopher Jencks (New York: Basic Books, 1972).

The Irony of Early School Reform by Michael B. Katz (Cambridge, Mass.: Harvard University Press, 1968).

Death at an Early Age by Jonathan Kozol (Boston: Houghton Mifflin, 1967).

110 Livingston Street by David Rogers (New York: Random House, 1968).

Crisis in the Classroom by C. Silberman (New York: Random House, 1970).

MICHAEL A. STEGMAN

The New Mythology of Housing

Good housing can make good people, even out of poor people. Such, cruelly compressed, was the cherished belief of housing reformers as they campaigned 30 years ago for low-rent public housing for the urban poor. By now, needless to say, that belief has been exposed as a myth. It has been shown to rest on faulty assumptions not only with respect to why poor people are poor, but also about what can be done to make them "better." As one student of urban affairs put it:

Once upon a time, we thought that if we could only get our problem families out of those dreadful slums, then papa would stop taking dope, mama would stop chasing around, and Junior would stop carrying a knife. Well, we've got them in a nice apartment with modern kitchens and a recreation center. And they're the same bunch of bastards they always were.

This is to state the disillusionment rather crudely, to be sure; but that is exactly the trouble with founding public policy on mythic grounds. The poor are held to be incurable. The reformers who helped spread the faulty gospel are crucified as false prophets or fade away as the public action they helped get going fails to solve the "problems." But, worse than this, their failures never seem to stimulate any attempts to correct the myths or modify the procedures. Rather, they serve only to weaken subsequent efforts to rally political support for further public action. In the case of low-rent public housing, the whole purpose of the program—the provision of decent shelter for the poor—was smeared along with the exposure of its guiding myth.

Today, the public housing program goes without its traditional liberal and intellectual support; it goes without union support; and it goes without any broad demand among the electorate. And as for the poor, they go without decent housing. As John P. Dean wrote 20 years ago in a review of our disappointing efforts in housing reform "... in the meantime, the patient has continued to sicken."

What I want to do here is take a hard look at what I believe are the *emerging* myths concerning community development and housing. It is only prudent to acknowledge that it would be much less risky to wait another decade or so to pass judgment. Yet by discussing the emerging

It is naive and seriously misleading to blame slumlords for the disaster in urban housing.

myths before they become crystalized, I may be able to raise some fundamental questions about their utility as a basis for public action. Moreover, the time seems particularly ripe now that the federal government has passed a multibillion dollar housing bill.

The Model Cities program provides a sophisticated example of current thinking about the complexities of the slum housing nexus. Its pronouncements at least indicate a heightened awareness that housing and social service needs are closely interrelated and might best be met simultaneously with a global attack. This is a far cry from the "good housing = good people" theory of years past, but I still get the nagging feeling that the emerging housing reform myths are going to be equally counter-productive.

The old myths developed as justifications for direct federal intervention in an area previously dominated by the private sector. The new myths are rationalizations for particular federal responses to housing problems that have remained unsolved in spite of earlier governmental involvement. These myths, which are concerned more with notions of how the problems can be solved than with their basic causes, can be summarized as follows:

■ Myths surrounding the nature of the owners of substandard housing.

■ Mythical explanations of the potential role of nonprofit sponsors in solving the nation's housing problems.

■ Myths involving the potential value of adopting a systems approach to neighborhood renewal.

■ Myths surrounding emerging efforts to involve unemployed ghetto manpower in the rehabilitation of slum housing.

■ Myths explaining why low-income *ownership* programs should be expected to solve those same social problems that the previous low-income minimum *rental* programs could not solve.

Myth #1: Slumlords

. . . the slumlord, that small body of landlords [who] are out to squeeze every last dollar out of the property as quickly as they can, regardless of the consequences in terms of human life, suffering and sickness. It is against this small minority that battle must be given—constant, unremitting and unrelenting battle.—*Former Mayor Robert Wagner of New York.*

Believers in this specimen myth frequently wind up their "argument" with the observation of David Hunter that all owners of substandard housing "look as though they had spent their childhoods drowning their playmates" and then grew up to play that same deadly game as an adult—only now in more subtle and painful ways.

This amateurish personality profile of the "typical slumlord" tends to confuse the real issues and has served to distort our national housing policy since the end of World War II. It has encouraged a myopic view of the housing problem, and it has demonstrably provided an outright faulty basis for public action. The stereotype of the slumlord strongly implies that the owners of substandard housing are largely responsible for our chronic housing problem, simply because they are evil men. This is not so for at least four reasons.

First, the stereotype doesn't stand up statistically. There are upwards of six million substandard housing units in our nation's cities and literally hundreds of thousands of individual landlords. Can *all* their owners match the above grotesque? Surely it is more reasonable to assume that their personal characteristics distribute in a pattern similar to that found in any large sample of population.

Second, slumlords and tenants enjoy, if that's the word, a perfectly symbiotic relationship; that is, they need each other. The owners need the poor and troubled because few others would consider living in depressed housing; and who but the poor and troubled must seek the cheapest possible shelter? Yet, this is no justification for blaming the owners for creating the shortages in decent low-rent housing that mark the inner cores of our cities. The notion

that owners of substandard units cause the sickness and suffering that plague the unfortunate families who dwell there sounds suspiciously like an inversion of the "good housing = good people" theory.

Third, the charge that most owners of slum properties are making excess profits may be seriously questioned, both within the real estate industry and in comparison with other major industries. While financial information on slums is extremely scarce, such relatively recent works as Woody Klein's *Let in the Sun* include some economic data that will disconcert liberal believers in the bloated slumlord myth. For example, the 36-unit tenement Klein wrote about grossed nearly one-half million dollars over a 60-year period ending in 1966. The New York City Planning Commission has estimated that such structures generally return around 36 percent of gross revenues on a net basis. With respect to the building in question, then, aggregate net revenues for the 60 years would have amounted to approximately $180,000, or an annual average of $3,000. Since fixed expenses (taxes, water and sewer charges and insurance) of such substandard tenements average 25 percent of gross revenues, it's obvious that when you then add on fuel and minimal maintenance costs, there will be little left over for major repairs. In fact, Klein estimates that in order to bring the tenement up to the standard specified in New York City's housing code, annual operating expenses would have to increase by $4,000 per year, which means an annual loss of $3,278. Undermaintenance therefore may be not only a rational, but a necessary means of survival in an industry beset with increased unionization and its concomitant, rising costs, as well as tenant incomes that remain either the same or fall over the years and the same or lower levels of occupancy.

Biased View of Landlords

Fourth, it is an incontrovertible fact that almost half (47 percent) of our national housing inventory was built before 1929. Our cities are getting older. And in housing, as in humans, aging causes problems, but it seems naive to place the responsibility for such problems at the feet of the landlord. Old structures are found in old neighborhoods, and more and more of them are becoming slums. Data from the South Los Angeles area show that the proportion of substandard units in that community increased from 18 percent to 34 percent between 1960 and 1965. In New York City the number of slum housing units went from 475,-000 in 1960 to an estimated 800,000 in late 1968. The Department of Labor estimates that 600,000 rural and semirural individuals are migrating into large urban areas each year. The housing crisis will surely increase as greater pressures are exerted upon an already aged and obsolete housing stock.

By adopting the myth of the slumlord, the public forecloses any consideration of an alliance with the owner of substandard housing in an attempt to find an enlightened approach to the problem. Also written off is much of the huge investment locked into the existing low-rent private housing stock.

Myth #2: Nonprofit Sponsors

Top housing officials have apparently accepted the myth of the slumlord. They have washed their hands of the individual low-rent property owner. A measure of their disenchantment is the increasing federal attention being paid to such nonprofit institutions as churches, foundations, fraternal organizations and labor unions in their low- and moderate-income housing efforts. In fact, a program was initiated in 1961 which could be interpreted as designed to stimulate such housing efforts. Known by the call letters 221(d)(3), it provides mortgage monies at low interest rates to nonprofit sponsors. Yet at this writing only 1,568 rental units have been rehabilitated under 221(d)(3), while only 46,565 new units have been built.

The meager contributions of 221(d)(3) can be readily explained. First, there has been an insufficient and uneven flow of federal funds to purchase below-market mortgages. Second, Congress cannot make up its mind whether the Federal Housing Authority should continue to broaden its social perspective, or model its role on that of a conservative Back Bay banker. Third and finally, the federal requirements for obtaining the financing are so complex and difficult to satisfy, that only the most energetic and well-staffed sponsors can succeed in getting any. The 221(d)(3) program requires filing forms for preapplication, application, precommitment processing, preinitial closing, initial closing and final closing stages—more than 40 forms in all. Urban America, Inc., recently published a guide to the program which is 359 pages long.

Simply put, the concept of nonprofit sponsors such as churches developing housing throughout the nation's urban areas on a scale large enough to have any measurable impact is basically ill conceived. When one considers the incredibly large number of steps involved in the residential development process, one has to conclude that the average church is just not prepared to carry the burden of solving even a fraction of our national housing problem. And as for the typical Negro church in the ghetto, the most appropriate potential sponsor for low-income housing, it unfortunately has even less resources and know-how.

It is true that some housing has been constructed under the 221(d)(3) program. The Kate Maramount Foundation in Chicago, the sponsor of nearly one-half of the 1,568 rental units rehabilitated under the program to date, has certainly mastered its technicalities. Yet, if Maramount were to concentrate all its future activities on Chicago's west side, and if it were able to rehabilitate 500 units a year under the program, which is highly unlikely, it would take 100 years to eliminate substandard housing in that community alone—assuming that no additional units became substandard in the interim. Obviously, there are not enough Maramounts, nor is there sufficient time for them to act. The scale of the problem is simply too great to be handled in the manner implied in the program.

There are two additional difficulties with this approach that do not show on paper, but which we must anticipate lest they pop up when unsuspecting organizations attempt to duplicate the work of Maramount. First, the open market is a hostile environment for anyone—private developer, church, non-profit institution or whoever—whose stated objective is to develop housing for black families outside the established ghettos. Frequently it becomes extremely difficult for indigenous institutions such as churches to secure appropriate project sites, sites that meet governmental specifications for mortgage insurance. Zoning, too, becomes a problem. It is most often necessary to secure changes in zoning laws before a project can be begun.

Second, the management of an efficient and financially sound housing development conflicts with the social goals of those institutions which might undertake such an enterprise. Management would have to screen potential tenants to avoid problem families, and it would have to evict families who could not pay their rent. If management begins to wink at rental arrears and is forced to downgrade its maintenance program, it would fall into a vicious cycle. Rental arrears lead to less maintenance. Less maintenance leads to infrequent occupancy. Infrequent occupancy leads to reduced revenue. Reduced revenue leads to still less maintenance. Q.E.D., the churches become the owners of tomorrow's slums.

The Maramount effort can never be sustained on more than a demonstration basis. The government will commit funds only to the most well-prepared groups to let them show the world what can be done. The irony of this lies in the assumption that this is supposed to highlight what others can do. In reality, when various organizations and institutions in low-income communities across the country hear about the program and become excited about its potential, they are forced to admit in time that they cannot possibly surround themselves with the personnel necessary to bring the needed housing into their communities. This is an illustrative example of the mythic quality of the nonprofit sponsor. On paper, anyone can do it; in reality, very few.

The role of the nonprofit institution in housing is still quite confused. The federal government has not loosened its purse strings, has not reduced the red tape, has not adjusted its mortgage insurance specifications, and has not helped the churches and other institutions prepare for a major role in the redevelopment it apparently wanted to stimulate.

What then is the true purpose of such a policy? Everyone would agree it is worthwhile to encourage such stable and committed institutions as churches to do their part in easing local housing problems—even though they are not yet well equipped for the job. But since the policy

The New Mythology of Housing

has not been enacted on any grand scale, the heart of the matter must lie elsewhere. It lies in the basic unwillingness of the federal government to give serious consideration to why private developers are not dealing in the low- and moderate-income sectors, and in its refusal to provide incentives to encourage such activity. The government has made a tradeoff—it has accepted the cleaner, less tainted nonprofit sponsor and has given up housing units.

Myth #3: Aerospace Systems Panaceas

There has been much recent speculation about how efficient community renewal might be if urbanologists and systems analysts jointly planned and implemented broad programs in our cities. Conceiving the neighborhood as a subsystem of interrelated physical, economic, social and political dimensions, which is related in turn to the larger urban system, the integrated approach obviously has value. Yet upon close examination, it reveals serious shortcomings and inaccuracies. The particular advantages of the aerospace systems approach to renewal are more managerial and administrative than they are substantive. Thus, the push for employing mutidisciplinary teams and large-scale computers in rebuilding the cities cannot be but one of the most flagrant of the emerging myths of housing reform.

The problem of renewal is money. In the eight major cities recently surveyed by the U.S. Civil Rights Commission, "almost half of the families surveyed received incomes solely from sources such as welfare, AFDC, unemployment compensation or other nonemployment sources." What improvements could come from a sophisticated, fully programmed, multidisciplinary approach to community renewal in those cities? There are hundreds of communities in 42 states where welfare payments fail to meet the states' own standards of the minimum income required for families to live? It is ludicrous to assert that we need a systems approach to reveal that a mother with three children needs $237 a month to live and can be provided through welfare with a maximum of only $126. The basic problem here is lack of money. That is obvious; yet there is no reason to suppose that Congress will show any more willingness to deal with the fundamental problems of poverty than it has in the past.

Another problem is racism. A sophisticated analytical framework cannot be expected to eliminate racial conflict. What could a systems approach accomplish in the Bayside District of Oakland, for example, where the under- and unemployment rate is more than 30 percent? One cannot use a managerial tool and expect to redistribute income. Without basic economic and social reforms, the glamorous aerospace approach to renewal cannot possibly accomplish the ends for which it is intended. Yet Congress has demonstrated that it is far more prepared to sponsor the development of a city technology under the auspices of the aerospace industry than it is to deal with the fact that the poor lack money, that they are the victims of racial discrimination, or that their "assistance programs" are falling apart.

Like the more familiar task forces and blue ribbon commissions empaneled to identify the obvious, the systems approach to community renewal promises to be used as a politically valuable delaying tactic by those who refuse to commit themselves to the necessity of righting wrongs and reversing social or economic injustices.

Systems analysis has of course made many unique, highly visible contributions in the amply funded, high priority realm of national defense. It is preposterous to expect that this expensive method will yield comparable results in a traditionally low-priority area where Congress is particularly tightfisted. The systems approach to the physical and human renewal of neighborhoods and communities promises to make much more efficient use of existing resources. It would avoid the piecemeal efforts of earlier renewal programs. Yet the Vietnam experience illustrates the system's failure to take into account the human and political variables. Racism and class conflict are the human and political variables of the cities; it can safely be predicted that systems analysis will be as little effective here as it has been in Vietnam.

Myth #4: Self-help Housing

The systems approach is being sold to Congress as the new urban panacea of the 1970s. It is an attractive panacea, suggesting the efficiency and reliability of moon shots and the like. But how well will it work in practice? While it is an obviously intelligent way to go about doing certain things, one may well wonder how well it will function on limited resources. Only time will tell.

As for public service and community facilities, the black ghettos have been the last to get the least. If one peruses a random sample of Model Cities program applications he will quickly learn that cities of all sizes are now quite willing to admit that their policies have been discriminatory. In response, the black community is now demanding direct and meaningful involvement in making policy and running programs designed to improve the quality of life in the ghettos. Most recently they have demanded the inclusion of low-income, low-skilled, unemployed ghetto men as workers in the construction and rehabilitation of low-income housing.

The myth is that housing programs can provide employment for the ghetto resident, and on paper it looks sound. Unemployed ghetto residents would be prepared for jobs in the building trades even as they are helping to alleviate the chronic housing problems in their neighborhoods. It would provide residents with a meaningful experience and a sense of contributing to neighborhood development. And maybe it would even reduce the vandalism in the houses being rehabilitated. All this is fine. Yet it is also, I think, naive to expect that a large share of the greater than six million substandard units in our metropolitan areas can be brought up to standard through such efforts.

Urban self-help housing has not yet assumed the stature of a major myth, but it is gaining increasing exposure and support as Model Cities monies become more available. I do not doubt that such efforts will result in rehabilitated housing; nor that unskilled labor can be trained in the building trades. However, as long as self-help housing is localized in the relatively few communities that have the talent and organizational base to push it, the number of units involved will remain small. And, as long as the rehabilitation efforts are headed by undercapitalized Negro contractors who do not pose overt threats to organized labor, it is a safe bet that direct involvement of black manpower in the rebuilding effort will fail to crack labor's stranglehold on the ghetto.

Localized self-help training programs seem too small a threat to the unions to warrant large mobilization against them. No better evidence need be sought than the fact that black workers themselves recognize the meagerness of these programs. Blacks are now demanding entry into the Chicago, Detroit and Pittsburgh construction unions. This marks the beginning of a much needed and long awaited national confrontation between the blacks and the buildings and trades unions. It also raises the conflict to a level beyond the point where training programs might have been an issue. Even were they to become an issue, the unions seems to have the procedural equipment to appear good guys. Consider the following scenario.

The unions select and deal with relatively small and isolated black contractors in scattered communities. They allow a certain number of trainees to work on the otherwise unionized rehabilitation jobs. If pressures for reform of the union arise, or if blacks make concerted efforts to penetrate the union ranks, the union local can then threaten to slow up or close down the rehabilitation job. As this would spell certain disaster to the usually undercapitalized black contractor, he would find ways to short-circuit the whole procedure. In the end, by permitting a scant few nonunion blacks to work on rehabilitation crews in a few ghetto communities, the unions appear progressive while still excluding blacks from where the main action is, in the unions themselves.

Yet, this issue seems to have the potential to escalate into a major conflict. A Negro contractor working in Cleveland's Hough district claims that "a union carpenter brought up in new construction is no better equipped for rehabilitation work than a raw man. . . . We can train a laborer to set up our prefab partitions in two hours. He can learn faster than a veteran carpenter because he isn't set in his ways and has no old work habits to overcome." If unskilled ghetto labor is capable of being trained to do rehabilitation work in significantly less time than the unions are willing to admit, and this appears to be the case, then massive training programs could be initiated. Such a new labor pool would be highly mobile and a threat to the unions. The unions would probably offer stiff resistance to such a development, so these self-help training programs may prove to be yet another false expectation.

With all these forces eddying around direct involvement in ghetto redevelopment, it is likely that a highly limited program will be enacted, which is tokenism at its worst. The myth is subtle. It plays upon the need and desires of the minority poor for a stake in the action. At the same time it guarantees that institutional changes in organized labor will be minimal or nonexistent, that the buildings and trades unions will not have to open their ranks to black labor on a large scale—because "they" will have their self-help training programs.

Myth #5: Home Ownership for the Poor

Congress recently considered more than 24 low income home-ownership bills; its action resulted in Section 235 of the Housing Act of 1968. The purpose of the program is to broaden the base of home ownership in an already predominantly home-owning nation through the provision of interest rate subsidies to low and moderate income families. The proponents of this program expect it to accomplish all the socially desirable ends that the welfare reformers of 30 years ago had hoped their public housing programs would achieve. Today public housing has come to represent a patronizing dole, they reason, while home ownership involves a stake in a piece of property, a sense of pride in one's home. Belief in this myth persists mainly because the public and the legislators see in home ownership a device to prevent more and greater rioting.

The myth of low-income home ownership is vulnerable on many counts. The most glaring error is that such programs are based on the projection of middle class values onto a non middle-class culture. Moreover, it is perceived as a solution, a salve to balm the wounds caused by discrimination, cultural starvation and the structural problems of our national labor market. But there are several difficulties with this romanticized notion of what ownership can accomplish.

There was and is nothing about a publicly supported low-rent housing program that would necessarily rob a man of his pride or sap him of his self-respect. Nor is there anything about owning one's home that guarantees that pride and self-respect will spontaneously spring up in the owner's breast. As far as the actual low-income ownership programs are concerned they may amount to little more than saying that everyone should have a title to his slum.

Realistically speaking, one cannot expect much more than a limited low-income home-ownership program. The entrenched and anachronistic National Association of Real Estate Boards (NAREB) is making visible efforts to avoid opening up the market to Negroes. A recent NAREB circular was distributed to presidents of local real estate boards entitled, "Some Questions (and their answers) suggested by a reading of Title VIII of Public Law No. 90-284 related to forced housing." It was an exploration of means to circumvent the provisions of the federal open-housing bill. In spite of recent federal legislation in this area, and the Supreme Court's ruling that an almost forgotten law enacted in 1866 is effectively a sweeping fair-housing bill, a truly open housing market seems highly unlikely in the foreseeable future.

Moreover, to stimulate hopes for home ownership without moving toward reducing levels of unemployment and underemployment might be the cruelest hoax yet perpetrated on the low-income population. Let us assume that the program provides for monthly carrying costs equal to 20 percent of monthly income. I feel the average low-income family participating in the program would find it extremely difficult to pay for its housing-related needs (operation, maintenance, taxes, water and insurance) as well as its nonhousing needs from its limited budget. Consequently, such a program might provide the family a piece of middle-class America, but only a little piece—a piece obtained at the cost of accepting the increased pressures that go along with internalizing middle-class values, with only a fraction of the economic resources with which to play the game.

It is of paramount importance to remember that the *style* in which a program is administered has direct impact upon the quality of life of the participants. For example, if a project is administered in a paternalistic manner, that is, if the local authority sits in judgment of the moral suasion of tenant families, the project becomes the enemy. As David Hunter has observed:

The projects in Harlem are hated. They are hated almost as much as policemen and this is saying a great deal. And they are hated for the same reasons; both reveal, unbearably, the real attitude of the white world. . . .

The way in which the program is administered could conceivably be as important as the housing it makes available to participating families. While the proponents of ownership for low-income families ceremonially chant incantations about the ideals that such an experience instills in one's soul, someone must begin to work out solutions to the many problems. How can the market be opened in the face of organized opposition? How can the low-income family be expected to absorb the hidden costs of ownership on a marginal budget? How can a home-ownership program improve the pride and self-respect of the participants? How can such a program be administered in a fashion that does not duplicate the inexcusably high-handed manner with which we have administered our low-rent housing programs throughout the country?

In the next generation we will have to build as many houses to accommodate population growth and normal replacement needs as we have built in our entire history as a nation. Yet we have seriously underestimated the extent and depth of our current housing crisis.

I cannot recommend a course that can eliminate existing inhuman housing conditions throughout the nation: I do not think that anyone can. The problem is too firmly rooted in our society. It is too much a part of our economic system. It is too closely related to such fundamental issues as the distribution of wealth and income to be dealt with in terms of housing alone. I would like to give serious consideration to several points that I believe are neither myths nor misconceptions, and that must be recognized in the development of any viable strategy to deal with the chronic shortage of decent housing.

First, uneven and under utilization of existing housing is a contributing factor to the perpetuation of the slum housing problem. Vacancy and abandonment rates are increasing in our small towns as well as in our large and congested cities. Therefore slum formation can no longer be equated solely with the unending crush of new arrivals forced to seek living space in already overcrowded and overutilized housing.

Second, the slumlord of myth does not exist. In his place is a many-headed hydra, the hundreds of thousands of individuals who own the slums. These people all have varying economic resources, motives for entering the slum market, and knowledge of the dynamics of the market. But the owner of slum property is not as sophisticated and professional as many of us have been led to believe, nor is he as unintelligent as many of us would like to think. In his study of slum properties in Newark, George Sternlieb found that "more than half the parcels are owned by people to whom real estate represents a trivial supplement to income . . . to a considerable degree this reflects the comparatively amateur kind of holder who predominates in the market . . . many are . . . owners by default rather than by purchase; are owners by inheritance, or lack of purchasers to buy unwanted properties; or by a relatively trivial investment which is not too meaningful in terms of overall capital or income."

The owner of substandard housing is aware that the government frequently provides meaningful incentives to stimulate housing programs. He is also aware that recent incentives have been largely limited to developing luxury housing or to aiding nonprofit sponsors. Until a meaningful program is developed for low-income housing, he will continue to shy away from government programs ostensibly designed to assist him to improve his housing but which will end up reducing the value of his investment, based upon existing market conditions.

Third, and in light of the above discussion, it is urgent that we devise a means for accumulating current and accurate information of the economics of slum ownership. Many owners of slum properties do not keep reliable financial records of their holdings. Without these, differences in the circumstances of various segments of the ownership pool makes it virtually impossible to devise meaningful programs to help renew our inner cities. Therefore I suggest that the public perform an audit or accounting function in the low-income sector of the market. We could require, as a possible way to do this, that every renter-occupied dwelling unit found to be substandard in the course of routine inspection, be subjected to financial analysis by independent auditors employed or secured by local licensing and inspection departments.

This information would allow us to develop a multiplicity of plans for the various sectors of the substandard market. Matching each plan to its appropriate situation seems to be the only meaningful way to renew the existing housing inventory. Obviously the needs of an elderly widow without any capital except a five-unit substandard tenement are not the same as those of a real estate broker who owns 60 parcels and maintains a work crew to service them. Nor, of course, are their motives or knowledge of the market the same. Governmental policies and programs must reach both extremes; families living in units owned by the widow must not be penalized because the government has chosen to assist the broker.

Furthermore, if we can obtain the economic data to build a repertoire of programs, we will then be in a position to penalize those owners who fail to respond to the offer of aid. Outright public purchase would be justified, as would government assistance in the transfer of ownership from a recalcitrant owner to one who will cooperate.

In brief, I suggest we develop a data-gathering mechanism for an analysis of the economic patterns of slum ownership, that we develop a repertoire of solutions to the various problems, and that we stimulate property improvement by enforcing penalties upon those owners who fail to respond to the offer of aid. Should this plan fail, and the rate of deterioration of the existing stock continue unabated or increases in the future, some emergency measures should be adopted. I propose that we give serious consideration to the multifaceted implications involved in declaring this nation's existing inventory of low-rent housing a public utility. The basis for such a declaration would be the nation's compelling interest in maintaining the health, safety and social well-being of hundreds of thousands of American families living in substandard housing in the cities and the nation at large.

Such a proposal obviously includes, among other things, consideration of the regulation of profits, subsidies to those owners who cannot earn a reasonable return on their investment, the movement of structures into and out of the regulated sector, and the problem of defining the sector of the inventory to be covered. I offer this suggestion as an alternative approach to safeguarding the shrinking supply of privately owned low-rent units. It is indicative of the gravity with which I view the housing crisis.

FURTHER READING

Behind Ghetto Walls by Lee Rainwater (Chicago: Aldine, 1970). A study of the infamous Pruitt-Igoe public housing project in Chicago.

Slums and Social Insecurity by Alvin Schorr (Washington, D.C.: Department of Health, Education and Welfare, Social Security Administration, 1966).

Housing Investment in the Inner City: The Dynamics of Decline by Michael Stegman (Cambridge, Mass.: M.I.T. Press, 1972).

Residential Abandonment: The Tenement Landlord Revisited by George Sternlieb (New Brunswick, N.J.: Center for Urban Policy and Research, Rutgers University, 1973).

Freedom To Build edited by John F. C. Turner and Robert Fichter (New York: Macmillan, 1932).

4. Racism and Repression

The National Commission on Civil Disorders (better known as the Kerner Commission) publicly condemned the United States as a racist society. In the wake of the riots which wracked American cities in the 1960s, most liberals were ready to admit that white society shared the blame for the deplorable conditions existing in the black ghettos and agreed that steps should be taken to correct these conditions.

Most liberals failed to recognize, however, that the eradication of racism in the United States required more than piecemeal reformist measures such as better schools, better housing, more jobs, etc., already familiar from the poverty program. Racism has long been a part of the institutional fabric of American society, with historical roots reaching back to colonial days. It is based on a doctrine of white supremacy, which is part of our Anglo-Saxon heritage and affects every aspect of American life. To eliminate it will require more than reformist measures designed to "integrate" a few blacks into the mainstream of white American society.

The "integrationalist" or "assimilationist" model has long dominated American ideology on the incorporation of diverse racial and ethnic groups into American society (cf. Milton Gordon, "Assimilation in American Life"). Assimilation rests on the basic assumption that all ethnic groups will submerge their own sense of identity in favor of a uniform set of values common to the entire society. Initially, this signified strict conformity to Anglo-American values and behavior, whereby the newcomer was to be stripped of his native cultural heritage and made over into a full "American." Later this notion of Anglo superiority was abandoned in favor of the "melting pot," the biological and cultural merger of diverse peoples into a new, indigenous American culture, different from any of its European forbears.

The process of assimilation worked quite well for European immigrants. Although some problems did emerge (cf. Sennett, Section 7), Europeans could become members of American society simply by surrendering their mother tongue and European cultural heritage. Blacks and other racial minorities in the United States, however, faced an additional obstacle—race. Absorption of American culture was not sufficient to integrate these groups because they differed racially from the dominant white society.

Because assimilation was ruled out, racial minorities in the United States adopted various strategies for survival in American society, ranging from total withdrawal to partial accommodation. American Indians were the first to encounter this problem, starting with the blatantly racist, exclusionary policies of the Puritans in New England. After fighting bitter wars against white settlers to retain their land and avoid constant "relocation," most Indians by the late nineteenth century were forced to retreat to reservations. Here they were allowed to maintain their traditional culture and "quaint" customs, which ironically became a source of curiosity and pride to some white Americans, especially anthropologists. Of course, many customs had to be abandoned because Indians on reservations lacked the resources to maintain them (e.g., buffalo hunting among the Plains Indians). Other customs which openly conflicted with the norms of the dominant white society were practiced secretly, such as the peyote cults of the Plains Indians.

Some Indian tribes, like the Cherokee, engaged in open conflict about their pattern of accommodation. In their article "Renaissance and Repression: The Oklahoma Cherokee" Wahrhaftig and Thomas describe how these Indians, after being forced to abandon their prosperous republic and title to all reservation land, split into two factions: those who adopted the norms of white society, intermarried with whites, and now constitute the "mixed bloods" at the pinnacle of Oklahoma society; and those who retreated into the Ozark flatlands where they could follow their traditional way of life relatively free of interference from whites. In short, like other ethnic groups in the United States and other parts of the world, the latter deliberately chose a marginal status in order to maintain their cultural heritage. Despite the existence of marginal unintegrated Cherokee groups, the image of the Cherokee that prevails in American society is of the assimilated mixed blood who has "made it" in white society and who is therefore living proof of the viability of the American dream.

Wahrhaftig and Thomas maintain that sociologists have tended to underrate the importance of ethnicity in their analysis of the social stratification patterns of American society, while in reality "American industrial economy caused a class-like structure to form on top of pre-existing ethnic communities." This is certainly true of the Mexican Americans of New Mexico, described by Love in "La Raza: Mexican Americans in Rebellion." Led by a charismatic leader, Tijerina, their basic demand has been for a return of lands lost to the Anglos and ceded to them centuries earlier by the Spanish Law of the Indies. Desire for land thus becomes the means by which these Mexican Americans assert their desire *not* to assimilate with the dominant Anglo society and to resist the breakdown of their traditional culture brought on by increasing removal from the land through taxation, forced sales, and the lure of the city. The Tijerina movement, based upon a utopian return to the land and the maintenance of traditional culture, differs considerably from the Chicano labor movement led by Cesar Chavez in California. The Chicano movement is made up of migrant farm workers whose basic demand is not for land but for better wages and working conditions. In an attempt to gain support for his union, Chavez has been forced to forge links with the wider white society and cannot seek a separatist solution like Tijerina.

The Chinese and Japanese minorities in the United States sought their own means of isolation from the dominant white society. As Hill describes in his article "Anti-Oriental Agitation and the Rise of Working-Class Racism," the Chinese, and later the Japanese, were brought in late in the nineteenth century as a source of cheap labor in railroad construction, mining, and other heavy manual work. This brought them into direct conflict with the fledgling union movement of the time, which accurately perceived the Orientals as a threat to their strenuous efforts to obtain better wages and working conditions. The Chinese were, in effect, used as scabs to break the union movement, much as Mexican *braceros* have been used to break Chavez' unionization efforts among migrant farm workers.

Since their work demanded urban residence and precluded geographic isolation, the Chinese retreated into their own communities (the famous "Chinatowns" of San Francisco, New York, Los Angeles, etc.) where they could speak their own language, establish their own schools, and, in some cases, even their own system of law and courts. As much as possible, they avoided contact with the white society and tended to marry within their own ethnic groups. Where possible, they also avoided the dependency of wage labor and opened their own small retail establishments—restaurants, laundries, groceries, and the like.

Though admired for their hard work, thrift, and patience—values embodied in the American Protestant ethic—the Chinese and Japanese were never regarded as first-class citizens. Thus, few Americans protested the internment of the entire Japanese community—both first and second generation—as a "protective measure" during World War II. Like the Jews of Nazi Germany, they learned from bitter experience how shallow their assimilation had been and how much latent hostility lurked behind their apparent acceptance into American society. The case of the Japanese makes clear that even where racial minorities apparently fully embrace the values of the dominant society, they may not be accepted by whites as their social equals.

The earlier struggles of American racial minorities for survival in American society were marked by basically conservative demands: to be left alone and to obtain a refuge where they could maintain their traditional culture relatively free from outside interference. Initially, this was also true of black Americans, who sought an accommodation with the white society which would not threaten the existing power structure. The blacks' first hope lay in emancipation from slavery and in the establishment of small family farms ("40 acres and a mule") following the Civil War. In the South they remained largely rural, more often as tenant farmers and sharecroppers than as small proprietors. Agricultural mechanization and the collapse of the Southern cotton crop gradually forced them off the land and they became increasingly urbanized, particularly following World War II and their great migration north.

In the Northern industrial cities, it was almost impossible for blacks to avoid open confrontation with the dominant white establishment. Relegated to the lowest-paying unskilled jobs in white-owned companies, they were totally dependent on wage labor, supplemented by public welfare, for their income and totally dependent on the larger society for schools, housing, medical aid, stores, etc. The article by Boesel et al., "White Institutions and Black Rage," amply demonstrates the degree of control exerted over the black community by whites, from teachers and social workers to politicians, policemen, and slum merchants. As the authors demonstrate, most of these agents of the white establishment in the black community share a belief that blacks are themselves responsible for their difficulties, that blacks are incompetent or unwilling to improve their lot. Among liberals, this basically racist belief is often cloaked in a benevolent paternalism which stresses the white society's need to "educate" the black and help him adapt to the white way of life—in short, to assimilate to American society.

It came as a shock to most liberals, therefore, when militant blacks rejected accommodation and assimilation with white society and advocated black power and black separatism. As we have seen, other racial minorities in the United States had also rejected white values, but in a far less open and hostile manner. Blacks could not adopt this more covert form of withdrawal because they are totally enmeshed in American industrial society and are also the most numerous, visible, and vulnerable oppressed minority. As a result, their forceful rejection of white values was the opening wedge in a more general attack on American institutions and values, not only by blacks, but by other racial and ethnic minorities, as well as dissident white groups, such as students and women.

Black Power did not erase internal dissension or differences in the black community; on the contrary, it drew attention to schisms in the community and strengthened the need to build a strong, unified black community which could withstand the "divide and rule" tactics of the white establishment. Though the civil rights movement, led by the highly respected Rev. Martin Luther King, Jr., originated in the South, the Black Power movement received its largest impetus in the North from black leaders like Stokely Carmichael, Eldridge Cleaver, and H. Rap Brown. The cleavage between "diffident rural blacks" and "Northern urban hustlers" was evident in Resurrection City, the last, mass public effort on the part of blacks and other oppressed minorities to make the government and the American people face up to poverty and racism in the United States. As Hunter points out in her article "On the Case in Resurrection City" the Poor People's Campaign suffered as much from internal conflicts as from external oppression and disdain. Hunter notes:

> Resurrection City was not really supposed to succeed as a city. It was supposed to succeed in dramatizing the plight of the poor in this country. And in doing so, it affirmed the view taken by black militants today—that before black people can make any meaningful progress in the United States of America, they have to, as the militants say, "get themselves together."

Yet American society persists in treating protest from dissident groups as a symptom of social pathology and disorganization. Our society is loathe to recognize that the root of these disorders may lie not in the group but in the external forces which oppress them and force them into violent outbursts. Protests are often their only means of making their problems visible to the larger society, since minorities are increasingly segregated both socially and physically from the surrounding community.

The establishment's methods for subverting and controlling these violent outbursts have become increasingly subtle. Though police, imprisonment, and other law and order techniques are still used in extreme cases, the emphasis is increasingly on preventive techniques, on methods to control or pacify the ghetto population long before disorders break out. One such method is described by Corey and Cohen in their article "Domestic Pacification." Operated by the Department of Defense, the program centers around the recruitment of black youth for summer camps and other recreational and educational activities where they are instilled wih patriotism, military discipline, individual initiative, and other American virtues. Ostensibly the program is designed to reduce poverty in the ghetto by providing education and alternative models to black youth, many of whom it is hoped will choose the army as a career. The authors conjecture, however, that the program's real aim is to maintain internal security by early indoctrination of the young. As Corey and Cohen note, the intrusion of the military into domestic internal security is especially ominous in the light of the tremendous growth of our military establishment because of our involvement in Vietnam and other imperialistic ventures abroad. Are we now reversing "technical aid" and using lessons learned abroad—like pacification—to be applied at home?

If this is our answer to the Kerner Report, if we are going to meet legitimate protest with repression or preventive control, then there is little hope we can ever eradicate racism from American society. Racism will not be eradicated by repression nor by facile reformist programs which integrate a few middle-class blacks into American society while leaving the mass of black poor in the ghetto. Racism is rooted in the basic structural inequalities of American society and will continue to produce mass riots or isolated acts of violence for which white society must pay the consequences.

It is still too early to judge the full effects of the Black Power movement and similar protests among other ethnic minorities in the United States. Though many would argue that the movement has been weakened by the brutal government repression of overtly radical groups such as the Black Panthers or the Black Liberation Army, the new sense of pride and dignity in their own cultural heritage which blacks now feel can never be erased. Black Power has provided the ultimate challenge to white supremacy and opened a new attack on power and privilege in American society.

ALBERT L. WAHRHAFTIG AND ROBERT K. THOMAS

Renaissance and Repression: The Oklahoma Cherokee

A week in eastern Oklahoma demonstrates to most outsiders that the Cherokee Indians are a populous and lively community: Indians *par excellence*. Still, whites in eastern Oklahoma unanimously declare the Cherokees to be a vanishing breed. Prominent whites say with pride, "we're all a little bit Indian here." They maintain that real Cherokees are about "bred out." Few Cherokees are left who can speak their native tongue, whites insist, and fewer still are learning their language. In twenty years, according to white myth, the Cherokee language and with it the separate and distinctive community that speaks it will fade into memory.

Astonishingly, this pervasive social fiction disguises the presence of one of the largest and most traditional tribes of American Indians. Six rural counties in northeastern Oklahoma contain more than fifty Cherokee settlements with a population of more than 9,500. An additional 2,000 Cherokees live in Indian enclaves in towns and small cities. Anthropologists visiting us in the field, men who thought their previous studies had taught them what a conservative tribe is like, were astonished by Cherokees. Seldom had they seen people who speak so little English, who are so unshakably traditional in outlook.

How can native whites overlook this very identifiable Indian community? The answers, we believe, will give us not only an intriguing insight into the nature of Oklahoma society, but also some general conclusions about the position of other ethnic groups in American society.

This myth of Cherokee assimilation gives sanction to the social system of which Cherokees are a part, and to the position Cherokees have within that system. This image of the vanishing Cherokee in some ways is reminiscent both of the conservative Southern mythology which asserts that "our colored folk are a contented and carefree lot," and of the liberal Northern mythology, which asserts that "Negroes are just like whites except for the color of their skins." The fiction serves to keep Cherokees in place as a docile and exploitable minority population; it gives an official rationale to an existing, historic social system; and it implies that when the Indian Territory, the last Indian refuge, was dissolved, no Indian was betrayed, but all were absorbed into the mainstream.

The roots of modern eastern Oklahoma are in the rural South. Cherokees, and whites, came from the South; Cherokees from Georgia and Tennessee; and whites from Tennessee, Kentucky, Arkansas and southern Illinois.

In the years immediately preceding 1840, Cherokees, forced out of their sacred homelands in Georgia and Tennessee, marched over an infamous "Trail of Tears," and relocated in a new Cherokee Nation in what is now the state of Oklahoma. They created an international wonder: an autonomous Cherokee Nation with its own national constitution, legislature, judiciary, school system, publishing house, international bilingual newspaper, and many other trappings of a prosperous Republic. The Cherokees, who as a people accomplished all this, along with their neighbors, the Creeks, Choctaws, Chicasaws and Seminoles, who followed similar paths, were called the five civilized tribes.

Promising as the Cherokee Nation's future might have seemed, it was plagued by internal controversy from birth. Bitterness between the traditional Ross Party and the Treaty Party was intense. The Ross Party resisted demands for relocating from the South until its followers were finally corralled by the Army; the Treaty Party believed cooperation with the United States Government was the more prudent course for all Cherokees.

The sons and daughters of the Ross Party kept their ancient villages together. They reestablished these in the hollows and rough "Ozark" country of the Indian territory. Hewing new log cabins and planting new garden spots, they hoped to live unmolested by their opponents. They are today's "fullbloods," that is, traditional and Cherokee speaking Cherokees. On the other hand, descendants of the Treaty Party, who concentrated in the flat bottomlands and prairies they preferred for farming, are now assimilated and functionally white Americans, though fiercely proud of their Cherokee blood.

The Ross Party was the core of the Cherokee tribes. It was an institution which emerged from the experience of people who lived communally in settlements of kinsmen. The Treaty Party was a composite of individuals splintered from the tribal body. There were of course great differences in life style among nineteenth century Cherokee citizens. The Ross men, often well-educated, directed the Cherokee legislators from backwoods settlements. Treaty Party men were more often plantation owners, merchants, entrepreneurs, and professionals—conventional southern gentlemen. The overriding difference between the two factions, however, was between men who lived for their community and men who lived for themselves.

During the 1880's this difference came to be associated

not with party but with blood. Geographically separated and ostracized by Ross men, members of the Treaty Party perforce married among the growing population of opportunistic whites who squatted on Indian land, defying U.S. and Cherokee law. The Treaty Party became known as the "mixed blood" faction of the tribe; the Ross Party as "full bloods." These terms imply that miscegenation caused a change of life style, a reversal of the historic events.

By 1907 when the Cherokee Nation was dissolved by Congressional fiat and the State of Oklahoma was created, the mixed bloods were already socially if not politically, part of the white population of the United States. The Ross Party settlements, now the whole of the functionally Cherokee population, are intact but surrounded by an assimilated population of mixed blood Cherokees integrated with white immigrants.

From the 1890s to 1920s, development of this area was astonishingly rapid. A flood of whites arrived. Land was populated by subsistence farmers, small town trade boomed, commercial farming expanded, railroads were built, timber exhausted, petroleum exploited and token industrialization established.

Already shorn of their nation, fullbloods were stunned and disadvantaged by the overnight expansion and growth. Change was rapid, the class system open. Future distinguished elders of small town society arrived as raggedy tots in the back of one-mule wagons. Not only was social mobility easy, few questions were asked about how the newly rich became rich. Incredible land swindles were commonplace. At the turn of the century, every square inch of

eastern Oklahoma was alloted to Cherokees; by the 1930s little acreage remained in Indian possession.

The result of this explosive development was a remarkably stratified society, characterized by highly personal relationships, old time rural political machines, Protestant fundamentalism, reverence of free enterprise, and unscrupulous exploitation; in short, a system typical of the rural south.

Superficially, this society appears to be one with the most resourceful at the top, and the unworthy, who let opportunity slip by, at the bottom. In reality, however, the system consists of ranked ethnic groups, rather than classes. The successful old mixed-blood families, now functionally "white," whose self-identification as "Cherokee" is taken as a claim to the venerable status of "original settlers," dominate. Below them are the prosperous whites who "made something of themselves," and at the bottom, beneath the poor country whites, Cherokee "full bloods."

In primitive tribes, myth is a sacred explanation of the creation of the tribe and of its subsequent history. Myth specifies the holy design within which man was set to live. The fiction of Cherokee assimilation illustrates that modern man still uses myth, though differently. For in Oklahoma, the myth of Cherokee assimilation validates the social conditions men themselves have created, justifying the rightness and inevitability of what was done. As Oklahomans see it, the demise of the Cherokee as a people was tragic, albeit necessary. For only thus were individual Cherokees able to share in the American dream. The Oklahoman conceives of his society as an aggregate of individuals ranked by class, with un-

limited opportunity for mobility regardless of individual ancestry. The high class position of the old Cherokee mixed-bloods signifies to the Oklahoman that the job of building Oklahoma was well done. The "responsible" Indians made it. The Cherokees, as a single historic people, died without heirs, and rightfully all those who settled on their estate now share in the distribution of its assets. For the culturally Indian individuals remaining, Oklahoma can only hope that they will do better in the future.

Even as the mythology serves to sanctify their high rank position, it insulates whites from the recognition of the Cherokee as a viable but low ranked ethnic community with unique collective aims and interests. Where a real community exists, Oklahomans see only a residue of low status individuals. The myth, by altering perceptions, becomes self-perpetuating.

Paradoxically, the myth of Cherokee assimilation has also contributed to the survival of the Cherokee as a people. To the extent that Cherokees believed the myth, and many did, it was not only an explanation of how the tribe came into the present but a cohesive force. Since the end of a tribal movement led by Redbird Smith, a half century ago, in response to the final pressures for Oklahoma statehood, Cherokees have seemed inert, hardly a living people. Nevertheless, Cherokee communal life persisted, and is in a surprisingly healthy state. Cherokee settlements remain isolated, and if what goes on in them is not hidden, it is calculatedly inconspicuous. For the freedom from interference that it afforded, Cherokees willingly acceded to the notion that the Cherokees no longer exist.

In addition to sanctioning the form of Oklahoma society, the myth also gives credence to basic social and economic institutions. The economy of the area depends on Cherokees and country whites as an inexpensive and permanent labor market. Cherokees are expected to do low paying manual work without complaint. In 1963, Cherokee median per capita income, approximately $500, was less than half the per capita income of neighboring rural whites. In some areas, Cherokees live in virtual peonage; in others, straw bosses recruit Cherokee laborers for irregular work at low pay. Even though Cherokee communities are relatively hidden, Cherokee labor has become an indispensable part of the local economy. Apparently one would think that daily contact of white workers and bosses with these Cherokee laborers might expose the myth of the well-off assimilated Cherokee. On the contrary, the myth prevails because the humble occupations practiced by Cherokees are seen as evidence that Cherokee character is indeed that which the myth of assimilation predicts.

White Blood Makes Good Indians

Imbedded in the Oklahoma concept of assimilation, is a glaring racism. Typical is the introductory page of a book published in 1938 entitled *A Political History of the Cherokee Nation,* written by Morris Wardell, a professor at the University of Oklahoma.

A selection: "Traders, soldiers, and treaty-makers came among the Cherokees to trade, compel and negotiate. Some of these visitors married Indian women and lived in the Indian villages the remainder of their days. Children born to such unions preferred the open and free life and here grew to manhood and womanhood, never going to the white settlements. This mixture of blood helped to produce strategy and cleverness which made formidable diplomats of many of the Indian leaders."

To white genes go the credit for Sequoyah's genius and John Ross's astuteness, whereas the remaining Cherokee genes contribute qualities that are endearing but less productive. Thus, in a history of the Cherokees published only six years ago, the author, an Oklahoman, says of modern "fullbloods": "They supplement their small income from farms and subsidies from the government with wage work or seasonal jobs in nearby towns or on farms belonging to white men. . . . Paid fair wages, this type of worker usually spends his money as quickly as he makes it on whisky, and on cars, washing machines, and other items that, uncared for, soon fall into necessitous disuse."

Oklahomans divide the contemporary Cherokees into two categories: those who are progressive and those who are not. The page just quoted continues, "this progressive type of Indian will not long remain in the background of the growing and thriving, and comparatively new, State of Oklahoma." That a viable Indian tribe exists is apparently inconceivable. Either Cherokees are worthy, responsible and assimilating, or they are the dregs; irresponsible, deculturated and racially inferior.

Through mythology, the exploitation of Cherokee labor is redefined into benevolent paternalism. Some patrons have Cherokees deliver their welfare checks to them, deduct from these housing and groceries. Afterwards the remainder is handed over to Cherokee tenants. Unknown to the welfare department, these same Cherokees receive stingy wages for working land and orchards belonging to the patron or to his kin. Patrons consider that they are providing employment and a steady paternal hand for unfortunate people who they contend could never manage themselves. The same ethic enables whites in good conscience to direct vestigal Cherokee tribal affairs; including the disbursement of well over two million dollars in funds left from a tribal land claim settlement.

Politicians Are Victims of Old Fears

It might seem odd that no one seeking to improve his position in the local establishment has ever tried to weaken these relationships. Why has no political figure taken cognizance of those thousands of Cherokee votes, and championed their cause? Instead politicians rely on the inefficient machinery of county patronage to collect Cherokee ballots. Unfortunately no one has yet dared, because fear binds the system. Older whites remember living in fear of a blood bath. The proposal to create Oklahoma meant a new state to whites; to Cherokees it meant the end of their own national existence. Their resistance to statehood was most desperate. Cherokees were a force to be contended with. They were feared as an ominously silent, chillingly mysterious people, unpredictable and violent. And Cherokees did organize into secret societies, much akin to the committees of twenty-five delegated in days past to murder collaborators who signed treaties. The reward of public office, politicians feel, does not justify the risk of rekindling that flame. To the extent that Oklahomans are aware of the numbers of Cherokees and the force they might generate, the myth of the assimilated Cherokee is a form of wishful thinking.

Finally, the myth protects the specific relationships of rank and power which determine the stability of the present eastern Oklahoma social system. It does this in the following ways: By preventing recognition by whites and Indians alike of the Cherokees as a permanent community of people whose demands and aspirations must be taken seriously, it allows whites to direct the affairs of the region as they see fit.

By causing Cherokee aspirations to be discounted as romantic and irrelevant, it prevents the emergence of a competitive Cherokee leadership and discourages Cherokees from taking action as a community. For example, by 1904 Cherokees were given what was thought of as an opportunity to develop individualism and responsibility. The U.S. Government divided their communally owned land and each Indian was given his own piece. Thus the efforts of the present day Cherokee Four Mothers Society to piece together individual land holdings, reestablish communal title, and develop cooperative productive enterprises, is smilingly dismissed as an atavistic retreat to "clannishness."

By fostering the notion that Cherokees are an aggregate of disoriented individuals, it allows whites to plan for Cherokees, to control Cherokee resources, and to reinforce their own power by directing programs devoted to Cherokee advancement.

By denying that there is a Cherokee community with which a Cherokee middle class could identify and to which a Cherokee middle class could be responsive, it draws off educated Cherokees into "white" society and leaves an educationally impoverished pool of Cherokees to perpetuate the image of Cherokee incompetence.

The myth prevents scholars, Indian interest organizations, and the like from becoming overly curious about the area. If Cherokees are assimilated and prosperous, as the myth implies, there is neither a problem nor a culture to study. For 40 years no social scientist has completed a major study of any of the five civilized tribes. For 40 years the spread of information which might cast doubt on the myth itself has been successfully impeded.

In all, the myth stabilizes and disguises the Oklahoma social system.

The stability of a local social system, such as that of eastern Oklahoma, is heavily influenced by events in the larger society. The past decade of civil rights activity shook Oklahoma. Gradually, Oklahomans are becoming aware that their society is not as virtuous, homogeneous, attractive, and open as they may have supposed. And Oklahomans will now have to deal with the old agrarian social system of Cherokees, hillbillies, mixed-blood Cherokees, and a new urban elite grafted onto the old.

Left behind in the rush of workers to industry and of power to industrialized areas, the Ozark east of Oklahoma is a shell, depopulated, and controlled by newly dominant cities, Tulsa and Oklahoma City. The area, quaint enough to attract tourists, is far too rustic for sophisticated Oklahoma urbanites to take seriously. Local politicians offer weak leadership. Beginning to suspect that the local establishment is no longer all powerful, Cherokees have begun to assert themselves as a tribal community. The Cherokees conceive of themselves as a civilized nation, waiting for the dark days of the foreigners' suppression and exploitation to end. Oklahomans regard Cherokees as an aggregate of disadvantaged people still in the background of an integrated state, a definition which Cherokees do not share. In fact, the Cherokees are flirting with political office and have entered the courts with a hunting rights case. In launching a "Five County Northeast Oklahoma

Cherokee Organization," they are gaining recognition as a legitimate community with rights, aspirations, resources and competence.

Consequently, the reappearance of assimilated Cherokees threatens the newly emergent regional power structure. Cherokees and the local establishment have begun jousting on a field of honor extending from county welfare offices (where the welfare-sponsored jobs of suspect members of the "Five County Organizations" are in jeopardy) to annual conventions of the National Congress of American Indians. Besides threatening an already shaky white power structure, the militant Cherokees are challenging the self esteem of the elderly and powerful "assimilated." Curiously, many white Oklahomans do not appear to be alarmed, but pleased, apparently, to relieve the tension that has developed between conflicting images of pretended assimilation and the reality of a workaday world.

The manner in which Oklahomans view their society is the manner in which American sociologists all too often view American society. Great emphasis is placed on class and on individual mobility. And, social description, in these terms, is seen very much as a product of the American ethos.

White Oklahomans consider themselves members of a class-stratified society in which any individual (Negroes excepted) has free access to any class. Descriptions of that system vary according to who is doing the describing. Generally, white Oklahomans conceive their society to be one in which the upper class is made up of prosperous whites and old Cherokee mixed-blood families, or their descendants; next in order is a layer of middle class whites and assimilated Cherokees; then, a lower class of poor, country whites, full-blood Cherokees and Negroes. Young liberals see a two-class system: A middle class of "decent" whites and Cherokees and socially unacceptable class of poor, country whites, Cherokees and Negroes.

How Mythical Is Mobility?

This latter classification suggests that younger people perceive a much more closed system than their elders. Everyone is viewed as part of the same *community*—a word Oklahomans are fond of using. Presumably all groups of people have an equal share in the life of the community. Nationality, the word Oklahomans use to denote ethnic origin, is a principal clue to class position. As evidence of how open their society is, eastern Oklahomans point to Cherokees and poor, country whites (although not yet to Negroes, to whom the system is closed) who occupy respected positions. These are store owners, bureaucrats, and entrepreneurs; Babbitts of the 1960's, though born of traditional Cherokee parents. Always, however, these have been individuals who followed the only approved channel of mobility by scrupulously conforming to standards of behavior defined by those in control of the system.

The classic sociological studies on class in America, such as those by W. Lloyd Warner and Robert Lynd, are essentially static descriptions of the rank position of aggregates of individuals similar to the native Oklahoman's conception of his society. These studies reflect a peculiarly American

bias. First, they examine the system that has formed rather than study how the system was formed. Americans are phenomenologists, more concerned with the things they have created than with the lengthy processes whereby these things have developed, more interested in ends than concerned with means.

Secondly, Americans do not stress ethnic considerations. In the American dream all individuals can "make it," regardless of nationality. For sociologists, class is a phenomenon in which individuals have social rank; ethnicity is treated as no more than an important clue in determining that rank. Thus, to be Irish was to be an outcast in nineteenth century Boston; not so today.

Thirdly, Americans, envisioning themselves as a nation of individualists, have assumed that social mobility for the most part rests on individual achievement. Immigrant groups are seen as having migrated into lower class positions in a relatively fixed class system through which individual immigrants rapidly became mobile. By contrast, Oklahoma's rapid entry into the formative American industrial economy caused a class-like structure to form on top of pre-existing ethnic communities.

A more balanced view shows that in the parts of the United States which industrialized earlier and more gradually, whole immigrant communities were successively imported into and butted one another through a social system which was in the process of formation and closure. The ways in which entire ethnic communities achieve mobility are overlooked.

Now it is becoming obvious that this mobility has slowed, even for those ethnic communities (like Poles) already "in the system." For communities which were brought into the system late (like Puerto Ricans) or at its territorial fringe (like Mexican-Americans in the Southwest) the situation is different.

Cherokees maintained technical independence as an autonomous nation until 1907, and in fact held America at arm's length until the 1890's. They provide an example of incorporation of an ethnic group into the industrial system in an area where no earlier group has paved the way. Thus, Cherokees are a "case type" which illustrated the modern dynamics of our system in pure form. Cherokees are now caught in our "historically mature" system of rank ethnic groups—a system which, for some, is rigid and closed, with little chance for individual and less for communal mobility. The total rank-structure of eastern Oklahoma is cemented by the mythology Americans use to obscure and rationalize their privileged position in a closed system.

In their conception of class, American sociologists are often as wedded to myth as are Oklahomans, and the resulting large areas of American social science they have created obediently subscribe to official fictions within the American world view.

Now, successive summers of violence have exploded some of the folk and scientific mythology shrouding the structure of our nation. The *Report of the National Advisory Commission on Civil Disorders* declares: "What white Americans have never fully understood—but what the Negro can never forget—is that white society is deeply implicated in the ghetto. White institutions created it, white

institutions maintain it, and white society condones it."
Yet throughout this unusually clear report the phenomenon
of white racism is barely alluded to, as though it were an
"attitude" born by an uninformed populace and unrelated
to the core of our national social system. That system, as
we see it in operation in Oklahoma, beneath its mythology
of assimilation, consists of a structure of ranked ethnic
groups, euphemistically called "classes" by American sociologists; a structure which is growing more stable and
more rigid. This kind of structure is general in America and,
of course, implied in the above quote from the Kerner
report. In Oklahoma such a system of relationships has
enabled aggressive entrepreneurs to harness and utilize the
resources of ethnic communities which are frozen into a
low ranked position by the dominant community's control
over channels of mobility and by the insistence that the
whole complex represents one single community differentiated only by personal capability. Thus, essentially
"racist" perceptions and relationships are the "motor"
driving the system and are embedded in the very day-to-day
relationships of middle class Oklahoma.

FURTHER READING

*When Shall They Rest? The Cherokee's Long Struggle
With America* by Peter Collier (New York: Holt, Rinehart and Winston, 1973). A brief and readable introduction to Cherokee history. It includes a discussion of Cherokees in the 1960s.

And Still the Waters Run by Angie Debo (Princeton,
N.J.: Princeton University Press, 1940). A historian's
meticulous account of the techniques through which the
Five Civilized Tribes were stripped of their resources at
the beginning of this century.

Custer Died for Your Sins by Vine Deloria, Jr. (New
York: Macmillan, 1968).

Four Centuries of Southern Indians edited by Charles
Hudson (Athens, Ga.: University of Georgia Press, 1974).
A collection of essays by historians and anthropologists
including a study of modern Cherokee community institutions by Albert Wahrhaftig.

The New Indians by Stan Steiner (New York: Harper &
Row, 1968). Chapter 1 presents a portrait of spokesmen
for the present community of traditional Cherokee Indians
and an account of their efforts to buck the Oklahoma
"establishment."

JOSEPH L. LOVE

La Raza: Mexican Americans in Rebellion

In early June, 1967 a group of Spanish-speaking Americans who call themselves the *Alianza Federal de Mercedes* (Federal Alliance of Land Grants) and claim that they are the legal and rightful owners of millions of acres of land in Central and Northern New Mexico, revolted against the governments of the United States of America, the State of New Mexico, and Rio Arriba (Up River) County, formally proclaiming the Republic of Rio Chama in that area.

On June 5 an armed band of forty or more *Aliancistas* attacked the Tierra Amarilla courthouse, released 11 of their members being held prisoner, and wounded a deputy sheriff and the jailer. They held the sheriff down on the floor with a rifle butt on his neck, searched for the District Attorney (who wasn't there) and for an hour and a half controlled the village (population 500). They took several hostages (later released when the getaway car stuck in the mud).

Despite some of the melodramatic and occasionally comic opera aspects of the affair, both the members of the *Alianza* and the local and state authorities take it very seriously. This is not the first time the Aliancistas have violated federal and state law, attempting to appropriate government property (in October, 1966, for instance, their militants tried to take over Kit Carson National Forest, and to expel the rangers found there as trespassers); nor is it the only time their activities have resulted in violence. In this case the state government reacted frantically, sending in armored tanks, 300 National Guardsmen and 200 state police. They rounded up dozens of Spanish-speaking persons, including many women and children, and held them in a detention camp, surrounded with guns and soldiers, for 48 hours. The raiders got away, but in several days all of them—including their fiery leader, former Pentecostal preacher Reies López Tijerina—were captured.

It has become common to associate these actions of the Alianza with other riots or revolts by poor, dark-skinned and disaffected Americans—with Watts, Newark and Detroit. Tijerina himself helps reinforce this impression by occasionally meeting with, and using the rhetoric of, some leaders of the black urban revolt. The fact is, however, that the Alianza movement is really a unique example in the United States of a "primitive revolt" as defined by Eric Hobsbawm, a kind almost always associated with developing nations, rather than advanced industrialized countries —and which includes such diverse phenomena as peasant anarchism, banditry, and millenarianism (the belief that divine justice and retribution is on the side of the rebels and that the millenium is at hand). The attack on the

courthouse, in fact, had more in common with the millenarian Sioux Ghost Dance cult of 1889-91 than with Watts.

As the Aliancistas see it, they are not violating any legitimate law. The territory around Rio Arriba belongs to them. They demand the return of lands—primarily common lands —taken from *Hispano* communities, most of which were founded in the Spanish colonial era. Their authority is the famous *Recopilación de leyes de los Reinos de Indias* (*Compilation of Laws of the Kingdoms of the Indies*, generally shortened to *The Laws of the Indies*) by which the Crown of Castile governed its New World possessions. They claim that according to these laws common lands

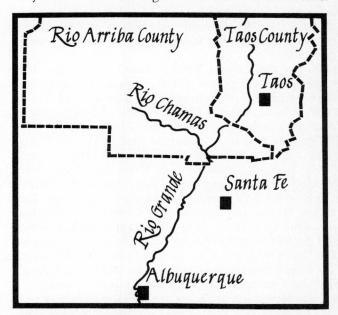

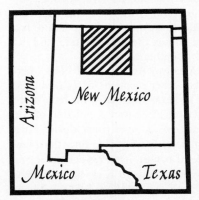

These maps show the location of Rio Arriba and Taos counties, where the Spanish-speaking population predominates. The average per capita income in these counties in 1967 was less than $1,000, compared to the state average of $2,310 and the national average of $2,940. About half of the residents are on welfare and unemployment is about 15 per cent—almost three times the state average.

were inalienable—could not be taken away. Since most of such lands were in existence when the Treaty of Guadalupe Hidalgo was signed in 1848—and since in that treaty the United States government pledged itself to respect property rights established under Mexican rule—the Alianza insists that those land grants remain valid. The members speak primarily of common lands, rather than individual heirs, and define the towns in question as "closed corporations, with membership restricted to the descendants and heirs of the founding fathers and mothers"—that is, themselves.

The Alianza's interpretations of law and history are, of course, selective, and tend to ignore inconvenient facts and other interpretations. It claims that *The Laws of the Indies* were not abrogated when "Mexico invaded and occupied New Mexico," nor when the United States did the same in 1846. The Aliancistas are the early settlers, the legitimate heirs.

The Maximum Leader

The Alianza and its actions cannot really be understood without knowledge of its background and its leader. First, the people from whom it draws its members and its strength—the Mexican-American minority in the US—and specifically New Mexico; second, the rapid economic changes throughout the area since World War II that have so greatly affected their lives; and last but surely not least the dynamism, determination and charisma of Reies Tijerina, without whom the movement would probably never have arisen.

In the 1960 census Mexican-Americans, though they made up only 2.3 percent of the population of the United States, constituted 12 percent of the population of Texas, New Mexico, Arizona, Colorado and California—almost three and a half million persons.

Generally they are a submerged minority that have only lately begun to articulate their demands. They formed "Viva Kennedy" committees in 1960; since then three Mexican-American Congressmen have gone to the House, and New Mexico's Joseph Montoya sits in the Senate. The end of the *bracero* program in 1964 opened the way to a successful unionization drive among agricultural workers; and the celebrated "Huelga" strike in Delano, California in 1965 was a symptom of and stimulus to the new awakening. The federal and state poverty programs, and the example of the Negro revolt, have also undoubtedly had their effects.

New Mexico is a distinctive area of Latin culture. It was the last state in the Southwest to be overwhelmed by Anglo-American civilization, and is the only one with two official languages. The Mexican-American population has been traditionally located along the Rio Grande and its tributaries, and extends into southern Colorado.

Until recent years, the Mexican Americans of New Mexico have been isolated from other members of *la raza* (the Mexican-American "race"). Texas and California have more than 80 percent of the Mexican-American population of the Southwest, yet most of these crossed over from Mexico after 1900, or descended from persons who did. But, the New Mexican *Hispanos* (the local name) have resided there for many generations, and some strains go back to the seventeenth century (Santa Fe was founded in 1609). More-

over, large numbers of English-speaking Americans only began to compete seriously for rural property in the 1880's, and appropriation continued into the 1920's.

In the 1960 census New Mexico had a higher percentage of "native born of native parents" than any other Southwestern state (87.4 percent). The mobility of Hispano males between 1955 and 1960 (defined in terms of changing residence) was lower in New Mexico than elsewhere. In 1960 New Mexico had the highest percentage of rural non-farm inhabitants with Spanish surnames.

In absolute numbers New Mexico's Anglo population was for many years roughly in balance with the Hispano. It is now surging ahead as a result of the economic boom which began with the atomic testing program of World War II. In no other Southwestern state was the disparity between the growth of Anglo and Latin populations greater from 1950 to 1960 than in New Mexico, where the former increased by 59.1 percent and the latter by a mere 8.1 percent. Yet in spite of this, New Mexico in 1960 still had a greater proportion of Mexican-Americans than any other state: about two-sevenths of its inhabitants had Spanish surnames, compared to one-seventh of Texans, and one-eleventh of Californians.

The job situation for the Hispanos of New Mexico has also worsened more rapidly than in other states. In 1950 male Mexican-Americans had a greater percentage of jobless in California, Colorado, and Arizona than in New Mexico; but ten years later the Hispanos of New Mexico had the dubious distinction of leading the list.

As some observers have noted, in certain ways New Mexico resembles Quebec: Both are centers of Latin culture founded in the seventeenth century, and both are subject to an increasing degree of Anglo domination. And like the Quebeckers, the New Mexicans have their fringe-group separatists—the *Alianza Federal de Mercedes.*

The Alianza was born in 1963, partly to combat the alienation and isolation of the Hispanos, but specifically to reclaim lands taken from the Spanish-speaking population since 1848. In colonial New Mexico (1598-1821), Spanish officials made land grants of indeterminate size to both individuals and to communities as commons, and the latter were respected through the era of Mexican rule (1821-1848). When Anglo-Americans began to enter New Mexico in significant numbers in the 1880's, they found it possible to wrest lands from the native inhabitants through the legal and financial devices of land taxes, mortgages, and litigation over disputed titles. By 1930, through legal and extralegal means, the Anglos had taken over most of the farming and ranching land in the state, and the state and federal governments appropriated much of the common lands that had previously belonged to the incorporated towns and villages. The Spanish-speaking population ultimately lost 1.7 million acres of community lands and two million acres in private holdings. The Hispanos sporadically reacted to this process by forming secret societies and vigilante groups; but at most this constituted harassment rather than effective resistance.

The Alianza now demands the return of these lands.

Yet in all probability, the Alianza would not exist but for the efforts of a single man, a leader who devotes his

The charismatic Reies López Tijerina, a former evangelist. Without his dynamic leadership the Alianza movement would probably never have arisen.

life to his cause, and inspires his followers to do likewise. Reies López Tijerina is a man of rare charisma who is most in his element when haranguing a large crowd. Of average height, he seems to have great physical strength as he grasps a microphone with one sinewy arm and gesticulates artfully and furiously with the other. He sometimes shouts violently as he asks rhetorical questions of his audience in Spanish—the language he uses by preference—and gets "Sí!" and "No!" bellowed back in appropriate cadences. The author witnessed a Tijerina performance last fall on the steps of the state capitol in Austin, Texas, where the Alianza leader told a group of Mexican-American Labor Day marchers he supported their demand for a state minimum wage of $1.25 an hour, but did so "with shame." Why should Mexican-Americans in Texas ask so little of the Anglos, whose government had repeatedly broken the Treaty of Guadalupe Hidalgo?

Reies Tijerina uses a demagogic style before a crowd, but he holds the tenets of his faith with unshakeable conviction: "It's something in me that must come out," Tijerina proclaims. His followers regard him with awe. He is "Caudillo" (leader) of the Alianza, but disclaims any desire to be dictator. He points out that a Supreme Council has ultimate control—though he, clearly, makes the decisions. It seems obvious that no one could step into his shoes, nor has anyone been groomed to do so. In any event Tijerina has no doubt that his followers require strong and able leadership. He justifies this by arguing that the Hispanos are a "young" race. They were "born," he explains, by virtue of a royal decree in 1514 allowing Spaniards to marry Indians; the term "Hispano" or "Spanish American" therefore can generally be equated with "mestizo." This young race is still learning, painfully, how to defend itself

and requires strong direction. It is not an ancient and clever people like the Jews, he says.

Recognizing the diverse historical experiences of Texas, New Mexico, and California, the Caudillo realizes that his constituency for the foreseeable future will be limited to New Mexico. He does believe, however, that the land grants to Mexican-Americans in California can still be identified and claimed like those of New Mexico.

It is no coincidence that Tijerina's style and language recall Pentecostal protestantism. He has been a minister in the Assembly of God, and was an itinerant revival preacher for many years to Mexican-Americans throughout the Southwest.

But, unlike the vast majority of his followers, he was not born in New Mexico but in Texas ("A prophet is not without honor save in his own country"). One of seven children of a migrant farm family, once so desperate that they were reduced to eating field rats, he picked crops and preached in Illinois and Michigan as well as in Texas and Arizona. He did not settle in New Mexico until 1960; and, with his five brothers, formed the Alianza three years later.

The quasi-religious fervor of Tijerina has strongly shaped the aspirations and style of the Alianza. However, there is greater emphasis on Old Testament justice than New Testament love. *Justicia* is a word frequently on the Caudillo's lips.

The Alianza now claims to have 30,000 dues-paying members paying at least $2.00 per month. A scholar guesses that 10,000 may be closer to the true figure. It seems clear that Tijerina's computation includes sympathizers or at least persons who have only occasionally contributed funds.

As with some sectors of the American Negro movement, the Alianza's programs began with an emphasis on litigation; and when that failed, frustration and a disposition toward violence emerged.

In April 1966 the "President and Founder" of the Alianza journeyed to Spain in order to gather materials on the registration of New Mexican land grants in the colonial era; from such documents he hoped to generate a strong legal case to present in federal courts.

In July Tijerina presented a petition to the Governor of New Mexico, Jack Campbell, and stated, "We do not demand anything. We just want a full investigation of the issue." Yet Governor Campbell would do little more than receive Tijerina and hear him out.

In January 1967, the Caudillo, one of his brothers, and a self-styled legal expert in the Alianza named Gerry Noll made a trip to Washington, D.C., where they "limited" their claims to 500,000 acres in the Kit Carson National Forest and to an area around the city of Albuquerque. He only obtained a brief hearing with a State Department attorney and a sympathetic interview with New Mexico's Senator Montoya.

In 1966 the Alianza had already begun to give up hope of legal redress. The Supreme Council of the Alianza "passed a resolution of non-confidence in the Courts of the State of New Mexico and of the United States of America" because of "corruption" and "low standards of knowledge of law."

Aliancistas Proclaim Independent Republic

On October 22, 1966 the Aliancistas proclaimed the existence of the Republic of San Joaquín del Río de Chama (in Rio Arriba County) with Tijerina as "city attorney" (*procurador*) of the community; they simultaneously attempted to take over Kit Carson Forest, which covers most of the county. They arrested U.S. Forest Rangers for trespassing, decided to print hunting and fishing licenses, and commandeered government vehicles. The rebels were quickly dispersed by local authorities, and Tijerina and four lieutenants were charged on counts of assault, converting government property to private use, and conspiracy.

Demonstrations and protest meetings continued. On January 15, 1967 the Alianza declared it would seek redress in the United Nations if the U.S. Congress failed to act. On April 17 several hundred Aliancistas paraded before the State House in Santa Fe, and Reies Tijerina, out on bond, delivered an ominous message: "We will . . . issue to the public and the federal government and the world the last human legal notice exposing the truth. . . . The government is being warned and advised if anybody is found trespassing on these land grants they will be arrested and punished. . . ."

At the beginning of June the District Attorney of Santa Fe, Alfonso Sánchez, expressed concern about the "communist philosophy" of the Alianza and alleged that Aliancistas were amassing "machine guns, M-1 rifles, and 15,000 rounds" of ammunition. Eleven members of the Alianza were promptly arrested and jailed in Tierra Amarilla, an Alianza stronghold and the seat of Rio Arriba County.

The reaction was swift and violent: On June 5, as noted, the Aliancistas launched their revolt and attacked the Tierra Amarilla courthouse. This time, when caught, the Caudillo and his principal aides were charged with kidnapping, three counts of conspiracy to commit murder, and bombing a public building (the courthouse). Despite the gravity of the charges, Tijerina and some of his men were released on bond after six weeks in prison. The failure of the attack by no means dampened the spirits of the Aliancistas.

In the months following, Tijerina traveled throughout the Southwest to gain backing. He found it, both in radical organizations of Mexican-Americans and Negroes, and in some Mexican-American associations with more traditional reformist leadership.

On October 15, Tijerina was in Los Angeles, linking his cause to the peace movement at an anti-war rally. Labeling the United States' involvement in Vietnam "the most criminal in the history of mankind," he contacted radical Negro and Mexican-American groups in the Los Angeles area. One week later, at a convention of the Alianza de Mercedes on October 21, Tijerina announced that a "Treaty of Peace, Harmony, and Mutual Assistance" had been contracted between his organization and SNCC, CORE, and the Black Panthers. The Caudillo also obtained statements of support from the Crusade for Justice, a Mexican-American organization of slumdwellers in Denver, and from MAPA, an important Mexican-American political action group in California.

While gathering support from non-Anglo groups outside New Mexico in the here and now, Tijerina and his deputies have not discouraged the movement's latent tendencies toward millenarianism and belief in special divine favor back home on the Upper Rio Grande. During the raid at Tierra Amarilla, several Aliancistas witnessed the appearance of a double rainbow, a sure sign of God's grace. According to others, the Caudillo is the prophet of Montezuma who will miraculously return in the imminent future to punish the Anglos for their appropriation of Hispano lands.

Another legend has it that a leader will come "from the east" and expel the foreigners who took the Mexican-Americans' lands. (Tijerina fits, since Texas is east of New Mexico.)

In the *"Corrido de Rio Arriba,"* which appeared shortly after the June raid, the balladeer told his audience that when bullets started flying *"Las mujeres y los niños/iban corriendo y llorando,*

Y en este instante pensamos/Que el mundo se iba acabando."

("Women and children / Ran about in tears

And at that moment we thought / The world was coming to an end.")

Although the "free city-states" which Tijerina hopes to erect are of this world, they clearly represent a sort of secular paradise, a recaptured golden age, somewhat along the lines prescribed in *The Laws of the Indies.* The inhabitants will be able to do any work they please, explains the Caudillo; but most will be herdsmen using the common lands (*ejidos*) of the pueblos. Tijerina himself will simply become City Attorney of the Republic of Chama.

If "la raza" is specially favored and will come into its millenium, why is it suffering so now? This is explained as the result of a "fall from grace" which occurred after the Anglo-American invasion of New Mexico in 1846 and the collusion of certain Hispanos with the alien conquerors. An allegorical mural at Alianza headquarters tells the story: A sacred temple in the center of the mural represents paradise entwined by a serpent, which also clutches three figures symbolizing the oppressed races—the Negro, the Indian, and the Hispano. The snake personifies the "Santa Fe Ring"—the Anglo and upper-class Hispano politicians who appropriated the poor Hispanos' lands in the 1880's and later. Figures on the right side, representing the People, begin to emerge from the Darkness and a reptile-devouring secretary bird, personifying Justice, arrives to attack the snake. At the top of the canvas is a rainbow (a symbol of God's blessing) and the phrase "Justicia." Just below this emblem is the City of Justice, which will once more be reconstituted on earth.

Yet there is a sinister element in the apocalypse which must precede the millenium: Anglos must be driven out. And Hispanos will be judged by whether they aided, stood aside from, or hindered the cause. Those who hindered will be treated harshly.

Gerry Noll, the Caudillo's lieutenant, has proclaimed as part of the Alianza creed:

. . . KNOW YE that We have exclusive and supreme jurisdiction within [New Mexico] over all persons and property situated therein. . . ."
We cannot afford to permit the present status quo to be maintained without actually destroying Our independence and autonomy. Consequently, We must take measures calculated to curtail the activities of any aggressors with the utmost dispatch . . . We shall enter troops into these territories to restore Our authority . . . woe to him who obeys the orders of the aggressor, for he shall be punished without mercy. . . .
THEREFORE KNOW YE that We shall commence to liberate Our kingdoms, realms, and dominions . . . We shall not take any prisoners of war, but shall take only war criminals and traitors and try [them] by a military tribunal and execute them.

At Tijerina's direction, the October 1967 convention of the Alianza unanimously set forth a weird dynastic claim: Gerry Noll was henceforth transformed into "Don Barne Quinto Cesar, King-Emperor of the Indies," the legitimate descendant of Ferdinand VII of Spain.

Dying Is Part of a King's Day's Work

In November Tijerina, "Don Barne," and several other Aliancistas stood trial for the charges stemming from the invasion of Kit Carson Forest in 1966. During the trial it was revealed that Noll's real name was Gerald Wayne Barnes, convicted of bank robbery in 1945, grand larceny in 1949, forgery in 1953, and third-degree assault in 1963. Found guilty, Noll and Tijerina were sentenced to three and two years respectively. At the trial Don Barne declared, "I am willing to die for my country and for my people. This is part of my job as king and all in a day's work." When sentenced in mid-December he retorted to the court, "It is I who make the laws—not the United States of America."

While waiting trial on the multiple charges of the June '67 raid and appealing against the decision in the first case,

Tijerina and his co-defendants were once more released on bond. On January 3, 1968, again in Tierra Amarilla, Deputy Sheriff Eulogio Salazar was kidnapped and beaten to death. Governor David Cargo, Campbell's successor, immediately revoked the bonds. Protests rapidly poured into the Governor's office from SNCC, MAPA, and other organizations, and a short time later Tijerina was out on bail again.

Since that time legal problems have necessarily absorbed most of Tijerina's energies, as he appealed the verdict of the first trial and prepared for the more serious set of charges (including kidnapping) stemming from the Tierra Amarilla affair. But the Caudillo found time to break into national headlines again in May and June when he led his followers at the Poor People's March on Washington. Alleging that the Negro leaders of the march refused to grant Mexican-Americans an adequate place in the sun, Tijerina cancelled Alianza participation in Resurrection City. Instead, he made use of his appearance in Washington to lecture State Department officials on the meaning of the Guadalupe Hidalgo Treaty—namely, the legitimacy of the Spanish land grants.

Tijerina had hoped to run for governor in the November 1968 elections, but the New Mexico Supreme Court disallowed his candidacy in October because of his conviction the previous year. Meanwhile the second (Tierra Amarilla) trial took place, during which Tijerina dramatically dismissed his lawyers and conducted his own defense. In mid-December his self-confidence was justified by his acquittal of kidnapping and two lesser counts. Other charges against him and nine other defendants had yet to come before the courts at the end of 1968.

But the real historical and sociological meaning of the Alianza cannot be solely understood in terms of its current embroilments or recent history in New Mexico. Most of the literature on the movement, so far, has dealt with the spectacular, bizarre, or violent elements involved; but the roots of primitive revolt go far back.

Since the enclosure movement began in Europe in the twelfth century, there have been scores of peasant revolts. Many sought the restoration of common lands taken by nobles and gentry.

In medieval Spain, many villages owned herds and land in common, and a number of these arrangements survived as late as the Spanish Civil War. These towns had once enjoyed special legal sanctions called *fueros,* by which they could themselves decide whether or not to enforce royal decrees and pay taxes.

One historian has written that "The village communities spontaneously developed an extensive system of municipal services, to the point of their sometimes reaching an advanced stage of communism." A scheme was proposed in 1631 to "nationalize all pasturage and establish each peasant with sufficient head of sheep and cattle to support him." In 1633 the Crown tried to implement this project by regulating tenancy and fixing rents in perpetuity, making leases irrevocable and hereditary, and setting up regulation commissions. Though the plan failed, the demands of shepherds for adequate grazing land were part of the

Hispanic tradition to which Tijerina appeals and went to Spain to study.

One student of Mexican-American culture, anthropologist Narcie González, writes that ". . . even now [1967] sheepherding remains an ideal way of life for the Hispano. . . . Virtually all contemporary accounts by social scientists comment upon the people's stated preference for this occupation. . . ." This preference explains why in Tijerina's Utopia the common lands are so highly valued. The Chama region, where the Tierra Amarilla revolt broke out, was principally a sheep-grazing area until after the Second World War.

What has occurred in New Mexico has been a breakdown of the traditional society, the ripping of the fabric of Hispano culture. In 1950, 41 percent of the Spanish-surname population in the state lived in urban areas; but by 1960, 61 percent did. Many of those moving to the cities (especially to Albuquerque) were ill prepared for their new way of life. In 1956 one investigator found that 834 out of 981 women in Albuquerque who received Aid to Dependent Children had Spanish surnames.

While the number of Anglo-Americans rapidly increased in New Mexico after World War II, the Mexican-American population was almost static, the high birth rate being offset by emigration to California. Consequently by 1960 the Anglo population in the state constituted almost two-thirds of the whole.

The legal structures of a modern capitalist society had by the late 1930's wrecked the traditional land-tenure patterns of the Upper Rio Grande. In 1940 Dr. George Sanchez reported that in Taos County "65 percent of the private lands represent land grants which have been subdivided or otherwise lost to the communities and families to which they were originally assigned. Of the original nine *mercedes* in Taos County, four were community grants and five were lands granted to individuals. . . . This cornerstone of Taos' economy has been destroyed by taxation and by uncontrolled exploitation." Furthermore, "Commercial livestock operators have acquired [the Hispano's] land grants and compete with him for grazing leases and permits on public lands. Exorbitant fees, taxes, and forced sales have crowded him out of his former grazing domain."

For a time the full impact of these changes were softened by the booming war and atomic energy economy in New Mexico, and by the fact that the National Forest Service seems to have acted as a surrogate patrón for the Hispano shepherd. Until drought in the 1960's forced a cutback, the Hispano could still obtain the use of federal lands for pasturing his livestock.

Rio Arriba County was one of the areas least affected by the state's economic growth. In 1960 it had the highest percentage of rural non-farm population of all New Mexico's counties (91.3 percent). It ranked high in native-born inhabitants, and low in the percentage of migrants. It had the third lowest median education and the fifth lowest median family income. In Rio Arriba and the other northern counties where the Spanish-speaking population predominates, the average per capita income in 1967 was less than $1,000, compared to the state average of $2,310 and the national average of $2,940. Furthermore, according to Governor Cargo, "11,000 of 23,000 residents of Rio Arriba County are on welfare rolls." The 1960 census showed that county with the state's highest rate of unemployment—15.1 percent—almost three times the state average.

Government Controls Grazing Lands

But it is not only unemployment that makes the residents of Rio Arriba dependent on federal and state largesse—72.1 percent of all land still available for grazing is owned by the US government in Kit Carson Forest. And what the government grants, it can, and sometimes does, also refuse.

The disintegration of the traditional Hispano community seems well underway, and Tijerina articulates widely-shared feelings that his people do not want to assimilate into Anglo culture. He also rejects relief as demoralizing to its recipients, stating again and again, "We will no longer take powdered milk in exchange for justice." Recent increases in welfare assistance may actually have aggravated the situation by raising the Hispanos' hopes for greater improvement.

Reaction to social disintegration can take many forms, and the Hispanic religious tradition—plus Tijerina's own background as a Pentecostal preacher—have helped channel it into millenarianism. In the 1930's a religious group called the Allelujahs, an Hispano version of the Holy Rollers, became popular, and before it faded out as many as half the people of some northern New Mexico communities had joined, taking part in religious services in which "Passages from the Revelation of St. John are favorite texts [according to a 1937 report], and lead to frenzies of religious ecstasy." The Allelujah experience has helped prepare the ground. So perhaps have the *Penitentes,* a lay brotherhood of Hispano mystics and self-flagellants that traces its origins back to the colonial era.

When the Alianza failed to obtain redress through the courts, the hope for and belief in extra-legal and supernatural means of relief—natural enough in the presence of the charismatic and fiery Tijerina—became exacerbated. When the National Forest Service recently cut back the use of grazing lands because of drought, the Hispanos were the hardest hit—and Tijerina was at hand to transform frustration into action. The frequency of millenarianism when belief in and identity with the dominant society are lost has been well documented in sociological literature. The Alianza constitutes an almost classic case.

Yet there is a "modern" dimension to the Alianza, and this is a direct outgrowth of its appearance in an industrial society with rapid transcontinental communications and ever-vigilant news media. The Alianza fits the requirements of a "primitive rebellion" or "revitalization movement," but its links with urban radical and reformist groups outside New Mexico show its potential for evolving into something more modern. Thus there are two distinct dimensions of the movement—the "primitive," rural, grass-roots constituency on the tributaries of the upper Rio Grande; and the "modern," urban, nationally-connected leadership in Albuquerque. The "visible" media-oriented sector is modern, but the "invisible" millenarian sector is not.

Tijerina's primary concern is still regaining lost community lands, as his action at the Poor People's March showed. The hunger for community lands—the *ejidos*—remains the basis for the "real" movement, despite manifestos of solidarity with the Black Panthers and denunciations of the war in Vietnam.

The ignorance of government officials of the basic nature of the movement is almost monumental. They tend to explain the Alianza away by easy, modern clichés. Some find in the references to common lands the spore of modern communism.

At the November 1967 trial, the prosecuting attorney declared, "This is not a social problem we're trying. This is a criminal problem." Even some sympathetic observers have used singularly inappropriate terms. Tom Wicker of the *New York Times* and Congressman Joseph Resnick, chairman of the House Agriculture Subcommittee on Rural Development, have both referred to Rio Arriba County as a "rural Watts."

But Rio Arriba has little in common with Watts. The majority of Aliancistas, the rural grassroots, are not industrial proletarians but primitive rebels—peasants reacting and striking back in millenarian fashion against the modernization that is tearing their society apart.

FURTHER READING

The Spanish Americans of New Mexico by Nancie L. Gonzalez (Albuquerque, N.M.: University of New Mexico Press, 1967).

Mexican American Youth: Forgotten at the Crossroads by Celia S. Heller (New York: Random House, 1966).

Awakening Minorities: American Indians, Mexican Americans, Puerto Ricans edited by John R. Howard (New Brunswick, N.J.: Transaction Books, 1972).

Primitive Rebels: Studies in Archaic Forms of Social Movement in the 19th and 20th Centuries by Eric J. Hobsbawn (New York: Norton, 1965). A basic source for theoretical and comparative purposes.

Reader in Comparative Religion by William A. Lessa and Evon Z. Vogt, ed. (New York: Harper & Row, 1965). Treats the sociological aspects of millenarianism, messianism, revitalization movements, and other religious phenomena.

Mexican Americans of South Texas by William Madsen (New York: Holt, Rinehart and Winston, 1964).

North From Mexico: The Spanish-Speaking People of the United States by Carey McWilliams (Philadelphia: J. B. Lippincott, 1948). An out-of-date but still indispensable work on the varieties of Mexican-American Culture.

Mexican Americans by J. W. Moore with A. Cuellar (Englewood Cliffs, N.J.: Prentice-Hall, 1970).

La Raza: Forgotten Americans edited by Julian Samora (Notre Dame, Ind.: University of Notre Dame Press, 1966). A wide-ranging contribution on Mexican-American society.

The Mexican Americans: An Awakening Minority by Manuel P. Servin (Beverly Hills, Calif.: Glencoe Press, 1970).

HERBERT HILL

Anti-Oriental Agitation and the Rise of Working-Class Racism

From the beginning of the new nation on the North American continent until our own time, each generation has been confronted by the question of who can be an American. The assumption that white Anglo-Saxons are the real "Americans" has permeated virtually the entire society. Conformity to Anglo-Saxon physical appear-

ance, religion, language, traditions and culture was long assumed to be the decisive factor in determining who could and who could not be considered an American.

From the colonial period through the early history of the United States, the white settlers developed policies that resulted in genocide, sequestration and slavery for the non-white populations. The Indians who survived the white man's slaughter were confined to limited territories or reservations. Most blacks were held in a condition of slavery that legally declared them to be subhuman property; and blacks who were not slaves were denied basic rights and could not achieve equal citizenship with the white population. But whatever difficulties successive waves of non-Anglo-Saxon white immigrants might face, they could eventually become naturalized and gain the rights of citizenship.

The Chinese immigration beginning in 1848 and the subsequent conflict between the forces of inclusion and exclusion are a prime example of the effect of racism on the "Americanization" process. For the first time a non-white population had arrived in this country for whose fate there was no precedent within the policies of the established system. The Chinese were not pressed into slavery nor sequestered on reservations. Because of new manpower needs that required a free but controlled and mobile work force, a different model for dealing with non-white labor had to be constructed—a model that encompassed a racial labor caste system together with rigid segregation for a non-slave but racially dintinct people. The Chinese were from the moment of their arrival a conflict population: though not slaves they were limited to certain categories of employment, denied basic rights, not considered as potential Americans and not allowed to become citizens. The Chinese were to be available for a very high degree of exploitation but were to be kept separate and apart from the rest of society. In part, this model of labor exploitation was derived from the earlier experience with a racially distinct slave labor force; in turn it provided a model that significantly influenced the treatment of blacks who were to be emancipated more than a decade later.

When the Chinese began to arrive in large numbers after 1850, the labor needs of the burgeoning urban factories and the vast railroad construction projects in the western part of the country could no longer be met by the existing white labor force. A slave system—which required a large capital outlay, ownership and resale and continuity of work over a long period—was not suited to these new conditions. The Chinese, easily exploitable as cheap labor by virtue of their endurance, skills and availability, were an excellent solution. They had an additional advantage for their white employers: since, unlike slaves, they were not property and since, unlike the white work force, they could not become citizens, no one had to take responsibility for them when their usefulness came to an end.

Still, the solution was only partial. The white workingman—faced with a racially separate work force that could be manipulated to the white worker's competitive disadvantage—had to come to terms with the crosscurrents of both class and racial conflict on a vast scale.

The choice made by labor organizations—their vigorous participation and leadership in the anti-Oriental agitation and their use of racial distinction to keep categories of workers outside their organizations—was an important factor in setting a pattern for the establishment of a racial labor caste system which was to develop into a major characteristic of the American labor movement. The relationship of racism to labor unionism, expressed in exclusionary and other discriminatory practices against Orientals and blacks, must be understood as part of a continuing historical process, rather than as one of direct causal effect.

For white labor these issues were not theoretical abstractions. They involved fundamental matters of work and social status. As successive generations of white immigrants effectively used labor unions to acculterate and become Americans, they acted through the same labor organizations to exclude non-whites from certain occupations and from society. Thus, organized labor has played an important role in the inclusion-exclusion process of Americanization.

Organized labor's role in the anti-Oriental agitation illustrates the process by which racism was institutionalized. From 1850 to 1875 the main thrust of the anti-Oriental movement was confined to California, Oregon and the state of Washington where the Chinese were sought out by entrepreneurs who saw great advantages in their industriousness and their capacity to work together in teams. They were simultaneously regarded as a threat by white workers who found it more and more difficult to compete against them. The Chinese settled overwhelmingly in the mining districts; they nearly always worked the abandoned or least desirable mines, making these mining operations profitable. As early as 1852 white miners in several areas forced Chinese workers out of mining operations and called for the prohibition of Chinese immigration. That year white miners in Marysville, California adopted a resolution denying mining claims to Chinese. Other communities passed laws excluding Chinese from mining and forced Chinese workers to leave mining camps. Not infrequently the expulsion of Chinese miners was accompanied by violence, as at Coal Creek Mine in King County, Washington, where the living quarters of Chinese were burned to the ground.

The Chinese, under pressure from white miners and special tax assessments against them levied by the state, began to leave the mining districts. Most of those forced to leave went to the cities, mainly San Francisco, Sacramento and Los Angeles. They later went to Wyoming, Oregon, Idaho and other states where the problem took on new and more ominous dimensions.

Chinese labor was also later used extensively in railroad construction. Historian Walton Bean writes:

The first experiment, with a crew of 50 Chinese in

1865, was so phenomenally successful that agents were soon recruiting them by the thousands, first in California and then in South China. At the peak of construction work, the Central Pacific would employ more than 10,000 Chinese laborers.... Labor unions in San Francisco protested, but as the railroad advanced into the mountains and construction continued throughout the year, white workers lost all interest in jobs that required the performance of hard and dangerous labor under the conditions of winter in the Sierras. Meanwhile, the state of California continued to punish the Chinese, preventing them from becoming citizens (even as they were accused of disdaining the privilege), excluding their children from public schools and attempting repeatedly to restrict their immigration (though white foreigners were encouraged to enter). Various anti-Chinese legislative measures, including special taxation, were eventually ruled illegal by the California courts. So long as the issue was confined to California, the racist attacks against the Chinese could simply be regarded as a response to regional conditions. But once the Chinese issue transcended the borders of California, its regional peculiarity could no longer be argued.

The enlargement of the obsession with the problem of Chinese labor corresponded roughly with the integration of the western mining economy into the national economic structure. Prior to the completion of the transcontinental railroad, influential eastern leaders, particularly politicians, businessmen and newspaper editors, had looked rather indulgently on the use of Chinese laborers in western mining and manufacturing. But during 1869 and 1870 this attitude shifted dramatically. The "problem" was spreading across the nation to the consciousness of the East. Henry George sounded the alarm against multitudes of cheap "coolie" labor in the New York *Tribune* on May 1, 1869. Southern planters at a meeting in Nashville in 1869 called for coolie labor to replace recently emancipated blacks (the call went unheeded), and 75 Chinese boot and shoe workers were introduced into the shoe factory of Calvin Sampson in North Adams, Massachusetts for the purpose of breaking a labor strike in 1870.

Because it involved the actual introduction of Chinese workers into eastern industry, the North Adams incident especially seemed to labor unions to be the opening trickle in a tidal wave of coolie labor that would overwhelm the East. Labor unions were then able to argue that the Chinese threatened the entire union movement and that only a national policy of exclusion could save the nation from destruction and contamination. At the moment when the Chinese were brought into North Adams the American economy was on the threshold of a protracted decline. With the depression of 1873, widespread unemployment provided a docile and readily available surplus work force. In essence, the depression destroyed organized labor's hope that without Chinese workers the labor supply would be small enough to allow trade unions to maintain control over wage scales in certain occupations. Both labor leaders and rank-and-file workers assumed a priori that the Chinese posed a definite economic threat to their interests, and that this cheap coolie labor was largely responsible for the depressed conditions of the American economy after 1873.

This "fact" soon became an unquestioned belief of the labor movement during the last part of the nineteenth century. For example, the Colorado Bureau of Labor Statistics' first report in 1887 solicited the general opinions and attitudes of Colorado workers in an effort to present rank-and-file views of "what labor wants." A white miner in Lake County, Colorado responded to the Bureau of Labor Statistics' questionnaire: "Laws should be passed compelling equal pay to each sex for equal work; making all manual labor no more than eight hours a day so workers can share in the gains and honors of advancing civilization; prohibiting any more Chinese coming to this country on account of physiological, labor, sanitary and other considerations, as the country would be happier without Chinamen and trusts." Note the automatic equation of Chinese labor and trusts, as if these were the twin (and equally dangerous) menaces that American labor had to combat. What makes this equation especially significant is the fact that there was not a single Chinese person living in Lake County, Colorado, either five years before or five years after the miner made that statement.

It should also be noted that since the Chinese numbered only 368 outside the West in 1870, even the most insistent labor politician could not factually argue that the depressed conditions of white workers were the result of competition from Chinese labor in that early period. Another problem with the apologies for labor's racism on economic grounds is that such a view ignores the ideological content of the anti-Chinese efforts within the labor movement. Selig Perlman, one of the writers at the forefront of that view, blatantly reveals the confusion of class interests with racial consciousness. Summing up what was obviously labor's own conception of its role in securing adoption of the Chinese Exclusion Act of 1882, Perlman writes that "the anti-Chinese agitation in California, culminating as it did in the Exclusion Law passed in 1882, was doubtless the most important single factor in the history of American labor, for without it the entire country might have been overrun by Mongolian labor, and the labor movement might have become a conflict of races instead of classes." These words, let it be emphasized, are quoted not because they are true but because they reflect the view held by organized labor and many of its academic apologists, even at the present time.

Three major factors after 1873 kept the Chinese question alive as a national issue: local western demagoguery, the fact that organized labor took up the anti-Chinese litany after 1870, and, in the wake of this, the recognition by both major national political parties that an anti-Chinese stand could win votes. The Democratic party, attempting to revive itself after the Civil War, used an anti-Chinese position to appeal to working men. The Democrats demonstrated an amazing resurgence in California and elsewhere on a labor platform that featured, above all else, attacks on Chinese labor and immigration. Soon the Republican party perceived the possibilities of the anti-Oriental agitation for its own purposes. The compromise of 1876 in effect dismissed the Negro as a factor in national politics and forced the Republicans to look elsewhere for political support. By then, the Republicans had come to understand that working men were important in building a successful national coalition and that the anti-Chinese position was winning politics.

Prior to 1876 and after 1882, the leadership of the anti-Chinese movement was held by the leaders of the craft unions—precisely those unions that had the least to fear in terms of economic competition with the Chinese. For the leaders of these unions the anti-Chinese movement became a means by which they could manipulate the political and organizational energy of the entire labor force, skilled and unskilled, thereby using the Chinese issue as a device to prevent an active challenge to their leadership and to their control of unionized occupations by unemployed and unskilled workers. This is not to say that at times hysterical xenophobia against the Chinese on the part of labor leaders was merely a convenient device. They were also vehemently asserting Caucasian superiority as an ideology. In 1906 Samuel Gompers went so far as to say that "Maintenance of the nation depended upon maintenance of racial purity," and that it was contrary to the national interest to permit the arrival of "cheap labor that could not be Americanized and could not be taught to render the same intelligent efficient service as was supplied by American workers." The equation of racism and Americanism was reaffirmed.

Given the great effort generated in the ranks of labor, passage of the Exclusion Act of 1882 could be regarded as only a partial victory. It of course barred all Chinese workers from entering the United States in the future, but it did not address itself to the 100,000-plus Chinese who were already here. As labor finally understood the act, it was not adequate, it was not a full solution, and labor had a mixed reaction to the passage of the law. Therefore, the anti-Chinese position was kept alive after 1882 by labor leadership. For example, Terrance Powderly of the Knights of Labor called for the total elimination of all Chinese in the United States at the end of 1882, even while he celebrated the passage of the Exclusion Act as a labor victory.

This new stage of anti-Chinese agitation corresponded to a period of national economic decline. The difference between 1876 and 1882 was not that the Chinese had flooded out of the West into eastern industry as had been feared in 1870 (there were still only 3,663 Chinese living outside the western states in 1880), but rather that the national political system in the seventies had given credence to labor's extreme anti-Chinese stance. The onset of the industrial depression in 1882 served as an excuse for labor to renew and extend its anti-Chinese campaign. The effects of the 1882-86 depression were borne largely by workers and consumers in terms of declining wage rates and high unemployment. As the ranks of the unemployed grew there was increasing pressure on labor leaders and politicians to give some direction to the discontent of both organized and unorganized workers. Anti-coolieism was their response. Anti-coolieism meant good politics in 1882 as it had in 1876, not only for the labor politicians but also for the trade union leaders who used the issue to divert pressure on them to make more meaningful or effective challenges to the political and economic order.

The politics of anti-coolieism was translated into direct action in the form of violence against Chinese along the Pacific Coast and in some areas of the mountain states during 1885 and 1886. The pattern of these attacks conformed to a standard pathology. In 1885 the nationwide depression reached its most severe stage. As this point was reached in a given locale, white workingmen, usually under the combined leadership of union officials and local politicians, often formed anti-Chinese organizations and sounded the call for the physical removal of the Chinese and their belongings from the area. The expulsion of Chinese usually followed one of three patterns. Often it took place very rapidly and spontaneously. Sometimes it followed a period of agitation which saw a rather intensive involvement of white workers in the local politics of anti-coolieism. Finally, agitation to expel Chinese would lead to savage violence, as in Rock Springs, Wyoming where some 30 Chinese were killed by white miners in 1885. Similar violence occurred in Eureka, California and in Tacoma and Seattle, Washington where entire Chinese populations were driven out by force in 1886.

Pogroms and organized actions against the Chinese were hardly new. There had been periodic outbreaks of violence against the Chinese in California, while they were blamed for everything from drought in San Francisco to the full-scale depression that struck California in 1877. The depression of 1877 in California is worth noting because it gave rise to the Workingman's Party of California—which combined a platform of idealism and compassion toward poor white workers with an extreme racism toward non-white workers. It was founded by one of the most interesting demagogues in American history, Denis Kearney. Kearney was a self-educated Irish drayman who had spent his early years as a poor lad in

Anti-Oriental Agitation and the Rise of Working-Class Racism

County Cork. Seizing his opportunity, he rose overnight from obscurity to national fame. He became so notorious that Lord Bryce, writing in the early 1880s, devoted an entire chapter of his great study of America to "Kearneyism in California."

The governing assumption of the Workingman's Party of California was that the rich and the Chinese were engaged in a tacit conspiracy to oppress white workers, small farmers, mechanics and struggling businessmen. The party's platform proposed a number of far-reaching economic reforms, including a system of progressive taxation, an extensive welfare state program "for the poor and unfortunate, the weak, the helpless and especially the young," the election of humble men to office and the destruction of "land monopoly." On the Chinese question, the platform was violently racist. "We propose to rid the country of cheap Chinese labor as soon as possible and by all means in our power, because it tends still more to degrade labor and aggrandize capital." They would "mark as public enemies" employers who refused to discharge their Chinese help. Throughout the winter of 1877, workingmen's clubs proliferated in the poorer neighborhoods of San Francisco. Having found their scapegoat, Germans, French, Scandinavians and Italians, socialists

and anti-socialists alike, all overcame their differences in their haste to join the new party.

Economic improvement sounded the death knell of the Workingmen's Party and eventually forced Kearney's retirement. Historically, radical or labor parties arise in the United States during periods of high unemployment; economic despair drives the workers to seek new political solutions. In prosperous times these parties disappear or merge with the two major parties. The Workingmen's Party of California suffered this fate. By mid-1880, it was finished in all but name, and Kearney's influence was gone.

During this period the California state legislature and various cities subjected the Chinese to extreme legal persecution. As early as 1870 the state legislature categorically outlawed the employment of Chinese in certain public works projects. Two years later it mounted a full-scale attack on them by prohibiting Chinese from owning real estate or securing business licenses.

Meanwhile San Francisco was imposing its own restrictions. For example, a license fee of $8.00 a year was demanded of one-horse laundry wagons. But those laundrymen who collected and delivered by foot (the Chinese) had to pay $60.00. The case of the vegetable peddlers was similar. The Chinese, who carried their

Racism and Repression

vegetables in baskets, were required to pay five times as much—$40.00 a year compared to $8.00—as those who used wagons. San Francisco also passed a Cubic Air Ordinance, which prohibited any tenant or factory worker from occupying a room that provided less than 500 cubic feet of air for him. So many Chinese were arrested that the jails were violating the law. Especially galling to the Chinese was the so-called Queue Ordinance, which stipulated that criminals must have their hair cropped. For the Chinese this meant loss of their pigtails—a form of sacrilege. Eventually all these ordinances were declared unconstitutional, but they caused much hardship during the years they were enforced.

And, as usual, whites often took matters into their own hands. No one knows how often the police looked away while the Chinese were violently attacked in the streets. It can be assumed that crimes against them were commonplace and almost always went unpunished. Generally, Chinese did not register formal complaints as they were legally prevented from testifying against whites. The most serious instance of organized violence against them took place in Los Angeles where a mob shot and hanged 20 Chinese, pillaged homes and stores and tortured Orientals.

With the return of prosperity and the decline of "Kearneyism," anti-Chinese agitation among the white workers of California entered a new phase. The cause was now taken up primarily by trade unions, representing the craftsmen and mechanics—the labor aristocracy. In April 1880, delegates from 40 labor unions met in San Francisco and established a so-called League of Deliverance (from the Chinese menace). The man most responsible for organizing the League—he was elected chairman—was one Frank Roney. Roney had been the leader of the anti-Kearney faction of the Workingmen's Party before becoming a socialist and a member of the violently racist San Francisco Seamen's Protective Union. Over the years he had assiduously built up support within the union movement to oust the Chinese from their jobs and, of course, keep them out of the country. His efforts had resulted in the formation of the League of Deliverance, which, within months after its founding, had 13 branches throughout the state and over 4,000 members. Persuading the public to boycott Chinese-made goods was the main tactic employed by the League, and it was a smashing success. Merchants refrained from buying commodities made by Chinese labor and many factories dismissed Chinese workers. How were the Chinese workers supposed to live? Leaders of the white labor organizations had no interest in such matters.

The League of Deliverance dissolved in 1882, its mission accomplished. In that year Congress enacted the Chinese Exclusion Law. The League's highly successful tactic of boycotting Chinese-made goods had actually been introduced earlier by white unionized cigarmakers.

From the start, the white cigarmakers marched in the forefront of the assault on the Chinese. It was the white cigarmakers, too, who discovered a most ingenious method of punishing their Chinese competitors. In 1874 they adopted a white label to indicate that they, the white union men, had produced the cigars. Accompanying the label was a certificate granted to those proprietors who sold only their cigars. The certificate contained the following message:

> Protect Home Industry. To All Whom It May Concern: This is to certify that the holder of this certificate has pledged himself to the Trades Union Mutual Alliance, neither to buy nor sell CHINESE MADE CIGARS, either wholesale or retail, and that he further pledges himself to assist in the fostering of Home Industry by the patronage of PACIFIC COAST LABEL CIGARS of which the above is a facsimile.

The facsimile of the label showed a dragon on one side, the union mark on the other, and the words, "White Labor, White Labor." The practice of issuing labels quickly caught on. In 1875 the St. Louis cigarmakers followed suit with a bright red one. Finally, in their general convention three years later, the Cigar Makers' International Union decided on a blue one. Thus, the great tradition of the union label began as a racist stratagem.

In California the proponents of the union label came not only from the ranks of organized labor but from

THE ARGUMENT OF NATIONALITY.

Excited Mob—"*We don't want any cheap-labor foreigners intruding upon us native-born citizens.*"

Anti-Oriental Agitation and the Rise of Working-Class Racism

small cigar producers, such as the White Cigar Makers' Association. By the mid-1880s the industry was becoming rapidly rationalized, meaning that the larger concerns, using a more refined division of labor, could manufacture cigars at a cheaper price than the smaller ones. Usually it was the larger concerns that employed Chinese who learned their trade quickly and well. The label thus "became a means of product differentiation by which small producers could cling to a toe-hold in the market." But the process of rationalization had gone so far that by 1885 almost seven-eighths of the cigarmakers of San Francisco were Chinese. The manufacturers hired them against prevailing public opinion because they had to meet the competition from the East or perish.

Precisely at this point the Cigar Makers' International Union (CMIU) entered the picture. Under the leadership of erstwhile Socialists like Adolph Strasser and Samuel Gompers the CMIU concentrated on securing higher wages and better working conditions for its skilled members, leaving the unskilled and disadvantaged to fend for themselves. In this way an aristocracy of labor emerged, enjoying increasing benefits while the rest of the work force, having no leverage in the open labor market, stagnated.

In 1884 the CMIU established Local 224 in San Francisco to drive Orientals out of the trade and give the unemployed white cigarmakers of the East (themselves casualties of rationalization) the jobs then held by the Chinese. The astonishing fact was that the whites were content to work at the same rate of pay—a complete reversal of roles. Now it was the whites who were entering into competition with the Chinese.

The Cigar Makers' International Union attacked the companies that employed the Chinese, and of course the Chinese themselves. The large manufacturers were the only major obstacle in the way of the union. The union's tactic was to persuade one large concern to hire just a few white workers. This occurred when the firm of Koeniger, Falk and Mayer took on a handful of whites. Soon the handful had turned into nearly half of the 160 man work force. The Chinese employees of Koeniger, Falk and Mayer knew that their days were numbered, and, with nothing to lose, organized a strike in protest against their displacement. The white community of San Francisco was shocked by this unprecedented show of audacity.

Other Chinese cigarmakers, employed elsewhere, stayed at their jobs. But the CMIU took advantage of the threat, now raised for the first time, of massive, industry-wide resistance by the Chinese. The Chinese were always regarded as servile and congenitally incapable of standing up for the rights of labor. Now the white cigarmakers union was claiming that its men were more compliant and trustworthy than the refractory Chinese. Once again the whites unhesitatingly reversed roles when it suited them to do so.

A WORD OF CAUTION TO OUR FRIENDS, THE CIGAR-MAKERS.
Through the smoke it is easy to see the approach of Chinese cheap labor.

In any case, the job walkout by the Chinese prompted the entire labor movement in San Francisco to take up the cause of the beleaguered white workers. The Knights of Labor and other organizations led a boycott of all brands of cigars except that of Koeniger, Falk and Mayer. The campaign was successful. By the end of November 1885 the large producers had agreed to the demands of the union. Jake Wolf, president of the San Francisco Cigar Makers' Union, extracted a promise from them that all of the Chinese would be removed from the industry the moment white workers replaced them. The target date was January 1, 1886. The target date was not met, but the Chinese were in time eliminated completely from the industry. A process of racial occupational eviction had begun that would soon be used by organized labor against black workers in many occupations.

Meanwhile organized labor in general responded to the controversy in the cigar trade by mounting a new attack on the Chinese. On November 30, 1885 delegates from 64 Pacific Coast organizations gathered at an extraordinary congress to frame a program against the Chinese "menace." Represented were trade unions, radical and conservatives alike, the Knights of Labor, the Anarcho-Communists of the International Working People's Association, and the Socialist Labor Party. "It was," said the chairman of the congress, "a queer combination of heterogenous elements." But on one thing they could all agree: that the Chinese must go. The question was how and when.

It did not take the congress long to take up the ques-

Racism and Repression

tion. One of the representatives of the Sailors' Union offered a resolution to expel the Chinese from San Francisco within 60 days. But the conservatives, consisting mainly of Knights of Labor delegates, thought labor should not lay down ultimatums which it could not enforce except by insurrectionary violence. Opposing the resolution too were the more principled members of the Socialist movement.

The advocates of immediate expulsion came from the left. Generally, those of the extreme left were the more intense in their desire to take up arms against the Chinese. One member of the International Working People's Association, a sailor named Alfred Fuhrman, maintained that the Chinese should be thrown out of the city at once. "By force," he asserted, "is the only way to remove the coolie and 20 days is enough to do it in." Under this kind of pressure, the congress passed the resolution by a vote of 60 to 47. Most of the representatives of the Knights of Labor then left the hall; they refused to be part of an organization openly advocating force and violence.

The other trade unions in the congress were perhaps as adverse as the Knights to force and violence, and they had no intention of honoring the resolution. But they wanted the Knights to leave the congress, and so used the militant radicals for their own ends. After the Knights left, the trade unions demanded that the resolution be reconsidered on the floor. Reference to an exact time period for the expulsion of the Chinese was deleted. In its final form the resolution merely expressed the sense of the congress that the Chinese should leave San Francisco and the Pacific Coast. The congress did, however, establish a trade union council for San Francisco (later the Federated Trades Council, then the San Francisco Labor Council) that over the next decades remained in the forward ranks of the crusade against the Oriental races in America.

The American Federation of Labor's predecessor and parent organization, the Federation of Organized Trades and Labor Unions, at its first convention in 1881, condemned the Chinese cigarmakers of California and recommended that only union label cigars be bought. But the leaders of the Federation (after 1886 the AFL) were not content merely to sanction, perhaps cynically, the movement against the Chinese. Instead, they became the most articulate champions of the anti-Oriental cause in America. No man was more persistent in providing leadership and support than Samuel Gompers, the president of the AFL (except for one year) from its inception to his death in 1924. He was himself an immigrant Jew who had early in his life embraced socialist ideals of brotherhood and the solidarity of the toiling class. But he later repudiated these ideas and became the major spokesman for concepts of racial and national superiority within organized labor.

What he really thought of Oriental workers—leaving aside his professions of "profound respect" for them in the autobiography he wrote in the last years of his life—is best revealed in a tract that he and another official of the AFL, Herman Gutstadt, co-authored at the turn of the century. Its title, *Some Reasons For Chinese Exclusion: Meat vs. Rice, American Manhood Against Asiatic Coolieism—Which Shall Survive?* will give an accurate enough idea of its content. First published in 1902, the pamphlet was written at the behest of the Chinese Exclusion Convention of 1901. Its purpose was to persuade Congress to renew the Exclusion Law, due to expire the following year. Gompers states that "...the racial dif-

Samuel Gompers was the major spokesman for the anti-Oriental view of organized labor.

ferences between American whites and Asiatics would never be overcome. The superior whites had to exclude the inferior Asiatics by law, or if necessary, by force of arms." The Chinese were congenitally immoral: "The Yellow Man found it natural to lie, cheat and murder and 99 out of every 100 Chinese are gamblers."

Gompers draws all the arguments that the anti-Chinese forces had been advancing since the 1850s. Only now they are decked out in new dress, for this is the period when the West trembled at the yellow peril and imagined that the dread Mongol hordes were about to march again. The Chinese conspire to overcome class differences, thereby placing white labor at a serious disadvantage. He stresses a familiar theme—the tendency of the Chinese to relentlessly degrade labor and create a new servile element in society.

Modeling himself on a Victorian dime novelist, Gompers conjures up a terrible picture of how the Chinese entice little white boys and girls into becoming "opium fiends." Condemned to spend their days in the back of laundry rooms, these tiny lost souls yield up their virgin bodies to their maniacal yellow captors. "What other crimes were committed in those dark fetid places," Gompers writes, "when these little innocent victims of the Chinamen's wiles were under the influence of the drug, are almost too horrible to imagine.... There are hundreds, aye, thousands, of our American girls and boys who have acquired this deathly habit and are doomed, hopelessly doomed, beyond a shadow of redemption."

Meat vs. Rice was reissued by the Asiatic Exclusion League in 1908, six years after it had been first published. Yet the Chinese question was long since closed, the third and final exclusion law having been enacted in 1902. Gompers and the labor federation arranged for its reissue because the "Mongolian menace" had suddenly reemerged. This time the enemy were the Japanese, several thousand of whom were immigrating to the United States every year. Accordingly, all that Gompers had said about the Chinese was applied with equal force to the Japanese. Having learned much from its experience in the attack upon the Chinese, organized labor once again assumed leadership of the campaign and did not rest until the Japanese too had been driven out of competing occupations and denied entry into the United States.

Before 1890 only a handful of Japanese had emigrated to the United States, less than 150 in all. Japan was closed to the world until 1853, when Admiral Perry's fleet opened Japan to the western world. Between 1886 and 1890, 3,000 Japanese came to America. During the next ten years the number rose to 27,000; and during the next eight to 127,000. In the period of the greatest immigration—1902 to 1908—the yearly total fluctuated between 11,000 and 30,000. At the beginning the *issei* (or first generation Japanese) faced little discrimination. Issei dressed and otherwise bore themselves like Western-

ers and were unfailingly "polite, courteous, smiling" as one newspaper put it. Most of them served as railroad men, as domestics, in some places as miners, lumbermen or fishermen, or they became storeowners catering to their own people. They quietly lived in their own communities, notably around San Francisco, Sacramento and the upper San Joaquin Valley. Later, the bulk of them moved to southern California.

Until 1905 attacks against the issei were sporadic and brief. As early as 1888 the San Francisco Trades Council called attention to a "recently developed phase of the Mongolian issue." Four years later, Denis Kearney came out of retirement to alert the public to "another breed of Asiatic slaves" who were filling the gap "made vacant by the Chinese." "We are paying out our money," he cried, so that "fully developed men who know no morals but vice (may) sit beside our... daughters to debauch (and) demoralize them. The Japs Must Go!" But Kearney's day was over. The public paid no heed to his ranting; nothing was heard of him again.

In 1900 a rather serious upsurge of anti-Japanese sentiment took place in San Francisco. It was instigated by the local labor unions and their friends, among them the mayor of San Francisco. He spoke a language which must have sounded familiar to many of his listeners. "The Chinese and Japanese are not bona fide citizens. They are not the stuff of which American citizens can be made." Later that same year the AFL took official notice of the Japanese and included them in demanding the total exclusion of "cheap coolie labor." And in 1901 the Chinese Exclusion Convention, which consisted largely of delegates from organized labor (800 out of 1,000) was told that it had better become aware of "the Japs," for they were "more intelligent and civilized... than the Chinamen."

By mid-1905 the labor unions of California had joined forces to establish the Asiatic Exclusion League. Four prominent San Francisco labor union executives were primarily responsible for launching the League's career; all four, it should be mentioned, were themselves immigrants (as were Kearney and Gompers). They were Patrick H. McCarthy (from Ireland), chief of the San Francisco Building Trades Council; his assistant, Olaf Tveitmoe (from Sweden), later to be convicted of participating in a plot to bomb the Los Angeles *Times;* Walter MacArthur (from Scotland) and Andrew Furuseth (from Norway), both representing the Sailors' Union.

Historians and biographers have duly acknowledged Furuseth's achievements. By the sheer force of his personality, he persuaded Congress to improve working conditions on American merchant ships. But beneath the aura that encircles his life and work lies the specter of racism. Improving the lot of seamen was less important to him than excluding "the Oriental" from American ships. The power of the white races, he claimed, rested on

PACIFIC RAILROAD COMPLETE.

its mastery of the seas. That control over the world which the white race—or a segment of it—had maintained unimpaired for 3,000 years now stood in jeopardy because "Oriental" seamen were replacing the whites. It followed that the law Furuseth wanted passed should include a provision forcing Asian seamen off the ships. Such a provision was indeed incorporated into the LaFollette Seamen's Act.

Such thinking was typical of the Asiatic Exclusion League. Its purpose was not only to stop all further Japanese immigration to America; it was also to deny or circumscribe their right to a livelihood. Usually the exclusionists depended on sweeping demagogic verbal attacks on the issei. The League, for example, declared in its statement of principles: 1) that the Japanese (like the Chinese) were unassimilable 2) that "foreigners so cocky, with such distinct racial, social and religious prejudices" would only cause "friction" 3) that Americans could not compete "with a people having a low standard of civilization, living and wage" 4) that American women must not be allowed to intermarry with "Asiatics" 5) that they must not be allowed to become citizens and 6) that if "the Jap" is not excluded how can the Chinese continue to be kept out?

During this period the AFL refused charters to agricultural worker's unions whose membership consisted mainly of Mexican and Japanese farm laborers in the sugar beet fields of California. There were Japanese trade unions in the early 1900s, but whenever they turned to their white "brethren" for help, they found none other than Samuel Gompers and the AFL in their path. In 1902-1903, the Japanese workers and contractors (middlemen who supplied labor and maintained discipline) of the Oxnard, California beet fields organized a strike after the owners, acting in concert, decided to eliminate the contractors and recruit the men themselves. The strike proved successful. More important, it resulted in the creation of the Sugar Beet and Farm Laborer's Union of Oxnard, its members consisting of Mexican as well as Japanese field hands. The Union promptly did what other unions were doing at the time—it applied to the American Federation of Labor for a charter.

In reply, Samuel Gompers wrote, "Your union must guarantee that it will under no circumstances accept membership of any Chinese or Japanese." In short, Gompers was asking the union to disband as the condition for securing a charter. J. H. Larraras, secretary of the Oxnard union, denounced Gompers' racism and inhumanity. He pointed out that "our Japanese here were the first to recognize the importance of cooperating and uniting in demanding a fair wage scale."

But Gompers refused to grant the charter. His blatant repudiation of earlier working class principles was excessive even for a number of unions within the Federation. The Los Angeles Labor Council resolved, in a show of solidarity with the Sugar Beet and Farm Laborers' Union, "that time has come to organize Japanese workers in fields into the Federation." And these sentiments were shared by the Chicago-based *American Labor Union Journal*. It wrote, in June 1903, that so long as non-whites were barred from membership in the AFL, just so long would it be impossible "to organize the wage workers of California for the protection of their interests."

As before with the Chinese, Gompers led the attacks upon the Japanese within organized labor. What Gompers thought of the prospect of organizing the Japanese can be gauged by his remarks at the 1904 convention of the American Federation of Labor. "The American God," he solemnly stated before his audience of delegates representing more than a million workers, "was not the God of the Japanese." The convention went on to give his anti-Japanese position its seal of approval by passing a resolution specifying that the "Japanese were as difficult to assimilate into the American culture as were the Chinese."

At the turn of the century, the American Federation of Labor was committed to a policy of racial superiority and national glorification and many of its affiliates engaged in a variety of overt discriminatory practices against Negroes and Orientals. This development, together with the refusal to organize the unskilled and mass-production workers, further alienated non-whites from organized labor. The discriminatory pattern was now firmly established and would continue for many decades.

Throughout the early months of 1906 tension continued to build in San Francisco as the Japanese were subject to one harassment after another. It was commonplace for them to be assaulted and beaten by gangs of hoodlums. Between May and November 290 cases of assault were reported; none of the white assailants was captured, but seven Japanese were arrested for defending themselves.

While Japanese individuals feared to walk the streets, Japanese restaurants were terrorized by a boycott organized by the labor-dominated Asiatic Exclusion League. In June 1906 the League's executive board concluded that too many "wage earners, laborers and mechanics" were eating in Japanese restaurants and ordered union members to cease eating in them or face penalties. The ban went into full effect four months later. Picket lines were formed around the restaurants and matchbooks were distributed with the label, "White men and women patronize your own race." The organizers frequently punctuated their racial admonitions by smashing windows and beating up owners. Again no arrests were made. The boycott illustrated the racism of the white trade unionists. Significantly, the Japanese restaurant workers applied for admission to the San Francisco Cooks' and Waiters' Union—the prime movers of the boycott—but were resoundingly turned down. The boycott also revealed the corruption to which racism naturally lent itself. When the Japanese consented to pay over $350 for "protection" the boycott was lifted. The union leaders had made a modest killing.

In 1920 the California State Federation of Labor helped form the Japanese Exclusion League of California; the other contributing charter organizations were the Native Sons of the Golden West, the American Legion, the California Federation of Women's Clubs, the California State Grange, the Farm Bureau and the Loyal Order of Moose. The old League had been led by San Francisco labor; this one was dominated by middle-class and small-town elements. It was the farmers, the small businessmen and other "respectable" citizens of California who were principally responsible for pressuring the legislature to enact a second Alien Land Law in 1920. More important, they were largely responsible for getting Congress—in the face of vigorous protests from the Japanese government—to pass an immigration law that barred all but a handful of Japanese (or members of any other non-white race) from entering the United States. The chapter was thus closed. The Japanese had officially joined the Chinese as a people declared unworthy of becoming American.

White working-class racism did not suddenly emerge full-blown. It gestated over a long period of time, advancing from stage to stage, incorporating the "Chinese question," the "Japanese question" and the "Negro question." Their success in excluding what they called "Mongolians" from the labor force suggested to the leadership of the American Labor movement how they could deal with the black worker. In each instance the objective was the same: to drive the workers of the offending "non-Caucasian" race from the job market, either (as in the case of the Chinese and the Japanese) by keeping them out of the country or (as in the case of blacks, Mexican-Americans and other "tainted" groups) by limiting them to low-paying, unskilled, non-mobile jobs outside of the mainstream of the American labor force.

It may be objected that the racial views of Gompers, Furuseth and other labor leaders should not be singled out for special notice or criticism, for as some have argued they merely reflected the zeitgeist. But the fallacy of the zeitgeist argument is that it receives its justification in retrospect from those labor historians who either eliminated or diminished the choices that confronted the major figures in the period under investigation. The zeitgeist did not command American labor organizations to embrace a policy of racism, and it certainly did not command the AFL, which spoke for the overwhelming majority of organized workers from the 1890s on, to be even more militantly racist than Americans in general.

The responsibility for what the AFL and its affiliated unions did lay with the AFL itself—it could have taken an alternative course at the time. It could have practiced what its leaders occasionally preached, namely, that all workers were equal, that no person should be treated as a commodity, that capital was the common enemy of all workers. Instead, the American Federation of Labor acted on the assumption that non-Caucasians were inferior, that they deserved to be used as commodities, that differences of race, not class or wealth, defined the important issues between men.

The ground rules that organized labor created made conflict between the races inevitable. Organized labor chose the path it walked in the years following the Civil War. In fact, it created its own zeitgeist. How different American Life might have been if organized labor had not repeatedly acted against the interests of non-Caucasian workers, both Oriental and black, who could have joined in a racially unified struggle for the equal rights of all working people.

FURTHER READING

Bitter Strength: A History of the Chinese in the United States, 1850–1870 by Gunther Barth (Cambridge, Mass.: Harvard University Press, 1964).

The Managed Casualty: The Japanese-American Family in World War II by Leonard Broom and John Kitsiese (Berkeley: University of California Press, 1956).

The Asian in the West by Stanford M. Lyman (Reno, Nev.: Western Studies Center, University of Nevada, 1970).

The Overseas Chinese by Lois Mitcheson (London: Bodley Head, 1961).

DAVID BOESEL, RICHARD BERK, W. EUGENE GROVES,
BETTYE EIDSON, AND PETER H. ROSSI

White Institutions and Black Rage

Five summers of black rebellion have made it clear that the United States is facing a crisis of proportions not seen since the Great Depression. And one of the root causes of this crisis, it has also become clear, is the performance of white institutions, especially those institutions in the ghetto. Some of these institutions—police and retail stores, for example —have done much to antagonize Negroes; others, such as welfare departments and black political organizations, have tried to help and have failed.

Why have these white institutions helped engender black rage? One way to find out might be to study the attitudes of the men working for them—to discover what their personnel think about the racial crisis itself, about their own responsibilities, about the work they are doing. Therefore, at the request of the National Advisory Commission on Civil Disorders (the riot commission), we at Johns Hop-

kins University visited 15 Northern cities and questioned men and women working for six different institutional groups: major employers, retail merchants, teachers, welfare workers, political workers (all Negro), and policemen. All of the people we questioned, except the employers, work right in the ghetto, and are rank-and-file employees—the cop on the beat, the social caseworker, and so on.

Employers' Social Responsibility

The "employers" we questioned were the managers or personnel officers of the ten institutions in each city that employed the most people, as well as an additional 20 managers or personnel officers of the next 100 institutions. As such, they represented the most economically progressive institutions in America. And in their employment policies we could see how some of America's dominant corporate institutions impinge on the everyday lives of urban Negroes.

Businessmen are in business to make a profit. Seldom do they run their enterprises for social objectives. But since it is fashionable these days, most of the managers and personnel officers we interviewed (86 percent, in fact) accepted the proposition that they "have a social responsibility to make strong efforts to provide employment for Negroes and other minority groups." This assertion, however, is contradicted by unemployment in the Negro community today, as well as by the hiring policies of the firms themselves.

Businessmen, as a whole, do not exhibit openly racist attitudes. Their position might best be described as one of "optimistic denial"—the gentlemanly white racism evident in a tacit, but often unwitting, acceptance of institutional practices that subordinate or exclude Negroes. One aspect of this optimistic denial is a nonrecognition of the seriousness of the problems that face black people. Only 21 percent of our sample thought that unemployment was a very serious problem in the nations' cities, yet 26 percent considered air pollution very serious and 31 percent considered traffic very serious. The employers' perspective is based upon their limited experience with blacks, and that experience does not give them a realistic picture of the plight of Negroes in this country. Employers don't even think that racial discrimination has much to do with the Negroes' plight; a majority (57 percent) felt that Negroes are treated at least as well as other people of the same income, and an additional 6 percent felt that Negroes are treated *better* than any other part of the population.

This optimistic denial on the part of employers ("things really aren't that bad for Negroes") is often combined with a negative image of Negroes as employees. Half of those employers interviewed (51 percent) said that Negroes are likely to have higher rates of absenteeism than whites, so that hiring many of them would probably upset production schedules. Almost a third thought that, because Negro crime rates are generally higher than white crime rates, hiring many Negroes could lead to increased theft and vandalism in their companies. About a fifth (22 percent) thought that hiring Negroes might bring "agitators and troublemakers" into their companies, and another one-fifth feared that production costs might rise because Negroes supposedly do not take orders well.

The employer's views may reflect not only traditional white prejudices, but also some occasional experience he himself has had with Negroes. Such experiences, however, may stem as much from the employer's own practices and misconceptions as from imputed cultural habits of Negroes. As Elliott Liebow observed in his study of Negro street-corner men *(Talley's Corner)*, blacks have learned to cope with life by treating menial, low-status, degrading jobs in the same way that the jobs treat them—with benign nonconcern.

Most of the employers believe that Negroes lack the preparation for anything but menial jobs. A full 83 percent said that few Negroes are qualified for professional jobs, and 69 percent thought that few are qualified for skilled positions. When it comes to unskilled jobs, of course, only 23 percent of the employers held this view.

The employers seem to share a widespread assumption—one frequently used as a cover for racism—that for historical and environmental reasons Negroes have been disabled to such an extent as to make them uncompetitive in a highly competitive society. And while it is certainly true that black people have suffered from a lack of educational and other opportunities, this line of thinking—especially among whites—has a tendency to blame the past and the ghetto environment for what is perceived as Negro incompetence, thus diverting attention from *present* institutional practices. So, many employers have developed a rhetoric of concern about upgrading the so-called "hard-core unemployed" in lieu of changing their employment policies.

To a considerable extent our respondents' assessment of Negro job qualifications reflects company policy, for the criteria used in hiring skilled and professional workers tend to exclude Negroes. The criteria are (1) previous experience and (2) recommendations. It is evident that because Negroes are unlikely to have *had* previous experience in positions from which they have long been excluded, and because they are unlikely to have had much contact with people in the best position to recommend them, the criteria for "qualification" make it probable that employers will consider most Negroes unqualified.

Negroes Get the Worst Jobs

In short, the employers' aversion to taking risks (at least with people), reinforced by the pressure of labor unions and more general discriminatory patterns in society, means that Negroes usually get the worst jobs.

Thus, although Negroes make up 20 percent of the unskilled workers in these large corporations, they fill only a median of one percent of the professional positions and only 2 percent of the skilled positions. Moreover, the few Negroes in the higher positions are unevenly distributed among the corporations. Thirty-two percent of the companies don't report Negroes in professional positions, and 24 percent do not report any in skilled positions. If these companies are set aside, in the remaining companies the median percentage of Negroes in the two positions rises to 3 percent and 6 percent respectively. Further, in these remaining companies an even larger percentage (8 percent in both cases) of *current* positions are being filled by Negroes—which indicates, among other things, that a breakthrough has been accomplished in some companies, while in others Negro employment in the upper levels remains minimal or nonexistent.

Even among those companies that hire blacks for skilled jobs, a Negro applicant's chances of getting the job are only one-fourth as good as those of his white counterpart. For professional positions, the chances are more nearly equal: Negro applicants are about three-fourths as likely to get these jobs as are white applicants. It seems that Negroes have come closest to breaking in at the top (though across all firms only about 4 percent of the applicants for professional positions are Negro). The real stumbling-block to equal employment opportunities seems to be at the skilled level, and here it may be that union policies—and especially those of the craft unions—augment the employers' resistance to hiring Negroes for and promoting Negroes to skilled positions.

What do urban Negroes themselves think of employers' hiring practices? A survey of the same 15 cities by Angus Campbell and Howard Schuman, for the riot commission, indicates that one-third (34 percent) of the Negro men interviewed reported having been refused jobs because of racial discrimination, and 72 percent believed that some or many other black applicants are turned down for the same reason. Almost as many (68 percent) think that some or many black people miss out on promotions because of prejudice. And even when companies do hire Negroes (presumably in professional positions), this is interpreted as tokenism: 77 percent of the black respondents thought that Negroes are hired by big companies for show purposes.

The companies we studied, which have little contact with the ghetto, are very different from the other institutions in our survey, whose contact with the ghetto is direct and immediate. The corporations are also up-to-date, well-financed, and innovative, while the white institutions inside the ghetto are outdated, underfinanced, and overloaded. In historical terms, the institutions in the ghetto represent another era of thought and organization.

Ghetto Merchants

The slum merchants illustrate the tendency of ghetto institutions to hark back to earlier forms. While large corporations cooperate with one another and with the government to exert substantial control over their market, the ghetto merchant still functions in the realm of traditional laissez-faire. He is likely to be a small operator, economically marginal and with almost no ability to control his market. His main advantage over the more efficient, modern retailer is his restricted competition, for the ghetto provides a captive market. The difficulty that many blacks have in getting transportation out of the ghetto, combined with a lack of experience in comparative shopping, seems to give the local merchant a competitive aid he sorely needs to survive against the lower prices and better goods sold in other areas of the city.

The merchants in our study also illustrate the free-enterprise character of ghetto merchandising. They run very small operations—grocery stores, restaurants, clothing and liquor stores, and so on, averaging a little over three employees per business. Almost half of them (45 percent) find it difficult to "keep up with their competition" (competition mainly *within* the ghetto). Since there are almost no requirements for becoming a merchant, this group is the most heterogeneous of all those studied. They have the widest age range (from 17 through 80), the highest percentage of immigrants (15 percent), and the lowest educational levels (only 16 percent finished college).

Again in contrast to the large corporations, the ghetto merchant must live with the harsh day-to-day realities of violence and poverty. His attitudes toward Negroes, different in degree from those of the employers, are at least partly a function of his objective evaluations of his customers.

Running a business in a ghetto means facing special kinds of "overhead." Theft is an especially worrisome problem for the merchants; respondents mentioned it more frequently than any other problem. There is, of course, some basis in fact for their concern. According to the riot commission, inventory losses—ordinarily under 2 percent of sales—may be twice as great in high-crime areas (most of which are in ghettos). And for these small businesses such losses may cut substantially into a slender margin of profit.

Thus it is not surprising that, of all the occupational groups interviewed in this study, the retail merchants were among the most likely to consider Negroes violent and criminal. For example, 61 percent said that Negroes are more likely to steal than whites, and 50 percent believed that Negroes are more likely to pass bad checks. No wonder, then, that black customers may encounter unusual surveillance and suspicion when they shop.

Less understandable is the ghetto merchant's apparent ignorance of the plight of ghetto blacks. Thus, 75 percent believe that blacks get medical treatment that is equal to or better than what whites get. A majority think that Negroes are not discriminated against with regard to treatment by the police, recreation facilities and so forth. Logically enough, 51 percent of the merchants feel that Negroes are making too many demands. This percentage is the second-highest measured (the police were the least sympathetic). So the merchants (like all other groups in the survey except the black politicians) are inclined to emphasize perceived defects in the black community as a major problem in their dealings with Negroes.

The shaky economic position of the merchants, their suspicion of their Negro customers, and the high "overhead" of doing business in the ghetto (because of theft, vandalism, bad credit risks) lead many merchants to sell inferior merchandise at higher prices—and to resort to other strategems for getting money out of their customers. To elicit responses from the merchants on such delicate matters, we drew up a series of very indirect questions. The responses we obtained, though they no doubt understate the extent to which ghetto merchants provide a poor dollar value per unit of goods, are nevertheless revealing. For example, we asked the merchants to recommend various ways of "keeping up with business competition." Some 44 percent said that you should offer extra services; over a third (36 percent) said you should raise prices to cover unusually high overhead; and the same number (36 percent) said that you should buy "bargain" goods at lower prices, then sell them at regular prices. (To a small merchant, "bargain goods" ordinarily means "seconds," or slightly spoiled merchandise, because he doesn't do enough volume to gain real discounts from a wholesaler.) A smaller but still significant segment (12 percent) said that one should "bargain the selling price with each customer and take whatever breaks you can get."

The Campbell-Schuman study indicates that 56 percent of the Negroes interviewed felt that they had been overcharged in neighborhood stores (24 percent said often); 42 percent felt that they had been sold spoiled or inferior goods (13 percent said often). Given the number of ghetto stores a customer may visit every week, these data are entirely compatible with ours. Since one-third of the merchants indicated that they were not averse to buying "bargain" goods for sale in their stores, it is understandable that 42 percent of the Negroes in these areas should say that at one time or another they have been sold inferior merchandise.

It is also understandable that during the recent civil disorders many Negroes, unable to affect merchants by routine methods, struck directly at the stores, looting and burning them.

Teachers in the Ghetto

Just as ghetto merchants are in a backwater of the economy, ghetto schools are in a backwater of the educational system, experimental efforts in some cities notwithstanding.

Negroes, of course, are most likely to be served by outmoded and inadequate schools, a fact that the Coleman Report has documented in considerable detail. In metropolitan regions of the Northeast, for example, 40 percent of the Negro pupils at the secondary level attended schools in buildings over 40 years old, but only 15 percent of the whites did; the average number of pupils per room was 35 for Negroes but 28 for whites.

The teachers covered in our survey (half of whom were Negro) taught in ghetto schools at all levels. Surprisingly, 88 percent said that they were satisfied with their jobs. Their rate of leaving, however, was not consistent with this. Half of the teachers had been in their present schools for no more than four years. Breaking the figures down year by year, we find that the largest percentage (17 percent) had been there only one year. In addition, the teachers' rate of leaving increased dramatically after they had taught for five years.

While the teachers thought that education was a major problem for the cities and especially for the ghettos, they did not think that ghetto schools were a source of the difficulty. A solid majority, comparing their own schools with others in the city, thought that theirs were average, above average, or superior in seven out of eight categories. The high quality of the teaching staff, so rated by 84 percent of the respondents, was rivaled only by the high quality of the textbooks (again 84 percent). The one doubtful area, according to the teachers, was the physical plant, which seemed to them to be just barely competitive; in this respect, 44 percent considered their own schools below average or inferior.

The teachers have less confidence in their students than in themselves or their schools. On the one hand, they strongly reject the view that in ghetto schools education is sacrificed to the sheer need for order: 85 percent said it was not true that pupils in their schools were uneducable, and that teachers could do little more than maintain discipline. On the other hand, the teachers as a group could not agree that their students were as educable as they might be. There was little consensus on whether their pupils were "about average" in interest and ability: 28 percent thought that their pupils were; 41 percent thought it was partially true that they were; and 31 percent thought it was not true. But the teachers had less difficulty agreeing that their students were *not* "above average in ability and . . . generally co-operative with teachers." Agreeing on this were

59 percent of the teachers, with another 33 percent in the middle.

The real problem with education in the ghetto, as the teachers see it, is the ghetto itself. The teachers have their own version of the "Negro disability" thesis: the "cultural deprivation" theory holds that the reason for bad education in the ghetto is the student's environment rather than the schools. (See "How Teachers Learn to Help Children Fail," by Estelle Fuchs, September, 1968.) Asked to name the major problems facing their schools, the teachers most frequently mentioned community apathy; the second most-mentioned problem, a derivation of the first, was an alleged lack of preparation and motivation in the students. Fifty-nine percent of the teachers agreed to some extent that "many communities provide such a terrible environment for the pupils that education doesn't do much good in the end."

Such views are no doubt detrimental to education in the ghetto, for they imply a decided fatalism as far as teaching is concerned. If the students are deficient—improperly motivated, distracted, and so on—and if the cause of this deficiency lies in the ghetto rather than in the schools themselves, then there is little reason for a teacher to exert herself to set high standards for her students.

There is considerable question, however, whether the students in ghetto schools are as distracted as the teachers think. Events in the last few years indicate that the schools, especially the high schools and the junior high schools, are one of the strongest focuses of the current black rebellion. The student strike at Detroit's Northern High School in 1966, for example, was cohesive and well-organized. A boycott by some 2,300 students, directed against a repressive school administration, lasted over two weeks and resulted in the dismissal of the principal and the formation of a committee, including students, to investigate school conditions. The ferment in the ghetto schools across the country is also leading to the formation of permanent and independent black students' groups, such as the Modern Strivers in Washington, D.C.'s Eastern High, intent on promoting black solidarity and bringing about changes in the educational system. In light of such developments, there is reason to think that the teachers in the survey have overestimated the corrosive effects of the ghetto environment on students—and underestimated the schools' responsibility for the state of education in the ghetto.

Social Workers and the Welfare Establishment

Public welfare is another area in which old ideas have been perpetuated beyond their time. The roots of the present welfare-department structure lie in the New Deal legislation of the 1930s. The public assistance provisions of the Social Security Act were designed to give aid to the helpless and the noncompetitive: the aged, the blind, the "permanently and totally" disabled, and dependent children. The assumption was that the recipient, because of personal disabilities or inadequacies, could not make his way in life without outside help.

The New Deal also provided work (e.g., the W.P.A.) for the able-bodied who were assumed to be unemployed only temporarily. But as the Depression gave way to the war years and to the return of prosperity, the massive work programs for the able-bodied poor were discontinued, leaving only those programs that were premised on the notion of personal disability. To a considerable extent today's Negro poor have had to rely on the latter. Chief among these programs, of course, is Aid for Dependent Children, which has become a mainstay of welfare. And because of racial discrimination, especially in education and employment, a large part of the Negro population also experiences poverty as a permanent state.

While most of the social workers in our survey showed considerable sympathy with the Negro cause, they too felt that the root of the problem lay in weaknesses in the Negro community; and they saw their primary task as making up the supposed deficiency. A hefty majority of the respondents (78 percent) thought that a large part of their responsibility was to "teach the poor how to live"—rather than to provide the means for them to live as they like. Assuming disability, welfare has fostered dependency.

The social workers, however, are unique among the groups surveyed in that they are quite critical of their own institution. The average welfare worker is not entirely at one with the establishment for which she works. She is likely to be a college graduate who regards her job as transitional. And her lack of expertise has its advantages as well as its disadvantages, for it means that she can take a more straightforward view of the situations she is confronted with. She is not committed to bureaucracy as a way of life.

The disparity between the welfare establishment and the average welfare worker is evident in the latter's complaints about her job. The complaints she voices the most deal *not* with her clients, but with the welfare department itself and the problems of working within its present structure—the difficulty of getting things done, the red tape, the lack of adequate funds, and so on. Of the five most-mentioned difficulties of welfare work, three dealt with such intra-agency problems; the other two dealt with the living conditions of the poor.

There is a good deal of evidence to support the social worker's complaints. She complains, for example, that welfare agencies are understaffed. The survey indicates that an average caseload is 177 people, each client being visited about once a month for about 50 minutes. Even the most conscientious of caseworkers must be overwhelmed by such client-to-worker ratios.

As in the case of the schools, welfare has engendered a countervailing force among the very people it is supposed to serve. Welfare clients have become increasingly hostile to the traditional structure and philosophy of welfare departments and have formed themselves into an outspoken movement. The welfare-rights movement at this stage has aims: to obtain a more nearly adequate living base for the clients, and to overload the system with demands, thus either forcing significant changes or clearing the way for new and more appropriate institutions.

Black Political Party Workers

Usually when segments of major social institutions become incapable of functioning adequately, the people whom the institutions are supposed to serve have recourse to pol-

itics. In the ghetto, however, the political machinery is no better off than the other institutions. Around the turn of the century Negroes began to carve out small niches for themselves in the politics of such cities as Chicago and New York. Had Negro political organizations developed along the same lines as those of white ethnic groups, they might today provide valuable leverage for the ghetto population. But this has not happened. For one thing, the decline of the big-city machine, and its replacement in many cities by "nonpolitical" reform governments supported by a growing middle class, began to close off a route traditionally open to minority groups. Second, black politicians have never been regarded as fullfledged political brokers by racist whites, and consequently the possibility of a Negro's becoming a powerful politician in a predominantly white city has been foreclosed (the recent election of Carl Stokes as Mayor of Cleveland and Richard D. Hatcher, Mayor of Gary, Indiana, would be exceptions). Whites have tended to put aside their differences when confronting Negro political efforts; to regard Negro demands, no matter how routine, as racial issues; and hence to severely limit the concessions made to black people.

Today the sphere of Negro politics is cramped and closely circumscribed. As Kenneth B. Clark has observed, most of the Negroes who have reached high public office have done so *not* within the context of Negro politics, but through competition in the larger society. In most cities Negro political organizations are outmoded and inadequate. Even if, as seems probable, more and more Negro mayors are elected, they will have to work within the antiquated structure of urban government, with sharply limited resources. Unless things change, the first Negro mayor of Newark, for example, will preside over a bankrupt city.

Our survey of Negro political workers in the 15 cities documents the inadequacy of Negro politics—and the inadequacy of the larger system of urban politics. The political workers, understandably, strongly sympathize with the aspirations of other black people. As ghetto politicians, they deal with the demands and frustrations of other blacks day after day. Of all the groups surveyed, they were the most closely in touch with life in the ghetto. Most of them work in the middle and lower levels of municipal politics; they talk with about 75 voters each week. These political workers are, of course, acutely aware of the precipitous rise in the demands made by the black community. Most (93 percent) agreed that in the last few years people in their districts have become more determined to get what they want. The strongest impetus of this new determination comes from the younger blacks: 92 percent of the political workers agreed that "young people have become more militant." Only a slight majority, however (56 percent), said the same of middle-aged people.

Against the pressure of rising Negro demands, urban political organizations formed in other times and on other assumptions, attentive to other interests, and constrained by severely limited resources, find themselves unable to respond satisfactorily. A majority of the political workers, in evaluating a variety of services available to people in their districts, thought that all except two—telephone service and the fire department—were either poor or fair. Worst of the lot, according to the political workers, were recreation, police protection, and building inspection.

In view of these respondents, the black community has no illusions about the ability of routine politics to meet its needs. While only 38 percent of the political workers thought that the people in their districts regarded their councilmen as friends fighting for them, 51 percent said that the people considered their councilmen "part of the city government which must be asked continually and repeatedly in order to get things done." (Since the political workers were probably talking about their fellow party members, their responses may have been more favorable than frank. A relatively high percentage of "don't know" responses supports this point.)

Almost all the Negro politicians said that they received various requests from the voters for help. Asked whether they could respond to these requests "almost always, usually, or just sometimes," the largest percentage (36 percent) chose "sometimes"—which, in context, is a way of saying "seldom." Another 31 percent said they "usually" could respond to such requests, and 19 percent said "almost always." Logically enough, 60 percent of the political workers agreed that in the last few years "people have become more fed up with the system, and are becoming unwilling to work with politicians." In effect, this is an admission that they as political workers, and the system of urban politics to which they devote themselves, are failing.

When economic and social institutions fail to provide the life-chances that a substantial part of a population wants, and when political institutions fail to provide a remedy, the aspirations of the people begin to spill over into forms of activity that the dominant society regards either as unacceptable or illegitimate—crime, vandalism, noncooperation, and various forms of political protest.

Robert M. Fogelson and Robert D. Hill, in the *Supplemental Studies* for the riot commission, have reported that 50 percent to 90 percent of the Negro males in ten cities studied had arrest records. Clearly, when the majority of men in a given population are defined as criminals—at least by the police—something more than "deviant" behaviour is involved. In effect, ghetto residents—and especially the youth—and the police are in a state of subdued warfare. On the one hand, the cities are experiencing a massive and as yet inchoate social rising of the Negro population. On the other hand, the police—devoted to the racial status quo and inclined to overlook the niceties of mere law in their quest for law and order—have found a variety of means, both conventional and otherwise, for countering the aims of Negroes. In doing so, they are not only adhering to the norms of their institution, but also furthering their personal goals as well. The average policeman, recruited from a lower- or middle-class white background, frequently of "ethnic" origins, comes from a group whose social position is marginal and who feel most threatened by Negro advances.

The high arrest rate in the Negro community thus mirrors both the push of Negroes and the determined resistance of the police. As the conflict intensifies, the police are more and more losing authority in the eyes of black people; the young Negroes are especially defiant. Any type of contact between police and black people can quickly lead to a situation in which the policeman gives an order and the Negro either defies it or fails to show sufficient respect in obeying it. This in turn can lead to the Negro's arrest on a disorderly conduct charge or on a variety of other charges. (Disorderly conduct accounted for about 17 percent of the arrests in the Fogelson-Hill study.)

Police Harassment Techniques

The police often resort to harassment as a means of keeping the Negro community off-balance. The riot commission noted that:

> Because youths commit a large and increasing proportion of crime, police are under growing pressure from their supervisors—and from the community—to deal with them forcefully. "Harassment of youths" may therefore be viewed by some police departments—and members even of the Negro community—as a proper crime prevention technique.

The Commission added that "many departments have adopted patrol practices which, in the words of one commentator, have 'replaced harassment by individual patrolmen with harassment by entire departments.' "

Among the most common of the cops' harassment techniques are breaking up street-corner groups and stop-and-frisk tactics. Our study found that 63 percent of the ghetto police reported that they "frequently" were called upon to disperse loitering groups. About a third say they "frequently" stop and frisk people. Obviously then, the law enforcer sometimes interferes with individuals and groups who consider their activities quite legitimate and necessary. Black people in the ghetto—in the absence of adequate parks, playgrounds, jobs, and recreation facilities, and unwilling to sit in sweltering and overcrowded houses with rats and bugs—are likely to make the streets their front yards. But this territory is often made uninhabitable by the police.

Nearly a third of the white policemen in our study thought that most of the residents of their precinct (largely Negro) were not industrious. Even more striking about the attitudes of the white police working in these neighborhoods is that many of them deny the fact of Negro inequality: 20 percent say the Negro is treated better than any other part of the population, and 14 percent say he is treated equally. As for their own treatment of Negroes, the Campbell-Schuman survey reported that 43 percent of the black men, who are on the streets more than the women, thought that police use insulting language in their neighborhoods. Only 17 percent of the white males held this belief. Of the Negro men, 20 percent reported that the police insulted them personally and 28 percent said they knew someone to whom this had happened; only 9 percent and 12 percent, respectively, of the whites reported the same. Similarly, many more blacks than whites thought that the police frisked and searched people without good reason (42 percent compared to 12 percent); and that the police roughed up people unnecessarily (37 percent as compared to 10 percent). Such reports of police misconduct were most frequent among the younger Negroes, who, after all, are on the receiving end most often.

The policeman's isolation in the ghetto is evident in a number of findings. We asked the police how many people —of various types—they knew well enough in the ghetto to greet when they saw them. Eighty-nine percent of the police said they knew six or more shopowners, managers, and clerks well enough to speak with, but only 38 percent said they knew this many teenage or youth leaders. At the same time, 39 percent said that most young adults, and 51 percent said that most adolescents, regard the police as enemies. And only 16 percent of the white policemen (37 percent of the blacks) either "often" or "sometimes" attended meetings in the neighborhood.

The police have wound up face to face with the social consequences of the problems in the ghetto created by the failure of other white institutions—though, as has been observed, they themselves have contributed to those problems in no small degree. The distant and gentlemanly white racism of employers, the discrimination of white parents who object to having their children go to school with Negroes, the disgruntlement of white taxpayers who deride the present welfare system as a sinkhole of public funds but are unwilling to see it replaced by anything more effective—the consequences of these and other forms of white racism have confronted the police with a massive control problem of the kind most evident in the riots.

In our survey, we found that the police were inclined to see the riots as the long range result of faults in the Negro community—disrespect for law, crime, broken families, etc.—rather than as responses to the stance of the white community. Indeed, nearly one-third of the white police saw the riots as the result of what they considered the basic violence and disrespect of Negroes in general, while only one-fourth attributed the riots to the failure of white institutions. More than three-fourths also regarded the riots as the immediate result of agitators and criminals—a suggestion contradicted by all the evidence accumulated by the riot commission. The police, then, share with the other groups—excepting the black politicians—a tendency to emphasize perceived defects in the black community as an explanation for the difficulties that they encounter in the ghetto.

The state of siege evident in many police departments is but an exaggerated version of a trend in the larger white society. It is the understandable, but unfortunate, response of people who are angry and confused about the widespread disruption of traditional racial patterns and who feel threatened by these changes. There is, of course, some basis for this feeling, because the Negro movement poses challenges of power and interest to many groups. To the extent that the movement is successful, the merchants, for example, will either have to reform their practices or go out of business—and for many it may be too late for reform. White suburbanites will have to cough up funds for the city, which provides most of them with employment. Police departments will have to be thoroughly restructured.

The broad social rising of Negroes is beginning to have a substantial effect upon all white institutions in the ghetto, as the situation of the merchants, the schools, and the welfare establishment illustrates. Ten years ago, these institutions (and the police, who have been affected differently) could operate pretty much unchecked by any countervailing power in the ghetto. Today, both their excesses and their inadequacies have run up against an increasingly militant black population, many of whom support violence as a means of redress. The evidence suggests that unless these institutions are transformed, the black community will make it increasingly difficult for them to function at all.

Members of the Group for Research on Social Policy at Johns Hopkins University are David Boesel, Richard Berk, W. Eugene Groves, Bettye K. Eidson, and Peter H. Rossi, chairman of the department of social relations at Johns Hopkins University and director of the Group for Research on Social Policy, under whose auspices this article was written.

The article is based on *Between White and Black: A Study of American Institutions in the Ghetto,* prepared for the National Advisory Commission on Civil Disorders, June 1968.

FURTHER READING

Cities Under Siege edited by David Boesel and Peter H. Rossi (New York: Basic Books, 1971). A collection of essays analyzing the reasons behind urban riots in the 1960s.

Dark Ghetto: Dilemmas of Social Power by Kenneth B. Clark (New York: Harper & Row, 1965). One of the best studies of the ghetto and its relation to white society.

Ghetto Crisis: Riots or Reconciliation? by Henry Etzkowitz and Gerald M. Schaflander (Boston: Little, Brown, 1969).

Supplemental Studies for the National Advisory Commission on Civil Disorders by Robert M. Fogelson and Robert D. Hill (Washington: U.S. Government Printing Office, 1968). Sociological studies of racial attitudes in 15 large cities, of white institutions in the ghettos of those cities, and of the characteristics of arrestees in major riots.

Life Styles in the Black Ghetto by William McCord, John Howard, Bernard Friedberg, and Edwin Harwood (New York: Norton, 1969).

The Moynihan Report and the Politics of Controversy by Lee Rainwater and William Yancey (Cambridge, Mass.: M.I.T. Press, 1973).

CHARLAYNE A. HUNTER

On the Case in Resurrection City

Resurrection City—where the poor had hoped to become visible and effective—is dead. And despite the contention of many people, both black and white, that it should never have been born, R.C. was, as its City Fathers had been quick to point out, a moment in history that may yet have a telling effect on the future of this country. For although Resurrection City was never really a city, per se, it functioned as a city, with all the elements of conflict that arise when public issues and private troubles come together.

The public issues were clear and could be articulated—at least in a general way—by most of the people who lived

there. Handbills had helped residents formulate their statement of purpose. "What will the Poor People's Campaign do in Washington?" read one handbill. "We will build powerful nonviolent demonstrations on the issues of jobs, income, welfare, health, housing, human rights. These massive demonstrations will be aimed at government centers of power and they will be expanded if necessary. We must make the government face up to poverty and racism." If such a statement was not specific enough, residents—who in all probability found it difficult to always know just what the leaders had in mind (as did the leaders themselves)—

would simply fend off the question with a statement like, "*We* know what the demands are." If pressed further, they would glare accusingly at the questioner, as if to further confirm his ignorance. (This technique of bluffing one's way into the offensive was initiated by the leader of the Poor People's Campaign, the Rev. Ralph Abernathy. The press was relentless in its efforts to get Mr. Abernathy to give out more specifics about his demands, but this was impossible for a long while simply because none had been formulated.)

The private troubles of those who came to live in R.C. were less clear, at least in the beginning. And as these troubles emerged—sometimes in the form of fights, rapes, thefts, and harassment—they became far more prominent than the cause or the individuals who came to fight for it. The outside world concerned itself with the disorganization and lack of leadership in the camp. And while this was certainly a valid concern, critics seemed to be missing one essential point—that the life styles of the poor vary, from individual to individual and from region to region. Long before coming to Resurrection City, leaders and followers had been conditioned by their backgrounds and the life styles they had established. That is why, for example, the first City Manager of R.C., Jesse Jackson—a 26-year-old Chicagoan and an official of the Southern Christian Leadership Conference (S.C.L.C.)—had more success with the Northern urban hustler than did Hosea Williams, the second City Manager, who came out of the South and had much more success with diffident rural blacks.

Most of the conflicts at the camp were caused by the ghetto youths whose lives in the asphalt jungles of the North led them to view Resurrection City as a camp-outing and an alfresco frolic. Surrounded by trees, grass, and open air, the Northern youths were among alien things, which (before the rain and mud) were hostile to them. The innocence of their Southern counterparts—for whom the trees, grass, open air, and mud are a way of life—was a challenge to the Northerners. With such easy, church-oriented prey, the hip cat from the North immediately went into his thing—taking advantage of the uninitiated. Southerners had the history of the movement behind them. They had produced the sit-ins, the Freedom Rides, the Bus Boycotts—the 1960's Direct Action Task Force. And yet much of the Southern mystique got beaten by the hard, hostile life style of the urban ghetto-dweller.

No one is quite sure how many people moved into Resurrection City, although there was an attempt to register people as they came in. The registration count was 6312, but the community was nothing if not mobile and there was no way to count the outflow.

The people came to the District from all sections of the country. They came in bus caravans and on trains. Some came from the South in the Mule Train (which was put into a regular train in Atlanta because the horses were giving out), some came from the nearby North in cars or on foot. They came representing the church. They came representing the community. They came representing street gangs—those that would fight and those that wouldn't. And many came representing themselves. Most came as followers. But, of necessity, a few emerged as leaders. Many came to partici-

On the Case in Resurrection City

pate in the campaign for as long as S.C.L.C. wanted them there, and then they planned to go home. Others came thinking of the North as a land of opportunity. And *they* came to stay forever.

Today, the site where Resurrection City stood is cleared. After the sun baked the mud dry, patches of growing grass were placed there, and although the land is not quite so green as it was before, it is just as it was when the architects began designing Resurrection City on paper back in April. Perhaps if they had it to do over, they would change a few things, because, by now, they would have learned about the differences in poverty—that poor people do not automatically respond positively to one another.

The design, on paper, had been impressive. Three architects (none of them Negroes), with the help of students of the Howard University School of Architecture (all of them Negroes), produced plans that called for modest A-frame structures, which could be built small enough for two and large enough for six or eight and which would house 3000 people for two to four months. The prefabricated units—25 percent of them A-frames and 75 percent of them dormitories—were to be assembled in Virginia by local white volunteers, then brought to Washington in trucks that would be unloaded next to the building sites, starting west and building eastward.

By the time the first stake for an A-frame was driven in by Mr. Abernathy, around a thousand people had already come into Washington and had been housed in coliseums and churches.

New Yorkers Go It Alone

During the first week, morale and energy and activity levels were high. But one of the first indications that the paper plans might not succeed came when the New York delegation insisted upon setting up shop in the most eastwardmost section of the site. New Yorkers, independent, fast-paced, and accustomed to protests (like rent strikes) that require organization, were going to do things their own way. Though this meant that they had to carry their own wood all the way from the front of the site to the back, they set up their structures with record-breaking speed. Where it sometimes took three men working together an hour to put up an A-frame, in the New York contingent three men produced an A-frame in 15 minutes. There was, among *everyone,* a feeling of distrust for larger communities: Provincialism had reared its head.

After a week and a half of more or less organized endeavor, there followed a long stretch of bad weather. It rained every day, and rivers of thick, brown mud stood in doorways and flowed along the walkways from one end of the camp to the other. But although the mud and rain sapped some of the energy of some of the assemblers, it seemed to inspire creativity in others—the majority, in fact, since they were eager to get their houses built so that they could move in. More people came to R.C. than left. And although many had been evacuated to churches and schools—often long distances away—the Mexican-Americans and the Indians were the only contingents that chose to stay on high ground.

When the rains did not let up, the last vestiges of formal organization at R.C. slid unceremoniously into the mud. But those who had left returned, and others joined them, and all waded through. Wood that had been lost turned up as porches for the A-frame houses—luxuries not called for in the paper plans. "It was interesting to see this mass-produced, prefab stuff developing into color and rambunctiousness," one of the planners said.

By the time most of the A-frames had been filled, what existed on the site of the planned city was a camp rather than a community, with some areas so compounded with picket fences or solid fences that no outsider could get in. Walking or wading through the camp, one saw not only simple, unadorned A-frames, but split-levels and duplexes. Some were unpainted; others were painted simply (usually with yellows and burgundy); and still others were both mildly and wildly, reverently and irreverently, decorated with slogans. One house bore on its side a verse from the Bible: "And they said one to another, behold, this dreamer cometh. Come now therefore, and let us slay him, and cast him into some pit, and we will say, some evil beast hath devoured him: and we shall see what will become of his dreams. Genesis 37. Martin Luther King, Jr., 1929-1968." Others had such slogans as "Black Power on Time," "Soul Power," "United People Power, Toledo, Ohio," "Soul City, U.S.A.," and "The Dirty Dozen," on a building I figured was a dormitory. And, of course, the inevitable "Flower Power." "I Have a Dream" stickers appeared in most places, as well as pictures of Martin Luther King—usually enshrined beside the canvas-and-wood cots inside the houses.

Just as the slogans varied widely, so did the inside appearance of the houses. While many looked like the wreck of the Hesperus, in others, by 9 A.M. when the camp was opened to visitors, beds were made, clothes were hung, floors were swept, and—in several houses—plank coffee-tables were adorned with greenery in tin-can vases.

The Coretta King Day Care Center was perhaps the most successful unit in the camp. A local church group contributed most of the materials, including books like *Alice in Wonderland, What Are You Looking At?, The Enormous Egg,* and Bennett Cerf's *Pop-Up Lyrics.* There were even toy cars and trucks, water colors, and jigsaw puzzles. And a hundred pairs of muddy boots. The children played games and sang songs such as "If You're Happy and You Know It, Clap Your Hands" and, of course, "We Shall Overcome." And they went on field trips—to the Smithsonian, the National Historical Wax Museum, and Georgetown University. Enrollment was about 75.

Improved Medical Care

Altogether, Resurrection City never contained more than the average American city—the bare-bone necessities. Still, many people received more medical attention than ever before in their lives. A young mother left Marks, Miss., with a baby whose chances of survival, she had been told, were very slim. He was dying of malnutrition. After three weeks of medical care—vitamins, milk, food—he began gaining weight and life. For others, teeth were saved.

Upper-respiratory infections—at one point a source of alarm to those outside the camp—were treated and curbed. And when one of the residents died while on a demonstration in the food line at the Agriculture Department, there was little doubt that it was not Resurrection City that killed him, but the lack of adequate medical attention back home. Most of the residents were also eating better. The menus were often a hodge-podge affair—sometimes consisting of beef stew, turnip greens, apple sauce, and an orange—but the food was nutritious. And you did not need food stamps to get it.

Residents of Resurrection City found it difficult to understand the outside world's reaction via the press to conditions within the camp. The stink from the toilets that filled one's nostrils whenever a breeze stirred was, as one observer put it, "the smell of poverty." Residents put it another way. "I appreciate the mud," a woman from Detroit said. "It might help get some of this disease out."

The mud of Resurrection City was seen by many as unifying, if not cleansing. Andy Young, an S.C.L.C. executive, trying to dispel rumors of disorganization in the camp, said one day: "We are a movement, not an organization. And we move when the spirit says move. Anything outside is God's business. We are incorporated by the Lord and baptized by all this rain."

Some Movers and Doers

While the camp was virtually leaderless from a formal, organizational standpoint (Mr. Abernathy was always off traveling with a large entourage of S.C.L.C. officials), it did not lack individual movers and doers. One day, a discussion of the mud revealed such a person. Standing attentively at a press conference on a sunny day, with an umbrella over her head, Mrs. Lila Mae Brooks of Sunflower County, Miss., said, to no one in particular, "We used to mud and us who have commodes are used to no sewers." A tall, thin, spirited woman, Mrs. Brooks talks with little or no prompting. Observing that I was interested, she went on: "We used to being sick, too. And we used to death. All my children [she has eight] born sickly. But in Sunflower County, sick folks sent from the hospital and told to come back in two months. They set up 27 rent houses—rent for $25—and they put you out when you don't pay. People got the health department over 'bout the sewers, but Mayor said they couldn't put in sewers until 1972." She is 47, and for years has worked in private homes, cotton fields, and churches. In 1964 she was fired from a job for helping Negroes register to vote. For a while, she was on the S.C.L.C. staff, teaching citizenship. When she had a sunstroke, and later a heart attack, she had to go on welfare. (She is also divorced.) For three years, she got $40-a-month child support, and finally $73. She left her children with her mother, who is 80, and sister to come to the campaign.

"People in Sunflower asked my friends was I sick 'cause they hadn't seen me. Then they saw me on TV in Washington and said I'd better head back before the first or they'd cut off my welfare check. You go out the state overnight and they cut off your welfare check. But that's OK. I had to come. When S.C.L.C. chose me from East-land's County, he met his match. I've seen so much. I've seen 'em selling food stamps and they tell you if you don't buy, they cut off your welfare check. And that stuff they sell there don't count—milk, tobacco, and washing powder. Well, how you gonna keep clean? All the welfare people know is what *they* need. I ain't raising no more white babies for them. Ain't goin' that road no more. I drug my own children through the cotton fields, now they talkin' 'bout not lettin' us go to Congress. Well, I'll stand on Eastland's toes. People from 12 months to 12 months without work. People with no money. Where the hell the money at? I say to myself, I'll go to Washington and find out. Talking about using it to build clinics. Then they make people pay so much at the clinics they get turned away. What the people gettin' ain't enough to say grace over. I done wrote to Washington so much they don't have to ask my name."

I asked Mrs. Brooks how long she planned to say here. "I don't know, honey," she said as she put her sunglasses on. "They just might have to 'posit my body in Washington."

There were other women organizing welfare groups and working in the lunch halls, and still others, like Miss Muriel Johnson, a social worker on loan to S.C.L.C. from other organizations. This was her first movement and she was in charge of holding "sensitivity" sessions. When I asked her what a sensitivity session was, she said, "Well, you just can't take a bunch of people out and march them down Independence Avenue. All they know is that they're hungry and want something done about it. We got 150 to 200 people out a day into nonviolent demonstrations. We got to teach them to protect themselves and prepare for whatever. We have to explain situations to people. And we have to talk with them, not down to them. If they get something out of this training, they'll go home and do something."

Leon and J.T.

Joining Mrs. Brooks and Miss Johnson were many other young men and women, among them college students who, like the students of the old movement (the early 1960s), believed that it was better for black boys and girls to give themselves immediately and fully to a worthwhile cause than to finish college. Many of them wore their hair natural and some wore buttons that said, "Doing it black." Young men like Leon and J.T., both S.C.L.C. organizers in the South, held no place in the movement hierarchy, but were, as the residents were fond of saying of anybody plugged in to what was going on, "on the case."

Leon and J.T. led demonstrations and boosted morale by taking part in the day-to-day problems and activities of Resurrection City. The difference between them and many of the other S.C.L.C. officials was that when R.C. residents were tired and smelly from marching eight miles to a demonstration and back, so were Leon and J.T. When residents went to bed wearing all their clothes and wrapped in blankets saturated with dampness, so did Leon and J.T. And if Leon and J.T. could still sing freedom songs the next day, then so could they. There were not, however, enough Leons and J.T.s. Many weeks had been spent building the Abernathy compound—a large frame structure surrounded by A-frames for his aides. But despite a ceremonial gesture of walking in with a suitcase and announcing that he was moving in, Mr. Abernathy never lived in R.C. Nor did his lieutenants.

One of the most effective communicators around Resurrection City was a man of a different breed from that of Leon or J.T.: Lance Watson, better (and perhaps solely) known as Sweet Willie Wine. Sweet Willie, 29, is the leader of the Memphis Invaders, the group accused of starting the riots in Memphis after the assassination of Martin Luther King. (Sweet Willie denies this.) He spent most of his time walking around the camp, wrapped in a colorful serapi, combing his heavy Afro. He condemns the Vietnam war as immoral, and of his own time in the army paratroops says, "In service I took the great white father's word. I thought it was all right to be half a man. Now it is time to question. We are questioning everything now."

When the campaign was over, most of the Invaders went home. Sweet Willie, however, is still walking the streets of Washington, occasionally plugging in to local militants, but more often holding down some corner in the black ghetto.

The Invaders bridged the gap between the diffident Southern blacks and the hustling ghetto youth from the North. Memphis, after all, is a kind of half-way place, with elements both of the Southern rural and the urban ghetto scenes. And it is perhaps because of this that they made it through to the end. The Blackstone Rangers, from Chicago, did not. Early on, they were sent home for causing trouble. Acting on the theory that if the tough guys were used as peace officers, they would be too busy keeping others out of trouble to get in trouble themselves, S.C.L.C. officials began using the Blackstone Rangers as marshals. It didn't work.

Yet most of the gangs there saw themselves more as protectors of the other black people in the camp than as participants in the campaign. The leader of St. Louis's Zulu 1200's, Clarence Guthrie, said that the Zulus did not pretend to be nonviolent, but "since this campaign concerns a lot of brothers and sisters who are working their thing, we'll use our resources to protect them."

With so many disparate elements in the camp, it only took a slight incident to cause a large group to assemble, with a great deal of fight potential. Most of the Southerners had come with an S.C.L.C. orientation, and as a result they were still singing "We Shall Overcome," including the verse "Black and white together." But few people from above the Mason-Dixon line were singing "We Shall Overcome," let alone "Black and white together." They usually ignored the whites inside the camp, who for the most part were either kids who would do all the dirty work or hippies off somewhere by themselves with their flowers. Still, any altercation outside the camp usually involved some white person. Such was the case when a fight broke out just outside the grounds. Police—mostly whites—appeared in large numbers. The Tent City Rangers, a group of older men formed as security offi-

cers, broke up the fight, but some of the boys whose adrenaline had risen headed for a white man wearing bermuda shorts and taking pictures. With dispatch, they relieved him of his camera and disappeared. The man wanted his camera back, he said, because it was expensive. But he added, "I think I understand. I come down here in my bermuda shorts taking pictures. And I guess I understand how this would make them angry."

Laurice Barksdale, a 24-year-old veteran from Atlanta, was angry, too. But he vented his frustrations in another way. From early in the morning to late in the afternoon, the sweet smell of baking bread joined the other scents in the air. In a small A-frame decorated with the motto "Unhung-up Bread," Barksdale spent every day baking bread for residents and visitors as well. The supplies had come from a white New Yorker who travels from community to community teaching people how to make bread. At R.C. he discovered Barksdale, who had learned to cook in his high school home-economics class, and set him up in business. After four years in the Marines, Barksdale had come home to Atlanta and had not been able to find a job. His mother, who worked for S.C.L.C., suggested that he go along on the Poor People's Campaign to see if he could help out. Barksdale says he's not really interested in making money. "I got a cause," he says. "And a lot of brothers and sisters around me."

Hosea's Gift of Rap

The one S.C.L.C. higher-up always on the case was Hosea Williams, who early in the campaign became the City Manager. One of Hosea's major assets was the gift of rap.

One Sunday morning he was stopped by three well-dressed white men, one of whom said he was running for Congress from Florida and had come to R.C. because he felt he and his people ought to know about it. Soon after the conversation began, the man asked Hosea about his background, and if he was a Communist. Hosea was not offended by the question, but moved into it slowly. He denied being a Communist.

"What is Resurrection City all about?" Hosea asked rhetorically. "This is what you have to know. We are asking for jobs. Not welfare. Check the cat on the welfare rolls and you'll find his mother and daddy were on welfare.

"What we've got to have is a redefinition of work. As Lillian Smith indicated in her book, I think *Killers of the Dream,* what we have is a conflicting ideology in our value system. The reason I loved Dr. King was that he made $600,000 in one year and died a pauper. We have got to let scientists go to work and create jobs. I know it can be done. I was working as a research chemist for 14 years trying to rid this country of insects. I was born in Attapulgus, Ga. My father was a field hand and my mother worked in the white folks' house. I raised myself while she raised the white folks' children. And we got to get some help for the old. And we got to do something about this educational system. That's what produced the hippies. White colleges. I got more respect for the hippies than I have for the hypocrites.

Racism and Repression

"R.C. is just a place we have to sleep and get some food to fight a war—a nonviolent war. We are here for an economic bill of rights. Congress's job is to solve the problems. We are political analysts and psychiatrists and Congress is the patient."

On that Sunday morning there was a sense of movement and activity throughout the camp. This was true on any given day. Near the entrance to the camp, young boys played checkers and whist, and some were getting haircuts. Over the P.A. system in City Hall, someone was calling for attention. "Will Cornbread please report to City Hall immediately? Attention. Will Cornbread please report to City Hall immediately?" Like Leon and J.T. most people didn't know any other name for Cornbread but Cornbread. But Cornbread was a household word because he was on the case.

Also on that morning, a tall, thin, white man looking like the church pictures of Jesus took up a position behind a table near the checkers game and began making predictions—that there would be a big snow in August; that there would be a Republican President in 1972; that people of America would one day eat one another.

"Are you open to question?" someone called out. He did not respond.

The thin man continued, saying that he had prophesied the burning in Washington. He was interrupted again, by another voice from what had become a building crowd. "Tell me what the number gon' be so I can be a rich man tomorrow." An elderly Negro man with a pair of crutches next to his chair called out, to no one in particular, "Hey, where are my cigars?"

I asked the crippled man where he came from. Coy, Ala. How long had he been at R.C.? "Since they drove the first nail," he answered. "What have you been doing?" "Well, I can't do much. I've got arthritis. I usually get up about 4 A.M. and just sit here. But I tried to organize a men's Bible class like at my church back home. Not too much success, though. I had a lovely time yesterday. Seven of us went out to a church and we had services. Then we had a wonderful dinner there—fried chicken, candied potatoes, and wrinkle steaks. You know what those are, don't you?" He smiled. "If I can hop a ride, I want to go back."

Sitting behind him were two young men. One was saying, "I got to fly home to court tomorrow. Charge of marihuana. Ain't had none." The young man was from New York. It was not the kind of thing one was likely to hear from his Southern counterpart. Narcotics is the traditional way out for many of the frustrated young in the asphalt jungles of the North. Somehow, this syndrome never hit the South. A young Southern black, eager to escape the lot of his father, has one way out—the army. And many of them, once they enlist, choose to stay.

Soon another announcement came over the P.A. system asking all residents who planned to take part in the day's demonstrations to report to the front gate.

The Day of the Tourist

On Sundays, Resurrection City—with all its diversity—was opened up to even more diversity. Sunday was tourist day and visitors began arriving sometime after breakfast. One particular Sunday, as the residents drifted out of the front gate to a demonstration, among the tourists coming in were many well-dressed Negroes from the District on their way home from church or elsewhere (as remote as they seemed to be from things, it didn't seem likely that they would have dressed up to come to R.C.). Some whites came, too. Mainly the tourists drove by in cars, slowing down long enough to snap a picture and continue on. To the Negro visitors (who almost never wore boots to protect their shoes from the mud), most residents (who did wear boots and slept in them at night to keep warm) were cordial, sometimes condescending (something of a unique turnabout in the scheme of things)—"Yes, *do* come in and have a look around. We're right proud of what we have here." Later, at a Lou Rawls concert, which was inadvertently set up before the demonstration, but which Hosea decided to let go on, Hosea addressed the crowd and concluded with a few well-chosen words for the Negro tourists: "The police want to use those billy clubs. But they ain't gonna bother you today. Today is Uncle Tom Day, and they don't whip up on Uncle Tom heads."

Demonstrations were the one constant in R.C. Each demonstration I attended was different from another, not so much because the body of demonstrators changed as because of their usual tendency to "do what the spirit say do."

Although R.C. residents had been there before—to present demands for changes in the welfare system—my first demonstration was at the Department of Health, Education, and Welfare. The 200 demonstrators marched into the auditorium of the building and sent word that they wanted to see "Brother Cohen"—Wilbur J. Cohen, Secretary of Health, Education, and Welfare. An otherwise impressive delegation—including Assistant Secretary Ralph K. Huitt and Harold Howe II of H.E.W.'s Office of Education—was sent in, but was given short shrift. Led by Hosea, the demonstrators began to chant "We want Cohen," and Hosea turned from the second-string officials and told the crowd: "You might as well get comfortable," and before he had finished a young boy in gray trousers and a green shirt had taken off his tennis shoes, rolled up his soiled brown jacket into a headrest, and stretched out on the floor. As he closed his eyes, the crowd, led by Hosea, began singing "Woke Up This Morning With My Mind Set on Freedom." In between songs the crowd would chant "We want Cohen." An elderly lady from New Orleans, who after the march obviously had little strength left to stand and yell and chant, simply shook her head in time with whatever she happened to be hearing at the moment.

The more pressure the officials put upon Hosea to relent, the stronger the support from the crowd. Given the demonstrators' vote of confidence, he began to rap. "I never lived in a democracy until I moved to Resurrection City. But it looks like the stuff is all right."

"Sock soul, brother!" the people yelled.

"Out here," he continued, "they got the gray matter to discover a cure for cancer, but can't."

"Sock soul, brother!"

Then, to the tune of the song "Ain't Gonna Let No-body Turn Me 'Round," Hosea led the group in singing, "Ain't Gonna Let the Lack of Health Facilities Turn Me 'Round." And at the end of the song—something like three hours after the demonstrators had demanded to see Cohen—the word spread through the auditorium: "Cohen's on the case."

Demonstrators who had spread throughout the building buttonholing anybody and everybody who looked important, demanding that they "go downstairs and get Cohen," filed back into the auditorium. And as Cohen appeared, an exultant cheer rose from the demonstrators—not for Cohen but for the point that they had won.

Before Cohen spoke, Huitt came to the microphone. He looked relieved. "I'd just like to say, before introducing the Secretary, that I haven't heard preaching and singing like that since I was a boy. Maybe that's what wrong with me." The crowd liked that and showed it. "Get on the case, brother," someone called. And as clenched black fists went into the air—a gesture that had come to stand for "Silence!" and succeeded in getting it—Cohen spoke:

"Welcome to your auditorium," he said, managing a smile. He proceeded to outline his response to the demonstrators' demands, which included changing the state-by-state system of welfare to a federally controlled one. When he had finished, he introduced a very polished, gray-haired, white matron sitting next to him as "our director of civil rights." A voice of a Negro woman in rags called out to her: "Get to work, baby."

At the Justice Department

The second demonstration I attended was at the Justice Department. Earlier in the day, as rumors grew of dissension between the Mexican-Americans and the blacks, Reiss Tiejerina, the leader of the Mexican-Americans, and Rodolfo ("Corky") Gonzales, his fiery lieutenant, appeared for a press conference to be held jointly with Hosea and the Indian leader, Hank Adams. Accompanying Tiejerina and Gonzales was a small contingent of Mexican-Americans with unmuddied feet (during the entire campaign, their group remained in the Hawthorne School, where there was not only hot food but hot showers as well), and a few Indians. Tiejerina had one major concern: regaining the land in New Mexico that, he claims, was illegally taken away from his people some 300 years ago in the Treaty of Guadalupe Hidalgo.

As the press conference broke up and the demonstrators made ready for the march, the Mexican-Americans boarded buses to take them to the Justice Department, while the preparations of the blacks consisted of a black demonstrator's shouting: "Get your feet in the street. We're marching today."

The Justice Department demonstration was officially under the direction of Corky Gonzales. His demands were that the Attorney General speak with 100 of the demonstrators, with all ethnic groups represented equally—which turned out to be 25 Mexican-Americans, 15 Indians, 20 poor whites, and 40 blacks. The Attorney General

agreed to speak with only 20 of the demonstrators, and this proved totally unacceptable to Gonzales. (Tiejerina was not there at the time.)

For several days, talk of getting arrested in some demonstration had become intense. Somehow, as the hours wore on during the Justice Department demonstration, it was decided that this might be the place. The question seemed to be, was it the time and was the cause broad enough?

There were some demonstrators who came prepared for any eventuality, regardless of the cause. As long as the order came from S.C.L.C. Ben Ownes, 52, widely known as Sunshine, was prepared. The crowd blocking the entrance to the Justice Department (a federal offense in itself), though led by Gonzales, was singing the S.C.L.C. songs: To the tune of "No More Weepin', No More Mourning," they sang, "No More Broken Treaties. . . ." Sunshine talked about his involvement in the movement.

"In Birmingham, in 1963, friends from my church were picketing. I went down. I didn't tote no signs, but my boss still told me when I got back to work not to tote. Then next time I went and toted. The third time I toted, I didn't have a job. But I'd heap more rather work for Dr. King for $25 a week than for $125. My house has been threatened. My mother has been threatened. But I registered a lot of people in Selma, Green County, Sumter County, and many others. Sometime I be sick, but I can't go home. I've gone too far now to turn 'round. I've been so close to so many things. Jimmy Lee Jackson got killed. James Reed got beat to death. Mrs. Liuzzo killed. September 15, 1963, six people were killed—two boys and four girls. If I die for *something* I don't mind. I've been in jail 17 or 18 times. But we really got to work in this town."

The police, however, did not seem to be in an arresting mood. They just stood in the street behind the demonstrators, more or less impassive. Suddenly Hosea took the bullhorn.

"Look at those cops!" he shouted.

The crowd turned. The cops shifted uneasily. "You see what they've done," he continued, his voice rising. The crowd looked. "They don't have on their badges, so that when they take you to jail and do whatever they're gon' do to you, you won't be able to identify them." The crowd was now facing the policemen and could see that not one of them was wearing a badge. Hosea started to rap about police brutality and the sickness of America. "Just look at that!" he cried, pointing an accusing finger. And no one had to be told, this time, what they were looking for. All could see that the shiny badges had been put back in their places—on the chests of the entire cadre of policemen standing behind them. But Hosea was now into his thing. "But look," he said, again pointing. "Just to show you how sick this country is—the sickness of America and racism—*look*." The crowd was baffled. What was he talking about now? Hosea, virtually overcome with rage, now shouted, "You see how sick this country is? Otherwise how come all the white cops are lined up on one side and all the black cops lined up further down the street? Just look at it!" The division in the line was distinct. Immediately behind the demonstrators was a line of white policemen. To the extreme left of the demonstrators a solid line of black faces in uniform. Hosea rapped a good long while.

As the evening wore on, and the Attorney General did not show up and the demonstrators did not get arrested, there seemed to be some indecision among the demonstration's leaders. Hosea, at times, seemed at a loss. Corky had tired of leading the group in songs, and the demonstrators had never quite caught all the words. Corky and Hosea huddled often, only to return and lead more singing. Father James Groppi of Milwaukee showed up, received wide applause, made an impassioned speech, and joined in the singing. At one point, Hosea broke off to consult with his lawyer, and Tiejerina showed up. "What's going on?" he asked innocently. Hosea explained that the Attorney General had refused to see 100, but would see 20. "That's fine. O.K., isn't it? We send the 20?"

Hosea looked confused. "Corky is holding out for 100." "I will talk to Corky," Tiejerina said, and good-naturedly bounced off.

The evening grew longer. The demonstrators grew tired. Few complained, but many were curious. They were not getting the usual positive vibrations from Hosea, who looked haggard and weary. Then, suddenly, as if he'd blown in on a fresh breeze, there stood Jesse Jackson, who has been described as being closer than anyone else to Dr. King in charisma and in his acceptance of nonviolence as a way of life. Jackson was wearing a white turtle-neck sweater, and he towered above the crowd. Reaching for the bullhorn, he began, "Brothers and sisters, we got business to take care of." "Sock soul, brother!" "We got a lot of work to do on this thing, and we gonna march now on over to the church where they're having the rally to help take care of this business." Corky looked stunned. Hosea looked relieved. And the crowd of demonstrators obediently lined up and marched away.

The conflict between the causes of the Mexican-Americans and those of the blacks had come to a head. The relationship had been strained all along, but the S.C.L.C. and Tiejerina had kept it going in the interest of unity and solidarity. Tiejerina's lieutenant, Corky Gonzales, had demanded that Hosea support the demonstration at the Justice Department, and really didn't seem interested in much else. Hosea didn't mind being arrested. In fact, he wanted to be arrested. But this cause—the release in California of a small group of Mexican-Americans charged with conspiracy—just didn't seem broad enough. Corky thought otherwise.

Jackson was not only fresher than Hosea that night—not having been on the demonstration in the hot sun all day—but he was better equipped to deal with Corky, whose orientation was closer to that of the urban hustlers Jesse Jackson was used to dealing with.

The around-the-clock demonstrations at the Agriculture Department were perhaps the most strenuous ordeals for the demonstrators. More people than usual were asleep during the day at R.C. because they had been up all night sitting on the steps of the Department. And they remained there, regardless of the weather.

One morning, as a weary group stood waiting to be replaced, the sky grew gray and a slight cool wind began to blow. As a heavy downpour of cold rain began, most of the group huddled together under army blankets and started singing.

Solidarity Day

The last demonstration I attended was on Solidarity Day. In that great mass of 50,000 or more people, I looked for the faces that I had come to know over the last few weeks. I saw only a few, and concluded that the veteran residents of R.C. just happened to be in places that I was not. Later, as the program dragged on and I became weary from the heat, I walked back into the city, expecting to find it empty. Instead I saw the people I had been looking for outside. J.T. and Leon and many others.

Harry Jackson, a cabinet-maker from Baltimore, sat in his usual place—inside the fenced-in compound of the Baltimore delegation. He was keeping watch over the two dormitories—women to the left, men to the right—and a frying pan of baked beans cooking on a small, portable grill. Since he was not out demonstrating, I asked him why he had come to R.C. in the first place. "We came because of the lack of association between the black man and the white man. If the system don't integrate itself, it will segregate itself all over again. Our group was integrated. We had one white fellow from the University of Massachussetts. But he hasn't been back."

This man, I thought, was probably typical of the majority of R.C. residents. They wanted things to get better, and felt that they would if people got together. The system didn't have to come down; it just needed overhauling. Still, the system had created the provincialism and distrust of larger communities that prompted Harry Jackson to remark as I was leaving, "I believe we should keep the people together who came together."

As I walked through Resurrection City, in the distance I could hear the sound of voices coming from the Lincoln Memorial—voices too distant to be understood. After a while, I ran across Leon and J.T. Leon said he was on the way to his A-frame.

"Why aren't you out at the demonstration?" I asked. And barely able to keep his eyes open, he replied weakly, "My demonstration was all night last night. Up at the Agriculture Department. And I'll be there again, all night tonight. That's why I've just got to get some sleep."

A few days later, Jackson and Leon and J.T. and every other resident of Resurrection City were either arrested (for civil disobedience) or tear-gassed (for convenience) by policemen from the District of Columbia. The structures came down in less than half the time it took to put them up. And Resurrection City was dead. Up on the hill, spokesmen for S.C.L.C. said they had achieved some of the goals of the campaign and were making progress toward achieving more. But the people were all—or mostly all—gone.

So, in the end, what did Resurrection City do? It certainly made the poor visible. But did it make them effective? Mr. Abernathy would have them believe that it did. And the people who believed him were, by and large, the ones who had come out of the same area that he had come from. An observer once said that Mr. Abernathy lived for the few hours when he could escape back to his church in Atlanta for Sunday services. This was home. Those who came out of that background were the ones who would have stayed in Washington until their leader said the job was done, working diligently all the while. But they, too, would be glad to get back home.

The confrontations of rural Negroes, not only with officials and the police but with urban blacks as well, may have engendered in them a bit of cynicism—perhaps even a bit of militancy. But one suspects that the talk, for years to come, will be of how they went to Washington and, for all practical purposes, "stood on Eastland's toes."

For the urban-rural types, who were in a transitional position to begin with, the frustrations inherent in the system became only more apparent. Already leaning toward urban-type militancy, their inclinations were reenforced by the treatment that even the nonviolent received when those in control grew weary of them and their cause.

The urban people did not learn anything that they hadn't already known. Except, perhaps, about the differences that exist between them and their Southern brothers. They expected nothing, they gave little, and they got the same in return.

Resurrection City was not really supposed to succeed as a city. It was supposed to succeed in dramatizing the plight of the poor in this country. Instead, its greatest success was in dramatizing what the system has done to the black community in this country. And in doing so, it affirmed the view taken by black militants today—that before black people can make any meaningful progress in the United States of America, they have to, as the militants say, "get themselves together."

FURTHER READING

The New American Revolution edited by Rodereck Aya and Norman Miller (New York: Free Press, 1971).

Protest, Reform, and Revolt: A Reader in Social Movements edited by Joseph R. Gusfield (New York: Wiley, 1970).

The Autobiography of Malcolm X by Malcolm X (New York: Grove, 1964).

Protest and Prejudice: A Study of Belief in the Black Community by Gary Marx (New York: Harper & Row, 1969).

Black Americans by A. Pinkney (Englewood Cliffs, N.J.: Prentice-Hall, 1969).

The Politics of Protest by Jerome Skolnick (New York: Simon & Schuster, 1969).

GEORGE D. COREY AND RICHARD A. COHEN

Domestic Pacification

Although the bus wouldn't pick them up until 8:30, many of them were there by six a.m. There was the normal quota of noisy playfulness that comes with any large group of pre-teens and young teenagers. But beyond that there was an air of tingling excitement—these kids were going to summer camp, many of them for the first time. The bus would eat away the 40 miles to the camp in no time. Then there would be swimming, fishing, softball, basketball, volleyball, boxing, cookouts. And talks on moral leadership, character guidance and citizenship; arms demonstrations, police demonstrations, military training films, marching instruction, patriotism and military discipline lectures. And maybe even a session or two on "The Communist Conspiracy."

No, this is not a privately funded camp, a church-affiliated camp, a YMCA camp, or even a camp run by a right-wing political group. It is a composite picture that would easily fit any of the thousands of summer camps for "disadvantaged" children run by the Department of Defense (DoD) under its rapidly expanding Domestic Action Program (DAP). Although on the surface the DoD claims its motives are altruistic, a careful examination of the program and a close reading of its readily available literature indicate otherwise. The key idea that recurs in a majority of the reports, pamphlets and brochures is that this program "will enhance [DoD's] ability to provide total national security." And while this somewhat vague concept is never clearly defined, it appears to translate into control or pacification of ghetto populations. Each year since 1968, the federal government has taken an increasingly large number (2.7 million in 1971) of impressionable ghetto children (primarily male and largely black) and attempted to mold them into right-thinking individuals—as defined by the Department of Defense with the blessings of President Richard Nixon:

The White House
Washington

April 11, 1969

Honorable Melvin R. Laird
Secretary of Defense
Washington, D.C.

Dear Mr. Secretary:

At a recent meeting of the Urban Affairs Council, I reviewed a presentation by Deputy Secretary of Defense David Packard and a member of his staff concerning ways in which the Department of Defense can participate in the alleviation of our Nation's serious domestic problems.

I concur with Secretary Packard's conclusion that the Department of Defense can make a meaningful contribution to our Administration's efforts in these areas without detracting from its primary mission of national security. I feel that the Department's traditional dedication to service and great talent for solving complex problems can and should be directed toward our domestic goals through coordination with the Urban Affairs Council.

I believe that your creation of the Department's Domestic Goals Action Council is an effective means of insuring continued emphasis on this subject. I know that your successful implementation of this concept will demonstrate to the public the Department of Defense's continued service to the Nation.

Sincerely yours,
(signed) Richard Nixon

With that letter President Nixon officially authorized the creation of a Domestic Action Program and a Domestic Action Council to direct an already ongoing effort. According to Colonel William Earl Brown, Jr., USAF, Special Assistant for the DAP:

April 1969 [was not] the initiation of domestic action activities by the Military Departments. . . .The history of our Armed Forces is one of military-civilian cooperation . . . .The establishment of the Domestic Action Program simply brought together, at DoD level, a body of men (the Domestic Action Council) to coordinate and organize such efforts.

Back in 1965, the Department of Labor in its publication *The Negro Family* (also known as *The Moynihan Report*) argued that at least one viable goal for black males might be to join the military. In fact, Daniel P. Moynihan reasoned that the military satisfies many of their psychological needs.

There is [a] special quality about military service for Negro men; it is an utterly masculine world. Given the strains of the disorganized and matrifocal family life in which so many Negro youth come of age, the Armed Forces are a dramatic and desperately needed change: a world away from women, a world run by strong men of unquestioned authority, where discipline, if harsh, is nonetheless orderly and predictable, and where rewards, if limited are granted on the basis of performances. The regimentation of the military according to this line of thought offers an alternative to their volatile existence. Moynihan portrays the family structure as the only significant determinant of a child's development. Actually, as Ulf Hannerz and other critics have shown, there is an interplay between the family and community environments; the community can and does provide the necessary male images that Moynihan contends the black family lacks.

Despite its inherent flaws, Moynihan's position filtered down into several military programs, most prominently into Jr. ROTC, which claims to offer:

> an excellent opportunity to give disadvantaged [male] children, at their option, a chance to make up for the opportunities many of them have missed because they come from broken homes, and have not had the advantages of parental attention, training, leadership and discipline.
>
> (1970 *Blue Ribbon Defense Report*)

The Blue Ribbon Defense Report not only suggests that Jr. ROTC had a rehabilitative effect on disadvantaged

youngsters, but adds that the program should actively seek to enlist these children because this would contribute to overall community betterment. This is in line with ROTC's stated goal of insuring the "community a well-groomed male body."

The attempt to regulate potentially rebellious youngsters by grounding them in military codes and training is nothing new. Some urban social workers have generally valued the rehabilitative function of the military. It is not uncommon, for instance, to find social workers in metropolitan areas arranging with military officials to induct poor black teenagers in order to prevent judges from sentencing them to training schools or jails. In such cases social workers become the undeputized agents of the armed services and channel the children of the poor into military life.

Plans for the establishment of a volunteer army will necessitate greatly augmented enlistment rates to maintain armed services manpower at effective levels. As the draft calls are eliminated, recruiting will take on more significance. New incentives will thus become necessary to encourage more people to enter the military service. With the unemployment level for black teenagers soaring, the manpower potential of the ghetto is overwhelming. Military public relations has thus aimed its sights toward the area. But a key factor in reducing the number of ghetto recruits has been their failure to pass mental and physical examinations. Something had to be done to increase the successful induction of this group.

The government's solution was to initiate in 1966 Project 100,000, which Pentagon spokesmen claimed would "salvage the poverty-scarred youth of our society" for military service and later civilian life. Called "the greatest contribution to the war on poverty," its original objective was to successfully enlist 100,000 men each year who had formerly failed to qualify. To accomplish this, the Selective Service lowered health and educational requirements. Its discriminatory application resulted in only 16 to 20 percent of black enlistees being disqualified for medical reasons compared to the 30 percent of the objectively healthier whites. With the phasing out of the draft, defense officials indicate that Project 100,000 quotas will be reduced but adds that when the volunteer army becomes a reality, "100,000" will merely take a different form.

From the government's point of view, channeling young blacks and other racial minorities into the military has a number of side benefits:

☐ It will reduce unemployment figures. Moynihan suggested this in his 1965 report when he noted that "if 100,000 unemployed Negro men were to have gone into the military, the Negro male unemployment rate would have been 7.0 percent in 1964 instead of 9.1 percent."

☐ Removing young blacks from the inner cities of the country will reduce juvenile delinquency rates. As the Katzenbach Commission on Law Enforcement and Administration of Justice (1967) reported, in ghettos considered to be "high delinquency rate" areas, well over half the boys under 18 appear in court. Consequently, indiscriminate mass relocation of ghetto youth could greatly reduce urban delinquency levels.

☐ Ghetto activism can be restrained. As juvenile gangs like the Young Lords begin to organize around political issues such as police relations, food programs or housing conditions, attempts to break up these gangs will become political actions designed to defuse minority political power.

Military programs such as Project 100,000 and Jr. ROTC deal only indirectly with the effects of poverty. DAP, on the other hand, is designed to deal directly with the problem—to provide welfare services to civilian populations, a role historically beyond the scope of DoD's responsibility. The largest of the welfare services is the Youth Opportunity Program (YOP). But DAP-YOP is significant for more than its size. While the DoD has previously concerned itself with civilian adults through the Selective Service, with the DAP it is becoming extensively involved in the welfare of children, that segment of the American population least capable of recognizing, articulating and defending its rights.

DAP's officially stated mission is to use the extensive resources of the Defense Department in cooperation with other governmental and private organizations in a national effort to overcome serious domestic problems and contribute to the constructive development of our society. In addition Domestic Action does satisfy a number of immediate military needs. Drastic troop reductions resulting from changes in our Vietnam War strategy are causing the military to look for new ways to maintain its dominant position in American society. The prospect of a volunteer army forces the armed forces to develop a positive image in order to secure enlistments. Two objectives are thus served by the military's entrance into the civilian sector via Domestic Action. While assuming its dominance in American life, the Defense Department can cultivate favorable attitudes towards the military among the young.

The Dod publicly claims that Domestic Action is an attempt to eradicate poverty. But privately it phrases its objectives in different terms. One Air Force report puts it this way:

> In military campaigns, it is important to know the enemy, define the objectives, form the strategy and tactics, and launch the offensive. So it is in the Domestic Action campaign. The "enemy" has been well defined by many people. He is the evil rampant in our society—and his offspring are the multifarious outgrowths of poverty, ignorance, and discrimination. It is difficult to spearate these three villains and the evils they spawn—crime, hate, fear, and destroyed lives.

The military imagines itself to be allied with the poor—primarily those urban non-white poor—in fighting their common enemy to achieve a better life. But the real objective is internal security against the dangerous consequences of an unrehabilitated poor. "For in the end," as Robert McNamara said in *The Essence of Security*, "poverty and social injustice may endanger our national security as much as any military threat."

David Packard, former Deputy Secretary of Defense has said, "The activities of the Defense Department's Domestic Action Program make a real contribution to the Nation's security. Of such activities, none are more important than those which give disadvantaged youth a chance to learn and work." Other DoD officials have found DAP's work vital to the "total national security." The reason is straightforward: national security is defined to include protection from

internal as well as external threats. And Colonel James A. Donavan, author of *Militarism USA*, has stated that DAP demonstrates the concern of the defense establishment "about the security of its rear, the Zone of the Interior."

Much of the DoD's official literature reflects this concern for security. The "First Six-Month Report on Domestic Action" (May-November, 1969), lists "Guidelines for Domestic Action" on the first page. The initial paragraph discusses the DoD's efforts to overcome "serious domestic problems" and adds, "By meeting this challenge, the Department will enhance its ability to provide total national security." DoD Directive 5030.37 (May 21, 1970) "provides guidelines and establishes policy" for DAP. Five major objectives are listed; number one reads: "Enhance DoD's ability to promote national security."

As of 1970, the total number of DAP activities involved 5,000 military institutions in all 50 states. Over 75 percent of the children in the summer programs were from "disadvantaged" families in poverty-stricken ghetto target areas. Since the council's formal inception of the Youth Programs in 1969, there has been more than a 300 percent increase in attendance each year. According to DoD statistics, DAP took 225,000 "disadvantaged youths" out of the ghetto in 1969. The number increased to 775,000 in 1970 (a 300 percent jump) and to 2,700,000 in 1971 (an increase of 347 percent).

Most of those attending are between the ages of ten to 21. This indicates a substantial overlap with the Kerner Commission's profile which describes a typical rioter as a "Negro, unmarried male between 15 and 24," although many studies, such as those of Robert M. Fogelson and others have subsequently challenged the validity of such profiles. Domestic Action, by reaching out to those children ages ten to 15, is attempting to divert them from becoming potential rioters by removing them from the frustrating and potentially explosive ghetto environment. It thus will curb ghetto riots rather than attacking their roots, the actual problems of poverty.

Evidently, while mouthing concern for individuals, the DoD is actually concerned with control of ghetto masses. In an article on DAP, *Commanders Digest* (a DoD publication) of July 12, 1969 stated "wherever possible, activities should be structured to provide measurable benefits within specific time limits." In light of Directive 5030.37, it is clear that while a quantity like cultural enrichment may be somewhat difficult to measure, the decreasing incidence of ghetto violence is easily measured.

DAP Linked to Riots

The inception of Camp Concern at Bainbridge, Maryland, is directly linked to the riots that followed the assassination of Martin Luther King, Jr.—by admission of the DoD. An official Naval press release reads:

> To fully understand the situation, it is necessary to go back to the spring of 1968. At that time the city of Baltimore was being torn by riots that left hundreds of inner city business establishments in smoking ruins. Something had to be done to direct the energies of the city's disadvantaged youth into constructive channels.

The Navy and the city of Baltimore concluded that a

Domestic Action Camp could help solve the problem. During Concern's nine-week summer schedule, 500 to 600 disadvantaged children were bussed 80 miles daily from Baltimore to Bainbridge in order to "prevent the scars [of riots] from being reopened during the hot summer months." During the first two years of Concern's operation, almost 11,000 youngsters were channeled out of Baltimore in the summer. Similarly, the Strategic Air Command Report on the Offut Air Force Base program in Omaha, Nebraska, credited the removal of children from Omaha with that city's peaceful summer.

A nationwide mobilization program using community agencies and groups to identify and recommend children for consideration such as that employed by DAP can isolate and segregate potentially rebellious members of society. Domestic Action's rate of growth over the last three years attests to the efficiency and speed with which this method of social control can be and has been effectuated. The negative aspects, of course, are that such a mechanism is tantamount to establishing preventive detention centers for children. When the risk of riot becomes the greatest during the summer months, the program is activated, effectively maintaining an artificial tranquility in the ghetto.

Concerning DAP-YOP, Dr. Curtis Tarr, Director of the Selective Service System, said:

The quality of the organization was impressive particularly on the part of the young people who acted as counselors. The experience is an exhilarating one, and I hope that we are somehow finding a way to influence the youngsters.

But in Boston, a Model Cities administrator who has worked with a local Domestic Action Project feels that the program influences the children adversely. Recalling last year's experience, he said:

Military camps are not designed for kids. It's too spread out. You have bused them from here to there and the kids in this neighborhood have been bused to hell. They're bused to school—to the countryside—everywhere. And just to take them out of the city is not enough. It's what you do with them that counts. In this program the welfare of the children is secondary. White counselors were hired from around the base. They told the white kids (at the camp) to keep away from the others (the black and Spanish children). The white counselors fostered racial tension. It spread to the kids—some riots broke out—some theft. Then it hit the newspapers.

Program Planning

One of the first military summer camps for children is located at Offut Air Force Base in Omaha, Nebraska. The camp's curriculum includes extensive tours of the installation, various military demonstrations, competitive sports, intermittent talks by military officers and officials on subjects like citizenship, patriotism and moral development, a counseling program and job placement. This camp served as a model for others.

At Offut, each Friday is devoted to learning how to be a patriot. A patriot is defined as one who "zealously fights" for his country and his country's interests. Police demonstrations, Defense Department films and proper flag care are used as teaching activities. These efforts to involve children in political indoctrination programs are, however, outside the officially stated scope of DAP-YOP, which is to provide counseling, vocational and remedial services to ghetto youths.

According to Captain E. P. Flynn, Jr. who initiated "Operation Shipmate" at the Charleston, South Carolina naval station, that program includes neither remedial education nor arts and crafts. While probably helpful to ghetto children and listed as an objective of DAP in Directive 5030.37, remedial education is not necessarily considered part of a typical summer camp program—but arts and crafts are. Instead, the program includes military fire-fighting demonstrations, tours of ships and fleet support units (including a tour of a mobile mine assembly unit) and flag-appreciation lectures. In addition, military films are shown, including "missions of Navy and various type ships" and "patriotism topic films."

Another typical program is the Summer Youth Activity Program of Fort Carson, Colorado. Serving 150 to 200 "disadvantaged youths" for the latter half of the summer of 1970, "Fort Carson sought to expose these youths to educational and recreational activities which would otherwise have been unavailable." Education is interpreted to mean vocational activities which include instruction in subjects like auto servicing. Recreational activities seek to take advantage of the Fort Carson environment, in terms of tours to Pike's Peak, Bust Rodeo and the Will Rogers Shrine. Organized athletics are supervised by Fort Carson soldiers, who also serve as guides, counselors, instructors and medics.

Although program content varies somewhat from base to base, it typically includes talks on moral guidance and patriotism. Some camps venture into politically controversial areas by adding sessions on "The Communist Conspiracy" and military discipline. Operation REAP of Fort McClellan, Alabama, includes "an arms demonstration. . . given by the Chemical Corps School." But virtually every program includes a heavy emphasis on athletics. And the highly competitive sporting event is one very effective method of controlling group violence. Through sports, camp counselors manage the children's aggressions. Physical combat is unbridled under strict rules, a practice common to both competitive games and military training. According to Willard Waller, all sports perform this function, but the military is one of the few environments which rewards planned physical aggressiveness. The even more disciplined format of military drills is also a major means of keeping order within the ranks of the youngsters. One DAP-YOP summer camp had a Marine instructor whose mission was stated as "the marching indoctrination of youth."

Military exercises are attuned to do more than develop merely physical discipline. Daily exposure to officers and soldiers creates ideal types for the children to emulate. After visiting a local DAP-YOP camp in 1970, a sportswriter from the *Baltimore News American* recounted:

Little boys and girls look up at the captain, whose handsome features and military bearing make him look like the perfect Naval officer Hollywood would cast in the role.

The captain added:

You can see how shy and withdrawn they are the first morning but they loosen up and relax. It's usually by the end of the week that they are giving me those playful salutes and calling me "Sergeant" and "Lieutenant."

At Domestic Action camps children actively seek to imitate their adult supervisors. A particularly striking example of this behavior is depicted in the Columbia Broadcasting System documentary "The Selling of the Pentagon" which appeared on national television in 1971. One segment shows children mimicking a military demonstration of hand-to-hand combat. Shortly after the airing of the film Vice-President Spiro Agnew commented:

I watched the films of the children romping around, playing at war. I didn't lose the obvious overtones that the Department of Defense was some sort of ogre for allowing encouragement of this type of play even though it's existed traditionally in history of all countries and will probably exist just as the western movie and the villain and the hero exist there.

In spite of the vice-president's rationalization, there is little justification for the DoD to actively expose children to institutional violence. The military, however, has deemed such conditioning to be in the interest of our national security.

Many of the DAP camps also include counseling programs which contribute to DAP-YOP job-placement services by identifying the aptitudes and impediments of each child, essential knowledge for job-placement functions. DAP-YOP employment placement is determined by the guidelines in Directive 5030.37, which requires that job placement or training be coordinated with local school systems and the nearest state employment office "to insure training compatible with expressed need of the local labor market." But such policy is repressive, for it is an institutionalized equivalent of the ghetto labor market, simply training youths in skills that confine them to the restrictive opportunities already available to ghetto residents. For example, the 1969 Tinker Air Force Base program trained 703 disadvantaged youths, two-thirds of whom were black, for clerical work (40 percent), typing (20 percent) and manual labor (30 percent). All of these are socially immobile labor roles. Only the 10 percent who were trained as skilled assistants in the Tinker program will have some chance of escaping the lower echelons of the labor market. Domestic Action policy implemented in this manner fails to ensure that participating youngsters get an equal opportunity through training in skills or by otherwise expanding their employment horizons.

Through talks on moral guidance, counseling and job placement, Domestic Action emphasizes that success is personally achieved. Poverty is described as the result of the individual's failure. Poverty becomes a state of mind rather than a condition of society. As William Ryan has charged, the victim is blamed for his circumstances. In promoting this philosophy, the military is stressing that individual motivation rather than institutional reform is the solution to poverty. The effect of this is the manipulation of individuals as directed by the military establishment toward illusory ameliorative goals.

The military camp in a very real sense is a symbolic representation of the ghetto. In neither environment can one expect to significantly improve one's life chances. Overt authority figures manifest themselves either as police or military officers. And in both the camp and the ghetto, gang or troop violence is a way of life.

Goal Assessment

There is a considerable discrepancy between what Domestic Action claims as its objectives and the methods employed to measure its success. The public mission of Domestic Action is as characterized by Secretary Laird, "solving some of the problems that afflict our urban area." Yet the youth programs under the council are not evaluated as to their impact upon any particular community's development. Required reports more or less give body counts of participants plus some commentary on how the program affected their attitudes towards the military. Under Defense Department Directive 5030.37, the only service-wide data that would lend itself to evaluation are "summaries of significant achievements or problems encountered within the program." Yet even this information is geared for increasing the efficiency of management rather than improving the community. Other reports are only suggested for submission: narrative summaries of youth activities accompanied by photographs, movies or slides intended for public relations. Since no service-wide evaluation of the program is made, nothing is known of the overall impact of Domestic Action.

The Domestic Action Council is thus unable to examine critically DAP's performance because it lacks evaluative data. It has not even planned effective mechanisms for evaluation. Apparently the Council does not want to know any more than whatever it needs for public relations. Moreover, information about the content of the children's programs is disseminated on a camp-to-camp basis, prohibiting the public from viewing the impact DAP-YOP has nationally. The structure of DAP's public relations promotes public acceptance but prevents public scrutiny.

Funding

The funding structure further frustrates public inquiry into the workings of Domestic Action. Each program generates its own unique funding after arrangements have been made with the local military post. The council simply authors directives, formulates policy and seeks departmental assistance from other federal agencies. In this fashion the council relieves itself from much of the paperwork involved in financing. At the same time, monitoring the funding becomes impossible to control or review because it is so diverse.

Most funding comes from a variety of government sources. Participating departments include Labor, Transportation, Agriculture, Commerce and Health, Education and Welfare. Agencies which also assist range from the Civil Service Commission to the Office of Economic Opportunity. Moreover, the military by law is not permitted to expend funds to support these programs. If military facilities and resources are used, the military is not reimbursed for these costs. Unenumerated military costs include men released from service to work in the programs, extra manpower assistance totaling in the hundreds of thousands of man-weeks per year, military hardware demonstration costs and public relations expenditures.

These hidden costs violate the Budget and Accounting Act Amendment of 1950, which explicitly requires full public disclosure of all government financial and management operations. Nowhere in the federal budget are the expenses for services rendered to DAP by the Department of Defense explicitly audited. What in fact occurs, with the diffusion of DAP funding and accountability, is a circumvention of the public's right to know. Congressional investigative committees are triply hamstrung in any congressional review of the Domestic Action Program; they lack evaluative data on 1) program results, 2) financial allocations and expenditures and 3) administrative responsibility.

But an even more insidious by-product of the diffusion of the Domestic Action Program is the encroachment of the Department of Defense into non-military federal functions. Under the Domestic Action Program, non-military funds from HEW, Labor and Agriculture for example, are administered within military contexts. The substantive result of this is an increasing tendency toward military usurpation and direction of non-military programs and functions. And other governmental agencies are ignoring this encroachment, or at least tacitly approving it by their silence. For example, the Office of Economic Opportunity, in Guidance Memorandum 6011-1 to its Community Action Agencies (CAAs), states its approval of DAP: "The objectives of the Department of Defense Domestic Action Program are consistent with the goals of the CAA's." It goes on to list, word for word, four of the five objectives stated in DoD 5030.37. But there is no mention of DoD's primary objective of national security.

The consequences of welfare services administered by military authorities could be nightmarish, recalling Kenneth Keniston's fantasy about the expansion of the DoD into "community mental health" maintenance. Military usurpation of civilian welfare functions is particularly serious in light of the relatively secretive way in which it has been carried out. Domestic Action must therefore be seen within the context of growing secrecy in the military.

The danger is clear and present. Who or what policies govern the governing? Without such checks in government, programs of social control such as Domestic Action are free to proliferate. From the discovery of Project Camelot—the Army's counterrevolutionary task force during the early 1960s—to the recent revelation that anthropological data is being used to manipulate primitive tribal groups for military purposes in Southeast Asia, it has been clear that coercive social research programs on the part of the armed forces are forging ahead. In a real sense, we may legitimately ask: What will check the expansion of the DoD's Domestic Action social welfare bureaucracy?

Even more alarming, from a social policy point of view, is why and how such a program came into existence. Domestic Action seems to have emerged out of a program vacuum. Those parts of the federal government which are responsible for the health and welfare of the civilian population—principally HEW—have failed to supply the country and specifically ghetto areas with the resources its young people need—resources like sufficient educational opportunity or adequate job training. At the same time the government has not been able to reduce the number of the poor. As their numbers and the consciousness of the need for some type of ameliorative programs grew, the problem became a crisis. Riots increased and delinquency escalated. The Department of Defense stepped in.

It was able to do so for a number of reasons. First, the armed services command a powerful and highly disciplined organization. If nothing else, they can manage the problem until some alternative arrangements can be made. In 1970 they were even encouraged in the Blue Ribbon Defense Panel Report to use pacification techniques developed in Vietnam with minority groups and ghetto areas.

As a public program, DAP-YOP is insidious. It is apparently in violation of significant statutes involving public accountability of executive programs. Its design ignores or subverts all regulations that require congressional investigation and public disclosure of data. DAP-YOP is a disturbing example of the creation of public policy by a bureaucratic structure outside the checks of elected representatives. It is a serious challenge to the efficacy of open democratic government.

And the YOP is only part of the total Domestic Action Program. DAP also includes Summer Hire, employing nearly 50,000 young people per year since 1969, over 75 percent of them considered "disadvantaged;" Assistance to Minority Business Enterprise, wherein DoD counsels "minority businessmen in the policies and procedures associated with doing business with DoD" and provides "technical management and other guidance;" and Project Value which trains "disadvantaged and hardcore unemployed persons for alternate employment within DoD or other agencies." These are just a few programs—there are many others.

Even more frightening, DoD think tanks may even now be involved in domestic areas. In a letter dated March 4, 1969, presumably addressed to the Secretary of HEW, Secretary of Defense Melvin Laird offered the use of "Federal Contract Research Centers (FCRC's), organizations such as RAND, Mitre Corporation and the Lincoln Laboratory of MIT" for "efforts to overcome our domestic problems." According to Laird, "the FCRC's have skills which might be used quite fruitfully by other departments of the Federal Government, as well as state and city governments."

Finally, DAP threatens the very basis of the distinction between the military and civilian sectors of American society. As the military gradually absorbs the functions of other executive departments, unnoticed by the public, the specter of an American society even more responsive to militarily defined priorities becomes frighteningly immediate.

FURTHER READING

Soul on Ice by Eldridge Cleaver (New York: Dell, 1968). A biographical statement by a well-known black militant.

Beyond the Planners by Robert Goodman (New York: Simon & Schuster, 1972). A scathing attack on planners' attempts to alleviate urban ills, accusing them of maintaining the status quo.

5. Violence: Individual and Institutional

Although we have become accustomed to thinking of violence as a peculiarly American problem, even the most cursory review of human history suggests that violence has always been a part of human life—although different cultures and different eras have exhibited not only very different rates but different kinds of violence as well. Moreover, while it is fashionable to discuss violence as an inevitable result of man's "violent nature" the variability in rates and kinds of violence among societies suggests that social and environmental forces play a more vital role than nature—both in stimulating and allaying human violence. Acceptance of a biological constant to explain variation is clearly bad science: it yields very little understanding of the situational contexts in which violence occurs and can offer as a cure only biological or medical means for control of violent behavior.

Conflict is a necessary aspect of human life, inevitable because we are social beings and because, of all species, humans are the most genetically and environmentally variable. The conditions under which conflict is transformed into violence, however, vary considerably. Emergence of violent behavior is associated with failures of culture—failures of our social institutions to resolve successfully interpersonal or intergroup hostilities. Violence between organized groups of armed men, for example—what we call warfare—is virtually nonexistent among hunting and gathering peoples though individual violence in the form of occasional assaults, murders, and rape certainly does occur. Full-fledged, long-term warfare is a relatively new invention. Its existence is dependent upon a society's ability to support large armies and a vast technology over relatively long periods of time. Such warfare demands surplus energy and the development of communications technology.

Feuding—interfamily violence that depends upon strong bonds of kinship—has virtually disappeared from all but a few societies. Its disappearance betokens no change in human nature, however, but rather indicates that the growth of the power of the state has eroded the power of the strong extended families who maintain feudal warfare.

As defined in the dictionary, violence is the exertion of physical force upon another human being. But a secondary definition indicates that violence is also injury done to that which is entitled to respect, reverence, or observation. We rarely refer to behavior sanctioned by the state, even if it constitutes an attack to do injury upon an individual, as violence. Our use of the term as well as its dictionary definition thus suggests that reverence or awe is owed to the state, while respect by the state for the individual is far more problematic. Thus we often conceptualize violent police acts as "law and order" and in our very definition of the word violence we tend to conceal from ourselves many of the institutional pressures that lead to violence—such as inequitable legal systems or vicious penal policies.

Our interest in violence appears to have increased during recent years because violence itself seems to be reaching epidemic proportions. Senseless murders, "thrill-killing," random and pointless attacks by snipers at anonymous victims, mass murders, and muggings all seem to be on the rise. We do not understand the reasons for this increase, except in a very general sense. We tend to find our explanations for such deviant behavior in individual psychology although there is mounting evidence that much maladjustment is sociogenic in origin.

Another kind of violence emerges when groups which have previously been isolated—either through custom or geographical or social distance—first make contact. When neither group is familiar with the rules governing the behavior of the other, conflict and violence arise out of misunderstanding. Thus, Indians who took objects from the homes of white men—because in their culture possessions were given for the asking—were branded as thieves and often killed or bound out as servants for "stealing."

Violence may also occur when one group, out of need or pride, sets out to steal the land, goods, or women of another. We are inclined to view such behaviors as evidence of a moral flaw or lack of ethical principle; but careful analysis of the conditions under which such violence occurs suggests that the values that make such behaviors possible are the result of economic changes or demographic alterations.

Social conflict also increases under conditions of rapid change. Change may derive from invention or from the introduction of new technologies or ideas, from peaceful contact as well as from invasion of one territory by another group. Such an invasion alters the complex, delicately balanced ecological relationships that previously existed and may lead to economic scarcity for both groups, or to the enrichment of one at the expense of the other.

Rapid change also leads to the development of new roles and statuses in which untested rule systems operate. Apparatus for the settlement of disputes must be developed; until it is, disputes often lead to violence. By focusing upon psychological, rather than sociological, causes of violence, we have succeeded in obscuring the relationship that exists between economics and social structure, and social structure and morality. As a result, we were shocked at the student riots and race demonstrations of the fifties and sixties. These disturbances may have been the result of sudden contact among groups within a society that have previously been isolated through housing segregation, division of labor, ethnic differences, racial barriers, or the like. The development of contact among such groups seems to derive from alterations in society's labor needs and the development of new modes of production which demand new methods of recruitment and an expanding labor pool.

Obviously, there are many aspects to the study of violence. In the section that follows we have focused our attention upon the relationship between individual violence and the social institutions which, designed to inhibit it, appear instead to nurture it.

Perhaps the most astonishing fact about violence today is increased public awareness of the threat it appears to pose to the public order. Some of this awareness is the result of better statistics, of alteration of definitions of violence, of the elimination of the frontier which absorbed deviants, adventurers, and failures and transformed them into mythical heroes, and of more efficient communications technology that brings into our living rooms an endless parade of riot, assault, murder, and assassination. Crimes which were once largely contained within our numerous ghettos. among the poor and disenfranchised have reached out to threaten the middle classes as well. Although victims of crime are far more likely to be found among the poor and the minorities, the middle class is no longer immune and can no longer safely ignore either the frustrated violence of the poor or their own increasing crime rates. More extensive police control, the breakdown of informal sanctions associated with the collapse of neighborhoods, and the increase in social and geographic mobility have placed larger numbers of middle-class members—particularly juveniles and young people—under police scrutiny.

Perhaps because they had been relatively well insulated against first-hand exposure to the possibility of violence, the American public responded with shock and horror to the assassination in 1963 of President John Kennedy. The wide TV coverage of the event and its dramatic aftermath shocked the nation and set the media to speculating on mystic theories of collective guilt. Of considerably more value than such idle speculation is Crotty's "Presidential Assassinations"—an analysis of the previous murders and assaults upon American presidents. His article indicates that while each assassination seems unique, common characteristics of assassins and would-be assassins indicate that they are primarily attacking the office or power of the president rather than the man himself. The assassins themselves share certain characteristics: lonely, rootless men with no strong family ties, few group associations, and easy access to lethal weapons— all were men with little power over their own lives. Increasing numbers of attacks on public figures may derive from an *absolute* increase in the number of citizens who have been divested of control of their own lives by current social and economic arrangements and who react by attempting to destroy the symbols of power.

Crotty's article suggests that assassinations are best understood as sociological rather than psychological phenomena, and he suggests that reduction in the actual power of the presidency could help reduce the risk of assassination. As the events of Watergate prove, this increase in executive power constitutes more than a threat to the lives of powerful presidents; it is a threat to individual freedom. By focusing on presidential power, Crotty points to what is actually a symptom of our institutional failure rather than its cause. Although presidential power is obvious, bureaucratic procedures have served more and more to conceal from view the processes of decision-making and the names of the decision-makers themselves. Decision-making in government no longer occurs in public, at open meetings or public forums; most decisions are made instead in private committees or in the insulated offices of thousands of bureaucrats (see Marcuse's article, Section 9). A more equitable distribution of power in government, through decentralization or through the reorganization of bureaucratic structures to clarify roles and responsibilities, and increased accountability, could begin to reduce the feeling of powerlessness that seems to be affecting more and more of our citizens. And the powerlessness is felt both by the public whose encounters with bureaucracy lead to fury and frustration, and the bureaucrats themselves who now number in the millions and represent the most rapidly growing segment of the labor force.

While we remain uneasily aware of the prospect of further assassinations, the debate on violence has focused attention on another area of American life—television programing. A steady parade of criminals and lawmen, thieves and gunmen, practitioners of karate, Kung Fu, and knife-throwing cast their doubtful images on the dark walls of our imaginations. Is their presence in our living rooms a major cause of real violence? Some researchers believe that it is, while others—some in the employ of TV networks—insist that television acts as a deterrent to violence by allowing people to express their rage through television fantasy rather than upon their fellow citizens. Rose Goldsen examines "NBC's Make-Believe Research on TV Violence" to point up the glaring errors in research design that led the network-sponsored studies to conclude that television violence had little to do with real violence. More objective studies indicate that both amounts and varieties of violence increase among children exposed to violent video programing. Even more significant was recent research which suggested that the exposure to television violence led to loss of capacity to empathize with victims.

Despite such studies, government has delayed action in funding research on media violence and has failed to act on information currently available. Some of this foot-dragging is the result of the presence of institutional lobbies and general consumer inability to recognize the nature of the problem or to organize its own pressure groups in order to provide a more balanced perspective for government policymakers. Violent programs, moreover, could prove to be a distinct boon to government officials because they not only provide audiences with a temporary respite from their problems but they increase passivity and dependency. The old Roman dictum which provided for "bread and circuses" may be as useful today as it was during the Pax Romana. It is the paradox posed by media violence that is most intriguing: on the one hand, the research suggests that the media does stimulate random individual violence which increases the demands for law and order and thus extends police power; on the other hand, the programs may increase passivity and thus deflect rightful anger and forestall organized activism which might effect real change.

Government censorship of the media represents one solution to the problem of media violence but that solution is probably worse than the disease it hopes to cure. Citizen action groups—like Action for Children's Television—have taken important initial steps in controlling TV violence by successfully lobbying against the selling on children's television programs of war toys or toys that encourage violent behavior. Listener-sponsored radio and viewer-sponsored television offer alternatives for viewers. The FCC, even now, has certain controls over television stations—particularly over commercials—which are rarely put in operation. And organized groups, if they wield sufficient purchasing power, can register their negative reactions with local television stations. These can be surprisingly responsive when their pocketbooks are involved.

Both the articles, Steinmetz and Straus' "The Family as Cradle of Violence" and Morris' "Psychological Miscarriage: An End to Mother Love," attest to increasing rates of intrafamilial violence in our society. Steinmetz and Straus emphasize the correlation between rates of intrafamilial violence and lack of economic and social resources. Morris emphasizes the role of individual maladjustment as the source of violent parental behavior.

Morris' emphasis is worthy of note because it represents the kind of thinking that until very recently governed much sociological literature: by focusing on the role of the individual she only dimly perceives the social context that governs interpersonal conflict. However, her recognition that disruption of mother-infant relationships is at least in part due to the impersonal procedures of modern hospitals and the social roles assigned to doctor and patient has broad implications for social scientists. Women have only recently become aware of their powerlessness, and many have focused upon the experience of childbirth in attempting to explain their struggle for equality. Casual commentators seem puzzled by the extent of female anguish over childbirth; but it is perhaps in the experience of modern childbirth that women realize most intensely how they have been alienated from their own bodies and stripped of the knowledge and feeling that would allow them to control this most meaningful event in their lives. Here, too, the poor, less educated female is at a greater disadvantage than her better educated sister: lacking information about hospital procedures, about her rights as a patient, about alternatives to anesthetics or instrument deliveries, she is even more likely to have her perception of herself as a helpless victim increased during childbirth.

Because women involved in child abuse are most often themselves victims of rejection, they are more vulnerable to a negative delivery experience. Morris calls for alteration of hospital procedures, counseling, establishment of social support groups, and adequate day care as well as economic aid that is given without subjecting such women to further humiliation. Women's groups have been circulating bulletins which outline "patients' rights"; they have encouraged midwifery, disseminated gynecological information, lobbied for abortion on demand, and are attempting through their liberation groups to sensitize medical schools to the need for psychology and social science in their curricula.

Ultimately, however, as Steinmetz and Straus point out, the solution to child abuse can be found only if we can develop a more humane society. Battered women produce battered children, and both are more frequent where men, unable to find work or to achieve sufficient self-esteem, utilize their wives or girl-friends as repositories for their most violent emotions. Steinmetz and Straus have also exposed the full extent of such powerlessness in our society. Their data indicates that intrafamily violence may well be as prevalent among middle-income and well-to-do families as it is among poor ones. If their assessment is correct, then we must assume that rage and frustration have spread beyond the bounds of the ghetto.

Sennett's "The Brutality of Modern Families" examines the effects of urban life upon the family and focuses primarily upon deteriorating interfamilial relationships which have been produced by the stratification of society. He is most concerned with the growing indifference of the middle class to problems of the poor—an indifference all the more ironic as both increasingly share similar problems. He attributes this indifference to the loss of family economic functions; stripped of its economic and social dependencies, the urban family hangs together because of its members' "need for intimacy." This need has grown more intense as the social context becomes more impersonal and bureaucratized. Held together only by fragile ties of affection, the family isolates itself from external pressure which threatens to rip apart the bonds of intimacy. The result is increased indifference to the problems of others and a rejection of political or institutional forces that might provide a power base from which to redress social wrongs.

Reduction in the brutality of middle-class families towards their neighbors depends upon our ability to diminish social barriers. Techniques that reduce spatial isolation and encourage group interaction could provide a broader setting for social intimacy. Economic incentives that would promote mixed housing and the provision of ombudsmen to provide continual on-site social support in racially or economically integrated housing developments have proven their effectiveness, but are rarely incorporated in planning proposals. Public awareness that family structure is profoundly affected by economic and political systems should lead to demands that we alter the dehumanizing aspects of our economic life, or at the very least consciously work at developing less stressful life-styles. New work arrangements that replace assembly-line structures with sociable organizations of labor could help to extend intimacy beyond the family and thus reduce both intrafamilial stress and violence and the interfamilial hostility and indifference that leads to political apathy and violence.

Throughout our society there exist a variety of social problems that provide a breeding ground for violent behavior. Alcoholism, drug addiction, child abuse, and increasing incidence of assault suggest that we are failing to socialize our citizens adequately. This failure appears to engender feelings of inadequacy and hopelessness that encourage escape through drugs, media, or assault.

Only as we realize that most individual violence is the result of social dislocations will we be able to create a psychology adequate to our problems. And we must also try to understand—and differentiate between—conflicts that are the signs of terminal disease and those that represent growing pains.

Black and white, male and female, rich and poor, American teenagers have the herding instinct. On streetcorners, in shopping centers, in the ghetto and in the suburbs, the boys and the girls hang out. Sometimes the kids get together for fun, sometimes for trouble, sometimes for political purposes. Mostly, they crave recognition, companionship and excitement. Gangs are a way of life for many adolescents—part of the ritual of growing up.

WILLIAM J. CHAMBLISS

The Saints and the Roughnecks

Eight promising young men—children of good, stable, white upper-middle-class families, active in school affairs, good pre-college students—were some of the most delinquent boys at Hanibal High School. While community residents and parents knew that these boys occasionally sowed a few wild oats, they were totally unaware that sowing wild oats completely occupied the daily routine of these young men. The Saints were constantly occupied with truancy, drinking, wild driving, petty theft and vandalism. Yet not one was officially arrested for any misdeed during the two years I observed them.

This record was particularly surprising in light of my observations during the same two years of another gang of Hanibal High School students, six lower-class white boys known as the Roughnecks. The Roughnecks were constantly in trouble with police and community even though their rate of delinquency was about equal with that of the Saints. What was the cause of this disparity? the result? The following consideration of the activities, social class and community perceptions of both gangs may provide some answers.

The Saints from Monday to Friday

The Saints' principal daily concern was with getting out of school as early as possible. The boys managed to get out of school with minimum danger that they would be accused of playing hookey through an elaborate procedure for obtaining "legitimate" release from class. The most common procedure was for one boy to obtain the release of another by fabricating a meeting of some committee, program or recognized club. Charles might raise his hand in his 9:00 chemistry class and asked to be excused—a euphemism for going to the bathroom. Charles would go to Ed's math class and inform the teacher that Ed was needed for a 9:30 rehearsal of the drama club play. The math teacher would recognize Ed and Charles as "good students" involved in numerous school activities and would permit Ed to leave at 9:30. Charles would return to his class, and Ed would go to Tom's English class to obtain his release. Tom would engineer Charles' escape. The strategy would continue until as many of the Saints as possible were freed. After a stealthy trip to the car (which had been parked in a strategic spot), the boys were off for a day of fun.

Over the two years I observed the Saints, this pattern was repeated nearly every day. There were variations on the theme, but in one form or another, the boys used this procedure for getting out of class and then off the school grounds. Rarely did all eight of the Saints manage to leave school at the same time. The average number avoiding school on the days I observed them was five.

Having escaped from the concrete corridors the boys usually went either to a pool hall on the other (lower-class) side of town or to a cafe in the suburbs. Both places were out of the way of people the boys were likely to know (family or school officials), and both provided a source of entertainment. The pool hall entertainment was the generally rough atmosphere, the occasional hustler, the sometimes drunk proprietor and, of course, the game of pool. The cafe's entertainment was provided by the owner. The boys would "accidentally" knock a glass on the floor or spill cola on the counter—not all the time, but enough to be sporting. They would also bend spoons, put salt in sugar bowls and generally tease whoever was working in the cafe. The owner had opened the cafe recently and was dependent on the boys' business which was, in fact, substantial since between the horsing around and the teasing they bought food and drinks.

The Saints on Weekends

On weekends the automobile was even more critical than during the week, for on weekends the Saints went to Big Town—a large city with a population of over a million 25 miles from Hanibal. Every Friday and Saturday night most of the Saints would meet between 8:00 and 8:30 and would go into Big Town. Big Town activities included drinking heavily in taverns or nightclubs, driving drunkenly through the streets, and committing acts of vandalism and playing pranks.

By midnight on Fridays and Saturdays the Saints were usually thoroughly high, and one or two of them were often so drunk they had to be carried to the cars. Then the boys drove around town, calling obscenities to women and girls; occasionally trying (unsuccessfully so far as I could tell) to pick girls up; and driving recklessly through red lights and at high speeds with their lights out. Occasionally they played "chicken." One boy would climb out the back window of the car and across the roof to the driver's side of the car while the car was moving at high speed (between 40 and 50 miles an hour); then the driver would move over and the boy who had just crawled across the car roof would take the driver's seat.

Searching for "fair game" for a prank was the boys' principal activity after they left the tavern. The boys would drive alongside a foot patrolman and ask directions to some street. If the policeman leaned on the car in the course of answering the question, the driver would speed away, causing him to lose his balance. The Saints were careful to play this prank only in an area where they were not going to spend much time and where they could quickly disappear around a corner to avoid having their license plate number taken.

Construction sites and road repair areas were the special province of the Saints' mischief. A soon-to-be-repaired hole in the road inevitably invited the Saints to remove lanterns and wooden barricades and put them in the car, leaving the hole unprotected. The boys would find a safe vantage point and wait for an unsuspecting motorist to drive into the hole. Often, though not always, the boys would go up to the motorist and commiserate with him about the dreadful way the city protected its citizenry.

Leaving the scene of the open hole and the motorist, the boys would then go searching for an appropriate place to erect the stolen barricade. An "appropriate place" was often a spot on a highway near a curve in the road where the barricade would not be seen by an on-coming motorist. The boys would wait to watch an unsuspecting motorist attempt to stop and (usually) crash into the wooden barricade. With saintly bearing the boys might offer help and understanding.

A stolen lantern might well find its way onto the back of a police car or hang from a street lamp. Once a lantern served as a prop for a reenactment of the "midnight ride of Paul Revere" until the "play," which was taking place at 2:00 AM in the center of a main street of Big Town, was interrupted by a police car several blocks away. The boys ran, leaving the lanterns on the street, and managed to avoid being apprehended.

Abandoned houses, especially if they were located in out-of-the-way places, were fair game for destruction and spontaneous vandalism. The boys would break windows, remove furniture to the yard and tear it apart, urinate on the walls and scrawl obscenities inside.

Through all the pranks, drinking and reckless driving the boys managed miraculously to avoid being stopped by police. Only twice in two years was I aware that they had been stopped by a Big City policeman. Once was for speeding (which they did every time they drove whether they were drunk or sober), and the driver managed to convince the policeman that it was simply an error. The second time they were stopped they had just left a nightclub and were walking through an alley. Aaron stopped to urinate and the boys began making obscene remarks. A foot patrolman came into the alley, lectured the boys and sent them home. Before the boys got to the car one began talking in a loud voice again. The policeman, who had followed them down the alley, arrested this boy for disturbing the peace and took him to the police station where the other Saints gathered. After paying a $5.00 fine, and with the assurance that there would be no permanent record of the arrest, the boy was released.

The boys had a spirit of frivolity and fun about their escapades. They did not view what they were engaged in as "delinquency," though it surely was by any reasonable definition of that word. They simply viewed themselves as having a little fun and who, they would ask, was really hurt by it? The answer had to be no one, although this fact remains one of the most difficult things to explain about the gang's behavior. Unlikely though it seems, in two years of drinking, driving, carousing and vandalism no one was seriously injured as a result of the Saints' activities.

The Saints in School

The Saints were highly successful in school. The average grade for the group was "B," with two of the boys having close to a straight "A" average. Almost all of the boys were popular and many of them held offices in the school. One of the boys was vice-president of the student body one year. Six of the boys played on athletic teams.

At the end of their senior year, the student body selected ten seniors for special recognition as the "school wheels"; four of the ten were Saints. Teachers and school officials saw no problem with any of these boys and anticipated that they would all "make something of themselves."

How the boys managed to maintain this impression is surprising in view of their actual behavior while in school. Their technique for covering truancy was so successful that teachers did not even realize that the boys were absent from school much of the time. Occasionally, of course, the system would backfire and then the boy was on his own. A boy who was caught would be most contrite, would plead guilty and ask for mercy. He inevitably got the mercy he sought.

Cheating on examinations was rampant, even to the point of orally communicating answers to exams as well as looking at one another's papers. Since none of the group studied, and since they were primarily dependent on one another for help, it is surprising that grades were so high. Teachers contributed to the deception in their admitted inclination to give these boys (and presumably others like them) the benefit of the doubt. When asked how the boys did in school, and when pressed on specific examinations, teachers might admit that they were disappointed in John's performance, but would quickly add that they "knew that he was capable of doing better," so John was given a higher grade than he had actually earned. How often this happened is impossible to know. During the time that I observed the group, I never saw any of the boys take homework home. Teachers may have been "understanding" very regularly.

One exception to the gang's generally good performance was Jerry, who had a "C" average in his junior year, experienced disaster the next year and failed to graduate. Jerry had always been a little more nonchalant than the others about the liberties he took in school. Rather than wait for someone to come get him from class, he would offer his own excuse and leave. Although he probably did not miss any more classes than most of the others in the group, he did not take the requisite pains to cover his absences. Jerry was the only Saint whom I ever heard talk back to a teacher. Although teachers often called him a "cut up" or a "smart kid," they never referred to him as a troublemaker or as a kid headed for trouble. It seems likely, then, that Jerry's failure his senior year and his mediocre performance his junior year were consequences of his not playing the game the proper way (possibly because he was disturbed by his parents' divorce). His teachers regarded him as "immature" and not quite ready to get out of high school.

The Police and the Saints

The local police saw the Saints as good boys who were among the leaders of the youth in the community. Rare-

ly, the boys might be stopped in town for speeding or for running a stop sign. When this happened the boys were always polite, contrite and pled for mercy. As in school, they received the mercy they asked for. None ever received a ticket or was taken into the precinct by the local police.

The situation in Big City, where the boys engaged in most of their delinquency, was only slightly different. The police there did not know the boys at all, although occasionally the boys were stopped by a patrolman. Once they were caught taking a lantern from a construction site. Another time they were stopped for running a stop sign, and on several occasions they were stopped for speeding. Their behavior was as before: contrite, polite and penitent. The urban police, like the local police, accepted their demeanor as sincere. More important, the urban police were convinced that these were good boys just out for a lark.

The Roughnecks

Hanibal townspeople never perceived the Saints' high level of delinquency. The Saints were good boys who just went in for an occasional prank. After all, they were well dressed, well mannered and had nice cars. The Roughnecks were a different story. Although the two gangs of boys were the same age, and both groups engaged in an equal amount of wild-oat sowing, everyone agreed that the not-so-well-dressed, not-so-well-mannered, not-so-rich boys were heading for trouble. Townspeople would say, "You can see the gang members at the drugstore, night after night, leaning against the storefront (sometimes drunk) or slouching around inside buying cokes, reading magazines, and probably stealing old Mr. Wall blind. When they are outside and girls walk by, even respectable girls, these boys make suggestive remarks. Sometimes their remarks are downright lewd."

From the community's viewpoint, the real indication that these kids were in for trouble was that they were constantly involved with the police. Some of them had been picked up for stealing, mostly small stuff, of course, "but still it's stealing small stuff that leads to big time crimes." "Too bad," people said. "Too bad that these boys couldn't behave like the other kids in town; stay out of trouble, be polite to adults, and look to their future."

The community's impression of the degree to which

Through all the pranks, drinking and reckless driving the Saints managed miraculously to avoid being stopped by the police. No one was ever seriously injured despite all the carousing and vandalism.

The Saints and the Roughnecks

this group of six boys (ranging in age from 16 to 19) engaged in delinquency was somewhat distorted. In some ways the gang was more delinquent than the community thought; in other ways they were less.

The fighting activities of the group were fairly readily and accurately perceived by almost everyone. At least once a month, the boys would get into some sort of fight, although most fights were scraps between members of the group or involved only one member of the group and some peripheral hanger-on. Only three times in the period of observation did the group fight together: once against a gang from across town, once against two blacks and once against a group of boys from another school. For the first two fights the group went out "looking for trouble"—and they found it both times. The third fight followed a football game and began spontaneously with an argument on the football field between one of the Roughnecks and a member of the opposition's football team.

Jack had a particular propensity for fighting and was involved in most of the brawls. He was a prime mover of the escalation of arguments into fights.

More serious than fighting, had the community been aware of it, was theft. Although almost everyone was aware that the boys occasionally stole things, they did not realize the extent of the activity. Petty stealing was a frequent event for the Roughnecks. Sometimes they stole as a group and coordinated their efforts; other times they stole in pairs. Rarely did they steal alone.

The thefts ranged from very small things like paperback books, comics and ballpoint pens to expensive items like watches. The nature of the thefts varied from time to time. The gang would go through a period of systematically shoplifting items from automobiles or school lockers. Types of thievery varied with the whim of the gang. Some forms of thievery were more profitable than others, but all thefts were for profit, not just thrills.

Roughnecks siphoned gasoline from cars as often as they had access to an automobile, which was not very often. Unlike the Saints, who owned their own cars, the Roughnecks would have to borrow their parents' cars, an event which occured only eight or nine times a year. The boys claimed to have stolen cars for joy rides from time to time.

Ron committed the most serious of the group's offenses. With an unidentified associate the boy attempted to burglarize a gasoline station. Although this station had been robbed twice previously in the same month, Ron denied any involvement in either of the other thefts. When Ron and his accomplice approached the station, the owner was hiding in the bushes beside the station. He fired both barrels of a double-barreled shotgun at the boys. Ron was severely injured; the other boy ran away and was never caught. Though he remained in critical condition for several months, Ron finally recovered and served six months of the following year in reform school. Upon release from reform school, Ron was put back a

grade in school, and began running around with a different gang of boys. The Roughnecks considered the new gang less delinquent than themselves, and during the following year Ron had no more trouble with the police.

The Roughnecks, then, engaged mainly in three types of delinquency: theft, drinking and fighting. Although community members perceived that this gang of kids was delinquent, they mistakenly believed that their illegal activities were primarily drinking, fighting and being a nuisance to passersby. Drinking was limited among the gang members, although it did occur, and theft was much more prevalent than anyone realized.

Drinking would doubtless have been more prevalent had the boys had ready access to liquor. Since they rarely had automobiles at their disposal, they could not travel very far, and the bars in town would not serve them. Most of the boys had little money, and this, too, inhibited their purchase of alcohol. Their major source of liquor was a local drunk who would buy them a fifth if they would give him enough extra to buy himself a pint of whiskey or a bottle of wine.

The community's perception of drinking as prevalent stemmed from the fact that it was the most obvious delinquency the boys engaged in. When one of the boys had been drinking, even a casual observer seeing him on the corner would suspect that he was high.

There was a high level of mutual distrust and dislike between the Roughnecks and the police. The boys felt very strongly that the police were unfair and corrupt. Some evidence existed that the boys were correct in their perception.

The main source of the boys' dislike for the police undoubtedly stemmed from the fact that the police would sporadically harass the group. From the standpoint of the boys, these acts of occasional enforcement of the law were whimsical and uncalled for. It made no sense to them, for example, that the police would come to the corner occasionally and threaten them with arrest for loitering when the night before the boys had been out siphoning gasoline from cars and the police had been nowhere in sight. To the boys, the police were stupid on the one hand, for not being where they should have been and catching the boys in a serious offense, and unfair on the other hand, for trumping up "loitering" charges against them.

From the viewpoint of the police, the situation was quite different. They knew, with all the confidence necessary to be a policeman, that these boys were engaged in criminal activities. They knew this partly from occasionally catching them, mostly from circumstantial evidence ("the boys were around when those tires were slashed"), and partly because the police shared the view of the community in general that this was a bad bunch of boys. The best the police could hope to do was to be sensitive to the fact that these boys were engaged in illegal acts and arrest them whenever there was some evidence that they had been involved. Whether or not the boys had in fact committed a particular act in a particular way was not especially important. The police had a broader view: their job was to stamp out these kids' crimes; the tactics were not as important as the end result.

Over the period that the group was under observation, each member was arrested at least once. Several of the boys were arrested a number of times and spent at least one night in jail. While most were never taken to court, two of the boys were sentenced to six months' incarceration in boys' schools.

The Roughnecks in School

The Roughnecks' behavior in school was not particularly disruptive. During school hours they did not all hang around together, but tended instead to spend most of their time with one or two other members of the gang who were their special buddies. Although every member of the gang attempted to avoid school as much as possible, they were not particularly successful and most of them attended school with surprising regularity. They considered school a burden—something to be gotten through with a minimum of conflict. If they were "bugged" by a particular teacher, it could lead to trouble. One of the boys, Al, once threatened to beat up a teacher and, according to the other boys, the teacher hid under a desk to escape him.

Teachers saw the boys the way the general community did, as heading for trouble, as being uninterested in making something of themselves. Some were also seen as being incapable of meeting the academic standards of the school. Most of the teachers expressed concern for this group of boys and were willing to pass them despite poor performance, in the belief that failing them would only aggravate the problem.

The group of boys had a grade point average just slightly above "C." No one in the group failed either grade, and no one had better than a "C" average. They were very consistent in their achievement or, at least, the teachers were consistent in their perception of the boys' achievement.

Two of the boys were good football players. Herb was acknowledged to be the best player in the school and Jack was almost as good. Both boys were criticized for their failure to abide by training rules, for refusing to come to practice as often as they should, and for not playing their best during practice. What they lacked in sportsmanship they made up for in skill, apparently, and played every game no matter how poorly they had performed in practice or how many practice sessions they had missed.

Two Questions

Why did the community, the school and the police react to the Saints as though they were good, upstanding, nondelinquent youths with bright futures but to the Roughnecks as though they were tough, young criminals who were headed for trouble? Why did the Roughnecks and the Saints in fact have quite different careers after high school—careers which, by and large, lived up to the expectations of the community?

The most obvious explanation for the differences in the community's and law enforcement agencies' reactions to the two gangs is that one group of boys was "more delinquent" than the other. Which group *was* more delinquent? The answer to this question will determine in part how we explain the differential responses to these groups by the members of the community and, particularly, by law enforcement and school officials.

In sheer number of illegal acts, the Saints were the more delinquent. They were truant from school for at least part of the day almost every day of the week. In addition, their drinking and vandalism occurred with surprising regularity. The Roughnecks, in contrast, engaged sporadically in delinquent episodes. While these episodes were frequent, they certainly did not occur on a daily or even a weekly basis.

The difference in frequency of offenses was probably caused by the Roughnecks' inability to obtain liquor and to manipulate legitimate excuses from school. Since the Roughnecks had less money than the Saints, and teachers carefully supervised their school activities, the Roughnecks' hearts may have been as black as the Saints', but their misdeeds were not nearly as frequent.

There are really no clear-cut criteria by which to measure qualitative differences in antisocial behavior. The most important dimension of the difference is generally referred to as the "seriousness" of the offenses.

If seriousness encompasses the relative economic costs of delinquent acts, then some assessment can be made. The Roughnecks probably stole an average of about $5.00 worth of goods a week. Some weeks the figure was considerably higher, but these times must be balanced against long periods when almost nothing was stolen.

The Saints were more continuously engaged in delinquency but their acts were not for the most part costly to property. Only their vandalism and occasional theft of gasoline would so qualify. Perhaps once or twice a month they would siphon a tankful of gas. The other costly items were street signs, construction lanterns and the like. All of these acts combined probably did not quite average $5.00 a week, partly because much of the stolen equipment was abandoned and presumably could be recovered. The difference in cost of stolen property between the two groups was trivial, but the Roughnecks probably had a slightly more expensive set of activities than did the Saints.

Another meaning of seriousness is the potential threat of physical harm to members of the community and to the boys themselves. The Roughnecks were more prone to physical violence; they not only welcomed an opportunity to fight; they went seeking it. In addition, they fought among themselves frequently. Although the fighting never included deadly weapons, it was still a menace, however minor, to the physical safety of those involved.

The Saints never fought. They avoided physical conflict both inside and outside the group. At the same time, though, the Saints frequently endangered their own and other people's lives. They did so almost every time they drove a car, especially if they had been drinking. Sober, their driving was risky; under the influence of alcohol it was horrendous. In addition, the Saints endangered the lives of others with their pranks. Street excavations left unmarked were a very serious hazard.

Evaluating the relative seriousness of the two gangs' activities is difficult. The community reacted as though the behavior of the Roughnecks was a problem, and they reacted as though the behavior of the Saints was not. But the members of the community were ignorant of the array of delinquent acts that characterized the Saints' behavior. Although concerned citizens were unaware of much of the Roughnecks' behavior as well, they were much better informed about the Roughnecks' involvement in delinquency than they were about the Saints'.

Visibility

Differential treatment of the two gangs resulted in part because one gang was infinitely more visible than the other. This differential visibility was a direct function of the economic standing of the families. The Saints had access to automobiles and were able to remove themselves from the sight of the community. In as routine a decision as to where to go to have a milkshake after school, the Saints stayed away from the mainstream of community life. Lacking transportation, the Roughnecks could not make it to the edge of town. The center of town was the only practical place for them to meet since their homes were scattered throughout the town and any noncentral meeting place put an undue hardship on some members. Through necessity the Roughnecks congregated in a crowded area where everyone in the community passed frequently, including teachers and law enforcement officers. They could easily see the Roughnecks hanging around the drugstore.

The Roughnecks, of course, made themselves even more visible by making remarks to passersby and by occasionally getting into fights on the corner. Meanwhile, just as regularly, the Saints were either at the cafe on one edge of town or in the pool hall at the other edge of town. Without any particular realization that they were making themselves inconspicuous, the Saints were able to hide their time-wasting. Not only were they removed from the mainstream of traffic, but they were almost always inside a building.

On their escapades the Saints were also relatively invisible, since they left Hanibal and travelled to Big City. Here, too, they were mobile, roaming the city, rarely going to the same area twice.

Demeanor

To the notion of visibility must be added the difference in the responses of group members to outside intervention with their activities. If one of the Saints was confronted with an accusing policeman, even if he felt he was truly innocent of a wrongdoing, his demeanor was apologetic and penitent. A Roughneck's attitude was almost the polar opposite. When confronted with a threatening adult authority, even one who tried to be pleasant, the Roughneck's hostility and disdain were clearly observable. Sometimes he might attempt to put up a veneer of respect, but it was thin and was not accepted as sincere by the authority.

School was no different from the community at large. The Saints could manipulate the system by feigning compliance with the school norms. The availability of cars at school meant that once free from the immediate sight of the teacher, the boys could disappear rapidly. And this escape was well enough planned that no administrator or teacher was nearby when the boys left. A Roughneck who wished to escape for a few hours was in a bind. If it were possible to get free from class, downtown was still a mile away, and even if he arrived there, he was still very visible. Truancy for the Roughnecks meant almost certain detection, while the Saints enjoyed almost complete immunity from sanctions.

Bias

Community members were not aware of the transgressions of the Saints. Even if the Saints had been less discreet, their favorite delinquencies would have been perceived as less serious than those of the Roughnecks.

In the eyes of the police and school officials, a boy who drinks in an alley and stands intoxicated on the street corner is committing a more serious offense than is a boy who drinks to inebriation in a nightclub or a tavern and drives around afterwards in a car. Similarly, a boy who steals a wallet from a store will be viewed as having committed a more serious offense than a boy who steals a lantern from a construction site.

Perceptual bias also operates with respect to the demeanor of the boys in the two groups when they are confronted by adults. It is not simply that adults dislike the posture affected by boys of the Roughneck ilk; more important is the conviction that the posture adopted by the Roughnecks is an indication of their devotion and commitment to deviance as a way of life. The posture becomes a cue, just as the type of the offense is a cue, to the degree to which the known transgressions are indicators of the youths' potential for other problems.

Visibility, demeanor and bias are surface variables which explain the day-to-day operations of the police. Why do these surface variables operate as they do? Why did the police choose to disregard the Saints' delinquencies while breathing down the backs of the Roughnecks?

The answer lies in the class structure of American society and the control of legal institutions by those at the top of the class structure. Obviously, no representative of the upper class drew up the operational chart for the police which led them to look in the ghettoes and on streetcorners—which led them to see the demeanor of lower-class youth as troublesome and that of upper-middle-class youth as tolerable. Rather, the procedures simply developed from experience—experience with irate and influential upper-middle-class parents insisting that their son's vandalism was simply a prank and his drunkenness only a momentary "sowing of wild oats" —experience with cooperative or indifferent, powerless, lower-class parents who acquiesced to the laws' definition of their son's behavior.

Adult Careers of the Saints and the Roughnecks

The community's confidence in the potential of the Saints and the Roughnecks apparently was justified. If anything, the community members underestimated the degree to which these youngsters would turn out "good" or "bad."

Seven of the eight members of the Saints went on to college immediately after high school. Five of the boys graduated from college in four years. The sixth one finished college after two years in the army, and the seventh spent four years in the air force before returning to college and receiving a B.A. degree. Of these seven college graduates, three went on for advanced degrees. One finished law school and is now active in state politics, one finished medical school and is practicing near Hanibal, and one boy is now working for a Ph.D. The other four college graduates entered submanagerial, managerial or executive training positions with larger firms.

The only Saint who did not complete college was Jerry. Jerry had failed to graduate from high school with the other Saints. During his second senior year, after the other Saints had gone on to college, Jerry began to hang around with what several teachers described as a "rough crowd"—the gang that was heir apparent to the Roughnecks. At the end of his second senior year, when he did graduate from high school, Jerry took a job as a used-car salesman, got married and quickly had a child. Although he made several abortive attempts to go to college by attending night school, when I last saw him (ten years after high school) Jerry was unemployed and had been living on unemployment for almost a year. His wife worked as a waitress.

Some of the Roughnecks have lived up to community expectations. A number of them were headed for trouble. A few were not.

Jack and Herb were the athletes among the Roughnecks and their athletic prowess paid off handsomely. Both boys received unsolicited athletic scholarships to college. After Herb received his scholarship (near the end of his senior year), he apparently did an about-face. His demeanor became very similar to that of the Saints. Although he remained a member in good standing of the Roughnecks, he stopped participating in most activities and did not hang on the corner as often.

Jack did not change. If anything, he became more prone to fighting. He even made excuses for accepting the scholarship. He told the other gang members that the school had guaranteed him a "C" average if he would come to play football—an idea that seems far-fetched, even in this day of highly competitive recruiting.

During the summer after graduation from high school, Jack attempted suicide by jumping from a tall building. The jump would certainly have killed most people trying it, but Jack survived. He entered college in the fall and played four years of football. He and Herb graduated in four years, and both are teaching and coaching in high schools. They are married and have stable families. If anything, Jack appears to have a more prestigious position in the community than does Herb, though both are well respected and secure in their positions.

Two of the boys never finished high school. Tommy left at the end of his junior year and went to another state. That summer he was arrested and placed on probation on a manslaughter charge. Three years later he was arrested for murder; he pleaded guilty to second degree murder and is serving a 30-year sentence in the state penitentiary.

Al, the other boy who did not finish high school, also left the state in his senior year. He is serving a life sentence in a state penitentiary for first degree murder.

Wes is a small-time gambler. He finished high school and "bummed around." After several years he made contact with a bookmaker who employed him as a runner. Later he acquired his own area and has been working it ever since. His position among the bookmakers is almost identical to the position he had in the gang; he is always around but no one is really aware of him. He makes no trouble and he does not get into any. Steady, reliable, capable of keeping his mouth closed, he plays the game by the rules, even though the game is an illegal one.

That leaves only Ron. Some of his former friends reported that they had heard he was "driving a truck up north," but no one could provide any concrete information.

Reinforcement

The community responded to the Roughnecks as boys in trouble, and the boys agreed with that perception. Their pattern of deviancy was reinforced, and breaking away from it became increasingly unlikely. Once the boys acquired an image of themselves as deviants, they selected new friends who affirmed that self-image. As that self-conception became more firmly entrenched, they also became willing to try new and more extreme deviances. With their growing alienation came freer expression of disrespect and hostility for representatives of the legitimate society. This disrespect increased the community's negativism, perpetuating the entire process of commitment to deviance. Lack of a commitment to deviance works the same way. In either case, the process will perpetuate itself unless some event (like a scholarship to college or a sudden failure) external to the established relationship intervenes. For two of the Roughnecks (Herb and Jack), receiving college athletic scholarships created new relations and culminated in a break with the established pattern of deviance. In the case of one of the Saints (Jerry), his parents' divorce and his failing to graduate from high school changed some of his other relations. Being held back in school for a year and losing his place among the Saints had sufficient impact on Jerry to alter his self-image and virtually to assure that he would not go on to college as his peers did. Although the experiments of life can rarely be reversed, it seems likely in view of the behavior of the other boys who did not enjoy this special treatment by the school that Jerry, too, would have "become something" had he graduated as anticipated. For Herb and Jack outside intervention worked to their advantage; for Jerry it was his undoing.

Selective perception and labelling—finding, processing and punishing some kinds of criminality and not others—means that visible, poor, nonmobile, outspoken, undiplomatic "tough" kids will be noticed, whether their actions are seriously delinquent or not. Other kids, who have established a reputation for being bright (even though underachieving), disciplined and involved in respectable activities, who are mobile and monied, will be

Truancy for the Roughnecks meant almost certain detection. The Saints' technique for covering truancy was so successful that teachers did not even realize that the boys were absent from school much of the time.

invisible when they deviate from sanctioned activities. They'll sow their wild oats—perhaps even wider and thicker than their lower-class cohorts—but they won't be noticed. When it's time to leave adolescence most will follow the expected path, settling into the ways of the middle class, remembering fondly the delinquent but unnoticed fling of their youth. The Roughnecks and others like them may turn around, too. It is more likely that their noticeable deviance will have been so reinforced by police and community that their lives will be effectively channelled into careers consistent with their adolescent background.

FURTHER READING

Whose Law, What Order? A Conflict Approach to Criminology by William J. Chambliss and Milton Mankoff (Andover, Mass.: Warner-Modular Publications, 1973).

The Vice Lords: Warriors of the Streets by R. Lincoln Keiser (New York: Holt, Rinehart and Winston, 1969).

"Matthew Washington Who Had Death in His Eyes" in *Social Control* edited by Peter Manning (New York: Free Press, 1973).

"White Gangs" by Walter B. Miller in *Transaction* V 6 (September 1969).

The Social Reality of Crime by Richard Quinney (Boston: Little, Brown, 1971).

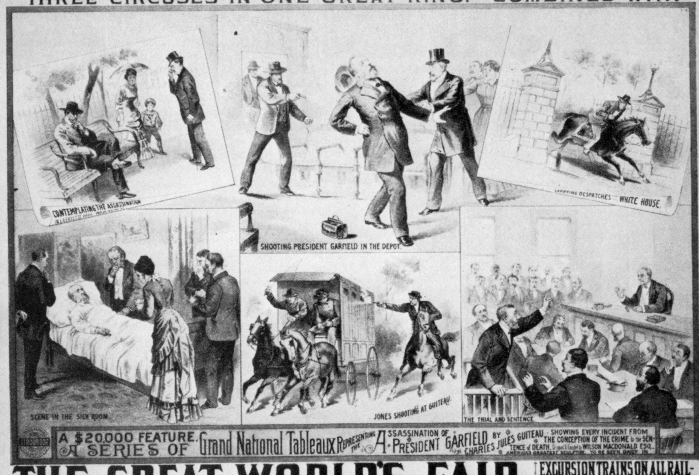

WILLIAM S. CROTTY

Presidential Assassinations

American exposure to assassination represents a recent occurrence, or so most would like to believe. On November 22, 1963 President John F. Kennedy was murdered while on a political trip to Dallas. People were shocked. The world's mightiest government momentarily staggered. An investigation was initiated into the events surrounding the act with the intention of fixing responsibility for the murder.

The Warren Commission Report, as it became known, was a comprehensive although not flawless examination of the assassination. The report's conclusions, despite a continuing controversy, were generally accepted by the American people. Within five years of John Kennedy's assassination, his brother Robert was murdered while seeking the Democratic nomination for the presidency. Robert Kennedy's assassination followed almost two months to the day the killing of the Reverend Martin Luther King, black civil

rights leader and the adaptor of Gandhian principles of non-violence to the turbulent racial crises of the 1960s. Between the deaths of the two Kennedys and Dr. King, at least two other political leaders representing polar extremes of political philosophy, Medgar Evers, the NAACP leader in Mississippi dedicated to achieving peaceful electoral participation of blacks, and Lincoln Rockwell, a fascist and outspoken head of the revived American-German Party, were assassinated.

The continuing assassinations in concert with a decade of seemingly endless violence brought serious concern to Americans. While assassinations, it turns out, are not unknown in the United States, these acts were new to the consciousness of the vast majority of living Americans.

The immediate outcry was one of confusion. Was America a sick society? Was some sinister long-range plot wreaking its vengeance? Was the United States headed toward a new era of open political warfare and potential police-state repression? Was the delicate fabric of American social and moral behavior collapsing?

Assassinations of political consequence can be defined as the murder of an individual, whether of public prominence or not, in an effort to achieve political gain. The classic conception of the assassination act is as a tactic in struggles for political power. Julius Caesar was assassinated by a group of friends and senators who feared the evil consequences of his great power; the legendary Rasputin was assassinated by Prince Felix Yusupov and a coconspirator who resented his evil influence over the Czar; two premiers of Japan, Hanaguchi and Inuiki, plus a number of cabinet officials were assassinated by political opponents in pre-World War II Japan. Each of these assassinations and the vast majority that stud the pages of history had explicitly political motives behind them.

This definition of assassination must be modified to have meaning within the American context. The statement assumes an element of rationality in the planning of the murder as it relates to the achievement of specified political objectives. Any assassin will deliberate on how to assault his victim—the time, the place, the weapon to be used, the nature of the encounter and so on. The concept of rationality is not intended to convey the idea of the preplanning of the details of the act. Rather, it means that the execution of the victim has a tangible relationship to a policy goal the conspirators wish to achieve. In other words it is motivated by political concerns. The chief factor isolating assassinations in the United States from those in other countries hinges on this distinction.

Lonely Figures

It can be argued with some limited support that the assassinations of prominent American political leaders, or at least of presidents, are best understood as individual acts that result from the pathological drives of the killer. All of the presidential assassins have been lonely figures, mentally unstable and through these murders have acted out inner fantasies. Such explanations may be partially acceptable for explaining simple acts; they are of little value for understanding the persistence of the murders over time or their broader implications. Why should an individual choose a public personage as his target if he is irrationally responding to internal needs? Why after seemingly peaceful interludes do assassinations reoccur? Why are assassinations more frequent in one nation than another? An approach that focuses on the peculiarities of a given assassination or number of assassinations cannot begin to address such questions. Assassinations are social acts with broad political consequences. They cannot be treated as isolated phenomena and thus not subject to systematic, comparative analysis or interpretation. Rather, they are acts that reflect a variety of cultural forces and social conditions, culminating in bizarre outlets for personal behavior.

A classification of assassinations can serve to explain patterns of assassination in the United States compared to other nations. Assassinations can be divided into five categories.

☐ *Anomic assassination* is the murder of a political figure for essentially private reasons. The justification for the act is couched in broadly political terms, but the relationship between the act and the advancement of the political objectives specified is impossible to draw on any rational basis. The connecting link then is assumed to be the fantasies of the assassin. This type of act is the most familiar to those concerned with presidential assassinations.

☐ *Elite substitution* is the murder of a political leader in order to replace him or those he represents in power with an opposing group at essentially the same level. The palace guard assassination of a dictator or the power struggle among groups for governmental leadership would result in this type of assassination. The continuing blood struggle between the Karageorgevich and Oberenovich dynasties in Serbia is a case in point. Transfer of power through elite assassination became almost a matter of court routine in nineteenth-century Turkey.

☐ *Tyrannicide* is one of the oldest forms of assassination and the one with the greatest philosophical justification—the murder of a despot in order to replace him with one more amenable to the people and needs of a nation. That assassination developed beyond the simple act to the preoccupation with tyrannicide and regicide in particular can be traced to the latter half of the nineteenth century. The struggles in Russia against the czar developed the systematic and tactical use of assassination as a broad-scale political weapon. The intention was to punish the government or its minions for specified acts, to decentralize and weaken it and eventually to incapacitate it. This in turn developed into a fourth type of assassination.

☐ *Terroristic assassination* can be employed on a mass basis to demonstrate a government's incapacity to deal with insurgents, to neutralize a populace's allegiance to a government, to enlist their support in a revolutionary movement or, more ambitiously, to allow a minority to suppress and subjugate a population. Examples of mass terror in history are many. The era associated with the French Revolution, the Inquisition, the Russian purges of the 1930s, the Mau Mau rebellion in Kenya during the 1950s, the Nazi persecutions, the American South following the Civil War and the terror used by the Viet Cong in the rural provinces of South Vietnam are examples of the systematic use of assassinations by an organized group within a population to achieve political goals.

The terror can be random, choosing targets for no reason indigenous to the victim. The intention is to erode any faith in the government and intimidate the population. In this, the terrorists are willing to deliberately murder innocents to achieve their broader objectives.

A case study in random mass terrorism was the Algerian nationalists' fight against the French. Reportedly in the first three years of the terrorism (November 1954 to November 1957) the Algerian rebels assassinated 8,429 civilians of whom only 1,126 were Europeans. The rest were brother Moslems. Curiously, the OAS (the Secret Army Organization of French Algerians) resorted to mass terror when it became apparent that the De Gaulle government was willing to accede to an independent Algeria. During the latter part of 1961 and early 1962, the OAS was credited with responsibility for 500 deaths in Algeria.

Terroristic assassinations directed toward specified categories of civilians or officials represents a more limited and systematic attempt to achieve the same ends as mass terror assassinations. The Viet Cong focused on village leaders, allegedly killing or kidnapping over 2,400 in the period 1957-1959, with an additional 7,982 civil officials assassinated and 40,282 abducted in the period 1961-1965. Macedonian, Armenian and Bulgarian terror directed against their Turkish rulers at the turn of the century are other examples of more discrete, highly specific assassination strategies.

☐ *Propaganda by deed* is a type of assassination employed to direct attention to a broader problem (for example, the subjugation of a people) with the hopes of bringing some alleviation. The assassinations during the 1950s by the Algerian nationalists were of this nature, although the volume of political murders would have to place them in the category of mass terror. The French colonial OAS organization in the early 1960s attempted to assassinate military figures and journalists in Paris to direct the attention of the French people to their difficulties. The assassination of Czar Alexander II was in part for propaganda purposes, as was the assassination attempt directed against President Truman and the explanation given for Senator Robert Kennedy's assassination. In Truman's case the Puerto Rican nationalists hoped to publicize their cause, independence for Puerto Rico, through their attack on the president. Sirhan Sirhan, the Jordanian immigrant who murdered Robert Kennedy, wanted to emphasize the plight of the Arab nations and the supposed favoritism shown Israel by Kennedy.

A comparison of the level of assassinations in the United States with other nations reveals a disquieting fact: the United States has a disturbingly high level of political assassinations. By virtually any measure, this country ranks near the top of any list of political assassinations. For the fifty-year period 1918-1968, information on assassinations and attempted assassinations reveals that the United States ranked thirtieth of the 89 nations studied. In another study of the frequency of assassinations for a more recent time period—the two decades immediately following the Second World War—the United States ranked fifth among the 84 nations analyzed.

Ivo Feierabend and his associates, in their comparative study of assassinations cross-nationally during this latter period, uncovered a number of interesting relationships. They demonstrated, for example, an association between a high incidence of political assassination and social disruption and political instability in a nation. Assassinations were also related to less developed nations and those in transitory economic situations, cases to which both France and the United States proved to be curious exceptions. There was a strong relationship between assassinations and politically violent acts more generally; in fact, the incidence of specified types of politically violent occurrences represented one of the most consistent predictors of assassination. The link with violence—both violent acts directed against other nations and internally violent events of political significance—was clearcut.

Carl Leiden and associates, in reviewing assassinations for the entire 50-year period, argue much the same relationship between political stress in a nation (as manifested in politically violent events) and a high level of assassinations. In noting that four periods accounted for 70 percent of the assassinations that took place over the entire

five decades, they point out that each was a time of unusual political turbulence. The years 1919-1923 represented the immediate post-World War I period; 1932-1934 encompassed the heart of the Great Depression; 1946-1951 witnessed the readjustment after World War II; and 1963-1966 highlighted the midpoint of a decade noted for its political unrest.

Many commonalities appear in the assassination attempts directed against American presidents or presidential candidates. A convenient way of examining those factors is to arbitrarily divide the assassination acts into similarities common to the intended victims and those associated with the assailants.

The Targets

One explanation for the assassinations that has enjoyed some vogue develops the assumption that certain types of politicians attract would-be assassins. The argument really breaks into two subthemes, one stressing a psychological interpretation of a politican's approach to life and the other dealing with the nature of political demands and the officeholder's reaction to these.

Some contend that certain personalities entertain an implicit death wish. These individuals are attracted to high-risk occupations. While politics does not compare to auto racing, it does represent a precarious calling and does prove attractive to adventuresome types. High-risk politicians are characterized by a willingness to extend themselves—actually overextend themselves—in seeking to advance their careers. They are willing to expose themselves to dangerous situations, possibly even subconsciously seek out such encounters, assumedly to satisfy internal psychological drives.

Robert Kennedy purportedly represents a prime example of this thesis. The senator's death wish, or at least his willingness to open himself to personal hurt, evidenced itself in private life in such treacherous pastimes as mountain climbing, navigating waterways such as the Amazon, and shooting dangerous rapids. He was known for his love of other physically taxing sports. In public life, the same drive surfaced in his pushing to the limits of physical stamina in the incessant campaigns, the tumultuous motorcades and the large and engulfing crowds regularly featured on the candidate's itinerary. This strain of argument contends that an individual places himself in situations that if not inviting attack permit the conditions that make it a possibility. Similar contentions were heard after John Kennedy's death. In retrospect, Theodore Roosevelt would fit this mold rather nicely also. After being shot by John Schrank when leaving a Milwaukee hotel to make a campaign speech, he insisted on making his speech although carrying the bullet in his chest and bleeding profusely.

The validity of such arguments cannot be easily assessed. They depend for verification upon an in-depth analysis by experts of the psychological mechanisms that motivate individual personalities. But it is unlikely that explanations of this nature can serve to develop a general understanding of political behavior as it relates to violent personal attacks. Whether such an explanation applies to the Kennedys is a moot point. McKinley, Garfield, Franklin Roosevelt and Truman do not appear to fit the theory.

At best, it is an explanation sufficient for understanding

individual cases one by one. It serves to divert attention from broader and more important themes that focus on an interlocking network of circumstantial and situational factors that at least offer hope of remedy.

A second type of argument emphasizes the image and intentions of the victim rather than his psychological drives. This school of thought claims that the presidents most prone to physical attack are those who challenge the status quo. The movers, the doers in office and those seeking election who associate themselves with change invite controversy and become targets for the frustrations of those inclined toward political murder.

Robert Kennedy as a leader of the New Politics and champion of the Negro, Mexican-American and the young appears to have been such an individual. John Kennedy may have seemed an innovator to his contemporaries. Franklin Roosevelt certainly introduced basic changes into American society. On the other extreme, Herbert Hoover and Dwight Eisenhower appeared to be complacent, less innovative presidents, and they were not attacked.

The argument claims a superficial credibility, but it does not hold up under examination. John Kennedy, while a personally glamorous figure, was not a particularly rash or disruptive president by present assessments. It appears that his reputed assassin, Lee Harvey Oswald, previously attempted to kill retired General Edwin Walker, a hero of the far Right. It is difficult to ascertain the link between Oswald's two targets, unless it lies within the killer rather than his victims. Indeed, Robert Kennedy was a product of the Old Politics more than the new, as was his brother. A more reasonable target, if this line of reasoning is extended to its logical end, was Eugene McCarthy. Senator McCarthy successfully mobilized and personified throughout his own 1968 presidential nomination campaign the politically charged elements of dissent within the United States. Further, Robert Kennedy's assassin, Sirhan, offered a different explanation for his attack. Senator Kennedy's support of Israel, a minor point in his prenomination campaign, was Sirhan's stimulus to attack. Beyond this, the love-hate relationship (as perceived by the murderer) with the politician offers another explanation of Sirhan's behavior, but again one that deals with the psychological workings of the assassin and is difficult to relate to his victim.

Franklin D. Roosevelt was an unquestioned mover, a prime molder of the domestic economic system of modern America. His achievements were profound, far outlasting his stewardship. Certainly he is the most powerful example to be offered in support of this line of contention.

Yet Giuseppe Zangara attacked Roosevelt after his election and prior to his inauguration, well in advance of any indications of the impact the president-elect would have on the country. The Democratic party platform Roosevelt had run on in the 1932 election was a conservative document and Roosevelt's campaign oratory was not designed to alarm anyone.

Zangara was concerned with the office, not the man. He believed it to be a symbol of oppression and disregard for the problems that beset the ordinary citizen. Zangara justified his action as striking a blow on behalf of the poor men of the world against capitalism. That Roosevelt, given

his place in history and the contemporary groups that opposed him, should symbolize the rejection of the common man is anomalous.

Zangara was an Italian immigrant. Before leaving Italy, by his own admission, he desired to assassinate King Victor Emmanuel III for the same reasons he later employed to justify his attack on Roosevelt. He also intended to assassinate Presidents Coolidge and Hoover, hardly symbols of change, but he never had the opportunity. The factor that distinguished Franklin Roosevelt as a target for assassination from either Hoover or Coolidge, or for that matter the king of Italy, was not his personality, his politics, or his potential impact on national politics, but the opportunity that he accidentally gave Zangara. Roosevelt happened to appear in Miami for a speech while Zangara was living there. While not a chief of state at the time, he was the president-elect, which was good enough for his assailant.

Zangara made the point unmistakably clear at his own trial. When asked if he would have attacked President Hoover he replied, "I see Mr. Hoover first I kill him first. Make no difference. President just the same bunch—all same. No make no difference who get that job. Run by big money. Makes no difference who he is."

It is difficult to envision Presidents Garfield or McKinley as significant threats to the status quo. The classification of Presidents Jackson and Truman and, at the time, presidential candidate Theodore Roosevelt, would depend on one's interpretation of their role in and contribution to the political development of the United States. Lincoln certainly must be regarded as a president who had a fundamental impact on his society. Overall, however, the evidence for this particular line of reasoning is not persuasive. The argument has an intrinsic popular appeal, but it is not substantiated by what is known concerning the assassinations.

The Assassins

Discernible patterns do emerge when the focus shifts from the victims to their assailants. First, and of greatest importance, only two of the nine attempts on the lives of presidents or presidential candidates can be considered the work of a conspiracy (see Table 1). And of these two, the Booth plot against President Lincoln was a pickup conspiracy involving friends and acquaintances of his, and the attempt on President Truman was little more. The attack against Lincoln was not known or supported by the southern Confederacy, which it was intended to help, and only conjectural evidence can be cited to implicate Lincoln's Secretary of War, Edwin M. Stanton, directly or indirectly in a coup d'etat.

The attempt by Oscar Collazo and Griselio Torresola to storm Blair House, the temporary residence of the president, and attack Harry Truman was a conspiracy, but a poorly conceived and ineptly executed one. The potential assassins were members of a Puerto Rican liberationist group centered in New York. They traveled to Washington with the intention of murdering the president as a symbolic propaganda act designed to draw attention to Puerto Rico's plight. The scheme was born of blind fanaticism. Truman had done more than any of his predecessors in recognizing

Table 1 — Presidential Assassinations and Assaults

Assailant	Target	Date of Attack	Outcome	Activity of Victim at Time of Attack	Age	Occupation	Assailant's Weapon	Place of Birth
ASSASSINATIONS:								
John Wilkes Booth	President **Abraham Lincoln**	4/14/1865	Lincoln's Death 4/15/1865	Attending "Our American Cousin" at Ford's Theatre, Washington, D.C.	26	Actor	Pistol	U.S. (1st generation born in U.S.)
Charles Julius Giteau	President **John Garfield**	7/2/1881	Garfield's Death 9/19/1881	Waiting to board train for vacation trip, Washington, D.C.	38	Lawyer, Lecturer, Evangelist	Pistol	U.S.
Leon F. Czolgosz	President **William McKinley**	9/6/1901	McKinley's Death 9/14/1901	Standing in receiving line, Pan-American Exposition, Buffalo, N.Y.	28	Mill Worker	Pistol	U.S. (1st generation born in U.S.)
Lee Harvey Oswald	President **John F. Kennedy**	11/22/1963	Kennedy's Death 11/22/1963	Motorcade through Dallas, Texas	24	Worker in Book Depository	Rifle	U.S.
Sirhan Sirhan	Senator **Robert F. Kennedy** Candidate for Democratic Presidential Nomination	6/5/1968	Kennedy's Death 6/5/1968	Returning from talk claiming victory in Calif. Democratic Primary, Los Angeles, Calif.	24	Stable boy, Clerk	Pistol	Jordan
ASSAULTS:								
Richard Lawrence	President **Andrew Jackson**	1/30/1835	Pistols misfired, Jackson unhurt	Leading funeral procession for deceased Congressman, Washington, D.C.	36	House Painter	Pistols	England
John Schrank	Presidential Candidate **Theodore Roosevelt**	10/14/1912	Roosevelt wounded, but survived	Leaving hotel to make campaign speech, Milwaukee, Wisc.	36	Bartender, Landlord	Pistol	Bavaria
Giuseppe Zangara	President-Elect **Franklin D. Roosevelt**	2/15/1933	Missed Roosevelt, killed Mayor Anton Cermak of Chicago standing near FDR	Speaking at political rally, Miami, Florida	32	Construction Worker	Pistol	Italy
Oscar Collazo and Griselio Torresola	President **Harry F. Truman**	10/31/1950	President unhurt; 1 Secret Service Agent killed, 2 wounded; Torresola killed; Collazo wounded	Assailants stormed Blair House, temporary residence of President, Washington, D.C.	36 25	Metal Polisher None	Pistols	Puerto Rico Puerto Rico

the island's difficulties and in attempting to stabilize its political and economic conditions. Nonetheless, he was the intended victim by virtue of the office he held. What tangible public benefit could be expected to accrue from the attack is difficult to conceive. The attempt was not designed to gain control of the government, quite obviously, or to give an opposition leader or party political advantage, classic objectives in traditional assassination conspiracies.

The conspirators themselves had only the most freewheeling of plans for gaining access to the president and engaged in the sketchiest of preparatory planning. The effort resulted in a wild gun battle leading to the deaths of Torresola, one Secret Service agent, and the wounding of two other agents and Collazo and the eventual imprisonment of the latter for life.

People find it difficult to understand how one lone, demented gunman can bring down the most powerful leader on earth. A pressing necessity exists to explain the murder in broader and more acceptable terms. Rather than a quirk happening, the act is reconstructed as part of a well-conceived plan with important ramifications. People want to believe that Oswald was a Communist agent, a representative of a right-wing hate group, or the tool of the CIA. Facets of his confused background could be interpreted to lend support to each of these possibilities. Richard Lawrence was accused of being the gunman of a Whig conspiracy designed to intimidate President Andrew Jackson. John Wilkes Booth and his accomplices were considered agents of the South. Charles Giteau supposedly represented the Republican party faction—the Stalwarts—that opposed Garfield. President McKinley's assassin, Leon Czolgosz, reportedly executed the wishes of the anarchists, a group that paid dearly for this asseumption. And Zangara was said to be carrying out the orders of mobsters—one rumor had it that his intended target was Mayor Anton Cermak of Chicago whom he did in fact kill and not President-elect Franklin Roosevelt.

An element of psychological reassurance resides in attempts to attribute assassinations to conspiracies. However, these speculations are fed by more than the individual's desire to relieve his mental anguish. The nature of the American presidency has grown in the mythology of the times far out of proportion to the presumed abilities of one man to fill it. The president assumes the attributes of a god, a king, a political leader without equal, the super-American in every respect. In contrast, the British divorce the traditional and symbolic roles (in the person of the king or queen) from the seat of actual political power, and they also discourage interpretations of the prime minister as the sole mover of events. While the American presidency has been humanized through media incredibly intrusive into every aspect of the occupant's life, paradoxically the president at the same time assumes almost superhuman dimensions.

The protective paraphernalia that surrounds the president reinforces an image of invincibility. All are familiar with the much publicized Secret Service and their role in providing for the safety of the president and his family. Television constantly exposes even the casual viewer to the presidential guardians in their supposedly unobtrusive execution of their duties. The president's car with its various gimmicks, including the famed (and as it later turns out) non-bulletproof bubble-top is well publicized, an object of curiosity every time he appears in a motorcade. Certainly with such an office, such a man and such protection, one sick gunman, it is thought, could not be the true explanation for assassination—a devilishly clever group of conspirators must have designed a plan to penetrate the impenetrable defenses around the president's life.

As with most erroneous beliefs that large numbers of people persist in subscribing to, there must be some credibility attached to them, some reason for believing. The ineptitude surrounding the immediate events following President Kennedy's assassination and the history of occurrences since then lend support to a wide range of conspiratorial theories. The events developing out of the assassination were poorly handled. Without straining, a variety of questions can be put forward for which no satisfactory answers exist. Why didn't a Secret Service man drive the route immediately preceding the presidential motorcade seeking trouble spots? Why didn't anyone of the spectators who saw Oswald with a rifle in the window awaiting the presidential party mention it to the police officers standing with them? Why did the president's car slow down after the first shot rather than speeding away? Why wasn't the hospital alerted to receive the mortally wounded president? Why weren't contingency plans immediately available for implementation? Why wasn't the Texas School Book Depository sealed off, if not immediately, then as soon as the police had an indication the shot had come from there? Why wasn't a record kept of Oswald's interrogation (in which the Secret Service, the FBI, the Texas Rangers, the county prosecutor's office and the Dallas police all participated)? Why wasn't Oswald allowed legal counsel? Why wasn't Oswald given over to the Dallas sheriff's office immediately after he was remanded to their custody in the hearing before the judge? Why were both of Oswald's preliminary hearings, one for Officer Tippett and the second for John Kennedy, held in camera? How could a civilian known to the police kill Oswald while he remained in police custody?

The later reluctance of the government to make available the full autopsy reports and the delicacy with which some witnesses were treated by the Warren Commission and others never requested to appear reveal a laudable but misplaced sympathy with the sensibilities of the individuals involved. A chief intention of the Warren Commission was to restore a sense of legitimacy and trust to the government. This concern also had to influence their deliberations. Placing the burden of the investigation into the assassination on the FBI, an agency facing judgment as to its own responsibilities in the sequence of events leading to the murder, invites distrust. The price paid for all this was high, a series of reflections made on the credibility of the official explanation put forward. Since such reports are always suspect, those who frame them should extend themselves to insure skeptics no basis for argument that can be avoided. The procedures employed and the evidence collected should be characterized by the greatest objectivity. The one intention should be to develop and make public the most comprehensive, accurate and impartial report of the events as they occurred. Anything less is totally unacceptable.

Within such a vortex of influences—the psychological need for reassurance, the overpublicized and personalized nature of the office, the invincible security arrangements and the official bungling in handling the murder and its ramifications—the desire to believe in a conspiracy appears not so unwarranted a response.

The assassins enjoyed several other things in common besides being non-conspirators. Most were fringe members

Giuseppe Zangara justified his attack on President-elect Franklin D. Roosevelt as striking a blow on behalf of the poor men of the world against capitalism. Roosevelt was not hit, but Mayor Anton Cernak of Chicago, who was standing near him at a political rally in Miami, Florida, was killed. (Giuseppe Zangara, left, his captors, right)

of society. Virtually all were mentally unstable. Few had succeeded in any walk of life. Oswald, Sirhan and Torresola worked irregularly at odd jobs; Czolgosz, a factory worker, quit his job three years prior to McKinley's assassination and did not work regularly after that. Giteau was an itinerant lawyer and lecturer of no great renown; Schrank, a bartender and tenement landlord, spent the bulk of his time reading, scribbling notes and wandering around Manhattan in the years preceding his attack on Theodore Roosevelt. John Wilkes Booth was a noted actor, although not of the calibre of his father or brothers, but one with declining opportunities to work and in jeopardy of losing his career altogether due to a throat ailment. Zangara was a bricklayer and contractor although holding no job for any length of time in the two years preceding his attack on FDR; Lawrence, a house painter, worked infrequently in the two years leading up to his attempted murder of Jackson. Collazo, the exception, held a variety of jobs but was employed steadily preceding his trip to Washington from New York City to make a strike for Puerto Rican independence.

Collazo was an exception in other respects. While each of the others had difficulty in establishing and maintaining mature emotional relationships, he had a wife and a settled family life. Collazo was proficient at his job and respected in his community—a type of recognition that eluded each of the others except Booth. Collazo's fanaticism, and again the parallel to Booth is appropriate, placed a cause above life. Excepting Collazo, each of the others gave demonstrable evidence of emotional instability in the years immediately prior to their assassination attempts.

Richard Lawrence, the would-be assassin of President Jackson, appears to have been totally irrational. He had threatened assassination before. He saw himself as a king, believed the United States was subtly persecuting him as he believed it had his father before him and that the country owed him large amounts of money.

Czolgosz felt McKinley "was the enemy of the good people—the good working people" and reported feeling no sorrow for his crime. Schrank coupled Theodore Roosevelt's try for a third term (actually Roosevelt served the major part of McKinley's second term after his death and

was elected to only one full term on his own) with an apparition of McKinley's ghost in a bizarre explanation. According to Schrank, "God . . . called me to be his instrument." Apparently the deceased McKinley did also, appearing before him in a dream and declaring, "This is my murderer [pointing at an image of Roosevelt], avenge my death." And finally, Schrank argued that "every third termer [must] be regarded as a traitor to the American cause . . . it is the right and duty of every citizen to forcibly remove a third termer."

Zangara wanted to strike a blow on behalf of the working man and to ease a pain in his abdomen, caused he felt by the capitalists, and for which no physical explanation could be found in his autopsy. In his words, "I have trouble with my stomach and that way, I make my idea to kill the president [President-elect Franklin Roosevelt] —kill any president, any king." Booth wished to gain immortality, to be remembered as the man who toppled the colossus. Vaguely, he intended his plan to aid the South also.

Two strains run through the Warren Commission assessment of Oswald's motive. One is that Oswald needed to overcome feelings of impotency, to assume the heroic proportions he fantasized for himself. The second is that he, as did Booth, craved historical notoriety.

One thing is clear: the assassins struck at the office, not the man. They had no personal relationships with their victims, no animosity directed against them as individuals and frequently even no knowledge of their personalities or policies when in office. Zangara typified the majority when he stated it made no difference to him whether he assassinated Coolidge or Hoover rather than Roosevelt, or for that matter, the king of Italy.

Most of the assailants felt they acted under divine inspiration. And although post facto diagnosis has its risks, most would have to be classified as patently unbalanced.

Public Revenge

The response of most Americans and the courts to the presidential assailants depended on whether their attempts on the lives of the presidents succeeded or not. If they failed in their attacks they were dealt with humanely.

Collazo, Schrank, Lawrence and Zangara (in his first trial which took place prior to Cermak's death) were institutionalized for life.

If the assassins succeeded, however, vengeance became the dominant public mood. Neither the courts specifically nor the legal safeguards provided by society as a whole have stood up well under the attack. Neither Oswald nor Booth came to trial. Both were killed. Oswald died within 48 hours of John Kennedy. Booth succumbed in a fiery barn within 12 days of Lincoln's death, killed either by his own hand or the bullet of a Union soldier. Four of Booth's co-conspirators were tried and hung, at least one on questionable evidence. Four others were imprisoned on the Florida Keys, one dying from disease before and one shortly after all were pardoned by Andrew Johnson in 1869. The lot included the boy who held Booth's horse outside of Ford's Theatre.

Zangara's second trial took place three days after Cermak's death. Within 24 hours he was judged guilty and 33 days after his attack he was electrocuted. Czolgosz was tried four days after McKinley's death. His trial lasted eight-and-one-half hours over a two-day period. The jury took 34 minutes to deliver the verdict and Czolgosz was electrocuted 40 days after McKinley's death. Sulfuric acid was poured into the coffin, apparently a custom of the time. Giteau's trial for the assassination of Garfield turned into a circus that lasted almost three months, although the results ultimately were the same.

Richard Lawrence's trial for his unsuccessful attack on President Jackson's life in 1835 represents a noteworthy gauge against which to assess the others because of the manner in which the law was applied to the case. In his introductory remarks the prosecutor, who was Francis Scott Key, drew attention to a British precedent as a basis for dismissing the prevailing criteria for determining legal responsibility for the crime, which was an individual's capacity to judge right from wrong. The prosecutor argued that a defendant who acted on the basis of a delusion should be judged insane and treated accordingly. The defense's responsibility was to prove the defendant suffered delusions that led to the attack against Jackson and this they did with ease. Lawrence pled insanity, was imprisoned for life and died in a mental institution.

None of the three sets of defense lawyers in the Giteau, Czolgosz or Zangara cases argued the precedent established in the Lawrence trial. Czolgosz had no legal representatives until two days before his trial, and then they put forward no defense witnesses on his behalf. The most eminent medical authorities concluded that Czolgosz was "unqualifiedly" sane, and the court assumed this was the case unless proven otherwise. The contention was not challenged. A thorough reanalysis of his life begun a year after his death by two highly competent psychiatrists, however, came to quite dissimilar conclusions.

In Zangara's case, a board of two court-appointed psychiatrists examined him but made no determination as to sanity. No psychiatric witnesses were called to testify on his behalf and his sanity was assumed, although one of the psychiatrists who examined him declared to author Robert Donovan 20 years later that "medically, he was not sane."

Giteau did plead insanity. He had a determined if unspectacular set of lawyers, testimony by experts was presented to the effect that he was insane, and his outbursts and consistently unpredictable behavior during the trial should have been sufficient to convince disbelievers of his illness. The court persisted in crediting him with being sane, partly because Giteau wanted to be judged mentally incapable and threatened God's personal intervention on the court if any other verdict was delivered. The public demanded blood in payment for President Garfield's assassination. The court convicted Giteau, an appeal to the Supreme Court was rejected, President Arthur refused clemency and, to the satisfaction of a large crowd of onlookers, Giteau was hung.

The office of presidency has been the target of assassins because of its power and visibility as the kingpin of American government. A depersonalization of the office and its incumbent would be helpful as would an emphasis on the complex responsibilities of competing centers of governmental power—the Congress, the state capitals and the mayors' offices.

Violence in America

A number of studies and presidential commissions have dealt with violence in American society with particular focus on some of its more unpleasant aspects—urban riots, crime, assassinations and death and disorders on college campuses. Main themes in all the reports are the need for greater tolerance and understanding, less rhetoric, more equitable distribution of the society's resources and truly representative governing bodies. The commissions have helped society to reexamine its past and they have done commendable jobs of explanation. But the net practical results measured in legislative gain and changed governmental procedures emanating from the work of the Warren, Kerner, Eisenhower and Scranton Commissions have been few. The public and its representatives content themselves with broad discussions of the problems involved and accept the recommendations of the commissions with grave reservations.

The public attitude toward political assassination is fatalistic. In 1963 the American people were deeply shocked by the assassination of President Kennedy and expected nothing of like nature to happen again. Five years later they were resigned to believing that assassination represents a necessary risk of political life.

In the nationwide poll on political violence conducted by Louis Harris and Associates, 51 percent of the respondents agreed with the statement that "if people go into politics they more or less have to accept the fact that they might get killed." Fifty-five percent agreed that "a lot more people in government and politics will probably be assassinated in the next few years."

Most discouraging of all has been the cautious response of public officials. Minor pieces of legislation are passed—such as weak gun control laws and increased Secret Service protection for presidential candidates. Commissions are appointed to study outbreaks of violence in order to defuse tense situations. But as long as no more serious solutions for dealing with the roots of the problem are offered, the results are predictable. A sober assessment of present conditions portends ominous future events.

216

SUZANNE K. STEINMETZ AND MURRAY A. STRAUS

The Family as Cradle of Violence

Although intrafamily violence like that attributed to Lizzie Borden is occasionally reported, such behavior is considered totally out of the ordinary—families are supposed to be oases of serenity where love and good feeling flow from each parent and child.

Unfortunately, that lovely picture is not accurate. In fact, the grizzly tale of Lizzie Borden may not be unique. Violence seems as typical of family relationships as love; and it would be hard to find a group or institution in American society in which violence is more of an everyday occurrence than it is within the family. Family members physically abuse each other far more often than do nonrelated individuals. Starting with slaps and going on to torture and murder, the family provides a prime setting for every degree of physical violence. So universal is the phenomenon that it is probable that some form of violence will occur in almost every family.

The most universal type of physical violence is corporal punishment by parents. Studies in England and the United States show that between 84 and 97 percent of all parents use physical punishment at some point in their child's life. Moreover, such use of physical force to maintain parental authority is not confined to early childhood. Data on students in three different regions of the United States show that half of the parents sampled either used or threatened their high school seniors with physical punishment.

Of course, physical punishment differs significantly from other violence. But it is violence, nonetheless. Despite its good intentions, it has some of the same consequences as other forms of violence. Research shows that parents who use physical punishment to control the aggressiveness of their children probably increase rather than decrease their child's aggressive tendencies. Violence begets violence, however peaceful and altruistic the motivation.

The violent tendencies thus reinforced may well be turned against the parents, as in the case of Lizzie Borden. Although most intrafamily violence is less bloody than that attributed to Lizzie, some family abuse does go as far as ax murder. Examination of relationships between murderer and victim proves that the largest single category of victim is that of family member or relative.

Homicide at Home

The magnitude of family violence became particularly obvious during the summer heat wave of 1972. Page 1 of the July 22, 1972 *New York Times* carried an article describing the increase in murders during the previous few days of extreme heat in New York City and summarizing the statistics for murder in New York during the previous six months. Page 2 held an article totalling deaths in Northern Ireland during three and a half years of disturbances. About as many people were murdered by their relatives in one six-month period in New York City as had been killed in three and a half years of political upheaval in Northern Ireland.

Murder, though relatively rare, gets far more attention than less violent abuse..Even though more murders are committed on family members than any other type of person, and even though the United States has a high degree of homicide, the rate is still only four or five per 100,000 population. What about non-lethal physical violence between husband and wife? While accurate statistics are hard to find, one way of estimating the magnitude of the phenomenon is through the eyes of the police.

Just as relatives are the largest single category of murder victim, so family fights are the largest single category of police calls. One legal researcher estimates that more police calls involve family conflict than do calls for all criminal incidents, including murders, rapes, non-family assaults, robberies and muggings. "Violence in the home" deserves at least as much public concern as "crime in the streets." The police hate and fear family conflict calls for several reasons. First, a family disturbance call lacks the glamour, prestige and public appreciation of a robbery or an accident summons. More important, such calls are extremely dangerous. Many a policeman coming to the aid of a wife who is being beaten has had a chair or a bottle thrown at him or has been stabbed or shot by a wife who suddenly becomes fearful of what is going to happen to her husband, or who abruptly turns her rage from her husband to the police. Twenty-two percent of all police fatalities come from investigating problems between husband and wife or parent and child.

One cannot tell from these data on police calls just what proportion of all husbands and wives have had physical fights, since it takes an unusual combination of events to have the police summoned. The closest published estimate is found in the research of George Levinger and John O'Brien. In studying applicants for divorce, O'Brien found that 17 percent of his cases

spontaneously mentioned overt violent behavior, and Levinger found that 23 percent of the middle-class couples and 40 percent of the working-class couples gave "physical abuse" as a major complaint.

Both of these figures probably underestimate the amount of physical violence between husbands and wives because there may well have been violent incidents which were not mentioned or which were not listed as a main cause of divorce. Even doubling the figure, however, leaves us far from knowing the extent of husband-wife violence. First, there is a discrepancy between the O'Brien and the Levinger figures. Second, these figures apply only to couples who have applied for divorce. It may be that there is a lower incidence of physical violence among a cross-section of couples; or it may be, as we suspect, that the difference is not very great.

A survey conducted for the National Commission of the Causes and Prevention of Violence deals with what violence people would approve. These data show that one out of four men and one out of six women approve of slapping a wife under certain conditions. As for a wife slapping a husband, 26 percent of the men and 19 percent of the women approve. Of course, some people who approve of slapping will never do it and some who disapprove *will* slap—or worse. Probably the latter group is larger. If that is true, we know that husband-wife violence at the minimal level of slapping occurs in at least one quarter of American families.

Our own pilot studies also give some indication of the high rate of violence in the family. Richard Gelles of the University of New Hampshire, who has done a series of in-depth case studies of a sample of 80 families, found that about 56 percent of the couples have used physical force on each other at some time.

In a second study, freshman college students responded to a series of questions about conflicts which occurred in their senior year in high school, and to further questions about how these conflicts were handled. Included in the conflict resolution section were questions on whether or not the parties to the disputes had ever hit, pushed, shoved, thrown things or kicked each other in the course of a quarrel.

The results show that during that one year 62 percent of the high school seniors had used physical force on a brother or sister and 16 percent of their parents had used physical force on each other. Since these figures are for a single year, the percentage who had *ever* used violence is probably much greater. How much greater is difficult to estimate because we cannot simply accumulate the 16 percent for one year over the total number of years married. Some couples will never have used violence and others will have used it repeatedly. Nevertheless, it seems safe to assume that it will not always be the same 16 percent. So, it is probably best to fall back on the 56 percent estimate from the 80 earlier interviews.

> The fact is that almost all everyday beating, slapping, kicking and throwing things is carried out by normal Americans rather than deranged persons.

Since a vast amount of family violence can be documented, what accounts for the myth of family non-violence? At least one basis for the rosy, if false, view is that the family is a tremendously important social institution, which must be preserved. In Western countries one supportive device is the ideology of familial love and gentleness, an ideology which helps encourage people to marry and to stay married. It tends to maintain satisfaction with the family system despite the stresses and strains of family life. From the viewpoint of preserving the integrity of a critical social institution, such a mythology is highly useful.

Other simplifications and generalizations also block knowledge and understanding of the nature of violence in the family. The psychopathology myth, the class myth, the sex myth and the catharsis myth must be exposed and examined if the true nature of intrafamily abuse is to emerge.

A growing number of sociologists and psychologists have suggested that a focus on conflict and violence may be a more revealing way of understanding the family than a focus on consensus and solidarity. Most members of this group, however, recognize that family conflict is legitimate, but still consider physical violence only as an abnormality—something which involves sick families. The facts do not support this *psychopathology myth*. According to Richard J. Gelles, only a tiny proportion of those using violence—even child abusers—can be considered mentally ill. Our own studies reveal that physically abusive husbands, wives and children are of overwhelmingly sound mind and body.

The fact that almost all family violence, including everyday beating, slapping, kicking and throwing things, is carried out by normal everyday Americans rather than deranged persons should not lead us to think of violence as being desirable or even acceptable. The important question is, Why is physical violence so common between members of the closest and most intimate of all human groups?

Although social scientists are still far from a full understanding of the causes of violence between family members, evidence is accumulating that family violence is learned—and learned in childhood in the home. This fact does not deny the importance of the human biological heritage. If the capacity for violence were not present in the human organism, learning and social patterning could not produce it.

If a child actually observes and experiences the effects of violence, he will learn to be violent. Husbands, wives and parents play out models of behavior which they learned in childhood from *their* parents and from friends and relatives. Rather than being deviant, they are conforming to patterns learned in childhood. Of course, in most cases they also learned the opposite message—that family violence is wrong. However, a message learned by experience and observation, rather than the message learned Sunday-school-style, has more force, especially when social stresses become great—and family stresses are often very great. The high level of interaction and commitment which is part of the pleasure of family life also produces great tensions.

Another widespread but hard-to-prove belief is the *class myth*, the idea that intrafamily violence occurs mainly in lower- and working-class families. Studying divorce applicants, George Levinger found that 40 percent of the working-class wives and 23 percent of the middle-class wives indicated "physical abuse" as a reason for seeking divorce. If almost one out of four middle-class women can report physical abuse, violence hardly seems absent from middle-class families. The nationwide sample survey conducted for the United States Commission on Violence reveals that over one-fifth of the respondents approve of slapping a spouse under certain conditions. There were no social-class differences in this *approval* of slapping, nor in reports of having ever spanked a child. At the same time, almost twice as many less educated respondents spank *frequently* (42 percent) as more educated respondents (22 percent).

Class Differences

Other research on physical punishment is also contradictory. Most studies report more use of physical punishment by working-class parents, but some find no difference. Howard S. Erlanger undertook a comprehensive review of studies of social-class differences in the use of physical punishment and concluded that, although the weight of the evidence supports the view of less use of this technique among the middle class, the differences are small. Sizeable differences between social classes show up only when the analysis takes into account differences within social classes of such things as race, the sex of the child and of the parent, parental ambition for the child and the specific nature of the father's occupation. Differences *within* social classes are at least as important as differences *between* classes.

Despite the mixed evidence, and despite the fact that there is a great deal of violence in middle-class families, we believe that research will eventually show that intrafamily violence is more common as one goes down the socioeconomic status ladder. Many social scientists attribute this to a lower-class "culture of violence" which encourages violent acts, and to an opposite middle-class culture which condemns violence. Although these cultural elements are well documented, we see them not as a cause, but as a response to fundamental social structural forces which affect families at all social levels but press harder and more frequently on the lower and working classes.

Compensatory Violence

Willingness and ability to use physical violence may compensate for lack of other resources such as money, knowledge and respect. If the social system does not provide an individual with the resources needed to maintain his or her family position, that individual will use violence if he is capable of it. John E. O'Brien asserts that ". . . there is considerable evidence that . . . husbands who . . . displayed violent behavior were severely inadequate in work, earner, or family support roles." While lack of the occupational and economic resources needed to fulfill the position of husband in our society is more characteristic of lower-class families than others, it is by no means confined to that stratum. The 1970-72 recession, with its high rates of unemployment among middle-class occupational groups (such as aerospace engineers) provides an opportunity to test this theory. The *resource theory* of violence would predict that unemployed husbands would engage in more intrafamily violence than comparable middle-class husbands who have not lost their jobs.

Some indication that the predicted results might be found is suggested by statistics for Birmingham, England, which showed a sharp rise in wife-beating during a six-month period when unemployment also rose sharply. A 1971 *Parade* report characterized these men as "frustrated, bored, unable to find a satisfying outlet for their energy, Britishers who are reduced to life on the dole meet adversity like men: they blame it on their wives. Then, pow!!!"

In a society such as ours, in which aggression is defined as a normal response to frustration, we can expect that the more frustrating the familial and occupational roles, the greater the amount of violence. Donald McKinley found that the lower the degree of self-direction a man has in his work, the greater the degree of aggressiveness in his relationship with his son. McKinley's data also show that the lower the job satisfaction, the higher the percentage using harsh punishment of children. The same relationship was found within each social class.

Both husbands and wives suffer from frustration, but since the main avenue of achievement for women has been in the family rather than in occupational roles, we must look within the family for the circumstances that are frustrating to women. Both residential crowding and too many children have been found to be related to the use of physical punishment. As with men, frustrations of this type are more common in the lower class, since lower-class wives are unlikely to have sufficient equipment and money for efficient, convenient housekeeping.

Although intrafamily violence probably is more common among lower-class families, it is incorrect to see it as only a lower-class or working-class phenomenon. What we have called the class myth overlooks the basic structural conditions (such as lack of adequate resources and frustrating life experiences) which are major causes of intrafamily violence and are present at all social levels, though to varying degrees. Some kinds of intrafamily violence are typical of all social classes—such as hitting children—even though the rate may be lower for middle class—while other kinds of intrafamily violence are typical of *neither* class—like severe wife-beating—even though the rate is probably greater for the working class and especially the lower class.

The *sex myth* is the idea that sexual drives are linked to violence by basic biological mechanisms developed in the course of human evolution. Violence in sex is directly related to violence in the family because the family is the main way in which sex is made legitimate. To the extent that there is an inherent connection between sex and violence, it would be part of the biological basis for violence within the family.

There is abundant evidence that sex and violence go together, at least in our society and in a number of others. At the extreme, sex and warfare have been associated in many ways, ranging from societies which view sex before a battle as a source of strength (or in

Frustrated, bored, unable to find a satisfying outlet for their energy Britishers who are reduced to life on the dole meet adversity like men: they blame it on their wives. Then, pow!!!

some tribes, as a weakness) to the almost universally high frequency of rape by soldiers, often accompanied by subsequent genital mutilation and murder. In the fighting following the independence of the Congo in the early 1960s, rape was so common that the Catholic church is said to have given a special dispensation so that nuns could take contraceptive pills. More recently, in the Pakistan civil war, rape and mutilation were everyday occurrences. In Vietnam, scattered reports suggest that rapes and sexual tortures have been widespread. Closer to home, we have the romantic view of the aggressive he-man who "takes his woman" as portrayed in westerns and James Bond-type novels. In both cases, sex and gunfights are liberally intertwined.

Sexual Repression

Then there are the sadists and masochists—individuals who can obtain sexual pleasure only by inflicting or receiving violent acts. We could dismiss such people as pathological exceptions, but it seems better to consider sadism and masochism as simply extreme forms of widespread behavior. The sex act itself typically is accompanied at least by mild violence and often by biting and scratching.

Nevertheless, despite all of this and much other evidence which could be cited, we feel that there is little biological linkage between sex and violence. It is true that in our society and in many other societies, sex and violence are linked. But there are enough instances of societies in which this is not the case to raise doubts about the biological linkage. What social conditions produce the association between violence and sex?

The most commonly offered explanation attributes the linkage between sex and violence to rules of the culture which limit or prevent sex. Empirical evidence supporting this sexual repression theory is difficult to establish. Societies which are high in restriction of extramarital intercourse are also societies which tend to be violent—particularly in emphasizing military glory, killing, torture and mutilation of an enemy. But just how this carries over to violence in the sex act is not clear. Our interpretation hinges on the fact that sexual restriction tends to be associated with a definition of sex as intrinsically evil. This combination sets in motion two powerful forces making sex violent in societies having such a sexual code. First, since sex is normally prohibited or restricted, engaging in sexual intercourse may imply license to disregard other normally prohibited or restricted aspects of interpersonal relations. Consequently, aggressively inclined persons will tend to express their aggressiveness when they express their sexuality. Second, since sex is defined as evil and base, this cultural definition of sex may create a label or an expectancy which tends to be acted out.

By contrast, in societies such as Mangaia, which impose minimal sex restrictions and in which sex is defined as something to be enjoyed by all from the time they are first capable until death, sex is nonviolent. In Mangaia, exactly the opposite of the two violence-producing mechanisms just listed seem to operate. First, since sex is a normal everyday activity, the normal standards for control of aggression apply. Second, since sex is defined as an act expressing the best in man, it is an occasion for altruistic behavior. Thus, Donald S. Marshall says of the Mangaia: "My several informants generally agreed that the really important thing in sexual intercourse—for the married man or for his unwed fellow—was to give pleasure to his partner; that her pleasure in orgasm was what gave the male partner a special thrill, separate from his own orgasm."

There is little evidence to show direct linkage between sex and violence. It is true that they are socially linked in many cultures, but there are enough societies where this is not the case to raise doubts about the biological linkage.

Socially patterned antagonism between men and women is at the heart of a related theory which can also account for the association of sex and violence. The sex antagonism and segregation theory suggests that the higher the level of antagonism between men and women, the greater the tendency to use violence in sexual acts. Since, by itself, this statement is open to a charge of circular reasoning, the theory must be backed up by related propositions which account for the sex role antagonism.

In societies such as ours, part of the explanation for antagonism between the sexes is probably traceable to the sexual restrictions and sexual denigration mentioned above. The curse God placed on all women when Eve sinned is the earliest example in our culture of the sexually restrictive ethic, the placing of the "blame" for sex on women, and the resulting negative definition of women—all of which tend to make women culturally legitimate objects of antagonism and aggression. The New Testament reveals much more antipathy to sex than the Old and contains many derogatory (and implicitly hostile) statements about women.

The present level of antagonism between the sexes is probably at least as great as that in biblical times. In novels, biographies and everyday speech, words indicating femaleness, especially in its sexual aspect (such as "bitch"), are used by men as terms of disparagement, and terms for sexual intercourse, such as "screw" and "fuck," are used to indicate an aggressive or harmful act. On the female side, women tend to see men as exploiters and to teach their daughters that men are out to take advantage of them.

It would be a colossal example of ethnocentrism, however, to attribute antagonism between the sexes to the Western Judeo-Christian tradition. Cultural definitions of women as evil are found in many societies. Obviously, more fundamental processes are at work, of which the Christian tradition is only one manifestation.

Catharsis Myth

A clue to a possibly universal process giving rise to antagonism between the sexes may be found in the cross-cultural studies which trace this hostility back to the division of labor between the sexes and other differences in the roles of men and women. This sex role segregation, gives rise to differences in child-rearing practices for boys and girls and to problems in establishing sexual identity. Beatrice Whiting, for example, concludes: "It would seem as if there were a never-ending circle. The separation of the sexes leads to a conflict of identity in the boy children, to unconscious fear of being feminine, which leads to protest masculinity, exaggeration of the differences between men and women, antagonism against and fear of women, male solidarity, and hence back to isolation of women and very young children." This process can also be observed in the matrifocal family of the urban slum and the Caribbean, the relationships between the sexes have been labeled by Jackson Toby as "compulsive masculinity" and vividly depicted in Eldridge Cleaver's "Allegory of the Black Eunuchs." Slightly more genteel forms of the same sexual antagonism are to be found among middle-class men, as illustrated by the character of Jonathan in the movie *Carnal Knowledge*.

Obviously, the linkages between sex and violence are extremely complex, and many other factors probably operate besides the degree of restrictiveness, the cultural definition of sexuality and antagonism between the sexes. But even these indicate sufficiently that it is incorrect to assume a direct connection between sexual drives and violence, since such an assumption disregards the sociocultural framework within which sexual relations take place. These social and cultural factors, rather than sex drives *per se*, give rise to the violent aspects of sexuality in so many societies.

The *catharsis myth* asserts that the expression of "normal" aggression between family members should not be bottled up: if normal aggression is allowed to be expressed, tension is released, and the likelihood of severe violence is therefore reduced. This view has a long and distinguished intellectual history. Aristotle used the term "catharsis" to refer to the purging of the passions or sufferings of spectators through vicarious participation in the suffering of a tragic hero. Both Freud's idea of "the liberation of affect" to enable reexperiencing blocked or inhibited emotions, and the view of John Dollard and his associates that "the occurrence of any act of aggression is assumed to reduce the instigation of aggression" are modern versions of this tradition.

Applying this approach to the family, Bettelheim urges that children should learn about violence in order to learn how to handle it. Under the present rules (at least for the middle class), we forbid a child to hit, yell or swear at us or his playmates. The child must also refrain from destroying property or even his own toys. In teaching this type of self-control, however, Bruno Bettelheim holds that we have denied the child outlets for the instinct of human violence and have failed to teach him how to deal with his violent feelings.

Proof of the catharsis theory is overwhelmingly negative. Exposure to vicariously experienced violence has been shown to increase rather than decrease both aggressive fantasy and aggressive acts. Similarly, experiments in which children are given the opportunity to express violence and aggression show that they express more aggression after the purported cathartic experience than do controls.

Theoretical arguments against the catharsis view are equally cogent. The instinct theory assumptions which underlie the idea of catharsis have long been discarded in social science. Modern social psychological theories—including social learning theory, symbolic interaction theory and labeling theory—all predict the opposite of the catharsis theory: the more frequently an act is performed, the greater the likelihood that it will become a standard part of the behavior repertory of the individual and of the expectations of others for that individual.

Cultural Beliefs

In light of largely negative evidence and cogent theoretical criticism, the sheer persistence of the catharsis theory becomes an interesting phenomenon. There seem to be several factors underlying the persistence of the catharsis myth:

□ *Prestige and influence of psychoanalytic theory*. Albert Bandura and Richard Walters suggest that the persistence of the catharsis view is partly the result of the extent to which psychoanalytic ideas have become part of both social science and popular culture. Granting this, one must also ask why this particular part of Freud's vast writing is unquestioned. After all, much of what Freud wrote has been ignored, and other parts have been dropped on the basis of contrary evidence.

Whenever an element of cultural belief persists in spite of seemingly sound reasons for discarding it, one should

Exposure to vicariously experienced violence has been shown to increase rather than decrease both aggressive fantasy and aggressive acts. Similarly, experiments in which children are given the opportunity to express violence and aggression show that they express more aggression after the purported cathartic experience.

look for ways in which the belief may be woven into a system of social behavior. Certain behavior may be least partially congruent with the "false" belief; various social patterns may be justified by such beliefs.

□ *Justification of existing patterns.* Intrafamily violence is a recurring feature of our society, despite the cultural commitment to nonviolence. It is not far-fetched to assume that, under the circumstances, the catharsis theory which in effect justifies sporadic violence will be attractive to a population engaged in occasional violence.

□ *Congruence with the positive value of violence in non-family spheres of life.* Although *familial* norms deprecate or forbid intrafamily violence, the larger value system of American society is hardly nonviolent. In fact, the overwhelming proportion of American parents consider it part of their role to train sons to be tough. The violence commission survey reveals that 70 percent of the respondents believed it is good for boys to have a few fist-fights. Thus, a social theory which justifies violence as being psychologically beneficial to the aggressor is likely to be well received.

□ *Congruence with the way familial violence often occurs.* Given the antiviolence norms, intrafamily physical abuse typically occurs as a climax to a repressed conflict. As Louis Coser points out:

> Closely knit groups in which there exists a high frequency of interaction and high personality involvement of the members have a tendency to suppress conflict. While they provide frequent occasions for hostility (since both sentiments of love and hatred are intensified through frequency of interaction), the acting out of such feelings is sensed as a danger to such intimate relationships, and hence there is a tendency to suppress rather than to allow expression of hostile feelings. In close-knit groups, feelings of hostility tend, therefore, to accumulate and hence to intensify.

At some point the repressed conflict has to be resolved. Frequently, the mechanism which forces the conflict into the open is a violent outburst. This is one of the social functions of violence listed by Coser. In this sense, intrafamily violence does have a cathartic effect. But the catharsis which takes place comes from getting the conflict into the open and resolving it—not the releasing effects of violent incidents *per se*, but on the ability to recognize these as warning signals and to deal with the underlying conflict honestly and with empathy.

□ *Confusion of immediate with long-term effects.* There can be little doubt that a sequence of violent activity is often followed by a sharp reduction of tension, an emotional release and even a feeling of quiescence. To the extent that tension release *is* produced by violence, this immediate cathartic effect is likely to powerfully reinforce the violence which preceded it. Having reduced tension in one instance, it becomes a mode of behavior likely to be repeated later in similar instances. An analogy with sexual orgasm seems plausible. Following orgasm, there is typically a sharp reduction in sexual drive, most obvious in the male's loss of erection. At the same time, however, the experience of orgasm is powerfully reinforcing and has the long-term effect of increasing the sex drive. We believe that violence and sex are similar in this respect. The short-term effect of violence is, in one sense, cathartic; but the long-term effect is a powerful force toward including violence as a standard mode of social interaction.

While the assumptions outlined in this article in some ways contribute to preserving the institution of family, they also keep us from taking a hard and realistic look at the family and taking steps to change it in ways which might correct the underlying problems. Such stereotypes contain a kernel of truth but are dangerous oversimplifications. Although there are differences between social classes in intrafamily violence, the class myth ignores the high level of family violence present in other social strata. The sex myth, although based on historically accurate observation of the link between sex and violence, tends to assume that this link is biologically determined and fails to take into account the social and cultural factors which associate sex and violence in many societies. The catharsis myth seems to have the smallest kernel of truth at its core, and its persistence, in the face of devastating evidence to the contrary, may be due to the subtle justification it gives to the violent nature of American society and to the fact that violent episodes in a family can have the positive function of forcing a repressed conflict into the open for nonviolent resolution.

This article is based on the general introduction to *Violence in the Family,* edited by Suzanne K. Steinmetz and Murray A. Straus, New York, Dodd, Mead, 1974.

ROSE K. GOLDSEN

NBC's Make-Believe Research on TV Violence

On April 20, 1971, Dr. Thomas E. Coffin, vice president for research of the National Broadcasting Company, held a press conference at which he unveiled Progress Report Number 1 of the network's Division of Environmental Study of Television and Violence. It reports preliminary results of a study that claims to investigate the effects of violence in television programs on antisocial and violent behavior in children.

The claim is unwarranted. The study does nothing of the sort. What it does do is provide a delaying tactic to maintain existing television fare unchanged.

It is a panel study, two years in progress with another three years to go. It conducts repeated interviews with 866 boys from seven to 18 years of age, half middle, half low

socioeconomic status. They live in "Mainland City" and "Frontier City" in "middle America."

Interviews began in June 1970, were repeated in November 1970 and again in February 1971. Wave four was scheduled for April 17, 1971. By the time the study is finished, the boys will have been interviewed two or three times per year over a five-year period. These interviews will be supplemented by intensive interviews with parents. Thus, say the researchers, long-term effects can be measured.

In this article, I shall analyze the research design to show why I say it is inadequate and why I think it serves as a delaying tactic. I choose this particular study because it is the most elaborate and ambitious execution of a style of research which has preempted the field of media research; and because it is being done by a large and powerful network. Later I shall suggest some alternative research designs that would address the questions this and much of the research in this field ignore.

Some Measures the Study Uses

I know that lists are a bore, but I am going to list the measures presented in the progress report because they will allow me to make my first point more easily. They are: Eron, Walder and Tioga's "Peer-rating measure," Wirt's "Personality inventory for children," Hollingshead's "Two-factor index," Crowne and Marlowe's "Social desirability scale," Rosenberg's "Scale of self-esteem," Devereaux and Bronfenbrenner's "Family authority structure measure" and Rokeach's "Dogmatism scale."

Certain new measures were devised just for this study: an "Index of family cohesiveness/integration," "Parental supervision scale," "Inventory of family disciplinary/ punishment practices," "Mother-son rejection scale," "Attempted parental domination scale," "Intra-familial sociability index" and "Teen-age boastfulness indices."

The progress report presents this listing only to give an *idea* of the kinds of factors in a child's background that the study wishes to consider. I suppose that there will be others: some sort of measure of social and economic status (SES), probably combining occupation, income and education of one or both parents. Perhaps some kind of religiosity measure—or maybe religious affiliation and attendance at services—will be used to "stand in" for a more detailed measure, and so on. But my point in spelling out these measures is to show the overwhelming emphasis the research is placing on measures of children and their sociological context.

The progress report stresses the multivariate nature of human behavior. You cannot study an audience's reactions, the report says, without taking into careful consideration the total setting in which the viewers find themselves. The design turns its penetrating searchlight of scientific inquiry upon the viewer and his setting—as the lists above begin to indicate.

I wish to stress that these are all factors about which a vast body of information is already on record. They are also factors over which programmers and broadcasters have no control.

Television Gets a Once-Over-Lightly

But the independent variable—the stimulus whose effects are to be studied—is not illuminated by that searchlight of scientific inquiry. The report says simply "television programs with high and low degree of violence." I looked through the report in vain for an equivalently detailed and complex specification of the components of these programs. All I find is "violent TV diet versus non-violent TV diet" and "exposure to aggressive content in television."

That is all.

This study is not set up to engage in research on American families, or urban problems, or school structure, or parental supervision, or dogmatism. It claims to study the effects of violence appearing in television programs.

That is the independent variable. That is what the study is about.

These are the factors which broadcasters *do* control.

Some of my colleagues have reminded me that there are always a number of ways to formulate a research question and while I am entitled to my preferences, so is NBC entitled to theirs. I claim that the margins of choice in this matter are limited for research which says it is directed to social policy. In this case, the social policy issue we have a right to do something about is, "What kind of television?" not "What kind of children?" Hence, NBC's phrasing of the research question is simply not relevant to the public issue.

We do not have a vast body of systematic and documented information about these television programs. The research team had a good opportunity to contribute new knowledge to the sociological record describing an important aspect of our society. They have assiduously not grasped it.

The progress report's introductory remarks stress the "myriads of influences, genetic and environmental" that the boy-viewers in this study are subject to. "Effect of any *one* is difficult to separate from the effects of all the others." This same comment could be made about any single act of violence on a television show. It does not occur in a vacuum either. Just as these boys come from certain types of families and certain sociological settings, so does a television act of violence belong in a total family of television acts.

A five-year study of violence on television. What a good opportunity to dissect television fare the way sociologists have dissected the myriads of sociological influences! For example, what kind of violence? Physical violence, emotional violence, violence to bodily integrity, violence to sense of self, violence by direct contact, violence by remote control, violence to one's peers, violence to one's superiors, violence by authority figures, violence by the powerful, violence by the deviant, violence by the frustrated, violence as a norm, violence as pathological behavior, violence for vengeance, violence to correct miscarriage of justice, violence by men to men, men to women, women to women, women to men, violence about sex, violence in sex, violence by animals or involving animals, violence by children or to children, violence whose consequences are shown, violence whose consequences are inferred, violence that is justified, violence in a measure appropriate to some previous injury, face-to-face acts of violence, institutional violence, violence in war, violence which redeems, violence which is directed to social change, violence as a means of conflict-resolution, violence as ideology . . . I could go on.

The NBC study is a panel study. That is, it makes the same measures of the same individuals at different time-points as they develop. When you mark your child's height on the wall from time to time to check his rate of growth, you are doing a modest panel study. This is obviously a good idea when you are studying a complex and changing phenomenon such as a human being.

But what about the television fare? It is similarly complex and changing over time. Bonanza at Time 1 is not the same as Bonanza at Time 2. Sometimes Hoss shoots down the bad guy, sometimes he protects an Indian from somebody else's violence. Sometimes the whole family is involved, sometimes not. I looked through NBC's progress report to see if the researchers planned to pay equivalent attention to development and change in the television stimuli—the thing the study is about, the thing the broadcasters control, the thing public policy is concerned about—and I found no such indication.

Then there are the structural factors. The child and his environment are studied dynamically and in detail. Structural factors are meticulously looked at. But what about the structural factors of the programs—the factors which "frame," so to speak, any given program: programs that occur in prime time versus the Saturday morning ghetto; programs that are interrupted by commercials versus programs in which commercials come only at the end versus programs without commercials; programs which demand passive watching by the viewer versus those which engage him in active participation; programs which provide for feedback by the audience; programs which permit the viewer to communicate directly with the protagonist at the end; programs which continue over time as an organic whole building toward some end-state viewed as desirable.

Now clearly, some of these variations do not exist in the world of television. Which brings me to my next point. I repeat Dr. Coffin's introductory remarks to the report, "myriads of influences, genetic and environmental," affect behavior. Not just television. True. Yet the research design bravely confronts this morass and plunges into it—another try at untangling the web of causality, *in vivo*. It launches its inadequate effort to reproduce more than a generation of research on delinquency, just ringing in a new variable: television.

In the face of these odds, the research question chosen is: "What is the effect of existing television programming on violent behavior in children, compared to innumerable other elements of a child's life that compete with television in producing or affecting behavior?" At the present stage of the art of sociological inquiry, this question is unanswerable.

An answerable question, germane to the social policy issue concerning television programming for children, must have been rejected. That question is: "What is the effect of television violence on children, compared with some other television fare, or compared with no television at all?"

The first question is the business of everyone in the society. The second question is the business specifically of broadcasters. The usual objection to research addressed to the second question is that there is virtually no "other television fare." In the United States you can scarcely find an appropriate control group of children *not* exposed to massive doses of television violence, who could be compared to similar children raised on television violence so that differences between the two groups might be measured.

That's a pretty accurate description of life in the United States today. But does this automatically limit research design? I submit that the answer is "no," and I shall specify why later.

But meanwhile, one thing is clear. The study takes for granted television fare as it is. It asks, "What is existing television fare doing to children in the audience, compared

with other weighty factors in their environment?" Such existing fare is subdivided, in some way not made clear in the progress report, into more violent and less violent programs.

This is not the usual procedure in research design. Let me digress a moment here for a brief look at how a researcher analyzes a problem at the point of design.

How Do You Design Research Anyway?

A researcher likes to know what the stimulus is whose effects he is curious about. This is known as "purifying the variable." It means he does a lot of fiddling with whatever it is that the test population is to be exposed to. If it had been done in this case, for instance, we would have a list of something like my long list of types of violence. And changes in types of violence.

Another thing the researcher likes is experimental logic. This is not necessarily a laboratory experiment—which the NBC research summarily rules out, by the way. It could be a "natural experiment," along the lines of an epidemiological model of exposed and not exposed populations. Or it could even be partial correlations (in a heterogeneous population of subjects, you look for subgroups exposed more versus those exposed less, just in the normal course of events).

The progress report mentions market-research on commercial messages as a model for this investigation. The analogy is not totally apt, since the behavior aimed for in testing commercials is specific: buying a product or producing positive attitudes. So-called entertainment television claims that it does not similarly aim for specified end-states in the viewers as outcomes.

But let's accept the analogy for the moment, anyway. If commercials did their testing by sticking only to one or two broad and globally defined formats and measuring *their* effects, and then controlling for all kinds of different proximate and remote sociological background characteristics and motivational structures, market research agencies would be out of business.

Market research on commercials is not very strong on the side of experimental logic. But it is very strong, indeed, on the side of detailing the stimulus to which test populations are exposed. When commercials are tested, messages and formats and cast and modes of presentation are tried all over the place. All elements of the message are examined in detail. Painstaking content analysis breaks the message down into its component parts. Not just the typed script, but the finished production. Each message unit is studied carefully and tested with target populations. Sometimes very imaginative variations of message-units and populations are built into the design. Placement is likewise tested. So is duration. So are visual and audio effects. So are a lot of other things about the commercial before it is put into mass production. All in the service of learning something about its probable effects on the audience.

I wish to recall here that Dr. Frank Stanton, now president of the Columbia Broadcasting System, broke into radio in the thirties by way of the Lazarsfeld-Stanton program-analyzer. This is a push button device that permits audiences to indicate affect-arousing parts of virtually infinitesimal elements of a program or broadcast message. It allows for subsequent interviewing, focussed on known elements of content, to determine what it was about these elements that aroused affective feelings in the respondent. Once this is known, subsequent study can follow up effects of the program in full detail.

In contrast to the design of the present study, the weighty investment of research effort when commercials are tested goes into analyzing the *stimulus* (independent variable) and the *outcome reaction* (dependent variable). And the desired outcome is certainly not defined negatively. Which takes me to my next point.

The study says the dependent variable is "boys' behavior," "violent and other anti-social and pro-social behavior . . . and their moral values and their desensitization to violence." "The definition of violent behavior . . . is . . . willful physical or verbal acts known to cause injury to person or property."

There are items on whether the subject "threatened to hurt others," "pushed, shoved or hit," "stole something," "got into physical fights," "damaged property," "occasionally uses marijuana or hashish," "put down or teased someone" and "got drunk." This list of behavior items is literally very close to the lone stimulus whose effects the study claims to investigate.

Again, I contrast the imaginative proliferation of the elements making up the child's sociological context with the lack of imagination and stark skeletonizing of the outcome variables in this study. For example: violence is the wielding of naked power and the abandonment of reason. As the child sees the world, then, what is the role of violence and naked power in—say—the way authority figures acquire or maintain their authority? To what degree are social order and social change dependent upon violence and the wielding of naked power? What role do violence and the exercise of naked power play when a minority tries to win over a majority? What is the relationship between violence, naked power, authority, prestige and individual worth? What is the meaning of triumph and defeat for one's sense of self-esteem?

My comments here are not directed to shortcomings of research design, but to shortcomings of sociological imagination. That is only my opinion, of course. The NBC researchers place particular emphasis on the study of behavioral acts as hypothesized effects of television violence. That is their privilege. I happen to think it is theoretically more important to examine attitudes, values, imagery, self-concept, world-views and mental constructs as proximate outcomes of exposure to current television. Television transmits—literally speaking—images, and I think it is those images which are likely to imbed themselves in the minds of our children. I think that these images are likely to be very important for our culture. (I do not think that the vast majority of whites actually turned loose dogs or set firehoses on peaceful protesters in, say, Birmingham, Alabama, in 1963; nor do I think that a majority of blacks in urban ghetto riots engage in the *acts* of looting or burning. Still, I think that something in the mental constructs of many of our black and white citizens of Birmingham and of our urban ghettos is relevant to any attempt to understand these occurrences.)

Alternative Research Designs

As the progress report points out, a major problem in research on human populations in natural settings lies in the difficulty of specifying which particular elements in a barrage of stimuli (television programs are only one set of these) produce or affect which activities of children, under the myriad conditions of life in which children find themselves.

It would be easier if otherwise similar children could be found, some of whom see violent television and others of whom do not. If unexposed children do exist, they are almost sure to be deviant in other ways and thus not comparable to the exposed children. Let's accept this for the moment. (But only for the moment.)

This is not an uncommon situation in research on society. When you study something that occurs in "the real environment," the thing you want to know about is often beyond your control. Or to control it would be unethical, or would change the name of the game.

The progress report refers respectfully to Paul F. Lazarsfeld as the father of the panel design used in this study. Reference is made to his studies of voting. Professor Lazarsfeld did not have the possibility of asking candidates to alter their appeals to voters to suit the purposes of his research design. He could not ask political parties to select one type of candidate rather than another, or to change the dates of their conventions, or to expose one town to the campaign and keep another isolated. He had no choice but to take the political campaign and the political environment as given and proceed from there.

But research on television programs is quite different—especially if you are the researcher employed by a national network. Here is where the classic research technique of designing the stimulus to meet the needs of the research question *can* be applied.

For example, epidemiological research faces the same complexities of highly varied populations in highly varied environments. Epidemiological researchers face up to the issue by using large populations and varying the stimulus. One group gets a vaccine, the other doesn't. They use the complexities of populations and conditions to refine the overall findings—to locate high risk cases for example and examine them in detail. The complexities work in the service of the research, not to confound it.

Now, academic research people usually cannot follow this model for television research. But networks can. They could make alternative programs incorporating specifically designed stimuli and present them in one area but not in another. For example, take an episode or even parts of episodes in Bonanza as is and beam them to one population. Remake the same show in a virtually identical manner, but resolve the conflict of the sequence or sequences by nonviolent rather than violent means and beam these materials to the other population. Then measure aggressive outcome in the viewers.

This idea can be expanded. A whole series of alternative programs can be made up for experimental purposes to be shown in one area but not in another. In the test area make before and after measures. A five-year panel study with repeated measures would be fine. Compare these measures to a control group not exposed to test programs.

This epidemiological model is already widely used in television and advertising circles. They call it product testing. A new product is introduced into a test market. Before-after measures give a reading on behavior change and attitude change in that market. A control group is not necessary, since marketing data normally available to businesses usually are available.

The major methodological requirement is that the stimulus must be varied as between test population and control population. Exposed and not exposed. Can this be done on television? It's easy.

Keep Violence In

On television, violence is highly stylized. Only certain kinds of people exercise it. Men against other men, usually young, vigorous and in the prime of life. They may be fathers, but their violence is usually extraneous to their father-role. Moreover, their violence is usually congruent with their principal occupations or style of life.

Such stylization makes it easy to manipulate the stimulus. You make a series of television programs in which those who exercise violence come from different spots on the sociological map. Women. Old people. Fathers exercising their fatherhood. People whose occupations are *not* appropriate to violent behavior (mother, grandmother, librarian, judge, legislator, businessman and so on). Then you follow the designs of the product test.

I pause briefly to wait for the sounds of outrage to subside. Do you object that this is a horrifying prospect, unethical, likely to produce unhealthy social consequences, and so on? But wait a minute! Similar decisions are made every season when next year's television fare is decided on.

If you feel that the manipulation of the independent variable in this manner cannot, in good conscience, be done for the sake of research, then I wonder why all the fuss about the need for research on the effects of violent television programs as a prior condition for changing children's programming? If I am willing to yield to social policy considerations and contain my zeal for research results, why shouldn't the same considerations apply to the networks?

Another objection to the above design could be that it would introduce a whole new type of program fare and thus is not relevant. Objection overruled: the research does not claim to study effects of existing programs: it claims to wonder about the effects of violence in television programs on children in the audience. The design I suggest would do precisely that. If something changes in girls who watch programs in which women engage in violence, but does not change in their counterparts who do not see such programs, then we have learned something about effects.

Would it be justified to extrapolate these conclusions to other populations and to other types of violence? That's a good question. Whether broadcasters would be willing to extrapolate the findings is one matter. Whether the general population of parents in the audience would be willing to do so is another matter. The question of what level of proof is convincing is not a scientific question. It is a social policy question. I suppose we would have a situation similar to the cigarette-lung cancer controversy with the tobacco industry.

Take Violence Out

Here's an alternative design. Introduce a new "product" —specially made programs without violence in a test market. Make your before-after and developmental measures over time and compare with a control market that does not see the programs.

I can envision both these designs executed with a carefully controlled bloc of time—say the Saturday morning children's ghetto or early prime time when lots of children watch. A five-year panel study would be great.

The experimental programs must be carefully constructed so that subsequent follow-ups with high-risk and low-risk cases would isolate precisely the contributions that specific elements of the programs are making to the results.

But how can we introduce programming? Isn't that beyond control? If NBC (and the other two networks) are serious about the need for research on television's impact on children, there is no compelling reason they cannot vary the stimulus they control to conform to the needs of the research. They can make the programs themselves, if they wish, or contract for them to be made.

The broadcasters have advantages that epidemiologists rarely have. They can block out the source of the contamination in test areas. In the case of television there is no reason for not doing this. (If NBC, for example, gets flak from their affiliates, they can do it on one or more of the five stations owned by the corporation in major markets.)

The same model could be followed on a more modest scale with smaller populations. Cable television offers a golden opportunity for this kind of research. The networks could select certain difficult reception areas that do not have cable television. Here they could combine their research aims with a social contribution, by constructing community antennae systems in selected areas. Then, wire up experimental homes which would receive test programs over a period of time—say five years—and compare what happens to the children in these homes with what happens to children in similar homes not so wired.

The same idea could be applied in areas that already have cable television, simply by using special incentives to plug people into the experimental channel or channels.

Another suggestion that would combine research with social uplift. Pick up matched groups of homeless children without families. Place them in favorable environments. Provide one group with experimentally contrived television programs over time, but do not do so for the others.

I could go on. Once you get the idea that the logic of an appropriate study follows the logic of the epidemiological and product-testing researches, and that it is the television which must be varied, it's not hard at all. Like a parlor game.

What About Costs?

What about the high costs of what I propose here? It's not at all clear that this kind of research would be any more costly than the present mammoth five-year panel study. Certainly, the analyzable returns, dollar for dollar, would put the cost-benefit advantage on the side of my suggestions.

I believe that the impediments to the kinds of studies I propose are likely to be not the dollar costs of the research but the cost of rocking the boat. The cost of introducing new programming. I do not mean production costs. I mean the possible reactions of advertisers who know that existing programs pull in audiences but do not know that new programming will do the same. The true cost that is feared is the potential dip in—or even loss of—mass audiences now attracted to the programs we know.

Ethological Model

Now I turn to the long-term effects that NBC's study design says it is designed to measure. The researchers plan a five-year follow-up, taking these particular respondents through ages 12-22. We can learn nothing about their citizenship behavior or the way these boys will reproduce and raise their children. Very important questions, in my judgment.

That kind of long-term follow-up is very tough when you deal with human populations. We still cannot produce genetically identical children and raise them in controlled environments and confine them to known television diets and follow them through a lifetime. This means that a perfect study design on long-term effects probably cannot be planned.

But it can be planned for primates. An experimental group of monkeys is exposed to a saturation diet of violent television fare. This could be either the kind of programming we are exposed to, or it could be specially produced programs with primates zonking and bopping and zapping each other. A control group is exposed to nonviolent television and a baseline group is exposed to no television. What happens to their social behavior? Their reproductive behavior? The way they raise their young? The way they resolve conflict? Their dominance and submission patterns?

This design is a very "clean" longitudinal study. It is also very useful from a cost-benefit point of view, since it would permit basic research that is badly needed. I am referring to the effects on the maturing individual of passive learning watching television versus involved and interactional learning with and without the set. But meanwhile, it would allow the study of the "long-term effects" the NBC study promises but will not be able to deliver.

Objection: primates are not people and how can you generalize findings based on animal populations to human populations? Same comment I made before applies here: level of proof is not a scientific question but a social policy question. Moreover, if there is a concerted push on a number of studies such as those I mention here, then the aggregate results reinforce the level of proof of each.

Studies of Television's Effects

Just a few more research designs that would concentrate on learning something about the effects of television on children, even though they would not set out to explicate the complex of causes leading to antisocial behavior. Use the Lazarsfeld-Stanton Program Analyzer simply to learn what elements of a program arouse affective reactions in children. Then interview them in detail on the whys and the wherefores. This would not tell us much about television's contribution to antisocial behavior, but it would reveal a great deal about what goes on inside the heads of children as they watch. Many parents would like to know this. I even think broadcasters might be interested.

Set up a stationary camera preferably (but not necessarily) with sound in selected living rooms to film children watching violent programs on television. Set up equivalent cameras in control group living rooms, filming children watching other types of programs. Analyze the film, using our well developed techniques of content analysis. Develop categories of analysis to describe the viewers' reactions. The analysis could include a panel of sociologists, anthropologists, psychiatrists, parents, even children and—why not?—broadcasters. (Edited, this film or tape could be sold as a documentary, thus reducing research costs.)

And those primates! The study of effects of passive learning through television versus active learning through television versus interactional learning without television is long overdue. Programs like "Sesame Street" would welcome such research. Underdeveloped countries, which are counting heavily on television to educate their illiterate masses, likewise.

Which brings me to my final proposal for needed research, perhaps the most important of all I have touched upon here. I am making certain charges in this article. I claim that these facts of omission justify inferences about the likelihood that the broadcasting industry will find out anything in this study that will move them to improve television programs for children in the next five years. Other pressures such as congressional committees, the FCC, citizens' lobbying and the recently issued report of the White House Conference on Children (June 1971) may have an impact leading to program changes.

I claim that if NBC is launching elaborate, expensive and exquisitely irrelevant research (and the other two networks are not doing any better) this is presumptive evidence that the industry a) does not plan to find out the effects of television on our children, and b) does not plan to change television fare following research results.

Some might say this is a charge about which reasonable men and women may disagree. I grant that it is based on inference, not on direct evidence, but I argue that the present paper offers some grounds, at least, for the claim.

Thus, my final research suggestion is for an investigation of the decision-making process on programming in the networks. How are programs created? What kinds of people order them made? What kinds of directives, both implicit and explicit, are issued? How do the decision-makers define the positive and negative aspects of these programs, leading to put some on and take some off? How does the whole process of program-production work? What programs are proposed but never made? What programs are made but never make it through to September opening? What are the comparative virtues of programs that finally do open in September over the rejects? How are these decisions justified?

These kinds of structural factors, once they are known, cannot predict effects; but knowing what options have been rejected informs us of possible effects that will never have a chance to occur because the option has been foreclosed at the source.

I cannot withdraw my charges against the broadcasting network until these and similar questions are answered. They cannot absolve themselves of my charges until these questions are answered.

MARIAN GENNARIA MORRIS

Psychological Miscarriage: An End to Mother Love

Not long ago a mother in the Midwest, while giving her baby its bath, held its head underwater until it drowned. She said that there was something wrong with the child. Its smell was strange and unpleasant; it drooled; it seemed dull and listless. It reminded her of a retarded relative, and the thought of having to spend the rest of her life caring for such a person terrified her. Her husband was out of work, and she was pregnant again. She said she "felt the walls closing in." When, in her confused and ignorant way, she had asked her husband, a neighbor, and a doctor for help, she got promises, preachments, and evasions. So she drowned the baby.

This mother said she had felt "so all alone." But, unfortunately, she had plenty of company. Many thousands of American women do not love or want their babies. Although few actually kill their infants, the crippling effects of early maternal rejection on children can hardly be exaggerated—or glossed over. The number directly involved is large. The social harm, for everybody, is great. An idea of the size of the problem can be gained from the following figures, taken from federal, state, and local sources:

■ 50-70,000 children neglected, battered, exploited annually;

■ 150,000 children in foster homes for these reasons;

■ over 300,000 children in foster care altogether;

■ 8 to 10 percent of all school children in one twenty-county study in need of psychiatric examination and some type of treatment for their problems.

But even these figures can hardly begin to describe the violence, deprivation, and dehumanization involved.

Recently we concluded a study of thirty rejecting mothers and their children, who can serve as examples. Our findings are supported by a number of other studies of parents and their children who have various physical and psychological disorders. Although the poor are hardest hit by family and emotional problems it should be noted that the majority of these families were not poverty-stricken. Psychological miscarriage of motherhood attacks all classes and levels.

Twenty-one of the thirty mothers demonstrated clearly from the time of delivery that they could not properly mother or care for their babies—could not even meet their basic needs. Yet no one who had had contact with them— neither doctors, nurses, nor social workers—had apparently

been able to help, effectively, any one of them, nor even seemed aware that severe problems existed.

The entire population of mothers was characterized by old troubles and hopelessness, stretching back to the previous generation—and in one-third of the cases, back to the third generation. Half the children were illegitimate, or conceived before marriage. Sixty percent of the families had been in juvenile, criminal or domestic courts at some earlier time. Two-thirds of the children were either first-borns, or first-borns of their sex—and lack of experience with children increased their mothers' insecurities.

All thirty children needed intensive psychiatric treatment. Only two of the thirty were "well" enough—from homes that were "stable" enough—for out-patient care to even be considered. The remaining twenty-eight were headed for institutions. Their prognoses are grave, their chances doubtful. They will cost us a great deal in the years to come, and their problems will be with us a long time. Some will never walk the streets as free men and women.

Actually, the children were so disturbed that they could not be diagnosed with great accuracy. For instance, it was impossible to tell how intelligent most really were because they were in such emotional turmoil that they could not function properly on tests, and seemed retarded. A fifth of them had been so beaten around the head that it is quite possible their brains were damaged. (One baby had been thrown across the room and allowed to stay where it fell.) Women who feel neglected and less than human in turn neglect their children and treat them as less than human.

Fear and Reality

In our supposedly interdependent society, we are close together in violence, but apathetic to each other's needs. But apathy to their needs constitutes a violence to women facing labor, delivery, and the early and bewildering adjustments of motherhood. And it is in these days and weeks that psychological miscarriage occurs.

During pregnancy, labor, and delivery the basic fears of childhood—mutilation, abandonment, and loss of love— are vividly revived for a woman, and with double force— for herself and the baby. Nor are these fears simply fantasies: mothers *are* frequently cut, torn, and injured, babies *are* born with congenital defects.

The entire pregnancy period, with its lowering of defenses, makes the mother more capable of loving and feeling for her baby. But whether she finds his needs pleasing or threatening depends on what happened to her in the past, and the support she gets in the present.

After delivery, still in physical and emotional stress, under great pressure, she must make the most important, difficult adjustments of all. She must "claim" her baby. That is, she must make it, emotionally, part of herself again; identify it with the qualities and values in herself and her life that she finds good, safe, reassuring, and rewarding. After all the dreams and fears of pregnancy, she now must face and cope with the reality—the baby and his needs. If she miscarries now and rejects the child as something bad that cannot be accepted, then the child cannot grow to be normal. Nor can its society be normal, since the mothers must hand down to each generation the values by which society survives.

In older days, when most women had their babies at home, these adjustments were made in familiar surroundings, with such family support as was available. Now they are made largely in the hospital. What actually happens to mothers in today's hospitals?

Childbirth, once a magnificent shared experience, has increasingly become a technical event. Administrative and physical needs get priority. Emotional needs and personalities tend to get in the way of efficiency. Administrators and medical personnel, like everyone else, respond most readily to those pressures which affect them. Since they are in charge, they pass them down to the patient, whether they help the patient or not.

The mothers of the poor in particular arrive faceless, knowing no one on the ward, with little personal, human contact from before birth until they leave. Increasingly, they arrive already in labor, so that the hospitals cannot turn them away. They also come at this late stage so that they can avoid the constant procession of doctors and the three and four-hour clinic waits, during which they are called "mother" because their names have been lost in the impersonal clinic protocols. In the wards, they may be referred to simply by their bed numbers.

Birth itself may be subordinated to the schedule: some doctors schedule their deliveries, and induce labor to keep them on time. Even "natural" labor may be slowed down or speeded up by drugs for convenience.

A Public Event

Mothers say that they are allowed little dignity or modesty. Doctors strange to them may, and do, examine them intimately, with little attempt at privacy. They say that without their permission they are often used as live lecture material, giving birth before interested audiences of young interns and students while the obstetrician meticulously describes each step and tissue. How apathetic we have become to the routine dehumanization of mothers is well illustrated by the story of an upper-middle-class woman I know. She was in labor, almost hidden by drapes preparatory to vaginal examination, light flooding her perineum (but not her face). Approached by a nurse and gloved physician she suddenly sat up in her short-tailed hospital gown and said, "I don't know who *you* are, doctor, but *I* am Mrs. Mullahy." Good for Mrs. Mullahy! She has a strong sense of personal identity, and is determined to preserve it.

"A mother enters the hospital prey to childhood insecurities, and stripped alike of defenses and clothes. Attitudes and cues from hospital personnel, and others, strongly affect her self-respect and her feelings about her baby's worth."

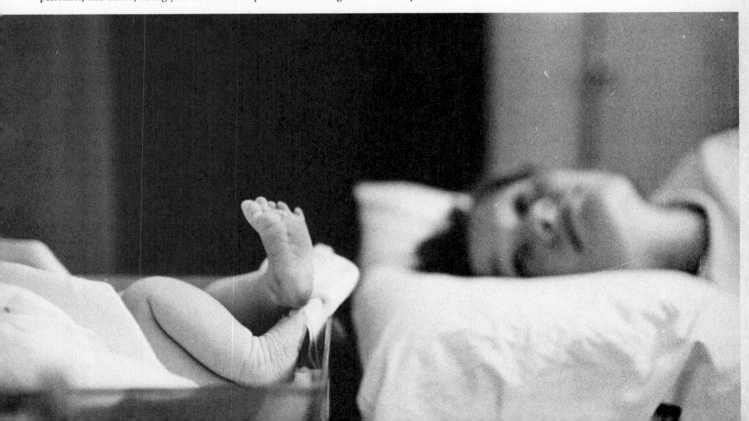

Mothers say they are isolated and humiliated. They say that in addition to their own anxieties they must worry about what their doctors think, and be careful to please and propitiate the staff members, who may have power of life and death over them and their babies.

They say that they are kept in stirrups for hours—shackled in what reduces them to something sub-human—yet afraid to complain.

Is it increasingly true, as mothers say, that babies are not presented to them for from four to twelve hours after birth? Social histories show that prompt presentation is necessary for the mental health of the mothers; studies of other mammals indicate that such delay interrupts mothering impulses and may bring on rejection of the young. Is this happening to human mothers and babies? How necessary, medically, is such a delay? Is it worth the price?

Many women become deeply depressed after childbirth. Is this at least partly a reaction to hospital experiences? Is it an early distress signal of psychological miscarriage? There is very little research that attempts to assess early maternal adaptation, and we need such research badly. Are the violent mothers, so brutal to their children, violent at least in part because of our faceless and impersonal birth practices? Clinical studies show that the less sense of identity and personal worth a mother has, the more easily she displaces her aggressions onto others—*any* others. Are we scapegoating our children?

Staking a Claim

To a mother, the birth of her baby is not a technical event. It starts in intimate contact with the father, and has deep roots in her feelings for and relationship with him, whether positive or negative. It reflects her personality, her state of maturity, the experiences of her most intimate anxieties and special hopes, and her associations with the adults who have had most influence on her. She enters the hospital prey to childhood insecurities, and stripped alike of defenses and clothes. Attitudes and cues from the hospital personnel, and from others, strongly affect her self-respect and her feelings about her own and her baby's worth.

It is difficult to observe most normal claiming behavior in a hospital. But some of it can be observed. Most mothers, for example, do find ways to make contact with their babies' bodies—touching and examining them all over delightedly, even to the tiny spaces between fingers and toes—cooing and listening to them, inhaling their odors, nuzzling and kissing them.

Socially, a major way to claim a child is to name it. Names suggest protective good magic; they establish identity and suggest personality; they emphasize masculinity or femininity; they affirm family continuity and the child's place in it.

Nevertheless, it is usually difficult to follow claiming behavior for two reasons. First, because hospital routines and tasks interfere. To the staff, the process of mothers becoming acquainted with infants is seen as merely cute, amusing, or inconvenient. Babies are presented briefly, pinned and blanketed tightly, making intimate fondling—for women who have carried these infants for months—difficult and sometimes even guilt-producing.

The second reason is related to the nature of normal motherhood. The well-adjusted mother is secure within herself, content to confine her communications mostly to her baby, rather than project them outward. As Tolstoy said of marriage, all happy ones tend to be happy in the same way, and relatively quiet. But the unhappy ones are different and dramatic—and it is by observing unhappy mothers that the pathological breakdown of maternal claiming can be most easily traced.

Let us consider a few examples:

Tim—Breakdown in Early Infancy

When Tim's mother first felt him move in her, and realized then that all evasion and doubt about her pregnancy was past, she blacked out (she said) and fell down a flight of stairs.

Tim was her second child. Her first pregnancy was difficult and lonely and, she had been told, both she and the baby had almost died during delivery. She suffered from migraine headaches, and was terrified of a second delivery.

For the first four months of Tim's life, she complained that he had virulent diarrhea and an ugly odor, and took him from doctor to doctor. Assured by each one that there was nothing wrong with the child (in the hospital the diarrhea cleared up in one day), she took this to mean that there was something wrong with *her*—so she sought another doctor. She took out thirteen different kinds of cancer insurance on Tim.

During an interview, she told a woman social worker that it was too bad that doctors could not look inside a baby and know he was *all* O.K.

The social worker decided to probe deeper: "You would have a hard time convincing me that you *deliberately* threw yourself down those stairs."

"Who, me? Why I told my mother all along that I would never *willingly* hurt a hair of one of my children's heads."

"But suppose you had, unwillingly. Would you blame someone else for doing it, under the circumstances?"

"No! I was sick and don't even know how it happened."

After that, the demon that had haunted her was in the open, and recovery began. She had felt that she was both criminal and victim, with the child as the instrument of her punishment. (Only a "good" mother deserves a good baby; a "bad" mother deserves a "bad"—damaged or sick—baby.) The implied criticisms of her mother and doctor had aggravated these feelings. She identified Tim not with the good in her but the "evil"—he was something faulty, something to be shunned.

Under treatment she learned to accept herself and regain her role of mother. She was not really the bad little girl her critical mother and doctor had implied; neither, therefore, was Tim bad—she could accept him. It was no longer dangerous to identify with her. She let Tim see her face; she held him comfortably for the first time; she did not mention his "ugly" smell; she stayed by his bed instead of restlessly patrolling the corridors. She referred to our hospital as the place she had "got him *at,*" instead of the hospital, ninety miles away, where he had actually been born.

Jack—Effects on an Older Child

Shortly after Jack was born, his mother asked her obstetrician whether Jack's head was all right. Gently touching the forceps marks, he said, *"These* will clear up." Thinking that she had been told delicately that she had a defective child, she did not talk to Jack for five-and-a-half years—

did not believe he could understand speech.

At five-and-a-half, approaching school, he had never spoken. A psychologist, thinking that the child was not essentially retarded, referred the mother to a child guidance clinic, where the social worker asked whether she had ever found out if the obstetrician had meant the *inside* of Jack's head. For the first time in all the years it occurred to her that there might have been a misunderstanding. Three months later Jack was talking—though many more months of treatment were still necessary before he could function adequately for his age.

Behind this, of course, was much more than a misunderstanding. Behind it was Jack's mother's feelings of guilt for having caused her own mother's death. Guilt went back many

---

Patterns of Rejection

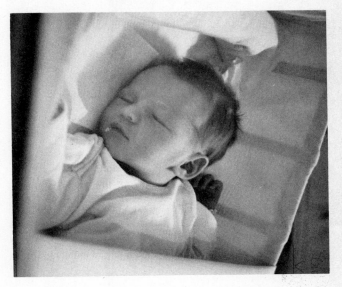

There are several criteria that can be used to assess the adequacy of a mother's behavior during the early weeks of an infant's life. Mother-infant unity can be said to be *satisfactory* when a mother can:

find pleasure in her infant and in tasks for and with him;
understand his emotional states and comfort him;
read his cues for new experience, sense his fatigue points.

Examples: she can receive his eye contact with pleasure; can promote his new learnings through use of her face, hands and objects; does not overstimulate him for her own pleasure.

In contrast, there are specific signs that mothers give when they are *not adapting* to their infants:
See their infants as ugly or unattractive.
Perceive the odor of their infants as revolting.
Are disgusted by their drooling and sucking sounds.
Become upset by vomiting, but seem fascinated by it.
Are revolted by any of the infants' body fluids which touch them, or which they touch.
Show annoyance at having to clean up infants' stools.
Become preoccupied with the odor, consistency and numbers of infants' stools.
Let infants' heads dangle, without support or concern.
Hold infants away from their own bodies.
Pick up infants without warning by touch or speech.
Juggle and play with infants, roughly, after feeding, even though they often vomit at this behavior.
Think infants' natural motor activity is unnatural.
Worry about infants' relaxation following feeding.
Avoid eye contact with infants, or stare fixedly into their eyes.
Do not coo or talk with infants.
Think that their infants do not love them.
Believe their infants expose them as unlovable, unloving parents.

Think of their infants as judging them and their efforts as an adult would.
Perceive their infants' natural dependent needs as dangerous. Fear death at appearance of mild diarrhea or cold.
Are convinced that infants have defects, in spite of repeated physical examinations which prove negative.
Often fear that infants have diseases connected with "eating": leukemia, or one of the other malignancies; diabetes; cystic fibrosis.
Constantly demand reassurance that no defect or disease exists, cannot believe relieving facts when they are given.
Demand that feared defects be found and relieved.
Cannot find in their infants any physical or psychological attribute which they value in themselves.
Cannot discriminate between infant signals of hunger, fatigue, need for soothing or stimulating speech, comforting body contact, or for eye contact.
Develop inappropriate responses to infant needs: over or under-feed; over or under-hold; tickle or bounce the baby when he is fatigued; talk too much, too little, and at the wrong time; force eye contact, or refuse it; leave infant alone in room; leave infant in noisy room and ignore him.
Develop paradoxical attitudes and behaviors.

Psychological Miscarriage: An End to Mother Love

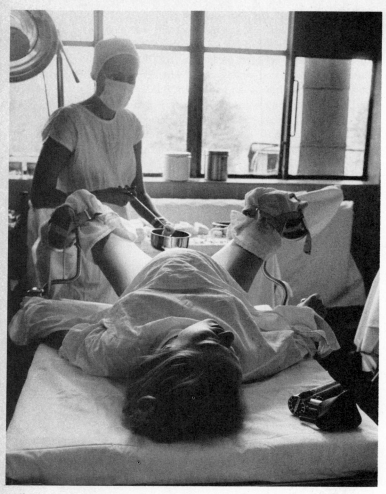

"Without their permission, mothers are often used as live lecture material, giving birth before interested audiences of young interns and students, while the obstetrician meticulously describes each step and tissue."

years. During an auto ride long ago, she had an accident in which her mother suffered a mild blow on the head. In the early months of pregnancy with Jack, she had found her mother dead in the tub. The cause was cancer, which had nothing to do with the bump. But deep down she could not believe this, and she developed the fear that Jack's head, too, was damaged—a fitting punishment for a woman who feared she had killed her mother. When her obstetrician seemed to confirm it, she did not question further.

For almost six years Jack was not so much an infant or child as a damaged head. Like her mother he was silent—from "brain injury." It was only under treatment that she accepted the possibility that she might have "misunderstood."

Babs—Hell Revisited

Babs was fourteen months old when she was flown to our hospital from South America, physically ill with diarrhea and dehydration, and emotionally badly withdrawn. In South America, her mother had trouble getting proper drugs

and talking effectively with Spanish-speaking doctors—and when she had had to face Babs's pleading eyes with little relief to offer, she had gone into acute panic. She hadn't been able to comfort her child, but had drawn away and could hardly look at her or touch her. From this rejection Babs had in turn withdrawn, and a mutual vicious cycle of rebuff and retreat had come about.

The mother felt that she had lived through all this before in her own childhood. When she was five, she had had a little brother, aged three. Her sick mother often left him in her charge. ("He was *my* baby.") One day both ate sprayed peaches from a tree. Both came down with severe diarrhea. She survived. She remembers vividly seeing him in "his little white coffin."

The pregnancy period with Babs had been stormy, full of family crises; she felt guilty about "not feeding Babs right." She could not accept the reassurances of her obstetrician. After Babs was born she was over-meticulous about cleaning her after bowel movements.

During treatment she shook visibly when asked whether Babs resembled her in any way. But when asked: "Could you have been Jim's *real* mother when you were only five?" she relaxed, and grew radiant. Later she said: "I know *now* that I couldn't have known that the peaches were poisoned."

"Nor that Babs would get sick with diarrhea if you went to South America to live with your husband?"

"No. I know now that the *place* is not good for any of us. I didn't know that before."

In a few days she was admiring in Babs the very qualities she had said she admired in herself—her sense of fun, and her determination. The positive identification between them had been made.

Mothers as Patients

How can we prevent such psychological miscarriages—and how can we limit their ravages once they have already occurred?

The dynamics of maternal rejection are not completely known—we need far more research, far more detailed and orderly observation of early maternal behavior. Nevertheless, enough is known already about the symptoms (detailed in the box on page 11) for us to be able to work up a reliable profile of the kind of woman who is most likely to suffer damage, and to take steps to make sure that help is offered in time. After all, the ultimate cause of maladaptation is lack of human sympathy, contact, and support, even though the roots may go back for more than one generation. We must, therefore, offer that support. We may not be able completely to heal old, festering wounds, but we can palliate their worst effects, and keep them from infecting new babies.

Mothers in our study identified the periods of greatest danger as just before and after delivery. It is then—and swiftly—that intervention by a psychiatric team should occur. What can be done?

■ We must have early recognition of trouble. Early signs

Violence: Individual and Institutional

of maternal maladaptation are evident in the mutual aversion of mother and child. But these signs have to be watched for—they cannot be ignored because of hospital routine that is "more important."

■ Let the mother have enough time to see and become acquainted with the hospital personnel with whom she will experience birth. Length of hospital stay is geared to technical requirements—five days for middle-class mothers, down (in some places) to twenty-four hours or less for the poor. Therefore, acquaintance should start before birth, at least with the physician, so that when delivery comes the mother will not be faced with a stranger in cap and gown, but a human being she already knows. Nurses and social workers should also be included. (The Hahnemann Medical College and Hospital in Philadelphia already assigns resident physicians to the pre-natal clinics to provide this continuity.)

■ Mothers of young infants suffer from geographical and psychological isolation. Services should work toward reducing both of these isolations. Ideally such services should come from a team, including not only the doctor and nurses, but a sympathetic pediatrician, psychiatric and medical social workers, of both sexes, who could also act as substitute parents. This help should be as available to the middle-class as to the poor (middle-class patients are sometimes denied hospital social services).

■ Help should carry over into home care. *Make sure that each mother has someone to care for her at home.* After their too brief hospital stay, poverty-stricken women, many without husband or family, are often more helpless and lost at home than in the hospital.

■ Mothers should not be left alone for long periods, whether under sedation or not. Schedules should and must be modified to allow them to have normal family support as long as possible. If they have none, substitutes—volunteers—should be found. Isolated mothers, cut off from support or even contact with their physicians, and treated as objects, much too often displace their loneliness, depression, resentment, bitterness, humiliation, rage, and pain onto their babies.

■ Get rid of the stirrups—and the practice of using them to hang mothers' legs in the air for hours! Find some other way to hold women on the delivery table until the last moments. Women often spend months recovering from backaches caused by stirrups.

■ Present the baby as soon as possible. The most frequent comment from mothers who remain conscious in the delivery room is, "The doctor gave him to me." This is psychologically very sound; when the father-image (doctor) presents the baby with the obvious approval of the mother-image (nurse), latent feelings of guilt about having a baby

and about the acceptability of the baby—and of motherhood—are lulled and dispelled. Too often, however, the nurse is cast, or casts herself, in the role of unwilling, stingy, critical giver of the baby—in fact the whole institution lends itself to this. Presentation should precede and not depend on feeding; it should be made gladly and willingly; it should allow time and ease of access for the mother to examine her baby's body.

■ Doctors, nurses, and aides should understand and come to know pregnancy, labor, delivery, and early growth as a continuing process, rather than in bits and pieces, a series of techniques. They need to understand and see it from the mothers' viewpoint, as well as in terms of bottles, diapers, rooms, instruments, and procedures.

■ Reassure mothers about their infants. This includes understanding the real meanings of their questions. If a mother continually discounts good reports, rejection may be underway, and psychological miscarriage imminent.

■ First-born children, and the first-borns of each sex, are the ones most commonly rejected; their mothers need special care—as do the mothers of the poor and those without family, husband, or outside human supports.

None of these proposals are radical—even administratively. Most are quite simple, and could be done directly in the wards and the private rooms.

Overall, we need more research. We do not know enough about the earliest signals of psychological miscarriage; we have not trained ourselves, nor taken the trouble, to watch for these early signs. Nor do we know enough about the long-term effects of maladaptation. Are the older children completely lost? Is the process irreversible? Cannot something be done to bring them back to productive life?

There is nothing more important in a maternity pavilion, nor in a home, than the experiences with which life begins. We must stop the dehumanization of mothers. We must give all children a chance for life.

FURTHER READING

Attachment and Loss by John Bowlby (New York: Basic Books, 1969).

Violence Against Children by David G. Gil (Cambridge, Mass.: Harvard University Press, 1970).

The Battered Child edited by Ray E. Hefler and Henry Kempe (Chicago: University of Chicago Press, 1968).

"Transition to Parenthood" by Danel F. Hobbs, Jr., *Journal of Marriage and the Family* 30. (August 1968): 413–417.

Wednesday's Children by Leontine Young (New York: McGraw-Hill, 1964).

RICHARD SENNETT

The Brutality of Modern Families

In the past ten years many middle-class children have tried to break out of the communities, the schools and the homes that their parents had spent so much of their own lives creating. If any one feeling can be said to run through the diverse groups and life styles of the youth movement, it is a feeling that these middle-class communities of the parents were like pens, like cages keeping the young from being free and alive. The source of the feeling lies in the perception that while these middle-class environments are secure and orderly regimes, people suffocate there for lack of the new, the unexpected, the diverse in their lives.

There is an irony in this accusation for it seems to run counter to widely held beliefs that, far from being more secure, the lives of metropolitans have become almost intolerably complex, wildly out of control. Yet what the kids have touched on in an oblique way is that what Lewis Mumford calls the "technics" of city life—the means by which people communicate with each other, work together or exchange services with each other, aided by machines and complex bureaucratic rules—are a cornucopia of tools with which metropolitan man is brutalizing his social relations into ever more simple, ever more controllable, ever less anarchic forms. In the process, the civilizing possibilities that a metropolis uniquely can offer are disappearing. The possibilities for unexpected and unplanned social encounter, the coexistence of diverse communities, the eccentricity and human variety that flourish when masses of people live without rules together—all these urbane qualities of community are on the wane. It is this urbanity the young are searching for but cannot find.

Indeed, it may appear in the future that men of this era balanced their energies in a peculiar way. The enthusiasm with which they invented machines for quick communication, rapid transport between communities and so on was balanced by a refusal to be social: all the labor-saving devices somehow left each man more and more alone.

This transformation of metropolitan life is profound and mystifying. It has taken a revolt of the children of middle-class affluence to awaken us to the fact that order and security can be destructive. Yet I fear we have much more to learn about the dimensions of this paradox

before we will be able to understand why we have willfully excluded a healthy disorder from our lives.

This paradox poses a question: is there a standard of urbanity by which we can judge metropolitan living today? It is not a utopian dream but history that affords us that standard, I believe, and history of a most ordinary sort. The life styles of civility and sophistication to which modern affluent urban life can be compared were found in the "low culture" of ethnic ghettos in our cities more than 70 years ago. For in those ethnic enclaves of the late nineteenth century, there were hidden threads of cooperation and communal association that gave people who lived there regions of identity beyond the fact of their own poverty.

On Halstead Street

Let us take a tour down Halstead Street, the center of Chicago's great immigrant ghetto, around 1900. The street was 22 miles long, most of it teeming with people. Were we to start at its northern end and move south, we would see that most of these people were "foreigners," but at any given point different kinds of foreigners, all mixed together. A native might tell us that a certain few blocks were Greek or Polish or Irish, but were one actually to look at particular houses or apartment buildings, one would find the ethnic groups jumbled together. Even on the Chinese blocks of the street—for the Chinese are supposed at this time to have been the most closed of ethnic societies—there would be numerous families from Ireland or eastern Europe.

The functioning of all these groups on Halstead Street would appear hopelessly tangled to modern observers. The apartments would be mixed in with the stores, the streets themselves crowded with vendors and brokers of all kinds; even factories, as we moved to the southern end of Halstead Street, would be intermixed with bars, brothels, synagogues, churches and apartment buildings. In the midst of this jumble, there were some hidden threads of a structured social existence.

Were we to follow one of the residents of Halstead Street through a typical day, the experience would be something like this: up at six in the morning, a long walk or streetcar ride to the factory and then ten or 11 hours of grueling work. With this much of his day we would be familiar. But when the whistle to stop work blew at six in the evening, his life would take on a dimension that is perhaps

The issues discussed in this article are dealt with at greater length in the author's book *The Uses of Disorder* (New York: Alfred A. Knopf, 1970).

not immediately recognizable. The path back home from the factory might be broken by an hour's relaxation at a tavern or coffeehouse. Halstead Street was crammed in 1900 with little cafés where men would come after work to let the tension drain out, talking to friends or reading a newspaper. Dinner would usually be at home, but after dinner the man, sometimes with his wife, would be out of the house again, attending a union meeting, caring for a sick member of a mutual-aid society to which he belonged or just visiting the apartment of friends. Occasionally, when the family needed some special help, there would be a glass of beer shared with the local political boss and a plea for assistance—a soft job for an infirm relative, help with a naturalization form, some influence in getting a friend out of jail. Religious responsibilities also pulled the man and woman out of the house, particularly if they were Jewish or practicing Catholics. Synagogues and churches had to be built in this strange city, and the money and organization to build them could come only from the little men who were their members.

The life of a child on Halstead Street in 1900 would also seem odd to us, not to say frightening. The child of ten or 11 would be wakened early in the morning, scrubbed and sent off to school. Until three in the afternoon he would sit at a high desk reciting and memorizing. This experience is not strange to us, but again, his life after school would be. For if he did not come home to work, and many did not, he would be out on Halstead Street selling or hawking in the stall of someone much older, who sold and cajoled the passing traffic just as he did. It is amazing to see in old photographs of Halstead Street the young and old, shoulder to shoulder in these stalls, shouting out the prices and the virtues of their wares. Many youths would, with the tacit consent of their parents, enter into the more profitable after-school activity of stealing—we read, for instance, in the letters of one Polish family of great religious piety, of the honor accorded to a little son who had stolen a large slab of beef from a butcher on the corner. Life was very hard, and everyone had to fight for his needs with whatever weapons were at hand.

This life on Halstead Street required an urbanity of outlook, and multiple, often conflicting points of social contact, for these desperately poor people to survive. They *had* to make this diversity in their lives, for no one or two or three institutions in which they lived could provide all their needs. The family depended on political favors, the escape valve of the coffee shops and bars, the inculcation of discipline of the *shuls* and churches and so forth. The political machines tended in turn to grow along personal lines, to interact with the shifting politics of church and synagogue. This necessary anarchy took the individuals of the city outside the ethnic "subcultures" that supposedly were snugly encasing them. Polish people who belonged to steel unions often came into conflict with Polish people who had joined the police. It is the mark of a sophisticated life style that loyalties become crossed in conflicting

forms, and this sophistication was the essence of these poor people's lives.

This condition has been carefully described by the great Chicago urbanist, Louis Wirth, in his essay "Urbanism as a Way of Life." He tried to show how the city of necessity broke apart the self-contained qualities of the various ethnic groups. The groups were not like little villages massed together in one spot on the map; rather they penetrated into each other, so that the daily life of an individual was a journey through various kinds of group life, each one different in its function and character from the others.

The subtlety of this idea can be seen by comparing a city subculture, as Wirth observed it, to the structure of village culture from which the ethnic groups came. In the small towns of southern Italy, in the *shtetl* of eastern Europe or the settlements of Anatolia, one finds what Robert Redfield has called a "village ethic": the accessibility of all village activities to all members of the village community. The village ethic is a web of cohesion: there are no disconnected or isolated social regions because, though different people might hold different rank or perform specialized activities, the character of the separate activities is known to everyone, and the differences add up to one organic whole. What made areas like Halstead Street in Chicago, New York's Lower East Side or London's East End seem so different to writers like Wirth was that the separate activities, or the different groups, depended on one another but were not harmoniously related. Each piece of the city mosaic had a distinct character, but the pieces were free of each other, they were not organically bound, they did not dovetail neatly. Individuals had to enter into a number of social regions in the course of daily life, even though the regions were not fluently organized and may even have been warring.

The Decline of Civility

It is the popular stereotype about "working-class" or "ethnic" culture that prohibits us from seeing the kind of density and sophistication that the city life of ordinary people possessed in the past. Writers such as William Whyte make that life into an image of a village when in fact it was more complex, less unitarily organized. No easy myth of solidarity could develop out of Halstead Street, no simplicity of the sort "I am who I am by what I do and what I believe." Nevertheless, this civility was bought at the price of much strain and economic anxiety; to recognize the complexity in these people's lives is not to glorify poverty —that would be a stroke of romantic cruelty—but to try to learn what strengths it is possible for city men to achieve.

In the last half-century, a majority of the ethnic groups in the city have achieved a state of prosperity for themselves far beyond what the first immigrants ever dreamed of. In the process, this necessary anarchy, this necessary sophistication, has died out; in its stead, social activities have become more coherent, more simple, and the social bond itself has become less compelling. The reason for this change is to be uncovered, I believe, in the transformation that family life has undergone as a majority of white urban Americans have achieved relative affluence. It is in the family lives of urban men today that one finds the expression of those forces that eroded the urbanity of city life in the past, eroded the necessary anarchy of the city and the complexities of feeling it exacted in ordinary experience.

When I first began to do research on the structure of city family life, I encountered over and over a popular stereotype: the idea that city conditions somehow contribute to the instability of the home. Evidently, the assumption is that the diversity of the city threatens the security and attachment family members feel for each other. Especially as suburban community life has come to dominate cities, there has grown up a mythological family image of affluent homes where Dad drinks too much, the kids are unloved and turn to drugs, divorce is rampant and breakdowns are routine. The good old rural families, by contrast, were supposedly loving and secure.

The trouble with this popular image is that it simply isn't true. Talcott Parsons has amassed evidence to show that the rate of divorce and desertion was much higher "in the good old days" at the turn of the century than it is now. William Goode has taken the idea a step further by showing how divorce is *less* frequent in affluent homes than in working-class homes. There may still be a great deal of unrest and tension in these suburban families, but it cannot be allied to their structural instability. In fact, we shall see, it is the juncture of great formal stability with deep and unresolved tension that now marks these families.

The idea of the city weakening the family has also come to express itself in the popular perversions of the Moynihan report on the family lives in the black ghettos. The phenomenon this document actually describes is the impact of unemployment on family structure. It has been misread, however, as a description of how northern city life has broken apart the black family, and, in its most distorted form, as a sign that there is something too "weak" in black culture to enable it to withstand the terrors of the city. What Moynihan describes occurs wherever unemployment or intermittent employment is a long-term family experience; one therefore finds a much higher rate of female-headed households, with shifting male partners and "illegitimate" children, among persecuted rural Catholics in Northern Ireland than among the blacks of New York City. But the myth remains: somehow it is the city that is the destroyer.

There is an important history to this stereotype of the city's threat to the home. At the turn of the century, the bulk of the population of American cities was working-class, people whose origins and urban experience was of a piece with the residents of Halstead Street. But there was a numerically smaller group of middle-class families in cities like Chicago whose family patterns were very different, much closer to the narrowness of the life of the affluent middle class in today's metropolitan areas. In *Families Against the City* I explored the lives of one such middle-class community and what the history of these people revealed was that the common stereotype of the city's impact on the family has to be reversed for middle-class homes. For the disorder and vigor of city life in the first decade of this century frightened middle-class families, but, unlike working-class people, they had the means to do something about their fears. They drew in upon themselves: there was little visiting outside the confines of home; voluntary groups like churches and political clubs claimed few bourgeois participants; in America, unlike France or Germany, the urban middle class shunned public forms of social life like cafés and banquet halls. The home became for these early middle-class city dwellers a sanctuary against the confusions of the outside world.

Family Intensity

That kind of family isolation has abated in modern times, particularly when a family is in crisis. But there was something about such urban middle-class families at the opening of the twentieth century that has survived over time. These families possessed a character that now typifies families in middle-class suburbs as well as the middle-class islands within the central city; it is a quality of living that unites newly middle-class families whose parents were immigrants with the native-born urban middle-class families that have always lived in large cities. This characteristic of family life is the intensity of family relations. It links the variety of groups and backgrounds of people lumped together as middle-class, and the reach of this phenomenon extends beyond the city proper into the suburb and the town.

What is meant by an "intense" family life? There are, I think, a state of mind and a style of living that define the family intensity now found in many if not most segments of the urban population. The state of mind is that family members believe the actions and feelings that transpire in the family are in fact a microcosm of the whole range of "meaningful" actions and feelings in the world at large. The belief is, as one middle-class mother in Queens explained to an interviewer recently, that nothing "really important" in human relationships occurs that cannot be experienced within the boundaries of the home. People who think in this way can therefore conceive of no reason for making social forays or social contacts that cannot be ultimately reconciled or absorbed in family life.

The style of living that makes for an intense family life is the reduction of family members to levels of equality. This characteristic is much more pronounced in American urban families than in European ones. The feeling consists, most vulgarly, in fathers wanting to be "pals" to their sons and mothers wanting to be sisters to their daughters;

there is a feeling of failure and dishonor if the parents are excluded from the circle of youth, as though they were tarnished by being adult. A good family of this sort is a family whose members talk to each other as equals, where the children presume to the lessons of experience and the parents try to forget them. That the dignity of all the family members might lie exactly in mutual respect for separateness and uniqueness is not conceived; dignity is conceived to lie in treating everyone equally. This brings the family members into a closer relation to each other—for there are taken to be, ideally, no unbridgeable gaps.

Both the state of mind and the life style have become in fact structures for limiting the sophistication and tolerance of the people who live in such homes.

The conviction that a family is the whole social arena in microcosm stifles parents and children both in an obvious and in a subtle way. Clearly, no band of four or five people represents the full spectrum of attitudes and human traits to be found in the wider society. The family as a world of its own can therefore become highly exclusive. Studies of intense family attitudes toward strangers reveal that the outsiders are judged to be "real," to be important and dealt with, only to the extent to which they reflect the particular attitudes and personalities found within a family circle. The most striking form of this can be seen in situations where middle-class neighborhoods have been successfully integrated racially. The black families have been accepted to the extent that people feel they are after all "just like us," or as a respondent in one study put it: "You wouldn't know from the way the Jones family acts they were Negroes." Accepting someone ineradicably different is not what occurs under these conditions.

Conflict Is a "No-No"

The subtle way in which families, feeling themselves a microcosm of the society, become self-limiting has to do with the base of stability on which such families rest. This base is the existence, or the belief in the existence, of long-term trust. For families to believe they are all-important there has to be the conviction that no betrayal and breakup will occur. People do not concentrate all their energies in one place and simultaneously believe it may one day shatter or betray them. Yet long-term situations of trust and reliability are rare in the larger social world. Not only in work but also in a variety of human affairs there are experiences of power and significance that cannot depend on a mutual commitment or trust for a long period. An intense family life must refuse to grant worth to that which is shifting, insecure or treacherous, and yet this is exactly what the diversity in society is built of.

When people in a family believe they must treat each other as equal in condition, the same self-blinding, the same limitation, occurs. A recent project made psychiatric interviews in homes of "normal," "just average" families in a modest suburb outside a large city. Over and over

again in these interviews adults expressed a sense of loss, sometimes amounting to feelings of annihilation, in the things in their lives they had wanted to do and could afford to do but refrained from doing for fear of leaving out the children. These sacrifices were not dictated by money; they were much more intimate, small-scale, yet important things: establishing a quiet spot in the day after work when a man and his wife were alone together, taking trips or vacations alone, eating dinner after the children were put to bed. In another frame, fathers spoke again and again of how they had failed their sons by not being able to understand them. When the interviewers asked what they meant, the response usually came as a version of "he doesn't open up to me the way he does to his friends." Such burdens are acquired, so many daily chances for diversity and change of routine are denied, out of the belief in the rightness of treating children as much as equals as possible, especially in early and middle adolescence.

In one way, the belief in the family as a microcosm of the world leads to this will to believe the family members all alike, all "pals." For if the family is a whole world, then somehow the conditions of friendship and comradeship must be established within its borders, and this can only be done by treating all the family members as comrades who can understand each other on the same grounds.

The idea just advanced may seem untrue to the experience of many—an experience of family tension and estrangement unlike what previous generations seemed to have known. But there is a perverse, hidden strain to this family intensity that may make sense of the phenomenon. Perhaps I can illustrate this from some professional work now being done by family researchers.

A few students of the family have recently been at pains to unravel what is awkwardly called "the guilt-over-conflict syndrome." This syndrome appears in the attitudes of many intense family members toward their families. The syndrome is simple to state, but not simple to overcome by people painfully caught up in it: to most people it appears that good families, upright families, ought to be happy, and it also appears that happy families ought to be tranquil, internally in harmony. What happens then when conflict or serious fights erupt? For many people, the emergence of conflict in their family lives seems to indicate some kind of moral failure; the family, and by reflection the individual, must be tarnished and no good. Until recently many therapists, too, thought family fighting was morally destructive. Like their clients, they imagined a healthy family to be one where differences were "resolved" without emotional heat. But a body of evidence about conflict and mental illness in families has accumulated sufficiently to make this middle-class notion untenable; the facts indicate that families in which abrasive conflicts are held down turn out to have much higher rates of deep emotional disorders than families in which hostilities are openly expressed, even though unresolved.

But the guilt-over-conflict syndrome is significant because it is so deeply held a presupposition about family life: people look, for example, at conflicts between generations as an evil, revealing some sort of rottenness in the familial social fabric, rather than as an inevitable and natural process of historical change. Sharp personality differences within the children's generation, leading to estrangements between brothers and sisters, are viewed as a sign of bad parental upbringing, and so on. Put another way, anxiety and guilt over family conflict really express the wish that for the sake of social order, diversity and ineradicable differences should not exist in the home.

Islands in Metropolis

But this guilt about conflict, produced by the desire for intense family relations, helps explain a much broader social phenomenon: the ways in which the family group brutalizes its members, both young and old, in their dealings with the larger society. The link between family life of this kind and the society beyond it can be understood by posing this question: is there any reason to call an intense family life, fearful of conflict, an "urban" condition? Could it not simply be the way in which families live today in America, and since most families live in urban areas, be an "urban" family trait by location only?

There is an intimate relation between the desire for family intensity, the guilt it produces over conflict or disorder in intimate affairs and the social structure of a city. For, as the intensity of family relations grows, freshening of one's perceptions through diverse experience in the outside world diminishes. Intense families wall in the consciousness men have of "significant" or "important" experiences in their lives. One special social institution—the family group—becomes the arena of what is real. Indeed, the guilt that family intensity produces about experiences of disorder or conflict makes this absorption into the home appear as a moral or healthy act. The diversity of the city world beyond, as an older generation of immigrants or blacks knew it, never fit together in an orderly way; men were continually becoming involved in messy situations or having to change the face they presented to the world. In the new order of affluence, significant social life can be more proper, more dignified, by virtue of a more narrow order. One affluent working-class father told me recently, "When I was a kid, I had to be on my toes all the time, see, because in the slums of Boston you couldn't take anything for granted if you wanted to survive. Now that I've got some money, I can live respectably, you know, take care of the house and kids and not worry about what's happening outside. Maybe I'm not as sharp, but I've got more respect."

The essence of intense family life is this absorptive capacity, a power to collect the interests and attention of the individual in the tight-knit band of kin. Historically,

the last half-century of city life has been marked exactly by such intimacy-making. This spells a decline in the sophisticated anarchy of association for most city men and the rise of an urban isolationism for the masses—an isolationism once encircling only the small, native-born, middle class.

Suburban Closeness

The vehicle for replacing the sophistication of an older urban life by the suffocation in the family today is the growth of middle-class suburbs in this country. The shrinking of diverse community life into the family is the hidden history of suburban places—which seem so empty of secrets; this history makes sense of their simplicity and their great appeal to Americans.

The classic pattern of industrial city-suburb arrangements up to the Second World War was the pattern still extant in Turin or Paris. Cities were arranged in rings of socioeconomic wealth, with the factories at the outskirts of town, workers' suburbs or quarters next to them and then increasingly more affluent belts of housing as one moved closer to the center of the city. There were exceptions to this pattern, to be sure, like Boston or Lyons, but the pattern seemed to apply to most of the great urban centers in the United States; New York, Philadelphia and Chicago showed in general such a pattern at the opening of the present century.

When the flight to the suburbs first began in massive numbers after the Second World War, it was commonly thought that its causes were related to the depression and to the population dislocation of the war. But this explanation is simply inadequate to explain the persistence of the event over the course of time.

Nor, in the United States, can the movement to the suburbs cannot be explained by the growing presence of Negroes in the urban centers after the Second World War. For one thing, these Negroes seldom moved close to areas where young middle-class people had lived; those poorer people whose neighborhoods were gradually taken over by Negroes did not move to far-lying suburbs but relocated only slightly farther away from the urban core. There are some exceptions to this latter pattern; there are some people in outer Queens who moved to avoid blacks, but few in Darien, Connecticut, did.

The historical circumstances of depression, war, land value and racial fear all have played a role, but they are offshoots of a more central change in the last decades that has led to the strength of suburban life. This deeper, more hidden element is a new attitude about the conduct of family life within and without the city.

A variety of recent books on suburbs, like Herbert Gans' *The Levittowners* or John Seeley's *Crestwood Heights,* reveal that people who now live in suburbs value their home settings because they feel that closer family ties are more possible there than in the city center. The closeness is not so much a material one—after all, families in city apartments are extremely close physically. Rather, as is now being learned, it is the simplification of the social environment in the suburbs that accounts for the belief that close family life will be more possible there than in the confusion of the city.

In most American suburbs, physical space has been rigidly divided into homogeneous areas: there are wide swatches of housing separated from swatches of commercial development concentrated in that unique institution, the shopping center; schools are similarly isolated, usually in a parklike setting. Within the housing sectors themselves, homes have been built at homogeneous socioeconomic levels. When critics of planning reproach developers for constructing the environment in this way, the developers reply truthfully that people want to live with people just like themselves; people think diversity in housing will be bad for social as well as economic reasons. In the new communal order made possible by affluence, the desire of people is for a functionally separated, internally homogeneous environment.

Homogenous Zones

I believe this homogeneous-zones idea in suburbs is a brutalizing community process, in contrast to the urban situation that preceded it in time. For the homogeneous zones of function in a suburb prohibit an overlay of different activities in the same place; each place has its own predefined function. What therefore results is a limitation on the chance combination of new situations, of unexpected events, of unlikely meetings between people that create diversity and a sense of complexity in individual lives. People have a vision of human variety and of the possibility of living in a different and better way only when they are challenged by situations they have not encountered before, when they step beyond being actors in a preordained, unchanging routine. This element of surprise is how human growth is different from the simple passage of time in a life; but the suburb is a settlement fitted only to muffle the unknown, by separating the zones of human activity into neat compartments.

This prohibition of diversity in the arrangement of suburban areas permits, instead, the intensity of family relations to gather full force. It is a means for creating that sense of long-term order and continuity on which family intensity must be based. In a stable family, where long-term trust between pretend-equals exists, the "intrusions" of the outside must be diminished, and such is the genius of the suburban mode. The hidden fear behind this family life in the suburbs is that the strength of the family bond might be weakened if the individual family members were exposed to a richer social condition, readily accessible outside the house.

When the suburbs began to grow rapidly after the Second World War, some observers, such as David Riesman, were moved to criticize them for an aimlessness and emptiness in communal relations. But there was and is a peculiar kind of social bond made possible by this very emptiness, this lack of confusion. The bond is a common determination to remain inviolate, to ensure the family's security and sanctity through exclusionary measures of race, religion, class.

Involved here was a new event in the idea of a "neighborhood," for such a place became much more definable in becoming more homogeneous. Social scientists used to spend a great deal of time fighting with each other about the meaning of "neighborhood" in cities, one of the principal points being that there was such a multiplicity of social contact that individuals could not be neatly categorized by where they lived. Now they can. The growth of intensive family life in the suburb has brought into being a metropolitan region where each neighborhood is all too identifiable in socioeconomic, racial and ethnic terms. Now people really are getting to know who their neighbors are: they are just like themselves.

This kind of family living in the suburbs surely is a little strange. Isn't the preference for suburbia as a setting for family life in reality an admission, tacit and unspoken to be sure, that the parents do not feel confident of their own human strengths to guide the child in the midst of an environment richer and more difficult than that of the neat lawns and tidy supermarkets of the suburbs? If a close, tight-knit family emerges because the other elements of the adult and child world are made purposely weak, if parents assume their children will be better human beings for being shielded or deprived of society outside the home and homelike schools, surely the family life that results is a forced and unnatural intimacy.

Of course there are many similar criticisms one could make of suburbs, all centered in some way on the fact that suburbanites are people who are afraid to live in a world they cannot control. This society of fear, this society willing to be dull and sterile in order that it not be confused or overwhelmed, has become as well a model for the rebuilding of inner-city spaces. It is often said that the differences are disappearing between the suburbs and such central-city developments as Lefrak City in New York or the urban renewal projects of inner Boston or the South Shore of Chicago. It would be more accurate to say that these inner-city, middle-class communities are becoming suburbanized in a historical sense: rigidly planned usage of space, an emphasis on security and warding off intrusions from the outside—in short, a simplification of the contacts and the environment in which the family lives. In the name of establishing the "decencies" of life as regnant, the scope of human variety and freedom of expression is drastically reduced. The emotions shaping the rebuilding of inner-city living-places run much deeper than protection from the blacks or from crime; the blacks and the criminals are a symbolic cover under which the family can turn inward,

The Brutality of Modern Families

and the family members withdraw from dealing with the complexities of people unlike themselves.

The Morality of Being Passive

This urban transformation has now a frightening impact on the social and political life of adult city men as citizens. In the collapsing of multiple, interwoven points of social contact as the majority of city families have come to live in intense situations, lies an urban crisis as important as the crises of life faced by city people who are still oppressed and without economic power.

It is common for "slum romantics" to bemoan the loss of intimate social space and small scale in modern city life. But from the vantage point of what has been set forth so far, the issue would appear to be the reverse. There has not been a loss of intimate small scale per se, but rather a loss of multiple foci of small scale. The urban family of this affluent era has developed a power to absorb activities and interests that were once played out in a variety of settings in the city. Indeed, it might best be said of city life during the past 25 years that the scale of life has become too intimate, too intense.

There has therefore grown up a change in the "morality" of participation in urban affairs. If one looks back to the ethnic ghettos of the turn of the century, one finds men and women forced to deal with each other, forced to deal with diverse and often strange social situations, in order to survive. In the suburbanized cities of our time men are not forced into association; each family has the means and the desire to provide for all its perceived needs within the borders of kin relations. But the ethos of intense family life works in a more forceful manner as well to make men passive in the larger society of the city.

This new configuration of polarized intimacy in the city provides the individual with a powerful moral tool in shutting out new or unknown social relations for himself. For if the suburbanized family is a little world of its own, and if the dignity of that family consists in creating bases of long-term stability and concord, then potentially diversifying experiences can be shut out with the feeling of performing a moral act. For the sake of "protecting the home" a man refuses to wander or to explore: this is the meaning of that curious self-satisfaction men derive in explaining what they gave up "for the sake of the children." It is to make impotence a virtue.

The glorification of passivity makes clearer the willful indifference or the hostility that most middle-class urbanites show toward programs aimed at eradicating conditions of poverty in the city. For this hostility, as people give voice to it, is more than a feeling of simple class interest or class conflict. I once interviewed a suburban mother about a school bussing program between her community and a part of the Brownsville ghetto in New York; she tried to explain her anger at the program by saying finally, "What I don't understand is why they don't let us alone; I didn't make them poor, they live totally different from me; why should I have to see their kids in my school?" It isn't that the poor are black that rankles so much, it isn't even that they are poor; what hurts is that middle-class people are asked by programs such as school bussing to be more than passive onlookers in the social process, they are asked to interact with people who are different, and that kind of interaction they find too painful. It is this same inner-turning little world of family affairs, unused to the daily shocks of confrontation and the expression of ineradicable differences, that reacts with such volatility when oppressed groups in the city become disorderly. It is a short step from concentrating on one's own home affairs to sanctioning terrible repression of disturbances from below: if the poor are silenced, then there need be no intrusions on the "meaningful" circle of one's own life, the intimate relationships between Pop, Mom and the kids.

In these ways, affluent city life has created a morality of isolationism. The new virtue, like the religious puritanism of old, is a ritual of purifying the self of diverse and conflicting avenues of experience. But where the first puritans engaged in this self-repression for the greater glory of God, the puritans of today repress themselves out of fear—fear of the unknown, the uncontrollable. The intense family is the *via regia* by which this fear operates: such a family creates in men's intimate lives the necessity for known functions and well-worn routines. It is this kind of family life that explains, I believe, why so many white Americans can accept with equanimity the remaining injustices and oppressive poverty faced by blacks and Puerto Ricans in our cities.

FURTHER READING

In the Country of the Young by John Aldridge (New York: Harper's Magazine Press, 1970). A long essay on the "smothering" that has occurred in the families of the suburbs during the last two decades.

The Levittowners by Herbert Gans (New York: Pantheon Books, 1967). An excellent community study of a suburb filled with people of immigrant background who are now lower-middle class. The same issues of family and communal togetherness are treated in a wholly different way.

The Promised City by Moses Rischin (Cambridge, Mass.: Harvard University Press, 1962). A moving account of immigrant life in New York at the turn of the century.

The Hidden Injuries of Class by Richard Sennett and Jonathan Cobb (New York: Vintage Books, 1973). An historical account of blue-collar families in a northeastern city.

6. Crime and Punishment: Police, Criminals, and the Courts

If any aspect of American life has been a traditional source of pride to most Americans it is our system of criminal justice. Protected by constitutional guarantees against self-incrimination and the invasion of privacy, guaranteed a fair trial before a jury of his peers, and assured that he will be considered innocent until proven guilty beyond a shadow of a doubt, the average American placed great faith in the equity of justice. Even the convicted criminal could be hopeful about his future—at least since the second half of the nineteenth century—when a system of prison reforms appeared to alter the character of penal institutions to focus upon rehabilitation rather than punishment. Until recently, most middle-class Americans appeared to believe that our system worked as advertised—to provide equality before the law for all citizens. The events of the last 15 years have revealed in our institutions of criminal justice not only outrageous forms of discrimination, but a level of brutality that belies both our Constitution and our values.

We have become aware of the breakdown in our system of criminal justice primarily as a result of the turbulent social protest of the sixties. During those years the growing militancy of minority groups was translated into legal and political confrontation: students rioted; young men resisted arrest as draft evaders; men and women experimenting with new life-styles ran afoul of the law and created a whole new class of criminal offenses. Middle-class kids caught smoking pot were put on probation, issued warnings, jailed for brief periods of time, or sent to prison for sentences of five, ten, or more years. The blindfold worn by Justice seemed to be slipping as judgments were made without regard to the merits of the case but with full deference to local prejudice or to the degree to which the clothing or manners of the defendants outraged the sensibilities of the court. Of course, this stereotyping was hardly news to members of minority groups or to the poor who often have spent time in jail because of their cultural "style," because they did not know their rights, because they lacked funds for bail, or because the legal help available to them had little sympathy or understanding of their plight.

If problems in the courtroom seemed insurmountable, those posed by the prisons appeared even worse. The institutions we had designed to resocialize criminals and make their re-entry into society possible were mired in brutality that eroded human confidence and ability. Instead of rehabilitating criminals, our prisons, in fact, provide training grounds for crime.

Even the police, once respected by the middle class—although always regarded with some suspicion by minority groups—developed a new image: one they earned in the head-breaking riots of the sixties.

Though many were shocked by these discoveries, the unrest of the sixties did at least expose some of the serious flaws in our system of crime and punishment, flaws that derive in good part from the workings of that system itself. The victims of the system are rarely numbered among the rich and powerful but comprise the most helpless groups among us. A graphic example is to be found in Lerman's "Delinquents Without Crimes" which indicates that children are often treated far more harshly than are adults for equivalent crimes. Moreover, most children are incarcerated for what are termed "juvenile status offenses"—behaviors like running away from home, truancy, lack of respect for adults—which are not crimes for adults. Children are sent to reformatories for such misbehavior primarily because we provide few social alternatives to these juvenile training schools. Children who run away from home frequently do so because their home situation is impossible; their behavior is treated as a crime primarily because we still regard children as possessions and the right of the parent as paramount over the interest of the child. Lerman calls for numerous reforms in our system of juvenile justice; primary among these is the elimination of juvenile status offenses and dependency and neglect cases from the jurisdiction of juvenile courts. Establishment of a new public agency which would include on its governing board adults from the community and a number of juveniles as well could free the court to handle more threatening cases with more care, and would serve to bring both the community and its social supports to the aid of these victims of society's indifference.

Like the children discussed by Lerman, poor people and members of minority groups are often punished far more harshly than are middle-class or wealthy criminals because the operation of the informal institutions, as well as formal prejudices, discriminate against them. In "The Saints and the Roughnecks" (in Section 5) Chambliss illustrates how the selective perception and labeling of poor teenagers increases the possibility that they will be sent to jail for behavior that goes virtually unnoticed when its practitioners come from the middle class. Almost all young Americans organize into groups and bands, and most appear to indulge in delinquent activities at some time or other. Poor delinquents appear to be much more visible to the authorities than are rich ones, in part because they lack automobiles which can remove them from their neighborhoods for their escapades, and in part because they lack information and access to power that allows middle-class kids to manipulate the system. The manners, behavior, and clothing of poor kids generally vary from the norm expected by the police or other authorities and these dress codes and codes of manners tend to stigmatize the poor and to call down upon them the fullest wrath of an outraged law. Programs designed to sensitize police to their own prejudices have been established by some communities. Others have attempted to create new agencies, or use existing community organizations, to intervene on behalf of many of these young men and young women who are guilty primarily of lack of sophistication, but who might otherwise be sent to reformatories for what is often little more than ordinary mischief.

In "Lawyers with Convictions" Blumberg focuses upon the informal networks and values that operate within the court system. All defendants in criminal proceedings have a right to counsel that is guaranteed them by the Supreme Court. However, the lawyers assigned to poor defendants have few incentives to force them to bring a case to trial, and the pressure of their work, the overcrowded court calendars, combine to increase the rate of plea-bargaining: whether his client is innocent or not, the lawyer often persuades him to plead guilty to a lesser charge rather than risk having the case come to trial. Since the lawyers get no more money for a lengthy defense than for a plea, there is no economic incentive for them to bring a case to trial. Moreover, because they are far more likely to be enmeshed in social relationships with court and police officials, the needs of the courts and of the police for speedy adjudication take primacy over the client's need for justice. Numerous reforms have been suggested to alter this situation: reorganization of the court system so that some cases now under criminal statutes could be handled in civil courts; elimination of "victimless crimes" like prostitution and homosexuality between consenting adults could reduce court case loads and reduce the pressure for plea-bargaining. Closer examination of the informal relationships of court personnel has led to attempts to reform law schools so that they educate young lawyers to their responsibility to the client. Most recently, young lawyers have banded together in attempts to counteract the influence of informal court networks by establishing community legal agencies where the lawyers can obtain community social support in their efforts to provide legal aid for poor clients.

Heyman's "Methadone Maintenance as Law and Order" raises several more disquieting points in her discussion of methods by which society attempts to maintain social order. Analysis of methadone programs has convinced her that society is more concerned with maintaining order than with rehabilitating individuals whose behavior contravenes established rules. The methadone maintenance program has been used primarily to keep addicts off the street by controlling their drug intake. At the same time little has been done to alter the lives of junkies or to cure the cause of their addiction. Recent laws which make sentences of life imprisonment mandatory for those who sell specific quantities of drugs end up by jailing pushers who are themselves, primarily, victims of the drug and who take up selling to support their "habits." Meanwhile, the major drug dealers remain at large. While methadone maintenance may inhibit some criminal activities, such reductions in crime are being purchased at a high cost; as Heyman points out, the methadone maintenance program may ultimately provide a precedent for the utilization of drugs to tranquilize troublesome citizens.

Faced with mounting prison costs, with rebellious prisoners, and with demands for law and order, the temptation towards brutality and towards the use of extra-legal devices has embroiled this country in a nightmare of listening devices and computer programs that provide highly personal data to a variety of economic institutions but are not now open for inspection by the subjects themselves. A bill to protect citizens from illegal invasions of privacy by governing the collection and dissemination of such information is currently being readied for congressional debate. It calls for establishment of an agency comprised of ordinary citizens in addition to representatives of federal and state law enforcement groups which would remove such "surveillance" systems from the exclusive control of police and criminal authorities.

Reiss' "Police Brutality—Answers to Key Questions" examines the increasing hostility of ghetto residents towards police and attempts to assess the validity of charges that police mistreatment of all citizens is increasing. Reiss is well aware that police brutality is not a new phenomenon—its former victims were generally the new immigrants to our cities. Today its victims are to be found principally among the poor, and black and Puerto Rican minorities. Reiss points to the difficulties in actually getting information on police activities and raises the question of police accountability. Citizen pressure for police accountability has led to establishment of civilian review boards to act as watchdogs over police behavior, the development of police-community programs in which police and community representatives participate as equals, and training that emphasizes the professionalization of workers so that they act in accordance with professional goals rather than personal prejudice. Massive neighborhood protest of specific police action has often led to the punishment of specific police for specific crimes. Some communities are debating the possibility of establishing residency rules for civil servants as part of the movement towards decentralization and to encourage recruitment of police personnel from the community in which they serve.

If police brutality poisons the relationship between citizens and law enforcement officials, the brutality of prison guards acts similarly to create a social nightmare in most of our country's prisons. Zimbardo, in an experiment which has since become a classic, explored the effects of life in a total institution on both prisoners and their guards. College students were placed in a simulated prison and played the roles of prisoners and guards. Although the experiment was extremely brief, both prisoners and guards suffered severe pathological disturbances. The former lost all dignity and self-esteem, the latter grew more and more brutal and indifferent to the suffering of the prisoners. Analyzing the situation, Zimbardo concluded that total institutions, like prisons, through the assignment of labels and stigma, strip both guards and inmates of their essential humanity. Prisoners learn to become dependent and devious or brutal and indifferent—hardly traits that are of value to them in the normal world. Once begun, the brutality of the guards led to increasingly disturbed behavior among the prisoners; and this behavior in turn increased the punishment inflicted by the guards. The numerous riots, of which Attica was probably the most famous, represent attempts by prisoners to alter this useless and destructive system of mutual hatred and dependency. Yet, despite investigations and recommendations for reform, our prisons have changed very little.

The low visibility of prisons—their locations in relatively inaccessible places and their restrictions on the flow of information into and out of the buildings—makes it difficult to sustain public interest in prison reform. In some cases, groups of prisoners have organized their own self-help groups with the aid of sympathetic prison personnel—conducted their own public relations campaigns and brought their grievances to the public via television or other mass media.

Money for extensive prison reform is in short supply, and funds are not likely to be increased as long as we regard the criminal as a pariah who is responsible for his own misbehavior. Some pilot projects in operation offer partial solutions. Programs that concentrate on altering the social organization of prisons by changing physical layouts or eliminating uniforms that mark the social distinctions between guards and prisoners are aimed at decreasing prisoner dependency and breaking the vicious cycle of prison brutality. Introduction of a variety of education programs provide training in skills that can be utilized by convicts after their release. Some prisons are experimenting with sexual visitation rights for their inmates; still others copy Swedish models which allow families to remain together in highly structured "prison villages." The development of halfway houses which ease the transition from prison to the outside world gathered impetus as a result of the success of such groups in the drug culture scene of a few years ago. Attempts are being made to establish minimal wages for prison labor. Payments made to convicts could be used as partial restitution to their victims or to supply financial security for the released prisoner. Other solutions based upon epidemiological models aim at segregation of various criminal types; better categorization of crimes could reduce recidivism by segregating minor offenders more carefully from hardened criminals.

Long before humans invented the complex apparatus of criminal justice man dealt with crime in other ways. Crime was prevented rather than punished through an elaborate system of social sanctions and pressures. When these failed, the accused criminal was brought to trial and forced to pay restitution, in goods or labor, for his crime. To pay his debt he often had to call upon the aid of friends and relatives for loans of goods or labor. Predictably, the members of his social network worked hard to keep him from further criminal activities. Moreover, men involved in minor infractions were often required to pay for drinks and entertainment in a community festivity designed both to ease the feelings of the victim and reincorporate the criminal into the group. Preventing crime was a community affair. Restoration of small neighborhoods as part of planning strategies, and strengthened community ties could revive such forms of social control. Some communities are in fact experimenting with informal systems of local "courts" which mete out penalties and provide local support for minor offenders.

Perhaps if we can begin to realize that crime and criminals are produced by social institutions rather than continuing to regard the criminal as a deviant, we will turn our attention to prevention and rehabilitation instead of punishment. The biblical injunction of "an eye for an eye and a tooth for a tooth" may have represented an ethical advance in a society which often exacted a penalty of death for adultery or mandated loss of a hand for minor theft. Today, however, such beliefs are perhaps a greater threat to justice and the social order than the criminals whose activities they propose to control.

PHILIP G. ZIMBARDO

Pathology of Imprisonment

I was recently released from solitary confinement after being held therein for 37 months [months!]. A silent system was imposed upon me and to even whisper to the man in the next cell resulted in being beaten by guards, sprayed with chemical mace, blackjacked, stomped and thrown into a strip-cell naked to sleep on a concrete floor without bedding, covering, wash basin or even a toilet. The floor served as toilet and bed, and even there the silent system was enforced. To let a moan escape your lips because of the pain and discomfort . . . resulted in another beating. I spent not days, but months there during my 37 months in solitary. . . . I have filed every writ possible against the administrative acts of brutality. The state courts have all denied the petitions. Because of my refusal to let the things die down and forget all that happened during my 37 months in solitary . . . I am the most hated prisoner in [this] penitentiary, and called a "hard-core incorrigible."

Maybe I am an incorrigible, but if true, it's because I would rather die than to accept being treated as less than a human being. I have never complained of my prison sentence as being unjustified except through legal means of appeals. I have never put a knife on a guard's throat and demanded my release. I know that thieves must be punished and I don't justify stealing, even though I am a thief myself. But now I don't think I will be a thief when I am released. No, I'm not rehabilitated. It's just that I no longer think of becoming wealthy by stealing. I now only think of killing—killing those who have beaten me and treated me as if I were a dog. I hope and pray for the sake of my own soul and future life of freedom that I am able to overcome the bitterness and hatred which eats daily at my soul, but I know to overcome it will not be easy.

This eloquent plea for prison reform—for humane treatment of human beings, for the basic dignity that is the right of every American—came to me secretly in a letter from a prisoner who cannot be identified because he is still in a state correctional institution. He sent it to me because he read of an experiment I recently conducted at Stanford University. In an attempt to understand just what it means psychologically to be a prisoner or a prison guard, Craig Haney, Curt Banks, Dave Jaffe and I created our own prison. We carefully screened over 70 volunteers who answered an ad in a Palo Alto city newspaper and ended up with about two dozen young men who were selected to be part of this study. They were mature, emotionally stable, normal, intelligent college students from middle-class homes throughout the United States and Canada. They appeared to represent the cream of the crop of this generation. None had any criminal record and all were relatively homogeneous on many dimensions initially.

Half were arbitrarily designated as prisoners by a flip of a coin, the others as guards. These were the roles they were to play in our simulated prison. The guards were made aware of the potential seriousness and danger of the situation and their own vulnerability. They made up their own formal rules for maintaining law, order and respect, and were generally free to improvise new ones during their eight-hour, three-man shifts. The prisoners were unexpectedly picked up at their homes by a city policeman in a squad car, searched, handcuffed, fingerprinted, booked at the Palo Alto station house and taken blindfolded to our jail. There they were stripped, deloused, put into a uniform, given a number and put into a cell with two other prisoners where they expected to live for the next two weeks. The pay was good ($15 a day) and their motivation was to make money.

We observed and recorded on videotape the events that occurred in the prison, and we interviewed and tested the prisoners and guards at various points throughout the study. Some of the videotapes of the actual encounters between the prisoners and guards were seen on the NBC News feature "Chronolog" on November 26, 1971.

At the end of only six days we had to close down our mock prison because what we saw was frightening. It was no longer apparent to most of the subjects (or to us) where reality ended and their roles began. The majority had indeed become prisoners or guards, no longer able to clearly differentiate between role playing and self. There were dramatic changes in virtually every aspect of their behavior, thinking and feeling. In less than a week the experience of imprisonment undid (temporarily) a lifetime of learning; human values were suspended, self-concepts were challenged and the ugliest, most base, pathological side of human nature surfaced. We were horrified because we saw some boys (guards) treat others as if they were despicable animals, taking pleasure in cruelty, while other boys (prisoners) became servile, dehumanized robots who thought only of escape, of their own individual survival and of their mounting hatred for the guards.

We had to release three prisoners in the first four days because they had such acute situational traumatic reactions as hysterical crying, confusion in thinking and severe depression. Others begged to be paroled, and all but three were willing to forfeit all the money they had earned if they could be paroled. By then (the fifth day) they had been so programmed to think of themselves as prisoners that when their request for parole was denied, they returned docilely to their cells. Now, had they been thinking as college students acting in an oppressive experiment, they would have quit once they no longer wanted the $15 a day we used as our only incentive. However, the reality was not quitting an experiment but "being paroled by the parole board from the Stanford County Jail." By the last days, the earlier solidarity among the prisoners (systematically broken by the guards) dissolved into "each man for himself." Finally, when one of their fellows was put in solitary confinement (a small closet) for refusing to eat, the prisoners were given a choice by one of the guards: give up their blankets and the incorrigible prisoner would be let out, or keep their blankets and he would be kept in all night. They voted to keep their blankets and to abandon their brother.

About a third of the guards became tyrannical in their arbitrary use of power, in enjoying their control over other people. They were corrupted by the power of their roles and became quite inventive in their techniques of breaking the spirit of the prisoners and making them feel they were worthless. Some of the guards merely did their jobs as tough but fair correctional officers, and several were good guards from the prisoners' point of view since they did them small favors and were friendly. However, no good guard ever interfered with a command by any of the bad guards; they never intervened on the side of the prisoners, they never told the others to ease off because it was only an experiment, and they never even came to me as prison superintendent or experimenter in charge to complain. In part, they were good because the others were bad; they needed the others to help establish their own egos in a positive light. In a sense, the good guards perpetuated the prison more than the other guards because their own needs to be liked prevented them from disobeying or violating the implicit guards' code. At the same time, the act of befriending the prisoners created a social reality which made the prisoners less likely to rebel.

By the end of the week the experiment had become a reality, as if it were a Pirandello play directed by Kafka that just keeps going after the audience has left. The consultant for our prison, Carlo Prescott, an ex-convict with 16 years of imprisonment in California's jails, would get so depressed and furious each time he visited our prison, because of its psychological similarity to his experiences, that he would have to leave. A Catholic priest who was a former prison chaplain in Washington, D. C. talked to our prisoners after four days and said they were just like the other first-timers he had seen.

But in the end, I called off the experiment not because of the horror I saw out there in the prison yard, but because of the horror of realizing that *I* could have easily traded places with the most brutal guard or become the weakest prisoner full of hatred at being so powerless that I could not eat, sleep or go to the toilet without permission of the authorities. *I* could have become Calley at My Lai, George Jackson at San Quentin, one of the men at Attica or the prisoner quoted at the beginning of this article.

Individual behavior is largely under the control of social forces and environmental contingencies rather than personality traits, character, will power or other empirically unvalidated constructs. Thus we create an illusion of freedom by attributing more internal control to ourselves, to the individual, than actually exists. We thus underestimate the power and pervasiveness of situational controls over behavior because: a) they are often non-obvious and subtle, b) we can often avoid entering situations where we might be so controlled, c) we label as "weak" or "deviant" people in those situations who do behave differently from how we believe we would.

Each of us carries around in our heads a favorable self-image in which we are essentially just, fair, humane and understanding. For example, we could not imagine inflicting pain on others without much provocation or hurting people who had done nothing to us, who in fact were even liked by us. However, there is a growing body of social psychological research which underscores the conclusion derived from this prison study. Many people, perhaps the majority, can be made to do almost anything when put into psychologically compelling situations— regardless of their morals, ethics, values, attitudes, beliefs or personal convictions. My colleague, Stanley Milgram, has shown that more than 60 percent of the population will deliver what they think is a series of painful electric shocks to another person even after the victim cries for mercy, begs them to stop and then apparently passes out. The subjects complained that they did not want to inflict more pain but blindly obeyed the command of the authority figure (the experimenter) who said that they must go on. In my own research on violence, I have seen mild-mannered co-eds repeatedly give shocks (which they thought were causing pain) to another girl, a stranger whom they had rated very favorably, simply by being made to feel anonymous and put in a situation where they were expected to engage in this activity.

Observers of these and similar experimental situations never predict their outcomes and estimate that it is unlikely that they themselves would behave similarly. They can be so confident only when they were outside the situation. However, since the majority of people in these studies do act in non-rational, non-obvious ways, it follows that the majority of observers would also succumb to the social psychological forces in the situation.

With regard to prisons, we can state that the mere act of assigning labels to people and putting them into a situation where those labels acquire validity and meaning is sufficient to elicit pathological behavior. This pathology is not predictable from any available diagnostic indicators we have in the social sciences, and is extreme enough to modify in very significant ways fundamental attitudes and behavior. The prison situation, as presently arranged, is guaranteed to generate severe enough pathological reactions in both guards and prisoners as to debase their humanity, lower their feelings of self-worth and make it difficult for them to be part of a society outside of their prison.

For years our national leaders have been pointing to the enemies of freedom, to the fascist or communist threat to the American way of life. In so doing they have overlooked the threat of social anarchy that is building within our own country without any outside agitation. As soon as a person comes to the realization that he is being imprisoned by his society or individuals in it, then, in the best American tradition, he demands liberty and rebels, accepting death as an alternative. The third alternative, however, is to allow oneself to become a good prisoner—docile, cooperative, uncomplaining, conforming in thought and complying in deed.

Our prison authorities now point to the militant agitators who are still vaguely referred to as part of some communist plot, as the irresponsible, incorrigible troublemakers. They imply that there would be no trouble, riots, hostages or deaths if it weren't for this small band of bad prisoners. In other words, then, everything would return to "normal" again in the life of our nation's prisons if they could break these men.

The riots in prison are coming from within—from within every man and woman who refuses to let the system turn them into an object, a number, a thing or a no-thing. It is not communist inspired, but inspired by the spirit of American freedom. No man wants to be enslaved. To be powerless, to be subject to the arbitrary exercise of power, to not be recognized as a human being is to be a slave.

To be a militant prisoner is to become aware that the physical jails are but more blatant extensions of the forms of social and psychological oppression experienced daily in the nation's ghettos. They are trying to awaken the conscience of the nation to the ways in which the American ideals are being perverted, apparently in the name of justice but actually under the banner of apathy, fear and hatred. If we do not listen to the pleas of the prisoners at Attica to be treated like human beings, then we have all become brutalized by our priorities for property rights over human rights. The consequence will not only be more prison riots but a loss of all those ideals on which this country was founded.

The public should be aware that they own the prisons and that their business is failing. The 70 percent recidivism rate and the escalation in severity of crimes committed by graduates of our prisons are evidence that current prisons fail to rehabilitate the inmates in any positive way. Rather, they are breeding grounds for hatred of the establishment, a hatred that makes every citizen a target of violent assault. Prisons are a bad investment for us taxpayers. Until now we have not cared, we have turned over to wardens and prison authorities the

unpleasant job of keeping people who threaten us out of our sight. Now we are shocked to learn that their management practices have failed to improve the product and instead turn petty thieves into murderers. We must insist upon new management or improved operating procedures.

The cloak of secrecy should be removed from the prisons. Prisoners claim they are brutalized by the guards, guards say it is a lie. Where is the impartial test of the truth in such a situation? Prison officials have forgotten that they work for us, that they are only public servants whose salaries are paid by our taxes. They act as if it is their prison, like a child with a toy he won't share. Neither lawyers, judges, the legislature nor the public is allowed into prisons to ascertain the truth unless the visit is sanctioned by authorities and until all is prepared for their visit. I was shocked to learn that my request to join a congressional investigating committee's tour of San Quentin and Soledad was refused, as was that of the news media.

There should be an ombudsman in every prison, not under the pay or control of the prison authority, and responsible only to the courts, state legislature and the public. Such a person could report on violations of constitutional and human rights.

Guards must be given better training than they now receive for the difficult job society imposes upon them. To be a prison guard as now constituted is to be put in a situation of constant threat from within the prison, with no social recognition from

the society at large. As was shown graphically at Attica, prison guards are also prisoners of the system who can be sacrificed to the demands of the public to be punitive and the needs of politicians to preserve an image. Social scientists and business administrators should be called upon to design and help carry out this training.

The relationship between the individual (who is sentenced by the courts to a prison term) and his community must be maintained. How can a prisoner return to a dynamically changing society that most of us cannot cope with after being out of it for a number of years? There should be more community involvement in these rehabilitation centers, more ties encouraged and promoted between the trainees and family and friends, more educational opportunities to prepare them for returning to their communities as more valuable members of it than they were before they left.

Finally, the main ingredient necessary to effect any change at all in prison reform, in the rehabilitation of a single prisoner or even in the optimal development of a child is caring. Reform must start with people—especially people with power—caring about the well-being of others. Underneath the toughest, society-hating convict, rebel or anarchist is a human being who wants his existence to be recognized by his fellows and who wants someone else to care about whether he lives or dies and to grieve if he lives imprisoned rather than lives free.

FURTHER READING

"Interpersonal Dynamics in a Simulated Prison" by C. Banks, C. Haney, and P. G. Zimbardo, *International Journal of Criminology and Penology 1* (1973): 69–97.

Asylums by Erving Goffman (Garden City, N.Y.: Anchor, 1961). Provides insights into the effect of total institutions on behavior and personality.

"The Socialization into Criminality: On Becoming a Prisoner and a Guard" by C. Haney and P. G. Zimbardo in *Issues of Law and Justice for Legal Socialization* edited by J. Tapp (in press).

"The Mock Ward: A Study in Simulation" by N. J. Orlando in *Behavior Disorders: Perspectives and Trends* edited by O. Milton and R. G. Wahler (Philadelphia: Lippincott, 1973).

"Six Characters in Search of an Author" by L. Pirandello in *Naked Masks: Five Plays* (New York: Dutton, 1952).

PAUL LERMAN

Delinquents Without Crimes

About 100 years ago, the state of New Jersey built a special correctional facility to save wayward girls from a life of crime and immorality. Over the years the ethnic and racial backgrounds of the institutionalized girls changed, the educational level of their cottage parent-custodians shifted upward, and the program of correction grew more humane. But the types of offenses that constitute the legal justification for their incarceration in the State Home for Girls have not changed, not appreciably.

The vast majority of the girls in the Home today, as in past years, were accused of misbehavior that would not be considered crimes if committed by adults. They were formally adjudicated and institutionalized as delinquents, but most of them have not committed real criminal acts. Over 80 percent of them in 1969 were institutionalized for the following misdeeds: running away from home, being incorrigible, ungovernable and beyond the control of parents, being truant, engaging in sexual relations, and becoming pregnant. Criminologists classify this mixture of noncriminal acts "juvenile status offenses," since only persons of a juvenile status can be accused, convicted and sentenced as delinquents for committing them. Juvenile status offenses apply to boys as well as girls, and they form the bases for juvenile court proceedings in all 50 states.

Most Americans are probably unaware that juveniles are subject to stricter laws than adults, and to more severe penalties for noncriminal acts than are many adults who commit felonies. This practice, so apparently antithetical to our national conceit of child-centeredness, began well before the Revolution. The Puritans of the Plymouth Bay Colony initiated the practice of defining and treating as criminal children who were "rude, stubborn, and unruly," or who behaved "disobediently and disorderly towards their parents, masters, and governors." In 1824, when the House of Refuge established the first American Juvenile correctional institution in New York City, the Board of Managers was granted

Crime and Punishment: Police, Criminals, and the Courts

explicit sanction by the state legislature to hold in custody and correct youths who were leading a "vicious or vagrant life," as well as those convicted of any crime. The first juvenile court statute, passed in Illinois in 1899, continued the tradition of treating juvenile status offenses as criminal by including this class of actions as part of the definition of "delinquency." Other states copied this legislative practice as they boarded the bandwagon of court reform.

My contention that juvenile status offenders are still handled through a *criminal* process will be disputed by many defenders of the current system who argue that the creation of the juvenile court marked a significant break with the past. They contend that juvenile courts were set up to deal with the child and his needs, rather than with his offense. In line with this benign aim, the offense was to be viewed as a symptom of a child's need for special assistance. The juvenile court was designed to save children—not punish them. Only "neglectful" parents were deemed appropriate targets of punishment.

Unfortunately, the laudable intentions of the founders of the court movement have yet to be translated into reality. The United States Supreme Court, in 1967, reached this conclusion; so, too, did the Task Force on Delinquency of the President's Commission on Law Enforcement and the Administration of Justice. Both governmental bodies ruled that juvenile court dispositions were, in effect, sentences that bore a remarkable resemblance to the outcomes of adult criminal proceedings. The Supreme Court was appalled at the idea that 15-year-old Gerald Gault could be deprived of his liberty for up to six years without the benefits of due process of law found in adult courts. The majority was persuaded that the consequences of judicial decisions should be considered, not just the ideals of the founders of the juvenile court.

Since the Supreme Court ruling in *Gault v. Arizona*, there has been increased concern and debate over the introduction of legal counsel and minimal procedural rights in the operation of the juvenile court. The preoccupation with legal rights in the courtroom has, however, obscured the fact that the sociolegal boundaries of delinquency statutes were unaffected by *Gault*. Nevertheless, some revision of the laws has been undertaken by the states, at least since 1960 when the Second United Nations Congress on the Prevention of Crime and the Treatment of Offenders recommended that juveniles should not be prosecuted as delinquents for behavior which, if exhibited by adults, would not be a matter of legal concern.

One state, New York, even approached a technical compliance with the United Nations standard. In New York, juvenile status offenders are adjudicated with a separate petition alleging a "person in need of supervision" (PINS); traditional criminal offenses use a petition that alleges "delinquency." However, true to American tradition, both types of petitioned young people are locked up in the same detention facilities and reform schools. One of the most "progressive" juvenile court laws in the country was initially enacted with restrictions on mixing, but this was soon amended to permit the change to be merely semantic, not substantive. Besides New York, six other states have amended their juvenile codes to establish a distinctive labeling procedure to distinguish criminal and noncriminal acts. Each of these states (California, Illinois, Kansas, Colorado, Oklahoma and Vermont) has banned *initial* commitment to

juvenile reformatories of children within the noncriminal jurisdiction of the court. Whether this ban will be continued in practice (and in the statutes) is uncertain. Meanwhile, young people can still be mixed in detention facilities, transfers to reformatories are technically possible, and subsequent commitments to delinquent institutions are apparently permitted. In addition, it is doubtful whether the public (including teachers and prospective employers) distinguishes between those "in need of supervision" and delinquents.

The Police as Dutch Uncles

If the letter and spirit of American juvenile statutes were rigorously enforced, our delinquency rates and facilities would be in even deeper trouble than they are today. For few American youth would reach adulthood without being liable to its stern proscriptions. However, mitigating devices are used to avoid further overcrowding court dockets and institutions, and to demonstrate that parents and enforcement officials can be humane and child-centered. Adult authorities are permitted to exercise discretionary behavior in processing actions by official petitions. The American system is notorious for its widespread use of unofficial police and judicial recording and supervision of juveniles, whether status offenders or real delinquents. As a matter of historical fact, the hallmark of the American system is the intriguing combination of limitless scope of our delinquency statutes and enormous discretion granted in their enforcement and administration. Our statutes appear to reflect the image of the stern Puritan father, but our officials are permitted to behave like Dutch uncles—if they are so inclined.

Discretionary decision making by law enforcement officials has often been justified on the grounds that it permits an "individualization" of offenders, as well as for reasons of pragmatic efficiency. While this may be true in some cases, it is difficult to read the historical record and not conclude that many juvenile status actions could have been defined as cultural differences and childhood play fads, as well as childhood troubles with home, school and sex. Using the same broad definition of delinquency, reasonable adults have differed—and continue to differ—over the sociolegal meaning of profanity, smoking, drinking, sexual congress, exploring abandoned buildings, playing in forbidden places, idling, hitching rides on buses, trucks and cars, sneaking into shows and subways and so forth. While many judgments about the seriousness of these offenses may appear to be based on the merits of the individual case, delinquency definitions, in practice, employ shifting cultural standards to distinguish between childhood troubles, play fads and neighborhood differences. Today, officials in many communities appear more tolerant of profanity and smoking than those of the 1920s, but there is continuing concern regarding female sexuality, male braggadocio and disrespect of adult authority. In brief, whether or not a youth is defined as delinquent may depend on the era, community and ethnic status of the official—as well as the moral guidelines of individual law enforcers.

National studies of the prevalence of the problem are not readily available. However, we can piece together data that indicate that the problem is not inconsequential. A conservative estimate, based upon analysis of national juvenile court statistics compiled by the United States Children's Bureau, indicates that juvenile status crimes comprise about 25 percent of the children's cases initially appearing before juvenile courts on a formal petition. About one out of every five boys' delinquency petitions and over one-half of all girls' cases are based on charges for which an adult would not be legally liable ever to appear in court.

The formal petitions have an impact on the composition of juvenile facilities, as indicated by the outcomes of legal processing. A review of state and local detention facilities disclosed that 40 to 50 percent of the cases in custody, pending dispositional hearings by judges, consisted of delinquents who had committed no crimes. A study of nearly 20 correctional institutions in various parts of the country revealed that between 25 and 30 percent of their resident delinquent population consisted of young people convicted of a juvenile status offense.

The figures cited do not, however, reveal the number of youths that are treated informally by the police and the courts. Many young people are released with their cases recorded as "station adjustments"; in a similar fashion, thousands of youths are informally dealt with at court intake or at an unofficial court hearing. Even though these cases are not formally adjudicated, unofficial records are maintained and can be used against the children if they have any future run-ins with the police or courts. The number of these official, but nonadjudicated, contacts is difficult to estimate, since our requirements for social bookkeeping are far less stringent than our demands for financial accountability.

One careful study of police contacts in a middle-sized city, cited approvingly by a task force of the President's Commission on Law Enforcement and the Administration of Justice, disclosed that the offense that ranked highest as a delinquent act was "incorrigible, runaway"; "disorderly conduct" was second; "contact suspicion, investigation, and information" ranked third; and "theft" was a poor fourth. In addition to revealing that the police spend a disproportionate amount of their time attending to noncriminal offenses, the study also provides evidence that the problem is most acute in low-income areas of the city. This kind of finding could probably be duplicated in any city—large, small or middle-sized—in the United States.

Legal Treatment of Delinquents without Crimes

A useful way of furthering our understanding of the American approach to dealing with delinquents without crimes is provided by comparing judicial decisions for different types of offenses. This can be done by reanalyzing recent data reported by the Children's Bureau, classifying offenses according to their degree of seriousness. If we use standard FBI terminology, the most serious crimes can be labeled "Part I" and are: homicide, forcible rape, armed robbery, burglary, aggravated assault and theft of more than $50. All other offenses that would be crimes if committed by an adult, but are less serious, can be termed "all other adult types" and labeled "Part II." The third type of offenses, the least serious, are those acts that are "juvenile status offenses." By using these classifications, data reported to the Children's Bureau by the largest cities are reanalyzed to provide the information depicted in the table. Three types of decisions are compared in this analysis: 1) whether or not an official petition is drawn after a complaint has been made; 2) whether or not the juvenile is found guilty, if brought before the court on an official petition; and 3) whether or not the offender is placed or committed to an institution, if convicted. The rates for each decision level are computed for each of the offense classifications.

Disposition of Juvenile Cases at Three Stages in the Judicial Process
19 of the 30 Largest Cities, 1965.

	Part I (Most Serious Adult Offenses)	Part II (All Other Adult Offenses)	Juvenile Status Offenses
% Court Petition after complaint	57% N=(37.420)	33% (52,862)	42% (33,046)
% Convicted — if brought into court	92% N=(21,386)	90% (17,319)	94% (13,857)
% Placed or Committed — if convicted	23% N=(19,667)	18% (15,524)	26% (12,989)

The table discloses a wide difference between offense classifications at the stage of deciding whether to draw up an official petition (57 percent versus 33 percent and 42 percent). Part I youth are far more likely to be brought into court on a petition, but juvenile status offenders are processed at a higher rate than all other adult types. At the conviction stage the differences are small, but the juvenile status offenders are found guilty more often. At the critical decision point, commitment to an institution, the least serious offenders are more likely to be sent away than are the two other types.

It is apparent that juvenile justice in America's large cities can mete out harsher dispositions for youth who have committed no crimes than for those who violate criminal statutes. Once the petitions are drawn up, juvenile judges appear to function as if degree of seriousness is not an important criterion of judicial decision making. If different types of offenders were sent to different types of institutions, it might be argued that the types of sentences actually varied. In fact, however, all three offender types are generally sent to the same institutions in a particular state—according to their age and sex—for an indeterminate length of time.

Length of Institutionalization

If American juvenile courts do not follow one of the basic components of justice—matching the degree of punishment with the degree of social harm—perhaps the correctional institutions themselves function differently. This outcome is unlikely, however, since the criteria for leaving institutions are not based on the nature of the offense. Length of stay is more likely to be determined by the adjustment to institutional rules and routine, the receptivity of parents or guardians to receiving the children back home, available bed space in cottages and the current treatment ideology. Juvenile status offenders tend to have more family troubles and may actually have greater difficulty in meeting the criteria for release than their delinquent peers. The result is that the delinquents without crimes probably spend more time in institutions designed for delinquent youth than "real" delinquents. Empirical support for this conclusion emerges from a special study of one juvenile jurisdiction, the Manhattan borough of New York City. In a pilot study that focused on a random sample of officially adjudicated male cases appearing in Manhattan Court in 1963, I gathered data on the range, median and average length of stay for boys sent to institutions. In New York, as noted earlier, juvenile status youth are called "PINS" (persons in need of supervision), so I use this classification in comparing this length of institutionalization with that of "delinquents."

The range of institutional stay was two to 28 months for delinquents and four to 48 months for PINS boys; the median was nine months for delinquents and 13 months for PINS; and the average length of stay was 10.7 months for delinquents and 16.3 months for PINS. Regardless of the mode of measurement, it is apparent that institutionalization was proportionately longer for boys convicted and sentenced for juvenile status offenses than for juveniles convicted for criminal-type offenses.

These results on length of stay do not include the detention period, the stage of correctional processing prior to placement in an institution. Analyses of recent detention figures for all five boroughs of New York City revealed the following patterns: 1) PINS boys and girls are more likely to be detained than are delinquents (54 to 31 percent); and 2) once PINS youth are detained they are twice as likely to be detained for more than 30 days than are regular delinquents (50 to 25 percent). It is apparent that juvenile status offenders who receive the special label of "persons in need of supervision" tend to spend more time in custodial facilities at *all* stages of their correctional experience than do delinquents.

Social Characteristics of Offenses and Offenders

The offenses that delinquents without crimes are charged with do not involve a clear victim, as is the case in classical crimes of theft, robbery, burglary and assault. Rather, they involve young people who are themselves liable to be victimized for having childhood troubles or growing up differently. Three major categories appear to be of primary concern: behavior at home, behavior at school and sexual experimentation. "Running away," "incorrigibility," "ungovernability" and "beyond the control of parental supervision" refer to troubles with parents, guardians or relatives. "Growing up in idleness," "truanting" and creating "disturbances" in classrooms refer to troubles with teachers, principals, guidance counselors and school routines. Sexual relations as "minors" and out-of-wedlock pregnancy reflect adult concern with the act and consequences of precocious sexual experimentation. In brief, juvenile status offenses primarily encompass the problems of growing up.

Certain young people in American society are more likely to have these types of troubles with adults: girls, poor youth, rural migrants to the city, underachievers and the less sophisticated. Historically, as well as today, a community's more disadvantaged children are most likely to have their troubles defined as "delinquent." In the 1830s the sons and daughters of Irish immigrants were over-represented in the House of Refuge, the nation's first

juvenile correctional institution. In 1971 the sons and daughters of black slum dwellers are disproportionately dealt with as delinquents for experiencing problems in "growing up."

Unlike regular delinquents, juvenile status offenders often find a parent, guardian, relative or teacher as the chief complainant in court. Since juvenile courts have traditionally employed family functioning and stability as primary considerations in rendering dispositions, poor youth with troubles are at a distinct disadvantage compared to their delinquent peers. Mothers and fathers rarely bring their children to courts for robbing or assaulting nonfamily members; however, if their own authority is challenged, many parents are willing to use the power of the state to correct their offspring. In effect, many poor and powerless parents cooperate with the state to stigmatize and punish their children for having problems in growing up.

At least since *Gault*, the system of juvenile justice has been undergoing sharp attacks by legal and social critics. Many of these have pertinence for the processing and handling of juvenile status offenders. The current system has been criticized for the following reasons:

☐ The broad scope of delinquency statutes and juvenile court jurisdictions has permitted the coercive imposition of middle-class standards of child rearing.

☐ A broad definition has enlarged the limits of discretionary authority so that virtually any child can be deemed a delinquent if officials are persuaded that he needs correction.

☐ The presence of juvenile status offenses, as part of the delinquency statutes, provides an easier basis for convicting and incarcerating young people because it is difficult to defend against the vagueness of terms like "incorrigible" and "ungovernable."

☐ The mixing together of delinquents without crimes and real delinquents in detention centers and reform schools helps to provide learning experiences for the non-delinquents on how to become real delinquents.

☐ The public is generally unaware of the differences between "persons in need of supervision" and youths who rob, steal and assault, and thereby is not sensitized to the special needs of status offenders.

☐ Statistics on delinquency are misleading because we are usually unable to differentiate how much of the volume reflects greater public and official concern regarding home, school and sex problems, and how much is actual criminal conduct by juveniles.

☐ Juvenile status offenses do not constitute examples of social harm and, therefore, should not even be the subject of criminal-type sanctions.

☐ Juvenile institutions that house noncriminal offenders constitute the state's human garbage dump for taking care of all kinds of problem children, especially the poor.

☐ Most policemen and judges who make critical decisions about children's troubles are ill equipped to understand their problems or make sound judgments on their behalf.

☐ The current correctional system does not rehabilitate these youths and is therefore a questionable approach.

Two Unintended Consequences

The Supreme Court in *Gault* found that the juvenile court of Arizona—and by implication the great majority of courts—was procedurally unfair. The court explicitly ruled out any consideration of the substantive issues of detention and incarceration. It may have chosen to do so because it sincerely believed that the soundest approach to ensuring substantive justice is making certain that juveniles are granted the constitutional safeguards of due process: the right to confront accusers and cross-examine, the right to counsel, the right to written charges and prior notice and the right against self-incrimination. Nevertheless, the inclusion of juvenile status offenders as liable to arrest, prosecution, detention and incarceration probably promotes the criminalization of disadvantaged youth. Earlier critics have indicated that incorrigible boys and girls sent to reform schools learn how to behave as homosexuals, thieves, drug users and burglars. But what is the impact at the community level, where young people initially learn the operational meaning of delinquency? From the child's point of view, he learns that occurrences that may be part of his daily life—squabbles at home, truancy and sexual precocity—are just as delinquent as thieving, robbing and assaulting. It must appear that nearly anyone he or she hangs around with is not only a "bad" kid but a delinquent one as well. In fact, there are studies that yield evidence that three-quarters of a generation of slum youth, ages ten to 17, have been officially noted as "delinquent" in a police or court file. It seems reasonable to infer that many of these records contain official legal definitions of essentially noncriminal acts that are done in the family, at school and with peers of the opposite sex.

It would be strange indeed if youth did not define themselves as "bad cats"—just as the officials undoubtedly do. It would be strange, too, if both the officials and the young people (and a segment of their parents) did not build on these invidious definitions by expecting further acts of "delinquency." As children grow older, they engage in a more consistent portrayal of their projected identity—and the officials dutifully record further notations to an expected social history of delinquency. What the officials prophesy is fulfilled in a process that criminalizes the young and justifies the prior actions of the official gatekeepers of the traditional system. Our societal responses unwittingly compound the problem we ostensibly desire to prevent and control—real delinquent behavior.

In the arena of social affairs it appears that negative consequences are more likely to occur when there is a large gap in status, power and resources between the "savers" and those to be "saved." Evidently, colonial-type relationships, cultural misunderstandings and unrestrained coercion can often exacerbate problems, despite the best of intentions. Given this state of affairs, it appears likely that continual coercive intrusion by the state into the lives of youthful ghetto residents can continue to backfire on a large scale.

We have probably been compounding our juvenile problem ever since 1824 when the New York State Legislature granted the Board of Managers of the House of Refuge broad discretionary authority to intervene coercively in the lives of youth until they become 21 years of age—even if they had not committed any criminal acts. Generations of reformers, professionals and academics have been too eager to praise the philanthropic and rehabilitative intentions of our treatment centers toward poor kids in trouble—and insufficiently sensitive to the actual consequences of an unjust system that aids and abets the criminalization of youth.

Sophisticated defenders of the traditional system are aware of many of these criticisms. They argue that the intent of all efforts in the juvenile field is to help, not to punish, the child. To extend this help they are prepared to use the authority of the state to coerce children who might otherwise be unwilling to make use of existing agencies. Not all acts of juvenile misbehavior that we currently label "status offenses" are attributable to cultural differences. Many youngsters do, in fact, experience troubles in growing up that should be of concern to a humane society. The fundamental issue revolves on how that concern can be expressed so as to yield the maximum social benefits and the minimum social costs. Thus, while the consequences of criminalizing the young and perpetuating an unjust system of juvenile justice should be accorded greater recognition than benign intentions, it would be a serious mistake to propose an alternative policy that did not incorporate a legitimate concern for the welfare of children.

New Policy Perspectives

The issue is worth posing in this fashion because of a recent policy proposal advanced by the President's Commission on Law Enforcement and the Administration of Justice. The commission suggested that "serious consideration should be given complete elimination from the court's jurisdiction of conduct illegal only for a child. Abandoning the possibility of coercive power over a child who is acting in a seriously self-destructive way would mean losing the opportunity of reclamation in a few cases."

Changing delinquency statutes and the jurisdictional scope of the juvenile court to exclude conduct illegal only for a child would certainly be a useful beginning. However, the evidence suggests that the cases of serious self-destructiveness are not "few" in number, and there is reason to believe that many adjudicated and institutionalized young people do require some assistance from a concerned society. By failing to suggest additional policy guidelines for providing the necessary services in a *civil* context, the commission advanced only half a policy and provided only a limited sense of historical perspective.

Traditional American practices towards children in trouble have not been amiss because of our humanitarian concern, but because we coupled this concern with the continuation of prior practices whereby disliked behavior was defined and treated as a criminal offense (that is, delinquent). Unfortunately, our concern has often been linked to the coercive authority of the police powers of the state. The problems of homeless and runaway youths, truants, sex experimenters and others with childhood troubles could have been more consistently defined as *child welfare* problems. Many private agencies did emerge to take care of such children, but they inevitably left the more

Crime and Punishment: Police, Criminals, and the Courts

difficult cases for the state to service as "delinquents." In addition, the private sector never provided the services to match the concern that underlay the excessive demand. The problem of the troublesome juvenile status offender has been inextricably linked to: 1) our failure to broaden governmental responsibility to take care of *all* child welfare problems that were not being cared for by private social agencies; and 2) our failure to hold private agencies accountable for those they did serve with public subsidies. We permitted the police, courts and correctional institutions to function as our residual agency for caring for children in trouble. Many state correctional agencies have become, unwittingly, modern versions of a poorhouse for juveniles. Our *systems* of child welfare and juvenile justice, not just our legal codes, are faulty.

The elimination of juvenile status offenses from the jurisdiction of the juvenile court would probably create an anomalous situation in juvenile jurisprudence if dependency and neglect cases were not also removed. It would be ironic if we left two categories that were clearly noncriminal within a delinquency adjudicatory structure. If they were removed, as they should be, then the juvenile court would be streamlined to deal with a primary function: the just adjudication and disposition of young people alleged to have committed acts that would be criminal if enacted by an adult. Adherence to this limited jurisdiction would aid the court in complying with recent Supreme Court rulings, for adversary proceedings are least suited to problems involving family and childhood troubles.

If these three categories were removed from the traditional system, we would have to evolve a way of thinking about a new public organization that would engage in a variety of functions: fact finding, hearing of complaints, regulatory dispositions and provision of general child care and family services. This new public agency could be empowered to combine many of the existing functions of the court and child welfare departments, with one major prohibition: transfers of temporary custody of children would have to be voluntary on the part of parents, and all contested cases would have to be adjudicated by a civil court. This prohibition would be in harmony with the modern child welfare view of keeping natural families intact, and acting otherwise only when all remedial efforts have clearly failed.

We have regulatory commissions in many areas of social concern in America, thereby sidestepping the usual judicial structure. If there is a legitimate concern in the area of child and family welfare, and society wants to ensure the maintenance of minimum services, then legally we can build on existing systems and traditions to evolve a new kind of regulatory service commission to carry out that end. To ensure that the critical legal rights of parents and children are protected, civil family courts—as in foster and adoption cases—would be available for contest and appeal. However, to ensure that the agencies did not become bureaucratic busybodies, additional thought would have to be given to their policy-making composition, staffing and location.

A major deficiency of many regulatory agencies in this country is that special interests often dominate the administration and proceedings, while affected consumers are only sparsely represented. To ensure that the residents most affected by proposed family and child welfare boards had a major voice in the administration and proceedings, they could be set up with a majority of citizen representatives (including adolescents). In addition, they could be decentralized to function within the geographical boundaries of areas the size of local elementary or junior high school districts. These local boards would be granted the legal rights to hire lay and professional staff, as well as to supervise the administration of hearings and field services.

The setting up of these local boards would require an extensive examination of city, county and state child welfare services to ensure effective cooperation and integration of effort. It is certainly conceivable that many existing family and child welfare services, which are generally administered without citizen advice, could also be incorporated into the activities of the local boards. The problems to be ironed out would of course be substantial, but the effort could force a reconceptualization of local and state responsibilities for providing acceptable, humane and effective family and child welfare services on a broad scale.

Citizen Involvement

The employment of interested local citizens in the daily operation of family and child welfare services is not a totally new idea. Sweden has used local welfare boards to provide a range of services to families and children, including the handling of delinquency cases. While we do not have to copy their broad jurisdictional scope or underrepresentation of blue-collar citizens, a great deal can be learned from this operation. Other Scandinavian countries also use local citizen boards to deal with a range of delinquency offenses. Informed observers indicate that the nonlegal systems in Scandinavia are less primitive and coercive. However, it is difficult to ascertain whether this outcome is due to cultural differences or to the social invention that excludes juvenile courts.

There exist analogues in this country for the use of local citizens in providing services to children in trouble. In recent years there has been an upsurge in the use of citizen-volunteers who function as house parents for home detention facilities, probation officers and intake workers. Besides this use of citizens, New Jersey, for example, has permitted each juvenile court jurisdiction to appoint citizens to Judicial Conference Committees, for the purpose of informally hearing and handling delinquency cases. Some New Jersey counties process up to 50 percent of their court petitions through this alternative to adjudication. All these programs, however, operate under the direct supervision and jurisdiction of the county juvenile court judges, with the cooperation of the chief probation officers. It should be possible to adapt these local innovations to a system that would be independent of the coercive aspects of even the most benign juvenile court operation.

Opposition to Innovation

Quite often it is the powerful opposition of special interest groups, rather than an inability to formulate new and viable proposals for change, that can block beneficial social change. Many judges, probation workers, correction officers, as well as religious and secular child care agencies, would strenuously oppose new social policies and alternatives for handling delinquents without crimes. Their opposition would certainly be understandable, since the proposed changes could have a profound impact on their work. In the process of limiting jurisdiction and altering traditional practices, they could lose status, influence and control over the use of existing resources. Very few interest groups suffer these kinds of losses gladly. Proponents of change should try to understand their problem and act accordingly. However, the differential benefits that might accrue to children and their families should serve as a reminder that the problems of youth and their official and unofficial adult caretakers are not always identical.

Experts' Claims

One proposal in particular can be expected to call forth the ire of these groups, and that is the use of citizens in the administration and provision of services in local boards. Many professional groups—psychiatrists, social workers, psychologists, group therapists and school guidance counselors—have staked out a claim of expertise for the treatment of any "acting out" behavior. The suggestion that citizens should play a significant role in offering assistance undermines that claim. In reply, the professionals might argue that experts—not laymen—should control, administer and staff any programs involving the remediation of childhood troubles. On what grounds might this kind of claim be reasonably questioned?

First, there is nothing about local citizens' control of child and family welfare activities that precludes the hiring of professionals for key tasks, and entrusting them with the operation of the board's program. Many private and public boards in the fields of correction and child welfare have functioned this way in the past.

Second, any claims about an expertise that can be termed a scientific approach to correction are quite premature. There does not now exist a clear-cut body of knowledge that can be ordered in a text or verbally transmitted that will direct any trained practitioner to diagnose and treat effectively such classic problems as truancy, running away and precocious sex experimentation. Unlike the field of medicine, there are no clear-cut prescriptions for professional behavior that can provide an intellectual rationale for expecting a remission of symptoms. There exist bits and pieces of knowledge and practical wisdom, but there is no correctional technology in any acceptable scientific sense.

Third, a reasonable appraisal of evaluations of current approaches to delinquents indicates that there are, in fact, no programs that can claim superiority. The studies do indicate that we can institutionalize far fewer children in treatment centers or reform schools without increasing the risks for individuals or communities; or, if we continue to use institutional programs, young people can be held for shorter periods of time without increasing the risk. The outcome of these appraisals provides a case for an expansion of humane child care activities—not for or against any specific repertoire of intervention techniques.

Fourth, many existing correctional programs are not now controlled by professionals. Untrained juvenile court judges are administratively responsible for detention programs and probation services in more than a majority of the

50 states. Many correctional programs have been headed by political appointees or nonprofessionals. And state legislatures, often dominated by rural legislators, have exercised a very strong influence in the permissible range of program alternatives.

Fifth, the professionalization of officials dealing with delinquent youth does not always lead to happy results. There are studies that indicate that many trained policemen and judges officially process and detain more young people than untrained officials, indicating that their definition of delinquency has been broadened by psychiatric knowledge. At this point in time, there is a distinct danger that excessive professionalization can lead to overintervention in the lives of children and their families.

Sixth, there is no assurance that professionals are any more responsive to the interests and desires of local residents than are untrained judges and probation officers. Citizens, sharing a similar life style and knowledgeable about the problems of growing up in a given community, may be in a better position to enact a *parens patrie* doctrine than are professionals or judges.

Seventh, in ghetto communities, reliance on professional expertise can mean continued dependence on white authority systems. Identification of family and child welfare boards as "our own" may compensate for any lack of expertise by removing the suspicion that any change of behavior by children and parents is for the benefit of the white establishment. The additional community benefits to be gained from caring for "our own" may also outweigh any loss of professional skills. The benefits accruing from indigenous control over local child welfare services would hold for other minority groups living in a discriminatory environment: Indians, Puerto Ricans, Mexicans, hillbillies and French Canadians.

Alternative Policy Proposals

The proposal to create family and child welfare boards to deal with juvenile status offenses may be appealing to many people. However, gaining political acceptance may be quite difficult, since the juvenile justice system would be giving up coercive power in an area that it has controlled for a long period of time. The proposal may appear reasonable, but it may constitute too radical a break with the past for a majority of state legislators. In addition, the interest groups that might push for it are not readily visible. Perhaps participants in the Women's Lib movement, student activists and black power groups might get interested in the issue of injustice against youth, but this is a hope more than a possibility. In the event of overwhelming opposition, there exist two policy proposals that might be more acceptable and could aid in the decriminalization of juvenile status offenses.

The two alternatives function at different ends of the traditional juvenile justice system. One proposal, suggested by the President's Task Force on Delinquency, would set up a Youth Service Bureau that would offer local field services and be operated by civil authorities as an alternative to formal adjudication; the second proposal, suggested by William Sheridan of the Department of Health, Education, and Welfare, would prohibit the mixing of juvenile status offenders and classic delinquents in the same institutions. The Youth Service Bureau would function after judicial disposition. Both proposals, separate or in concert, could aid in the decriminalization of our current practices.

However, both proposals would still leave open the possibility of stigmatization of youth who had committed no crimes. The Youth Service Bureau would provide an array of services at the community level, but the court would still have ultimate jurisdiction over its case load, and any competition over jurisdiction would probably be won by the traditional court system. The prohibition of mixing in institutions would, of course, not change the fact that young people were still being adjudicated in the same court as delinquents, even though they had committed no crimes. In addition, the proposal, as currently conceived, does not affect mixing in detention facilities. These limitations are evident in the statutes of states that have recently changed their definitions of "delinquency" (New York, California, Illinois, Colorado, Kansas, Oklahoma and Vermont).

Both proposals deserve support, but they clearly leave the traditional system intact. It is possible that Youth Service Bureaus could be organized with a significant role for citizen participation, thus paving the way for an eventual take-over of legal jurisdiction from the juvenile court for juvenile status offenses (and dependency and neglect cases, too). It is conceivable, too, that any prohibitions of mixing could lead to the increased placement of children in trouble in foster homes and group homes, instead of reform schools, and to the provision of homemaker services and educational programs for harried parents unable to cope with the problems of children. Both short-range proposals could, in practice, evolve a different mode of handling delinquents without crimes.

The adaptation of these two reasonable proposals into an evolutionary strategy is conceivable. But it is also likely they will just be added to the system, without altering its jurisdiction and its stigmatic practices. In the event this occurs, new reformers might entertain the radical strategy that some European countries achieved many years ago— removal of juvenile status offenders from the jurisdiction of the judicial-correctional system and their inclusion into the family and child welfare system.

New Definitions

What is the guarantee that young people will be serviced any more effectively by their removal from the traditional correctional system? The question is valid, but perhaps it underestimates the potency of social definitions. Children, as well as adults, are liable to be treated according to the social category to which they have been assigned. Any shift in the categorization of youth that yields a more positive image can influence such authorities as teachers, employers, military recruiters and housing authority managers. For there is abundant evidence that the stigma of delinquency can have negative consequences for an individual as an adult, as well as during childhood.

It is evident, too, that our old social definitions of what constitutes delinquency have led us to construct a system of juvenile justice that is quite unjust. By failing to make

reasonable distinctions and define them precisely, we not only treat juvenile status offenders more harshly but undermine any semblance of ordered justice for *all* illegal behavior committed by juveniles. Maintenance of existing jurisdictional and definitional boundaries helps to perpetuate an unjust system for treating children. That this unjust system may also be a self-defeating one that compounds the original problem should also be taken into account before prematurely concluding that a shift in social labeling procedures is but a minor reform.

We would agree, however, with the conclusion that a mere semantic shift in the social definition of children in trouble is not sufficient. The experience of New York in providing a social label of "person in need of supervision" (PINS)—without providing alternative civil modes for responding to this new distinction—indicates that reform can sometimes take the guise of "word magic." Children are often accused of believing in the intrinsic power of words and oaths; adults can play the game on an even larger scale.

We need alternative social resources for responding to our change in social definitions, if we are at all serious about dealing with the problem. Whether we are willing to pay the financial costs for these alternatives is, of course, problematic. While we have not conducted a financial cost-benefit analysis, it is conceivable that the old system might be cheaper, even though its social costs outweigh any social benefits. Whether we will be willing to tax ourselves to support a more reasonable and moral social policy may turn out to be a critical issue. Perceived in this manner, the problem of children in trouble is as much financial as it is political. This, too, is part of the American approach to juvenile status offenders.

FURTHER READING

Borderland of Criminal Justice: Essays in Law and Criminology by Frances A. Allen (Chicago: University of Chicago Press, 1964). Frequently cited by the U.S. Supreme Court in the *Gault* decision, this perceptive legal scholar examines the legal and social consequences of the American predeliction for attempting to criminalize social problems.

"Youthful Offenders" by R. Coles, *The New Republic* 12 (October 4, 1969).

After Conviction: A Review of the American Correction System by Ronald L. Goldfarb and Linda R. Singer (New York: Simon & Schuster, 1969).

Juvenile Court: Social Action and Legal Change: Revisions Within the Juvenile Court by Edwin M. Lemert (Chicago: Aldine, 1970).

Delinquency and Social Policy edited by Paul Lerman (New York: Praeger, 1970). Presents further evidence and discussion of injustice, ineffective corrections, police discretion, and other pertinent topics concerning adult behavior vis-à-vis youngsters.

The Child-Savers: The Invention of Delinquency by Anthony M. Platt (Chicago: University of Chicago Press, 1969).

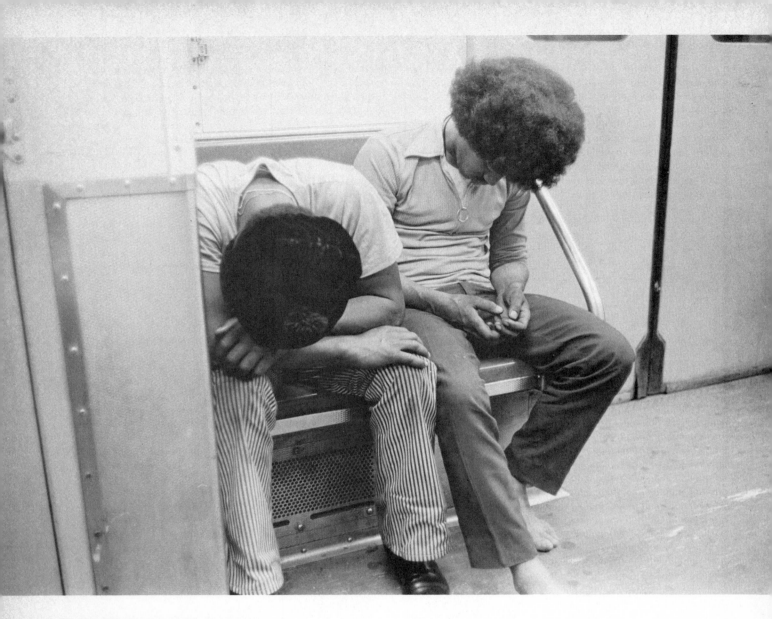

FLORENCE HEYMAN

Methadone Maintenance as Law and Order

The drug treatment business has entered the major leagues in the United States. It is now proposed that the federal government alone spend about $1 billion over the next three years in an effort to stem the tide of the urban drug crisis. Its major treatment approach will be the widespread use of methadone, a typically American answer to a large-scale American problem—the use of a synthetic chemical to cure a complex, socially rooted disease. Methadone has the benefit of being cheap and easy to administer, but it also is the basis for a new bureaucracy

with a whole new field in which to create a bureaucratic empire. For the addict it is a substitute addiction. Correctly administered it can be the beginning of a new life for him, but only if methadone is recognized as a first step in the treatment process instead of a final solution—a legal addiction to replace an illegal one.

Even a cursory examination of the Philadelphia Methadone Drug Treatment Program makes it clear that the potential for social rehabilitation for the addicts is not being explored. A careful reading of its literature also

Crime and Punishment: Police, Criminals, and the Courts

clearly shows that the descriptions of the program and the program itself parted company very early in the history of the clinic. Rather than a cooperative rehabilitative effort, there appears to be a silent war waged between clients and staff. The clinic setting is in a walled-off, barren and Kafkaesque section of a general hospital and a community health center. The addicts are impressed with the idea that they are social lepers who are to use the back entrance and stay away from people. They retaliate by stealing from the clinics that are supposed to be helping them, by cheating (using other drugs) and by dealing in drugs on the clinic grounds and even inside the clinic itself.

Since there are careers and reputations to be made in the drug treatment business, reports of successful treatment are a necessity for program directors. Despite the allocation of unheard-of sums in this field, there is fierce competition among local programs both for recognition and funding. It would be easy to dismiss the flaws in the Philadelphia program as well-intended mistakes and its reports of success as overenthusiasm. However, to do so would be to overlook the potential in the use of methadone as a means of social control.

While the aims of the program designers and directors are personal advancement and power, they just happen to coincide with the aims of social policy in dealing with the addict population. Addicts are a threat to the community because of the crimes they commit to support their habits. The drug dealers are a source of pervasive corruption of the entire police establishment. These conditions are what concern the community, and their amelioration is the measure that is used for judging the success of drug treatment programs.

Lowering the Crime Rate

What has occurred in Philadelphia fits into the model of social policy that is described by Martin Rein of MIT and Richard A. Cloward and Frances Fox Piven of Columbia University as the "compliance and achievement model." Their position is that no matter how humane these programs set out to be, they ultimately promote compliance and achievement but actually achieve only compliance. Seen in this context, the course of the Philadelphia program cannot be viewed as an accident. Instead says Rein:

> To define social policy as responsive to human need often reveals more rhetoric than reality and can contribute little to our understanding of the actual functioning of social policy in our society. The disparity between the intent and the performance is so apparent that it must be accepted not as an aberration but as a norm.

In fact the crime rate of the addict-patients in the Philadelphia Drug Treatment Program has been reduced sharply. However, the program only provides free drugs which means it addresses itself to only one aspect of the addict's problems. It does not attempt to treat what addiction represents to the addict: a way of life, an identity, excitement, activities which the addict calls "the hustle." To treat this and to attempt social rehabilitation would call for the establishment of a network of rehabilitative programs which are costly and do not exist at present.

While it's true that such programs cost less than addicts steal, they also require a social orientation in which addicts are considered as people and programs which are concerned with their welfare as well as that of the general community.

Measures of the success of such programs would deal with issues of social rehabilitation as well as reduced criminality. Methadone programs never address problems like the emptiness of the addicts' lives, their lack of personal identity, the absence of a sense of mastery and meaningfulness in their lives. The hustle and the negative junkie identity are the addict's way of meeting these problems. A drug treatment program must devise substitutes for these social-psychological disabilities as well as provide for controlled support of drug intake. The methadone program in Philadelphia does not even do the latter. And it measures success by reduced criminaltiy rate only.

Addicts as Expendable People

According to the 1971 *Public Health Service Bulletin*, the stated philosophy and aims of the federally funded drug treatment program should "consist of a full range of rehabilitative services. . . . Counselling, job retraining and the building of a new way of life must be combined with methadone maintenance treatment." The problem is not a lack of knowledge in this area. Rather, we need a basic philosophy which does not treat addicts as expendable people coupled with real opportunities for an exercise of the skills the addict learns.

To meet the urban drug crisis, the president convened the Task Force on Narcotics and Drug Abuse as part of his Commission on Law Enforcement and Administration of Justice. After reviewing all treatment programs and modalities, the Task Force did come up with an ideal program model which met the requirements for social rehabilitation insofar as it is a possibility for the individual addict. The report it published recognized a number of hard realities about the drug addiction problem. There are a large number of addicts who may never be able to get off drugs but who can be reintegrated into the society and lead more fulfilling lives. There is another group for which even this goal is impossible; they require drug maintenance as a primary treatment method. But in Philadelphia at present the use of methadone in a clinical setting—only the precondition for addict rehabilitation—is the major treatment approach and even that is not doing too well.

In the course of its review, the Task Force took particular note of the Dole-Nyswander methadone program in New York City. This program reports (as of March 1968) an 87 percent retention rate of its patients among its considerable successes. By retention rate Vincent Dole and Marie Nyswander meant that they had lost only 13 percent of the program's clients since it opened its doors in January of 1964. By "success" both the program and the Task Force do not necessarily mean abstinence from all narcotic drugs. They do mean social rehabilitation and a transfer of the addiction to methadone. Rehabilitation includes the ability to hold a job or go to school, to abstain from criminal activities and to assume and maintain personal and social relationships. In terms of accountability by the patient, the Dole-Nyswander program is outstanding: 55 percent of its patients never cheated (used drugs other than methadone) and only 15 percent of them continued to cheat but only sporadically.

The Dole-Nyswander program has consistently claimed outcomes far better than any other, including those which administer methadone. However, by its own account, it also has a patient population which is carefully selected and which cannot be compared to the average street addict. Of the first 1,007 persons interviewed for admission to the program, 35 percent were dropped for failing to meet admission criteria and another 5 percent did not return after the first interview. Data in its March 1968 review concern only the remaining 755 persons. A comparison of the Dole-Nyswander patients with street addicts shows the following:

	Dole-Nyswander Patients	New York City Register of Addicts
Mean Age:	33	28
Over 30:	68%	34%
Ethnic Composition		
White:	48%	25%
Negro:	33%	47%
Puerto Rican:	18%	27%

About half of both populations did not finish high school, but the highest number of years is in the Dole-Nyswander group. The pretreatment conviction rate of the Dole-Nyswander patients was 52 per hundred patient years for all offenses. The conviction rate during treatment was 5.4 per hundred patient years for all offenses, a reduction to a tenth of the former rate.

Older addicts (with a more stable home life, more years of education, more years of successful work experience prior to addiction and more marketable skills) and white addicts tend to do better in treatment programs, a fact not emphasized by the program publications even though Drs. Dole and Nyswander themselves have stated that their outcomes are not applicable to all addicts. There is a self-selection factor present in all programs (and among addicts who never seek treatment) as well as screening by program criteria which makes such generalizations suspect if not impossible.

The Commonwealth of Pennsylvania has some other concepts of what drug treatment programs ought to be like. Official guidelines were published in the summer of 1971, but the thinking that went into them appears to have been operating for a long time. The stated major objectives of methadone programs are 1) to evaluate the effect of methadone in the treatment and rehabilitation of drug dependent patients, 2) to protect the patients and society from the harmful effects of the drug (heroin), 3) to bring about the eventual withdrawal of patients from drug dependency and 4) to enable the patients to become productive citizens. There follows a list of persons who may not become patients in such programs which includes pregnant women and psychotic patients.

Objective number one reveals a basic misunderstanding about methadone. It has no rehabilitative or treatment value in itself but only blocks the effect of heroin. A dissocial person has as many problems on methadone as he does on heroin. The basic advantage of methadone is that it does not provide the euphoric high that heroin does. However, after the first few months or at most one year of heroin use, heroin no longer produces euphoria either. Another advantage of methadone is that it is somewhat less difficult to withdraw from if the goal of treatment is abstinence. But actually, it would be equally logical to treat addicts with regulated doses of heroin.

Objective number two is made more difficult to realize by the policy of not admitting addicts into hospitals as inpatients for the purpose of detoxification. Although the Philadelphia program has worked within this restriction, it is probably one of the major reasons it is failing to wean its clients off heroin. Objective number three cannot apply to all addicts across the board and runs counter to all considered opinion in the field. The Task Force noted that nothing is gained if one detoxifies a heroin addict only to have him reappear as an alcoholic skid row derelict. Without rehabilitative efforts these are the most likely alternatives for addicts. The aim is to reintegrate him into society whether or not he is using drugs. Objective number four, which calls for making the addict productive, is interesting because all drug treatment programs throughout the world use it as a rationale for treatment. What they do not mention is the existence of a market for the addict's productivity. At present, there is widespread unemployment among the population of the Philadelphia clinics. Aside from market considerations, the addict might be interested in development of any potential he may have, enjoying more fulfilling human relationships and feeling better about himself. These goals are not included in the program concept of the State of Pennsylvania.

The section barring pregnant women from the program is indefensible. One of the positive outcomes added to the Philadelphia program was the treatment of 25 pregnant women. Seventeen of them delivered last year at Philadelphia General Hospital with far fewer complications than addicted mothers not on the program. The babies were all withdrawn successfully and are being studied in a special project on infant feeding.

As for barring psychotic patients, under some definitions of that term at least half of the clinic's clients would not be admissible. Last year a survey of one satellite clinic revealed that over 50 percent of its population could be categorized as either borderline state, schizophrenic or depressive. The clinic administered methadone in combination with psychotropic drugs to maintain these individuals. Only 38 percent of them were employed. This is the group of patients for whom little enough is being done and who have very few options outside of hospitalization. To remove them from the program would increase the risk that they would require even costlier care in both human and economic terms. There is no reason, aside from bureaucratic regulations, why they should be ineligible for treatment.

The last section of the rules is titled "patient detoxification or processing." "Heroin use" say the rules, "should cease immediately." Inpatient detoxification should not exceed seven days and outpatient detoxification should not exceed six weeks.

There is no outpatient program in the United States that can return detoxified addicts to the community in either seven days or six weeks without expecting them to relapse almost immediately. It takes up to two weeks—in a hospital—for withdrawal symptoms to disappear. Since 1968, the Dole-Nyswander program has not attempted to detoxify patients because of the high failure rate.

The record of Lexington and Fort Worth which not only achieved inpatient abstinence but kept patients in the hospital for up to six months is a testimony to the futility of this approach. Both methadone and abstinence may be more appropriately considered preconditions for resocialization of the addict, not treatment modalities in themselves.

The issue of detoxification continues to plague the Philadelphia program. It undertook to detoxify patients on a large scale but by this year reported that only 4 percent of the patients are now in the program because of the large numbers of relapses. However, it published a paper on its detoxification efforts in which it claimed success with 25 percent of the patients. Although it has long since been demonstrated that these patients either never were or did not remain off narcotics, brochures describing the program (distributed to drug educators and clinicians) and articles about the program still make this false claim. The program is presently under fire from state and federal agencies for its failure.

Most recently, Dole has stated that in the proposed large-scale national methadone program there may be a dropout rate as high as 25 percent. If that program is as deficient as the one in Philadelphia that would be a most optimistic figure.

A small test program directed by Alfred M. Freedman at Metropolitan Hosptal in New York City has had only a 55 percent success rate with methadone. The program consists of intensive social rehabilitation and pharmacological intervention. It says nothing about wishing to make addicts productive citizens or helping them understand the underlying pathology which motivates the addiction. It seeks, instead, to restore them to a more fulfilling and satisfying life.

Morris E. Chafetz, writing on alcoholism, reviewed the literature over an 11 year span and concluded "We are unable to form a conclusive opinion as to the value of the psychotherapeutic method in the treatment of alcoholism." A review of the literature written 25 years earlier said the same thing. Jonathan O. Cole in reviewing all the drug treatment modalities involving some form of psychotherapy concluded that there was no evidence favoring the use of one over another (individual, group, milieu, aggressive case work). Dole, who holds the view that addicts resemble the base population from which they are drawn, has little use for psychotherapy in treatment programs. His own program does not use it as a matter of choice, although facilities are available and each patient is interviewed on intake by a psychiatrist. Chafetz calls addiction a preverbal disorder which requires a doing rather than a talking therapy. Addicts, he notes "have a peculiar sensitivity to rejection" and low self-esteem. Programs then should be devised to improve this self-image, not to help the addict explore it.

The psychological profiles of alcoholics, psychedelic drug users and heroin addicts as measured by the widely used psychological test, the MMPI (Minnesota Multiphasic Personality Inventory), are very similar. The peaks may be higher in MMPI profiles of heroin addicts than psychedelic drug users, but both will be very high on scores for depression and psychopathic personality. It is the latter score which rules out any therapy which is based on establishing a meaningful dyadic relationship with a therapist. Stephen Pittel and his group are developing a theory that ego defects are basic to addiction. This concept of the addict as lacking inner resources does not encourage the use of a therapy which involves talking about or understanding one's problems. Pittel's population was 250 subjects, 85 percent of whom were of middle-class origin and presumably more verbally oriented than those seen in heroin or alcohol treatment programs. Yet he felt that the use of a talking therapy was a waste of time and effort.

A doing therapy (one based on activities and skill development) is recommended not only in the case of addiction, but in a wider range of disorders manifested by antisocial behavior. In every case these analyses and recommendations point to programs which are based not on self-understanding but on ego-building and ego-satisfying experiences. The addict, after all, is often taking drugs to deaden those conflicts and thoughts which therapy might expose. It is not that he has no psychiatric disability; but it is a kind which requires covering in order to diminish his potential anxiety and the re-creation of a real personality with real mastery in lieu of the synthetic and fragile self he presents. Cole, in reviewing existing programs, noted:

Most addicts do not cooperate well in formal, interview type dynamic therapy . . . but have a large array of needs . . . no money, no place to live, no marketable skills . . . little motivation to solve any of these problems and little trust in professional therapists.

A doing therapy need not involve a therapeutic clinic as demonstrated by the 75 percent of Dole-Nyswander patients who are at work or in school. It does address the problem of removing the addict from the streets where he used to hang out with fellow addicts and where drugs are not only available but socially acceptable. By working in a sheltered workshop or at a real job the addict begins to form a new identity to replace the negative junkie image.

Defects of Philadelphia Program

There are about two dozen programs in the Philadelphia area for the treatment of heroin addiction. None of them in any way resembles the suggested design of the Task Force. Public facilities for referral and ancillary service are grossly inadequate. Supposedly there are 20 beds at Philadelphia General Hospital set aside for the treatment of addicts, but it is almost impossible for the methadone program to get any of its patients into that or any other hospital for detoxification. (Last year, two of its 756 clients were hospitalized and not necessarily for detoxification.) There are no day-treatment programs, no half-way houses, no sheltered workshops, inadequate vocational training and not enough jobs for the trained patients. The Philadelphia Methadone Program is one of about five offering methadone; all offer some kind of psychotherapy or counseling; one offers substitute activities to replace heroin.

The Philadelphia program has a number of medical residents on its staff and did have social work students. But

The Philadelphia program started treatment of 13 patients in hospital and 19 patients out of hospital in August 1966. In a footnote we are informed that there were originally 40 patients, but five of the inpatients and three of the outpatients dropped out. Already the results are less successful than those of the Dole-Nyswander program. Since in this test admission criteria were chosen to be comparable to those of Dole-Nyswander, this 20 percent loss of patients would appear to merit more than a footnote. Even if the two groups responded similarly for the period of the test, the sample is so small as to nearly invalidate the statistics used. In addition, the program directors knew that the selection of patients had been biased by referring doctors, producing a far higher proportion of white subjects than the clinic ever saw again (or than resides in Philadelphia for that matter).

Outpatient indoctrination was supposed to be beneficial because the existing shortage of treatment space and personnel could be better used and "a large amount of money would be released to provide expanded concurrent services . . . a greater number of treating facilities . . . many more addicts could be treated." Concurrent services have not been expanded. The program does include more facilities and larger numbers of patients. Criteria for success were clinical improvement (as subjectively experienced and reported by the patient), employment, lack of heroin cheating and reduced criminality.

Both inpatient and outpatient groups had similar results: 78.1 percent felt better, 78.1 percent had jobs once in the program as opposed to one-third prior to it; very few cheated with heroin and very few were arrested while in the program. But this outcome cannot be generalized to the entire addict population. The patients in this small study were well-integrated and highly motivated individuals. Outpatient treatment may be a viable modality for selected patients, but not for the clients the Philadelphia program normally treats.

Other study findings are also questionable. The study observed that holding a job and cheating with heroin were unrelated. This has not held up in subsequent studies. The researchers stated that patients receiving high or low doses cheated or refrained from cheating equally. This, too, is no longer considered to be the case.

In a paper entitled "Outpatient Detoxification of Narcotic Addiction" by William F. Wieland and Carl D. Chambers, the authors describe a program which started in October of 1967, for "well integrated and highly motivated" addicts or those newly addicted. A comparison of this group of 162 patients with the original 32 reveals that by many measures the larger group appeared to be less likely to succeed in a detoxification program. Unlike the small group, which had manifested very little cheating while on methadone, the cheating rate for the larger group was so high as to make the goal of detoxification seem most unlikely. We are here discussing the 162 patients in active treatment, not the "long term addicts whose histories and present attitudes indicate that the chances for success are close to zero" who were not put in this program, the 101 "crisis cases" who terminated after only one or two visits, the 186 who terminated after three or more visits nor the 105 who failed to detoxify and were transferred to

since the program is so lacking in resocialization facilities, those workers are trained to talk about problems—precisely what Pittel, Chafetz and other researchers have claimed is a waste of time. To put together a resocialization program of the nature it claims to have, the program would have to demand a host of currently non-existent services in behalf of its clients.

The Philadelphia program opened its doors to the street addict in 1968. Unfortunately, its program design was based on a statistical fallacy: the test group it selected or acquired by referral was uniquely different from the street addicts it subsequently treated on a far larger scale. As a result, just about none of the findings from the test group study have held up over time—yet the program carries on as though they had. It originally set out to demonstrate, contrary to the findings of the successful Dole-Nyswander program, that a first treatment phase on an outpatient basis was as effective, in the long run, as inpatient methadone stabilization.

The Dole-Nyswander program consists of three phases: 1) an inpatient six-week stabilization phase, 2) outpatient clinic treatments daily and urine checks for the detection of drugs other than methadone and 3) methadone maintenance with less frequent clinic visits. By this time the addict is most usually at work or in school and able to live in the community comfortably and without drug problems.

Crime and Punishment: Police, Criminals, and the Courts

maintenance. These terminations occurred "early in the treatment program when staff was inexperienced and the temporary facilities were physically and esthetically inadequate." No one could imagine a setting more esthetically inadequate than exists at present. But, more important, if these terminations occurred early in the program and the program began in October of 1967 and was formalized by September of 1968, then how is it possible that only 20 terminations (nine involuntary) occurred up to February 1968?

Table 1 — A Comparison of Three Addict Populations
In the Philadelphia Program

Characteristic	I The Original 32 Patients	II The "Highly Motivated" 162 Patients	III The 756 Clinic Population reported in the Budget, 1971-72
Number	32	162	756
Race:			
White	84.4%	`34%	56.5%
Negro	15.6%	66%	43.5%
Employed	78.1%	62.2%	50%
Education: High School Grad. or more	56.3%	32%	28.7%
Sex: Male	87.5%	80%	84.1%
Married: Intact	59.4%	36%	28.7%
Years of Use: Mean	13.9	8	5.6
Age: Mean	32.1	31	28
Total with Arrest Record	90.6%	86%	77.7%

1. The decrease in intact marriages is symptomatic of the changing clinic population and is particularly noteworthy in view of the decreased mean age of the clinic population.
2. The decreased years of use indicates that the decreased age of the clients shows that they are coming into treatment sooner than former populations, not that they began using sooner and are seeking to get out of the life that much sooner. This decreased age statistic is hopeful in that it shows the impact of treatment programs, even when they are far short of ideal. It also poses a challenge to the clinic since younger addicts are more difficult to treat.

The data in the "Detoxification" paper are presented in a most confusing manner. "Successfully detoxified" patients who left the program are lumped together with those leaving against medical advice (AMA) under the rubric "terminations." Sixty-two patients were readmitted to the program but we are not told whether they terminated as "abstinent" or "AMA." Of all 385 terminations (79.2 percent of the total), 95 (24.7 percent) were abstinent, 186 (48.3 percent) left against medical advice and 105 (27.3 percent) were transferred to maintenance. Less than 15 percent of the entire population (162 plus 486) were abstinent when discharged. Less than 19 percent of terminated patients were abstinent temporarily, the authors chose to use 385 as the base for estimating the 24.7 percent abstinent. These data are the source of the subsequently repeated claim that this program can successfully detoxify a fourth of its patients. It "detoxified" a fourth of its "terminations after three or more visits," not

of its population as a whole nor even of its terminations as a whole. And these patients did not remain detoxified.

Subsequent studies showed that at least two-thirds of them returned to heroin use. From studies performed elsewhere, this is a very low estimate of relapse. The budget for fiscal 1971-72 claims that a "reconceptualization" has occurred and this entire program has been dropped. Out of the then 756 patients, 30 (or four percent) were in a detoxification program. The reason given for dropping it was the high failure rate. The results of these follow-up studies are known to the authors, yet they continue to distribute a brochure describing the program which makes the claim (that was never true) that the program detoxifies a fourth of its patients. Further, *Social Work* published an article in July of 1971 repeating this statement.

In its study of the 32 test patients, the authors did not include among criteria for success a retention rate, although it claimed one equal to the Dole-Nyswander program. It did include cheating with other drugs. In this study the goal has shifted markedly (for no reason that the data support) and the authors state "Cheating with heroin is fairly common. . . . Most of the cheaters are using considerably less than previously, which is at least a step in the right direction." They then present a tabulation of cheating rates which has categories so large as to obscure its meaning and has no column headings so that the reader is left to decode it:

Heroin Cheating During a One-Month Period
(4-20 specimens per patient)

0 - 15% positive specimens:	24.4%
26 - 50% positive specimens:	22.7%
51 - 100% positive specimens:	52.9%

More than half the 162 patients had specimens positive for heroin more than half the time. Presumably some patients never cheated, and some always cheated, but this information is obscured by the manner of presentation.

The authors conclude that "in addition to the achievement of abstinence . . . *there are two other successful outcomes* (my emphasis): those who use the program as a pretreatment phase for methadone maintenance and . . . those who are functioning well on very low doses of methadone. . . ." In other words, having failed to achieve the goal of the program (detoxification) the addict may successfully enter another program, one which the authors have always supported as more reasonable. In between these papers, Wieland published a paper describing 60 patients he maintained on methadone, in which, the authors say, his statistics are "almost identical" to those of Dole and Nyswander. In this article, Wieland pleaded for the acceptance of methadone maintenance as a legitimate treatment modality and medical breakthrough. He compared its discovery to that of lithium, asepsis and free association. He wrote:

The unanswered question [is] whether patients will have to be maintained on methadone for the rest of their lives or whether they will eventually be able to be withdrawn. . . . *Only a few patients have attempted withdrawal to date, and all have become readdicted to heroin.* It is possible that intensive group therapy may permit some patients to withdraw successfully . . . one can do worse than to take methadone for the rest of one's life. . . .

The "Detoxification" paper was presented to the National Research Council in 1970. It made no reference to large scale failures to achieve abstinence or a prior commitment to maintenance. It closed by saying it had experienced some unspecified failures, ascribing them to inexperience, not to an absence of enough or intense enough group therapy. This particular reference is puzzling since the program has not offered intensive group therapy in the past and does not do so now. Insufficient therapy is an excellent excuse for failure. No one has ever determined how much is enough. (And just what is intensive group therapy?)

Another "success" the program has reported in its recent budget request is that of vocational counseling. They now have two counselors and have requested two more. The counselors have seen 100 people in the past year. They have successfully placed 36 of them in jobs or training programs. When this was written there were 756 patients in the program of whom half were unemployed. The counselors have succeeded in placing less than 10 percent of the clinic's unemployed population.

The authors repeatedly refer to the program as a reward and punishment model. If a patient fails to achieve abstinence he is transferred to the methadone maintenance program where his dosage is most likely increased. Is he being rewarded or punished?

In all its discussions of the necessity of making careful checks through urinalysis no statement is ever made as to what will be done when persistent cheating is detected. The program has never developed a clear and consistent position on this issue. It has threatened to suspend or even remove patients (thus increasing its termination rate) but since no other similar treatment facility exists in the city, there is no program to transfer the miscreant to.

Few, if any, treatment decisions are made on the basis of data from urinalysis reports. In the most recent study of the program most of the staff claimed that the urinalysis monitoring is not helpful to them or needs to be improved. Twenty-one percent said it was not vital to their counseling; 43 percent said it had some value but needed improving; 36 percent said it had no value at all. Yet the testing program costs $200,000 and its importance is reiterated in every document this or any other methadone program puts out. Testing has become a source of mutual hostility between patients and staff. Harrisburg sent down a ruling that staff must observe patients in toilets. They do not do so even though patients are suspected (and probably with good cause) of selling specimens to each other.

Urinalysis reports can be useful only if the counselor can receive them in time to prevent the addict from taking methadone on top of some other illicit drug. Even with computerization this is not possible. It is possible that merely from observation and experience the counselor could determine if the patient was taking some other drug. This method is inexact, but it might work if the counselor saw the patient daily. The authors have claimed in several articles that the patient is seen for counseling every day for 20 to 30 minutes. But according to the most recent study of the clinic, the addict actually spends 10 to 15 minutes in the clinic, just long enough to get his medication. It's up to the nurse who hands him the methadone to determine if he already has had something else. How poorly this system works is revealed by the cheating record of the patients. There is no way that counselors could see their clients so frequently and for so long as the authors claim; the average case load is 50 (35 to 60) and counselors have responsibilities other than interviewing patients.

Comparing the cheating rates of the three populations, it was found that in:

Group I (the original 32)—After 20 months of treatment, nine of the patients cheated with heroin. No other tests were done (for other drugs). This is a 28 percent rate; in a 60-day test period, each of the nine cheated an average of two times.

Group II (the "highly motivated" 162)—After an average of six months of treatment, 4 to 20 urine specimens per patient were tested during a one-month period.

Times cheated	Patients
0 - 25%	24.4%
25 - 50%	22.7%
51 - 100%	52.9%

Group III (the 756 clinic population reported in the Budget 1971-72)—Only 4 percent never cheated.

1 - 35%	44%
36 - 70%	24%
71 - 100%	28%

During the period 1970-71, an independent check of patients' cheating patterns was conducted and reported in the New York Times. A random sample of 40 patients was selected from those in treatment over six months and receiving over 60 mg. of methadone (high dose) per day. It was found that 82.5 percent used other detectable drugs, excluding marijuana and psychedelics; 77.5 percent used heroin; 73 percent used barbiturates; 25 percent used amphetamines; 22.5 percent used all three of the preceding.

When this study was expanded for the detection of cocaine five months later and 39 of the above group retested, it was found that now 97.4 percent used other detectable drugs; 43.6 percent of the group used cocaine and 51.3 percent took heroin and barbiturates, amphetamines or cocaine. Incidence per patient of other drug use was not given.

In other words, the longer on the program, the more the patients cheated! This fact alone, no matter what the percentages, should have alerted the clinic staff that

Table 2 — A Comparison of Drug Use Prior to and After Entry into the Program (from the Budget, 1971-72; based on the 756 clinic population)

Drug	Prior	Post
Marijuana	90%	not given
Amphetamines	50.9%	68%
Barbiturate-Sedatives	62%	22%
Psychedelics	18%	not given
Heroin	100%	0-96%

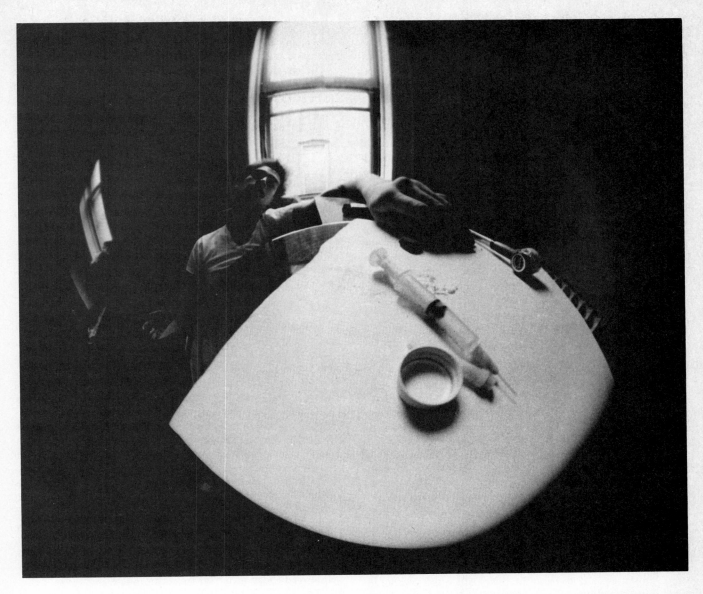

something was seriously amiss and rethinking of goals and methods was required. The authors explained the increased numbers of persons using amphetamines after entering the program as efforts of patients to lose weight. A side effect of methadone is increased appetite and weight gain in some patients. However, many more showed up using amphetamines than gained weight. If tests had been made for alcohol use, cheating rates would have been even higher.

By the time the budget for 1971-72 was written, it was impossible to tease out the retention rate of patients from the data presentation. The director claimed it was 55 percent. In all, 1350 patients have been treated, the current enrollment is 756, ergo . . . 55 percent. According to the same report's Summary of Admissions and Terminations, however, only 83 of these 756 are retained from last year. There were 673 new admissions or readmissions this year. As of last year, same date, the program had an enrollment of 314 patients. The 83 retained of these makes the retention rate 27 percent per annum.

In March 1971 Dr. Wieland coauthored an article about his program which was published in *Clinical Medicine.* The abstract the authors present states:

Methadone maintenance . . . ambulatory . . . can greatly reduce the need for costly, largely unavailable treatment of addiction and enable rehabilitation programs to manage a larger proportion of narcotics addicts.

Very early in this series of publications, economy and management of large numbers of addicts emerged as *the* concern of this program. The paucity of treatment facilities is accepted as a fact of life in this statement just as the lack of facilities and options for the programs was accepted. The authors again compare their work to that of Dole and Nyswander, with by now no justification whatsoever. They have dropped references to detoxification.

Another journal article describing the Philadelphia program appeared in *Social Work* in July 1971. A number of treatment approaches are suggested including inpatient detoxification and day treatment or residential treatment centers for recalcitrant patients. Among the suggested modalities they include a detoxification program. "Ideally, when the client has ceased cheating... the daily dose of methadone is decreased by 10 mg." The article then reviews the Synanon experience where the dropout rate is 50 percent in the first few weeks and 72 percent afterwards. This information makes the goals and claims for the Philadelphia program appear even more unrealistic.

The Philadelphia Methadone Treatment Program distributes a brochure bearing as the authors' names Dr. Robert L. Leopold, director of the West Philadelphia Mental Health Consortium and Dr. William Wieland, former director of the methadone program. The booklet is distributed to drug educators who come to the Eastern Pennsylvania Psychiatric Institute for indoctrination and training. It repeats all of the misstatements and incorrect facts contained in previous articles describing the program. Drug educators are being sold a bill of goods about a non-existent treatment which claims that "most patients enter the detoxification program" and that "25 percent of them achieve abstinence" while "another 35 percent are transferred to methadone maintenance and remain in active treatment." The source for the 35 percent figure is a mystery. In the "Detoxification" paper the authors claimed that less than 25 percent of the patients were transferred to methadone maintenance. We have no evidence that patients remain in treatment very long.

The cheating rate of the Philadelphia addict-patient represents a far more serious threat to his well-being than merely a failure to cooperate with a treatment program. He is given a dose of methadone on the basis of his heroin habit. If he takes even more narcotics on top of that, he is increasing his habit and increasing the difficulty of ever becoming abstinent. While abstinence is not a feasible goal for the majority of the clients of the program, it is possible for addicts over the age of 35 or 40. A great many addicts spontaneously improve in that age group. Studies of addicts released from Lexington over several decades showed that half of the survivors after five years were abstinent. Immediately after release almost all of them had gone back to drug use. Another group of addicts that were studied were chosen at random from the roster of a public school in St. Louis. Ten percent of the former students had become heroin addicts but over 80 percent of these addicts had given up heroin use by the age of 33. What we have no way of knowing is how many addicts in the general population have done the same. Clinics do attract specific types of individuals who may not represent the addict population at large. It is therefore a matter of real concern that free drugs are widely available via clinic treatment programs. It is still a debatable issue because of the role that easy availability does seem to play in the promulgation of addiction. The patient population at Lexington contains eight times the number of medical professionals and paraprofessionals than proportionately exists in the general population. In these cases it was felt that not only did the availability of drugs play a role but that the medical addict was not as psychologically disabled as the street addict. In other words, it took less personal pathology to become an addict under those circumstances than is the norm. Another conclusion that must be drawn from studies such as these is that any treatment program's outcomes cannot be compared to a hypothetical "no change" without treatment, since there is ample evidence that addicts can and do improve spontaneously (if they survive physically).

What the Philadelphia Methadone Treatment Program can prove unequivocally is that it reduces the incidence of criminal activity among its clients and does so sharply. There is a widely used statistic which claims that each addict steals about $50,000 worth of goods each year. The reduction in delinquent behavior achieved by the program represents an enormous saving to the community and is an excellent selling point for support of the program.

Although half the clinic population is unemployed and the unemployment is greatest among patients with psychiatric diagnoses, the employment rate as a whole is a reflection of the general employment picture among the population the addict is drawn from. A recent study indicates that the clinic population as a whole is not any worse off than the base population in terms of education or job experience prior to addiction.

In the first year of its existence, 12.5 percent of the clinic's patients were on welfare. This figure rapidly grew to 21 percent and now it is closer to 50 percent. The program is hoping to cut its costs to $1,000 per patient per annum when it expands to include 1,200 patients. In addition to the financial costs of maintaining its population on welfare, the future for the program as a whole does not look bright; it is lacking all the kinds of services and real opportunities for its clients that would make rehabilitation a possibility for them. Meanwhile, the pharmaceutical industry keeps searching for chemical answers to the chemical addiction problem. In the *New York Times* of November 23, 1971 it was reported that the Pharmaceutical Manufacturers Association may have found a heroin antagonist among the chemicals it developed for the Defense Department. It claimed that the industry is searching for a non-addictive tranquilizer and an anti-euphoric heroin antagonist. This sounds dangerously close to an ideal police-state weapon for the tranquilization of a potentially troublesome ghetto population. And the manner in which methadone is being employed today is not far from this image.

FURTHER READING

Law and Order: The Scales of Justice edited by Abraham S. Blumberg (Chicago: Aldine, 1971).

The Road to "H" by Isidor Chein et al. (New York: Basic Books, 1964). A standard text presenting all the relevant issues. His data are supported by subsequent studies.

Marijuana: The New Prohibition by John Kaplan (New York: World, 1971).

The Drug Addict as Patient by Marie Nyswander (New York: Grune & Stratton, 1956). An easily read account of the issues and history of drug treatment.

Federal Involvement in the Use of Behavior Modification Drugs on Grammar School Children, of the Right to Privacy Inquiry, Hearings before a Subcommittee of the Committee on Government Operations, House of Representatives, 91st Congress, Second Session, September 29, 1970 (Washington, D.C.: USGPO), 654.

ABRAHAM S. BLUMBERG

Lawyers with Convictions

The criminal trial—in a vision based not only on plays and novels, but also on a number of Supreme Court decisions—is believed to be a kind of highly civilized trial by combat. Two attorneys—one championing the people, the other championing the accused—robe themselves in the majesty of the law and battle before a stern impartial judge who considers their performances in light of the special rules of the law and grants victory to the best man.

This is a dramatic picture. But if we look closely at the reality of a large number of criminal trials, we find drama of a decidedly different kind. It may be a miracle play or a farce or a tragedy, depending on the point of view.

The defendant in a criminal court almost always loses. Most often—nine times out of ten is a good rough measure—he is found guilty. Does the prosecution have the best men, or are the police amazingly efficient? The prosecution does have good men, and the police do have competent investigators, but still we must look a little deeper to find out why losers lose.

Often, the source of their defeat has been sought in deprivations and social disabilities such as race, poverty, and social class. Researchers have attempted to learn how the deprived regard the legal system and how the system regards the deprived. But what of the legal system itself? What are the values of the judges and lawyers who work in the criminal courts? What is their thrust, purpose, and direction?

I am most concerned here with the "lawyer regulars"—those defense lawyers, including public defenders, who represent the bulk of defendants—and not with those lawyers who come to court occasionally because someone for whom they have written a will or deed has gotten into trouble. These clients end up in the hands of the regulars when their troubles are serious.

The private regulars are highly visible in the major urban centers of the nation; their offices—at times shared with bondsmen—line the back streets near courthouses. They are also visible politically, with clubhouse ties reaching into judicial chambers and the prosecutor's office. The regulars make no effort to conceal their dependence upon police, bondsmen, jail personnel, as well as bailiffs, stenographers, prosecutors, and judges. These informal relations are essential to maintaining and building a practice. Some lawyers are almost entirely dependent on such contacts to find clients, and a few even rely on an "in" with judges to obtain state-paid appointments which become the backbone of their practices.

A defense lawyer willing to go to trial can accomplish a great deal for his client, even a client technically guilty of some crime. Say the man has been arrested with a roomful of stolen furs, a satchel filled with burglar tools, a burglary record, and no alibi for the night of the crime. If the prosecution charges him with burglary, but the defense can show there was no forcible entry, then no burglary has been committed. The prosecution might try to convict on a number of lesser charges—theft, possession of stolen property, or possession of burglar tools—but in the process, the defense lawyer may have thrown up so much reasonable doubt as to get his man off. The prosecution is liable to other mistakes as well. They may have used faulty search warrants or attempted to introduce other illegal evidence; they may tamper with the witnesses or the jury; they may simply put on a bad case.

In order to accomplish these gains for his client, the defense lawyer must go to trial. However, going to trial is out of character with his role as a member of the court system. This holds true for both public and private attorneys. As members of a bureaucratic system the defense lawyers become committed to rational, impersonal goals based on saving time, labor, and expense and on attaining maximum output for the system. For the defense lawyer this means choosing strategies which will lead to working out a plea of guilty, assuring a fee, and shrouding these acts with legitimacy. The accused and his kin, as outsiders, cannot perceive the mutual dependence of the prosecutor and the defense lawyer, himself often a former prosecutor. These two need each other's cooperation for their continued professional existence. Even in bargaining over guilty pleas, their combat tends to be reasonable rather than fierce.

The Confidence Game

The defense lawyer in many ways plays the confidence man. The client is cast as the mark. The lawyer convinces him that pleading guilty will lead to a lesser charge or a lesser sentence, and the eager client agrees, forgetting that in pleading guilty, he is forfeiting his right to a trial by jury and getting a presentence hearing before a judge.

The lawyer's problem is different. He is not concerned with guilt or innocence, but rather with giving the client something for his money. Usually a plumber can show that he has performed a service by pointing to the unstopped drain or the no longer leaky faucet as proof that he merits his fee. A physician who has not performed surgery, advised a low-starch diet, or otherwise engaged in some readily discernible procedure may be deemed by the patient to have done nothing for him. Thus, doctors may order a sugar pill or water injection to overcome the patient's dissatisfaction in paying a fee "for nothing."

The practice of law has a special problem in this regard. Much legal work is intangible: a few words of advice, a telephone call, a form filled out and filed, a hurried conference with another attorney or a government official, a

---

"The defense lawyer chooses strategies which will lead to working out a plea of guilty, assuring a fee, and shrouding these acts with legitimacy."

---

letter or brief, or some other seemingly innocuous or even prosaic activity. These are the basic activities, apart from any possible court appearance, of almost all lawyers at all levels of practice. The client is not looking for this, but rather for the exercise of the traditional, precise, and professional skills of the attorney: legal research and oral argument on appeals; court motions; trial work; drafting of opinions, memoranda, contracts, and other complex documents and agreements.

Despite the client's expectations, whether the lawyer has offices on Wall Street or in his hat, most legal activity more closely resembles the work of a broker, salesman, lobbyist, or agent. The product is intangible.

The members of a large-scale law firm may not speak as openly of their contacts, their fixing abilities, as does the hustling, lone-wolf lawyer. The firms trade instead upon thick carpeting, walnut paneling, genteel low pressure, and superficialities of traditional legal professionalism. There are occasions when even the large firm is defensive about the fees because the services or results do not appear substantial. Therefore, the recurrent problem in the legal profession is setting and justifying the fee.

Although the fee at times amounts to what the traffic and the conscience of the lawyer will bear, one further observation must be made about the size of the fee and its collection. The criminal defendant and his presumed loot are soon parted. Frequently the defense lawyer gets it in payment of his fee. Inevitably, the dollar value of the crime committed affects the fee, which is frequently set with precision at a sum which bears an uncanny relationship to that of the net proceeds of the crime. On occasion, defendants have been known to commit additional offenses

while out on bail in order to meet their obligations for payment of legal fees. Defense lawyers teach even the most obtuse clients that there is a firm connection between paying up and the zealous application of professional expertise, secret knowledge, and organizational connections. Lawyers, therefore, seek to keep their clients at the precise emotional pitch necessary to encourage prompt fee payment. Consequently, the client treats his lawyer with hostility, mistrust, dependence, and sychophancy in precarious mixture. By keeping his client's anxieties aroused and establishing a relationship between the fee and ultimate extrication, the lawyer assures a minimum of haggling over the fee and its eventual payment.

As a consequence, all law practice in some degree involves a manipulation of the client and a stage management of the lawyer-client relationship so that there will be at least an *appearance* of help and service. At the outset, the lawyer employs with suitable variation a measure of puffery which may range from unbounded self-confidence, adequacy, and dominion over events to complete arrogance. This is supplemented by the affectation of a studied, faultless mode of personal attire. In larger firms the furnishings and office trappings will serve as the backdrop to help in impressing and intimidating the client. In all firms, solo or large scale, an access to secret knowledge and to the seats of power is implied.

Fees and Finances

The lack of a visible end product offers a special complication for the professional criminal lawyer. The plain fact is that the accused in a criminal case almost always loses, even when he has been freed by the court. All the hostility resulting from arrest, incarceration, possible loss of job, and legal expense then is directed toward the lawyer. Thus, it can also be said that the criminal lawyer never really wins a case. The really satisfied client is rare, since even vindication leaves him feeling hostile and dissatisfied. He didn't want to be arrested in the first place. Even the rare defendant who sees himself as a professional criminal and views legal fees as business expenses thinks that the overhead should be cut down. It is this state of affairs that reinforces the casting of the lawyer as a con man.

The risks of nonpayment of the fee are high. Most of the clients are poor, and most of them are likely to end up in jail, where their gratitude will be muted. It is no surprise that criminal lawyers collect their fees in advance. The fee is one of three major problems the lawyer must solve. The second is preparing the client for defeat and then cooling him out when it comes, as it is likely to do. Third, he must satisfy the court that his performance in negotiating the plea was adequate. Appellate courts are more and more looking over the trial judge's shoulder. Even the most unlikely cases may be finally decided by the Supreme Court. The next drifter accused of breaking and entering might be another Clarence Gideon.

To be sure of getting his fee, the criminal lawyer will very often enter into negotiations with various members of the accused's family. In many instances, the accused himself is unable to pay any sort of fee or anything more than a token fee. It then becomes important to involve as many of his relatives as possible. This is especially so if the attorney hopes to collect a substantial fee. It is not uncommon for several relatives to contribute toward the fee. The larger the group, the greater the possibility that the lawyer will collect a sizable fee.

A fee for a felony case which results in a plea, rather than a trial, may range anywhere from $500 to $1,500. Should the case go to trial, the fee will be larger, depending upon the length of the trial. But the larger the fee the lawyer wishes to exact, the more impressive his performance must be. Court personnel are keenly aware of the extent to which a lawyer's stock in trade involves precarious staging of a role which goes beyond the usual professional flamboyance. For this reason alone the lawyer is bound in to the court system. Therefore, court personnel will aid the lawyer in the creation and maintenance of that impression. There is a tacit commitment to the lawyer by the court organization, apart from formal etiquette, to aid him. This augmentation of the lawyer's stage-managed image is the partial basis for the quid pro quo which exists between the lawyer and the court organization. It tends to serve as the continuing basis for the higher loyalty of the lawyer to the court organization while his relationship with his client, in contrast, is transient, ephemeral, and often superficial.

The lawyer has often been accused of stirring up unnecessary litigation, especially in the field of negligence. He is said to acquire a vested interest in a cause of action or claim which was initially his client's. The strong incentive of possible fee motivates the lawyer to promote litigation which would otherwise never have developed. The lawyers have even encoded two crimes with fine medieval names to limit this activity. *Barratry* is persistent incitement of litigation, and *champerty* is taking part in a suit without justification in exchange for a cut of the proceeds. The criminal lawyer develops a vested interest of an entirely different nature in his client's case: not to promote the litigation, but to limit its scope and duration. Only in this way can a case be profitable. Thus, he enlists the aid of relatives not only to assure payment of his fee, but to help him in his agent-mediator role of convincing the accused to plead guilty, and ultimately to help him in the "cooling out" if necessary.

It is at this point that an accused defendant may experience his first sense of betrayal. While he had perceived the police and prosecutor to be adversaries, and possibly even the judge, the accused is wholly unprepared for his counsel's role as an agent-mediator. In the same vein, it is even less likely to occur to an accused that members of his own family may become agents. Usually it will be the law-

yer who will activate the family in this role, his ostensible motive being to arrange for his fee. But soon the latent and unstated motives will assert themselves. The lawyer asks the family to convince the accused to "help himself" by pleading guilty. Appeals to sentiment are exploited by a defense lawyer (or even by a district attorney) to achieve the specific end of concluding a particular matter with all possible dispatch.

The fee is often collected in installments, usually payable prior to each court appearance. In his interviews and communications with the accused or with members of his family, the lawyer employs an air of professional confidence and inside-dopesterism to assuage all anxieties. He makes the necessary bland assurances and manipulates his client, who is usually willing to do and say things, true or not, which his attorney says will help him. Since what he is selling—influence and expertise—cannot be measured by the client, the lawyer can make extravagant claims of influence and secret knowledge with impunity. Lawyers frequently claim to have inside knowledge in connection with information in the hands of the prosecutor, police, or probation officials. They often do have access to them and need only to exaggerate the nature of their relationships to impress the client. But in the confidence game, the victim who has participated is loath to do anything which will upset the lesser plea which his lawyer has conned him into accepting.

Copping Out

The question has never been raised as to whether "copping" a plea, or justice by negotiation, is a constitutional process. Although it has become the most central aspect of the process of criminal law administration, it has received virtually no close scrutiny by the appellate courts. As a consequence it is relatively free of legal control and supervision. But, apart from any questions of the legality of bargaining, in terms of the pressures and devices that are employed which tend to violate due process of law, there remain ethical and practical questions. Much of the danger of the system of bargain-counter justice is concealed in secret negotiations and its least alarming feature, the final plea, is the only one presented to public view.

In effect, in his role as double agent the criminal lawyer performs a vital and delicate mission for the court organization and the accused. Both principals are anxious to terminate the litigation with a minimum of expense and damage to each other. There is no one else in the court structure more strategically located or more ideally suited

"The bureaucratic system cannot rely on idiosyncratic police pressure for confessions. The defense counsel is a far more reliable source of guilty pleas."

to handle this than the defense lawyer. In recognition of this, judges will cooperate with attorneys in many important ways. For example, they will continue the case of an accused in jail awaiting plea or sentence if the attorney requests it. This may be done for some innocuous and seemingly valid public reason, but the real purpose is pressure by the attorney for the collection of his fee, which he knows he may lose if the case is concluded. Judges know of this none too subtle method of dunning a client. The judges will go along on the ground that important ends are being served. Often, however, the only end being served is to protect a lawyer's fee.

Another way the judge can help an accused's lawyer is by lending the official aura of the bench as a backdrop to an all-out performance for the accused in justification of his fee. The judge and other court personnel will serve as supporting players for a dramatic scene in which the defense lawyer makes a stirring appeal in his behalf. With a show of restrained passion, the lawyer will intone the virtues of the accused and recite the social deprivations which have reduced him to his present state. The speech varies somewhat, depending on whether the accused has been convicted after trial or has pleaded guilty. The incongruity, superficiality, and ritualistic character of the performance is underscored by a visibly impassive, almost bored reaction on the part of the judge and other members of the court retinue. Afterward there is a hearty exchange of pleasantries between the lawyer and district attorney, wholly out of the context of the adversary nature of the hearing. The courtroom players are not "method" actors.

The fiery passion of the defense is gone, and lawyers for both sides resume their offstage relations, chatting amiably and perhaps even including the judge in their restrained banter. Even a casual observer is put on notice; these individuals have claims upon each other.

Criminal law practice is unique since it really only appears to be private practice but is actually bureaucratic practice. Private practice is supposed to involve an organized, disciplined body of knowledge and learning. Individual practitioners are imbued with a spirit of autonomy and service. Earning a livelihood is incidental. But the lawyer in the criminal court serves as a double agent, serving organizational rather than professional ends. To some extent the lawyer-client confidence game serves to conceal this fact.

The "cop-out" ceremony is not only invaluable for redefining the defendant's perspectives of himself, but also in reiterating his guilt in a public ritual. The accused is made to assert his guilt of a specific crime, including a complete recital of its details. He is further made to say that he is entering his plea of guilty freely and that he is not doing so because of any promises that may have been made to him. This last is intended as a blanket statement to shield the court bureaucrats from any charges of coercion. This cuts off any appellate review on grounds that due process was denied as well as cutting off any second thoughts the defendant may have about his plea.

This affirmation of guilt is not a simple affair. Most of those who plead guilty are guilty and may be willing or even eager to say so in order to be charged with a lesser crime or receive a lesser sentence. The system serves the guilty better because they are glad to get half a loaf in return for playing along. But the innocent—subject to precisely the same pressures—get no reward from a negotiated plea. In any case, the defendant's conception of himself as guilty is ephemeral; in private he will quickly reassert his innocence. The "cop-out" is not comparable to Harold Garfinkel's "status degradation ceremony" because it has no lasting effect on the interrelations of the defendant and society. Rather, it is a charade. The accused projects the appropriate amount of guilt, penance, and remorse; his hearers engage in the fantasy that he is contrite and merits a lesser punishment.

Pleas of Innocence

Defendants begin dropping the guilty role very soon. Many do so in their interviews with the probation officer immediately after the plea but before sentencing. The first question the probation officer routinely asks is: "Are you guilty of the crime to which you pleaded?" I have gathered the responses of 724 male defendants to this question. The research was done in 1962, 1963, and 1964 in a large metropolitan court handling only felonies. The men were charged with crimes ranging from homicide to forgery, but most of them pleaded guilty to misdemeanors after negotiation. At this early stage, 51.4 percent claimed innocence in some fashion. In practice when a prisoner claims innocence, the probation officer will ask him to withdraw his plea and stand trial on the original charges. This threat is normally sufficient to provide the system with a second affirmation of guilt.

Very few choose to go on trial again. They are very likely to be convicted if they do. Between 1950 and 1964 in the court I studied, from 75 to 90 percent of the actual adversary trials ended in conviction. In all years less than 5 percent of all indictments ended in adversary trials.

In the present system it would appear that once an individual is indicted, there is very little chance of escaping conviction.

The unrehearsed responses to the probation officer tell us a great deal about how defendants feel about their negotiated pleas. Only 13.2 percent straightforwardly admitted their guilt and of these, 10.3 percent added exculpatory statements such as, "But I should have gotten a better deal (from the lawyer, prosecutor, police, judge)." The large group claiming innocence, 373 men, were for the most part interested in underscoring their "goodness" for the probation officer.

These innocent respondents employed varying degrees of fervor, solemnity, and credibility. In the main they were pragmatic, saying, "I wanted to get it over with," or "You can't beat the system," or "They have you over a barrel when you have a record." This pragmatic response covered 20.3 percent of the sample. "I followed my lawyer's advice," was the claim of 12.7 percent. Nearly as many defendants—11.8 percent—said they had been manipulated or conned by lawyer, judge, police, or prosecutor. The smallest number—2.1 percent—traced their plea to a "bad report" by the probation officer or psychiatrist in investigations before hearing the plea. Only a very few were defiant outright; just 4.5 percent (or 33) claimed that they had been framed or betrayed.

By far the largest grouping in the sample were those who were fatalistic, neither pressing their innocence nor admitting their guilt. This 34.8 percent (248) explained their pleas by saying, "I did it for convenience," or "My lawyer told me it was the only thing I could do," or "I did it because it was the best way out." This last group seemed to feel that they, like Joseph K. in Kafka's *The Trial,* are caught up in a monstrous apparatus which may turn on them no matter what they do, no matter whether they say they are innocent or guilty. These men adopt a stance of passivity, resignation, and acceptance. Interestingly, in most instances it was their lawyer who crystallized the alternatives for them and who was therefore the critical element in their decision to plead guilty.

In order to determine the critical elements in all 724 cases, the men were asked who first suggested the plea of guilty and who most influenced their final decision to enter this plea. The results are listed in Table I:

TABLE I—DECISIONS TO PLEAD GUILTY

Agent-Mediator	First Suggestion		Most Influence	
	No.	%	No.	%
Judge	4	0.6	26	3.6
Prosecutor	67	9.3	116	16.0
Defense counsel	407	56.2	411	56.8
Probation officer	14	1.9	3	0.4
Psychiatrist	8	1.1	1	0.1
Wife	34	4.7	120	16.6
Friends and relatives	21	2.9	14	1.9
Police	14	1.9	4	0.6
Fellow inmates	119	16.4	14	1.9
Others	28	3.9	5	0.7
No response	8	1.1	10	1.4

It is popularly assumed that most guilty pleas are a result of pressure to confess from the police or more elaborate coercion from the prosecutor. In my sample, however, only 43 men, or 5.94 percent, had confessed before they were indicted, and as Table I shows, the defense attorney was by far the most potent source of guilty pleas, particularly if it is recalled that most of the pressure from family and friends to plead this way is likely to be generated by the defense attorney. The bureaucratic system cannot rely on idiosyncratic police pressures for confessions and retain its efficiency, high production, and rational-legal character. The defense counsel is a far more effective source of pleas,

living as he does astride the world of the court and the world of the defendant. Even though fellow inmates were frequently the first to mention such a plea, defendants still tended to rely strongly on their counsel as the ultimate source of influence for a final decision.

Therefore, I asked the 724 defendants at what point in their relationship the defense counsel first suggested a guilty plea. Although these men cited many sources of influence, they all had lawyers, and of course they were not likely to plead without concurrence by or at least consultation with their lawyers. In the court I studied there are three basic kinds of defense counsel: private, legal-aid (a private defender system which receives public funds and has taken on the coloration of a public defender system), and court-assigned (who may later be privately retained).

The overwhelming majority related a specific incident of an early suggestion that they plead guilty to a lesser charge if this could be arranged. Of all the agent-mediators, it is the lawyer who is most effective in manipulating the defendant, notwithstanding possible pressures by police, prosecutor, judge, or others. Legal-aid and assigned counsel

TABLE II—STAGE AT WHICH PLEA WAS FIRST SUGGESTED OR DISCUSSED

Meeting	Private	Legal-Aid	Assigned	All	%
First	66	237	28	331	45.7
Second	83	142	8	233	32.2
Third	29	63	4	96	13.3
Fourth or later	12	31	5	48	6.6
No response	0	14	2	16	2.2
TOTAL NUMBER OF CASES	190	487	47	724	100.0%

are apparently more likely to suggest the plea in the initial interview, perhaps as a response to pressures of time and, in the case of the assigned counsel, the strong possibility that there is no fee involved. In addition, there is some further evidence in Table II of the perfunctory character of criminal courts. Little real effort is made to individualize the defendant. Although the defense lawyer is an officer of the court he mediates between the court organization and the defendant; his duties to each are rent by conflicts of interest. Too often these must be resolved in favor of the organization which provides him with his professional existence. In order to reduce the strains and conflicts imposed, the lawyer engages in the lawyer-client confidence game so as to make his situation more palatable.

Based on data which are admittedly tentative and fragmentary, the furor over confessions, whether forced or voluntary, is not statistically meaningful. Criminal law enforcement has always depended, and will continue to do so in the foreseeable future, on judicial confessions—that is, pleas of guilty—rather than confessions hammered out in the squeal room of a police station.

The Gideon, Miranda, and Escobedo decisions were greeted with such lively delight or anguished dismay that outsiders must have thought that the Supreme Court had wrought some magnificent transformation in the defense lawyer. Actually, the court in these cases was perpetuating the Perry Mason myth of an adversary trial, while in the lesser courts of the nation, the dreary succession of 90 percent negotiated pleas continued. These "trials" are highly reminiscent of what George Feifer described in *Justice in Moscow*. The Soviet trial has been termed "an appeal from the pre-trial investigation." All notions of the presumption of innocence are completely alien, and as Feifer states: ". . . the closer the investigation resembles the finished script, the better. . . ."

I do not mean to be pejorative. Feifer finds the Soviet trial preferable in some ways because it judges the criminal and not the crime, but in the American form, the "irrelevant" factors of background and record are considered only after the finding of guilty, not before as in Russia and much of Europe.

The Escobedo and Miranda decisions protecting against defendant confusion in the hands of the police and the Gideon decision assuring counsel for felony defendants are popular in and out of legal circles, but my experiences and observations suggest that a poor defendant with a lawyer may not be much better off than a poor defendant without a lawyer. These decisions have not changed the nature of the court bureaucracy and, if anything, the pressure for guilty pleas and the drive for efficient production may grow even stronger, and the position of the defendant as a bureaucratic client further hampered by race, poverty, and class may become weaker and weaker.

Courts, like many other large modern organizations, possess a monstrous appetite not only for individuals, but for entire professions. Almost all those coming under an organizational authority find their definitions, perceptions, and values have been refurbished in terms largely favorable to the particular organization and its goals.

Thus, the Supreme Court decisions extending the right to counsel may have an effect which is radically different from that intended or anticipated. The libertarian rules will tend to augment the existing organizational arrangements, enriching court organizations with more personnel and elaborate structure, and making them an even more sophisticated apparatus for processing defendants toward a guilty finding.

FURTHER READING

Lawyers' Ethics by Jerome E. Carlin (New York: Russell Sage, 1966).

Gideon's Trumpet by Anthony Lewis (New York: Random House, 1964).

Prosecution: The Decision to Charge a Suspect with a Crime by Frank W. Miller (Boston: Little, Brown, 1969).

Equal Justice for the Accused by the Special Committee of the Association of the Bar of the City of New York and The National Legal Aid and Defender Association. (Garden City, N.Y.: Doubleday, 1959).

Criminal Lawyer by Arthur Lewis Wood (New Haven, Conn.: College & University Press, 1967).

Lawyers and Their Society by Dietrich Rueschemeyer (Cambridge, Mass.: Harvard University Press, 1973).

ALBERT J. REISS, JR.

Police Brutality—
Answers to Key Questions

"For three years, there has been through the courts and the streets a dreary procession of citizens with broken heads and bruised bodies against few of whom was violence needed to effect an arrest. Many of them had done nothing to deserve an arrest. In a majority of such cases, no complaint was made. If the victim complains, his charge is generally dismissed. The police are practically above the law."

This statement was published in 1903, and its author was the Hon. Frank Moss, a former police commissioner of New York City. Clearly, today's charges of police brutality and mistreatment of citizens have a precedent in American history—but never before has the issue of police brutality assumed the public urgency it has today. In Newark, in Detroit, in Watts, in Harlem, and, in fact, in practically every city that has had a civil disturbance, "deep hostility between police and ghetto" was, reports the Kerner Commission, "a primary cause of the riots."

Whether or not the police accept the words "police brutality," the public now wants some plain answers to some plain questions. How widespread is police mistreatment of citizens? Is it on the increase? Why do policemen mistreat citizens? Do the police mistreat Negroes more than whites?

To find some answers, 36 people working for the Center of Research on Social Organization observed police-citizen encounters in the cities of Boston, Chicago, and Washington, D.C. For seven days a week, for seven weeks during the summer of 1966, these observers, with police permission, sat in patrol cars and monitored booking and lockup procedures in high-crime precincts.

Obtaining information about police mistreatment of citizens is no simple matter. National and state civil-rights commissions receive hundreds of complaints charging mistreatment—but proving these allegations is difficult. The few local civilian-review boards, such as the one in Philadelphia, have not produced any significant volume of complaints leading to the dismissal or disciplining of policemen for alleged brutality. Generally, police chiefs are silent on the matter, or answer charges of brutality with vague statements that they will investigate any complaints brought to their attention. Rank-and-file policemen are usually more outspoken: They often insinuate that charges of brutality are part of a conspiracy against them, and against law and order.

The Meaning of Brutality

What citizens mean by police brutality covers the full range of police practices. These practices, contrary to the impression of many civil-rights activists, are not newly devised to deal with Negroes in our urban ghettos. They are ways in which the police have traditionally behaved in dealing with certain citizens, particularly those in the lower classes. The most common of these practices are:

—the use of profane and abusive language,

—commands to move on or get home,

—stopping and questioning people on the street or searching them and their cars,

—threats to use force if not obeyed,

—prodding with a nightstick or approaching with a pistol, and

—the actual use of physical force or violence itself.

Citizens and the police do not always agree on what constitutes proper police practice. What is "proper," or what is "brutal," it need hardly be pointed out, is more a matter of judgment about what someone did than a description of what police do. What is important is not the practice itself but what it means to the citizen. What citizens object to and call "police brutality" is really the judgment that they have not been treated with the full rights and dignity owing citizens in a democratic society. Any practice that degrades their status, that restricts their freedom, that annoys or harasses them, or that uses physical force is frequently seen as unnecessary and unwarranted. More often than not, they are probably right.

Many police practices serve only to degrade the citizen's sense of himself and his status. This is particularly true with regard to the way the police use language. Most citizens who have contact with the police object less to their use of four-letter words than to *how* the policeman talks to them. Particularly objectionable is the habit policemen have of "talking down" to citizens, of calling them names that deprecate them in their own eyes and those of others. More than one Negro citizen has complained: "They talk down to me as if I had no name—like 'boy' or 'man' or whatever, or they call me 'Jack' or by my first name. They don't show me no respect."

Members of minority groups and those seen as nonconformists, for whatever reason, are the most likely targets of status degradation. Someone who has been drinking may be told he is a "bum" or a "shitty wino." A woman walking alone may be called a "whore." And a man who doesn't happen to meet a policeman's standard of how one should look or dress may be met with the remark, "What's the matter, you a queer?" A white migrant from the South may be called a "hillbilly" or "shitkicker"; a Puerto Rican, a "pork chop"; a young boy, a "punk kid." When the policeman does not use words of status degradation, his manner may be degrading. Citizens want to be treated as people, not as "nonpersons" who are talked about as if they were not present.

That many Negroes believe that the police have degraded their status is clear from surveys in Watts, Newark, and Detroit. One out of every five Negroes in our center's post-riot survey in Detroit reports that the police have "talked down to him." More than one in ten says a policeman has "called me a bad name."

To be treated as "suspicious" is not only degrading, but is also a form of harassment and a restriction on the right to move freely. The harassing tactics of the police—dispersing social street-gatherings, the indiscriminate stopping of Negroes on foot or in cars, and commands to move on or go home—are particularly common in ghetto areas.

Young people are the most likely targets of harassing orders to disperse or move on. Particularly in summer, ghetto youths are likely to spend lots of time in public places. Given the inadequacy of their housing and the absence of community facilities, the street corner is often their social center. As the police cruise the busy streets of the ghetto, they frequently shout at groups of teenagers to "get going" or "get home." Our observations of police practices show that *white as well as Negro youths* are often harassed in this way.

Frequently the policeman may leave the car and threaten or force youths to move on. For example, one summer evening as the scout car cruised a busy street of a white slum, the patrolmen observed three white boys and a girl on a corner. When told to move on, they mumbled and grumbled in undertones, angering the police by their failure to comply. As they slowly moved off, the officers pushed them along the street. Suddenly one of the white patrolmen took a lighted cigarette from a 15-year-old boy and stuck it in his face, pushing him forward as he did so. When the youngsters did move on, one policeman remarked to the observer that the girl was "nothing but a whore." Such tactics can only intensify resentment toward the police.

Police harassment is not confined to youth. One in every four adult Negroes in Detroit claims he has been stopped and questioned by the police without good reason. The same proportion claim they have been stopped in their cars. One in five says he has been searched unnecessarily; and one in six says that his car was searched for no good reason. The members of an interracial couple, particularly a Negro man accompanying a white woman, are perhaps the most vulnerable to harassment.

What citizens regard as police brutality many policemen consider necessary for law enforcement. While degrading epithets and abusive language may no longer be considered proper by either police commanders or citizens, they often disagree about other practices related to law enforcement. For example, although many citizens see "stop and question" or "stop and frisk" procedures as harassment, police commanders usually regard them merely as "aggressive prevention" to curb crime.

Physical Force—or Self-Defense?

The nub of the police-brutality issue seems to lie in police use of physical force. By law, the police have the right to use such force if necessary to make an arrest, to keep the peace, or to maintain public order. But just how much force is necessary or proper?

This was the crucial problem we attempted to answer by placing observers in the patrol cars and in the precincts. Our 36 observers, divided equally between Chicago, Boston, and Washington, were responsible for reporting the details of all situations where police used physical force against a citizen. To ensure the observation of a large number of encounters, two high-crime police precincts were monitored in Boston and Chicago; four in Washington. At least one precinct was composed of primarily Negro residents, another primarily of whites. Where possible, we also tried to select precincts with considerable variation in social-class composition. Given the criterion of a high-crime rate, however, people of low socio-economic status predominated in most of the areas surveyed.

The law fails to provide simple rules about what—and how much—force that policemen can properly use. The American Bar Foundation's study *Arrest*, by Wayne La Fave, put the matter rather well, stating that the courts of all states would undoubtedly agree that in making an arrest a policeman should use only that amount of force he reasonably believes necessary. But La Fave also pointed out that there is no agreement on the question of when it is better to let the suspect escape than to employ "deadly" force.

Even in those states where the use of deadly force is limited by law, the kinds of physical force a policeman may use are not clearly defined. No kind of force is categorically denied a policeman, since he is always permitted to use deadly force in self-defense.

This right to protect himself often leads the policeman to argue self-defense whenever he uses force. We found that many policemen, whether or not the facts justify it, regularly follow their use of force with the charge that the citizen was assaulting a policeman or resisting arrest. Our observers also found that some policemen even carry pistols and knives that they have confiscated while searching citizens; they carry them so they may be placed at a scene should it be necessary to establish a case of self-defense.

Of course, not all cases of force involve the use of *unnecessary* force. Each instance of force reported by our observers was examined and judged to be either necessary or unnecessary. Cases involving simple restraint—holding a man by the arm—were deliberately excluded from consideration, even though a policeman's right to do so can, in many instances, be challenged. In judging when police force is "unwarranted," "unreasonable," or "undue," we rather deliberately selected only those cases in which a policeman struck the citizen with his hands, fist, feet, or body, or where he used a weapon of some kind—such as a nightstick or a pistol. In these cases, had the policeman been found to have used physical force improperly, he could have been arrested on complaint and, like any other citizen, charged with a simple or aggravated assault. A physical assault on a citizen was judged to be "improper" or "unnecessary" only if force was used in one or more of the following ways:

■ If a policeman physically assaulted a citizen and then failed to make an arrest; proper use involves an arrest.

■ If the citizen being arrested did not, by word or deed, resist the policeman; force should be used only if it is necessary to make the arrest.

■ If the policeman, even though there was resistance to the arrest, could easily have restrained the citizen in other ways.

■ If a large number of policemen were present and could have assisted in subduing the citizen in the station, in lockup, and in the interrogation rooms.

■ If an offender was handcuffed and made no attempt to flee or offer violent resistance.

■ If the citizen resisted arrest, but the use of force continued even after the citizen was subdued.

In the seven-week period, we found 37 cases in which force was used improperly. In all, 44 citizens had been assaulted. In 15 of these cases, no one was arrested. Of these, 8 had offered no verbal or physical resistance whatsoever, while 7 had.

An arrest was made in 22 of the cases. In 13, force was exercised in the station house when at least four other policemen were present. In two cases, there was no verbal or physical resistance to the arrest, but force was still applied. In two other cases, the police applied force to a handcuffed offender in a field setting. And in five situations, the offender did resist arrest, but the policeman continued to use force even after he had been subdued.

Just how serious was the improper use of force in these 44 cases? Naturally there were differences in degree of injury. In about one-half of the cases, the citizen appeared little more than physically bruised; in three cases, the amount of force was so great that the citizen had to be hospitalized. Despite the fact that cases can easily be selected for their dramatic rather than their representative quality, I want to present a few to give a sense of what the observers saw and reported as undue use of force.

Observing on Patrol

In the following two cases, the citizens offered no physical or verbal resistance, and the two white policemen made no arrest. It is the only instance in which the observers saw the same two policemen using force improperly more than once.

The police precinct in which these incidents occurred is typical of those found in some of our larger cities, where the patrolmen move routinely from gold coast to slum. There are little islands of the rich and poor, of old Americans and new, of recent migrants and old settlers. One moves from high-rise areas of middle- and upper-income whites through an area of the really old Americans—Indians—to an enclave of the recently arrived. The recently arrived are primarily those the policemen call "hillbillies" (migrants from Kentucky and Tennessee) and "porkchops" (Puerto Ricans). There are ethnic islands of Germans and Swedes. Although there is a small area where Negroes live, it is principally a precinct of whites. The police in the district are, with one exception, white.

On a Friday in the middle of July, the observer arrived for the 4 to 12 midnight watch. The beat car that had been randomly chosen carried two white patrolmen—one with 14 years of experience in the precinct, the other with three.

The watch began rather routinely as the policemen cruised the district. Their first radio dispatch came at about 5:30 P.M. They were told to investigate two drunks in a cemetery. On arriving they found two white men "sleeping one off." Without questioning the men, the older policeman began to search one of them, ripping his shirt and hitting him in the groin with a nightstick. The younger policeman, as he searched the second, ripped away the seat of his trousers, exposing his buttocks. The policemen then prodded the men toward the cemetery fence and forced them to climb it, laughing at the plight of the drunk with the exposed buttocks. As the drunks went over the fence, one policemen shouted, "I ought to run you

fuckers in!" The other remarked to the observer, "Those assholes won't be back; a bunch of shitty winos."

Not long after they returned to their car, the policemen stopped a woman who had made a left turn improperly. She was treated very politely, and the younger policeman, who wrote the ticket, later commented to the observer, "Nice lady." At 7:30 they were dispatched to check a suspicious auto. After a quick check, the car was marked abandoned.

Shortly after a 30-minute break for a 7:30 "lunch," the two policemen received a dispatch to take a burglary report. Arriving at a slum walkup, the police entered a room where an obviously drunk white man in his late 40s insisted that someone had entered and stolen his food and liquor. He kept insisting that it had been taken and that he had been forced to borrow money to buy beer. The younger policeman, who took the report, kept harassing the man, alternating between mocking and badgering him rhetorical questions. "You say your name is Half-A-Wit [for Hathaway]? Do you sleep with niggers? How did you vote on the bond issue? Are you sure that's all that's missing? Are you a virgin yet?" The man responded to all of this with the seeming vagueness and joviality of the intoxicated, expressing gratitude for the policemen's help as they left. The older policeman remarked to the observer as they left, "Ain't drunks funny?"

For the next hour little happened, but as the two were moving across the precinct shortly after 10 P.M., a white man and a woman in their 50s flagged them down. Since they were obviously "substantial" middle-class citizens of the district, the policemen listened to their complaints that a Negro man was causing trouble inside the public-transport station from which they had just emerged. The woman said that he had sworn at her. The older policeman remarked, "What's a nigger doing up here? He should be down on Franklin Road!"

With that, they ran into the station and grabbed the Negro man who was inside. Without questioning him, they shoved him into a phone booth and began beating him with their fists and a flashlight. They also hit him in the groin. Then they dragged him out and kept him on his knees. He pleaded that he had just been released from a mental hospital that day and, begging not to be hit again, asked them to let him return to the hospital. One policeman said: "Don't you like us, nigger? I like to beat niggers and rip out their eyes." They took him outside to their patrol car. Then they decided to put him on a bus, telling him that he was returning to the hospital; they deliberately put him on a bus going in the opposite direction. Just before the Negro boarded the bus, he said, "You police just like to shoot and beat people." The first policeman replied, "Get moving, nigger, or I'll shoot you." The man was crying and bleeding as he was put on the bus. Leaving the scene, the younger policeman commented, "He won't be back."

For the rest of the evening, the two policemen kept looking for drunks and harassing any they found. They concluded the evening by being dispatched to an address where, they were told, a man was being held for the police. No one answered their knock. They left.

The station house has long been suspected of harboring questionable police practices. Interrogation-room procedures have been attacked, particularly because of the methods the police have used to get confessions. The drama of the confession in the interrogation room has been complete with bright lights and physical torture. Whether or not such practices have ever existed on the scale suggested by popular accounts, confessions in recent years, even by accounts of offenders, have rarely been accompanied by such high drama. But recently the interrogation room has come under fire again for its failure to protect the constitutional rights of the suspect to remain silent and to have legal counsel.

Backstage at the Station

The police station, however, is more than just a series of cubicles called interrogation rooms. There are other rooms and usually a lockup as well. Many of these are also hidden from public view. It is not surprising, then, that one-third of all the observations of the undue use of force occurred within the station.

In any station there normally are several policemen present who should be able to deal with almost any situation requiring force that arises. In many of the situations that were observed, as many as seven and eight policemen were present, most of whom simply stood by and watched force being used. The custom among policemen, it appeared, is that you intervene only if a fellow policeman needs help, or if you have been personally offended or affronted by those involved.

Force is used unnecessarily at many different points and places in the station. The citizen who is not cooperative during the booking process may be pushed or shoved, have his handcuffs twisted with a nightstick, have his foot stomped, or be pulled by the hair. All of these practices were reported by policemen as ways of obtaining "cooperation." But it was clear that the booking could have been completed without any of this harassment.

The lockup was the scene of some of the most severe applications of force. Two of the three cases requiring hospitalization came about when an offender was "worked over" in the lockup. To be sure, the arrested are not always cooperative when they get in the lockup, and force may be necessary to place them in a cell. But the amount of force observed hardly seemed necessary.

One evening an observer was present in the lockup when two white policemen came in with a white man. The suspect had been handcuffed and brought to the station because he had proved obstreperous after being arrested for a traffic violation. Apparently he had been drinking. While waiting in the lockup, the man began to urinate on the floor. In response, the policemen began to beat the man. They jumped him, knocked him down, and beat his head against the concrete floor. He required emergency treatment at a nearby hospital.

At times a policeman may be involved in a kind of escalation of force. Using force appropriately for an arrest in the field seemingly sets the stage for its later use, improperly, in the station. The following case illustrates how such a situation may develop:

Within a large city's high-crime rate precinct, occupied mostly by Negroes, the police responded to an "officer in trouble" call. It is difficult to imagine a call that brings a more immediate response, so a large number of police cars immediately converged at an intersection of a busy public street where a bus had been stopped. Near the bus, a white policeman was holding two young Negroes at gun point. The policeman reported that he had responded to a summons from the white bus-driver complaining that the boys had refused to pay their fares and had used obscene language. The policeman also reported that the boys swore at him, and one swung at him while the other drew a screwdriver and started toward him. At that point, he said, he drew his pistol.

The policemen placed one of the offenders in handcuffs and began to transport both of them to the station. While driving to the station, the driver of one car noted that the other policeman, transporting the other boy, was struggling with him. The first policeman stopped and entered the other patrol car. The observer reported that he kept hitting the boy who was handcuffed until the boy appeared completely subdued. The boy kept saying, "You don't have any right to beat me. I don't care if you kill me."

After the policemen got the offenders to the station, although the boys no longer resisted them, the police began to beat them while they were handcuffed in an interrogation room. One of the boys hollered: "You can't beat me like this! I'm only a kid, and my hands are tied." Later one of the policemen commented to the observer: "On the street you can't beat them. But when you get to the station, you can instill some respect in them."

Cases where the offender resists an arrest provide

perhaps the most difficulty in judging the legitimacy of the force applied. An encounter that began as a dispatch to a disturbance at a private residence was one case about which there could be honest difference in judgment. On arrival, the policemen—one white, the other Negro—met a white woman who claimed that her husband, who was in the back yard and drunk, had beaten her. She asked the policemen to "take him in." The observer reported that the police found the man in the house. When they attempted to take him, he resisted by placing his hands between the door jamb. Both policemen then grabbed him. The Negro policeman said, "We're going to have trouble, so let's finish it right here." He grabbed the offender and knocked him down. Both policemen then wrestled with the man, handcuffed him, and took him to the station. As they did so, one of the policemen remarked, "These sons of bitches want to fight, so you have to break them quick."

A Minimal Picture?

The reader, as well as most police administrators, may be skeptical about reports that policemen used force in the presence of observers. Indeed, one police administrator, indignant over reports of undue use of force in his department, seemed more concerned that the policemen had permitted themselves to be observed behaving improperly than he was about their improper behavior. When demanding to know the names of the policemen who had used force improperly so he could discharge them—a demand we could not meet, since we were bound to protect our sources of information —he remarked, "Any officer who is stupid enough to behave that way in the presence of outsiders deserves to be fired."

There were and are a number of reasons why our observers were able to see policemen behaving improperly. We entered each department with the full cooperation of the top administrators. So far as the men in the line were concerned, our chief interest was in how citizens behave toward the police, a main object of our study. Many policemen, given their strong feelings against citizens, fail to see that their own behavior is equally open to observation. Furthermore, our observers are trained to fit into a role of trust— one that is genuine, since most observers are actually sympathetic to the plight of the policeman, if not to his behavior.

Finally, and this is a fact all too easily forgotten, people cannot change their behavior in the presence of others as easily as many think. This is particularly true when people become deeply involved in certain situations. The policeman not only comes to "trust" the observer in the law-enforcement situation—regarding him as a source of additional help if necessary— but, when he becomes involved in a dispute with a citizen, he easily forgets that an observer is present. Partly because he does not know what else to do, in such situations the policeman behaves "normally." But should one cling to the notion that most policemen modify their behavior in the presence of outsiders, one is left with the uncomfortable conclusion that our cases represent a minimal picture of actual misbehavior.

Superficially it might seem that the use of an excessive amount of force against citizens is low. In only 37 of 3826 encounters observed did the police use undue force. Of the 4604 white citizens in these encounters, 27 experienced an excessive amount of force —a rate of 5.9 for every 1000 citizens involved. The comparable rate for 5960 Negroes, of whom 17 experienced an excessive amount of force, is 2.8. Thus, whether one considers these rates high or low, the fact is that the *rate of excessive force for all white citizens in encounters with the police is twice that for Negro citizens.*

A rate depends, however, upon selecting a population that is logically the target of force. What we have just given is a rate for *all* citizens involved in encounters with the police. But many of these citizens are not logical targets of force. Many, for example, simply call the police to complain about crimes against themselves or their property. And others are merely witnesses to crimes.

The more logical target population consists of citizens whom the police allege to be offenders—a population of suspects. In our study, there were 643 white suspects, 27 of whom experienced undue use of force. This yields an abuse rate of 41.9 per 1000 white suspects. The comparable rate for 751 Negro suspects, of whom 17 experienced undue use of force, is 22.6 per 1000. If one accepts these rates as reasonably reliable estimates of the undue force against suspects, then there should be little doubt that in major metropolitan areas the sort of behavior commonly called "police brutality" is far from rare.

Popular impression casts police brutality as a racial matter—white police mistreating Negro citizens. The fact is that white suspects are more liable to being treated improperly by the police than Negro suspects are. This, however, should not be confused with the chances a citizen takes of being mistreated. In two of the cities we studied, Negroes are a minority. The chances, then, that any Negro has of being treated improperly are, perhaps, more nearly comparable to that for whites. If the rates are comparable, then one might say that the application of force unnecessarily by the police operates without respect to the race of an offender.

Many people believe that the race of the policeman

Crime and Punishment: Police, Criminals, and the Courts

must affect his use of force, particularly since many white policemen express prejudice against Negroes. Our own work shows that in the police precincts made up largely of Negro citizens, over three-fourths of the policemen express prejudice against Negroes. Only 1 percent express sympathetic attitudes. But as sociologists and social psychologists have often shown, prejudice and attitudes do not necessarily carry over into discriminatory actions.

Our findings show that there is little difference between the rate of force used by white and by Negro policemen. Of the 54 policemen observed using too much force, 45 were white and 9 were Negro. For every 100 white policemen, 8.7 will use force; for every 100 Negro policemen, 9.8 will. What this really means, though, is that about one in every 10 policemen in high-crime rate areas of cities sometimes uses force unnecessarily.

Yet, one may ask, doesn't prejudice enter into the use of force? Didn't some of the policemen who were observed utter prejudiced statements toward Negroes and other minority-group members? Of course they did. But the question of whether it was their prejudice or some other factor that motivated them to mistreat Negroes is not so easily answered.

Still, even though our figures show that a white suspect is more liable to encounter violence, one may ask whether white policemen victimize Negroes more than whites. We found, for the most part, that they do not. Policemen, both Negro and white, are most likely to exercise force against members of their *own* race:

—67 percent of the citizens victimized by white policemen were white.

—71 percent of the citizens victimized by Negro policemen were Negro.

To interpret these statistics correctly, however, one should take into account the differences in opportunity policemen have to use force against members of their own and other races. Negro policemen, in the three cities we studied, were far *less* likely to police white citizens than white policemen were to police Negroes. Negro policemen usually policed other Negroes, while white policemen policed both whites and Negroes about equally. In total numbers, then, more white policemen than Negro policemen used force against Negroes. But this is explained by the fact that whites make up 85 percent of the police force, and more than 50 percent of all policemen policing Negroes.

Though no precise estimates are possible, the facts just given suggest that white policemen, even though they are prejudiced toward Negroes, do not discriminate against Negroes in the excessive use of force. The use of force by the police is more readily explained by police culture than it is by the policeman's race. Indeed, in the few cases where we observed a Negro policeman using unnecessary force against white citizens, there was no evidence that he did so because of his race.

The disparity between our findings and the public's sense that Negroes are the main victims of police brutality can easily be resolved if one asks how the public becomes aware of the police misusing force.

The Victims and the Turf

Fifty years ago, the immigrants to our cities—Eastern and Southern Europeans such as the Poles and the Italians—complained about police brutality. Today the new immigrants to our cities—mostly Negroes from the rural South—raise their voices through the civil-rights movement, through black-nationalist and other race-conscious organizations. There is no comparable voice for white citizens since, except for the Puerto Ricans, they now lack the nationality organizations that were once formed to promote and protect the interests of their immigrant forbears.

Although policemen do not seem to select their victims according to race, two facts stand out. All victims were offenders, and all were from the lower class. Concentrating as we did on high-crime rate areas of cities, we do not have a representative sample of residents in any city. Nonetheless, we observed a sizable minority of middle- and upper-status citizens, some of whom were offenders. But since no middle- or upper-class offender, white or Negro, was the victim of an excessive amount of force, it appears that the lower class bears the brunt of victimization by the police.

The most likely victim of excessive force is a lower-class man of either race. No white woman and only two Negro women were victimized. The difference between the risk assumed by white and by Negro women can be accounted for by the fact that far more Negro women are processed as suspects or offenders.

Whether or not a policeman uses force unnecessarily depends upon the social setting in which the encounter takes place. Of the 37 instances of excessive force, 37 percent took place in police-controlled settings, such as the patrol car or the precinct station. Public places, usually streets, accounted for 41 percent, and 16 percent took place in a private residence. The remaining 6 percent occurred in commercial settings. This is not, of course, a random sample of settings where the police encounter suspects.

What is most obvious, and most disturbing, is that the police are very likely to use force in settings that they control. Although only 18 percent of all situations involving suspects ever ended up at the station house, 32 percent of all situations where an excessive amount of force was used took place in the police station.

No one who accepts the fact that the police sometimes use an excessive amount of force should be surprised by our finding that they often select their own turf. What should be apparent to the nation's police administrators, however, is that these settings are under their command and control. Controlling the police in the field, where the policeman is away from direct supervision, is understandably difficult. But the station house is the police administrator's domain. The fact that one in three instances of excessive force took place in settings that can be directly controlled should cause concern among police officials.

The presence of citizens who might serve as witnesses against a policeman should deter him from undue use of force. Indeed, procedures for the review of police conduct are based on the presumption that one can get this kind of testimony. Otherwise, one is left simply with a citizen complaint and contrary testimony by the policeman—a situation in which it is very difficult to prove the citizen's allegation.

In most situations involving the use of excessive force, there were witnesses. In our 37 cases, there were bystanders present three-fourths of the time. But in only one situation did the group present sympathize with the citizen and threaten to report the policeman. A complaint was filed on that incident—the only one of the 37 observed instances of undue force in which a formal complaint was filed.

All in all, the situations where excessive force was used were devoid of bystanders who did not have a stake in being "against" the offender. Generally, they were fellow policemen, or fellow offenders whose truthfulness could be easily challenged. When a policeman uses undue force, then, he usually does not risk a complaint against himself or testimony from witnesses who favor the complainant against the policeman. This, as much as anything, probably accounts for the low rate of formal complaints against policemen who use force unnecessarily.

A striking fact is that in more than one-half of all instances of undue coercion, at least one other policeman was present who did not participate in the use of force. This shows that, for the most part, the police do not restrain their fellow policemen. On the contrary, there were times when their very presence encouraged the use of force. One man brought into the lockup for threatening a policeman with a pistol was so severely beaten by this policeman that he required hospitalization. During the beating, some fellow policemen propped the man up, while others shouted encouragement. Though the official police code does not legitimate this practice, police culture does.

Victims—Defiant or Deviant

Now, are there characteristics of the offender or his behavior that precipitate the use of excessive force by the police? Superficially, yes. Almost one-half of the cases involved open defiance of police authority (39 percent) or resisting arrest (9 percent). Open defiance of police authority, however, is what the policeman defines as *his* authority, not necessarily "official" authority. Indeed in 40 percent of the cases that the police considered open defiance, the policeman never executed an arrest—a somewhat surprising fact for those who assume that policemen generally "cover" improper use of force with a "bona-fide" arrest and a charge of resisting arrest.

But it is still of interest to know what a policeman *sees* as defiance. Often he seems threatened by a simple refusal to acquiesce to his own authority. A policeman beat a handcuffed offender because, when told to sit, the offender did not sit down. One Negro woman was soundly slapped for her refusal to approach the police car and identify herself.

Important as a threat to his authority may appear to the policeman, there were many more of these instances in which the policeman did *not* respond with the use of force. The important issue seems to be whether the policeman manages to assert his authority despite the threat to it. I suspect that policemen are more likely to respond with excessive force when they define the situation as one in which there remains a question as to who is "in charge."

Similarly, some evidence indicates that harassment of deviants plays a role in the undue use of force. Incidents involving drunks made up 27 percent of all incidents of improper use of force; an additional 5 percent involved homosexuals or narcotics users. Since deviants generally remain silent victims to avoid public exposure of their deviance, they are particularly susceptible to the use of excessive force.

It is clear, though, that the police encounter many situations involving deviants where no force is used. Generally they respond to them routinely. What is surprising, then, is that the police do not mistreat deviants more than they do. The explanation may lie in the kind of relationships the police have with deviants. Many are valuable to the police because they serve as informers. To mistreat them severely would be to cut off a major source of police intelligence. At the same time, deviants are easily controlled by harassment.

Clearly, we have seen that police mistreatment of citizens exists. It is, however, on the increase?

Citizen complaints against the police are common, and allegations that the police use force improperly are frequent. There is evidence that physical brutality exists today. But there is also evidence, from the history of our cities, that the police have long engaged in the use of unnecessary physical force. No one can say with confidence whether there is more or less of it today than there was at the turn of the century.

What we lack is evidence that would permit us to calculate comparative rates of police misuse of force for different periods of American history. Only recently have we begun to count and report the volume of complaints against the police. And the research reported in this article represents the only attempt to estimate the amount of police mistreatment by actual observation of what the police do to citizens.

Lack of Information

Police chiefs are notoriously reluctant to disclose information that would allow us to assess the nature and volume of complaints against the police. Only a few departments have begun to report something about citizen complaints. And these give us very little information.

Consider, for example, the 1966 Annual Report released by the New Orleans Police Department. It tells us that there were 208 cases of "alleged police misconduct on which action was taken." It fails to tell us whether there were any allegations that are *not* included among these cases. Are these all the allegations that came to the attention of the department? Or are they only those the department chose to review as "police disciplinary matters"? Of the 208 cases the department considered "disciplinary matters," the report tells us that no disciplinary action was taken in 106 cases. There were 11 cases that resulted in 14 dismissals; 56 cases that resulted in 72 suspensions, fines, or loss of days; and 35 cases involving 52 written or verbal "reprimands" or "cautionings."

The failure of the report to tell us the charge against the policeman is a significant omission. We cannot tell how many of these allegations involved improper use of force, how many involved verbal abuse or harassment, how many involved police felonies or misdemeanors, and so on. In such reports, the defensive posture of the nation's police departments is all too apparent. Although the 1966 report of the New Orleans Police Department tells us much about what the police allege were the felonies and misdemeanors by citizens of New Orleans, it tells us nothing about what citizens allege was misconduct by the police!

Many responsible people believe that the use of physical brutality by the police is on the wane. They point to the fact that, at least outside the South, there are more reports of other forms of police mistreatment of citizens than reports of undue physical coercion. They also suggest that third-degree interrogations and curbstone justice with the nightstick are less common. It does not seem unreasonable, then, to assume that police practices that degrade a citizen's status or that harass him and restrict his freedom are more common than police misuse of force. But that may have always been so.

Whether or not the policeman's "sense of justice" and his use of unnecessary force have changed remains an open question. Forms may change while practices go on. To move misuse from the street to the station house, or from the interrogation room to the lockup, changes the place but not the practice itself.

Our ignorance of just what goes on between police and citizens poses one of the central issues in policing today: How can we make the police accountable to the citizenry in a democratic society and yet not hamstring them in their legitimate pursuit of law and order? There are no simple answers.

Police departments are organizations that process people. All people-processing organizations face certain common problems. But the police administrator faces a problem in controlling practice with clients that is not found in most other organizations. The problem is that police contact with citizens occurs in the community, where direct supervision is not possible. Assuming our unwillingness to spend resources for almost one-to-one supervision, the problem for the police commander is to make policemen behave properly when they are not under direct supervision. He also faces the problem of making them behave properly in the station house as well.

Historically, we have found but one way—apart from supervision—that deals with this problem. That solution is professionalization of workers. Perhaps only through the professionalization of the police can we hope to solve the problem of police malpractice.

But lest anyone optimistically assume that professionalization will eliminate police malpractice altogether, we should keep in mind that problems of malpractice also occur regularly in both law and medicine.

FURTHER READING

Serpico by Peter Maas (New York: Viking, 1968).

Varieties of Police Behavior by James Q. Wilson (Cambridge, Mass.: Harvard University Press, 1968).

7. The Changing Economy

Even a cursory survey of the evolution of human societies suggests that changes in the organization of energy systems—changes in the ways in which man exploits his environment for his subsistence needs—are always accompanied by changes in social and political organization, in value systems and religious beliefs, and in family structure and individual personality. When human beings gave up hunting and gathering for agriculture, they altered more than their subsistence because they had to organize society to meet very different demands posed by farming and herding. People settled in villages, replacing their roving, mobile life with less active pursuits. Sedentary life offered new opportunities, but it also placed new restrictions on human behavior. No longer could an individual solve his conflicts by leaving his band to join another. People were now tied to the land that supported them, and had to develop new methods of adjudicating personal disputes. Sedentary life also permitted an increase in population, partly because its agricultural base provided a more predictable food supply; partly because the need for mobility which had severely restricted the number of children in a band had been eliminated; and partly because agricultural requirements for larger numbers of cooperative persons to plant or harvest encouraged large families.

Clearly, subsistence needs and the methods by which societies are organized to provide for them affect every dimension of human life, and these effects have not diminished because today's world is so much bigger and more complex than the world of peasants or hunters and gatherers. We face similar problems: like hunters and gatherers we exploit energy systems, produce, manufacture, and consume goods, and distribute—however inequitably—the fruits of our labor throughout society. However, unlike hunters and gatherers, we do not provide equality of access to resources for all members of our group. A resource may become scarce or nonexistent because of thoughtless waste, or greed, or even as the result of natural processes. As one group gains ascendancy over another, it tends to exploit that group both for its raw materials and labor power. As a result, our society has moved far from the relatively egalitarian society of hunters and gatherers to develop a highly stratified class system in which different groups possess differential access to vital resources.

Throughout history economic conditions have created interdependencies as well as interpersonal conflicts among men. The degree of that conflict has increased at an exponential rate in recent years. Conflict increases as a function of change: in altering our modes of reproduction, we must also change many of the other rules by which we live. Sennett's "Genteel Backlash: Chicago 1886" describes the dislocations created in Chicago as the result of changes in the organization of family life brought on by industrialization and urbanization. Describing the Haymarket riots as an inevitable outcome of the paranoia engendered in privatistic nuclear families, Sennett suggested that the fear of immigrants and unions exhibited during the riots was a projection of "a hysterical belief in hidden, unknown threats ready to strike at a man at almost any time." Unable to move up the status ladder primarily because their methods of socialization precluded the necessary abilities, these families lived in dread of falling back into poverty. Meanwhile, as the pace of urban life around them grew more confusing—in response to the rapid pace of industrial change—the families retreated further into isolation and privatism.

Similar forces may be at work in today's cities. Piven's "Militant Civil Servants in New York City" offers a modern parallel to the Chicago of 1886. Instead of viewing recent militancy by civil service workers as a contest between the unions and the public, she sees the strikes as a struggle between the largely white civil servants and the largely black ghetto residents. Motivating the strikes today, as in the past, is middle-class uneasiness over the prospect of sharing its jobs, its successes, its achievements with the black poor.

Clearly the fear of scarcity is the major motivation behind both the Haymarket riots and civil servant militancy. Lacking assurance that there is enough for all and lacking the entrepreneurial opportunities once afforded by the frontier, small businesses, and an expanding need for hand labor, civil servants have consistently moved towards maintenance of the status quo. Piven notes that the struggle between black and white in the city is misplaced, if understandable. But what could prevent such clashes? For one thing, the polarization of civil servants and the black poor is the result of channeling practices that have barred many qualified blacks from the training necessary for civil service jobs. The establishment of open enrollment programs in city colleges, special programs in ghetto high schools, more responsive counseling services, and school decentralization provide some hope for future equalization of the educational opportunity necessary for qualification. Minority groups may also enter the civil service labor pool if they are successful in altering job requirements to reflect job needs realistically. Substitution of work experience for credentials, community residence requirements for community civil service jobs, and the use of minority quotas to ensure minority representation in the civil service are valid strategies currently being tested or debated.

Moreover, since civil service jobs are actually increasing, white perception of a limited job market derives primarily from the changing picture within civil service where the number of teaching jobs is declining while the number of jobs in the medical field, in special education, and in administration is increasing. Rational programs to retrain obsolete civil servants combined with better coordination of educational institutions to job needs could open the way for a more realistic perception of the civil service by the white majority.

The Changing Economy

If civil servants are acting to retain their positions, industrial unions have also responded to workers' demands by becoming conservative forces dedicated to maintenance of the status quo. Glaberman discusses the changing role of the union in American life in "Unions vs. Workers in the Seventies: The Rise of Militancy in the Auto Industry." Not only have unions been accused of segregationist policies, but all too often in recent years the union has failed to represent the workers' interests and instead has aided management in disciplining workers in production. Many current union demands for "featherbedding," for example, are demands for maintenance of union jobs within family lines. Like the protectionist legal devices of civil servants, contracts worked out on such principles assure union members considerable security. At the same time, such policies mortgage the future of nonunion members by shutting them out of future jobs. Glaberman suggests that current worker demands, aimed ultimately at the control of productive processes themselves, are often ignored by union management because they can never be met within the current corporate structure. Legal requirements for incorporation could be altered so that the managerial structure of corporations had to include representatives of labor. Government could offer economic incentives or tax breaks to companies which engaged in extensive profit-sharing with their workers. Labor unions have the power to persuade Congress to introduce legislation that would give labor a greater share both in profits and decision making. Whether union leadership will rise to meet the challenge involved in altering current economic arrangements is a real and very troubling question.

Economic problems affect every segment of the economy and every group within it. Many of our problems may derive from the shift from an industrial to a postindustrial society. Perhaps a simpler way of putting it is to describe it as a shift from a labor-intensive to a capital-intensive technology. Such a shift has led to a tremendous growth in the service, or tertiary, sector and has produced more unemployment among unskilled, and even skilled, workers in obsolescent technologies. Although we are only dimly aware of it, one aspect of this change—the shift from a production to a consumption ethic—has already occurred. The old Protestant work ethic has been replaced by a leisure ethic. One effect of this change—a shortage of jobs for the unskilled—has irrationally increased the importance of credentials. Increased pressure for education keeps workers off the labor market for longer periods of time. Americans are starting work at a later age and retiring earlier. Moreover, as a result of population increase and demands for work made by minority and women's groups, the labor pool has expanded even further.

Shifts in areas of economic focus have expanded opportunities for some kinds of workers: government bureaucracies at both the state and national level have grown rapidly during the past decades; health professions are currently expanding. At the same time, demands for teachers have diminished as the effects of the baby boom that followed World War II have subsided. Farming is almost totally industrialized; only the harvesting done by migrant workers remains a hand operation. Even war—defense—production needs have changed. The relative proportion of money spent on weaponry has decreased but the output has increased. Changing technology, however, has thrown a great many skilled, specialized professionals out of work. Construction of new housing has slowed: inflation, shortage of mortgage money, high prices of raw materials, legal confusion over land-use codes and inadequate subsidization of low- and middle-income housing are all involved.

The effects of economic dislocations have been most sharply felt by the poor and by the minorities. Despite an alphabet soup of government programs, unemployment continues to increase, and remains proportionately greater among the poor and the minorities. Frequently the victims, rather than the social institutions that create unemployment, are blamed for their failure to find work. Wellman's case history "The *Wrong* Way to Find Jobs for Negroes" analyzes a job program that failed. The failure did not derive from the inability of black youths to learn or from black "shiftlessness"; the program neglected to produce jobs or provide training in skills or necessary social support. The program simply tried to show black youths how to get nonexistent jobs.

Our sanguine belief in education and in the ability of a virtuous middle class to rise above adversity is questioned in Powell and Driscoll's "Middle-Class Professionals Face Unemployment." Powell and Driscoll discovered that unemployment produced behavior patterns among the middle class that were virtually identical to patterns believed to be characteristic of the poor. The subjects of the study had all lost jobs in highly skilled professions. At first they reacted optimistically and made considerable effort towards finding work. When they failed to find new positions, they first became doubtful of their abilities. Rage accompanied doubt. Finally a sense of powerlessness replaced both rage and doubt. Most of the men ceased searching for jobs. Although we hesitate before calling such former pillars of the community "lazy" or "shiftless," their behavior was identical to behavior similarly labeled in minority communities.

Another problem created by a changing economy is the increasing discontinuity between systems of education and the roles for which such systems are designed to train us. Once again a problem that was endemic among the poor has now emerged among the middle classes. In years past, the middle class looked down upon the vocational education programs because of their blue-collar status. The aim of the working-class parent was to send his child to college for liberal arts training. Today, however, with an increasing surplus of college-trained personnel, trade and technical schools are assuming greater importance. At the same time, the college degree has been devalued and more and more jobs now require postgraduate training. In "Rich Man's Qualifications for Poor Man's Jobs" Berg explores the effect on the labor market of the increasing demand for college credentials. Upgrading of job requirements occurs regardless of necessity. And this upgrading makes even the lowest level job unavailable to those who lack credentials, just as it increases job dissatisfaction among job holders who are overtrained, overqualified, and overexpectant for the positions they ultimately obtain. As educational costs soar and government subsidization declines, demands for credentials increase the problems of nonwhites and those too poor to afford higher education. As the author suggests, it is not education that is at fault but the value that equates credentials with job eligibility. Periodic gluts or shortages of personnel are inevitable as long as education is governed by a market model and rational planning for labor needs is avoided.

Berg stresses the development of action programs that might provide more equal access to jobs. His focus on changes in institutions that mold behavior rather than changes in behavior itself is strongly reiterated by Gans in "More Equality: Income and Taxes." He surveys the various suggestions offered over the years to reduce the inequities in income distribution. Unlike many of the articles in this reader, which analyze problems, Gans' piece surveys a variety of solutions to inequitable income distribution: tax reform, welfare systems, national health insurance or social security, subsidized educational programs that provide job training, and government programs to create new jobs. Almost any of the plans suggested by Gans would provide at least minimal subsistence to all families without requiring them to submit to the degrading processes of our current welfare system.

Such plans could go a long way toward eliminating absolute poverty, as well as the self-destructive behaviors that result from adaptation to a welfare system. Until recently, for example, it was assumed that the breakdown of welfare families was due to some failure in the family itself. Studies have clearly shown, however, that the welfare system which interferes with the male feeling of self-esteem hastens family dissolution. Many other problems of welfare families have been traced to legal demands and procedures of the system itself. Although everyone agrees that the current welfare system must go, there is at present no one definitive program with which to replace it. Most programs suggested so far move towards income distribution but do little to level the relative distinctions that currently exist between economic classes. Far more needs to be done to close tax loopholes—for corporations as well as individuals—and to eliminate government subsidies for big business, such as oil depletion allowances and farm subsidies (which have benefitted agri-business far more than the small farmer). Our progress in these areas has been very slow, as the defeat of Nixon's modest family assistance plan amply demonstrates.

Jacob's "Winners and Losers: Garnishment and Bankruptcy in Wisconsin" provides another example of government policy that enriches the well-to-do at the expense of the poor. Bankruptcy proceedings, utilized primarily by businessmen, protect the bankrupt from loss of income, and if their lawyers have done their homework, allow the bankrupt person or company to renege on its financial obligations even while maintaining considerable cash reserves. Garnishment, on the other hand, is a weapon used by creditors against the less affluent. Frequently it is a financial credit company charging exorbitant interest rates which attaches the basic income of an employed debtor. The debtor is allowed a small sum for living expenses; the remainder goes to the creditor to pay off the interest charges and later the capital. Because legal processes are required for both procedures government has become a partner in the inequitable distribution of debt. If bankruptcy does not make the rich richer (and it sometimes does), garnishment certainly guarantees further impoverishment of the poor. Jacob's piece is directed towards an analysis of the processes that make such economic discrimination possible, and he calls for further analyses of the frequently informal institutions that allow government coercive powers to be used for personal enrichment.

Suelzle, in her ironic and aptly titled "Women in Labor," underscores the problems faced by women currently struggling for equality on the labor market. The exploitation of women is based on a series of myths which assert that women are less productive, less reliable, less serious, and less suited by nature or temperament for positions which are demanding and stimulating. A number of feminists have analyzed the reasons for the prevalence of such myths and the exploitation of women in our society. Their data suggest that subjugation of women is closely linked to the nature of the economic system. "Women in Labor" attacks the myths which help keep women in their place. Despite numerous statistical studies proving otherwise, the myths persist, maintained by a bewildering variety of social forces. Socialization processes create feelings of female inadequacy that inhibit the achievement drive; lack of female role models makes it difficult for girls to learn behavior appropriate to a variety of professions; academic requirements geared to male rather than female life cycles make advanced education more difficult for girls; economic and other barriers to the development of informal channels of support and communication prevent female cooperation in hiring or promotions. Women are working to change these legal barriers to achievement and to make government more responsive to their needs by establishing day-care centers, legislating equal pay for equal work, and establishing programs in woman's studies that correct for male bias in a number of fields. Optimistic though they are, most feminists recognize as does Suelzle that women will not achieve true equality until they as well as other disadvantaged groups unite to overcome discrimination against them. So far the process has gathered most momentum among professional, middle-class women, but the emphasis upon bread-and-butter issues is winning increased support from working-class and black women as well.

Our problems in production and distribution have been further compounded during the past few years by our awareness of impending ecological disaster and the energy crisis. Formerly, exploitation of a needed resource occurred as soon as that resource was located and manpower was available to extract it. Today, antipollution legislation, development of strict land-use codes, and time-consuming suits have slowed down the development of fossil fuel resources, atomic energy plants, and certain kinds of mining operations. While social scientists continue to debate the extent of the danger of pollution and of the energy crisis, we are adjusting to power cutbacks, fuel shortages, severe price increases in virtually all consumer goods, and even the annoyance of mosquitoes currently left to proliferate undeterred by DDT. To what extent the power shortages reflect a true ecological crisis is not certain. Many other forces are at work creating domestic scarcities such as the oil embargo, trade deals which have increased export of our raw materials to other countries, and inefficient planning. Most of these problems are the result of monopolistic control over vital resources by a few large corporations. Government reluctance to control the profits of large companies has enriched these concerns at the expense of the consumer.

The oil companies' financial profits have been accompanied by another kind of profit: fuel shortages have increased pressure on the government to license business to exploit off-shore oil reserves, to allow strip mining with its attendant social and environmental evils, and to decrease the number of independent merchants currently in the fuel markets. The beneficiaries are primarily the large multinational oil conglomerates; the hardships weigh most heavily upon the poor.

By focusing their attention on environmental degradation and limitations of natural resources rather than upon the role of business in overexploitation or upon the institutional causes of scarcity, many conservationists have expended valuable energy, money, and time in public relations campaigns to persuade people to clean up their neighborhoods or cut fuel consumption. Although conservationists are zealous supporters of government planning, they represent an élite group which has done little to educate the public about the workings of the economic and political institutions that have generated today's environmental crises.

Boulding's "Ecology and Environment" makes a strong case for increasing general attention to current ecological problems. He stresses the need for a universal détente—a recognition that we all live and depend upon "spaceship earth." Increased awareness of the claims of all people to the resources of the earth should make us more cautious about our environment. As long as we were a privileged nation and could utilize worldwide resources for ourselves, we achieved for a portion of our population a high standard of living. Population increase, plus the rightful demands of other nations, has curtailed the supply of available wealth. Also crucial in this environmental equation have been the unanticipated effects of technology. The green revolution which promised so much and initially resulted in high yields of grain and other products has proven disappointing. Demands for a high level of technology and capitalization could not be met by small farmers who increasingly were forced to surrender their land to large companies or to individuals who could afford the capital investments for seed and machinery. By replacing agricultural techniques which emphasized variety and maintained soil fertility by techniques which emphasized single crops, the green revolution demanded increased use of chemical fertilizers. Many of these have been proven dangerous to men and animals and created demands for further innovations to replace them. Some new kinds of fertilizers may be in the offing but they are expensive to discover and produce. Meanwhile, societies may be expected to be more cautious about accepting new processes without adequate testing.

Until now, America has attempted to overcome all challenges to its economy by concentrating upon technological solutions and ignoring the institutional framework within which our technology functions. Under the illusion that a free market can adequately control production and distribution, we consistently affirm the virtues of laissez-faire. In reality, however, markets are not free, government interferes consistently to protect business interests, and our access to vital resources is manipulated daily by corporations founded not to enhance the public good but to increase their own profits. Because of our failure to recognize and to deal with the reality of our economic institutions, we have created a continual series of crises which have affected us all.

RICHARD SENNETT

Genteel Backlash: Chicago 1886

A bomb exploded in Chicago's Haymarket Square on May 4, 1886, killing seven people and setting off what may have been the first police riot in that city's history. The neighborhood in which this violence broke out was hardly what one would call a high crime area today. The quiet residential district adjacent to the Haymarket was considered so nondescript, so ordinary, that it had never even been given a special name. Richer and poorer neighborhoods had names; Union Park, as I shall call it here, was anonymous, like most other middle- and lower middle-class communities in the industrial cities of nineteenth century America.

The people of Union Park were the forgotten men of that era, neither poor enough to be rebels like the Socialist workingmen who assembled that day in Haymarket Square, nor affluent enough to count in the affairs of the city. For a quarter of the century, from 1865 to 1890, Union Park

epitomized that tawdry respectability of native-born, lower middle-class Americans that Dreiser was to capture in *Sister Carrie,* or that Farrell would later rediscover in the bourgeois life of Catholic Chicago.

The beginnings of Union Park, when Chicago was a commercial town rather than a diverse manufacturing city, were much grander. In the 1830s and 1840s it was a fashionable western suburb, separated by open land from the bustle of the business district and the noisome unhealthy river at the heart of the city. Then, in the years after the Civil War, a change in the pattern of commercial land investment, the filling in of a swamp on the edge of Lake Michigan by Potter Palmer and the growth of a manufacturing district to the south of Union Park led fashionable people to desert the old suburb for newer, more magnificent residences along the lake shore of Chicago. In their place, in the 1870s, came people of much lesser means,

The Des Plaines Street Police Station, Chicago, May 4, 1886, after the Haymarket riot (from a painting of the period).

Genteel Backlash: Chicago 1886

seeking a respectable place to live where rents and land were becoming cheap. Union Park for these new people was a neighborhood where they could enjoy the prestige of a once-fashionable address, and even pretend to be a little grander than they were. "The social Brooklyn of Chicago," Mayor Harrison called it; "a place where modest women become immodest in their pretentions," wrote another contemporary observer. For 25 years the old holdings were gradually divided up into little plots, and native-born Americans—who were the bulk of the migrants to the cities of the Midwest before the 1880s—rented small brick houses or a half floor in one of the converted mansions.

It was here, in this modest, cheerless community, that a series of unexpected events took place in the late 1880s, beginning with the bloody encounter between police and workingmen in nearby Haymarket Square. That riot was followed 18 months later by a series of highly expert robberies in the community, a crime wave that culminated in the murder of a leading Union Park resident. The striking feature of all this violence lay not in the events themselves but in the reaction of shopkeepers, store clerks, accountants and highly skilled laborers to the disorder suddenly rampant among their sedate homes. Their reaction to the violence was impassioned to an extent that in retrospect seems unwarranted by events; the character of their reaction will, however, seem familiar to students of urban backlash in our own time. The forgotten men of Union Park responded to violence by holding a whole class—the poor, and especially the immigrant poor—responsible for the course of these violent eruptions. For a modern observer, the puzzle is what made them react this way.

The Haymarket Bombing

> Certain people, mostly foreigners of brief residence among us, whose ideas of government were derived from their experience in despotic Germany, sought by means of violence and murder to inaugurate a carnival of crime. *F. H. Head, official orator at the unveiling of the Haymarket Square Statue for policemen slain in the riot, reported in the* Chicago Daily Tribune, May 31, 1889.

Chicago's haymarket constituted the dividing line between the residences and neighborhood stores of Union Park and the warehouses of the growing central city. Haymarket Square itself was enclosed by large buildings and the Des Plaines Street Police Station was just off the Square. It was hardly a place to engage in clandestine activity, but, for a peaceful meeting, the Square was an ideal forum, since it could accommodate roughly 20,000 people.

The common notion of what happened on May 4, 1886, is that a group of labor unionists assembled in Haymarket Square to listen to speeches and that, when the police moved in to break up the meeting, someone in the crowd threw a bomb, killing and wounding many policemen and bystanders. This account is true as far as it goes, but ex-

plains little of what determined the event's effect on the community and city in the aftermath.

The people who came to the meeting were the elite of the working class, those who belonged to the most skilled crafts; they were hardly the "dregs" of society. The crowd itself was small, although it had been supposed that events in Chicago during the preceding days would have drawn a large gathering. On May 3, demonstrations had been organized in the southwestern part of the city against the McCormick Works, where a lockout of some union members had occurred. The police had responded with brutal force to disperse the crowd. Later that same night, at a number of prescheduled union meetings, it was resolved to hold a mass meeting at some neutral place in the city.

A small group of Socialist union leaders, led by August Spies and Albert Parsons, decided the time was ripe for a mass uprising of laboring men; the moment seemed perfect for an expression of labor solidarity, when large numbers of people might be expected to rally to the cause as Spies and Parsons understood it—the growth of Socialist power. Haymarket Square was the obvious choice for a neutral site. Posters were printed in the early hours of the next day and spread throughout the city.

When Parsons and Spies mounted the speakers' rostrum the next night in Haymarket Square, they must have been appalled. Instead of vast crowds of militants, there were only a thousand or so people in the Square, and as speaker after speaker took his turn the crowd dwindled steadily. The audience was silent and unmoved as the explanations of the workers' role in socialism were expounded, though there was respect for the speakers of the kind one would feel for a friend whose opinions grew out of a different sphere of life. Yet as the meeting was about to die out, a phalanx of policemen suddenly appeared on the scene to disperse the crowd.

Why the police intruded is the beginning of the puzzle we have to understand. Their reaction was totally inappropriate to the character of what was occurring before their eyes; they ought rather to have breathed a sigh of relief that the meeting was such a peaceful fiasco. But, as the civil riots of a later chapter in Chicago's history show, it is sometimes more difficult for the police to "cool off" than it is for the demonstrators. In any event, just as the Haymarket meeting was falling apart, the police moved in to disperse it by force, and thus brought back to life the temporary spirit of unity and of outrage against the violence at McCormick Works that had drawn the crowd and orators together.

The knots of men moved back from the lines of police advancing toward the speaker's stand, so that the police gained the area in front of the rostrum without incident. Then, suddenly, someone in the crowd threw a powerful bomb into the midst of the policemen, and pandemonium broke loose. The wounded police and people in the crowd dragged themselves or were carried into the hallways of buildings in the eastern end of Union Park; drugstores, like Ebert's at Madison and Halstead and Barker's on West Madison, suddenly became hospitals with bleeding men stretched out on the floors, while police combed the residences and grounds of Union Park looking for wounded members of the crowd who had managed to find shelter under stoops or in sheds from the police guns booming in the Square.

As the news spread, small riots with aimless energy broke out in the southwestern part of the city, but they were soon dispersed. By the morning of May 5, the working-class quarters were quiet, though the police were not. They, and the middle-class people of Chicago, especially those living in Union Park, were in a fever, a fever compounded of fear, a desire for vengeance, and simple bewilderment.

It is this reaction that must be explored to gauge the true impact of the Haymarket incident on the Union Park community. The first characteristic of this reaction was how swiftly an interpretation, communally shared, was formed; the middle-class people of Union Park, and elsewhere in Chicago, were immediately moved by the incident to draw a clearly defined picture of what had happened, and they held onto their interpretation tenaciously. Today it is easy to recognize, from the location of the meeting next to a police station, from the apathy of the crowd, from the sequence of events that preceded the bombing, that the Haymarket incident was not a planned sequence of disorder or a riot by an enraged mob, but rather the work of an isolated man, someone who might have thrown the bomb no matter who was there. But the day after the bombing, these objective considerations were not the reality "respectable" people perceived. Middle-class people of Chicago believed instead that "the immigrant anarchists" were spilling out of the slums to kill the police, in order to destroy the security of the middle classes themselves. "Respectable" people felt some kind of need to believe in the enormity of the threat, and in this way the community quickly arrived at a common interpretation of what had happened.

The enormity of the threat was itself the second characteristic of their reaction. The color red, which was taken as a revolutionary incitement, was "cut out of street advertisements and replaced with a less suggestive color." On the day after the riot a coroner's jury returned a verdict that all prisoners in the hands of the police were guilty of murder, because Socialism as such led to murderous anarchy, and anyone who attended the meeting must have been a Socialist. Yet this same jury observed that it was "troublesome" that none of those detained could be determined to have thrown the bomb. Anarchism itself was generalized to a more sweeping scope by its identification with foreign birth; the "agitators" were poor foreigners, and this fact could explain their lawlessness. For example, the *Tribune* reported that on the day after the Haymarket Riot police closed two saloons

Courtesy Chicago Historical Society

that were the headquarters of the foreign-speaking population, which flaunts and marches under the red flag, and heretofore they were the centers of a great throng of men who did little but drink beer and attend the meetings in the halls above.

On May 5 and 6, the police were engaged in a strenuous effort to determine where the "anarchist" groups lived, so that the population as a whole might be controlled. On May 7, and this was the view to prevail henceforth, they announced that the residences of most anarchists must be in the southwestern portion of the city, the immigrant, working-class area.

In Union Park the assigning of the responsible parties to the general category of "foreigner" excited even more panic. The *Tribune* of May 7 reported that the community was gripped by a fear that lawless marauders would again erupt out of the proletarian sector of the city and terrorize people in the neighborhood of the riot. These fears were sustained by two events in the next week.

First were reports of the deaths, day after day, of policemen and innocent bystanders who had been seriously

The intersection of Washington Boulevard and Ogden Avenue as seen from Union Park in the nineties.

wounded by the bomb on May 4, coupled with a massive newspaper campaign to raise money for the families of the victims. Second, and by far more important, fear of renewed bombing was kept alive by the fantasies of a Captain Schaack of the Chicago police who day by day discovered and foiled anarchist plots, plans to bomb churches and homes, attempts on the lives of eminent citizens. Such were the scare stories with which the middle-class people of Chicago horrified themselves for weeks.

The same deep communal force that immediately led the people of Union Park to interpret an objectively confused event in a very similar and very simplistic fashion also led them to use increasingly horrific metaphors to describe the nature of the threat and challenge. But as events a year later were to show, this force also prevented the men of Union Park from being able to deal effectively with the future violence.

Crime in the Streets

On Thursday, February 9, 1888, the *Chicago Tribune* gave its lead space to the following story:

Amos J. Snell, a millionaire who lived at the corner of Washington Boulevard and Ada Street, was shot to death by two burglars who entered his house and made off with $1,600 worth of county warrants and $5,000 in checks. The murder was committed at about 2 A.M. and discovered by a servant at about 6:30 A.M.

Snell had been a resident of the area since 1867, when he built a home in Union Park and bought up many blocks of desirable real estate around it.

The murder of Snell climaxed a tense situation in Union Park that had existed since the beginning of the year 1888. Since New Year's Day, "between forty and fifty burglaries

have been committed within a radius of half a mile from the intersection of Adams and Ashland Avenues," the editor of the *Tribune* wrote the day after Snell's death. Though the police counted half this number, it appears that the burglars had a simple and systematic scheme: to loot any household goods, such as furs, silver plate, jewelry or bonds left in unlocked drawers. Occasionally some of the property was recovered, and occasionally a thief was arrested who seemed to have been involved, but the operation itself was remarkably smooth and successful.

How did people in Union Park react to these burglaries, and what did they do to try to stop them? The reaction of the community was much like their reaction to the Haymarket bombing: they felt caught up at once in a "reign of terror," as the *Tribune* said, "that was none of their doing —they didn't know when the danger would strike again or who would be hurt. Most of all, they didn't know how to stop it." Once again, community fear was escalated to a general, sweeping and impersonal terror.

Before the Snell murder, the citizens of the community had tried two means of foiling the robbers, and so of quieting the fears of their families. One was to make reports to the police, reports which the editor of the *Tribune* claimed the police did not heed. The citizens then resorted to fortifying their homes, to hiring elderly men as private guards but the thieves were professional enough to deal with this: "somehow or other the burglars evaded all the precautions that were taken to prevent their nocturnal visits."

The Neighborhood as Garrison State

The Snell murder brought public discussion of the robberies, and how to stop them, to a high pitch. Especially in Union Park, the vicinity of Snell's residence, the com-

The Changing Economy

munity was "so aroused that the people talked of little else than vigilance committees and frequent holdings of court . . . as a panacea for the lawless era that had come upon them." Gradually, the small-town vigilante idea gave way to a new attitude toward the police, and how the police should operate in a large city. "It is no use," said one member of the Grant Club, the West Side club to which Snell himself had belonged, "to attempt to run a cosmopolitan city as you would run a New England village." He meant that the police had up to that time concentrated on closing down gambling houses and beer parlors as a major part of their effort to keep the town "respectable" and "proper." Thus they didn't deal effectively with serious crimes like robbery and murder because they spent too much time trying to clean up petty offenses; the main thing was to keep the criminal elements confined to their own quarters in the city. In all these discussions, the fact of being burglarized had been forgotten. The search turned to a means of separatism, of protection against the threatening "otherness" of the populace outside the community.

Such views were striking, considering the position of Union Park. The community's own physical character, in its parks and playgrounds, was nonurban, designed in the traditions of Olmstead and Vaux; the people, as was pointed out repeatedly in the newspaper account, were themselves among the most respectable and staid, if not the most fashionable in the city. Yet here were the most respectable among the respectable arguing for abandoning the enforcement of a common morality throughout the city. The petty criminals outside the community's borders ought to be left in peace, but out of sight. Union Park existed in a milieu too cosmopolitan for every act of the lower classes to be controlled; the police ought to abandon attempts to be the guardians of all morality and instead concentrate on

assuring the basic security of the citizens against outbursts of major crime.

What Union Park wanted instead, and what it got, was a garrison of police to make the community riotproof and crimeproof. For the police did indeed abandon the search for the killers, and concentrated on holding the security of Union Park, like an area under siege. In this way, the original totally suburban tone of the parks and mansions was transformed; this respectable neighborhood felt its own existence to be so threatened that only rigid barriers, enforced by a semimilitary state of curfew and surveillance, would permit it to continue functioning.

The characteristics of their reaction to violence could only lead to such a voluntary isolation: everyone "knew" immediately what was wrong; and what was wrong was overwhelming: it was nothing less than the power of the "foreigner," the outsider who had suddenly become dominant in the city. Isolation, through garrisons and police patrols, was the only solution.

Union Park held onto its middle-class character until the middle of the 1890s; there was no immediate desertion by respectable people of the area in the wake of the violence: where else in a great city, asked one citizen, was it safe to go? Everywhere the same terror was possible.

The contrast between the limited character of civil disturbance and the immediate perception of that disturbance as the harbinger of an unnameable threat coming from a generalized enemy is a theme that binds together much research on urban disorders.

Until a few years ago, riots were taken to be the expression of irrational and directionless aggression. "Irrationality of crowds" and similar explanations of crowd behavior as an innate disorder were first given a cogent interpretation in the industrial era in the writings of Le Bon,

Courtesy Chicago Historical Society

for whom the irrational brutality of crowds was a sign of how the "psychology" of the individual becomes transformed when the individual acts in concert with other people. This image of crowds was as congenial to many of the syndicalists on the Left as it was to the fears of bourgeois people like those in Union Park. The difficulty with the image is that, for the nineteenth century at least and for the Haymarket Riots certainly, it does not seem to fit the facts of crowd behavior.

Nevertheless, expecting "seething passions" to erupt hysterically, the middle-class people of Chicago and their police were somehow blind to a spectacle they should have enjoyed, that of the workers' increasing boredom with the inflammatory talk of their supposed leaders. The expectations of a seething rabble had somehow to be fulfilled, and so the police themselves took the first step. After the shooting was over, the respectable people of Chicago became inflamed. This blind passion in the name of defending the city from blind passion is the phenomenon that needs to be explained. A similar contradiction occurred in the series of robberies 18 months later as well. As in the riot, the facts of the rationality of the enemy and his limited purpose, although acknowledged, were not absorbed; he was felt to be something else—a nameless, elusive terror, all-threatening—and the people reacted with a passion equal to his.

This mystifying condition, familiar now in the voices heard from the "New Right," is what I should like to explain, not through a sweeping theory that binds the past to the present, but through a theory that explains this peculiar reaction in terms of strains in the family life of the Union Park people. What I would like to explore—and I certainly do not pretend to prove it—is how, in an early industrial city, the fears of the foreign masses held by a middle-class group may have reflected something other than the actual state of interaction between bourgeoisie and proletariat. These fears may have reflected instead the impact of family life on the way the people like those in Union Park understood their places in the city society.

If it is true that in the character one ascribes to one's enemy lies a description of something in one's own experience, the nature of the fear of lower-class foreigners among Union Park families might tell something about the Union Park community itself. The Union Park men, during the time of the riot and robberies, accused their chosen enemies of being lawless anarchists whose base passions pushed them outside the bounds of acceptable behavior, which finally, sent them emotionally out of control. If the poor were reasonable, if they were temperate, ran the argument, these violent things would not have come to pass.

What about the Union Park people themselves, then? Were they masters of themselves? A study I have recently completed on the family patterns of the Union Park people during the decades of the 1870s and 1880s may throw some light on the question of stability and purposefulness

in their lives: it is the dimension of stability in these family patterns, I believe, that shaped their reaction to violence in their city.

A Close and Happy Home?

In 1880, on a 40-square-block territory of Union Park, there lived 12,000 individuals in approximately 3,000 family units. The latter were of three kinship types: single-member families, where one person lived alone without any other kin; nuclear families, consisting of a husband and wife and their unmarried children; and extended families, where to the nuclear unit was added some other relative—a brother or sister of the parents, a member of a third generation, or a son or daughter who was married and lived with his spouse in the parental home. The most common form of the extended family in Union Park was that containing "collateral kin," that is, unmarried relatives of the same generation as the husband or wife.

The dominant form of family life in Union Park was nuclear, for 80 percent of the population lived in such homes, with 10 percent of the population living alone in single-member families, and the remaining 10 percent living in extended family situations. A father and mother living alone with their growing children in an apartment or house was the pervasive household condition. There were few widowed parents living with their children in either nuclear or extended homes, and though the census manuscripts on which my study of the year 1880 is based were inexact at this point, there appeared to be few groups of related families living in the same neighborhood but in separate dwellings.

Family Sizes

The size of the Union Park family was small. Most families had one or two children; it was rare for a family to have more. And, the size of poorer families was in its contours similar to the size of the wealthier ones: few families were larger than six members.

Over the course of time internal conditions of family structure and of family size tended to lead to similar family histories. Nuclear families had characteristic histories similar to the experience of smaller families having from two to four kin members in the 1870s and 1880s. Extended families, on the other hand, had histories similar to the experience of the minority of families with four to six kin members during these decades. What made this process subtle was that nuclear families did not tend to be smaller, or extended larger. Family size and family kinship structure seemed rather to be independent structures with parallel internal differences in functioning.

Why and how this was so can be understood by assessing the patterns of the generations of the dominant group.

The nuclear, small-size families during the year 1880 were very cohesive in relations between husbands and wives, parents and children. Whether rich or poor—and about 25 percent of the community fell into a working class category—the young men and women from such homes rarely broke away to live on their own until they themselves were ready to marry and found families, usually when the man was in his early thirties. The families of Union Park, observers of the time noted, were extremely self-contained, did little entertaining, and rarely left the home even to enjoy such modest pleasures as a church social or, for the men, a beer at the local tavern. The small family, containing only parents and their immediate children, resisted the diverse influences either of other relatives or extensive community contacts. These intensive families would seem to epitomize stability among the people of Union Park.

Mobility and Family Stability

Nevertheless, my study of intergenerational mobility in work and residence from 1872 to 1890 did reveal a complicated, but highly significant pattern of insecurity in the dominant intensive families as compared to the smaller group of less intensive families.

The first insecurity of these families was in the rate of desertion. While divorce was rare—it was an act carrying a terrible stigma a hundred years ago—practical divorce in the form of desertion did occur. In Union Park, the rate of desertion was twice as high as that of *poorer* communities—in nearly one out of ten families husband or wife had deserted. A more subtle pattern of insecurity was at work as well.

In the nuclear-family homes and in the smaller families the fathers were stable job holders, as a group, over the course of the 18 years studied; roughly the same proportions of unskilled, skilled and white-collar workers of various kinds composed the labor force of these nuclear fathers in 1890 as in 1872. Given the enormous growth of Chicago's industrial production, its banking and financial capital, retail trade volume, as well as the increase of the population (100 percent increase each ten years) and the greatly increasing proportion of white-collar pursuits during this time, such stability in job distribution is truly puzzling.

But equally puzzling is the fact that this pattern of job holding among the fathers of intensive families was not shared by the fathers in extended families or fathers of larger families living in Union Park. For, unlike their neighbors, fathers of these more complex and extensive families were mobile up into exclusively bureaucratic, white-collar pursuits—so much so that by 1890 virtually none of these fathers worked with their hands. They gradually concentrated in executive and other lesser managerial pursuits and decreased their numbers in shopkeeping, toward which, stereotypically, they are supposed to gravitate.

Even more striking were the differences between fathers and sons in each of these family groups. The sons in the dominant family homes were, unlike their fathers, very unstable in their patterns of job holding. As many moved down into manual pursuits over the course of the 18 years as moved up into the white-collar occupations. One is tempted to explain this simply as a regression toward the mean of higher status groups in time. But the sons of extended and large families did not move in this mixed direction. Rather, they followed the footsteps of their fathers into good white-collar positions, with almost total elimination of manual labor in their ranks as well. This pattern occurred in small-family sons versus large-family sons and in nuclear-family sons versus extended-family sons. The difference in the groups of sons was especially striking in that the starting points of the sons in the occupational work force had virtually the *same* distribution in all types of families. Stephan Thernstrom has pointed out that economic aid between generations of workers is more likely to manifest itself at the outset of a young person's career than when the older generation has retired and the young have become the principal breadwinners. But the fact is that in Union Park, both extended-family and nuclear-family sons, both large- and small-family sons, began to work in virtually the same pursuits as their fathers, then became distinctively different in their patterns of achievement. This strongly suggests that something *beyond* monetary help was at work in these families to produce divergences in the work experiences of the different groups of sons.

The residence patterns of the generations of the intensive and less intensive families also bears on the issues of stability and instability in the lives of the people of Union Park. Up to the time of violence in the Union Park area, the residence patterns of the two kinds of families, in both the parents' and the sons' generations, were rather similar. In the wake of the violence, however, it appears that within the parents' generation there was significant movement back into the Union Park area, whereas for the half decade preceding the disturbances there was a general movement out to other parts of Chicago. It is in the generation of the sons that differences between the two family groups appeared. In the wake of the violence, the sons of large families and of extended families continued the exodus from Union Park that began in the early 1880s. The sons from intensive families did not; in the years following the violence they stopped migrating beyond the boundaries of the community they had known as children, and instead kept closer to their first homes.

Family Background and Making It

These observations have an obvious bearing on an important debate over what form of bourgeois family life best nurtures the kind of children who can cope with the immensely dynamic and risky world of the industrial city. Talcott Parsons has argued that the small nuclear family is a kinship form well adapted to the industrial order; the lack of extensive kin obligations and a wide kin circle in this family type means, Parsons has contended, that the kinship unit does not serve as a binding private world of its own, but rather frees the individual to participate in "universalized" bureaucratic structures that are urban-wide and dynamic.

The cultural historian Phillippe Aries, in *Centuries of Childhood,* has challenged this theory by amassing a body of historical evidence to show that the extended kinship relationships in large families, at least during an earlier era, were actually less sheltering, more likely to push the individual out into the world where he would have to act like a full man on his own at an early age, than the intense, intimate conditions of the nineteenth-century home. In intensive homes, the young person spent a long time in a state of dependence under the protection and guidance of his elders. Consequently, argues Aries, the capacity of the young adult from small nuclear homes to deal with the world about him was blunted, for he passed from a period of total shelter to a state in which he was expected to be entirely competent on his own.

The data I collected on Union Park clearly are in line with the argument made by Aries. The young from homes of small scale or from homes where the structure of the family was nuclear and "privatistic," in Aries' phrase, had an ineptness in the work world, and a rootedness to the place of their childhood not found to the same degree among the more complex, or larger-family situations. (I have no desire to argue the moral virtues of this rootedness to community or failure to "make it" in the city; these simply happened to be the conditions that existed.) But the conditions that faced Union Park families in a new kind of city, a city at once disorganized and anarchic, set the stability of the family against adaptation to city life. For it is clear that the nineteenth-century, privatistic, sheltering homes Aries depicts, homes that Frank Lloyd Wright describes in his *Autobiography* of his early years in Chicago, homes that observers of the time pointed to as a basic element in the composition of the "dull respectability" of Union Park, could themselves have easily served as a refuge from the confusing, dynamic city that was taking shape all around the confines of Union Park.

And what is more natural than that middle-class people should try to hold onto the status position they had in such a disrupting, growing milieu, make few entrepreneurial ventures outside their established jobs, and withdraw into the comfort and intimacy of their families. Here is the source of that job "freeze" to be seen in the mobility patterns of fathers in intense-family situations; the bourgeois intensive family in this way became a shelter from the work pressures of the industrial city, a place where men tried to institute some control and establish some comforting intimacies in the shape of their lives, while withdrawing to the sidelines as the new opportunities of the city industries opened up. Such an interpretation of these middle-class families complements Richard Hofstadter's interpretation of middle-class political attitudes in the latter part of the nineteenth century. He characterizes the middle-class as feeling that the new industrial order had passed them by and left them powerless. It is this peculiar feeling of social helplessness on the part of the fathers that explains what use they made of their family lives.

But the late nineteenth century was also the world of Horatio Alger, of "luck and pluck"; it was no time for withdrawal. The idea of seizing opportunities, the idea of instability of job tenure for the sake of rising higher and higher, constituted, as John Cawelti has described it, the commonly agreed-upon notion among respectable people of the road to success. One should be mobile in work, then, for this was the meaning of "opportunity" and "free enterprise," but in fact the overwhelming dislocations of the giant cities seem to have urged many men to retreat into the circle of their own families, to try simply to hold onto jobs they knew they could perform.

Conditions of privacy and comfort in the home weakened the desire to get ahead in the world, to conquer it; since the fathers of the intensive families were retreating from the confusions of city life, their preparation of their sons for work in Chicago became ambiguous, in that they wanted, surely, success for their sons, yet shielded the young, and did not themselves serve as models of successful adaptation. The result of these ambiguities can be seen directly in the work experience of the sons, when contrasted to the group of sons from families which, by virtue either of family form or size, were more complex or less intense. Overlaid on these family patterns was a relatively high rate of hidden marital breakdown in Union Park—one in every ten homes—while the expectation was, again, that such breakdowns must not occur, that they were a disgrace.

Because the goals of these middle-class people were bred of contradictory desires to escape from and succeed in the city, the possibility of a wholly satisfying pattern of achievement for them was denied. The family purposes were innately contradictory. A family impulse in one direction inevitably defeated another image of what was wanted. This meant that the sources of defeat were nameless for the families involved; surely these families were not aware of the web of self-contradictions in which in retrospect they seem to have been enmeshed; they knew only that things never seemed to work out to the end planned, that they suffered defeats in a systematic way. It is this specific kind of frustration that would lead to a sense of being overwhelmed, which, in this community's family system, led easily to a hysterical belief in hidden, unknown threats ready to strike at a man at almost any time.

What I would like to suggest is that this complex pattern of self-defeat explains the character of the Union Park reaction to violence. For the dread of the unknown that the middle classes projected onto their supposed enemies among the poor expressed exactly the condition of self-instituted defeat that was the central feature of the family system in Union Park. And this dread was overwhelming precisely because men's own contradictory responses to living in such a city were overwhelming. They had defined a set of conditions for their lives that inevitably left them out of control. The fact that in Union Park there was a desire to destroy the "immigrant anarchists" or to garrison the neighborhood against them, as a result of the incidents of violence, was important in that it offered an outlet for personal defeats, not just for anger against lawbreakers. This response to violence refused to center on particular people, but rather followed the "path of hysterical reaction," in Freud's phrase, and centered on an abstract class of evildoers. The fear of being suddenly overwhelmed from the outside was really a sign that one was in fact in one's own life being continually overwhelmed by the unintended consequences of what one did.

The terrible fear of attack from the unbridled masses was also related to the fear of falling into deep poverty that grew up in urban middle-class families of this time. To judge from a wide range of novels in the latter half of the nineteenth century there was a dread among respectable people of suddenly and uncontrollably falling into abject poverty; the Sidwells in Thackeray's *Vanity Fair* plummet from wealth to disorganized penury in a short space of time; In Edith Wharton's *Age of Innocence,* Lily Bart's father is similarly struck down by the symbol of entrepreneurial chance in the industrial city, the stock market. This feeling of threat from the impersonal, unpredictable workings of the city economy was much like the sense of threat that existed in the Union Park families, because the dangers encountered in both cases were not a person or persons one could grapple with, but an abstract condition, poverty, or family disorder that was unintended, impersonal and swift to come if the family should once falter. Yet what one *should* do was framed in such a self-contradictory way that it seemed that oneself and one's family were always on the edge of survival. In this way, the growth of the new industrial city, with its uncertainties and immense wastes in human poverty, not all victims of which were easily dismissed as personal failures, could surely produce in the minds of middle-class citizens who were uneasy about their own class position and lived out from the center of town, the feeling that some terrible force from below symbolized by the poor, the foreigner, was about to strike out and destroy them unless they did something drastic.

The reaction among most of the families to the eruption of violence bears out this interpretation of events. With the exception of the upwardly mobile, extended-family sons, most family members did not try to flee the community as a response to the threats of riot and the organized wave of crime. There was a renewed feeling of community solidarity in the face of violence, a solidarity created by fear and a common dread of those below.

The relations between family life and the perception of violence in this Chicago community could be formed into the following general propositions. These were middle-class families enormously confused in what they wanted for themselves in the city, both in terms of their achievements in the society at large and in terms of their emotional needs for shelter and intimacy. Their schema of values and life goals was in fact formed around the issues of stability and instability as goals in a self-contradictory way. The result of this inner contradiction was a feeling of frustration, of not really being satisfied, in the activities of family members to achieve *either* patterns of stability or mobility for themselves. The self-defeat involved in this process naturally led these families to feel themselves threatened by overwhelming, nameless forces they could not control, regardless of what they did. The outbreak of violence was a catalyst for them, giving them in the figure of the "other," the stranger, the foreigner, a generalized agent of disorder and disruption.

It is this process that explains logically why the people of Union Park so quickly found a communally acceptable villain responsible for violence, despite all the ambiguities perceived in the actual outbreaks of the disorders themselves. This is why the villain so quickly identified, was a generalized, nonspecific human force, the embodiment of the unknown, the outside, the foreign. This is why the people of Union Park clung so tenaciously to their interpretation, seemed so willing to be terrorized and distraught.

Then and Now

If the complex processes of family and social mobility in Union Park are of any use in understanding the great fear of disorder among respectable, middle-class urbanites of our own time, their import is surely disturbing. For the nature of the disease that produced this reaction to violence among the industrial middle classes was not simply a matter of "ignorance" or failure to understand the problems of the poor; the fear was the consequence, rather, of structural processes in the lives of the Union Park families themselves. Thus for attitudes of people like the Union Park dwellers to change, and a more tolerant view of those below to be achieved, nothing so simple as more education about poor people, or to put the matter in contemporary terms, more knowledge about Negroes, would have sufficed. The whole fabric of the city, in its impact on staid white-collar workers, would have to have been changed. The complexity and the diversity of the city itself would need to have been stilled for events to take another course. But were the disorder of the city absent, the principal characteristic of the industrial city as we know it would also have been absent. These cities were powerful agents of change, precisely because they replaced the controlled social space of village and farm life with a kind of human settlement too dense and too various to be controlled.

And it comes to mind that the New Right fears of the present time are as deeply endemic to the structure of complex city life as was the violent reaction to violence in Union Park. Perhaps, out of patterns of self-defeat in the modern middle classes, it is bootless to expect right-wing, middle-class repression to abate simply through resolves of goodwill, "education about Negroes," or a change of heart. The experience of bourgeois people of Chicago 100 years ago may finally make us a great deal more pessimistic about the chances for reason and tolerance to survive in a complex and pluralistic urban society.

This article is from *Nineteenth-Century Cities: Essay in the New Urban History* edited by Stephan Thernstrom and Richard Sennett (New Haven and London: Yale University Press, 1969). Copyright © 1969 by Yale University.

FURTHER READING

Centuries of Childhood by Phillippe Aries, translated from the French by Robert Baldick (New York: Knopf, 1962). Probably the finest book on the history of family life.

Aries concludes his work with an attack on the "ethical narrowness" of intense families.

World Revolution and Family Patterns by William J. Goode (New York: Free Press, 1963).

Parents and Children in History by David Hunt (New York: Basic Books, 1970).

"From Shantytown to Public Housing: A Comparison of Family Life in Two Urban Neighborhoods in Puerto Rico" by Helen Safa, *Caribbean Studies* 4 (1964): 3–12.

Families Against the City: Middle Class Homes of Industrial Chicago by Richard Sennett (Cambridge, Mass.: Harvard University Press, 1970).

The Uses of Disorder: Personal Identity and City Life by Richard Sennett (New York: Knopf, 1970).

"Urbanism as a Way of Life" by Louis Wirth, *American Journal of Sociology* 44 (July 1938):1–24.

FRANCES FOX PIVEN

Militant Civil Servants in New York City

Not long ago, thousands of people massed in front of New York's City Hall and sang "Solidarity Forever." The image was of workers marching against Pinkertons. But the ranks were middle-class civil servants, and their solidarity was directed against the black and Puerto Rican poor. The issue on this occasion was school decentralization, but that is only one of a host of issues currently galvanizing white civil servants and dividing them from the enlarging minorities in the cities.

The rising militancy of public employees needs no documenting here. New York's 60,000 school teachers have been shutting down the school system regularly; this fall it was the Day Care Center workers; slowdowns by police and firemen are becoming commonplace. And if public employees are more militant in New York, where they are the most numerous and best organized, public unions across the country are catching up. Teachers prevented schools from opening this fall in Illinois, Ohio, Indiana, Massachusetts, Pennsylvania, New Hampshire, Michigan, New York, Pennsylvania, Connecticut, Rhode Island, Wisconsin, Minnesota, Utah and Tennessee. Last year Detroit's police were hit by the "blue flu"; while Cleveland's police threatened outright rebellion against Mayor Carl B. Stokes. In Atlanta the firemen went on strike; in Newark the police and firemen simultaneously called in sick.

These events are not, as they are sometimes described, simply contests between unions and the "general public." The keenest struggle is with residents of the central-city ghettos (who in any case now form a substantial segment of the "general public" in most big cities). Police, firemen, teachers and public-welfare workers increasingly com-

plain about "harassment" in the ghettos. For their part, growing numbers of the black poor view police, firemen, teachers, public-welfare workers and other city employees as their oppressors.

The emerging conflict is not difficult to explain. Whites and blacks are pitted against each other in a struggle for the occupational and political benefits attached to public employment. Whites now have the bulk of these benefits, and blacks want a greater share of them. Nor is it only jobs that are at stake. Organized public employees have become a powerful force shaping the policies of municipal agencies, but the policies that suit employees often run counter to ghetto interests. We may be entering another phase in the long and tragic history of antagonism between the black poor and the white working class in America.

The Ethnic Stake-out

Municipal jobs have always been an important resource in the cultivation of political power. As successive waves of immigrants settled in the cities, their votes were exchanged for jobs and other favors, permitting established party leaders to develop and maintain control despite the disruptive potential of new and unaffiliated populations. The exchange also facilitated the integration of immigrant groups into the economic and political structures of the city, yielding them both a measure of influence and some occupational rewards. Public employment was a major channel of mobility for the Italian, the Irish and the Jew, each of whom, by successively taking over whole sectors of the public services, gave various municipal agencies their distinctly ethnic coloration. Now blacks are the newcomers. But they come at a time when public employment has been preempted by older groups and is held fast through civil-service provisions and collective-bargaining contracts. Most public jobs are no longer allocated in exchange for political allegiance, but through a "merit" system based on formal qualifications.

The development of the civil-service merit system in municipalities at the turn of the century (the federal government adopted it in 1883) is usually credited to the efforts of reformers who sought to improve the quality of municipal services, to eliminate graft and to dislodge machine leaders. At least some of the employees in all cities with more than 500,000 inhabitants are now under civil service; in about half of these cities, virtually all employees have such protections.

Although the civil service originated in the struggle between party leaders and reformers for control of public employment, it launched municipal employees as an independent force. As municipal services expanded, the enlarging numbers of public employees began to form associations. Often these originated as benevolent societies, such as New York's Patrolmen's Benevolent Association which formed in the 1890s. Protected by the merit system, these organizations of public employees gradually gained some influence in their own right, and they exerted that influence at both the municipal and the state level to shape legislation and to monitor personnel policies so as to protect and advance their occupational interests.

Shortly after World War I, when the trade union movement was growing rapidly, public employees made their first major thrust toward unionization in the famous Boston police strike. About 1,100 of the 1,400-man force struck, goaded by the refusal of city officials to grant pay raises despite rapid inflation and despite the favorable recommendations of a commission appointed to appraise police demands. The strike precipitated widespread disorder in the streets of Boston. Official reactions were swift and savage. Calvin Coolidge, then governor, became a national hero as he moved to break the strike under the banner, "There is no right to strike against the public safety by anybody, anywhere, anytime." Virtually the entire police force was fired (and the few loyal men were granted pay raises). More important, the numerous police unions that had sprouted up in other cities, many of them affiliated with the American Federation of Labor, were scuttled. Public unionism did not recover its impetus until well after World War II.

In the meantime, civil-service associations relied mainly on lobbying to press their interests and, as their membership grew, they became an effective force in party politics. Although the mode of their involvement in party politics varied from place to place and from time to time, the sheer numbers of organized public employees made political leaders loath to ignore them. One measure of their impact is the number of major party leaders who rose from their ranks. In New York City, for example, Mayor William O'Dwyer was a former policeman; Abe Beame, the Democratic candidate for mayor in 1965, was a former schoolteacher, and Paul Screvane, his competitor for the Democratic mayoralty nomination in that same year, began as a sanitation worker.

Public Unionism

Now unionism is on the rise again, signalling a new phase in the political development of public employee groups. It is even spreading rapidly to the more professional services, such as education and welfare, whose employees have traditionally resisted the working-class connotation of unionism. The American Federation of Teachers has organized so many teachers as to force the National Educational Association, which considers itself a professional association, into a militant stance (including endorsing boycotts and strikes by its members). In New York, firemen last year successfully wrested the right to strike from their parent International Association of Firefighters, and the Patrolmen's Benevolent Association is exploring the possibility of an affiliation with the AFL-CIO. The American Federation of State, County, and Municipal Employees—half of whose members work for municipalities—is one of the fastest-growing affiliates of the AFL-CIO, having increased its membership by 70 percent in the last

four years. Overall, unions of public employees are adding 1,000 new members every working day, according to a member of the National Labor Relations Board.

By becoming part of the labor movement, public employees are augmenting their influence in two ways. First, they can call for support from other unions, and that support can be a substantial force. New York's teachers were backed in the struggle against school decentralization by the Central Labor Council, which represents 1.2 million workers. (The Central Labor Council, headed by a top official from the electricians' union, and with an overwhelmingly white membership, also had its own interest in the school issue: the Board of Education disperses over $1 billion annually for maintenance and construction. Under a system of community control, contracts might be awarded to black businesses or to contractors who hire black workers. Some black labor officials, seeing themselves allied against their own communities, broke ranks with the Central Labor Council over the decentralization issue.)

Unionism also means that public employees feel justified in using the disruptive leverage of the strike. Transit workers bring a metropolis to a standstill; teachers close down the schools; sanitation men bury a city under mounds of garbage. With each such crisis, the cry goes up for new legislative controls. But it is hard to see how laws will prevent strikes, unless the political climate becomes much more repressive. So far political leaders have been reluctant to invoke the full penalties permitted by existing law for fear of alienating organized labor. Thus New York State's Condon-Wadlin Law, enacted in 1947, was not used and was finally replaced by the "model" Taylor law which, as the experience of the last three years shows, works no better. Theodore Kheel, one of the nation's most noted labor arbitrators, in pronouncing the failure of the new law, pointed out that the state Public Employment Relations Board, established under the Taylor law to arbitrate disputes, took no action on either of the New York City teacher strikes. The *New York Times* concluded with alarm that "The virus of irresponsibility is racing through New York's unionized civil service," and "There is no end, short of draining the municipal treasury and turning taxpayers into refugees or relief recipients. . . ."

Public unions must be controlled, so the argument goes, because they are uniquely capable of paralyzing the cities and gouging the public as the price of restoring services. In a recent decision, New York's highest court held that a legislative classification differentiating between public and private industry was reasonable and constitutional, thus justifying prohibitions on the right of public employees to strike. The courts unanimously held that public employees could "by the exercise of naked power" obtain gains "wholly disproportionate to the services rendered by them."

As a practical matter, however, these distinctions between public and private employees do not hold up. Strikes in the public and private sectors rely on the same forms of leverage, though in varying degrees. Private-sector strikes result in economic losses, but so do strikes in the municipal services (for example, transit stoppages). Even teachers and welfare workers exert some economic pressure, although they rely more heavily on another form of leverage—the cries of a severely inconvenienced and discomfitted populace—to force government to settle their grievances. But private strikes of milk or fuel deliveries, of steel workers or transportation workers, also discomfit large sectors of the population and generate pressure for government to intervene and force a settlement.

Nor is it true that the coercive power of municipal unions enables them to obtain more favorable settlements than private unions. If, under the pressure of a strike in municipal services, the public is often unmindful of the impact of settlements on taxes, the public is equally unmindful of the eventual costs to consumers of settlements in the private sector. Industrial strikes are by no means necessarily less disruptive than public strikes or less coercive in pressing for a greater share of the public's dollar.

Blanket Security

Despite the continuing controversy over the right to strike, it is not the root of the trouble over municipal employment. Rather it is that the gains won by employees after long years of struggle now seem to be in jeopardy.

In fact, some groups of public employees had managed to secure substantial control over their working conditions long before they began to unionize, and in many cases long before comparable gains had been secured by workers in the private sector. These victories were won by intensive lobbying and by the assiduous cultivation of influence in the political parties at the municipal and state levels.

In the past, except where wages were concerned, other groups in the cities rarely became sufficiently aroused to block efforts by public employees to advance their interests. On issues such as tenure of working conditions or career advancement, and even retirement (which does not involve immediate costs) the civil services associations were able to make substantial strides by using conventional means of political influence.

First, with their jobs secured by the merit system, public workers in many agencies went on to win the principle of "promotion from within." This principle, together with promotion criteria that favored longevity, assured the career advancement of those already employed. But such a system of promotion, because it has the consequence of restricting outsiders to the bottom rank of public employment, is being opposed by new groups. When proponents of school decentralization insist that these requirements be waived to place black people in supervisory or administrative positions, spokesmen for the New York school supervisors' association answer that it will "turn the clock back 100 years and reinstate the spoils system."

In some municipal agencies, moreover, newcomers are even barred from lower-level jobs. Building inspectors in New York City are required to have five years' experience in the building trades, but few black people can get into the building trades. Police associations oppose any "lowering" of hiring standards, proposed as a way of facilitating entrance by minority groups, arguing that the complexity of modern law enforcement calls for even higher educational standards. (Police have even objected to lowering the physical height requirement, which now excludes many Puerto Ricans.) When New York City recently announced that impoverished people would be granted up to 12 extra points on civil-service tests for 50 low-paying jobs in anti-poverty agencies, the very meagerness of the concession cast in relief the system of exclusion it was to modify.

Public employees have also been successful in preempting some of the future resources of the city. Demands for improved retirement and pension plans, for example, are prominent: New York's transit workers recently settled for a contract that awarded pension pay on the basis of a time-and-a-half provision during their last year of employment, and the police are demanding the right to retire after 15 years. Such benefits are often won more easily than wage demands, for it is less onerous for a mayor to make concessions payable under a later administration.

Obviously, elaborate entrance and promotion requirements now limit access by blacks to municipal jobs. Indeed, one can almost measure the strength of public employee associations in different cities by their success in securing such requirements, and in keeping minority members out. In New York, where municipal workers are numerous and well organized, 90 percent of the teachers are white; in Detroit, Philadelphia, and Chicago, where municipal employees are not well organized, 25 to 40 percent of the teachers are black.

Mortgaged Treasuries

The number of jobs at stake is vast, and black demands are mounting. New York City employs 325,000 people, and personnel costs naturally account for the lion's share (about 60 percent) of a municipal budget topping $6 billion. And the share is growing: the number of public employees continues to rise (up 60 percent in New York City since the end of World War II), and wages and benefits are also rising. The question is not whether these costs are legitimate—but who will benefit by them. For as blacks become more numerous in cities, they will come to power only to find the treasuries mortgaged to earlier groups.

Unionization has been important mainly (but not exclusively) in the area of wages, where public employees often lagged behind organized private workers. Relying as they did on political influence, they were blocked by taxpayer groups who usually opposed higher municipal salaries. However, with unionization and strike power, public employees are no longer dependent on the vicissitudes of interest-group politics to get higher wages, and

so, as the *New York Times* notes with horror, they have begun to "leap frog" each other in salary demands.

Unionization is also enabling large numbers of municipal workers who hold less coveted jobs to move forward. By and large, hospital workers, clerks and janitors, for example, were left behind in the process of advancement through the civil services and through party politics. In New York City, many of these workers have now been organized by District 37 of the State, County and Municipal Employees Union. Furthermore, because these are low-paid, low-prestige jobs, they are often held by blacks who constitute about 25 percent of District 37s membership. (This helps to explain why Victor Gotbaum, the outspoken head of District Council 37, bucked the Central Labor Council in the school decentralization fight.) And following the path of earlier public employee groups, District 37 is beginning to press for a series of civil service reforms to enable its members to move up the muncipal career ladder. The much publicized struggles of the garbage workers in Memphis, and the hospital workers in Charlotte are efforts by low-paid blacks who, by using militant union tactics, are making their first advances.

Competition for jobs and money is by no means the worst of the struggle between the ghetto and public employees. In the course of securing their occupational interests, some groups of public employees have come to exercise substantial control over their agencies, and that control is now being challenged, too. The struggle over school decentralization in a number of cities is a prime example.

Public employees have been able to win considerable influence over the tasks they perform and other conditions of work. Many civil-service positions are now enshrined in codified descriptions which make both the job-holder and the work he performs relatively invulnerable to outside interference, even by political leaders. Furthermore, substantial discretion is inherent in many civil-service tasks, partly because legislative mandates are obscure, and partly because many civil-service positions require the occupants to be "professionals," enabling them to resist interference on the ground that they are "experts."

Public employees often use both the codified protection of their jobs and their powers of discretion to resist policy changes that alter the nature of their work. When former Mayor Robert Wagner asked the police department to patrol housing projects, the police refused and were supported by the police commissioner. School personnel effectively defeated desegregation policies by simply failing to inform ghetto parents of their right to enroll their children in white schools, and by discouraging those parents who tried to do so. The combined effect of procedural safeguards and professional discretion is suggested by the often-noted dilemma of a board of education that is simultaneously too centralized and too decentralized: it is hamstrung by regulations that seem to limit policy options, while its personnel retain the license to undermine central directives.

If some public employees have always had the ability to undermine policies, they now want the right to set policies, usually on the ground that as professionals they know what's best. Thus teachers recently demanded that the New York City Board of Education expand the "More Effective Schools" program, and that they be granted the right to remove "disruptive" children from their classrooms. Threatened by the efforts of ghetto parents to free their children from an unresponsive educational system, the union became the major force opposing school decentralization. Similarly, New York's striking welfare workers bargained for (but have not yet won) the right to join the commissioner in formulating agency policies, arguing that 8,000 case workers ought to have a say in policy decisions. The Patrolmen's Benevolent Association has begun issuing its own instructions to policemen on how the law should be enforced, to countermand Mayor John Lindsay's presumed indulgence of looters and demonstrators. And only through a full-scale public campaign was the mayor able to override the PBA's stubborn resistance to a "fourth platoon" permitting heavier scheduling of policemen during high crime hours. All of these ventures by the unions represent incursions on matters of municipal policy. That they are made under the banner of professional commitment to public service should not obscure the fact that they will entrench and enhance the position of the public employees involved.

In part, demands in the policy area are being provoked by the feeling among public employees that they must defend their agencies against black assailants. The black masses are very dependent on public services, but these services have been conspicuously unresponsive to them, and have even become instruments of white antagonism, as when police services take on the character of an army of occupation in the ghetto. The fierce fight waged by the New York Patrolmen's Benevolent Association against a civilian review board reveals the intensity of the conflict over the control of municipal agencies. In education and public welfare, the effects of cleavage between white staff and black recipients are even more pervasive and tragic, for by blocking and distorting the delivery of these services white staffs virtually fix the life chances of the black poor.

Jobs and services have always been the grist of urban politics. By entrenching and enlarging control over municipal agencies, white-controlled public-employee unions are also blocking a traditional avenue by which newcomers become assimilated into the urban political and economic system. Politicians who depend on the black vote have not been oblivious to this obstruction. One response has been to generate new systems of services to be staffed by blacks. By establishing these services under separate administrative auspices and by calling them "experimental," political leaders have tried to avoid aggravating white public employees.

Thus the national Democratic administration which took office in 1960 created a series of new programs for the inner city in the fields of delinquency, mental health, poverty, education and the like. Federal guidelines required that blacks have a large share of the new jobs and policy positions (e.g., "maximum feasible participation of the poor"). In general, these "demonstration" programs have been more responsive than traditional municipal agencies to black interests. Of course, the white-dominated city bureaucracies fought for control of the new programs and sometimes won: at the least, they obtained a substantial share of the new funds as compensation. But regardless of who has control, the new programs are miniscule compared with existing municipal programs. If anything, the antipoverty program has made more visible just how little blacks do control, thus precipitating some of the current wrangles over control of traditional municipal programs.

Ironies of History

There are ironies in these developments. Reformers struggled to free municipal services from the vicissitudes of party politics; now some politicians are struggling to free municipal services from the vicissitudes of employee control. The advent and (at this writing) likely defeat of the Lindsay administration in New York City is a good illustration, for it exposed and escalated the conflict between blacks and whites. Lindsay campaigned against the old Democratic regime to which the unions were tied. His election was made possible by the defection of almost half of the black voters from Democratic ranks, and by middle- and upper-class support. It was to these groups that he appealed in his campaign and to which he is now trying to respond through his public posture and policies. To the black voter, he has been a politician who walked in the ghetto streets, who allowed the welfare rolls to rise, who attempted to assert control over the police force and to decentralize the school system; to the middle and upper classes, he has been a reformer and innovator who revamped the city's bureaucratic structures and appointed prestigious outsiders to high administrative posts. Appeals to both constituencies led him to do battle with the public unions regularly, for these moves threaten the control exerted by employee groups over municipal services. These battle have activated race and ethnic loyalties so fierce as to seem to rupture the city; and the possibility that Lindsay has even alienated the largely liberal Jewish vote exposes the intensity of the struggles for control of municipal benefits. Similar alliances between the black poor and affluent whites are also appearing in other cities (Cleveland, Detroit, Gary) with similar reactions from public employees, and white ethnic groups generally.

There is still another irony, for the militancy and radical rhetoric of the rapidly growing public unions have led some observers to define them as the vanguard of a reawakened labor movement. Bayard Rustin and A. Philip

Randolph were recently moved to applaud the New York teachers' union for "having clearly demonstrated that trade unionism can play a useful part in obtaining needed facilities for . . . radically improving the quality of education for all children." One could wish the applause were justified; one could wish that white workers were allies of the black masses. But it is turning out that most advances by the public unions are being made at the expense of the black masses. As it now stands, there is only so much in the way of jobs, services and control over policy to be divided up. As one black spokesman said of the struggle between the UFT and the Ocean Hill-Brownsville governing board, "The name of the game is money and power for blacks!" Or, he might have added, for whites.

But the bitterest irony of all is that the struggle between whites and blacks is being played out within the narrow limits of the resources available in municipalities. There is nothing unreasonable in white employees' pressing to hold and expand the gains they have won, which in any case are not so munificent. What is unreasonable is that their gains are being made at the expense of blacks, not at the expense of affluent and powerful sectors of the society. How to shift the struggle from the arena of municipal jobs and services to the arena in which national and corporate wealth are divvied up is hardly clear. But one thing is clear. The burden of shifting the struggle should not fall on blacks, for they are only now getting their first chance at a share of what the city has to offer. Confined to the municipal sphere, blacks will oppose the advances of the white unions and fight for what others got before them. And they may have cause to worry—not only that the stakes of municipal politics are limited, but that all of the stakes may be claimed before they have joined the game.

FURTHER READING

City Politics by Edward C. Banfield and James Q. Wilson (Cambridge, Mass.: Harvard University Press and M.I.T. Press, 1963).

Confrontation at Ocean Hill-Brownsville: The New York School Strikes of 1968 edited by Maurice R. Berube and Marilyn Gittell. (New York: Praeger, 1969).

"The Urban Crisis: Who Got What and Why?" by Frances Fox Piven in *1984 Revisited*, edited by Robert Paul Wolff (New York: Random House, 1973).

Governing New York City by Wallace S. Sayre and Herbert Kaufman (New York: Russell Sage, 1960).

MARTIN GLABERMAN

Unions vs. Workers in the Seventies: The Rise of Militancy in the Auto Industry

On the morning of July 16, 1970 the *Detroit Free Press* featured on its front page a large five-column picture of General Motors Vice President Earl Bramblett and UAW President Leonard Woodcock shaking hands as they opened negotiations for a new contract. The headline beneath the picture read: "Negotiations Begin; Auto Talk Key: Living Costs."

The banner headline that morning, overshadowing the ritual start of negotiations, was: "Ousted Worker Kills Three in Chrysler Plant Shooting; 2 Foremen, Bystander Are Slain." A black worker at Chrysler's Elden Avenue Axle Plant, suspended for insubordination, had killed two foremen (one black, one white) and a Polish setup man.

The timing of the events was coincidental—but it is the kind of coincidence that lends a special insight. What is at issue—not only in the auto negotiations but in most relations involving American workers, unions and management—is not living costs but living. Involved is not just dollars and cents, important as always to workers, but an entire way of life.

Take a close look at the union's demands. The UAW

left out only one thing: the demand to turn the plants over to the workers. Apart from the usual wage increases and financial improvements, some of the issues raised by the UAW bargaining teams included: pensions after 30 years instead of after a specific age; restoration of the escalator cost-of-living clause to its original form; ending time clocks and putting production workers on salary; inverting seniority so that older workers could take the time off at nearly full pay in the event of layoffs; the problem of pollution, both in the plants and in the community; changing production to deal with boredom on the assembly line. Many of these issues were raised purely for propaganda effect with little intent to bargain seriously over them. But taken as a whole, they provide an interesting picture that reflects, if only in a distorted way, the extent of the worker's concern for the nature of his workplace.

Public Show of Militancy

This technique in bargaining was developed by Walter Reuther and is being continued by Woodcock. It gives the public appearance of great militancy but it means something very different. While the leadership of the union goes through the motions of accepting all the workers' demands and pressing them on the companies, the tactic of publicly demanding almost everything that could be thought of at the beginning of negotiations is intended to get the workers off their backs and keep them quiet when the serious negotiating begins in secret sessions. It leaves the union leadership free to work out any settlement it thinks reasonable and to establish its own priorities in the negotiations.

The range of union demands in the auto negotiations also reflects something else. It is a sign that unionism in the United States is reaching its limit. Not because they will win so little, but because they will win so much and it will prove to be so little. It will not make the life of the black worker at the Eldon Avenue plant of Chrysler or the white worker at the GM Chevrolet plant in Flint one bit more tolerable.

That is one of the reasons that the union leadership has such a hard time with the new generation of young workers in the plants. They tell the workers about the great victories of the union in the past and what it was like in open shop days. They tell the truth—those were genuine victories. But they have become transformed into their opposite by virture of becoming incorporated into contracts and the whole process of what is called labor relations. (Labor relations, it should be noted, has nothing to do with workers; it has to do with relations between company representatives and union representatives.)

The *Detroit Free Press* published the following report in August 1970:

Some 46 percent of General Motors' hourly workers are below age 35. They have never known a depression, they have had more schooling than the man who lived through the last one, and they aren't impressed by the old Spartan idea that hard, repetitive work is a virtue.

They are less responsive to authority than even the men who seized the Flint GM plants in the historic 1936-1937 sit-down strikes.

That is precisely the background against which discontent is surfacing throughout the industry today, discontent that has reached its most advanced stage in the auto industry.

At the time of the dispute at the Chevrolet Vega plant in Lordstown, Ohio, production on the assembly line had been rationalized to the point where a job took 35 seconds. There are two categories of time that are difficult to visualize from outside the factory. One is 35 seconds. You cannot light a cigarette or get a drink of water in 35 seconds without a car going by on the assembly line. The other category is the rest of your life. This is where the worker expects to be for all of his working life—accumulating seniority. How can one express the tensions that are inherent in such a situation—doing a job that takes 35 seconds for the rest of your life?

The formation of the CIO in the 1930s settled once and for all the idea that owners or managers or stockholders had the right to run their plants any way they saw fit. Sit-downs, strikes, wildcats, direct on-the-job action, sabotage and violence established the power of workers in the plants. The tactics used and the extent of that power varied from plant to plant and from industry to industry.

Sabotage and violence have long been a part of the auto industry. There were reports of the murder or disappearance of foremen at the Ford Rouge plants in the days before the union; the recent murder of two foremen at a Chrysler plant is not an especially new development. Other forms of sabotage are less severe but nonetheless effective. On some assembly lines where the links are exposed, an occasional rest period or slow down is achieved by the simple (and virtually undetectable) tactic of putting the handle of a long open-end wrench into the chain to shear the pin and stop the line. Sometimes the light bulb that signals the line breakdown is unscrewed or broken so that an extra few minutes are gained before the stoppage is discovered.

Not uncommon is the sabotage of the product. Sometimes this increases the amount of the repair work coming off the lines. Sometimes this saddles a customer with a built-in rattle in a high-priced car because some worker welded a wrench or some bolts into a closed compartment.

The nature of violence and sabotage as a tool of American workers provides an insight into the problems caused by the extensive technological changes of the past 20 years. Although generally called automation, something else is involved: the first and basic reason for technological change is the struggle against workers' power by the employers. Technological advance is designed, directly or indirectly, to eliminate workers or to make them more subservient to the machine. And most changes made in plants are made solely to increase production rather than out of any concern for the workers.

For example, Chrysler stamping operations are now centered in the Sterling Township Stamping Plant, about 15 miles outside Detroit. The plant now does operations that were formerly done at the Dodge, Plymouth and Chrysler plants. Separating 4,000 or so workers from most of their fellows seriously reduced the power and effectiveness of the workers. The shutting down of old plants means that formal and informal organizations are broken up or abandoned. And it takes time for new relations and new organizations to be worked out. Workers at Sterling have indicated that it took approximately four years for the plant to be transformed from just an accidental combination of workers to a relatively well organized and disciplined force.

In the early days of the union the power of the workers could be wielded more openly and more directly. Workers negotiated directly with the lower levels of management and were able to settle things right on the shop floor. How easily they were able to do this depended, of course, on their relative strength and the nature of the technology involved among other things. As an example, the workers in the heat-treat department at the Buick plant in Flint had an especially strong position. One time, shortly after the union was established, they felt themselves strongly aggrieved. But the early contracts did not rigidly define the grievance procedure. So instead of locating the violated clause and leaving their fate to a bureaucracy, they simply sent the steward to see the general foreman. Since their interest in this discussion was very great, they accompanied the steward and stood around outside the foreman's office while the discussion was going on. The time they picked for this meeting was just after they had loaded a heat into the furnace. The heat was scheduled to emerge from the other end of the furnace 20 minutes later. If the heat was not pulled at that time the damage to both the steel being treated and to the furnace itself would have been irreparable.

In the early stages of the discussion the foreman was adamant. He would not accede to the demands—"and you'd better get those guys back to work." As the minutes sped by, the foreman became less and less adamant until, finally, with a couple of minutes left to go, he capitulated. The steward then signalled the workers standing outside and the heat was pulled.

That might be an extreme situation but it was not an unusual one. Workers are very aware of how their jobs fit into the total process of production. To change the scale and to change the time: almost 30 years later, during a wildcat at the Sterling Stamping Plant of the Chrysler Corporation in 1969, the workers made clear their awareness of how their plant fit into the scheduling of Chrysler plants in Detroit, Windsor, Ontario, St. Louis and elsewhere. They knew when and in what order the Sterling strike would shut down other Chrysler plants. The knowledge of the workers' importance in the overall framework is both an instrument in the day-to-day struggle and the essential basis for a new society.

Unions vs. Workers

The instinctive assertion of their own power on the shop floor that workers managed in the thirties was extended in the forties when war production requirements and the labor shortage forced the government and the corporations to make concessions to workers' control. But that was also the period during which the

separation of workers from the union structure began. The last major organizing success marks the turn to bureaucracy.

When Ford fell to the union in 1941, both the check-off and full time for union committeemen were incorporated into the contract. But the apparent victories only created more problems. Workers wanted full time for union representatives to get them out from under company pressures and discrimination. Getting elected steward often got you the worst job in a department and stuck away in a corner where you couldn't see what was happening. But full time for stewards did more than relieve union representatives from company pressure — it ended up by relieving representatives from workers' pressure. The steward is less available than he was before, and you have to have your foreman go looking for him should you happen to need him.

The check-off produced a similar situation. Designed to keep the company from pressuring weaker workers to stay out of the union even though they were sharing in its benefits, the check-off ended up reducing worker pressure on the union officials. No longer does the steward have to listen to workers' complaints each month as he goes around collecting the dues. Once a month the dues are delivered in one huge check from the company to the union and the worker never sees his dues payment.

One-Party Governments

American entry into World War II finished what the Ford contract had begun. The top layers of the union leadership were incorporated into the government boards and agencies that managed and controlled war production. In return certain concessions were made in terms of union organization. Union recognition was often arranged from above without the participation of the workers in strike or other action. At this point in time the lower levels of the union leadership were still pretty close to the workers and very often local union officials participated in and supported the numerous wildcat strikes that took place.

This process of bureaucratization was completed with Walter Reuther's victory and his substitution of the "one-party state" in control of the union for the democratic kind of factionalism that had been the norm in the UAW before. And with the Reuther administration the union moved to participate directly in the management and discipline of workers in production. All through the fifties, with intensive automation and decentralization going on in the auto industry, the union collaborated in crushing the numerous wildcat strikes, in getting rid of the most militant workers, in establishing labor peace in the industry.

In the other industrial unions the pace of bureaucratization was much more advanced. In steel, for example, Phil Murray kept a tight and undemocratic hold on the

Steel Workers Organizing Committee until after the basic contracts had been negotiated with United States Steel. It was only then that the Organizing Committee appointed from the top was replaced by an autonomous union which could vote on its own officers or contracts. Any worker can illustrate the bureaucratic history of his own union.

The grievance procedure became virtually worthless to the workers. In 1955 at the termination of a contract presumably designed to provide a grievance procedure, there were in some GM plants as many as 10,000 unresolved grievances. The situation has not improved since then. GM complains that the number of grievances in its plants has grown from 106,000 in 1960 to 256,000 in 1969 or 60 for each 100 workers.

What are these specific local grievances? They involve production standards: the speed of a line, the rate on a machine, the number of workers assigned to a given job, the allowable variations in jobs on a given line. They involve health and safety standards: unsafe machines, cluttered or oily floors, rates of production which prevent the taking of reasonable precautions, the absence or misuse of hoists or cranes, protection from flames or furnaces, protection from sharp, unfinished metal, protection from welding or other dangerous chemicals or fumes, the right to shut an unsafe job down until the condition is changed.

They involve the quality of life in the plant: the authoritarian company rules which treat workers like a combination of prison inmate and kindergarten child, the right to move about the plant, the right to relieve yourself physically without having to get the foreman's permission or the presence of a relief man, the right to reasonable breaks in the work, the right to a reasonable level of heat in the winter or reasonable ventilation in the summer. And on and on.

The grievances that crowd the dockets of General Motors and of other companies cover the total range of life in the factory. The fact that they are called grievances helps to conceal what they really are—a reflection of the total dissatisfaction of the workers in the way production is run and of the desire of the workers to impose their own will in the factory. The UAW and the Ford Motor Company recently have been discussing the problem of boredom on the assembly line. The only reason they are discussing it at all—it is by no means a new development—is because more and more workers are refusing to accept factory discipline as a law of nature. And it is not boredom but power which is at stake.

The same worker who for eight hours a day attaches belts to a motor and can't wait to get out of the plant will spend his weekends tinkering with his car and consider it rewarding work. The difference is in who controls the work.

It might be worth noting a couple of things. All workers are exploited to one degree or another. But office workers on the whole do not have to walk past armed guards going to and from work and have a certain amount of freedom in scheduling their work on the job. The coffee break is not a blue-collar institution. It is clear that historically bosses never thought that workers would work without the severest external discipline and control. And they still don't.

In addition, no matter what all the theoreticians of capitalism may say, workers are treated very differently from anyone else. The Industrial Division of American Standard has a plant in Dearborn, Michigan which manufactures industrial air conditioning. The company places ads in trade journals urging employers to air condition their facilities. The office section of the facility is air conditioned. The plant is not. The only thing that makes this situation unusual is that the company manufactures the equipment. But even that isn't enough to get them to provide for blue-collar workers what office workers, engineers, managers and professionals now take as a matter of course.

In 1958 a major depression in the auto industry marked a new stage. Packard, Hudson, Murray Body and other auto companies went down the drain. Employment began to drop considerably and led to the development of new theories about the impending disappearance of the industrial working class and the elimination of the black American from gainful employment. The actual developments were quite different.

The reorganization, technological change and decentralization that characterized the fifties and culminated in the depression gave way to a new expansion which brought significant numbers of blacks and young workers into the industry. These are workers, as the *Detroit Free Press* noted, who couldn't care less about what the union won in 1937. They are not more backward (as the UAW bureaucrats like to pretend) but more advanced. They are attuned to the need to change the nature of work, to the need of human beings to find satisfaction in what they do.

It is this new and changing working class that was the basis for the new level of wildcat strikes, for a doubled rate of absenteeism, for an increased amount of violence in plants where guns are often openly carried. It is a new working class that no conceivable contract settlement can control or immobilize.

Both unions and industry are aware of their problem to some degree. The union wants management to contribute to a Training and Education Fund that the union will use to educate and develop a new corps of porkchoppers. "The UAW believes," says the *Free Press*, "that a better-trained corps of union stewards would be better equipped to cope with these issues and with gut plant problems like narcotics, alchoholism, loan-sharking, weapon-packing, pilfering and gambling. 'A bunch of armed guards isn't the only answer,' said one committeeman."

After 33 years of unionism, they have suddenly discovered that armed guards are not the answer. To put it plainly, they have suddenly discovered that armed guards are not enough.

The slowdown of automation in the sixties (a consequence of the shortage of capital) has led to a relative stabilization. That is, workers in new installations and in old ones that have been reorganized have now had a few years to work out new forms of organization. The complaints against the young workers who make up a crucial force in the factories indicate that the wildcats of the past may be replaced, or at least supplemented, by something new.

The tightly knit structures of the big industrial unions leave no room for maneuvering. There is no reasonable way in which young workers can use the union constitution to overturn and overhaul the union structure. The constitution is against them; the money and jobs available to union bureaucrats are against them. And if these fail, the forces of law and order of city, state and federal governments are against them. If that were not enough, the young workers in the factories today are expressing the instinctive knowledge that even if they gained control of the unions and reformed them completely, they would still end up with unions—organizations which owe their existence to capitalist relations of productions.

The impossibility of transforming the unions has been argued by a number of obervers. Clark Kerr has noted, without disapproval, that "unions and corporations alike are, with very few exceptions, one-party governments." That is the phrase usually reserved for Stalinist or fascist totalitarian governments. But it is not overdrawn. Paul Jacobs has documented this in the case of the unions:

A study of 70 international union constitutions, the formal instruments that rule a membership of al-most 16,000,000 workers, shows among other things that in most of these 70 unions power is generally concentrated in the hands of the international presidents, with few restraints placed upon them, that discipline may be enforced against union members with little regard for due process, and that opposition to the incumbent administration is almost impossible.

And all of this is what young workers are revolting against.

That means that the course of future developments in the factories of America has to be sought outside the unions. Caucuses and factions will still be built and, here and there, will have temporary and minor successes. But the explosions that are still to come are likely to have the appearance of new revolutionary forms, organizations which are not simply organs of struggle but organs of control of production. They are a sign of the future.

FURTHER READING

False Promises by Stanley Aronowitz (New York: McGraw-Hill, 1973).

Autocracy and Insurgency in Organized Labor edited by Burton H. Hall (New Brunswick, N.J.: Transaction Books, 1972). Excellent in documenting autocracy in specific unions, but the concept of insurgency tends to be limited to formally organized union oppositions and much spontaneous activity is ignored.

Class, Race and Labor by John C. Leggett (New York: Oxford University Press, 1968).

The Company and the Union by William Serrin (New York: Knopf, 1973).

Working by Studs Terkel (New York: Pantheon Books, 1974).

Counter-Planning on the Shop Floor by Bill Watson (*Radical America*, 1972). The positive aspects of worker resistance to management control of production.

DAVID WELLMAN

The *Wrong* Way to Find Jobs for Negroes

In the summer of 1966 I studied a Federal government program designed to help lower-class youths find jobs. The program was known as TIDE. It was run by the California Department of Employment, and classes were held five days a week in the Youth Opportunities Center of West Oakland.

The TIDE program was anything but a success. "I guess these kids just don't want jobs," one of the teacher-counselors told me. "The clothes they wear are loud. They won't talk decent English. They're boisterous. And they constantly fool around. They refuse to take the program seriously."

"But isn't there a job shortage in Oakland?" I asked. "Does it really *matter* how the kids act?"

"There's plenty of jobs. They're just not interested."

The students were 25 young men and 25 young women selected by poverty-program workers in the Bay Area. Their ages ranged from 16 to 22, and most were Negroes. The government paid them $5 a day to participate. Men and women usually met separately. I sat in on the men's classes.

The young men who took part in TIDE had a distinctive style. They were "cool." Their hair was "processed." All sported sunglasses—very lightly tinted, with small frames. They called them "pimp's glasses." Their clothes, while usually inexpensive, were loud and ingeniously altered to express style and individuality. They spoke in a "hip" vernacular. Their vocabularies were small but very expressive. These young men, as part of the "cool world" of the ghetto, represent a distinctively black working-class culture.

To most liberals these young men are "culturally deprived" or "social dropouts." Most had flunked or been kicked out of school. Few had any intention of getting a high-school degree. They seemed uninterested in "making it." They had long and serious arrest and prison records. They were skeptical and critical of both the TIDE program and white society in general.

The TIDE workers were liberals. They assumed that if the young men would only act a little less "cool" and learn to smooth over some of their encounters with white authorities, they too could become full-fledged, working members of society. The aim of TIDE was not to train them for jobs, but to train them how to *apply* for jobs—how to take tests, how to make a good impression during a job interview, how to speak well, how to fill out an application form properly. They would play games, like dominoes, to ease the pain associated with numbers and arithmetic; they would conduct mock interviews, take mock tests, meet with management representatives, and tour places where jobs might be available. They were told to consider the TIDE program itself as a job—to be at the Youth Opportunities Center office on time, dressed as if they were at work. If they were late or made trouble, they would be docked. But if they took the program seriously and did well, they were told, they stood a pretty good chance of getting a job at the end of four weeks. The unexpressed aim of TIDE, then, was to prepare Negro youngsters for white society. The government would serve as an employment agency for white, private enterprise.

The program aimed to change the youngsters by making them more acceptable to employers. Their grammar and pronunciation were constantly corrected. They were indirectly told that, in order to get a job, their appearance would have to be altered: For example, "Don't you think you could shine your shoes?" Promptness, a virtue few of the youngsters possessed, was lauded. The penalty for tardiness was being put on a clean-up committee, or being docked.

For the TIDE workers, the program was a four-week exercise in futility. They felt they weren't asking very much of the youngsters—just that they learn to make a good impression on white society. And yet the young men were uncooperative. The only conclusion the TIDE workers could arrive at was: "They just don't want jobs."

Yet most of the youngsters took *actual* job possibilities very seriously. Every day they would pump the Youth Opportunities Center staff about job openings. When told there was a job at such-and-such a factory and that a particular test was required, the young men studied hard and applied for the job in earnest. The TIDE program *itself,* however, seemed to be viewed as only distantly related to getting a job. The youngsters wanted jobs, but to them their inability to take tests and fill out forms was *not* the problem. Instead, they talked about the shortage of jobs available to people without skills.

Their desire for work was not the problem. The real problem was what the program demanded of the young men. It asked that they change their manner of speech and dress, that they ignore their lack of skills and society's lack of jobs, and that they act as if their arrest records were of no consequence in obtaining a job. It asked, most important, that they pretend *they,* and not society, bore the responsibility for their being unemployed. TIDE didn't demand much of the men: Only that they become white.

Putting On the Program

What took place during the four-week program was a daily struggle between white, middle-class ideals of conduct and behavior and the mores and folkways of the black community. The men handled TIDE the way the black community in America has always treated white threats to Negro self-respect. They used subtle forms of subversion and deception. Historians and sociologists have pointed to slave subversion, to the content and ritual of Negro spirituals, and to the blues as forms of covert black resistance to white mores.

Today, "putting someone on," "putting the hype on someone," or "running a game on a cat" seem to be important devices used by Negroes to maintain their integrity. "Putting someone on," which is used as much with black people as with whites, allows a person to maintain his integrity in a hostile or threatening situation. To put someone on is to publicly lead him to believe that you are going along with what he has to offer or say, while privately rejecting the offer and subtly subverting it. The tactic fails if the other person recognizes what is happening. For one aim of putting someone on is to take pride in feeling that you have put something over on him, often at his expense. (Putting someone on differs from "putting someone down," which means active defiance and public confrontation.)

TIDE was evidently interpreted by the men as a threat to their self-respect, and this was the way they responded to it. Sometimes TIDE was put on. Sometimes it was put down. It was taken seriously only when it met the men's own needs.

There was almost no open hostility toward those in charge of TIDE, but two things quickly led me to believe that if the men accepted the program, they did so only on their own terms.

First, all of them appeared to have a "tuning-out" mechanism. They just didn't hear certain things. One young man was a constant joker and talked incessantly, even if someone else was speaking or if the group was supposed to be working. When told to knock it off, he never heard the command. Yet when he was interested in a program, he could hear perfectly.

Tuning-out was often a collective phenomenon. For instance, there was a radio in the room where the youngsters worked, and they would play it during lunch and coffee breaks. When the instructor would enter and tell them to begin work, they would continue listening and dancing to the music as if there were no one else in the room. When *they* were finished listening, the radio went off and the session began. The youngsters were going along with the program—in a way. They weren't challenging it. But they were undermining its effectiveness.

A second way in which the young men undermined the program was by playing dumb. Much of the program consisted of teaching the youngsters how to fill out employment applications. They were given lengthy lectures on the importance of neatness and lettering. After having filled out such forms a number of times, however, some students suddenly didn't know their mother's name, the school they last attended, or their telephone number.

This "stupidity" was sometimes duplicated during the mock job interviews. Five or more of the students would interview their fellow trainees for an imaginary job. These interviewers usually took their job seriously. But after it became apparent that the interview was a game, many of the interviewees suddenly became incredibly incompetent. They didn't have social-security numbers, they couldn't remember their last job, they didn't know what school they went to, they didn't know if they really wanted the job—to the absolute frustration of interviewers and instructors alike. Interestingly enough, when an instructor told them one morning that *this* time those who did well on the interview would actually be sent out on a real job interview with a real firm, the stupid and incompetent were suddenly transformed into model job applicants.

The same thing happened when the youngsters were given job-preference tests, intelligence tests, aptitude tests, and tests for driver's licenses. The first few times the youngsters took these tests, most worked hard to master them. But after they had gotten the knack, and still found themselves without jobs and taking the same tests, their response changed. Some of them no longer knew how to do the test. Others found it necessary to cheat by looking over someone's shoulder. Still others flunked tests they had passed the day before. Yet when they were informed of actual job possibilities at the naval ship yard or with the post office, they insisted on giving and taking the tests themselves. In one instance, some of them read up on which tests were relevant for a particular job, then practiced that test for a couple of hours by themselves.

Tuning-out and playing stupid were only two of the many ways the TIDE program was "put-on." Still another way: Insisting on work "breaks." The young men "employed" by TIDE were well-acquainted with this ritual, and demanded that it be included as part of their job. Since they had been given a voice in deciding the content of the program, they insisted that breaks become part of their daily routine. And no matter what the activity, or who was addressing them, the young men religiously adhered to the breaks.

The program started at 9:30 A.M. The youngsters decided that their first break would be for coffee at 10:30. This break was to last until 11. And while work was never allowed to proceed a minute past 10:30, it was usually 11:15 or so before the young men actually got back to work. Lunch began exactly at 12. Theoretically, work resumed at 1. This usually meant 1:15, since they had to listen to "one more song" on the radio. The next break was to last from 2:30 to 3. However, because they were finished at 3:30 and because it took another 10 minutes to get them back to work, the fellows could often talk their way out of the remaining half hour. Considering they were being paid $5 a day for five hours' work, of which almost half were regularly devoted to breaks, they didn't have a bad hustle.

Trips and Games

Games were another part of the TIDE program subverted by the put-on. Early in the program an instructor told the students that it might be helpful if they mastered arithmetic and language by playing games—dominoes, Scrabble, and various card games. The students considered this a fine idea. But what their instructor had intended for a pastime during the breaks, involving at most an hour a day, they rapidly turned into a major part of the instruction. They set aside 45 minutes in the morning and 45 minutes in the afternoon for games. But they participated in these games during their breaks as well, so that the games soon became a stumbling block to getting sessions back in order after breaks. When the instructor would say, "Okay, let's get back to work," the men would sometimes reply, "But we're already working on our math—we're playing dominoes, and you said that would help us with our math."

To familiarize the students with the kinds of jobs potentially available, the TIDE instructors took them on excursions to various work situations. These excursions were another opportunity for a put-on. It hardly seemed to matter what kind of company they visited so long as the visit took all day. On a trip to the Oakland Supply Naval Station, the men spent most of their time putting the make on a cute young WAVE who was their guide. One thing this tour did produce, however, was a great deal of discussion about the war in Vietnam. Almost none of the men wanted to serve in the armed forces. Through the bus windows some of them would yell at passing sailors: "Vietnam, baby!" or "Have a good time in Vietnam, man!"

The men would agree to half-day trips only if there was no alternative, or if the company would give away samples. Although they knew that the Coca-Cola Company was not hiring, they wanted to go anyway, for the free Cokes. They also wanted to go to many candy and cookie factories. Yet they turned down a trip to a local steel mill that they knew was hiring. TIDE, after all, was not designed to get them an interview—its purpose was to show them what sorts of jobs might be available. Given the circumstances, they reasoned, why not see what was *enjoyable* as well?

When the men were not putting-on the TIDE program and staff, they might be putting them down. When someone is put-down, he knows it. The tactic's success *depends* on his knowing it, whereas a put-on is successful only when its victim is unaware of it.

The Interview Technique

Among the fiercest put-downs I witnessed were those aimed at jobs the students were learning to apply for. These jobs were usually for unskilled labor: post-office, assembly-line, warehouse, and longshore workers, truck drivers, chauffeurs, janitors, bus boys, and so on.

The reaction of most of the students was best expressed by a question I heard one young man ask an instructor: "How about some tests for I.B.M.?" The room broke into an uproar of hysterical laughter. The instructor's response was typically bureaucratic, yet disarming: "Say, that's a good suggestion. Why don't you put it in the suggestion box?" The students didn't seem able to cope with that retort, so things got back to normal.

Actual employers, usually those representing companies that hired people only for unskilled labor, came to TIDE to demonstrate to the men what a good interview would be like. They did *not* come to interview men for real jobs. It was sort of a helpful-hints-for-successful-interviews session. Usually one of the more socially mobile youths was chosen to play the role of job applicant. The entire interview situation was played through. Some employers even went so far as to have the "applicant" go outside and knock on the door to begin the interview. The students thought this was both odd and funny, and one said to the employer: "Man, you've already *seen* the cat. How come you making him walk out and then walk back in?"

With a look of incredulity, the employer replied: "But that's how you get a job. You have to sell yourself from the moment you walk in that door."

The employer put on a real act, beginning the interview with the usual small talk.

"I see from your application that you played football in high school."

"Yeah."

"Did you like it?"

"Yeah."

"Football really makes men and teaches you teamwork."

"Yeah."

At this point, the men got impatient: "Man, the cat's here to get a job, not talk about football!"

A wisecracker chimed in: "Maybe he's interviewing for a job with the Oakland Raiders."

Usually the employer got the point. He would then ask about the "applicant's" job experience, draft status, school record, interests, skills, and so on. The young man being interviewed usually took the questions seriously and answered frankly. But after a while, the rest of the group would tire of the game and (unrecognized, from the floor) begin to ask about the specifics of a real job:

"Say man, how much does this job pay?"

"What kind of experience do you need?"

"What if you got a record?"

It didn't take long to completely rattle an interviewer. The instructor might intervene and tell the students that the gentleman was there to help them, but this would stifle revolt for only a short while. During one interview, several of the fellows began loudly playing dominoes. That got the response they were looking for.

"Look!" shouted the employer. "If you're not interested in learning how to sell yourself, why don't you just leave the room so that others who are interested can benefit from this?"

"Oh no!" responded the ringleaders. "We work here. If you don't dig us, then *you* leave!"

Not much later, he did.

Sometimes during these mock interviews, the very nature of the work being considered was put-down. During one mock interview for a truck-driving job, some of the men asked the employer about openings for salesmen. Others asked him about executive positions. At one point the employer himself was asked point-blank how much he was paid, and what his experience was. They had turned the tables and were enjoying the opportunity to interview the interviewer. Regardless of a potential employer's status, the young men treated him as they would their peers. On one tour of a factory, the students were escorted by the vice-president in charge of hiring. To the TIDE participants, he was just another guide. After he had informed the students of the large number of unskilled positions available, they asked him if he would hire some of them, on the spot. He replied that this was just a tour and that he was in no position to hire anyone immediately. One youth looked at him and said: "Then you're just wasting our time, aren't you?"

Although shaken, the executive persisted. Throughout his talk, however, he innocently referred to his audience as "boys," which obviously bothered the students. Finally one of the more articulate men spoke up firmly: "We are young *men,* not boys!"

The vice-president blushed and apologized. He made a brave attempt to avoid repeating the phrase. But habit was victorious, and the word slipped in again and again. Each time he said "you boys" he was corrected, loudly, and with increasing hostility.

The students treated State Assemblyman Byron Rumford, a Negro, the same way. The meeting with Rumford was an opportunity for them to speak with an elected official about the job situation in the state. The meeting was also meant to air differences and to propose solutions. At the time, in fact, the men were quite angry about their rate of pay at TIDE. An instructor had suggested that they take the matter up with Rumford.

The meeting was attended by both the young men and women in the TIDE program. The young women were very well-dressed and well-groomed. Their clothes were not expensive, but were well cared for and in "good taste." Their hair was done in high-fashion styles. They looked, in short, like aspiring career women. The young men wore their usual dungarees or tight trousers, brightly colored shirts and sweaters, pointed shoes, and sunglasses.

The women sat quietly and listened politely. The men spoke loudly whenever they felt like it, and constantly talked among themselves.

Rumford, instead of speaking about the job situation in the Bay Area, chose to talk about his own career. It was a Negro Horatio Alger story. The moral was that if you work hard, you too can put yourself through college, become a successful druggist, then run for public office.

The moment Rumford finished speaking and asked for questions, one of the men jumped up and asked, "Hey man, how do we get a raise?" A male chorus of "Yeah!" followed. Before Rumford could complete a garbled answer (something like, "Well, I don't really know much about the procedures of a federally sponsored program"), the battle of the sexes had been joined. The women scolded the men for their "disrespectful behavior" toward an elected official. One said: "Here he is trying to help us and you-all acting a fool. You talking and laughing and carrying on while he talking, and then when he finishes you want to know about a raise. Damn!"

"Shit," was a male response. "You don't know what you talking about. We got a *right* to ask the cat about a raise. We elected him."

"We supposed to be talking about jobs," said another. "And we're talking about *our* job. If y'all like the pay, that's your business. We want more!"

The debate was heated. Neither group paid any attention to Rumford, who wisely slipped out of the room.

Battle of Sexes—or Class Conflict?

During the exchanges it became clear to me that the differences in clothing and style between the sexes reflected their different orientations toward the dominant society and its values. In the minds of the young women, respect and respectability seemed paramount. At one point, a young woman said to the men, "You acting just like a bunch of *niggers.*" She seemed to identify herself as a Negro, not as a "nigger." For the men, on the other hand, becoming a Negro (as opposed to a "nigger") meant giving up much that they considered positive. As one young man said in answer to the above, "You just ain't got no soul, bitch."

The women's identification with the values of white society became even clearer when the debate moved from what constituted respect and respectability to a direct attack on a personal level: "Do you all expect to get a job looking the way you do?" "Shit, I wouldn't wear clothes like that if I was on welfare."

The direction of the female attack corresponded closely with the basic assumptions of the TIDE program: People are without jobs because of themselves. This barrage hit the young men pretty hard. Their response was typical of any outraged male whose manhood has been threatened. In fact, when one young woman gibed, "You ain't no kinda man," some of the fellows had to be physically restrained from hitting her.

One of the men explained that "maybe the reason cats dress the way they do is because they can't afford anything else. Did you ever think of that?"

The woman's response was one I had not heard since the third or fourth grade: "Well, it doesn't matter what you wear as long as it's clean, pressed, and tucked-in. But hell, you guys don't even shine your shoes."

The battle of the sexes in the black community seems to be almost a class conflict. Many observers have noted that the black woman succeeds more readily in school than the black man. Women are also favored by parents, especially mothers. Moreover, the black woman has been for some time the most stable force and the major breadwinner of the Negro family. All these things put Negro women in harmony with the major values attached to work and success in our society. Black men, however, have been estranged from society, and a culture has developed around this estrangement— a male Negro culture often antagonistic to the dominant white society. The black woman stands in much the same relation to black men as white society does.

Even including Rumford, no group of officials was put down quite so hard as the Oakland police. Police brutality was constantly on the youngsters' minds. A day didn't pass without at least one being absent because he was in jail, or one coming in with a story about mistreatment by the police. A meeting was arranged with a sergeant from the Community Relations Bureau of the Oakland police. The students seemed excited about meeting the officer on their own turf and with the protection provided by the program.

In anticipation of his arrival, the fellows rearranged the room, placing all the separate tables together. Then they sat down in a group at one end of the table, waiting for the officer.

Putting Down the Police

Sergeant McCormack was an older man. And while obviously a cop, he could also pass for a middle-aged businessman or a young grandfather.

"Hi boys," he said as he sat down. His first mistake. He began with the five-minute speech he must give to every community group. The talk was factual, uninteresting, and noncontroversial: how the department is run, what the qualifications for policemen are, and how difficult it is for police to do their work and still please everyone. His talk was greeted with complete silence.

"I understand you have some questions," McCormack finally said.

"What about police brutality?" asked one man.

"What is your definition of police brutality?" the sergeant countered.

"How long you been a cop?" someone shouted.

"Over 20 years."

"And you got the nerve to come on sounding like you don't know what we talking about. Don't be jiving us. Shit, if you've been a cop *that* long, you *got* to know what we talking about."

"Righteous on that, brother!" someone chimed in.

"Well, I've been around a while, all right, but I've never seen any brutality. But what about it?"

"What *about* it?" There was a tone of disbelief mixed with anger in the young man's voice. "Shit man, we want to know why you cats always kicking other cats' asses."

The officer tried to draw a distinction between necessary and unnecessary police violence. The fellows weren't buying that. They claimed the police systematically beat the hell out of them for no reason. The officer asked for examples and the fellows obliged with long, involved, and detailed personal experiences with the Oakland Police Department. The sergeant listened patiently, periodically interrupting to check details and inconsistencies. He tried to offer a police interpretation of the incident. But the fellows were simply not in a mood to listen. In desperation the sergeant finally said, "Don't you want to hear *our* side of the story?"

"Hell no, motherfucker, we *see* your side of the story every night on 14th Street."

One young man stood up, his back to the officer, and addressed his contemporaries: "We *tired* of talking! We want some action! There's a new generation now. We ain't like the old folks who took all this shit off the cops." He turned to the sergeant and said, "You take that back to your goddamn Chief Preston and tell him."

McCormack had a silly smile on his face.

Another youngster jumped up and hollered, "You all ain't going to be smiling when we put dynamite in your police station!"

The officer said simply, "You guys don't want to talk."

"You see," someone yelled, "the cat's trying to be slick, trying to run a game on us. First he comes in here all nice-talking, all that shit about how they run the police and the police is to protect us. And then when we tell him how they treat us he wants to say we don't want to talk. Shit! We want to talk, he don't want to listen."

From this point on, they ran over him mercilessly. I, with all my biases against the police, could not help feeling compassion for the sergeant. If the police are an authority figure in the black community, then this episode must be viewed as a revolt against authority— *all* authority. There was nothing about the man's life, both private and public, that wasn't attacked.

"How much money you get paid?"

"About $12,000 a year."

"For being a cop? Wow!"

"What do you do?"

"I work in the Community Relations Department."

"Naw, stupid, what *kind* of work?"

"I answer the telephone, speak to groups, and try to see if the police treat the citizens wrong."

"Shit, we could do that and we don't even have a high-school education. Is that all you do? And get that much money for it?"

"Where do you live?"

"I'll bet he lives up in the hills."

"I live in the east side of Oakland. And I want you to know that my next-door neighbor is a colored man. I've got nothing against colored people."

"You got any kids?"

"Yeah, two boys and a girl."

"Shit, bet they all went to college and got good jobs. Any of your kids been in trouble?"

"No, not really."

"What do they do?"

"My oldest boy is a fighter pilot in Vietnam."

"What the hell is he doing over there? That's pretty stupid."

"Yeah man, what are we fighting in Vietnam for?

Is that your way of getting rid of us?"

"Well, the government says we have to be there and it's the duty of every citizen to do what his country tells him to do."

"We don't want to hear all that old bullshit, man."

"Hey, how come you wear such funny clothes? You even look like a goddam cop."

"Yeah baby, and he smells like one too!"

The barrage continued for almost half an hour. The instructor finally called a halt: "Sergeant McCormack has to get back, fellows. Is there anything specific that you'd like to ask him?"

"Yeah. How come Chief Preston ain't here? He's always talking to other people all over the country about how good the Oakland cops are and how there ain't going to be no riot here. Why don't he come and tell us that? We want to talk with the chief."

The next day, Deputy Chief Gain came—accompanied by the captain of the Youth Division, the lieutenant of that division, and a Negro sergeant. It was a formidable display of police authority. The youngsters were noticeably taken aback.

Chief Gain is a no-nonsense, businesslike cop. He takes no static from anyone, vigorously defends what he thinks is correct, and makes no apologies for what he considers incorrect. He is an honest man in the sense that he makes no attempt to cover up or smooth over unpleasant things. He immediately got down to business: "All right now, I understand you guys have some beefs with the department. What's the story?"

The fellows started right in talking about the ways they had been mistreated by the police. The chief began asking specific questions: where it happened, when it happened, what the officer looked like, and so on. He never denied the existence of brutality. That almost seemed to be assumed. He did want details, however. He always asked whether the youth had filed a complaint with the department. The response was always No. He then lectured them about the need to file such complaints if the situation was to be changed.

He explained the situation as he saw it: "Look fellows, we run a police force of 654 men. Most of them are good men, but there's bound to be a few rotten apples in the basket. I know that there's a couple of men who mistreat people, but it's only a few and we're trying our best to change that."

"Shit, I know of a case where a cop killed a cat and now he's back on the beat."

"Now wait a minute—"

"No more waiting a minute!" someone interrupted. "You had two cops got caught taking bribes. One was black and the other Caucasian. The black cat was kicked off the force and the white cat is back on."

"Yeah, and what about that cat who killed somebody off-duty, what about him?"

"Hold on," Gain said firmly. "Let's take these things one at a time." He didn't get very far before he was back to the "few rotten apples" argument.

"If it's only a few cops, how come it happens all the time?"

The deputy chief told them that he thought it was the same few cops who were causing all the problems. "Unless you file complaints each time you feel you've been mistreated, we can't do anything about it. So it's up to you as much as it is up to us."

For the first time in weeks, I intruded into the discussion. I pointed out to Gain that he was asking citizens to police their own police force. He had argued that in most situations the department had a good deal of control over its own men—the same argument the police had used against a civilian-review board. Now he was saying the opposite: that it was up to the citizens. This seemed to break the impasse, and the students howled with delight.

"What happens if a cop beats my ass and I file a complaint?" demanded one. "Whose word does the judge take?"

"The judge takes the evidence and evaluates it objectively and comes to a decision."

"Yeah, but it's usually two cops against one of us, and if both testify against me, what happens? Do you think the judge is going to listen to me?"

"Bring some witnesses."

"That ain't going to do anything."

"That's your problem. If you don't like the legal system in this country, work to change it."

"Okay man," one fellow said to Gain, "You pretty smart. If I smack my buddy here upside the head and he files a complaint, what you gonna do?"

"Arrest you."

"Cool. Now let's say one of your ugly cops smacks *me* upside the head and I file a complaint—what you gonna do?"

"Investigate the complaint, and if there's anything to it, why we'll take action—probably suspend him."

"Why do *we* get arrested and *you* investigated?"

The deputy chief's response was that most private companies with internal difficulties don't want to be investigated by outside agencies. The fellows retorted: "Police are *not* a private business. You're supposed to work for the people!"

"And shit, you cats get to carry guns. No businessman carries guns. It's a different scene, man."

"How come you got all kinds of squad cars in this neighborhood every night? And have two and three cops in each of them?"

"The crime rate is high in this area," replied Gain, "and we get a lot of calls and complaints about it."

"Yeah, and you smart enough to know that when you come around here, you better be wearing helmets and carrying shotguns. If you that clever, you got to be smart enough to handle your own goddamn cops.

At this point the fellows all jumped on the deputy chief the same way they had jumped on the sergeant the day before:

"Why don't you just let us run our own damn community?"

"Yeah. There should be people on the force who've been in jail because they the only people who know what it means to be busted. People in West Oakland should be police because they know their community; you don't."

"Why do we get all the speeding tickets?"

"How come we got to fight in Vietnam?"

"Why the judges so hard on us? They don't treat white cats—I mean dudes—the way they do us."

The chief began assembling his papers and stood up. "You guys aren't interested in talking. You want to yell. When you want to talk, come down to my office and if I'm free we'll talk."

But the fellows had the last word. While he was leaving they peppered him with gibes about how *they* were tired of talking; promised to dynamite his office; and called the police chief a coward for not coming down to speak with them.

When the deputy chief had gone, the instructor asked the fellows why they insisted on ganging up on people like the police. The answer provides a lot of insight into the young men's actions toward the police, businessmen, and public officials:

"These people just trying to run a game on us. If we give them time to think about answers, they gonna put us in a trick. We've *got* to gang up on them because they gang up on us. Did you dig the way that cat brought three other cats with him? Besides, how else could we put them down?"

A Subtle Form of Racism

In effect, the young men had inverted the meaning and aims of the TIDE program. It was supposed to be an opportunity for them to plan careers and prepare themselves for their life's work. The immediate goal was to help them get started by showing them how to get a job. The youngsters had a different view. The program was a way to play some games and take some outings—an interesting diversion from the bore-

dom and frustration of ghetto life in the summer. In some respects it was also a means of confronting, on equal terms, high-status people normally unavailable to them—and of venting on them their anger and hostility. But primarily they saw it as a $5-a-day job.

The program simply did not meet the needs of these young men. In fact, it was not really meant to. The Great Society was trying to "run a game on" black youth. TIDE asked them to stop being what they are. It tried to lead them into white middle-class America by showing that America was interested in getting them jobs. But America does not provide many jobs—let alone attractive jobs—for those with police records, with few skills, with black skins. The youths knew that; TIDE workers knew that, too. They did not train youths for work, but tried to make them believe that if they knew *how* to get a job, they could. The young men saw through the sham.

Ironically, the view that Negro youths, rather than society, are responsible for the employment problem is very similar to the familiar line of white racism. Negroes will not work because they are lazy and shiftless, the old Southern bigot would say. The Northern liberal today would put it a little differently: Negroes cannot get jobs because of their psychological and cultural impediments; what they need is cultural improvement, a proper attitude, the ability to sell themselves. Both views suggest that inequities in the job and opportunity structure of America are minor compared to the deficiencies of Negroes themselves. In the end, Northern liberals and Southern racists agree: The problem is mainly with Negroes, not with our society. This fallacy underlies much of the war on poverty's approach and is indicative of the subtle forms racism is taking in America today.

FURTHER READING

Shadow and Act by Ralph Ellison (New York: Signet Books, 1972).

Dying Colonialism by F. Fanon (New York: Grove Press, 1967).

"The Hero, the Sambo and the Operator: Three Characterizations of the Oppressed" by R. S. Warner, D. T. Wellman and L. J. Weitzman, *Urban life and Culture* 2 (April 1973): 53–85.

DOUGLAS H. POWELL AND PAUL F. DRISCOLL

Middle-Class Professionals Face Unemployment

"I knew it was coming....For over a year I hadn't been sleeping very well because I could see business falling off and knew they didn't need me. When I was finally laid off I stopped worrying...for a while, anyway." Many unemployed professionals share the feelings of this purchasing agent when faced with the prospect of joblessness. The actual layoff comes as a relief from the anxiety and tension of anticipation and they do not begin to look for a job immediately. One man went to Europe for a month's vacation and others expressed guarded optimism: "I don't feel unemployed," and "No question in my mind I'll be employed in a few months."

We began to understand the feelings and attitudes of these unemployed professionals while meeting with groups of out-of-work scientists, engineers and technical people at an experimental Professional Service Center in Massachusetts. While we knew of several studies dealing with the reactions of lower-class and minority workers to unemployment, we had little information about the feelings and behavior of middle-class men facing lengthy periods of unemployment. From our research and discussions with these middle-class professionals we constructed a four stage description of their difficulties and responses to a situation which threatens to become increasingly widespread.

Stage I: Period of Relaxation and Relief

Most of the men in our survey reacted to the initial period of unemployment with a sense of relief. Like the purchasing agent, they had seen their companies failing to find new business, contracts terminating and their friends laid off. The period following layoff became one of relaxation and relief. Sometimes they are bitter to-

How the Study of Middle-class Unemployed Men was Made

Our initial impressions of how middle-class men feel and act during a period of lengthy unemployment came in the course of 30 discussions with groups of about 25 unemployed scientists and engineers at an experimental Professional Service Center in Massachusetts. The intent of the meetings was the development of job-seeking skills and remotivation, but our preliminary observations encouraged us to look more carefully. We interviewed an additional 50 men picked randomly from among those coming to the job center. The men in our sample had these characteristics:

	Mean	Range
Age	41 years	25-53
Education	16 years	14-20
Length of Unemployment	9.5 months	2-18 months

Our open-ended interviews with these unemployed men were not viewed as a test of the theoretical scheme. They were intended to provide data which would illuminate our initial impressions as well as to suggest new directions for inquiry. We treated the interview data inductively, tabulating reports of changing patterns of job-seeking behavior, feelings and attitudes, and relationships with others when they occurred. The result is the clinical description in this article—supported by the evidence of our interview material—of the four stages which unemployed middle-class people seem to go through if they are not able to find a job within a short time. The stages are progressive and appear to have characteristic emotional and behavioral patterns related to how long the individuals have been out of work. Among our sample of unemployed scientists and engineers, each man reported going through at least two of the stages, and most of them had been through three or four. At the time of the interviews five men were in Stage I, nine of the men were classified in Stage II, ten in Stage III and 26 in Stage IV.

ward their employer, but most men understand why they are laid off. The intellectual awareness of the reasons for their unemployment tends to dampen anger or bitterness—or even depression—they may feel when first fired.

During this time, the unemployed scientists and engineers don't like to think much about being out of work. There is a sense of being "between jobs;" they feel confident and hopeful of finding a job as soon as they are "ready" to go back to work. Although most of the men make at least one clearcut effort to look for work at this stage, they do so on a casual basis: "I feel I know people and can get into places." They call a friend or agency or respond to an ad.

The newly unemployed seize gladly upon any excuse not to look for work. "I stopped looking because I figured no work was coming for the holidays," explained a quality control engineer; one physicist said, "I wanted to have companies get over their summer doldrums before I looked." They spend time very much as they would on a vacation at home—being with the family, sleeping late, reading or tinkering in the workshop. Sometimes they travel, but they all tend to find some release to recuperate and prepare for intensive job-seeking.

Relationships with others do not change much during this period of relief and relaxation. Family relationships remain normal. Neither husband nor wife openly airs their mutual concerns at this time and family equilibrium is maintained.

Newly unemployed men talk openly about their situation to co-workers and friends in other divisions of their companies (contacts who know their situation as a matter of course). But they do not initiate contacts with friends who wouldn't know about their situation unless told.

Stage II: Period of Concerted Effort

After a period of approximately 25 days, the individual begins to feel rested, often somewhat bored and edgy. Now he starts to make a systematic and usually well-organized attempt to find work. This is a period of concerted effort. The individual relies on job-finding strategies which have been successful in the past, including calling friends, sending resumes to blind ads and going back to the university placement center. He tries to follow the advice of job counselors who say, "You have a full-time job. Your full-time job is to find a full-time job!" More time is spent actually looking for work or thinking about it than in other activity.

This is a time of optimism and planning. Among the scientists and engineers we talked with these descriptions were common:

"I do my homework. When I have an interview I study everything concerning the company that I can get my hands on."
"I went door-to-door, private agencies, resume send-outs."
"I'd literally memorize the want ads."
"I'm pushing, trying to hit all bases."

During this stage a logical, consistent approach is followed:

"I laid out my plan of action, contacted all friends, agencies and ads."

"I get up every morning at 7, get the paper, check to see what I have to do for the day."

"I keep a notebook of contacts. Keep close tabs on where I've been, where I have to go."

If an unemployed man finds himself blocked in one area —for example, the local want ads—he looks elsewhere. He shows flexibility. He contacts other sources of potential jobs such as employment agencies and the Division of Employment Security. He is willing to make "cold calls."

Though the average amount of time devoted to these activities was about three months, individual variation was substantial. There was evidence that this period could be very short indeed—a matter of days for some—and rather lengthy for others. The length of time an unemployed person was able to sustain his confidence seemed to depend on several factors. The men we interviewed who were able to maintain themselves three months or longer mentioned these reasons:

Just didn't think about failure; financial security from pension or savings; received reinforcement from job market and support from family and friends.

Critical to the maintenance of a concerted effort is the capacity to avoid becoming overly depressed or anxious in the face of rejection letters from potential employers —or worse, no response at all. The unemployed person must bounce back quickly to remain active. He tries not to think about how tough it is to find jobs or why he failed in his last attempt. Any encouragement from the market place helps immensely: a note indicating that an application is being processed, a call from a friend saying a company had called for a reference or a letter asking for more information results in renewed optimism.

Having savings or other money to tide the family over while the individual is out of work is vitally important to maintaining a sustained effort. Those with greater financial resources continue to look for work in a positive, organized manner much longer than those who do not.

This appears to be a time of maximum support and encouragement from family and friends. To the extent he receives support, the unemployed scientist and engineer's capacity to maintain a concerted effort is enhanced.

Overall, family relations during this period are good. The wife helps in the job search by taking care of the secretarial chores often necessary to finding a job and giving moral support and encouragement. Often she becomes as emotionally involved as her husband is about his getting a particular job—if he fails she becomes very upset too. Her ability to maintain her resiliency and optimism directly influences her husband's continuing efforts.

So, too, do friends provide maximum support. As one engineer said, "I opened up a bit. I don't plead, just tell them the facts. My company has been hit by the layoffs. If you know of anybody looking for a good guy, I'm available." Most men we talked with reported a cordial response from friends and neighbors whom they told about their problem. Friends took resumes, made phone calls, gave advice, volunteered to talk to people they know who might be able to help. It appears that friends are motivated to help because the unemployed person is actively looking for a job.

But this is not a time when the unemployed individual likes being in the presence of other unemployed people. Usually he avoids them. "I'm not like *them*," one engineer said, "They are out of a job. I am waiting for an offer from Corning Glass." When he met other unemployed men, he would often greet them with the enthusiasm he would normally show a leper—afraid that whatever they have might be catching.

Men who have a prior history of being laid off seem to adjust better to unemployment than those who have never been out of work. They spent less time in the stage of relaxation, were more open in telling others about their unemployment, and were more appropriate in their job-seeking strategies. Furthermore, these men had saved a greater proportion of their salary while they were working, and when it was possible for the wives to work this reversal of roles was handled smoothly.

Stage III: Period of Vacillation and Doubt

At this point the individual usually has been unemployed longer than he has been out of work before, or it becomes clear to him that the usual ways of finding a job are inadequate. His mood is characterized by vacillation in many areas. Job-seeking behavior is sporadic, a less than half-time process with alternating periods of intense activity and lying fallow. Doubt begins to undermine the process of decision making. He becomes intensely moody. Relationships with family and friends deteriorate.

With repeatedly unsuccessful encounters with the job market, the controlled optimism which produced earlier efforts starts to erode. The unemployed man begins doubting his judgment, second-guessing himself and becoming more self-critical. Fears and doubts—earlier suppressed by working hard, looking for work and trying not to think about the last unsuccessful attempt— trouble the unemployed scientist and engineer much more than before. Anxiety surrounding these feelings intensifies.

Preparation and organization, the unifying strategies of previous efforts, are gradually discarded. Much of the individual's job-searching strategy is aimed at reducing anxiety. One way was to "do" something. One chemical engineer said, "I was sitting around, getting edgier and edgier....So I just went down to the Northwest Industrial Park and went from door to door." Another reported almost the same behavior. He looked at the parking lot first and dropped in on only those companies where the lot was filled with cars.

Identity problems become a serious issue as the scientist or engineer tries to decide which aspects of his occupational experience and skill he should feature in order to find a job. The men have a tendency to lose a sense of who they are vocationally, allowing the market to define their abilities. Some men write four resumes which describe four different people. They are ripe to be taken in by unscrupulous job placement agencies who seem to promise jobs at enormous cost but are not in fact helpful. But most men don't complain. They are ready to grab at anything promising relief for their anxiety.

This was the time many men said they began to think seriously about making a significant change in their careers. A number actually began to pursue a specific alternative, the most common being taking the civil service exam, and going back to college for a teaching certificate. But unemployed scientists and engineers at higher levels of technical proficiency appear to be resistant to changing fields, while those who have climbed the management ladder seem more willing to shift careers. A project manager for a large defense contractor with an M.S. in physics justified his attempts to switch fields with the comment, "Managing people is the same regardless of the business product." His administrative experience offered him a number of options which he pursued early in his unemployment.

During this third stage many men develop an increasing sense of being past their prime. The majority of unemployed scientists and engineers over 35 said in one way or another, "They're looking for a younger man," to explain why they could not find a job. There is some truth in the statement—younger men are cheaper. But it also appears to be true that unemployed men in this period of vacillation and doubt have a premature sense of not being the men they once were.

Part of the problem is that engineering and technology fields condition men to feel obsolete quickly when they are out of work. Procedures and techniques change so rapidly that it is difficult for a man to begin working at the same level of responsibility if he has been unemployed and not in close contact with his field for a year or more.

Particularly hard hit are men in the aerospace industry who have had marginal formal education, but have grown through on-the-job training into positions usually requiring a degree in engineering. So long as they remain within a company they have no problems. Their co-workers know what they can do. But when the layoffs come these men with lots of experience but no degree find it more difficult than degree holders to get a job. For some non-degree holders this means returning to technician status again. Sometimes it is not the financial regression that hurts but the loss of the hard-earned professional status.

Extreme moodiness characterizes men in this stage. A young unemployed personnel manager put his feelings this way:

It's like being on a roller coaster of mental attitude, a yo-yo of mental attitude. Sometimes I feel depressed —I mean *really* depressed, and wonder if I'll ever snap out of it. After a while I begin to feel really agitated... you know, filled with energy. Then I'm really hyper! I spend a lot of energy, though I don't seem to get much done. I race through want ads but don't get much (from them)...then I go to the unemployment (sic) office for help...I only have pieces of conversation there, cutting short any help they might be, acting as if I have to go somewhere important in a hurry. I know what I'm doing is not helping....Yet, it feels better when you're on the move.

Frustration builds and keeping cool is increasingly difficult. Several men reported they lost jobs they were qualified for because they couldn't restrain themselves from badgering the potential employer for a decision.

Violent Rage

During this period most unemployed men feel extremely angry. They censure the government for breaking up the aerospace industry and are furious at the universities for training men for jobs that no longer exist. They feel a violent rage that sometimes turns back on them in the form of a deep depression. Unable to find a suitable external object to direct their anger against, some men internalize these intense feelings of fury and accumulated frustration. The despair and sense of panic they feel is at its greatest point and during this period men who commit suicide are likely to decide to do it.

Relations with others are severely impaired and the strain weighs heavily on marital relations. The men described two common family problems. Some felt they were a burden on their family, "I'm moody, beginning to pick on my wife for small things;" others said their wives annoyed them a great deal, "Her worrying bothers me" or "She's questioning me and I don't like it." Seeing her husband fail to obtain a job and then apparently fall into periods of no activity at all, a wife badgers her husband to try harder or begins to doubt his ability and transmits these concerns to him. Already doubting himself and wondering if he will ever find a job, the husband often responds acrimoniously to well-intended queries about how things are going, and what should be done if he doesn't soon find a job. Problems at home are further exacerbated in those cases where the unemployed man is not actively looking for a job, yet expects his wife to continue to do all the household work. In homes where the roles are strictly defined, the difficulties were most severe. These problems are intensified when the wife actively considers going back to work.

Relations with friends sometimes change in this phase.

About one man in four said they felt their friends began to avoid them when their concerted efforts to find work were not productive. A substantial minority reported their friends offered money or other support. Reactions to these offers ranged from tearful appreciation to hostile rejection because of the implication that a man out of a job needs charity.

After an average of six weeks of sporadic activity (it varies between three and nine weeks), there is a definite winding down of job hunting. Describing themselves toward the end of this stage, the scientists and engineers in our sample commented: "I'm not looking for a job as much any more." "I've stopped using certain approaches like sending out resumes. They don't pay off." "It's sporadic. I push a little harder only when an opportunity comes up." These statements reflect a gradual constriction of continuing efforts to find work, and movement toward the stage of malaise and cynicism.

Stage IV: Period of Malaise and Cynicism

Now looking for a job becomes an infrequent endeavor. Job-seeking strategies are often oriented toward protecting self-esteem. Moods stabilize as do relationships with others. As opposed to the transition from Stage II to Stage III which is marked by a great deal of anxiety and depression, the transition from Stage III to Stage IV appears to be a smoother one.

The individual goes longer and longer between positive attempts to secure a job, substantial efforts to change his job strategy, or active consideration of retraining. We found that one of the clearest indications that the individual has given up completely is where he has not had personal contact with a potential employer, job counselor, agency or college placement group in a 60-day period.

When the unemployed scientist or engineer looks for a job he often does so in a manner designed to cushion himself against the pain which could come from a possible refusal rather than adopting a more aggressive strategy and opening himself to disappointment if he is turned down. He protects his self-esteem by responding mostly to blind ads which ask for applicants to send their resumes, but don't require a personal contact. In this impersonal exchange, no response is the worst thing that can happen. There isn't much of an investment in getting the job—and not much chance of getting it either. Scientists and engineers responding to a blind ad typically face odds of 100 to 1 or worse against their being considered.

The men look for perfect matches as a way of guarding against getting turned down. Many unemployed scientists and engineers won't seek a position unless the job description fits their experience and training exactly. A systems engineer in our sample with sub-specialties in radar communication and automatic test equipment looked for openings that required his primary, secondary and tertiary skills. It appears that the longer a man remains in this fourth period, the more rigidly he holds to this highly differentiated view of himself. By holding on to this narrow vocational self-image he, in effect, avoids looking for a job.

The reasons men give for not looking for work are interesting: "I've lost all my drive and don't care." "What's the use of looking? I'll just get turned down." "I'm sick of being humiliated by people who act like they're doing you a favor just talking to you." Unemployed men in our sample described themselves as apathetic and listless in most aspects of their lives. One unemployed mechanical engineer described his behavior to us this way: "Not only have I lost my drive (looking for a job), but I'm not doing much of anything. I'm just staying around the house." Sentiments like this were expressed by two-thirds of the scientists and engineers.

In this stage most unemployed scientists and engineers start to lose the sense they are in control of their own vocational lives or futures. Luck seems more important in getting a job than anything he can do. As one scientist said, "No matter what I do it just doesn't make any difference. It's just a throw of the dice, whether I'll get the job or not." The feeling of powerlessness and pessimism are also characteristic of men in this stage. "Why go in for an interview," a physicist said, "I'll never get past the secretary anyway."

There is an enormous amount of cynicism in the ranks of the out-of-work scientists and engineers during this fourth stage. Programs designed to retrain out-of-work professionals are often greeted with superficial sarcasm about their real purpose being to keep bureaucrats busy and the minds of the unemployed off their troubles. At a deeper level there is frequently the conviction that nothing can really help.

This cynicism seemed to be a way of avoiding a very painful confrontation with the necessity of making a major change in life style in order to be able to return to work. This was illustrated by a conversation with an engineer who had been out of work for 15 months. He had not pursued any job opening in the last nine months. He recounted his several initial efforts to find work which turned up nothing. Noting he had several education courses in college, a job counselor suggested he might retrain in that field and plan to teach math or science. His initial response was, "Who's going to pay for the education I am going to have to get to retrain?" When it was determined he could capitalize on some veteran's benefits which would support much of the cost, he said, "Hell, there's no money in education anyway!" The job counselor responded that there were many jobs in education which paid as well as most jobs paid in his field. His final response was, "Well, even if I get a job in education I'll never get one of those high-paying jobs because everything is all political anyway."

The psychological mood of unemployed scientists and engineers becomes typically more quiet and stable than in the previous period. Most individuals don't feel as upset and anxious as they did earlier. The desperate feelings that are so intense in Stage III are tempered by helplessness and quiescence.

In this fourth period of unemployment, relations between husband and wife become markedly better. The wife stops asking her husband why he isn't actively looking for work anymore. Roles begin to be shifted or shared more equally. Mindful of financial realities the unemployed man faces the need for his wife to find work if she can. As many scientists and engineers marry close to their own educational background, their spouses are able to find work rather easily.

Relationships with others are more limited, largely restricted to a few very close friends and relatives. This constriction in interpersonal relationships cannot be explained solely on the basis of limited funds for entertainment or that the husband has lost contact with colleagues at work. In fact, most unemployed individuals report that they and their wives turned down a number of social invitations. Though the reasons vary, a major factor is that the family altered their life style to accommodate the husband's unemployment. It was easier for them to stay at home than to be with acquaintances whose way of life is now very different from theirs. Here the cycle comes to a close and the future depends upon the vagaries of the job market and the willingness of the professional to consider a change in career fields.

Several intriguing questions arise about the fate of the unemployed professionals in Stage IV and beyond. We would like to know more about how they find their way back to work and what the effect of lengthy unemployment has been on their careers.

In our sample some of the men were remotivated by special training programs. Others were sought out by previous employers or colleagues. Individuals who were more future oriented in their job-seeking strategy found these efforts paid off many months later. Men who made a number of contacts with potential employers who did not have openings at the time, or with whom the application process was lengthy, often were surprised later on by a job offer when they had nearly abandoned hope. One scientist in Stage IV was finally called back to his old company because when he was making a concerted effort to find work he had reinitiated contact with them, expressed his continued interest when a position opened up and attempted to keep them aware of his availability even though he was sure nothing would materialize immediately. An engineer finally received a civil service appointment even though it had been several months since he had contact with the potential employer. The individual realized at the time he initiated this contact that it might not pay off but went ahead anyway.

Interestingly, both of these men said they would not have made contacts of this type in Stage IV. Their limited job-seeking activity was mainly present oriented. This sentiment was shared by many men in Stage IV with whom we talked.

We think these ideas about progressive stages of unemployment, each with unique behavioral and emotional characteristics, are likely to apply to any unemployed middle-class group. But to what extent these observations differentiate the upper-middle-class engineer from a working-class laborer is not clear. Much behavior characteristic of unemployed scientists and professional groups in Stage IV—malaise, cynicism, a sense of powerlessness—has been described as typical of the poor and minority group workers as well as of workers in other countries. Our suspicion, therefore, is that these characteristics are human reactions to unemployment and the frustrations associated with it, and are not restricted to a specific group of individuals.

The success of programs designed to help unemployed groups such as scientists and engineers as well as men in other occupations might be enhanced by an understanding that these men have very different needs depending upon which stage of unemployment they are in. These needs and related patterns of behavior make them responsive to specific kinds of help and indifferent or hostile to others. For example, a man in Stage II doesn't need counseling, he needs job openings to pursue; a man in Stage III may require a good deal of counseling before he is ready to look for a position; and giving a man in Stage IV a list of job openings is not likely to be very helpful. Often they will require a good deal of outside help aimed at restoring self-confidence and changing job-seeking strategies before they will take a job interview.

The image of competent and energetic men reduced to listless discouragement highlights the personal tragedy and the loss of valuable resources when there is substantial unemployment. It presses us to seek more thorough and intensive methods of remotivation and more dignified avenues of return to the world of work. Perhaps more significantly, the situation of these middle-class unemployed further dramatizes the plight of the larger number of unemployed non-skilled workers whose fate is to deal with unemployment often during their lifetime.

FURTHER READING

The Meaning of Work and Retirement by Eugene Freedman and Robert J. Havighurst (Chicago: University of Chicago Press, 1954).

"The Engineer and His Work: A Sociological Perspective" by Alvin Rudoff and Dorothy Lucken, *Science*, 172 (1971): 1103–1108.

The Stress of Life by Hans Selyn (New York: McGraw-Hill, 1956).

IVAR BERG

Rich Man's Qualifications for Poor Man's Jobs

It is now a well-known fact that America offers more and more jobs to skilled workers while the increase in unskilled jobs has slowed down. Newspaper articles regularly remind us that we have a shortage of computer programmers, and, at the same time, too many unskilled laborers. The conventional solution is to correct the shortcomings of the labor force by educating more of the unemployed. Apart from its practical difficulties, this solution begs the important question: Are academic credentials important for *doing* the job—or just for *getting* it?

My studies of manpower use indicate that although in recent years requirements for many jobs have been upgraded because of technological and other changes, in many cases education requirements have been raised arbitrarily. In short, *many employers demand too much education for the jobs they offer.*

Education has become the most popular solution to America's social and economic ills. Our faith in education as *the* cure for unemployment, partly reflects our inclination as a society to diagnose problems in individualistic terms. Both current and classical economic theories merely reinforce these attitudes; both assume that the labor supply can be significantly changed by investments in education and health. Meanwhile private employers, on the other side of the law of supply and demand, are held to be merely reacting to the imperatives that generate the need for better educated manpower.

Certainly the government cannot force private employers to hire people who have limited educations. Throughout our history and supported by our economic theory, we have limited the government's power to deal with private employers. According to law and the sentiments that support it, the rights of property owners and the protection of their property are essential functions of government, and cannot or should not be tampered with. In received economic doctrine, business stands apart as an independent variable. As such, business activity controls the demand for labor, and the best way the government has to reduce unemployment is by stimulating business growth.

Some of the methods the government uses to do this are direct subsidies, depreciation allowances, zoning regulations, fair-trade laws, tax holidays, and credit guarantees. In return for these benefits, governments at all levels ultimately expect more jobs will be generated and more people employed. But when the market for labor does not work out according to theory, when employer demand does not increase to match the number of job seekers, attention shifts to the supply of labor. The educational, emotional, social, and even moral shortcomings of those who stand outside the boundaries of the social system have to be eliminated, we are told—and education seems to be the best way of doing it.

Unfortunately, economists and public planners usually assume that the education that employers require for the jobs they offer is altogether beneficial to the firm. Higher education, it is thought, means better performance on the job. A close look at the data, however, shows that here reality does not usually correspond with theory.

In recent years, the number of higher-level jobs has not increased as much as personnel directors lead us to believe. The big increase, rather, has been in middle-level jobs—for high-school graduates and college dropouts. This becomes clear when the percentages of jobs requiring the three different levels of education are compared with the percentages of the labor force that roughly match these categories. The comparison of census data with the U.S. Employment Service's descriptions of 4,000 different jobs also shows that (1) high-education jobs have expanded somewhat faster for men than for women; (2) those jobs in the middle have expanded faster for women than for men; and (3) that highly educated people are employed in jobs that require *less* education than these people actually have.

The fact is that our highly educated people are competing with lesser educated people for the jobs in the middle. In Monroe County, N.Y. (which includes Buffalo), the National Industrial Conference Board has graphically demonstrated this fact. Educational requirements for most jobs, the board has reported, vary with the academic calendar: Thus, requirements rise as the end of the school year approaches and new graduates flood the market. Employers whose job openings fall in the middle category believe that by employing people with higher-than-necessary educations they are benefiting from the increasing educational achievements of the work force. Yet the data suggest that there is a "shortage" of high-school graduates and of people with post high school educations short of college degrees while there is a "surplus" of college graduates, especially females.

The economic and sociological theories that pour out of university computers have given more and more support to the idea that we, as a society, have more options in dealing with the supply side of employment —with the characteristics of the work force—than with demand.

These studies try to relate education to higher salaries; they assume that the income a person earns is a valid measure of his job performance. The salaries of better-educated people, however, may not be closely related to the work they do. Female college graduates are often employed as secretaries; many teachers and social workers earn less than plumbers and others who belong to effective unions. What these rate-of-return studies lack is productivity data isolated according to job and the specific person performing the job.

In any event, it is circular reasoning to relate wage and salary data to educational achievements. Education is often, after all, the most important criterion for a person's getting a job in the first place! The argument that salaries may be used to measure the value of education and to measure the "value added" to the firm by employees of different educational backgrounds, may simply confirm what it sets out to prove. In jobs for which educational requirements have not been thoughtfully studied, the argument is not an argument at all, but a self-fulfilling prophecy.

Despite the many attempts to relate a person's achievements to the wages he receives, researchers usually find that the traits, aptitudes, and educational achievements of workers vary as greatly *within* job categories as they do *between* them. That is, people in job A differ as much from one another as they differ from people in job B. Only a small percentage of the labor force—those in the highest and those in the lowest job levels—are exceptions. And once workers become members of the labor force, personal virtues at even the lower job levels do not account for wage dif-

ferences—intelligent, well-educated, low-level workers don't necessarily earn more than others at the bottom of the ladder. Marcia Freedman's study of employment patterns for Columbia's Conservation of Human Resources project, indicates that, although many rungs of the organizational ladder are linked to differences in pay, these rungs are not closely related to differences in the employees' skills and training.

Educational requirements continue to go up, yet most employers have made no effort to find out whether people with better educations make better workers than people with inferior educations. Using data collected from private firms, the military, the federal civil service, and public-educational systems, and some collected from scratch, I have concentrated on this one basic question.

Business managers, supported by government leaders and academics interested in employment problems, have well-developed ideas about the value of a worker's educational achievement. They assert that with each increment of education—especially those associated with a certificate, diploma, or degree—the worker's attitude is better, his trainability is greater, his capacity for adaptation is more developed, and his prospects for promotions are rosier. At the same time, those workers with more modest educations, and especially those who drop out of school, are held to be less intelligent, less adaptable, less self-disciplined, less personable, and less articulate.

The findings in my studies do not support these assertions.

A comparison of 4,000 insurance agents in a major company in the Greater New York area showed that an employee's productivity—measured by the dollar value of the policies he sold—did not vary in any systematic way with his years of formal education. In other words, those salesmen with less education brought as much money into the company as their better educated peers. When an employee's experience was taken into account, it was clear that those with *less* education and *more* experience sold the most policies. Thus, even an employer whose success in business depends on the social and psychological intangibles of a customer-client relationship may not benefit from having highly educated employees. Other factors such as the influence of colleagues and family obligations were more significant in explaining the productivity of agents.

In another insurance agency, the job performances of 200 young female clerks were gauged from the number of merit-salary increases they had received. Researchers discovered that there were *no* differences in the performance records of these women that could easily be attributed to differences in their educational backgrounds. Once again, focusing on the educational achievements of job applicants actually diverted at-

tention from characteristics that are really relevant to job performance.

At a major weekly news magazine, the variation in educational achievement among over 100 employees was greater than among the insurance clerks. The magazine hired female college graduates, as well as high-school graduates, for clerical-secretarial positions. While the employers argued that the girls needed their college degrees to qualify for future editorial jobs, most editorial positions were *not* filled by former secretaries, whether college graduates or not, but by college graduates who directly entered into those positions. And although the personnel director was skeptical of supervisors' evaluations of the secretaries, the supervisors determined the salary increases, and as many selective merit-pay increases were awarded to the lesser-educated secretaries as to the better-educated secretaries.

Executives of a larger well-known chemical company in New York told me that the best technicians in their research laboratory were those with the highest educational achievement. Therefore, in screening job applicants, they gave greater weight to a person's educational background than to his other characteristics. Yet, statistical analysis of relevant data revealed that the rate of turnover in the firm was positively associated with the employees' educational achievement. And a close look at the "reasons for leaving" given by the departing technicians showed that they intended to continue their educations. Furthermore, lesser-educated technicians earned higher performance evaluations than did their better-educated peers. Understandably, the employer was shocked by these findings.

Over Educated Are Less Productive

The New York State Department of Labor's 1964 survey of employers suggests that technicians often possess educational achievements far beyond what employers themselves think is ideal for effective performance. Thousands of companies reported their minimal educational requirements to the Labor Department, along with their ideal requirements and the actual educators of the technicians they employed. In many industries and in respect to most types of technicians, the workers were better educated than they were required to be; in 10 out of 16 technical categories they were even better educated than their employers dared hope, exceeding the "ideal" requirements set down by the employers.

Upper- and middle-level employees are not the only ones who are overqualified for their jobs. Nor is the phenomenon only to be observed in metropolitan New York. In a study of eight Mississippi trouser plants, researchers found that the more education an employee had, the less productive she was. Several hundred female operators were paid by "piece work" and their wages therefore were a valid test of workers' productivity. Furthermore this study showed that educational achievement was positively associated with turnover: The better-educated employee was more likely to quit her job.

Education's negative relationship to jobs can be measured not only by the productivity and turnover of personnel, but also by worker satisfaction. It may be argued that dissatisfaction among workers leads to a desirable measure of labor mobility, but the funds a company spends to improve employee morale and make managerial personnel more sensitive to the needs of their subordinates strongly suggest that employers are aware of the harm caused by worker dissatisfaction. Roper Associates once took a representative sample of 3,000 blue-collar workers in 16 industries in all parts of the United States. Among workers in lower-skilled jobs, dissatisfaction was found to increase as their educational achievements increased.

These studies of private firms suggest that many better-educated workers are assigned to jobs requiring low skills and that among the results are high turnover rates, low productivity, and worker dissatisfaction. Nonetheless, the disadvantages of "overeducation" are best illustrated by employment practices of public-school systems.

Educated Teachers Opt Out

Many school districts, to encourage their teachers to be highly educated, base teachers' salaries upon the number of credits they earn toward higher degrees. However, data from the National Opinion Research Center and the National Science Foundation's 1962 study of 4,000 teachers show that, like employees elsewhere, teachers become restless as their educational achievements rise. Elementary and secondary school teachers who have master's degrees are less likely to stay in their jobs than teachers with bachelor's degrees. And in a similar study done by Columbia Teachers College, it was evident that teachers with master's degrees were likely to have held jobs in more than one school system.

Thus, for school systems to tie pay increases to extra credits seems to be self-defeating. Teachers who earn extra credits apparently feel that their educational achievements reach a point beyond which they are overtrained for their jobs, and they then want to get administrative jobs or leave education for better paying jobs in industry. The school districts are, in a sense, encouraging teachers not to teach. This practice impedes the upgrading of teacher qualifications in another

way. Thanks to the extra-credit system, schools of education have a steady supply of students and therefore are under little pressure to furnish better and more relevant courses.

For the most part, though, employers in the public sector do not suffer from problems of unrealistic educational requirements. For a variety of reasons, they do not enjoy favored positions in the labor market and consequently have not been able to raise educational requirements nearly so fast as the private employer has. But for this reason alone, the experiences of government agencies are significant. How well do their employees with low-education backgrounds perform their jobs?

The pressure on the armed forces to make do with "what they get" has forced them to study their experiences with personnel. Their investigations clearly show that a person's educational achievement is not a good clue to his performance. Indeed, general tests developed for technical, military classifications and aptitude tests designed to screen individual candidates for training programs have turned out to be far better indicators of a person's performance.

In a 1948 study of Air Force personnel, high-school graduates were compared with nongraduates in their performance on the Army Classification Tests and on 13 tests that later became part of the Airman Classification Battery. The military's conclusion: "High-school graduates were not uniformly and markedly superior to non-graduates. . . . High-school graduation, unless supplemented by other screening measures such as tests or the careful review of the actual high-school record, does not insure that a basic trainee will be of high potential usefulness to the Air Force."

In 1963, the Air Force studied 4,458 graduates of eight technical courses. Comparing their performances in such courses as Reciprocating Engine Mechanic, Weather Observer, Accounting, and Finance Specialist with the education they received before entering the service, the Air Force found that a high-school diploma only modestly predicted the grades the airmen got in the Air Force courses. In other Air Force studies, aptitude tests were consistently found to correlate well with a person's proficiency and performance, while educational achievement rarely accounted for more than 4 percent of the variations.

These Air Force data do not conclude that education is unimportant, or that formal learning experiences are irrelevant. Rather, it points out the folly of confusing a man's driver's license with his driving ability. Just as different communities have different safety standards, so schools and school systems employ different kinds of teachers and practices. It should surprise no one that a person's credentials, by themselves, predict his performance so poorly.

Rich Man's Qualifications for Poor Man's Jobs

Army and Navy studies confirm the Air Force findings. When 415 electronic technicians' scores on 17 concrete tasks were analyzed in conjunction with their age, pay grades, and education, education was found to be negatively associated with performance. When the Navy updated this study, the outcome was the same. For high performance in repairing complicated electronic testing equipment, experience proved more significant than formal education.

Perhaps the military's most impressive data came from its experiments with "salvage" programs, in which illiterates and men who earn low scores on military classification tests are given remedial training. According to research reports, these efforts have been uniformly successful—as many graduates of these programs develop into useful servicemen as the average, normal members of groups with which they have been regularly compared.

Naval Manpower Salvage

In a 1955 study done for the Navy, educational achievements were not found to be related to the performance of 1,370 recruits who attended "recruit preparatory training" courses. Neither were educational achievements related to the grades the recruits received from their company commanders and their instructors, nor to their success or failure in completing recruit training. In some instances, the low-scoring candidates with modest educational backgrounds performed at higher levels than better-educated men with high General Classification Test scores. The military recently expanded its "salvage" program with Project 100,000, and preliminary results tend to confirm the fact that training on the job is more important than educational credentials.

Military findings also parallel civilian studies of turnover rates. Reenlistment in the Navy is nearly twice as high among those men who have completed fewer than 12 years of school. But reenlistment in the military, of course, is related to the fact that the civilian economy does not particularly favor ex-servicemen who have modest educational achievements.

Wartime employment trends make the same point. During World War II, when demand for labor was high, both public and private employers adapted their recruiting and training to the labor supply. Productivity soared while a wide range of people mastered skills almost entirely without regard to their personal characteristics or previous circumstances. Labor's rapid adjustment on the job was considered surprising; after the war, it was also considered to be expensive. Labor costs, it was argued, had gone up during the war, and unit productivity figures were cited as evidence. These figures, however, may have been misleading. Since the majority of wartime laborers were employed in industries with "cost-plus" contracts—where the government agreed to reimburse the contractor for all costs, plus a certain percentage of profit—such arrangements may have reduced the employer's incentives to control costs. The important lesson from the war period seems to be that people quickly adjust to work requirements once they are on the job.

A 5 percent sample of 180,000 men in the federal civil service shows that while the number of promotions a person gets is associated with his years of education, the link is far from complete. Education has a greater bearing on a person's rank at *entry* into the civil service than on his prospects for a promotion. Except for grades 11-15, in accounting for the promotion rates of civil servants, length of service and age are far more significant than education. A closer look at one government agency will perhaps clarify these points.

Few organizations in the United States have had to adapt to major technological changes as much as the Federal Aviation Agency has. Responsible among other things for the direction and control of all flights in the United States, it operates the control-tower facilities at all public airports. With the advent of jet-powered flights, the F.A.A. had to handle very quickly the horrendous technical problems posed by faster aircraft and more flights. Since no civilian employer requires the services needed by the F.A.A. in this area, the agency must train its own technicians and control-tower people. The agency inventively confronted the challenge by hiring and training many new people and promoting those trained personnel it already had. Working with the background data on 507 men—all the air-traffic controllers who had attained grade 14 or above—it would seem that, at this high level, education would surely prove its worth.

On the Job Training for Tower Controllers

Yet in fact these men had received very little formal education, and almost no technical managerial training except for the rigorous on-the-job training given by the F.A.A. itself. Of the 507 men in the sample, 211, or 42 percent, had no education or training beyond high school. An additional 48, or 10 percent, were high-school graduates who had had executive-training courses. Thus, more than half of the men had had no academic training beyond high school. There were, however, no patterns in the differences among the men in grades 13 or 15 with respect to education. That is, education and training were *not* related to the higher grade.

The F.A.A.'s amazing safety record and the honors and awards given to the tower controllers are good indicators of the men's performance. The F.A.A.'s Executive Selection and Inventory System records 21 different kinds of honors or awards. Only one-third of the men have never received any award at all. Half of the 77 percent who have been honored have been honored more than once. And a relatively high percentage of those with no education beyond high school received four or more awards; those with a B.A. degree were least likely to receive these many honors. Other breakdowns of the data confirm that education is not a factor in the daily performance of one of the truly demanding decision-making jobs in America.

The findings reported in these pages raise serious questions about the usefulness of raising educational requirements for jobs. They suggest that the use of formal education as a sovereign screening device for jobs adequately performed by people of lower educational achievements may result in serious costs—high turnover, employee dissatisfactions, and poorer performance. Programs calculated to improve employees' educations probably aim at the wrong targets, while programs calculated to reward better-educated people are likely to miss their targets. It would be more useful to aim at employers' policies and practices that block organizational mobility and seal off entry jobs.

There Are More Job Openings in the Middle

Given the facts that there are more job openings in the middle, and that many people are overqualified for the jobs they do have, policies aimed at upgrading the educational achievements of the low-income population seem at best naïve. It would make better sense to upgrade people in the middle to higher jobs and upgrade those in lower-level jobs to middle positions, providing each group with an education appropriate to their age, needs, and ambitions. The competition for lower-level jobs would then be reduced, and large numbers of drop-outs could move into them. (Only after young people, accustomed to a good income, develop middle-class aspirations are they apparently interested in pursuing the balance of their educations.) Current attempts to upgrade the labor supply also seem questionable in light of what psychologists and sociologists have to say. Changing people's attitudes, self-images, and achievements is either enormously time-consuming—sometimes requiring half a generation—or it is impossible. At any rate, it is always risky.

If the much-maligned attitudes of low-income Americans were changed without establishing a full-employment economy, we might simply be adding fuel to the smoldering hatreds of the more ambitious, more frustrated groups in our urban ghettos. And if we wish to do something about the supposed shortcomings in the low-income Negro families, it will clearly require changes in those welfare arrangements that now contribute to family dissolution. The point is that rather than concentrate on the supply of labor, we must reconsider our reluctance to alter the *demand* for labor. We must have more realistic employment requirements.

Unfortunately, attempts to change people through education have been supported by liberal-intellectuals who place great value upon education and look appreciatively upon the economic benefits accruing to better-educated Americans. Indeed, one of the few elements of consensus in present-day American politics may well be the reduction of the gap between the conservative and liberal estimate of the worth of education.

Obviously, the myths perpetuated about society's need for highly-educated citizens work to the disadvantage of less-educated people, particularly nonwhites who are handicapped whatever the state of the economy. Information obtained by economist Dale Hiestand of Columbia does not increase one's confidence that educational programs designed to help disadvantaged people over 14 years old will prove dramatically beneficial. Hiestand's studies show that even though the best-educated nonwhites tend to have more job mobility, they are more likely to enter occupations that are *vacated* by whites than to compete with whites for *new* jobs. Since the competition for middle-education jobs is already very intense, it will be difficult to leapfrog Negroes into jobs not yet vacated by whites, or into new jobs that whites are likely to monopolize.

Now, nothing in the foregoing analysis should be construed as suggesting that education is a waste of time. Many jobs, as was stated at the outset, have changed, and the need for education undoubtedly grows quite aside from the monetary benefits individuals derive from their educations. But I think it is fundamentally subversive of education and of democratic values not to see that, in relation to jobs, education has its limits.

As the burden of evidence in this article suggests, the crucial employment issue is not the "quality of the work force." It is the overall level of employment and the demand for labor in a less than full-employment economy.

FURTHER READING

Making the Grade: The Academic Side of Life by Howard S. Becker, Blanche Geer, and Everett C. Hughes (New York: Wiley, 1968). A study of the grading system in our colleges and its effects upon student and teacher. The authors recommend dispensing with grades.

Education, Structure and Society by B. R. Cosin (Baltimore, Md.: Penguin Books, 1972).

"Creaming the Poor" by S. M. Miller, Pamela Roby, and Alwine A. de Vos van Steenwijk, *Transaction* 7 (June 1970). Reveals how antipoverty programs are ineffective in helping the real poor and more efficient in helping those who do not need help as much.

Income redistribution—a thoroughly controversial topic—received initial nationwide political exposure in the ill-fated presidential campaign of George McGovern. To be sure, the senator borrowed the idea from Fred Harris's own brief presidential stand and gave it little prominence in his campaigning, but he did place it on the country's political agenda. Even though income redistribution was buried along with everything else in the Nixon landslide, I suspect it will reappear in future presidential campaigns and may someday become the law of the land. Some current trends in the American economy and in people's attitudes toward it suggest that income redistribution is an idea whose time has just about arrived.

Toward Income Redistribution

Trends toward income redistribution were set in motion by the rising expectations for a higher standard of living that developed among moderate-income Middle Americans as a result of the affluence that followed World War II. Although the expectations have been frustrated by the economic downturn following the escalation of the Indochinese War, they have not been given up; instead, many Americans believe that government should step in to preserve their standard of living and intervene in the economy for this purpose. Moreover, the everheightening fear that automation and other technological changes are reducing the supply of jobs encourages the belief that government must ensure the existence of jobs, particularly in an era when the opportunity to go into business for oneself is also declining for the average American.

In addition, people who once believed that as long as the economy continued to grow their own incomes would rise accordingly are now having some doubts, because of the absorption of much of that growth by the large corporations, including multinational ones, the recent decline of growth and the increase in foreign competition, and of course, inflation and the energy crisis.

All these doubts about the ability of the economy—and particularly of private enterprise—to guarantee the achievement of economic expectations are beginning to make people aware of the unequal distribution of wealth and income in America, which in turn made it possible for Senators Harris and McGovern to include redistributional proposals in their 1972 campaigns. At present, this awareness is limited to the fact that many rich individuals and corporations escape the payment of taxes through tax preferences and loopholes; but if current economic trends continue, more people will become aware of other economic inequalities, and eventually will begin to realize that they can best achieve their own expectations if income and wealth are shared more equally. When a politically significant number of Americans

HERBERT GANS

More Equality:

come to this realization, serious political pressure for income redistribution will begin to develop.

Possibilities for Tax Reform

Income can be redistributed from the rich to the rest of the population in several ways: through tax reform; by government programs and subsidies that go to the less affluent but are paid for by the more affluent, such as welfare benefits; by tax-funded government programs such as national health insurance, which replace expensive commercial ones; through educational programs that enable people to obtain better jobs; and through the creation of new jobs, which is especially effective in redistributing income to the unemployed and underpaid. Although the federal income tax has long been viewed as a logical device for redistributing income, it has not functioned that way. There is virtually no difference between before-tax and after-tax income distributions. Over the years, several attempts at progressive tax reform have all come to naught, because of political opposition by affluent individual and corporate taxpayers; Presidents Kennedy and Nixon contributed further to inequality by corporate tax reductions and new depreciation allowances.

Nevertheless, tax reform has remained the kingpin of most recent redistributive schemes, and closing the tax loopholes of the rich has been on the agenda of liberals for many years. Despite this, the first fledgling moves toward income redistribution were made to help the poor without taking from the rich. Antipoverty warriors looking for a substitute for the welfare system took up Milton Friedman's idea of the Negative Income Tax (NIT) to be paid out as a cash grant to the nontaxpaying poor, which eventually became part of President Nixon's ill-fated Family Assistance Plan (FAP). Despite Daniel Patrick Moynihan's claim that FAP was a radical redistributive scheme, it did not call for higher taxes on the rich, and it proposed a mere $2,400 minimum grant for a family of four without other income—so that it would have raised the income of welfare recipients in only

Income and Taxes

about eight states. Although FAP also provided a grant to the many working poor who labor full time at jobs without earning enough, that grant would have ended at $3,940 for a four-person family, an income still below the 1972 federal poverty line of $4,140.

Senator McGovern came up with two redistributive ideas during his campaign. One was his proposal for taxing "unearned" income in the same way as "earned," thus eliminating the tax preferences that come with capital gains, tax-exempt municipal bonds, and tax shelters for real estate, among others, all of which primarily benefit the rich. His second proposal was to give every American a tax credit of $1,000 a year, but he stated his plan so badly that the resulting political protest forced him to withdraw it shortly afterwards. Actually, that proposal was for an entirely new system of collecting taxes, the Credit Income Tax (CIT), first invented in England during World War II by Lady Rhys Williams, then reinvented here by Berkeley economist Earl Rolph, and further developed by James Tobin, who later became a McGovern adviser.

The basic idea behind the CIT is simple: it proposes to tax all income, whether from salaries, capital gains or any other source, at the same flat rate, thus eliminating both the tax loopholes for the wealthy and the personal exemption now claimed by every taxpayer. Instead the CIT would provide everyone with a tax credit, such as the $1,000 per person Senator McGovern suggested, which would be paid in cash to those persons whose credit exceeded their tax bills, and which would provide a guaranteed minimum-income grant to people without other income. The CIT differs from the NIT in that it applies to everyone, not just the poor and working poor, and it is also more progressive, for the combination of a universal credit and a flat tax rate exempts many moderate-income people from the payment of income taxes and even reduces the tax burden of the slightly more affluent.

For example, a CIT plan grounded on the original McGovern proposal presented to the 1972 Democratic Party Platform Hearings by Harold Watts, the University of Wisconsin economist, called for a tax credit of $3,720 for the prototypical family of four and a basic tax rate of 33.3 percent on all income. Under the Watts plan, the minimal grant in lieu of welfare would have come to $3,720, and the wage earner with $3,940 who would have received nothing further from FAP would have received another $2,407 from CIT, for a total income of $6,347, or 56 percent more than his income from wages. (His tax credit would have been $3,720 minus $1,313, the 33.3 percent tax on his $3,940 income, which would have been added to his income from wages.) A $6,000 earner would have been eligible for an additional $1,720 which, with the elimination of the $300 income tax he now pays, would have given him a 33 percent increase in income; an $8,000 earner would have received $1,054 and a 22 percent increase in income.

The median-income earner, who now gets just above $10,000 and pays about $1,000 in federal taxes, would have been eligible for $420 in tax credits, producing a 14 percent increase in total income; and all families earning up to $11,160, at which point the $3,720 is exactly equal to the 33.3 percent tax on earnings, would have received some cash payments, as well as relief from present taxes. Since the Watts plan was designed for implementation in 1975 and the median family income is expected to reach $11,000 at that time, roughly half of all Americans would have been freed from paying income taxes and eligible for some tax credit in cash.

The resulting losses in tax receipts would have been made up by the more affluent parts of the population, particularly those who earned most or part of their income from capital gains, tax shelters and other tax-preferred sources, but also those with high salaries. For example, a family with a $50,000 income, half of which is derived from capital gains, would have been paying nearly $13,000 in taxes as compared with $8,200 now, and a family with $100,000, nearly $30,000 instead of $24,000. Still, not even the very rich would have been "soaked."

The CIT has a number of important virtues in addition to its redistributive potential. First, it would considerably simplify taxpaying and tax collection, since tax-payers would list all their income and then pay the flat rate amount minus the credit. Second, it is flexible, for not only can the flat rate be adjusted to meet national needs, but it can be raised at higher incomes. (Watts, for example, proposed a 40 percent rate for incomes over $50,000 and a 50 percent rate for incomes over $100,000.) Also, socially desirable deductions can be retained, such as those for medical and charitable contributions, which Watts kept in his plan. Third, it avoids a major drawback of the NIT, which economists call the "notch problem." Since NIT is tied to the existing tax structure, a tax inequity arises at the income point where NIT stops, for the family with that income pays no tax; but the family with just one dollar more in income pays the regular income tax, thus making its after-tax income considerably less. Although this problem would not have arisen with FAP because, like the $3,940 earner, the $3,941 earner is exempt from the income tax as a result of tax reforms passed in 1969, it would arise with an NIT which ends at $4,500 or $5,000, and requires setting up a "tax break-even line" with a reduced tax rate to iron out the inequity. Under the CIT, such inequities do not exist, since everyone is taxed at the same rate.

Like all good ideas, the CIT also has some disadvantages. For one thing, it relies on an absolute figure for the minimal grant, which remains static as other people's incomes rise, and would thus further increase the inequality gap between the poor and other Americans. To prevent this, some poverty researchers have advocated that both the poverty line and minimum grants be set at a percentage of median income so that they would rise with increases in median income. Adapting this notion to the Watts plan, the universal tax credit would be set at 37 percent of median income, but this is about $400 below even the current poverty line. Consequently, I would favor a more redistributive CIT plan to begin with a tax credit equal to 60 percent of median income, or about $6,000 in today's income figures as determined by the census—and more if other definitions of income and other data-gathering methods are used. Such a plan would also redistribute more money to moderate-income people, for with a flat tax rate of 33.3 percent, the $6,000 earner would receive $10,000; the $8,000 earner, $11,334; and the $10,000 earner, $12,667.

Even a high minimal-income grant is still a substitute for welfare, and while it would eliminate poverty and reduce inequality, people who are unable to work would continue to be dependent on the government for their income. This dependency is unpopular not only with tax-payers but with most welfare recipients as well; in America, almost everyone believes that income ought to be derived from work. Consequently, the minimum-income grant built into the CIT should be paid only to people clearly unable to work for reasons of ill-health,

old age or familial responsibilities; for the rest of the population, the minimum income, whether set at $3,720 or at 60 percent of median income, should come from a job. The best income-redistribution scheme, particularly for the poor, is therefore a full-employment program, which provides funds to private enterprise to create new and well-paying jobs, and uses the government as an employer of "later resort" until the unemployment rate is down to 2 percent, the standard in most European countries.

A job-based income-redistribution scheme would in effect mean an end not only to unemployment but also to underemployment and low-wage labor in general. It would require a shift from the present capital-intensive trend in industry to a labor-intensive one, but since the job-creating potential of industry has been poor in recent years, most of the new jobs would have to be in the public services, whether privately or publicly administered. It would be possible to create such jobs in many services—education, health, mental health and recreation—as well as to raise the quality of other public services, from garbage pickup to cleaning up America's polluted rivers.

At the same time, however, wages would have to be increased in many existing private firms and public agencies, and those among the former which can only survive with low-wage labor would either have to raise their prices to the consumer or go out of business. Consequently, it may be impossible to redistribute income solely through the creation of better jobs and what is in effect a much higher minimal wage; most likely, some combination of job-creation and tax-credit schemes would be necessary, the latter then functioning as a kind of wage supplement. And if not all able-bodied people who wanted to work could find jobs, they would have to receive a minimal-income grant instead.

Economic Effects of Income Redistribution

Income redistribution cannot be treated as an end in itself; it is only a means to the improvement of society and the general welfare, and one must therefore consider whether it would in fact lead to the needed improvement, or whether it would have other effects that would only make things worse. Could the economy afford either the Watts plan or the more redistributive proposal that combines jobs with a minimal grant set at 60 percent of median income (hereafter to be called the 60 percent plan); and if so, who would be benefitted and who would be hurt, and most important, what would happen to incentives to work and to invest?

That the economy can afford income redistribution in the abstract is not difficult to document, for if national Total Personal Income were divided equally, the prototypical family of four would receive close to $17,000, more than half again the current median income. More concretely, Watts has shown that his plan would be entirely feasible: after tax credits had been paid, it would raise $129 billion in taxes, which, together with the savings of $18 billion from the elimination of public assistance and other transfer payments, would yield $147 billion dollars, enough to meet the Brookings Institution estimate of $144 billion dollars to be raised from personal income taxes in 1975. The 60 percent plan is another matter; it would cost about $100 billion more in additional taxes, and while some funds could be raised by increasing the flat tax rate on high incomes, the rest would have to come from a redistribution of wealth, and not just annual income.

In reality, of course, tax reform does not "cost" anything extra; it only redistributes existing tax bills, and while the new tax bills would be considered costs by the affluent, they would be benefits for the rest of the population. Job-creation programs however, would require higher governmental expenditures, and these would have to come out of somebody's taxes, but some of the initial expenditures would come back to the government as the taxes resulting from the higher productivity generated by full employment. Even service jobs would have such an effect; for example, a higher level of health services would alleviate one cause of industry absenteeism and thus increase productivity in manufacturing.

The principal beneficiaries of CIT would be poor and moderate-income Americans; as already indicated, the Watts plan would relieve almost half the population of federal income taxes and provide it with some cash benefits from the tax credit. The principal losers would be people who derived most of their income from capital gains and other tax-preferred sources, for example, those making their living playing the stock market. The very rich among them would pay the highest tax increase, but it would constitute a modest proportion of their income. Conversely, such people in the $25,000 to $50,000 income bracket might lose a more sizable proportion of their income to the tax collector. Their number is small, however; projecting from a 1962 study, families in that income bracket receive only about 12 percent of their total income from property ownership and not all of it would be affected by the Watts plan. Census data for 1970 showed that only 0.8 percent of families then in that income bracket—17,000 families in the entire country—reported obtaining their income entirely from sources other than salaries, and again, many of these sources would not be affected by the CIT reform.

The prime question about income redistribution has to do with its impact on the economy, and particularly on incentives of the poor to work if they could make a living from a $3,720 or $6,000 tax credit, and on the incentives

of the rich to work and invest if taxes ate up more of their incomes. McGovern's tax-reform proposals predictably set off a series of gloomy predictions on all these questions from Wall Street, rich campaign contributors, and conservative journalists and intellectuals. Their main worry was that incentives would be so seriously damaged that the economy would be plunged into a major depression; in fact, Pierre Renfret, an economic pollster who sometimes advises President Nixon, quickly reported that 43 percent of the businessmen he sampled said that they would reduce their capital-investment plans after hearing the McGovern proposals.

These reactions should not be surprising, for the beneficiaries of the current tax system would sustain some losses, and their understandable opposition is easily translated into dire predictions. They might even be right in the short run, insofar as tax reform would set off a panic on their part, creating fears about the future that would become a self-fulfilling prophecy by affecting their actions in the present. But since no tax reform schemes with income-redistribution potential could be implemented without a long political struggle, its opponents could, if they were not able to prevent it, make preparations for living with it, and learn that in the long run, at least, their fears were not justified.

Conventional economic thinking would of course argue that these fears are justified even for the long run, for the economic rationality that underlies such thinking assumes that people do not like to work, would not work if they could obtain a CIT income grant instead, and would not work as hard if their after-tax incomes went down or invest if their after-tax profits were cut. Conversely, common sense and a good deal of sociological research have suggested that people work also to feel socially useful and to obtain self-respect, that the poor share these feelings, that even welfare recipients want to work, and that their work incentive is increased when they are given economic aid.

Their incentive to take underpaid, insecure and dirty jobs would, however, be considerably reduced if they could obtain an equivalent and more secure income from a tax-credit grant. Indeed, during the congressional debate on FAP, Senator Russell Long was quoted in the press as asking who would launder his shirts if his laundress could get a $2,400 FAP grant instead, and the Nixon administration included a workfare provision in FAP in order to force poor people to take such jobs.

As for the affluent, studies indicate that tax increases make people work harder and longer to bring their take-home pay back up to the previous level. Work incentives among the affluent would therefore not be reduced by redistributive tax reform, except perhaps among people whose higher income is earned by extraordinary effort, for example, some self-employed businessmen and professionals who already work long hours, or workers who make extra money through overtime and moonlighting. Older people might not work so hard if they could not pass as much of their fortune on to their children, but this should not affect productivity, for owners of family firms would just pass the reins on to their children at a younger age and corporation presidents would retire a little earlier.

Occupations that cater largely to the rich might suffer from tax reform, not in the loss of incentive, but in the loss of reward; painters and sculptors, for example, would lose some sales if the rich had to pay higher taxes. While this would not discourage people from entering the arts, since their motivation for doing so is not primarily economic, it would force the few who can now make a living from their work to take other jobs, as most artists do even today, although a wise society would increase public subsidies to museums so as to compensate artists for the loss of private customers.

The incentive to take risks with one's money is more affected by rational economic motives than work, but even investment is a social process. Private investors invest not only to make a profit but to make more profit than other private investors, and as long as the opportunity to make more profit than anyone else is available, investors will continue to invest, even if the over-all level of profit is reduced by tax reform. In addition, being an investor is an occupation in itself and is thus governed by some of the social and emotional motives that go with work.

Nevertheless, if a CIT plan were adopted and tax preferences for capital gains were eliminated, people earning less than $50,000 a year would have less incentive—and less money—to invest, and more of their income would go into consumer goods. The very rich, who are the most important private investors, cannot consume much more than they already do, and they would have to continue to be investors, even if they were unhappy about a lower after-tax profit. They might look instead for new sources of high-profit investment, including foreign and illegitimate ones, and the government would have to make sure that such sources were either taxed more heavily or otherwise restricted.

The stock market would undoubtedly decline with the onset of the CIT and the fear that the rich would stop investing, but stock prices would rise again, if not to their present levels, once this fear was shown to be groundless. Moreover, with only 5 percent of corporate capital requirements now coming from the stock market, even a temporary panic in the stock market would not endanger the economy as a whole. Still, that market plays an important symbolic role in the economy, providing a simple if not exactly reliable indicator of economic health, and before tax reform could be instituted, private enterprise and government would have to develop a new index to replace the Dow-Jones and other stock-market indicators by which investors could gauge the national economic health and the profit potential of their investment alternatives.

Corporate incentives to invest would not be significantly reduced by the CIT because corporations need to continue to grow and to prevent their competitors from obtaining a larger share of the market. Among small and family-owned firms, the CIT might depress investment incentives, but among large oligopolistic corporations, the major effect would be some reluctance to make extremely risky investments. This can be counteracted by appropriate increases in selected depreciation allowances, by additional government investment subsidies, and even by over-all reductions in the corporate tax rate, as long as such reductions were made only to ensure against a loss of productivity and employment.

Tax reform might, however, discourage some nonprofit investment, that is, donations to nonprofit institutions such as museums and universities, particularly on the part of people earning less than $50,000, who would presumably offset their higher taxes by cutting down on charitable contributions rather than by giving up luxuries to which they have become accustomed. Nonprofit and charitable institutions that depend heavily on the largesse of such people might be hurt, but since the CIT does not require the repeal of the tax deduction for charitable contributions, it seems unlikely that the very rich would forego the prestige—and also the immortality—that accompanies large donations to cultural institutions. In fact, they might be encouraged to give more if the CIT were complemented by a more stringent inheritance tax.

Yet even if such donations should decrease, one can argue that privately owned nonprofit institutions are in reality public, and should be financed by the public through the federal government rather than be dependent on the whims of rich philanthropists. Admittedly, the federal government will not be eager to fund private universities or museums while public agencies are demanding more money; also, in a society with as high an infant mortality rate as ours, one can argue that government funds for further museum acquisitions are less urgent than better health care. Besides, inheritance and other tax laws could be rewritten so that monies from the very rich and from old fortunes would flow into foundations like those established by the Fords, Rockefellers, Carnegies, and others, particularly to finance cultural and other activities that are too controversial or politically unprofitable for government financing.

Finally, the deflationary effects of higher taxes on the rich would be offset by the additional economic activity generated by the beneficiaries of the CIT and of job-creation programs. Not only is full employment a better stimulus to investment than income inequality, but both poor and moderate-income consumers will generate additional economic activity by buying more goods and services, and the latter will put some money into savings which can be invested in place of the reluctant capital of the rich. No one can estimate now the additional GNP, tax receipts, and new jobs which would be created as multiplier effects from the CIT alone, but while Seventh Avenue might sell fewer $500 dresses, it would sell many more at $25.

Social Effects of Income Redistribution

The effects of income redistribution on American society would probably be more dramatic than those on the economy, for even the Watts plan would free the approximately 7 million families now earning less than $3,720, and the 2 million individuals earning less than the $1,320 tax credit Watts has proposed for individuals, from much of the constant worry, stress, and depression that go with being poor, enabling them to live with somewhat more joy, dignity, and self-respect. This in turn would reduce some of the current tension and conflict between the haves and the have-nots. At first, these effects might be less visible than complaints about higher taxes by rich speechmakers and columnists, but as the morale of the poor began to rise, so would that of the rest of the population, particularly in communities with sizable poor populations. The Watts plan would also make possible the elimination of public welfare, and thus liberate its recipients from the harsh regulations and the stigma under which they now live, and it might even reunite some broken families now separated by AFDC regulations. Even so, the total number of female-headed families, black and white, would probably not change, since the $3,720 minimum income would give other mothers enough economic independence not to marry, especially if job opportunities for poor males were not improved at the same time.

The most startling impact of the Watts plan would be felt in the nonurban sections of America, the South and other poor regions, for there the economic gap between the poor and their neighbors would be narrowed. In the South, for example, where the median income is $1,500 less than that of the nation, a poor person receiving $3,720 would now obtain over 40 percent of the median income, as compared with about one-tenth to one-fourth the median obtained by welfare recipients at present. Consequently, many of the poor would be able to improve their standard of living and spruce up their homes, or to move out of the slums, particularly in areas where rents are still low. In addition, the recipients of CIT grants would funnel additional monies into the economies of nonurban and poor regions, and thus contribute to their general economic improvement.

These improvements should in turn stem the migration of the poor to the cities, lessening some of the city's financial problems and social tensions. (The Puerto Rican migration to the United States would, however, rise to fantastic heights, unless the Watts plan were also implemented there.) Some urban welfare recipients might even return "home," where their $3,720 would provide a higher standard of living. Narrowing the inequality gap between the poor and the more affluent residents of these areas could create new social conflict, however, for the latter might feel that as the poor improved their living conditions they would also become "uppity" and no longer pay them the deference they now receive. For example, since added income usually results in more political influence, the beneficiaries of the CIT might seek to participate in community activities from which they are now excluded and demand a greater say in community politics. The resulting tensions would be particularly strong in the South, where many of the beneficiaries would be blacks, and it is possible that more affluent white Southerners would make life so unpleasant for them that they would move North, even at some economic disadvantage.

In the large cities that now pay liberal welfare benefits, the Watts plan would not significantly increase the incomes of welfare recipients; in New York, for example, some recipients already get over $4,000 a year—although most cities are not that generous. The CIT would, however, increase the incomes of those poor people who are not eligible for welfare or who, despite their eligibility, are not receiving it because of the cutback on welfare expenditures. Consequently, CIT should contribute to rising standards of living among the urban poor as well. This should be accompanied by some improvements in their health, though only if current health programs for the poor are maintained or if national health insurance replaces them; $3,720 is not enough to enable anyone to buy decent medical care in the private market. Similarly, some people would be able to leave the slums, though fewer than in small cities, but again, only if subsidized housing programs were continued and enlarged, for in the big cities $3,720 is not enough income to pay the rent outside (or inside) the slums.

Both in and out of the cities, reductions in some of the pathologies associated with poverty—alcoholism, drug addiction and mental illness—could be expected, and crime motivated by economic need alone should drop. Higher incomes, combined with recent improvements in drug treatment, might make it possible to reduce the number of drug addicts and alcoholics, although many of the addicted—as of the mentally ill—are probably beyond help. The major effect of the Watts proposal would be to lessen the despair that recruits people into escape-seeking addictions and illnesses, and the number of new addicts should decline. Fewer addicts would also result in less crime, both in the slums and in more affluent neighborhoods, and it is even possible that the streets

More Equality: Income and Taxes

and parks of the city would be somewhat safer than they have been for a long time.

Nevertheless, the redistribution called for by the Watts plan would not be enough to bring about a significant decline in these pathologies. A $3,720 income would enable mothers to buy their children the kind of clothing they need to go to school without feeling inferior, but it would not be enough to reduce other, more serious inequalities or the feelings about them. Pathology and crime would probably decline significantly only with full employment and the more drastic redistributive scheme I described as the 60 percent plan, and even then progress would be slow, for not only would it take some time to heal the emotional ravages of a heritage of inequality, but more equality would generate higher expectations and demands for the removal of other sources of inequality.

Moderate-income families would, as already indicated, benefit from the Watts plan both through the tax credit and through relief from present taxes, ranging from a net increase in income of 33 percent among $6,000 earners to 8 percent among $12,000 earners. The Watts plan would thus enable them to raise their standard of living by the same proportion, although it would not be enough for a major change in life-style, except among the $6,000 to $8,000 earners. Besides, more money alone will not lead working-class families to stop entertaining the relatives around the kitchen table or in the family room and hold formal cocktail parties instead. Ambitious families might be able to send one of their children to a better college than originally planned, thus enabling some of them to move into the professional middle class, but many more would put the extra money into various consumer goods and better housing. Many of the remaining city dwellers would try to join the suburban trek, although a greater degree of income redistribution would be necessary before most were able to afford suburbia's ever more costly housing.

Black moderate-income families would perhaps benefit from the same tax credit more than whites, for many would use it to escape the slums, and those who could head for the suburbs would have easier access to the better jobs located there. Although they would undoubtedly wind up in new suburban ghettos, their higher incomes would also increase the size of the black middle class, and this, together with the benefits going to the poor, might begin to lessen the racial discrimination among whites which is based on fears of lower-class pathology and rests on the now accurate generalization that many blacks are lower class. Nevertheless, a black middle class of sufficient size to make real inroads into discrimination could come only with a higher degree of redistribution.

Among the affluent, the effects of the Watts plan would be felt only by people who can now buy extra luxuries with the profits from capital gains and other tax-preferred sources. Some would have to give up some of these luxuries, particularly people in the $25,000 to $50,000 brackets who depend on tax-preferred income for the luxuries they can afford, and they might have to forego an extra European trip or a more expensive summer home. The tax increases they would experience under the CIT would not be high enough to affect their over-all style of life, however; they would not have to take their children out of private schools or give up the second or third car. The very rich would pay much higher taxes, of course, but since they can afford them, their style of life would not be touched at all. Perhaps high and café society would become a little more austere, additional large mansions might be sold to suburban developers, and some gentlemen farmers might have to give up their rural holdings if these no longer served as tax shelters.

Still, these changes would be noticed mainly on the society pages and among some of the fanciest stores. Indeed, the principal impact of the Watts CIT scheme on the rich would most likely be psychological; some might panic that they were henceforth condemned to relative poverty, even if their panic was groundless. They might also feel that their social and political influence on American society would decline sharply, although that feeling would be groundless as well. Only a much higher degree of income redistribution could have such an effect.

Political Prospects of Redistribution

Neither the economic nor the social effects of income redistribution, particularly that called for by the Watts plan, are likely to result in serious or long-term problems, but the fears of economic decline which income redistribution is already evoking suggest that even as moderate a scheme as Watts's would arouse considerable political opposition. The rich will argue strenuously that they should not be required to share their hard-earned wealth, and that income redistribution poses a threat to everyone, rich or poor, who still has hopes of becoming rich. They may even suggest that government has no right to interfere with anyone's pursuit of wealth, even though government already interferes, by tax preferences and by subsidizing college educations, housing mortgages, and other goods and services which add to people's income, especially that of the rich.

Consequently, when income redistribution returns to the political agenda, it is doubtful that the poor, who would be its major beneficiaries, will be able to put enough pressure on Congress to overcome the objections of the rich or to quiet the fears about the economy. Most labor unions, in the past the most stalwart lobbyists for progressive domestic legislation, would probably support a scheme like the Watts plan, and so would many liberals, but they are not politically strong enough to exert the needed pressure, either alone or in coalition with organizations of the poor.

As a result, the fate of income redistribution lies in the hands of the people who constitute the moderate-income majority. When they are actively interested in a piece of legislation, they can pass or defeat almost anything, but at present, income redistribution is so new an idea in America that most of them are completely unfamiliar with it. When Senator McGovern first issued his tax-credit proposal, their unfamiliarity quickly turned to hostility; Senator McGovern's failure to explain the proposal and Senator Humphrey's misrepresentation of it were persuasive enough that even potential beneficiaries perceived it only as a new and higher dole to welfare recipients for which they would bear the costs. Their reaction was not entirely irrational; many moderate-income people are opposed to higher benefits for the nonworking poor, and they are even opposed to tax reform per se, for they fear that they will have to pay the largest share of the new taxes, as they often have in the past.

Consequently, it is impossible to predict how the majority of Americans will react to income redistribution until it again becomes a political issue and they have become familiar with it. At this point, its fate will depend also on how the news media deal with it, for not only will most Americans get their knowledge of income redistribution from these media, but politicians often measure the public reaction to an idea by how they report it and editorialize about it. Owners of newspapers and television stations, most of whom are rich or Republican or both, are unlikely to favor income redistribution, and even many journalists, most of whom have only recently become affluent enough to play the stock market, are not likely to be enthusiastic. Despite their unquestioned allegiance to objectivity and fairness in reporting the news, they could unconsciously insert their own misgivings into the questions they ask of their sources, or find the opponents of redistribution more dramatic and newsworthy than its advocates.

Nevertheless, uncomplimentary news stories and hostile editorials will not prevent moderate-income people from supporting income redistribution once they realize that it will mean additional money in their pockets. At the same time, it is perfectly possible that they will not support a plan that increased the income of the poor or ameliorates the harsh conditions under which welfare is given out. This is suggested by the defeat of FAP and the continuing indication in opinion polls that many people still feel the poor are to blame for their own poverty and that too much is already being done for blacks. On the other hand, a recent study by Lee Rainwater of popular reaction to FAP among Bostonians found that many members of his sample not only favored it but came out for a higher minimal grant than anyone has yet proposed, and were even willing to pay higher taxes for it. Their generosity was based on the notion "that FAP would provide higher benefits for families than is now the case and therefore truly assist them to have a decent life, provide strong incentives to work and therefore discourage welfare chiseling and laziness, and do so in a straightforward and nonstigmatizing manner." Of course, answers to a sociologist's interview questions do not always predict how people will feel when an idea is actually up before Congress, and besides, those who support it may not exert as much political pressure as its opponents. Consequently, a politically feasible income-redistribution scheme is likely to favor moderate-income Americans and the working poor, providing the unemployed and unemployable poor a modest guaranteed income at best, and a continuation of welfare and workfare at worst.

Even the prospects of that kind of redistribution scheme depend on the economic and political conditions prevailing when the idea resurfaces as an issue, and on the leadership provided by its advocates. If President Nixon follows the normal Republican modus operandi during the rest of his second term and opts for a deflationary economic policy that will increase unemployment, particularly among Middle Americans, and if he cannot stop the continuing increases in the cost of living, political pressure for income redistribution is likely to develop faster than it would in prosperous times. In fact, the next Democratic presidential candidate might then give redistribution a central place in his campaign.

Nevertheless, the urgent needs of the poor will have to be met in other ways. As long as most Americans believe that income should be derived from work and as long as they favor policies which put people to work rather than on the dole, the poor are most likely to obtain higher incomes through programs for full employment and deliberate job creation. Such programs must therefore be part of the legislative package when the time comes for America to adopt income redistribution.

From a longer perspective, that legislative package is still only a first step, for eventually America must also consider the redistribution of wealth. Unequal income rests on a foundation of unequal wealth, and some day that foundation must be dismantled by such policies as the breakup of old fortunes, the levying of stricter inheritance taxes, the sharing of unredistributed corporate wealth, and the dispersion of stock ownership. If income redistribution ever becomes politically feasible, the need for greater sharing of the wealth will soon be apparent, and if Americans feel that wealth which is not derived from work does not deserve the same protection as income which *is* derived from work, policies for redistributing wealth may gain a more widespread political acceptance than policies for redistributing income.

HERBERT JACOB

Winners and Losers: Garnishment and Bankruptcy in Wisconsin

The prospect of being dragged into court for not paying one's debts or else pleading bankruptcy in order to evade them looms in the future of thousands of Americans every year. But whether the courts will be the last resort of debt collectors and debt dodgers depends on numerous influences ranging from the attitude of individual communities regarding indebtedness to the life-styles of debtors and creditors.

The courts are the most important contact many citizens have with the government. But whether this political instrument is used to seize wages of those owing money or to help others evade payment by declaring them bankrupt is related to income, the type of debt incurred, job status, to some degree race, and the manner in which the community where the action is taking place views itself.

To find out who uses the courts for garnishment and bankruptcy proceedings, we searched the court records of four Wisconsin cities—Madison, Racine, Kenosha, and Green Bay. In Green Bay, where the number of such proceedings was small, all debtor-creditor cases for a year were recorded. A random sample was taken from the other cities' files.

In all, 454 debtors were interviewed. Another 336 creditors and 401 employers returned completed questionnaires. Interviews with selected attorneys, creditors, collection agencies, and court officials added to the information. From these sources emerged profiles of creditors and debtors and their use of the courts.

Debtor-creditor conflicts usually involve the refusal of the debtor to pay what the creditor feels is due him. The debtor may feel he was cheated or that the creditor didn't live up to the agreement. Unemployment, ill health, a family emergency, or pressure from other creditors to repay them first are other common reasons that people don't pay bills. Sometimes, the debtor simply forgets or no longer wants to pay. In each case, the probability of conflict is high, for most creditors pursue the debtor until he pays. Only when collection costs rise above the amount owed, will most creditors write off the loss.

The typical creditor is a finance company, department store, service station, television repair shop, landlord, hos-

pital, doctor, or even lawyer. A few creditors are personally involved insofar as they themselves extend credit, lend money, or have extensive personal relations with their customers and make a personal effort to collect the loan. Most collectors do not make loans, but are employees of large collection organizations and view collecting as a routine matter.

When most private actions to collect debts fail, the courts stand ready to help creditors: (1) If an article were purchased through a conditional sales contract, the creditor may repossess, sell it, and get a deficiency judgment for the difference between the resale price and the amount still owed on the item from the debtor. (2) The creditor may obtain a judgment so that he can use the sheriff's office in collecting the amount due. The sheriff can seize for sale any articles not exempt under the state law. (3) When, as in many cases, the debtor owns no goods that satisfy the judgment, most states allow the creditor to attach the debtor's wages through wage garnishment. In some states like Wisconsin, creditors may seize the debtor's wages through garnishment even before they obtain a judgment against the debtor.

Under garnishment proceedings, a summons is sent to the debtor's employer, who is then obligated to report whether he owes the debtor any wages. If he does, he must send those wages to court. The debtor may recover some of his wages for living expenses but the bulk of the funds satisfies the debt. A creditor may garnishee his debtor's wages repeatedly until the debt is paid.

Debtors, in turn, have a number of extralegal remedies they can use. In a country where there is free movement and different state laws regarding creditor-debtor relations, the easiest thing for a debtor to do may be to move. Or he may defend his nonpayment in the judgment suit, though this is expensive and rarely successful. But debtors increasingly use a more successful legal measure—promising repayment through a court-approved amortization plan.

Such plans may be available under state law (as in Wisconsin) or through Chapter 13 of the Federal bankruptcy statute. Under the Wisconsin statute, a debtor earning less than $7,500 per year may arrange to repay his debts in full within two years if his creditors consent. During this time, he is protected from wage garnishments and other court actions that seek to collect the debts listed. New debts, however, may be collected as before through judgments or wage garnishments. Under Chapter 13 of the Bankruptcy Act, amortization usually allows the debtor three years to pay. During this time, interest accumulation is stopped and all creditor actions against the debtor are prohibited. New debts as well as old ones may be included in the repayment plan although new debts may be incurred only with the approval of a court-appointed trustee. Chapter 13 also provides for partial payment in satisfaction of the debt.

Bankruptcy provides the final legal escape for the debtor. Bankruptcy is available under Federal law to both the business and nonbusiness debtor. A debtor need not be penniless; he only needs to have debts which he cannot pay as they fall due. Under bankruptcy proceedings, the debtor makes available to the court all nonexempt assets that he possesses for repayment to his creditors.

Nonbusiness bankruptcies usually involve no assets that can be distributed to creditors. After this has been established, the Federal court discharges the debts of the bankrupt and he is no longer legally obligated to repay. (Tax debts, alimony, and child support payments as well as debts incurred through fraud cannot be discharged.) The only limitation to this remedy for debtors is that it may be used only once every six years.

Only a tiny proportion of credit transactions turn into conflicts between creditor and debtor and only a small proportion of those are eventually brought to court. It is therefore important to identify the conditions under which some people seek to invoke governmental sanctions in their efforts to collect or evade debts. *Four sets of conditions* are readily identifiable and are the subject of analysis here.

■ *Socioeconomic conditions:* A recession (even if slight and local) following a period when credit was freely extended is likely to produce more creditor-debtor conflicts than continued prosperity or a long recession. Likewise, the type of economy in an area is important. Subsistence economies, either in rural or urban slums, do not involve much consumer credit. Factory workers whose employment or earnings are erratic are more likely to be in credit difficulties than white-collar workers whose employment is steadier and whose wages, although lower, are more regular. The availability of credit is also significant. Those living in small towns or cities with few banks and lending institutions may find it more difficult to get credit and also find themselves less tempted to borrow than those living amidst a plethora of lending institutions, constantly inviting them to borrow.

■ *"Civic" or "public" culture of a community:* Some communities have more conservative lending policies than others. Large blocs of citizens may not borrow because they are older and not used to it or because they come from ethnic groups unaccustomed to living on credit. Alternatively, some communities are composed of groups who borrow heavily. In some communities, using the courts comes easily; in others, it involves a morally and culturally difficult decision.

■ *Availability of court action:* In some communities, court action is unlikely because no court sits in the town—all actions must be started in a distant town making litigation

inconvenient as well as expensive. Also, some courts are more stringent about requiring representation by lawyers than others. In one town, attorneys may be more available for collection work than in others. Finally, litigation costs vary from town to town, as local judges interpret state laws regarding fees in different ways.

■ *Ability of potential litigants to use remedies:* Different members of a community vary considerably in their ability to use available remedies. They need to know about them. They need the requisite financial resources. They need to be convinced that court action is really appropriate in their situation and to be free of the psychological restraint of shame and the social restraint of retaliation.

Creditor Use of the Courts

In the cities studied, money lenders (principally finance companies), and retailers were the heaviest users of wage garnishments. Hospitals, doctors, and dentists were the third most frequent users in three cities, while in the fourth, landlords were. All other creditors accounted for less than one-third of the wage garnishments docketed in small-claims court.

Creditors, however, do not use wage garnishments in identical ways. Their readiness to use the courts occurs under very different conditions. Finance companies, for example, have the most developed collection system. Ten days after a payment is due, they consider the debtor delinquent and begin efforts to collect. A large repertoire of collection methods are called into play, including overdue notices, telephone calls to the debtor, personal calls to his home, telephone calls to his employer, calls to co-signers of his note (if any), seizure of the collateral for the loan (if any), and wage garnishment. Most of these steps are carried out with minimal assistance by outsiders since their internal organization is structured to accommodate them. Consequently, finance companies almost never use collection agencies. And although they garnishee frequently, they do so only after a long chain of attempts to collect.

Doctors and hospitals are in a different position. Medical ethics downgrade commercial success, and patients reinforce this de-emphasis. Most patients expect a bill; few expect a bill collector to follow. Medical services are something they feel entitled to, regardless of their ability to pay, and therefore even when medical clinics and hospitals have business offices, they do not usually use them for extensive bill-collecting purposes.

Most doctors are not organized for nor do they depend on credit profits. Yet collectively, they probably extend as much credit as finance companies do. As professionals, they dislike spending time collecting delinquent bills. Generally, they wait three months before they consider a bill delinquent. They then send one or two reminders to the patient. They do not call him at home or at work. They have no co-signer through whom to exert pressure; they have

no purchases to repossess. They do not even have the time to go to court themselves, so they usually turn delinquent accounts over to a collection agency or attorney. One or two more impersonal attempts are made to collect before the issue goes to court for a judgment and/or wage garnishment. Typically, the doctor and the hospital receive only half the proceeds collected by the agency, the other half being the agency's fee. Most maintain that they pay little attention to what the collection agency does to collect a bill and are unaware that they are garnisheeing their patients' wages. Some say they resort to collection agencies for tax reasons only, since they believe the Internal Revenue Service does not permit them to write off a delinquent account as uncollectable unless court action was attempted.

Retail merchants stand between finance companies and medical men in their use of wage garnishments. Large stores with thousands of accounts have about the same organizational capability of collecting debts as finance companies. Small merchants have to use collection agencies. Like doctors, most retailers do not consider accounts delinquent until 90 days after payment is due and they also have no collateral to repossess since most retail sales are for soft goods. When hard goods such as TVs and refrigerators are sold on credit, the notes are sold by the retailer to a finance company. Retailers, moreover, are sensitive to their customers' opinions of them. Nearly 25 percent of the retailers interviewed were afraid that if they were frequently involved in direct wage garnishments they would lose customers. Almost 50 percent of the doctors expressed similar fears, but no finance company and very few banks and credit unions mentioned this as a reason for not using garnishments more often.

Willingness to use government help in collecting delinquent accounts thus seems to depend, in part, on the organizational resources of creditors, on their dependence on credit for profits, and on restraints produced by customer or patient alienation. Finance companies frequently use the courts because they possess the organizational resources, depend entirely on credit profits, and have little to fear since their customers generally have no other place to borrow. Doctors, hospitals, and retailers differ on all these points from finance companies and, insofar as they differ, are less likely to use the courts. Many, however, are indirectly drawn into court actions by the collection agencies they employ because collection agencies have the same characteristics as finance companies: the organizational resources to sue, their existence depends on collecting, and they have no fear of customer alienation.

The size of the debt is another important variable in the use of the courts. Most bills leading to wage garnishments are relatively large. Only 16 percent involved less than $50. Most were $50-$99, the median was $100-$149. About 20 percent were between $400 and $500, the upper limit of small-claims actions.

Most creditors find that costs are too high for debts of

Persons from previously deprived backgrounds are more susceptible to hardsell techniques, overpurchasing and indebtedness than those from more affluent backgrounds.

less than $50 to risk wage garnishment proceedings. It costs up to $35 (half in court fees and half in attorney's fees) to collect a bill by garnishment. If the creditor is successful in assessing the garnishment, the debtor pays the court fees. But if the garnishment is unsuccessful—if the creditor puts the wrong employer down on the summons or if he garnishes when the employer does not owe his employee any wages (for example, the day *after* payday rather than the day before)—the creditor must pay the full costs.

Since most debtors earn less than $100 a week, most debts far exceed the amount that can be collected by a single garnishment. Under Wisconsin law, the employer must usually pay the debtor $25 if he is single and $40 if he has dependents before he turns wages over to the court for payment to the creditor. Thus, most garnishments capture $60 or less out of which both the original debt and the court and attorney fees must be paid. In many cases it would take at least three garnishments to satisfy the debt and few debtors are likely to remain on their job beyond two such proceedings. Either they are fired because of the garnishments or quit in order to escape them. Most creditors therefore use wage garnishment to force the debtor to

come in and make an arrangement to repay more gradually. As we shall see later, however, these generalizations about the users of garnishment proceedings are not entirely accurate for every city studied, with the locale making a considerable difference.

Debtor Use of the Courts

While creditors are often organizations, the debtors we studied were always individuals. Bankrupts had most often purchased large items such as cars (generally, used cars), appliances, TVs, furniture, and encyclopedias in the three years before going bankrupt. Garnishees, however, reported such purchases far less frequently, mentioning only two luxury items with consistency—home freezers and air conditioners. Medical debts were common to all; 82 percent of the bankrupts and 92 percent of the garnishees reported they were behind in their medical bills. Garnishees were more often protected by medical insurance. While 84 percent said some of their medical bills were paid by insurance, only 66 percent of the Chapter 13's and 57 percent of the bankrupts had similar protection.

Significantly, debtors in our sample who sought court relief were very similar to those who did not. Although

Table I

INDEBTEDNESS OF BANKRUPTS, CHAPTER 13's AND GARNISHEES

Indebtedness	Bankrupts *(N = 196)	Chapter 13's (N = 72)	Garnishees (N = 168)
Up to $999	.5	9.7	25.6
$1000-4999	56.6	73.6	52.4
$5000-9999	20.4	12.4	10.1
Over $10000	22.9	4.2	11.9

* Number of cases

garnishees generally had a lower level of indebtedness, and many bankrupts were hopelessly mired in the quicksand of credit, most owed about the same amount of money —between $1,000 and $5,000. (See Table I)

■ Slightly more than half the bankrupts had incomes below $6,000, less than the median family income for the four Wisconsin cities in 1959. Like the garnishees, the vast majority were above the official "poverty" line of $3,000. Most of the Chapter 13's and garnishees reported incomes above $6,000. (See Table II) The most striking difference between the three groups is the frequency of home ownership, with garnishees owning homes more often. This difference may in part be attributed to the loss of homes by bankrupts in the bankruptcy proceedings.

■ As Table III indicates, garnishees who did not go through bankruptcy court often had larger numbers of wage garnishments levied against them than did bankrupts or Chapter 13's. In fact, many of the bankrupts and Chapter 13's reported neither actual garnishment nor threatened garnishment prior to court relief from their debts.

What then distinguishes those who seek government aid to evade debts from those who don't? Indebtedness and assets do not clearly differentiate the three groups, nor do education and occupation. Most debtors, 84 percent to 87 percent, had at least some high-school education. Most were blue-collar workers—craftsmen, foremen, factory workers, or laborers. A small proportion, ranging from 10 percent of the Chapter 13's to 15 percent of the bankrupts were white-collar workers.

Age, however, separates the three groups. Younger debtors go bankrupt more frequently than older ones. Sixty-two percent of the bankrupts were less than 30 years old. Only 43 percent of the Chapter 13's and 37 percent of the gar-

Table II

SELECTED ASSETS OF DEBTORS: TOTAL FAMILY INCOME, HOME OWNERSHIP

Income	Bankrupts	Chapter 13's	Garnishees
Less than $3000	6.2%	6.1%	5.4%
$3000-5999	47.4%	30.7%	33.9%
$6000-9999	40.7%	57.0%	48.2%
Over $10000	5.7%	6.1%	12.5%
Number of cases	209	65	168
Home Ownership			
Own or buying	21.2%	36.4%	42.1%
Number of cases	212	66	171

nishees were so young. *A majority of the bankrupts were young men in the early years of their family life who had built up high levels of debt, purchasing most of the items needed to establish a household.* Most did not have more than two children living with them. By contrast, the garnishees were a much older group with well-established homes; often their children had already left home so that they too were usually supporting households with two children or less.

Moreover, a relatively high proportion of the debtors were Negroes. While only 2.5 percent of the total population were black, 16 percent of the garnishees, 12 percent of the Chapter 13's, and 9 percent of the bankrupts were Negroes. This is not surprising given the generally high

Table III

ACTUAL AND THREATENED GARNISHMENT

Actual Garnishment	Bankrupts	Chapter 13's	Garnishees
None	44.3%	45.3%	—
1-2	28.8%	22.7%	58.1%
3-5	15.6%	17.3%	30.4%
More than 5	11.3%	14.6%	11.5%
Number of cases	214	75	174
Threatened Garnishment			
Yes	55.6%	72.7%	50.3%
Number of cases	214	77	176

income of Negroes in the four cities and the likelihood that Negroes are more tempted to overpurchase, because of their previously deprived status and because of the hard-sell techniques. That fewer Negroes take advantage of court relief from their debts results from their being among the least efficacious members of society and that they may know courts only from criminal proceedings.

Neither indebtedness, income, education, nor age distinguish Negroes who seek court relief from debts from those who don't. The difference is principally occupational status, with craftsmen and foremen going to bankruptcy court and mainly factory workers being garnished.

A number of characteristics seemingly related to the occupational status of Negroes are present among the whole sample of debtors. High-job status Negroes are relatively well-integrated at their work place and probably better integrated into the general community than lower-occupation status Negroes. Furthermore, they are probably better linked in communication networks through which they may learn about bankruptcy than are lower-status Negroes. These inferences can't be tested here because the number of Negroes in the sample is too small for more detailed analysis. But these hypotheses should also hold true for the entire group of debtors.

The data indicate that there are significant differences between garnishees and bankrupts in the quantity of information they had and the direction of advice they received about their financial distress. Bankrupts were apparently much better integrated into the legal system than garnishees since twice as many bankrupts as garnishees saw an attorney about a previous garnishment. In addition, those who saw an attorney in the two groups received different advice. Only half the bankrupts were advised to make arrangements to pay their creditors while 75 percent of the garnishees were given that advice. More than 40 percent of the bankrupts were advised by their attorney to go into bankruptcy; less than 20 percent of the garnishees received such advice. Combining the effects of the propensity to see a lawyer and the advice lawyers gave, we find that almost half of the bankrupts were told to take advantage of bankruptcy, while only 5 percent of the garnishees received such advice from a lawyer.

Bankrupts also received different advice from their friends than the garnishees. Far fewer bankrupts reported that their friends advised "doing nothing" or paying their creditors off. Many more reported being advised to see an attorney about their garnishment and a significant proportion (17 percent) were told about bankruptcy, whereas not a single garnishee reported being told about bankruptcy by a friend.

Other data also indicate the importance of integration into a communication network which facilitates the decision to go into bankruptcy. The second most frequent response to "Why did you decide to go into bankruptcy?" was advice from various quarters—most often that advice came from their attorney. In addition, when we asked them where they learned about bankruptcy, lawyers were the most frequently mentioned source of information. Friends, relatives, and people at their place of work followed. The overwhelming proportion of our sample learned about bankruptcy from personal sources rather than from impersonal communications. Indeed, the media were not specifically mentioned by a single one of the almost 200 bankrupt respondents. A final indicator of the importance of personal communications comes from the fact that more than half the bankrupts knew someone else who had gone through bankruptcy.

These data indicate that bankrupts were integrated into the legal system by a communication network which was conversant with bankruptcy proceedings. Although bankrupts varied greatly in their socioeconomic characteristics, they were linked in a loose communication network. They apparently learned about bankruptcy with relative ease and received support from the various people from whom they heard about bankruptcy. All of this contrasts sharply with the experience of garnishees. Garnishees, although in financial difficulty, were shut out of that network. Thus they did not learn about bankruptcy, were not encouraged to use it, and were not in contact with the professionals who might facilitate their use of it.

Inter-City Variations in Garnishment

Neither creditors nor debtors used the courts to the same extent in the four cities studied. Nor did the variation in

Table IV

GARNISHMENT AND BANKRUPTCY ACTIONS FOR 12 MONTH PERIOD:

	Madison	Racine	Kenosha	Green Bay
Garnishments	2860	2740	813	130
per 1000 pop.	22.6	30.7	12.0	2.1
Bankruptcies	112	100	63	32
Chapter 13's	37	18	5	7
Total BK-13 per 1000 pop.	1.17	1.32	1.0	.62

garnishment and bankruptcy rates in the four cities conform to social, economic, or partisan factors. (See Table IV) Each of the cities had approximately the same degree of prosperity during the period studied. The proportion of families with incomes in the range where garnishment and bankruptcy most frequently occurs ($3,000-$10,000) was almost identical for Madison, Racine, and Kenosha. Green Bay had slightly more such families but this scarcely explains its *lower* garnishment and bankruptcy rate. All cities had small nonwhite populations. Racine has the largest Negro community consisting of 5.4 percent of its population. Only .9 percent of Green Bay's population was nonwhite, principally Indian. And though there are no available figures on the amount of credit extended in the four cities, the differences in retail sales for the four do not explain the differences in garnishment and bankruptcy rates.

The only factor clearly explaining the different rates of garnishment and bankruptcy in the four cities might be called the "public" or "legal" culture. Excluding garnishment and bankruptcy, the frequency with which civil court cases are initiated in the four cities closely follows debtor case rates. (See Table V) The highest rate occurs in Racine, with Madison, Kenosha, and Green Bay following. As expected, the criminal rates differ since they are initiated by public officials. Civil cases, for the most part, are initiated by private citizens. All civil litigation reflects, it then seems, a set of peculiar institutional and cultural patterns that are not evident in the standard socioeconomic indexes ordinarily applied to these cities.

Robert Alford and Harry M. Scoble's study of these four cities and their municipal decision-making processes

Table V

CIVIL AND CRIMINAL CASES IN FOUR COUNTIES, JULY 1, 1964-JULY 1, 1965

Civil Cases	Dane (Madison)	Racine	Kenosha	Brown (Green Bay)
County and Circuit Court	1691	817	1203	803
Small Claims Court (minus garnishment)	4203	3024	743	233
Civil Case Rate 1000 pop.	26.5	27.0	19.5	8.2
Criminal Cases (excluding ordinance)	3195	1020	867	722
Rate/1000 pop.	15.8	7.2	8.6	5.8

suggests that they represent distinct political cultures. They label these cultures as (1) *traditional conservatism* (Green Bay), government is essentially passive, a caretaker of law and order, not an active instrument for social or private goals; (2) *traditional liberalism* (Kenosha), "the bargaining process may even extend to traditional services . . .;" (3) *modern conservatism* (Racine), government is legitimately active, but furthering private economic interests that are in the long range public interest, and (4) *modern liberalism* (Madison), "a high level of political involvement . . . may itself exacerbate conflicts. . . ." Alford and Scoble concentrate on the liberal-conservative dimensions of the four cities, by focusing on the kinds of public decisions made and the range of participation in the decision-making process. When we examine litigation rates, however, the cities cluster on the traditional-modern dimension. It appears that Green Bay and Kenosha share low litigation rates because of more traditional public cultures, while Racine and Madison share higher litigation rates because of their more modern public culture. Data from our interviews provide supporting evidence for this conclusion.

Less frequent use of public facilities to settle private conflicts is congruent with the concept of a traditional American public culture. Depending more on personal and less on bureaucratic ways of settling disputes, the traditional culture leads to dependence on personal contact between the principals.

Taking a debtor to court is a highly impersonal proceeding involving the use of public officials as intermediaries and arbiters. Interview data indicate that in Green Bay and Kenosha firms and professionals collecting delinquent accounts depend more on the use of personal contacts, telephone calls to the debtor, or informal arrangements with employers. In Green Bay, where the garnishment rate is lowest, attorneys and creditors often asserted that the city was small enough for everyone to know everyone else, making court action unnecessary. But Green Bay has only 5,000 fewer inhabitants than Kenosha (where no respondents mentioned the intimacy of the town) and is only one-third smaller than Racine which has the highest garnishment rate. Nevertheless, the exaggeration of its small size is significant, since the perception of Green Bay as a small town fits the description of its traditional culture.

The lower garnishment rate also fits Alford's description of these traditional cities as ones in which the business elite does not look upon government as an instrument to obtain private objectives. Passive government and informal bargaining typify many public situations in Green Bay and Kenosha, with the debt-collection process being just one manifestation. In Madison and Racine, creditor-debtor conflicts, like public disputes, more frequently reach official government agencies—in this case, the court—for formal adjudication.

Alford's characterization of these cities leads us to look for differences in the degree to which the people are fiscally traditional.

For the most part, these expectations are confirmed by the debtor interviews. Slightly more debtors in Green Bay than elsewhere thought banks were the best place to borrow money and an overwhelming proportion thought finance companies the worst source of loans.

But Kenosha does not fit the expected pattern, falling instead between Madison and Racine in both ratings. The same is true for actual behavior of the debtors: Fewer Green Bay debtors reported finance companies as their biggest source of loans; the highest proportion using finance companies was in Racine. On another behavioral indicator, more Madison debtors showed an inclination to approve borrowing for a wider range of items than Racine, Kenosha, or Green Bay debtors. The ordering of the cities followed our expectation closely though not exactly: Madison, Racine, Kenosha, Green Bay. Finally, a related indicator showed Green Bay debtors to be more aware of interest rates on their loans than Madison, Kenosha, and Racine debtors—traditional norms of consumer behavior emphasize cost rather than immediacy of purchase. These data support Alford and Scoble's characterization of Green Bay and Kenosha as traditional and Madison and Racine as modern. The patterns distinguishing the public decision-making styles of these cities apparently spill over to private use of judicial agencies by both creditors and debtors.

Traditionalism also affects the legal culture. Only in Green Bay did most of the attorneys handling garnishment cases send out letters to the debtors prior to initiating the court action despite the cases having been extensively worked over by the creditor's collection department or a collection agency. Attorneys in Green Bay were more concerned about avoiding formal court action than attorneys in the other three cities, who reported that they immediately filed for court action unless they knew there had not been an active effort to collect.

Everything cannot be explained by cultural differences between the communities. The higher incidence of Chapter 13 proceedings as compared to bankruptcies in some of the cities is due to different evaluations of Chapter 13 by attorneys and to pressure exerted by the referees in bankruptcy. Where Chapter 13 proceedings are most frequent (in Madison and Racine), debtors report that lawyers often give them a real choice between it and bankruptcy. In Kenosha and Green Bay, lawyers rarely talk about Chapter 13 to bankruptcy clients and since these clients rarely heard of Chapter 13 from other sources, fewer used it.

Differences in attorney behavior are largely accounted for by the pressures they feel from the referee in bankruptcy and their relation to the Chapter 13 trustee, who handles the debtors affairs while he is under the plan. In Madison, the lawyer's preference for Chapter 13 proceedings can be traced to active campaigning in favor of it by the Madison Referee in Bankruptcy. Racine's higher Chapter 13 rate reflects the fact that the trustee was a fellow Racine attorney, readily available on the telephone for consultation. Kenosha attorneys who also had to use the Racine trustee felt that Chapter 13 cases were beyond their control. They hesitated to incur the slight charge for a call to neighboring Racine. They preferred amortization under state law (although it provided less protection for the debtor) because they could maintain control over the proceedings and keep in close contact with the debtor who might later bring them higher fees in an accident or divorce case. Green Bay and Madison attorneys almost never

Is Garnishment Law Constitutional?

The constitutionality of the Wisconsin garnishment statute permitting the seizure of wages without any prior hearing in order to pay a bad debt has been appealed to the United States Supreme Court. The NAACP Defense and Educational Fund, which is the counsel in the case of Sniadash vs. Family Finance Corporation, contends such practice is a violation of due process. The original suit involved the seizure of $32.50 from the $65 weekly pay of Sniadash to pay on a debt of $420.

Under Wisconsin law, the first wage garnishment may be instituted without a hearing, although a hearing must be held before the money is given to the creditor. There must also be a judgment before subsequent garnishments will be ordered by the court. Sixteen other states have laws on the books similar to this.

used Wisconsin's amortization proceeding and did not speak of it as a lure to attract clients in better paying cases.

With only four cities, it is statistically impossible to estimate how much of the variation is explained by the political culture, by the legal culture, and by what appear to be accidental variations. Nevertheless, the wide variations discovered among four cities are significant.

This exploration of court usage in wage garnishment and consumer bankruptcy actions shows none of the usual political links between governmental action and private demands. To look for partisan biases of the judges (or referees), for evidence of other attitudinal biases in their decisions, for the linkage between the judicial selection process and court decisions, for the role of other political activities in this process, we would come away convinced that wage garnishment and bankruptcy are totally nonpolitical processes. Only an examination of patronage shows political processes at work, since the referees may appoint at will Chapter 13 trustees and trustees for all bankrupt estates. But Chapter 13 cases don't generate a great deal of revenue for the trustees and most straight bankruptcies by consumers involve either no or very limited assets so that the trustees benefit little from the cases. In the usual *partisan* sense, the processes examined are indeed nonpolitical.

Nevertheless, the courts are very political. Garnishment and bankruptcy cases invoke government power for private ends. Garnishment redistributes millions of dollars each year from the wages of debtors to the accounts of creditors. Bankruptcy results in the cancellation of other millions of dollars of indebtedness. The use of these court procedures also involves frequent harassment and considerable stigmatization. Although garnishment and bankruptcy are considered "private" proceedings, they significantly affect the distribution of material and symbolic values by government in the United States.

Thus it is politically significant that only a few of all eligible creditors and debtors use garnishment and bankruptcy proceedings. It means that government power is used to buoy what many consider to be the socially least desirable form of consumer credit—that extended by finance companies. The experience of wage earners with garnishment is likely to undermine their confidence in the courts as institutions which treat them justly and fairly. On the other hand, the use of bankruptcy by the minority of those eligible for it limits its benefits to the small group which happens to be well integrated into the legal system. Translating these findings to larger cities, it seems likely that in ghetto areas garnishment has even more disadvantageous effects in supporting undesirable credit and bankruptcy is even less used by the masses of alienated consumers who crowd the inner core.

The political process described is quite different from the electoral or legislative political processes political scientists ordinarily study. Instead, it resembles the administrative process which is becoming increasingly significant. The use of agricultural extension services, the use of counseling and educational services by the poor, the use of higher-education facilities by the young raise problems similar to those of court usage. None of these, however, involve, as wage garnishment and bankruptcy do, the dramatic use of the government coercive power for private objectives.

Government power can be invoked through far more routine ways than campaigning in elections. The consumption of government services is based on far different objectives than the ordinary use of government power through partisan means. Court actions, as well as other administrative decisions, frequently affect the core of people's personal behavior, their life-style, or fortune. They can color people's perception of the government and generate support for or alienation from it. We need to know what individuals and groups use such services and how they use them.

FURTHER READING

Buy Now, Pay Later by Hillel Black (New York: Pocket Books, 1961). An exposé of credit schemes.

The Poor Pay More by David Caplovitz (New York: Macmillan, 1963). Describes the credit problems of impecunious consumers.

MARIJEAN SUELZLE

Women in Labor

To read the newspapers one would think that the top jobs in public life are opening up for women and that our occupational status was rising generally: Interstate Commerce Commissioner Virginia Mae Brown became the first woman to head an independent federal administrative agency; Helen D. Bentley became chairman of the Maritime Commission; the first four female scientists explored the Antarctic; Barbara J. Rubin, a jockey, was the first woman to win a pari-mutuel race; and a 13-year-old girl, Alice De Rivera, integrated the all-male Stuyvesant High School in New York. While publicity on the "breakthroughs" does break down some psychological barriers, it exaggerates and misrepresents the real occupational changes. In order to find out what these real changes are, we must look at social trends that affect the changing profile of women in the labor force and at some myths and stereotypes that surround the working woman.

In 1920 the average woman worker in this country was 28 years old and single. Today she is 39 years old, married and living with her husband. In 1920 she was most likely to be a factory worker or other operative, but large numbers of women were also clerical workers, private household workers and farm workers. Her occupational choice was extremely limited. Today the average woman in the labor force is most likely to be a clerical worker, with other large numbers of women being service workers outside the home, factory workers or other operatives and professional or technical workers. She may be working in any one of 479 individual occupations, but most women are concentrated in a relatively small number of occupations.

Times of Life and Work

Caroline Bird has identified five factors influencing the changing profile of the woman worker. First, the vital statistics of birth, marriage and death have changed so that women have more years of life when they are not bearing or rearing children. One of the most important factors effecting the change is greater longevity, especially for women. The baby girl born in 1900 (that is, the grandmother of many women entering the labor force today) had a life expectancy of 48 years, whereas the baby girl born today has a life expectancy of 74 years, a figure that can be expected to go higher. About half today's women marry by age 20, and more marry at age 18 than at any other age. On the average, they will have had their last child by age 30 and will be in their mid-thirties by the time their youngest child is in school. The mother will have about 40 years, or one-half, of her life ahead of her, freed from child-rearing responsibilities.

A second important factor affecting the profile of the woman worker is education. Girls have consistently outnumbered boys among high school graduates, although the difference has narrowed. In 1900, girls were approximately 60 percent of all high school graduates, whereas recently the number of girls graduating from high school is only slightly higher than the number of boys—50.4 and 49.6 percent respectively in 1968. During this period, of course, the number of both girls and boys graduating from high school has been growing steadily. Each year more women enroll in and graduate from institutions of higher education, but women still lag behind men in pursuing education beyond high school, and, according to Dean Knudsen, the lag is *increasing*. Women earned 19 percent of the bachelor's or first professional degrees awarded in 1900, as against 41 percent in 1965; 19 percent of the master's degrees awarded in 1900, as against 32 percent in 1965; and 6 percent of the doctor's degrees awarded in 1900, as against 11 percent in 1965. But if we take the period 1940 to 1964 and asked what proportion of girls were enrolled for degree credit, Dean Knudsen has shown that the proportion of girls has declined by 5.5 percent.

A third factor is the experience of employment itself. In 1900, women were only 18 percent of all workers; in 1940, about 25 percent. The proportion reached a high of 36 percent during World War II, dropped back to 28 percent with the return of male veterans to civilian jobs, before beginning to climb again to 37 percent today. The shift in production from home to factory has influenced the rise in the numbers and proportion of women in the labor force. The work ethic, self-fulfillment and the right of each individual to happiness have increasingly become associated with educational and career attainment, the paycheck and its rate of increase. Thus, the homemaker role as the only role capable of meeting the cultural ideals is called into question. Far from a shameful necessity reflecting the inadequacy of the husband as provider, earnings have become a point of pride for wives of men who are obviously able to "support" them adequately.

A fourth minor factor affecting the profile of the woman worker is the increasing desegregation of work. Sex-typing of jobs, however, remains the norm. The woman worker is concentrated in a relatively small number of occupations. One-third of all working women are employed in seven occupations—secretary, saleswoman, general private household worker, teacher in elementary school, bookkeeper, waitress and professional nurse. This can be contrasted to the scarcity of women in such professional positions as physician, engineer, and scientist despite the increased job openings created by the tremendous interest in research and development. Job channeling and labeling come about through custom, an unquestioning acceptance of certain assumptions about masculinity and feminity. The question asked is often "Is it fitting and proper?" rather than "Is she qualified?"

The fifth and final factor affecting the profile of the woman worker is a general desegregation of the sexes—in the professions, the church, education, recreation and public accommodation.

To the above five factors identified by Caroline Bird, a sixth can be added, that of an increasing awareness of and concern over the population explosion. Although population predictions are necessarily tentative, Dr. Richard S. Miller, a Yale University ecologist, projects the current doubling time of the world's human population as 36 years into the next century, 20 years beginning in 2000 and 16 years beginning in 2020. The total world population by his projection is 28 billion people in 2036, an obvious impossi-

Women and Careers

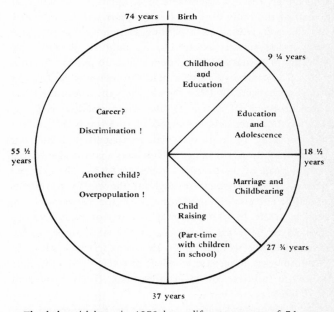

The baby girl born in 1970 has a life expectancy of 74 years. About half of today's women marry by age 20, and more marry at age 18 than at any other age. On the average, they will have had their last child by age 30 and will be in their mid-thirties by the time their youngest child is in school. The mother will have about one-half of her life ahead of her. If she decides to reenter the job market after a period of absence for childrearing, she will face difficulty in upgrading her skills and discrimination in an occupational structure geared to continuous (male) employment. At the same time, an increased concern with the population explosion will influence her not to have more than two children.

bility. Some women today are aware not only that motherhood is not enough but also that, for the first time in history, it is actually socially irresponsible to have as many children as one would like. The efforts of such social movements as Zero Population Growth, with their goal of one adult, one child, have already caused some women to report negative social reactions when they are expecting their third (or more) child. Such social criticism is leading many women to seek career alternatives rather than bearing more than two (or in some cases any) children.

Changing Profile of Women in the Labor Force

According to the U. S. Department of Labor Women's Bureau, there have been some startling changes in the profile of women in the labor force, as there have been in the profile of the woman who actually works. However, the changes have *not* all been unidirectional and do not bear out the "onward and upward ideology" reflected in the media. While the rate of labor force participation has expanded, earnings relative to males are down, as are the rates of women employed in most higher status occupations. Factors pushing and attracting women into the labor force are increasing while, at the same time, rewards for so participating are declining.

Fifty years ago, in 1920, less than one-fourth of all women 20 to 60 years of age in the population were workers (23 percent). Today almost half of all women 18 to 64 years of age in the population are workers (49 percent). The age at which women were most apt to be working has remained the same over the last 50 years although the rate has changed. During both periods women were most apt to be working at ages 20 to 24; but only 38 percent were working in January 1920, as opposed to 56 percent in April 1969. The pattern of employment throughout the life cycle has also changed. In 1920 female participation in the labor force dropped off at age 25, decreased steadily with age, and by the time they were aged 45 to 54 only 18 percent were working. In contrast, female participation in the labor force today drops off at age 25 but rises again at age 35 to a second peak of 54 percent at ages 45 to 54. The changed pattern of employment throughout the life cycle reflects the different employment outlook of the 35-year-old woman in 1920. In 1920 less than one out of every five women 35 to 64 years of age was in the labor force. Today almost half the women at age 35 can expect to work 24 to 31 more years. More than one-half of today's young women will work full-time for 25 or more years. Today 37 percent of all workers are women.

As I mentioned earlier, women are concentrated in a relatively small number of occupations. The number of occupations in which 100,000 or more women were employed increased between 1950 and the present time by the addition of seven occupations--baby-sitter, charwoman and cleaner, counter and fountain worker, file clerk, housekeeper (apart from private household) and stewardess, musician and music teacher and receptionist--hardly impressive additions when one bears in mind the increased educational attainment of women during this period.

Another example of the clear sex-typing of (underpriced) "women's work" shows up if we examine sex ratios in the major occupational categories. In more than half of the 36 occupations in which 100,000 or more women were employed in 1960, at least three out of four workers were women; in at least one-third, nine out of ten were women.

Women have been gaining status in some sectors of the economy, but they have been losing it in others. For example, in the executive branch of the Federal Civilian Service, increasing numbers of young women are taking the Federal Service Entrance Examination and being appointed to professional positions at entrance levels. Their numbers have doubled between 1963 and 1967 (rising from 18 to 35 percent). In addition, 29 percent of those selected as management interns in 1967 were women, as compared to only 14 percent in 1965. At the same time, however, the proportion of women teachers at the college and university level has declined. Only 22 percent of the faculty and other professional staff in institutions of higher education were women in 1964, down from the proportion in 1940 (28 percent), 1930 (27 percent) or 1920 (26 percent).

When averages are computed separately for men and for women in the labor force, women are consistently shown to be the disadvantaged group. Women workers are concentrated in lower-paying jobs, they earn less than men in all kinds of jobs, and their unemployment rate is higher. Furthermore, the gap between the earnings of women and of men has been steadily widening since 1956 (see table). Thus, the status of women in the labor force relative to the status of men has been declining for at least the past 15 years. Furthermore, the areas in which women have been making positive occupational gains are more than being offset by those areas in which opportunities have been decreasing.

The increase in women's employment is a case of moving in, not up. Top positions for women are too few relative to their increased educational attainments over the past 50 years. There are many reasons for the pay and status differentials, most of them based on hoary stereotypes concerning women's work. But these attitudes and practices are fostered not only by the employer but the woman employee herself. For even though many of these myths have been shattered by serious investigation, there are few truths that make their way easily and quickly into public knowledge to become new myths. Some of the current myths are these:

Myth 1: Women naturally don't want careers, they just want jobs.

As a generalization about women entering or in the job market in 1970, the statement may or may not be accurate. It is a myth because of the "naturally." There is nothing natural about the low aspirations of women, any more than the low aspirations of ethnic minorities in public life. To assume that "ambition" is unfeminine is to admit no individual variability: it depends on the person, not the sex.

In a recent study Matina Horner administered a story completion test to female and male undergraduates. Women were asked to write a story based on the sentence "After first-term finals, Anne finds herself at the top of her medical-school class." (Men were given the same task, but with the word "John" replacing the word "Anne" in the sentence.) Over 65 percent of the girls told stories which reflected strong fears of social rejection, fears about definitions of womanhood or denial of the possibility that any mere woman could be so successful:

Anne is pretty darn proud of herself, but everyone hates and envies her.

Anne is pleased. She had worked extraordinarily hard, and her grades showed it. "It is not enough," Anne thinks. "I am not happy." She didn't even want to be a doctor. She is not sure what she wants. Anne says to hell with the whole business and goes into social work—not hardly as glamorous, prestigious or lucrative; but she is happy.

It was luck that Anne came out on top because she didn't want to go to medical school anyway.

In contrast, less than 10 percent of the boys showed any signs of wanting to avoid success. Rather, they were delighted at John's triumph and predicted a great career for him.

Generalized statements about women's ambivalence about ambition, based on findings such as the above, become part of a myth system when they are used to make predictions and decisions about individual women. It is al-

ways necessary to allow for individual differences no matter how true the generalization. Nearly 10 percent of the boys in Horner's study *did* show a tendency to avoid success. And nearly 35 percent of the girls *did not* as the following story indicates:

Anne is quite a lady—not only is she tops academically, but she is liked and admired by her fellow students— quite a trick in a man-dominated field. She is brilliant— but she is also a woman. She will continue to be at or near the top. And . . . always a lady.

Especially pernicious is the tendency to take a generalization beyond the level of description to make assumptions that the differences are biologically determined. This amounts to blindness to the statistical probability that most women will work for a large part of their adult lives.

Women's Image

At the present time there is an elaborate educational system designed to teach women to underestimate themselves. Society's expectations enter the teaching process before girls reach school, but once they do, school textbooks continue to keep a ceiling on the aspirations of little girls. A recent study of five social studies textbooks written for grades one to three revealed that men were shown or described in over 100 different jobs and women in less than 30. Almost all the women's jobs are those traditionally associated with women. Women are shown as having so few jobs of interest available to them that they might as well stay home and have children. But even their work at home is downplayed. Women are not shown teaching or disciplining their children, baking complicated dishes or handling money in a knowledgeable way. Because the father is

Women in Labor

making money and therefore the more important member of the family, a house is where Mr. Brown "and his family live." Even pictures show men or boys seven times as often as women or girls.

Moreover, examination of any toy catalog will show page after page of dolls and household appliances for little girls, but no little girls' outfits for engineer, chemist, lawyer or astronaut. TV commercials (bear in mind the length of time the average American child spends before the TV set) endlessly show women helpless before a pile of soiled laundry until the male voice of authority overrides hers to tell how brand X with its fast-acting enzymes will get her clothes cleaner than clean.

If a woman desires or has to work, and if her early socialization hasn't "taken," then for the mature woman there are such venerable institutions as Dr. Spock to make her feel guilty for doing so, especially if she has children.

"Why can't a woman," asked Dr. Benjamin M. Spock, "be less like a man? . . .

"The absurd thing is that men go into pediatrics and obstetrics because they find them interesting and creative, and American women shun childbearing and childrearing because they don't. . . .

"Man is the fighter, the builder, the trap-maker, the one who thinks mechanically and abstractly. Woman has stayed realistic, personal, more conservative.

"Everybody can disprove me by saying these are culturally determined, but I can disprove them by saying that these are emotionally determined."

This type of rhetoric, reinforcing male vanity, has been used until recently to prevent Third World people from taking themselves seriously in occupational terms also, as the following paraphrase by Karen Oppenheim illustrates:

"Why can't a Negro," asked Dr. Benjamin M. Spock, "be less like a white? . . .

"The absurd thing is that whites go into agricultural science and overseeing because they find them interesting and creative, and American Negroes shun cotton picking and plant pruning because they don't. . . .

"Whites are the fighters, the builders, the leaders, the ones who think mechanically and abstractly. Negroes have stayed rhythmic, personal, more happy-go-lucky.

"Everybody can disprove me by saying these are culturally determined, but I can disprove them by saying that these are emotionally determined."

To the influence of textbooks, the media and books on child care we can add the fact that many young women have never had the experience of dealing with a woman in a responsible position of authority. School guidance counsellors assist in the cooling-out process by discouraging women from entering nontraditional fields of employment.

Myth 2: If women do pursue a career they tend to be more interested in personal development than in a career as a way of life.

Another form of this myth is "She will only get married, have children and drop out of the labor force anyway." Figures from the Women's Bureau show the fallacy in this line of reasoning. *One-tenth* of *all* women remain single, and these women work for most of their lives. In fact, those who enter the labor force by age 20 and remain unmarried will work 45 years on the average—*longer* than the 43-year average for men. In addition, *one-tenth* of all *married* women do not have children. If they enter the labor force by age 20, they will work 35 years on the average, eight years less than men. Although it is difficult to estimate the average time spent in the labor force by women with children (the tendency is to work, drop out when the children are small and then reenter), the average woman today will be in her mid-thirties by the time her youngest child is in school. If she reenters the labor force at age 35 and has no more children, she will average another 24 years of work. Women in the labor force who are widowed, separated or divorced at age 35 will work on the average another 28 years (17 percent of women in the population aged 16 or over were widowed or divorced in 1967; 15 percent of those were in the labor force).

Apart from those women who are single, widowed, divorced, married with no children or married with their youngest child in school, there are women with pre-school age children who are motivated to work either due to financial necessity or to the desire for a continuous career pattern. For all of these women it is not only (or perhaps not even primarily) their lack of motivation that prevents their career advancement so much as it is institutionalized assumptions concerning the normality of marriage, motherhood and the inevitability of withdrawal from the labor force. A striking example of this was reported by journalist Jane Harriman who wrote in a recent *Atlantic* article that she was fired from her job when she asked her boss to give her leave to have a baby. That the baby was to be illegitimate only underscores the assumptions and expectations that people have about motherhood. Why, for that matter, shouldn't there be paternity leaves, or paternity firings?

A related, equally serious, result of assuming women to be a marginal and uncommitted work force is the lack of adequate day care facilities. In 1965 the Census Bureau conducted a national study of women who had worked 27 weeks or more in 1964, either full- or part-time, and who had at least one child under 14 years of age living at home. The 6.1 million mothers surveyed had 12.3 million children under 14 years of age, of whom 3.8 million were under six years. But licensed public and private day care facilities available three years later could provide for only about half a million of those children!

The California Advisory Commission on the Status of Women, for example, had to report that the actual unmet need for children's center services was an unknown quantity. Most districts reported waiting lists from 50 to 100 percent of their present capacity. A two-year delay after being placed on a waiting list was not unusual. One out of every five poverty level residents not in the labor force, but

who wanted a regular job, listed inability to obtain child care as the primary reason for not looking for work. Even the available facilities were found to be inadequate. The problems encountered in existing programs and services included obsolete and unsafe facilities, lack of a state-level child care coordinating council, staff shortages, lack of continuity of funding, segregation of children by economic class, lack of adequate licensing standards, transportation and lack of facilities for children under two, for school-aged children up to the age of 12 years and for sick children.

Myth 3: There will be a higher absenteeism and turnover rate amongst women than amongst men, due to the restrictions imposed by children on working mothers.

The third myth is used to rationalize discriminatory employment practices related to women. However, in a 1969 study the Women's Bureau found labor turnover rates more influenced by the skill level of the job, the age of the worker, the worker's record of job stability and the worker's length of service with the employer than by the sex of the worker. Indeed a study of occupational mobility of individuals 18 years of age and over showed that men changed occupations more frequently than women. Between January 1965 and January 1966, 10 percent of the men, as against 7 percent of the women, were employed in different occupations. Similarly, women on the average lose more workdays due to acute conditions than do men, but men lose more workdays due to chronic conditions such as

heart trouble, arthritis, rheumatism and orthopedic impairment. Considering both conditions, during a one-year period, *women lost less time* than men because of illness or injury (5.3 days for women versus 5.4 days for men 17 years of age and over).

Myth 4: Women are only working for pin money, for extras.

The fourth myth is used to justify discrimination in employment when a job is given to a less qualified man because "she didn't need the money anyway." The Women's Bureau found 1.5 million female family heads—more than one-tenth of all families were headed by a woman in 1966—were the sole breadwinners for their families. Moreover, families headed by women were the most economically deprived: in 1967 almost one-third of such families lived in poverty, and they were the most persistently poor. Their median income was only $4,010 rising to $5,614 if the woman head was a year-round full-time worker. The income is substantially lower than the $8,168 median income of male-head families in which the male head worked full-time year-round but the wife was not in the labor force. Even where both husband and wife are working, the woman's income is often not for frivolous luxuries but means the difference between economic survival or not. In March 1967, 43 percent of those wives whose husbands' incomes were between $5,000 and $7,000 were in the labor force; 41 percent where husbands' incomes were between $3,000

Women in Labor

and $5,000; 33 percent between $2,000 and $3,000; 27 percent between $1,000 and $2,000; and 37 percent when husbands' incomes were under $1,000.

At the state level, the California Advisory Commission on the Status of Women found nearly one in ten families in California headed by a woman. Similar to the national findings, in California economic need is the most compelling reason to work for the great majority of women with young children. The two factors most responsible for the need are the amount and the regularity of the husband's earnings. Women's earnings are not supplementary but basic to the maintenance of their family. Women comprise 35.7 percent of the California labor force, and the California economy depends significantly on women workers.

Myth 5: Women control most of the power and wealth in American society.

The inference that is supposed to be drawn from this notion is that women are "the power behind the throne," the major controllers of economic wealth even though they do not earn it. A weak form of the argument, for example, is that women are the major American stockholders. The argument is false. The Women's Bureau found 18 percent of the total number of shares of stock reported by public corporations were owned individually by women, 24 percent individually by men. The remaining 58 percent were held or owned by institutions, brokers and dealers. In estimated market value, stock registered in women's names was 18 percent of the total, in men's names 20 percent. A glance at the board of directors of public corporations will reveal an almost totally male membership, casting great doubt on how much social control women have, even over the stock they do own.

Women may spend a major portion of their husbands' earnings, but the expenditures are typically for the smaller consumer items. Major purchases such as those of a house or a car will be decided by the husband or by the husband and wife together, rarely by the wife alone. Most women do not even know the exact amount of their husbands' income, so it is he who has the ultimate power over how much of it she can spend. In any event, the amount of power over expenditure is nonexistent when the most important buying decision to be made is that between brand X and brand Y of detergent. Job discrimination, the inability to realize one's true potential, is a high price to pay for the dubious privilege of deciding what color socks he will wear.

Myth 6: It will be too disruptive to an efficient work orientation if women and men are permitted to mingle on the job.

Studies have repeatedly shown that traditional attitudes such as these are illogical, based on bias and prejudice, rather than on fact. With respect to the ego threat implied by a woman co-worker or supervisor, men are likely to report that they would feel their masculinity threatened, if they do not have a working wife or if they have never worked for a female supervisor. If they have had the experience, however, their view changes to the positive. Relevant here is the fact that it is much harder for women to get the title than to get the work. Too often, women end up in clerical dead-end jobs, keep getting assigned more and more authority and responsibility as their experience and competence increase, but with no corresponding title or salary increase. They may run the office, but it will be in the old "helpmate" pattern, in the private sense of adjunct to the boss rather than in the public sense of official recognition (social or economic) from others.

The problem of women entering male fields is similar, especially if the field is one of higher status than women are usually allowed to enter. Women and men work compatibly without disruptive sexual involvement as graduate students, laboratory technicians and bank tellers. The real problem with women entering the male-dominated trades or professions, or with men entering the clerical field, would seem to be the salaries. This would create the problem of women being paid "too much" and men "too little" for what has come to be defined as appropriate for women and men.

In brief, myths concerning sexuality on the job are mostly invoked when there is a danger of a crossing-over of female and male status and pay differentials on the job. Although the principle of "equal pay for equal work" is widely accepted and sometimes even legally enforced, great care is taken to ensure that women and men are not given the same job titles and corresponding opportunities for advancement.

Myth 7: Women are more "human-oriented," less mechanical, and they are better at tedious, boring or repetitive tasks than men are.

The myth embodies the dual notion that women's place is in the (human-oriented) home and that women are innately inferior to men in intellectual capacity. When feminists were demanding the right to an education in the last century, educators such as Dr. Edward H. Clarke in a book entitled *Sex in Education* published in 1873, expressed learned judgments that the demand for equality in education was physically impossible. A boy could study six hours a day, according to Dr. Clarke, but if a girl spent more than four the "brain or special apparatus will suffer . . . leading to those grievous maladies which torture a woman's earthly existence, called leucorrhoea, amenorrhoea, dysmenorrhoea, chronic and acute ovaritis, prolapsus uteri, hysteria, neuralgia, and the like." While this quaint wording makes us smile at the ignorance of an earlier generation, it should be noted that Dr. Clarke was only painfully seeking a rationalization for making the value judgment that "what is" must inevitably, innately, biologically —and therefore logically—"continue to be so." Dr. Clarke was Professor of Materia Medica at Harvard from 1855 to 1872 and for five succeeding years an Overseer. He opposed the suggestion that women be admitted to Harvard College.

The Changing Economy

Women were not educated equally with men; women could not be educated equally with men.

Yet few people today smile at the ignorance of today's generation in denying women equal access to a scientific education. The young woman who wants to be an engineer, astronaut, or scientist will be ridiculed out of her decision by her family, school counselors, textbooks, and teachers, and by her peers. The woman who wants a technical education will find many colleges and trade schools do not accept women in pre-employment apprenticeship courses in fields such as carpentry and electronics. The woman who works in a factory will find herself assigned to the tedious, repetitive, boring jobs, denied on-the-job training, placed on a separate seniority list than men (last hired, last promoted, first fired) and, of course, paid less. Women are not educated equally with men; women cannot be educated equally with men. The scientific and technical arena is the last hold out of Dr. Clarke's earlier philosophy. The woman who is unable to become an engineer or a carpenter and the woman who is assigned to the tedious factory position are both being discriminated against by the same myth.

Employers still advertise in separate male and female help wanted columns; unions still advertise for journeywomen and journeymen. The journeywoman is given less training, her promotional ladder is shorter or non-existent, and she is paid less. The woman in the factory, i.e., the woman at the lowest level in the hierarchy of this form of discrimination, suffers the greatest economic deprivation. She is the least educated, most unskilled, and often her job is necessary for her sheer physical survival. Union leadership is often absent or unresponsive to her plight. If she has a family to support or is a single head of household, she does not have the time to attend union meetings that a man, because he also has a wife who is his caretaker, does. The lack of opportunity for on-the-job training and her social education to a more passive role than her male counterpart

also militate against her organizing in her own self-interest as long as her wages remain at the survival level, i.e., as long as she has something—anything—to lose.

As Marjorie B. Turner points out, we know nothing about the comparative propensity of women and men to join unions on an industry-wide basis. The Women's Bureau reports that 1 out of 7 women in the nation's labor force, but 1 out of 4 men workers, belonged to a union in 1966. Whether this is a reflection of sex labelling in jobs, discrimination, segregated locals, or difficulty or disinterest in organizing women is unknown.

The evidence regarding innate sex differences in mechanical and verbal aptitudes is sufficiently contradictory that no generalizations are warranted. Through the preschool and early school years, girls exceed boys in both verbal performance and ability with numbers. By high school, boys fairly consistently excel at mathematics. In addition, boys more accurately assess their abilities and performance by high school, whereas girls seem to show an earlier decline in tested performance. Such differences could, of course, be genetic. However, it seems equally or more plausible to suggest that they are related to social pressures operating differently on women and men to mold them into the adult roles they are assigned by tradition to play. As children, girls are taught to be passive and submissive, and this is conducive to grade school performance. By high school, boys are taught to prepare for careers, and this is conducive to high school performance. The cultural interpretation is consistent with Matina Horner's findings regarding the stronger motive to avoid success in college women than in college men. Until a culture evolves in which both sexes are treated as *people* with equal opportunities and expectations, the question of genetic differences in intellectual functioning will have to remain moot.

Even granting that sex differences may have a genetic

base, the statistical picture that emerges is still one of highly overlapping curves for women and men, rather than separate ones. We would be led to predict perhaps a 60:40 or smaller split in the sexes among certain occupations, but not one that is 100:0. Clearly, whether or not sex differences in mechanical aptitude are genetically determined, the current labor market certainly assumes that they are. But evidence to support the opposite conclusion was provided by the demonstrated competence of women in a wide range of occupations during World Wars I and II. Even today, the Women's Bureau reports that by mid-1968 women were being or had been trained as apprentices in 47 skilled occupations. Many of the apprenticeships, such as that of cosmetologist or dressmaker, reflected traditional roles. But some women were being trained as clock and watch repairman, electronic technician, engraver, optical mechanic, precision lens grinder, machinist, plumber, draftsman, electrical equipment repairer, electronic subassembly repairer and compositor.

Women's entry into traditionally male apprenticeship fields illustrates the fallacy of the myth that women are better than men at tedious, boring or repetitive tasks. It is doubtful whether the boredom, repetitiveness or tediousness differs greatly between a clock and watch repairman (male) and a typist (female) or between a precision lens grinder (male) and a dental technician (female). As Caroline Bird has documented, women's work in one part of the world or at one historical period may be man's work in another part of the world or at another time. What doesn't change is that whatever men do is regarded as more important, and gets more rewards, than what women do. The boundaries are defined by status, not aptitude, for even in traditionally female fields the persons in the highest positions of authority are most likely to be male.

Myth 8: Women need to be "protected" because of their smaller size.

There is no question but that women are physically smaller on the average than are men, but the inferences drawn from, and the restrictions imposed by, the biological fact are socially determined. In other cultures and at other times it has been women who have pulled the plows or carried burdens on their heads because of their presumed superior physical strength. Today it is men who suffer from hernias, back troubles and a shorter life expectancy because of the heavier physical tasks they are expected to assume. The industrial revolution made most, if not all, heavy physical work unnecessary, providing employers are willing to invest in the necessary laborsaving equipment. As long as there is a marginal, exploitable, male labor force (as has been the case with Third World peoples in America), it is often cheaper for the employer to use manual labor than to provide the requisite equipment.

Protective laws with respect to lifting should be extended to cover all *people* not restricted to one sex. Where lifting is required, a person's physical ability to hold the job should be medically, not sexually, determined. There may be some jobs involving lifting which only a few women—or men—

would be able to perform. At the present time there seems little inclination for women to enter such fields as professional football. (There is one exception, and she may truly prove the rule: she was squashed by an opposing guard.) There has, however, been much resistance to women jockeys, whose smaller size is a decided asset.

As long as there are protective laws governing women only, and not protective laws for workers in general, such laws can be used to perpetuate discrimination. A job requiring heavy lifting can be placed in the lower rung of a promotional hierarchy, even if experience at that job bears no relation to subsequent positions in the hierarchy. It has the effect of preventing women from entering *any* of the positions in the hierarchy because they are not allowed to enter the one with the weight-lifting restriction at the bottom.

With respect to restrictions on night work ostensibly concerning the safety of women going to and from their jobs, the rationalization only seems to occur when the overtime or shift work involved would place her in a higher status occupational category as well. As baby-sitter, as charwoman, as librarian, as telephone operator, as nurse, as keypuncher, the woman working at night is considered perfectly capable of looking after her own safety. It is well worth remembering that men often place women on pedestals only so they do not have to look us in the eye!

Vicious Circle

The myth systems that perpetuate sexual discrimination bring us round full circle. Women are stereotyped as lacking in aggressive and managerial qualities; if they do have the qualities or the opportunity to learn them, laws and customs are invoked to prevent their being used. Women and men are not judged as individuals based on demonstrated competence, but on the basis of sexual stereotypes. Moreover, women's underestimation of their own abilities combines with others' underestimation of their abilities to produce the declining status of women in today's labor force.

As Cynthia Fuchs Epstein points out, success is difficult for women because of the nature of informal channels of support and communication. Breaking a color, ethnic or sex occupational barrier means that the newcomers have not shared the same worlds as their colleagues. Casual chats, informal rituals, jokes, shared experiences—all become strained and serve to keep the newcomer in the psychological position of "the stranger."

It is true that women are becoming more emancipated, but it is an emancipation from the home and not towards higher status in the labor force. Although the mass media provide great fanfare for women as they become "firsts" in traditionally male fields, the publicity obscures the overall decline in women's status in the labor force. The Horatio Alger myth of American society was always a cruel hoax. Perpetuated with respect to women, it is simply laughable, when the average woman with five years of college can expect to earn the equivalent of a man with a high school education.

KENNETH E. BOULDING

Ecology and Environment

Recently I came upon the reassuring news that the year 1910 was a crucial one in human history because this was the year when the medical profession began to do more good than harm. I wonder whether the teaching profession has reached this watershed yet. I am almost certain that government hasn't; every time Congress adjourns I sigh with relief that a damaging process has been temporarily suspended. Yet, as a teacher, I must ask whether I am doing any better.

With respect to doing better than Congress, let that be as it may. But with respect to doing better than past performance, teaching could and must be improved—of this I am sure. My thesis here is that the principal task of education in this day is to convey from one generation to the next a rich image of the total earth, that is, the idea of the earth as a total system.

We can start with the concept of the earth as a series of approximately concentric spheres: the lithosphere, the hydrosphere, the atmosphere, the biosphere and finally the sociosphere, or (more awkwardly) the anthroposphere. This last, of course, is the sphere of man and all his activities, and in our time it increasingly dominates all the others, for good and ill. Thanks to it, the evolution of the elements is now continuing where it seems to have left off four or six billion years ago. Thanks to it, the evolution of life seems on the point of being purposefully altered, as man gets his busy little fingers ever more deeply into the business of genetic programming. This is the kind of world we have to prepare children for.

Toward a Unified Social Science

If we look closely at the various social sciences, it becomes clear that they are all studying the same thing and are all operating at the same systems level. This is not true of all the sciences: the crystallographer studies the world at a different systems level from that of the physiologist and the physiologist from that of the social scientist. But the economist, the political scientist, the anthropologist, the sociologist and the social psychologist, even the historian and the human geographer, are all really studying the same thing, which is the sociosphere, that is, the three billion human beings, all their inputs, outputs, interactions, organizations, communications and transactions.

The different social scientists, of course, study the sociosphere from different points of view. We also carve up the sets of organizations and institutions: economists study banks, anthropologists tribes, political scientists governments, sociologists families and so on. In this matter we should do some trading around. It would be fun to have anthropologists study banking on the ground that bankers are really a savage tribe. The economist has already been moving in on the family, which we call a spending unit. Political scientists have already begun to look at the political structure of the corporation, and the game theorists have even begun to move in on moral philosophy. All this is much to the good, but it has not yet affected our teaching very much, and the way we divide up the field can easily result in a misapprehension by students who do not see that all institutions are part of the totality.

In short, I agree with several observers that we are moving very rapidly toward a unified social science, simply because we are all coming to realize that the sociosphere itself is a unity and offers a single system to be studied. This does not deny the usefulness of such abstractions as economic systems, the international system or the integrative system, which is that aspect of the sociosphere which deals with such matters as status, community, identity, legitimacy, loyalty and love. We must somehow manage to teach the students that all these systems have a certain structure and dynamics of their own, that they also all interact very strongly with each other and that they are all indeed abstractions from a total system of reality.

What I am arguing for is, frankly, a general systems approach to education. But I think of general systems not so much as a body of doctrine as a way of looking at things which permits the perception of the world as a totality and fosters communication among the specialized disciplines.

A system can be defined as anything which is not chaos, and by this definition earth is clearly a system in spite of large random elements. The task of learning is to perceive what is chaos and what is not chaos in the world. It is important both to perceive order where it exists and not to perceive it where it does not, for that leads us into superstition.

The Dynamics of Systems

All real systems are dynamic; that is, they exist in four dimensions, three of space and one of time. What we are trying to do in the learning process is to try to perceive the continuing patterns in this four-dimensional solid. This is really what education is all about.

We cannot of course visualize four dimensions directly. It is very useful, however, to visualize two dimensions of space and one of time. So we visualize the earth going around the sun as a kind of spiral tapeworm, the cross section of which is roughly circular in the plane of space.

There are four easily distinguishable types of pattern in the space-time continuum which correspond to four types of dynamics. The simplest kind is Newtonian celestial mechanics, which really involves the perception of stable relationships between today and tomorrow or between today, tomorrow and the next day. If regularity of this kind persists, we can easily project it into the future as we perceive it in the past. Thus, if we have a stable relationship between today and tomorrow, then if we know the state of the system today we know it tomorrow; and if we know it tomorrow we know it the day after and so on indefinitely into the future. In social systems we have to be careful about such projections however. The astronomer is fortunate in that the planets are moved by extremely well behaved angels, whereas in social systems things are moved by people who are not well behaved, and if our projections are mistaken for predictions we can be led badly astray.

A famous example of projections that were proven false is the projections of the U.S. Bureau of the Census in the middle 1940s according to which the United States would have a stable population of about 180 million by the 1980s. Between 1945 and 1947, however, we had a "system break," in which the basic parameters of the demographic system shifted in such a manner as to give us a much larger rate of population expansion than had been expected. Almost everybody in the 1950s found themselves with much larger numbers of children to educate than they expected. Thus, when constants are not constant, as they frequently are not in social systems, we have to learn to take predictions based on constant parameters with a great deal of reserve.

The Life Cycle Pattern

A second dynamic pattern can be seen in the homely analogy of wallpaper. If we see a wallpaper with a regular pattern, we have a good deal of confidence that the pattern continues under the mirror and behind the furniture or even beyond our field of vision. Similarly, we can see the space-time continuum as a four-dimensional wallpaper in which our field of vision is cut off abruptly at the present. If, however, we perceive the beginnings of past patterns, we may reasonably expect them to be projected into the future.

Perhaps the best example of this principle is the life cycle. Up to now, at any rate, man has shared with all other living creatures a very regular life pattern. A person's age is probably the most important single piece of information we can know about him. If he is one year old we know he will look like a baby, and if he is 90 he will look like an old man. This pattern may, of course, be upset by the growth of biological knowledge in the next generation or so, and we may be in great danger of immortality. This would present the human race with probably the greatest crisis it has ever had to face. Who, for instance, would want to be an assistant professor for 500 years? What makes life tolerable, especially for the young, is death, and if we do away with it, we are in real trouble.

Life cycle patterns are also found in human artifacts, such as automobiles, buildings and so on. The concept is less applicable to social organizations which often have the capacity for self-renewal. Neither organizations nor civilizations are under the necessity of aging, although this does sometimes happen. The fact that people die, however, means that organizations can renew their youth as the old occupants of powerful positions die off and younger occupants take their place. We do not seem to be able to do this with neurons.

Mutation and Selection

A third type of dynamic system is that of evolution and learning. These can be put together because they are essentially the same thing. Even biological evolution is a learning process by which matter is "taught" to form itself into more and more improbable structures as time goes on. Similarly, human learning involves the construction of more and more improbable images in the mind. Both these processes take place by mutation and selection.

One of the difficulties with evolutionary theory is that it is hard to put content into it. It is a beautiful vision, but it has extraordinarily little predictive power. There is a good reason for this, for any dynamic system which has information or knowledge in it as a fundamental element is inherently unpredictable. It has to have what I call fundamental surprise. Thus, if we could predict what we are going to know in 25 years we would know it now, and if we could predict the result of a research project there would be no need to do it and you could not get any money for it.

The Decision System

The fourth dynamic process is of peculiar importance in social systems and might be called the decision system. We can see the movement of the social system through time as a kind of "decision tree" in which we keep coming to decision points where there are a number of possible futures and of which we select only one. Our decisions, however, depend on values, and in man values are almost wholly learned. Instincts are quite literally for the birds. A decision tree, therefore, is a curiously unstable dynamic structure which is hard to predict. Decision theory states that everybody does what he thinks best at the time, which is hard to deny. The tricky problem is how do we learn not only what the real alternatives are, but also what values we place on them. It is true that we move toward what we think are the higher payoffs, but the trick is that we learn what the payoffs are only by moving toward them. The economist tends to assume that decision-making is a maximization process, like getting to the top of a mountain.

Yet, if we had to deduce the mountain from the behavior of people who climb it, which is the theory of revealed preference, the theory becomes dangerously close to the proposition that people do what they do, and it does not require much theory to tell us this, no matter how elegant the mathematical language in which it is wrapped. The situation is even worse than this because in actual decisions we are not climbing a real mountain, but an imaginary mountain, and a mountain, furthermore, which is like a featherbed and falls in as we get to the top of it. We learn to like what we get as well as to get what we like.

One way out of this morass is to look for structures which determine decisions because perhaps they determine the information flows and corrupt or purify information as it flows up through an organization. Lawrence Senesh wrote a delightful poem about cities once, the last verse of which reads, in part, as follows:

If cities will be
Rich, exciting and bold

. . .

For work and for play,
The people who live there
Must make them that way.

I could not help adding a verse to it as I felt that his was a little too Pollyannish. Here is my version:

The reason why cities are ugly and sad
Is not that the people who live there are bad;
It's that most of the people who really decide
What goes on in the city live somewhere outside.

This simple structural fact throws a great deal of light on the whole dynamics of urban decay. At this level we have to admit that we do not know very much, although there do seem to be possibilities of knowing a great deal more in the future.

How does this apply to teaching about social systems?

I have been neglectful of equilibrium systems up to this point simply because a realistic appraisal must regard them as special cases of the general dynamic process. Nevertheless, as a teacher of economics I cannot throw them away because in many cases they are all we have, and in any case they are a useful intellectual steppingstone to an appreciation of a more complex dynamics. Somewhere in the teaching business, therefore, we have to tell people about equilibrium systems, and we can even point to actual phenomena in society and also in the biosphere, perhaps even in the atmosphere, where something like a quasi equilibrium exists. Thus, the notion of ecological equilibrium is a tremendously important concept which we must get over to the student at some point. Here I endorse Alfred Kuhn's theory that ecology is the beginning of wisdom in a great many spheres.

Somewhere in the schools we must get the idea across that society is a great pond, and just as in a fish pond (if it's unpolluted) frogs, vegetation and chemicals all interact to form a reasonably stable equilibrium of populations, so in society we have rough equilibrium at any one moment of interacting populations of criminals, police, automobiles, schools, churches, supermarkets, nations, armies, corporations, laws, universities and ideas. The ideal time for formalizing this concept would seem to be in high school algebra when the student is studying simultaneous equations. The essential proposition of ecological equilibrium is that if everything depends on everything else and if there is one equation of equilibrium for each population, we have n-equations and n-unknowns which with a bit of luck may have a solution in which the equilibrium size of each population is consistent with the size of all the others. The fact that ecological systems do exist in nature means that sometimes these equations can be solved. Boulding's first law is that anything which exists is possible. It is surprising how many people do not believe it. There must be some ecological equations, therefore, which have a solution, and this is worked out in the pond and the prairie and the forest and likewise in the city, the nation and the world. Even in the primary grades we could get something of this idea across.

It is a big step from the concept of ecological equilibrium to the concepts of homeostasis and cybernetics by which equilibrium conditions are maintained through a dynamic process. But even in grade school children can understand the thermostat and go on to see that the body regulates many processes in a similar way. Social organizations are similarly full of homeostatic mechanisms by which disruptive change is resisted and role occupants are replaced.

Recently in Poland I saw an example of the homeostatis of beauty. Many ancient buildings in Poland that were destroyed during the war have been rebuilt exactly as they were before; large parts of Warsaw have been rebuilt stone by stone, street by street, house by house, church by church and palace by palace. The Russians did the same thing with Leningrad. Here the image of a city perpetuates itself in society because decisions are made on the basis of an idea of beauty from the past. The astonishing recovery of nations such as Japan and Germany after a destructive war is a good example of how an old equilibrium reasserts itself.

The next concept beyond that of ecological equilibrium and homeostasis is that of ecological succession in which the equilibrium is gradually changed by irreversible movements. This gets us right into the developmental process

and into the theory of evolution, both biological and social. Mutation is a process by which new equations are introduced into the ecological system; selection is the process by which these equations result either in a new solution or in a rejection of the new populations. Likewise, in the learning process information put into the old structure of ideas, either coming from outside or generated from within, is a mutation which may be rejected or which may restructure the mind into a new ecological pattern.

We still have a long way to go before we can begin to understand the human learning process even though real progress is being made in this direction. We have even further to go before we can understand the process of education, which is by no means the same thing as learning. One of the things that is most puzzling is why some people survive the educational process and some do not—in the sense that after they have gone through formal education they never seem to learn anything again. The main object of formal education should be to teach people how to continue learning, yet as educators we fall very far short of this idea.

The most depressing experience I ever had as a teacher was while standing one day in the commencement procession at a little college where I was teaching. I overheard one senior say to another, both of them splendid in their caps and gowns, "Well, that is the last time I am ever going to have to crack a book." I almost tore my hair in despair. How often, with our grades and quizzes and exams, assignments and curricula do we destroy the learning process in our attempts at forced feeding?

Priorities in the Social Sciences

I would like to conclude by looking at some possible content areas of high priority in the social sciences which could contribute toward the larger ends we have in view.

My first suggestion as to content is the comparative study of relatively stable cultures, most of which, of course, comes out of anthropology. A good deal of anthropology is at the level of natural history rather than analysis—interesting stories about strange people—but it does at least give the student the idea that there are many ways of doing things besides his own and so opens up worlds of culture beyond his own backyard. It is important for young children to have a feeling that there are a great many ways of doing things. I am convinced that if a thing is worth doing it is worth doing wrong, or at least worth doing in many ways. The curse of the British educational system in which I grew up was the idea that there is a right way to do everything. I have a vivid memory of a British mother at a swimming pool making her children absolutely miserable by saying all the time, "Swim properly, swim properly," while our children just swam cheerfully. The Russians are even worse than the British when it comes to the appalling concept of propriety, for there even ideas have to be "correct." Anthropology undermines propriety because it

shows there are many different kinds of stable systems.

Even in complex social systems the student should be able to perceive certain stabilities and capacities for regeneration. Students can be made to see that the recovery of a society after a disaster, the regeneration of a limb of a starfish and even the return of the liquor industry after Prohibition are all examples of similar systems of regeneration and homeostasis. Once we have established the idea that there are stabilities in equilibria we can then go on to dynamics, to developmental systems and into concepts of economic and political development and ideological change. One of the unfortunate effects of Marxism and the cold war has been a polarization of views on the matter of dialectics. Most Communists cannot admit that there are any non-dialectical systems, and we find it hard to admit that there are dialectical ones. This is disastrous because obviously there are both, and we need to see the total social dynamic process as a complex interaction of dialectical and non-dialectical elements. As a result of our polarization of this matter, both parties have developed unrealistic attitudes towards conflict. The dialecticians idealize it, whereas in this country we tend to suppress it because of our lack of confidence in our ability to manage it. We ought to be able to train people to feel that a well-managed conflict is a beautiful thing and should not be suppressed. On the other hand, a badly managed conflict can be disastrous for all parties. We see this in all areas of social life. It is well-managed conflicts, not the absence of conflicts that make for success in marriage, in industrial relations, and in party politics, and underlie almost all creativity in both art and science. This is something that formal education does not seem to teach very well.

One final question which puzzles me a good deal about formal education is what people should know in the way of plain old facts. General principles are obviously not enough. If you live in California you need to know that Sacramento is the capital, although you may not need to recall immediately what is the capital of Chad. We have never asked ourselves seriously what is the minimum that people need to know in the way of factual material. In the light of the knowledge explosion this question becomes more important all the time, for it becomes almost criminal to teach people things they do not really need to know if this prevents them from learning things they do need to know. On this point I have four very tentative suggestions.

Facts: How Many and What Kind

In the first place, we need to know something about the order of magnitude of the factual world. It is often more important to know orders of magnitude than it is to know about particular details. Thus, people ought to know that in this country agriculture is only 5 percent of the gross national product. We ought to know that the world war industry is equal to the total income of the poorest half of the human race. We ought to know that Japan in recent years has had a rate of economic development of 8 percent per annum per capita, whereas the United States has had about 2½ percent. We ought to have some idea as to what the "real maps" of the world look like. We even ought to know a lot of things that nobody knows, such as the rate at which the real resources of planet earth are being depleted, and the rate at which the basic metabolic processes of the biosphere are being upset. We often stuff students with names and dates and general principles, but there is an intermediate area of orders of magnitude. Even in universities there is an incredible ignorance about the orders of magnitude of the world.

The second point is that it is often more important to know where to find information than to have it in your head. This is one point where my own formal training was sadly deficient. When I was at Oxford, for instance, the catalogue of the Bodleian Library was written in elegant eighteenth-century longhand in enormous and rather inaccessible volumes. This no doubt accounts for the fundamental Oxford principle that it is much easier to think something up than to look it up. In this day and age, however, we must teach people how to search for information. Computers and information retrieval are going to revolutionize the process of search. But in order to use information systems, one must have a certain amount of information to start with.

A third suggestion is that we need to give people factual information—at least on an order-of-magnitude basis—about the shape of the space-time continuum in which they live. This is history-geography, which to my mind should be the same subject, history being only geography in four dimensions. From the point of view of total earth, formal education does a poor job on this, mainly because it is deliberately distorted to create an artificial national image. Thus, students are surprised when they learn that medieval Europe was a peninsula on the edge of the civilized world and that even at the time of the Roman Empire the Han Empire in China was probably superior in knowledge and technology. After about 700 A.D. there is little doubt that the most developed country was China, that Islam was the second layer of development and Europe, the third. In that period most advances in technology started in China and came to Europe by way of Islam. This is not the impression that we produce in our school system, and white Americans, at any rate, ought to know that their European ancestors were by no means top dogs and that in the Middle Ages it would not be wholly unfair to categorize them as slowly emerging hillbillies.

My fourth objective for formal education is to develop a lively appreciation of the nature and necessity of sampling and a distrust of purely personal experience. One of the fatal weaknesses of Deweyism is that while theoretical-ly it emphasized starting from where the student is, in practice it often resulted in an emphasis on *being* where the student is. If where he is is in a backyard at West Lafayette, Indiana, where is that? The really interesting thing is not where you are but where you are not, and the purpose of education is to get you from where you are to where you aren't. This is why a purely empirical bias in the culture can be very dangerous because it results in a bias of the attention toward what exists for one, whereas the things that do not exist for one are much more numerous and perhaps more important. Even in the evolutionary process many of the most interesting things were those which did not survive, and we need to know why they did not.

One of the greatest political problems arises from the tendency of people to generalize from their own personal experience to propositions about society as a whole. Formal education should teach people that their personal experience, important as it is to them, is a very imperfect sample of the totality, and we must give people an idea of *how* to sample this totality. Errors of sampling are even commoner in literature and the arts than they are in the sciences and a widespread understanding of the nature of sampling error might preserve us from the literally deadly seriousness of the cults of youth, radicalism and the avant-garde.

What formal education has to do is to produce people who are fit to be inhabitants of the planet. This has become an urgent necessity because for the first time in human history we have reached the boundaries of our planet and found that it is a small one at that. This generation of young people have to be prepared to live in a very small and crowded spaceship. Otherwise they are going to get a terrible shock when they grow up and discover that we have taught them how to live in a world long gone. The nightmare of the educator is what Veblen called "trained incapacity," and we have to be constantly on the watch that this does not become one of our main products.

From *Social Science: A Search for Rationale*, Irving Morrissett and W. W. Stevens, Jr. Editor, New York: Holt, Rinehart & Winston, 1971. © 1970 by Holt, Rinehart & Winston.

FURTHER READING

"From Social System to Eco-System" by Otis Dudley Duncan, *Sociological Inquiry*, Spring 1961.

The Social Costs of Private Enterprise by K. William Knapp (New York: Schocken Books, 1971).

Conflict in Man-Made Environment by Anatole Rapoport (Baltimore, Md.: Penguin, 1973).

8. Changing Life-Styles

Though rarely defined in the texts or in the popular press in which it is so liberally used, the term "life-style" has become a well-worn coin in our linguistic currency. Like the term "culture," it is a global concept that encompasses a total set of behavioral items as well as artifacts. Unlike the concept of culture, however, which implies the existence of a relatively enduring set of behaviors, the term life-style suggests rapid change, transient customs with little temporal, and perhaps little emotional, depth. Used most often in the plural, the term indicates the existence of considerable variation in the way of life of present-day Americans. That such a variation should exist in a society as complex and hierarchically organized as is our own should be no surprise. What is surprising, and provides us with some insight into the ways in which language alters our conceptions of reality, is the fact that the term life-style is used to refer both to evanescent behavior patterns of socially mobile groups in our society, and to relatively enduring patterns of adaptation found among our ethnic groups, our poor, our racial and religious minorities. Use of the term in this way suggests that all groups are currently sharing in economic progress. By utilizing the term life-style we help to maintain our belief in the evanescence of group-linked behavior patterns so that we may cling to the American myth of the melting pot even as we celebrate group differences. The global use of the term thus tends to obscure the fact that social mobility is not available to everyone. Moreover, because we tend to think in terms of "changing" life-styles, we are often unaware of the degree to which some life-styles, although they arise in response to political and economic changes, often support the status quo.

Like the concept of culture, the concept of life-style implies adaptation. Life-styles do not arise accidentally, nor are they the result of personal whim or charismatic influence-peddlers. A changing life-style is a response to changes in the basic organization of human societies, and changes in the organization of human societies seem to derive principally from changes in the organization of energy systems. Like the relationships that exist among social animals, most human relationships—and the rules that govern role and status—are structured on the need to maintain the life of the group.

By his constant invention of new environments, man has far surpassed the variety found in nature; hence the rules of human social relationships are far more complex and bewildering than those found among animals. As men reorganize their lives to meet the demands of their work they alter their cultures. Culture is responsive to environmental change, but it changes more slowly than life-style. Thus less important changes—adjustments in the relationships of groups to each other, changes in sources of goods or technology of distribution, changes which result from exhaustion of resources in one place or discovery of new resources elsewhere—seem to be reflected in changing life-styles. Life-styles appear to exist within a more general cultural context—a context in which they may function either as mechanisms of experimentation and potential change or as mechanisms of adaptation and maintenance of the status quo.

However one regards life-styles—as mechanisms of change or stalwart supports of currently existing social arrangements—there seems little doubt that our own society is characterized by a bewildering variety of styles. It also appears likely that the sudden eruption of new life-styles in the decades since World War II, particularly during the decade of the 1960s, is linked to some kind of change in our society. It is Rainwater's thesis in "Post-1984 America" that the changes in life-style are a result of growing affluence which allows for some degree of experimentation in new social arrangements. Underlying this belief in affluence as the flywheel of social experiment is the concept of surplus, often used to explain the sudden development of art, monumental architecture, and new forms of social and political organization which heralded the dawn of civilization in the ancient civilizations of the Near East. The concept asserts that social experimentation can only take place where surplus energy can support groups in creative exercises that do not contribute directly to the subsistence needs of the society.

Such surplus energy may be provided by the labor of the underclasses, but its benefits are not distributed equally among the members of society; thus *changes* in life-style have affected only a portion of the population. The poor, the blacks, migrant workers, a variety of ethnic groups, and much of the working class have not benefitted or participated in these changes. Members of the underclass have their own life-styles—these have remained relatively stable although the influence of new communications technology that has brought variety and possibility into virtually everybody's living room has tended to sharpen awareness of the disparity between rich and poor, black and white, lower and upper classes.

It is among the middle and upper-middle classes that the most significant experimentation is taking place. Women, for example, who once could not envision life without marriage and who were taught to choose early marriage and large families, may now choose between marriage and career; or they may choose to marry late or early, to have none or few children, to divorce, and to remarry, or to remain free of permanent liaisons. Men, who were once raised to follow in their families' professions, or to attend schools in order to better themselves, have fewer options; but increasingly they too may choose to drop out, to alter careers in mid-life without fear of social ostracism.

While there is a heady vigor to new life-styles, the pressure that accompanies the self-conscious creation of new rules, new behaviors, and new relationships brings its share of pain. Weissman and Paykel explore the effects upon women of the geographical mobility that so often in our society is the ticket to social mobility. In "Moving and Depression in Women" they expose the depression, apathy, and hopelessness frequently engendered by constant moving, and the sharp wrench from familiar persons and places. Considered among the most fortunate members of our society, wives of upwardly mobile men are, in reality, victims of a system which ignores their needs to satisfy corporation requirements for male personnel.

Another group generally viewed as fortunate, but which has also been subjected to new strains as a result of our changing economic needs, is described by Starr and Carns in "Singles in the City." Popular opinion, buttressed by media puffery, calls them "the swinging singles." But most young people in the city do not live lives of sexual abandon or total freedom. Instead, they have been cast adrift in an alien urban environment that does not meet their needs for sociability and intimacy. These largely college-educated members of the middle class, a privileged group among us, suffer from feelings of powerlessness and alienation. Because they are not expected to remain either "swinging" or "single," planners have largely ignored their needs for specific kinds of housing or settings for social activity. But changing patterns of family life and demands by women for equality suggest that singles may become more important in the future; hence, attention to their needs is due. The tragic murders of young women who frequent singles bars in search of companionship are but a symptom of this failure of planning that has placed so many of our young people in physical—as well as emotional—jeopardy.

Equally ignored, though for different reasons, are the aged. In "Timing of Our Lives" Browning analyzes the conflict between increased life expectancy and an economic system that emphasizes the talents of youth. His article suggests that problems of age are due less to the aging processes than to cultural values which deny the elderly a meaningful role in society.

While there is much support for the theory that changing life-styles depend upon affluence, another view suggests that, on the contrary, new life-styles are attempts at adaptation—determined rather than free choices. A phenomenon like "swinging" or switching marital partners may, in this view, be an adaptive response to specific social pressures. In "Swinging in Wedlock" the Palsons note that swinging does not undermine marriage. Swingers report that their sexual experimentation romanticizes and, paradoxically, seems to strengthen their marriages. A clue to the function of swinging may be found in the term used to describe it. Swinging is an interesting euphemism once used in the gay world to describe bisexuality. Swinging suggests freedom; the swinger literally has his head in the clouds and his feet off the ground. Swinging does not, however, change anything: swingers move back and forth in a condition of moving equilibrium.

Those who engage in swinging see their behavior as freely chosen. Their comments and observations suggest that swinging increases the sense of individuation of the partners and allows them to give new meaning and functions to the institution of marriage at precisely the time when birth control, the collapse of the family farm and business, and social welfare programs have absorbed two of the family's major functions—child care and economic interdependence. Today marriage appears to have evolved into an institution devoted primarily to the development of personality: it is a relationship between a man and a woman which allows each to grow more fully. The Palsons point out that swinging led to a decline in wish fantasy and an increase in recollection. Shared memories are important in holding individuals, as well as groups, together. Swinging appears to be a method by which the old institution of marriage has been given a new function and meaning more appropriate in a society in which few interpersonal bonds remain and there are few social supports to maintenance of close personal ties.

Among those in our society who seem to be experimenting most with new institutions, women and homosexuals have been most vocal in their demands. Freeman's "The Social Construction of the Second Sex" attacks the current rigid and discriminatory definitions of sex roles. Recognizing that sexual characteristics are not biologically given but develop in response to the division of labor within society, Freeman views male and female personality differences primarily as the result of socialization processes. Such learned behaviors may change rapidly but they seem to change most easily as a result of changes in basic social institutions. Full equality for men and women will require alterations in division of labor, in roles and role training, and in socialization processes. Women are thus addressing their demands to inequities in hiring and firing practices, to discrimination in schooling, and to patterns, particularly within the family, which encourage strict separation between male and female roles.

Making a similar connection between economy and sexual repression of homosexuals, Humphreys describes "New Styles in Homosexual Manliness" as an emergent development of an ideal of virility, of ambisexuality, and openness in sexual relationships that is opposed to more traditional feminized and secret homosexual practice. Humphreys views the older form of homosexual behavior as a direct reflection of the ideals of the capitalist market place in which human relationships are specific, depersonalized, short-term, and contractual. The new, open gay scene, which insists upon honesty, individualization, deep personal trust, and long-term loyalty may represent one form of rebellion against capitalist values.

Humphreys links the new gay militancy with the forces that nurtured the counterculture of the sixties. In one sense the counterculture can be understood as a form of experimentation with different life-styles conducted by young members of the affluent middle class. A dialectic model would suggest that the counterculture is an inevitable reaction to the social pressures of a capitalist society. But it is also possible to comprehend the counterculture in more functional terms.

An emphasis upon leisure rather than work, on immediate rather than delayed gratification, on personal relationships rather than rules, and, for some, on communal life rather than privacy may derive from changes in our economy which has already moved some distance away from its previous emphasis upon labor-intensive production toward provision of services and consumption. Increased sensitivity to others rather than adherence to precise rules demanded by mechanized factory work could be a useful talent for much of our future labor force. Moreover, if automation freed a significant number of people from the need to work as long and as hard as they previously have, personal satisfaction might have to depend more upon both leisure activities and personal relationships. Increased tolerance toward aberrant sexual behavior, emphasis upon male/female role exchange, and growing—if grudging—acceptance of demands made by women for jobs and equality may well depend upon changing work needs. Both gay and women's liberation may owe their success, thus far, not only to their militancy but to the expansion of work opportunities that demand so-called "feminine" talents of interpersonal communication. Militancy itself may derive from society's need for female talents. Also within the realm of possibility, although the mechanism by which it works has not been clearly explicated, is the fact that both female equality and homosexuality help to restrict population growth and may represent a systemic response to clear needs for population control.

Although the functional explanation of new life-styles is attractive, it can lead to false optimism and feelings of complacency. Brown's "The

Condemnation and Persecution of Hippies" offers some sobering insights into government's ability to destroy beneficial social movements in order to maintain the status quo. The dangers of official persecution, as he points out, are not limited to dissidents like hippies but may extend to all forms of "deviance." Whether we regard deviance as functional or as part of an inevitable dynamic of change, such governmental power threatens us with destruction by inhibiting adaptability. The hippie life-style, with its emphasis upon intimacy, informality, immediate gratification, and egalitarianism, could not be tolerated by a bureaucracy.

If government has reached out quickly to crush some kinds of deviance, it has rather significantly ignored and even embraced others. The emergence of a variety of new religious movements, although it has caused much personal alarm among parents of children who have chosen to follow the tenets of Buddha, Krishna, Jesus, or some current charismatic leader, has received relatively little government attention. This indifference may be due to the fact that all these groups seem to take a passive stance towards current social affairs. Analyzing the Jesus Freaks and the even younger Jesus Boppers, Adams and Fox suggest that such movements are agents of social repression—institutions which resocialize into the establishment the many middle-class youngsters who joined in search of new values. Although the less familiar Oriental sects are not quite as acceptable in Christian America, they too have not aroused official repression, possibly because they refrain from social action. These groups do little social planning, many of their members work, and though they profess ideals close to those professed by hippies they tend to isolate themselves and remain indifferent to political activity. These expanding sects seem to act as a safety valve, alleviating many of the strains that might lead to conflict and change. As "Mainlining Jesus: The New Trip" points out, adolescents who enter the Jesus movement are assured of "the necessary peers, rituals, creeds, and programs to maintain their childhood morality." The Jesus trip thus solves some culturally constituted problems of emerging sexuality by replacing sexuality with asceticism. Because many of these religious groups recruit their membership primarily among middle-class youngsters who once indulged in heavy drug use, they provide a socially safe alternative for former addicts. As a result they appear to have gained tolerance and, in some cases, the active support of the larger society.

In sum, new life-styles like other social changes offer both problems and promise for the future. Some deriving from militant liberation movements appear to offer genuine prospects for change; many others, like religious movements or swinging, despite an appearance of novelty, seem to function to maintain the status quo. While we like to believe that new life-styles are freely chosen experiments in new social arrangements, the links between life-style and economy and life-style and government suggest that their development derives less from changes in ideology than from changes in technology and political organization. New life-styles do not necessarily represent progress; sometimes they owe their success to the degree to which they allow people to avoid genuine change. Only by carefully analyzing each case can we determine whether we are being lulled into complacent belief in a nonexistent social mobility, or a spurious sense of "progress," or are actually participating in experiments towards a more humane society—responsive to human needs rather than economic imperatives.

LEE RAINWATER

Post-1984 America

The way of life of Americans changes constantly yet somehow over long periods of time is recognizably the same. Indeed, whether the life style of particular groups of Americans is seen as changing or stable is somewhat a matter of emphasis and purpose. Moreover, when predicting what life styles will be in a decade or so, the issue of change versus stability, of emergence versus repetition, is a complex one. Demographic and economic analysis shows that there will be striking changes in these objective indicators of socioeconomic position. On the other hand, during the past two or three decades—during which there have been similarly striking socioeconomic changes—the life styles of the various social classes have been remarkably stable despite all the technological innovation and socioeconomic progress.

Changes in life style and values in the future are likely to be subtle, or even superficial, in the sense that they represent adaptations to basic core values and patterns of interpersonal relationships to a new social, economic and ecological situation. The stability of life style is maintained in exactly this way—by constant reinterpretation of the meanings and use of particular products and services to make them consistent with the basic themes of various life styles.

The Next 15 Years

We are often misled into thinking about social problems by fastening too much on the present and the immediate past in developing the paradigms by which we seek to understand and control problems. As antidote for that let us look at what seems to be the most likely course of development of the broad segments of the American society over the period of the next 15 years.

The nation is now heavily urban in its pattern of settlement; by the mid-1980s it will be slightly more urban, the proportion of the population in metropolitan areas having increased from 68 percent to 71 percent. But there is another side to this increased urbanization. Because of the transportation revolution brought on by the automobile and the superhighway, within the urban areas the population is less and less densely settled—the population per square mile in urbanized areas will have decreased from 6,580 in 1920 to around 3,800 in 1985. And the proportion of the population living in the suburban areas will have increased from 39 percent to 45 percent. This is what suburbanization is all about; it is a trend that can be expected to continue into the future. This means that more and more land will be subject to the stresses of suburbanized development.

The population will grow, but current indications are that the growth will not be nearly as great as has been previously thought. The rate of population growth seems to be slowing down and some of the most experienced demographers believe that somewhat greater perfection of contraceptive technology will lead to zero population growth without any special need for exhortation. The population of the mid-1980s is likely to include some 240 million Americans—about 35 million more than today.

This growth is not particularly dramatic although it will certainly require a great deal in the way of new facilities. The most dramatic aspect of population change is the change in the age distribution. If the sixties and early seventies have been the generation of youth—of the teenager and early twenties adult—the late 1970s and 1980s will be the era of the young marrieds. The number of men and women between the ages of 24 and 34 will increase by 60 percent; the younger group will increase less than 10 percent. There will be a 37 percent increase in the number of adults between 35 and 45, a small decrease in the number 45 to 54, and a 27 percent increase at the over-65 level. The big demographic impact on the society, then, will be in the years of youthful maturity.

Most indications are that the economy will grow fairly steadily through the 1970s and 1980s. This will result in an increase in the size of the GNP from one to 1.7 trillion dollars. It is expected that the service sector of the economy will grow much more rapidly than the goods sector but the growth in the latter will not be inconsiderable.

In the daily life of members of the society the concomitant impact of this growth is a very large increase in personal income. The median income for families is expected to grow from around $10,000 to over $16,000 (in dollars of 1970 purchasing power).

However, there are no indications to suggest that this income will be distributed more equitably in the future than it is at present. As has been true for the post-World War II period it seems likely that, although each income class will participate in the rising personal income, those at the bottom will not be increasing their share of the pie. That would mean that in the future as today the richest 20 percent of families would still be receiving over 40 percent of all of the personal income, and the poorest 20 percent would still be receiving less than 5 percent of the money income.

Of these various changes, two principal ones seem likely to have the greatest import for life style changes that have taken place over the past decades and that will take place (in all likelihood with increasing intensity) in the next two decades. The first of these is economic and the second cultural.

We are so used to the steady increase in affluence

(despite occasional periods of two or three years of relative stagnation) and we adapt so rapidly to each successive level of affluence, that it is often difficult to realize how very large the shifts in personal income are. For example, the median income of families and unrelated individuals is projected to increase by $6700 from 1971 to 1985 (1970 dollars). One way of looking at this increase is to say that over a 17-year period median income will increase as much as it has over the previous 50 years. Thus, although the proportionate increase in income year by year, decade by decade is projected to be about the same over the next few years as it has been over the past half-century, the absolute increase is much larger because of the larger base on which the constant proportionate increase takes place. The result of these increases will be that by the mid-1980s half of the population will enjoy the level of living that characterized only the top 3 percent of the population in 1947 or the top 15 percent of the population in 1970. The very large bundle of goods and services that goes with this very large absolute increase in median income can be expected to have important interactions with the emerging life styles of the 1980s, both affecting and being affected by those styles. The table presents comparative data for 1968 and 1985.

Comparing Actual 1968 with Predicted 1985 Family and Individual Income in the United States.

Income levels	Families		Families and Individuals	
	1968	1985	1968	1985
Number (millions)	50.5	66.7	64.3	85.9
Percent	100	100	100	100
Under $3,000	10	4	19	9
$3,000 to $4,999	12	6	14	8
$5,000 to $9,999	38	18	34	19
$10,000 to $14,999	25	23	21	21
$15,000 to $24,999	12	33	10	29
$25,000 and over	3	16	2	15
Aggregate income (billions)	$486	$1,074	$544	$1,277
Percent	100	100	100	100
Under $3,000	2	1	4	1
$3,000 to $4,999	5	1	6	2
$5,000 to $9,999	29	8	30	9
$10,000 to $14,999	31	18	30	17
$15,000 to $24,999	23	37	21	35
$25,000 and over	10	35	9	36
Mean income	$9,600	$16,100	$8,500	$14,900
Median income	$8,600	$14,700	$7,400	$13,500

The median educational attainment of the population is expected to grow to only 12.6 years by 1985, and the proportion who attend college is projected to increase to 31.5 percent, with 18.8 percent completing college.

While these upward shifts in educational attainment are not particularly dramatic, the small increases there, in addition to numerous other forces expanding the knowledgeability of the population (and shifting its values and tastes in a more sophisticated and cosmopolitan direction) will combine to make important changes in the world view of consumers in the 1980s. The continuing urbanization of the population and the impact of modern communications have the effect of exposing the average citizen to a much wider range of information, and a much wider range of perspectives for interpreting that information, than has ever been true in the past. The citizen in the 1980s is therefore likely to be less insulated from national and worldwide trends in taste, style and innovation than has ever been true.

Life styles will increasingly be built out of a rapidly expanding multiplicity of choices—choices made possible by the interaction of affluence and cosmopolitanism. One of the most striking things about American society since World War II (or longer than that) has been the extent to which the lives of most Americans involve what they put together out of the choices available to them rather than to what they are constrained to do by their socioeconomic situation. Much of the conflict and turmoil in the society probably has as much to do with anxiety and uncertainty engendered by continuing massive increases in the range of choices available to people as with more frequently cited factors. Indeed the "oppression" that many of those who "protest" feel (aside from blacks and other minorities) is probably more the oppression of having many choices and not knowing how to choose among them than of being "forced" to do things one does not wish to do.

Out of the current ferment about life styles is very likely to come the institutionalization of a set of pluralistic standards which legitimate a far wider range of ways of living in American society than has previously been the case. From the various liberation movements (black, brown, red, women, gay men, gay women, youth) will probably come a more widespread ethic of pluralism in life styles. (And this will be more than toleration in that it will involve recognition of the legitimacy of different kinds of identities and life styles.)

The ability to pursue a life style more tailored to individual choice (and less constrained by standards as to what a respectable conforming person should be like) is tremendously enhanced by the increases in material affluence and cultural sophistication. Because of higher incomes one can afford to take up and put aside different styles of living without regretting the capital investment that each may take. The security about the future which goes with steady increases in prosperity allows for the deferral of more permanent life style choices to the future; without this kind of security individuals feel they must make the permanent commitments relatively early in life. To the extent that sanctions against what has been nonconforming behavior decline, individuals are paradoxically less likely to be fixed in nonconforming identities and styles once chosen, since the "road back" is not blocked by discrimination or the necessity to repent. And by the same token, the nonconforming life style can be pursued more fully and more vigorously because of less need for secretiveness if a respectable future is desired.

For the most part these shifts in opportunity for choice will not involve dramatic changes in life for the great bulk of Americans because their exercise of choice will tend to be in the direction of elaborating and perfecting the existing class-related life styles. However, given the resources available to them it is likely that their particular version of those life styles will become increasingly distinc-

Shifts in life style for the bulk of Americans will tend to be in the direction of elaborating and perfecting existing class-related life styles.

Changing Life-Styles

tive, increasingly tailored to the needs and identities which they bring to their life situation and which evolve out of its year to year development. It is likely that more and more individuals and families will find it possible to elaborate particular arenas in which they can indulge one or another special taste or interest in a major kind of way. As in the past the increasing level of affluence and sophistication will allow the great middle majority of the population to increase their psychological and financial investment in leisure time activities, and there will be a broadening range of the kinds of activities chosen by different families of equal resources for this kind of investment.

At the level above the middle majority, where the absolute dollar amounts of the increase are even greater, one can expect to find, as in the past, even more highly specialized interests and pursuits. The "class mass" will be in the vanguard of the development of new styles—styles which as time goes on will tend to filter down, be reinterpreted and assimilated to the ongoing middle majority styles.

More of the Same

In the post-World War II period the life styles of each of the major social classes have evolved in terms of a logic dictated by the values and needs of families in each class as these interact with the increasing resources and possibilities available. The dominant trends of each class can be expected to continue to be important as families from these classes use the resources that come to them to further accomplish their goals and aspirations.

For the working class the dominant theme has been the solidification of the nuclear family base. Traditionally the working class has been very much enmeshed in kinship, ethnic and peer group ties, and the nuclear family has tended to be relatively "porous" to influences from the outside. Already in the early 1960s the affluence of the post-World War II period had produced a modern working-class family in which husband and wife interacted in a closer and less rigid way, and in which they directed themselves together toward the goal of perfecting a secure, comfortable and pleasant home as the central focus of their lives. Their relationships, particularly the father's, with the children also reflected this sharp focus on the home as opposed to previous external ties. This development was central to the consumer goals of the modern working-class family which were strongly oriented toward investment in the home to perfect it as a secure, comfortable, cozy place. In many ways this modern working-class family seemed to be adopting the styles of the lower-middle class. But that class also was in the process of change.

The lower-middle class has traditionally centered its life style on a necessity to achieve and maintain respectability. (This has been a lesser point of elaboration for the working class. Even as the modern working class developed in ways that made it seem superficially similar to the lower-middle class in day-to-day life, the importance of the striving after

respectability was not so apparent.) While respectability certainly continues to be a touchstone for the lower-white-collar way of life, it is increasingly taken for granted and decreasingly an issue of preoccupation for lower-middle-class men and women.

The growing economic affluence and the wider horizons that come from higher education and constant attention to the messages of the mass media have highlighted the striving after wider horizons as perhaps the central theme in the development of a modern lower-middle-class life style. Affluence allows the working-class family to turn in on itself since it no longer has to be so deeply enmeshed in a mutual aid network of community and peers. Affluence allows a lower-middle-class family to reach outward to experience and make use of a wider slice of the world outside the family. This is true both for lower-middle-class individuals who move toward expression of personal interests and for the lower-middle-class family as a whole, which is able to increasingly define as central to family interaction the experiences they have as individuals or together in the outside world. These wider horizons, however, are pursued from a very solid family-oriented base, and with the assumption that the experiences of the wider world will not change the members in any essential way or change their relationships to each other. Therefore the traditional base of family togetherness as a core goal of the lower-middle-class life style is not challenged. Thus lower-middle-class people come to have a wider range of experiences and possessions that have previously been considered characteristic of the upper-middle-class taste and way of life. Here too, however, the reinterpretation of new life style elements and the changes in the social class above them result in a continued distinctiveness about the life style.

In the upper-middle class the push out to the larger world is intensified. The central characteristics of the upper-middle-class orientation towards living have always been self-sufficiency and the pursuit of self-gratification. It is a more egocentric class in that the claims of respectability and of membership in diffusely obligating groups such as kindred are subordinated to personal goals and desires. Increasing resources and knowledgeability intensify the striving after exploration and fuller self-realization. This is particularly apparent among upper-middle-class youth where parental indulgence, current life situation and family resources combine to maximize the possibilities for fullest realization. At the level of older upper-middle-class persons the experimental approach to perfecting life styles is more subdued but is also often pursued with greater resources. Upper-middle-class people are in a position to afford, and are likely to have the knowledge to select, major new additions to their way of life—whether this be a vacation home and the frequent use of it to develop an alternative social world, or the development of a fairly systematic plan of vacation travel that, for example, allows one to see the U.S.A., then Europe, then Asia, with in-between excursions to the Caribbean and Latin America. Because of the extremely large absolute increase in income that will accrue to this group, one can expect a considerable strengthening in the 1980s of this propensity toward elaborate life style innovations. Thus while the median increase in family income projected for 1970 to 1985 is $6700, the median increase for the upper-middle class will more likely be on

the order of $17,000 to $20,000. Such a large absolute increase obviously provides a very rich resource for upper-middle-class experimentation with new life styles without the necessity of sacrificing the material base that supports the more traditional life style.

In addition to the unfinished agenda of the social classes discussed above, one can expect life style changes in response to the changing circumstances that future developments will bring. In some cases (as in fertility) these changes represent a reversal of previous trends, in other cases simply an intensification of changes that have been taking place over a longer period of time.

Changes in Family Living

Adults will spend less time in the "full nest" stage of the family life cycle. This will come about through a later age at marriage and birth of the first child, an unchanging age at the birth of the last child and an unchanging or perhaps slightly declining age at which the child ceases to live at home.

As a lasting legacy of youth and Women's Liberation thinking we are likely to find that young people marry somewhat later than they have in the past. There is no evidence of a major revolution in the extent of premarital sexual relations—the Kinsey Institute study of college youth completed in the mid-1960s showed essentially no change over the first Kinsey study in the proportion of women who had had premarital relations. In both cases approximately half the women had had premarital sexual relations. However, there do seem to be important changes in the pattern of sexual relations for that portion of the female population that has premarital sexual relations at all. Sexual relationships are likely to be more frequent and more institutionalized, more open and more accepted within the peer group than was true in the 1930s. Since there is reason to believe that the post-World War II trend toward earlier marriage in the middle class (the lower and working class had always married young) was in large part responsive to an effort on the part of young people to establish their maturity and adult status, the development of alternate modes of being "grown up" should mean less of a rush to marriage. The beginning of legitimation of premarital sexual relations in the context of youth peer group relations (rather than as furtive and hidden activities) should go a long way toward reducing pressure for marriage to establish legitimate adulthood. (For that matter the 18-year-old vote and the consequent courting by politicians may bring somewhat the same result.)

It seems likely that at the level of the class mass (as least the highly urban and more cosmopolitan portion of it) relationships that involve young couples living together will become fairly widespread. Under these circumstances marriage will come when the couple decide to settle down either to have children or to begin seriously to build incrementally a career and its related family base. For large numbers of other young men and women, less institutionalized patterns of heterosexual relationships may serve to allow a sense of adulthood without marriage. We have already seen the development in a few cities, particularly on the West Coast, of a wide range of singles institutions. One can expect this pattern to continue to spread across the country and to become more elaborate as the level of

Changing Life-Styles

affluence of young adults permits this.

Social and heterosexual relationships of the kind sketched above (involving as a common, though not majority pattern, reasonably regular participation in sexual relationships) depend, of course, on a high possibility of preventing unwanted births. The continued development of more and more effective contraceptive devices (and in the 1980s a once-a-month technique such as the prostaglandins should be well established) means that the technical base for this pattern of social relationships will be available. Legalization of abortion on demand (which should be the case by the 1980s in the states with the great majority of the population) allows for the clearing up of "mistakes" which often currently precipitate marriages (apparently about one-quarter of all brides are pregnant at marriage). While there is ample evidence that the availability of contraception does not have much impact on women's willingness to give up their virginity, the willingness to establish a regular premarital sexual relationship is much more responsive to the possibility of effective and interpersonally simple contraception.

Of course the same contraceptive techniques and the availability of abortion which make possible lower rates of premarital fertility also allow couples to space births and to have exactly the number of children they want. Analysis of surveys already conducted suggests that if couples had only the children they chose to have—that is, if pregnancy was completely voluntary—the average completed fertility of married couples would be on the order of 2.6 children (whereas in fact average completed fertility has been running more on the order of 3.3 children).

We have almost no information as to why there seems to be a shift towards smaller family ideals during the past decade. There is no way of predicting with much assurance what fertility desires will be in the late 1970s and 80s. However, according to fertility survey data, even in a period of fairly high fertility a great deal of the expressed preference for medium and large families may well have been a rationalization of "accidents" and unplanned pregnancies. This makes it seem most reasonable to predict a continued trend toward lower fertility.

The results of these various changes in mating behavior are that women would be likely to complete their fertility in the late twenties as they do now, having (again on the average) started their families somewhat later than they do now. The children would be grown and old enough to leave home while the parents are on the average somewhat younger than they are now. For example, the median case might be one in which the mother marries at 22 or 23 and has 2 children. The last one is born when she is 27 or 28 and, the children leave home for college or a job and "singles" living when the mother is not yet 50. Whereas the typical time period between the marriage and the last child leaving home is now between 25 and 30 years, given these patterns of marriage and fertility the more typical range in the 1980s might be 20 or 25 years. The life style elaborations both prior to marriage—the various "singles" styles—and those after the children leave home would loom larger than is presently the case.

Changing Role of Women

The new feminism seems to contain two strains of thought for women, one of which may very well have a pervasive effect and the other a more limited effect. The first involves a greater self-consciousness on the part of women about their subordinate status within the family and in the larger world, and a drive for more autonomy, self-respect and self-expression.

The second involves a challenge to the still established notion that a woman's place is (really) in the home. The implications of the new feminism are easy to misconstrue because of a peculiarity of the interests of the leaders versus the subjects of the movement. By definition women who seek leadership or elite positions within the Women's Liberation Movement are persons whose major identity goals are bound up with activities in the public world, and often also with career aspirations. Such interests, aspirations and the relevant skills are entailed in the elite roles. Therefore the leaders of the Women's Liberation Movement will probably consistently underplay the importance of equality goals and aspirations that do not relate in one way or another to the larger, more public, world. More specifically, the leaders will tend not to regard as legitimate the homemaker role as a major commitment on the part of women. The mass of the followers, however, will be much concerned with their ability to fulfill the homemaker role in a way that is personally gratifying, in a way that allows for the development of autonomy, self-respect, and a sense of valid identity within the narrower and more private worlds that they themselves construct. Even though they will often find the public level of discussion of feminine equality frustrating because it does not take these aspirations as fully legitimate, they probably will prove remarkably tenacious (as people do generally in such a situation) in pursuing their own interests by reinterpreting a great deal of the public ideology of the movement to support the actual roles that they play in their private worlds.

As quickly becomes apparent in any discussion between men and women on this subject, the liberation of women also involves a very significant change in attitudes on the part of men and in relationships between men and women. The kind of thinking that is apparent in the new feminism (except in its more radical version) clearly assumes the viability of marriage but points in the direction of greater equality between husbands and wives in their functioning. This amounts to a strengthening of trends apparent over the last several decades in the middle-class family towards more sharing of power and duties and a less sharply defined division of labor. It has in the past been a point of considerable ambivalence among middle-class women as to whether they are the servants of their families, the hidden bosses of their families, or persons of equal status whose duties happen to be those of keeping things running smoothly within the home. It is the latter definition which is likely to be strengthened by the new feminism.

As incomes rise, the need for the woman's management of the home, and the complexity of that activity of manager, purchasing agent and doer of tasks also rise. If more and more goods and services are brought into and used within the home the woman's work there becomes more valuable rather than less. Yet women have the problem that the values of the society do not define the wife's work as general manager of the home as productive and worthwhile in the same sense that paid-for labor is regarded as productive and worthwhile. Thus women can define themselves as oppressed and "underpaid" for their valuable work for other members of the family. Many women's first impulse is to get out of the home and to earn self-respect and respect from others by work in the labor market. Such work not only earns a clear-cut status, but the demands in jobs are more specific and less diffuse than are homemakers' tasks. Women sometimes find it easier to feel that they are doing a good job at those more specifically defined tasks than at home where a woman's work is never done—nor is it unambiguously judged. Yet with the rise in affluence and productivity in the commodity sector, the kinds of services that a woman might buy to take care of her home become increasingly expensive so that women will be loath to buy on the outside market much of the labor that will be necessary to maintain the home.

There may well be a class difference in response to the combination of affluence and a continuing emphasis on feminine equality. Very likely at the working- and lower-middle-class level, the two will combine to give women a greater sense of worth and to encourage them toward more autonomous functioning within the homemaker role. At the upper-middle-class level, however, there may be an increasing emphasis on career for purely self-expressive goals. (At all class levels there may be some increase in the proportion of women in the work force—because of the decline in fertility and the fewer years in which a woman has children in the home.) Upper-middle-class women have always included activities outside the home (either in voluntary activities or at jobs) as a central part of their role definition. They will certainly expect, as part of rising affluence, to be able to engage in these self-enhancing and self-validating activities more fully. This will put a strong premium on work organization and homemaking products which facilitate labor and timesaving. While on the one hand the home will be a more elaborate and complex place, on the other hand the woman will want to spend less time there. This will create a great demand for innovations which make homes easier to keep clean and neat, meals quicker to prepare and so forth.

Since families are smaller it is likely that there will be greater opportunities for the development of individual interests and activities on the part of all members of the family. The lesser burden of child care and rearing certainly enhances these possibilities for the mother, and for the father. The children too, because of greater resources available and a lessened tendency to treat the children as "a group," will be more likely to move in individualistic directions. (During the height of the large-family enthusiasm of the 1950s this potentiality was viewed negatively, as encouraging the "selfishness" of both parents and children.)

For the same reasons the family as a group becomes more "portable." The smaller family can more easily leave the home base for travel—both short-run travel as to a weekend cottage, and longer-run vacations. The heavy home-centeredness that was a concomitant of the large-family enthusiasm of the 1950s can be expected to decline as families feel themselves less space-bound.

Modern communications combined with the greater sophistication of the audience have the effect of bringing the world in on the average citizen in more and more forceful terms as the years go on. He reacts to what he sees in various ways—sometimes with fright and intimidation and other times with interest, approval and fascination. Both of these responses can be expected to be at least as characteristic of the 1980s citizen as of today's, assuming that all the world's problems are not solved between now and then. But the need to pull back, to disengage from exposure to the world's events (not just the large scale events seen on the evening news but also those observed and important in one's day-to-day life at work, on the street, in the local community and elsewhere) strengthens people's commitment to home as their castle, as well as encouraging them toward seeking to relax and vacation in other locales which are tranquil, isolated, private. The feeling that the world is too much with us leads to an interest in getting away from it all, getting "back to nature."

There Won't be Enough Time to Spend All the Money

People become busier the more affluent they are. Paradoxically, people whose affluence is increasing tend to make choices which result in their having less free or uncommitted time rather than more. There is considerable evidence to suggest that, with increasing affluence, workers do not choose greater leisure rather than more income; work hours tend either not to decrease at all or to decrease very slightly. None of the predictions made in the early 1950s concerning significantly shorter working hours seem to have held up. Indeed, in the few cases where unions have bargained for a short work week the slack seems to have been taken up for a fair number of the workers by more moonlighting. This makes good economic sense. After all, a man doesn't have to have anything extraordinarily interesting to do with his leisure time if his only choice is earning 50 cents an hour. On the other hand, at ten dollars an hour the leisure time needs to be pretty gratifying to cause him to forego his money.

With increasing affluence people are able to buy more and more goods and services, but then they run into the hard fact that the using of the products and services requires time. And the time available for consumption does not change. One cannot really buy time; all one can do is try to buy more efficient use of time. This fact has profound implications for life styles—many of these implications are discussed within the framework of economic theory by Steffan Linder in *The Harried Leisure Class* (Columbia University Press, 1970).

In general, when there are so many products to use and things to do and gratifications to be derived from both, people will tend to become impatient with routine, purely instrumental activities which seem to consume a great deal of time and effort relative to the gratification they produce. Similarly, people will tend to shift their commitments in the direction of activities that seem to provide more gratification per time unit and away from those which seem time-consuming in relation to the amount of gratification they provide.

The principal effect of this time/affluence dynamic is to make daily life more "commodity and service intensive." That is, people will tend to use more and more products and services in ways that maximize the satisfaction in a given period of time. Linder argues that with rising incomes pure leisure time (that is time in which you do nothing much) tends to decline because the degree of gratification that is available from goods and services, that were previously too expensive, is now greater than the gratification that is available from leisure and from one's own efforts to turn leisure into gratifying activity. Similarly, activities that are less productive of gratification tend to be given up or the time devoted to them sharply curtailed in favor of activities that are more productive and more expensive. The less time goods take per unit of satisfaction provided, the more in demand they will be. The cheapness of the product in terms of time becomes more and more important as the importance of their cheapness in terms of money declines. Individuals tend to give up relatively less productive activities such as reading or taking long walks in familiar territory or leisurely engagement in lovemaking in favor of activities that require less less time investment per unit of gratification. The same activities may be pursued in more exotic settings as a way of heightening satisfaction through the use of economic resources—thus the man who would hardly waste his time to view nature in the city park a few blocks away from his home may be ecstatic about the beauties of the Scottish countryside. People are notorious in not being tourists in their own cities because they are "too busy," but they will spend a great deal of money to visit a distant city and end up knowing more about its interesting sights than they do about the ones in their own home town.

These trends, coupled with the trends toward freeing women even more from their household duties, will tend to heighten awareness of the home as a "system" involving shelter, furnishings, production processes and their maintenance, a view in line with at least one economic theory of how households operate (Gary S. Becker, "A Theory of the Allocation of Time," *American Economic Review*, September, 1965). The home will become a more and more capital-intensive place as the cost of both externally supplied labor and household labor increases.

The Consumption of Services Will Grow and Broaden

A large segment of the multiplicity of choices that become available to people as their affluence rises has to do with the wide range of services which they can afford. People are able to buy expensive services which they previously had to forego (like regular medical care) or perform for themselves. As their own time becomes more and more valuable they are more willing to pay others to do things for them, if those others can perform the task more efficiently (often at the cost of possession of special equipment) or in a more satisfying way. This trend toward having others do work previously performed by household members is most dramatically evident in the rapid growth of franchise food operations. In the future one would expect an increase in the proportion of the family food budget used for meals away from home.

A second area in which a large expansion of services is likely has to do with the public sector. If the current national consensus toward disengagement from worldwide empire becomes a more or less permanent feature of the nation's stance towards the larger world, then one can expect an even greater rate of growth in public sector services than has been apparent over the last decade. The basis of support of demand for a broader and more fully developed range of public sector services is provided both by increasing affluence and by the broad exposure of most of the population to "informed opinion" through the mass media. Also, a higher proportion of the population attends college and is exposed there to welfare-oriented teaching which emphasizes public sector services of all kinds.

Future of the Underclass

So much for likely life style developments affecting the fortunate majority of Americans who are above the level of economic marginality. But what of the groups that have occupied so much of the public attention during the decade just finished—the poor and the oppressed minorities?

All of the income projections currently made predict no change in the distribution of income. Thus from 1947 (and very likely for much longer than that) through 1985 there is no present reason to imagine a major change in the distribution of income among families. In 1985, as at present and as in past decades, it is projected that slightly less than 20 percent of families will be living on incomes that are less than half of the median family income.

By 1985 the income that marks the top of the underclass will stand at $8,200 a year, an increase of $3,400—even larger than the absolute increase since 1947. However the constant dollar gap between the underclass income and that of the man in the mainstream also grows—from $2,800 in 1947 to $5,600 in 1971 to $8,400 in 1985.

There are obviously two ways to look at what happens to disadvantaged groups under these economic circumstances. If one focuses on the absolute changes, one can say that they are far better off than today. If one focuses on changes relative to the majority segments of the society, one can say that they are not at all or only slightly better off.

The people we would have called poor on the basis of an examination of their way of life in 1950 we would very likely call poor in 1970 because their way of life is much the same despite the fact that it includes slightly more in the way of material goods. Their affluence has increased somewhat but in absolute amounts the affluence of the bulk of the population has increased even more and they will find themselves further away from the going standard of American life now than they did in 1960. The issue of poverty then and the apparent progress toward eliminating it has concealed all along the issue of inequality and the fact of no progress toward eliminating it.

If membership is the key issue in the human's effort to find a meaningful life and if in affluent industrial societies membership can be achieved only through the command over the goods and services that are required for mainstream participation, then it follows that we will continue to have poor people and oppressed minorities so long as a significant proportion of Americans have incomes far removed from that of the average man. It follows that the underclass will be alive and well in 1985. And all of the pathologies of the city which are generated by the oppression and deprivation which produce the underclass will also still be with us.

Just as there are reasons for predicting no change in the income distribution, there are good reasons for predicting only small changes in the relative incomes of white and black families by 1985. The 1960s saw a significant increase in black family incomes relative to whites—from around 53 percent of white income to around 63 percent of white income. However, there has been no improvement in that figure in the last couple of years—emphasizing again the crucial role of high unemployment rates in black economic oppression. Indeed, an economist, Harold W. Guthrie, has projected the comparative experience of white and non-white families from 1947 through 1968 into the future by calculating the number of years required for equality of family income between the two races under various employment conditions. His results suggest that at current unemployment rates equality of income between black and white families would take well over 100 years to achieve.

At the so-called full employment rate of 4 percent it would still require 30 years to achieve equality of income. Only with a sustained unemployment rate lower than 3½ percent would black and white incomes be equal by 1985. Given the kinds of swings in unemployment experienced in the 1960s we could perhaps expect black family incomes to increase to between 70 and 75 percent of white family income. At 75 percent of white family income, blacks would be enjoying the standard of living purchased by over $12,000 a year, significantly better than the median family income for whites today. Their incomes would have almost doubled. Yet relative to whites the absolute difference in income would be slightly larger than it is today.

As we have seen, without marked improvements in their economic situation the black underclass will continue to grow in numbers. Because the black migration from the rural South to the major metropolitan areas does not seem to be abating very fast, it is likely that the size of the urban ghettos will continue to grow, in some cities spilling over into the suburbs. In any case the ghettos will remain the locales of concentrated trouble and violence that they are today.

Because the underclass will still be there, and because of the much higher level of affluence, property crime rates will probably continue to increase, and crimes of violence will probably not decrease very much. There may or may not be recurrent periods of urban rioting—but then the riots are really less important to the day-to-day lives of people living in the ghetto than the more random and individual violence to which they are subjected. One can expect larger and larger areas of the city to deteriorate and become abandoned, and one can expect more no-man's-lands to develop in cities, areas where no one wants to go for any legitimate purpose, and which are abandoned to whatever use marginal persons may want to put them. Again, although the financial cost to individuals with whose commercial or residential investments in the areas of deterioration may be great, the net cost of the deterioration of the cities will continue to be fairly small relative to the general level of affluence, and relative to the opportunities that the expanding suburban and exurban rings provide.

Finally, while one can expect to see a very large growth in the "human service" industries—with perhaps a large part of that growth directed toward doing something about the problems of the underclass—it seems likely that these service-oriented programs will continue to prove to be failures. They will provide opportunities for middle-class professionals and hopefully for a few mobile persons from the underclass to earn a good and steady income but will not do much in fact to improve life for the "clients" of these services.

Only if there is a very major shift in the way Americans think about and cope with the problems of poverty, race, urban distress and the like is 1985 likely to appear much better to us in these respects than 1972.

FURTHER READING

The Coming of Post-Industrial Society by Daniel Bell (New York: Basic Books, 1973).

Rich Man, Poor Man by Herman P. Miller (New York: T. Y. Crowell, 1971). Projects income and consumption to 1985 and relates shifting consumption behavior to changes in the age distribution of the population.

The Future of Inequality by S. M. Miller and Pamela Roby (New York: Basic Books, 1970). Discusses unchanging patterns of inequality in American society and their implications for the future.

Future Shock by Alvin Toffler (New York: Bantam Books, 1970).

MYRNA M. WEISSMAN AND EUGENE S. PAYKEL

Moving and Depression in Women

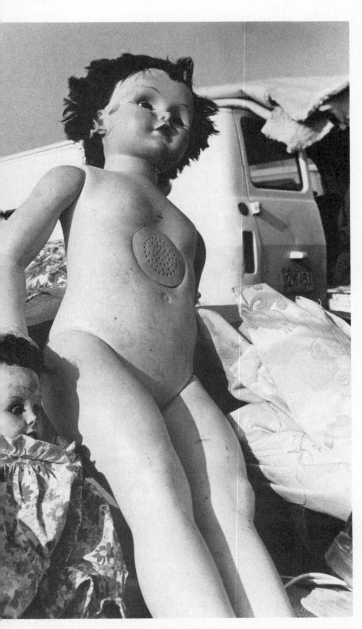

It is generally believed that most Americans have adapted to the geographical mobility of contemporary life with relative ease and little anxiety. Unfortunately, reality does not coincide with expectation—in fact, moves quite often generate a great deal of stress. But social pressures inhibit personal acceptance of this stress, and difficulties in coping with the problems of moving come to be regarded as personal inadequacies and failures. And while moving can be beneficial, it can also mean multiple losses to the individual—loss of important social ties, familiar living patterns, security and even income. It is these losses that contribute to the development of depression.

It is noteworthy that sociological and psychiatric studies have focused on moves in working-class subjects. It is rarely noted in the reports of researchers, most of whom are aspirants in the upward ladder of university and professional career activities, that the geographical moves which are usually part of their own lives may be stressful both to them and their families. The particular components of that stressfulness may be different in any move. Nevertheless, it would appear that as universal as the experience of moving is in American society, it is also a considerable universal stress and challenge.

During the course of studying a group of depressed women in New Haven, Connecticut, we noted in a number of them temporal relationships between their depressive symptoms and recent moves. These women often did not relate their illnesses to the moves but more often attributed them to other events in their lives such as financial problems, increased loneliness, increased marital friction, problems with children, career frustrations, identity confusion. In most cases, however, these other events were the by-products of faulty adaptation to the stresses and changes created by moving. We suspected that these women did not associate their symptoms with moving, since it is such an accepted part of American life that it is almost taken for granted. These women instead internalized the stresses and blamed themselves for their problems. The result was an emergence of depressive symptoms.

Most of the women were patients in a research clinic and were being treated for depressive episodes. They showed the usual symptoms of depression including feelings of helplessness and futility, hopelessness about the future and persistent sadness, impaired capacity to perform their work and other usual activities and a loss of interest in friends and family. We were led to examine their experience of moving in more detail and we found that in some cases the move was the last straw in a series of stressful events and interpersonal difficulties. In other cases moving represented an abortive effort to solve other problems, often financial or marital. However, in some cases the move itself created new stresses and interpersonal difficulties which had not previously existed. This pattern of depression occurred even though the moves were voluntary and related to presumably desirable circumstances, such as improved housing and financial status. This sharply contrasts with reports suggesting that moves produce detrimental effects only if they are involuntary or undesirable.

The circumstances surrounding the moves and the reasons they occurred showed wide variation and we proceeded to classify them. The following represent some of the different types we encountered and probably cover

the most common kinds of moves made each year. Although our examples (drawn primarily from the research clinic which treated only women) are depressed women, we believe that moving also creates stresses for men. Equally, the impact extends beyond the narrow bounds of the depression clinic. We believe we are documenting here a stress which is extremely common, although often ignored or underestimated. Although most studies of the psychological effects of mobility have focused on groups that make up only a small portion of the people who move—such as working-class families who are forced out of their homes by urban renewal or military families who are regularly reassigned to new posts—our study covered a wider socioeconomic range of families. Rather than being confined to lower-class and military families the impact of moving, we found, was stressful to women of all classes.

The effects of forced dislocation from an urban slum through urban renewal has been well described by Marc Fried in his study of the working-class residents of the West End of Boston. His subjects were people who had a strong and positive attachment to their homes and community, strong interpersonal relations and ties and a group identity based on availability and contact with familiar groups of people. When the West End homes were torn down for redevelopment and the residents relocated, a majority of the individuals experienced the reaction Fried described as "grieving for a lost home." This grief was manifested in feelings of painful loss, continued longing, helplessness, depressive tone and a tendency to idealize the lost place. The researcher concluded that while relocation may increase the rate of social mobility and create new opportunities for some people, for most of the working class dislocation leads to intense personal suffering which is not easily alleviated by larger or newer apartments or by home ownership. Similar experiences have been reported in studies made in England.

In our New Haven study, we found fewer urban renewal victims. But when we did, our findings were consistent with the Boston study.

Miss T., a 54-year-old, single woman born and raised in Italy, lived with her single brother. She worked as a machine operator and had held this job for the last 14 years. She had lived in central New Haven since she was the age of fifteen and in the same home her father had purchased. After her parents' death she and her brother had stayed on in the house. One year prior to her depressive illness, she and her brother were forced to move out of the house because of the City Redevelopment Program. Together, they purchased a small house in a semi-rural area, without public transportation, about eight miles from the city. She began to feel isolated, extremely lonely and bored in her new home. It was difficult for her to see her friends and relatives, as she did not drive. She missed the familiar neighbors she had known as a youngster, the short walk to the downtown shops and seeing her girlfriends whom she had previously gone out with at least two nights a week. She also had to give up her weekly social club because of lack of transportation. She was not able to warm up to the new parish church which she described as "more beautiful than the old but not so cozy." At first she was enraged towards the city officials for forcing the family to move. Then her anger shifted towards her brother and other family members for their willingness to adapt. Finally, her rage turned inward, when her siblings kept insisting that she should snap out of her depression and adjust as they had. She became fatigued and weepy, lost weight and developed difficulty sleeping. She would come home from work exhausted and go immediately to sleep. She began to feel she would be better off dead.

Decent housing is invariably a major problem for the poor, particularly people on welfare. Welfare recipients are often moved from one place to another against their will. They are often not as concerned about the breakup of their old neighborhoods as about what the new one will be like, realizing that their stay in the neighborhood will probably be short.

Mrs. L., a 29-year-old woman with five young children, was forced to go on welfare when her husband was arrested for drunkenness and beating up the children. He never had been able to support the family in a sustained fashion and when they separated, she assumed all financial support of the children. She lived in a pleasant semi-suburban area when she was not on welfare. Eventually she had to go to an old apartment, in the center of an urban slum, when welfare began to pay the rent. The neighborhood was noisy and there was much crime, fighting and drunkenness. She became extremely apprehensive and nervous for herself and her children. Three weeks prior to her coming for treatment for depression, her 17-month-old son was hospitalized for lead poisoning. She developed insomnia, became hopeless and pessimistic and blamed herself for the difficulties. These feelings continued until she was moved by welfare to a new housing project in a safer neighborhood.

Many of our patients had moved to find new employment—frequently without prior investigation into the housing, living costs or employment opportunities. They chose a place on the basis of hearsay, magazine ads or other fantasies of golden opportunity (as if moving would suddenly solve their lack of skills or poor work references). They drained their savings to get to the new location and find housing. Further, since the move was often viewed by those left behind as a courageous act or an exciting adventure, the family was embarrassed to ask for help when the plan did not work. They turned to public agencies for the financial and emotional assistance they might have requested from their relatives. Often the disruption of the move created breakdown in the behavior of individual family members. Children had trouble adjusting in school, and without the social control of nearby families or peers they could more easily stop attending. Some women began extramarital affairs for the first time under these circumstances. In these families, the move had been an attempt to halt a process of downward mobility. If it failed, additional family breakdown occurred.

The M.'s were a fairly stable, hardworking couple in their mid-40s with six children aged seven to 16. Mr. M., an unskilled laborer, had worked for many years on a factory assembly line. He lost his job because of plant automation. He had difficulties finding another job that paid as well. One day he struck up a conversation with a casual acquaintance in a bar, and he described his unemployment plight. The man told him about "big money to be made in construction in Florida" and gave him the name of someone to contact. Florida seemed like the magic solution to his problems. Within three weeks he packed up the family and possessions, took his small savings and after a flurry of gay farewell parties with relatives, the family drove to Florida. Mr. M. called his friend's contact who turned out to be a construction supervisor, not the owner of the company. He was hired as a construction laborer, a job he had never done before

and within six weeks he was laid off. He was unable to find any other work. The family savings were soon spent and they had to move to a smaller apartment. At one point they did not have enough food to eat and their electricity was turned off. They finally received aid from the Salvation Army and were humiliated when turned down for assistance by many agencies because of residency requirements. Mrs. M. found a part-time job as a nurse's aide. Mr. M. began drinking and became abusive and Mrs. M. sought the company of a male employee at her job, who consoled her. She actually left her husband for four weeks to live with this man and began divorce proceedings. In conflict, guilty and depressed, she made a suicide gesture before returning home. Her oldest two daughters missed their friends and were doing poorly in school. They left Florida and returned to their former home to live with their aunt. They never returned to high school. The family finally all moved back North but Mrs. M. was too disgraced and embarrassed to reunite with her relatives. Her daughters resented her and there was considerable parent-child friction. She stopped attending church, withdrew from family and friends, took to bed and became extremely depressed.

It is easier to change your address than yourself. Some of our patients became depressed when they found that moving did not solve interpersonal problems but created additional ones.

Frequently the problem was related to a conflict-ridden sexual relationship. One woman was carrying on an extramarital affair which her husband presumably did not know about. When the relationship deepened she was faced with the possibility of having to make a choice between her husband and her lover. She demanded that her husband buy the family a new home in the country, away from the urban duplex housing they had always occupied. The spouse was perplexed by his wife's demands but succumbed to them, although they could hardly afford to move. In the country, the patient's *Better Homes and Gardens* fantasies of homemaking rapidly evaporated. She was lonely, missed the constant visiting back and forth of her friends and had no money or energy to devote to making the home beautiful. She took to bed, lost 15 pounds, felt depressed, trapped, hopeless and suicidal.

A few people were observed to use moving as a lifelong quest for solution to personal difficulties. In one case, an intelligent, highly educated couple had made seven moves in five years searching for more comfortable jobs. Instead they found each new job less desirable than the previous one, and their financial status had declined further because of the cost of moving. The search for a dream house became a substitute ambition. The patient and spouse spent endless hours with real estate agents searching for houses which they were increasingly less able to afford. As the marriage deteriorated with their vanishing dreams the woman began to feel disillusioned and depressed.

A lovely private home, grass in which the children can play, clean air, birds and peace motivate a significant number of Americans each year to voluntarily leave multi-family urban homes and move to the suburbs. Unlike the previous moves we described which were mostly involuntary and undesirable, the move to the suburbs from the city, from a rented apartment to a private home, symbolizes the family's prosperity and success and is usually considered a joyous event. While opinions differ on the desirability of such a life style, some researchers have found that suburban life itself had little ill effect on mental health. They did note, however, that certain groups of people find the suburbs stressful. Among them are adolescents who are consumers of the urban activities and become bored with the lack of activities in the suburbs, working-class women who find it difficult to deal with the social demands of the new environment, urban cosmopolitan individuals who miss the city and feel isolated and educated women who want to work.

Herbert Gans concludes that people who have problems in the city bring them to the suburbs. We certainly would agree with this conclusion; however, we did find some women who did not fall into any of these groups described as having difficulty in the suburbs. These women could not adapt even though the move was considered desirable by the family. In these cases, it seems that the depressive illness was intensified or exacerbated by the suburban life style. For example, the low population density and the loss of natural daily social gatherings on the porch, the street or the corner drug store made sharing experiences and ventilating problems more difficult. Thus more emotional demands were put on the nuclear family, especially on the husband. If the marriage was shaky, the husband unavailable because of long hours at work or emotional disentanglement, the woman felt isolated and alone. Often people of similar age and income lived in the community, especially in the new developments, and no older baby sitters, or bearers of grandmotherly wisdom were available to the young mother. This was especially difficult for the woman if she had depended on her own mother for support and advice and the move had made daily contacts with her family less possible.

Mrs. Z. was a 37-year-old married woman with two small children. She had married late, in her early 30s, and helped her husband better himself by working herself, so that he could return to college. The couple worked hard together and saved money so that they could someday purchase their own home. After graduation her husband's success as an accountant continued and he received enough of a salary increase so that their dream could be realized. The family moved to a new ranch home in the suburbs about 15 miles from the urban area where they had lived. With the cost of moving and setting up their new home they could not afford a second car so that Mrs. Z. was unable to leave the home during the day and visit her mother or sisters whom she had been used to seeing daily. She had always been a shy and insecure woman and found it difficult to establish friendships with her neighbors. In the past when she had felt blue or lonesome she would go to her local pharmacist, an older kindly man, sit on a stool in his drug store and talk to him. Now, alone in the house, without her family in daily contact and with her neighbors occupied with their own young families, she felt alone and unable to cope with the new house or her children. When she complained to her parents they scolded her for being ungrateful and not appreciating her new home. Her husband saw the house as a symbol of

his "arriving" and became obsessed with it, seeking out more chores in his spare time in order to maintain and improve the house. Mrs. Z. felt she was slipping into second place as he became annoyed with her complaints.

In some cases, the move to the suburbs put unanticipated financial burdens on the family which considerably increased the tension in the home. In purchasing the home, the extra cost of commuting, the second car, baby sitters who previously had been neighbors or family in the building the care of the grass and recreation for the children had not been considered. While some families thrived on the shared chores in the new home, for some families it was a burden which frequently fell to the woman, leading to her feelings of resentment and futility.

The R.'s had been married five years when they decided to move to the suburbs. Their marriage had gone fairly well those first five years. However, financial problems began to mount as a result of this move, as unanticipated problems with the house occurred—the water supply was inadequate and they had to dig another well. Even after that the water was poor. They incurred many bills and couldn't afford furniture for the house or recreation. Mrs. R. found living out in the country isolating. She missed her neighbors and friends and as a result had more expectations and desire of companionship from her husband than he was able to supply. Her nagging was beginning to drive him away and she feared that he was unfaithful.

Career advancement in many professions and in academia often depends on the individual's willingness to move to a better job. In fact, the middle-class professional has become a new migrant worker, especially during the early years of his career. One recent study of 280 university faculty wives indicated that the typical family moved on the average of three times in ten years and that two-thirds of these moves meant an upward step for the husband's career. For his wife it can have considerably different implications. One research group has reported on the discrepancy between spouses in the perception of moving. They considered why a group of similar persons, in this instance the husbands of depressed women who were subjected to the same stress of moving, did not develop the same symptoms of depression. They noted that the event of moving, necessitated by a job change, was usually initiated by the husband who viewed it quite differently from his wife. The husband felt he was initiator, but the wife felt helpless and a victim. This discrepancy in perception may be less frequent in families who have fallen on hard times and who see the move as an active solution to an already poor situation. But in the middle-class family the wife may not see enough tangible financial or social improvement to offset the disruption of moving. Further, if the man is preoccupied with his career he may not assist in the move and the burden of selling the house, finding a new one and making friends falls to his wife.

The B.'s were a prosperous couple in their late 30s with two children of school age. Mr. B. was an insurance executive who had risen steadily in the company from selling insurance to a responsible administrative job. His advancement had necessitated four moves in the past five years, in most cases to a new state. The pattern of the moves was always the same. Mr. B. would go ahead of the family. Mrs. B. would stay behind, check the children out of school, sell the house, and move. She resented being left behind with all the work to do. With her last move she felt physically exhausted and found it difficult to make friends. The demanding responsibilities of her husband's new job required that he be away from home often. Mrs. B. missed the friends she had made in the part-time job she had before the move. She was unable to easily find another job in the new community and was too busy unpacking and settling the children in the new school to explore many possibilities. She began to feel hopeless and despondent.

Overlapping the problems described by professional white-collar workers are those of educated housewives, a rapidly increasing group. In many instances, the educated housewife is married to the professional or academic man whose career in the early years requires that he move. Though some young couples firmly decide that each will pursue independent careers and will only plan moves that are accordingly desirable for both, more often the woman's career assumes a minor role in her life—especially during the eight to ten years when her children are small. She may have given up her education or career, taken secondary jobs to earn extra spending money for the family or to assist her husband during his training, or she may have pursued her career on a part-time basis. In most cases, her career has been disrupted during the period of life when the pressures for its development are usually the greatest, ages 28 to 35. Until alternate career styles are accepted and available, many educated women, especially as they mature and have their child rearing behind them, will find themselves in a dilemma. A fragmental work or educational history often precludes an interesting job. This fragmentation, along with geographical discontinuities, excludes her from being socialized into a profession, a process considered essential not only for learning occupational skills but for developing a clearer image of oneself as competent and adequate in a particular field. As a result we found a number of educated and sometimes talented women who had held a multitude of jobs often below their training. They felt hopeless and discouraged about their own chances of ever doing gratifying work in their field of training. The majority of these women felt that their husbands would have to relocate in the next five years. Their husbands were often successful in their chosen profession, considered on the way up and the family had already experienced multiple moves.

Mrs. E., a 27-year-old medical resident's wife, had major career disruptions herself because of her husband's career. Because of his training, they had four moves in five years. Her husband was soon to begin a full-time job and was frequently not available to her. She was jealous of her husband's involvement in his work. She had not worked professionally since she received her master's degree in psychology and had given up going on for a doctoral degree because of the moves. She lacked confidence, felt rusty and had no relevant work experience.

The evidence from our clinical experience, although anecdotal, suggests that in a variety of ways moves in modern America tend to be a good deal more stressful than is generally believed because they are shaded by cultural expectations. Scattered observations in the literature tend to support this conclusion.

Several studies suggest a relationship with clinical depression. Melitta Leff and others studied the occurrence of stressful events prior to the development of a serious depressive illness in 40 patients. Of the 20 events studied, geographic move was the third most frequent event. Of the 40 patients, 18 (45 percent) had moved in the year preceding the illness. Eugene S. Paykel and other researchers studied the occurrence of 33 events in 185 depressed patients and 185 matched controls from the general population during the six months preceding the onset of the depression. Depressed patients reported substantially more moves than did the controls, just failing to reach statistical significance but ranking high in the list of events in magnitude of patient-control differences. Exits or separations from persons in the immediate social field of the respondent showed a particularly high relationship to depression. Richard W. Hudgens and his research associates, who compared 40 hospitalized depressives with 40 medical controls, also found that depressed patients reported more frequent changes of residence in the year prior to hospitalization, although the relationship was not regarded as clearly causative.

These studies all refer to treated depressives. In a non-clinical situation, Fried noted a high incidence of severe and persistent depressive symptoms in a group of working-class people who were being moved out of their homes because of urban renewal. Gans concluded that even the opportunity for better housing could not make up for the social advantages of being near old friends. The anguish experienced by many of the former residents was so great that they would return on weekends to walk through their old neighborhood and its rubble-strewn streets.

It would seem that the stressful effects of American geographical mobility have been underestimated. Moving often places inordinate demands on the individual to adapt and raises continued challenges to his identity. While many people move each year and experience no problems or only transient ones, there are a substantial number of persons who do experience incapacitating suffering.

This study was supported by U.S.P.H.S. Grant MH13738 from NIMH.

FURTHER READING

Depression by Aaron T. Beck (New York: Harper & Row, 1967). A scholarly book describing clinical, experimental, and theoretical aspects of depression.

The Urban Condition edited by Leonard J. Duhl (New York: Basic Books, 1963). A series of studies on problems encountered in moving; contains an excellent article by Marc Fried "Grieving for a Lost Home."

The Split Level Trap by R. E. Gordon, K. K. Gordon, and M. Gunther (New York: Dell, 1962). A sociological study of isolation and conformity in suburbia.

"The Faculty Wife: Talent Unused" by Katherine Nelson, Myrna Weissman, Judith Hackman et al. *Yale Alumni Magazine* 35 (January 1972):340.

JOYCE R. STARR AND DONALD E. CARNS

Singles in the City

In increasing numbers the young college graduate has come to expect more from life than immediate security. For many, social and financial independence and career mobility have replaced early marriage as immediate postgraduation goals. Since the romantic image of the city as the place of flourishing ambitions has changed little during the past century, the urban setting has a magnetic pull on young people of all persuasions. Such has been the function of the city in a tradition which has held from Theodore Dreiser's nineteenth-century innocent *Sister Carrie* to the jaded twentieth-century heroine of *Darling.*

But never before has the city seemed so organized in its readiness to accommodate the young. Most cities appear to have an abundance of singles bars; some have co-ed singles apartment houses. Ads for singles weekends and excursions pad out the travel sections of big city newspapers. All this would seem to suggest an unprecedented institutionalization of this new life style in cities. But does it become a reality? Or is it just another media-created fantasy profitable only to those businessmen involved in its promotion?

The question is significant in the same way any challenge to or test of a stereotype is socially meaningful, whether it relates to blacks, women, students, Communists or whomever. The question has further meaning since a large proportion of these elite middle-class singles are the product of our advanced educational system. The degree to which preurban socialization (in school, at home and so forth) prepared them for the realities of urban living—or conversely for its image—is crucial because it provides a partial test of the efficacy of these institutions. Are these people fulfilled, hopeful, nostalgic, sad, lonely or what?

Finally, since this population will in a few years help swell the familiar ranks of married, middle-class suburbanites, to what degree do men and women anticipate this probable future state? What are their attitudes toward marriage, monogamy, security, responsibility?

It is not possible in this brief article to address all these issues. Our discussion will focus on the three major (basic) tasks involved in successful urban adjustment: finding and maintaining a place to live; finding, keeping or changing jobs; and meeting friends, dates and potential mates (whether legal or consensual).

Our findings are based upon approximately 70 face-to-face interviews which are structured but essentially open-ended. Our subjects are never-married college graduates of both sexes who are in their early- to mid-twenties, who have not done graduate work and who have opted to come to or remain in Chicago to work. We conducted our interviews during 1970 and the first half of 1971 and are still interviewing. Ruling out the feasibility of a sampling method, we substituted a "snowball" technique (one contact leading to the next), attempting to include a variety of occupations, living arrangements, locations and other aspects of urban life style.

Chicago's Singles Community

Chicago's North Side singles community extends approximately eight miles north of the Loop, roughly two-and-one-half miles to the west and is bounded on the east by Lake Michigan. This general area encompasses four fairly distinct subareas, each of which is home to a wide range of life styles. The Near North, which lies closest to the Loop, is a city planner's horror—a patchwork of 20-story apartment buildings and renovated brownstones seeded with a number of stand-up style singles bars in the Rush Street area.

Moving farther north we find Chicago's Old Town, a subarea characterized by aging brownstones, occasional duplexes and a few high rises, whose alarmingly rapid encroachment on the scene is altering the fundamental character of the neighborhoods. Wells Street, one of the Old Town's major arteries, is a potpourri of fun houses, ice cream palaces, "head-shops" and strip joints to which tourists and teeny-boppers gravitate and which singles generally avoid.

Old Town merges into the Mid-North—a dense concentration of back-to-back high rises and four-plus-ones (cheaply built four-story apartment buildings—four stories plus a parking level—that took advantage of a loophole in Chicago's otherwise stringent building code and are now illegal). The Mid-North has only a smattering of night spots and retail establishments. At the loosely defined boundaries of the Mid-North, New Town begins. This subarea managed without a specific name until the advent of the commercial boom that began to move north along Broadway and Clark streets. In its wake it spawned a profusion of easy-entry stores and boutiques purveying antiques, waterbeds and ethnic cuisine. There are also a number of sit-down bars ("that give you a chance to talk") and a small sprinkling of Chicago's own "off-Broadway" and out-of-the-Loop playhouses. An area of mixed housing types—four-plus-ones, brownstones and occasional high rises in the vicinity of Lake Michigan—New Town also contains Homo-Heights, which is exactly what the name implies.

The proportion of young college graduates is by no means equally distributed among these areas but it tends to increase as one moves northward to the lower rental sections of the Mid-North and New Town. The young, unattached graduates, contrary to the mass media's image of the "singles scene," are clearly outnumbered by other kinds of people living in the area. Older persons, particular-ly widows, comprise a significant proportion of this less newsworthy population. There are also a number of married couples (with or without children), who have either returned to the city after an unsuccessful brush with the suburbs or who are unwilling to leave it. Other residents include divorcées, bachelors over 30 and students. The bond among these disparate groups is neither age nor life style but expedience—the desire to live close to the city's central business district.

The typical graduate arriving in Chicago has little or no awareness of Chicago's singles scene. The decision to move to Chicago after finishing college, then, is rarely a function of informed expectations concerning social life in the city. For the majority of those who were raised in Chicago or its environs, their return is usually based on no more substantial criteria than "it seemed like the natural thing to do." The decision of other graduates appears even more haphazard. "I wanted to get away from home and Chicago is the nearest big city." "A few of my close friends from college were coming here, and I had no place else to go, so . . ." "My boy (or girl) friend had decided to move here." "I figured the job market would be better here than New York or San Francisco." "The job I was offered just happened to be based in this city." Women typically offer one of the first three responses while men are more likely to respond with one of the last two.

Governed by such social motives, a woman moves only to that city where friends and/or family may serve her needs. Because the man's decision is more often work related, he will frequently move to a city where he has neither family nor friends. He therefore is more likely to find an apartment by himself, to live alone when he first comes into the city. Also contributing to this pattern, of course, is the fact that male graduates, earning higher salaries, can better afford to live alone.

The out-of-town female, on the other hand, tends to establish living arrangements with one or two college friends. Having no car at her disposal, the typical woman is primarily concerned that her new living quarters be close to transportation and involve a reasonably short commute to her place of work. Her second concern is for safety, both in terms of the building itself and the surrounding area. Many women consequently restrict their apartment hunt to buildings equipped with doormen or buzzer systems; they are more likely than men to move initially into a high rise or four-plus-one.

By contrast, the typical male graduate moving to Chicago usually has access to a car and is largely unconcerned with safety. Faced with high expenses and automobile payments (not to mention astronomical urban insurance costs), he generally chooses to economize on rent and therefore tends to seek an older building. Moreover, because of these different considerations, men frequently seek apartments in blue-collar and migrant neighborhoods along the western border of Chicago's singles community.

Both men and women soon learn that desirable apartments are at a premium. With their search usually limited to the span of one weekend, most out-of-town graduates settle on a building (and consequently on a neighborhood) merely because "the apartment was available." Chicago's tradition of May-to-October leasing periods exacerbates the shortage

by making relatively fewer apartments available at other times of the year. Furthermore, many graduates never suffer the rigors of apartment hunting; they either move in with a friend (or a friend of a friend) who already has an apartment or they let their roommate(s)-to-be do the hunting and deciding.

Neighbors Avoided

Unlike cities in California and some other states, Chicago has few, if any, "singles only" buildings or complexes; there are none in the North Side (this area does contain one megacomplex which rose from the rubble of urban blight under the rubric and financing of "middle-income housing," but which has actually done little to serve that population. Housing about six thousand people, it bears a reputation as a miniature "swingle's city"—an undeserved reputation in that the majority of its residents are not under 25 and single.)

Our data suggest that the majority of graduates, especially the men, prefer not to live in a building that fabricates and formalizes the meeting and dating process. To be sure, many have fond recollections of the communal type of living arrangements of their college years. "I knew 90 percent of the people living in my building; here I don't even know my next-door neighbor." But the kind of living situations they seek is exemplified by such key terms as spontaneous, casual and not forced. The majority of those interviewed were uncomfortable or openly disdainful about living arrangements that focus on or exploit their single status. However, given a climate that permits year-round outdoor facilities (such as swimming pools and tennis courts) this population would probably find such arrangements more acceptable in natural settings, such as California. (The party rooms and mixing lounges that abound in cold-climate buildings bent on attracting single populations are anathema to them. Clearly this climate variable merits future research.)

It should be kept in mind that the college student spends the bulk of his day alone whether in classes or studying. In classrooms even when surrounded by peers, the student is not actually interacting with anyone in an active and meaningful way; nor is college performance dependent upon such interactions. Although unlikely, it is quite possible to complete four years of college successfully and earn a bachelor's degree without ever having spoken to a fellow student or, sad to say, to a professor.

The world of work, on the other hand, places a high premium on interpersonal skills—a fact that graduates soon discover. (Ironically, when asked how, if at all, college prepared them for the experience of working, the typical response is "it taught me how to get along with people.") Because the average working graduate in this sample finds himself (or herself) interacting with people eight or more hours per day, frequently in pressure situations which could hardly be characterized as purely social, his need for privacy and solitude is a real one. While the modal graduate laments the city's coldness and unfriendliness, nostalgically recalling his school days, the majority sheepishly admit that they have in fact expended little effort to alter the situation; few have ever overtly initiated a friendship and most have not followed through on overtures made by others. Clearly, they cherish their house as a haven of privacy in an environment of functional and personal interaction.

Averted Eyes

The home-as-haven concept persists in the face of neighborhoods with strong concentrations of people with similar ages and educational backgrounds. We must seriously question whether such homogeneity is a sufficient condition for meaningful social interaction. Our data suggest that neighborhood- and housing-based interactions do not significantly contribute to the formation of friendships and dating relationships.

Several reasons are offered for this lack of neighborhood-based interaction. Some blame themselves, but with little remorse: "I just never think about it" or "I know enough people." Others cite lack of time rather than a lack of interest. But the majority attribute it to the hostile, impersonal and secondary nature of the big city milieu where "everyone is in a hurry," or is "concerned with

Changing Life-Styles

making it" and is "so self-centered." Chicago's long dreary winters are blamed for creating their own unfriendliness as well as the standoffishness of others.

The warm weather of spring and summer seems to usher in a moratorium on distrust and aloofness (and, ironically, a simultaneous increase in forcible rapes, burglaries and other criminal acts). People emerge from indoors to bicycle through Chicago's extensive lake front parks, meander through shops, sunbathe at the beach and attend outdoor concerts. Not only do the seasons have a bearing on actual behavior, they are very much a part of the consciousness of these graduates. (Warm weather will be a time "when I'll find out who my neighbors are.")

Our data indicate, however, that despite this dramatic seasonal shift in casual street behavior—from stares and averted eyes to smiles—only rare encounters develop beyond a quick "hi." Only one male respondent followed up a street meeting by asking the girl out, and in this instance both persons recognized each other as tenants of the same building. The few relationships that had evolved from casual neighborhood meetings—in shops or laundromats or through a street encounter—were viewed as eventful because they were so atypical. Unlike the college community where it is tacitly assumed that socioeconomic background and social motives converge, in the city one has only the appearance of youth as a common bond, and even that may be highly suspect.

Making a Living

For the most part males appear to have a solid cultural understanding and acceptance of work, the preparation necessary for a lifetime work role and the behavior essential for successful on-the-job performance. Some educated women share this orientation, but many do not. Based on our data, females may be placed in three categories (with some overlap): 1) the career girl, that is, one who aspires to developing her work role into a career; 2) the female who views working as an "experience," who wants to gain satisfaction from her work and feel responsible, but who does not regard this role as an end in itself, that is, as a lifetime career. She is likely to consider it as either temporary (until she marries) or as a secondary commitment to her primary future role as wife and mother. The career-committed girl, on the other hand, tends to view the two roles as either comparable or complementary; 3) the girl who begrudges her work role. She would prefer not to have to work either because she envisions herself as a wife/mother and not a worker or simply because at present (and possibly for the rest of her life) she is not ready to settle down to the responsibility of a job. This category includes girls who have not yet decided what they want to do with their lives. They may seek jobs that prolong the freedom from decision-making which characterized their college years; they may, for example, work as waitresses or receptionists, earning enough to keep the body together.

The males in our sample also fall into three categories with regard to their work orientation: 1) the conventional career-oriented male who strives for success within the corporate world or who at least subscribes to the traditional definition of success as prestige and financial gain; 2) the man who consciously rejects traditional work options and values. Working at temporary jobs (cab driver, construction worker) that provide for minimal necessities, he most closely resembles the third female above. Also in this category are those young men who seek satisfaction in non-middle-class work situations, especially those involving craftsmanship—carpentry, mechanics, leatherwork and the like; 3) the male who straddles both worlds but belongs to neither. Typically craving material success, he lacks either talent, skill or motivation. This young graduate is most likely to be frustrated because the type of job he lands or can qualify for cannot begin to satisfy his material cravings.

The straddler's plight is shared, although to a lesser degree, by all of our young newcomers to the city, whether male or female. Some may be more, others less, concerned with "the freedom only money can buy," but quite soon after graduation, the majority confront the hard economic fact that a bachelor's degree is at best an admission card to, not a guarantee of, the fruits of upward mobility.

According to Ivar Berg's research reported in *The Great Training Robbery*, the typical college graduate is awakening to the fact that a great disparity exists between the number of educated persons in the United States and the number of jobs that make full use of their background. He discovers that although his undergraduate degree is not without value, his college experience with its relatively free and unstructured environment and its emphasis on creativity and responsibility did little to prepare him for a work world in which creative and responsible positions are the exception rather than the rule. This realization both challenges and threatens the ego of the more highly motivated graduates; it reveals above all the mediocrity of the rest. Attending college had been adequate testimony of personal worth; but simply going to work, on the contrary, often provides evidence of abject failure.

Finding far less satisfaction and/or challenge than he had hoped for and even expected, the young urban graduate (like his counterpart in blue-collar work) reports personal associations as the major source of job satisfaction. Involvement in the meeting-mating process, then, becomes an important compensating factor, both for ego gratification and as a diversion from workaday routine.

Friends and Dates

Based on the inordinate amount of attention devoted by the media to singles bars, one mistakenly assumes that the bar scene is the exclusive social setting for the casual relationships established by young unmarried graduates; here, we have been led to believe, lie the underpinnings of the "sexual revolution:" one-night stands in which liberated females display the same sexuality as males.

Our data indicate that the typical graduate frequents singles bars only one or two nights a week, if that often. These bars are usually noisy; sitting is actively discouraged by an arrangement of narrow counters and a dearth of seats; interaction especially during initial contact tends to be nonverbal. Attendance at such places appears to vary inversely with the amount of time one has lived in the city. One female commented, "I made the Rush Street scene at first, but it seemed so desperate;" another, "You head there in the beginning. What else is there to do?" It is a rare woman who, after six months in Chicago, continues to seek

social contacts at singles bars. Certainly by the time she is approaching 25—the upper age point in this sample—the typical female has little use for this scene.

Males may continue to frequent swinging singles bars for a longer period of time. The rhetoric of the sexual revolution notwithstanding, it is the male who seeks sex or at least an environment which feeds his psychosexual fantasies. Although tending to marry at or above their social level, men are willing to have sex with females who are their social inferiors, for example, with the many high-school-educated habitués of swingers bars. In a complementary fashion such females appear to use the bar scene for husband-hunting probably with a very low chance of success. Swinging bars serve their purpose in the long run only if everyone is committed to swinging or—in the case of marriage-minded women—they aspire to a payoff from casual sex in the form of a more permanent relationship.

Sit-down style bars, which abound in the more northerly parts of Chicago's North Side singles area, draw more steady customers but receive less play in the media because the setting is not frankly sexual. Most of the women in our sample who reported frequenting one or more of these bars tended to define the crowd in terms of friends rather than potential dates. A place to talk is the main attraction for the many young graduates in groups, with a date or with a person of the same sex.

One could argue that both styles of bars offer a nostalgic re-creation of the college years in a peer-concentrated setting but unlike the undergraduate scene, the personal return is more in terms of a feeling of security rather than actual dating relationships. Such a feeling, however, is apt

to elude those who visit the Rush Street bars where the ambience is one of contrived artificiality—interaction is forced and conviviality strained. "You watch people . . . they don't talk. Hell, they can't! The noise in the place is fantastic."

Each bar has its following and thus its in-group which is a kind of heterosexual fraternity. Among the regulars are persons with odd working hours—stewardesses and bartenders/waiters who maintain the fellowship of their clique in other settings, as for example, sunbathing during the week in "their" section of Lake Michigan's Oak Street beach. However, the nighttime regulars generally do not see each other socially outside of the bar setting. Describing this scene as a "meat market" and the bar clientele as "plastic," most graduates (accustomed to the informality of the college atmosphere where "making it" just happened or involved only minimal effort) find its requirements for survival and success totally repugnant.

If young urban graduates cannot establish dating relationships in the bars to any significant degree, where do they go? We have already discounted housing as a primary meeting-dating nexus. For a working person who spends his or her day at the office, interaction at home is likely to be restricted to the elevator or laundry room, the latter being the only facility in many buildings which could lend itself to this activity. But as one female graduate put it, "I could go down there with all the beautiful people, but I like to get my laundry done in a hurry; I want to get it over with." Furthermore, because singles are a transient population their chances for establishing lasting relationships in a building are reduced. But most significantly the majority of

Changing Life-Styles

graduates consider home as a private and inviolate place; they do not welcome intrusions and they avoid making their apartments overly accessible. Many respondents reported that intrabuilding dating was "too close to home," that discontinued relationships could be awkward. More often they reported finding friends rather than dates at or near their home bases.

Similarly, organizations do not appear to be significant sources of dating relationships. Persons in this age group are not volunteers to any great degree; even those who were active in college find themselves unmotivated when it comes to seeking out organizations in the city. Comments such as "never get around to it" and "always seem to be busy" are common. Many perceive no great personal reward from such associations, especially when compared to the satisfactions gained in college from fraternities, student government and the like.

A kind of powerless alienation is frequently evident; many feel that organizational activity cannot duplicate the standing and involvement they enjoyed as members of the college community. More importantly, whereas participation in college activities brought instant peer recognition, no such immediate approval exists in the city where friends have scattered interests. Finally, formal voluntary organizations in a city like Chicago—be they political, cultural or environmental—tend to have a mixed membership including large numbers of married people; in short, they are not ideal ways to make dates and meet prospective mates.

Organizations—like apartment buildings and singles bars—do not provide the spontaneity that most young people require of a setting for meeting dates. The excitement which accompanies the American meeting-dating encounter seems centered on its accidental character. For the first 21 years of their lives these graduates have been surrounded by their age peers and have rarely been forced to seek companionship. To do so now would involve violating these values—a step that many are simply unprepared to take.

To illustrate, one male graduate commented on his recent visit to a "singles only" dance, the advertisement for which promised "over 300 young, single Chicagoans." "I tell you—there were greasers and very straight types, varnished hairdos, 45-year-old divorcées. Dance steps were five years out of date. I split after 15 minutes. It embarrassed me." Clearly such self-conscious seekings of companionship would force the graduate back into a junior high-school world of after-the-game dances and acute awkwardness.

In passing, we should mention that parties are seldom cited as a setting for meeting dates, partly because it takes time to establish enough contacts to guarantee invitations. But more important, the majority of the graduates, including those who have lived in the city for a period of time, either do not go to parties or find that they already know most of the people attending them. (The number of comments about Chicago's cliquishness simply underscores the patterned nature of urban social interaction.)

Having eliminated most of the possible ways to meet dates, we are left with only one major alternative—the work situation. Work was the most frequently cited institutional setting for making friends and (indirectly) meeting persons of the opposite sex. This should not be surprising since the average person spends most of his waking day at work, and it is also the setting most likely to facilitate familiarity and emotional intimacy. By no means, however, does work guarantee that the graduate will meet people; the work situation must be such that the graduate makes contact with persons who are not only close to his age but also single. Where the modal graduate finds himself in the exclusive company of coworkers who are older and/or married, he seldom is able to develop close friendships. Such is the predicament of stewardesses and along with their odd working hours, it may account for their patronage of singles bars.

The relationship between work and dating is frequently a two-stage process. Most graduates form friendships on the job (a pattern conforming to the view of the city as constellations of functionally rather than spatially interrelated people); generally, they do not date persons from the office because eligibles are in short supply and because they tend to avoid intimacy with people whom they must face every day whether the relationship succeeds or fails. The typical graduate, however, has dates arranged through office friends in a "friend-of-a-friend" pattern.

Two predominant themes emerge from our discussion of young single college graduates in the city. First, the popular image of the "swinging singles" spawned and nurtured by the media is clearly false. There is little in the bars to attract these people, especially the women. Most of them do not lead lives of wild sensual abandon. Their apartment buildings are not re-creations of co-educational dormitories without housemothers. They are people coping with the same problems we all face: finding a place to live, searching for satisfaction from their jobs and seeking friends, dates and ultimately mates in an environment for which they have been ill-prepared and which does not easily lend itself to the formation of stable human relationships. That they are coping at all is significant; that they are doing it as well as they are is a testimony to their resiliency in the face of considerable odds. These people are among those on the front line of urban existence, aspiring to the goals of middle-class America—financial security, mating and the like—but lacking many of the usual institutional supports for their activities.

Second, we must reorient our thinking about the city away from the housing environment and the neighborhood (the classic focus of many urban studies) and toward the world of work. It is the adjustment these graduates make to the world of work and their patterns of forming and dissolving friendships outside of work that provide their significant connections and sense of self in the urban milieu.

FURTHER READING

Education and Jobs: The Great Training Robbery by Ivar E. Berg (New York: Praeger, 1970). An in-depth analysis of the actual relationship between education and opportunity in the United States.

Status Passage: A Formal Theory by Barney G. Glaser and Anselm L. Strauss (Chicago: Aldine-Atherton, 1971). A systematic study of changes in status including careers.

Singles in the City

HARLEY L. BROWNING

Timing of Our Lives

Only quite recently in his history has man been able to exercise any important and lasting influence on the control of his mortality. In Western Europe mortality declines have been documented for periods ranging up to several hundred years, but this accomplishment recently has been overshadowed by the spectacular drops in mortality in many developing countries. They are now accomplishing in a few decades what the European countries took many generations to achieve. In Mexico, to cite one remarkable example, male life expectancy at birth has nearly doubled within the span of a single generation (1930-1965). During this period, the life expectancy of Mexican men rose from 32 to 62 years.

Man's great leap forward in mortality control, which now permits so large a proportion of those born in advanced societies to pass through virtually all important stages in the life cycle, must surely be counted among his most impressive accomplishments. Yet, there has been no systematic effort to follow out all the ramifications of this relatively new condition. If a Mexican boy born in 1965 can expect to live twice as long as his father born in 1930, can he not also expect to pass through a life cycle markedly different in quality and content from that of his father?

One would think that a man who had little chance of living beyond 35 would want to cram all the important stages of his life into a brief period. Conversely, one might expect that if given twice the time in which to live out his life cycle, an individual might plan and space out the major events in his life such as education, marriage, birth of his children and beginning of his work career and so on—to gain the optimal advantage of all this additional time. But, in reality, little intelligent use is being made of the extension of life expectancy in terms of the spacing of key events in the life cycle.

Here, for purposes of exploring the possibilities opened up by recent advances in mortality control, I want first to document the astonishing increase in life expectancy of recent times. From there we can examine some of the implications that can be drawn from it and consider the potential consequences of increased longevity in altering the timing of events in the life cycle. Finally, I shall comment on the feasibility of planning changes in the life cycle to better utilize the advantages of reduced mortality rates. Since my purpose is to set forth a perspective for the linking of life expectancy and life cycle, I have not attempted systematically to provide data for all of my generalizations. Therefore, my conclusions must be taken as exploratory and tentative.

In the investigation of the relationship of changes in life expectancy to changes in the life cycle, it is worthwhile to consider two groupings of countries—the developed countries, where life expectancy has been increasing over a considerable period of time, and the developing countries, with their recent and very rapid increases.

For the developing countries, an important question for which we have little evidence as yet is how much people are aware at all social levels of the dramatic change in life expectancy. Perhaps it is not generally "perceived" because the change has not had time to manifest itself in the lifetime of many persons. The fact that in Mexico there is now so great a generational difference in life expectancy that the son may expect to live almost twice as long as his father surely will have considerable impact upon the family and other institutions. But we can only know these changes for certain as the son passes through his life span, well into the next century, a time when all of us will be dead.

Mexico is a striking case but by no means an isolated one. A number of other developing countries will achieve much the same record within a fifty-year period or less. Thus, for a substantial part of the world's population, the mortality experience of succeeding generations will differ markedly and to an extent unparalleled in any other historical period.

There are striking extremes between conditions in primitive and pre-industrial countries with unusually high death rates and the situation that many countries in Western Europe and Anglo-America either have already reached or are closely approaching. For instance, India between 1901 and 1911 represented the conditions of extremely high mortality under which mankind has lived during most of his time on this earth. A male child born in this period and locale had a life expectancy of slightly less than 23 years. Today such conditions are extremely rare. At the other extreme, a boy born in the United States in 1950, for example, could expect to live almost to age 74.

As is well-known, the greatest improvement in mortality control has come about through the reduction of deaths in infancy and early childhood. In India around 1901, nearly one-half of those born were lost by age five. By contrast, under the conditions prevailing in the United States in 1950, 98.5 per cent of male children were still living five years after birth.

For the purposes of relating life expectancy to life cycle, however, it is not the losses in the early years that are of the most importance. Death at any time, including the first few years of life, is of course a "waste," but the loss on "investment" at these ages for both parents and society is not nearly so great as for those persons who die at just about the time they are ready to assume adult responsibilities. This is when such significant events in the life cycle as higher education, work career, marriage and family take place. For this reason, the focus of this article is upon the fifty-year span from age 15 to 65. By age 15 the boy is in the process of becoming a man and is preparing himself either for college or entry into the labor force. Fifty years later, at age 65, the man is either retired or, if not, his productivity is beginning to decline noticeably in most cases.

But what are the consequences of these changes that have recently permitted a substantial part of the world's population for the first time to live what Jean Fourastie has called "a biologically complete life." What can be the meaning of death in a society where nearly everyone lives out his allotted threescore and ten years? Is death beyond the age of 65 or 70 really a "tragic" occurrence? The specter of early and unexpected death manifested itself symbolically in countless ways in societies with high mortality. Of France in the twelth century, Fourastie writes, "In traditional times, death was at the center of life, just as the cemetery was at the center of the village."

Not everyone believes that the great increase in life expectancy is entirely favorable in its consequences. Some argue that perhaps advanced societies now allow too high a proportion of those born into them to pass through to advanced ages. "Natural selection" no longer works effectively to eliminate the weak and the infirm. In other words, these people maintain that one consequence of improved mortality is that the biological "quality" of the population declines.

While we can grant that a number of individuals now survive to old age who are incapable of making any contribution to their society, the real question is how numerically important a group they are. My impression is that their numbers have generally been exaggerated by some eugenicists. The cost of maintaining these relatively few individuals is far outweighed by the many benefits deriving from high survivorship. In any event, the strong ethical supports for the preservation of life under virtually all conditions are not likely to be dramatically altered within the next generation or so.

Whatever the problems occasioned by the great rise in

natural increase, no one would want to give up the very real gains that derive from the control of mortality man now possesses. One of the most interesting features is the biological continuity of the nuclear family (parents and children) during the period when childbearing and child-rearing take place. In most societies the crucial period, for men at least, is between ages 25 and 55. But only a little more than a third of the males born under very backward conditions survive from age 15 to age 55. By contrast, almost 94 percent in Europe and Anglo-America reach this age. The fact that until relatively recently it was highly probable that one or both parents would die before their children reached maturity had a profound effect upon family institutions. In "functional" terms, the survival of the society depended upon early marriages and early and frequent conceptions within those marriages. Andrew Collver has shown this very effectively in his comparative study of the family cycle in India and the United States:

> In the United States, the married couple, assured of a long span of life together, can take on long-term responsibilities for starting a new household, rearing children and setting aside some provisions for their old age. In India, by contrast, the existence of the nuclear family is too precarious for it to be entrusted entirely with these important functions. The joint household alone has a good prospect for continuity.

Not all societies with high mortality are also characterized by the importance of joint households. But all societies of the past in one way or another had to provide for children who were orphaned before they reached maturity. One largely uncelebrated consequence of greatly reduced mortality in Western countries, for example, has been the virtual disappearance of orphanages. In the United States, the number of complete orphans declined from 750,000 in 1920 to 66,000 in 1953. In this way a favorite theme of novelists a century or so ago has largely disappeared. Were Dickens writing today he would have to shift his attention from orphans to the children of divorced or separated parents. The psychological and economic consequences of whether homes are broken by divorce or separation rather than by the death of one or both parents obviously may be quite different.

I need not elaborate the obvious advantages of increased life expectancy both for the individual and his society in terms of advanced education and professional career. Under present conditions it is now possible for an individual realistically to plan his entire education and work life with little fear of dying before he can carry out his plans. In this respect, the developed countries have a considerable advantage over developing countries, for the former do not suffer many losses on their investments in the training and education of their youth. But under conditions that are still typical of a large number of countries, a third of those who have reached the age of 15 never reach age 45, the peak productive period of an educated person's life.

In such countries, primary education for everyone may be desirable but a part of the investment will be lost for the substantial number who will die during their most productive period.

Another consequence, perhaps overlooked, of the improvement of life expectancy in advanced countries is the fact that while even the rich and powerful were likely to die at early ages in older societies, now everyone, including the poor, can expect to pass through most of the life span. Considerable attention in America is now concentrated on conditions of social inequality, and clearly very large differences exist for characteristics such as education, occupation, and income. But in a society where about eighty-five of every one hundred persons can expect to reach their 65th birthday, extreme differences in longevity among the social strata do not exist. This is not to say that mortality differentials do not exist; they do, but not nearly to the degree found for other major socioeconomic variables. For the poor, unfortunately, increased longevity may be at best a mixed blessing. Too frequently it can only mean a prolongation of ill health, joblessness, and dependency.

What is still not well-appreciated are the consequences of the prolongation of life for the spacing of key events in the life cycle. Obviously, wholesale transformation of the life cycle is impossible because most of the events of importance are to one degree or another associated with age. Retirement cannot precede first job. Nevertheless, the timing of such events or stages as education, beginning of work career, marriage and birth of first and last child is subject to changes that can have marked repercussions on both the individual and the society.

One of the difficulties of dealing with the life cycle is that it is rarely seen in its entirety. Specialists on child development concentrate only on the early years, while the period of adolescence has its own "youth culture" specialists, and so on.

But another important reason why changes in the life cycle itself have not received much attention is the lack of data. Ideally, life histories are required so that the timing of each event can be specified, but until quite recently the technical problems in gathering and especially in processing detailed life histories on a large scale were so great as to make the task unfeasible. Now, however, with the help of computers, many of these problems can be overcome.

Let's examine one particular instance—age at first marriage in the United States—in which one might expect increased life expectancy to have some effect either actual or potential on the life cycle. The data are reasonably good, at least for the last seventy years, and age at first marriage is an event subject to a fair amount of variation in its timing. More interestingly, age at first marriage can greatly affect the subsequent course of a person's life and is indicative of changes in social structure.

In the time period of concern to us, 1890-1960, the generational life expectancy in the United States at age 20 increased 13 years for males and 11 years for females. This is not so great an increase as is now occurring in developing countries but it is still an impressive gain. With an appreciable extension in his life expectancy, a person might reasonably be expected to alter the spacing of key events in his life cycle in order to take advantage of the greater "space" available. In particular, we might expect him to marry at a somewhat later age. But exactly the opposite has happened! Between 1890 and 1960 the median age at first marriage for males declined about four years, a very significant change. For females, the decline was only two years, but their age at first marriage in 1890 (22) already was quite low.

Isn't this strange? During the period of an important extension in life expectancy, a substantial decline in age at first marriage has occurred. Unquestionably, many factors go into an adequate explanation of this phenomenon. One of the reasons why age at first marriage was high around the turn of the century was the numbers of foreign-born, most of them from Europe where marriage at a later age was characteristic, even among the lower strata. Immigrants who arrived as single men had some difficulty finding wives and this delayed their first marriage. In addition, around the turn of the century, middle-class men were not expected to marry until they had completed their education, established themselves in their careers and accumulated sufficient assets to finance the marriage and a proper style of living.

The greatest drop in age at first marriage occurred between 1940 and 1960, especially for females. During this period a great many changes took place in society that worked to facilitate early marriages. "Going steady" throughout a good part of adolescence became accepted practice. Parents adopted more permissive attitudes toward early marriage and often helped young couples to get started. The reduced threat of military conscription after 1946 for married men with children was also a big factor along with a period of general prosperity and easy credit that enabled newlyweds to have a house, furnishings and car, all with a minimal down payment. And not only is marriage easier to get into, it is now easier to get out of; divorce no longer carries the stigma once attached to it.

Of course, many early marriages are not wholly voluntary and in a substantial number of cases the couple either would never have married or they would have married at a later age. David Goldberg has estimated, on the basis of a Detroit survey, that as high as 25 percent of white, first births are conceived outside of marriage, with a fifth of these being illegitimate. As he puts it:

We have been accustomed to thinking of the sequence marriage, conception and birth. It is apparent that for a very substantial part of the population the current sequence is conception followed by birth, with marriage intervening, following birth or not occurring at all. This may represent a fundamental change in marriage and fertility patterns, but historical patterns are lacking. An increase in illegitimate conceptions may be largely responsible for the decline in marriage age in the postwar period.

Unfortunately, there is no way to determine if the proportion of illegitimate conceptions has risen substantially since 1890.

The causes of early first marriage are not so important for the purposes of this article as their consequences for subsequent events of the life cycle. For one thing, age at first marriage is closely related to the stability of the marriage. The high dissolution of teenage marriages by divorce or other means is notorious. One may or may not consider this as "wastage" but there is no question about the costs of these unsuccessful unions to the couples involved, to their children and often to society in the form of greater welfare expenditures.

Not only has age at first marriage trended downward, especially since World War II, but family formation patterns have also changed. For the woman, the interval between first marriage and birth of her first child has diminished somewhat and the intervals between subsequent births also have been reduced. As a result, most women complete their childbearing period by the time they reach age 30.

Marriage, Work and Babies

The effects of these changes on the family cycle are as yet not very well understood. But the lowering of age at first marriage among men encompasses within the brief span of the early twenties many of the most important events of the life cycle—advanced education, marriage, first stages of work career and family formation. This is particularly true for the college-educated. Since at least four of every ten college-age males will have some college training, this is an important segment of the population. Each important stage of the life cycle requires commitment and involvement of the individual. If he crowds them together, he reduces both the time he can devote to each of them and his chances for success in any or all of them.

From our discussion of increased life expectancy and the timing of one particular aspect of the life cycle, age at first marriage, we might conclude that there is little relationship between the two. Man has been able to push back the threat of death both in developing and developed societies but he has not seen fit to make much use of this increased longevity. Must this be? Would not the "quality" of the populations in both developing and developed countries be improved by a wider spacing of key events in the life cycle? I believe a good argument can be made that it would.

First, take the situation in the developing countries. What would be the consequences of raising the age at marriage several years and of widening the interval between births? The demographic consequences would be very important, for, independent of any reduction of completed family size, these changes would substantially reduce fertility rates. Raising age at marriage would delay births as a short-run effect and in the long run it would lengthen the span of a generation. At a time when there is much concern to slow down the rate of population growth in most developing countries, this would be particularly effective when coupled with a concomitant reduction in completed family size.

A second effect of the raising of age at marriage and widening the spacing of births would be to allow these societies to better gear themselves to the requirements of a modernized and highly-trained population. A later age at marriage for women could permit more of them to enter the labor force. This in itself would probably result in lowered fertility. In most developing societies, the role and position of the woman *outside* of the home must be encouraged and strengthened.

Accommodating the Sex Drive

The case of the developed countries, particularly the United States, is somewhat different. I see very few advantages either for the individual, the couple or the society in the recent practice of squeezing the terminal stages of education, early work career and marriage and family formation into the period of the early twenties. There simply isn't time enough to do justice to all of these events. The negative effects are often felt most by the women. If a woman is married by age 20, completes her childbearing before 30 and sees her children leave home before she reaches 50, she is left with a long thirty years to fill in some manner. We know that many women have difficulty finding meaningful activities to occupy themselves. True, the shortening of generations will permit people the opportunity of watching their great-grandchildren grow up, but does this compensate for the earlier disadvantages of this arrangement? From the standpoint of the society, there are few if any advantages.

If an argument can be made that little intelligent use is being made of the extension of life expectancy in terms of timing key events in the life cycle, what can be done about it? In any direct way, probably very little. "Licensing" people to do certain things at certain ages is, to my mind, appropriate only in totalitarian societies. So far as I am aware, contemporary totalitarian societies have made rela-

tively little effort to actively regulate the timing of events in the life cycle. The Chinese, for example, have only "suggested" that males defer marriage until age 30. But if the state is not to force people to do things at specified ages, at least it might educate them as to the advantages of proper spacing and also make them aware of the handicaps generated by early marriage and, particularly, early family formation. Both in developing and developed countries there probably is very little direct awareness of how spacing will affect one's life chances and how something might be done about it.

Obviously, if marriage is delayed, then something must be done to accommodate the sex drive. Fifty years ago the resolution of this problem was for men to frequent prostitutes while women had fainting spells, but neither alternative is likely to gain favor with today's generation. Perhaps Margaret Mead has once again come to our rescue with her proposal that two kinds of marriages be sanctioned, those with and those without children. Under her "individual" marriage young people could enter into and leave unions relatively freely as long as they did not have children. This, of course, would require effective contraception. Such a union would provide sexual satisfaction, companionship, and assuming the women is employed, two contributors to household expenses. This arrangement would not markedly interfere with the careers of either sex. Marriages with the purpose of having children would be made more difficult to enter into, but presumably many couples would pass from the individual into the family marriage. This suggestion, of course, will affront the conventional morality, but so do most features of social change.

FURTHER READING

From Generation to Generation by S. N. Eisenstadt (Glencoe, Ill.: Free Press, 1956). Sets forth the normative approach to the life cycle and its key events.

The Urban Villagers by Herbert Gans (New York: Free Press, 1963).

American Families by Paul Glick (New York: Wiley, 1957). Represents the demographic approach to the family life cycle.

Marriage and the Family: A Comprehensive Reader edited by Jeffrey K. Hadden and Marie L. Borgatta (Itasca, Ill.: F. E. Peacock, 1969). Has a number of good articles on the family life cycle.

CHARLES AND REBECCA PALSON

Swinging in Wedlock

Since the later 1960s, an increasing number of middle-class couples have turned to mate swapping or "swinging" as an alternative to strictly monogamous marriage. That is, married couples (or unmarried couples with an apparently stable relationship) willingly and knowingly relinquish sexual rights to their own mates so that others may temporarily enjoy these rights. This phenomenon, which is fairly recent in its openness and proportions, provides an opportunity of testing, on a large scale, the traditional theories about the consequences of extramarital sexual activity. It has often been assumed that sexual infidelity, where all the concerned parties know of it, results to some degree in jealousy. The intensity of jealousy is thought to increase in proportion to the amount of real or imagined emotional involvement on the part of the unfaithful member of the couple. Conversely, the more "purely physical" the infidelity, the less likely that there will be any jealousy. Thus it is often hypothesized that where marital stability coexists with infidelity, the character of the extramarital involvement is relatively depersonalized.

In the film *Bob and Carol and Ted and Alice,* Bob finds Carol, his wife, entertaining another man in their bedroom. Although he had previously told her that he was having an affair, and they had agreed in principle that she too could have affairs, he is obviously shaken by the reality. Nervously trying to reassure himself, he asks, "Well, it's just *sex,* isn't it? I mean, you don't *love* him?" In other words, Bob attempts to avoid feelings of jealousy by believing that Carol's affair involves only depersonalized sex in contrast to their own relationship of love.

In his book, *Group Sex,* Gilbert Bartell offers the same hypothesis about those people he calls "organization swingers:"

> They are terrified of the idea that involvement might take .place. They take comfort from the fact that if they swing with a couple only once or at most twice, the chances of running into a marriage-threatening involvement are small.

These swingers, who can be described as organizational only in the sense that they tend to use swinger magazines or special swinging nightclubs to make their contacts, are mostly beginners who *may* act in ways that approximate Bartell's description. Near the end of the book, however, he mentions some couples he interviewed whom he calls dropouts. These people either had never desired depersonalized swinging or had passed through a depersonalized stage but now preferred some degree of emotional involvement and long-term friendship from their swinging relationships. Bartell does not explain how these couples continue to keep stable relationships and can remain free of jealousy, but the fact that such couples exist indicates that depersonalization is not the only way to jealousy-free swinging.

Our involvement with the subject has been partly a personal one, and this requires some introductory explanation. In September 1969, we read an article about swinging and became fascinated by the questions it raised about sex and the American family. Did this practice signal the beginning of the breakup of the family? Or was it a way to inject new life into marriage as the authors of the article suggested? How do people go about swinging and why? We contemplated these and many other questions but, not knowing any swingers, we could arrive at only very limited answers. It seemed to us that the only way to find out what we wanted to know was to participate ourselves. In one way this seemed natural because anthropologists have traditionally lived with the people they have studied. But our curiosity about swinging at that time was more personal than professional, and we knew that ultimately our participation would have personal consequences, although we had no idea what their nature might be. We had to decide whether exploration of this particular unknown was worth the risk of changing the perfectly sound and gratifying relationship which we had built during the previous three-and-a-half years. Finally, our misgivings gave way to curiosity and we wrote off to some couples who advertised in a national swinger's magazine.

Although, like most beginners, we were excited about swinging, we were nervous too. We didn't know what swinging in reality was like or what "rules" there were, if any. In general, however, we found those first experiences not only enjoyable from a personal point of view, but stimulating intellectually. It was then that we decided to study swinging as anthropologists. But, like many anthropologists who use participant observation as a method of study, we could never completely divorce ourselves from the personal aspects of our subject.

The method of participant observation is sometimes criticized as being too subjective. In an area such as sex, where experiences are highly individual and personal, we feel that participant observation can yield results even more thorough and disciplined than the more so-called objective methods. Most of our important insights into the nature of swinging could only have been found by actually experiencing some of the same things that our informants did. Had we not participated, we would not have known how to question them about many central aspects of their experience.

This article presents the results of our 18-month, participant observation study of 136 swingers. We made our contacts in three ways. First, we reached couples through swinger magazines. These are magazines devoted almost exclusively to ads placed by swingers for the purpose of contacting other interested couples and/or singles. Many, although not all, of the couples we contacted in this way seemed to be beginners who had not yet found people with whom they were interested in forming long-term relationships. Second, we were introduced to couples through personal networks. Couples whom we knew would pass our name on to others, sometimes explicitly because they wanted our study to be a success. Third, some couples contacted us as a result of lectures or papers we presented, to volunteer themselves as informants. It should be noted that we did not investigate the swingers' bars, although second-hand reports from couples we met who had used them for making contacts seem to indicate that these couples did not significantly differ from those who do not use the bars. Our informants came from Pennsylvania, New Jersey, New York, Massachusetts, Louisiana, California, Florida and Illinois. They were mostly middle class, although ten could be classified as working class.

Usually we interviewed couples in very informal settings, and these interviews were often indistinguishable from ordinary conversation that swingers might have about themselves and their activities. After each session we would return home, discuss the conversation and write notes on our observations. Later several couples volunteered to tape interviews, enabling us to check the accuracy of the field notes we had taken previously.

In spite of our efforts to find informants from as many different sources as possible, we can in no way guarantee the representativeness of our sample. It should be emphasized that statistics are practically useless in the study of swingers because of insurmountable sampling problems. We therefore avoided the statistical approach and instead focused the investigation on problems of a nonstatistical nature. The information we obtained enabled us to understand and describe the kinds of cultural symbols—a "symbolic calculus," if you will—that swingers must use to effectively navigate social situations with other swingers. This symbolic calculus organizes widely varying experiences into a coherent whole, enabling swingers to understand and evaluate each social situation in which they find themselves. They can thereby define the choices available to them and the desirability of each. Our research goal, then, was to describe the symbols that infuse meaning into the experiences of all the swingers that we contacted.

Unlike Bartell, we had no difficulty finding couples who either wanted to have or had succeeded in having some degree of emotional involvement and long-term friendship within a swinging context. In fact, many of them explained to us that depersonalization simply brought them no satisfaction. In observing such couples with their friends it was evident that they had formed close and enduring relationships. They host each other's children on weekends, celebrate birthdays together, take vacations together and, in general, do what close friends usually do. It should be noted that there is no way of ascertaining the numbers of couples who have actually succeeded in finding close friends through swinging. In fact, they may be underrepresented because they tend to retreat into their own small circle of friends and dislike using swinger magazines to find other couples. Thus they are more difficult to contact.

In order to see how swingers are able to form such relationships it is necessary to understand not how they avoid jealousy, but how they deal with its causes. Insecurity and fear of being replaced are the major ingredients in any experience with jealousy. An effective defense against jealousy, then, would include a way to guarantee one's irreplaceability as a mate. If, for example, a wife knows that she is unlike any other woman her husband has ever met or ever will meet, and if they have a satisfying relationship in which they have invested much time and emotion, she can rest assured that no other relationship her husband has can threaten her. If, on the other hand, a woman feels that the continuance of her marital relationship depends on how well she cooks, cleans and makes love, jealousy is more likely to occur, because she realizes that any number of women could fill the same role, perhaps better than she.

Similarly, a man who feels that the continuance of his wife's loyalty depends on how well he provides financial security will be apt to feel more jealousy because many men could perform the same function. To one degree or another, many swingers naturally develop towards a more secure kind of marital relationship, a tendency we call *individuation.* Among the couples we contacted, individuation was achieved for the most part at a level that precluded jealousy. And we found that, to the extent that couples did not individuate, either jealousy occurred or swinging had to take other, less flexible forms in order to prevent it.

We found evidence of individuation in two areas. First, we found that patterns of behavior at gatherings of swingers who had passed the beginning stages were thoroughly pervaded by individuation. Second, we found that by following changes in a couple's attitudes toward themselves, both as individuals and as a couple and toward other swingers, a trend of increasing individuation could be observed.

Individuating Behavior at Gatherings

When we first entered the swinging scene, we hypothesized that swinging must be characterized by a set of implicit and explicit rules or patterns of behavior. But every time we thought we had discovered a pattern, another encounter quickly invalidated it. We finally had to conclude that any particular swinging gathering is characterized by any one of a number of forms, whatever best suits the individuals involved. The ideal, as in nonswinging situations, is for the initiation of sexual interaction to appear to develop naturally—preferably in a nonverbal way. But with four or more people involved and all the signaling and cross-signaling of intentions that must take place, this ideal can only be approached in most cases. The initiation may begin with little or no socializing, much socializing with sex later on as a natural outgrowth of the good feelings thus created, or some mixture in-between. Socializing is of the variety found at many types of nonswinging gatherings. The sexual interaction itself may be "open" where couples participate in the same room or "closet" where couples pair off in separate rooms. In open swinging, a "pretzel," "flesh pile" or "scene" may take place, all terms which signify groups of more than two people having sex with each other. Like Bartell, we found that females are much more likely to participate in homosexuality—probably near 100 percent— while very few men participate in homosexuality. Younger people tend to be much more accepting about the latter.

All of this flexibility can be summed up by saying that swingers consider an ideal gathering one in which everyone can express themselves as individuals *and* appreciate others for doing the same. If even one person fails to have an enjoyable experience in these terms, the gathering is that much less enjoyable for everyone.

An important consequence of this "do your own thing" ethic is that sexual experiences are talked about as a primarily personal matter. Conversely they are not evaluated according to a general standard. Thus one hears about "bad experiences" rather than "bad swingers." This is not to say that swingers are not aware of general sexual competence, but only that it is largely irrelevant to their appreciation of other people. As one informant said:

Technique is not that much. If she's all right, I don't care if she's technically terrible—if I think she's a beautiful person, she can't be that bad.

Beginners may make certain mistakes if they do not individuate. They may, for example, take on the "social director" role. This kind of person insists that a party become the materialization of his own fantasies without regard for anyone else's wishes. This can make the situation very uncomfortable for everyone else unless someone can get him to stop. Or, a nervous beginner may feel compelled to look around to find out what to do and, as a result, will imitate someone else. This imitation can be disturbing to others for two reasons. First, the imitator may not be enjoying himself. Second, he may be competing with someone else by comparing the effects of the same activity on their different partners. In either case, he is not involved with perceiving and satisfying the individual needs of his own partner. This would also be true in the case of the person who regularly imitates his or her own previous behavior, making an unchanging formula for interaction, no matter who he is with. Swingers generally consider such behavior insensitive and/or insincere.

Modification of Attitudes

Beginners tend to approximate the popular stereotype of sex-starved deviates. A 50-year-old woman described one of her beginning experiences this way:

It was one after another, and really, after a point it didn't make any difference *who* it was. It was just one great big prick after another. And I *never* experienced anything like that in my whole life. I have never had an experience like that with quite so many. I think in the course of three hours I must have had 11 or 12 men, and one greater than the next. It just kept on getting better every time. It snowballed.

The manner in which she describes her experience exemplifies the attitudes of both male and female beginners. They are not likely to develop a long lasting friendship with one or a small number of couples, and they focus much more on sex than the personalities involved. Frequently, they will be more interested in larger parties where individual personality differences are blurred by the number of people.

Simple curiosity seems to be the reason for this attitude. As one beginner told us, "Sometimes, we get titillated with them as people, knowing in the long run that it won't work out." It seems that because the beginner has been prevented so often from satisfying his curiosity through sexual liaisons in "straight" life, an important goal of early swinging is to satisfy this curiosity about people in general. This goal is apt to take precedence over any other for quite some time. Thus, even if a couple sincerely hopes to find long-lasting friendships, their desire to "move on" is apt to win out at first.

Bartell has asserted that both personality shallowness and jealousy are always responsible for this focus on sex and the search for new faces. For the most part, neither of these factors is necessarily responsible. First, the very same couples who appear shallow in fact may develop friendships later on. Second, as we shall see below, some couples who focus almost exclusively on sex nevertheless experience jealousy and must take certain precautions. On the other hand, some swingers *do* couple-hop because of jealousy. The Races, for example, dislike swinging with a couple more than once or twice because of the jealousy that arises each time. Very often only one member is jealous of the other's involvement but the jealousy will be hidden. Pride

continued on page 401

FIVE TYPES OF SWINGING COUPLES:
The Eversearches, the Closefriends, the Snares, the Races and the Successes

The following are composite case histories of five swinging couples. Although each case history is closely tied to one couple whom we knew fairly well, the case itself is more generalized to represent at least a few couples we have met. To check the accuracy of our perceptions of these different types of couples, we showed these case histories to five couples. All recognized other swinging couples whom they had also met.

Two problems present themselves here—the representativeness of the individual cases and the comprehensiveness of the five cases taken as a whole. In regard to the former, there is no way to know what proportion of swingers represent each case. In fact, to judge proportions from our sample might very well be misleading. This is because couples such as the Eversearches use swinging media and are therefore more visible and easier to contact, while couples like the Closefriends are very difficult to locate because they stay within their own circle of close friends. Hence, even though the Eversearches probably represent a higher proportion of our sample, this in no way tells us about the actual proportion of Eversearch types. In regard to the question of comprehensiveness, these case histories are only meant to intuitively represent the possible range of types. Many couples may better be seen as a mixture of types, and some types of couples may not be represented at all.

Jack and Jeanine Eversearch

Jack and Jeanine grew up in the same small town. They went to the same schools and the same church. In their sophomore year of high school they began to go steady. Just before she was to graduate, Jeanine, to her dismay, became pregnant, and her parents, experiencing a similar reaction, finally decided on abortion. They wanted her to go to college, enlarge her experiences, and perhaps find some other marriage prospect than the rather placid Jack.

At college, however, the two continued to see each other frequently. Jeanine occasionally went out with other men, but never felt as comfortable with them as she did with Jack. Jack never went out with anyone but Jeanine, mainly because his shyness prevented him from meeting other girls. It was predictable that the two would marry the June they graduated.

Five years and two children later, Jack and Jeanine were living much as they always had, in a new suburban home, close to their families. Life had become a routine of barbecues and bridge parties on weekends and children to get ready for school during the week, marked by occasional special events like a church social or a ride in the country. To all appearances, they seemed to have a model marriage.

But their marriage had actually changed, so gradually that the shift was almost imperceptible. Like most married couples, they had experienced a waning of sexual interest from time to time. But in their case, the troughs had lengthened until sex had become a perfunctory gesture, something they did just because they were married. As Jeanine said, "We didn't fight, because there was nothing to fight about. We just felt the inevitability of being together for the rest of our lives—something like brother and sister without the blood."

They had used the church before in a social way; they turned to it now for inspiration. Their congregation had recently acquired a new pastor, a sincere and intelligent man, whom almost everyone liked.

But the home situation continued to disintegrate. Jeanine, on her own most of the day, found the situation intolerable and decided to seek help from the pastor:

I knew something was wrong but it was too vague to talk about very clearly. I just kept stammering about how . . . things weren't what they used to be. But I couldn't say exactly why. In fact, I was so fuzzy that I was afraid he'd misunderstand me and that instead of advice I'd get a lecture about how God is the source of all meaning in life or something like that. So, when he started telling me about the problems that he and his wife had, I was quite surprised but also delighted.

They continued to meet as friends, and it became apparent that the pastor needed Jeanine for personal comfort and support as much as she needed him. This led to an affair, which lasted until Jack came home unexpectedly early from work one day three months later.

After the initial shock faded, Jack was left with a feeling of total inadequacy:

I guess I thought that if Jeanine wanted to sleep with someone else, that meant I had disappointed her. I felt that my inability to rise in the company reflected on our marriage and on her choice of me as a husband—which didn't do my ego any good.

The episode proved fortunate, because it provided them with a reason to talk about their problems, and with the channels of communication open once more, their marriage began to seem fulfilling again. Their sexual interest in each other returned:

We started doing things in bed that we'd always been curious about but had never bothered to try or had been too embarrassed to mention. There were many nights when we couldn't wait to get into bed.

About a year after Jeanine's affair ended, they started discussing the possibility of swinging. But when they thought of it seriously, they realized that not one other couple they knew would be willing partners. Jack had heard of swingers' magazines, gave the local smut peddler a try, and brought one home.

They examined the magazine for hours, wondering about the people who had placed the ads and looking at the pictures. Finally, caution gave way to curiosity, and they answered four of the more conservative ads. Within a few weeks they had received encouraging answers from all four.

Jack and Jeanine found their first swinging experience very pleasant. They felt nervous at first when they were greeted at the door by the other couple because they did not know what to expect. Nevertheless, they enjoyed themselves enough to agree to swing when it was suggested by their hosts. Having their fantasies and desires come true in the bedroom was intensely pleasurable to them both, and when they returned home they longed to share their elation with someone else, but could think of no one who would not be shocked. So they called the other couple back and told *them* what a good time they'd had.

Encouraged by this first happy experience, the Eversearches began to swing with practically every couple they could contact. Lately, they have become more selective, but they still devote some time to contacting and meeting new people.

Looking back, both feel that swinging has changed them. Before, Jack had always gone along with the men he knew, accepting, at least verbally, their values, attitudes and behavior:

It bugs me now that I have to play some kind of he-man role all the time. I never used to notice it. You know how guys are always talking about this girl and how they would like to get her in bed? Well . . . I'm not interested in just sex anymore—I mean, I want to have someone I like, not just a writhing body.

Jeanine feels similarly:

All of a sudden it seems I have more insight into everybody, into how they interact with each other. Maybe because we've met so many different kinds of people. And I have to be very careful that I don't express some of my liberal views. Sometimes, I really want to tell our nonswinging friends about our new life—but then I'm sure they wouldn't understand.

Mike and Maryann Closefriend

Mike and Maryann are 30 and 25 years old and have been married five years. They originally met when Mike, then an advanced graduate student, gave a lecture about inner-city family structure to a group of volunteer social workers. Maryann was in the audience and asked several penetrating questions. After the talk, she approached him to find out more. They were immediately attracted to each other and started going out frequently. After about six months they rented an apartment together, and when Mike got his Ph.D. in social science a year later, they married and moved to the East Coast, where he had obtained a teaching post.

Their early life together seemed an experience of endless enjoyment. They went camping on weekends, took pottery classes, and were lucky in meeting several people whose outlook on life was similar to theirs, with whom they developed close relationships. These friends have helped not only in practical things, such as moving or house painting, but in emotional crises. When, for example, Mike and Maryann seemed to be on the verge of breaking up about two years ago, their friends helped to smooth things over by acting as amateur psychologists.

The Closefriends don't remember exactly how they started swinging. Mike says it was "just a natural consequence of our friendship—our feeling for our friends." They remember some nudity at their parties before they swung, mostly unplanned. People took off their clothes because of the heat or just because they felt more comfortable that way. Sometimes they engaged in sexual play of various kinds, and this led to intercourse as a natural part of these occasions. Sometimes just two people felt like swinging, and sometimes everyone. If the former was the case, people could just watch, or if the couple wanted privacy, they went to another room. And sometimes no one felt like swinging, and the subject was never brought up.

For the Closefriends, swinging seems to be a natural outgrowth of the way they approached marriage and friendship, and the way they feel about and relate to people in general. As Maryann puts it:

I guess it has to do with our basic belief in the totality of sharing and the kind of dialogue that we have with each other. Our no-holds-barred, no secrets kind of relationship produces such a lovely kind of glow that we just naturally like to share it with our friends. Our having close relationships with people is actually like having a second marriage. Not that we would all want to live together, although that might be possible some day. Some of the men, for example, couldn't live with me—we would be incompatible—but that doesn't make us any less desirable to each other.

Paul and Georgia Snare

When Paul met Georgia, he had been married about a year and was beginning to find his wife Serita both boring and demanding. A handsome young man, Paul had led an exciting life as a bachelor and found the daily routine of marriage very depressing:

I felt awfully trapped. . . . It just got worse and worse until I couldn't see going home anymore. I bought a motorcycle and joined up with a bunch of guys pretty much like me. We'd ride around all night so we wouldn't have to go home to our old ladies.

Georgia was a salesgirl in the drugstore next door to the camera shop where Paul worked. He used to drop by daily for cigarettes and a chat, and they became friendly. Paul even made a few passes, but Georgia knew he already had a wife and refused his attentions. Unused to this kind of treatment, Paul took her refusals as a challenge and became quite serious in his efforts to persuade her to go out with him. Finally, when Paul and Serita got a formal separation, Georgia accepted his invitations, and they began to date steadily.

Georgia became pregnant about three months before Paul's divorce was due to come through, so they were married the week after the decree became final. At first things went well. Georgia stayed home and took care of the small house in the suburbs that Paul had bought for her, and the marriage ran smoothly for about six months, until the baby came. Then Paul began to feel trapped again, "going to work every day, coming home to dinner and going to bed. I didn't want it to happen again but it did."

Paul resorted to outside affairs, but found them unsatisfactory because they took too much time and money, and "it just wasn't worth all the lying." He suggested to Georgia the possibility of swinging with some friends of theirs, pointing out that he loved her but that "every man needs a bit of variety." Georgia initially thought the idea was crazy, but Paul persisted and finally persuaded her to try it.

Persuading their friends, however, was another matter. They didn't want to come right out and proposition them, so they decided on seduction as the method of persuasion. They would "date" a couple each weekend, and go dancing to provide an excuse for body contact. Paul would get increasingly intimate with the wife, and if the husband followed his example, Georgia would accept his advances.

They decided their first couple would be their old friends Bill and Jean. Everything went as planned for a while until Bill became suspicious and asked Paul to explain his attentions to Jean. When Paul did so, the couple became upset and left almost immediately.

Somewhat depressed by the loss of their friends, Paul and Georgia tried another couple they knew, but this time they enacted their plan more slowly. It took about six months, but it worked, and they continued to swing with the couple exclusively for about a year, until they discovered swinging magazines and began making new contacts through them.

Neither of the Snares have any problems with jealousy, and agree that this is because "we are so good in bed with each other that no one could really compete." From time to time Paul even brings home girls he has met; Georgia doesn't get jealous "just so long as he introduces them to me first and they do their thing in my house." For her part, Georgia has discovered that she likes women too and regularly brings home girls from a nearby homosexual bar. "Men," she says, "are good for sex, but it isn't in their nature to be able to give the kind of affection a woman needs." Georgia's activities don't worry Paul a bit:

> A woman couldn't provide the kind of support I do. They just don't know how to get along in the world without a man. A lot of these lesbians she meets are really irresponsible and would never be able to take care of the kid.

Swinging has affected Georgia's self-confidence as well as changing her sex habits. She now feels much more confident in social situations, a change that occurred after she began making her own choices about whom she would swing with. At first, she had let Paul make all the decisions:

> If he liked the woman, then I would swing with the man. But it got so I couldn't stand it anymore. I had to make it with so many creeps! I just got sick of it after a while. Paul kept getting the good deals and I never found anybody I liked. Finally, I just had to insist on my rights!

Paul agrees that this is good and points out that one swinger they know constantly forces his wife to swing with men she has no desire for, and as a result their marriage is slowly disintegrating. He credits swinging with saving his own marriage with Georgia and thinks that, had he known about it before, it could have saved his first marriage too.

Frank and Helen Race

Frank and Helen met at a well-known West Coast university where both were top-ranked graduate students in biochemistry. Both were from Jewish backgrounds, strongly oriented toward academic achievement.

Frank, largely because of his parents' urging, had excelled in high school, both academically and in extracurricular activities. After high school, he enlisted in the marines, was commissioned after OCS training and commanded one of the best units on his base. Ultimately, he became dissatisfied with the life of a marine officer and left to attend college, where he finished his bachelor degree in three years, graduated with honors and went on to graduate school.

As a child, Helen had experienced much the same kind of pressure. Her father, an excellent musician, dominated the family and drove her endlessly. She began piano lessons at age four and remembers that he was always at her shoulder to scold her when she made a mistake. She was able to end music lessons only because she attended a college where no facilities were available, leaving her free to devote all her time to the study of biochemistry, which she much preferred.

Helen and Frank married during their third year of graduate school. It seemed a perfect match—two fine scholars with identical interests, who could work as a team. For the next four years they did work closely together on their respective Ph.D. dissertations, which were published and became well known in the field. Despite this success, however, they could not find jobs with prestige schools and had to take posts at a less well known institution.

They settled into their professional lives, both publishing as much as possible in the hope of eventually gaining positions at a more prestigious university. They worked together closely, constantly seeking each other's help and proffering severe criticisms. If either published more than the other during the year, the "underpublished" one would experience intense jealousy. Realizing this disruptive competition was a serious threat to their marriage, they sought help from a psychotherapist and from group therapy sessions.

The most important thing Frank and Helen learned about themselves in therapy was that by making their relationship competitive they had forfeited their appreciation of each other as individuals. They also discovered another element in their lives, which Frank links directly to their decision to take up swinging:

> I told Helen that I missed terribly the experiences that other men had as kids. I was always too busy with school to ever have a good time dating. I only had a date once in high school, for the senior prom, and I had only had one girl friend in college. I felt that a whole stage of my life was totally absent. I wanted to do those things that I had missed out on—then maybe I'd feel more able to cope with our problems. Much to my surprise, Helen felt she too had missed out.

Like the Eversearches, the Races met their first couple through an ad in a swinger publication. Their first meeting, however, was somewhat unpleasant. Frank felt jealous because he feared the man might be sexually better than he. He did not tell Helen this, however, but simply refused to return, on the grounds that he had not enjoyed the woman. Helen suspected Frank was in fact jealous, and many arguments ensued.

The Races have been swinging for about three years and average one contact every two or three months, a rate of frequency considerably lower than usual. Both agree that they have a lot of difficulty with jealousy. If, for example, they meet a couple and Helen is very attracted to the man, Frank will invariably insist he does not find the woman desirable. They have come to realize that the one who exercises the veto is probably jealous of the good time the other has had or is about to have and thus insists on breaking off the threatening relationship. They also realize that swinging may not be the best way to use their leisure time—but somehow they can't give up the hope that they may find the experiences they missed as young people.

Glen and Andrea Success

Glen and Andrea were married shortly before the end of the war, immediately after Glen graduated with a Ph.D. in biology. Because he felt that teaching at a university would be financially limiting, he found a job with a medical supply manufacturing company, which promised him a high-ranking executive position in the future. He has stayed with the company for nearly 20 years, rising to positions of increased responsibility.

Five years after he had begun work, Andrea and Glen were able to afford a luxurious suburban home. Well settled into their house and community, they started their family. Andrea enjoyed motherhood and raised her two boys and a girl as model children:

> There wasn't a thing we couldn't do. Glen and I traveled all over the States and Europe. We even went to Australia. We had bought ourselves a lovely house, we had a fine marriage and wonderful, healthy children. We had many fine friends too.

Glen claims it was this unusual good luck that eventually turned them to swinging. About seven years ago, they began to feel they had achieved everything that people usually want and anything else would be anticlimactic:

> We knew one couple with whom we could talk about anything and everything, and we did! One conversation especially, I think, led to our considering swinging. We were talking about success and trying to define exactly what it meant. Andrea and I thought it was something like having all the money you

need and a good marriage. They said that if that was true, then we already had everything we would ever want.... Later on, when I thought about what he'd said, I got a funny kind of hollow feeling. Forty-five, I said to myself, and at the end of the line.

In this state of mind Glen got the idea that swinging might be a way out. He and Andrea spent about a month discussing the possibility and finally decided to try it out. Their first meeting with another couple was disturbing for them both, but they continued to look for more satisfactory people. If the second meeting had been equally bad, they probably would have given up the whole idea. But it ended pleasantly in a friendship that lasted about three years.

At first they had to rely on contacts from the *National Enquirer,* but about a year after they started swinging their local newspaper began running ads on the lines of "Modern couple interested in meeting the same. Box 1023." About ten of these ads

appeared during the brief period before the paper found out what they were for and ceased to accept any more. By then Glen and Andrea had contacted all the couples who had advertised. These people, in turn, knew other swingers whom they had either met through national publications or had initiated themselves. Soon a large network began to form.

Glen applied his organizational talents to the swinging scene and was soon arranging parties for couples he felt would be compatible, spending his own money to rent halls for get-togethers. Many couples started coming to him with their problems, and to help them out, he arranged for a doctor to direct group discussions dealing with typical swinging problems. He even contacted lawyers whom he knew personally to protect "his swingers," as he was beginning to call them, should they have any difficulties with the law. In fact, the Successes knew so many couples that other swingers began to rely on them as a kind of dating

service that could arrange for either quiet evenings or major parties.

The Successes feel that in swinging they have finally found an activity which offers lasting interest and stimulation. Says Andrea:

Glen and I have done everything—I don't just mean sex. Just doing things doesn't really appeal to us anymore. But swinging has managed to hold our attention for a long time. If you give me a choice between going to South America, nightclubbing or swinging, I think swinging is the most satisfying and interesting.

Why? Glen says:

I think it's because in swinging you can see people for who they really are—as individuals, without the masks they have to wear most of the time. In a way, I guess I never knew people before, and I'm amazed at the variety. Maybe that's why swinging holds my interest—everybody is different, a challenge to get to know.

continued

may prevent each from admitting jealousy for quite some time. Each partner may feel that to admit jealousy would be to admit a weakness and instead will feign disinterest in a particular couple to avoid another meeting.

This stage of swinging eventually stops in almost all cases we know of, probably because the superficial curiosity about people in general is satisfied. Women are usually responsible for the change, probably because they have been raised to reject superficial sexual relationships. Sometimes this is precipitated by a bad experience when, for example, a man is particularly rough or inconsiderate in some way. Sometimes a man will be the first to suggest a change because of erection problems which seem to be caused in some cases by a general lack of interest in superficial sexual contacts. In other words, once his general curiosity is satisfied, he can no longer sustain enough interest to be aroused.

The termination of the curiosity stage and the beginning of a stage of relative selectivity is characterized by increasing individuation of self and others. Among men this change manifests itself in the nature of fantasies that give interest to the sexual experience. The statement of one male informant exemplifies the change:

Now, I don't fantasize much. There's too much reality to fantasize, too much sex and sex realities we've experienced. So there is not too much that I *can* fantasize with. I just remember the good times we've actually had.

Instead of fantasies being what one would wish to happen, they are instead a kind of reliving of pleasant past experiences with particular people. Also, some informants

have noticed that where their previous fantasies had been impersonal, they eventually became tied to specific people with whom pleasant sexual experiences had been shared.

Increasing individuation is also noticeable in beginners' changing perceptions of certain problems that arise in swinging situations. Many male swingers have difficulty with erections at one time or another. Initially, this can be quite ego shattering. The reason for this trauma is not difficult to understand. Most Americans believe that the mere sight of a nude, sexually available woman should arouse a man almost instantly. A male who fails to be aroused may interpret this as a sign of his hitherto unknown impotency. But if he is not too discouraged by this first experience he may eventually find the real reasons. He may realize that he does not find some women attractive mentally and/or physically even though they are sexually available. He learns to recognize when he is being deliberately though subtly discouraged by a woman. He may discover that he dislikes certain situational factors. For example, he may find that he likes only open or only closet swinging or that he cannot relax sufficiently to perform after a hard day's work. Once a swinger realizes that his physical responses may very well be due to elements that inhere to the individual relationship rather than to an innate sexual inadequacy, he has arrived at a very different conception of sexual relationships. He is better able to see women as human beings to whom he may be attracted as personalities rather than as objects to be exploited for their sexual potential. In our terms, he can now more successfully individuate his relationships with women.

Women must cope with problems of a slightly different

nature when they begin to swing. Their difficulties develop mostly because of their tendency to place decorum above the expression of their own individual desires in social situations. This tendency manifests itself from the time the husband suggests swinging. Many women seem to swing merely because their husbands want to rather than because of their own positive feelings on the matter. This should not be interpreted to mean that wives participate against their will, but only that as in most recreational activity, the male provides the initial impetus that she can then choose to go along with or reject. Her lack of positive initiative may express itself in the quality of her interaction. She is apt to swing with a man not because he manifests particular attributes that she appreciates, but because he lacks any traits that she finds outright objectionable. One woman describes one of her first experiences this way:

As I recall, I did not find him particularly appealing, but he was nice, and that was OK. He actually embarrassed me a bit because he was so shy and such a kind of nonperson.

This is not to say that women do not enjoy their experiences once they begin participating. The same woman remarks about her first experience in this way:

Somehow, it was the situation that made the demand. I got turned on, although I hadn't anticipated a thing up to that point. In fact, I still have a hard time accounting for my excitement that first time and the good time which I did actually have.

In fact, it sometimes happens at this stage that women become more enthusiastic about swinging than men, much to the latter's embarrassment.

Their enjoyment, however, seems to result from the same kind of psychology that is likely to propel them into swinging in the first place, the desire to please men. Hence, like her nonswinging counterparts, a woman in swinging will judge herself in terms of her desirability and her attractiveness to men much more than thinking about her own individuality in relation to others.

After swinging for awhile, however, her wish to be desired and to satisfy can no longer be as generalized because it becomes apparent that she is indeed desired by many men, and thus she has no need to prove it to herself. In order to make the experience meaningful, she arrives at a point where she feels that she must begin to actually refuse the advances of many men. This means that she must learn to define her own preferences more clearly and to learn to act on these preferences, an experience that many women rarely have because they have learned to rely on their husbands to make these kinds of decisions in social situations. In short, a woman learns to individuate both herself and others in the second stage of swinging.

Another change that swingers mention concerns their feelings towards their mates. They say that since they started swinging they communicate better than they did before. Such couples, who previously had a stable but uninteresting or stale marriage ("like brother and sister without the blood"), say that swinging has recreated the romantic feelings they once had for each other. These feelings seem to find concrete expression in an increasing satisfaction with the sexual aspects of the marital relationship, if not in an actual increase in sexual intercourse. This

is almost always experienced by older couples in terms of feeling younger.

An explanation for this change, again, involves the individuation process. Marriage can grow stale if a couple loses a sense of appreciation of each other's individuality. A husband may look too much like an ordinary husband, a wife like an ordinary wife. This can happen easily especially when a couple's circumstances (job, children and so forth) necessitate a great deal of routinization of their life together. Such couples find in swinging the rare opportunity to escape from the routine roles that must be assumed in everyday life. In this setting individual differences receive attention and appreciation and, because of this, married couples can again see and appreciate their own distinct individuality, thus reactivating their romantic feelings for each other.

It is interesting to note that, those couples who do not answer in this way almost always experience jealousy, not romanticization, as a result of swinging. This is the case with one couple we interviewed, each of whom insists that the other is "better than anyone else," although it was clear by their jealousy of each other that neither was entirely confident of this.

Individuation, then, pervades the swinging scene and plays an important role in minimizing jealousy. But it alone cannot guarantee the control of jealousy—because there is always the possibility that a person will appreciate and be equally attracted to two unique individuals. Clearly, individuation must be complemented with something more if the marriage is to be effectively distinguished from other extramarital relationships.

This "something else" is compatibility. Two individuals who perceive and appreciate each other's individuality may nevertheless make poor living mates unless they are compatible. Compatibility is a kind of superindividuation. It requires not only the perception and appreciation of uniqueness, but the inclusion of this in the solutions to any problems that confront the relationship. Each partner must have the willingness and the ability to consider his or her mate's needs, desires and attitudes, when making the basic decisions that affect them both. This is viewed as something that people must work to achieve, as indicated by the phrase, "He failed in his marriage."

Unlike swinging, then, marriage requires a great deal of day-to-day giving and taking, and an emotional investment that increases with the years. Because such an investment is not given up easily, it provides another important safeguard against jealousy.

The dimension of marital compatibility often shows itself in swinging situations. If and when serious problems are encountered by one marriage partner, it is expected that the other partner will take primary responsibility for doing what is necessary. One couple, for example, was at a gathering, each sitting with their swinging partners. It was the first time they had ever tried pot, and the wife suddenly became hysterical. The man she was with quickly relinquished his place to her husband, who was expected to take primary responsibility for comforting his wife, although everyone was concerned about her. Another example can occur when a man has erection problems. If he is obviously miserable, it is considered wrong for his wife to ignore his condition, although we have heard of a few cases where this has happened. His wife may go to his side and they will decide to go home or she may simply act worried and less than completely enthusiastic, thus evincing some minimal concern for her husband. In other words, the married couple is still distinguished as the most compatible partners and remains therefore the primary problem-solving unit.

The importance of compatibility also shows up in certain situations where a couple decides that they must stop swinging. In several cases reported to us, couples who had been married two years or less found that swinging tended to disrupt their marital relationship. We ourselves encountered three couples who had been married for under one year and had not lived together before marriage. All three had difficulties as a result of swinging, and one is now divorced. These couples evidently had not had the time to build up the emotional investment so necessary to a compatible marriage.

It is clear, then, that to the degree that couples individuate and are compatible, jealousy presents no major problems. Conversely, when these conditions are not satisfied, disruptive jealousy can result.

There are, however, some interesting exceptions. For a few couples who seem to place little emphasis on individuation, marital compatibility is an issue which remains chronically unresolved. Compatibility for them is a quality to be constantly demonstrated rather than a fact of life to be more or less taken for granted. Hence, every give-and-take becomes an issue.

These couples focus on the mechanics of sexual competence rather than on personal relationships. These are the people who will talk about "good swingers" and "bad swingers" rather than good and bad experiences. One of these husbands once commented:

Some people say there's no such thing as a good lay and a bad lay. But in my experience that just isn't true. I remember this one woman I went with for a long time. She was just a bad lay. No matter what I did, she was just lousy!

In other words, his bad lay is everyone's bad lay. One of his friends expressed it differently. He didn't understand why some swingers were so concerned with compatibility; he felt it was the sex that was important—and simply "having a good time."

Because they do not consider individuation important, these couples tend to approximate most closely the popular stereotypes of swingers as desiring only "pure sex." Swinging for these couples is primarily a matter of sexual interaction. Consequently, they are chiefly interested in seeing how sexually competent a couple is before they decide whether or not to develop a friendship. Competence may be defined in any or all of a number of ways. Endurance, size of penis, foreplay competence—all may be used to assess competence during the actual sexual interaction whether it be a large open party or a smaller gathering.

It is clear, then, that such couples perceive sex in a way that individuators find uncongenial or even repugnant. When we first observed and interviewed them, we interpreted their behavior as the beginning stage of promiscuity that new couples may go through. But when we asked, we would find that they had been swinging frequently for a period of two years, much too long to be considered inexperienced. How, we asked ourselves, could such couples avoid jealousy, if they regularly evaluated sexual partners against a common standard? It seemed to us that a husband or wife in such a situation could conceivably be replaced some day by a "better lay," especially if the issue of marital compatibility remained somewhat unresolved. Yet these couples did not appear to experience any disruptive jealousy as a result of swinging. We found that they are able to accomplish this by instituting special, somewhat less flexible arrangements for swinging. First, they are invariably exclusive open swingers. That is, sexual interaction must take place in the same room. This tends to reduce any emotional involvement in one interaction. They think that closet swinging (swinging in separate rooms) is "no better than cheating." They clearly worry about the possibility of emotional infidelity more than individuators. An insistence on open swinging reduces the possibility of emotional involvement, and with it, the reason for jealousy. Second, they try to control the swinging situation as much as possible. So, for example, they are much more likely to insist on being hosts. And they also desire to state their sexual preferences ahead of time, thereby insuring that nothing very spontaneous and unpredictable can happen. Third, the women are more likely to desire female homosexuality and more aggressively so. This often results in the women experiencing more emotional involvement with each other than with the men, which is more acceptable because it does not threaten the marital relationship.

Sexual Revolution?

We are now at the point where we can answer some of the questions with which we began our research. Contrary to many who have assumed that any extramarital activity results in at least some jealousy and possibly even marital breakup, especially when there is emotional involvement, we have found that swinging often succeeds in solidifying a marriage. It does this by reromanticizing marriage, thereby making it tolerable, even enjoyable to be married. In a very important way, then, swinging is a conservative institution.

It is usually assumed that the present "sexual revolution" of which swinging is a part will continue. Bartell, reflecting this view, points out that an increasing number of people are becoming interested in swinging. Basing his prediction on a projection of present trends, he believes that swinging will probably grow in popularity and become in some way a permanent part of American culture. A similar view is expressed by James and Lynne Smith. Although they do not believe that it will become a universal form in marriage, they believe that eventually as many as 15 to 25 percent of married couples will adopt swinging.

But predictions based on projection are inadequate because they do not consider the causal processes involved and therefore cannot account for future deviations. In other words, in order to predict increasing sexual freedom, one must first understand what caused it to appear in the first place.

Although we cannot at this time make rigorous scientific statements amenable to disciplined criticism, a glance at

American history in this century reveals trends that suggest some tentative answers. Since the 1920s, greater sexual freedom has always been followed by periods of relatively greater sexual repression. The flappers of the 1920s were followed by the more conservative women of the 1930s, and the freer women of World War II were followed by an era where women flocked back to conservative roles in the home. And finally, of course, we have the counterculture which expresses an unprecedented height of sexual freedom in this century. An important factor present in all of these periods seems to be the economic ebb and flow. Economic depressions and recessions have preceded all years of more conservative sexual norms. And it is probably no accident that the present summit of sexual freedom has taken place in the longest run of prosperity this country has ever experienced. With increased economic independence, women have gained sexual privileges more nearly equal to those of men. Even homosexuality has become more acceptable. Further evidence that economic ebbs and flows may directly affect sexual norms can be seen by comparing class differences in sexual behavior. For example, working-class attitudes towards sex tend to be more conservative than those of the middle and upper classes. In general it would seem that as economic resources become more plentiful so do acceptable alternative norms of sexual behavior.

If this is so, given the present decline of economic prosperity, we should find the numbers of acceptable alternative norms shrinking. One of the more obvious indications of this is the back-to-Jesus trend which is attracting increasing numbers of young people who would have formerly been drawn to the rock-drug counterculture.

It is possible, then, that swinging and sexual freedom in general is a function of factors that are beyond the immediate control of individuals. Such factors as investment flows, limited resources, fluctuations in world markets and so forth, all events that seem isolated from the arena of intimacy which people carve out for themselves are in fact very much a part of their most personal relationships. These superstructural events are critical in that they regulate the resources at the disposal of groups of people, thereby limiting the alternatives available to any one individual in his social relations including his sexual relations.

Given economic prosperity as a necessary condition for increasing sexual freedom, it is quite possible that with the economic difficulties this country is now facing the number of available acceptable sexual alternatives will decline and swinging may all but disappear from the American scene.

FURTHER READING

Group Sex by Gilbert D. Bartell (New York: New American Library, 1971).

Intimate Life Styles: Marriage and Its Alternatives by Jack and JoAnn De Lara (Pacific Palisades, Calif.: Goodyear, 1972).

The Sexual Scene edited by John Gagnon and William Simon (Chicago: Aldine, 1970).

Open Marriage by Nina and George O'Neill (New York: Avon, 1972).

LAUD HUMPHREYS

New Styles in Homosexual Manliness

Near the heart of a metropolis on the eastern seaboard, there is a historic park where homosexuals have been cruising for at least a hundred years. As an aging man told me:

Back around 1930, when I was a very young man, I had sex with a really old fellow who was nearly 80. He told me that when he was a youngster—around the end of the Civil War—he would make spending money by hustling in that very park. Wealthy men would come down from the Hill in their carriages to pick up boys who waited in the shadows of the tree-lined walks at night.

In our motorized age, I have observed car drivers circling this park and adjoining residential blocks for the same sexual purposes. On a Friday night, unless the weather is bitter cold, a solid line of cars moves slowly along the one-way streets of this area, bumper to bumper, from 9:00 P.M. until 5:00 in the morning. The drivers pause in their rounds only long enough to exchange a few words with a young

man on the sidewalk or to admit a willing passenger. There is no need to name this park. A knowledgeable person can find such pickup activity, both homosexual and heterosexual, in every major city of the Western world.

Cruising for "one-night-stands" is a major feature of the market economy in sex. In *The Wealth of Nations* Adam Smith postulated the ideal form of human relationship as being specific, depersonalized, short-term and contractual. This capitalist ideal is realized in the sex exchange of the homosexual underworld perhaps more fully than in any other social group, and the cruising scene of the gay world may continue for another hundred years or more. There are indications, however, that in the affluent, highly industrialized centers of our civilization the popularity of this sort of activity is declining. No one, of course, could make an up-to-date count of all the participants in even a single segment of the sexual market, and no base is available from which to estimate variations in such activity over time. One can only depend on careful observers of the scene, chief among whom are the participants themselves. I can report, then, what respondents tell me, checking their observations against my own of the past six years.

Decline of Cruising

Even with this limited source of data, it is still possible to discern a trend away from the traditional cruising for pickups as the major activity of the homosexual market. Men still make sexual contracts with other men along the curbstones of our cities and in the shadowy places of public parks, but at least three social factors are acting to alter and curtail those operations and to increase the popularity of other forms of sexual exchange.

The most obvious factor affecting the cruising scene along this nation's roadways is perhaps the least important: the matter of crime in the streets. As a criminologist, I am yet to be convinced that the streets are actually less safe than they were 10, 30 or 100 years ago. American streets have been the scenes of assaults and robberies for generations. Slums expand into certain areas, making some streets more dangerous than they were; but slums also contract, leaving once dangerous streets more safe. I doubt, however, that it is any more dangerous to pick up a hitchhiker in 1970 than it was in 1940.

Moreover, anyone seeking deviant sex is engaged in a risky activity, and usually knows it. Indeed, risk in the pursuit of sex simply increases the appeal of the homosexual markets for millions of American men. The chances they take add an element of adventure to the gaming encounters and, for many participants, serve as an aphrodisiac. In fact, of course, most of the moral risk—and much of the physical danger—encountered by homosexuals comes from vice squad operations. The mugger is no more to be feared than the violent policeman. When I interviewed him, the man I quoted above was still recuperating from a severe beating at the hands of a patrolman. Two years ago, an active member of the homophile movement was shot to death by a vice squad detective in a Berkeley, California, park. But such attacks by police and youthful toughs are nothing new in homosexual marketplaces.

Nevertheless, crime in the streets is of importance in curtailing homosexual cruising, if only because it is perceived and publicized as being on the increase. It thus becomes more an excuse than a deterrent. Since the man who cruises for sex has always been vulnerable to such victimization, that alone does not serve as a major factor in his decision to switch to another form of sexual exchange. But, if he is driven by other social forces to a new market place, he may use the widely perceived threat of violence as an excuse for changing.

Another factor in contemporary society that does effectively turn men away from this sort of sexual liaison is the growing scarcity of time. To cruise for sex requires leisure. The successful cruiser must have plenty of time to devote to his favorite sport. As with fishing, one dare not be hurried. It takes a great deal of time to size up a trick, to convince him that you are a legitimate score, for both parties to signal their intentions and to effect a contract. More time is required to find a safe locale for the sexual act—an out-of-the-way place to park, an apartment or hotel room, a *pied-a-terre* maintained for this purpose. For cruising, expressways and fast cars are scarcely more advantageous than cobblestone streets and carriages; in this as in so many things, technological advance represents no gain because it has not been accompanied by increased leisure. The plague of anomie, caused by a people with too much time on its hands, has yet to descend on us.

The Swedish economist Staffan B. Linder discusses the actual fate of *The Harried Leisure Class*:

> We had always expected one of the beneficent results of economic affluence to be a tranquil and harmonious manner of life, a life in Arcadia. What has happened is the exact opposite. The pace is quickening, and our lives in fact are becoming steadily more hectic.

The clock on the cover of a paperback edition of Thorstein Veblen's *The Theory of the Leisure Class* has no hands. But Veblen was careful to point out that he used the term "leisure" not to "connote indolence or quiescence. What it connotes is non-productive consumption of time." As Veblen indicated, it is consumption, not production, that is inefficient and time wasting. Indeed, so much time is consumed in our society, Linder says, that there is an increasing scarcity of it. The upper stratum of society that Veblen defined as the Leisure Class at the end of the nineteenth century must now be defined as the Jet Set: "Superficial people in the rich countries [who] are often in a greater hurry than anyone else. They are enormously busy, even if it is sometimes difficult to see with what."

There was a time when a man of means could dally with a maid in a Victorian attic room or spend a leisurely afternoon with his mistress. He could afford to cruise for a pickup or manage a tryst in some sylvan glade. As Linder states, "To court and love someone in a satisfactory manner is a game with many and time-consuming phases." The pleasures of the bed are declining, he continues, in three ways: "Affairs, which by their very nature occupy a great deal of time, become less attractive; the time spent on each occasion of lovemaking is being reduced; the total number of sexual encounters is declining."

Among the evidence that tends to support Linder's hypotheses is that gathered in a recent study of the sexual behavior of Frenchmen. Jacques Baroche notes that the fabled Gallic lover is leaving his mistress and turning to the fleeting sex act. One man interviewed in the research states that "only one thing counts in love—it is the brief encounter."

Impersonalization

Cruising operations may have led to the ideal type of relationship for a laissez faire capitalist of a century ago, but the market economy has since produced social factors necessitating transformation of its own sexual adjunct. It is no longer sufficient for human relationships to be depersonalized, short-term and contractual, such as that which might be expected to result from a pickup on the streets. In the sexual sphere, at least, relationships must now be utterly impersonal, highly expedient, fleeting in nature. The capitalist criteria have become more demanding.

In my study of the impersonal sex that occurs in public rest rooms, *Tearoom Trade* I wrote:

What the covert deviant needs is a sexual machine—collapsible to hip-pocket size, silent in operation—plus the excitement of a risk-taking encounter. In tearoom sex he has the closest thing to such a device. This encounter functions, for the sex market, as does the automat for the culinary, providing a low-cost, impersonal, democratic means of commodity distribution.

The sexual encounter in the tearoom constitutes the epitome of libidinal enterprise for the contemporary, consuming society. An old man on the toilet stool, serving as habitual insertee in fellatio with a succession of commuters, could better meet the standards of Madison Avenue only if he were an antiseptic machine with a coin slot in his forehead and stereo speakers for ears.

Approaching the phenomena of impersonal sex from a psychoanalytic standpoint rather than a socioeconomic one, Rollo May says in "Love and Will:" "The Victorian person sought to have love without falling into sex; the modern person seeks to have sex without falling into love." My objection to May's analysis (other than his apparent ignorance of Steven Marcus' "Other Victorians") is its implication that modern man knows what he seeks. We pursue what we have been conditioned to seek, what is expedient for members of the consuming society. We are subject to the subliminal suggestion that love and sex are essentially indistinguishable and any distinctions irrelevant. As with Coca-Cola, things go better with sex.

The increasing scarcity of time has differing effects upon the various segments of American society. As Linder suggests, some men simply find it more expedient to take their sex at home. Millions of others, however, limited or lacking in the conjugal exchange of goods and services, are turning to market places of impersonal sex, such as the tearooms. For instance, my data indicate that Roman Catholic religious affiliation is a causal factor in tearoom participation, because that church's prohibition of the use of artificial contraceptives limits the sexual outlet in marriage. Of the married men in my sample of tearoom participants, 50 percent are Roman Catholic or married to a Roman Catholic, as compared to 26 percent of married men in the control sample. For some single men, primarily those with higher educational levels, masturbation provides a sufficiently expedient sexual outlet. Others must turn to impersonal sexual exchanges to meet these needs.

The overall effect is the increasing impersonalization of the sexual markets. Prostitutes are now offering five-minute "blow jobs" in the parking garages of major cities, while the free service of tearooms increases in popularity. As more "straight" men, those lacking in homosexual identity and self-image, turn to impersonal sexual outlets provided by the gay world, others who seek homosexual relationships find the tearooms more rewarding than cruising the streets. America's sexual answer to the increasing scarcity of time, tearoom activity, seems to counter Linder's prediction that "the total number of sexual encounters is declining." Perhaps Sweden is lacking in such facilities.

Virilization

If the scarcity of time in our society were the only factor influencing homosexual market operations, why aren't all men with homosexual interests crowding into the nation's public toilets to satisfy their growing demand for what can be found there? There is, however, another social factor acting upon the gay world to produce a countertendency. The cruising scene, so familiar to those interested in the homosexual subculture, is yielding to attacks from two sides: it is not sufficiently impersonal and expedient for some, and too much so for others. Sexual exchanges in the gay underworld are experiencing a polarization, torn between a growing impersonalization on the one hand and increasing virilization on the other.

By virilization, I refer to the increasingly masculine image of the gay scene. Few gay bars are now distinguished by the presence of limp wrists and falsetto voices. Increasingly, these centers for the homosexual subculture are indistinguishable from other hangouts for youths of college age. Girls are now common among the patrons in gay bars. Beards, leather vests, letter jackets and boots have their place alongside the more traditional blue jeans and T-shirts. If any style predominates, it is that of the turned-on, hip generation.

As Tom Burke pointed out in *Esquire* a year ago, just when the public seemed ready to accept the sort of homosexual portrayed in *The Boys in the Band* that life style began to fade away: "That the public's information vis-a-vis the new deviate is now hopelessly outdated is not the public's fault. It cannot examine him on its own because, from a polite distance, he is indistinguishable from the heterosexual hippie." Although this "new homosexuality" is increasingly evident on both coasts, as well as on campuses across the country, it is just beginning to appear in the gay bars and coffeehouses of Denver, Omaha and St. Louis. The hip, masculine image for homosexuals is not yet as universal, the transformation not so dramatic, as Burke would have us believe. "The majority of contemporary homosexuals under forty," he claims, "are confirmed potheads and at least occasional acid-trippers." Such a statement makes good copy, but there is no evidence for it. My sample of tearoom participants included fewer drug users than the control samples indicates are in the nondeviant population. But my research subjects were, by definition, only those who seek the impersonal sex of tearooms. My current research in the homosexual ecology of a sample of cities throughout the nation indicates a far higher proportion of pot smokers, perhaps 20 percent, among the population who engage in homosexual activity than I encountered during my field research six years ago. Clearly, the youth counterculture with its attendant styles of dress and drug use has spawned a young, virile set to coexist with the effete martini sippers of the traditional gay world.

The new emphasis in the homosexual subculture, then, is upon virility: not the hypermasculinity of Muscle Beach and the motorcycle set, for these are part of the old gay world's parody on heterosexuality, but the youthful masculinity of bare chests and beads, long hair, mustaches and hip-hugging pants. The new generation in gay society is more apt to sleep with a girl than to mock her speech or mannerisms. Many of these young men (along with the older ones who imitate their style) frown upon an exclusive orientation to homosexual or heterosexual activity. The ideal is to be a "swinger," sensitive to ambisexual pleasures, capable of turning on sexually with both men and women.

In a crowded gay bar in Boston I recently watched this new facet of the subculture in action. Neither the young men nor the girls scattered throughout the room were at all distinguishable from any other college-age group in the taverns of that city. There were fewer women, to be sure, but the dress, appearance and conversations were typical of any campus quadrangle. A handsome youth in a denim jacket and pants introduced an attractive young girl to a group standing at the bar as his fiancee. One man remarked, with a grin, that he was jealous. The young man, whom I shall call Jack, placed an arm around the shoulders of his fiancee, and, pulling her head toward his, explained: "Tom here is an old lover of mine." "Aren't we all!" another member of the party added, upon which all within earshot laughed.

After the bar closed, I was invited, along with the young couple, to join a number of patrons for "some group action" in a nearby apartment. A rather common, two-room pad with little furniture but many pillows and posters, the apartment was illuminated by only a single light-bulb suspended from the kitchen ceiling. Once our eyes had adjusted to the darkness of the other room, we could see about a dozen men, stretched in a number of stages of undress and sexual activity over the mattress and floor at the far end of the room. Excusing himself, Jack joined the orgy. In a few minutes, I could discern that he was necking with one man while being fellated by another.

Having explained my research purposes on the way to the apartment, I sought to explore the girl's reactions to her lover's apparent infidelity. I asked whether it bothered her. "Does it arouse me sexually, do you mean?" she replied. "No. Like, does Jack's behavior upset you?" With a laugh, she answered, "No, not at all. Like, I love Jack for what he is. You know, like, he swings both ways. If that's his thing, I groove on it. He could have left me home, you know—that's what some guys do. They leave their chicks home

and, like, feed them a lot of shit so they can slip out and get their kicks. One of the things I dig most about Jack is that he shares everything with me. Having secrets just leads to hangups." "But don't you feel even a bit jealous?" I probed. "Like, wouldn't you rather be making love to him than standing here rapping with me?" "Why should I?" she said. "Like, Jack and I'll go home and ball after this is over. He's a beautiful person. Being able to share himself with so many different people makes him more beautiful!"

Later, Jack and his fiancee left those of us who were bound for an all-night restaurant. Arm in arm, they headed for the subway and a pad in Cambridge. Their story, I think, is an accurate reflection of the morality of the youth counterculture, both in its easy acceptance of a variety of sexual expressions and its nondefensive trust that the deeper, personal relationships are the more important ones.

Subcultural Diversity

Like the scarcity of time, such norms of the counterculture have differing effects upon the sexual markets and life styles of the gay world, depending upon the permeability of various segments of the homosexual society. In order to outline and gauge these changes, it is necessary to construct a taxonomy of the homosexual community. Once we are able to consider its diverse segments in relation to each other, we can compare their reactions to some of the forces of contemporary society.

In my study of tearoom sex, I delineated four basic types of participants in these impersonal encounters: trade, ambisexuals, the gay and closet queens. These men are differentiated most clearly by the relative autonomy afforded them by their marital and occupational statuses. When one engages in sexual behavior against which the society has erected strong negative sanctions, his resources for control of information carry a determining relationship to his life style, as well as to his self-image and the adaptations he makes to his own discreditable behavior. An example of this principle of classification would be that married men who are bound hand and foot to their jobs have more to fear—and less to enjoy—from their clandestine encounters because they have relatively fewer means of countering exposure than men of greater autonomy.

I have chosen the word "trade" from the argot of the homosexual community because it best describes that largest class of my respondents, the married men with little occupational autonomy. In its most inclusive sense in the gay vocabulary, this term refers to all men, married or single, who think they are heterosexual but who will take the insertor role in homosexual acts. Except for hustlers, who will be discussed later, most of these men are married. As participants in homosexual activity, they are nonsubcultural, lacking both the sources of information and the rationalization for their behavior that the gay circles provide. Generally, the trade are of lower-middle or upper-lower socioeconomic status. They are machinists, truck drivers, teachers, sales and clerical workers, invariably masculine in appearance, mannerisms and self-image. Single men, I have found, are generally less stable in sexual identification. Once they begin to participate in homosexual relations, therefore, their straight self-image is threatened, and they tend to drift into the less heterosexual world of the closet queens or gay bar crowd. Apart from an exclusive concern with tearoom operations, however, I think it preferable to allow for the inclusion of some single men in the trade classification.

Moving into the upper strata of society, it is difficult to find participants in homosexual activity who think of themselves as strictly heterosexual. Americans with the higher educational level of the upper-middle and upper classes tend to find literary justification for their ventures into deviant sexual activity. The greater occupational autonomy of these men enables them to join in friendship networks with others who share their sexual interests. If these men are married, they tend to define themselves as "ambi-sexual," identifying with a distinguished company of men (Alexander the Great, Julius Caesar, Shakespeare, Walt Whitman and a number of movie stars) who are said to have enjoyed the pleasures of both sexual worlds. In this classification are to be found business executives, salesmen with little direct supervision, doctors, lawyers and interior decorators.

College students join with artists, the self-employed and a few professional men to constitute the more autonomous, unmarried segment of the gay society. These men share enough resources for information control that they are unafraid to be active in the more visible portions of the homosexual subculture. In the tearoom study, I refer to them as "the gay," because they are the most clearly definable, in the sociological sense, as being homosexual. They are apt to have been labeled as such by their friends, associates and even families. Their self-identification is strongly homosexual. Because their subcultural life centers in the gay bars, coffeehouses and baths of the community, I will refer to them here as the "gay bar crowd."

The fourth type identified in my previous research are the "closet queens." In the homosexual argot this term has meanings with varying degrees of specificity. Occasionally, trade who fear their own homosexual tendencies are called closet queens. Again, the term may be used in referring to those in the subculture who feel that they are too good or proper to patronize the gay bars. In its most general sense, however, it is employed to designate those men who know they are gay but fear involvement in the more overt, bar-centered activities of the homosexual world. Because they avoid overt participation in the subculture, the married ambisexuals often receive the closet queen label from the gay bar crowd. I should like to maintain the distinctions I have outlined between ambisexuals and closet queens, however, because of the contrasting marital and socioeconomic statuses of the two groups. As I employ the term in my tearoom typology, the closet queens are unmarried

teachers, clerks, salesmen and factory workers. Living in fear that their deviance might be discovered, they tend to patterns of self-hatred, social isolation and lone-wolf sexual forays.

There is a fifth type of man who is seldom found in tearooms, where money does not change hands, but who plays an important role in the homosexual markets. I mean the hustlers, homosexual prostitutes who operate from the streets, theaters and certain bars, coffeehouses and restaurants of the urban centers. The majority of these "midnight cowboys" share a heterosexual self-image. Indeed, since relatively few of them make a living from sexual activity, there is strong evidence that, for most hustlers, the exchange of money functions more to neutralize the societal norms, to justify the deviant sexual behavior, than to meet economic needs.

My observations suggest that there are at least three subdivisions among male prostitutes. One large, relatively amorphous group might properly be called "pseudo-hustlers." For them the amount of money received holds little importance, a pack of cigarettes or a handful of change sufficing to justify their involvement in the forbidden behavior, which is what they really wanted. Another large number of young men would be called "semiprofessionals." This type includes members of delinquent peer groups who hustle for money and thrills. Unlike the pseudo-hustlers, these young men receive support and training from other members of the hustling subculture. They are apt to frequent a particular set of bars and coffeehouses where a strict code of hustling standards is adhered to. Although a minority of these boys rely upon their earnings for support, the majority gain from their hustling only enough to supplement allowances, using their take to finance autos and heterosexual dates.

New to the sexual markets are the "call boys." Advertis-

ing in the underground papers of such cities as Los Angeles, San Francisco and New York as "models," these young men charge an average fee of $100 for a night or $25 an hour. I have seen a catalogue distributed by one agency for such hustlers that provides frontal nude, full-page photographs of the "models," complete with telephone numbers. In general, the call boys share a gay or ambisexual identity and take pride in their professional status. The appearance of these handsome, masculine youngsters on the gay scene is an important manifestation of the virilization of the homosexual market.

These five, basic types constitute the personnel of the gay world. The hustlers and trade, few of whom think of themselves as homosexual, are the straight world's contribution to the gay scene. Without their participation, the sex exchanges would atrophy, becoming stale and ingrown. The ambisexual enjoys the benefits of his status, with a well-shod foot firmly planted in each sexual world. He need not be as covert as either the closet queen or trade and, when out of town on a business trip, may become very overt indeed. The open, visible members of the homosexual community are the hustlers and those I have called, for the purposes of this taxonomy, the gay bar crowd. With this classification in mind, it is possible to see how the contemporary social forces are diffused and filtered through interaction with each class of persons in the gay community.

Polarization of Market Activity

As the growing scarcity of time drives an increasing number of American males from every walk of life into one-night-stand sexuality, the impersonalized sex exchange thrives. Rest stops along the expressways, older tearooms in transportation terminals, subways, parks and public buildings—all enjoy popularity as trysting places for "instant sex." The more expedient an encounter's structure and the greater the variety of participants, as is the case with tearoom sex, the less attractive are the time-demanding liaisons of the cruising grounds.

The trade and closet queens, in particular, find their needs met in the impersonal sex market of our consuming society. Here they can find sex without commitment, an activity sufficiently swift to fit into the lunch hour or a brief stop on the way home from work. The ambisexuals—many of them harried business executives—prefer the tearooms, not only for the speed and anonymity they offer, but also for the kicks they add to the daily routine.

Covert members of the gay society provide impetus to the impersonalization of the homosexual market. My study of tearoom participants revealed that trade, closet queens and ambisexuals share highly conservative social and political views, surrounding themselves with an aura of respectability that I call the breastplate of righteousness. In life style, they epitomize the consuming man of the affluent society. In tearooms, they fill the role of sexual consumers, exchanging goods and services in every spare moment they can wring from the demands of computerized offices and automated homes. At the same time, however, their conservatism makes them nearly impervious to the pressures of the youth counterculture.

On the overt side of the gay world, the virile influence of hip culture is having profound effects. Already poorly represented in the tearoom scene, the gay bar crowd is preconditioned to embrace some of the stronger norms of the flower people. At least in word, if not always in deed, these overt leaders of the gay community espouse the deeper, more personal type of relationship. Theirs is a search for lovers, for men with whom they may build abiding relationships. Moreover, like hippies, these men flaunt some of the more sacrosanct mores of the straight society. With the hustlers, they share a sense of being an oppressed minority. On the whole, they are happy to discard the effeminate mannerisms and vocabulary of low camp in return for the influx of the new blood, the turned-on generation.

Arrival of the new bold masculinity on the gay bar scene has made the bars more suitable for hustlers of drinking age. As recently as 1967, I have seen hustlers ejected from a midwestern bar that now plays host to many of them. In those days, they were too easily identified by their rough, masculine appearance that contrasted with the neat effeminacy of the other customers. On both coasts, and increasingly in other parts of the country, bars and coffeehouses are now replacing the streets as sexual markets for hustlers and their scores.

One might surmise that the meeting of hustlers and the gay bar crowd in the same branch of the sexual market would signify a countertendency to what I see as a personalization of sex on the more virile side of the sexual exchange. But this, I think, is to misunderstand prostitution, both heterosexual and homosexual. Hustling involves many deeply personal relationships, often accompanied by a sense of commitment. Admittedly with much futility, prostitutes generally seek love and hope for the lover who will keep them. Persons who lack knowledge of the tearooms and other scenes of thoroughly impersonal sex fall victim to the stereotype of the frigid prostitute who values the customer only for his money. In reality, prostitution is at the corner grocery end of the market economy spectrum. Tearoom sex ranks near the public utility extreme of the continuum.

The addition of the hip set with its virile, drug-using, ambisexual life style has transformed the gay bar into a swinging, far less inhibited setting for sexual contact. The old bar is familiar from gay novels: a florid, clannish milieu for high-pitched flirtation. Patrons of the new bars are justifiably suspicious of possible narcotics agents; but black, white, lesbian, straight women, heterosexual couples, old and young mix with an abandon unknown a decade ago.

Gay bathhouses, once little more than shabby shelters for group sex, although still active as sexual exchanges, are now becoming true centers for recreation. The underground press, along with homophile publications such as the *Los Angeles Advocate,* provide a medium for such facilities to compete in advertising their expanding services. Such advertisements, limited as they may be to underground newspapers, are distinctive marks of the new virilized sex exchanges. By advertising, bars, baths and even hustlers proclaim their openness. It is as if this overt portion of the homosexual community were announcing: "Look, we're really men! Mod men, to be sure, children of the Age of Aquarius; but we are real men, with all the proper equipment, looking for love." In the 1970s it will be very difficult for a society to put that down as deviant.

Radicalization

The new generation's counterculture has also had its impact on the homophile movement, a loose federation of civil rights organizations that reached adolescence about the same time as the flower children. Beginning with the Mattachine Foundation, established around 1950 in Los Angeles, the homophile movement has produced a history remarkably parallel to that of the black freedom movement. Frightened by the spirit of McCarthyism, its first decade was devoted primarily to sponsoring educational forums and publications, along with mutual encouragement for members of an oppressed minority.

During the sixties, with the leadership of attorneys and other professional men, it began to enlist the support of the American Civil Liberties Union in using the courts to assure and defend the civil rights of homosexuals. About the time ministers marched in Selma, clergymen (inspired, perhaps, by the stand of the Church of England in support of homosexual law reform in that nation) began to join the movement as "concerned outsiders." The National Council on Religion and the Homosexual was formed, and, with clergy as sponsors and spokesmen, members of the movement entered into dialogues with straights.

With the proliferation of organizations for the homosexual, a variety of social services were initiated for the gay community: bulletins announcing social events; referral services to counselors, lawyers and doctors; venereal disease clinics; legal guides for those who might suffer arrest; lonely hearts clubs. As they gained strength, the organizations began to foster changes in legislation and to organize gay bar owners for defense against pressures from both the police and organized crime.

In the mid-sixties, the first homosexual pickets began to appear, and the North American Conference of Homophile Organizations (NACHO) held its first national meeting. San Francisco's Society for Individual Rights (SIR), now the largest homophile group, was created and soon began to use picketing and techniques of applying political pressure. "Equal" signs in lavender and white appeared on lapels. But the new militancy began, significantly enough, with demonstrations by Columbia University's Student Homophile League in 1968. At that year's NACHO meetings, the movement's official slogan was adopted: "Gay is Good!"

Radicalization of the movement seems to have peaked in 1969. In that year, homosexuals rioted in New York, shouting "Gay Power!", and the Gay Liberation Front was organized. Student homophile organizations were recognized on half a dozen campuses. By the end of 1970, such groups were recognized on about 30 campuses.

The Backlash—Normalization

Meanwhile, older leaders who had felt the sting of public sanctions recoiled in fear. Not only did the shouts of "Gay Power!" threaten to unleash a backlash of negative sentiment from a puritanical society, but the militants began to disrupt meetings, such as that of NACHO in San Francisco in the fall of 1970. As one homophile leader states: "The youngsters are demanding too much, too fast, and threatening to destroy all that has been gained over 20 painful years." Countless closet queens, who had joined when the movement was safer and more respectable, began to pressure the old militants to return to the early principles and activities of the movement.

An example of such reaction took place in St. Louis early in 1970. The campus-activist founders of the newly formed but thriving Mandrake Society were voted out of office and replaced by a conservative slate. Pages of the Mandrake newsletter, formerly occupied with items of national news interest, warnings about police activity and exhortations for homosexuals to band together in self-defense, have since been filled with notices of forthcoming social events. A Gay Liberation front has been formed in that city during the past few months.

In his report to the membership on the year 1969, SIR's president criticized the "developing determined and very vocal viewpoint that the homosexual movement must be 'radicalized' " by aligning with the New Left on such issues as draft resistance, Vietnam, the Grape Boycott, student strikes and abortion. He replied to this demand: "SIR is a one issue organization limiting itself to a concern for the welfare and rights of the homosexual as a homosexual. The SIR position has to be more like the American Civil Liberties Union than to be like a political club." While SIR's members recovered from the St. Valentine's Sweetheart Dance, the Gay Liberation Front at San Francisco State College threatened to take over all men's rooms on campus unless the administration grant them a charter.

As the process of normalization, with its emphasis on respectable causes, like social events and educational programs, asserts itself in established organizations of the gay world, more closet queens may be expected to join the movement. At the same time, Gay Liberation groups, cheered on by others of the New Left, should be expected to form on all the larger campuses of the nation. This marks a distinct rift in the homophile movement. At present, one finds an alignment of loyalties, chiefly along the dimensions of age and occupational status. Younger homophiles who enjoy relatively high autonomy follow a red banner with "Gay Power!" emblazoned upon it. (The motto of the recent Gay Liberation Conference was "Blatant Is Beautiful!") Older men—and those whose occupations require a style of covert behavior—sit beneath a lavender standard, neatly lettered "Gay Is Good!"

Sensitive to the need for unity, some leaders of the older homophile organizations plead for the changes needed to keep the young "Gayrevs" within the established groups. One such appeal is found in the April, 1969, issue of *Vector*:

It's time that we took some long, hard looks. If we want a retreat for middle-aged bitchery. A television room for tired cock-suckers. An eating club and community theatre—then let us admit it and work toward that.

If we are, as we say we are, interested in social change —then let's get on the ball. Let's throw some youth into our midst. But I warn you . . . they don't want to live in 1956 (and neither do I).

Unity in Adversity

In August of 1970, SIR began picketing Macy's in San Francisco to protest the arrest of 40 men in that store's restrooms. Young men in sandals demonstrated alongside the middle-aged in business suits, together suffering the insults and threats of passersby. Recently, they have called for a nation-wide boycott of the Macy's chain by homosexuals. Resulting internal struggle brought the resignation of Tom Maurer, SIR's conservative president. Present indications are that this large organization is successfully maintaining communication with both sides of the activist rift.

Meanwhile, New York's Gay Activists Alliance, dedicated to nonviolent protest, has provided youthful leadership for homophiles of varying ideological persuasions in the campaign to reform that state's sodomy, fair employment and solicitation statutes. In both Albany and San Diego, organizations with reformist emphases have taken the name of Gay Liberation Front.

Although severe enough to confound social scientists who attempt to describe or analyze *the* homophile movement, the rift between homophile groups has yet to diminish their effectiveness. Much anger was generated when invading radicals disrupted the 1970 meetings of NACHO, but that organization has yet to enjoy what anyone would call a successful conference anyway. Meanwhile, the hotline maintained by the Homophile Union of Boston serves as a center of communication for the nine, varied homophile groups that have developed in that city during the past 18 months.

Three factors promote cooperation between the conservative, reform and radical branches of the homophile movement. First, instances of police brutality in such widely scattered cities as New York, Los Angeles, San Francisco and New Orleans have brought thousands of homosexuals together in protest marches during the past year. Nothing heals an ailing movement like martyrs, and the police seem pleased to provide them. Because a vice squad crusade is apt to strike baths and bars, parks and tearooms, all sectors of the homosexual market are subject to victimization in the form of arrests, extortion, assaults and prosecution. There is a vice squad behind every active homophile group in America. With a common enemy in plain clothes, differences in ideology and life style become irrelevant.

Second, the *Los Angeles Advocate* has emerged as the homosexual grapevine in print. With up-to-date, thorough news coverage rivaling that of the *Christian Science Monitor* and a moderate-activist editorial policy, this biweekly is, as it claims, the "Newspaper of America's Homophile Community." With communication provided by the *Advocate* and inspiration gained from the successes of the Women's Liberation Movement, the larger homophile organizations appear to be moving into a position best described as moderately activist.

Finally, a truly charismatic leader has appeared on the homophile scene. The Rev. Troy Perry, founder of the Metropolitan Community Church, a congregation for homosexuals in Los Angeles, was arrested during a fast in front of that city's Federal Building in June of 1970. The fast coincided with "Gay Liberation Day" marches of 2,000 persons in New York and 1,200 in Los Angeles. An articulate, moving speaker, Perry began to tour the nation for his cause. I have seen him honored by a standing ovation from an audience of a hundred main-line Protestant and Catholic clergy in Boston. Because he commands general respect from both gay libs and liberals in the movement, it is impossible not to draw a parallel between this minister and Martin Luther King. When I suggested that he was "the Martin Luther King of the homophile movement," he countered that "Martin Luther *Queen* might be more appropriate." As an evangelical religious movement spreads from the West coast, replacing drugs as a source of enthusiasm for many in the youth counterculture, Perry's position of leadership should increase in importance.

Just as the world of female homosexuals should benefit from the trend towards liberation of women, so the male homosexual world of the 1970s should thrive. Divisions of the movement may provide the advantages of diversification. The new blood provided by the Gay Liberation Front, alarming as it may be to some traditionalists, is much healthier than the bad blood that has existed between a number of NACHO leaders.

Concurrently, the same social forces that are dividing and transforming the homophile movement have polarized and strengthened the homosexual markets. By now, the consuming American should know that diversification in places and styles of exchange is a healthy indicator in the market economy. Both virilization and impersonalization will attract more participants to the market places of the gay world. At the same time, traditionalists will continue to cruise the streets and patronize the remaining sedate and elegant bars. When threatened by the forces of social control, however, even the closet queens should profit from the movement's newly-found militance.

JO FREEMAN

The Social Construction of the Second Sex

The passivity that is the essential characteristic of the "feminine" woman is a trait that develops in her from the earliest years. But it is wrong to assert a biological datum is concerned; it is in fact a destiny imposed upon her by her teachers and by society.

Simone de Beauvoir

During the last 30 years social science has paid scant attention to women, confining its explorations of humanity to the male. Research has generally reinforced the popular mythology that women are essentially nurturant, expressive, passive and men instrumental, active, aggressive. Social scientists have tended to justify these stereotypes rather than analyze their origins, their value or their effect.

The result of this trend has been a social science that is more a mechanism of social control than of social inquiry. Rather than trying to analyze why, it has only described what. Rather than exploring how men and women came to be the way they are, it has taken their condition as irrevocably given and sought to explain this on the basis of "biological" differences.

Nonetheless, the assumption that psychology recapitulates physiology has begun to crack. William Masters and Virginia Johnson shattered the myth of woman's natural sexual passivity—on which her psychological passivity was claimed to rest. Research is just beginning in other areas, and while evidence is being accumulated, new interpretations of the old data are being explored. What these new interpretations say is that women are the way they are because they've been trained to be that way—their motivations as well as their alternatives have been channelled by society.

This motivation is controlled through the socialization process. Women are raised to want to fill the social roles in which society needs them. They are trained to model themselves after the accepted image and to meet as individuals the expectations that are held for women as a group. Therefore, to understand how most women are socialized we must first understand how they see themselves and are seen by others. Several studies have been done on this.

One thorough study asked men and women to choose out of a long list of adjectives those that most closely applied to themselves. The results showed that women strongly felt that they could accurately be described as uncertain, anxious, nervous, hasty, careless, fearful, dull, childish, helpless, sorry, timid, clumsy, stupid, silly and domestic. On the more positive side women felt they were understanding, tender, sympathetic, pure, generous, affectionate, loving, moral, kind, grateful and patient. This is not a very favorable self-image, but it does correspond fairly well to the myths about what women are like. The image has some "nice" qualities, but they are not the ones normally required for the kinds of achievement to which society gives its highest rewards.

Gross Distortions

Now, one can justifiably question both the idea of achievement and the qualities necessary for it, but this is not the place to do so. The fact remains that these standards are widely accepted and that women have been told they do not meet them. My purpose here, then, is to look at the socialization process as a mechanism to keep them from doing so. All people are socialized to meet the social expectations held for them, and only when this process fails to work (as is currently happening on several fronts) is it at all questioned.

When we look at the *results* of female socialization we find a strong similarity between what our society labels, even extols, as the typical "feminine" character structure and that of oppressed peoples in this country and elsewhere. In his classic study on *The Nature of Prejudice*, Gordon Allport devotes a chapter to "Traits Due to Victimization." Included are such personality characteristics as sensitivity, submission, fantasies of power, desire for protection, indirectness, ingratiation, petty revenge and sabotage, sympathy, extremes of both self and group hatred and self and group glorification, display of flashy status symbols, compassion for the underprivileged, identification with the dominant group's norms and passivity. Allport was primarily concerned with Jews and Negroes, but his characterization is disturbingly congruent with the general profile of girls that Lewis Terman and Leona Tyler draw after a very thorough review of the literature on sex differences among young children. For girls, they listed such traits as sensitivity, conformity to social pressures, response to environment, ease of social control, ingratiation, sympathy, low levels of aspiration, compassion for the underprivileged and anxiety. They found that girls compared to boys were more nervous, unstable, neurotic, socially dependent, submissive, had less self-confidence, lower opinions of themselves and of girls in general, and were more timid, emotional, ministrative, fearful and passive.

Girls' perceptions of themselves were also distorted. Although girls make consistently better school grades than boys until late high school, their opinion of themselves grows progressively worse with age and their opinion of boys and boys' abilities grows better. Boys, however, have an increasingly better opinion of themselves and worse opinion of girls as they grow older.

These distortions become so gross that, according to Phillip Goldberg in an article in this magazine, by the time girls reach college they have become prejudiced against women. He gave college girls sets of booklets containing six identical professional articles in traditional male, female and neutral fields. The articles were identical, but the names of the authors were not. For example, an article in one set would bear the name John T. McKay, and in another set the same article would be by-lined Joan T. McKay. Each booklet contained three articles by "women" and three by "men." Questions at the end of each article asked the students to rate the articles on value, persuasiveness and profundity and the authors for style and competence. The male authors fared better on every dimension, even such "feminine" areas as art history and dietetics. Goldberg concluded that "women are prejudiced against female professionals and, regardless of the actual accomplishments of these professionals, will firmly refuse to recognize them as the equals of their male colleagues."

This combination of group self-hate and a distortion of perceptions to justify that group self-hate is precisely typical of a minority group character structure. It has been noted time and time again. Kenneth and Mamie Clark's finding of the same pattern in Negro children in segregated schools contributed to the 1954 Supreme Court decision that outlawed such schools. These traits, as well as the others typical of the "feminine" stereotype, have been found in the Indians under British rule, in the Algerians under the French and in black Americans. It would seem, then, that being "feminine" is related to low social status.

This pattern repeats itself even within cultures. In giving Thematic Apperception Tests to women in Japanese villages, George De Vos discovered that those from fishing villages, where the status position of women was higher than in farming communities, were more assertive, not as guilt-ridden and were more willing to ignore the traditional pattern of arranged marriages in favor of love marriages.

In Terman's famous 50-year study of the gifted, a comparison of those men who conspicuously failed to fulfill their early promise with those who did, showed that the successful had more self-confidence, fewer background disabilities and were less nervous and emotionally unstable. But, he concluded, "the disadvantages associated with lower social home status appeared to present the outstanding handicap."

Sexual Characteristics

The fact that women do have lower social status than men in our society and that both sexes tend to value men, and male characteristics, values and activities more highly than those of women, has been noted by many authorities. What has not been done is to make the connection between this status and its accompanying personality. The failure to analyze the effects and the causes of lower social status among women is surprising in light of the many efforts that have been made to uncover distinct psychological differences between men and women to account for the tremendous disparity in their social production and creativity. The Goldberg study implies that even if women did achieve on a par with men it would not be perceived or accepted as such and that a woman's work must be of a much higher quality than that of a man to be given the same recognition. But these circumstances alone, or the fact that it is the male definition of achievement which is applied, are not sufficient to account for the relative failure of women to achieve. So research has turned to male-female differences.

Most of this research, in the Freudian tradition, has focused on finding the psychological and developmental differences supposedly inherent in feminine nature and function. Despite all these efforts, the general findings of psychological testing indicate only that individual differences are greater than sex differences. In other words, sex is just one of the many characteristics that define a human being.

An examination of the work done on intellectual differences between the sexes discloses some interesting patterns, however. First of all, the statistics themselves show some regularity. Most conclusions of what is typical of one sex or the other are founded upon the performances of two-thirds of the subjects. For example, two-thirds of all boys do better on the math section of the College Board Exam than they do on the verbal section, and two-thirds of the girls do better on the verbal than the math. Robert Bales' studies show a similar distribution when he concludes that in small groups men are the task-oriented leaders and women are the social-emotional leaders. Not all tests show this two-thirds differential, but it is the mean about which most results of the ability tests cluster. Sex is an easily visible, differentiable and testable criterion on which to draw conclusions; but it doesn't explain the one-third that do not fit. The only characteristic virtually all women seem to have in common, besides their anatomy, is their lower social status.

Secondly, girls get off to a very good start. They begin speaking, reading and counting sooner. They articulate more clearly and put words into sentences earlier. They have fewer reading and stuttering problems. Girls are even better in math in the early school years. Consistent sex differences in favor of boys do not appear until high school age. Here another pattern begins to develop.

During high school, girls' performance in school and on ability tests begins to drop, sometimes drastically. Although well over half of all high-school graduates are girls, significantly less than half of all college students are girls. Presumably, this should mean that a higher percentage of the better female students go on to higher education, but their performance vis-a-vis boys' continues to decline.

Only Men Excel

Girls start off better than boys and end up worse. This change in their performance occurs at a very significant point in time. It happens when their status changes or, to be more precise, when girls become aware of what their adult status is supposed to be. It is during adolescence that peer group pressures to be "feminine" or "masculine" increase and the conceptions of what is "feminine" and "masculine" become more narrow. It is also at this time that there is a personal drive for conformity. And one of the norms of our culture to which a girl learns to conform is that only men excel. This was evident in Beatrice Lipinski's study on *Sex-Role Conflict and Achievement Motivation in College Women* which showed that thematic pictures depicting males as central characters elicited significantly more achievement imagery than those with females in them. One need only recall Asch's experiments to see how peer group pressures, armed only with our rigid ideas about "feminity" and "masculinity" could lead to a decline in girls' performance. Asch found that some 33 percent of his subjects would go contrary to the evidence of their own senses about something as tangible as the comparative length of two lines when their judgements were at variance with those made by the other group members. All but a handful of the other 67 percent experienced tremendous trauma in trying to stick to their correct perceptions.

When we move to something as intangible as sex role behavior and to social sanctions far greater than the displeasure of a group of unknown experimental stooges we can get an idea of how stifling social expectations can be. A corollary of the notion that only men can excel is the cultural norm that a girl should not appear too smart or surpass boys in anything. Again, the pressures to conform, so prevalent in adolescence, prompt girls to believe that the development of their minds will have only negative results. These pressures even affect the supposedly unchangeable IQ scores. Corresponding with the drive for social acceptance, girls' IQs drop below those of boys during high school, rise slightly if they go to college and go into a steady and consistent decline when and if they become full-time housewives.

These are not the only consequences. Negative self-conceptions have negative effects. They stifle motivation and channel energies into areas more likely to get some positive social rewards. The clincher comes when the very people (women) who have been subjected to these pressures are condemned for not having striven for the highest rewards society has to offer.

A good example of this double bind is what psychologists call the "need for achievement." Achievement motivation in male college sophomores has been studied extensively. In women it has barely been looked at. The reason for this is that women didn't fit the model social scientists set up to explain achievement in men. Nonetheless, some theories have been put forward which suggest that the real situation is not that women do not have achievement motivation but that this motivation is directed differently than that of men. In fact, the achievement orientation of both sexes goes precisely where it is socially directed—educational achievement for boys and marriage achievement for girls.

After considerable research on the question James Pierce concluded that "girls see that to achieve in life as adult

females they need to achieve in non-academic ways, that is, attaining the social graces, achieving beauty in person and dress, finding a desirable social status, marrying the right man. This is the successful adult woman . . . Their achievement motivations are directed toward realizing personal goals through their relationship with men . . . Girls who are following the normal course of development are most likely to seek adult status through marriage at an early age."

Achievement for women is adult status through marriage, not success in the usual use of the word. One might postulate that both kinds of success might be possible, particularly for the highly achievement-oriented woman. But in fact the two are more often perceived as contradictory; success in one is seen to preclude success in the other.

Matina Horner recently completed a study at the University of Michigan from which she postulated a psychological barrier to achievement in women. She administered a test in which she asked undergraduates to complete the sentence, "After first term finals Anne finds herself at the top of her medical school class," with a story of their own. A similar one for a male control group used a masculine name. The results were scored for imagery of fear of success and

Horner found that 65 percent of the women and only 10 percent of the men demonstrated a definite "motive to avoid success." She explained the results by hypothesizing that the prospect of success, or situations in which success or failure is a relevant dimension, are perceived as, and in fact do, have negative consequences for women.

While many of the choices and attitudes of woman are determined by peer and cultural pressures, many other sex differences appear too early to be much affected by peer groups and are not directly related to sex role attributes.

Analytic Children

One such sex difference is spatial perception, or the ability to visualize objects out of their context. This is a test in which boys do better, though differences are usually not discernible before the early school years. Other tests, such as the Embedded Figures and the Rod and Frame Tests, likewise favor boys. They indicate that boys perceive more analytically while girls are more contextual. Again, however, this ability to "break set" or be "field independent" also does not seem to appear until after the fourth or fifth year.

According to Eleanor Maccoby, this contextual mode of perception common to women is a distinct disadvantage for scientific production: "Girls on the average develop a somewhat different way of handling incoming information—their thinking is less analytic, more global, and more perservative[sic]—and this kind of thinking may serve very well for many kinds of functioning but it is not the kind of thinking most conducive to high-level intellectual productivity, especially in science."

Several social psychologists have postulated that the key developmental characteristic of analytic thinking is what is called early "independence and mastery training," or as one group of researchers put it, "whether and how soon a child is encouraged to assume initiative, to take responsibility for himself, and to solve problems by himself, rather than rely on others for the direction of his activities." In other words, analytically inclined children are those who have not been subject to what Urie Bronfenbrenner calls "oversocialization," and there is a good deal of indirect evidence that such is the case. D.M. Levy has observed that "overprotected" boys tend to develop intellectually like girls. Bing found that those girls who were good at spatial tasks were those whose mothers left them alone to solve the problems by themselves while the mothers of verbally inclined daughters insisted on helping them. H.A. Witkin similarly found that mothers of analytic children had encouraged their initiative while mothers of nonanalytic children had encouraged dependence and discouraged self-assertion. One writer commented on these studies that "this is to be expected, for the independent child is less likely to accept superficial appearances of objects without exploring them for himself, while the dependent child will be afraid to reach out on his own, and will accept appearances without question. In other words, the independent child is likely to be more active, not only psychologically but physically, and the physically active child will naturally have more kinesthetic experience with spatial relationships in his environment."

The qualities associated with independence training also have an effect on IQ. I.W. Sontag did a longitudinal study in which he compared children whose IQs had improved with those whose IQs had declined with age. He discovered that the child with increasing IQ was competitive, self-assertive, independent and dominant in interaction with other children. Children with declining IQs were passive, shy and dependent.

Maccoby commented on this study that "the characteristics associated with a rising IQ are not very feminine characteristics." When one of the people working on the Sontag study was asked about what kind of developmental history was necessary to make a girl into an intellectual person, he replied, "The simplest way to put it is that she must be a tomboy at some point in her childhood."

However, analytic abilities are not the only ones that are valued in our society. Being person-oriented and contextual in perception are very valuable attributes for many fields where, nevertheless, very few women are found. Such characteristics are also valuable in the arts and some of the social sciences. But while women do succeed here more than in the sciences, their achievement is still not equivalent to that of men. One explanation of this, of course, is the study by Horner which established a "motive to avoid success" among women. But when one looks further it appears that there is an earlier cause here as well.

Sons and Daughters

The very same early independence and mastery training which has such a beneficial effect on analytic thinking also determines the extent of one's achievement orientation. Although comparative studies of parental treatment of boys and girls are not extensive, those that have been made indicate that the traditional practices applied to girls are very different from those applied to boys. Girls receive more affection, more protectiveness, more control and more restrictions. Boys are subjected to more achievement demands and higher expectations. In short, while girls are not always encouraged to be dependent per se, they are usually not encouraged to be independent and physically active. As Bronfenbrenner put it, "Such findings indicate that the differential treatment of the two sexes reflects in part a difference in goals. With sons, socialization seems to focus primarily on directing and constraining the boys' impact on the environment. With daughters, the aim is rather to protect the girl from the impact of environment. The boy is being prepared to mold his world, the girl to be molded by it."

Bronfenbrenner concludes that the crucial variable is the differential treatment by the father, and "in fact, it is the father who is especially likely to treat children of the two sexes differently." His extremes of affection and of authority are both deleterious. Not only do his high degrees of nurturance and protectiveness toward girls result in "oversocialization" but "the presence of strong paternal . . . power, is particularly debilitating. In short, boys thrive in a patriarchal context, girls in a matriarchal one."

Bronfenbrenner's observations receive indirect support from Elizabeth Douvan who noted that "part-time jobs of mothers have a beneficial effect on adolescent children, particularly daughters. This reflects the fact that adolescents may receive too much mothering."

Anxiety

The importance of mothers, as well as mothering, was pointed out by Kagan and Moss. In looking at the kinds of role models that mothers provide for developing daughters, they discovered that it is those women who are looked upon as unfeminine whose daughters tend to achieve intellectually. These mothers are "aggressive and competitive women who were critical of their daughters and presented themselves to their daughters as intellectually competitive and aggressive role models. It is reasonable to assume that the girls identified with these intellectually aggressive women who valued mastery behavior."

To sum up, there seems to be some evidence that the sexes have been differentially socialized with different training practices, for different goals and with different results. If David McClelland is right in all the relationships he finds between child-rearing practices, in particular independence and mastery training, achievement motivations scores of individuals tested, actual achievement of individuals and, indeed, the economic growth of whole societies, there is no longer much question as to why the historical achievement of women has been so low. In fact, with the dependency training they receive so early in life, the wonder is that they have achieved so much.

But this is not the whole story. Maccoby, in her discussion of the relationship of independence training to analytic abilities, notes that the girl who does not succumb to overprotection and develop the appropriate personality and behavior for her sex has a major price to pay—a price in anxiety. Some anxiety is beneficial to creative thinking, but high or sustained levels of it are damaging. Anxiety is particularly manifest in college women, and of course they are the ones who experience the most conflict between their current—intellectual—activities and expectations about their future—unintellectual—careers.

Maccoby feels that "it is this anxiety which helps to account for the lack of productivity among those women who do make intellectual careers." The combination of social pressures, role expectations and parental training together tells "something of a horror story. It would appear that even when a woman is suitably endowed intellectually and develops the right temperament and habits of thought to make use of her endowment, she must be fleet of foot indeed to scale the hurdles society has erected for her and to remain a whole and happy person while continuing to follow her intellectual bent."

The reasons for this horror story must by now be clearly evident. Traditionally, women have been defined as passive creatures, sexually, physically and mentally. Their roles have been limited to the passive, dependent, auxiliary ones, and they have been trained from birth to fit these roles. However, those qualities by which one succeeds in this society are active ones. Achievement orientation, intellectuality, analytic ability all require a certain amount of aggression.

As long as women were convinced that these qualities were beyond them, that they would be much happier if they stayed in their place, they remained quiescent under the paternalistic system of Western civilization. But paternalism was a pre-industrial scheme of life, and its yoke was partially broken by the industrial revolution. With this loosening up of the social order, the talents of women began to appear.

In the eighteenth century it was held that no woman had ever produced anything worthwhile in literature with the possible exception of Sappho. But in the first half of the nineteenth century, feminine writers of genius flooded the literary scene. It wasn't until the end of the nineteenth century that women scientists of note appeared and still later that women philosophers were found.

Lords at Home

In pre-industrial societies, the family was the basic unit of social and economic organization, and women held a significant and functional role within it. This, coupled with the high birth and death rates of those times, gave women more than enough to do within the home. It was the center of production, and women could be both at home and in the world at the same time. But the industrial revolution, along with decreased infant mortality, increased life span and changes in economic organization, has all but destroyed the family as the economic unit. Technological advances have taken men out of the home, and now those functions traditionally defined as female are being taken out also. For the first time in human history women have had to devote themselves to being full-time mothers in order to have enough to do.

Conceptions of society have also changed. At one time, authoritiarian hierarchies were the norm, and paternalism was reflective of a general social authoritarian attitude. While it is impossible to do retroactive studies on feudalistic society, we do know that authoritarianism as a personality trait does correlate strongly with a rigid conception of sex roles, and with ethnocentrism. We also know from ethnological data that, As W.N. Stephens wrote, there is a "parallel between family relationships and the larger social hierarchy. Autocratic societies have autocratic families. As the king rules his subjects and the nobles subjugate and exploit the commoners, so does husband tend to lord it over wife, father rule over son."

According to Roy D'Andrade, "another variable that appears to affect the distribution of authority and deference between the sexes is the degree to which men rather than women control and mediate property." He presented evidence that showed a direct correlation between the extent to which inheritance, succession and descent-group membership were patrilineal and the degree of subjection of women.

Even today, the equality of the sexes in the family is often reflective of the economic quality of the partners. In a Detroit sample, Robert Blood and D.M. Wolfe found that the relative power of the wife was low if she did not work and increased with her economic contribution to the family. "The employment of women affects the power structure of the family by equalizing the resources of husband and wife. A working wife's husband listens to her more, and she listens to herself more. She expresses herself and has more opinions. Instead of looking up into her husband's eyes and worshipping him, she levels with him, compromising on the issues at hand. Thus her power increases and, relatively speaking, the husband's falls."

William J. Goode also noted this pattern but said it varied inversely with class status. Toward the upper strata wives are not only less likely to work but when they do they contribute a smaller percentage of the total family income than is true in the lower classes. Reuben Hill went so far as to say "Money is a source of power that supports male dominance in the family . . . Money belongs to him who earns it not to her who spends it, since he who earns it may withhold it." Phyllis Hallenbeck feels more than just economic resources are involved but does conclude that there is a balance of power in every family which affects "every other aspect of the marriage—division of labor, amount of adaptation necessary for either spouse, methods used to resolve conflicts, and so forth." Blood feels the economic situation affects the whole family structure. "Daughters of working mothers are more independent, more self-reliant, more aggressive, more dominant, and more disobedient. Such girls are no longer meek, mild, submissive, and feminine like 'little ladies' ought to be. They are rough and tough, actively express their ideas, and refuse to take anything from anybody else . . . Because their mothers have set an example, the daughters get up the courage and the desire to earn money as well. They take more part-time jobs after school and more jobs during summer vacation."

Sex and Work

Herbert Barry, M.K. Bacon and Irvin Child did an ethnohistoriographic analysis which provides some further insights into the origins of male dominance. After examining the ethnographic reports of 110 cultures, they concluded that large sexual differentiation and male superiority occur concurrently and in "an economy that places a high premium on the superior strength and superior development of motor skills requiring strength, which characterize the male." It is those societies in which great physical strength and mobility are required for survival, in which hunting and herding, or warfare, play an important role, that the male, as the physically stronger and more mobile sex, tends to dominate.

Although there are a few tasks which virtually every society assigns only to men or women, there is a great deal of overlap for most jobs. Virtually every task, even in the most primitive societies, can be performed by either men or women. Equally important, what is defined as a man's task in one society may well be classified as a woman's job in another. Nonetheless, the sexual division of labor is much more narrow than dictated by physical limitations, and what any one culture defines as a woman's job will seldom be performed by a man and vice versa. It seems that what originated as a division of labor based upon the necessities of survival has spilled over into many other areas and lasted long past the time of its social value. Where male strength and mobility have been crucial to social survival, male dominance and the aura of male superiority have been the strongest. The latter has been incorporated into the value structure and attained an existence of its own.

Thus, male superiority has not ceased with an end to the need for male strength. As Goode pointed out, there is one consistent element in the assignment of jobs to the sexes, even in modern societies: "Whatever the strictly male tasks are, they are defined as *more honorific* [emphasis his] . . .Moreover, the tasks of control, management, decision, appeals to the gods—in short the higher level jobs that typically do not require strength, speed or traveling far from home—are male jobs."

He goes on to comment that "this element suggests that the sexual divisions of labor within family and society, come perilously close to the racial or caste restrictions in some modern countries. That is, the low-ranking race, caste, or sex is defined as not being able to do certain types of prestigious work, but it is also considered a violation of propriety if they do. Obviously, if women really cannot do various kinds of male tasks, no moral or ethical prohibition would be necessary to keep them from it."

Companionship

These sex role differences may have served a natural function at one time, but it is doubtful that they still do so. The characteristics we observe in women and men today are a result of socialization practices developed for the survival of a primitive society. The value structure of male superiority is a reflection of the primitive orientations and values. But social and economic conditions have changed drastically since these values were developed. Technology has reduced to almost nothing the importance of muscular strength. In fact, the warlike attitude that goes along with an idealization of physical strength and dominance is coming to be seen as dreadfully dangerous. The value of large families has also come to be questioned. The result of all these changes is that the traditional sex roles and the traditional family structures have become dysfunctional.

To some extent, patterns of child rearing have also changed. Bronfenbrenner reports that at least middle-class parents are raising both boys and girls much the same. He noted that over a 50-year period middle-class parents have been developing a "more acceptant, equalitarian relationship with their children." With an increase in the family's social position, the patterns of parental treatment of children begin to converge. He likewise noted that a similar phenomenon is beginning to develop in lower-class parents and that equality of treatment is slowly working its way down the social ladder.

These changes in patterns of child rearing correlate with changes in relationships within the family. Both are moving toward a less hierarchical and more egalitarian pattern of living. As Blood has pointed out, "today we may be on the verge of a new phase in American family history, when the companionship family is beginning to manifest itself. One distinguishing characteristic of this family is the dual employment of husband and wife . . . Employment emancipates women from domination by their husbands and, secondarily, raises their daughters from inferiority to their brothers . . . The classic differences between masculinity and femininity are disappearing as both sexes in the adult generation take on the same roles in the labor market . . . The roles of men and women are converging for both adults and children. As a result the family will be far less segregated internally, far less stratified into different age generations and different sexes. The old asymmetry of male dominated, female-serviced family life is being replaced by a new symmetry."

Leftover Definitions

All these data indicate that several trends are converging at about the same time. Our value structure has changed from an authoritarian one to a more democratic one, though our social structure has not yet caught up. Social attitudes begin in the family; only a democratic family can raise children to be citizens in a democratic society. The social and economic organization of society which kept women in the home has likewise changed. The home is no longer the center of society. The primary male and female functions have left it, and there is no longer any major reason for maintaining the large sex role differentiations that the home supported. The value placed on physical strength, which reinforced the dominance of men, and the male superiority attitudes that this generated have also become dysfunctional. It is the mind, not the body, that society needs now, and woman's mind is the equal of man's. The pill has liberated women from the uncertainty of childbearing, and with it the necessity of being attached to a man for economic support. But our attitudes toward women, and toward the family, have not changed. There is a distinct "cultural lag." Definitions of the family, conceptions of women and ideas about social function are left over from an era when they were necessary for social survival. They have persisted into an era in which they are no longer viable. The result can only be called severe role dysfunctionality for women.

The necessary relief for this dysfunctionality must come through changes in the social and economic organization of society and in social attitudes that will permit women to play a full and equal part in the social order. With this must come changes in the family, so that men and women are not only equal but can raise their children in a democratic atmosphere. These changes will not come easily, nor will they come through the simple evolution of social trends. Trends do not move all in the same direction or at the same rate. To the extent that changes are dysfunctional with each other they create problems. These problems will be solved not by complacency but by conscious human direction. Only in this way can we have a real say in the shape of our future and the shape of our lives.

This article is taken from *Roles Women Play: Readings Towards Women's Liberation*, edited by Michele Hoffnung Garskof, Monterey, Calif.: Brooks/Cole Publishing Co., 1971.

FURTHER READING

Roles Women Play: Readings Toward Women's Liberation edited by Michelle Garskof (Monterey, Calif.: Brooks-Cole, 1971).

"Current Patterns in Sex Roles: Children's Perceptives" by Ruth E. Hartley, *Journal of the National Association of Women Deans and Counselors*, 25 (October 1961): 3–13.

"Sex-Role Identification' A Symposium" by Ruth E. Hartley, *Merrill-Palmer Quarterly* 10 (1964):3–16.

Women in a Man-Made World edited by Nona Glazer Malbin and Helen Youngelson Waehrer (Skokie, Ill.:Rand McNally, 1972).

Men in Groups by Lionel Tiger (New York: Random House, 1969). A controversial interpretation of sex roles and male bonding from an evolutionary perspective.

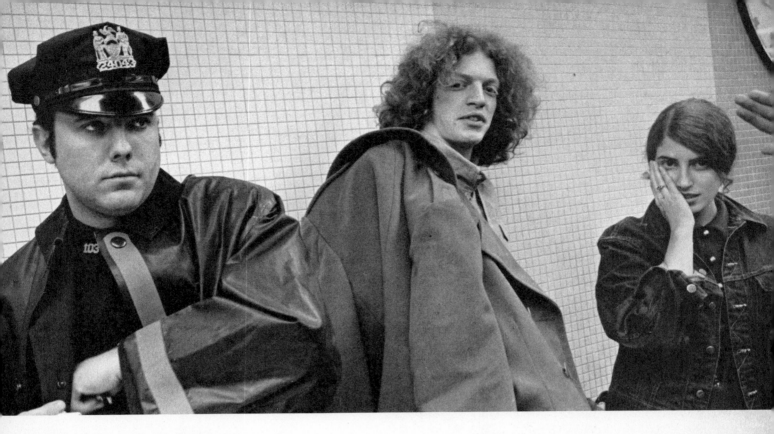

MICHAEL E. BROWN

The Condemnation and Persecution of Hippies

This article is about persecution and terror. It speaks of the Hippie and the temptations of intimacy that the myth of Hippie has made poignant, and it does this to discuss the institutionalization of repression in the United States.

When people are attacked as a group, they change. Individuals in the group may or may not change, but the organization and expression of their collective life will be transformed. When the members of a gathering believe that there is a grave danger imminent and that opportunities for escape are rapidly diminishing, the group loses its organizational quality. It becomes transformed in panic. This type of change can also occur outside a situation of strict urgency: When opportunities for mobility or access to needed resources are cut off, people may engage in desperate collective actions. In both cases, the conversion of social form occurs when members of a collectivity are about to be hopelessly locked into undesired and undesirable positions.

The process is not, however, automatic. The essential ingredient for conversion is social control exercised by external agents on the collectivity itself. The result can be.

benign, as a panic mob can be converted into a crowd that makes an orderly exit from danger. Or it can be cruel.

The transformation of groups under pressure is of general interest; but there are special cases that are morally critical to any epoch. Such critical cases occur when pressure is persecution, and transformation is destruction. The growth of repressive mechanisms and institutions is a key concern in this time of administrative cruelty. Such is the justification for the present study.

Social Control as Terror

Four aspects of repressive social control such as that experienced by Hippies are important. First, the administration of control is suspicious. It projects a dangerous future and guards against it. It also refuses the risk of inadequate coverage by enlarging the controlled population to include all who might be active in any capacity. Control may or may not be administered with a heavy hand, but it is always a generalization applied to specific instances. It is a rule and thus ends by pulling many fringe innocents into its bailiwick; it creates as it destroys.

Second, the administration of control is a technical problem which, depending on its site and object, requires the bringing together of many different agencies that are ordinarily dissociated or mutually hostile. A conglomerate of educational, legal, social welfare, and police organizations is highly efficient. The German case demonstrates that. Even more important, it is virtually impossible to oppose control administered under the auspices of such a conglomerate since it includes the countervailing institutions ordinarily available. When this happens control is not only efficient and widespread, but also legitimate, commanding a practical, moral and ideological realm that is truly "one-dimensional."

Third, as time passes, control is applied to a wider and wider range of details, ultimately blanketing its objects' lives. At that point, as Hilberg suggests in his *The Destruction of the European Jews,* the extermination of the forms of lives leads easily to the extermination of the lives themselves. The line between persecution and terror is thin. For the oppressed, life is purged of personal style as every act becomes inexpressive, part of the strug-

Changing Life-Styles

gle for survival. The options of a life-style are eliminated at the same time that its proponents are locked into it.

Fourth, control is relentless. It develops momentum as organization accumulates, as audiences develop, and as unofficial collaborators assume the definition of tasks, expression and ideology. This, according to W. A. Westley's "The Escalation of Violence Through Legitimation," is the culture of control. It not only limits the be-

haviors, styles, individuals and groups toward whom it is directed, it suppresses all unsanctioned efforts. As struggle itself is destroyed, motivation vanishes or is turned inward.

These are the effects of repressive control. We may contrast them with the criminal law, which merely prohibits the performance of specific acts (with the exception, of course, of the "crime without victims"—homosexuality, abortion, and drug use). Repres-

sion converts or destroys an entire social form, whether that form is embodied in a group, a style or an idea. In this sense, it is terror.

These general principles are especially relevant to our understanding of tendencies that are ripening in the United States day by day. Stated in terms that magnify it so that it can be seen despite ourselves, this is the persecution of the Hippies, a particularly vulnerable group of people who are the cultural wing of a way of life recently emerged from its quiet and individualistic quarters. Theodore Roszak, describing the Hippies in terms of their relationship to the culture and politics of dissent, notes that "the underlying unity of youthful dissent consists . . . in the effort of beat-hip bohemianism to work out the personality structure, the total life-style that follows from New Left social criticism." This life-style is currently bearing the brunt of the assault on what Roszak calls a "counter-culture"; it is an assault that is becoming more concentrated and savage every day. There are lessons for the American future to be drawn from this story.

Persecution

Near Boulder, Colorado, a restaurant sign says "Hippies not served here." Large billboards in upstate New York carry slogans like "Keep America Clean: Take a Bath." and "Keep America Clean: Get a Haircut." These would be as amusing as ethnic jokes if they did not represent a more systematic repression.

The street sweeps so common in San Francisco and Berkeley in 1968 and 1969 were one of the first lines of attack. People were brutally scattered by club-wielding policemen who first closed exits from the assaulted area and then began systematically to beat and arrest those who were trapped. This form of place terror, like surveillance in Negro areas and defoliation in Vietnam, curbs freedom and forces people to fight or submit to minute inspection by hostile forces. There have also been one-shot neighborhood pogroms, such as the police assault on the Tompkins Square Park gathering in New York's Lower East Side on Memorial Day, 1967: "Sadistic glee was written on the faces of several officers," wrote the *East Village Other*. Some women became hysterical. The police slugged Frank Wise, and dragged him off, handcuffed and bloody, crying, "My God, my God, where is this happening? Is this America?" The police also plowed into a group of Hippies, Yippies, and straights at the April, 1968, "Yip-in" at Grand Central Station. The brutality was as clear in this action as it had been in the Tompkins Square bust. In both cases, the major newspapers editorialized against the police tactics, and in the first the Mayor apologized for the "free wielding of nightsticks." But by the summer of 1968, street sweeps and busts and the continuous presence of New York's Tactical Police Force had given the Lower East Side an ominous atmosphere. Arrests were regularly accompanied by beatings and charges of "resistance to arrest." It became clear that arrests rather than subsequent procedures were the way in which control was to be exercised. The summer lost its street theaters, the relaxed circulation of people in the neighborhood and the easy park gatherings.

Official action legitimizes nonofficial action. Private citizens take up the cudgel of law and order newly freed from the boundaries of due process and respect. After Tompkins Square, rapes and assaults became common as local toughs

assumed the role, with the police, of defender of the faith. In Cambridge, Massachusetts, following a virulent attack on Hippies by the Mayor, *Newsweek* reported that vigilantes attacked Hippie neighborhoods in force.

Ultimately more damaging are the attacks on centers of security. Police raids on "Hippie pads," crash pads, churches and movement centers have become daily occurrences in New York and California over the past two and a half years. The usual excuses for raids are drugs, runaways and housing violations, but many incidents of unlawful entry by police and the expressions of a more generalized hostility by the responsible officials suggests that something deeper is involved. The Chief of Police in San Francisco put it bluntly; quoted in *The New York Times* magazine in May, 1967, he said:

Hippies are no asset to the community. These people do not have the courage to face the reality of life. They are trying to escape. Nobody should let their young children take part in this hippy thing.

The Director of Health for San Francisco gave teeth to this counsel when he sent a task force of inspectors on a door-to-door sweep of the Haight-Ashbury—"a two-day blitz" that ended with a strange result, again according to *The Times:* Very few of the Hippies were guilty of housing violations.

Harassment arrests and calculated degradation have been two of the most effective devices for introducing uncertainty to the day-to-day lives of the Hippies. Cambridge's Mayor's attack on the "hipbos" (the suffix stands for body odor) included, said *Newsweek* of Oct. 30, 1967, a raid on a "hippie pad" by the Mayor and "a platoon of television cameramen." They "seized a pile of diaries and personal letters and flushed a partially clad girl from the closet." In Wyoming, *The Times* reported that two "pacifists" were "jailed and shaved" for hitchhiking. This is a fairly common hazard, though Wyoming officials are perhaps more sadistic than most. A young couple whom I interviewed were also arrested in Wyoming during the summer of 1968. They were placed in solitary confinement for a week during which they were not permitted to place phone calls and were not told when or whether they would be charged or released. These are not exceptional cases. During the summer of 1968, I interviewed young hitchhikers throughout the country; most of them had similar stories to tell.

In the East Village of New York, one hears countless stories of apartment destruction by police (occasionally reported in the newspapers), insults from the police when rapes or robberies are reported, and cruel speeches and even crueler bails set by judges for arrested Hippies.

In the light of this, San Francisco writer Mark Harris' indictment of the Hippies as paranoid seems peculiar. In the September 1967 issue of *The Atlantic,* he wrote,

The most obvious failure of perception was the hippies' failure to discriminate among elements of the Establishment, whether in the Haight-Ashbury or in San Francisco in general. Their paranoia was the paranoia of all youthful heretics. . . .

This is like the demand of some white liberals that Negroes acknowledge that they (the liberals) are not the power structure, or that black people must distinguish between the good and the bad whites despite the fact that the black experience of white people in the United States has been, as the President's Commission on Civil Disorder suggested, fairly monolithic and racist.

Most journalists reviewing the "Hippie scene" with any sympathy at all seem to agree with *Newsweek* that "the hippies do seem natural prey for publicity-hungry politicians—if not overzealous police," and that they have been subjected to varieties of cruelty that ought to be intolerable. This tactic was later elaborated in the massive para-military assault on Berkeley residents and students during a demonstration in support of Telegraph Avenue's street people and their People's Park. The terror of police violence, a constant in the lives of street people everywhere, in California carries the additional threat of martial law under a still-active state of extreme emergency. The whole structure of repression was given legitimacy and reluctant support by University of California officials. Step by step, they became allies of Reagan's "dogs of war." Roger W. Heyns, chancellor of the Berkeley campus, found himself belatedly reasserting the university's property in the lot. It was the law and the rights of university that trapped the chancellor in the network of control and performed the vital function of providing justification and legitimacy for Sheriff Madigan and the National Guard. Heyns said: "We will have to put up a fence to re-establish the conveniently forgotten fact that this field is indeed the university's, and to exclude unauthorized personnel from the site. . . . The fence will give us time to plan and consult. We tried to get this time some other way and failed—hence the fence." And hence "Bloody Thursday" and the new regime.

And what of the Hippies? They have come far since those balmy days of 1966-67, days of flowers, street-cleaning, free stores, decoration and love. Many have fled to the hills of Northern California to join their brethren who had set up camps there several years ago. Others have fled to communes outside the large cities and in the Middle West. After the Tompkins Square assault, many of the East Village Hippies refused to follow the lead of those who were more political. They refused to develop organizations of defense and to accept a hostile relationship with the police and neighborhood. Instead, they discussed at meeting after meeting, how they could show their attackers love. Many of those spirits have fled; others have been beaten or jailed too many times; and still others have modified their outlook in ways that reflect the struggle. Guerrilla theater, Up Against the Wall Mother Fucker, the Yippies, the urban communes; these are some of the more recent manifestations of the alternative culture. One could

see these trends growing in the demonstrations mounted by Hippies against arrests of runaways or pot smokers, the community organizations, such as grew in Berkeley for self-defense and politics, and the beginnings of the will to fight back when trapped in street sweeps.

It is my impression that the Hippie culture is growing as it recedes from the eye of the media. As a consequence of the destruction of their urban places, there has been a redistribution of types. The flower people have left for the hills and become more communal; those who remained in the city were better adapted to terror, secretive or confrontative. The Hippie culture is one of the forms radicalism can take in this society. The youngsters, 5,000 of them, who came to Washington to counter-demonstrate against the Nixon inaugural showed the growing amalgamation of the New Left and its cultural wing. The Yippies who went to Chicago for guerrilla theater and learned about "pigs" were the multi-generational expression of the new wave. A UAWMF (Up Against the Wall Mother Fucker) drama, played at Lincoln Center during the New York City garbage strike—they carted garbage from the neglected Lower East Side and dumped it at the spic 'n' span cultural center—reflected another interpretation of the struggle, one that could include the politically militant as well as the culturally defiant. Many Hippies have gone underground—in an older sense of the word. They have shaved their beards, cut their hair, and taken straight jobs, like the secret Jews of Spain; but unlike those Jews, they are consciously an underground, a resistance.

What is most interesting and, I believe, a direct effect of the persecution, is the enormous divergence of forms that are still recognizable by the outsider as Hippie and are still experienced as a shared identity. "The Yippies," says Abbie Hoffman, "are like Hippies, only fiercer and more fun." The "hippie types" described in newspaper accounts of drug raids on colleges turn out, in many cases, to be New Leftists.

The dimensions by which these various forms are classified are quite conventional: religious-political, visible-secret, urban-hill, communal-individualistic. As their struggle intensifies, there will be more efforts for unity and more militant approaches to the society that gave birth to a real alternative only to turn against it with a mindless savagery. Yippie leader Jerry Rubin, in an "emergency letter to my brothers and sisters in the movement" summed up:

Huey Newton is in prison.

Eldridge Cleaver is in exile.

Oakland Seven are accused of conspiracy.

Tim Leary is up for 30 years and how many of our brothers are in court and jail for getting high?

. . .

Camp activists are expelled and arrested.

War resisters are behind bars.

Add it up!

Rubin preambles his summary with:

From the Bay Area to New York, we are suffering the greatest depression in our history. People are taking bitterness in their coffee instead of sugar. The hippie-yippie-SDS movement is a "white nigger" movement. The American economy no longer needs young whites and blacks. We are waste material. We fulfill our destiny in life by rejecting a system which rejects us.

He advocates organizing "massive mobilizations for the spring, nationally coordinated and very theatrical, taking place near courts, jails, and military stockades."

An article published in a Black Panther magazine is entitled "The Hippies Are Not Our Enemies." White radicals have also overcome their initial rejection of cultural radicals. Something clearly is happening, and it is being fed, finally, by youth, the artists, the politicos and the realization, through struggle, that America is not beautiful.

Some Historical Analogies

The persecution of the Jews destroyed both a particular social form and the individuals who qualified for the Jewish fate by reason of birth. Looking at the process in the aggregate, Hilberg describes it as a gradual coming together of a multitude of loose laws, institutions, and intentions, rather than a program born mature. The control conglomerate that resulted was a refined engine "whose devices," Hilbert writes, "not only trap a larger number of victims; they also require a greater degree of specialization, and with that division of labor, the moral burden too is fragmented among the participants. The perpetrator can now kill his victims without touching them, without hearing them, without seeing them. . . . This ever growing capacity for destruction cannot be arrested anywhere." Ultimately, the persecution of the Jews was a mixture of piety, repression and mobilization directed against those who were in the society but suddenly not of it.

The early Christians were also faced with a refined and elaborate administrative structure whose harsh measures were ultimately directed at their ways of life: their social forms and their spiritual claims. The rationale was, and is, that certain deviant behaviors endanger society. Therefore, officials are obligated to use whatever means of control or persuasion they consider necessary to strike these forms from the list of human possibilities. This is the classical administrative rationale for the suppression of alternative values and world views.

As options closed and Christians found the opportunities to lead and explore Christian lives rapidly struck down, Christian life itself had to become rigid, prematurely closed and obsessed with survival.

The persecution of the early Christians presents analogies to the persecution of European Jews. The German assault affected the quality of Jewish organizations no less than it affected the lives of individual Jews, distorting communities long before it destroyed them. Hilberg documents some of the ways in which efforts to escape the oppression led on occasion to a subordination of energies to the problem of simply staying alive—of finding some social options within the racial castle. The escapist mentality that dominated the response to oppression and distorted relationships can be seen in some Jewish leaders in Vienna. They exchanged individuals for promises. This is what persecution and terror do. As options close and all parts of the life of the oppressed are touched by procedure, surveillance and control, behavior is transformed. The oppressed rarely retaliate (especially where they have internalized the very ethic that rejects them), simply because nothing is left untouched by the persecution. No energy is available for hostility, and, in any case, it is impossible to know where to begin. Bravery is stoicism. One sings to the cell or gas chamber.

The persecution of Hippies in the United States involves, regardless of the original intentions of the agencies concerned, an assault on a way of life, an assault no less concentrated for its immaturity and occasional ambivalence. Social, cultural and political resources have been mobilized to bring a group of individuals into line and to prevent others from refusing to toe the line.

The attractiveness of the Hippie forms and the pathos of their persecution have together brought into being an impressive array of defenders. Nevertheless theirs has been a defense of gestures, outside the realm of politics and social action essential to any real protection. It has been verbal, scholarly and appreciative, with occasional expressions of horror at official actions and attitudes. But unfortunately the arena of conflict within which the Hippies, willy-nilly, must try to survive is dominated not by the likes of Susan Sontag, but by the likes of Daniel Patrick Moynihan whose apparent compassion for the Hippies will probably never be translated into action. For even as he writes (in the *American Scholar*, Autumn, 1967) that these youths are "trying to tell us something" and that they are one test of our "ability to survive," he rejects them firmly, and not a little *ex cathedra*, as a "truth gone astray." The Hippie remains helpless and more affected by the repressive forces (who will probably quote Moynihan) than by his own creative capacity or the sympathizers who support him in the journals. As John Kifner reported in *The Times*, " 'This scene is not the same anymore,' said the tall, thin Negro called Gypsy. . . . There are some very bad vibrations.' "

Social Form and Cultural Heresy

But it's just another murder. A hippie being killed is just like a housewife being killed or a career girl being killed or a hoodlum being killed. None of these people, notice, are persons; they're labels. Who cares who Groovy was; if you know he was a 'hippie,' then already you know more about him than he did about himself.

See, it's hard to explain to a lot of you what a hippie is because a lot of you really think a hippie IS something. You don't realize that the word is just a convenience

Changing Life-Styles

picked up by the press to personify a social change thing beginning to happen to young people. *(Paul William, in an article entitled "Label Dies—But Not Philosophy," Open City, Los Angeles, November 17-23, 1967.)*

Because the mass media have publicized the growth of a fairly well-articulated Hippie culture, it now bears the status of a social form. Variously identified as "counter-culture," "Hippie-dom," "Youth" or "Underground," the phenomenon centers on a philosophy of the present and takes the personal and public forms appropriate to that philosophy. Its values constitute a heresy in a society that consecrates the values of competition, social manipulation and functionalism, a society that defines ethical quality by long-range and general consequences, and that honors only those attitudes and institutions that affirm the primacy of the future and large-scale over the local and immediately present. It is a heresy in a society that eschews the primary value of intimacy for the sake of impersonal service to large and enduring organizations, a society that is essentialist rather than existentialist, a society that prizes biography over interactive quality. It is a heresy in a country whose President could be praised for crying, "Ask not what your country can do for you, but what you can do for your country!" Most important, however, it is heresy in a society whose official values, principles of operation and officials themselves are threatened domestically and abroad.

For these reasons the Hippie is available for persecution. When official authority is threatened, social and political deviants are readily conjured up as demons requiring collective exorcism and thus a reaffirmation of that authority. Where exorcism is the exclusive province of government, the government's power is reinforced by the adoption of a scapegoat. Deviant style and ideals make a group vulnerable to exploitation as a scapegoat, but it is official action which translates vulnerability into actionable heresy.

By contrast, recent political developments within black communities and the accommodations reached through bargaining with various official agencies have placed the blacks alongside the Viet Cong as an official enemy, but not as a scapegoat. As an enemy, the black is not a symbol but a source of society's troubles. It is a preferable position. The Hippie's threat lies in the lure of his way of life rather than in his political potential. His vulnerability as well as his proven capacity to develop a real alternative life permits his selection as scapegoat. A threatened officialdom is all too likely to take the final step that "brings on the judge." At the same time, by defining its attack as moderate, it reaffirms its moral superiority in the very field of hate it cultivates.

A Plausible Force

We are speaking of that which claims the lives, totally or in part, of perhaps hundreds of thousands of people of all ages throughout the United States and elsewhere. The number is not inconsiderable.

The plausibility of the Hippie culture and its charisma can be argued on several grounds. Their outlook derives from a profound mobilizing idea: Quality resides in the present. Therefore, one seeks the local in all its social detail—not indulgently and alone, but openly and creatively. Vulnerability and improvisation are principles of action, repudiating the "rational" hierarchy of plans and stages that defines, for the grounded culture, all events as incidents of passage and means to an indefinitely postponable end—as transition. The allocation of reality to the past and the future is rejected in favor of the present, and a present that is known and felt immediately, not judged by external standards. The long run is the result rather than the goal of the present. "Psychical distance," the orientation of the insulated tourist to whom the environment is something forever foreign or of the administrator for whom the world is an object of administration, is repudiated as a relational principle. It is replaced by a principal of absorption. In this, relationships are more like play, dance or jazz. Intimacy derives from absorption, from spontaneous involvement, to use Erving Goffman's phrase, rather than from frequent contact or attraction, as social psychologists have long argued.

This vision of social reality makes assumptions about human nature. It sees man as only a part of a present that depends on all its parts. To be a "part" is not to play a stereotyped role or to plan one's behavior prior to entering the scene. It is to be of a momentum. Collaboration, the overt manifestation of absorption, is critical to any social arrangement because the present, as experience, is essentially social. Love and charisma are the reflected properties of the plausible whole that results from mutual absorption. "To swing" or "to groove" is to be of the scene rather than simply at or in the scene. "Rapping," an improvised, expansive, and collaborative conversational form, is an active embodiment of the more general ethos. Its craft is humor, devotion, trust, openness to events in the process of formation, and the capacity to be relevant. Identity is neither strictly personal nor something to be maintained, but something always to be discovered. The individual body is the origin of sounds and motions, but behavior, ideas, images, and reflective thought stem from interaction itself. Development is not of personalities but of situations that include many bodies but, in effect, one mind. Various activities, such as smoking marijuana, are disciplines that serve the function of bringing people together and making them deeply interesting to each other.

The development of an authentic "counter-culture," or, better, "alternative culture," has some striking implications. For one, information and stress are processed through what amounts to a new conceptual system—a culture that replaces, in the committed, the intrapersonal structures that Western personality theories have assumed to account for intrapersonal order. For example, in 1966, young Hippies often turned against their friends and their experience after a bad acid trip. But that was the year during which "the Hippie thing" was merely one constructive expression of dissent. It was not, at that point, an alternative culture. As a result, the imagery cued in by the trauma was the imagery of the superego, the distant and punitive authority of the Western family and its macrocosmic social system. Guilt, self-hatred and the rejection of experience was the result. Many youngsters returned home filled with a humiliation that could be forgotten, or converted to a seedy and defensive hatred of the dangerously deviant. By 1968 the bad trip, while still an occasion for reconversion for some, had for others become something to be guarded against and coped with in a context of care and experienced guidance. The atmosphere of trust and new language of stress-inspired dependence rather than recoil as the initial stage of cure. One could "get high with a little help from my friends." Conscience was purged of "authority."

Although the ethos depends on personal contact, it is carried by underground media (hundreds of newspapers claiming hundreds of thousands of readers), rock music, and collective activities, artistic and political, which deliver and duplicate the message; and it is processed through a generational flow. It is no longer simply a constructive expression of dissent and thus attractive because it is a vital answer to a system that destroys vitality; it is culture, and the young are growing up under the wisdom of its older generations. The ethos is realized most fully in the small communes that dot the American urbscape and constitute

an important counter-institution of the Hippies.

This complex of population, culture, social form, and ideology is both a reinforcing environment for individuals and a context for the growth and elaboration of the complex itself. In it, life not only begins, it goes on; and, indeed, it must go on for those who are committed to it. Abbie Hoffman's *Revolution for the Hell of It* assumes the autonomy of this cultural frame of reference. It assumes that the individual has entered and has burned his bridges.

As the heresy takes an official definition and as the institutions of persecution form, a they-mentality emerges in the language which expresses the relationship between the oppressor and the oppressed. For the oppressed, it distinguishes life from nonlife so that living can go on. The they-mentality of the oppressed temporarily relieves them of the struggle by acknowledging the threat, identifying its agent, and compressing both into a quasi-poetic image, a cliche that can accomodate absurdity. One young man said, while coming down from an amphetamine high: "I'm simply going to continue to do what I want until they stop me."

But persecution is also structured by the they-mentality of the persecutors. This mentality draws lines around its objects as it fits them conceptually for full-scale social action. The particular uses of the term "hippie" in the mass media—like "Jew," "Communist," "Black Muslim," or "Black Panther"—cultivates not only disapproval and rejection but a climate of

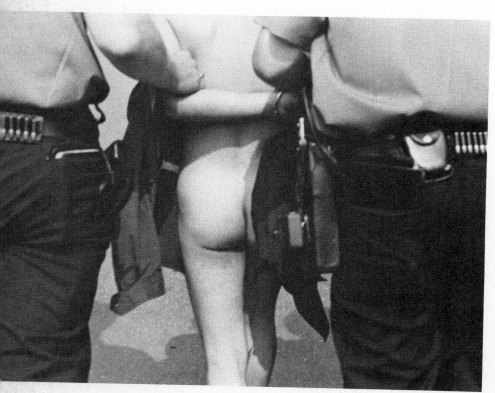

Changing Life-Styles

opinion capable of excluding Hippies from the moral order altogether. This is one phase of a subtle process that begins by locating and isolating a group, tying it to the criminal, sinful or obscene, developing and displaying referential symbols at a high level of abstraction which depersonalize and objectify the group, defining the stigmata by which members are to be known and placing the symbols in the context of ideology and readiness for action.

At this point, the symbols come to define public issues and are, consequently, sources of strength. The maintenance of power—the next phase of the story—depends less on the instruction of reading and viewing publics than on the elaboration of the persecutory institutions which demonstrate and justify power. The relationship between institution and public ceases to be one of expression or extension (of a public to an institution) and becomes one of transaction or dominance (of a public with or by an institution). The total dynamic is similar to advertising or the growth of the military as domestic powers in America.

An explosion of Hippie stories appeared in the mass media during the summer of 1967. Almost every large-circulation magazine featured articles on the Hippie "fad" or "subculture." *Life*'s "The Other Culture" set the tone. The theme was repeated in *The New York Times Magazine,* May 14, 1967, where Hunter Thompson wrote that "The 'Hashbury' (Haight-Asbury in San Francisco) is the new capital of what is rapidly becoming a drug culture." *Time*'s "wholly new subculture" was "a cult whose mystique derives essentially from the influences of hallucinogenic drugs." By fall, while maintaining the emphasis on drugs as the cornerstone of the culture, the articles had shifted from the culturological to a "national character" approach, reminiscent of the World War II anti-Japanese propaganda, as personal traits were piled into the body of the symbol and objectification began. The Hippies

Some of the Hippies have fled to the hills and built their own communal homesteads.

were "acid heads," "generally dirty," and "visible, audible and sometimes smellable young rebels."

As "hippie" and its associated terms ("long-haired," "bearded") accumulated pejorative connotation, they began to be useful concepts and were featured regularly in news headlines: for example, "Hippie Mother Held in Slaying of Son, 2" (*The New York Times,* Nov. 22, 1967); "S Squad Hits Four Pads" (*San Francisco Chronicle,* July 27, 1967). The articles themselves solidified usage by dwelling on "hippie types," "wild drug parties" and "long-haired, bearded" youths (see, for example, *The New York Times* of Feb. 13, 1968, Sept. 16, 1968 and Nov. 3, 1967).

This is a phenomenon that R. H. Turner and S. J. Surace described in 1956 in order to account for the role of media in the development of hostile consciousness toward Mexicans. The presentation of certain symbols can remove their referents from the constraints of the conventional moral order so that extralegal and extramoral action can be used against them. Political cartoonists have used the same device with less powerful results. To call Mexican-Americans "zootsuiters" in Los Angeles, in 1943, was to free hostility from the limits of the conventional, though fragile, antiracism required by liberal ideology. The result was a wave of brutal anti-Mexican assaults. Turner and Surace hypothesized that:

To the degree, then, to which any symbol evokes only one consistent set of connotations throughout the community, only one general course of action with respect to that ob-

ject will be indicated, and the union of diverse members of the community into an acting crowd will be facilitated . . . or it will be an audience prepared to accept novel forms of official action.

First the symbol, then the accumulation of hostile connotations, and finally the action-issue: Such a sequence appears in the news coverage of Hippies from the beginning of 1967 to the present. The amount of coverage has decreased in the past year, but this seems less a result of sympathy or sophistication and more one of certainty: The issue is decided and certain truths can be taken for granted. As this public consciousness finds official representation in the formation of a control conglomerate, it heralds the final and institutional stage in the growth of repressive force, persecution and terror.

The growth of this control conglomerate, the mark of any repressive system, depends on the development of new techniques and organizations. But its momentum requires an ideological head of steam. In the case of the Hippie life the ideological condemnation is based on several counts: that it is dangerous and irresponsible, subversive to authority, immoral, and psychopathological.

Commenting on the relationship between beliefs and the development of the persecutory institutions for witch-control in the 16th century, Trevor-Roper, in an essay on "Witches and Witchcraft," states:

In a climate of fear, it is easy to see how this process could happen: how individual deviations could be associated with a central pattern. We have seen it happen in our own time. The "McCarthyite" experience of the United States in the 1950's was exactly comparable: Social fear, the fear of an incompatible system of society, was given intellectual form as a heretical ideology and suspect individuals were persecuted by reference to that heresy.

The same fear finds its ideological expression against the Hippies in the statement of Dr. Stanley F. Yolles, director of the National Institute of Mental Health, that "alienation," which he called a major underlying cause of drug abuse, "was wider, deeper and more diffuse now than it has been in any other period in American history." The rejection of dissent in the name of mental health rather than moral values or social or political interest is a modern characteristic. Dr. Yolles suggested that if urgent attention is not given the problem:

there are serious dangers that large proportions of current and future generations will reach adulthood embittered towards the larger society, unequipped to take on parental, vocational and other citizen roles, and involved in some form of socially deviant behavior. . . .

Dr. Seymour L. Halleck, director of student psychiatry at the University of Wisconsin, also tied the heresy to various sources of sin: affluence, lack of contact with adults, and an excess of freedom. Dr. Henry Brill, director of Pilgrim State Hospital on Long Island and a consultant on drug use to federal and state agencies, is quoted in *The New York*

Times, Sept. 26, 1967:

It is my opinion that the unrestricted use of marijuana type substances produces a significant amount of vagabondage, dependency, and psychiatric disability.

Drs. Yolles, Halleck, and Brill are probably fairly representative of psychiatric opinion. Psychiatry has long defined normality and health in terms of each other in a "scientific" avoidance of serious value questions. Psychiatrists agree in principle on several related points which could constitute a medical rational foundation for the persecution of Hippies: They define the normal and healthy individual as patient and instrumental. He plans for the long range and pursues his goals temperately and economically. He is an individual with a need for privacy and his contacts are moderate and respectful. He is stable in style and identity, reasonably competitive and optimistic. Finally, he accepts reality and participates in the social forms which constitutes the givens of his life. Drug use, sexual pleasure, a repudiation of clear long-range goals, the insistence on intimacy and self-affirmation, distrust of official authority and radical dissent are all part of the abnormality that colors the Hippies "alienated" or "disturbed" or "neurotic."

This ideology characterizes the heresy in technical terms. Mental illness is a scientific and medical problem, and isolation and treatment are recommended. Youth, alienation and drug use are the discrediting characteristics of those who are unqualified for due process, discussion or conflict. The genius of the ideology has been to separate the phenomenon under review from consideration of law and value. In this way the mutual hostilities that ordinarily divide the various agencies of control are bypassed and the issue endowed with ethical and political neutrality. Haurek and Clark, in their "Variants of Integration of Social Control Agencies," described two opposing orientations among social control agencies, the authoritarian-punitive (the police, the courts) and the humanitarian-welfare (private agencies, social workers), with the latter holding the former in low esteem. The Hippies have brought them together.

The designation of the Hippie impulse as heresy on the grounds of psychopathology not only bypasses traditional enmity among various agencies of social control, but its corollaries activate each agency. It is the eventual coordination of their efforts that constitutes the control conglomerate. We will briefly discuss several of these corollaries before examining the impact of the conglomerate. Youth, danger and disobedience are the major themes.

Dominating the study of adolescence is a general theory which holds that the adolescent is a psychosexual type. Due to an awakening of the instincts after a time of relative quiescence, he is readily overwhelmed by them. Consequently, his behavior may be viewed as the working out of intense intrapsychic conflict—it is symptomatic or expressive rather than rational and realistic. He is idealistic, easily influenced, and magical. The idealism is the expression of a threatened superego; the susceptibility to influence is an attempt to find support for an identity in danger of diffusion; the magic, reflected in adolescent romance and its rituals, is an attempt to get a grip on a reality that shifts and turns too much for comfort. By virtue of his entrance into the youth culture, he joins in the collective expression of emotional immaturity. At heart, he is the youth of Golding's *Lord of the Flies,* a fledgling adult living out a transitional status. His idealism may be sentimentally touching, but in truth he is morally irresponsible and dangerous.

Youth

As the idealism of the young is processed through the youth culture, it becomes radical ideology, and even radical practice. The attempts by parents and educators to break the youth culture by rejecting its symbols and limiting the opportunities for its expression (ranging from dress regulations in school to the censorship of youth music on the air) are justified as a response to the dangerous political implications of the ideology of developed and ingrown immaturity. That these same parents and educators find their efforts to conventionalize the youth culture (through moderate imitations of youthful dress and attempts to "get together with the kids") rejected encourages them further to see the young as hostile, unreasonable and intransigent. The danger of extremism (the New Left and the Hippies) animates their criticism, and all intrusions on the normal are read as pointing in that direction. The ensuing conflict between the wise and the unreasonable is called (largely by the wise) the "generation gap."

From this it follows that radicalism is the peculiar propensity of the young and, as Christopher Jencks and David Riesman have pointed out in *The Academic Revolution,* of those who identify with the young. At its best it is not considered serious; at its worst it is the "counter-culture." The myth of the generation gap, a myth that is all the more strongly held as we find less and less evidence for it, reinforces this view by holding that radicalism ends, or should end, when the gap is bridged—when the young grow older and wiser. While this lays the groundwork for tolerance or more likely, forbearance, it is a tolerance limited to youthful radicalism. It also lays the groundwork for a more thorough rejection of the radicalism of the not-so-young and the "extreme."

Thus, the theory of youth classifies radicalism as immature and, when cultivated, dangerous or pathological. Alienation is the explanation used to account for the extension of youthful idealism and paranoia into the realm of the politically and culturally adult. Its wrongness is temporary and trivial. If it persists, it becomes a structural defect requiring capture and treatment rather than due process and argument.

Danger

Once a life-style and its practices are declared illegal, its proponents are by definition criminal and subversive. On the one hand, the very dangers presupposed by the legal proscriptions immediately become clear and present. The illegal life-style becomes the living demonstration of its alleged dangers. The ragged vagabondage of the Hippie is proof that drugs and promiscuity are alienating, and the attempts to sleep in parks, gather and roam are the new "violence" of which we have been reading. Crime certainly is crime, and the Hippies commit crime by their very existence. The dangers are: (1) crime and the temptation to commit crime; (2) alienation and the temptation to drop out. The behaviors that, if unchecked, become imbedded in the personality of the susceptible are, among others, drug use (in particular marijuana), apparel deviance, dropping out (usually of school), sexual promiscuity, communal living, nudity, hair deviance, draft resistance, demonstrating against the feudal oligarchies in cities and colleges, gathering, roaming, doing strange art and being psychedelic. Many of these are defused by campaigns of definition; they become topical and in fashion. To wear bell-bottom pants, long side-burns, flowers on your car and beads, is, if done with taste and among the right people, stylish and eccentric rather than another step toward the brink or a way of lending aid and comfort to the enemy. The disintegration of a form by co-opting only its parts is a familiar phenomenon. It is tearing an argument apart by confronting each proposition as if it had no context, treating a message like an intellectual game.

Drugs, communalism, gathering, roaming, resisting and demonstrating, and certain styles of hair have not been defused. In fact, the drug scene is the site of the greatest concentration of justificatory energy and the banner under which the agencies of the control conglomerate unite. That their use is so widespread through the straight society indicates the role of drugs as temptation. That drugs have been pinned so clearly (despite the fact that many Hippies are nonusers) and so gladly to the Hippies, engages the institutions of persecution in the task of destroying the Hippie thing.

The antimarijuana lobby has postulated a complex of violence, mental illness, genetic damage, apathy and alienation, all arising out of the ashes of smoked pot. The hypothesis justifies a set of laws and practices of great harshness and discrimination, and the President recently recommended that they be made even more so. The number of arrests for use, possession or sale of marijuana has soared in recent years: Between 1964 and 1966 yearly arrests doubled, from 7,000 to 15,000. The United States Narcotics Commissioner attributed the problem to "certain groups" which give marijuana to young people, and to "false information" about the danger of the drug.

Drug raids ordinarily net "hippie-type youths" although

lately news reports refer to "youths from good homes." The use of spies on campuses, one of the bases for the original protest demonstrations at Nanterre prior to the May revolution, has become common, with all its socially destructive implications. Extensive spy operations were behind many of the police raids of college campuses during 1967, 1968 and 1969. Among those hit were Long Island University's Southampton College (twice), State University College at Oswego, New York, the Hun School of Princeton, Bard College, Syracuse University, Stony Brook College and Franconia College in New Hampshire; the list could go on.

It is the "certain groups" that the Commissioner spoke of who bear the brunt of the condemnation and the harshest penalties. The laws themselves are peculiar enough, having been strengthened largely since the Hippies became visible, but they are enforced with obvious discrimination. Teenagers arrested in a "good residential section" of Naugatuck, Connecticut, were treated gently by the circuit court judge:

I suspect that many of these youngsters should not have been arrested. . . . I'm not going to have these youngsters bouncing around with these charges hanging over them.

They were later released and the charges dismissed. In contrast, after a "mass arrest" in which 15 of the 25 arrested were charged with being in a place where they knew that others were smoking marijuana, Washington's Judge Halleck underscored his determination "to show these long-haired ne'er-do-wells that society will not tolerate their conduct" (*Washington Post,* May 21, 1967).

The incidents of arrest and the exuberance with which the laws are discriminatorily enforced are justified, although not explained, by the magnifying judgment of "danger." At a meeting of agents from 74 police departments in Connecticut and New York, Westchester County Sheriff John E. Hoy, "in a dramatic stage whisper," said, "It is a frightening situation, my friends . . . marijuana is creeping up on us."

One assistant district attorney stated that "the problem is staggering." A county executive agreed that "the use of marijuana is vicious," while a school superintendent argued that "marijuana is a plague-like disease, slowly but surely strangling our young people." Harvard freshmen were warned against the "social influences" that surround drugs and one chief of police attributed drug use and social deviance to permissiveness in a slogan which has since become more common (*St. Louis Post-Dispatch,* Aug. 22, 1968).

Bennett Berger has pointed out that the issue of danger is an ideological ploy (*Denver Post,* April 19, 1968): "The real issue of marijuana is ethical and political, touching the core of cultural values.' " *The New York Times* of Jan. 11, 1968, reports "Students and high school and college officials agree that 'drug use has increased sharply since the intensive coverage given to drugs and the Hip-

pies last summer by the mass media.' " It is also supported by other attempts to tie drugs to heresy: *The New York Times* of Nov. 17, 1968, notes a Veterans Administration course for doctors on the Hippies which ties Hippies, drugs, and alienation together and suggests that the search for potential victims might begin in the seventh or eighth grades.

The dynamic relationship between ideology, organization and practice is revealed both in President Johnson's "Message on Crime to Insure Public Safety" (delivered to Congress on February 7, 1968) and in the gradual internationalizing of the persecution. The President recommended "strong new laws," an increase in the number of enforcement agents, and the centralization of federal enforcement machinery. At the same time, the United Nations Economic and Social Council considered a resolution asking that governments "deal effectively with publicity which advocates legalization or tolerance of the non-medical use of cannabis as a harmless drug." The resolution was consistent with President Johnson's plan to have the Federal Government of the United States "maintain worldwide operations . . . to suppress the trade in illicit narcotics and marijuana." The reasons for the international campaign were clarified by a World Health Organization panel's affirmation of its intent to prevent the use or sale of marijuana because it is "a drug of dependence, producing health and social problems." At the same time that scientific researchers at Harvard and Boston University were exonerating the substance, the penalties increased and the efforts to proscribe it reached international proportions. A number of countries, including Laos and Thailand, have barred Hippies, and Mexico has made it difficult for those with long hair and serious eyes to cross its border.

Disobedience

The assumption that society is held together by formal law and authority implies in principle that the habit of obedience must be reinforced. The details of the Hippie culture are, in relation to the grounded culture, disobedient. From that perspective, too, their values and ideology are also explicitly disobedient. The disobedience goes far beyond the forms of social organization and personal presentation to the conventional systems of healing, dietary practice and environmental use. There is virtually no system of authority that is not thrown into question. Methodologically, the situationalism of pornography, guerrilla theater and place conversion is not only profoundly subversive in itself; it turns the grounded culture around. By coating conventional behavioral norms with ridicule and obscenity, by tying radically different meanings to old routines, it challenges our sentiments. By raising the level of our self-consciousness it allows us to become moral in the areas we had allowed to degenerate into habit (apathy or gluttony). When the rock group, the Fugs, sings and dances "Group Grope" or any of their other songs devoted brutally to "love" and "taste," they pin our tender routines to a humiliating obscenity. We can no longer take our behavior and our intentions for granted. The confrontation enables us to disobey or to reconsider or to choose simply by forcing into consciousness the patterns of behavior and belief of which we have become victims. The confrontation is manly because it exposes both sides in an arena of conflict.

When questions are posed in ways that permit us to disengage ourselves from their meaning to our lives, we tolerate the questions as a moderate and decent form of dissent. And we congratulate ourselves for our tolerance. But when people refuse to know their place, and, what is worse, our place, and they insist on themselves openly and demand that we re-decide our own lives, we are willing to have them knocked down. Consciousness permits disobedience. As a result, systems threatened from within often begin the work of reassertion by an attack on consciousness and chosen forms of life.

Youth, danger and disobedience define the heresy in terms that activate the host of agencies that, together, comprise the control conglomerate. Each agency, wrote Trevor-Roper, was ready: "The engine of persecution was set up before its future victims were legally subject to it." The conglomerate has its target. But it is a potential of the social system as much as it is an actor. Trevor-Roper comments further that:

> once we see the persecution of heresy as social intolerance, the intellectual difference between one heresy and another becomes less significant.

And the difference, one might add, between one persecutor and another becomes less significant. Someone it does not matter who tells Mr. Blue (in Tom Paxton's song): "What will it take to whip you into line?"

How have I ended here? The article is an analysis of the institutionalization of persecution and the relationship between the control conglomerate which is the advanced form of official persecution and the Hippies as an alternative culture, the target of control. But an analysis must work within a vision if it is to move beyond analysis into action. The tragedy of America may be that it completed the technology of control before it developed compassion and tolerance. It never learned to tolerate history, and now it is finally capable of ending history by ending the change that political sociologists and undergroups understand. The struggle has always gone on in the mind. Only now, for this society, is it going on in the open among people. Only now is it beginning to shape lives rather than simply shaping individuals. Whether it is too late or not will be worked out in the attempts to transcend the one-dimensionality that Marcuse described. That the alternative culture is here seems difficult to doubt. Whether it becomes

revolutionary fast enough to supersede an officialdom bent on its destruction may be an important part of the story of America.

As an exercise in over-estimation, this essay proposes a methodological tool for going from analysis to action in areas which are too easily absorbed by a larger picture but which are at the same time too critical to be viewed outside the context of political action.

The analysis suggests several conclusions:

■ Control usually transcends itself both in its selection of targets and in its organization.

■ At some point in its development, control is readily institutionalized and finally institutional. The control conglomerate represents a new stage in social organization and is an authentic change-inducing force for social systems.

■ The hallmark of an advanced system of control (and the key to its beginning) is an ideology that unites otherwise highly differing agencies.

■ Persecution and terror go in our society. The Hippies, as a genuine heresy, have engaged official opposition to a growing cultural-social-political tendency. The organization of control has both eliminated countervailing official forces and begun to place all deviance in the category of heresy. This pattern may soon become endemic to the society.

FURTHER READING

Collective Behavior by Michael Brown and Amy Goldin (Pacific Palisades, Calif.: Goodyear, 1973).

Freak Culture by Daniel Foss (New York: New Critics Press, 1971).

The Destruction of the European Jews by Raul Hilberg (New York: Quadrangle, 1961).

Revolution for the Hell of It by Abbie Hoffman (New York: Dial, 1968).

The Religions of the Oppressed by Vittorio Lanternari (New York: Knopf, 1963). Deals with the emergence of political and cultural underlife.

Bomb Culture by Jeff Nuttall (London: MacGibbon and Kee, 1968). An historical description of the emergence of the underground currents of the sixties.

The Hippie Ghetto by William Partridge (New York: Holt, Rinehart and Winston, 1973).

The Making of a Counter Culture by Theodore Roszak (Garden City, N.Y.: Doubleday Anchor Books, 1969).

The Politics of Protest (The Report to the National Commission on the Causes and Prevention of Violence) by Jerome H. Skolnick (New York: Simon & Schuster, 1969).

The Seamy Side of Democracy: Repression in America by Alan Wolfe (New York: McKay, 1973).

ROBERT LYNN ADAMS AND ROBERT JON FOX

Mainlining Jesus: The New Trip

"It's the greatest rush I've ever had," commented one hip young man describing his experience in turning on to Jesus. Similar drug culture metaphors are used by other former drug users who have joined the spreading movement of evangelical religion among the young—a movement that originated largely in Southern California. The ranks of the "Jesus people" or "Jesus freaks," as some call them, have grown considerably during 1970. Thousands have been baptized off the beaches of Southern California, and the movement has spread across the country trailing colorful publicity in its wake.

"We made *Time*!" exulted a young prophet of the movement recently. Bumper stickers substitute "Have a Nice Forever" for the familiar California expression, "Have a Nice Day;" the Jesus-oriented *Free Paper* is sent to 50 states and 11 foreign countries—a biweekly, it claims a circulation of 260,000. In new recordings featuring "Jesus rock" the composers search for spiritual guidance and direction. Musical groups such as The J.C. Power Outlet and

The Love Song proliferate. A new social system blends the hip style of dress, music and speech into the "Jesus culture"—something new, yet something old indeed! The Jesus trip is The Great Awakening of 1740 (Jonathan Edwards) revisited; it is American frontier religion revisited with Volkswagens and amplifiers supplanting the horses, wagons and saddlebacks of Cane Ridge, Kentucky, 1801.

The young whites of middle-class background turning toward revivalist religion come from two rather distinct groups. From observations of crowds at religious services, one of these groups consists largely of teenagers whom we call "Jesus-boppers." In them, rock groups turned on to Jesus have a ready-made audience from the large ranks of rock music fans. Free concerts followed by an invitation to accept Jesus Christ attract large youth audiences.

The other element in the Jesus movement is a smaller and more intense group of young adults (usually in their twenties) who have opted out of the drug culture. Many are former peace movement activists who have dropped out of

Changing Life-Styles

society over the past four or five years. For them, the Jesus movement constitutes a ritual of re-entry into the system.

In our investigation of the Jesus movement we used both observations and interviews. We attended many religious services, interviewing the ministers of the church in Orange County, where the movement is largely centered, visited religious communes, using a formal questionnaire to interview 89 young people. Although the sample is small, it served to add validity to the observations and unstructured interviews, the latter being taped for analysis. We encountered great resistance in the communes to the questionnaire; some attributed their reluctance to an unwillingness to mull over the past. One respondent mentioned that talking about one's past was actually forbidden in the San Francisco commune where he had formerly lived.

A Trip to the Chapel

As an institution, Gethsemane Chapel is three years old. It is an independent, nondenominational congregation whose basically conservative Baptist theology is a blend of holiness and pentecostalism. Its ministry is anti-establishment in its rejection of the theology and social positions of the major Protestant denominations. The main minister is a hawk on the Vietnam war, decrying the no-win policy which has been pursued by the government.

Sunday morning and evening as well as several week nights are Bible study sessions, attended mainly by older persons. Some week-night meetings find Gethsemane Chapel jammed with youth, but the big youth night is Wednesday, when a number of musical groups are featured. The church is packed two hours prior to the service—crowd estimates range from 1,300 to 1,400 persons; about one-third are outside listening on loudspeakers and participating visually through the chapel's glass walls. Approximately 80 percent of the audience is female; and less than 5 percent are what could be called hippies. Yet the style of dress is informal—jeans and hip garb and long hair abounds. Over half the crowd consists of early teens and less than 15 percent are over twenty.

A 22-year-old lay minister—a former drug user, with flowing robe, long hair and beard—leads this service. Later, in an "afterglow" he leads a smaller group in receiving the baptism of the Holy Spirit—speaking in tongues. The interaction style in the worship and in the entire movement is intensely personal, a kind of "Gospel Anonymous," with pastors and members first-naming each other.

Gethsemane's services are more holiness than pentecostal in that they follow a definite order, eschewing the freewheeling "do your thing" style of the latter. The young minister mentioned above, whom we shall call Rennie, has been known to silence persons who interrupt to speak in tongues during the service. Informal songs are sung by the congregation, mostly centering around the person of Jesus and his imminent return to earth. Prayers for the sick are offered and testimonies are heard. The ubiquitous "one way" sign (extended index finger with clenched fist) shows the congregation's approval of various elements of the services. Rennie affirms that God desires to heal anything from "warts to cancer." The "flashes" from previous LSD trips can also be cured. One woman (older than most present) testifies that she has been cured of dandruff.

"Praise the Lord!" says Rennie. An examination of her head reveals no trace of dandruff.

Following the singing, testimonies and music groups, Rennie reads from the Bible and gives a sermon—often a defense of speaking in tongues. At the close, an invitation is given to accept Jesus. On an average Wednesday night, about 100 young persons come forward, affirm their faith in unison, and are then led to another part of the church to be presented with a Bible. When there were fewer converts, individual counseling was also conducted. Many of the converts are later baptized in the ocean, although apparently no set plan is announced for doing so immediately.

In the afterglow, another Bible study is conducted, after which Rennie invites those who want the baptism of the Spirit to come forward. A flute player provides an eerie background (he "plays by the Spirit") while Rennie assists those who wish to receive the Spirit, with such blandishments as, "you may kneel, if you wish," or "you may extend your arms toward heaven, if you wish."

Rennie moves in and out among those standing on the platform, touching and speaking to them. Eventually a cadence of people speaking in a babble and singing in tongues intertwines with the mystic tones of the flute. (Many Jesus-boppers report receiving this baptism.) For this part of the service the church is full, but the aisles and the grounds are empty of people; some teenage girls attempt to sit in the aisle to get close to the platform where Rennie is leading the service. Following the afterglow, which is terminated at Rennie's command, certain individuals remain fixed in apparent hysterical stupor. "Counselors" help them to "give in" to the Spirit, some of whom are unable to pull out of their babbling and hysteria.

On Friday nights there are no music groups, although the service is supposedly programmed for youth. Another young lay minister—more square than Rennie—leads this service. The attendance is about one-third of the Wednesday night assemblage, with fewer teenagers present. This difference is likely due to the drawing power of the professional gospel rock groups on Wednesday plus the charisma of Rennie.

The Jesus Commune

The leaders of Gethsemane Chapel, being interested in reaching young people in the drug culture for Jesus, developed the idea of adopting the commune as a service-oriented institution. And the movement appears to be very successful. Scores of Jesus-oriented houses have sprung up along the entire West Coast under the sponsorship of Gethsemane Chapel.

Visits to these communes reveal a rigid separation of male and female living quarters, with a strict affirmation of asceticism. Many of the occupants have been members of drug-oriented communes, where sexual relations were available. The same individuals appear to move toward early marriage after being saved. Their frequently idealistic conception of marriage is exemplified by the response of one young man, who when asked if he thought sex could be misused in marriage, said, "Certainly not." (He believed that he had misused it out of marriage.)

The communes visited had approximately 20 to 30 permanent residents, although their turnover appears high.

When one commune becomes fairly large, another is established; when one is overpopulated, members move to another which has space. The commune also serves as a type of crash pad where anyone is welcome to eat and/or sleep.

Money earned by members is given to a central treasury, although one's worldly wealth is not demanded (as was the case in the traditional monastery movement). Yard and gardening work is done for local residents to earn money to support the house as well as to learn to work and live together. Several deacons are in charge of finances plus the physical and spiritual nurture of the house. The leaders deny that there are rules, saying everyone is to follow God's will. Emphasis on cooperation rather than rules appears to be effective in accomplishing the day's tasks. There is a minimum of scheduling, although a list of those preparing breakfast is posted. The diet, which has a heavy starch content, is augmented by fruit and vegetable discards donated by local grocery stores. The direction of the Spirit is sought in all matters, including remodeling and obtaining materials for a new roof, for example.

Persons visiting a commune receive an open and friendly welcome. Such was the case at Mansion Messiah. A tour of the premises may reveal a young man speaking in tongues in the garden, a modest "prayer house" in the back yard, with another young man just leaving it to return to the main building. Just recently the "family" had added the eating room. There were no contractors hired to build the addition, and the plywood and materials for the roof were all donated. "The Lord just showed us where to lay the beams," and the members built the roof. The garage was converted into a bedroom by the members also and holes in the walls were left for the windows. "The Lord provided us with windows to fit the holes." In this bedroom at least nine men sleep, in three bunk-beds, three high, that the men had made themselves.

The girls (about ten in number) do all the cooking, mending, serving, washing and other housework and hold no outside jobs. The men do the yard work, gardening, repairs around the house, building of furniture and some hold outside jobs. It costs about $2,000 per month to run the house. Donations and contributions help to pay the expenses that are not covered by the men's pay.

Many individuals in the commune appear for the first time in their lives to be learning how to work and live with others. The leaders do not deny that conflicts arise in the house; such conflicts, they emphasize, are a creative opportunity for individuals to learn to live together. The nightly Bible study time is used to deal with such problems; leaders of the evening frequently pick a New Testament passage dealing with mutual sharing and responsibility.

Life in the Jesus movement is ruled by two norms: the Bible and the direct guidance of the Holy Spirit. As their former lives have been physically sensate in relation to drugs and sex, so their "born-again" lives tend to be spiritually sensate. Thus it is difficult to gather information on such mundane topics as finances either at Gethsemane Chapel or in the communes. "The Lord provides" and "right on!" are the expressions one elicits upon bringing up the problem of money. Since all problems are dealt with by the direct guidance of the Spirit (unless explicit Biblical instructions can be found), it is not surprising to find commune members and ministers of the church extremely spiritually sensate in regard to budgets.

During the study of the communes, it became evident that the wide publicity given the movement in the press and on television was affecting the communes' image. These problems and others were observed by a student researcher during her visit to what we term Christus House:

I went to the Christus House on a Friday night. Everyone was sitting around talking and drinking either coffee or tea, waiting for the meeting to start. At about 7:00 p.m. every night the house has a meeting with people who live outside. These are carefully screened by the leader, a deacon named John. The meeting lasts between two and three hours.

While I was waiting for the meeting to begin I talked with several people who were very open to introduce themselves, but very hesitant to carry on a conversation. The first question they asked was "Have you been saved?" I overheard a conversation between two members of the house, one male and one female. The female, Jane, was expressing her previous concern (before being saved) and anxiety about getting married. She said she was glad she didn't have to worry about that any more because it was now in God's hands. The meeting began with guitar music and singing by everyone present. John led the meeting, but everyone was given a chance to talk. This they referred to as "sharing."

At first they shared different encounters they had had during the day. The main topic of discussion was a program on television that afternoon in which John, a girl named June and several people from another commune participated. They had spent the time talking about God and Christ. John had cut his hair for the program and had suffered "trials" throughout the week because he was afraid the devil was making him do it. They both expressed how upset they had been because they might misrepresent the Lord. However, they were both at ease when they discovered, while on the air, that they didn't really even speak but "it was the Lord speaking through them." They expressed concern with changing their image from that of long-haired, former drug users to conservative, clean-cut citizens. In fact, they showed hostility at the image they thought the public had of them. Others mentioned having individual problems and the Lord leading them to a specific chapter in the Bible that solved the problem. They discussed what the phrase "I love someone but I don't like them" means, as John had just found out from a minister at Gethsemane that afternoon. One member expressed how thrilled he was because it was his first day working for Jesus.

Experience in the communes is dichotomous: one is led either by the Lord or the devil. It was thus very difficult to get very detailed answers to questions. The public (i.e., the "world") is likewise viewed in authoritarian, either-or terms: as in "darkness" and "searching for the light." After the meeting, members left for a theater to witness to people waiting in line. John tends to use scare tactics in a gentle way, illustrated by the fact that he very calmly asked me if I died on the way home, which I might, would I go to heaven? He had also mentioned in the meeting that in the studio that day he had asked someone else the same question.

The Jesus-boppers

Most of the members of the Jesus movement in Orange County seem to be teenage youth—the "Jesus-boppers." Their motivation for being in the movement is apparently twofold, stemming both from a desire for peer-group approval and a need for resolving the identity crisis. According to Erik Erikson's analysis of the teenage years as a period of identity vs. role confusion, puberty marks the beginning of the developmental stage crisis. The physiological revolution within and the tangible adult tasks ahead of them cause youth to be primarily concerned with how they appear to others rather than with what they feel they are. Erikson writes:

> The adolescent mind is essentially a mind of *moratorium,* a psycho-sexual stage between childhood and adulthood, and between the morality learned by the child, and the ethics to be developed by the adult. It is an ideological mind—and, indeed, it is the ideological outlook of a society that speaks most clearly to the adolescent who is eager to be affirmed by his peers and is ready to be confirmed by rituals, creeds and programs which at the same time define what is evil, uncanny, and inimical.

The Jesus trip seems tailor-made for adolescents. Not only does commitment to Jesus preserve childhood morality with its absolutistic definitions of right and wrong, but it also provides an ideology based on personal, internal and, for the most part, unexplainable experience rather than on critical, rational or realistic analysis. Indeed, the ideology is unchallengeable and thereby not available for analysis by the uninitiated.

The Jesus trip also provides adolescents with the necessary peers, rituals, creeds and programs—brothers, baptisms, speaking in tongues and a source for the ideology, the Bible. Approval and affirmation by peers are guaranteed within the movement. To the droves of young teens who fill Gethsemane Chapel on the nights that the professional music groups perform, Rennie issues the invitation in these words, "Accept Jesus Christ. Don't get left out. Come right now."

The Jesus trip can be seen as an attempt to resolve the crisis of the onset of sexuality by denying sexual feelings. Previous to puberty, the individual has developed to some degree an identity based upon his or her experiences and needs. With the onset of the physiological revolution within and with the growing awareness of adult roles, this identity is threatened; suddenly he must accept a new aspect of identity—sexuality. Successful growth depends on the individual's ability to meet his new needs and expand his identity without threatening the self. Rather than risk the trauma of this adjustment, the individual may resolve the crisis in neurotic fashion: by establishing an ideal by which to deny his feelings. Adolescent idealism represents one such attempt to keep oneself separate from one's real feelings. An example of such denial is this statement by a 16-year-old who had been on drugs and sexually active prior to his conversion:

I am free, free from the garbage of the world—the kind of stuff that you're a slave to. Jesus said, "Whoever commits sin is a servant of sin." I've quit taking drugs, I've quit getting it on the girls—I've changed, man! Don't you understand? I'm free, free, free—all the time and not just for six to eight hours—all the time. I still have problems, but I don't hassle with them, because I'm free!

We believe that religion as represented in this movement is a step backwards. The Jesus trip, like drugs, appears to be used in such a way as to avoid coming to terms with the anxieties related to the identity crisis. In normal development the new dimensions of identity are added to the previously established identity, modifying it to some degree; some parts of one's previous identity will be discarded, submerged or eradicated by new behavior. Instead of progressing toward adult ethics, the Jesus person clutches tenaciously to childhood morality, with its simplistic black-and-white, right-and-wrong judgments. Rather than developing behavior oriented towards reality, he flies into ideational, ideological abstractions to numb his awareness of his newly arisen needs. Spurning a reality that begins with individual feelings, he subordinates himself to peer approval. For these reasons we term the Jesus trip a pseudo-solution to the identity vs. role confusion crisis.

Comparing Drug and Jesus Cultures

Members of the Jesus movement have a high incidence of past drug use, with 62 percent of those over 18 and 44 percent of those under 18 having used dope. Only a few individuals were extremely light users, usually of marijuana.

Continuities between the drug and Jesus experiences are as follows: 1) both are outside the modal American life style, in fact, both are anti-establishment in their attempts to create alternatives to the American middle-class life style. Middle-class denominational religion, in the words of one pastor, "is as phony as it can be." 2) Both are subjective and experientially oriented, as opposed to the dominant cultural style, which is objective, scientific and rationally oriented. 3) The nature of the religious experience at Gethsemane Chapel and other holiness-type congregations is wholly consonant with previously experienced drug highs. A common description of the conversion experienced is: "It's a rush like speed."

We found a number of discontinuities between the dope and Jesus trips. As compared with the drug culture, the Jesus trip offers an extremely limited repertoire for action. For the Jesus person, life revolves entirely around Jesus, his acceptance and mission. All events are either of the Lord or of the devil. Brothers and sisters of the faith meet each other with religiously-infused greetings, and "God bless" substitutes for "goodbye." The drug culture as a whole exhibits a much greater variety. Certainly there are drug users whose lives center solely around dope, its procurement and use, but drug use has become quite generalized among a wide variety of people many of whom have a broader range of action alternatives in dealing with reality than the Jesus people.

The Jesus trip represents an almost violent ideological swing from far left to far right, a type of "reaction formation." A shift toward a conservative position in solving world problems is reported by 76 percent of those interviewed. Only two persons have changed toward the left. Of those who reported no change in position, none were "drop-outs" in the usual sense of the word. They represent a more consistent ideological history—no rebellion against parents, a continuity between their childhood religious faith and the adult Jesus movement. Their feelings toward American society, for example, are that it is "pagan like the Roman Empire at the time of Christ" or it is "too complex" for an opinion to have been formed. A slightly more liberal outlook was articulated by one respondent who observed that "the system is great, but people pervert justice." The focus here is still typically on the individual rather than on system change.

Four out of five of those reporting a shift in outlook state that the change coincided with their religious conversion. World problems, they now believe, "can only be solved through finding Christ;" "We can't have peace on the outside if we don't on the inside;" "If everyone was a Christian there wouldn't be any world problems."

However, certain Jesus publications in the area encourage a more worldly approach to political and social problems, indeed a very conservative one. For example, the *Hollywood Free Paper* routinely attacks the peace movement. *For Real* made the following comments in the May 1971 edition in an article entitled "The Real Lesson of the Calley Trial:"

> The fact is, too many people are bad. Because people are bad, they must be restrained by force. Because they must be restrained by force, police are necessary. Armies, navies and air forces are necessary. Wars are inevitable. Killing is necessary. That's the real lesson of the William Calley trial.

For Jesus people, sexual behavior also undergoes profound alteration when they leave the drug culture. Although 62 percent of the Jesus people in the sample report premarital sex prior to conversion, in most cases asceticism has become the dominant rule since being saved. A few slips are reported "once after conversion," but these can hardly be classified as libertine. Less than 5 percent openly differ with the sexual ethics of the movement and continue to practice premarital sex after their conversion. Another divergency is that the Jesus culture entails re-entering the system, returning to a middle-class work ethic and closing the generation gap. After coming from middle-class backgrounds (72 percent of those reporting father's occupation are from white-collar homes and over two-thirds of these are clearly upper-middle-class occupations), dropping out represents downward mobility; these youth are now re-entering the system, preparing to participate in the work force.

The movement's strong anti-intellectualism, however, is prompting some young people to drop out of college at a time when their re-entry into the system requires additional training. Many Jesus people, however, are still involved in routine educational programs while at the same time they hold anti-intellectual views. Of the 89 young people who answered the questionnaire, 17 had completed high school, 19 were still in college, three had some college, two were college graduates, and many were young high school students.

Several in the sample, who had dropped out of college, cite their religious experience as the motivating force in this decision. A songwriter-itinerant singer for gospel causes asserts that "The more education one has, the less likely one is to join (the) Jesus movement . . . (the) less one becomes childlike . . . becomes hardened." He elaborates that school teaches that science is God, that truth is relative, and that there can be good and evil at the same time, but this is not true.

College graduates are included among the ranks of commune dwellers who tend gardens as a livelihood. Generally, though, the older persons in the movement had dropped out during or after high school and now represent a most interesting sociological phenomenon: downward mobility and movement from church to sect (many come from church-affiliated families). Thus in closing the gap between themselves and their parents by rejoining the system, they have created fresh conflict over their education and religion. However, many parents are so pleased with their return to the system that they are financing their offspring's stay in the commune. One youth mentioned the possibility of going to Europe to an evangelical convention, explaining that his father would pay his expenses.

Preachers at Gethsemane Chapel admonish the audience to "honor thy father and thy mother." Many youth noted their conscious attempts to help them rebuild relationships with their families. Prayers in communes often concern members of the family who have problems and "need to be saved."

Whereas the drug trip represents a quest, the Jesus trip is a panacea. Despite its attendant problems, the drug culture is admirable in its affirmation of the individual's quest for experience and discovery of truth; in this it is not unlike the basis of modern liberal education. The Jesus trip, however, is a cure-all. No problem is too great to be answered easily; the believer desists from solving problems, "leaves it up to the Lord."

Another difference between the two cultures relates to authoritarianism. The free-lance drug culture is by definition nonauthoritarian. The Jesus culture, on the other hand, sees the world in either-or terms. No experience is free from being of God or of the devil. This unequivocal embracing of authoritarianism may be a by-product of the scanty education of many young believers combined with a background of family conflict.

The Jesus culture escapes the leadership problem posed by the individualism of the drug culture. Lewis Yablonski observes how the individualism of the drug scene often leads to a lack of leadership—a vacuum which sometimes allows "deviants" from the scene to wreak havoc on the peace and tranquility desired by the majority. Although leadership in the Jesus movement is attributed to God, there is no want of self-anointed human leaders around to make suggestions: the hierarchy ranges from the deacons in the commune (often young Christians with less than one year's experience of being saved) to the ministers of Gethsemane Church. The ministers are consulted on Biblical and other problems which the deacons in the commune cannot solve.

Before undertaking this study, the writers had theorized that Jesus people who are ex-dopers had participated in a succession of social movements: they began in the peace movement, had dropped out into the drug scene and finally joined the religious revival. The data, however, refute this assumption about the sequence of membership in the various movements, for the use of drugs almost always had preceded participation in the peace movement. We find the mean age of 25 former drug-and-peace people to be 20.3, while the mean age of nondrug-nonpeace participants (Jesus-boppers) is 17.4. Another segment in the sample consists of ex-dopers who were not in the peace movement (16 individuals with a mean age of 20.2, similar to the drug-and-peace group). Only four persons participated in the peace movement, but not in drugs; their mean age is 18.2.

Since the mean ages of the two ex-dope groups is similar, a contrast between them is fruitful. The drug-peace contingent is more likely to report (79 percent) dropping out of society than the nonpeace group (55 percent). However, contrary to popular opinion, their dropping out did not mean total absorption in the quest for individual experience; it did not interfere with New Left political participation by 32 Jesus people in the survey.

If the movements are so dissimilar, why the switch from dope to Jesus? One possibility is the faddishness of the Jesus trip; the same quest for novelty had motivated some to join the drug scene. The hippie faddist finds that drugs and sex are not "where it's at." Those of middle-class background may be torn between their former values and those of the drug scene; they may welcome the Jesus trip as an expedient means of returning to middle-class values, while retaining peer approval. The religious fervor of the Jesus movement provides a more socially acceptable way for them to resolve their conflict; its life style is as much a drop in as a drop out. One can gradually become reoriented to the larger segments of the population without really going too straight. In fact, few changes in life style are required in the move from dope to Jesus.

Criticisms of the Movement

The Jesus culture bears watching in the future because of several ironic twists: It is a victim of area right-wing politics, and we foresee its steadily increasing exploitation by reactionary political forces. Pamphlets distributed by the Jesus people are beginning to contain familiar attacks on one-world government, the ecumenical movement among liberal denominations, and other favorite targets of local conservative politicians. Disaffection of the movement's adherents (who generally interpret the teachings of Jesus as condemning all wars) may be expected when they discover that their leaders are militarists. The "true believer" psyche in the Jesus people, however, may well make it possible to rationalize their loyalty to their leaders.

The movement is insular—a cop-out from the realities of social change which face America. A basically white movement, it has no program for reaching the members of another race or less affluent economic groups than those in its area. The attempt to equate denominational religion with the establishment is presently successful; however, when the youth see that the denominational church has stood against racism, war and poverty, the Jesus movement may well fade. As one liberal, establishment, campus minister put it:

I think the kind of world in which we live leads to some kind of escape. And some of the same kids who were escaping through heroin are now mainlining Jesus, and confusing Jesus with a way of withdrawing from the world and its problems. I can sympathize with them. There are times when I would like to withdraw too.

Jesus to them is a kind of spirit that they have a union with. Whereas Jesus, for the early Christians, was a man of flesh and blood who took history seriously, and whose concern [was] about the whole man, not just his spirit, not just his soul. Jesus will push someone back into those problems, back into the world, only if they stay with him.

The movement denies the complexity of human nature. It abrogates the psycho-socio-sexual nature of man by dividing the self into physical and spiritual entities; the individual is indoctrinated to anticipate "rapture" when the soul is delivered from the body. Many Judeo-Christian theologians would label this as heresy, citing that the Bible teaches the unity of man's nature.

The movement's faithful show a rapid turnover. This may be related to their return to middle-class society. Some young teens who were in the movement have lessened in religious fervor considerably as they approach the middle-teen years.

The movement denies the future by turning its back on the temporal world. The apocalyptic feature of the movement dissuades young people from rejoining society because they are led to believe that the second coming of Christ is imminent. They need not concern themselves with improving our decaying cities, solving the problems of poverty, war and disease—all can be left up to God. A new pamphlet says the ecology movement is irrelevant because Jesus is coming soon anyway. Similarly the individual has no need for long-range plans; his exclusive concern is with the immediacy of his personal needs. Such myopia will certainly obstruct attempts to bridge the generation gap. (The movement's dropouts will undoubtedly become more oriented toward the future.)

Among the potential trouble spots uncovered in our data is the gap between the ministers' beliefs and those of their followers. For example, the ministers interviewed saw nothing contradictory in being both Christian and economically successful; the young people, particularly the commune members, take the antimaterialism of Jesus seriously. The main minister, as already mentioned, supports the presence of the U.S. fighting forces in Vietnam (his associate—not Rennie—did not dispute his view); but the young people, although no longer participating in the peace movement, nevertheless do not support the war as a just cause. Only two of 89 persons thought the war just, while eight felt it definitely unjust; 23 had no opinion or did not answer; 33 percent of the sample gave a generalized answer that it is wrong to kill; others saw providence or prophecy working in the war; one felt "he would go to Vietnam and try to change the people spiritually," and two persons said Jesus would not be involved—either as hawk or dove.

The communes are the most impressive part of the Jesus movement. The contribution made by their members lies in the simplicity of their life style, their easy acceptance of themselves, their genuine attempts at learning to get along with others and participate in communal tasks. Although they have kicked the drug habit, their abstinence has been too brief to predict how successful they will be at giving up drugs permanently. We may wonder what will happen if and when they are no longer high on Jesus. The potential psychological difficulties could be enormous, for in large measure they have channeled their anxieties about their problems into displays of religious fervor rather than coming to terms with the realities of the identity crisis.

FURTHER READING

A Rumor of Angels by Peter L. Berger (Garden City, N.Y.: Doubleday, 1969).

The Jesus People, Old Time Religion in the Age of Aquarius by Ronald M. Enroth (Grand Rapids, Mich.: Eerdmans, 1972).

That New Time Religion, the Jesus Revival in America by Erling Jorstad (Minneapolis, Minn.: Augsburg, 1972).

New Gods in America by Peter Rowley (New York: McKay, 1971).

9. The Burden of Responsibility: Politics and the Power Structure

When Auguste Comte first proclaimed the establishment of social science he saw as its aim the prediction and control of human behavior. In the optimistic climate of "progress" that followed, few questioned either the desirability of control or the possibility that the "aims" of social scientists might not result in the greatest good for the greatest number. Social scientists, confident that science was truth, were not overly concerned with responsibility for their theories or their research behavior. Besides, although social scientists wished very much to play a role in politics, their involvement in policymaking was peripheral. Often mistaken for "socialists," sociologists found themselves opposing much government policy. And anthropologists, as a rule, were too engaged in gathering data about the rapidly vanishing peoples of the earth to pay much heed to their role in the disappearance of their subjects. Not much given to philosophical discourse, American sociology by and large ignored the promise provided by Karl Mannheim's sociology of knowledge, and even today few universities offer courses that analyze the development of sociological thought or link past social science models to larger social issues. Firmly entrenched in a belief in the existence of an objective science, social scientists ignored and denied both the social cause and social effects of their theorizing.

Since World War II, however, social scientists have become more thoughtful, more aware of their power, the limitations of power exerted by government, and the responsibility they owe to each other, to science, and to their subjects. Increased knowledge about the nature of science has shaken belief in the existence of a value-free (or culture-free) objectivity, and with this doubt has come skepticism that scientific findings must necessarily alter human life for the better.

The ethical and moral questions faced by social science today range from the pragmatic to the ideological. At one extreme is the problem of theory. Like all other aspects of culture, our scientific models rest firmly on the values of those who create them. Since model building rests with social scientists, and social scientists generally derive from Western, middle-class cultures, their models, too, tend to perpetuate and validate the values of this culture. Although there have been great debates in social science over theories, both evolutionism (despite its accent on the normalcy of change) and functionalism tend to strive either towards maintenance of the status quo or towards gradual reform. Evolutionary models, with their emphasis upon adaptation, measure success in terms of existence, and also suggest that since change is inevitable, man need do little about it. Both evolutionism and functionalism can thus create theories that preclude active human intervention or sudden change, and both tend to reduce the sense of responsibility of the scientists holding them.

At another level, the social scientist must face a more pragmatic problem—the fact that his presence alters the lives and behaviors of his subjects. This may seem like a small thing, but we have learned from bitter experience that even the most innocent interference by well-meaning researchers can create cultural disaster. In an experiment that has since become famous, "Steel Axes for Stone Age Australians," Sharp described the effect upon a group of simple hunters of the gift of a few steel axes. The introduction of the steel axe to a few individuals provided them with power and prestige, and preferential access to a valuable resource—and created hostility, violence, and eventual collapse of social relations that had previously centered upon the making and distribution of stone tools. Dozens of such stories abound in the literature. Today the problems have been further exacerbated by growing literacy and wider dissemination of information. Although the social scientist usually conceals from a broader public the identity of the group he is studying by the use of fictional names and addresses, publication of his research data and dissemination of its results are no longer confined to the sociological audience. Instead, his books get back to his subjects, who often discover that their revelations now threaten relationships with neighbors and community.

Such unwitting interference with other cultures is hardly desirable; even worse, is the use of social science by government to exploit, acculturate, or destroy subject peoples. Although American social scientists have not explicitly allied themselves with government forces to impose American colonialism on subject peoples, or maintain exploitation of minorities, their research has often been used by policymakers for the manipulation of these minority groups and subject peoples. Social science funding comes from government and big business, including university contracts and grants. How can social scientists know which agencies are legitimate, which might use information for counterinsurgency? How can a social scientist ensure the safety and freedom of his research subjects when the data he has gathered may be used by his employer for any purpose he wishes?

Even if a particular researcher declines to work for suspect agencies, how can he—or should he—apply sanctions to prevent other colleagues from doing so? Aside from the thorny question of ethics, social scientists face a more practical problem: the behavior of such researchers often makes it impossible for others to work. As our experience with Project Camelot demonstrates, a country whose citizens have once been injured, or whose integrity has been undermined as the result of social science culture brokers, is hardly likely to open its arms to other researchers no matter how well intentioned.

Another problem very much disturbing social science today is the role played by research in forming attitudes. Social science information can affect attitudes, and attitudes eventually affect politicians and policymakers.

Social science research thus can play a large, indirect role in policymaking. More and more, social scientists are being employed directly by government in planning and policy positions. They are thus directly responsible for programs that affect the health, education, and welfare of the country and must learn to use this power wisely.

The articles included in this section flesh out some of these problems or provide a somewhat different perspective about them. In his classic article "The Pentagon Papers and Social Science" Horowitz assesses the impact of the disclosure of the Pentagon Papers on social science. The Pentagon Papers revealed both the degree of participation of social science in policy and the limits of power of the social scientists when shrouded in government secrecy. Social science must assert its responsibility for its research by calling for an end to the kind of government secrecy that has heretofore utilized power without public consent.

In "Scientists, Partisans and Social Conscience" Edel raises many of the questions about the relationship between theory and action mentioned in this introduction. He provides a brief historical overview of sociology and calls for action by social scientists against those forces which threaten not only the pursuit of science itself but the right of all peoples to a decent and dignified life.

Two somewhat more specific problems (Kelman's "Deception in Social Research" and Toch's "The Convict as Researcher") touch on yet another issue: the need for cooperation and participation by subjects in ongoing research. Because models and theories are likely to generate action programs, social scientists are now seeking a broader source for theory. The call for participation in research and planning by those who are ultimately the subjects of such planning is aimed at providing input from a variety of minority groups. Kelman's article indicates how deception in social research has been used to inhibit active participation by the subjects. Toch's piece underscores the value—both to the convict employed and to his research—of using the subjects themselves as researchers. In such a way research programs not only provide different input; they are themselves action programs and provide both income and training for their subjects.

Finally, Wolfson analyzes the effects of social science procedures and group structures on research. In his discussion of the Rand Corporation in "In the Hawk's Nest" he raises important questions about the current institutional framework in which much research occurs. His article underscores the danger of closed institutions: the selection processes guarantee that only certain kinds of scientists will participate; the social structure precludes contact with the outside world; and the result is that the norms and expectations of researchers are never questioned—instead, they are strengthened and solidified. Wolfson also indicates how some of the techniques used by Rand—like war games—ultimately desensitize their participants to reality. Played as a game by Rand participants, war may come to be treated as a game, and real people to be regarded as counters, numbers, statistics, or objects to be manipulated in order to win.

Like Horowitz, Wolfson hopes to arouse social scientists to the danger which closed systems pose to processes of scientific growth and development. Most important, however, he delineates the processes by which such systems separate analysis and responsibility. The result is the creation of fantasy worlds in which the most heinous crimes may be committed under the guise of "games" and in which neither morality nor adaptability is put to the test.

While Wolfson and Horowitz point to the growing importance of the military establishment in American society and its increasing involvement with social science research, Hightower documents the profound impact corporate interests have had on the direction and outcome of scientific research in the United States. In his searing indictment of the land grant colleges in "Hard Tomatoes, Hard Times: Failure of the Land Grant College Complex" Hightower analyzes how research and extension services in these colleges are almost exclusively directed to the benefit of corporate conglomerates, who ". . . sit on boards of trustees, purchase research from experiment stations and colleges, hire land grant academics as private consultants," and in other ways heavily influence, if not control, priorities for agricultural research. The result has been the collapse of the family farm, the exodus of the rural population to urban ghettos, and the decline and decay of rural communities all over America, as they are taken over by these modern "factories in the field." The collapse of liberal capitalism is epitomized in the transformation of our rural population from small, independent entrepreneurs to wage earners in agri-business conglomerates.

The impact of monopoly capitalism on federal policy is shown in Graham's article "Amphetamine Politics on Capitol Hill." He documents the way in which powerful pharmaceutical lobbies in Washington, with the support of the Nixon administration, have been able to forestall the legislative curtailment of the production and distribution of amphetamines, widely used by white, middle-class Americans. While recent legislation has somewhat curtailed the unprescribed use of amphetamines, it would seem that the federal government has been more reluctant to act in the case of amphetamines than in the case of hard drugs like heroin or even much less harmful drugs like marijuana. The struggle for the restriction of amphetamines is reminiscent of the control of cigarettes, which was also staunchly opposed by powerful corporate interests who are more interested in high profits than in public welfare.

The use (or abuse) of state power by corporate and other interest groups is amply demonstrated by Burnham in his far-reaching article "Crisis of American Political Legitimacy." Burnham shows how interest group liberalism or pluralism has given rise to a vast new syndicalist complex consisting of the leading corporations, the formulators of foreign policy around the president, in the universities, in Congress and in the Pentagon, and to a lesser extent, organized labor. Major groups left out of this coalition—youth, the poor, blacks and other minorities, and now women—have been putting increasing pressure upon this Establishment for incorporation into the political process, as the 1972 Democratic convention dramatically illustrates. Burnham predicts that if these groups are not incorporated, the alternative will be violent revolution—which is almost certain to fail—or the growth of fascist authoritarianism. Certainly the extent of moral decadance and political corruption revealed by Watergate and Agnew's resignation would appear to support the latter ominous outcome.

Marcuse's brief comments on Watergate, included here, sum up much of what we have been delineating in this book: the postwar change from liberal capitalism to monopolistic competition and imperialistic expansion in increasing collusion with the state. However, Marcuse notes that the extent of corruption revealed by Watergate has aroused protest, not only from the traditional critics of the New Left, but ". . . from those conservative and liberal forces which are still committed to the progressive ideas of the Republic." Hopefully this broadened opposition may lead to a redefinition of the role of government and the reinstitution of the rule of law, so that no one, not even the president, may declare himself above it.

Clearly the problem is no longer whether the government should intervene in such matters as the control of the economy or the provision of social welfare services, although some die-hard conservatives would have us return to this laissez-faire approach. Both Burnham, and Schick in his article, "The Cybernetic State," present cogent proof of the increasing powers of the federal government not only to regulate but also to replace private enterprise in areas such as education, health, transportation, and other public services. The cybernetic state, Schick informs us, is based upon a systems model guided by sociostatic norms in areas such as employment, poverty, or education set by "systems engineers, planners, and other generalists whose perspectives transcend the functional specialities." Schick's implicit faith in technology and scientific expertise minimizes the political issues involved in the control of the cybernetic state and the vast new possibilities for power which it opens.

The issue is not whether the government should intervene but who controls the government's increasing powers to regulate and allocate the nation's public as well as private resources. If government policies continue to be dominated by corporations, the military, and other powerful interest groups, then we are clearly moving toward a state governed by a "narrow executive-military élite" which cannot possibly pretend to represent the broad public interest, much less respond to the needs of the poor, racial minorities, women, youth, or other marginal groups in our society.

The demand for recognition from these groups grows daily, for they realize that it is only through the political process that they can hope to make their voices heard in American society. The middle class, too, grows increasingly restive as issues such as pollution, unemployment, drug use, crime, and now the energy crisis begin to threaten their well-being. The burden of responsibility for responding to these demands clearly lies with the government, for no other institution in our society has the leverage to curtail the growing power of the military-industrial complex. It remains to be seen whether the government will respond to these challenges or whether it will continue to place big business and private profits above the public welfare.

IRVING LOUIS HOROWITZ

The Pentagon Papers
and
Social Science

Today, no major political event, particularly one so directly linked to the forging of American foreign policy as the publication of the Pentagon Papers by the *New York Times* and the *Washington Post* can be fully described without accounting for the role of the social scientist. In this case, the economists clearly performed a major role. From the straightforward hawkish prescriptions offered in 1961 by Walt W. Rostow to the dovishly motivated release of secret documents on the conduct of the war in 1971 by Daniel Ellsberg, the contributions of social scientists were central. As a consequence, it is fitting, nay imperative, that the import of these monumental events be made plain for those of us involved in the production and dissemination of social science information and insight.

The publication of the Pentagon Papers is of central importance to the social science community in at least two respects: social scientists participated in the development of a posture and position toward the Vietnam involvement; and at a more abstract level, the publication of these papers provides lessons about political participation and policy-making for the social sciences.

We live in an age in which the social sciences perform a special and unique role in the lives of men and in the fates of government, whatever be the status of social science theory. And because the questions of laymen are no longer "is social science scientific," but "what kinds of recommendations are offered in the name of social science," it is important that social scientists inquire as to any special meaning of the Pentagon Papers and documents, over and above the general and broad-ranging discussions that take place in the mass media. Thus, my effort here is not to be construed as a general discussion of issues, but rather a specific discussion of results.

I. Findings

The Pentagon's project director for a *History of United States Decision-Making Process on Vietnam Policy* (now simply known as *The Pentagon Papers*), economist Leslie H. Gelb now of Brookings, remarked: "Writing history, especially where it blends into current events, especially where the current event is Vietnam, is a treacherous exercise." Former Secretary of Defense Robert S. McNamara authorized this treacherous exercise of a treacherous conflict in 1967. In initiation and execution this was to be "encyclopedic and objective." The actual compilation runs to 2.5 million words and 47 volumes of narrative and documents. And from what has thus far been made public, it is evident that this project was prepared with the same bloodless, bureaucratic approach that characterizes so much federally inspired social science and history. The Pentagon Papers attempt no original hypothesis, provide no insights into the behavior of the "other side," make scant effort to select important from trivial factors in the escalation process; they present no real continuity with past American foreign policy and in general eschew any sort of systematic survey research or interviewing of the participants and proponents. Yet, with all these shortcomings, these materials offer a fascinating and unique account of how peace-keeping

> In the absence of the governmental checks and balances present in other areas of our national life, the only effective restraint upon executive policy and power in the areas of national defense and international affairs may lie in an enlightened citizenry. Without an informed and free press there cannot be an enlightened people.
>
> *Justice Potter Stewart*

agencies became transformed into policy-making agencies. That this record was prepared by 36 political scientists, economists, systems analysts, inside dopesters and outside social science research agencies provides an additional fascination: how the government has learned to entrust its official records to mandarin types, who in exchange for the cloak of anonymity are willing to prepare an official record of events. An alarming oddity is that, in part at least, the chronicle was prepared by analysts who were formerly participants.

For those who have neither the time nor the patience to examine every document thus far released, it might be worthwhile to simply summarize what they contain. In so doing, it becomes clear that the Vietnam War was neither a Democratic nor a Republican war, but a war conducted by the political elite, often without regard to basic technical advice and considerations, and for reasons that had far less to do with curbing communism than with the failure of the other arms of government in their responsibility to curb executive egotism. The publication of these papers has chronicled this country's overseas involvement with a precision never before available to the American public. Indeed, we now know more about decision-making in Vietnam than about the processes by which we became involved in the Korean War. For instance, we have learned that:

1. The United States ignored eight direct appeals for aid from Ho Chi Minh in the first half-year following World War II. Underlying the American refusal to deal with the Vietnamese leader was the growth of the cold war and the opposition to assisting a communist leadership.

2. The Truman administration by 1949 had already accepted the "domino principle," after the National Security Council was told early in 1950 that the neighboring countries of Thailand and Burma could be expected to fall under communist control if Vietnam were controlled by a communist dominated regime.

3. The Eisenhower administration, particularly under the leadership of Secretary of State John Foster Dulles, refused to accept the Geneva accords ending the French-Indochina war on the grounds that it permitted this country "only a limited influence" in the affairs of the fledgling South Vietnam. Indeed, the Joint Chiefs of Staff opted in favor of displacing France as the key influence rather than assisting the termination of hostilities.

4. The final years of the Eisenhower administration were characterized by a decision to commit a relatively small number of United States military personnel to maintain the Diem regime in Saigon and to prevent a détente between Hanoi and Saigon.

5. The Kennedy administration transformed the limited risk gamble into an unlimited commitment. Although the troop levels were indeed still quite limited, the Kennedy administration moved special forces units into Vietnam, Laos and Cambodia—thus broadening the conflict to the area as a whole.

6. The Kennedy administration knew about and approved of plans for the military coup d'état that overthrew President Diem. The United States gave its support to an army group commited to military dictatorship and no compromise with the Hanoi regime.

7. The Johnson administration extended the unlimited commitment to the military regime of Saigon. Under this administration between 1965 and 1968, troop levels surpassed 500,000 and United States participation was to include the management of the conflict and the training of the ARVN.

8. After the Tet offensive began in January 1968, Johnson, under strong prodding from the military Chiefs of Staff, and from his field commanders, moved toward full scale mobilization, including the call-up of reserves. By the termination of the Johnson administration, the United States had been placed on a full-scale war footing.

Among the most important facts revealed by the Papers is that the United States first opposed a settlement based on the Geneva accords, signed by all belligerents; that the United States had escalated the conflict far in advance of the Gulf of Tonkin incident and had used congressional approval for legitimating commitments already undertaken rather than as a response to new communist provocations; and finally that in the face of internal opposition from the same Department of Defense that at first had sanctioned the war, the executive decided to disregard its own policy advisers and plunge ahead in a war already lost.

II. Decisions

Impressive in this enumeration of policy decisions is the clinical way decisions were made. The substitution of war game thinking for any real political thinking, the total submission of the Department of State to the Department of Defense in the making of foreign policy, and the utter collapse of any faith in compromise, consensus or cooperation between nations, and the ludicrous pursuit of victory (or at least non-defeat) in Vietnam, all are so forcefully illustrated in these Pentagon Papers, that the vigor with which their release was opposed by the Attorney General's office and the executive branch of government generally, can well be appreciated.

Ten years ago in writing *The War Game* I had occasion to say in a chapter concerning "American Politics and Military Risks" that "a major difficulty with the thinking of the new civilian militarists is that they study war while ignoring politics." The recent disclosure of the Pentagon Papers bears out that contention with a vengeance; a kind of hot house scientology emerges, in which the ends of foreign policy are neatly separated from the instruments of immediate destruction. That a certain shock and cynicism have emerged as a result of the revelations in these papers is more attributable to the loss of a war than to the novelty of the revelations. The cast of characters that have dragged us through the mire of a bloody conflict in Southeast Asia, from Walt W. Rostow to Henry A. Kissinger, remain to haunt us and taunt us. They move in and out of administrations with an ease that belies political party differences and underscores the existence of not merely a set of "experts," but rather a well defined ruling class dedicated to manufacturing and manipulating political formulas.

The great volume of materials thus far revealed is characterized by few obvious themes: but one of the more evident is the utter separation of the purposes of devastation from comprehension of the effects of such devastation. A kind of Howard Johnson sanitized vision of conflict emerges that reveals a gulf between the policy-makers and battlefield soldiers that is even wider and longer than the distance between Saigon and Washington. If the concept of war gaming is shocking in retrospect, this is probably due more to its utter and contemptible failure to provide battlefield victories than to any real development in social and behavioral science beyond the shibboleths of decision theory and game theory.

III. "Scientists"

A number of researchers as well as analysts of the Pentagon Papers were themselves social scientists. There were political scientists of considerable distinction, such as Morton Halperin and Melvin Gurtov; economists of great renown, such as Walt W. Rostow and Daniel Ellsberg; and systems analysts, such as Alain Enthoven. And then there was an assorted group of people, often trained in law, such as Roger Fisher and Carl Kaysen, weaving in and out of the Papers, providing both point and counterpoint. There are the thoroughly hawkish views of Walt Rostow; and the cautionary perspective of Alain Enthoven; and the more liberal recommendations of people like Roger Fisher. But it is clear that social scientists descend in importance as they move from hawk to dove. Walt Rostow is a central figure, and people like Carl Kaysen and Roger Fisher are at most peripheral consultants—who in fact, seem to have been more often conservatized and impressed by the pressurized

Washington atmosphere than to have had an impact on the liberalization or softening of the Vietnam posture.

The social scientific contingency in the Pentagon, whom I christened the "new civilian militarists" a decade ago, were by no means uniform in their reactions to the quagmire in Vietnam. Political scientists like Morton H. Halperin and economists like Alain C. Enthoven did provide cautionary responses, if not outright criticisms of the repeated and incessant requests for troop build-ups. The Tet offensive, which made incontrovertible the vulnerability of the American posture, called forth demands for higher troop levels on the part of Generals William C. Westmoreland and Maxwell Taylor. Enthoven, in particular, opposed this emphatically and courageously:

> Our strategy of attrition has not worked. Adding 206,000 more U.S. men to a force of 525,000, gaining only 27 additional maneuver battalions and 270 tactical fighters at an added cost to the U.S. of $10 billion per year raises the question of who is making it costly for whom. . . . We know that despite a massive influx of 500,000 U.S. troops, 1.2 million tons of bombs a year, 200,000 enemy killed in action in three years, 20,000 U.S. killed in action in three years, 200,000 U.S. wounded in action, etc., our control of the countryside and the defense of the urban areas is now essentially at pre-August 1965 levels. We have achieved stalemate at a high commitment. A new strategy must be sought.

Interestingly, in the same month, March 1968, when Enthoven prepared this critical and obviously sane report, he wrote a curious paper on "Thomism and the Concept of Just and Unjust Warfare," which, in retrospect, seemed to be Enthoven's way of letting people like myself know that he was a dissenting voice despite his earlier commitment to war game ideology and whiz-kid strategy.

As a result of these memoranda, Assistant Defense Secretary Paul Warnke argued against increased bombing and for a bombing pause. He and Assistant Secretary of Defense for Public Affairs, Phil G. Goulding, were then simply directed to write a draft that "would deal only with the troop issue;" hence forcing them to abandon the internal fight against an "expansion of the air war." And as it finally went to the White House, the report was bleached of any criticism. The mandarin role of the social scientists was reaffirmed: President Johnson's commitments went unchallenged. The final memo advocated deployment of 22,000 more troops, reserved judgment on the deployments of the remaining 185,000 troops and approved a 262,000 troop reserve build-up; it urged no new peace initiatives and simply declared that a division of opinion existed on the bombing policy, making it appear that the division in opinion was only tactical in nature. As the Pentagon Papers declared:

> Faced with a fork in the road of our Vietnam policy, the working group failed to seize the opportunity to change directions. Indeed, they seemed to recommend that we continue rather haltingly down the same road, meanwhile, consulting the map more frequently and in greater detail to insure that we were still on the right road.

One strange aspect of this war game strategy is how little the moves and motives of the so-called "other side" were

The time has come for the public to form its own opinion.
It has the opportunity. It can only do that by reading the
words of their public servants themselves and make their
own decisions on how well they have been served and how
well they want to be served in the future.

Daniel Ellsberg

ever taken into account. There is no real appreciation of the distinction between North Vietnam and the National Liberation Front of South Vietnam. There is not the slightest account taken of the actual decisions made by General Giap or Chairman Ho. The Tet offensive seems to have taken our grand strategists by as much surprise as the political elites whom they were planning for. While they were beginning to recognize the actual balance of military forces, Wilfred Burchett had already declared, in 1967 to be exact, that the consequences of the war were no longer in doubt—United States involvement could not forestall a victory of the communist factions North and South. Thus, not only do the Pentagon Papers reveal the usual ignorance of the customs, languages and habits of the people being so brutally treated, but also the unanticipated arrogance of assuming throughout that logistics would conquer all. Even the doves like George W. Ball never doubted for a moment that an influx of a certain number of United States troops would in fact swing the tide of battle the way that General Westmoreland said it would. The argument was rather over tactics: is such a heavy investment worth the end results? In fact, not one inner circle "wise man" raised the issue that the size of the troop commitment might be basically irrelevant to the negative (from an American viewpoint) outcome of the Southeast Asian operations. One no longer expects good history or decent ethnography from those who advise the rulers, but when this is compounded with a heavy dose of impoverished war gaming and strategic thinking in the void, then the question of "science for whom" might well be converted into the question of "what science and by whom."

All of this points up a tragic flaw in policy-making by social science experts. Their failure to generate or to reflect a larger constituency outside of themselves made them continually vulnerable to assaults from the military and from the more conservative sectors of the Pentagon. This vulnerability was so great that throughout the Pentagon Papers, one senses that the hawk position is always and uniformly outspoken and direct, while the dove position is always and uniformly ubiquitous and indirect. The basis of democratic politics has always been the mass participation of an informed electorate. Yet it was precisely this informed public, where a consensus against the war had been building, that was cut off from the policy-planners and recommenders. Consequently they were left in pristine

isolation to pit their logic against the crackpot realism of their military adversaries within the bowels of government.

IV. Disclosures

Certain serious problems arose precisely because of the secrecy tag: for example, former Vice President Hubert Humphrey and Secretary of State Dean Rusk have both denied having any knowledge whatsoever of these papers. Dean Rusk went so far as to say that the research methodology was handled poorly: "I'm rather curious about why the analysts who put this study together did not interview us, particularly when they were attributing attitudes and motives to us." (*New York Times,* Saturday, July 3, 1971.) Perhaps more telling is Dean Rusk's suggestion that the Pentagon Papers have the characteristics of an anonymous letter. Along with Dean Rusk, I too believe that the names of the roughly 40 scholars connected with the production of these papers should be published. To do otherwise would not only prevent the people involved from checking the veracity of the stories attributed to them, but more important, would keep the social science community from gaining a clearer insight into the multiple roles of scholars, researchers, professors and government analysts and policy-makers. The nature of science requires that the human authorities behind these multi-volumes be identified, as in the precedent established by the identification of the authors of the various bombing surveys done after World War II and the Korean War.

One serendipitous consequence of the Pentagon Papers has been to provide a more meaningful perspective toward the proposed "Code of Ethics" being advanced by so many social science professional associations. They all deal with the sanctity of the "subject's rights." All sorts of words guarding privacy are used: "rights of privacy and dignity," "protection of subjects from personal harm," "preservation of confidentiality of research data." The American Sociological Association proposals for example are typical:

Confidential information provided by a research subject must be treated as such by the sociologist. Even though research information is not a privileged communication under the law, the sociologist must, as far as possible, protect subjects and informants. Any promises made to such persons must be honored. . . . If an informant or other subject should wish, however, he can formally release the promise of confidentiality.

The Burden of Responsibility: Politics and the Power Structure

While the purpose of this code of ethics is sincerely geared to the protection of individuals under study, if taken literally, a man like Daniel Ellsberg would be subject to penalty, if not outright expulsion, on the grounds that he was never allowed by the individuals concerned to make his information public. What so many professional societies forget is that the right to full disclosure is also a principle, just as significant as the right of the private subject to confidentiality, and far more germane to the tasks of a social scientific learned society. The truly difficult ethical question comes not with the idea of maintaining confidentiality, but with determining what would be confidential, and when such confidentiality should be violated in terms of a higher principle. All social science codes of ethics presume an ethical standpoint which limits scientific endeavor, but when it is expedient to ignore or forget this ethical code, as in the case of the Pentagon Papers, the profession embarrassingly chooses to exhibit such a memory lapse. The publication of the Pentagon Papers should once again point the way to the highest obligation of social science organizations: to the truth, plain and simple, rather than the preservation of confidentiality, high and mighty. And unless this lesson is fully drawn, a dichotomous arrangement will be made between making public the documents of public servants whose policies they disapprove of and keeping private the documentation on deviants whom supposedly the social scientists are concerned with protecting. This is not an ethical approach but an opportunistic approach. It rests on political and professional expediency. The need therefore is to reassert the requisites of science for full disclosure, and the ethics of full disclosure as the only possible ethics for any group of professional scientists. If the release of the Pentagon Papers had done nothing else, it has reaffirmed the highest principle of all science: full disclosure, full review of the data, full responsibility for what is done, by those who do the research.

V. Secrets

Another area that deeply concerns the social scientist and that is highlighted in the Pentagon Papers is the government's established norms of secrecy. While most officials in government have a series of work norms with which to guide their behavior, few forms of anticipatory socialization have applied to social scientists who advise government agencies. The professionalization of social scientists has normally been directed toward publicity rather than secrecy. This fosters sharp differences in opinion and attitudes between the polity and the academy, since the reward system for career advancement is so clearly polarized.

The question of secrecy is intimately connected with matters of policy, because the standing assumption of policy-makers (particularly in the field of foreign affairs) is not to reveal themselves entirely. No government in the game of international politics feels that its policies can be candidly revealed for full public review; therefore, operational research done in connection with policy considerations is customarily bound by the canons of government privacy. But while scientists have a fetish for publicizing their information as a mechanism for professional advancement no less than as a definition of their essential role in the society, the political branches of society have as their fetish the protection of private documents and privileged information. Therefore, the polity places a premium not only on acquiring vital information, but on maintaining silence about such information precisely to the degree that the data might be of high decisional value. This leads to differing premiums between analysts and policy-makers and to tensions between them.

Social scientists complain that the norm of secrecy oftentimes involves yielding their own essential work premises. A critical factor reinforcing an unwilling acceptance of the norm of secrecy by social scientists is the allocation of most government research funds for military or semi-military purposes. Senate testimony has shown that 70 percent of federal funds targeted for the social sciences involve such restrictions.

The real wonder turns out to be not the existence of the secrecy norm but the relative availability of large chunks of information. Indeed, the classification of materials is so inept that documents (such as the Pax America research) designated as confidential or secret by one agency may often be made available as a public service by another agency. There are also occasions when documents placed in a classified category by sponsoring government agencies can be gotten without charge from the private research institute doing the work.

But the main point is that the norm of secrecy makes it extremely difficult to separate science from patriotism and

William Shirer has commented on the fact that government papers are so often made available to history only through the fact of a revolution or change in regime. He did not relate the present revelations to a situation which, if by no means revolutionary, involves an extremely serious erosion of the legitimacy of the government. In this sense, the sociological implications of the publishing of the Pentagon Papers may be as much of a landmark as their political reverberations.

Peter Steinfels

hence makes it that much more difficult to question the research design itself. Social scientists often express the nagging doubt that accepting the first stage—the right of the government to maintain secrecy—often carries with it acquiescence in a later stage—the necessity for silence on the part of social researchers who may disagree with the political uses of their efforts.

Steinfels quote goes here

The demand for government secrecy has a telling impact on the methodology of the social sciences. Presumably social scientists are employed because they, as a group, represent objectivity and honesty. Social scientists like to envision themselves as a wall of truth off which policy-makers may bounce their premises. They also like to think that they provide information which cannot be derived from sheer public opinion. Thus, to some degree social scientists consider that they are hired or utilized by government agencies because they will say things that may be unpopular but nonetheless significant. However, since secrecy exists, the premises upon which most social scientists seek to work are strained by the very agencies which contract out their need to know.

The terms of research and conditions of work tend to demand an initial compromise with social science methodology. The social scientist is placed in a cognitive bind. He is conditioned not to reveal maximum information lest he become victimized by the federal agencies that employ his services. Yet he is employed precisely because of his presumed thoroughness, impartiality and candor. The social scientist who survives in government service becomes circumspect or learns to play the game. His value to social science becomes seriously jeopardized. On the other hand, once he raises these considerations, his usefulness to the policy-making sector is likewise jeopardized.

Social scientists believe that openness is more than meeting formal requirements of scientific canons; it is also a matter of making information universally available. The norm of secrecy leads to selective presentation of data. The social scientist is impeded by the policy-maker because of contrasting notions about the significance of data and the general need for replication elsewhere and by others. The policy-maker who demands differential access to findings considers this a normal return for the initial expenditure of risk capital. Since this utilitarian concept of data is alien to the scientific standpoint, the schism between the social

scientist and the policy-maker becomes pronounced precisely at the level of openness of information and accessibility to the work achieved. The social scientist's general attitude is that sponsorship of research does not entitle any one sector to benefit unduly from the findings—that sponsorship by federal agencies ought not place greater limitations on the use of work done than sponsorship by either private agencies or universities.

VI. Loyalties

A major area that deeply concerns social scientists is that of dual allegiance. The Pentagon Papers have such specific requirements and goal-oriented tasks that they intrude upon the autonomy of the social scientist by forcing upon him choices between dual allegiances. The researcher is compelled to choose between participating fully in the world of the federal bureaucracy or remaining in more familiar academic confines. He does not want the former to create isolation in the latter. Thus, he often criticizes the federal bureaucracy's unwillingness to recognize his basic needs: 1) the need to teach and retain full academic identity; 2) the need to publicize information; and above all 3) the need to place scientific responsibility above the call of patriotic obligation—when they may happen to clash. In short, he does not want to be plagued by dual or competing allegiances.

The norm of secrecy exacerbates this problem. Although many of the social scientists who become involved with federal research are intrigued by the opportunity to address important issues, they are confronted by some bureaucracies which oftentimes do not share their passion for resolving social problems. For example, federal obligations commit the bureaucracy to assign high priority to items having military potential and effectiveness and low priorities to many supposedly idealistic and far-fetched themes in which social scientists are interested.

Those social scientists, either as employees or as consultants connected with the government, are hamstrung by federal agencies which are in turn limited by political circumstances beyond their control. A federal bureaucracy must manage cumbersome, overgrown committees and data gathering agencies. Federal agencies often protect a status quo merely for the sake of rational functioning. They must conceive of academicians in their midst as a standard bureaucratic type entitled to rise to certain federal ranks.

Federal agencies limit innovating concepts to what is immediately useful, not out of choice and certainly not out of resentment of the social sciences but from what is deemed as impersonal necessity. This has the effect of reducing the social scientist's role in the government to that of ally or advocate rather than innovator or designer. Social scientists begin to feel that their enthusiasm for rapid change is unrealistic, considering how little can be done by the government bureaucracy. And they come to resent involvement in theoryless application to immediacy foisted on them by the "new utopians," surrendering in the process the value of confronting men with the wide range of choices of what might be done. The schism, then, between autonomy and involvement is as thorough as that between secrecy and publicity, for it cuts to the quick well-intentioned pretensions at human engineering.

The problem of competing allegiances is not made simpler by the fact that many high ranking federal bureaucrats have strong nationalistic and conservative political ideologies. This contrasts markedly with the social scientist, who comes to Washington not only with a belief in the primacy of science over patriotism but also with a definition of patriotism that is more open-ended and consciously liberal than that of most appointed officials. Hence, he often perceives the conflict to extend beyond research design and social applicability into one of the incompatible ideologies held respectively by the social scientist and entrenched Washington bureaucrats. He comes to resent the proprietary attitude of the bureaucrat toward "his" government processes. The social scientist is likely to consider his social science biases a necessary buffer against the federal bureaucracy.

VII. Elitists

The publication of the Pentagon Papers sheds new light on political pluralist and power concentrationist hypotheses. When push finally did turn to shove, President Nixon and the government officials behaved as members of a ruling class and not as leaders of their political party. President Nixon might easily have chosen to let the Democratic party take the burn and bear the brunt of the assaults for the betrayal of a public trust. Indeed the Nixon administration might have chosen to join the chorus of those arguing that the Democratic party is indeed the war party, as revealed in these documents; whereas the Republican party emerges as the party of restraint—if not exactly principle. Here was a stunning opportunity for Mr. Nixon to make political capital at a no risk basis: by simply drawing attention to the fact that the war was constantly escalated by President Truman, who refused to bargain in good faith with Ho Chi Minh despite repeated requests, by President Kennedy, who moved far beyond anything President Eisenhower had in mind for the area, by making the fatal committment not just to land troops but to adopt a domino theory of winning the war, by President Johnson, whose role can well be considered as nefarious: coming before the American people as a peace candidate when he had already made the fatal series of committments to continuing escalation and warfare. That the president chose not to do so illustrates the sense of class solidarity that the political elites in this country manifest; a sense of collective betrayal of the priesthood, rather than a sense of obligation

to score political points and gain political trophies. And that too should be a lesson in terms of the actual power within the political structure of a small ruling elite. Surely this must be considered a fascinating episode in its own right: the reasons are complex, but surely among them must rank the belief that Mr. Nixon behaved as a member of the ruling elite, an elite that had transcendent obligations far beyond the call of party, and that was the call of class.

One fact made clear by the Pentagon Papers is the extent to which presidentialism has become the ideology and the style in American political life. The infrequency of any reference to the judicial situation with respect to the war in Southeast Asia and the virtual absence of any reference to congressional sentiments are startling confirmations of an utter change in the American political style. If any proof was needed of the emerging imbalance between the executive and other branches of government, these papers should put such doubt to rest. The theory of checks and balances works only when there are, in fact, groups such as senators or stubborn judges who believe in the responsibility of the judiciary and legislative branches to do just that, namely, establish check and balance. In the absence of such vigor, the war in Southeast Asia became very much a series of executive actions. And this itself should give pause to the advocates of consensus theory in political science.

The failure of the Vietnam episode has resulted in a reconsideration of presidentialism as the specific contemporary variant of power elite theory. The renewed vigor of Congress, the willingness, albeit cautionary willingness, of the Supreme Court to rule on fundamental points of constitutional law, are indicative of the resurgence of pluralism. In this sense, the darkest hour of liberalism as a political style has witnessed a liberal regrouping around the theme of mass politics. Even the domestic notions of community organization and states rights are indicative of the limits of presidentialism—so that Mr. Nixon, at one and the same time, is reluctantly presiding over the swan song of presidentialism in foreign affairs, while celebrating its demise in domestic affairs. The collapse of the Vietnam War and the trends toward neo-isolationism are in fact simply the reappearance of political pluralism in a context where to go further in the concentration of political power in the presidency would in all likelihood mean the upsurge of fascism, American style. If the concept of a power elite was reconfirmed in the Pentagon Papers, so too, strangely, was the concept of political pluralism in the public response to them. The countervailing influence of the Supreme Court was clearly manifested in the ringing affirmation of the First Amendment, in the denial of the concept of prior restraint and prior punitive actions, and in the very rapidity of the decision itself. This action by the judiciary, coupled with a show of muscle on the part of the Senate and House concerning the conduct of the war, military appropriations, boondoggles and special privileges for a select handful of aircraft industries in their own way served to underscore the continued importance of the open society and the pluralistic basis of power. Even executives, such as Hubert H. Humphrey, have declared in favor of full disclosure and reiterated the principles guiding the publication of the Pentagon Papers.

Power elites operate behind a cloak of anonymity. When that cloak is lifted, an obvious impairment in the operational efficiency of elites occurs. What has happened with the release of the Pentagon Papers is precisely this collapse of anonymity, no less than secrecy. As a result, the formal apparatus of government can assert its prerogatives. This does not mean that the executive branch of government will be unable to recover from this blow at its prestige, or that it will no longer attempt to play its trump card: decision-making by executive fiat. It does mean, however, that the optimal conditions under which power elites operate have been seriously hampered. The degree of this impairment and the length of time it will obtain depend exclusively on the politics of awareness and participation, no less than the continuing pressures for lowering the secrecy levels in high level international decision-making.

Probably the most compelling set of reasons given for President Nixon's bitter opposition to the release of the Pentagon Papers is that provided by Melvin Gurtov, one of the authors of the secret Pentagon study and an outstanding political scientist specializing in Asian affairs. He speaks of three deceits in current American Vietnamese policy: "The first and most basic deceit is the Administration's contention that we're winding down and getting out of the war." In fact, Vietnamization is a "domestic political ploy that really involves the substitution of air power for ground power." The second deceit is that "we're truly interested in seeing the prisoners of war released." Gurtov notes that "as far as this administration is concerned the prisoners of war are a political device, a device for rationalizing escalation, by saying these are acts that are necessary to show our concern for the prisoners." The third deceit "is that under the Nixon Doctrine the United States is not interested in making new committments in Asia." In fact, the administration used the Cambodia coup "as an opportunity for creating for itself a new commitment in Southeast Asia, namely the survival of a non-Communist regime in Pnompenh." This outspoken position indicates that the defense of the power elite of the past by President Nixon might just as well be construed as a self-defense of the power elite in the present.

VIII. Conspiracies

The Pentagon Papers provide much new light on theories of power elite and power diffusion and also provide an equal measure of information on conspiracy theory. And while it is still true that conspiracy *theory* is bad theory, it is false to assert that no conspiracies exist or are not perpetrated by the government. It might indeed be the case that all governments, insofar as they are formal organizations, have secrets; and we call these secrets, conspiracies. From this point of view, the interesting question is how so few leaks resulted from an effort of such magnitude and involving so many people as setting policy in the Vietnam War. Rather than be surprised that these papers reached the public domain four to six years after the fact, one should wonder how the government was able to maintain silence on matters of such far-ranging and far-reaching consequence.

Cyrus Eaton, American industrialist and confidant of many communist leaders, indicates that the Vietnamese almost instantaneously were made aware of United States policy decisions. But I seriously doubt that they actually had copies of these materials. Rather, like the American public itself, they were informed about the decisions but not the cogitations and agitations that went into the final decision. Perhaps this is the way all governments operate; nonetheless, it is fascinating—at least this once—to be privy to the process and not simply the outcome, and to see the foibles of powerful men and not just the fables manufactured for these men after the fact.

These papers tend to underwrite the common-sensical point of view that governments are not to be trusted, and to undermine the more sophisticated interpretation that governments are dedicated to the task of maintaining democracy at home and peace abroad. As bitter as it may seem, common sense cynicism has more to recommend it than the sophisticated, well elaborated viewpoints which take literally the formal structure of government and so readily tend to dismiss the informal response to power and pressure from men at the top. The constant wavering of Lyndon B. Johnson, his bellicose defiance of all evidence and information that the bombings were not having the intended effect, followed by shock that his lieutenants like Robert McNamara changed their position at midstream (which almost constituted a betrayal in the eyes of the president) were in turn followed by a more relaxed posture and a final decision not to seek the presidency. All of this forms a human drama that makes the political process at once fascinating and frightful; fascinating because we can see the psychology of politics in action, and frightful because the presumed rationality is by no means uniformly present.

The publication of the Pentagon Papers, while a considerable victory for the rights of a free press and of special significance to all scientists who still uphold the principle of full disclosure as the norm of all political as well as scientific endeavor, is not yet a total victory for a democratic society—that can only happen when the concept of secrecy is itself probed and penetrated, and when the concept of undeclared warfare is finally and fully repudiated by the public and its representatives. The behavior of the government in its effort to suppress publication of the Pentagon Papers cannot simply be viewed as idiosyncratic, but rather as part of the structure of the American political processes in which the expert displaces the politician, and the politicians themselves become so beholden to the class of experts for information, that they dare not turn for guidance to the people they serve. For years, critics of the Vietnam War have been silenced and intimidated by the policy makers' insistence that when all the facts were known the hawk position would be vindicated and the dove position would be violated. Many of the facts are now revealed—and the bankruptcy of the advocates of continued escalation is plain for all to see. Hopefully, this will strengthen the prospects for peace, and firm up those who, as an automatic reflex, assume the correctness of the government's position on all things military. It is to be hoped that the principle of democracy, of every person counting as one, once more becomes the source of fundamental decision-making and political discourse.

ABRAHAM EDEL

Scientists, Partisans and Social Conscience

Nearly every group in our society—from businessmen to policemen to teachers—finds no difficulty in talking about social responsibilities. Why has there been confusion about it in the case of the scientific enterprise? At least one reason, apart from historical and sociological considerations, has been the conception of science—the strange mixture of the timorous and the lordly stance—which attempted to give a single answer in terms of a particular conception of the lone scientist as intrinsically a truth-seeker. This is both narrow and wide—narrow because it ignores the understanding of the scientific enterprise in terms of its changing historical relations, and wide because the very pursuit of truth itself, if faced as a path in the contemporary world, carries its practitioner much farther than he may think on empirical and historical grounds.

In a time of crisis the problem of the responsibilities of scientists as scientists should constantly recur. What is surprising is that it should keep coming back in the same old terms and with the same old dichotomies, and—in spite of twentieth-century philosophy having been characterized as an Age of Analysis—without a clearer analysis of the questions themselves and their presuppositions. It is as if we started with some fixed definition of the scientist, whether the layman's image of a father-figure in white coat or the philosopher's fallibilistic doubter, and set it against an equally fixed concept of a social conscience embodying the usual hard-line division between individual and social responsibility. And it is as if we simply held up and compared the two pictures and reported that there was or was not a path between the two conceptions.

There is something very wrong with this procedure and its results. Science is a historically changing enterprise and its responsibilities flow not only from its perennial features but from its place in a given time and level of social development. A sense of social responsibility does not take its character from the perennial features of the human conscience alone, but from the whole sociocultural complex in its historical development. Hence any picture of the relations of the two rests on assumed pictures of the whole of the human world in its operations in our age. Once we realize this we can see how complex is the scope of our problem.

I shall therefore discuss at the outset the changing character of the scientific enterprise, go on to the changing character of social conscience, and finally draw conclusions about the contemporary social responsibilities of science.

The Scientific Enterprise

The material and sociological changes in the scientific enterprise are familiar enough. There are more scientists now alive and at work than the past total in all human history. Science is also more systematically organized. It has large resources. Basic research is now encouraged and subsidized. Sociologically, science is not a self-determining field. In spite of the occasional dreams of technocracy or the occasional entry of a scientist into the directory of ruling classes, science is the servant, not the Platonic guardian. It has many masters and many strings by which it is pulled, even in the freer atmosphere of the better university where its practitioners can soothe themselves with a truth-for-truth's-sake ideology. We know that some scientists have shifted from physics to theoretical biology, despairing of any physical research outside the grasp of a war machine. By contrast, the relation of the scientific enterprise to business and the search for profits seemed almost benign, till sociology produced the concept of the "military-industrial complex." But at this point I want to explore the internal changes in the scientific enterprise—both in the theory of knowledge and in the practical attitudes of men—that the progress of science has brought about; it is these changes that determine the responsibility of scientists in the contemporary world. I want to distinguish four such changes:

☐ A shift in the view of human interference in the course of events.

☐ The growing scope of the scientific enterprise.

☐ The development of what may be called an "ecological mode of thought."

☐ An apparent change in the relation of practice to theory in the scientific enterprise.

1) *The model of human interference.* Men have always wanted to extend their control of the world and themselves, but the ideal of science has not always been associated with that of control. In ancient Greek philosophy the ideal of science was the intellectual grasp of the eternal; the purer the science, therefore, the less the extent of human control. The idea of knowledge as power had a

slow growth. We can see this clearly in the human attitudes to crisis. First there is a kind of weather-model; you wait till the crisis blows over, if you are lucky. Economic crises were treated in this way till quite recently. Then there is the intervention-model: you intervene only to remove obstacles, so that nature can take its course. This was the medical model under the older teleological approach that nature works for the best. With the Cartesian view of the body as a machine, the idea of interfering to control came to the fore; now some see the body as a mechanism with replaceable, even improvable parts.

In the social field, resistance to intervention is old. We may recall Aristotle's story, in his *Politics*, of the society in which a person who moved a change in the laws had a halter put around his neck, and if his motion lost, he was hanged on the spot. The adulation of tradition has an almost parallel character—to try consciously to remake, to plan the whole, is to exhibit the height of folly. The contemporary attitude is one of the control-model permeating all fields. It reflects not only the vast expansion of science, but also the desperate state of many of our problems, in which a weather-model would mean the acceptance of disasters. Of course even the attitude to the weather is changing: the next generation may think such a name for a resignation-model rather queer and inaccurate.

2) *The growing scope of the scientific enterprise.* It was barely yesterday that arguments were still popular about the inherent limitations of science. First a sharp line was drawn between the physical and the human-social, and the latter declared out of bounds. Then parts of psychology and the social were surrendered, but the cultural and the historical were ideographic, empathetic, value-ridden. We need not track down all the barriers that were thrust aside. Of course, the conception of science changed in the process; it ceased being the universalistic, mechanical-quantitative in the nineteenth-century sense; probability and statistics made their sweep into the human field; generalized and refined mathematical conceptions of order upset the sharp distinction of quantity and quality; and so on. The outcome is that the whole domain of knowledge lies open to the attempts of science. To attempt is not to succeed, but *a priori* and metaphysical limitations seem to be a thing of the past. The domain of ignorance is and will be indefinitely vast. But from a practical point of view it can no longer be used as an *a priori* veto on attempts at knowledge and control. In more-stable days, it could be said that no experimental ventures should be made in human life which involved a plunge into the unknown, because disasters might result. Now the same argument often can be urged against *not* making experimental ventures; for the consequences of continuing in the old ways in a rapidly changing world may be quite as unknowable and quite as disastrous. This argument does not justify recklessness in experiment; we are learning how reckless we have been. But it underlines the recklessness of conservatism too. In short, the emphasis falls on responsible attempts at control. The burden of responsibility falls with increasing weight on the scientific enterprise.

3) *The ecological mode of thought.* Part of the recklessness has come not from ignorance but from neglect of knowl-edge in other fields. There is arising a changed mode of thought which we may call "ecological" because it is so sharply illustrated in ecological studies. We have become very sensitive to the way in which attempts at control in one direction have upset the balance of nature in others, as in the case of insecticides and the disposal of industrial wastes. So we now demand that the application of knowledge be carried out in terms of the whole range of relevant knowledge available. In a column in the *New York Times* James Reston quotes Prime Minister Clement Attlee's remark that, when he concurred in President Harry Truman's decision to drop the atomic bomb on Hiroshima, they knew nothing about the genetic effects of fallout, though in fact, as Reston points out, H.J. Muller had won the Nobel Prize in 1927 for his evidence of the genetic effects of radiation.

Another aspect in the shift in outlook is a demand that one-sided evaluation should not dominate policy; for example, when offshore oil drilling springs a leak, the oil industry may worry about the seepage of salt water into oil, and the seashore population about dispersing the oil lest it cover the beaches. But the chemical used to disperse the oil may have a more deleterious effect on marine life than the oil itself.

On the theoretical side, an ecological mode of thought involves a systems approach, in which there is not only a meeting of different sciences in relation to a particular problem, but there may be a recasting of formulations in the hitherto isolated disciplines. This approach may in part constitute a critique of isolated abstract formulation of knowledge itself in an unduly narrowed domain—the fallacy, for example, of the presidential candidate in the late 1920s who argued that the American economy was in fine shape but something happened abroad and it spread to cause the Great Depression. He failed to realize that the description of an economy in the modern world should be as part of a world-system.

It is probably space research which best dramatizes the need for a full picture which combines the work of many sciences. Applied to the whole of human life, we begin to think of the planet itself as a spaceship, a relatively closed system in which the cyclical processes maintaining a balance have to be known and reckoned with if disaster is to be avoided.

4) *The relation of practice to theory in the scientific enterprise.* Practical questions are playing a greater role in scientific work today. Experiment itself requires more extended use and organization of resources. In part it is because developed sciences experiment over a broader field. Nuclear tests involve a wide geographic area; medical experiments may require a large population of subjects; economic and political experiments have to take place in the on-going life of a society. In part it is because the very tools of testing and observation become large and complex technological achievements, whether it be the telescopes of astronomy or the standardization of tests in psychology and the use of computers in behavioral science generally. In part it is because the field of practical application may itself be furnishing a test in experience which adds weight for or against a theoretical position. For example, the collapse of a bridge brings to a test the strength of the materials, the

appearance of side-effects tests the safety of a drug, the day-by-day sessions of the psychoanalyst constitute some kind of check on the theory of therapy, and so on. And in part it is because the subject matter of experiment, especially in social science, may itself be the practical issue of human well-being, so that the experiment is one of how to diminish crime or use of drugs or to achieve fewer family breakups. In fact this is so widespread that some theoretical attempts have been made to redefine the social sciences by human objectives, for instance, economics as the science of securing high productivity and wide distribution without depressions.

In much of this, where the scientific study is of human beings, the integration of practical application and experiment becomes so close that they seem almost two different ways of saying the same thing. Thus in medicine the line grows thin between the experimental effect of a drug and its medical efficacy. In recent governmental hearings on the contraceptive pill, one outcome was a recommendation that every doctor regard every use of it by a patient as an experiment. One could draw an interesting parallel from the history of thought between the integration of the empirical element in science and the symptoms of integration of the practical element now taking place. In its early history, the model of science was wholly mathematical-conceptual and experience had merely an outside suggestive role. In time, not only did the areas that were "merely empirical" achieve respectability as fit subjects for science, but science itself became thought of as "empirical science." Practical application too has been traditionally conceived as having merely an illustrative or facilitating role. But its closer relations seem to bring it near to occupying the place of an insider in the scientific enterprise. The integration of practical application within the complex of theory and experience may mean that the concept of the scientific enterprise is itself being refashioned.

If these four tendencies constitute a trend in our understanding of the scientific enterprise, there will as a consequence be serious inroads on the traditional view that the scientist as individual or the scientist as citizen may have social responsibilities, but not as scientist. How is such a view of science possible when the scientific enterprise has come to take a control-stance, to range over the whole of human life, to adopt an ecological mode of thought, and to bring practical application within the scope of its work? Does not such an emerging view of the scientific enterprise itself demand a social conscience?

It is possible to invoke the metaphysical dogma of the sharp separation of value and fact as an *a priori* barrier to this demand. But it must not be assumed that science is equivalent to fact in such a dichotomy; science may very well involve some facts and some values, no matter how strongly the dogma be held to. If the scientific enterprise is allowed an internal value of the pursuit of truth, it becomes an empirical matter how far into the value domain this carries the scientist. For he is committed to defending the pursuit of truth as scientist, not merely as citizen or individual. And if the picture of the world should happen to be that only a particular political policy will preserve the pursuit of truth, and all others will subvert it, he may find himself as scientist committed to political action. Of course, there is the possibility of drawing back.

It might be said that while the scientific enterprise, as a human affair, involves values, science as an ideal type of activity does not. But this argument is, I suspect, a desperate move. It will end up by holding that the aim of science is not the discovery of truth, but only the discovery of theoretical systems to fit accumulated data—that the aim is only to show which theoretical formulations are assigned with what degrees of probability on the basis of what evidence. This can, I think, be worked out to a refined extent. But the result will bear little resemblance to what we think of as the scientific enterprise; it is rather a particular redefinition of science. And it would be question-begging to argue that it is justified because it would preserve the value-free character of science.

Social Conscience

The social conscience of a society can be described as a pattern of assumed and felt responsibility for others, a concern for the well-being of people and for the solution of dominant social problems. Every society has some such pattern. Individuals may differ in the extent and intensity in which they exhibit responsibility. But the scope of social conscience, its mode of expression, the kinds of topics on which it is directed, are historically variable and can be seen as sociocultural formations. The only way to understand the present character of our social conscience is to see it as the outcome of a historical development of the last few centuries.

By the seventeenth century, a new pattern of conscience was in the making. We need not enter into the background of the emerging economic order in which an acquisitive individualism became dominant nor the religious break with the older authoritarian church as a result of which the lone individual directly faced his God. Soon the individual was no longer enmeshed in the guilt of original sin with its weight of obligations. He became increasingly an atomic will, exercising his choice and recognizing no obligation that did not issue from his will. This *moral voluntarism* or, in interpersonal and social relations, *moral contractualism*, became enshrined as an individualistic pattern of obligations and responsibilities. It is clearly marked in political, legal and moral theory. In politics the very state was conceived as contractual in origin: atomic individuals entered with an initial capital of natural rights, and took on burdens only by consent, for the effective maintenance and expression of their rights. In law, the field of contract increasingly took over human relations that had been the subject of institutional regulation; in Maine's familiar phrase, the movement of progressive societies was from status to contract. In the theory of tort and crime, men went far toward shedding fault and responsibility for anything that could not be traced by direct connection to their intentional acts or by indirect connection to their negligence.

It is perhaps the abstract regions of ethical theory that show most starkly the character of the shift. The older pattern of duties imposed on men by God's will and applied by derivation from natural law, without consulting individual will or consent, gives way to a primary dichotomy between self and other. In the "other" are telescoped all the intermediate kinds of ties—family, kin, small group, as well as society at large. Moral philosophers in the eighteenth century, faced with Hobbes' stern egoism, attempted to justify benevolence, that is, to persuade the individual to stretch out his hand toward others, his non-self. They seemed to think, as Hobbes himself had done, that a sober rationality would take a man beyond himself, even if only to protect himself, that a greater wisdom would find an identity of interest with others, that beneficence would be a good investment yielding appropriate return, or that private profit pursued would redound to public well-being through greater productivity.

These roundabout routes for mustering a social conscience are familiar enough. Nor were they questions of abstract theory alone. For their anxious character reflected the breakdown in traditional ways of handling widespread poverty, suffering and social displacement. The career of parish relief and poor laws in England, supplemented by Dickens' novels and the bitter history of trade-union organizational struggles, is evidence enough. When the twentieth-century outburst of industrial progress faced men with the familiar dislocation—industrial accidents, unemployment, poverty, social insecurity—the intellectual equipment for social responsibility was utterly inadequate, and justification for what was socially unavoidable and socially desirable had to be fashioned almost afresh.

I need not recapitulate the familiar story of the growth of social responsibility and the struggles in this century, both theoretical and practical, that were waged to secure workmen's compensation, unemployment insurance, social security, welfare support, medical care, extension of educational opportunity, and so on. It is a somber paradox that human treatment was often argued for *not* because of any sense of the fellowship of man, but because the worker was seen as a factor in production, whose depreciation should be borne by those who gain from using it, just as they had to stand the losses in the wear and tear of machinery. But of course this presupposed that men, unlike worn-out machines, could not simply be thrown on the scrap-heap or would not endure being so thrown. Nowadays even the scrap-heap has become a problem of social responsibility and the debate goes on whether pollution is to be faced as a social problem met through the tax fund or through throwing the burden as "external costs" on the enterprises that produce the pollution as a normal part of their operation. But perhaps the best example of how far we have moved in developing a pattern of social responsibility is the current consideration of a guaranteed minimum annual income.

The growth of a social conscience in all these ways does not, however, spell the end of the individualistic tradition in morality. Strangely enough, it is becoming more not less powerful and taking over provinces hitherto marked as social. Perhaps the most extreme form of individualist reconstruction is seen in the rise of individual responsibility *against* authority and the state, as contrasted with the older social conception of patriotism, obedience and loyalty. A number of diverse forces have fed this growth of individual judgment. One is no doubt the weakening of patriotism as a dominant binding relation, in the development of the wider loyalties of an increasingly

unified humanity. A great share of causal responsibility goes to the discrediting of the mystique of the state in the evidence of Hitlerism and its deeds; this is best seen in the outcome of the Nuremberg trials in which even disobedience to military commands is enjoined where basically immoral action is commanded. I think that a third factor in elevating individual judgment lies in the lessons of experience with intellectual repression—for example, such impositions of ideological dogmatism in the Soviet Union as the notorious Lysenko affair and its domination of genetics, or our own experience of the drive for conformity in the so-called McCarthy period of the 1950s.

In the 1960s a fourth factor was added to our experience—the civil rights movement, in which legality was on the side of discrimination, and, later, the opposition to the Vietnam War. The growth of civil disobedience as a technique of social change has thus been rapid, and the movement to give greater legal scope to conscience is a serious one; for example, to allow conscientious opposition to a particular war, not merely to war itself, as a ground for draft-exemption.

The ambivalent attitude to individual judgment in contemporary society reflects, I believe, two conflicting forces. On the one hand, the growth of corporate enterprise and large-scale organization presses for conformity. On the other, the complexity of technological and social organization and the weight of problems and the rapidity of change in all fields of life demand a high degree of inventiveness, individual initiative in thought, a constant stream of new ideas. And so we have almost the paradox of nonconformity becoming a conformist demand. The weight of individual decision and the lack of social guidance for decision in many areas of life are greater than ever before.

On the theoretical side, too, the individualistic form of morality has been growing rather than receding. And yet, though individual decision and responsibility are the central focus of theoretical developments, this is no longer the old individualism of the atomic self, cut off by initial stipulation from society as its opposite. Dewey's individualism proposes the rich development of the person as a social goal for education and morals and social institutions. And Sartre's intensely individual focus has him assume responsibility for all that is immoral around him. A man cannot, says Sartre, shift off responsibility for a war that he had no part in making, for he could always be asked what he has done to stop it. The depth of social responsibility for the individual conscience in the moral philosophies of today is central, no longer peripheral or a good business transaction.

What is happening is a long overdue breakdown of the individual-social dichotomy. Both the growth of our knowledge of man and the development of our complex, interrelated modern life make this dichotomy less significant for understanding what kind of self a man develops and what his obligations and responsibilities are. It is not yet clear what kind of categories will emerge as central in ethics and human understanding. That of the active or creative, as against the fixed, currently looms large, but this too may reflect the intensity of change. Yet it does contain the permanent lesson that man's self-knowledge is an active point of self-reconstruction rather than a learning of what is already fixed by nature. This lesson was already clear in the nineteenth century. In historical terms it is found in the Marxian conception of freedom as the growth of human awareness of the laws of the world and man, which enables man to make greater progress in the attainment of his human values. In individualistic subjective terms it is clearly stated by Kierkegaard when in his *Either/Or* he contrasts the Socratic moral maxim of "know thyself" with his own maxim of "choose thyself."

Morality is self-making and society-making and there is no cut between the two. The growth of social conscience in the contemporary world represents a profound transformation in the life of men, breaking into their consciousness, reshaping thought and sentiment, and creating the opportunity for a freer reconstruction. Whatever historical and social sources, it has a growing firmness which imparts to it the voice of judgment. It is with this conscience and its demands that the scientist must reckon as he attempts to shape—whether to expand or limit—the responsibilities of his profession.

The Scientific Enterprise and Social Conscience

Let us now ask what role the scientist should take in relation to the social conscience, what specific pattern of responsibilities he should assume. On the one hand, the scope of scientific knowledge suggests the greater share in the social conscience; on the other, the high standards of evidence and the disinterested character of scientific inquiry suggest distinguishing sharply between the scientist and the citizen and assigning responsibility to a man as citizen or as individual, not as scientist.

There are two ways to deal with this line of argument. One is basically revolutionary in the sphere of thought, for it upsets the categories and dichotomies in terms of which the question is framed. Thus it may be said that the role-playing which distinguishes the man as scientist, as citizen, as individual, is becoming an increasingly meaningless game, that it will go the way of the older distinctions between the economic man and the moral man, or the self as individual and the self as social. There are particular moral problems of conflict in different relationships, but no general partitioning of the person and his responsibility; man and human life are becoming too integrated for that, and even in the past such distinctions were never more than relative isolation of systems and practices in a basically unified human life. The second path is less drastic: it is the argument that even if one wishes to preserve the distinctions between the various roles, the decision about what social responsibilities fall within which role is itself a scientific or empirical one, contextual rather than general. I want to pursue the second path here, though I think in the long run the first is the more profound. Yet to be more than a general insight it will have to work out its detailed modes of assigning responsibilities.

Suppose then that the scientist argues against taking a policy stand on social matters because as scientist he is aware of the vast amount of justifying evidence needed in authoritative judgment; one has fewer cognitive responsibilities if he judges social matters as a citizen or as an individual, since it permits more subjective judgment. The difficulty is, however, that on many questions the scientist knows the central evidence only as a scientist—the genetic effects of nuclear fallout as a biologist, the inflationary effects of the Vietnam War as an economist, the psychological effects of ghetto life as a social psychologist, and so on. As a private citizen he might have had quite aberrant notions. Of course, part of the evidence may come from other scientific fields than his own. And part may indeed be just his belief as a layman. If these scruples stand in the way of expressing a scientific social judgment, the scientific thing to do is not to plead subjectivity and individual bias, but to be more precise about the extent of his evidence and specify its credentials. Thus, a particular social stand by biologists might be advanced with the addendum: 70 percent as biologist, 10 percent as relying on economists, 12 percent as general intellectual (all intellectuals presum-

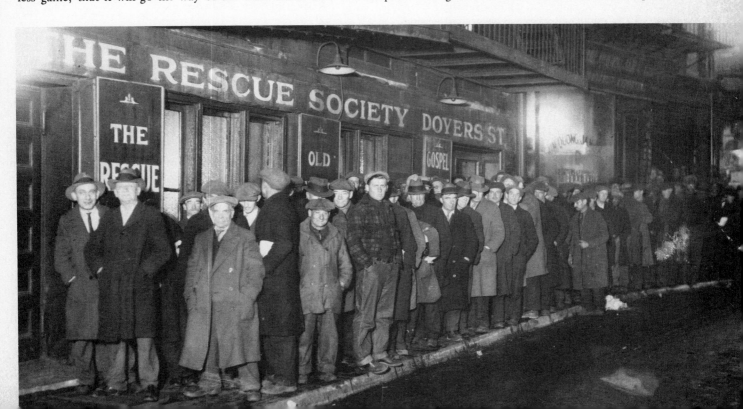

ably having a more sharpened sense of evidence or relevance), 5 percent as citizen (in terms of accepted social obligations), and 3 percent as individual subjective conviction.

Think of the generally educative effect of such pronouncements. If a classification were developed for social judgments, think of the height of sophistication if the public could respond to a flaming headline—"Political Scientists Issue 4D Condemnation of Federal Pollution Policy; Ecologists Concur with 2A Resolution."

Sometimes I have the impression that the scientists' plea for exemption from social judgment as scientists is a normative judgment parallel to an occupation's plea for automatic draft exemption on the grounds of its social importance. Scientists are too busy for political activism or incipient rebellion. Yet here again, the answer is unfortunately not open to antecedent determination. Whether or how much rebellion is involved is an empirical matter and depends on the state of the country and the character of the issues. In Nazi Germany, to make a biological assertion about the lack of evidence for Aryan superiority was probably equivalent to revolt. And in the Oppenheimer case, as we recall, it was a scientific hesitation about the feasibility of the hydrogen bomb that played some part, as well as moral consideration of the consequences of pushing on with its development.

But a large part of social action that can fall into the province of scientists is scarcely of this dramatic kind. Many social questions are not a matter of introducing new and revolutionary categories, but of shifting mutually acceptable categories. Thus if ecologists want a nationally directed water policy or economists and sociologists want a governmental housing industry, they need not be voting on socialism versus capitalism. The categories exist within our society: for example, our army is a collective institution, but we do not advertise for a war to be waged by the lowest private bidder. Nor was the recent suggestion in New York, that subway rides should be free, an anarchistic-collectivist aspiration: it was simply saying that subways should be the same kind of municipal service as garbage collection.

Certainly these are social-science issues in large part. I am reminded of the clarity with which, if I recall a newspaper account correctly, Milton Friedman, when he was testifying for the negative income tax, cut through the remark of a senator to the effect that at least people who got public money in this way should forfeit their right to vote; he replied that if putting one's hand in the public trough warranted loss of the vote, businessmen would be the first to lose it.

A number of different types of social responsibility for the scientific enterprise may be distinguished. Some would fall on individual scientists, some would more effectively be carried out by scientists in associated groups. There are, first, obligations that arise in the professional and public milieu with respect to the scientific work itself. For example, Bentley Glass, in his *Science and Ethical Values*, lists such obligations as: to publish one's methods and results in such a way that another may confirm and extend the results; to see that one's work is properly abstracted and indexed; to write critical reviews in the field; to communicate to the general public the new revelations of

science; to transmit the knowledge to the succeeding generation. Such obligations follow from the state of the field as well as the general objectives of the enterprise; thus proper indexing rises to importance because of the stream of contributions in the contemporary world, so that the dangers of work being lost are very real in some fields. Again, the obligation to ensure communication to the general public reflects the tremendous importance of a wide base of public understanding if the lessons of science are to play a part in the advance of culture and social life; this obligation is distorted if scientists think of it only as a way of ensuring financial support for science. It is not implied of course that every scientist has to be busy on all these fronts. Some of the obligations can be carried out in an organized professional or even institutional way, for example, the rise of scientific journalism as a profession itself, rather than as an additional burden to a scientist who may not be gifted in this respect. While there is no scientific obligation to be polemical about conflicting theories and approaches, the obligation to do critical reviews seems to suggest not only the wider purview of the field but participation in the sharpening of theoretical approaches.

There are, in the second place, direct social responsibilities to others who are involved in the work or come within its ambit. Familiar examples of such responsibilities are those of medical researchers to subjects; psychological experiments which involve lying to or misleading the subjects (the extreme case of the Milgram electric shock tests, in which the subject is told to increase an alleged electric shock in order to see when the subject will revolt and draw the line as he watches the faked tortured response); relations of anthropologists to informants in native villages whose ordinary relations may be quite upset after the researcher's departure; questions of invasion of privacy of informants in modes of research and modes of publication; participant observation as a technique and its effects.

Responsibilities of Science

There is further the general responsibility of maintaining the conditions under which science can be continued. This may become a matter of direct political participation when general freedom of inquiry is threatened. Other issues may have a comparable status. For example, the imposition of secrecy on research projects where they are connected with military or political applications has been much opposed by scientists as a hindrance to the free flow of scientific communication. The imposition of political qualifications on scientists as a condition of engaging in research is often seen as disruptive of the community of science and its professional criteria. There is no advance way of knowing what kinds of conditions may turn out to interfere with scientific work and progress, but when scientists individually or in organized fashion oppose these conditions, it is as a scientific responsibility or an exercise of a scientific social conscience.

Moving gradually into the context of scientific work, it would seem to be a scientist's responsibility to know or be aware of the various social relations of his scientific work—how it is supported and financed, what practical purposes motivate the support and the work, what applications are likely to be made of it, who will benefit and who will be affected in what way. So far I speak merely of the obligations not to remain in the dark on these matters. But knowledge about one's scientific work and its context would seem to carry some responsibility for decision—whether to abandon the research under these conditions, to do it but make public or agitate against its intended applications, to work out alternative ways of carrying it on. With the development of such large-scale problems in our scientific culture, paradigms may well be established in the ethical code of the profession. For example, research in biological warfare might well have been banned by scientists even before its recent partial rejection by national edict. Many fuzzy borderlines still remain to be dealt with. It is not inconceivable that a union of engineers should include, in its bargaining with a given corporation, provision of nonpolluting processes of waste disposal, just as a teachers' union may include in its bargaining the provision of school breakfasts or lunches for children—in part because of the help this gives to the educational process, in part because of the general obligation for the welfare of those affected.

Where there are crucial problems affecting the whole life of the society, it may well be a responsibility of all intellectual, scientific and cultural leadership in the community to ask itself what it can do to help face the problems. Thus, in our contemporary world one could pinpoint the problems of war, discrimination in its various forms, overpopulation, pollution of the environment and exhaustion of natural resources as the four great threats to mankind. Hence there would be no question about the scope of social conscience in general with respect to them and about the obligation of scientists to ask themselves what their fields could do to ameliorate the situation. In fact, the obligation of scientists here is directly greater because of the part science has played in generating the situation, even where its action was directly beneficial as, for example, in increasing life expectancy by reducing infant mortality. Two excellent examples of the exercise of this obligation of science to crucial problems and threats are the reaction of anthropologists in the 1930s to Nazi racism and the agitation by atomic scientists in the 1940s and 1950s for controls of nuclear power against war uses. The geneticists nowadays are much worried about the impending breakthrough in their field and the questions of control over human biological development it may raise.

Let me conclude with a few reflections on the modes of action a sense of social responsibility among scientists may call for. Again there is no simple answer. We may distinguish individual action, informal group action, and action in structured associational groups. Individual action may take the form of public criticism, withdrawal from a field of work, or engagement in some form of political action. Informal group action has tended to be ad hoc; it is a familiar feature of our society to see advertisements of scientists speaking on the question of the Vietnam War or on overpopulation or occasionally even on some particular flagrant injustice.

Organized group action is less developed. We may distinguish briefly three types. One is the exercise of negative fighting functions, parallel to strikes by unions for specific demands; this has not been employed very much by organized scientists but is quite conceivable in the present state of things. The second is the exercise of what we may call a ferment-function, to generate all sorts of new ideas and plans and intensify consciousness of the problems and possible solutions. The third is what we may think of as institution-making, which has been more common than we may think. Thus the development of insurance as an idea was a mathematical discovery which underlies vast social transformation in modern societies, though not directly applied by scientists themselves. Group medicine was an invention of medical practitioners. The development of clinics for psychotherapy and the growth of schools for mentally ill children arose from the work of professionals and readily passed into government programs. Recent attempts to organize the poor to take part in a concerted pursuit of their own welfare also had professional origins.

There is nothing implausible in current suggestions that organized scientists market their own discoveries for public welfare, for example, in drugs or even in certain industries. We may compare the fostering of housing and banks by certain unions, or even the suggestion that Harold Ickes made after World War II that what the government had built up for industry during war production should be turned over to a corporation with all veterans as shareholders, instead of being sold at a cheap price to industrial corporations.

Of course such suggestions run up against the realities of basic power. But the amount of free play in our society would be tested by social experiments along these lines. My point is simply that there are avenues for the legitimate exercise of the social conscience of scientists, far beyond the mere expression of a collective voice where there is one. There could very well be sections of the scientific societies on institution-making and on international scientific cooperation, for example, on implementing the abolition of biological warfare. It may not even be too early to think about the possibilities of international citizenship for scientists.

FURTHER READING

The Social Functions of Science by J. P. Bernal (New York: Macmillan, 1939). Represents a Marxist attempt to set ideas in a sociohistorical context of development, a task which Marxism was the first major philosophy to undertake.

Science and Ethical Values by Bentley Glass (Chapel Hill, N.C.: University of North Carolina Press, 1965). Deals with the values of science and the obligations of the scientist.

Reinventing Anthropology edited by Dell Hymes (New York: Random House, 1972).

The New Sociology by Irving Louis Horowitz (New York: Oxford University Press, 1964). Confronts the question of values and scientific work.

The Structure of Scientific Revolution by Thomas Kuhn (Chicago: University of Chicago Press, 1962).

"Steel Axes for Stone Age Australians" by Lauriston Sharp, in Edward H. Spicer (ed.), *Human Problems in Technological Changes: A Casebook* (New York: Russell Sage, 1952).

The Sociological Imagination by C. Wright Mills (New York: Oxford University Press, 1959). Shows twists and turns of schools in social science as value-bulging, not merely value-laden.

HERBERT C. KELMAN

Deception in Social Research

In order to advance the understanding of human behavior, psychologists regularly use human beings as subjects in a wide variety of experiments. In many of these experiments, the subject is kept in the dark or misinformed about the true purpose of the experiment. Sometimes the deception exposes him to embarrassing, disturbing, or potentially harmful experiences that he had not bargained for.

There is generally a good reason for the use of deception. Many of the phenomena that the psychologist wishes to study would be altered if the subject knew the purpose of the experiment—if he knew, for example, what psychological processes the experimenter is trying to activate and what reactions he is hoping to observe. And yet the use of deception, even when it is done for a scientifically valid reason, poses ethical questions.

These questions are fairly obvious when the deception has potentially harmful consequences for the subject; they are more subtle, but nonetheless important, even in experiments where there is little danger of harmful effects. The issue is: How can we strike a proper balance between the interests of science and the considerate treatment of people who make themselves available as the raw material of research?

The problem of deception has taken on increasingly serious proportions in recent years as its use has become almost a standard feature in psychological experiments. Deception has been turned into a game, often played with great skill and virtuosity. A considerable amount of creativity and ingenuity by social psychologists is given to the development of increasingly elaborate deception situations.

For example, the potentially harmful effects of deception are dramatized in some recent studies of obedience. One volunteer was "smiling and confident" when he entered the laboratory. "Within 20 minutes," the experimenter reported, "he was reduced to a twitching, stuttering wreck, who was rapidly approaching a point of nervous collapse." What caused him to become a "wreck" was an experiment in which subjects were led to believe that they were participating in a learning study. They were instructed to administer increasingly severe shocks to another person, who after a while began to protest vehemently. In fact, of course, the "victim" was an accomplice of the experimenter and did not receive any real shocks. But in some cases, the experimenter instructed the subject to continue to "shock" the "victim" up to the maximum level, which

the subject believed to be extremely painful when the victim writhed in pain and pounded his head against the wall.

Not surprisingly, both obedient and defiant (those who refused to administer shocks) subjects exhibited a great deal of stress. And there is surely good reason to believe that at least some of the obedient subjects came away from this experience with lowered self-esteem, realizing that they yielded to authority to the point of inflicting extreme pain on a fellow human being. The fact that, in the experimenter's words, they had "an opportunity to learn something of importance about themselves, and more generally, about the conditions of human action" is beside the point.

If this were a lesson *from life,* it would constitute an instructive confrontation and provide a valuable insight. But do researchers, for purposes of experimentation, have the right to provide such potentially disturbing insights to subjects who do not know that this is what they volunteered for?

And yet, this same research illustrates the complexity of the issues raised by the use of deception. These studies of obedience have produced significant and challenging findings which have posed some basic questions about human behavior and social life. Without deception, this line of investigation could probably not have been pursued.

A GENERATION OF DECEIVERS

It is easy to view the situation with alarm, but it is much more difficult to formulate an unambiguous position on this problem. As a working experimental social psychologist, I know that there are good reasons for using deception in many experiments. There are many significant problems, like the study of obedience, that probably cannot be investigated without the use of deception—at least, given the present level of development of our experimental techniques. Thus, researchers are always confronted with a conflict of values. If they regard the acquisition of scientific knowledge about human behavior as a positive value, and if an experiment using deception constitutes a significant contribution to such knowledge which could not be achieved by other means, then it is difficult to rule out the experiment unequivocally. The question is not simply whether or not to use deception, but whether the amount and type of deception are justified by the significance of the study and the unavailability of alternative procedures.

What concerns me most, then, is not so much that deception is used, but that it is used without question. I sometimes feel that a whole generation of psychologists now in training will not know there is any other way of doing experiments. Too often deception is used, not as a last resort, but as a matter of course. The attitude seems to be: If you can deceive, why tell the truth?

What are some of the major problems posed by the use of this dangerously doubled-edged tool? There are three areas to consider:

■ the ethical implications;
■ the real effectiveness of deception;
■ the implications for the future of psycho-social research in our society.

ETHICAL IMPLICATIONS. Ethical problems of a rather obvious nature arise in those experiments in which deception has potentially harmful consequences for the subject. For example, a brilliant experiment was recently designed to observe the effects of threat on group solidarity and the need for strong leadership. In this study (one of the very rare examples of an experiment conducted in a natural setting) independent food merchants in a number of Dutch towns were brought together for group meetings and informed that a large organization would soon open a chain of supermarkets in the Netherlands. In a "high threat" condition, the subjects were told that their towns would probably be selected as sites for such markets, which would cause a considerable drop in their business. On the advice of the executives of the shopkeepers' organizations who had helped to arrange the group meetings, the investigators never revealed, even after the experiment was over, that the supermarket threat was a fiction.

I have been worried about those Dutch merchants ever since I first heard about this study. Did some of them go out of business in anticipation of the heavy competition? Do some of them have an anxiety reaction every time they see a bulldozer? Chances are that they soon forgot about this threat (unless, of course, supermarkets actually did move into town) and that it became just one of the many little moments of anxiety that occur in every shopkeeper's life. But do investigators have the right to add to life's little anxieties and to risk the possibility of more extensive anxiety purely for the purposes of such experiments?

Two other recent studies provide further example of potentially harmful effects arising from the use of deception. In one set of studies, male college students were led to believe that they had been homosexually aroused by photographs of men. In the other study, subjects of both sexes were given disturbing information about their levels of masculinity or femininity, presumably based on an elaborate series of psychological tests they had taken. In all of these studies, the deception was explained to the subjects at the end of the experiment. One wonders, however, whether this explanation removes the possibility of harmful effects. For many persons in this age group, sexual identity is a live and sensitive issue, and the self-doubts generated by this laboratory experience could linger.

What about the less obvious cases, in which there is little danger of harmful effects? Serious ethical issues are also raised by such deception per se, and the kind of use of human beings that it implies. In other inter-human relationships, most psychologists would never think of doing the things that they do to their subjects—exposing them to lies and tricks, deliberately misleading them, and making promises or giving assurances that they intend to disregard. They would view such behavior as a violation of the respect to which all fellow humans are entitled. Yet they seem to forget that the experimenter-subject relationship—whatever else it is—is a *real* inter-human relationship, in which the experimenter has a responsibility towards the subject as another human being whose dignity he must respect. The difference between the experimenter's behavior in everyday life and his behavior in the laboratory is so marked that one wonders why there has been so little concern with this problem.

The broader ethical problem of the very use of deception becomes even more important when we view it in the present-day historical context. We are living in an age of mass societies, in which the transformation of man into an object, to be manipulated at will, occurs on a mass scale, in a systematic way, and under the aegis of specialized institutions deliberately assigned to this task. In institutionalizing the use of deception in psychological experiments we are contributing to a historical trend that threatens the values most of us cherish.

METHODOLOGICAL IMPLICATIONS. I have increasing doubts about the effectiveness of deception as a method for social research.

A basic assumption in the use of deception is that a subject's awareness of what the experimenter is really trying to find out would affect the subject's behavior in such a way that the experimenter could not draw valid conclusions from it. For example, if the experimenter is interested in studying the effects of failure on conformity, he must create a situation in which subjects actually feel that they have failed, and in which they can be kept unaware of his interest in observing conformity. In short, it is important to keep the subjects naive about the purposes of the experiment so that they can respond spontaneously.

How long, however, will it be possible to find naive subjects? Among college students it is already very difficult. They may not know the exact purposes of the particular experiment in which they are participating, but many of them know that it is *not* what the experimenter says it is. As one subject pithily put it, "Psychologists always lie!"

There are, of course, other sources of human subjects that have not been tapped, but even here it is only a matter of time until word about psychological experiments gets around and sophistication increases. Whether or not a subject knows the true purpose of the experiment, if he does not believe what the experimenter tells him, then he is likely to make an effort to figure out the purpose of the experiment and to act accordingly. This may lead him to do what he thinks the experimenter wants him to do. Conversely, if he resents the experimenter's attempt to deceive him, he may try to throw a monkey wrench into the works. Whichever course the subject uses, however, he is operating in terms of his own conception of the nature of the situation, rather than in terms of the conception that the experimenter is trying to induce. In short, the experimenter can no longer assume that the conditions that he is trying to create are the ones that actually define the situation for the subject. Thus, the use of deception, while it is designed to give the experimenter control over the subject's perceptions and motivations, may actually produce an unspecifiable mixture of intended and unintended stimuli that make it difficult to know just what the subject is responding to. Therefore, is there any future in the use of deception?

IMPLICATIONS FOR THE FUTURE. My third main concern about the use of deception is that, from a long-range point of view, there is obviously something self-defeating about it. As experiments of this kind continue, potential subjects become more and more sophisticated, and scientists become less and less able to meet the conditions that their experimental procedures require. Moreover, potential subjects become increasingly distrustful, and future relations between subjects and experimenters upon which successful research depends are likely to be undermined. Thus, we are confronted with the anomalous circumstance that, the more this research is carried on, the more difficult and questionable it becomes.

The use of deception also involves a contradiction between experimental procedures and the long-range aims of scientists and teachers. In order to be able to carry out experiments, they are concerned with maintaining the naiveté of the population from which they draw subjects. This perfectly understandable desire to keep procedures secret go counter to the traditional desire of the scientist and teacher to inform and enlighten the public. For the long run, it even suggests the possible emergence of a special class, in possession of secret knowledge—a possibility that is clearly antagonistic to the principle of open communication to which scientists and intellectuals are so fervently committed.

ENRICHMENT THROUGH EXPERIMENT

If my concerns about the use of deception are justified—and I think that they are—what are some of the ways they can be dealt with? I would like to suggest two basic remedies:

- exploring ways of counteracting and minimizing the negative efforts of deception;
- giving careful attention to the development of new experimental techniques that can dispense with the use of deception altogether.

In those experiments in which deception could have harmful effects, there is an obvious requirement to build protections into every phase of the process. Subjects must be selected in a way that will exclude individuals who are especially vulnerable; the potentially harmful manipulation (such as the induction of stress) must be kept at a moderate level of intensity; the experimenter must be sensitive to danger signals in the reactions of his subjects and be prepared to deal with crises when they arise; and, at the conclusion of the session, the experimenter must take time, not only to reassure the subject, but also to help him work through his feelings about the experience to whatever degree may be required.

In general, a good principle to follow is that a subject ought not to leave the laboratory with greater anxiety or lower self-esteem than he came with. I would go beyond it to argue that the subject should in some positive way be enriched by the experience—he should come away from it with the feeling that he has learned something, understood something, or grown in some way. And this adds special importance to the kind of feedback—about what was really being done—that is given to the subject at the end of the experimental session.

This post-experimental feedback is also the primary way of counteracting negative effects in those experiments in which the issue is deception as such, rather than possible threats to the subject's well-being. If the subject is deceived, then he must be given a full and detailed explanation of what has been done and of the reasons for doing it. It is not enough to give the subject perfunctory feedback. These explanations should be meaningful and instructive for the subject and helpful in rebuilding his relationship with the experimenter. I feel very strongly that, to accomplish these purposes, the experimenter must keep the feedback itself inviolate and under no circumstance give the subject false feedback, or pretend to be giving him feedback while in fact introducing another experimental manipulation.

THE CASE FOR COOPERATION

My second suggestion is that scientists invest some of the creativity and ingenuity now being devoted to the construction of elaborate deceptions to the search for alternative experimental techniques that do not rely on the use of deception. They would be based on the principle of eliciting the subject's positive motivations to contribute to the experimental enterprise. They would draw on the subject's active participation and involvement in the proceedings and encourage him to cooperate in making the experiment a success by conscientiously taking the roles and carrying out the tasks that the experimenter assigns to him. In short, the kind of techniques I have in mind would be designed to involve the subject as an active participant in a joint effort with the experimenter.

Perhaps the most promising sources of alternative experimental approaches are procedures using some sort of role-playing—that is, procedures in which the experimenter asks the subject to act *as though* he were in a certain situation rather than actually creating that situation experimentally as a "real" one. I have been impressed, for example, with the role-playing that I have observed in the Inter-Nation Simulation, a laboratory procedure in which the subjects take the roles of decision-makers of various nations. This situation seems to create a high level of emotional involvement and to elicit motivations that have a real-life quality to them. (See "The Study of Man," March/April *Trans-action*.)

In general, the results of role-playing experiments have been very encouraging. Despite the fact that they know it is all make-believe, subjects usually react realistically to the experimental stimuli, and these reactions follow an orderly pattern.

There are other types of procedure, in addition to role-playing, that are worth exploring. For example, it may be possible to conduct more experiments in a natural non-laboratory setting in which, with the full cooperation of the subjects, specific experimental variations are introduced. The advantages of dealing with motivations at a real-life level of intensity might well outweigh the disadvantages of subjects' knowing the general purpose of the experiment. A much simpler alterative, also worth exploring, would be for experimenters to inform the subjects at the beginning of a laboratory experiment that they will not receive full information about what is going on, but ask them to suspend judgment until the experiment is over.

Whatever alternative approaches are tried, there is no doubt that they will have their own problems and complexities. Procedures effective for some purposes may be quite ineffective for others, and it may well turn out that for certain kinds of problems there is no adequate substitute for the use of deception. But there *are* alternative procedures that, for many purposes, may be as effective or even more effective than procedures built on deception.

These approaches often involve a radically changed set of assumptions about the role of the subject in the experiment: *the subject's motivation to cooperate is utilized rather than by-passed.* These new procedures may even call for increasing the sophistication of potential subjects, rather than maintaining their naiveté.

FURTHER READING

The Use and Abuse of Social Science: Behavioral Science and National Policy-Making edited by Irving Louis Horowitz (New Brunswick, N.J.: Transaction Books, 1971).

The Uneasy Partnership: Social Science and the Federal Government in the Twentieth Century by Gene M. Lyons (New York: Russell Sage, 1969).

Obedience to Authority by Stanley Milgram (New York: Harper & Row, 1974).

HANS TOCH

The Convict as Researcher

J. Douglas Grant and I recently concluded a study on the social psychology of violence. In studying violence inside prisons we operated with a resident research staff that combined sophistication, practical experience, and the ability to inspire confidence in our informants. Our group in San Quentin prison, for instance, consisted of six men whose graduate training added up to 83 years of confinement. Their competence to study violence in prisons is obvious since five of them also qualified as subjects.

Our top researcher was an interdisciplinary social scientist for whom I cannot find enough praise. His name is Manuel Rodriguez, and his academic background consists of an eighth grade education, a term in the U. S. Army Supply School, and a short course in automobile repair.

But Rodriguez has other qualifications. Before the age of 18 he was arrested for malicious mischief and assault. Later he was sentenced for such offenses as armed robbery, burglary, firearms possession, narcotic addiction, and drunk driving. (I might confess that since joining us he has been arrested again, this time for driving without a license while engaged in research.)

Rodriguez has spent 15 of his 36 years behind bars, mostly in the California State Prison at San Quentin. As an inmate Rodriguez became interested in our research subject. He describes the beginning of his interest:

I was assigned to the weight-lifting section of the gymnasium. Most of the more violence-prone inmates come here to blow off steam at one time or another. It is also sort of a refuge where an inmate can get away from the pressures of staff scrutiny and the yards. We try to keep violence nonexistent, if possible, in this section. This was part of my job, although it was not explicit. In many cases—as a peacemaker—I had to convince both would-be combatants that they could retreat without losing face or pride. Most inmates contemplating violence will usually go to a respected member of the prison community for advice on "Shall I kill this guy or not?" I and a friend of mine were two of these persons so respected. When these guys who are straddling the fence between violence and nonviolence came to us we began to actively prescribe nonviolence. . . .

Rodriguez started out as an informed layman, with a completely pragmatic concern with violence. Today he is a sophisticated researcher, and he is an expert on the subject.

His transmutation began in early 1965 when he became a trainee in the New Careers Development Project directed by my collaborator, J. Douglas Grant. This revolutionary program is aimed at converting standard clients of professional services (such as Manuel) into dispensers of professional services—or at least into intermediaries between clients and professionals. Research work seemed one obvious target for this effort. Inmate Rodriguez was thus put to work, during his training period in prison, on the first stage of our study. His work included research design, as well as code construction, interviewing, and coding. After Rodriguez was released on parole, we were happy to hire him as a staff member.

Outside, Rodriguez has acted as our principal interviewer. He has interviewed parolees with violent records and citizens who have assaulted police officers. He is not only a sympathetic and incisive interviewer, but became unusually successful in stimulating interest among potential subjects. He is 5 feet 10 inches tall and weighs 175 pounds. He generally wears shirts that allow an unimpeded view of two arms full of tattoos. In addition, when we began the police assaulter interviews, Manual grew a bushy moustache to make himself look—as he put it—more "subculture." This prop undergirded an invitation to participate that started with the words, "We are not a snitch outfit," but then proceeded to a thoughtful, honest exposition of our objective.

We have tried to blur the line between the observer and the observed. Each of our interviewees is invited to sit down with us to conceptualize the data obtained from him. Each one is asked to help find common denominators in the particulars obtained in the interview. Each one gets the same opportunity we do to play scientist and becomes a minor partner in our enterprise. We obtain some material of extraordinary sophistication from these nonprofessional collaborators.

Results and Rapport

Why do we choose to rely on these nonprofessionals? How do they serve us better than the usual research associates and assistants with the conventional technical and academic credentials?

First, and most obviously, the empirical reason: They bring us better results. They are able to establish trust where we are not, to get data that we could not get, and to obtain it in the subjects' own language. I think I can best illustrate this advantage by excerpting a brief passage out of one of our prison interviews. The respondent here is a seasoned inmate whose reputation is solidly based on a long record of violent involvements. The interviewer is one of our nonprofessional researchers—another inmate:

Q: Was it the next day that you were going through the kitchen line and that he approached you and said he was coming down and wanted his stuff, and you better be there with it?

A: He said he was coming to get me, and I better be ready. The inference was—Was I going to be ready?

Q: So you went back to the kitchen and got a shank [knife] and then went to your pad. Now this dude who was doing the talking to you now, this is the one who you were playing coon can [a card game] with? The next morning one of the dudes approached you?

A: The next morning. The same dude. When I came out of my cell in the wing this guy approached me. He lived in the wing.

Q: What is his message?

A: His message is just a play, and they were playing a pat hand. It wasn't anything different from the day before. I told him. . . .

This excerpt fits into a standardized interview schedule that was designed to tease out sequences of interpersonal events leading to violence. But it also is a snatch of conversation between two persons discussing a subject of mutual interest in the most natural and appropriate language possible. In this type of interaction, data collection occurs with no constraint, and without translations designed to please or to educate the researcher.

Another advantage to be obtained in the use of nonprofessionals is the benefit of their unique perspective in data interpretation. A well-chosen lay researcher can often be in a position to correct naive inferences by less experienced professionals. In one dramatic experience one of my research partners, inmate Hallinan of San Quentin, chided me (in writing) for drawing a hasty and incorrect conclusion from an interview we had conducted:

Your interpretation seems to be influenced by the subject's storied loquaciousness rather than the incidents themselves. Is the subject's behavior, as he claims, the result of his being an Indian leader, and having to intercede in their behalf, or is it because of his need to establish a personal reputation as a prison tough guy? I choose the latter interpretation; an interpretation based on how the subject has behaved, not how he thinks he has behaved. . . .

An Indian functions within the rigid framework of rules. "There are family codes, tribal codes, and Indian laws," is how he puts it. But there is also . . . a joint code that he is well aware of: "The cons have their own rules, and one of them is that they step on the weak." . . .

The first incident that the subject becomes involved in is the rat-packing of an Indian child molester in order to ostracize and punish the molester, and also to solidify his position among the low-riders. So, rather than being a leader of these Indians, he is using his Indian blood to further his own ends. He wants to be a tough con, someone to be feared and respected. "The new guys that come in, no one knows about them." "Once you get a reputation you have to protect it." The above statements, and others similar in nature, were made by the subject during the course of the interview. [Their] significance is self-evident.

How does the subject go about building a reputation? As he says, fighting for home boys, and interceding for other Indians? No. Of the ten incidents—actually nine, because No. 1 and No. 9 are the same—No. 6 no violence occurred; No. 2 involved helping a friend, although the details were vague; No. 7 was a fight of his own making; No. 9 he was attacked; and No. 10 was the rat-packing incident. The remaining four involved custody. He was proudest of No. 8. In regards to this incident the following dialogue occurred:

Q: Do you think this incident helped your reputation?

A: It sure as hell did. I knocked down the Captain.

Q: How did you feel just before you knocked him down?

A: Like a big man.

Q: During?

A: I sure am doing it right this time.

The subject is also proud of the fact that at one time he had spat on the warden. . . . Obviously the subject feels that these things scare people. . . .

The word circulates that he has fought with the "bulls," implying that he will jump on a convict with little provocation. The facts are never pursued, but accepted prima facie, because those who pass on these rumors and exaggerations are the very ones who are most impressed by them. The rumor returns and the subject begins to believe his own yard reputation. . . .

Our subject has completed the building of his reputation, petty though it is, and now he and his low-rider friends can observe and honor it. Not that the cons on the yard do, but the subject feels that they do, and this is all that really matters. If anything he is tolerated, not respected and feared as he would like.

It is obvious that inmate Hallinan is not only furnishing me with a lesson in perspective, but is also demonstrating that he can compete with professionals in his methodological acumen and his ability to vividly summarize and communicate research conclusions. And although this analysis is unusually literate, because inmate Hallinan has invested much prison time in creative writing courses, much can be learned even from our most unlettered collaborators.

There is another aspect to the use of nonprofessionals which relates to a less tangible and more general advantage. Most social researchers sense some difficulty in the initial approach to subject populations of vastly different backgrounds from our own. Some of us react at this juncture with an elaborate process of ingratiation or "gaining of rapport" in which we, and the research, are presented in the (presumably) best light. This posturing is often transparently insincere and always wasteful. Worse, it usually achieves merely a wary and delicate stalemate, during which only a hit-and-run raid for data is possible before the subjects discover what has happened to them.

Avoiding Exploitation

During rare moments of honesty, we may admit that even when we induce subjects to cooperate, our dealings with them are seldom the exciting adventure we tell our students about. I say this because I suspect that the real problem is not one of communication and social distance at all—it may have nothing to do with habits or dress or the use of most vivid vocabulary. It may be that our subjects understand us only too well—that what we ask is unreasonable and unfair. After all, at best we are supplicants, and at worst, invaders demanding booty of captive audiences. In return for a vague promise or a modest remuneration we expect a fellow human being to bare his soul or to make controversial and potentially incriminating statements. The "communication" is one way—the researcher maintains his position as an "objective" recipient of non-reciprocated information.

We also make our informant aware that we are not interested in him as a person but as a "subject"—a representative of a type, or a case, or an item in a sample. He knows this because he knows who he is and who we are. He knows that he is being approached because he is the inhabitant of a ghetto or a prison, because he is a "consumer," or because he acts as an informer. And he knows that his aims are being subordinated to our own. How can he share our objectives, after all, if he cannot even see the results of the efforts in which he has participated?

I speak with considerable humility here, because I almost once again made the mistake of taking my Viennese accent and my parochial concerns into prison cells and police stations, expecting to secure frank answers to prying questions. I have done this sort of thing often in the past. This strategy strikes me now not only as naive but as offensive.

Therefore, Grant and I followed an alternative course in our violence project, such as I have briefly described. This has supplied us with linkage across cultural gaps, with highly motivated informants, with substantive expertise, with heightened analytic power, and with the feeling that we have been fair.

I shall not pretend that these benefits are automatic and free of risk. Like professional researchers, nonprofessional participants in research must be selected with care. Unintelligent or completely illiterate persons would be of limited use, as would social isolates. A cynical, exploitive, or immature outlook can create a poor prospect for programs that have the usual training resources. This is also true of rigidly held preconceptions, though to a lesser extent.

On the other hand, too close attention to selection criteria may produce a staff of quasi-professional nonprofessionals—which is also bad. They may be rejected by the subjects and even be considered a species of Uncle Tom. Not being trusted, they may have relatively limited useful knowledge or insight, contribute little, discover they are marginal members of the team, develop poor motivation.

Even careful selection will not altogether eliminate these possibilities. The nonprofessional must get training that is not only directly related to research but also can provide him with incentives, support, and a meaningful self-concept. Some of this training may be of the sort routinely encountered in graduate schools; some may be more characteristic of social movements. The nonprofessional researcher must be, in a sense, a *convert*. He must acquire a new role, a new set of values, and new models and friends while remaining in close touch with his old associates. The professional merely places others under the microscope; but the nonprofessional must convert his own life experiences into data. While the rest of us can view research as a job, the nonprofessional must see the involvement as a mission or a crusade—or he will have trouble doing it at all.

What training then should these nonprofessionals get? First, research indoctrination, in the purest sense of the word, that aims directly at awakening curiosity and at the desire to reach latent meanings or patterns. It must try to inculcate suspicion of the unrepresentative and unique and a phobia against premature interpretation. Obviously, it must also provide tools—intensive practical instruction in the use of steps to be employed, including interviewing techniques, content analysis, survey problems, and data processing. This training must not only include general background information and acquaintance with the content of the research but also self-corrective and social skill training of the kind necessary to work with sensitive groups.

But the most critical challenge is ours. Will we treat the trained nonprofessional as a partner and colleague and respect his integrity and abilities? We must preserve the nature of our own contribution; but we must also be prepared to become members of our own team.

Nonprofessionals, if given the opportunity, can help us shape ideas, formulate designs, and analyze results. We should continue to provide intellectual discipline and a sense of perspective. For the rest, we may find ourselves in the unaccustomed position of being students to spirited and able teachers—and the benefits will be reflected in the quality of research, as well as in the resolution of ethical dilemmas that currently often leave social researchers with a bitter taste in the mouth.

ROBERT J. WOLFSON

In the Hawk's Nest

From early summer 1963 until late summer 1965, I was a member of the research staff of the RAND Corporation in Santa Monica, California. It was a particularly interesting time to be there because during that period the RAND staff members began to differ significantly among themselves over public policy matters that had their roots in the organization's work. Both the impending détente of the early 1960s (the nuclear test ban treaty was under discussion when I started work at RAND) and the escalation of the Vietnam War (the bombing of North Vietnam and the United States troop buildup in the South were already well established by the time I left) generated sharp divisions within the corporation, although in both cases the majority was on the side of the military. Dissatisfaction about Vietnam, however, persisted and apparently extended within the staff as it has among the general population of this country, and last year it resulted in the desperate and risky action taken by Daniel Ellsberg, formerly one of RAND's brightest staff members, in releasing the Pentagon Papers to the press.

This is an account of how RAND looked and felt to one of the relatively few doves on its professional staff in that earlier, crucial period.

It is now apparent that until the mid-sixties Ellsberg, like almost all those at RAND, was perfectly satisfied with the main thrust of United States foreign policy. He accepted the notion that the use or threat of using force throughout the world was a legitimate means to the attainment of United States ends abroad. And it is yet unclear whether he

now feels differently except in specific circumstances. In 1965, when he was in Vietnam for the Department of Defense, he wrote to friends that the Vietnamese were beautiful people and that the United States must continue to help them. This was at a time when we were already using napalm freely, destroying villages and setting up free-fire zones, as Ellsberg has since told us he was then beginning to learn.

In some ways, an understanding of Ellsberg is extremely helpful in understanding the RAND Corporation itself. His attitudes and his way of approaching the problems of the United States and its relationship to the world are characteristic of the most important people at RAND. He would not otherwise have won such esteem there—and later at the Pentagon.

Ellsberg's act of releasing the Pentagon Papers to the public took immense personal courage on his part—courage of a particularly unusual sort. We are impressed from childhood onward with the importance of being courageous in both the physical and spiritual sense, but we are strongly impressed with the heinousness of acting against society. And for Ellsberg, as for many of us, society and the government of the United States have been indistinguishable. Yet even in taking this extraordinary step he still seems to have been unable to shed some of the former habits which he shared with other jingoists like himself at RAND. They appeared always to know they were right. They had no visible reservations. They believed that ends justified means. The word "zealot" has been used recently to describe Ellsberg and it seems to fit. When he emerged from the courthouse after being released in the summer of 1971, he was asked by a reporter if he wasn't concerned about having to go to prison. His response was most revealing: "Wouldn't you be glad to go to prison to end this terrible war?" His reply had all the conviction of the newly converted St. Augustine realizing the errors of his former ways and expecting everyone else to follow him.

In addition, Ellsberg's position is incomplete. What seems to be bothering him primarily is that the American people were treated contemptuously by their government. That is a profoundly serious matter; but by underemphasis he seems to be saying that if the American people had been taken into their government's confidence and had approved the policy, then the war itself would have been all right. Ellsberg's opinion has not been heard on our Dominican adventure in May 1965. There was a case in which the government was more honest, although not completely so. But the public did not object and we won—and quickly. Was it, then, an acceptable move?

By comparison with the way the American people were dealt with by the Johnson administration, it could almost be said that the German people were honestly dealt with by their leaders in the 1930s and most seemed to go along with them—but that is no basis for justification of Nazi policies. Democracy is not simply a set of procedures; it must be based on some moral foundation. It was this reading of democracy as procedures and not much more—procedures that could be suspended in times judged (by some elite) to be sufficiently serious—which was characteristic of the so-called defense intellectuals who played important roles in the White House, the Pentagon, Saigon and RAND.

What was it about RAND itself or the people at RAND that generated such attitudes? That question is my central concern here, and I will also attempt to explore the danger inherent in supposing that value-free analysis of social policy can be carried out by value-free analysts in the employ of power wielders.

The nature of the danger is that, as the relationship is prolonged, the thinking of both the analysts and their employers comes to resemble one another's. Their expectations of each other, especially the employers' expectations of the analysts, change subtly. Less and less do the employers really want cool levelheaded analysis. More and more they want support for the means and objectives to which they are already committed on other grounds—perhaps irrational, perhaps unconscious, perhaps impossible to reveal for any number of reasons.

In general, analysts long in the employ of the military establishment find themselves under irresistible pressure to weight the balance in favor of the exercise of military power. This exercise may range from showing the flag threateningly all the way to thermonuclear exchange. But the military worries that without such occasional exercises its chances of maintaining position and power inside the United States are threatened. So conclusions are reached under these pressures which might not have been reached in their absence.

This relationship and these pressures—most of them subtle but powerful—are worth exploring. To do so we turn to RAND—its history, its people and its ways of doing business.

RAND was originally formed as a special group inside the Douglas Aircraft Corporation during World War II. It was established as an independent corporate entity in 1947. Its initial commitment was to the development of analytical techniques for the formulation of air-war tactics and strategy. As time passed, it expanded its concerns into air-weapons design and testing for the Atomic Energy Commission (AEC), the formulation of quantitative analyses of bombing plans and logistical procedures, and the quantitative and nonquantitative analysis of global strategy. At the same time it was being encouraged by the air force to do basic scientific work in a number of areas related to staff interests. However, as time went on, less and less of this was acceptable to the air force and, at an accelerating pace, more and more of the air force prime contract with RAND was devoted to air force operations analyses.

RAND's staff was usually classified into two broad categories: research or scientific personnel and the so-called support staff. The former were the professional personnel who conducted the analyses, wrote the reports, held the advanced degrees—mathematicians, physicists, economists, computer scientists, meteorologists, earth scientists, astronomers, statisticians, operations analysts, engineers, philosophers and social scientists. A few of these were retired air force colonels. In the second group were the secretaries, clerks, typists, computer operators, maintenance and repair people and the security guards. A group which fell between these two included computer programmers, technical writers and librarians, editors and research assistants (most of whom, in this typical American institution, were attractive, bright, young women). Apart from these groups were the executives and administrators, most of whom had once been members of the research staff. Significantly, neither the man who was president of the corporation for its first 20 years of operation nor its sole senior vice-president had ever been members of any research staff; they had been managers at Douglas before RAND was formed.

The research staff is of primary interest for it was this work which justified RAND's existence at the Pentagon, in the White House and in the planning rooms of air commands and the aerospace industry.

Most RAND people came from one of two places—the aerospace industry or the academic world. The former were largely engineers and the latter had either come directly from academic work or tended to think of it as their long-run alternative opportunity. Many people served as academic consultants at RAND for periods of a few weeks or months at a time, especially in the summer. A significant proportion of RAND's regular full-time staff had originally come there as summer consultants or as summer interns while they were graduate students.

Until the mid-sixties, a job or consultantship at RAND was, for an academician, financially advantageous, paying better than an equivalent academic post would pay on a full-year basis and better than an equivalent government job. By the mid-sixties both academic and government salaries had undergone significant improvement, both relative and absolute, so that people were easily able to leave RAND for academic or government jobs and do as well or better financially. For the engineers, RAND salaries have always been competitive with those in the aerospace industry. However, the work at RAND tended to be more interesting, and working conditions better. For example, with almost no exceptions, it was unheard of in the aerospace industry for nonexecutive engineers to have their own offices. They worked in large groups in so-called bullpens. At RAND, however, each research staff member had his own office.

Thus, for most members of the research staff, RAND was a place that offered solid professional advantages. There were frequent tough illuminating seminars. Publication in professional journals and trips to professional meetings were encouraged. University people were constantly visiting RAND, and in many academic fields it was considered a favorable professional qualification to have worked there. RAND was spoken of as a quasi-academic institution. Indeed, there was talk for years (which appears now to be coming to fruition) of RAND's offering a doctorate in the field of policy analysis.

Security at RAND

RAND has always been operated as a so-called secure facility. That is, it has had to observe rules laid down by Defense Department security personnel concerning entry and egress, eligibility of personnel and the handling of files and documents. As a condition of employment, all employees of RAND were required to apply for a top secret Department of Defense security clearance. Until they had been granted a secret clearance they could not have free access to the main RAND facility but worked in the small uncleared facility and were allowed into the rest of the building only with an escort. Some people I knew spent more than a year languishing in the uncleared facility before receiving a clearance. In one case the problem was an uncle who was believed to have been a Communist 25 years earlier. If it turned out that the Defense Department security people were unwilling, even under RAND pressure, to grant a top secret clearance, then employment was terminated. These conditions also applied to most consultants.

The granting of security clearance to an individual comes after a lengthy investigation by military security. Granting the clearance implies that the recipient is judged by military security to be personally and politically reliable, emotionally stable, patriotic and not subject to blackmail, and that he is to be trusted with classified military secrets up to and including the level of sensitivity of the clearance granted.

Access to classified information is granted only if two conditions are met. First, the person requesting access must hold a clearance of at least the level of classification of the information. Second, he must formally establish, in writing and to the satisfaction of the security personnel controlling the information, the basis for his need to know the classified information. The need to know must be established in terms of objectives or interests of the United States which would thereby be furthered, as interpreted by those same security personnel.

The need to know was presumed to exist for any person employed or consulting at RAND who had the proper clearance for any piece of information at RAND. So far as I know RAND was unique in this respect. This universal, presumptively established need to know appears to have been terminated by the Secretary of Defense on July 2, 1971 after the Pentagon Papers leak was traced to RAND—despite the fact it would seem to be the Defense Department's own secretiveness that was basically at fault. Ellsberg, on leave from RAND, was assigned by the Defense Department to the team writing the history of U.S. involvement in Vietnam, now known as the Pentagon Papers. His increasing criticism of the United States role in Vietnam led the Defense Department to remove him from the project and give him other duties, but they did not inform RAND of this. Hence, after his return to RAND no question was raised about his access to RAND's copy of the papers.

The reconsideration of the need to know is probably the most serious revision of RAND security procedures that has taken place, although RAND staff members are already being subjected to frequent unannounced shakedowns and inspections, both covert and overt, and the RAND security office and its procedures are undoubtedly being turned upside down by air force security people. That these changes are quite sweeping is attested to by the unexpectedly early resignation—obviously under pressure—of RAND's second president, Henry Rowen, in November 1971, apparently for reasons related to the Ellsberg episode.

What this unusual past procedure meant was that any RAND staff member who was curious about a classified document, whether or not it had anything to do with the work he was engaged in, had a good chance of seeing it simply by requesting a copy. Of course he had to know that it existed and was inside RAND. This was easy if it was a document which had originally been produced at RAND and had been formally entered into the RAND publication process. Sometimes items in this process were actually published in the usual sense, but of course they were not classified. Other items were classified and assigned a publication number and would be mentioned on the list of RAND publications circulated to everyone two or three times a month. This list was itself frequently classified because some of the titles on it were classified (though usually at a lower level than the documents they described).

However, if the classified item had been brought into RAND from another agency or if it was produced at RAND but kept in unpublished memo or letter form, then the uninvolved person would learn about it only unofficially and might have a bit of difficulty getting a look at it. Still, it was frequently possible to see someone else's copy, and a person could get one of his own if he persisted.

Thus it was possible, because there was a great deal of fairly free lunch-hour and coffee-break conversation among RAND staff members, for someone to find out a great deal about what sorts of things were being worked on and what sorts of documents were entering or being generated at RAND.

At RAND, as at any other secure facility, visitors had to be under escort at all times. Once an acquaintance of mine brought a girl friend to his office for a few hours one evening while he worked. At one point he had to use the men's room but spent nearly a half-hour agonizing over how to handle the situation. The girl could not enter the men's room with him, he felt, and yet he had to see that she remained escorted. After a long painful period he remembered that he could leave her at the entrance to the building which was manned 24 hours a day, seven days a week, by members of the security guard.

The security guard, like a good, well-educated mannerly police force appeared to know everyone at RAND by name. Apparently the guards' jobs required that they immediately familiarize themselves with the faces of all new people as they arrived and with the entire staff of some 1,200 in short order after their own arrival. The head of the security guard was a top-sergeant type who, on one particularly hot day, came up with a dress code: no shorts for research staff. This generated a high-school type of dress-code revolt wherein many of us went home at lunch time and returned in shorts. He lost. The chief security officer and his chief assistant, both retired naval officers, were decent, unimaginative bureaucrats. They could not have done well at military installations for they were too intelligent, but they were ideal for dealing with RAND's collection of prima donnas.

RAND Liberals

Most RAND people, when it came to domestic political and social concerns, were liberals. Recently the term has come into some disrepute and with reason. But in those days it still connoted opposition in principle to discrimination, concern for the poor, support for some significant downward redistribution of power and wealth, and a corresponding antagonism toward the concentration of power and income by the rich and by corporations. It also carried a distrust (however vague) of Neanderthalism among the military—a concern over the amount of killing power in the hands of the major world military leaders. Most of all, to be a liberal placed one squarely in the pragmatic rationalist tradition—a liberal could rest comfortably when logic and analysis were being applied to human problems.

Many RAND people belonged to clubs of the California Democratic Council, the left wing of the Democratic Party in California. Many others were active in the regular Democratic Party. Only a very few considered themselves right of center. During the 1964 election campaign there were a few Goldwater bumper strips in the RAND parking lot, most of them on cars belonging to members of the support staff. The research staff had a small number of hardliners. They felt outnumbered and subject to silent ridicule, and they expressed themselves vociferously on occasion. One might have expected that it would be these people who would be staffing studies of first strike (preemptive) nuclear war strategy but this was not the case. The majority of people working on such studies called themselves liberals. This sort of discovery was particularly shocking.

In the Los Angeles metropolitan area the semi-informed general public spoke of RAND in hushed tones and tended automatically to regard its staff as geniuses. In truth, as a group RAND people were as brilliant and as dull, as responsible and as irresponsible, as honorable and as dishonest, as the faculty of an average large American university. The difference was that as a group they have always had more obvious and more efficient channels for transmission of their ideas into the real centers of American power. Occasionally we would encounter people who saw

RAND as a keystone in the structure of Defense Department planning, who would speak in very hostile tones—and in retrospect who could blame them? In such circumstances my response was to try to explain that not all of us were planning wars, but that, while true, was not very persuasive.

A particular critic of the United States cold-war commitments, who was pleased at the development of the détente and disturbed about Vietnam, was the man in charge of public relations for RAND—although the way in which he handled his job and kept the organization out of the papers led me to describe him as RAND's public nonrelations chief. One of his activities was to invite people from the academic world and from the left who were in the Santa Monica area to come and speak at RAND and then meet with small groups. The idea was to convince them that RAND people did not necessarily each have horns and a tail. Among those who got this treatment was Sidney Lens, the left-wing union leader who subsequently became a co-chairman of the New Mobe which organized several of the most successful antiwar marches between 1967 and 1969. Norman Thomas also came and delivered a quiet but sharp attack on the war. After his speech there was an ovation and near demonstration for him in the lecture hall; I cannot recall any other person getting such a reception. Of course, it was not for his speech, but because he was Norman Thomas. For most of the RAND liberals and welfare statists he was a household symbol, impotent but important.

RAND people tended to work and play together. And their play reflected attitudes and skills carried over from their work. Competition between tennis players as well as skill at the game were at higher levels than I can recall at a half-dozen large university campuses. Extended relationships were conducted across chessboards and bridge and poker tables. Some RAND people made a near fetish of playing poker skillfully and for high stakes—the use of the bluff and high stakes was not just a part of the poker game but consciously reflected the use of the bluff and high stakes in the international strategy so many RAND people were analyzing and planning.

At noontime many of the staff members would eat lunch in several of the conference rooms. One was traditionally set aside for bridge players, another for players of Kriegspiel, a game based on chess, but in which neither player can see his opponent. Each has his own board, and the men and boards are separated by a barrier. A referee, whose job is no mean trick of visualization and analysis, checks each board and decides if a player's move is, by chess rules, legal or not. Small amounts of information are given: whether or not someone has been placed in check and if so, from what direction; whether a pawn or a piece (not further identified) has been lost and if so on what square; whether or not there are opportunities for capture

"Ellsberg's act of releasing the Pentagon Papers to the public took immense personal courage on his part. Yet even in taking this extraordinary step he still seems to have been unable to shed some of the former habits which he shared with other jingoists like himself at RAND. They appeared always to know they were right. They had no visible reservations. They believed that ends justified means. The word "zealot" has been used recently to describe Ellsberg and it seems to fit." (Daniel Ellsberg, left, with Anthony Russo)

The Burden of Responsibility: Politics and the Power Structure

by pawns and if so, on what squares. Aside from this each player is forced to hypothesize and run risks by testing his hypotheses. (Some skillful shoulder-readers used what body movement was visible over a shoulder-high barrier to generate hypotheses, so the barrier was raised.) The result is a much faster game than chess and one very different from it. It is particularly impressive to the novice observer. If there was a visitor in the house during the lunch hour he would be brought into the Kriegspiel room to watch us as we played and presumably would go out dazzled by the "geniuses" at RAND.

The RAND Corporation is almost invariably coupled in the popular mind with the theory of games. This is somewhat misleading. Game theory, strictly speaking, is a mathematical theory dealing with the behavior of competitive players under a very specific set of behavioral assumptions. It happens that there were at RAND a number of mathematicians concerned with the theory of games in this very restricted sense. However, other methods of analysis and other problems were the basis of most people's work there. RAND dealt, in a wide variety of contexts and with a range of methods, with problems of conflict. At the most abstract level game theory and extensions of it were explored to see if it might be possible, by developing a sufficiently rich range of conditions under which abstract mathematical models of conflict could lead to solutions, to deal with real problems of war and threat. In fact, after 20 years of this sort of research at RAND and elsewhere, game theory has yielded up few useful results.

War gaming, which is a variety of role playing with a skeletal script built around a real or hypothetical international conflict situation, has been used at RAND. In this procedure each of several persons is given a description of a role he is to play, a description of the relevant features of the situation at the beginning of play, and some information about those with and against whom he is playing. Each player makes decisions within the competence of his role in response to information he receives about the effects of his and his fellow players' decisions. In a particular game the characters would usually include high military and political figures of two opposing countries, and the cast occasionally included high-ranking civilians or military people from the Pentagon. The objectives of such a game can be both instructional for potential decision-makers and exploratory for researchers who are trying to gain insight into the structure of decision making in particular circumstances.

Most significant at RAND in the study of conflict situations has been historical and literary analysis which consciously attempts to be rigorously (albeit not formally) logical in drawing implications of various stances of the United States and other world powers. The logical underpinnings of the entire strategy of nuclear deterrence, the face we have presented to other world superpowers for over 20 years, were worked out in this fashion, and to a significant degree at RAND. RAND's work in the planning and justification of counterinsurgency tactics and pacification programs carried out in Vietnam was also conducted with these techniques.

The remainder of RAND's military work has been concerned chiefly with economizing on air force procurement and operations, given the strategic commitments

already worked out. These economizing studies have dealt with a wide range of matters from weapons design and testing through weapons procurement, maintenance, repair and supply. One of RAND's major studies in the fifties was concerned with such a question: Would it be better for the air force to continue to operate its Strategic Air Command bombers from overseas bases in Spain, Okinawa, North Africa and Turkey or to develop airborne refueling and other techniques to allow SAC to operate from much less vulnerable North American bases? The study concluded that the latter course made more sense on the basis of detailed and abstract cost analyses. The air force significantly modified earlier plans it had made in response to the results.

A small fraction of RAND's work, some 10 to 15 percent when I was there, was for other government agencies or for other United States armed forces. Approximately 7 percent was sponsored by foundations and by RAND itself and was concerned with such matters as urban transportation and planning problems, aspects of theoretical biology, computer-language development and computer system design and application, computer simulation of human problem-solving activity, earth science and meteorology, international economic relations and mathematics.

RAND's only output was, as someone put it, paper—that is, reports. There were no laboratories there and all work done was theoretical, historical or computational.

Power Trips at RAND

Throughout my stay at RAND I was aware that for some people the real kick in being there came from the feeling of being involved in making important decisions. These were the relatively few people who made a trip or two to the Pentagon each month to brief high-ranking officials on the results of their studies. Some of these people would return and speak casually of "when I saw Curt LeMay last week" or "the last time I briefed the Secretary." Being at RAND was a real power trip for them. Most were working on studies of preemptive war, the use of nuclear threats against entire nations or the use of civilian populations as pawns in counterinsurgency situations. When asked how they could morally justify doing such work, several sorts of answers were forthcoming. One was the classic Eichmann excuse: "I was only doing my job, someone has to do it;" another was that these were simply contingency plans—although I never did receive an explanation of what the contingency was that could justify starting a thermonuclear war.

Not all of RAND's military work was to such ends. On an earlier brief visit to RAND I spent time with two men who went on to become subcabinet officials in Defense and in the Bureau of the Budget during the Kennedy-Johnson period. One of them has since returned to RAND in a senior capacity. These two men told me that almost accidentally they had learned a year or more before of the air force's plans for a 24-hour airborne alert strategic bombing force. The plan called for a flight of B-52s, loaded with thermonuclear warheads, to be aloft at all times. Each flight would head toward the North Pole from a United States base, to reach a certain point in the Arctic region by a specified time. If by then they had not received a coded radio signal calling them back, they were to cut off radio contact, open their sealed bombing orders and proceed to bomb their designated targets. The two staff men described their horror at learning this. By pointing out that not only was the reliability of this plan dangerously dependent on satisfactory radio reception in an area (near a magnetic pole) of great radio interference, but that it placed far too great a burden of power in the hands of one man, the flight commander, they succeeded (although with difficulty) in getting the air force to convert this plan into the well-known "fail-safe" one in which planes were to proceed only if ordered by coded radio signal to do so. The possibility of accidental thermonuclear war has no doubt been reduced as a result of their success.

Herman Kahn was at RAND for many years. More than any other single person, he should probably be given major credit for persuading senior military people in the late fifties and early sixties that they should not think casually of "nuking" as the first response to any radar anomaly in a time of international tension. For his pains, and because he was heavily in favor of a large fallout shelter program (which the air force objected to because of not being able to claim jurisdiction over it), Kahn was apparently given the polite bum's rush from RAND in 1961.

Most of RAND's work was based on a premise which can best be described as a perverse compound of positivism and arrogance. A careful positivist might say that in principle, most human processes might be shown to operate according to a number of fundamental regularities or laws; very few of those laws could now be described and almost no computations could confidently be conducted on their basis now or in the foreseeable future. But RAND and a few other groups tended to operate as if these laws were sufficiently in our grasp for significant decisions, involving vast amounts of human and material resources to be made on the basis of that knowledge.

How was this assumption of such a reliable basis for action made in the first place, and how was it used?

RAND was the first major organization wholly formed by an intellectual movement using systems analysis—the application of probability theory and logic and a sense of urgency to the study of systems of moderate complexity and of a middle range of articulatedness. Thus, systems analysis of the progress of a submarine through a known body of water, of the pursuit of one aircraft with known flight characteristics, of the impact on a particular landscape or seascape of the detonation at a specified altitude of a particular size and type of nuclear weapon, of the flow through a network, the pileup and/or depletion of material at various points in the network when the layout and capacity of the components of the network are known, were typical of problems handled in the early days by systems analysts at RAND and elsewhere. Characteristically, these analysts were not specialists in aircraft or naval tactics, bombing analysis or traffic management. They tended to think of themselves as generalists, that is, as experts in the use of analytical techniques. As generalists they accepted objectives or goals (or what are known in larger contexts as values) from their employers or clients, and worked out techniques for maximal approach to them with minimum expenditures of effort or resources.

So long as the limitations of this sort of generalist

analysis were understood—when the importance of errors arising from unfamiliarity with empirical detail was minimized by the relatively tight articulation of the system, and when the cost of error was confined by the relatively confined character of the problem—then systems analysis was useful and safe both for military and nonmilitary systems. However, the normal arrogance of the technician who has had successes where others have had failures led to the assertion of competence in much larger, less confined, less well articulated processes. The result has been a greater admixture of failures with successes. And the failures have been more spectacular and costly. Moreover, they have been met all too frequently by the "well, back to the drawing board" attitude of the technician, which, in really catastrophic situations, is an acceptance of no responsibility at all.

This transfer of abstract analysis to real cosmic threat situations (such as the Cuban missile crisis) is characteristic of the RAND systems-analysis approach to human problems. Similar such extensions of generalist competence can be found in and out of RAND. Daniel Ellsberg had spent a few years at RAND doing studies of deterrence and war-threat crises in a world of nuclear powers before he began occasionally briefing people on the White House War Room staff and in the Office of the Secretary of Defense on the subject of crisis management.

A specialist expert in high-altitude photography—Amron Katz—became a generalist expert in the politics of disarmament. A specialist expert in the testing of high-yield nuclear weapons—Herman Kahn—became a generalist expert in the politics of escalation and in almost any other subject in which he was interested. Specialist experts in cost analysis—the group that moved with Charles Hitch from RAND into the Office of the Comptroller and the Office of Systems Analysis in the Office of the Secretary of Defense under Robert McNamara—became generalist experts and enunciated design principles for a supersonic fighter-bomber for the air force and the navy, counter to the strong opinion of experienced procurement and flight officers in both services. Using program budgeting and cost-effectiveness analysis, they planned the entire force structure of the United States defense system.

This sort of thinking—generalizing, often successfully, on the basis of intellectual skill in handling limited, simple problems to the treatment of more complex, less confined, more bloody problems, while at the same time not really accepting responsibility; seeing human problems as games which can be replayed, again without acceptance of responsibility—came out of RAND and a few other places (such as the Institute for Defense Analyses, Harvard and MIT) and lodged in the White House, the Pentagon and the State Department in the persons of McNamara and his whiz kids, the Bundy brothers, W. W. Rostow and others. Vietnam, the Dominican adventure, the missile crisis and F-111 should all be understood as the fruits of that sort of thinking.

Within RAND there has always been a kind of recognized order of brilliance, and admiration for it as a quality. Those who were especially opposed to the war in Vietnam and who were therefore most frequently subject to criticisms that they were being unpatriotic or were confused were not regarded within the organization as brilliant. The question that naturally comes to mind, now that it is generally agreed that something has been rotten in Vietnam all along, is this: What is brilliance and what value is it if it is associated with dimness in recognizing such a state of affairs, especially with so much more information available than the general public has?

Brilliance, of course, must be understood as a flashy, narrow, technical facility. The keen mind that can weave its way through complex technical issues is considered brilliant. But wisdom is yet another quality, different from brilliance. Wisdom involves making ethical judgments and reasoning from ethical positions, while brilliance does not. RAND has had lots of brilliance and very little wisdom.

What is a Nice Boy Like You. . .

After all this, it is reasonable to ask why I was at RAND. All told, I worked in RAND-like situations for five years, although the two years before I came to RAND and the one year after I left were spent at places that only vaguely resembled it. They did work for the Department of Defense but almost exclusively in logistics. Still, clearances were required. I regarded that five-year episode as a potentially interesting experience, a sort of trial by ordeal, and went into it at a time when I was ready to leave the academic situation in which I then found myself. When I was invited to join RAND in 1963 I set only one condition: that I not be pressed to do war-connected work. This condition was accepted, but shortly after I arrived the promise began to be eroded. I resisted and during the two years I was there my superiors and I fought constantly. I'm sure that RAND did not get its money's worth from me because I kept insisting on the original bargain. Finally, in the midst of a financial debacle and a sizeable reduction in personnel, I was fired. I felt relieved. I had joined RAND believing I could stay uninvolved with those things which I vaguely knew were going on there. I stayed because I was fascinated and horrified, as was probably the case with others. Still others have stayed because they felt that they might make some difference and yet others because RAND was one of the few places in which they can do their own non-war-related work. Most, of course, have stayed because a RAND job is, by most indices, a good job and because the work is not sufficiently disturbing to cause them to leave.

What is apparent to me now—and it is at the heart of the tragedy of the Ellsbergs and all the other whiz kids and men who ever went to Washington from RAND or anywhere else—is that defense think tanks engender habits of thought which are amoral because they appear to separate analysis and responsibility. When minds that are morally relaxed grapple with problems that are loaded with moral freight, they are likely to come up with immoral policies. Only the burden of responsibility can be depended on to make people face the implications of their work. It is easier for the bomber pilot to unleash death on thousands of civilians than for the rifleman to do the same to dozens.

Moreover, RAND has not simply generated such solutions within its own walls and by means of its alumni in Washington. It has been emulated in a wide variety of ways. There are, first of all, a number of other defense think tanks which were and are patterned after RAND, but because it was the first and the most successful it is still the most influential. Secondly, whenever a proposal is made for an institute to be set up which will use highly trained technical skill to deal in a detached abstract way with any of a wide range of nonmilitary problems or tasks of society, the image of RAND is invoked as a reference image, frequently as a goal. Thirdly, RAND was for many years and may still be a large influence on university campuses. It has spent significant sums of money for work done on those campuses and, even more important, it brings many university faculty members and dozens of graduate students to its quarters for extended stays each year. RAND money buys their time and services and may well affect them, although probably less intensively, in ways which are similar to the ways in which I have suggested it affects its own full-time people. Hence RAND and the other defense think tanks may be a source of moral infection which ought to be taken seriously.

Ought we to continue to operate research institutes and research-funding institutes which purport to conduct or support value-neutral analyses of important value-laden policy questions? Should we continue to place brilliant minds in positions where they can influence or bring about important decisions without responsibly facing their implications and without the restraint of fundamental moral commitments? The price has been very high and not all the bills are in yet.

FURTHER READING

Studies of War, Nuclear and Conventional by P. M. S. Blackett (New York: Hill & Wang, 1962).

Militarism, U.S.A. by James Donovan (New York: Scribner, 1970).

War: The Anthropology of Armed Conflict and Aggression, edited by Morton Fried, Marvin Harris, and Robert Murphy (Garden City, N.Y.: Natural History Press, 1965).

The American Military, 2d ed., edited by Martin Oppenheimer (New Brunswick, N.J.: Transaction Books, 1974).

Systems Analysis and Policy Planning by E. S. Quade (New York: Elsevier, 1968).

The RAND Corporation: A Case Study of a Nonprofit Advisory Corporation by B. L. R. Smith (Cambridge, Mass.: Harvard University Press, 1966).

The Military Establishment by A. Yarmolinsky (New York: Harper & Row, 1971).

JIM HIGHTOWER

Hard Tomatoes, Hard Times: Failure of the Land Grant College Complex

Corporate agriculture's preoccupation with scientific and business efficiency has produced a radical restructuring of rural America that has been carried into urban America. There has been more than a green revolution out there—in the last 30 years there literally has been a social and economic upheaval in the American countryside. It is a protracted, violent revolution, and it continues today.

The land grant college complex has been the scientific and intellectual father of that revolution. This public complex has put its tax dollars, its facilities, its manpower, its energies and its thoughts almost solely into efforts that have worked to the advantage and profit of large corporations involved in agriculture.

The consumer is hailed as the greatest beneficiary of the land grant college effort, but in fact consumer interests are considered secondarily if at all, and in many cases, the complex works directly against the consumer. Rural people, including the vast majority of farmers, farm workers, small town businessmen and residents, and the rural poor, either are ignored or directly abused by the land grant effort. Each year about a million of these people pour out of rural America into the cities. They are the waste products of an agricultural revolution designed within the land grant complex. Today's urban crisis is a consequence of failure in rural America. The land grant complex cannot shoulder all the blame for that failure, but no single institution—private or public—has played a more crucial role.

The complex has been eager to work with farm machinery manufacturers and well-capitalized farming operations to mechanize all agricultural labor, but it has accepted no responsibility for the farm laborer who is put out of work by the machine. It has worked hand-in-hand with seed companies to develop high-yield seed strains, but it has not noticed that rural America is yielding up practically all of its young people. It has been available day and night to help non-farming corporations develop schemes of vertical integration, while offering independent family farmers little more comfort than "adapt or die." It has devoted hours to the creation of adequate water systems for fruit and vegetable processors and canners, but 30,000 rural communities still have no central water systems. It has tampered with the gene structure of tomatoes, strawberries, asparagus and other foods to prepare them for the steel grasp of mechanical harvesters, but it has sat still while the American food supply has been laced with carcinogenic substances.

The land grant college complex is made up of three interrelated units, all of which are attached to the land grant college campuses. The first unit is comprised of the Colleges of Agriculture, created in 1862 by the Morrill Act. The State Agricultural Experiment Stations are the second unit. They were created in 1887 by the Hatch Act for the purpose of conducting agricultural and rural research in cooperation with the Colleges of Agriculture.

Excerpted from Jim Hightower, *Hard Tomatoes, Hard Times: The Failure of the Land Grant College Complex* © 1972 by Agribusiness Accountability Project.

The Extension Service, created in 1914 by the Smith-Lever Act completes the picture. It was designed to bring the fruits of research to all rural people.

Reaching into all 50 states, the complex is huge, intricate and expensive. It is estimated that the total complex spends three-quarters of a billion tax dollars appropriated each year from federal, state and county governments. The public's total investment in this complex, including assets, comes to several billion dollars in any given year, paying for everything from test tubes to experimental farms, from chalk to carpeting in the dean's office. But this public investment is being misspent. The land grant complex has wandered a long way from its origins, abandoning its historic mission to serve rural people and American consumers.

The Agribusiness Accountability Project, a public-interest research and advocacy organization based in Washington, D.C., created the Task Force on the Land Grant Complex to look into this issue. In addition to research done in Washington and by correspondence, studies were conducted on the campuses of the University of California, Cornell University, University of Florida, Iowa State University, University of Maryland, Michigan State University, North Carolina State University, Purdue University and Texas A & M University.

It is practically impossible to talk with anyone in the land grant college complex or to read anything about the complex without confronting the staggering achievements wrought by agricultural research. There is no doubt that American agriculture is enormously productive and that agriculture's surge in productivity is largely the result of mechanical, chemical, genetical and managerial research conducted through the land grant college complex. But the question is whether the achievements outweigh the failures, whether benefits are overwhelmed by costs. Ask a family farmer or any rural American about the costs. There is a crisis in the countryside. While the agribusiness conglomerates continue to grow because of agricultural research, the independent farmer is pushed out of the way or, worst of all, just forgotten. Tragically, the land grant complex, the public's primary investment of intellectual and scientific resources in rural America, has not only failed to respond—it has contributed to the problems. There is an obvious failure. You don't even need the readily available statistics to see that rural America is crumbling. And not just the family farm, but every aspect of life is crumbling—entire communities, schools, churches, business and a way of life. For example:

☐ 47.1 percent of the farm families in this country have annual incomes below $3,000.

☐ More than half of the farms in the country have sales of less than $5,000 a year; together, this majority of farmers accounted for only 7.8 percent of farm sales.

☐ Since 1940, more than 3 million farms have folded, and farms continue to fold at a rate of 2,000 a week.

☐ The number of black farm operators fell from 272,541 in 1959 to 98,000 in 1970.

☐ For the first time since the nation was settled coast to coast, the farm population has fallen below 10 million.

☐ During the 1960s, the proportion of farm people over 55 years of age rose by a third, while the proportion of those under 14 years of age declined by half.

☐ Hired farm workers in 1970 averaged an income of $1,083 if they did farm work only, while those who also did some non-farm work averaged an income of $2,461.

☐ 14 million rural Americans exist below a poverty income, with millions more clinging just on the edge of poverty.

☐ Independent, small-town businesses are closing at a rate of more than 16,000 a year.

☐ 132 rural counties have no doctor.

☐ 30,000 rural communities are without central water systems; 30,000 are without sewer systems.

☐ 2.5 million substandard houses—60 percent of the bad housing in America—are occupied by rural families.

☐ 64 percent of all rural counties lost population during the sixties.

☐ Since 1940, 30 million people have left their rural homes for urban areas, and this migration continues at a rate of 800,000 a year.

☐ More than 73 percent of the American people live now on less than 2 percent of the land.

Despite the obvious need, the land grant complex has not provided the answers. For example, in the fiscal year 1969, a total of nearly 6,000 scientific man-years (smy) were spent doing research on all projects at all state-agricultural experiment stations. Based on USDA's research classifications, only 289 of those scientific man-years were expended specifically on "people-oriented" research. That is an allocation to rural people of less than 5 percent of the total research effort at the state agricultural experiment stations. And the experiment stations were doing less of this type of research in 1969 than they were in 1966.

The focus of agricultural research is warped by the land grant community's fascination with technology, integrated food processes and the like. Strict economic efficiency is the goal. The distorted research priorities are striking:

☐ 1,129 scientific man-years on improving the biological efficiency of crops, and only 18 smy on improving rural income.

☐ 842 smy on control of insects, diseases and weeds in crops, and 95 smy to insure food products free from toxic residues from agricultural sources.

☐ 200 smy on ornamentals, turf and trees for natural beauty, and a sad seven smy on rural housing.

☐ 88 smy on improving management systems for livestock and poultry production, and 45 smy for improving rural institutions.

☐ 68 smy on marketing firm and system efficiency, and

17 smy on causes and remedies of poverty among rural people.

A close analysis of these research projects reveals even less of a commitment to the needs of people in rural America than appears on the surface. In rural housing, the major share of research has been directed not to those who live in them but to those who profit from the construction and maintenance of houses—architects, builders, lumber companies and service industries.

Other people-oriented projects tend to be irrelevant studies of characteristics, seemingly stemming more from curiosity than a desire to change conditions. At Cornell, for example, a study found that "employed homemakers have less time for housekeeping tasks than non-employed homemakers." Other projects are just about as "useful."

☐ Mississippi State University researchers discovered "that families in poverty are not of a single, homogeneous type."

☐ The University of Nebraska is at work on a study of "factors affecting age at marriage."

☐ A cooperative Regional Research study unveiled two findings of such significance that Dr. Roy Lovvorn included them in CSRS' 1970 presentation to Congress: "the rural population is dichotomous in racial composition" and "pre-retirement family incomes have a direct bearing upon economic expectations for retirement."

☐ Back at Mississippi State, researchers concluded that "the better educated young individuals are able to recognize and take advantage of economic opportunities attainable through migration."

☐ University of Nebraska researchers surveyed football coaches in the state and got 60 percent agreement "that introduction of a federally sponsored school breakfast program would benefit the nutritional health of teenage athletes."

For the most part, then, even this small amount of people-oriented research done by the land grant complex, is nothing more than useless poking into the behavior and life styles of rural people.

Mechanization Research

The agribusiness corporations envision rural America as a factory that will produce food, fiber and profits on a corporate assembly line extending from the fields through the supermarket checkout counters. It is through mechanization research that the land grant colleges are coming closest to this agribusiness ideal.

Mechanization has been a key element in the cycle of bigness: enough capital can buy machinery, which can handle more acreage, which will produce greater volume, which can mean more profits, which will buy more machinery. Mechanization has not been pressed by the land grant complex as an alternative, but as an imperative.

Once again, those who most need the help of the land grant complex are its primary victims. If mechanization research has been a boon to agribusiness interests, it has been a bane to millions of rural Americans. The cost has been staggering.

Farm workers were the first to get the axe. Again and again the message is hammered home—machines either exist or are on the way to replace farm labor. There were 4.3 million hired farm workers in 1950. Twenty years later, that number has fallen to 2.5 million. As a group, those laborers averaged $1,083 for doing farm work in 1970, making them among the very poorest of America's employed poor. The great majority of these workers were hired by the largest farms, which are the same farms moving as swiftly as possible to mechanize their operations.

Farm workers have not been compensated for jobs lost to mechanization research. They were not consulted when that research was designed, and their needs were not a part of the research package that resulted. They simply were left to fend on their own—no retraining, no effort to find new jobs for them, no research to help them adjust to the changes that came out of the land grant colleges. Corporate agribusiness received machines with the tax-payer's help, but the workers who are replaced are not even entitled to unemployment compensation.

Independent, family farmers are also hard hit. Designed to the specifications of the largest-scale producers, mechanization has not been much of a blessing to those who are lacking capital, acreage or management capabilities. Small- and medium-scale farmers, making annual sales under $20,000, (which includes 87 percent of all farmers in the United States), simply are not able to make much use of $25,000 harvesting equipment. Even the great majority of large-scale farmers, with sales ranging up to $100,000 a year, have not been well served by the mechanization research of land grant colleges.

The rapidly increasing cost of farming, in combination with perennially low farm prices, is driving farmers off the land. Tractor prices range from about $7,000 for a small one to $36,000 for huge crawler tractors. A tractor is useless without plows, rakes, harrows and other essential attachments. These cost extra, and dearly. Harvesting equipment is tremendously expensive—for example, a cotton picker costs $26,000 to $30,000 and a tomato harvester runs $23,000. More sophisticated pieces, with electronic sensors and other gadgets developed by land grant scientists, simply are out of the question for all but the very well heeled. Operator of his own 600-acre Nebraska farm, Elmer Zeis told a newspaper interviewer about these costs:

You can't get a piece of small equipment for under $1,000. The combine I bought this fall cost $20,000; I pay all that and use it one month out of the year. Then I have to trade a piece or two each year just to keep current.

Zeis estimated that he had $50,000 tied up in machinery and another $25,000 in storage buildings and bins.

Like the farm worker, the average farmer is not invited into the land grant laboratories to design research. If he were, the research package would include machines useful on smaller acreages, it would include assistance to develop cooperative ownership systems, it would include efforts to develop low-cost and simpler machinery, it would include a heavy emphasis on new credit schemes, and it would include special extension to spread knowledge about the purchase, operation and maintenance of machinery. These efforts do not exist, or exist only in a token way. Mechanization research has left the great majority of farmers to "get big" on their own, or to get out of farming altogether.

Who then benefits from mechanization research? The largest-scale growers, the farm machinery and chemical input companies and the processors are the primary beneficiaries. Big business interests are called upon by land grant staffs to participate directly in the planning, research and development stages of mechanization projects. The interests of agribusiness literally are designed into the product. No one else is consulted.

Obviously, farm machinery and chemical companies are direct beneficiaries of this research, since they can expect to market products that are developed. Machinery companies such as John Deere, International Harvester, Massey-Ferguson, Allis-Chalmers and J. I. Case almost continually engage in cooperative research efforts at land grant colleges. These corporations contribute money and some of their own research personnel to help land grant scientists develop machinery; in return, they are able to incorporate technological advances in their own products. In some cases they actually receive exclusive license to manufacture and sell the product of tax-paid research.

But mechanization means more than machinery for planting, thinning, weeding and harvesting. It also means improving on nature's design—breeding new food varieties that are better adapted to mechanical harvesting. Having built machines, the land grant research teams found it necessary to build a tomato that is hard enough to survive the grip of mechanical "fingers"; necessary to redesign the grape so that all the fruit has the good sense to ripen at the same time; and necessary to restructure the apple tree so that it grows shorter, leaving the apples less distance to fall to the mechanical catcher.

Mechanization of fruits and vegetables has been focused first on crops used by the processing industries. Brand name processors—such as Del Monte, Heinz, Hunt, Stokely Van-Camp, Campbell's and Green Giant —are direct beneficiaries of mechanization research. Many of these corporations have been directly involved in the development of mechanization projects.

The University of Florida, for example, recently has developed a new fresh market tomato (the MH-1) for machine harvesting. In describing the characteristics that make this tomato so desirable for machine harvest, the university pointed to "the thick walls, firm flesh, and freedom from cracks." It may be a little tough for the consumer, but agricultural research can't please everyone. The MH-1, which will eliminate the jobs of thousands of Florida farm workers who now handpick tomatoes for the fresh market, is designed to be harvested green and to be "ripened" in storage by application of ethylene gas. Michigan State University, in a proud report on "tailor-made" vegetables, notes that their scientists are at work on broccoli, cauliflower, cucumbers, snapbeans, lima beans, carrots and asparagus. And the processors have benefitted because mechanization has been able to lower the costs of production.

If produce cannot be redesigned by manipulating genes, land grant scientists reach into their chemical cabinet. Louisiana State University has experimented with the chemical "Ethrel" to cause hot peppers to ripen at the same time for "onceover" mechanical harvesting; scientists at Michigan State University are using chemicals to reduce the cherry's resistance to the tug of the mechanical picker; and a combination of ferric ammonia citrate and erythorbic acid is being used at Texas A&M to loosen fruit before machine harvesting. This benefits both the chemical input firms on one end and the processors on the other.

Large-scale farming operations, many of them major corporate farms, are also directly in line to receive the rewards of mechanization research. In the first place, it is these farms that hire the overwhelming percentage of farm labor, thus having an economic incentive to mechanize. Secondly, these are the massive farms, spreading over thousands of acres, a scale of operation which warrants an investment in machinery. Thirdly, these are heavily-capitalized producers, including processing corporations, vertically integrated input and output industries and conglomerate enterprises. Such farming ventures are financially able and managerially inclined to mechanize the food system—that 1 percent of American farms with annual sales of $100,000 or more.

These are the "farmers" who are welcome in the land grant research labs. They bring grants and equipment to those labs, but, more importantly, they also bring a shared vision of assembly-line food production. In turn, they get research to implement that vision. These huge growers are more than clients of the land grant system— they are colleagues.

Genetically redesigned, mechanically planted, thinned and weeded, chemically readied and mechanically harvested and sorted, food products move out of the field and into the processing and marketing stages—untouched by human hands.

The agricultural colleges also are engaged in "selling" the consumer on products he neither wants or needs, and they are using tax money for food research and development that should be privately financed. There are many projects that analyze consumer behavior. Typically these involve consumer surveys to determine what influences the shopper's decision-making. If this research is useful to anyone, it is food marketers and advertisers—and reports on this research make clear that those firms are the primary recipients of the results.

The result of this research is not better food but "better looking" food. These public laboratories have researched and developed food cosmetics in an effort to confirm the consumer's preconceptions about food appearances. Chickens have been fed the plant compound Xanthophyll to give their skin "a pleasing yellow tinge," and several projects have been undertaken to develop spray-on coatings to enhance the appearance of apples, peaches, citrus and tomatoes. Other cosmetic research projects are underway at land grant colleges:

□ Iowa State University is conducting packaging studies which indicate that color stays bright longer when bacon is vacuum-packed or sealed in a package containing carbon dioxide in place of air, thus contributing to "more consumer appeal."

□ Scientists at South Carolina's agricultural experiment station have shown that red flourescent light treatment can increase the red color in green, machine-packed tomatoes and can cause their texture and taste to be "similar to vine-ripened tomatoes."

□ Kansas State University Extension Service, noting that apples sell on the basis of appearance rather than nutrition, urged growers to have a beautiful product. To make the produce more appealing, mirrors and lights in supermarket produce cases were cited as effective selling techniques.

Convenience to the processor often outweighs concern for the consumer, both as a motive for and as an end result of such research. For example, University of Wisconsin researchers have developed a process of making mozarella cheese in five-and-a-half minutes compared to the usual time of four hours. The flavor of the final product is reported to be "mild, but satisfactory for the normal uses." While this is relatively harmless, there is evidence that some aspects of food engineering at land grant colleges are directly counter to the interests of the consumer. For instance, when ethylene gas is used to ripen tomatoes, in addition to inferior taste, color and firmness, the amounts of vitamin A and vitamin C are known to decrease.

Even more insidious, there is strong evidence the DES, a growth hormone fed to cattle to make them grow faster, causes cancer in man. Yet DES has added some $2.9 million to the treasury of Iowa State University, where the use of the drug was discovered, developed, patented and promoted—all with tax dollars. Eli Lilly and Company, which was exclusively licensed by Iowa State to manufacture and sell the drug, has enjoyed profits on some $60 million in DES sales to date.

More and more, chemicals are playing a role in the processing phase. Ohio State University reports that "chemical peeling of tomatoes with wetting agents and caustic soda reduces labor by 75 percent and increases product recovery." One wonders if the consumer will recover. Lovers of catfish might be distressed to know that this tasty meat now is being skinned chemically for commercial packaging.

At the same time, some of the research products are deceptively harmless—to the point of absurdity. At Cornell a critical issue has been how hard to squeeze a grapefruit in the supermarket:

Should you squeeze a product firmly or softly to determine its freshness, such as is commonly done with bread and some fruits? By using a universal testing machine, scientists have determined that a gentle squeeze, or more scientifically, a small deformation force, is much more precise in comparing textural differences than a firm squeeze or large deformation force.

Among other mind-boggling land grant college projects, Auburn and Penn State have used tax dollars to study "heat-retaining properties" of Astroturf; the University of Wisconsin has turned to camping for a research challenge; and Purdue has spent years and untold tax dollars on athletic turfs for football fields and golf courses. Except for agribusiness, land grant college research has been no bargain. Hard tomatoes and hard times is too much to pay.

The Extension Service (ES) is the outreach arm of the land grant college complex. Its mandate is to go among the people of rural America to help them "identify and solve their farm, home and community problems through use of research findings of the Department of Agriculture and the State Land Grant Colleges." As with the rest of the complex, the ES has hardly lived up to its mandate.

The focus of ES is primarily on "clients" who need it least, ignoring the obvious needs of the vast majority of rural Americans. The service devotes more than half of its total work to just one-quarter of the farmers in this country—those with sales of more than $10,000 annually. That leaves 2.4 million farmers—75 percent of the total according to ES figures—without the attention that their need and numbers warrant. Included are hundreds of thousands of marginal farmers, with "net incomes insufficient for levels of living acceptable even for rural areas."

Three hundred thirty-one million dollars were available to the Extension Service in 1971. Like the other parts of the land grant complex, Extension has been preoccupied with efficiency and production—a focus that has contributed much to the largest producers. And while the rural poor get little attention from ES professionals, they receive band-aid assistance from highly-visible but marginally helpful programs like nutrition aids.

The poor get even less attention than appears on the surface. 4-H—that social club for youth—received $72 million in 1971 and accounted for the largest allocation of extension agents' time—over one-third of the total. And with this time and money 4-H helps the rural poor by conducting litter clean-up days and awarding ribbons to everybody.

In 1955, a Special Needs Section was added to Extension legislation, setting aside a sum of money to assist disadvantaged areas. But Extension has failed to make use of it. Policy-making within ES fails to involve most rural people, and USDA has failed utterly to exercise its power to redirect the priorities and programs of the state extension services.

Who does the ES serve? Like their research and teaching colleagues in the land grant complex, extension agents walk hand in hand with agribusiness. To an alarming degree, extension agents are little more than salesmen. A recent article in *Farm Technology*, the magazine for county agents, offers this insight into corporate ties to Extension:

We are impressed with the fact that much time is spent working closely with industry agrifieldmen and other company representatives. Nearly all states reported that this type of cooperation is increasing.

A good example of this can be found in Arizona where weed specialists "hit the road" with the chemical company representatives and are involved in cooperative field tests and demonstrations.

Moreover, the Extension Service's historical and current affiliation with the American Farm Bureau Federation, the nation's largest, most powerful and affluent farm organization, casts a deep shadow over its claim that it can ever be part of the solution of the problems of rural America.

The civil rights record of ES comes close to being the worst in government. In three states suits have been brought against the Extension Service for overt and flagrant discrimination in hiring and service. Median income figures from 1970 show that white farm families averaged $7,016 per year, while black farm families averaged $3,037. Yet of all the rural poor, blacks can expect the least assistance from ES.

This is not the only case of institutional racism within the land grant complex. When the Morrill Act created land grant colleges in 1862, most of America's black population was in slavery. After the Civil War, blacks were barred from admission both by custom and by law. In 1890 a second Morrill Act was passed to obtain more operating money for the colleges. This act also included a "separate but equal" provision authorizing the establishment of colleges for blacks. Seventeen southern and border states took advantage of this provision. But these black colleges have been less than full partners in the land grant complex. Resource allocations have been blatantly discriminatory. In 1971, of the $76,800,000 in United States Department of Agriculture funds allocated to those 16 states with both white and black land grant colleges, 99.5 percent went to the white colleges, leaving only 0.5 percent for the black colleges. Less than one percent of the research money distributed by the Cooperative State Research Service in 1971 went to black land grant colleges. This disparity is not by accident, but by law.

Making Research Policy

Land grant policy is the product of a closed community. The administrators, academics and scientists, along with USDA officials and corporate executives, have locked themselves into an inbred and even incestuous complex, and they are incapable of thinking beyond their self-interest and traditional concepts of agricultural research.

The short range research policy of the land grant system is the product of the annual budgeting process and the substance of that research budget is determined by the Agricultural Research Policy Advisory Committee (ARP-AC), which reports directly to the Secretary of Agriculture. Its members are the agricultural research establishment taken from USDA and the land grant community.

The National Association of State Universities and Land Grant Colleges is the home of the land grant establishment. Their particular corner in the Association is the Division of Agriculture, composed of all deans of agriculture, all heads of state experiment stations and all deans of extension. With eight members on the 24-man ARPAC board, NASULGC's Agricultural Division plays a major role in the determination of research priorities and budgets. The division also represents the land grant college complex before Congress on budget matters.

The top rung on the advisory ladder is USDA's National Agricultural Research Advisory Committee. This 11-member structure currently includes representatives from the Del Monte Corporation, the Crown Zellerbach Corporation, AGWAY, Peavey Company Flour Mills, the industry-sponsored Nutrition Foundation and the American Farm Bureau Federation.

Most national advisory structures are dominated by land grant scientists and officials, but whenever an "outsider" is selected, chances are overwhelming that the person will come from industry. A series of national task forces, formed from 1965-1969 to prepare a national program of agricultural research, were classic examples of this pattern. Out of 32 task forces, 17 listed advisory committees containing non-USDA, non-land grant people. All but one of the outside slots on those 17 committees were filled with representatives of industry, including General Foods on the rice committee, U.S. Sugar on sugar, Quaker Oats on wheat, Pioneer Corn on corn, Liggitt & Myers on tobacco, Procter & Gamble on soybeans and Ralston Purina on dairy. Only on the "soil and land use" task force was there an adviser representing an interest other than industrial, but even there, the National Wildlife Federation was carefully balanced by an adviser from International Minerals and Chemical Corporation.

Agribusiness Links to Land Grant Campuses

The giant agribusiness corporations and the land grant complex are linked in an extensive interlocking web. Corporate executives sit on boards of trustees, purchase research from experiment stations and colleges, hire land grant academics as private consultants, advise and are advised by land grant officials: they go to Washington to help a college or an experiment station get more public money for its work, publish and distribute the writings of academics, provide scholarships and other educational support, invite land grant participation in their industrial conferences and sponsor foundations that extend both grants and recognition to the land grant community.

Money is the catalyst for this tight web of relationships. It is not that a huge sum of money is given—industry gave only $12 million directly to state agricultural experiment stations for research in 1969. Rather it is that enough money is given to influence research done with public funds.

Corporate money goes to meet corporate needs and whims, and these needs and whims largely determine the research program of land grant colleges. A small grant for specific research is just good business. The grant is tax deductible either as an education contribution or, if the research is directly related to the work of the corporation, as a necessary business expense. Not only is the product wrapped and delivered to the corporation, but with it comes the college's stamp of legitimacy and maybe even an endorsement by the scientist who conducted the research. If it is a new product, the corporation can expect to be licensed, perhaps exclusively, as the producer and marketer. Everything considered, it amounts to a hefty return on a meager investment.

There is a long list of satisfied, corporate customers. Prime contributors are chemical, drug and oil corporations. Again and again the same names appear—American Cyanamid, Chevron, Dow Chemical, Esso, Eli Lilly, Geigy, FMC-Niagra, IMC Corporation, Shell, Stauffer, Union Carbide and The Upjohn Company are just a few of the giants that gave research grants to each of three colleges checked (University of Florida, North Carolina State University and Purdue University). Chemical, drug and oil companies invested $227,158 in research at Florida's Institute of Food and Agricultural Science, for example, accounting for 54 percent of research sponsored there by private industry in 1970.

Land Grant Research Foundations

At least 23 land grant colleges have established foundations to handle grants and contracts coming into their institutions for research. These quasi-public foundations are curious mechanisms, handling large sums of money from a wide array of private and public donors, but under practically no burden of public disclosure.

A funding source can give money to a private research foundation, which then funnels the money to a public university to conduct research. By this shell game, industry-financed research can be undertaken without obligation to make public the terms of the agreement. The foundation need not report to anyone the names of corporations that are making research grants, the amounts of those grants, the purpose of those grants or the terms under which the grants are made.

These foundations also handle patents for the colleges. When a corporation invests in research through a foundation, it is done normally with the understanding that the corporation will have first shot at a license on any patented process or product resulting from the research. On research patents that do not result from corporate grants, the procedure for licensing is just as cozy. At Purdue University, for example, a list is drawn of "responsible" companies that might have an interest in the process or product developed, and the companies are approached one by one until there is a taker.

Because of these complex and tangled funding procedures it is often difficult to discover exactly what the land grant complex is doing. For example, most agricultural experiment stations offer an annual report in compliance with the Hatch Act disclosure provisions, but these reports are less than enlightening. Some do not list all research projects, but merely list highlights. Most do not include money figures with the individual projects, and very few reveal the source of the money. Instead they contain only a very general financial breakdown, listing state, federal and "other" funds received and expended. Few offer any breakdown of industry contributions, naming the industry, the contribution and the project funded; and none of the reports contain any element of project continuity to show the total tax investment over the years in a particular investigation.

Data are not supplied uniformly, are not collected in a central location and either are not reported or reported in a form that cannot be easily obtained or understood. Even more significant is the fact that many fundamental questions go unasked and fundamental facts go unreported.

The land grant college complex has been able to get by with a minimum of public disclosure—and with a minimum of public accountability. Millions of tax dollars annually are being spent by an agricultural complex that effectively operates in the dark. The farmer, the consumer, the rural poor and others with a direct interest in the work of the land grant complex can get no adequate picture of its work.

Congress is no help; it does not take the time to probe the system, to understand it in detail and to direct its work in the public interest. It is here that the public might expect some serious questions of research focus—and some assertion of public rather than private interests. But it just does not happen. Congress has relinquished its responsibility and authority to single-minded officials at USDA and within the land grant community. Like spokesmen of the military-industrial complex, these officials and their allies come to the Capitol at appropriations time to assure a docile Congress that its investment in agricultural hardware is buying "progress" and that rural pacification is proceeding nicely.

There is nothing inevitable about the growth of agribusiness in rural America. While this country enjoys an abundance of relatively cheap food, it is not more food, not cheaper food and certainly not better food than that which can be produced by a system of family agriculture. And more than food rolls off the agribusiness assembly line—including rural refugees, boarded-up businesses, deserted churches, abandoned towns, broiling urban ghettoes and dozens of other tragic social and cultural costs.

The solution to the problems of rural America is not a return to the hand plow. Rather, land grant colleges researchers must get out of the comfortable chairs of corporate board rooms and get back to serving the independent producer and the common man of rural America. It means returning to the historic mission of taking the technological revolution to all who need it, rather than smugly assuming that they will be unable to keep pace. Instead of adopting the morally bankrupt posture that millions of people must "inevitably" be squeezed out of agriculture and out of rural America, land grant colleges must turn their thoughts, energies and resources to the task of keeping people on the farm, in the small towns and out of cities. It means turning from the erroneous assumption that big is good, that what serves Ralston Purina serves rural America. It means research for the consumer rather than for the processor. In short, it means putting the research focus on people first—not as a trickle-down afterthought.

It is the objective of the Task Force on the Land Grant College Complex to provoke a public response that will help realign that complex with the public interest. In a recent speech concerned with reordering agricultural research priorities, Dr. Ned Bayley, Director of Science and Education for the USDA said that, "the first giant steps are open discussion and full recognition of the need." The Task Force report has recognized the need and is prompting an open discussion. The time for action is at hand.

FURTHER READING

Dollar Harvest by Samuel R. Berger (Lexington, Mass.: Heath, 1971). The Farm Bureau's ties to corporate agribusiness.

Eat This Book: How the Department of Agriculture Serves Corporations Instead of Farmers by Martha M. Hamilton (Washington, D.C.: Agribusiness Accountability Project, 1972). The international grain trade and federal food procurement.

Let Them Eat Promises: The Politics of Hunger in America by Nick Kotz (Garden City, N.Y.: Doubleday Anchor Books, 1971).

Factories in the Field by Carey McWilliams (New York: Barnes & Noble, 1967).

Corporate Power in America edited by Ralph Nader and Mark Green (New York: Grossman, 1973).

The Closed Corporation: American Universities in Crisis by James Ridgeway (New York: Ballantine, 1968).

Sowing the Wind: A Report for Ralph Nader's Center for Study of Responsive Law on Food Safety and the Chemical Harvest by Harrison Wellford (New York: Grossman, 1972).

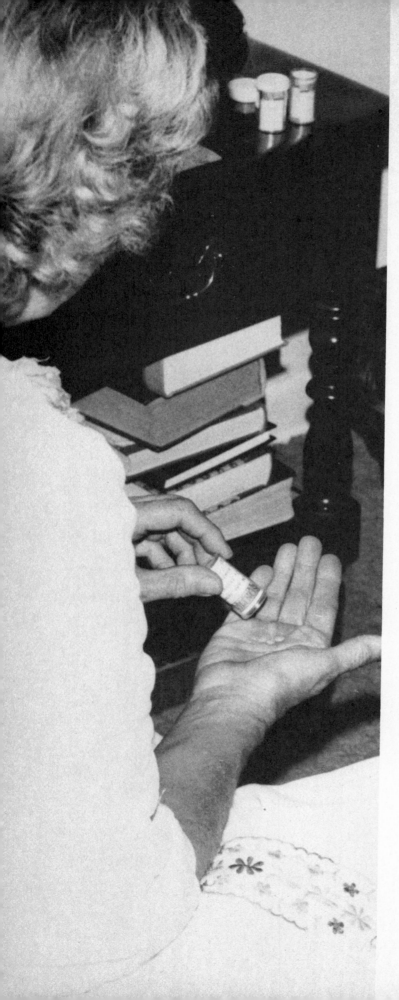

JAMES M. GRAHAM

Amphetamine Politics on Capitol Hill

The American pharmaceutical industry annually manufactures enough amphetamines to provide a month's supply to every man, woman and child in the country. Eight, perhaps ten, billion pills are lawfully produced, packaged, retailed and consumed each year. Precise figures are unavailable. We must be content with estimates because until 1970, no law required an exact accounting of total amphetamine production.

Amphetamines are the drug of the white American with money to spend. Street use, contrary to the popular myths, accounts for a small percentage of the total consumption. Most of the pills are eaten by housewives, businessmen, students, physicians, truck drivers and athletes. Those who inject large doses of "speed" intravenously are but a tiny fragment of the total. Aside from the needle and the dose, the "speed freak" is distinguishable because his use has been branded as illegal. A doctor's signature supplies the ordinary user with lawful pills.

All regular amphetamine users expose themselves to varying degrees of potential harm. Speed doesn't kill, but high sustained dosages can and do result in serious mental and physical injury, depending on how the drug is taken. The weight-conscious housewife, misled by the opinion-makers into believing that amphetamines can control weight, eventually may rely on the drug to alter her mood in order to face her monotonous tasks. Too frequently an amphetamine prescription amounts to a synthetic substitute for attention to emotional and institutional problems.

Despite their differences, all amphetamine users, whether on the street or in the kitchen, share one important thing in common—the initial source of supply. For both, it is largely the American pharmaceutical industry. That industry has skillfully managed to convert a chemical, with meager medical justification and considerable potential for harm, into multihundred-million-dollar profits in less than 40 years. High profits, reaped from such vulnerable products, require extensive, sustained political efforts for their continued existence. The lawmakers who have declared that possession of marijuana is a serious crime have simultaneously defended and protected the profits of the amphetamine pill-makers. The Comprehensive Drug Abuse Prevention and Control Act of 1970 in its final form constitutes a victory for that alliance over compelling, contrary evidence on the issue of amphetamines. The victory could not have been secured without the firm support of the Nixon Administration. The end result is a national policy which declares an all-out war on drugs which are *not* a source of corporate income. Meanwhile, under the protection of the law, billions of amphetamines are overproduced without medical justification.

Hearings in the Senate

The Senate was the first house to hold hearings on the administration's bill to curb drug abuse, The Controlled Dangerous Substances Act (S-3246). Beginning on September 15, 1969 and consuming most of that month, the hearings before Senator Thomas Dodd's Subcommittee to Investigate Juvenile Delinquency of the Committee on the Judiciary would finally conclude on October 20, 1969.

The first witness was John Mitchell, attorney general of the United States, who recalled President Nixon's ten-point program to combat drug abuse announced on July 14, 1969. Although that program advocated tighter controls on imports and exports of dangerous drugs and promised new efforts to encourage foreign governments to crack down on production of illicit drugs, there was not a single reference to the control of domestic manufacture of dangerous drugs. The president's bill when it first reached the Senate placed the entire "amphetamine family" in Schedule III, where they were exempt from any quotas and had the benefit of lesser penalties and controls. Hoffman-LaRoche, Inc. had already been at work; their depressants, Librium and Valium, were completely exempt from any control whatsoever.

In his opening statement, Attorney General Mitchell set the tone of administrative policy related to amphetamines. Certainly, these drugs were "subject to increasing abuse"; however, they have "widespread medical uses" and therefore are appropriately classed under the administration guidelines in Schedule III. Tight-mouthed John Ingersoll, director of the Bureau of Narcotics and Dangerous Drugs (BNDD), reaffirmed the policy, even though a Bureau study over the last year (which showed that 92 percent of the amphetamines and barbiturates in the illicit market were legitimately manufactured) led him to conclude that drug companies have "lax security and recordkeeping."

Senator Dodd was no novice at dealing with the pharmaceutical interests. In 1965 he had steered a drug abuse bill through the Senate with the drug industry fighting every step of the way. Early in the hearings he recalled that the industry "vigorously opposed the passage of (the 1965) act. I know very well because I lived with it, and they gave me fits and they gave all of us fits in trying to get it through."

The medical position on amphetamine use was first presented by the National Institute of Mental Health's Dr. Sidney Cohen, a widely recognized authority on drug use and abuse. He advised the subcommittee that 50 percent of the lawfully manufactured pep pills were diverted at some point to illicit channels. Some of the pills, though, were the result of unlawful manufacture as evidenced by the fact that 33 clandestine laboratories had been seized in the last 18 months.

Dr. Cohen recognized three categories of amphetamine abuse, all of which deserved the attention of the government. First was their "infrequent ingestion" by students, businessmen, truck drivers and athletes. Second were those

people who swallowed 50-75 milligrams daily without medical supervision. Finally, there were the speed freaks who injected the drug intravenously over long periods of time. Physical addiction truly occurs, said Dr. Cohen, when there is prolonged use in high doses. Such use, he continued, may result in malnutrition, prolonged psychotic states, heart irregularities, convulsions, hepatitis and with an even chance of sustained brain damage.

As the hearings progressed, the first two classes of abusers described by Dr. Cohen would receive less and less attention, while the third category—the speed freaks—would receive increasing emphasis. The amphetamine industry was not at all unhappy with this emphasis. In fact, they would encourage it.

Ingersoll had already said that BNDD statistics indicated that only 8 percent of illicit speed was illegally manufactured. Thomas Lynch, attorney general of California, testified that his agents had in 1967 successfully negotiated a deal for one-half million amphetamine tablets with a "Tijuana café man." Actual delivery was taken from a California warehouse. All of the tablets seized originated with a Chicago company which had not bothered to question the authenticity of the retailer or the pharmacy. Prior to the 1965 hearings, the Food and Drug Administration completed a ten-year study involving 1,658 criminal cases for the illegal sale of amphetamines and barbiturates. Seventy-eight percent of all convictions involved pharmacists, and of these convictions 60 percent were for illicit traffic in amphetamines.

The pharmacists were not the source of illicit diversion, according to the National Association of Retail Druggists (NARD) and the National Association of Chain Drug Stores. Indeed, NARD had conducted an extensive educational program combating drug abuse for years, and, as proof of it, introduced its booklet, "Never Abuse—Respect Drugs," into the record. Annual inventories were acceptable for Schedule I and II drugs, NARD continued, but were unwarranted for the remaining two schedules which coincidently included most of their wares—unwarranted because diversion resulted from forged prescriptions, theft and placebo (false) inventories.

The amphetamine wholesalers were not questioned in any detail about diversion. Brief statements by the National Wholesale Druggists Association and McKesson Robbins Drug Co. opposed separate inventories for dangerous drugs because they were currently comingled with other drugs. Finally, the massive volume of the drugs involved—primarily in Schedule III—was just too great for records to be filed with the attorney general.

Dodging the Diversion Issue

The representative of the prescription drug developers was also not pressed on the question of illicit diversion. Instead, the Pharmaceutical Manufacturers' Association requested clarifications on the definitional sections, argued for formal administrative hearings on control decisions and on any action revoking or suspending registration, and endorsed a complete exemption for over-the-counter non-narcotic drugs.

With some misgivings, Carter-Wallace Inc. endorsed the administration bill providing, of course, the Senate would accept the president's recommendation that meprobamate not be subjected to any control pending a decision of the Fourth Circuit as to whether the drug had a dangerously depressant effect on the central nervous system. On a similar special mission, Hoffman-LaRoche Inc. sent two of its vice-presidents to urge the committee to agree with the president's recommendation that their "minor tranquilizers" (Librium and Valium) remain uncontrolled. Senator Dodd was convinced that both required inclusion in one of the schedules. The Senator referred to a BNDD investigation which had shown that from January 1968 to February 1969, three drug stores were on the average over 30,000 dosage units short. In addition, five inspected New York City pharmacies had unexplained shortages ranging from 12 to 50 percent of their total stock in Librium and Valium. Not only were the drugs being diverted, but Bureau of Narcotics information revealed that Librium and Valium, alone or in combination with other drugs, were involved in 36 suicides and 750 attempted suicides.

The drug company representatives persisted in dodging or contradicting Dodd's inquiries. Angry and impatient, Senator Dodd squarely asked the vice-presidents, "Why do you worry about putting this drug under control?" The response was as evasive as the question was direct: There are hearings pending in HEW, and Congress should await the outcome when the two drugs might be placed in Schedule III. (The hearings had begun in 1966; no final administrative decision had been reached and Hoffman-LaRoche had yet to exercise its right to judicial review.)

In the middle of the hearings, BNDD Director Ingersoll returned to the subcommittee to discuss issues raised chiefly by drug industry spokesmen. He provided the industry with several comforting administrative interpretations. The fact that he did not even mention amphetamines is indicative of the low level of controversy that the hearings had aroused on the issue. Ingersoll did frankly admit that his staff had met informally with industry representatives in the interim. Of course, this had been true from the very beginning.

The president of the American Pharmaceutical Association, the professional society for pharmacists, confirmed this fact: His staff participated in "several" Justice Department conferences when the bill was being drafted. (Subsequent testimony in the House would reveal that industry participation was extensive and widespread.) All the same, the inventory, registration and inspection (primarily "no-knock") provisions were still "unreasonable, unnecessary and costly administrative burden(s)" which would result in an even greater "paper work explosion."

For the most part, however, the administration bill had industry support. It was acceptable for the simple reason that, to an unknown degree, the "administration bill" was a "drug company bill" and was doubtless the final product of considerable compromise. Illustrative of that give-and-take process is the comparative absence of industry opposition to the transfer of drug-classification decision and research for HEW to Justice. The industry had already swallowed this and other provisions in exchange for the many things the bill could have but did not cover. Moreover, the subsequent windy opposition of the pill-makers allowed the administration to boast of a bill the companies objected to.

When the bill was reported out of the Committee on the Judiciary, the amphetamine family, some 6,000 strong, remained in Schedule III. Senator Dodd apparently had done some strong convincing because Librium, Valium and meprobamate were now controlled in Schedule III. A commission on marijuana and a declining penalty structure (based on what schedule the drug is in and whether or not the offense concerned trafficking or possession) were added.

Debate in the Senate—Round I

The Senate began consideration of the bill on January 23, 1970. This time around, the amphetamine issue would inspire neither debate or amendment. The energies of the Senate liberals were consumed instead by unsuccessful attempts to alter the declared law enforcement nature of the administration bill.

Senator Dodd's opening remarks, however, were squarely directed at the prescription pill industry. Dodd declared that the present federal laws had failed to control the illicit diversion of lawfully manufactured dangerous drugs. The senator also recognized the ways in which all Americans had become increasingly involved in drug use and that the people's fascination with pills was by no means an "accidental development": "Multihundred million dollar advertising budgets, frequently the most costly ingredient in the price of a pill, have, pill by pill, led, coaxed and seduced post-World War II generations into the 'freaked-out' drug culture.... Detail men employed by drug companies propagandize harried and harassed doctors into pushing their special brand of palliative. Free samples in the doctor's office are as common nowadays as inflated fees." In the version adopted by the Senate, Valium, Librium and meprobamate joined the amphetamines in Schedule III.

Hearings in the House

On February 3, 1970, within a week of the Senate's passage of S-3246, the House began its hearings. The testimony would continue for a month. Although the Senate would prove in the end to be less vulnerable to the drug lobby, the issue of amphetamines—their danger and medical justification—would be aired primarily in the hearings of the Subcommittee on Public Health of the Committee on Interstate and Foreign Commerce. The administration bill (HR 13743), introduced by the chairman of the parent committee, made no mention of Librium or Valium and classified amphetamines in Schedule III.

As in the Senate, the attorney general was scheduled to be the first witness, but instead John Ingersoll of the BNDD was the administration's representative. On the question of amphetamine diversion, Ingersoll gave the administration's response: "Registration is... the most effective and least cumbersome way" to prevent the unlawful traffic. This coupled with biennial inventories of all stocks of controlled dangerous drugs and the attorney general's authority to suspend, revoke or deny registration would go a long way in solving the problem. In addition, the administration was proposing stronger controls on imports and exports. For Schedules I and II, but not III or IV, a permit from the attorney general would be required for exportation. Quotas for Schedules I and II, but not III or IV, would "maximize" government control. For Schedules III and IV, no approval is required, but a supplier must send an advance notice on triple invoice to the attorney general in order to export drugs such as amphetamines. A prescription could be filled only five times in a six-month period and thereafter a new prescription would be required, whereas previously such prescriptions could be refilled as long as a pharmacist would honor them.

The deputy chief counsel for the BNDD, Michael R. Sonnenreich, was asked on what basis the attorney general would decide to control a particular drug. Sonnenreich replied that the bill provides one of two ways: Either the attorney general "finds *actual street abuse* or an interested party (such as HEW) feels that a drug should be controlled." (Speed-freaks out on the street are the trigger, according to Sonnenreich; lawful abuse is not an apparent criterion.)

The registration fee schedule would be reasonable ($10.00—physician or pharmacist; $25.00—wholesalers; $50.00—manufacturers). However, the administration did not want a formal administrative hearing on questions of registration and classification, and a less formal rule-making procedure was provided for in the bill.

Returning to the matter of diversion, Sonnenreich disclosed that from July 1, 1968 to June 30, 1969 the BNDD had conducted full-scale compliance investigations of 908 "establishments." Of this total, 329 (or about 36 percent) required further action, which included surrender of order forms (162), admonition letters (38), seizures (36) and hearings (31). In addition to these full-scale investigations, the Bureau made 930 "visits." (It later came to light that when the BNDD had information that a large supply of drugs was unlawfully being sold, the Bureau's policy was to warn those involved and "90 percent of them do take care of this matter.") Furthermore, 574 robberies involving dangerous drugs had been reported to the Bureau.

Eight billion amphetamine tablets are produced annually, according to Dr. Stanley Yolles, director of the National Institute of Mental Health, and although the worst abuse is by intravenous injection, an NIMH study found that 21 percent of all college students had taken amphetamines with the family medicine cabinet acting as the primary source—not surprising in light of the estimate that 1.1 billion prescriptions were issued in 1967 at a consumer cost of $3.9 billion. Of this total, 178 million prescriptions for amphetamines were filled at a retail cost of $692 million. No one knew the statistics better than the drug industry.

Representing the prescription-writers, the American Medical Association also recognized that amphetamines were among those drugs "used daily in practically every physician's armamentarium." This casual admission of massive lawful distribution was immediately followed by a flat denial that physicians were the source of "any significant diversion."

The next witness was Donald Fletcher, manager of distribution protection, Smith Kline & French Laboratories, one of the leading producers of amphetamines. Fletcher, who was formerly with the Texas state police, said his company favored "comprehensive controls" to fight diversion and stressed the company's "educational effort." Smith Kline & French favored federal registration and tighter controls over exports (by licensing the exporter, *not* the shipment). However, no change in present record-keeping requirements on distribution, production or inventory should be made, and full hearings on the decisions by the attorney general should be guaranteed.

The committee did not ask the leading producer of amphetamines a single question about illicit diversion. Upon conclusion of the testimony, Subcommittee Chairman John Jarman of Oklahoma commented, "Certainly, Smith Kline & French is to be commended for the constructive and vigorous and hard-hitting role that you have played in the fight against drug abuse."

Dr. William Apple, executive director of the American Pharmaceutical Association (APhA), was the subject of lengthy questioning and his responses were largely typical. Like the entire industry, the APhA was engaged in a massive public education program. Apple opposed the inventory provisions, warning that the cost would be ultimately passed to the consumer. He was worried about the attorney general's power to revoke registrations ("without advance notice") because it could result in cutting off necessary drugs to patients.

Apple admitted organizational involvement "in the draft stage of the bill" but all the same, the APhA had a "very good and constructive working relationship" with HEW. Apple argued that if the functions are transferred to Justice, "We have a whole new ball game in terms of people. While some of the experienced people were transferred from HEW to Justice, there are. many new people, and they are law-enforcement oriented. We are health-care oriented." Surely the entire industry shared this sentiment, but few opposed the transfer as strongly as did the APhA.

Apple reasoned that since the pharmacists were not the source of diversion, why should they be "penalized by costly overburdensome administrative requirements." The source of the drugs, Apple said, were either clandestine laboratories or burglaries. The 1965 Act, which required only those "records maintained in the ordinary course of business" be kept, was sufficient. Anyway, diversion at the pharmacy level was the responsibility of the pharmacists—a responsibility which the APhA takes "seriously and (is) going to do a better job (with) in the future."

Congress should instead ban the 60 mail-order houses which are not presently included in the bill. (One subcommittee member said this was a "loophole big enough to drive a truck through.") The corner druggist simply was not involved in "large-scale diversionary efforts."

The Pharmaceutical Manufacturers' Association (PMA) was questioned a bit more carefully in the House than in the Senate. PMA talked at length about its "long and honorable history" in fighting drug abuse. Its representative echoed the concern of the membership over the lack of formal hearings and requested that a representative of the manufacturing interests be appointed to the Scientific Advisory Committee. Significantly, the PMA declined to take a position on the issue of transfer from HEW to Justice. The PMA endorsed the administration bill. PMA Vice-President Brennan was asked whether the federal government should initiate a campaign, similar to the one against cigarettes, "to warn people that perhaps they should be careful not to use drugs excessively." Brennan's response to this cautious suggestion is worth quoting in full:

> I think this is probably not warranted because it would have the additional effect of giving concern to people over very useful commodities. . . . There is a very useful side to any medicant and to give people pause as to whether or not they should take that medication, particularly those we are talking about which are only given by prescription, I think the negative effect would outweigh any sociological benefit on keeping people from using drugs.

"Limited Medical Use"

There was universal agreement that amphetamines are medically justified for the treatment of two very rare diseases, hyperkinesis and narcolepsy. Dr. John D. Griffith of the Vanderbilt University School of Medicine testified that amphetamine production should be limited to the needs created by those conditions: "A few thousand tablets (of amphetamines) would supply the whole medical needs of the country. In fact, it would be possible for the government to make and distribute the tablets at very little cost. This way there would be no outside commercial interests involved." Like a previous suggestion that Congress impose a one cent per tablet tax on drugs subject to abuse, no action was taken on the proposal.

The very next day, Dr. John Jennings, acting director of the Food and Drug Administration (FDA), testified that amphetamines had a "limited medical use" and their usefulness in control of obesity was of "doubtful value." Dr. Dorothy Dobbs, director of the Marketed Drug Division of the FDA further stated that there was now no warning on the prescriptions to patients, but that the FDA was proposing that amphetamines be labeled indicating among other things that a user subjects himself to "extreme psychological dependence" and the possibility of "extreme personality changes. . . (and) the most severe manifestation of amphetamine intoxication is a psychosis." Dr. Dobbs thought that psychological dependence even under a physician's prescription was "quite possible."

Congressman Claude Pepper of Florida, who from this point on would be the recognized leader of the anti-amphetamine forces, testified concerning a series of hearings which his Select Committee on Crime had held in the fall of 1969 on the question of stimulant use.

Pepper's committee had surveyed medical deans and health organizations on the medical use of amphetamines. Of 53 responses, only one suggested that the drug was useful "for *early* stages of a diet program." (Dr. Sidney Cohen of NIMH estimated that 99 percent of the total legal prescriptions for amphetamines were ostensibly for dietary control.) Pepper's investigation also confirmed a high degree of laxness by the drug companies. A special agent for the BNDD testified that by impersonating a physician, he was able to get large quantities of amphetamines from two mail-order houses in New York. One company, upon receiving an order for 25,000 units, asked for further verification of medical practice. Two days after the agent declined to reply, the units arrived. Before Pepper's committee, Dr. Cohen of NIMH testified that amphetamines were a factor in trucking accidents due to their hallucinatory effects.

Dr. John D. Griffith from Vanderbilt Medical School, in his carefully documented statement on the toxicity of amphetamines, concluded "amphetamine addiction is more widespread, more incapacitating, more dangerous and socially disrupting than narcotic addiction." Considering that 8 percent of all prescriptions are for amphetamines and that the drug companies make only one-tenth of one cent a tablet, Dr. Griffith was not surprised that there was so little scrutiny by manufacturers. Only a large output would produce a large profit.

Treatment for stimulant abuse was no easier than for heroin addiction and was limited to mild tranquilization, total abstinence and psychiatric therapy. But, heroin has not been the subject of years of positive public "education" programs nor has it been widely prescribed by physicians or lawfully produced. A health specialist from the University of Utah pointed out that the industry's propaganda had made amphetamines: "One of the major ironies of the whole field of drug abuse. We continue to insist that they are good drugs when used under medical supervision, but their greatest use turns out to be frivolous, illegal and highly destructive to the user. People who are working in the field of drug abuse are finding it most difficult to control the problem, partly because they have the reputation of being legal and good drugs."

The thrust of Pepper's presentation was not obvious from the questioning that followed, because the subcommittee discussions skirted the issue. Pepper's impact could be felt in the subsequent testimony of the executive director of the National Association of Boards of Pharmacy. The NABP objected to the use of the word "dangerous" in the bill's title because it "does little to enhance the legal acts of the physician and pharmacist in diagnosing and dispensing this type of medication." (The Controlled Dangerous Substances Act would later become the Comprehensive Drug Abuse Prevention and Control Act of 1970.)

As in the Senate hearings, Ingersoll of the BNDD returned for a second appearance and, this time, he was the last witness. Ingersoll stated that he wished "to place. . . in their proper perspective" some "of the apparent controversies" which arose in the course of testimony. A substantial controversy had arisen over amphetamines, but there was not a single word on that subject in Ingersoll's prepared statement. Later, he did admit that there was an "overproduction" of amphetamines and estimated that 75 percent to 90 percent of the amphetamines found in illicit traffic came from the American drug companies.

Several drug companies chose to append written statements rather than testifying.

Abbott Laboratories stated that it "basically" supported the administration bills and argued that because fat people had higher mortality rates than others, amphetamines were important to the public welfare, ignoring the charge that amphetamines were not useful in controlling weight. Abbott then argued that because their products were in a sustained-release tablet, they were "of little interest to abusers," suggesting that "meth" tablets per se cannot be abused and ignoring the fact that they can be easily diluted.

Eli Lilly & Co. also endorsed "many of the concepts" in

the president's proposals. They as well had "participated in a number of conferences sponsored by the (BNDD) and...joined in both formal and informal discussions with the Bureau personnel regarding" the bill. Hoffman-LaRoche had surely watched, with alarm, the Senate's inclusion of Librium and Valium in Schedule III. They were now willing to accept all the controls applying to Schedule III drugs, including the requirements of record-keeping, inventory, prescription limits and registration as long as their "minor tranquilizers" were not grouped with amphetamines. Perhaps, the company suggested, a separate schedule between III and IV was the answer. The crucial point was that they did not want the negative association with speed and they quoted a physician to clarify this: "If in the minds of my patients a drug which I prescribe for them has been listed or branded by the government in the same category as 'goofballs' and 'pep pills' it would interfere with my ability to prescribe...and could create a mental obstacle to their...taking the drug at all."

When the bill was reported out of committee to the House, the amphetamine family was in Schedule III, and Hoffman-LaRoche's "minor tranquilizers" remained free from control.

Debate in the House—Round I

On September 23, 1970, the House moved into Committee of the Whole for opening speeches on the administration bill now known as HR 18583. The following day, the anti-amphetamine forces led by Congressman Pepper carried their arguments onto the floor of the House by way of an amendment transfering the amphetamine family from Schedule III into Schedule II. If successful, amphetamines would be subject to stricter import and export controls, higher penalties for illegal sale and possession and the possibility that the attorney general could impose quotas on production and distribution. (In Schedule III, amphetamines were exempt from quotas entirely.) Also, if placed in Schedule II, the prescriptions could be filled only once. Pepper was convinced from previous experience that until quotas were established by law the drug industry would not voluntarily restrict production.

Now the lines were clearly drawn. The House hearings had provided considerable testimony to the effect that massive amphetamine production coupled with illegal diversion posed a major threat to the public health. No congressman would argue that this was not the case. The House would instead divide between those who faithfully served the administration and the drug industry and those who argued that Congress must act or no action could be expected. The industry representatives dodged the merits of the opposition's arguments, contending that a floor amendment was inappropriate for such "far reaching" decisions.

"Legislating on the floor...concerning very technical and scientific matters," said subcommittee member Tim Lee Carter of Kentucky, "can cause a great deal of trouble. It can open a Pandora's Box" and the amendment which affected 6,100 drugs "would be disastrous to many companies throughout the land."

Paul G. Rogers of Florida (another subcommittee member) stated that the bill's provisions were based on expert scientific and law enforcement advice, and that the "whole process of manufacture and distribution had been tightened up." Robert McClory of Illinois, though not a member of the subcommittee, revealed the source of his opposition to the amendment:

Frankly...there are large pharmaceutical manufacturing interests centered in my congressional district.... I am proud to say that the well-known firms of Abbott Laboratories and Baxter Laboratories have large plants in my (district). It is my expectation that C.D. Searl & Co. may soon establish a large part of its organization (there). Last Saturday, the American Hospital Supply Co. dedicated its new building complex in Lake County... where its principal research and related operations will be conducted.

Control of drug abuse, continued McClory, should not be accomplished at the cost of imposing "undue burdens or (by taking) punitive or economically unfair steps adversely affecting the highly successful and extremely valuable pharmaceutical industries which contribute so much to the health and welfare of mankind."

Not everyone was as honest as McClory. A parent committee member, William L. Springer of Illinois, thought the dispute was basically between Pepper's special committee on crime and the subcommittee on health and medicine chaired by John Jarman of Oklahoma. Thus phrased, the latter was simply more credible than the former. "There is no problem here of economics having to do with any drug industry."

But economics had everything to do with the issue according to Representative Jerome R. Waldie of California: "(T)he only opposition to this amendment that has come across my desk has come from the manufacturers of amphetamines." He reasoned that since the House was always ready to combat crime in the streets, a "crime that involved a corporation and its profits" logically merits equal attention. Waldie concluded that the administration's decision "to favor the profits (of the industry) over the children is a cruel decision, the consequences of which will be suffered by thousands of our young people." Pepper and his supporters had compiled and introduced considerable evidence on scientific and medical opinions on the use and abuse of amphetamines. It was now fully apparent that the evidence would be ignored because of purely economic and political considerations. In the closing minutes of debate, Congressman Robert Giaimo of Connecticut, who sat on neither committee, recognized the real issue: "Why should we allow the legitimate drug manufacturers to indirectly supply the (sic) organized crime and pushers by producing more drugs than are necessary? When profits are made while people suffer, what difference does it make where the profits go?"

Pepper's amendment was then defeated by a voice vote. The bill passed by a vote of 341 to 6. The amphetamine industry had won in the House. In two days of debate, Librium and Valium went unmentioned and remained uncontrolled.

Debate in the Senate—Round II

Two weeks after the House passed HR 18583, the Senate began consideration of the House bill. (The Senate bill, passed eight months before, continued to languish in a House committee.) On October 7, 1970, Senator Thomas Eagleton of Missouri moved to amend HR 18583 to place amphetamines in Schedule II. Although he reiterated the arguments used by Pepper in the House, Eagleton stated that his interest in the amendment was not solely motivated by the abuse by speed freaks. If the amendment carried, it would "also cut back on abuse by the weight-conscious housewife, the weary long-haul truck driver and the young student trying to study all night for his exams."

The industry strategy from the beginning was to center congressional outrage on the small minority of persons who injected large doses of diluted amphetamines into their veins. By encouraging this emphasis, the drug companies had to face questioning about illicit diversion to the "speed community," but they were able to successfully avoid any rigorous scrutiny of the much larger problem of lawful abuse. The effort had its success. Senator Thomas J. McIntyre of New Hampshire, while noting the general abuse of the drugs, stated that the real abuse resulted from large doses either being swallowed, snorted or injected.

Senator Roman Hruska of Nebraska was not suprisingly the administration and industry spokesman. He echoed the arguments that had been used successfully in the House: The amendment seeks to transfer between 4,000 and 6,000 products of the amphetamine family; "some of them are very dangerous" but the bill provides a mechanism for administrative reclassification; administration and "HEW experts" support the present classification and oppose the amendment; and, finally, the Senate should defer to the executive where a complete study is promised.

It would take three to five years to move a drug into Schedule II by administrative action, responded Eagleton. Meanwhile amphetamines would continue to be "sold with reckless abandon to the public detriment." Rather than placing the burden on the government, Eagleton argued that amphetamines should be classed in Schedule II and those who "are making money out of the misery of many individuals" should carry the burden to downgrade the classification.

Following Eagleton's statement, an unexpected endorsement came from the man who had steered two drug control bills through the Senate in five years. Senator Dodd stated that Eagleton had made "a good case for the amendment." Senator John Pastore was sufficiently astonished to ask Dodd pointedly whether he favored the amendment. Dodd unequivocally affirmed his support. Dodd's endorsement was clearly a turning point in the Senate debate. Hruska's plea that the Senate should defer to the "superior knowledge" of the attorney general, HEW and BNDD was met with Dodd's response that, if amphetamines were found not to be harmful, the attorney general could easily move them back into Schedule III. In Schedule II, Dodd continued, "only the big powerful manufacturers of these pills may find a reduction in their profits. The people will not be harmed." With that, the debate was over and the amendment carried by a vote of 40 in favor, 16 against and 44 not voting.

Dodd may have been roused by the House's failure, without debate, to subject Librium and Valium to controls which he had supported from the beginning. Prior to Eagleton's amendment, Dodd had moved to place these depressants in Schedule IV. In that dispute, Dodd knew that economics was the source of the opposition: "It is clearly evident. . . that (the industry) objections to the inclusion of Librium and Valium are not so much based on sound medical practice as they are on the slippery surface of unethical profits." Hoffman-LaRoche annually reaped 40 million dollars in profits—"a tidy sum which (they have) done a great deal to protect." Senator Dodd went on to say that Hoffman-LaRoche reportedly paid a Washington law firm three times the annual budget of the Senate subcommittee staff to assure that their drugs would remain uncontrolled. "No wonder," exclaimed Dodd, "that the Senate first, and then the House, was overrun by Hoffman-LaRoche lobbyists," despite convincing evidence that they were connected with suicides and attempted suicides and were diverted in large amounts into illicit channels.

By voice vote Hoffman-LaRoche's "minor tranquilizers" were brought within the control provisions of Schedule IV. Even Senator Hruska stated that he did not oppose this amendment, and that it was "very appropriate" that it be adopted so that a "discussion of it and decision upon it (be) made in the conference."

The fate of the minor tranquilizers and the amphetamine family would now be decided by the conferees of the two houses.

In Conference

The conferees from the Senate were fairly equally divided on the issue of amphetamine classification. Of the eleven Senate managers, at least six were in favor of the transfer to Schedule II. The remaining five supported the administration position. Although Eagleton was not appointed, Dodd and Harold Hughes would represent his position. Hruska and Strom Thurmond, both of whom had spoken against the amendment, would act as administration spokesmen.

On October 8, 1970, before the House appointed its conferees, Pepper rose to remind his colleagues that the Senate had reclassified amphetamines. Although he stated that he favored an instruction to the conferees to support the amendment, he inexplicably declined to so move. Instead, Pepper asked the conferees "to view this matter as sympathetically as they think the facts and the evidence they have before them will permit." Congressman Rogers, an outspoken opponent of the Pepper amendment, promised "sympathetic understanding" for the position of the minority.

Indeed, the minority would have to be content with that and little else. All seven House managers were members of the parent committee, and four were members of the originating subcommittee. Of the seven, only one would match support with "sympathetic understanding." The other six were not only against Schedule II classification, but they had led the opposition to it in floor debate: Jarman, Rogers, Carter, Staggers and Nelsen. Congressman Springer, who had declared in debate that economics had nothing to do with this issue, completed the House representation. Not a single member of Pepper's Select Committee on Crime was appointed as a conferee. On the question of reclassification, the pharmaceutical industry would be well represented.

Hoffman-LaRoche, as well, was undoubtedly comforted by the presence of the four House subcommittee conferees: The subcommittee had never made any attempt to include Valium and Librium in the bill. On that question, it is fair to say that the Senate managers were divided. The administration continued to support no controls for these depressants.

At dispute were six substantive Senate amendments to the House bill: Three concerned amphetamines, Librium and Valium; one required an annual report to Congress on advisory councils; the fifth lessened the penalty for persons who gratuitously distributed a small amount of marijuana; and the sixth, introduced by Senator Hughes, altered the thrust of the bill and placed greater emphasis on drug education, research, rehabilitation and training. To support these new programs, the Senate had appropriated $26 million more than the House.

The House, officially, opposed all of the Senate amendments.

From the final compromises, it is apparent that the Senate liberals expended much of their energy on behalf of the Hughes amendment. Although the Senate's proposed educational effort was largely gutted in favor of the original House version, an additional 25 million dollars was appropriated. The bill would also now require the inclusion in state public health plans of "comprehensive programs" to combat drug abuse and the scope of grants for addicts and drug-dependent persons was increased. The House then accepted the amendments on annual reports and the possession charge for gratuitous marijuana distributors.

The administration and industry representative gave but an inch on the amphetamine amendment: Only the liquid injectible methamphetamines, speed, would be transferred to Schedule II. All the pills would remain in Schedule III. In the end, amphetamine abuse was restricted to the mainlining speed freak. The conference report reiterated the notion that further administrative action on amphetamines by the attorney general would be initiated. Finally, Librium and Valium would not be included in the bill. The report noted that "final administrative action" (begun in 1966) was expected "in a matter of weeks." Congress was contented to await the outcome of those proceedings.

Adoption of the Conference Report

Pepper and his supporters were on their feet when the agreement on amphetamines was reported to the House on October 14, 1970. Conferee Springer, faithful to the industry's tactical line, declared that the compromise is a good one because it "singles out the worst of these substances, which are the liquid, injectible methamphetamines and puts them in Schedule II." If amphetamine injection warranted such attention, why, asked Congressman Charles Wiggins, were the easily diluted amphetamine and methamphetamine pills left in Schedule III? Springer responded that there had been "much discussion," yes and "some argument" over that issue, but the conferees felt it was best to leave the rest of the amphetamine family to administrative action.

Few could have been fooled by the conference agreement. The managers claimed to have taken the most dangerous and abused member of the family and subjected it to more rigorous controls. In fact, as the minority pointed out, the compromise affected the least abused amphetamine: Lawfully manufactured "liquid meth" was sold strictly to hospitals, not in the streets, and there was no evidence of any illicit diversion. More importantly, from the perspective of the drug manufacturers, only five of the 6,000 member amphetamine family fell into this category. Indeed, liquid meth was but an insignificant part of the total methamphetamine, not to mention amphetamine, production. Pepper characterized the new provision as "virtually meaningless." It was an easy pill for the industry to swallow. The Senate accepted the report on the same day as the House.

Only Eagleton, the sponsor of the successful Senate reclassification amendment, would address the amphetamine issue. To him, the new amendment "accomplish(ed) next to nothing." The reason for the timid, limpid compromise was also obvious to Eagleton: "When the chips were down, the power of the drug companies was simply more compelling" than any appeal to the public welfare.

A week before, when Dodd had successfully classified Librium and Valium in the bill, he had remarked (in reference to the House's inaction): "Hoffman-LaRoche, at least for the moment, have reason to celebrate a singular triumph, the triumph of money over conscience. It is a triumph. . . which I hope will be shortlived."

The Bill Becomes Law

Richard Nixon appropriately chose the Bureau of Narcotics and Dangerous Drugs offices for the signing of the bill on November 2, 1970. Flanked by Mitchell and Ingersoll, the president had before him substantially the same measure that had been introduced 15 months earlier. Nixon declared that America faced a major crisis of drug abuse, reaching even into the junior high schools, which constituted a "major cause of street crime." To combat this alarming rise, the president now had 300 new agents. Also, the federal government's jurisdiction was expanded: "The jurisdiction of the attorney general will go far beyond, for example, heroin. It will cover the new types of drugs, the barbiturates and amphetamines that have become so common *and are even more dangerous because of their use"* (author emphasis).

The president recognized amphetamines were "even more dangerous" than heroin, although he carefully attached the qualifier that this was a result "of their use." The implication is clear: The president viewed only the large dosage user of amphetamines as an abuser. The fact that his full statement refers only to abuse by "young people" (and not physicians, truck drivers, housewives or businessmen) affirms the implication. The president's remarks contained no mention of the pharmaceutical industry, nor did they refer to any future review of amphetamine classification. After a final reference to the destruction that drug abuse was causing, the president signed the bill into law.

WALTER DEAN BURNHAM

Crisis of American Political Legitimacy

The American political system was organized and achieved its concrete behavioral reality under social, economic and international conditions which have ceased to exist in our time. The whole system is based upon several primordial elements, elements which may well be sine qua non for its survival in recognizable form. The first of these was a belief, revolutionary in its time and for many decades thereafter, in the inherent equality and dignity of the individual. Associated with this was a political machinery developed by the founders which explicitly denied that sovereign power existed anywhere within it in domestic affairs, while concentrating such sovereignty in the president so far as the country's relations with foreign powers were concerned. This denial of internal sovereignty is of course enshrined in two key elements of the Constitution: the separation of powers at the center and the centrifugal force of federalism.

Thirdly, the whole enterprise was based upon the development and maintenance of a very broad consensus within society on fundamentals involving the place of organized religion in the political system and the place of private initiative and the private sector generally in the political economy. Without such a consensus the

cumbersome machinery would have collapsed; but that is another way of saying that sovereign power in the state develops historically in response to fundamental conflicts among sharply discrete social groups over control of society through politics. It represents the victory of one coalition of such groups over another and the positive use of state power to consolidate the control of the new group over the social system—for example, the bourgeoisie over pre-modern feudal and clerical elements.

In the American case, we find one spectacular example of this in the Civil War. And it is precisely here for a short season that we find the collapse of the Constitution and the development of sovereign power to an astonishing degree. The episode was temporary, though leaving some permanent residues, but it is also exceptionally instructive. Otherwise, however, the social consensus survived, changing in emphasis and shape as the society was transformed by industrialization. This consensus was essentially the ideology of liberal capitalism, coupled after the 1870s by an increasingly explicit racism which justified the reduction of the southern black to a limbo halfway between the slavery of old and genuine citizenship.

When we find ourselves in a political crisis, it is extraordinary to see how often older theorists of American politics—particularly those steeped in a juristic-institutional tradition—can illuminate the problem. An individualist, liberal-capitalist theory and practice of politics assumes by definition that the state, and above that the public, has no collective business to transact apart from the most marginal welfare and police-keeping functions. In turn this presupposes a socioeconomic system which is not dominated by collectivist concentrations of power. It also presupposes, far more than we have realized until recently, that American involvement with the outside world is episodic rather than permanent: a lack of external empire and the power structures which go with imperial world involvement.

In 1941 the late E.S. Corwin made precisely this point and coupled it with a warning for the future of American politics—and of constitutional liberty in this country, as that term had hitherto been understood. He identified two changes in the contexts of American politics which had arisen since 1929 and whose implications profoundly disturbed him. The first, of course, was the emergence of a permanent federal presence in the private sector necessitated by the collapse of free-market capitalism in the Great Depression. The second was the permanent mobilization of the United States in world politics—in a context of acute military threat.

Naturally, Corwin approached these issues from a juristic perspective which many today would describe as conservative if not reactionary. The same is even more true of the warnings which Herbert Hoover continually issued in the 1930s about the dangers of the kind of corporatist syndicalism which the New Deal was bringing into being. Yet in our own day such warnings may well be taken more and more seriously. While we cannot review all of these issues, we can give some indication of their relevance to the current crisis of political legitimacy which grips the United States.

We have argued that the American political system was set up according to a certain conception of liberty which denied the normal existence of sovereign governmental power in domestic affairs. This implied the lack of need for permanent public regulation of or intervention into the private sector. Yet during industrialization this sector had elaborated one of the great collectivist organizations of all time—the business corporation; and the corporation became and remains the dominant form of social organization in the United States. It was not long after the turn of this century that the leaders of corporate capitalism discovered the uses of public authority to achieve some rationalization of their competitive activities and to avoid some of the more ruinous implications of truly free competition.

But the Great Depression which began in 1929 revealed that such marginal public-sector efforts were not enough even to protect the basic interests of entre-

"The flaw in the pluralist heaven is that the heavenly choir sings with a markedly upper-class accent." (Republican National Convention, August 1972)

"In a larger, perhaps almost mystical sense, the struggle is for the American soul." (Republican National Convention, August 1972)

preneurs and management, not to mention those of the rest of society. So permanent public-sector involvement came with the New Deal but it came without any basic change in the political system. That system remained, as before, the kind of essentially non-sovereign collection of middle-class economic and political feudalities which it had been since the end of Reconstruction.

The interaction between this archaic political system and an overwhelming demand, which it could not resist without courting social and political revolution, produced the hybrid phenomenon known as "interest-group liberalism." This in turn promptly received an ideological support base from political scientists and others who celebrated the virtures of pluralism and veto groups in the political process and of incremental change in policy outputs. Yet there were two significant problems in this rewriting of Locke, this recasting of atomistic individualism from the level of the individual to the level of the group. The first was that such a huge proportion of the American people were not actually included in the new groupist system. They belonged to no groups with political leverage, and—if not subject to outright disfranchisement and political persecution, as were the southern blacks—were excluded from the most elemental mode of participation, that is, voting.

Throughout the New Deal and down to the present time, these excluded people formed not less than two-fifths of the total adult population—concentrated, of course, at the bottom of the socioeconomic system. As the late E.E. Schattschneider pithily observed, "The flaw in the pluralist heaven is that the heavenly choir sings with a markedly upper-class accent." It is virtually impossible to overstate the importance of this steep class bias in our politics for the workings of interest-group liberalism since the New Deal.

The second major problem in interest-group liberalism was accurately pinpointed by Herbert Hoover, of all people. Such liberalism amounts to a kind of unresponsive syndicalism which can work oppression on individual human beings in several different ways. Such syndicalism rests upon the creation of very large-scale or "peak" organizations and ultimately upon power transactions between the top leadership of these organizations and the top leadership of Congress, executive agencies and independent regulatory commissions. Needless to say, the interests of the ordinary individual can and very often do get lost in this process at all levels—in the private-sector organizations themselves, in the interface transactions between peak groups and government, in the shaping of public policy and in the ordinary transactions between individual citizens and bureaucracies. This, of course, applies to individuals who are fortunate enough to be covered by the umbrellas provided by the corporation, the labor union or other group active in the pressure system. How much more forcefully does it apply to the very large fraction of the population which is outside these groups.

"Power speaks to power;" if there is any part of the "old politics" which has generated more passionate opposition among Americans than any other, it is this. Such opposition is crystallized implicitly or explicitly around the belief that there is a common public interest which trancends group negotiations; that this interest is somehow grossly violated by the power game played by peak associations and top-level government people and that legislation is or of right ought to be the product of more than the temporary balance of power among these organized groups.

Pluralists either ignore or categorically deny the existence of such a public interest at home, though they find it easy enough to discover an American national interest abroad. But this rejection of the notion of a public interest reveals the true extent to which pluralism is bourgeois ideology—a logic of justification for an established order of things. The trouble with this line of argument is that it enshrines naked power relationships among group and political elites while arguing that these processes are beneficial because of social harmony. It is laissez-faire ideology writ large. But it is vulnerable when and to the extent that individuals come to disbelieve in this harmony; and in fact, the long-term workings of this syndicalism destroy, almost dialectically, public belief in the justness of political solutions and the legitimacy of government itself. At the "end of liberalism," as Theodore Lowi has precisely argued, is a felt lack of justice, of simple human equity in the political system.

It is no wonder that academic pluralism has been so hostile to the notion of a public interest. The existence of a public interest presupposes that there is collective business to transact at home. It necessarily presupposes a fundamental opposition to the theory and practice of corporate syndicalism. To the extent that such collective business is perceived to exist, a first and very long step has been taken toward the creation of a government which is responsible not merely to the leadership of private power concentrations but to the people of the United States. The struggle to create such a government is a basic ingredient in today's political turmoil. It will go on for the foreseeable future. Only such a government is likely in the long run to generate the moral authority necessary to function effectively without resort to armed force.

Corwin was also apprehensive about the political implications of permanent mobilization of the United States in international politics. In his farewell address in 1961, President Eisenhower voiced a very similar concern when he warned against the acquisition of influence, sought or unsought, by the military-industrial complex. It is a pity that all of his successors have been so patently insensitive to this warning.

Crisis of American Political Legitimacy

The reason for this worry is inherent in the American constitutional structure. It cannot be said often enough that the American political system is extremely archaic by comparative standards and that in foreign and military affairs it presupposes that the president will act very much like a seventeenth-century patriot king. Not only does sweepingly sovereign power exist so far as foreign and military affairs are concerned; in practice the power has been concentrated even beyond the Constitution's very broad grant in a very narrow executive elite.

Since World War II a well-known combination of factors—contextual (military threat from the Communist world), ideological (reflexive anti-communism) and economic (the possibility of large Keynesian public-sector expenditures without competition with private enterprise)—have contributed to the development of a colossal military and defense-related organizational structure. This structure ramifies throughout the political system. Four-fifths of all congressional districts now have defense installations or plants which are of more or less significance to the local economy. Perhaps one way to capture graphically the change which has occurred since Corwin wrote is to present the per capita expenditures on defense, space and military-assis-

tance programs. In current dollars, these amounted to $4.19 per capita in 1935, $89.18 in 1950, $245.97 in 1960 and $387.75 in 1970. Even taking inflation into account, the burden of empire for the average American has grown enormously in the past generation.

The political implications of this immense proliferation in military activity and expenditure have been fundamental. In the first place, a vast new syndicalist complex has come into existence since the New Deal era. It is based squarely upon the top management of the leading industrial corporations, the political foreign-policy establishment around the president and in leading universities, the top Pentagon elite and the armed services and appropriations committees of Congress. It has been actively supported by another major element in the New Deal syndicalist coalition, the top leadership of organized labor—not only on grounds of international anti-communist ideology, but above all because where defense is, there are jobs also. Any effort to organize a domestic political movement calling for reallocation of our scarce resources and budget priorities must recognize the pervasiveness of this complex and the multitude of very large material and ideological interests which are permanently mobilized around it.

Granted the realities of international power configurations since World War II, it would be unrealistic to argue that defense and related burdens on American resources can be done away with or that they are not needed. But even if we cannot dismantle the military-industrial-academic complex if we would, the future of American domestic politics depends in a very real sense upon whether this immense set of power concentrations can be tamed and made politically accountable. This complex represents at its highest point of development the syndicalist interest-group liberalism which has dominated American politics. Perhaps the supreme example of the coercions which play upon the little man who is subject to power he cannot begin to control is the drafting of young men to fight in a war which was initiated entirely by the president and his narrow elite of military, civilian and academic advisers.

It is not possible to devote much time here to the Vietnam War. It has vastly accelerated the domestic political crisis in the United States and may even come to be viewed in retrospect as the most durably influential such experience since the Civil War itself. The decision to make war in Vietnam captures the essence of Corwin's worries about the operation of this political system under conditions of permanent imperial involvement in the outside world. It was an executive decision. It was made by a president who had campaigned a few months earlier on a pledge not to do so. The president so acted with the advice and consent not of the Senate but of a rarified elite of advisers who were accountable to no one but themselves and the chief executive. But it was also a decision which ordinary people had to pay for—in the case of 50,000 young men, with their lives. Naturally, the latter point, not less than the barbarously inhumane methods by which this war was and is being carried on, contributed immensely to the volcanic alienation of college youth and others in the late 1960s. But these considerations, however important, should not deflect our view from the core of the issue which the war has raised. This issue, baldly put, involves the ascendancy of a narrow executive-military elite in our politics and the absence of any organized institutional means for restraining the exercise of that power.

Lurking just beneath the once calm surface of American politics is a fundamental constitutional crisis, the gravest indeed since the Civil War a century ago. On the domestic scene the syndicalist politics of groups has produced in dialectical contradiction waves of antagonistic mobilizations and countermobilizations. The final product of the old politics of interest-group liberalism is the wavelike spread of acute relative deprivation feelings among more and more people. This is so not only because such a system "lacks justice" in Lowi's abstract sense, but because concretely it tends to operate only in response to organized pressures and protests. Action and reaction lead to ever wider senses of frustration and alienation; power groups proliferate at all levels; and the system jams in its practical operation while its very legitimacy suffers cumulative erosion. On the international front we find ourselves half-republic, half-empire; and one may doubt that this house divided can indefinitely survive divided any more successfully than did the house of which Lincoln spoke a century ago.

A number of revolutions have been unfolding during the past generation and pushing us toward and beyond the present political crisis. We have discussed the two most basic—the post-1929 revolution in political economy and the imperium revolution. But there have been others.

1) The demographic revolution. This involves the social and political effects of an enormous exchange of population since 1945: the urbanization of American blacks (and other groups such as Puerto Ricans and Chicanos) and the massive middle-class white flight from central cities to suburbs.

2) The civil-rights revolution and the political mobilization of the black and the poor, a revolution which, by destablilizing race relations and destroying the repressive compromise of 1877, has also effectively destroyed the old New Deal political coalition.

3) The combined education and media revolutions, themselves the product of increased economic affluence in American society. The education revolution has in a sense created the conditions, at least, for the emergence of a college-based class for itself among young people with common concerns and political values. But the media revolution may prove at least as important. In a very curious way, it has permitted people who are physically separated but have common interests and problems to find one another. Moreover, it has drastically reduced the costs of political information and—even more subversively, from an official point of view—has permitted ordinary people to judge for themselves the falsity of official pronouncements about such basic events as the Vietnam War. The two revolutions together are producing a very large group of Americans who are well educated, who are politically committed and who are independent actors in the political arena.

4) Closely associated with both preceding revolutions—and the industrial affluence which underlies both—is a very far-reaching cultural revolution. One need not accept all of Charles Reich's pieties or naivetes in *The Greening of America* to realize that, among growing numbers of people—young and not so young—the traditional bonds and moral imperatives of such elemental social groupings as organized religion and the family, not to mention those of the old puritan work ethic, are rapidly dissolving. A worldwide crisis of authority is going on: as J. H. Plumb has pointed out, basic social institutions which in one form or another go back to the Neolithic era have suddenly become visibly fragile if not evanescent.

One primary feature of this cultural revolution is that—with all its bizarre and even repellent manifestations—an active search is going on for a new meaning in the lives of individuals. When old social myths and mazeways collapse, when they lose their coercive moral authority, predictably strange things happen to people in society. Group struggles and personal anxieties increase drastically. Some people move into politics with the kind of "Puritan saint" commitment of which Michael Walzer has written. Cults flourish, along with chiliastic and millenarian movements; "the end of the world" in one form or another seems remarkably close at hand to many. Ultimately, the quest is for revitalization: for some new set of social myths and routines which, because people come to believe in them, have the power to reintegrate this social chaos in some new and acceptable order.

Unhappily such conditions are not the stuff of which political pluralism or incremental bargaining in the policy process are made. They appear in fact to be essential ingredients of every truly revolutionary situation; and that is because, consciously or not, increasing numbers of people are searching for a reconstruction of themselves through a reconstruction of the social order itself. What they seek they will find, though not necessarily in the form that any individual might either foresee or desire a priori. At the same time, what makes revolutions what they are is the fact that this drive for revitalization, for political and social reconstruction, always encounters increasingly desperate resistance not only from established elites but from very broad masses of the population. Revolutions are virtually never matters of unanimous consent: the very revitalization which becomes psychically necessary to the person who supports the revolution becomes psychically intolerable to the person who cannot imagine his survival without his traditional beliefs.

If all the foregoing has some relationship to today's reality, several propositions can be made about the near future of American politics:

The overall thrust of our revolutions, especially the last, is to rediscover the worth and dignity of the individual, be his social estate never so low. It is also to attack the fundamental legitimacy of political decisions based upon syndicalist bargains among elites and of the political processes by which such decisions are made.

The political thrust of these revolutions is aimed squarely against the coercive power of Big Organization, whether nominally public or nominally private. One very difficult question is the extent to which such attacks can proceed before they compromise or destroy the capacity of these organizations to perform their functions. In any case, the political organization of prisoners in jails, the emergence of storefront lawyers and many other signs of the times have come into being to give the little man the elemental leverage on his life that interest-group liberalism has denied him.

To the extent that the contemporary crisis in American politics is founded in a far-reaching if uneven collapse in traditionally held values, it can be resolved only through revitalizations of some sort. Whatever this revitalization turns out to be at the end, one thing is certain: it will not be liberal, for Lowi is quite right in claiming that liberalism has really come to an end.

Because of this, it seems increasingly certain that American political processes and structures will undergo profound transformation before the end of this century. It is possible that this change, when it occurs, will be revolutionary (or counter-revolutionary); it will in any case be sweeping in practical operation, even though the forms of the Constitution itself may not change very much. In view of the tremendous durability of this archaic political system, such a prediction seems rash, to say the least. But it is based upon certain basic propositions: first, that the system cannot operate without consensus on social fundamentals; second, that such consensus is now very rapidly disappearing; and third, that political involvement with both the value and operational problems of American society will of necessity create permanent sovereign political power resources in its national government. To the extent that the existing operation of American politics is based upon the denial of such sovereign power, it can hardly survive such a transition in recognizable form. There is no reason to suppose with Charles Reich

that the cultural revolution must succeed or that revitalization centered around its rediscovery of the individual's human, social and political needs must prevail. Indeed, it is very unlikely to prevail without political organizations which collectively concentrate the power of individuals and which will therefore articulate new needs in an organizationally familiar way. Every revolution has its counter-revolution, and counter-revolutions sometimes succeed.

The genius of American politics, as its past history abundantly demonstrates, has lain in the capacity of the system as a whole to undergo renewal and revitalization through critical realignments in the electorate and in the policy structure. Thus far the revolutionary thrust of the present-day changes we have discussed has been contained remarkably well through the existing instrumentalities of politics. But a trade-off is required sooner or later: at some point the old must yield at least partially to the new or resort to force, to breaking the system in the name of its preservation, and the preservation of the ascendancy of the old. If one thinks as a whole about all of the revolutions we have discussed, the most striking thing about them is that they point in increasingly polar-opposite directions. The older revolutions in political economy and world politics taken together point to a state with an explicitly clearly defined ruling class based upon an oligarchy of sydicalist elites and one whose leaders deal with revolutions abroad and discontent at home in an increasingly militarized, technocratic way.

The newer revolutions in media, education and culture have served to mobilize groups whose former passivity and non-participation have been essential preconditions for the smooth operation of the syndicalist welfare-warfare state. The Vietnam War somehow crystallizes for the newer America what has gone wrong with our national life under its bipartisan ruling class. It spells out for this newer America how far the syndicalist leadership of the old order has been prepared to drift away from the humane premises of the Republic in their pursuit of ideology, interest and, it may be, Empire. It is the dialectical polarization which our revolutions have generated, taken together in the same period of time, which has fueled the present crisis and which has eroded the legitimacy of the existing political order.

Now few sensible people seriously think that all the ills or dysfunctions of a social order undergoing such massive doses of change can be resolved by politics. But few would doubt either that politics is somehow integrally related to redefining the terms of conflict and compromise among major social forces. It seems to me that we have about reached the point in our national life where a clear breakthrough of the newer forces in American politics cannot be longer deferred without catastrophic intermediate-run consequences for the

The Burden of Responsibility: Politics and the Power Structure

prospects of political freedom in the United States. Realignments have been the price which American politics pays for timely change which does not foreclose future options and which does not short-circuit the system into authoritarianism. A realignment is obviously due if not overdue: and this is clearly what the political struggles of 1968 and 1972 have been all about. If the old America, working through its entrenched syndicalist groups, can effectively choke off this peaceful revolutionary upsurge, I would regard the future of the Republic as very dim indeed.

Political forces such as those which are now on the move represent objective conflicts in society; these conflicts are long-term; and very broadly, they can be settled only by peaceful if rapid change, by violent revolution or by authoritarian reaction with clearly fascist overtones. The first alternative presupposes that the rot of syndicalism at home and of imperialism abroad has not gone so far that democratic revitalization has become excluded as a practical option. It presupposes that we have not yet crossed the point of no return on the march to the construction of the *Imperium Americanum*. This may seem to some an heroic assumption, but all the returns are not quite in yet. The second alternative is virtually certain to fail as such: but the danger is very real that newer America may be driven by desperation to violent collisions with the established political order if they cannot gain access to it peacefully. Such collisions would serve, in all probability; to speed up the processes involved in the third solution, one which carries out the implications of syndicalism and militarized

foreign policy to their logical extreme. To the extent that manifest destiny dominates the political-economy and foreign-policy revolutions of our time—as an orthodox Marxist, for example, might well argue—it must candidly be said that this third option would clearly be the most likely one.

But this is to foreclose a future which has not yet occurred, in the name of a social and political determinism which cannot rest upon an adequate scientific basis. The precise point is that struggle is going on. This struggle is over peaceful penetration of democratic elements into an elite-controlled political system. But in a larger, perhaps almost mystical sense, the struggle is for the American soul. On its outcome, in my view, literally hangs the future of human freedom in United States.

FURTHER READING

Hopes and Fears of the American People by Albert H. Cantril and Charles W. Roll, Jr. (New York: Universe Books, 1971).

Why Men Rebel by Ted Robert Gurr (Princeton, N.J.: Princeton University Press, 1970).

The End of Liberalism by Theodore J. Lowi (New York: Norton, 1969).

Pentagon Capitalism by Seymour Melman (New York: McGraw-Hill, 1970).

Crisis in American Institutions by J. Skolnick and E. Currie (Boston: Little, Brown, 1970).

HERBERT MARCUSE

When Law and Morality Stand in the Way

The treatment of the Watergate scandal has concealed more than it has revealed. With rare exceptions, mainly in the "underground press," the significance of the events has been hidden or minimized by publicizing it as an extraordinary case of corruption in the highest circles of the government — extraordinary because of its bungling brutality, its violation of elementary constitutional rights. However, this sort of treatment isolates the scandal from the context which makes the extraordinary an ordinary event, not an aberration but the extreme political form of the normal state of affairs.

This context is the present state of American capitalism. It seems that it cannot function, cannot grow any more without the use of illegal, illegitimate means, without the practice of violence in the various branches of the material and intellectual culture. The rule of law, and the political morality stipulated by it, were appropriate to the period of liberal capitalism: the age of free competition and free enterprise. On the open market, certain legal safeguards, generally observed, sufficed to protect private enterprise from undesirable interference; their observance did not unduly hamper good business, nor was free competition under the rule of law altogether detrimental to progress: the competing powers developed the productive forces and provided the goods and services to satisfy the basic needs of an increasing part of the population.

But the picture begins to change with the period of the world wars. Competition generates oligopolies and monopolies; gradual saturation of the capital market at home leads to an aggressive imperialist policy, and the rapid rise of giant corporate interests transforms even independent enterprises into direct or indirect dependencies. At the same time, the growing power of organized labor threatens the corporate dominion, and the sharpening conflicts now demand the intervention of the state which the liberal phase restricted to a minimum: politics becomes part of business, and vice versa.

The rule of law, the morals of legitimacy, based on the relative equality of competitors and on their general and common interests, becomes, under the changed conditions, an obstacle to business and power, on the one hand, and an inadequate safeguard for the weak on the other. Monopolistic competition and imperialistic expansion become the vehicles of growth on the national as well as international levels; the economy functions through a series of conspiratorial agreements, and its political counterpart operates through latent or manifest intervention in foreign countries—surreptitious or overt entry.

These tendencies change the composition, function and behavior of the ruling class. To the degree to which it no longer develops but rather distorts and destroys the productive forces, it turns into a vast network (or chain) of rackets, cliques and gangs, powerful enough to bend the law or to break it where existing legislation is not already made or interpreted in their favor. In terms of liberal economics, today's conglomerates and multinational corporations would, by their very structure, exercise conspiratorial and illegitimate power. The difference between the Mafia and legitimate business becomes blurred. The purveyors of violence, as entertainment or as part of the job to be done, find sympathetic response among the underlying population whose character they have shaped.

There is no reason why the political sphere should remain immune from these developments. A wave of political assassinations and assassination attempts has swept the country. The previously progressive institutions of the Republic have been made into barriers against social change, stabilizers of the status quo. The electoral process has long since been dominated by the power of big money, the separation of powers turned into a presidential dictatorship. The distinction between the office and the officeholder, one of the most liberating achievements of Western civilization, has collapsed. Now, not the office of the President, the President himself is taboo; he defines and implements national securi-

American capitalism...cannot grow any more without the use of illegal, illegitimate means, without the practice of violence in the various branches of the material and intellectual culture.

ty. Above right and wrong, his definition and implementation override dissent. He is also above logic; his statements are neither true nor false, they are "operative" or "inoperative."

"Operative" means having force, being in effect; it is neutral to moral values and legal norms. Watergate would have been operative if it had worked; since it has been bungled, it has become inoperative. And this means that it disrupts the cohesion of the political system. As (and only as) a bungled undertaking, it becomes dangerous, compromising: it comes under the jurisdiction of moral and legal norms; it becomes a series of crimes, offenses. They must be publicized, televised, punished, because at stake are not only the prestige and the efficiency of the government but also of the society as a whole—of its "normal" behavior.

But what remains "operative" and unscathed by revelations and exposures of abuse is the notion of national security. The White House insists, understandably, on rigid secrecy to protect sensitive government documents—insists understandably, for it is precisely this secrecy which protects not only such documents of the government but also its policy from being revealed in its paranoic aggressiveness. The national security of this country is not now, nor in a foreseeable future, threatened by anyone anywhere in the world—neither at home nor abroad. What may indeed be threatened is the further expansion of the American world empire, and secrecy serves to prevent the people from finding out what is being done to them under a false flag.

Popular awareness of these facts is combatted by the vast intelligence network which makes spying a normal activity. Its extent, its means and its targets stand in no relation to national security; they are an insult to the sanity of the people. Reading the documents on the planning and organization of the super-intelligence agency, one must assume that in 1970, students, Panthers, Arabs, etc., were about to take over the country.

No, the vast, secret, illegal intelligence apparatus would not and could not suppress any real threat to national security, but well it could (and indeed did) suppress a threat against the established policy, domestic and foreign. While Congress was surrendering ever more of its balancing and controlling powers to the executive, while intimidation and self-censorship of the media became ever more noticeable, while inflation and unemployment continued unabated, while the power to wage war anywhere in the world was handed over to the President, the militant opposition was concentrated in the New Left.

Even without the full-scale implementation of the "game plan" to hunt down suspects and enemies all over the place, the operation was at least temporarily successful. The student movement has been broken up; the opposition has retreated. Temporarily, because the spirit of 1968-70 lives on, all over the nation, and not only among the young and the intelligentsia. And here, the all but irresistible protest against the Watergaters and the Gestapo mentality on the most august levels of government may well indicate the possibility of changing the course.

This opposition does not come from the Left: it comes from those conservative and liberal forces which are still committed to the progressive ideas of the Republic.

It is too early to write the obituary on Watergate, too early to say which side will win. The powers responsible for Watergate may survive; basic tendencies in the capitalist society support them, especially the increasing concentration of power, the amalgamation of big business and politics, the repression of radical dissent fostered by the aggravating economic difficulties.

FURTHER READING

Who Rules America? by G. William Domhoff (Englewood Cliffs, N.J.: Prentice-Hall, 1967).

How the Government Breaks the Law by Jethro K. Leiberman (Baltimore, Md.: Penguin, 1974).

The White House Transcripts (New York: Bantam, 1974).

ALLEN SCHICK

The Cybernetic State

Visions of the cybernetic age always have been of two sorts. Some have foreseen a period of unparalleled freedom, with man possessing the autonomy and leisure he has sought for ages. The cybernetic state would care for many of man's needs but would not exact a loss of freedom and selfhood; freed from the bonds of necessity and collective action, man would attain new command over himself and the world. The other version sees man as inevitably enslaved by the state, surrendering to powerful and uncontrollable institutions the freedoms that mark his selfhood. He will be controlled by the seeing hand which dictates his actions and thoughts. Man will be programmed—genetically or through thought control. He will be free to obey.

One can make a plausible case for either version or for both. Certainly both potentials are latent in cybernetics, though the actualities of history lend scant encouragement to the hope that the potentials will be used only for good. The story has always been the same. Man discovers fire for warmth and sustenance, but he also uses it to burn and destroy. Prometheus unbound is not always beneficent.

The Constitution of the United States might not quite endure for the ages, but it has survived great transformations in the conduct of public affairs. In few sectors have the changes been more pronounced or portentous than in the creation of the vast administrative structures that dominate the economy and the polity of the country today. The entire administrative staff of George Washington's government could be fitted comfortably into the offices of a medium-size bureau. As a government we have undergone several critical changes in the relationship between the administrative and the political. At the start the United States was designed as a political state; the growth of industry and public regulation in the nineteenth century led to the emergence of an administrative state; New Deal activism opened the door to the bureaucratic state; now, according to some expectations, we stand at the threshold of the cybernetic state.

Though it is possible to place each of these states into time zones, aspects of each appear in all periods of American history. The political, which was prominent in the earliest times, still carries over in the main representative theatre—the Congress—as well as in other national institutions. The cybernetic, which appears to be the emergent form today, certainly was operative in Alexander Hamilton's day through some of the accounting controls maintained over financial transactions. What characterizes an age is the dominance of one form of political-administrative relation, not the total absence of the others. The computer may be the logo of the cybernetic age, but the dawn of this period was portrayed in various artistic and scholarly works long before the first computer was constructed. Moreover, long after a particular form has been replaced, certain of its characteristics continue to show vigor and growth. Even if bureaucratics is displaced by cybernetics, we can anticipate the further development of large-scale bureaucracies for particular functions.

The cybernetic state of 1984 is not a product of the constitutional decisions of 1787. The Framers were occupied with building a political state, that is, with creating representative institutions through which power would be exercised and controlled. They did not—and could not—look to administrative or bureaucratic structures for the power or the controls, nor could they deal with the myriad of administrative details pertaining to the operation of the new government. Thus, there is scarcely a hint in the Constitution of the great organizational machines that would be created in the nineteenth and twentieth centuries and which ultimately would recast the distribution of powers and rights into something other than was envisioned originally.

From the Political to the Administrative State

In designing the political state, therefore, the constitutional architects concentrated on rules of representation, qualifications for office, the scope and powers of the several branches, the allocations between national and state jurisdictions and the establishment of limits on political action. These limits were aimed, for the most part, at the

The Burden of Responsibility: Politics and the Power Structure

representative institutions, and primarily at the national legislature. "Congress shall make no law" was the First Amendment formula for protecting political rights; trial by jury, along with its associated procedures, was the formula for guarding judicial rights. No explicit protection was incorporated into the Bill of Rights against infringement by administrative fiat or proceeding. Of the basic rights, only the "search and seizure" prohibition was generalized to cover all public actions, though its actual intent was to curb police power.

The passage from the political to the administrative state was due largely to the growth of national industry, the creation of new regulatory instruments and agencies prompted by that growth and the mobilization of administrative expertise to manage public activities. Whatever power Congress gave to administrators, it gave away voluntarily, and often with the blessing or the prodding of the president. The first national regulatory instrument, the Interstate Commerce Commission (ICC) was established in 1887, and three years later the Sherman antitrust controls were enacted. Resistance came from a different quarter, the judiciary, which insisted on applying the established constitutional standards to the new administrative structures.

One initial judicial response was to apply A.V. Dicey's "rule of law" doctrine to the administrative arena: ". . . no man is punishable or can be lawfully made to suffer in body or goods except for a distinct breach of law established in the ordinary courts of the land. In this sense the rule of law is contrasted with every system of government based on the exercise by persons in authority of wide, arbitrary, or discretionary powers of constraint." Applied strictly, this rule would have barred virtually all administrative adjudication, but it ultimately came to mean that the fundamental procedures of law (notice, hearing, examination, etc.) would have to be adhered to in administrative proceedings.

In striking out against the emergent administrative state, the courts relied on a parochial reading of the commerce clause and a stretched version of the 14th Amendment's due process clause. National power over the economy was curtailed in the Sugar Trust case (1895), the Child Labor cases (1918, 1922) and various New Deal cases. Much economic activity was deemed beyond the reach of the police powers of the states. For this view the courts found bountiful constitutional support by converting the 14th Amendment, which had been stripped of its Negro rights functions by the Slaughterhouse and Civil Rights cases (1873 and 1883), into a protection against state regulation of business activity.

But the emergence of the administrative state was to be determined in the legislative and executive arenas, and though the courts could harass and delay, they could not prevent the establishment of powerful regulatory instruments that were only feebly controlled by their creators. Following a spate of anti-New Deal decisions in the mid-1930s, the Supreme Court abruptly abandoned the review of economic legislation and began to concentrate on other areas of constitutional agitation. Since 1936 not a single piece of federal legislation has been invalidated as an unwarranted delegation of power to an administrative body.

Though it has some operating responsibilities of its own, the basic purpose of the administrative state is to regulate the new corporate concentrations of wealth and power. The administrative state, thus, continues to abide by the doctrines of the separation of public and private and of the basic soundness of the private market. Its task is not to impose a political solution, but to make use of specialized skills to correct for certain market defects or improprieties. To accomplish this requires a separation of the administrative from the political, a separation which was built into the major regulatory agencies and accepted as the cardinal precept by the intellectual fathers of the administrative state— Frank Goodnow, Woodrow Wilson, William F. Willoughby and others. By means of this separation, administration is made superior to politics, and efficiency replaces representation as the key operational norm of public policy. The fundamental constitutional rules of representation continue to apply to the political sphere, but not to membership on regulatory agencies, advisory boards and other appointive institutions. Regulatory agencies are made exempt from the sacred doctrine of separation of powers and are assigned substantial judicial, legislative and executive powers. As larger and more diffuse grants of power are turned over to efficiency experts and new concentrations of functional expertise are established within the cabinet structure, executive departments, particularly their bureaus and subunits, gain a good deal of de facto independence for the political institutions. They are also liberated from the president, who is no longer capable of directing their regular affairs, and from Congress, which no longer can exercise close supervision of their actions.

From the Administrative to the Bureaucratic State

The bureaucratic state began to displace the administrative state when the primary function of government changed from regulation to operation of business. Though the federal government had assumed a *doing* role in selected programs many years earlier, the New Deal era can be regarded as the great leap to bureaucratics. The bureaucratic state was designed to replace the market with public enterprises, not merely to correct for its deficiencies. It represented a refusal to accept the market's verdict that millions of elderly people must be poor, that rural communities must lack electric power lines, that the housing supply must be substandard and unable to meet demand, that farm incomes must sink below subsistence levels. The regulatory commissions that marked the administrative state have come to pale by every comparison with the operating bureaus of the federal government. Federal bureaucrats in the Bureau of Public Roads pass judgment on the location and design of federally aided but locally constructed highways and thereby exercise far greater sway over transportation policy than does the ICC; federal SST (supersonic transport) decisions probably will have greater air travel implications than will the combined regulatory actions of the Federal Aeronautics Administration and Civil Aeronautics Board.

Federal jurisdictions sweep over state and local boundaries, for a bureaucracy must always be structured according to its functions rather than according to local tradition. This movement is fueled by massive grants-in-aid and by federal involvement in functions long reserved for local action, such as law enforcement, poor relief and basic education.

In the bureaucratic state, the administrative and political are joined, united by interest-group brokers who traffic between the bureaucracies and the people and weave complex clientele–congressional bureau relationships for the purpose of channeling the public enterprises into the service of private interests. A new public market thus is created, resembling the private one in certain aspects, but lacking both the ultimate test of profit and the unremitting competition of adversaries. Interests bargain with one another at the public trough, but they also form coalitions and drive out competition when it suits their objectives. Politics and adminstration sometimes seem to be split again—in a divorce of convenience—as when advisory groups are comprised of functional specialists and community leaders in order to keep the program free of politics. But it all is for the sake of enhancing interest politics, and efficiency becomes the instrument of established group interests rather than a value in itself.

Interest groups form and begin to dominate the political-administrative process because in the bureaucratic state enormous interests are at stake, and the rewards for public success often far exceed what can be obtained in the private market. Moreover, all the political-administrative actors benefit in some way from the brokerage services provided by groups. Voters do not have an electoral mechanism for transacting their public business directly with the bureaucracy, nor do they often possess the skill or resources for doing so. Bureaucrats use the

groups for stirring clientele support for their demands on the president and Congress and for protecting themselves from executive and legislative supervision. Congress looks to the groups for learning about what the public wants and for gaining electoral support. The president uses the groups for mobilizing the electorate and for communicating his policies to the masses. Each one must pay a fee for the brokerage services, and as a result, the interest groups govern the terms

of the politics-administration process. Hence, the unification of politics and administration does not restore the constitutional representatives to their original political positions. As a matter of fact, each is further debilitated by the commanding role of the interest groups.

Of primary importance is the need to find constitutional support for the legitimacy of interest politics. Political writers rediscover Madison's *Federalist* No. 10 and elevate it to a status su-

The Burden of Responsibility: Politics and the Power Structure

perior to the constitutional scriptures themselves. In providing an intellectual justification for group politics, this discovery establishes competition in the political arena as a desirable substitute for market competition. It enables social checks and balances to take the place of legal checks and balances. It provides a substitute for electoral representation. It satisfies the requirement for external control of administration. Congress doesn't do the job well any more, but the groups do. They distribute the benefits of public activity widely, at least among those within the ambit of group operations.

The courts lose interest in administrative regulation and become concerned with the nationalization of civil rights and the granting of constitutional status to the rights of association. Operating under the Frothingham rule, which bars taxpayer challenges to federal programs, the vast programmatic development of the New Deal through the Great Society period escaped judicial review. The courts nationalize the Bill of Rights and apply federal standards to a widening group of police and criminal actions. They nationalize racial policies in the schools and in other public programs. They nationalize representation and apply strict one-man, one-vote rules to state legislatures and municipal councils.

Interest groups gain constitutional status, but they thereby become affected with a public interest and become subject to public controls. In *Thornhill* v. *Alabama* (1940), the Supreme Court extends free speech protection to peaceful picketing in labor disputes. Almost two decades later, with the 1959 Labor-Management Reporting and Disclosure Act, Congress adopts a bill of rights for union members. The integrated bar (which means requiring membership in a state bar as a condition for eligibility to practice law) was upheld in *Lathrop* v. *Donohoe* (1961), and the courts frequently have upheld group-licensing requirements for particular professions. In a series of cases involving the NAACP, the Supreme Court affirmed the right of association. Certain interest group activities were brought under public control in the Federal Regulation of Lobbying Act of 1946 which was upheld in *United States* v. *Harriss* (1954).

Still another judicial response occurs when the bureaucratic state reaches its full form and the cybernetic age begins to dawn. Unlike previous eras in which the courts told governments what they must not do, the courts now begin to instruct governments as to what they must do. Thus, recent court decisions in the welfare field have required bureaucrats to provide welfare benefits to indigents who have not satisfied local residence requirements, to families which have a man in the house and to pay benefits above ceilings enacted by the state legislature.

As the bureaucracy grows and creates the technological skills for its operation, certain critical transformations begin to occur in its character. The lines between public and private begin to break down, efforts are made to break away from the lockstep of functional bureaucracies, gov-

ernment regulation tends to become insular. These and many smaller and larger changes signal the beginning of the cybernetic state. And as the character of the state changes, so too does the focus of constitutional development, as it is expressed in the case law and in agitation for constitutional reform.

From Bureaucratics to Cybernetics

In the postindustrial cybernetic state, government functions as a servomechanism, concerting the polity and the economy to achieve public objectives. As a result, government changes from a *doer* of public activities to a distributor of public benefits, and the kinds of programs it operates reflect this change. For example, welfare has been one of the key programs of the bureaucratic state involving a large-scale welfare bureaucracy with thousands of governments and millions of people. As welfare becomes cybernated, it shifts to some form of guaranteed income, adjusted automatically as the income of the recipient rises or falls. (It doesn't matter for our purposes whether the guarantee is in the form of family allowances, negative tax or other means, though of course each form carries a different set of costs and benefits.) Government action is triggered automatically by changes in the economic condition of the individual. Government writes the "program" (in the computer sense of the word), establishes sociostatic norms (such as the "poverty level"), monitors the system and activates the money-disbursing machines. This is far different from the conventional welfare bureaucracy in which eligibility and benefits are determined by corps of case workers in accord with overall legislative and administrative rules.

Embryonic cybernetic-type programs have been established in health where Medicaid and Medicare now far exceed in cost the standard health programs such as local health clinics, public hospitals, Hill-Burton grants, publicly aided research and so forth. But the new health pro-

grams are only imperfectly cybernated because government lacks the means of controlling medical costs or for monitoring the demands on the system made by its clients. We can anticipate that aspects of program cybernation will bloom in other functional areas—education, public transportation and housing seem to be attractive possibilities.

In the public sector, perhaps the greatest advances have occurred in the macroeconomy where the refinement of national income accounts over the past 30 years has given federal authorities a substantial capability to guide the economy and to make quick adjustments as economic conditions change. But the macroeconomy is not yet fully cybernated. The accounts are not perfected to a reliability where governments can use servomechanistic controls; that is, it cannot fine-tune the economy and be sure that it will get the results it expects. Furthermore, Congress has not shown much enthusiasm for proposals to empower the executive to take nonlegislative corrective action. For example, it is not likely to adopt in the near future Herbert Stein's proposal for a permanent surtax that is adjusted upwards or downwards as rates of employment and other economic barometers fluctuate. Yet we should not underestimate the capabilities gained over the past generation, and it is possible that a cybernated macroeconomy is nearer than we think.

Cybernetic development lags behind in the microeconomy, partly because the accounts still are in a primitive condition, and partly because the resistances to cybernation are stronger here. Some first steps have been taken, as the recent publication of *Towards a Social Report* shows, but we will have to progress a long way before we have social indicators comparable in scope and reliability to the basic economic indicators. Cybernation cannot operate under uncertainty, for in this condition corrective action must always be tentative and discretionary. Moreover, there is little current evaluation of public programs and, hence, little feedback from results to decisions. The introduction of Program-

Planning Budgeting (PPB) and related types of policy systems gives evidence of the directions in which reformers would like to move, but it is now four full years since PPB was launched in Washington, and its meager accomplishments demonstrate that the job is not easy. Furthermore, in the macroeconomy, adjustments could be made for the benefit of all, and though the relative shares might be altered as a consequence of public action (not everyone benefits equally from economic growth), almost everyone gains. In the microeconomy, however, adjustments mean taking from some to give to others. Government action has to be redistributive. Hence, it is likely that this will be one of the last policy

functions surrendered by the representative institutions.

In the cybernetic state, the lines between public and private crumble. Government enters markets previously reserved for private entrepreneurs, but new private institutions enter arenas hitherto dominated by public bureaucracies. The penetration of government into private spheres is especially revolutionary in certain service areas such as doctor-patient and lawyer-client relationships. But as the lines between public and private erode, private institutions recapture some of the functions long regarded as public. Thus, in some instances, elementary education is turned over to private contractors, usually operating with public funds

and always under public control. The market is rediscovered, but it is harnessed to public purposes, and its behavior little resembles that of the traditional form.

As public and private commingle, distinctions between them become meaningless. Private institutions acquire legal status as "public accommodations," as provided in the Civil Rights Act of 1964 and sustained by the Supreme Court in *Heart of Atlanta Motel Inc.* v. *United States* (1964). Some recent court rulings have brought private clubs, perhaps the last bastion of privatedom, within the orbit of public control. It is no longer possible to tell where the private ends and the public begins as public and private funds and workers flow and work side by side in SST development, job training and countless other programs. In the basic social accounts, the public-private distinction no longer is significant; more and more, the accounts concentrate on the aggregate social input and output, regardless of its public or private character.

A similar amalgam occurs in the political and bureaucratic spheres. Administrative actions become politicized, and political actions become bureaucratized. Consider these two examples from the storehouse of current events. The supreme political act of determining legislative districts has been turned over to computer specialists, sometimes under court order, sometimes by legislative acquiescence. When this happens, legislative districting ceases being a political act, however great its political consequences are. Administrative actions have been politicized in the "maximum feasible participation" arenas as the floodgates of political activity, including formalized election procedures, have been opened to policy decisions that previously were made bureaucratically.

The regulatory functions of government which loomed so large in the administrative state, turn inward as government develops self-regulatory devices essential for its servo-mechanistic role. Corps of federal regulators man the guidelines in the Departments of Housing and Urban Development, Health, Education and Welfare (HEW), Labor and the Office of Economic Opportunity and regulate other public officials (mostly state and local) through a network of grant controls. Moreover, departments begin to use the computer to extend their program reporting, auditing and evaluating procedures to their own operations.

From Efficiency to Effectiveness

Yet even as government regulation turns inward, its policy perspectives turn outward. In the bureaucratic state, decision-making tends to be insular, concerned with the internal dynamics of the organization rather than with the effects on the citizenry. For preparation of his programs, the public official looks to his files and from there to the reports and accounts they contain, not to the hospital ward or the classroom. In drawing up his claim on public resources, he looks to last year's records and decides what to add and what to subtract. The cybernetic state, however, is goal-oriented. It is concerned with the income of families, the condition of the economy, the health of mothers, the intelligence of children. Efficiency norms which are relevant to the internal operation of organizations no longer hold the commanding positions they once had. Effectiveness criteria take their place as the guiding determinants of public policy.

To achieve this looking outward, the cybernetic state must be systemic rather than functional. In the development of the bureaucratic state, the functional arrangement was useful because it promoted efficiency, mobilized the use of specialists and gave representation to professional interest. For a goal-directed cybernetic institution, the functional form is an encumbrance, for it allows the interests of the functionalists to get in the way of the results. To take a common case: An education bureaucrat in HEW cooperates with a contact in the National Education Association (NEA) and obtains agreement that 25,000 volumes is the appropriate minimum for a high school library. This standard is transmitted via the state functional bureaucracies to school boards and via NEA publications to school administrators. Soon the 25,000 minimum gets adopted by the accreditation agencies as one of the conditions for holding accreditation. While this numbers game is being

played, it is hard to keep in mind how many books high schoolers read, what they read, what they learn from the books and whether other forms of communications can substitute for books. In other words, the function gets in the way of the goal.

The cybernetic form of organization is based on systems such as model cities in which functional specialists may continue to operate, but not as the key policy makers. The system is guided by systems engineers, planners and other generalists whose perspectives transcend the functional specialties.

In a full-blown cybernetic state, politics and bureaucracy would wither away, though their forms might remain. That is, there still might be contests for public office, but the process would not have its old importance. To the extent that sociostatic norms limit conflict, the scope of politics would be narrowed. Whether or not we ever reach the "political fiction" world of genetic or thought control, there will be less disagreement in the future than existed in the past. Already, in the macroeconomic sphere where the cybernetic condition is most advanced, differences between Democrats and Republicans now are mini-mal, despite the great stakes involved and the history of party controversy.

As government becomes self-regulative, with its actions guided by goal criteria, the bureaucracy also might begin to shrink in size and importance. Government will have nuclear "central guidance clusters," such as the Council of Economic Advisors, but it will not have the need for armies of bureaucratic doers. Thus, as welfare shifts from poor relief to income maintenance, the logic of maintaining thousands of social workers on the public payrolls decreases.

In similar fashion, the interest groupings which dominated the bureaucratic state no longer retain their central position. If it operates by means of cybernetic systems, government no longer requires the intermediation of these groups for communicating its goals, receiving policy preferences from the public and controlling the actions of the bureaus and representative institutions. The president can use the mass communications media to reach the public more effectively than through group exertions. Mass, class and individual identities become more important than group associations.

In the cybernetic state, there is both a massive collectivization of action, continuing the trends established in the earlier administrative period, as well as increasing privatization of life. Among the recent straws in the wind, we can point to the growing penetration of the hospital market by national corporations, the institutionalization of research and the dominance of contemporary philanthropy by the foundations. At the same time, life is increasingly privatized; that is, individuals are more isolated from one another and have greater liberty in personal behavior. Individuals are freed from traditional social and communal bonds: the Pill enables them to engage in private sexual practice free of effective social sanction; a television in each room allows each member of the family to watch his program without obtaining approval from others; a multi-car family can send the husband to his club and the wife to her group with both maintaining contact with one another via remote communications. The combination of collectivization and privatization is what gives the cybernetic state its Janus-like character, capable of elevating the individual to new levels of personal autonomy or of crushing him under the yoke of public oppression.

As the character of the state changes, so too do the methodologies for studying it. Political science is transformed into policy science, not merely a change in semantics, but in focus as well. For politics ceases to be the central concern; after all, if politics withers away, why study it? The policy sciences deal with the purposes of government and with the organization of intelligence for their attainment. They encompass both public and private spheres and concentrate on the content of policy rather than on the processes of choice. The analytic constructs also change —from processes and institutions to systems and communications nets.

At this point in the development, it is difficult to gauge how far we have moved from the bureaucratic to the cybernetic or to predict whether the cybernetic state will in fact be realized. The bureaucratic state has not yet reached its final development, and some of the current reform proposals are relevant to it rather than to the emergent cybernetic form. We do not know whether all the (good and bad) dreams of the future are technologically feasible or whether all that is feasible will be done. Perhaps there will be a Luddite uprising against cybernation and its systems. But our task here is not to foretell the future—there are enough year 2000 wizards on the market already—but to comment on the current state of affairs. Enough cybernetic tendencies have surfaced to have bestirred the minds and actions of reformers and to have created new kinds of constitutional issues.

Constitutional Issues in a Cybernetic State

Examination of the potential character of the cybernetic state suggests the kinds of things that will stop being constitutionally active or will be less significant than they once were. Probably the greatest wane will be in the area of civil liberties, for as the political processes diminish in salience, there will be less incentive to try to stretch these rights through constitutional action. The traditional First Amendment rights, such as free speech, might be more important to individuals who are concerned about their personal lives than to those concerned about marshaling political resources to influence public action. Of what use will be the right to speak if the speaker has little ability to challenge the dominance of the experts and systems engineers and little ability to sway the course of public policy by his vote?

Yet it is possible to foresee agitation for two types of political rights in the cybernetic age. First might be the right *not* to engage in political activity, not to be part of the collective mass that is politicized in the service of the state. Though Supreme Court rulings stand in the way, the right to remain silent, the right not to speak or to answer, might once again become defensible on First Amendment grounds. Second, the concept of *speech plus* might be further stretched to provide constitutional protection for overt political actions above and beyond the protection conventionally afforded the expression of ideas. Search and seizure litigation will have a prominent place on court dockets as new cybernetic technologies are used for surveillance. But many of the hot criminal procedure issues of the 1960s probably will diminish in importance, and if this occurs, a chapter on the great constitutional battles of the bureaucratic period will be concluded.

In every age the list of constitutionally active issues consists of the things we want to gain and the things we want to avert. In the cybernetic age, four types of constitutional issues might move to the forefront: the protection of personal rights; control of the cybernetic system; forms of political participation; and the structure of government.

The protection of personal rights. We have already noted that in a cybernetic state the distinction between public and private tends to dissolve and that, as institutions become more collective, the individual finds his life more privatized. For many future-gazers, the stereotype of the cybernetic tomorrow is of Big Brother watching over you, possessing the means to monitor every move and thought and constantly guiding your actions. Whether or not this fear is justified, constitutional guardians are already on the alert against moves that might bring us closer to 1984. The recent uproar over the questions to be asked in the 1970 census gives one indication of the sensitivity to governmental invasions of privacy. Still another indication was the opposition in Congress and elsewhere to proposals for a national data center. Despite all protestations of being misunderstood and despite the offering of assurances that privacy would be protected, the scientific and governmental proponents of the data bank were unable to sell their pet project to Congress.

Privacy already is a big issue in the courts, and it prob-

ably will get bigger. Until recent years the courts viewed the right of privacy as a derivative of protections against self-incrimination and unreasonable search. But in two landmark decisions, the Supreme Court established privacy as a fundamental constitutional right. In *Griswold* v. *Connecticut* (1965), a state law prohibiting the use of contraceptives was overturned. "We deal with a right of privacy older than the Bill of Rights—older than our political parties, older than our school system." The second decision, in *Stanley* v. *Georgia* (1969), voided a conviction for possession of obscene films. "If the First Amendment means anything, it means that a state has no business telling a man, sitting alone in his own house, what books he may read or what films he may watch." And in a clear reference to that awful cybernetic tomorrow, the Court declared: "Our whole constitutional heritage rebels at the thought of giving government the

power to control men's minds."

It is unlikely that we have seen the end of privacy cases. Many new circumstances could bring the issue to the courts time and again: security checks, census questionnaires, rights of public employees, students or inmates protesting the use of TV monitors, the use of drugs in the home, the sexual conduct of consenting adults, invasion of privacy by private groups.

Privacy will perhaps be only one form of the coming constitutional issue: what is the state's and what is the individual's? As the lines between public and private become blurred and as the tensions between the state's thrust for collective action and the individual's quest for autonomous behavior increase, we can anticipate heightened uncertainty and controversy over the respective spheres of the state and the individual. For example, can the state compel an individual not to smoke? Can it require

adults to work? Can it force mothers to send three-year-olds to school? None of these issues is distinctively new; but what is new is the ground on which they are being fought and will be decided. Prohibition was a moral issue, but smoking is already a scientific one.

Control of the cybernetic systems. Two types of visionaries want to control the cybernetic state; the first, to ensure the realization of its noble capabilities; the second, to avert its coming.

Inasmuch as the cybernetic system is fueled by the communications that course through its networks, carrying messages from command posts and feedback from monitors, control is often desired over the communications apparatus, both the network and the content of the messages. We have mentioned recent objections to census probes and central data systems. In addition to these attempts to withhold data from the state, control is exer-

privacy is not always compatible with the right to know. The government that gives away information under the Freedom of Information statute might be taking away another man's privacy. Man can be manipulated by being kept in the dark or by being exhibited in the open. How these two rights are reconciled will be one of the critical constitutional tests of the cybernetic age.

A cybernetic state operates under sociostatic norms: employment rates, poverty levels, educational criteria. Traditionally, we have been willing to entrust the establishment of these standards to professional interests. Economists tell us what an acceptable rate of unemployment is; doctors tell us what the normal life expectancy is; school administrators decide norms of educational achievement. But as these norms come to be the servomechanistic trigger of public action, it is possible that the competence of professionals to set the standards will be challenged. Perhaps the Orshansky scale used by the Social Security Administration to define the level and incidence of poverty in the United States will be challenged in a "Brandeis" brief which demonstrates that it costs much more than $3400 a year for a family of four to subsist in New York City. Just as individuals quarrel over the setting of the thermostat in their homes, so they may begin to contest the official policy norms. The due process and equal protection clauses have the elasticity to do the job.

Many of the challenges are likely to come from those most affected by government action, especially recipients of public benefits and public employees. Welfare recipients have carried their case to the courts, the streets and government offices, sometimes with conspicuous success. Groups of public employees such as FEDS (Federal Employees for a Democratic Society) have agitated for "the creation of a genuine participatory democracy' both within our Federal agencies and within our society-at-large."

The notion that those who benefit most from government control should have the greatest control over its policy seems to be a conflict of interest, but it is merely a new twist on the standard interest group ideology that

cised by opening up publicly held information to outsiders. If information gives power, its possession should not be monopolized by the state. This is the ethos of the Freedom of Information Act which became operative in 1967. The act enables an individual to sue a federal agency for access to information which has been denied to him. The initial experience under this act gives little encouragement to the hope that the government will eagerly open its books to public exam-

ination. It might be that only the confrontation tactics of "Nader's Raiders" and like groups can wrest the secrets from the state.

As the distinction between public and private narrows, the right to know also is applied to the private sector. The recent spate of truth-in-lending and truth-in-packaging legislation gives evidence of the ferment in this sector.

But the duality of rights sought in the cybernetic age reflects the dualism of visions of the future. The right of those whose interests are most at stake legitimately have the largest voice in shaping the policy. Cross out welfare recipients and put in television stations, and the notion is neither revolutionary nor absurd.

Forms of political participation. The basic form of political participation was molded for the political state, a system of free elections for public representatives. This system has persisted through two centuries of change, but it no longer possesses the relevance it once had, at least not for those who are dissatisfied with the shape of things. As the character of the state changed, new forms of participation grew up, interest and functional representation in particular. The cybernetic state probably will continue the old rituals of participation, but it might add some new forms suited to the problem of controlling the cybernetic apparatus.

Judging from the activism of the New Left—and that might not be a reliable guide—we can expect both withdrawal from politics and political confrontation, with the same persons vacillating between the two patterns. "Woodstock," as one participant put it, "was just like government and politics and law just didn't exist."

The belief that what is important is not changing government but changing yourself might be one of the romances of youth, but it seems to enjoy wide currency today. Yet youth has also marched in the peace moratoriums, worked in the ghettos, blocked entrances and challenged authority. Though they have no confidence in the efficacy of representative politics, the New Left does believe in direct political action. Yet the cry of "participatory democracy" so loud and clear at Port Huron seven years ago is muted these days. To participate is to offer oneself for co-optation, to join the establishment, and to surrender a commitment to radical change. Whether through withdrawal or confrontation, the challengers do not seek change through the Constitution.

The structure of government. The cybernetic age opens up two thrusts for change in government organization: new forms of community government and new structures for cybernetic guidance; the former to enhance the opportunities for participation, the latter to create a government that functions cybernetically.

Participation can be as part of a mass—faceless, remote, not able to relate to the central institutions. Or it can be in institutions that are cut down to man's size. Mass participation exists when man is politicized in the service of the state. Personal participation for most citizens, however, can only be within a community, the scope of which is immediate to their life wants. For the first time in many years, political scientists are concerned with the optimal size of cities, and government reformers want to reduce rather than expand the scale of local government. Maximum feasible participation, whatever its virtues or defects, can only occur in the neighborhood where one lives and transacts his personal life. Obstacles to community government exist at both the state and municipal levels. Dillon's rule has never been repealed: the state continues to enjoy constitutional preeminence over its subdivisions. Proposals for a constitutional structure that vests political status in the community have been voiced by several writers. Viewed from the perspective of the neighborhood, City Hall might be a bigger obstacle than the State House; indeed, enterprising community leaders now negotiate agreements with state officials to bypass the formal municipal structures. It is not likely that community recognition will come de jure; rather, through the operation of grant programs and government policy, neighborhood units might be able to gain a measure of political autonomy.

Community government is valued by minorities because it offers them some self-government apart from the larger majority. Blacks are approximately 10 percent of the national population, but their proportions and strength grow as the scale of government shrinks. Community control is a modern version of Calhoun's concurrent majority, and, accordingly, there are areas in the country where it can be made to work against the interests of blacks and others. But few among the minority—whether the blacks or the poor or the dissidents—take comfort in the minorities rule assurances of the pluralists; only members of the majority seem to benefit from that kind of minority rule. Blacks see metropolitan consolidation—once the darling of the liberal set—as still another means of robbing them of the municipal power that their numerical status within the city entitles them to.

The second restructuring of the state is to provide for the conduct of its cybernetic functions. If government is to serve as the central guidance structure, it must be vested with that capability. While we would not rule out the possibility of constitutional overhaul to accomplish this, the more probable path to change will be through a buildup of the presidential capability to govern without undue dependence on the functional bureaucracies. We can expect a continued enlargement of presidential staff and perhaps a reorientation of the executive office to serve a policy development and evaluation role in the interdepartmental and intergovernmental arenas.

Thus, the two lines of development will be at the bottom and at the top, the community and the presidency. Whether these changes can be concordant—most reformers today believe that they are, that the president is more a friend of the ghetto than either the mayor or governor—we do not know. Much depends on which version of the cybernetic state triumphs.

The changes from the political state to the emergent cybernetic state have been linear, with few reversals or zigzags. There has been a virtually continual closing of the gap between public and private and expansion of the scope of governmental jurisdiction.

But though the changes can be explained, they cannot always be predicted. In retrospect the cybernetic state might turn out to have been fantasy, compounded of fears and hopes. Much of the expectation of the coming cybernetic age is grounded on the capabilities of technology, not on the behavior of humans and organizations. Yet these latter, neglected factors might prove to be decisive. Citizens might resist the cybernetic penetration of their lives. Bureaucracies might refuse to wither away. Indeed, we have no precedent for such a dismantling to occur. President Nixon's new welfare scheme moved toward cybernation of benefits, but it also gave the welfare bureaucracy additional responsibilities for the determination of eligibility.

FURTHER READING

Discretionary Justice by Kenneth Culp Davis (Baton Rouge, La.: Louisiana State University Press, 1969).

The Age of Discontinuity by Peter Drucker (New York: Harper & Row, 1969).

The Technological Society by Jacques Ellul (New York: Knopf, 1964).

The New Industrial State by J. Kenneth Galbraith (New York: Signet, 1967).

The Administrative State by Dwight Waldo (New York: Ronald, 1948).

Notes on Editors

HELEN M. ICKEN SAFA, coeditor of *Social Problems in Corporate America*, is presently New Brunswick Chairperson and Graduate Director of Anthropology at Rutgers, The State University, as well as Director of the Latin American Institute at Rutgers. As a social anthropologist, Dr. Safa has done extensive research into the problems of low-income families in the United States, Puerto Rico, and Latin America. Among the nineteen articles she has written are "The Female-Based Household in Public Housing: A Case Study in Puerto Rico"; "The Case for Negro Separatism: The Crisis of Identity in the Black Community"; "The Poor are Like Everyone Else, Oscar"; and "The Social Isolation of the Urban Poor: Life in a Puerto Rican Shanty Town." Dr. Safa is the author of *The Urban Poor of Puerto Rico* and coeditor of a book on migration change and development to be published in the spring of 1975.

GLORIA LEVITAS, coeditor of *Social Problems in Corporate America*, is a 1975 candidate for a Ph.D. in anthropology at Rutgers, The State University, and is a professor at Queens College, City University of New York. She has worked with the Institute for Architecture and Urban Planning and was Director of Publications at the New York City Ethical Culture Society. Her books include *The World of Psychology, The World of Psychoanalysis*, and *Culture and Consciousness*. Ms. Levitas is coeditor of *Poetry and Prose of the American Indians: We Wait in the Darkness*, to be published in the fall of 1975.

Notes on Authors

ADAMS, ROBERT LYNN ("Mainlining Jesus: The New Trip"), is associate professor of sociology at Chapman College in Orange, California. Coauthor of articles on marriage and mobility in church and sect and on conflict over charges of heresy in American Protestant seminaries, he is currently working on a book on conflict and change in Appalachia.

BERG, IVAR ("Rich Man's Qualifications for Poor Man's Jobs"), is professor of sociology and associate dean of faculties at the Columbia University Graduate School of Business. His books include *Education Credentials for Jobs in a Democratic Society* and *Sociology and the Business Establishment*, with David Rogers.

BERK, RICHARD ("White Institutions and Black Rage"), lecturer in sociology at Goucher College, is currently studying the relation of black militancy and civil disorders to the actions of city officials and major institutions. He has conducted research on politics and the poor, and now he is finishing a study of ghetto retail merchants.

BLUMBERG, ABRAHAM S. ("Lawyers With Convictions"), is associate dean of faculty and professor of sociology and law at John Jay College of Criminal Justice. He has written extensively on criminal law, including *Current Perspectives on Criminal Behavior*, and is currently completing two books: *Private Troubles and Public Issues* and *Secret Police*.

BOESEL, DAVID ("White Institutions and Black Rage"), is research analyst with the Office of Economic Opportunity, Washington, D.C. His book *The Ghetto Riots: 1964–68* is based on the data he collected while an analyst for the Kerner Commission.

BOULDING, KENNETH E. ("Ecology and Environment"), professor of economics at the University of Colorado, is president of the Association for the Study of the Grants Economy and the International Studies Association. He is author of many books in the social sciences, most recently, *The Economy of Love and Fear: A Preface to Grants Economics*.

BOWLES, SAMUEL ("Unequal Education and the Reproduction of the Class Structure"), is associate professor of economics at Harvard University. He is an active member of the Union of Radical Political Economists.

BROWN, MICHAEL E. ("The Condemnation and Persecution of Hippies"), associate professor of sociology at Queens College, City University of New York, is presently active in the Labor Caucus of the Professional Staff Congress, C.U.N.Y., and is part of the collective teaching in the critical studies program. He is coauthor of *Collective Behavior*, written with Amy Golden.

BROWNING, HARLEY L. ("Timing of Our Lives"), is associate professor of sociology at the University of Texas at Austin and director of the Population Research Center. His major interests are the modernization process, particularly urbanization and internal migration in Latin America, and explorations in social demography.

BURNHAM, WALTER DEAN ("Crisis of American Political Legitimacy"), is professor of political science at MIT. He has written extensively on American politics and his primary research interest is American voting behavior and electoral politics. His latest book is *Critical Elections and the Mainsprings of American Politics*.

CARNS, DONALD E. ("Singles in the City"), is associate professor of sociology at the University of Nevada in Las Vegas. Currently he is conducting research on the cocktail waitress as part-time prostitute within the context of casino organizations.

CHAMBLISS, WILLIAM J. ("The Saints and the Roughnecks"), is a professor of sociology at the University of California, Santa Barbara. He is currently involved with work on a monograph on organized crime and professional theft. His most recent publication is *Whose Law, What Order?*

CLOWARD, RICHARD A. ("The Relief of Welfare"), professor at the Columbia University School of Social Work, has authored many books and articles on major social problems. He coauthored *Regulating the Poor: The Functions of Public Welfare*, which won the C. Wright Mills Award of the Society for the Study of Social Problems. He is now working on a book about political movements of the poor.

COHEN, RICHARD ("Domestic Pacification"), a graduate student in the city planning department at the University of Pennsylvania, Philadelphia, is also the editor of a transportation newsletter. He was formerly on the research staff of the Student Advisory Group on International Affairs.

CONFORTI, JOSEPH M. ("Newark: Ghetto or City?"), is assistant professor of sociology and director of the urban studies program at Rutgers University, Newark. His current interests include urban change as an American cultural phenomenon, the demographic and ecological consequences of city size and popular music as an arena for racial conflict. At present he is working on a book entitled *The Urban World*.

COREY, GEORGE D. ("Domestic Pacification"), a law student at American University Law School, has worked for the Small Claims Court Study Group, a Ralph Nader Project. Previously a law clerk to U.S. Senator Thomas J. McIntyre, Corey is now a judicial law clerk on the New Hampshire State Supreme Court.

CROTTY, WILLIAM S. ("Presidential Assassination"), is associate professor of political science at Northwestern University. Coauthor of two books on assassination, he was co-director of the Task Force on Assassination and Political Violence of the National Commission on the Causes and Prevention of Violence.

DRISCOLL, PAUL F. ("Middle-Class Professionals Face Unemployment"), is a counselor with the Massachusetts Division of Employment Security. While continuing his research in the area of unemployment he is also working with state correctional inmates. He has been associated with programs for lower-class workers and with the Professional Service Center.

EDEL, ABRAHAM ("Scientists, Partisans and Social Conscience"), is professor of philosophy at the graduate center of the City University of New York. He is the author of several works on ethics and science, including *Ethical Judgment: The Use of Science in Ethics, Science and the Structure of Ethics* and *Method in Ethical Theory*.

EIDSON, BETTYE K. ("White Institutions and Black Rage"), is associate professor of sociology at the University of Michigan. She previously worked at the Bureau of Social Science Research and has conducted research on government programs for the unemployed as well as study of community structure and conflict in 15 U.S. cities.

FOX, ROBERT JON ("Mainlining Jesus: The New Trip"), coauthored this article while a master's degree candidate in counseling psychology at Chapman College, Orange, California.

FREEMAN, JO ("The Social Construction of the Second Sex"), is assistant professor of sociology at the State University of New York, College of Old Westbury.

FRENCH, ROBERT M. ("Black Rule in the Urban South?"), is associate professor of sociology at Florida State University and editor of *The Community: A Comparative Perspective*.

GANS, HERBERT J. ("More Equality: Income and Taxes"), professor of sociology at Columbia University, is senior research associate, Center for Policy Research. His research interests include urban and community studies, planning and its social aspects, urban poverty and segregation and the mass media. *More Equality* and *High Culture and Popular Culture* are his most recent books.

GLABERMAN, MARTIN ("Unions vs. Workers"), is presently teaching at Wayne State University. He will spend a year as visiting lecturer at the Free University of Berlin.

GOLDSEN, ROSE K. ("NBC's Make-Believe Research on TV Violence"), is associate professor of sociology at Cornell University. She is also program advisor in the social sciences to the Ford Foundation for Latin America, especially Columbia, Venezuela, and Peru. Her works include *Puerto Rican Journey*, with C. Wright Mills and Clarence Senior, and *What College Students Think*.

GRAHAM, JAMES M. ("Amphetamine Politics on Capitol Hill"), is supervising instructor of the legal writing program at the University of Wisconsin Law School. He received his law degree from the University of Michigan in 1971.

GREER, EDWARD ("The 'Liberation' of Gary, Indiana"), is director of the urban affairs program at Wheaton College, Norton, Massachusetts. This article was based on research done when he was director of the Office of Program Coordination in Gary during Mayor Richard Hatcher's administration. He is editor of the reader *Black Liberation Politics*.

GROVES, W. EUGENE ("White Institutions and Black Rage"), a member of the group for Research on Social Policy at Johns Hopkins University, is presently conducting a detailed analysis of policing in the ghetto, and with Peter H. Rossi is planning to survey the social conflict arising from drug use on college campuses.

GUTMAN, HERBERT G. ("Industrial Invasion of the Village Green"), chairman and professor, department of history at the City College of the City University of New York, is also a member of the graduate faculty at C.U.N.Y. He has a forthcoming book, *Afro-Americans and Their Families During and After Enslavement, 1750–1830*, to be published in the fall of 1975.

HEILBRONER, ROBERT L. ("Benign Neglect in the United States"), is the chairman of the department of economics, graduate faculty at the New School of Social Research. He is the author of numerous books, including *Between Capitalism and Socialism*.

HEYMAN, FLORENCE ("Methadone Maintenance as Law and Order"), has studied criminology at the University of California, Berkeley, and is a doctoral candidate in social work at Bryn Mawr. Currently in the department of family psychiatry at Eastern Pennsylvania Psychiatric Institute, she has worked in the Haight Ashbury and Berkeley free clinics and the Philadelphia Methadone Treatment Program.

HIGHTOWER, JIM ("Hard Tomatoes, Hard Times"), a free-lance writer on politics and rural affairs, was formerly a legislative assistant to Senator Ralph Yarborough.

HILL, HERBERT ("Anti-Oriental Agitation and the Rise of Working-Class Racism"), is author of *Black Labor and the American Legal System* and other books. He has taught at the University of Wisconsin, Princeton University, and elsewhere in the U.S. and abroad. Mr. Hill is National Labor Director of the NAACP.

HOROWITZ, IRVING LOUIS ("The Pentagon Papers and Social Science"), is distinguished professor of sociology and political science at Rutgers University, director of Studies in Comparative International Development and editor in chief of *Society* magazine. He is the author of

numerous books, including *The Rise and Fall of Project Camelot* and *Israeli Ectasies* and *Jewish Agonies*.

HUMPHREYS, LAUD ("New Styles in Homosexual Manliness"), is associate professor of criminal justice at the State University at Albany. He is the author of *Tearoom Trade*, winner of the 1970 C. Wright Mills award. He is currently working on a book *Gay Libs and Liberals*, the sociology of the homophile movement in America.

HUNTER, CHARLAYNE A. ("On the Case in Resurrection City"), covered the Poor People's Campaign on a grant from the Russell Sage Foundation. She has worked for *The New Yorker*, *The New York Times*, and she was a Russell Sage Fellow at *Society* magazine (formerly *Transaction*) while studying sociology and political science at Washington University.

JACKSON, BRUCE ("In the Valley of the Shadows: Kentucky"), is a writer and photographer, currently associate professor at the State University of New York at Buffalo where he teaches literature, folklore and criminology. He is director of the Newport Folk Festival and author of *Wake Up Dead Man*, a collection and analysis of Texas convict worksongs.

JACOB, HERBERT ("Winners and Losers: Garnishment and Bankruptcy in Wisconsin"), a professor at Northwestern University, has been a fellow for the Center for Study in the Behavioral Sciences. His numerous publications most recently include *The Potential for Reform of Criminal Justice* (ed.) and *Urban Justice*.

KELMAN, HERBERT C. ("Deception in Social Research"), is professor of psychology and research psychologist at the Center for Research on Conflict Resolution at the University of Michigan. His recent books are *A Time to Speak on Human Values* and *Social Research and Cross-National Encounters: The Personal Impact of an Exchange Program for Broadcasters*.

LERMAN, PAUL ("Delinquents Without Crimes"), is associate professor of social work at the Graduate School of Social Work, Rutgers University, where he teaches courses on delinquency and social policy, social welfare policy and research. His major interest is in understanding societal responses to youthful deviance.

LEWIS, OSCAR ("The Death of Dolores"), conducted family studies in Mexico, New York, Puerto Rico and Cuba, where he attempted to discover whether the culture of poverty has been eradicated in the Socialist society. He was the author of *Five Families*, *The Children of Sánchez*, *Pedro Martínez*, *La Vida* and other ethnographic and theoretic studies.

LOVE, JOSEPH L. ("La Raza: Mexican Americans in Rebellion"), is associate professor of history at the University of Illinois at Champaign-Urbana. His research interests include regionalism in modern Brazilian history and peasant movements in Brazil and elsewhere in Latin America. He has published a book entitled *Rio Grande do Sul and Brazilian Regionalism 1882–1930*.

MARCUSE, HERBERT ("When Law and Morality Stand in the Way"), professor of philosophy at the University of California at San Diego, is the author of *Reason and Revolution*, *Eros and Civilization*, *One-Dimensional Man*, and other well-known works.

MARKSON, ELIZABETH W. ("A Hiding Place To Die"), is director of the Mental Health Research Unit of the New York State Department of Mental Hygiene. Markson, who has written extensively, is currently doing research in the areas of psychiatric sociology and the life cycle.

MORRIS, MARIAN GENNERIA ("Psychological Miscarriage: An End to Mother Love"), has graduate degrees in both nursing and social work and was research associate at Hahnemann Medical College and Hospital in Philadelphia. At the Children's Hospital of Los Angeles, Department of Psychiatry, she has done work on abusive parents.

NELKIN, DOROTHY ("Invisible Migrant Workers"), is associate professor in the Cornell Program on Science, Technology and Society and the department of urban planning and development. Among her many publications are *The University and Military Research: Moral Politics at M.I.T.*, *Methadone Maintenance—A Technological Fix* and most recently *Jetport: The Boston Airport Controversy*.

PALSON, CHARLES ("Swinging in Wedlock"), is a doctoral candidate in anthropology at the University of Chicago. At present he is teaching marriage and family relations at Immaculata College, Immaculata, Pennsylvania. He is national president of the Student Evaluation Project (STEP) which publishes student evaluations of graduate departments of anthropology.

PALSON, REBECCA ("Swinging in Wedlock"), has studied anthropology and art. Coauthor with her husband of several articles on the culture of sex and the structure of swingers' relationships, she is working with him on a book, *Friends and Lovers: A Study in the Use and Meaning of Sex*.

PAYKEL, EUGENE S. ("Moving and Depression in Women"), is consultant psychiatrist at St. George Hospital in London. Former director of the Depression Research Unit at Yale University School of Medicine, he is foundation member of the Royal College of Psychiatrists of London.

PIVEN, FRANCES FOX ("Militant Civil Servants" and "The Relief of Welfare"), professor of political science at Boston University and a Guggenheim fellow, is the author of many books and articles on urban politics. She coauthored *Regulating the Poor: The Functions of Public Welfare* and is presently at work on a book, *Recent Movements of the Poor and Why They Failed*.

POWELL, DOUGLAS H. ("Middle-Class Professionals Face Unemployment"), is chief of the psychology service at the Harvard University Health Services. A lecturer on social psychology, he has long been interested in the psychology of career development.

RAINWATER, LEE ("Post-1984 America"), is professor in the department of sociology and the John F. Kennedy school of government at Harvard University. Among his many publications are *Behind Ghetto Walls* and *Family Design*. Research for this article was supported by grant no. 1-PO-MH-15567 from the National Institute of Mental Health.

REISS, ALBERT J. ("Police Brutality: Answers to Key Questions"), is professor and chairman of the department of sociology at Yale University as well as professor at the Institute for Social and Policy Studies. He has authored numerous books and articles on urban problems and has served on the editorial boards of various professional journals.

ROSSI, PETER R. ("White Institutions and Black Rage"), is professor of sociology at the University of Massachusetts, Amherst. Formerly chairman of the department of social relations at Johns Hopkins University and director of the Group for Research on Social Policy, his recent books include *The Education of Catholic Americans* (with A. M. Greely) and *The New Media and Education* (with B. Biddle).

SCHICK, ALLEN ("The Cybernetic State"), is a research associate at the Brookings Institution. He has served as a consultant to the United States Commission on Civil Rights, the U.S. Bureau of the Budget, the Rand Corporation and the President's Advisory Council on Government Organization. He has written numerous works on American politics.

SENNETT, RICHARD ("The Brutality of Modern Families" and "Genteel Backlash: Chicago 1886"), associate professor of sociology at New York University, is the editor of *Middle-Class Families and Urban Violence: The Experience of a Chicago Community in the Nineteenth Century*, the author of *Uses of Disorder: Personal Identity and City Life*, and coauthor with Jonathan Cobb of *The Hidden Injuries of Class*.

SLOAN, LEE ("Black Rule in the Urban South?"), is associate professor of sociology at Brooklyn College, City University of New York. Sloan is currently at work on a study of ethnic conflict in Newark, New Jersey, and a longitudinal study of linkages between the military-industrial complex and the university.

STARR, JOYCE R. ("Singles in the City"), a doctoral candidate in sociology at Northwestern University, is currently a consultant for the Drug Abuse Council in Washington, D.C. Her main research interests are in evaluation research and young-adult life-styles.

STEGMAN, MICHAEL A. ("The New Mythology of Housing"), professor in the department of city and regional planning at the University of North Carolina, is the director of the North Carolina Housing Market Study. He has published extensively on the problems of urban housing and has served as housing consultant on various research projects. His publications include *Relocating the Dispossessed Elderly* with Julie Reich and Nancy Stegman.

STEINER, GILBERT. Y. ("Day Care Centers: Hype or

Hope?"), is senior fellow and director of the Governmental Studies Program at the Brookings Institution. He has long been a consultant to state and local governments and has written many books and articles, including *Social Insecurity: The Politics of Welfare* and *The State of Welfare.*

STEINMETZ, SUZANNE K. ("The Family as Cradle of Violence"), is a doctoral candidate at Temple University. Coeditor (with Murray A. Straus) of *Violence in the Family*, she was a delegate to the NATO conference on "Determinants and Origins of Aggressive Behavior" and is currently studying conflict resolution methods in the family using samples in both the United States and Finland.

STRAUS, MURRAY A. ("The Family as Cradle of Violence"), is the author of over 60 articles on rural sociology, South Asia and the sociology of the family. A professor of sociology at the University of New Hampshire and coeditor of *Violence in the Family* (with Suzanne K. Steinmetz), he is completing a book on class and family in Bombay, San Juan, and Minneapolis.

SUCZEK, BARBARA ("Chronic Medicare"), is a doctoral candidate at the University of California at San Francisco. Her major areas of interest include symbolic systems, social worlds, and deviant behavior. The renal failure study was made under a grant given to Anselm Strauss by the Russell Sage Foundation and is part of a forthcoming book.

SUELZLE, MARIJEAN ("Women in Labor"), is a research associate at the Survey Research Center, University of California, Berkeley. Her current research interests include the effect of family structure on the development of achievement motivation and the influence of cognitive explanatory structures on discrimination against minorities.

SUTTLES, GERALD ("Anatomy of a Chicago Slum"), is assistant professor of sociology at the University of Chicago. His article is an excerpt from his recent book, *The Social Order of the Slum: Ethnicity and Territoriality in the Inner City.*

THOMAS, ROBERT ("Renaissance and Repression: The Oklahoma Cherokee"), is associate professor at the Science of Society Division at Wayne State University,

Michigan. With Sol Tax, he directed the Carnegie Cross-Cultural Education Project, which was primarily based upon the Cherokee Indians of Oklahoma.

TOCH, HANS ("The Convict as Researcher"), is professor of psychology at Michigan State University. He edited *Legal and Criminal Psychology* and is the author of *The Social Psychology of Social Movements.* This article is based on research done with J.D. Grant for a book on violence.

WAHRAFTIG, ALBERT ("Renaissance and Repression: The Oklahoma Cherokee"), is assistant professor of anthropology at Sonoma College. He has done considerable research among Cherokees, most recently as part of a comparative study of economic development in Indian communities.

WEISSMAN, MYRNA M. ("Moving and Depression in Women"), is an assistant professor of psychiatry at Yale University School of Medicine and director of the Depression Research Unit. She has recently coauthored a book entitled *The Depressed Woman: A Study of Social Relationships.*

WELLMAN, DAVID ("The *Wrong* Way to Find Jobs for Negroes"), is assistant professor of sociology at the University of Oregon where he teaches the sociology of race relations and ethnic groups. He has published articles on the politics of social research and is working on a study that analyzes white racism as a defense of privilege.

WHITT, J. ALLEN ("Californians, Cars and Technological Death"), an organizer of Energy Expo '74, is especially interested in urban planning, sociology of the environment, critical theory, and political sociology.

WOLFSON, ROBERT J. ("In the Hawk's Nest"), is a professor of economics at Syracuse University. He is currently engaged in research on the development of social performance indicators for public sector organizations and is planning, with others, some interdisciplinary work on the philosophical foundations of policy analysis.

ZIMBARDO, PHILIP G. ("Pathology of Imprisonment"), is a professor of psychology at Stanford University where he conducts research on a variety of social psychological issues related to the social and cognitive control of human behavior. He is currently active in trying to encourage reform of the prison system.

WITHDRAWN

DATE DUE			
GAYLORD			PRINTED IN U.S.A.

75 76 77 9 8 7 6 5 4 3 2 1